10/2/1979

For Mother:

According to the Sages (hitherto unknown source) life and love really begin at 80, as the accompanying volume makes clear.

Love,

Noel

SONG OF SONGS

THE ANCHOR BIBLE is a fresh approach to the world's greatest classic. Its object is to make the Bible accessible to the modern reader; its method is to arrive at the meaning of biblical literature through exact translation and extended exposition, and to reconstruct the ancient setting of the biblical story, as well as the circumstances of its transcription and the characteristics of its transcribers.

THE ANCHOR BIBLE is a project of international and interfaith scope: Protestant, Catholic, and Jewish scholars from many countries contribute individual volumes. The project is not sponsored by any ecclesiastical organization and is not intended to reflect any particular theological doctrine. Prepared under our joint supervision, THE ANCHOR BIBLE is an effort to make available all the significant historical and linguistic knowledge which bears on the interpretation of the biblical record.

THE ANCHOR BIBLE is aimed at the general reader with no special formal training in biblical studies; yet, it is written with the most exacting standards of scholarship, reflecting the highest technical accomplishment.

This project marks the beginning of a new era of co-operation among scholars in biblical research, thus forming a common body of knowledge to be shared by all.

William Foxwell Albright
David Noel Freedman
GENERAL EDITORS

Following the death of senior editor W. F. Albright, The Anchor Bible Editorial Board was established to advise and assist David Noel Freedman in his continuing capacity as general editor. The members of the Editorial Board are among the contributors to The Anchor Bible. They have been associated with the series for a number of years and are familiar with its methods and objectives. Each is a distinguished authority in his area of specialization, and in concert with the others, will provide counsel and judgment as the series continues.

כיונים על אפיקי מים רוחצות בחלב ישבות על מלאת לחיו כערוגת הבשם מגדלות
שיר השירים אשר לשלמה
שיר

THE ANCHOR BIBLE

SONG OF SONGS

A New Translation
with
Introduction and Commentary

by
Marvin H. Pope

DOUBLEDAY & COMPANY, INC.
GARDEN CITY, NEW YORK
1977

Grateful acknowledgment is given to the following for permission to reprint:
Excerpts from *The Literature of Ancient Egypt,* Part 4: Songs, Poetry and Hymns, the Love Songs and the Song of the Harper, by W. K. Simpson, 1972. Reprinted by permission of Yale University Press.
Lines of translation of Sumerian poetry from *The Exaltation of Inanna* by W. W. Hallo and J. J. A. Van Dijk, 1968. Reprinted by permission of Yale University Press.
Excerpts from "The Interpretation and Use of the Song of Songs," by Robert B. Dempsey, 1963. Dissertation, Boston University School of Theology. Reprinted by permission of the author.
Summary of material in *Le plus beau chant de la creation* by Daniel Lys, 1968, Editions du Cerf. Used by permission of the author.
Excerpts from *Ancient Near Eastern Texts Relating to the Old Testament,* edited by James B. Pritchard, 3d edition with Supplement. Copyright © 1969 by Princeton University Press. Used by permission of Princeton University Press.
Excerpts from "The Sacred Marriage and Solomon's Song of Songs," by S. N. Kramer in *The Sacred Marriage Rite, Aspects of Faith, Myth, and Ritual in Ancient Sumer,* 1969. Reprinted by permission of Indiana University Press.
Excerpts from *Some Poetical and Structural Features of the Song of Songs,* by R. Kessler, 1957. Leeds University Oriental Society Monograph Series, no. 8. Reprinted by permission of The University of Leeds.
Excerpts from *Sophocles: The Antigone Translated into English Rhyming Verse,* by Gilbert Murray, 1941. Reprinted by permission of George Allen & Unwin, Ltd.
Excerpts from "A Drinking Song," in *Collected Poems* by William Butler Yeats. Copyright 1912 by Macmillan Publishing Co., Inc., renewed 1940 by Bertha Georgie Yeats. Reprinted by permission of Macmillan Publishing Co., Inc.
Excerpts from W. G. Lambert's translation of Akkadian love poetry from "The Problem of the Love Lyrics," in *Unity and Diversity,* edited by H. Geodicke and J. J. Roberts. Copyright © 1975 by The Johns Hopkins University Press. Reprinted by permission of The Johns Hopkins University Press.
"Apologetic Motifs in the Targum to the Song of Songs," by Raphael Loewe, condensed by permission of the author and publishers from *Biblical Motifs: Origins and Transformations,* Alexander Altmann, editor, Lown Institute Studies and Texts, III, Cambridge, Mass.: Harvard University Press. Copyright © 1966 by the President and Fellows of Harvard College.
Excerpts from *The Hebrew Goddess* by Raphael Patai. Copyright © 1967 by Raphael Patai. Reprinted by permission of Ktav Publishing House.
Excerpts from "Bilingual Selections from Sophocles' *Antigone,*" translated by Joan O'Brien, 1977. Courtesy of Southern Illinois University Press.

Library of Congress Cataloging in Publication Data

Bible. O.T. Song of Solomon. English. Pope. 1977.
Song of songs.

(The Anchor Bible; 7C)
Includes bibliographies and indexes.
1. Bible. O.T. Song of Solomon—Commentaries.
I. Pope, Marvin H. II. Title. III. Series.
BS192.2.A1 1964.G3 vol. 7c [BS1485.3] 220.6'6s [223'.9'066]
ISBN 0-385-00569-5
Library of Congress Catalog Card Number 72-79417

Printed in the United States of America
First Edition

To Helen
whose love is strong as Death

PREFACE

Apologies are in order for the protraction of this project, both temporally and verbally. The work dragged on longer than expected, despite the generous help of friends. The relevant literature turned out to be more extensive than an educated guess would anticipate, too much to be catalogued completely, to say nothing of any hope of perusing the whole.

Thanks are due to more people than can be listed. First and foremost, I am beholden to Mr. Gary Tuttle who has been most helpful in reading major portions of the manuscript; his editorial skills and experience, exacting attention to detail and vigilance against discrepancies, combined with thorough knowledge of Ugaritic language and literature, led to the elimination of many errors. I am also especially indebted to Mr. Bruce Zuckerman who helped with the present work, as he had done also with the last edition of the Job commentary. Special thanks are also due to my colleague, Professor Sid Leiman, who was ever willing and able to confirm, correct, or supply references in the field of classical Judaica. Dr. Ann Matter gave expert assistance with early and medieval Christian literature. Professor Stanley Insler kindly provided the translation from Sanskrit of Kalidasa's description of the goddess Parvati's beauty. Among those who perused portions of the manuscript and offered constructive criticisms are Professor Robert Wilson, Dr. Cheryl Exum, Dr. Alan Cooper, Dr. Peter Knobel, Rabbi David Wortman, and Mr. Robert Good. Dr. Exum is also to be thanked for permission to summarize her treatment of the question of literary structure and unity of the Song of Songs.

Particular expressions of appreciation and gratitude are directed to Professors S. N. Kramer, W. G. Lambert, Raphael Loewe, and Raphael Patai for assent to my liberal use of their work and to their publishers for leniency in granting permissions for quotations and summaries. Thanks also are given to Professor Chaim Rabin for assent to the summary of his article on the Song of Songs and Tamil Literature and to Dr. Robert B. Dempsey for allowing quotation from his investigation of contemporary attitudes toward Solomon's Song. Acknowledgment also is given for the contribution of Professor Phyllis Trible in her application of the Song of Songs to the process of biblical depatriarchalization. I am grateful to Dr. Max Pusin for permission to quote his letter describing the use of the Song of Songs in his teaching of a course on Freud and women's dreams. To Dr. Yasin al-Khalesi I am indebted for permission to reproduce the photograph of a Mesopotamian figurine treated in his master's thesis written at the University of Baghdad.

The chariot scene illustrative of Song of Songs 1:9 was drawn by Mrs. Virginia Simon, Director of the Department of Medical Illustration at Yale-New Haven Hospital and Miss Beverly Pope of the same department prepared other line drawings and photographs.

Thanks are again due to Dr. David Noel Freedman for his scholarly perusal and critique of the present work and for his advice and encouragement over the years. A special note of appreciation is addressed to Mr. Robert Hewetson for the skill, patience, and care given to the preparation of this work for printing. My admiration for his expertise has grown through his processing of three editions of the Job commentary and especially in this latest experience with Solomon's Song; it has been a pleasure and privilege to work with him.

For the typing of the manuscript thanks go mainly to Mrs. Janice Tuttle and Mrs. Maureen Draicchio. The indexes were prepared by Mr. Thomas McAlpine, to whom I am exceedingly grateful.

The indexes will serve to indicate the heavy debt to others, particularly to Christian David Ginsburg for his sketch of the history of exegesis up to his day when he thought the truth had dawned in the melodramatic interpretation of the Song as a manifesto for women's liberation (limited somewhat by Victorian ideals and perceptions).

It proved necessary to prune the burgeoning manuscript in order to compass it in a single volume and thus many elaborations and excurses were excised. Some readers may judge even more drastic surgery indicated. In the interest of even-handed ecumenism, samples of traditional Jewish and Christian interpretations are cited for each verse of the Song. The suggestion that our Song is related to the ancient funeral feast may repel moderns reluctant to reflect on the mysterious bond of Love and Death. It has been for me a moving experience to ponder what sages and saints have seen in the Sublime Song and to join the quest for the allegedly lost key of which Saadia spoke. Since reverence is the master key to knowledge, apologies are offered for apparent disrespect in dealing with flights of allegorical fancy which have their own germ of goodness and truth apart from any reasonable basis in the sacred text. If any are offended by materials adduced here, I beg pardon and trust that time and the God who laughs will mitigate the scandal. If the "slothful down on pampered ignorance" is ruffled, it may serve to ventilate vital issues long evaded or suppressed.

The flaws, deficiencies, and excesses which remain in this study, despite friendly help and advice, are the fault of the writer.

MARVIN POPE

CONTENTS

Preface ix
List of Illustrations xv
Principal Abbreviations xvii

The SONG OF SONGS – translation of chapters 1–8 1

INTRODUCTION

Proem 17
The Position of the Song of Songs in the Scripture 18
Canonicity 18
The Versions 19
    The Septuagint 19
    The Vulgate 20
    The Peshitta 20
    The Ethiopic 20
    The Targum 21
The State of the Text 21
The Date of the Book 22
The Language 33
Literary Classification—drama; idyl; cantata; anthology 34
Prosody 37
Literary Integrity 40
Form Criticism and Canticles; Praise of Pulchritude and Parallel Love Poetry 54
Gita-Govinda, the so-called "Indian Song of Songs" 85
Interpretations of the Sublime Song 89
    The Targum and Subsequent Jewish Interpretations 93
    Christian Interpretations 112

Dream Theories, Melodrama 132
The Wedding Week Theory 141
Cultic Interpretation 145
Jewish Mysticism 153
The Shekinah 158
Shekinah-Matronit in Qabbalah 161
Historical Allegory 179
Mystical Marriage 183
Mariology and the Lady of the Canticle 188
Humanizing the Sublime Song 192
Catholic Views of Canticles as Songs of Human Love 199
A French Protestant View: Sacred and Sexual 201
The Song of Songs and Women's Liberation 205
Love and Death 210

BIBLIOGRAPHIES

I. Texts and Versions 233
II. Chronological, pre-1800 236
III. Alphabetical, post-1800 252

TRANSLATION and NOTES

I. The First Chapter (1:1–17) 291
II. The Second Chapter (2:1–17) 364
III. The Third Chapter (3:1–11) 412
IV. The Fourth Chapter (4:1–16) 452
V. The Fifth Chapter (5:1–16) 501
VI. The Sixth Chapter (6:1–12) 551
VII. The Seventh Chapter (7:1–14) 593
VIII. The Eighth Chapter (8:1–14) 653

INDEXES

Authors 703
Topics 712
Words 717
Scriptural references 722
Post-biblical Jewish references 740
Ugaritic references 742

LIST OF ILLUSTRATIONS

Text of the Song of Songs arranged as a floral design, for a wedding. Shalom Asch Collection. Courtesy of The Beinecke Rare Book and Manuscript Library, Yale University. *Frontispiece*

LINE DRAWINGS

1–4. *Love, death, and dogs*

1. Early Mesopotamian "sacred marriage" scene with dog under couch. H. Frankfort, *Stratified Seals from the Diyala Region,* Oriental Library Publications, LXXII, pl. 34, no. 340. Courtesy of The University of Chicago Press. (See p. 212)

2. Anatolian tomb relief. Drawing by Beverly Pope. (See p. 212)

3. Funerary relief from Piraeus. Drawing by Beverly Pope. (See p. 215)

4. Corinthian crater (mixing bowl) showing leashed dogs under banquet couches. Drawing by Beverly Pope. (See p. 215)

5. Ramses II charges the Hittites at Qadesh. A. C. Th. E. Prisse D'Avennes, *Histoire de l'Art égyptien,* I, Paris, 1878. Drawing by V. Simon. (See p. 292)

6. Ashurbanipal and consort in ceremonial wine-bibbing. Relief from Kuyunjuk. British Museum. (See p. 366)

7. Terracotta figurines of goddess with layered necklace. After G. Dales, *RA* 57 (1963), 21–40, figs. 8 and 34. Courtesy of George F. Dales. (See p. 454)

8. Gazelles feeding among lotus. W. H. Goodyear, *The Grammar of the Lotus,* 1891, pp. xxxviii, 251. (See p. 455)

9. Eye-idols from Tell Brak, Syria. From O. G. S. Crawford, *The Eye Goddess.* Courtesy of J. M. Dent & Sons Ltd., London. (See p. 456)

10. Festal scenes from ancient Mesopotamian glyptic featuring feasting, music, dance, and sexual congress. After P. Amiet, *La glyptique mésopotamienne archaique,* 1961. Courtesy of Centre National de la Recherche Scientifique. (See p. 503)

11. Mesopotamian cultic chariot scenes. From P. Amiet, *La glyptique mésopotamienne archaique,* 1961, p. 92. Courtesy of Centre National de la Recherche Scientifique. (See p. 552)

12. Mandrakes, male and female. From HORTUS SANITATUS (Deutsch) by Peter Schöffer, Mainz, 1485 (no page numbers). Courtesy of the Medical Library of Yale University. (See p. 594)

Plates

following p. 360

I. Mold from palace kitchen at Mari, for making cakes in form of the love-goddess, Ishtar, queen of Heaven. A. Parrot, *Mission archéologique de Mari II,* 1959, pl. XIX. Courtesy of Librairie Orientaliste Paul Geuthner. (See p. 379.)

II. Ivory inlay of love scene from bed of king of Ugarit. C. F.-A. Schaeffer, *Syria* 31 (1954), 1–2, pl. VII. Courtesy of Professor C. F.-A. Schaeffer-Forrer. (See p. 445.)

III. Terracotta figurine. Courtesy of the Babylonian Collection, Yale University (NBC 4466). (See pp. 465–469.)

IV. Terracotta figurine from Iraq Museum. Courtesy of Dr. Yasin al-Khalesi. (See p. 377.)

V. Terracotta plaque from Nippur described as "female figure with a necklace." Oriental Institute Publications, LXXVIII, Nippur I, pl. 137, fig. 6. Courtesy of The University of Chicago Press. (See p. 517.)

VI. Title page of Dr. Sibs' sermons on Canticles. Courtesy of Yale Medical Library. (See p. 519.)

VII. Statuette of Baal from Ugarit composed of five materials. Cf. *Syria* 17 (1936), fig. 25 and pl. 21. The Louvre. (See p. 77.)

VIII. Ivory head from the palace of Ugarit. Its gender is uncertain, but C. F.-A. Schaeffer inclines to the view that it represents a queen of Ugarit. Cf. C. F.-A. Schaeffer, *Ugaritica,* IV, 1963, 25, fig. 24. Copyright by Professor C. F.-A. Schaeffer-Forrer. (See p. 625.)

IX. The Goddess as Destroyer in union with her husband, the two aspects of Shiva, in the cremation-ground. Painting of the Bengal School, twentieth century. After P. Rawson, *Erotic Art of the East,* 1968, fig. 111. Courtesy of the Gulbenkian Museum of Oriental Art, the University of Durham. (See p. 608.)

X. The goddess Artemis/Diana of Ephesus with protuberances of uncertain character usually taken to represent breasts. (See p. 633.)

XI. Goddess suckling two godlings or princelings. Ivory panel from the bed of the king of Ugarit. C. F.-A. Schaeffer, *Syria* 31 (1954), 1–2, pl. VII. Courtesy of Professor C. F.-A. Schaeffer-Forrer. (See pp. 445 and 657.)

XII. Etruscan sarcophagous lid of alabaster, fourth century B.C. Museum of Fine Arts, Boston, gift of Mrs. Gardner Brewer. Courtesy of the Museum of Fine Arts, Boston. (See pp. x, 17, 210–229.)

XIII. Winged Athena carrying corpse (human or divine?). Cf. D. Le Lasseur, *Les déesses armées dans l'art classique grec et leurs origenes orientales,* 1919, fig. 126, p. 336. Courtesy of Librairie Hachette. (See pp. 161*f.*)

XIV. St. Teresa receives the shaft of love. Sculpture of Giovanni Bernini, S. Maria della Vittoria, Rome. Courtesy of Alinari/Scala. (See p. 188.)

PRINCIPAL ABBREVIATIONS

AASOR	Annual of the American Schools of Oriental Research
AB	Anchor Bible, 1964–
AcOr	*Acta orientalia*
AER	*American Ecclesiastical Review*
AfO	*Archiv für Orientforschung*
AJSL	*American Journal of Semitic Languages and Literature*
ANEP	*Ancient Near East in Pictures,* ed. J. B. Pritchard, 1954
ANET	*Ancient Near Eastern Texts,* ed. J. B. Pritchard, 2d ed., 1955
AOAT	Alter Orient und Altes Testament
APOT	*Apocrypha and Pseudepigrapha of the Old Testament,* ed. R. H. Charles, 2 vols., 1913
ArOr	*Archiv orientální*
ASTI	Annual of the Swedish Theological Institute
AT	*The Bible: An American Translation,* 1931
ATh	*L'Année theologique*
BA	*Biblical Archaeologist*
BASOR	*Bulletin of the American Schools of Oriental Research*
BDB	F. Brown, S. R. Driver, and C. A. Briggs, eds., of W. Geseniush *Hebrew and English Lexicon of the Old Testament,* 2d ed., 1952
BHK	*Biblia hebraica,* eds. R. Kittel et al., 7th ed., 1951
Biggs	Robert D. Biggs, *ŠÀ.ZI.GA. Ancient Mesopotamian Potency Incantations,* Texts from Cuneiform Sources, II, 1967
BT	*The Bible Translator*
BVC	*Bible et vie chrétienne*
BW	*Biblical World*
BWL	*Babylonian Wisdom Literature,* by W. G. Lambert, 1960
B-Y	Eliezer Ben-Yehuda, *Dictionary and Thesaurus of the Hebrew Language,* 17 vols., 1908–59
BZ	*Biblische Zeitschrift*
BZAW	Beihefte zur *ZAW*
CAD	*The Assyrian Dictionary of the Oriental Institute of the University of Chicago,* 1956–
CBQ	*Catholic Biblical Quarterly*
CIS	*Corpus inscriptionum semiticarum*

CP	*Comparative Philology of the Text of the Old Testament,* by James Barr, 1968
DISO	*Dictionnaire des inscriptions sémitiques de l'ouest,* by C.-F. Jean and J. Hoftijzer, 1960
DT	*Divus Thomas*
ÉBib	Études bibliques
Ehrlich	Ehrlich, A. B., *Randglossen zur hebräischen Bibel,* VII, 1914
EM	Ephemerides Mariologicae
ERE	*Encyclopaedia of Religion and Ethics*
ErJb	*Eranos Jahrbuch*
ETL	*Ephemerides theologicae lovanienses*
ÉTR	*Études théologiques et religieuses*
EUT	*El in the Ugaritic Texts,* by Marvin H. Pope, VTS, II, 1955
EvQ	*Evangelical Quarterly*
ExpT	*Expository Times*
FJ	*Die Flora der Juden,* by Immanuel Löw, 4 vols., 1924–34
FuF	*Forschungen und Fortschritte*
GCS	Griechische christliche Schriftsteller
Ginsburg	C. D. Ginsburg, *The Song of Songs,* 1857. Reprint, 1970: see S. H. Blank, Bibliography III
GKC	*Gesenius' Hebrew Grammar,* ed. E. Kautzsch, tr. and rev. by A. E. Cowley, 2d ed., 1910
HAHAT	*Hebräisches und Aramäisches Handwörterbuch über des Alte Testament,* by W. Gesenius, 21st ed., ed. E. Robinson, 1880
HR	*History of Religions*
HTR	*Harvard Theological Review*
HUCA	*Hebrew Union College Annual*
IB	*Interpreter's Bible,* eds. G. A. Buttrick et al., 12 vols., 1952–57
ICC	International Critical Commentary
IDB	*Interpreter's Dictionary of the Bible,* eds. G. A. Buttrick et al., 4 vols., 1962
IEJ	*Israel Exploration Journal*
ILOT	*Introduction to the Literature of the Old Testament,* by S. R. Driver, 1910
JA	*Journal asiatique*
JAAR	*Journal of the American Academy of Religion*
JAC	Jahrbuch für Antike und Christentum
JANES	*Journal of the Ancient Near Eastern Society of Columbia University*
JAOS	*Journal of the American Oriental Society*
JB	*The Jerusalem Bible,* 1966
JBC	*The Jerome Biblical Commentary,* eds. R. E. Brown et al., 1968

JBL	*Journal of Biblical Literature*
JCS	*Journal of Cuneiform Studies*
JEA	*Journal of Egyptian Archaeology*
JEPG	*Journal of English and German Philology*
JNES	*Journal of Near Eastern Studies*
Joüon	Paul Joüon, *Grammaire de l'Hébreu Biblique,* 2d ed., 1947
JPOS	*Journal of the Palestine Oriental Society*
JPSV	*Jewish Publication Society Version:* The Five Megilloth and Jonah, 1969
JQR	*Jewish Quarterly Review*
JRAS	*Journal of the Royal Asiatic Society*
JS	*Journal des savants*
JSS	*Journal of Semitic Studies*
JTS	*Journal of Theological Studies*
KAI	*Kanaanäische und aramäische Inschriften,* by H. Donner and W. Röllig, 3d ed., 3 vols., 1969–73
KAR	*Keilschrifttexte aus Assur religiösen Inhalts*
KAV	*Keilschrifttexte aus Assur verschiedenen Inhalts*
KB	L. Koehler and W. Baumgartner, *Lexicon in Veteris Testamenti libros,* 1953
KJ	The *King James,* or *Authorized Version,* 1611
KUB	*Keilschrifturkunden aus Boghazköi*
LCL	Loeb Classical Library
Littledale	R. F. Littledale, *A Commentary on the Song of Songs. From Ancient and Mediaeval Sources,* 1869
LOT	*Literature of the Old Testament in Its Historical Development,* by J. A. Bewer, 1922
MAD	Materials for the Assyrian Dictionary
MAOG	Mitteilungen der altorientalischen Gesellschaft
MGWJ	*Monatsschrift für Geschichte und Wissenschaft des Judentums*
MIOF	Mitteilungen des Instituts für Orientforschung
MVAG	Mitteilungen der vorderasiatisch-ägyptischen Gesellschaft
NAB	*New American Bible,* 1970
NEB	*New English Bible,* 1961, 1970
NKZ	*Neue kirchliche Zeitschrift*
NRT	*La nouvelle revue théologique*
OIP	Oriental Institute Publications
OLZ	*Orientalistische Literaturzeitung*
OrAnt	*Oriens antiquus*
PAAAS	*Proceedings of the American Academy of Arts and Sciences*
PAPS	*Proceedings of the American Philosophical Society*
Patai	Raphael Patai, *The Hebrew Goddess,* 1967
PBA	*Proceedings of the British Academy*
PEQ	*Palestine Exploration Quarterly*

PG	*Patrologia graeca.* J. Migne
PL	*Patrologia latina.* J. Migne
PNWSP	*Proverbs and Northwest Semitic Philology,* by M. Dahood, 1963
PRU	*Le Palais royal d'Ugarit*
PS I, II, III	*Psalms I, 1–50; Psalms II, 51–100; Psalms III, 101–150,* by M. Dahood, AB 16, 17, 17A, 1965, 1968, 1970
PW	A. Pauly (1839*ff*) and G. von Wissowa et al. (1894*ff*), *Real-Enzyklopädie der classischen Altertumswissenschaft*
RA	*Revue d'assyriologie et d'archéologie orientale*
RB	*Revue biblique*
RBén	*Revue bénédictine de critique, d'histoire et de littérature religieuses*
RÉA	*Revue des études Augustiniennes*
RevQ	*Revue de Qumrân*
RevSém	*Revue sémitique*
RGG	*Religion in Geschichte und Gegenwart*
RHA	*Revue hittite et asianique*
RHPR	*Revue d'histoire et de philosophie religieuses*
RivB	*Rivista Biblica*
RLV	*Reallexikon der Vorgeschichte*
ROL	*Revue de l'Orient Latin*
Rowley	H. H. Rowley, "The Interpretation of the Song of Songs," in *The Servant of the Lord and Other Essays,* 1952, pp. 189–234
RSR	*Recherches de science religieuse*
RSV	*Revised Standard Version,* 1946, 1952
RTF	A. Robert, R. Tournay, and A. Feuillet, *Le Cantique des Cantiques: traduction et commentaire,* ÉBib, 1963
RThom	*Revue Thomiste*
SAOC	Studies in Ancient Oriental Civilizations
SH	*Scripta Hierosolymitana*
SKIZ	*Sumerische Königshymnen der Isin-Zeit,* by W. H. Ph. Römer, 1965
SMR	*The Sacred Marriage Rite: Aspects of Faith, Myth, and Ritual in Ancient Sumer,* by S. N. Kramer, 1969
SR	*Studies in Religion/Sciences religieuses*
SRT	*Sumerian Religious Texts,* ed. E. Chiera, 1924
SSS	*A Symposium on the Song of Songs,* ed. W. H. Schoff, 1924. (For other participants—F. Edgerton, W. W. Hyde, M. L. Margolis, T. J. Meek, J. A. Montgomery—see Bibliography III.)
StOr	Studia orientalia
TB	Talmud Babli

TCL	Textes cunéiformes du Louvre
TD	*Theology Digest*
Tenses	*A Treatise on the Use of the Tenses in Hebrew,* by S. R. Driver, 3d ed., 1892
TGl	*Theologie und Glaube*
Thespis	*Thespis: Ritual, Myth and Drama in the Ancient Near East,* by T. H. Gaster, 1950
TLZ	*Theologische Literaturzeitung*
TQ	*Theologische Quartalschrift*
TRu	*Theologische Rundschau*
TZ	*Theologische Zeitschrift*
UF	*Ugarit-Forschungen*
UT	*Ugaritic Textbook,* by C. H. Gordon, 4th ed., 1965
UUA	Uppsala universitetsårsskrift
VAB	Vorderasiatiche Bibliothek
VT	*Vetus Testamentum*
VTS	Vetus Testamentum Supplements
WbM	*Wörterbuch der Mythologie,* ed. W. H. Haussig, 1962–
WUS	*Wörterbuch des ugaritischen Sprache,* by J. Aistleitner, 1963
WZKM	*Wiener Zeitschrift für die Kunde des Morgenlandes*
YGC	*Yahweh and the Gods of Canaan,* by W. F. Albright, 1968
ZA	*Zeitschrift für Assyriologie*
ZAW	*Zeitschrift für die alttestamentliche Wissenschaft*
ZDMG	*Zeitschrift der deutschen morgenländischen Gesellschaft*
ZDPV	*Zeitschrift des deutschen Palästina-Vereins*
ZE	*Zeitschrift für Ethnologie*
ZKT	*Zeitschrift für katholische Theologie*
ZRGG	*Zeitschrift für Religions- und Geistesgeschichte*
ZS	*Zeitschrift für Semitistik und verwandte Gebiete*
ZTK	*Zeitschrift für Theologie und Kirche*

SONG OF SONGS

THE SONG OF SONGS

I
(1:1–17)

1 The Sublime Song of Solomon
2 a Let him kiss me with his mouth's kisses!
b Truly, sweeter is your love than wine,
3 a Than the smell of your precious oil.
b Turaq oil is your name.
c Therefore girls love you.
4 a Draw me after you, let us run!
b The king brought me to his chambers.
c We will exult and joy in you.
d We will savor your love above wine.
e Rightly do they love you.
5 a Black am I and beautiful,
b O Jerusalem girls,
c Like the tents of Qedar,
d Like the pavilions of Salmah.
6 a Stare not at me that I am swart,
b That the sun has blackened me.
c My mother's sons were incensed at me,
d They made me a vineyard guard;
e My own vineyard I did not guard.
7 a Tell me, my true love,
b Where do you pasture?
c Where do you fold at noon?
d Lest I be as one veiled
e Among your comrades' flocks.
8 a If you do not know,
b O fairest of women,

c Follow the sheep tracks,
d And graze your kids
e Close to the shepherds' huts.
9 a To a mare among Pharaoh's cavalry
b Would I compare you, my darling.
10 a Your cheeks adorned with bangles,
b Your neck with beads.
11 a Bangles of gold we will make you,
b With spangles of silver.
12 a While the king was on his couch,
b My nard yielded its scent.
13 a A bundle of myrrh is my love to me,
b Between my breasts he lodges.
14 a A cluster of cypress is my love to me,
b From the gardens of En Gedi.
15 a Indeed you are fair, my darling,
b Indeed you are fair.
c Your eyes are doves.
16 a Indeed you are fair my love,
b Yea pleasant.
c Our couch is luxuriant.
17 a Our bower's beams are cedars,
b Our rafters cypresses.

II
(2:1–17)

1 a I am the crocus of the plain,
b The lotus of the valley.
2 a Like a lotus among brambles,
b So is my darling among girls.
3 a Like the apple in the wild wood,
b So is my love among boys.
c In his shade I love to sit,
d And his fruit is sweet to my palate.
4 a He brought me into the wine house,
b His intent toward me Love.

5 a Sustain me with raisin cakes,
b Brace me with apples,
c For faint from love am I.
6 a His left hand under my head,
b His right hand clasps me
7 a I adjure you, Jerusalem girls,
b By the gazelles or hinds of the steppe
c That you neither incite nor excite
d Love until it is eager.
8 a Hark my love,
b There he comes,
c Leaping over mountains,
d Bounding o'er hills.
9 a My love resembles a buck,
b Or a young stag.
c Lo, there he stands at our wall,
d Peeking in the window,
e Peering through the lattice.
10 a My love spoke and said to me,
b Arise, my darling,
c My fair one, come.
11 a For, lo, the winter is past,
b The rain is over, gone.
12 a Blossoms appear in the land,
b Pruning-time has come.
c The voice of the turtledove
d Is heard in our land.
13 a The fig ripens her fruits,
b The vines in bloom give scent.
c Arise, come, my darling,
d My fair one, come away.
14 a My dove in the cliff crannies,
b In the covert steep,
c Show me your form,
d Let me hear your voice;
e For your voice is pleasant,
f Your form fair.

15 a Catch us foxes,
b Little foxes,
c Vineyard spoilers,
d Our vineyards in bloom.
16 a My love is mine
b And I am his
c Who browses on the lotus.
17 a Until the day breathes,
b And the shadows flee,
c Turn and be, my love,
d Like a buck, or young stag,
e On the cleft mountains.

III
(3:1–11)

1 a On my bed at night
b I sought him whom I love.
c I sought, but did not find him.
2 a I will rise and roam the city,
b In the streets and squares.
c I will seek him whom I love.
d I sought, but did not find him.
3 a The guards found me
b They who patrol the city.
c Have you seen the one I love?
4 a Scarce had I passed them by
b When I found the one I love.
c I grasped and would not loose him
d Till I brought him to my mother's house,
e To the chamber of her who conceived me.
5 a I adjure you, Jerusalem girls,
b By the gazelles or hinds of the steppe,
c That you neither incite or excite
d Love until it is eager.
6 a Who is this ascending from the steppe,
b Like columns of smoke,

c Redolent with myrrh and incense,
d All the pedlar's powders?
7 a Behold Solomon's bed,
b Sixty heroes round it,
c Valiants of Israel,
8 a All of them war-skilled,
b Battle taught,
c Each with sword at his side
d Against night terror.
9 a A litter he made for himself,
b Did King Solomon,
c From wood of Lebanon.
10 a He made its posts silver,
b Its bolster gold,
c Its cushion purple wool,
d Its sides love inlaid.
11 a Jerusalem girls come out
b Look, O Zion's girls,
c At King Solomon,
d At the crown his mother gave him
e On his wedding day,
f On the day of his heart's delight.

IV
(4:1–16)

1 a Behold you are fair, my darling,
b Behold you are fair.
c Your eyes are doves
d Behind your veil.
e Your hair like a flock of shorn goats
f Streaming down Mount Gilead.
2 a Your teeth like a flock of ewes
b Coming up from washing,
c All of them twinning,
d None bereft among them.

3 a Like a scarlet fillet your lips,
b Your mouth comely.
c Like a pomegranate slice your brow
d Behind your veil.
4 a Like David's tower your neck,
b Built in courses.
c A thousand shields hung on it,
d All bucklers of heroes.
5 a Your breasts like two fawns,
b Twins of a gazelle,
c Browsing on the lotus.
6 a While the day breathes
b And the shadows flee,
c I will hie me to the myrrh mountain,
d To the frankincense hill.
7 a You are all fair, my darling.
b Blemish there is none in you.
8 a Come from Lebanon, bride,
b Come from Lebanon, come.
c Come from the peak of Amana,
d From the peak of Senir and Hermon,
e From the lions' dens,
f From the panthers' lairs.
9 a You ravish my mind, my sister, bride,
b You ravish my mind with one of your eyes,
c With a single gem of your necklace.
10 a How fair your love,
b My sister, bride.
c Sweeter your love than wine,
d The scent of your perfume than any spice.
11 a Your lips drip honey, bride,
b Honey and milk under your tongue,
c And the scent of your robes
d Is like the scent of Lebanon.
12 a A garden locked is my sister, bride,
b A pool locked, a fountain sealed.
13 a Your groove a pomegranate grove

b With fruits delectable,
c Cypress with nard,
14 a Nard and saffron,
b Cane and cinnamon,
c With all fragrant woods,
d Myrrh and aloes,
e With all prime perfumes.
15 a A garden fountain,
b A well of living water,
c Cascading from Lebanon.
16 a Stir, O North-wind,
b Come, O South-wind!
c Breathe on my garden.
d Let its spices flow.
e Let my love enter his garden.
f Let him eat its delectable fruits.

V
(5:1–16)

1 a I entered my garden, my sister, bride;
b I plucked my myrrh with my spice;
c I ate my honeycomb with my honey;
d I drank my wine with my milk.
e Eat, friends, drink,
f Be drunk with love!
2 a I slept, but my mind was alert.
b Hark, my love knocks.
c Open to me, my sister,
d My darling, my dove, my perfect one!
e For my head is drenched with dew,
f My locks with the night mist.
3 a I have removed my tunic
b How shall I put it on?
c I have washed my feet
d How shall I soil them?

4 a My love thrust his "hand" into the hole,
b And my inwards seethed for him.
5 a I rose to open for my love,
b And my hands dripped myrrh,
c My fingers liquid myrrh,
d On the handles of the bolt.
6 a I opened to my love,
b But my love had turned and gone.
c My soul sank at his flight.
d I sought, but could not find him.
e I called him, but he did not answer me.
7 a The guards found me,
b They who patrol the city;
c They struck me, they wounded me,
d Took my veil from me,
e They who guard the wall.
8 a I adjure you, Jerusalem girls,
b If you find my love,
c What will you tell him?
d That I am sick with love.
9 a What is your beloved above another,
b O fairest of women,
c What is your beloved above another,
d That you thus adjure us?
10 a My love is radiant and ruddy,
b Conspicuous above a myriad.
11 a His head finest gold,
b His locks luxuriant,
c Black as the raven.
12 a His eyes like doves by waterducts,
b Splashing in milky spray,
c Sitting by brimming pools.
13 a His cheeks like spice beds,
b Burgeoning aromatics.
c His lips lotuses,
d Dripping liquid myrrh.
14 a His arms rods of gold,

b Studded with gems;
c His loins smoothest ivory,
d Encrusted with sapphires.
15 a His legs marble pillars,
b Based on sockets of gold.
c His aspect like the Lebanon,
d Choice as the cedars.
16 a His mouth is sweet,
b And all of him desirable.
c This is my love, this my mate,
d O Jerusalem girls.

VI
(6:1–12)

1 a Whither has your love gone,
b O fairest among women?
c Whither has your love turned
d That we may seek him with you?
2 a My love has gone down to his garden,
b To the balsam beds,
c To browse in the gardens,
d To pluck lotuses.
3 a I am my love's and my love is mine,
b He who feeds on the lotus.
4 a Fair you are, my darling, verily pleasing,
b Beautiful as Jerusalem,
c Awesome with trophies.
5 a Avert your eyes from me,
b For they drive me wild.
c Your hair is like a flock of goats
d Streaming down Gilead.
6 a Your teeth like a flock of ewes
b Coming up from the washing;
c Each one has its twin,
d None bereft among them.

7 a Like a slice of pomegranate your cheeks
b Behind your veil.
8 a Sixty queens are they,
b Eighty concubines,
c Girls without number.
9 a Unique is my dove, my perfect one,
b Unique she to her mother,
c Favorite of her parent.
d The girls saw and praised her,
e Queens and concubines lauded her.
10 a Who is this that looks forth as the dawn,
b Fair as the moon,
c Bright as the sun,
d Awesome as with trophies?
11 a To the walnut grove I went down
b To view the valley verdure,
c To see if the vines had blossomed,
d If the pomegranates had bloomed.
12 a Unawares I was set
b In the chariot with the prince.

VII
(7:1–14)

1 a Leap, leap, O Shulamite!
b Leap, leap, and let us gaze on you.
c How will you gaze on Shulamite
d In the Dance of the two Camps?
2 a How beautiful your sandaled feet,
b O prince's daughter!
c Your curvy thighs like ornaments
d Crafted by artist hands.
3 a Your vulva a rounded crater;
b May it never lack punch!
c Your belly a mound of wheat
d Hedged with lotuses.

4 a Your breasts like two fawns,
b Twins of a gazelle.
5 a Your neck like an ivory tower,
b Your eyes the pools in Heshbon
c By the gate of Bat-Rabbim.
d Your nose like towering Lebanon
e Overlooking Damascus.
6 a Your head on you like Carmel,
b The locks of your head like purple,
c A king captive in the tresses.
7 a How fair, how pleasant you are!
b O Love, daughter of delights.
8 a Your stature resembles the palm,
b Your breasts the clusters.
9 a Methinks I'll climb the palm,
b I'll grasp its branches.
c Let your breasts be like grape clusters,
d The scent of your vulva like apples,
10 a Your palate like the best wine
b Flowing (for my love) smoothly,
c Stirring sleepers' lips.
11 a I belong to my beloved,
b And for me is his desire.
12 a Come, my love,
b Let us hie to the field,
c Let us lie in the cypress,
13 a Let us get to the vineyards.
b We will see if the vine sprouts,
c If the blossoms bud,
d If the pomegranate flowers.
e There will I give you my love.
14 a The mandrakes give scent,
b At our door is every delicacy;
c Things both new and old,
d My love, I have stored for you.

VIII
(8:1–14)

1 a O that you were as my brother
b Who sucked the breasts of my mother!
c I would find you in the street and kiss you,
d And none would scorn me.
2 a I would lead you to my mother's house,
b Bring you to the chamber of her who bore me.
c I would make you drink spiced wine,
d The juice of my pomegranate
3 a His left hand under my head,
b His right hand clasps me.
4 a I adjure you,
b Jerusalem girls,
c That you neither incite nor excite
d Love until it is eager.
5 a Who is this ascending from the steppe,
b Leaning on her lover?
c Under the apple tree I aroused you;
d There your mother conceived you,
e There she who bore you conceived.
6 a Set me as a signet on your heart,
b As a signet on your arm.
c For Love is strong as Death,
d Passion fierce as Hell.
e Its darts are darts of fire,
f Its flames — — —
7 a Mighty waters cannot quench Love,
b No torrents can sweep it away.
c [If a man gave all the wealth of
d his house for love, would he be despised?]
8 a Our sister is young
b And breasts she has none.
c What will we do for our sister
d On the day she is bespoken?

9 a If she be a wall,
b We will build on her a silver buttress.
c If she be a door,
d We will close her with a cedar board.
10 a I am a wall,
b And my breasts like towers.
c Thus have I become in his eyes
d As one producing peace.
11 a Solomon had vineyard
b In Baal Hamon.
c He gave the vineyard to keepers.
d A man would offer for its fruit
e A thousand silver pieces.
12 a My own vineyard is before me.
b The thousand is yours, O Solomon,
c And two hundred for those who guard its fruit.
13 a You who dwell in gardens,
b Companions are attentive.
c Make me hear your voice.
14 a Bolt, my love,
b Be like a buck,
c Or a young stag,
d On the spice mountains.

INTRODUCTION

PROEM

No composition of comparable size in world literature has provoked and inspired such a volume and variety of comment and interpretation as the biblical Song of Songs. In adding to the already bloated body of literature, no claim is made that the present study supplies the master key to the inner sanctum of the mysteries of Solomon's superb Song which the savant Saadia long ago likened to a lock for which the key had been lost. The quest for the supposedly lost key has been futile, for the door to the understanding of the Song was not locked, nor even shut, but has been wide open to any who dared to see and enter. The barrier has been a psychological aversion to the obvious, somewhat like the Emperor's New Clothes. The trouble has been that interpreters who dared acknowledge the plain sense of the Song were assailed as enemies of truth and decency. The allegorical charade thus persisted for centuries with only sporadic protests.

In recent decades there has been a general and growing tendency to reject allegory and freely admit the application of the Song to human physical love. In a conversation with Père de Vaux a few months before his death, that learned and devoted churchman confided that he had just revised the captions of Cantique des Cantiques for the new edition of *La Bible de Jérusalem* eliminating allegorical interpretation in favor of human love. This, admittedly, is a move in the right direction, in keeping with the rabbinic dictum that the words of Scripture are human language. Nevertheless, the instincts and insights that from the beginning led both Christian and Jewish exegetes to relate the language of the Song to divine and superhuman love were based on internal evidence largely ignored by recent interpreters. Modern research has tended to relate the origins and background of the Songs to the sacral sexual rites of ancient Near Eastern fertility cults wherein the issues of life and death were the crucial concern. In working through the Song word by word and verse by verse, and in reviewing the interpretations that have been imposed upon it, the impression has grown to conviction that the cultic interpretation, which has been vehemently resisted from its beginnings, is best able to account for the erotic imagery. Sexuality is a basic human interest and the affirmation that "God is Love" includes all meanings of both words. Sex is so significant that it has been mythologized as a divine prerogative, too good to be permitted mankind (cf. Gen 3:5). But our blessed Mother Eve filched the forbidden fruit of the Tree of Knowledge of Good and Evil and shared it with her less venturesome mate, thus bestowing the bittersweet blessing and curse of sexuality on humanity and with it the final dread Death.

These twin realities, Love and Death, which haunt every sentient soul, are mentioned together toward the end of the Canticle. The asseveration that "Love is strong as Death," 8:6, must be the climax and immortal message of the Sublime Song. The sepulchral love scene (Plate XII) proposed as the jacket of this volume speaks to this suggestion more eloquently than words.

THE POSITION OF THE SONG OF SONGS IN THE SCRIPTURE

In the Hebrew Bible the Song of Songs is placed among the Writings, *kĕṯûḇîm,* following Job as the first of the Five Scrolls (Song of Songs, Ruth, Lamentations, Ecclesiastes, Esther). This order corresponds to the sequence of their use in the liturgy, the Songs of Songs being read on the eighth day of Passover, Ruth at the Feast of Weeks (Pentecost), Lamentations on the ninth day of Ab (mourning the destruction of the Temple), Ecclesiastes at the Feast of Tabernacles, and Esther at Purim. This order may be a secondary development since the Talmud (Baba Bathra 14b, 15a), some Spanish MSS, and the Massora indicate that the older order was Proverbs, Ecclesiastes, Song of Songs, putting the putative Solomonic compositions together.

CANONICITY

The propriety of inclusion of the Song of Songs in the Canon was apparently questioned from the start and has been vigorously protested in modern times.* Yet it must be said that the evidence for its early acceptance, in spite of the objections, is as well attested as that for any other portion of the Jewish-Christian Scripture. It has been regarded and transmitted as canonical by both the Synagogue and the Church.

Whether the allusion to Solomon's writings in Eccles 47:15b includes the Song of Songs is doubtful; it is probably no more than a poetic allusion to I Kings 5:12. Similarly, Josephus' enumeration of the sacred books (*Against Apion* I 8) does not make clear whether the Song of Songs was counted among the "four books which contain hymns to God and precepts for the conduct of human life." It is, however, included in the list of sacred books in

* Writers on the Song of Songs from the second through the eighteenth centuries may be found in the chronologically ordered BIBLIOGRAPHY II at p. 236; those after 1800, in the alphabetically listed BIBLIOGRAPHY III at p. 252.

the Talmud (Baba Bathra 14) and in the Canon of Melito, Bishop of Sardis, who in the latter part of the second century traveled to Palestine to discover what books were considered canonical there. It was translated into Greek by Aquila between ca. A.D. 90 and 130 and later by Symmachus and Theodotion before the end of the second century.

From rabbinic sources we gather that there was some dissension about the canonicity of the Song of Songs at the council of Yabneh (Jamnia) and that Aqiba took an active part in the controversy. This need not mean, as some scholars (notably Graetz) have supposed, that the book had remained outside the Canon until that time. The issue was not whether the book was included in the Canon, but whether it should have been. The dispute arose in connection with another book attributed to Solomon, viz. Qohelet (Ecclesiastes). Rabbi Judah opined (Mishnah, Yadayim III 5) that the Song of Songs defiles the hands (i.e. is tabu or sacred, hence canonical), but Qohelet does not defile the hands, while Rabbi Jose said that the Song of Songs is disputed. Aqiba, however, said, "Perish the thought! No man of Israel ever disputed about the Song of Songs, that it did not defile the hands. The whole world is not worth the day on which the Song of Songs was given to Israel, for all the Scriptures are holy, but the Song of Songs is the Holy of Holies; if they disagreed, it was only about Qohelet that they disagreed." Rabbi Aqiba's regard for the Song of Songs as the veritable Holy of Holies moved him also to protest what he regarded as its profanation in the "Banquet Houses." "He who trills his voice in chanting the Song of Songs in the banquet house and treats it as a sort of song (*zĕmîr*) has no part in the world to come" (Tosefta, Sanhedrin XII 10). A similar view is expressed elsewhere, anonymously, "He who pronounces a verse of the Song of Songs and makes it a sort of song and pronounces a verse in a banquet house not in its time brings evil to the world" (TB Sanhedrin 101a). We will ponder elsewhere the question of the nature of the usage which Aqiba found objectionable. It is clear that Aqiba must have understood the Song allegorically and we have some samples of his interpretation of selected verses which will be noted in other connections.

THE VERSIONS†

The Septuagint

The Greek translation of the Old Testament, the Septuagint, conventionally designated by the Roman numerals LXX, is the starting point for the history of Jewish interpretation of Scripture. The Pentateuch was translated into

† See BIBLIOGRAPHY I, p. 233.

Greek about 250 B.C., the Prophets about a century later, and "the rest of the books" perhaps another century or more later. It is likely that the Greek translation of the Song of Songs was completed by 100 B.C., probably in Alexandria. The translation strives to render the Hebrew text as literally as possible. What may seem at first glance to be additions are often found to be the result of transpositions of words or phrases which appear elsewhere in the Hebrew text as we now have it. There is no clear evidence that the translator was influenced by the allegorical interpretation which the Synagogue and Church later applied to the text. The translation of the name of the mountain Amana as meaning "faith" in 4:8 is scant basis for assuming allegorical intention.

The Vulgate

The Vulgate Canticum Canticorum was produced by Saint Jerome in a few days in the year 398. His purpose was to render into Latin the *Hebraica veritas,* "the Hebrew truth," to give the sense rather than merely the words. This commendable goal inevitably allowed considerable freedom in judging truth. In places where the Vulgate appears to depart from the Hebrew as we now have it and to be influenced by the Greek, we have to bear in mind that Jerome was working with an unvocalized Hebrew which could be read in different ways. It is clear that Jerome translated a Hebrew text of the Song of Songs very close to the text we now have.

The Peshitta

The translation of the Song of Songs into Syriac was made from the Hebrew text about A.D. 200 apparently in Christian rather than Jewish circles. As with the Vulgate, there are a number of instances where the agreement is with the Greek rather than the Hebrew. Whether this derives from a different Hebrew original or from accommodation to the Greek text is not immediately clear. A critical edition by J. A. Emerton of the Peshitta of the Song of Songs in Syriac was published in 1966.

The Ethiopic

The Ethiopic version of the Song of Songs was based on the LXX rather than on the Hebrew. The Ethiopic text with an English translation is presented by H. C. Gleave, 1951.

The Targum

The Targum to the Song of Songs is a version only in the sense that it is an indirect witness to the Hebrew text which it interprets, but it could hardly be called a translation. The Targum turns the Song into a Haggadah, or Narrative, spanning the history of Israel from the Exodus to the messianic age to come. The Targumist used words and phrases from the Hebrew text as a springboard or launching pad, but it is not always immediately obvious just what it was in the original text that served as the point of departure. Discussion of the ingenious connections between the Hebrew text and the Targum to the Song of Songs would be an interesting exercise, but cannot be undertaken here. Some samples are given in the dissertation by J. L. Miller (1957, 221–257). A translation of the Targum is given with each verse in the NOTES of this commentary, along with a few samples from the Midrash Rabbah and from the Church Fathers and later Christian expositions, to illustrate modes of allegorical interpretation.

THE STATE OF THE TEXT

Some critics have complained of the supposed sorry state of the text of the Canticles. T. K. Cheyne, e.g., opined that "The Song of Songs suffers from many often most unfortunate corruptions of the text; some dislocations of passages have added to the difficulties of the interpreter" (1889, col. 694). It is generally conceded, however, that the text is in excellent state of preservation, particularly as compared with some other pieces of biblical poetry. T. J. Meek suggested (1956, 97) that the poem was kept in tune with the language of the common people, as folks songs and similar compositions usually are, and that this may be another argument in favor of the liturgical interpretation. "In any case, whether secular songs or liturgies accompanying dances and masques, they were kept alive by continual recitation, which accounts for any marks of late style and for the splendid preservation of the text so that the whole book requires remarkably few emendations." Similarly, M. H. Segal suggested (1962, 478) that the poems continued to be recited and sung by the people long after they had been fixed in writing, and thus suffered changes which may be reflected in the present text through interpolations and mutilations introduced by editors and scribes. We know from Rabbi Aqiba's outrage that snatches of the Song were sung in his day in a way which the good rabbi found objectionable. The Song was probably familiar to the common people so that radical changes could not be made by censors, official or self-appointed. Modern emendations of the text have been dictated more by theories of interpretation than by valid grammatical considerations.

Two fragments of the Song of Songs among the manuscripts discovered in Cave 1V at Qumran appear on cursory examination to offer no notable deviations from the MT (cf. M. Burrows, 1958, 145).

THE DATE OF THE BOOK

Opinions on the date of composition of the Song of Songs have not been as numerous or as varied as the theories of interpretation, but they also differ widely. The connection with the name of Solomon in the superscription and elsewhere in the Song (3:7,9,11, 8:11,12) have been taken both as genuine contemporary allusions and as examples of the pseudepigraphic technique of relating late compositions to the names of ancient worthies. Up to the rise of modern criticism in the nineteenth century, the common view among both Jews and Christians ascribed the composition to Solomon, son of David. Some Talmudists, however, assigned the work to Hezekiah, while Qimḥi and a few others attributed it to Isaiah. The traditional ascription to Solomon was held by some modern critics to be supported by internal evidence. The reference to Tirzah in 6:4, the capital of the Northern Kingdom under Jeroboam I and his successors, I Kings 14:17, would not have been set in parallelism with Jerusalem by a poet of either Israel or Judah, it was argued, after the revolt of the Ten Tribes. Thus, the latest possible date was considered to be the outbreak of war between Jeroboam and Abijam ca. 915–913 B.C. (I Kings 15:7). The reference in 6:8 to sixty queens and eighty concubines was put in contrast to the figures of I Kings 11:3, "seven hundred wives, princesses, and three hundred concubines," to show that the Song must have been written early in Solomon's reign before he had fallen into the extravagant excesses of his old age. This argument would appear to be somewhat shaken by the climactic mention of "girls innumerable" in 6:8c. Solomon's penchant for collecting women appears to have been a constant and the statistics are neither precise nor dated. Solomon's literary productivity, I Kings 5:12[4:32E], three thousand similitudes and a thousand and five songs, has also been argued in support of his authorship of the Canticles on the assumption that some of this output would have been preserved. Again, Solomon's interests as a naturalist and a poet in the flora and fauna of his world, I Kings 5:13[4:32E], and the Canticles' profusion of natural imagery and names of plants and animals have been alleged in favor of the traditional view of Solomon's authorship.

Some recent critics, with widely different theories of interpretation, have assigned the book to the Solomonic period, or not long thereafter. Tur-Sinai (1950–51, 356) ascribed the songs essentially to the time of Solomon, interpreting the superscription to mean a song by the poets laureate (*haššay-yārîm*) in the court of Solomon. Thus the song is not by Solomon but about Solomon and by Solomon's court poets.

Similarly, M. H. Segal (1962) assigned the Song to the age of Solomon. The Song, according to Segal, although not the work of Solomon, had a very close association with Solomon and "the whole contents of the Song breathe the particular atmosphere of the Solomonic age with its worldliness, its wealth and its luxury" (p. 481). Some of the tokens of luxury adduced by Segal are: that the damsel, contrary to the isolated picture of her as a vineyard keeper and shepherdess (1:6,8), appears throughout as living in considerable comfort, in a house of cedar and fir (1:17), with walls, windows, and lattices (2:19) and a special room for her mother (3:4); she wears shoes (7:2) and washes her feet before going to bed (5:3); she wears ornaments (1:10), a veil or shawl (5:7) such as worn by the luxurious girls of Jerusalem (Isa 3:23); she uses a great variety of spices and perfumes (1:12–14; 3:6; 5:5); her home is not in the country (7:12), but in a city with walls, broad streets, and night watchmen (3:2–3; 5:7). This city, according to Segal (p. 482) can only be the Jerusalem of Solomon, since no other period will match the various details of the picture. "Only in the age of Solomon could a poet speak of Solomon's curtains as familiar to him as the black tents of Kedar, and of the company of horses in Pharaoh's chariots to serve him as a comparison with the attractions of his beloved (i 5, 9). The horses in Pharaoh's chariots which aroused the poet's admiration must have appeared in Jerusalem on a friendly visit in honour of King Solomon as an escort of the daughter of the Pharaoh, Solomon's queen (I Kings iii 1), or perhaps as a force to conquer the city of Gezer for Solomon (I Kings ix 16). Only a contemporary of Solomon could invite the daughters of Zion to 'go forth and behold king Solomon with the crown wherewith his mother crowned him in the day of his espousals' (iii 11), or to talk to Solomon in person about the produce of his vineyard (viii 12)." Other details adduced by Segal as best fitting the age of Solomon are the armory in David's tower with the thousand shields (iv 4) which recall the gold shields made by Solomon (I Kings x 16–17) and looted by Shishak (I Kings xiv 26); the frequent reference to cedar wood (i 17; iii 9) so plentiful in the days of Solomon (I Kings x 27), and the profusion of perfumes and spices (I Kings x 10). "And when," asked Segal (p. 483), "could a Jerusalem poet have seen 'gold rollers set with beryl,' 'bright ivory overlaid with sapphires,' 'pillars of marble set upon sockets of gold' (v 14–15) except in the days of Solomon when there was a large inflow into Jerusalem of costly metals and precious stones (I Kings ix 28; x 10–11)?"

To these details Segal added the wide topographical horizon of the Song, from Damascus and the peaks of Lebanon in the north to En Gedi in the south, and from the Moabite Heshbon in the east to Mount Carmel in the west (6:5; 4:8; 1:14; 4:1; 7:5,6, etc.) which for a Jerusalem poet best suits the age of Solomon (I Kings 5:1,4). Tirzah, too, as a rival of Jerusalem's beauty (6:4), best suits the age of Solomon before the city disappeared. And lastly, according to Segal, "the whole tone of the Song with its happy youthfulness, its worldliness, its delight in love and in good living and in pleasant things suit best the rein of Solomon, the only really happy reign of an Israelite king, when 'Judah and Israel were many . . . eating and drinking and making merry' (I Kings iv 20). The happiness of the people in that reign, described under the figure of Judah and Israel dwelling 'safely every man under his vine and under his fig tree' (I Kings v 5[iv 25E]), was so rare a thing in the long and mournful story of Israel as to become an ideal for the messianic age (Micah iv 4; Zech iii 10). It is the felicitous reign of King Solomon which must have produced in Israel such a thing of happiness as the Song of Songs" (p. 483).

G. Gerleman also assigned the Song to the age of Solomon, but on grounds quite different from those of Segal. In Gerleman's view the author of the Song shows familiarity with Egyptian graphic arts, especially in those lyrics in which the lovers describe each others physical charms. The models for these descriptions were not from life, according to Gerleman, but from such paintings or sculptures as could be seen in the palace of a pharaoh, painted, polished, inlaid with jewels, gold and silver plated (cf. 5:10), with features more reminiscent of portraits than living people, eyes, e.g., in the shape of doves like those of Egyptian art (1:15, 4:1, 5:12). The bizarre language of the Canticles thus finds its explanation in the art of Egypt (cf. Gerleman, 1962, and his commentary, 1965). The likely period for this influence to have been exercised was in Gerleman's view the age of "Solomonic Humanism" (1965, 76).

Critics who regarded the Song as a polemic against Solomon, an attack on his morals or his ultimately disastrous political policies, set the date close to Solomon's time. C. D. Ginsburg, e.g., who regarded it as a drama celebrating the victory of a humble shepherdess' virtue over Solomon's determined effort to seduce her, placed the date "in the most flourishing age of the Hebrew language, and about the time of Solomon" (p. 125). Leroy Waterman (1948) interpreted the book as a political polemic reflecting the bitterness of the Northern Kingdom against the South following Solomon's death and the rupture of the union.

Interpreters of the Song as a fertility cult liturgy have tended to date it early rather than late. W. Wittekindt (1926), e.g., dated the Song to the reign of Manasseh in the first half of the seventh century B.C. H. Schmökel, however, (1956, 124*f*), was unable to set any approximate date but felt sure that this sort of poetry was not produced in post-exilic Judaism. In view of the development of the sacred marriage in Mesopotamian religion in the third millennium and the close contacts between Mesopotamia and Syria-Palestine, Schmökel felt that acquaintance with the basic mythic material and its dramatization (*kultisch-mimisch Agierung*) in Canaan need not be younger. Nothing stands in the way of the assumption of an "Ur-Hoheslied" in the second millennium in Canaan and indeed the entire mythical content of the Canticle is in the Canaanite rather than the Israelite realm. Thus a pre-Israelite origin may be presumed, with many modifications in the process of syncretism and modification before it was accepted in the Jewish canon.

A number of critics have met the tricky issue of dating the book with the judicious concession that it may be a mixed bag with not all the materials from the same period. Julius Bewer, e.g. (1922, 393), viewed the book as a Jerusalem recension perhaps as late as the third century, but containing older materials of diverse origins, some pre-exilic and from the north. Max Haller (1940, 21–24) adopted a post-exilic date for the writing down of the Songs, but a much earlier date for their composition, before the eighth century. N. K. Gottwald (1962) suggested that 3:6–11 may have been composed for one or more of Solomon's many marriages, even though the book as a whole was "edited" in the fifth century. Roland Murphy (1968, 506) subscribed to a date "after the exile," but conceded that parts may be earlier, such as the reference to Tirzah in 6:4. H. Graetz (1871) devoted some fifty pages (40–91) of his commentary to the question of the date of composition of the Song of Songs which he considered as perhaps the most interesting point. Graetz credited A. Hartmann with having put an end to the Solomonic Splendor as the background of the Song, properly setting the date in the third century B.C., nearly seven centuries later than most previous commentators had done. Graetz proceeded then to detailed consideration of the data with treatments of (1) Aramaisms and Neohebraisms, (2) Persian Linguistic Elements, (3) Greek Linguistic Elements, (4) Greek Customs and Attitudes, (5) Parallels in the Song of Songs and in the Greek Poets. In view of the alleged Greek elements and parallels with the idyls of Theocritus, who was a court poet to Ptolemy Philadephus in Alexandria (284–275 B.C.) and could very well have been known to the nobility of the Palestinian Jews, Graetz narrowed the date for the composition of the Canticles to the latest and most precise yet assigned it—to the period between 230 and 218 B.C.! The great poet thus flourished in the last quarter of the third century. He knew the Greek language, Greek literature, the Greek mores and immoralities, and he wished to neutralize the venom of the incipient decline of morality in Judea with the antidote of a seemingly erotic poem. It dissipated, however, through the abscess of the apostate Hellenists (Graetz, 90*f*).

R. Gordis (1954, 23*f*), opined that most of the songs, being lyrical and without historical allusions, are undatable. There are, however, a few exceptions such as the song which mentions Tirzah (6:4) and thus must predate Omri's building of Samaria as the capital of the Northern Kingdom in 876 B.C., or the verse which uses the Persian word *pardēs* (4:13) and thus can hardly antedate the sixth century. But even this latter inference, Gordis judiciously noted, must be qualified by the consideration that folk songs often undergo changes in the course of time, with later words and expressions inserted into older material. The epithalamium of 3:6–11 Gordis had already appraised as suited to a wedding of great luxury and even national significance best explained by the assumption "that we have here a song composed on the occasion of one of Solomon's marriages to a foreign princess" (p. 20). Thus, according to Gordis, the datable material in the Song spans five centuries, from Solomon's accession to the throne, ca. 960 B.C., to the Persian era. The variations in language and in geographical locales, the change from rustic simplicity in some lyrics to urban sophistication in others, suggested to Gordis different provenance in time and locale for the various songs. The bulk of the material, however, appeared to Gordis to be pre-exilic rather than post-exilic, but the book was redacted in the Persian period, not later than the fifth century.

S. H. Blank in the Prolegomenon to the reissue of Ginsburg's commentaries on the Song of Songs and Coheleth noted (1970, xxviii*f*) that "Except for fragments of a manuscript of the Song found in Qumran (cf. Patrick W. Skehan, [1965, 88]), there is no external evidence of the existence of the book in pre-Christian times." This could also be said of a number of other books of the Hebrew Bible which we are reasonably sure were in existence long before the Qumran Community copied them. The absence of the Book of Esther among the Scriptures of the Qumran sect, we may assume does not mean that the book did not yet exist but rather that the sect did not consider it edifying, as they apparently did the Song of Songs. Blank, without committing himself, concluded his "Considerations Relative to the Origin and Date of the Song of Songs" with reference to the view of the German Spinozist Carl Gebhardt (1931, 19) who compared the Song to the mimed Idyls of Theocritus and suggested the third century B.C. as the date. In this he was anticipated more than a century before by A. T. Hartmann and only a little later by H. Graetz (1871, 41n, and 90*f*). "And this indeed is the tendency among interpreters today," according to Blank.

In the absence of reliable historical evidence within the book for the date of the Song, commentators have invoked linguistic data, and the majority incline to a late post-exilic period. H. L. Ginsberg (1969, 3) whose knowledge of the biblical languages is unsurpassed, asserted that, "The language of the Song of Songs shows that in its present form it is late, perhaps as late as the third century B.C.E." It is important to note Ginsberg's qualification, "in its present form," and to bear in mind Gordis's observation (pp. 23*f*) "that folk songs often undergo many changes with time, so that later words and expressions may well be inserted into such older material." We know from Rabbi Aqiba's protest that verses of the Song were trilled in the Banquet Houses and we may surmise that the singing was from memory rather than from a written text.

W. F. Albright (1963, 1) balanced the striking archaisms, detected by comparison with Ugaritic, against a few Iranian loanwords and concluded that "A date in the fifth-fourth century B.C. for the collection and editing of Canticles thus appears to be certain." According to Albright, there is not a single Greek loanword in Canticles and therefore no evidence of the frequently assumed Hellenistic date. The "archaic survivals" recognized by Albright are authenticated as such by the parallels in the Ugaritic texts which are more than half a millennium earlier than the age of Solomon. Thus the background of the Song is at least a millennium older than the date assigned by Albright for the collection and editing. No matter how late one places the final editorial operations, the antiquity of at least parts of the Songs cannot be doubted in light of the Ugaritic parallels.

The dating game as played with biblical books like Job and the Song of Songs, as well as with many of the Psalms, remains imprecise and the score is difficult to compute. There are grounds for both the oldest and youngest estimates.

The Song of Songs has quite recently (1973) been assigned to the time of Solomon by a distinguished Hebraist, Professor Chaim Rabin of the Hebrew University in Jerusalem. For more than forty years now evidence has been accumulating for some kind of relationship between the cities of the Harrapan civilization of the Indus Valley and lower Mesopotamia during the latter part of the third millennium B.C. and into the second (cf. C. J. Gadd, *PBA*, 1932). Rabin (205) called attention to the few dozen typical Indus culture seals which have been found in various places in Mesopotamia, some of which seem to be local imitations. He suggested that these objects were imported not as knickknacks, but because of their religious symbolism by people who had been impressed by Indus religion. To the examples of Indus type seals in Mesopotamia cited by Rabin (217n2), we may add a dated document from the Yale Babylonian Collection, an unusual seal impression found on an inscribed tablet dated to the tenth year of Gungunum, king of Larsa, in Southern Babylonia, which according to the commonly accepted "middle" chronology would be 1923 B.C. (B. Buchanan, 1967).

Another instance of intercourse between the Indus civilization and Mesopotamia was the importation of monkeys. A Sumerian proverb mentions the monkey of the Great Music House sitting on the garbage-heap (cf. Rabin, 203 and 218n5) and a school text represents a monkey as writing a letter to his mother complaining about the garbage he has to eat. R. D. Barnett ("Monkey Business," 1973) suggests that the idea of monkeys acting like humans may have come to Sumer from India.

Rabin cited a story from the Buddhist Jātakas, the Bāveru Jātaka, which tells of Indian merchants delivering a trained peacock to the kingdom of Bāveru, the bird having been conditioned to scream at the snapping of fingers and to dance at the clapping of hands. Since maritime connection between Mesopotamia and India lapsed after the destruction of the Indus civilization, and since the name Bāveru (i.e. Bābel, Babylon) would hardly have been known in the later period when trade with India went via South Arabia, Rabin concluded that the Jātaka story about the peacock must ultimately date before 2000, an example of the tenacity of Indian tradition (p. 206). Ivory statuettes of peacocks found in Mesopotamia suggest that the birds themselves may also have been imported before 2000 B.C. (cf. W. F. Leemans, 1960, 161, 166), and Rabin (206) wondered whether the selection of monkeys and peacocks for export may not have derived from the Indian tendency to honor guests by presenting them with objects of religious significance. Imports of apes and peacocks are mentioned in connection with Solomon's maritime trade in I Kings 10:22[=II Chron 9:21], the round trip taking three years. The word for "peacocks," *tukkiyyîm,* singular *tukkî,* has since the eighteenth century been explained as a borrowing of the Tamil term for "peacock," *tōkai.* Tamil is a Dravidian language which in ancient times was spoken throughout South India, and is now spoken in the East of South India. Scandinavian scholars claim to have deciphered the script of the Indus culture as representing the Tamil language (cf. Rabin, 208, 218n20). Further evidence of contact with Tamils early in the first millennium B.C. is found in the names of Indian products in Hebrew and in other Semitic languages. In particular Rabin cites the word *'ăhālôṯ* for the spice wood "aloes," Greek *agallochon,* Sanskrit *aghal,* English agal-wood, eagle-wood, or aloes, the fragrant *Aquilaria agallocha* which flourishes in India and Indochina. The Tamil word is *akil,* now pronounced *ahal.* Its use for perfuming clothing and bedding is mentioned in Ps 45:9[8E] and Prov 7:17 and Rabin surmised that the method was one still current in India, the powdered wood being burned on a metal plate and the clothing or bedding held over the plate to absorb the incense. Rabin supposed that it was necessary to have observed this practice in India in order to learn the use of the substance (p. 209). Aloes are mentioned in 4:14 among the aromatics which grace the bride's body. The method of perfuming bedding and clothing by burning powdered aloes beneath them may clarify the puzzling references to columns of smoke, incense, and pedlar's powders in connection with the epiphany of "Solomon's" splendiferous wedding couch ascending from the steppes (3:6–10), bearing it seems (cf. 8:5) the (divine?) bride and her royal mate. Myrrh and frankincense only are mentioned, but "all the pedlar's powders" presumably included the precious aloes from India.

Opportunity to observe Indian usages would have been afforded visitors to India in the nature of the case, since the outward journey from the West had to be made during the summer monsoon and the return trip during the winter monsoon, so that the visitor would have an enforced stay in India of some three months. Repeated visits with such layovers would provide merchant seamen with the opportunity to learn a great deal about local customs, beliefs, and arts.

After a brief critique of modern views about the Song of Songs, none of which has so far found general acceptance, Rabin ventured to propound a new theory based on Israel's commercial contacts with India during Solomon's reign.

There are three features which, in Rabin's view (pp. 210*f*), set the Song of Songs apart from other ancient oriental love poetry. Though occasional traces of these may be found elsewhere, Rabin alleged that they do not recur in the same measure or in this combination:

1. The woman expresses her feelings of love, and appears as the chief person in the Song. Fifty-six verses are clearly put into the woman's mouth as against thirty-six into the man's (omitting debatable cases).
2. The role of nature in the similes of the Song and the constant reference to the phenomena of growth and renewal as the background against which the emotional life of the lovers moves, Rabin regarded as reflecting an attitude toward nature which was achieved in the West only in the eighteenth century.
3. The lover, whether a person or a dream figure, speaks with appropriate masculine aggressiveness, but the dominant note of the woman's utterances is longing. She reaches out for a lover who is remote and who approaches her only in her dreams. She is aware that her longing is sinful and will bring her into contempt (8:1) and in her dream the "watchmen" put her to shame by taking away her mantle (5:7). Ancient eastern love poetry, according to Rabin, generally expresses desire, not longing, and to find parallels one has to go to seventeenth-century Arab poetry and to the troubadours, but even there it is the man who longs and the woman who is unattainable.

These three exceptional features which Rabin attributed to the Song of Songs he found also in another body of ancient poetry, in the Sangam poetry of the Tamils. In three samples, chosen from the *Golden Anthology of Ancient Tamil Literature* by Nalladai R. Balakrishna Mudaliar, Rabin stressed the common theme of women in love expressing longing for the object of their affection, for their betrothed or for men with whom they have fallen in love, sometimes without the men even being aware of their love. The cause of the separation is rarely stated in the poem itself, but this is rooted in the Tamil social system and code of honor in which the man must acquire wealth or glory, or fulfil some duty to his feudal lord or to his people, and thus marriage is delayed. There is conflict between the man's world and the woman's and her desire to have her man with her. This conflict is poignantly expressed in one of the poems cited (Rabin, 212) in which a young woman whose beloved has left her in search of wealth complains:

> I did his manhood wrong by assuming that he would not part from me. Likewise he did my womanhood wrong by thinking that I would not languish at being separated from him. As a result of the tussle between two such great fortitudes of ours, my languishing heart whirls in agony, like suffering caused by the bite of a cobra.

In the Tamil poems the lovelorn maiden speaks to her confidante and discusses her problems with her mother, as the maiden of the Song of Songs appeals to the Jerusalem maids and mentions her mother and her lover's mother; but neither in the Tamil poems nor the Song of Songs is there mention of the maiden's father. In Rabin's view the world of men is represented by "King Solomon," surrounded by his soldiers, afraid of the night (3:7–8), with many wives and concubines (6:8), and engaged in economic enterprises (8:11). Significantly, however, according to Rabin (p. 213), Solomon's values seem to be mentioned only to be refuted or ridiculed: "his military power is worth less than the crown his mother(!) put on him on his wedding day; the queens and concubines have to concede first rank to the heroine of the Song; and she disdainfully tells Solomon (viii 12) to keep his money."

Since the Sangam poetry is the only source of information for the period with which it deals, Rabin plausibly surmised that the recurring theme of young men leaving home to seek fortune and fame, leaving their women to languish, corresponded to reality, i.e. the theme of longing and yearning of the frustrated women grew out of conditions of the society which produced these poems. Accordingly, the cause for the lover's absence need not be explicitly mentioned in the Tamil poems and is only intimated in elaborate symbolic language. Similarly, Rabin finds hints of the non-availability of the lover in the Song of Songs. The references to fleeing shadows in 2:17, 4:6–8, and 8:14 Rabin takes to mean wintertime when the shadows grow long. The invitation to the bride to come from Lebanon, from the peaks of Amana, Senir, and Hermon in 4:6–8 means merely that the lover suggests that she think of him when he traverses those places. The dreamlike quality of these verses need not, in Rabin's view, prevent us from extracting the hard information they contain. The crossing of mountains on which or beyond which are myrrh, incense, and perfumes all lead to South Arabia, the land of myrrh and incense. Thus the young man was absent on a caravan trip. Even though he did not have to traverse Amana or Hermon to reach Jerusalem from any direction, he did have to traverse mountains on the trip and in South Arabia he had to pass mountain roads between steep crags ("cleft mountains") and it was on the slopes of such mountains that the aromatic woods grew ("mountains of perfume"). Coming from South Arabia, however, one had to cross Mount Scopus, "the mountain of those who look out," from which it is possible to see a caravan approaching at a considerable distance. In 3:6 "Who is she that is coming up from the desert, like pillars of smoke, perfumed with myrrh and incense, and all the powders of the perfume merchant?" is taken to refer to the caravan, the unexpressed word for "caravan" *šayyārāh,* being feminine (Rabin, 214 and 219n29). "The dust raised by the caravan rises like smoke from a fire, but the sight of the smoke also raises the association of the scent a caravan spreads around it as it halts in the market and unpacks its wares."

The enigmatic passage 1:7–8 Rabin also related to a camel caravan despite the pastoral terminology. Rabin's theory encounters difficulty with the repeated use of the verb *rʿy,* "pasture," and its participle, "pastor, shepherd" in view of which commentators commonly regard the Song as a pastoral idyl. His solution is to suggest that the term may have some technical meaning connected with the management of camels.

The list of rare and expensive spices in 4:12–14 reads so much like the bill of goods of a South Arabian caravan merchant that Rabin is tempted to believe that the author put it in as a clue.

> Be it what it may, it provides the atmosphere of a period when Indian goods like spikenard, curcuma, and cinnamon, as well as South Arabian goods like incense and myrrh, passed through Judaea in a steady flow of trade. This can hardly relate to the Hellenistic period, when Indian goods were carried by ship and did not pass through Palestine: it sets the Song of Songs squarely in the First Temple period (Rabin, 215).

As for the argument that the Song contains linguistic forms indicating a date in the Hellenistic period, Rabin points out that the alleged Greek origins of *'appiryôn* in 3:9 and *talpiyyôṯ* in 4:4, the former word supposedly related to *phoreion,* "sedan chair," and the later to *telopia,* "looking into the distance," are dubious.

> The phonetic similarity between the Greek and Hebrew words is somewhat vague, and this writer considers both attributions to be unlikely, but even acceptance of these words as Greek does not necessitate a late dating for the Song of Songs, since Mycenaean Greek antedates the Exodus. Neither word occurs elsewhere in the Bible, so that we cannot say whether in Hebrew itself these words were late. In contrast to this, *pardēs* "garden, plantation," occurs, apart from 4:13, only in Nehemiah 2:8, where the Persian king's "keeper of the *pardēs*" delivers wood for building, and in Ecclesiastes 2:5 next to "gardens." The word is generally agreed to be Persian, though the ancient Persian original is not quite clear. If the word is really of Persian origin, it would necessitate post-exilic dating. It seems to me, however, that this word, to which also Greek *paradeisos* belongs, may be of different origin.

In a brief discussion of the argument that certain linguistic features of the Song have been thought to connect it with Mishnaic Hebrew, Rabin concentrates on the subordinating particle *še* which is used throughout the Song, except in the title which is not part of the original work. Noting that this particle also occurs in one of the earliest extant documents of Hebrew, the Song of Deborah, Judg 5:7, Rabin commented that

> It seems to have been current over part of the Hebrew language area, and to have persisted as a form used in familiar language and in dialects, being ousted from the written idiom only with the emergence of the official Classical Hebrew of the time of David and Solomon. Its appearance in the Song of Songs is thus more likely to be a stylistic matter than an indication for dating. Besides, the difference between *asher* and *she-* was well known in later times, and it can hardly be believed that a poet who wanted to give his work the appearance of having been

written in the time of Solomon would have spoiled this by introducing an easily identified word betraying his own speech. It is not impossible, however, that our entire system of linguistic criteria for the dating of Hebrew texts needs revision (p. 216).

Rabin's summation of his view of the Song of Songs is of such interest and significance as to warrant citation of his concluding paragraphs (pp. 216*f*):

It is thus possible to suggest that the Song of Songs was written in the heyday of Judaean trade with South Arabia and beyond (and this may include the lifetime of King Solomon) by someone who had himself travelled to South Arabia and to South India and had there become acquainted with Tamil poetry. He took over one of its recurrent themes, as well as certain stylistic features. The literary form of developing a theme by dialogue could have been familiar to this man from Babylonian-Assyrian sources (where it is frequent) and Egyptian literature (where it is rare). He was thus prepared by his experience for making a decisive departure from the Tamil practice by building what in Sangam poetry were short dialogue poems into a long work, though we may possibly discern in the Song of Songs shorter units more resembling the Tamil pieces. Instead of the vague cases for separation underlying the moods expressed in Tamil poetry, he chose an experience familiar to him and presumably common enough to be recognized by his public, the long absences of young men on commercial expeditions.

I think that so far our theory is justified by the interpretations we have put forward for various details in the text of the Song of Songs. In asking what were the motives and intentions of our author in writing this poem, we must needs move into the sphere of speculation. He might, of course, have been moved by witnessing the suffering of a young woman pining for her lover or husband, and got the idea of writing up this experience by learning that Tamil poets were currently dealing with the same theme. But I think we are ascribing to our author too modern an outlook on literature. In the light of what we know of the intellectual climate of ancient Israel, it is more probable that he had in mind a contribution to religious or wisdom literature, in other words that he planned his work as an allegory for the pining of the people of Israel, or perhaps of the human soul, for God. He saw the erotic longing of the maiden as a simile for the need of man for God. In this he expressed by a different simile a sentiment found, for instance, in Psalm 42:2–4: "Like a hind that craves for brooks of water, so my soul craves for thee, O God. My soul is athirst for God, the living god: when shall I come and show myself before the face of God? My tears are to me instead of food by day and by night, when they say to me day by day: Where is your god?" This religious attitude seems to be typical of those psalms that are now generally ascribed to the First Temple period, and, as far as I am aware, has no clear parallel in the later periods to which the Song of Songs is usually ascribed.

Rabin considered the possibility of moving a step further in speculation about Indian influence.

In Indian legend love of human women for gods, particularly Krishna, is found as a theme. Tamil legend, in particular, has amongst its best known items the story of a young village girl who loved Krishna so much that in her erotic moods she adorned herself for him with the flower-chains prepared for offering to the god's statue. When this was noticed, and she was upbraided by her father, she was taken by Krishna into heaven. Expressions of intensive love for the god are a prominent feature of mediaeval Tamil Shaivite poetry. The use of such themes to express the relation of man to god may thus have been familiar to Indians also in more ancient times, and our hypothetical Judaean poet could have been aware of it. Thus the use of the genre of love poetry of this kind for the expression of religious longing may itself have been borrowed from India.

Rabin's provocative article came to the writer's attention after most of the present study had been written. It is of particular interest in the light of other Indian affinities of the Song adduced elsewhere in this commentary.

THE LANGUAGE

The language of the Song of Songs presents a number of dialectal peculiarities. A striking feature is the use of the relative particle *še* throughout the book, except in the title which is an editorial contribution. No other biblical book consistently uses this particle, although it occurs a number of times elsewhere, e.g. Gen 6:3; Judg 6:17, 7:12, 8:26; II Kings 6:11. It has been frequently taken as a token of late origin, but wrongly so. It occurs in the Song of Deborah, Judg 5:7, one of the oldest pieces of biblical poetry. It is manifestly cognate with the Akkadian form *ša,* but it is also to be equated with the variant orthographic forms of other Semitic dialects, Arabic *ḏū,* Ugaritic *d* and *ḏ,* and Aramaic *dī,* all going back to the troublesome Proto-Semitic interdental *ḏ* which was variously pronounced and spelled. The connection between the spellings with *š, d, ḏ, z* is suggested by the sporadic use of a special symbol in Ugaritic for the interdental which was for a long time assumed to represent *ś* because of the similarity of the form of the symbol with that which represents *š*. The present writer has suggested that the fluctuation in representation of the interdental, however it was pronounced, is involved in the variant spellings of the word for a type of wheat, Arabic *ḏurrat,* which appears in Ugaritic as *drt* but in Isa 28:25 and in the Panammu II inscription is spelled with *š* or *ś* as the representation of the original interdental preserved in the Arabic form of the word (cf. M. H. Pope, 1966, 456). The use of *še* as the relative particle in the Canticle is thus to be correlated not only with Akkadian *ša* but with Ugaritic *d* and *ḏ,* Canaanite *z,* Aramaic *d,* and Arabic *ḏū*. The use of *še* in the Canticle is one of the features generally cited as indicative of the northerly dialectical affinity.

Several details of the language of the Song have been characterized as Aramaisms and adduced as evidence for a late date. It must be remembered, however, that Aramaic is as old as Hebrew and that the dialectology of

Northwest Semitic gets more complicated as our data increase. Ugaritic has a number of features that appear also in later Aramaic. The spelling *nṭr,* instead of the usual Hebrew orthography *nṣr,* in 1:6, 8:11,12, could be regarded as an Aramaism since Aramaic spelled the word with *ṭ*. The matter, however, is complicated by peculiar Ugaritic spelling of this word as *nġr* instead of *nẓr*. In any case, this representation of original *ẓ* by *ṭ* is confined to this word in the Canticle and other instances of original *ẓ* are spelled with *ṣ,* as in Hebrew. The spelling of the word for "cypress" with *t* instead *š* in 1:17 also agrees with the Aramaic orthography, but this also is the only instance in the Canticle where original *ṯ* is represented by *t* rather than *š*. Otherwise, the representation of permuted polyphonous consonants in the Canticle follows regular Canaanite (Hebrew) practice rather than Aramaic.

The vocabulary of the Song of Songs is also unusual in the proportion of words unique or rare elsewhere in Scripture. No other book approaches it in this regard. In the brief span of little more than a hundred verses there are almost fifty hapax legomena and an even greater number of words only rarely found elsewhere in Scripture. Discussions of some of these words will be found in the NOTES and there is little point in merely listing them here. One of them may be singled out for special attention here. The word *kōp̄er* which occurs thrice in the Canticle (1:14, 4:13, 7:12) had been regarded as a loanword *from* Greek, but Meek (*IB,* V, 99) rightly regarded it as a loanword *in* Greek. The occurrence of the word in Ugaritic with reference to the perfume of the goddess Anat takes it out of the category of "late-known" terms, whatever its origin may be. Similarly the verb *'ry* which occurs in 5:1 and elsewhere only in Ps 80:13 is elucidated by the Ugaritic noun *ary,* "sibling," and the meaning of the cognate verb in Arabic, "eat at a common manger." At the same time this connection supplies a plausible etymology for the common biblical word for "lion" and a clue to the hidden wordplay in Samson's riddle, Judg 14:14.

LITERARY CLASSIFICATION

The classification of the Canticle as to literary genre, like almost every other aspect of the book, is a vexed question.

From early times the Song was regarded as dramatic. Origen, in the third century, considered it a nuptial poem in dramatic form. Two of the Greek translations, Codex Sinaiticus of the fourth century, and Codex Alexandrinus of the fifth century, supplied marginal notes to the text indicating the speakers and the persons addressed. The Ethiopic translation divided the book into five parts, perhaps on the assumption that it is a drama in five acts. After the Protestant Reformation, the dramatic hypothesis gained ground.

John Milton, in his treatise *The Reason of Church Government urg'd against Prelatry,* endorsed Origen's view: "The Scripture also affords us a Divine pastoral Drama in the Song of Solomon consisting of two persons, and a double Chorus, as Origen rightly judges." The dramatic theory was elaborated with great imagination and ingenuity in the nineteenth century. The learned and devout Franz Delitzsch developed (1885) the simplest form with two characters and an uncomplicated plot: Solomon saw Shulamith (on this word and its transliterations, see NOTE on 7:1), fell in love with her at first sight, took her from her rural home to his court and by her was lifted from mere physical attraction, to pure love. This simple plot, however, was not wholly convincing since there were those who had trouble supposing that a reputed voluptuary like Solomon could be transformed and raised to the heights of pure love by the beauty and virtue of a rustic maiden. In spite of the alleged dramatic form, Delitzsch did not regard the Song as a theatrical piece.

The two-character hypothesis had extremely limited potential for dramatic movement or development and was eclipsed by the three-character scheme which had been suggested by Ibn Ezra in the twelfth century, revived by Jacobi and Löwisohn in the eighteenth century, and developed by H. Ewald in the nineteenth century. The three-character plot presents a pair of rustic lovers and a royal lecher who tries to get the girl from her shepherd swain. Ginsburg made this plot into a veritable Victorian melodrama celebrating the triumph of true love and virtue over every temptation. Ernest Renan developed a cast of ten characters plus a double chorus, male and female. In the present century, A. Hazan prepared a rendition of the Song in dramatic verse for stage presentation, featuring the Beauty and the Shepherd (La Belle et le Pâtre) with a supporting cast of the king and his favorite harem lady and assorted minor characters (1936).

It has been urged against the dramatic view that drama was unknown in Semitic literature and was not cultivated among the Jews. When Herod built a theatre (Josephus *Antiquities* xv 81), it was regarded as an affront by pious Jews. Liturgy and litany, however, are closely related to drama. S. R. Driver (1910, 444) speaks of the different parts of the Song as "personated by different characters." As for dramatic action, Driver observed that "even the varied gesture and voice of a single reciter might perhaps be sufficient to enable a sympathetic circle of hearers to apprehend its purport."

The grounds for the dramatic view consist of the fact that the book presents speakers and dialogue without introductory statements or transitional directions and that where action or account of speech are given in the third person, as in 3:1*ff*,6*ff*, 5:2*ff*, 8:8*ff*, the narrator appears to be one of the actors. The poet-author nowhere appears. Thus if the book is a unity, and if there is a plot, we have the basic features of drama.

Against the dramatic view is the consideration that there is no general agreement among its exponents as to the number of the *dramatis personae,* the action, nor the assignment of speeches to speakers. A response to this criticism has been (cf. A. Harper, 1907, xix) that if an act of one of Shakespeare's plays were stripped of outward indications of the speakers, attempts to restore them would differ. Proponents of other views of the Song also differ with respect to detail, Harper noted.

Although there is dialogue in the Canticle, much of it appears to be monologue and exponents of dramatic schemes with several characters have to subdivide sections in order to supply bit parts to the cast. As modern analogues to the lyrical monologues of the Canticle, Harper (p. xx) adduced the dramatic lyrics of Robert Browning, in particular "James Lee's Wife" and "In a Gondola," the former featuring a single speaker and the latter several. "In a Gondola" provides the best parallel, according to Harper, with dialogue, monologue, musings, and a historic background which suddenly becomes apparent at the tragic end. Browning supplied indications of the changes of speakers with formulae such as He/She sings/speaks/muses, but even without these the attentive reader would usually be able to identify the speaker. It was, however, in response to complaints about obscurity that Browning furnished notations to some of his poems. Harper (Appendix I, pp. 63–73) placed notations in the margin of his own translation to identify the speakers, e.g. for 1:2–3 "The daughters of Jerusalem addressing or speaking of Solomon"; for 1:4a,b "The Shulammite muses, mentally addressing her absent lover"; the second half of the verse is ascribed to "Daughters of Jerusalem addressing Solomon." Efforts to present the Song as drama generally require a supply of directions and explanations almost equal to the brief text, and still more by way of commentary to try to make the conversation sensible.

Scholars of the highest repute accepted the dramatic view of the Song, as noted by H. H. Rowley (1952, 204*f*) who emphasized that it was adopted by S. R. Driver in *ILOT* which served as the standard English textbook for more than a generation.

The Canticle has been classed as an idyl, in the sense of a composition describing pastoral or bucolic scenes, or any charmingly simple episode or appealing event, like idyls of Theocritus, Bion, or Moschus. There is much in the outdoor atmosphere and pastoral imagery to support this classification. R. G. Moulton (1930, viii) termed the Song a lyric idyl. There are, however, non-pastoral scenes in royal chambers and city streets. It has been objected that it cannot be called an idyl since it is composed of speeches by different persons without connecting narrative (W. E. Adeney, 1895, 5). D. Castelli (1892), however, termed it an idyl in dialogue (cf. Cheyne, 1889, col. 685). Despite idyllic qualities, the classification as such is far from satisfactory. Gebhardt (1931, 17*f*,21) regarded the Song as mime rather than drama, not mere folk poetry, but a work of art best understood in the light of the idyls of Theocritus which were not acted out by a company but either read by different voices or mimed by a single reader with nuances to indicate different characters. Thus it was aural rather than visual play, not "Schau-Spiel," but "Hör-Spiel."

The superscript title of the book plainly presents it as a song, a song par excellence. Ewald (1826) termed it a cantata, a designation which combines both lyric and dramatic features. The term cantata, however, originally designated a metrical narrative set to recitative. The narrative elements of the Song, however, are scattered and sporadic, the longest being 5:2–8, and there is no continuity except in the imagination of those who read between the lines. K. Kohler (1878) characterized the Song as a Jerusalemite operetta, "Ein Jerusalemisches Singspiel." Quite recently the Song has been represented and produced both in book form and on the stage as an oratorio by Calvin Seerveld (1967). This oratorio was twice performed before large audiences in Palos Heights, Illinois, and near Toronto, with a cast representing the Shulamite, Solomon, and the shepherd, with faculty wives as the chorus of harem women. "As preface to the oratorio and in between the rhapsodies, a narration was held which tried to project the spirit of faith in which the Song was being proclaimed" (Seerveld, p. 102).

The characterization of the Song as an anthology is not especially helpful, apart from consideration of the question of the purpose and unifying theme of the collection and whether the poetic posies are arranged in a special way for a special intention. R. Murphy mentioned one professor of Scripture who half-humorously characterized the collection thus: "it is as if one were to reach into a piano bench and come up with a group of songs that have been published together" (1955, 96n7). The refrains sprinkled throughout the Song have been adduced as argument both for unity and compositeness. Even those who regard the Song as a haphazard collection are at least agreed that the subject matter of the poems is love. The crucial question is what kind of love and for what purpose.

PROSODY

The meter of the Songs, as Meek noted (*IB,* V, 97), is predominantly the *qînāh,* i.e. the 3+2 beat, as in 1:9

lĕsûsāṯî́ bĕriḵḇế p̄ar'ṓh	To a mare among Pharaoh's cavalry
dimmîṯî́ḵ ra'yāṯî́	Would I compare you, my darling

The syllable count in this verse is nine for the first line and six for the second. O. Loretz (1971) gives the count of the consonants for each line, which varies from a minimum of six consonants to a maximum of eighteen. In the present instance the consonant count is fourteen and eleven. It will be immediately obvious that the number of consonants is less significant than the syllable count for metrical analysis. Meek noted that occasionally we get a 2+3 line, as in 1:12

'aḏ-šehammélek bimsibbố	While the king was on his couch
nardî́ nā́ṯan rêḥố	My nard yielded its scent.

It will be seen, however, from the syllable count, seven or eight in the first and six in the second line, that the balance is more even than the counting of accents or consonants indicates. Occasionally, according to Meek, we get a 2+2 line and as an example he cited 2:8b. It seems better to look at the whole verse to appreciate the meter which suggests the quick, strong movements of the leaping lover:

qôl dôḏî	Hark my love,
hinnēh-zeh bā'	There he comes
mĕḏallēḡ 'al-hehārîm	Leaping over mountains
mĕqappēṣ 'al-haggĕḇā'ôṯ	Bounding o'er hills.

If one combines the first two lines, then there are seven syllables in each line. It seems better, however, to divide the first part into two short staccato lines in keeping with the saltation.

According to Meek, the only exception to the *qînāh* meter is 1:2–4 which is 3+3, with its variant 3+3+3 in 1:3. Again it will be more instructive to see the lines in transliteration:

		Syllables
1:2a	*yiššāqēnî minnĕšîqôṯ pîhû*	10
b	*kî-ṭôḇîm dôḏeḵā miyyāyin*	9
3a	*lĕrēaḥ šĕmāneḵā ṭôḇîm*	9/8
b	*šemen tûraq šĕmeḵā*	7
c	*'al-kēn 'ălāmôṯ 'ăhēḇûḵā*	9
4a	*moškēnî 'aḥăreḵā nārûṣāh*	10
b	*hĕḇî'anî hammeleḵ ḥăḏārāyw*	10
c	*nāḡîlāh wĕniśmĕḥāh bāḵ*	8
d	*nazkîrāh dôḏeḵā miyyayin*	8
e	*mêšārîm 'ăhēḇûḵā*	7

One has to agree with Meek that each line has three beats, except for the last which contains only two words. The number of syllables, however, varies from seven to ten. This series of ten lines raises the question of stichometry and the arrangement of the lines in series, in distichs and tristichs, or bicola and tricola, and even longer series. Meek observed that "more frequently than in any other book we have a tristich instead of the usual distich," and he cited as examples 1:7a (3+2+3) and 1:8b (3+2+2), with a whole series of tristichs or tricola in 4:9–5:1a. The statement with regard to frequency of tricola is probably true, but needs clarification. Job certainly offers more tricola than does the Song of Songs; but then Job is a much larger book, and the Song of Songs may have more tricola in proportion to its size. Loretz noted (1971, 57*f*) that bicola predominate in the Canticle and he listed 134 bicola to only 24 tricola. The present writer finds only 18 examples of tricola in the Canticle and there is no need to list them since they will be readily recognized as such in the arrangement of the translation. There is no need to argue over a half-dozen tricola, but note that Loretz obtains his first example, 1:5a,c–d, by the dubious device of deleting the apostrophe to the Jerusalem girls in 1:5b. In 4:10a–c both Meek and Loretz find a tricolon, but it seems better to make 4:10a a bicolon of 2+2 beats:

mah-yyāp̄û dôḏayiḵ	How fair your love,
'ăḥôṯî ḵallāh	My sister, bride!

Stanislav Segert (1956) has devoted special attention to the prosody of the Canticle, subsequent to a resurvey of the problem in search of a new solution (1953). Segert, on the basis of content, divided the Song into thirty-two smaller poems and presented four metrical analyses for each of the short units: I Word-meter (Wortmetrik), II and III Accentual meter (Akzentuierende Metrik) according to the systems of Sievers (1901) and Haller (1940), IV Alternating meter (Alternierende Metrik), based on the alternating of long and short or heavy and light syllables, a principle recommended by G. Hölscher in 1920 for application to Psalms, Proverbs, Job, Song of Songs, Lamentations, and Sirach (p. 99). For the analysis according to alternating meter, Segert conceded that it would have been better to give the text in transliteration, or at least to employ schemata, but for economy of space he adduced only numbers. The figures for the first unit, 1:2–4, dubbed "Lied der Braut" (Song of the Bride), are as follows:

		Akzentuierende Metrik		Alternierende
	Wortmetrik	Sievers, 1901	Haller, 1940	Metrik
2:	3+3	3:3	3+3	4, 4
3a:	3	3:	3+2!	4
3b:	3+3	:3, an 2	3+3	3, 3?
4a:	3+3	3:3	3+3	4, 4?
4b:	3+3	3:3	3+3	4, 4
4c:	2	2	dl	3/4

It will be seen at a glance, as Segert noted (1956, 287), that the regular verse structure for the first three columns is double threes and for the alternating meter double fours. For a better view of what the figures represent, we give the verses in syllables with the chief accents marked

2 *yiš-šā-qḗ-nî min-nĕ-šî-qốṯ pî́-hû kî-ṭô-ḇî́m dô-ḏé-ḵā miy-yá-yin*

3a *lĕ-rḗ-aḥ šĕ-mā-né-ḵā ṭô-ḇî́m*

3b *šé-men tû-ráq šĕ-mé-ḵā 'al-kḗn 'ă-lā-mốṯ 'ă-hē-ḇû́-ḵā*

4a *moš-ḵḗ-nî 'a-ḥă-rḗ-ḵā nā-rū́-ṣāh hĕ-bî-'ā́-nî ham-mḗ-leḵ ḥa-ḏā-rā́yw*

4b *nā-ḡî-lāh wĕ-niś-mĕ-hā́h bā́k naz-kî-rāh dô-ḏḗ-ḵā miy-yā́-yin*

4c *mē-šā-rī́m 'ă-hē-ḇū́-ḵā*

The remaining thirty-one poems present a similar picture, with mostly double threes in the word and accent lists, but with greater irregularity in the alternating meter. The interested reader may study Segert's figures, but it does not seem expedient to repeat them here or to juxtapose a transliteration of the text or a schematization which would make the figures more meaningful. It is clear that further investigation of biblical prosody is needed.

LITERARY INTEGRITY

The question of literary unity or integrity is bound up with the problems of form and purpose of the book and on all these points there has been and remains a wide variation of opinion. The conventional division into eight chapters of somewhat uneven length was perhaps based on some vague notions of transition, but, as with other books, is useful only for text reference. The notion that the Songs were intended to be sung during the seven days of marriage celebrations, proposed by Bossuet (Prefatio, in *Canticum Canticorum,* 1683) dictated a sevenfold division, but this has been generally regarded as much too small a number of songs. A fifteenth-century poetic paraphrase in Middle High German divided the book into forty-four parts, using the Vulgate incipits as headings. The poet and critic J. G. von Herder (d. 1803) called attention to this interesting work and printed it as a supplement to his essay on the Song of Songs as "vier und vierzig alten Minneliedern," but in his own treatment Herder reduced the subdivisions by more than half, finding an even score of songs.

The Dramatic Theory of interpretation necessarily assumes a basic unity, but each producer or director in this *Spiel* is free to introduce as many acts, scenes, actors, and speeches as fancy may dictate. Delitzsch, e.g., divided the Song into six two-scene acts, with two main characters, Solomon and Shulamith. Ginsburg, Harper, W. W. Cannon, Waterman, and others introduced a third main character, the maiden's rustic lover whom Waterman dubbed Dodai. Cannon divided the "Dramatic Poem" (1913) into thirteen lyrics. K. Budde (1894a, 70,72,74), although relating the songs to the wedding week, judged that the collection had been handed down without designation of sources or distinction of separate songs and that a redactor thinking he had a whole work before him, rather than a collection, put it all together. The uniformity of speech and style was attributable to uniformity of place, time, and occasion, rather than unity of authorship. Paul Haupt regarded the Canticles as "simply a collection of popular love-ditties, and these erotic songs are not at all complete . . . neither are they given in their proper order." Haupt cited Goethe's characterization of the Canticles as the most tender and inimitable expression of passionate yet graceful love that has yet come down to us, but which, unfortunately, cannot be fully enjoyed because they are fragmentary, telescoped or driven into one another, and mixed up (1902b, 205*f*). Haupt "thought repeatedly of selecting and arranging something out of this charming confusion, but this enigmatic and inextricable condition invests those few leaves with a peculiar charm. Many a time well-meaning methodical minds have been tempted to find or establish an intelligible connection, but a subsequent student must do the work all over again." While admitting the impossibility of recovering the original songs or retracing the plan of the collector, Haupt could not resist the temptation to rearrange and "improve" the Received Text with the object of restoring the individual songs rather than the restoration of the sequence of the original collection. "It makes very little difference in what order the various songs follow each other." Haupt supposed that the "charming confusion" of the Received Text may have been the result of a desire to make certain passages less objectionable. By way of example, Haupt suggested that in the present sequence of 4:16b and 5:1 the erotic imagery is not plain; but if 7:12–14 and 6:11 be inserted between and then 5:1 followed by 6:2, "the erotic allusions can hardly be misunderstood." Haupt was obviously concerned lest the unimaginative reader miss some of the erotic allusions and for this interest he has been frequently criticized by interpreters anxious to spiritualize the songs.

M. Jastrow, Jr. regarded the book as an anthology of folk songs from different times and places and he isolated twenty-three lyrics and some fragments. Jastrow detected "evidence of and endeavor on the part of editors to connect the songs by taking a 'refrain' from one poem where it is in place and transferring it to another." Accordingly, Jastrow considered it "within the range of possibility that a more or less definite scheme was followed in the sequence of the poems." If one seeks hard enough, Jastrow conceded, some associations of ideas may be detected to explain the sequence,

> but such possible associations do not suffice to outweigh the fact that for the arrangement as a whole no guiding principle can be found which will satisfactorily explain the order. It seems more natural to assume that the collection represents a natural growth. One compiler began the process by putting together some songs that had attained wide popularity, others followed by adding their favorites, and so in the course of time the little anthology arose (1921, 137).

N. Schmidt (1911, 230*ff*) isolated nineteen poems from the same author, setting aside later additions and interpolations. Israel Bettan (1950, 10) reduced the number of songs to eighteen.

Gordis (1954, 16–18,24) regarded the book as a collection of twenty-eight love poems dating from the time of Solomon to the Persian period. O. Eissfeldt found some twenty-five profane love and wedding songs for which "a principle of arrangement is only observable here and there, for sometimes the order seems to be based on catchwords" (1965, 485,489*f*).

Franz Landsberger (1954) agreed with those who see in the Song of Songs "not a connected whole, but a collection of several poems" (p. 203). With regard to the number of poems, Landsberger regarded Eissfeldt's "estimate of about 25 songs" as erroneous and suggested that the number is "far, far greater." Most of these are short epigrams (p. 212).

There certainly are some of considerable length: the two dream poems, or the repeated and detailed descriptions of the man or maid. But apart from that, short and very short poems abound. It appears that the reader of those days quite particularly valued the latter, just as—to choose a simile from the Song of Songs—the lover is delighted with as much as one bead from the beloved's necklace (p. 216).

Segal (1962, 477*f*) found the book to be

a collection of love poetry of varied character, love poems addressed by the lovers to each other, love poems spoken by the lovers in the hearing of an audience, duplicate poems and fragments of love poems and of extraneous material, . . . The collector made . . . a brave effort to arrange his varied material in a methodical fashion, placing some of his material at the beginning and some at the conclusion of his main work. And in the main body itself he seems to have divided his poems into two groups, placing first the group which contained the earlier version of poems and which culminated in the consumation of the love (1:9 – 5:2), and then the group which contained the later version of poems (5:2*ff*).

The material, in Segal's opinion, was drawn from oral rather than written sources and in the course of generations of oral transmission "the poems were subject to changes and adaptations until they all assumed a more or less uniform style and language." Later editors and scribes introduced changes, interpolations, and mutilations.

Proponents of varieties of the Cultic Theory of interpretation also differ among themselves as to the structural integrity of the Song. According to Meek (*IB,* V, 96*f*), "No serious scholar today believes that Solomon was the author, and there are few who believe that the book was the work of a single hand. It is too repetitious for that and too disorderly in its content." The disorderliness from Wittekindt's point of view (1926) is seen at a glance from the key to his treatment of various passages (Stellenverzeichnis) in which the first verse is treated on p. 212 and the last on p. 73. The Canticle Wittekindt saw as a syncretistic torrent from a variety of springs from different cult areas, Canaanite, Byblian, and Babylonian (p. 192).

Schmökel (1956, 42) assumed that the original structure of the Canticle as the liturgy for a Sacred Marriage, sometime, somewhere in Israelite Palestine, had been deliberately destroyed. In keeping with this theory Schmökel reconstituted the text as a ritual drama in three scenes (pp. 45*ff*):

SCENE ONE

"Appear, O Goddess"	(Men's chorus)	8:13
Inquiry about Goddess' Nature	(Women's chorus)	6:10,5a
Ishtar's Answer	(Priestess)	1:5–6
Question about the Haunt of the Beloved	(Women's chorus)	6:1
Response of the Goddess	(Priestess)	6:2
Appearance of Goddess after Spring	(Priestess)	6:11–12
The Trip to the Netherworld	(Priestess)	3:1–2, 5:7, 3:4
Yearning Dream	(Priestess)	5:2–6, 3:3, 5:8
Question of the Chorus about the Nature of the Beloved	(Women's chorus)	5:9
Descriptive Song	(Priestess)	5:10–16
Request of the Goddess for a Tryst	(Priestess)	1:7
Choral Response	(Men's chorus)	1:8
Yearning of the Goddess	(Priestess)	8:1–2

SCENE TWO

Reception Song	(Priestess and Women's chorus)	4:8
Choral Query at Epiphany of the Divine Pair	(Chorus)	8:59
Response of the Goddess:	(Priestess)	8:5b–7
Praise of Love		
1. Wooing Song of the Beloved	(Priest)	7:7–10
2. Wooing Song of the Beloved	(Priest)	2:10b–14
Response of the Goddess	(Priestess)	2:17
"Seduction Call"		
1. Song of Praise about the Beloved (Female)	(Priest)	4:9–11
Responsorium, Adjuration of Love	(Priestess and Women's chorus)	2:16
2. Song of Praise about the Beloved (Female)	(Priest)	6:4,5b–9
Responsorium	(Priestess and Women's chorus)	6:3
3. Song of Praise about the Beloved (female)	(Priest)	4:1–5,7
Responsorium	(Priestess and Women's chorus)	7:11

SCENE THREE

Hymns at the Entry of Tammuz as Royal Bridegroom	(Women's chorus)	3:6–11

Dance Song	(Men's chorus)	7:1–6
Three Love Conversations during the Symposium	(Priest and Priestess)	1:9–14, 2:1–3, 4:12–6
At the Entry of Tammuz into the Bridal Chamber	(Priestess)	2:8–9
1. Wedding Song	(Priestess)	7:12–14
Responsorium (Adjuration)	(Women's chorus)	2:6–7
2. Wedding Song	(Priestess)	1:2–4
Responsorium	(Women's chorus)	3:5
3. Wedding Song	(Priestess)	2:4–5
Responsorium	(Women's chorus)	8:3–4
4. Wedding Song	(Priestess and chorus)	1:16–17

Schmökel commented on the text according to the scheme above.

In opposition to the view that the Canticles are a haphazard collection of love songs, there have been concerted efforts to find methodological principles for determining the structure and poetic divisions of the Song. D. Buzy (1940b; 1947) seized on the use of initial and final themes to isolate seven poems, each of which begins with the theme of desire and ends with the fulfillment of the desire in mutual possession of the lovers. Within the poems there is progression, from desire to the realization of desire, but no progression from poem to poem. (Criticism by R. Murphy, 1949, 385*f*,n14.) A. Robert accepted the pattern of initial and final refrains as discerned by Buzy and found the leitmotiv in the refrain of 2:7, 3:5, and 8:4. Robert, moreover, discerned constant progression in the Song consisting of five poems and the dénouement, the last six verses being appendixes (cf. A. Robert and R. Tournay in RTF, 18*ff*). Their Tableau Analytique (pp. 56*f*) presented the following scheme:

Title	(1:1)
Prologue: The exilee calls the Absent One	(1:2–4)
First poem	(1:5–2:7)
The Bride	(1:5–7)
in the ordeal she retains her charms	(1:5–6)
she is anxious to know if she will be able to find the Absent One	(1:7)
Response of the Chorus	(1:8)
The Groom formulates some promises	(1:9–11)
The dialogue of the spouses	(1:12–2:5)
Is the union restored?	(2:6)
No, the Bride sleeps	(2:7)
Second Poem	(2:8–3:3)
The Bride sought by the Beloved	(2:8–16)
She sets out in quest of the Beloved	(2:17–3:3)
Is the union restored?	(3:4)
No, the Bride sleeps	(3:5)

Third Poem (3:6–5:1)
  Triumphal return of the exiles and the messianic advent (3:6–11)
  The Groom describes the charms of the Beloved (4:1–8)
  New admiring description (4:9–15)
  She addresses her invitation to the Groom (4:16)
  Is the union restored? (5:1)

Fourth Poem (5:2–6:3)
  The Bride:
    How she hesitated to open the door to the Beloved (5:2–5)
    How she hastened to the search (5:6–8)
  Solicited by the Chorus, she describes the beauty of the Beloved (5:9–16)
  New question of the Chorus (6:1)
  The Bride sees the union realized (6:2–3)

Fifth Poem (6:4–8:5)
  Monologue of the Groom:
    he details anew the charms of the Beloved (6:4–12)
  The Chorus invites the Beloved to come back (7:1a)
  The Groom begins to speak:
    he sees her come back (7:1b)
    he contemplates her beauty (7:2–6)
    his passionate desires (7:7–10)
  The Bride:
    her reciprocal protestation (7:10b–14)
    the messianic vow (8:4)
    could this be at last the mutual possession? (8:3)
  The Groom:
    it depends on no one but her (8:4)
  The Chorus announces the return from exile (8:5a)
 The dénouement (8:5b–7)
  The Groom himself awakens her (8:5b)
  He makes a final request (8:6–7a)
  Aphorisms of a sage (8:7b)
 Appendices (8:8–14)
  Two epigrams (8:8–12)
    Useless precaution (8:8–10)
    The two Solomons (8:11–12)
  Last additions (8:13–14)
    Prayer to Wisdom (8:13)
    Response to Wisdom (8:14)

J. Angénieux in a series of articles (1965, 1966, 1968) faulted the method of Buzy and Robert who based their analyses on the presumed sense of the Song and came out with differing divisions because their views of the sense differed. Angénieux endeavored to base his analysis on form rather than sense and arrived at a classification of the refrains under five types: (1) The refrain of the embrace, found twice in identical terms 2:6 and 8:3. (2) The refrain of possession, found twice in 2:16 and 6:3, in the last instance with inversion of the two members of the first stich. (3) The refrain of movement, twice, in identical terms, in 2:7, 3:5, and 8:4. (4) and (5) secondary refrains, of house and of beauty, are found four times each, the house in 1:4, 2:4, 3:4, and 8:2, beauty in 1:15, 4:1, 4:7, 7:7. The refrains of movement and awakening are initial refrains, those of embracing and possession are final. The alternation of these initial and final refrains in Angénieux's analysis delineates eight poems or songs, with some juggling of the Received Text. This scheme is presented in a series of charts too complex to be summarized or reproduced here.

J. C. Exum (1973) acknowledged the importance of Angénieux's work for "the use of form as a guide to meaning and the establishment of methodological principles for the poetic division of the Song," but she regarded it as "extremely unfortunate that in rigid application of his method, Angénieux distorts the text almost beyond recognition" (p. 48). Her method in analysis of the structure of the Song was to attempt "the isolation of the poetic units, the examination of the form and stylistic characteristics of each poem, and the establishment of parallels among the poems. The criteria used to determine the limits of the poems, are the repetition of key phrases, words, and motifs, and the contextual coherence of the poems" (p. 49). Exum's analysis proceeded from the discovery that 2:7 – 3:5 and 5:2 – 6:3 are "carefully constructed parallel poems." On this basis, the search was made for structural parallels in other units within the Song. The result was the discernment of other pairs of parallel poems:

2:7 – 3:5 // 5:2 – 6:3
3:6 – 5:1 // 6:4 – 8:3
1:2 – 2:6 // 8:4–14

Thus the Song was found to consist of six poems, the first and the last forming an inclusio within which the others occur in the order A B A′ B′, thus:

I	1:2 – 2:6 containing (A) 1:2–11 and (B) 1:12 – 2:6, 2:1–6 being a transitional element
II	2:7 – 3:5
III	3:6 – 5:1, containing (A′) 4:10 – 5:1, which also serves as a transitional element
IV	5:2 – 6:3
V	6:4 – 8:3, containing (B′) 7:7 – 8:3
VI	8:4–14

"Since the proper articulation of form serves as an indication of the proper understanding of meaning," the results of this analysis, Exum affirmed, "will have implications for the interpretation of the Song of Songs in general" (p. 78). Without attempting to apply these results immediately to the exegetical problems of the Song, two conclusions were alleged to follow from this structural analysis: "a unity of authorship with an intentional design, and a sophistication of poetic style" (p. 78). The structure thus delineated "proves untenable the theory that the Song is an anthology or collection" (p. 78). Further, this analysis has implications for the dramatic theory which assumes a basic unity in the Song but meets criticism for the need to supply speakers, scenes, and plots. This analysis "argues against the division of the poems on the basis of scenes and speakers and in favor of isolation of poetic units guided by stylistic considerations" (p. 79). Dialogue here does not serve as a key to structure, but structure may serve as a key to dialogue. Despite the limited scope of the investigation, the author felt that indications were given that the artistry of the Song is even more intricate than indicated and that further study will be required "to relate the intricate workings of the poet's style to the problems of the over-all interpretation and exegesis of the Song" (p. 79). The present writer will have to reserve judgment on the exegetical implications of this mode of structural analysis, pending further study. Even if it proves to be well based, exegetical ingenuity, of which the Song has seen more than any other opus of comparable size, will be able to turn it to a variety of uses in support of different interpretations.

The study by R. Kessler (1957) has unfortunately been overlooked in recent treatments of the structure of the Song of Songs. This study was originally part of a projected book, but the author died before the work could be published. The study explored various types of repetition in the Song, reiterated sound sequences, rhyme, alliteration and paronomasia, and in particular those peculiar repetitions of whole phrases and even whole verses and groups of verses which have puzzled every student of the Song. In Kessler's view, they were not to be highly regarded as a means of poetical expression, but were appreciated as indicative of structural peculiarities, revealing the craftmanship behind the Song's poetry.

Kessler's study of the love epithets of the Song and their distribution reveals an interesting fact that might have otherwise passed unnoticed. The epithets used of the male are:

1) *dôḏî* (my beloved one): 1:13,14,16, 2:3,8,9,10,16,17, 4:16, 5:2,4,5,6(twice), 8,10,16, 6:2,3(twice), 7:10,11,12,14, 8:14. In 5:9, 6:1, and 8:5 the "Daughters of Jerusalem" use the same epithet with appropriate change of suffixes.
2) *rēʿî* (my friend): 5:16.
3) *še 'ahăḇāh napšî* (Whom my soul loves): 1:7, 3:1,2,3,4 (cf. *Odyssey* IV 71).

The epithets directed to, or used about, the female are:

4) *hayyāp̄āh bannāšîm* (fairest among women): 1:8, 5:9, 6:1.
5) *raʿyāṯî* (my beloved one): 1:9,15, 2:10,13, 4:1,7, 5:2, 6:4.
6) *yāp̄āṯî* (my fair one): 12:10,13.

7) *yônāṯî* (my dove): 2:14, 5:2, 6:9.
8) *'ăḥôṯî* (my sister): 4:9,10,12, 5:1,2.
9) *kallāh* (Bride): 4:8,9,10,11,12, 5:1.
10) *tammāṯî* (my perfect one/my spotless one): 5:2, 6:9.
11) *haššûlāmmîṯ* (Maid of Shulem): twice in 7:1. This, according to Kessler, is not really a pet-name, though it is used almost as if it were.
12) *bāṯ-nāḏîḇ* (daughter of a prince/noble maiden): 8:2.

In 2:7, 3:7 *'ahăḇāh* (love) is translated as a pet-name by some commentators and so would belong to the second group.

After a discussion in some detail of the distribution and gaps in the use of the various love-epithets, Kessler was unable to detect any rules or principles governing their use, but suggested that

The fact of their being crowded in certain parts and scarce in others, the prevalence of some of them in one chapter to the exclusion of all others, and their absence in all or most of the remaining chapters, cannot fail to create the impression of irregularity or lack of system, . . . This phenomenon can best be explained by the assumption of more or less loosely connected poems of different origin having been joined together into one book; in other words by the compilation theory. . . . All things considered, the way the love-epithets are used in the Song appears as a strong argument against the unity theory (pp. 8*f*).

A study of the comparisons (pp. 9–13) provided an additional argument in favor of the compilation theory. Some twenty-five pages were devoted by Kessler to Repetitions of Sound Combinations, Alliterations, and Rhymes in Ancient Hebrew Poetry, with a schematic listing of these features in the Song of Songs. Not surprisingly, "it seems that the Song is particularly rich in sequences of sound-combinations." These are spread rather evenly over the eight chapters. "Some kind of blank occurs only within the comparatively small space of chapter v which, as a compensation, so to speak, is distinguished by alliteration and rhyme." The rather uniform distribution of sound sequences cannot, however, be taken as an argument in favor of unity of authorship, according to Kessler (p. 36).

Of special interest are the sections of Kessler's study on "Repetition of Phrases in the Song and its Four Parts" (pp. 38–50) and "Repetitive Parallelism in the Song" (pp. 50–60). On the question of the major divisions of the Song, "the major incision exists behind verse v 1" (p. 42) which divides the Song into two almost equal halves. The Song, however, according to Kessler,

seems to consist not of two parts only, but of four. This is strongly suggested by the very fact that there are four love-dreams with four adjurations at their ends, although there is no intrinsic necessity for this multiplicity. And apart from the three eulogies in praise of a girl or woman (iv 1–7, vi 4–7, and vii 2–7) there may have existed also a fourth eulogy, now lost, commencing with verse i 15: "Behold thou art fair, my love, behold thou art fair, thine eyes are doves," for these words are exactly the same as those introducing eulogy iv 1–7 (p. 43).

Similarly, Kessler pointed out, v *2ff* has a parallel in iii *1ff* and the last verse of the Song has its counterpart in ii 17. Thus Kessler arrived at the fourfold division:

i 2	//	ii 17
iii 1	//	v 1
v 2	//	vii 1
vii 2	//	viii 14

Each division comprises roughly two chapters and has a nearly equal number of verses (33, 28, 28, and 27 verses respectively). Having established the quarterly division, Kessler reverted to the instances of "distant repetitions" which were the starting point of his analysis. Fifteen instances were noted, a few of which are attested in triplicate:

1) thy caresses are better than wine (1:2 and 4:10).
2) behold thou art fair, my love, behold thou art fair, thine eyes are doves (1:15 and 4:1).
3) I am sick with love (2:5 and 5:8).
4) his left hand under my head and his right hand embraces me (3:6 and 8:3, both being part of the day-reveries).
5) I adjure you, Daughters of Jerusalem, by the gazelles or by the hinds of the field (not to rouse and not to stir up the beloved until she pleases) (2:7, 3:5, 5:8, and 8:4, all four being conclusions of love-dreams).
6) voice of my beloved (2:8 and 5:2).
7) my beloved is mine and I am his who feeds (his flock) among the lilies (or roses) (2:16 and 6:3) and similarly "I am my beloved's" (7:11).
8) until the day breathes forth and the shadows flee away (2:17 and 4:6).
9) be like a gazelle or a young hart upon mountains of spice (Bether) (2:17 and 8:14).
10) I sought him but I found him not. The watchmen that go about the city found me (3:*2ff* and 5:*6ff*, both being part of the night dreams).
11) to my mother's house (3:4 and 8:2).
12) Who is she, coming up from the country . . . ? (3:6 and 8:5) and similarly "Who is she who looks forth as the dawn . . . ?" (6:10).
13) Thy hair is like a flock of goats that come down from Gilead. Thy teeth are like a flock of shorn (mother) sheep which have come up from the washing; whereof every one has twins and none is barren among them. . . . Thy temples are like a piece of pomegranate behind thy veil (4:1b–2 and 3b and 6:5b–7).
14) Thy two breasts are like twin fawns of the gazelle (4:5 and 7:4).
15) . . . see whether the vine has budded . . . and the pomegranates are in flower (6:11 and 7:13).

The list shows that if a phrase or sentence is repeated, either literally or with variation, the repetition is never found in the section where the phrase or sentence first occurred, but always in another part. In the effort to explain these "distant" parallels, an analogy was drawn with the repetitions in the different divisions of the Psalter, and the possibility was broached that the four parts of the Song might represent originally independent collections later merged. But the difference was not overlooked that the major repetitions of the Psalter are rather extensive, once a whole Psalm, in other cases groups of many verses, while in the Song the repetitions are brief, a few verses, a single verse, or only a few words. Further, since the Song's four parts are so short, it would be difficult to regard them as originally separate collections. The brevity of the parts, Kessler suggested, might be due to

> extensive, even ruthless expurgation; only a diminutive bit, a skeleton as it were, of the original volume may have been spared. . . . Another explanation of the curious distribution of the "distant" repetitions could be that the redactors who gave the Song its final shape may have inserted some of them, above all the love-dreams with their adjurations, for reasons of symmetry or to make the Song conform to allegorical interpretation which was in almost general use for many centuries. Unmistakable similarities of arrangement, especially of parts two and three, may betray some purposeful hand (p. 49).

"The impression of artificiality is enhanced," Kessler suggested,

> if, dismissing for a moment the idea of the Song's comprising four amalgamations or simply four parts, we cut it up, somewhat arbitrarily, in four two-chapter pieces, combining each odd-number chapter with the following even-number chapter. Still, we would be confronted with the phenomenon that phrases or verses appearing in one of these two-chapter pieces would never be repeated in the same, but always in another two-chapter piece. It almost looks as if somebody would have (*sic*) sprinkled repetitions throughout the Song in a planned way.

Kessler was unable to offer any reasonable solution to this puzzle and had to content himself "with a mere exposition of facts and phenomena" (p. 49).

The similarities and also the differences between the analyses of Kessler and Exum are striking. The two have been cited at some length to highlight the point that efforts to deal with biblical poetry without recourse to the Ugaritic mythological texts are futile. The Ugaritic mythological texts are replete with clichés, which could be regarded as refrains or distant repetitions analogous to the phenomena which are seized by analysts of the structure of Canticles as evidence of literary unity or compositeness. The significance of Ugaritic parallel passages was signaled long ago by Franz Rosenthal (1939), but both Ugaritologists and biblical scholars still have not given adequate attention to the varieties and ramifications of the parallels within the Ugaritic texts and the implications and applications with respect to biblical poetry. Here it should suffice simply to cite some examples from a single Ugaritic hymn which deals with fertility rites and divine marriage. The poem often called "The Birth of the Beautiful Gods" (23[52]) presents in the lines 1 and 23 the refrain "I invoke the beautiful gods," in lines 13 and 28 "the field is the field of the gods, the field Asherah-and-Raḥmay," in lines 24 and 59 "suckers of the nipple of the breast of Asherah/the Lady." In lines 24 and 59 the designation of the gods as "suckers of the nipple of the breast of Asherah/the Lady," while not a refrain, would qualify as an example of "distant" repetition of the sort Kessler noted in Canticles. When the distance is reduced we have what is called "repetitive parallelism" which is a feature common to the Canticle and the Ugaritic hymn cited.

The distinctive feature of repetitive parallelism common to early Hebrew poetry and Ugaritic poetry was first appreciated by W. F. Albright, who generalized that it was "most popular in Israelite literature during the thirteenth and twelfth centuries B.C. and that it rapidly lost ground thereafter, being abandoned entirely by the tenth century, except where older Canaanite poems were adapted to Israelite purposes and where single poetic passages or lines were re-used in archaizing verse" (1949, 232). Some samples from early Hebrew poetry will illustrate. The Song of the Sea, Exod 15:6,

Your right hand, O Yahweh, is glorious in power,
Your right hand, O Yahweh, smashed the foe.

The Song of Deborah, Judg 5:7,

The warriors grew plump
In Israel they grew plump again
Because you arose, O Deborah,
Because you arose, a mother in Israel!

and 5:21:

The Wadi Qishon swept them away
The Wadi overwhelmed them—the Wadi Qishon.

(As translated by R. G. Boling in AB 6A; see NOTES ad loc.)

Ps 92:9,

Behold, your enemies, O Yahweh,
Behold, your enemies shall perish,
All evil doers shall be scattered.

A notable parallel for this latter instance occurs in Ugaritic (2:4[68].9–10):

Behold, your enemies, O Baal,
Behold, your enemies you will smite.
You will take your eternal kingship,
Your dominion of generations.

A number of examples of such repetitive parallelism occur in the Canticle.

Indeed you are fair, my darling,
Indeed you are fair.
Your eyes are doves. 1:15

What is your beloved above another,
O fairest of women,
What is your beloved above another,
That you thus adjure us? 5:9

Unique is my dove, my perfect one,
Unique she to her mother,
Favorite of her parent. 6:9

Leap, leap, O Shulamite!
Leap, leap, and let us gaze on you. 7:1

Under the apple tree I aroused you;
There your mother conceived you,
There she who bore you conceived. 8:5c,d,e

An extended series of repetitive parallels occurs in 4:8*ff*.

Come from Lebanon, bride,
Come from Lebanon, come.
Come from the peak of Amana
From the peak of Senir and Hermon,
From the lions' dens,
From the panthers' lairs.

You ravish my mind, my sister, bride,
You ravish my mind, with one of your eyes,

How fair your love,
My sister, bride.
Sweeter your love than wine . . .

Similar series of repetitive parallelisms occur in the Ugaritic poem "The Beautiful Gods" (23[52].32*ff*),

Now they cry, "Daddy, daddy,"
Now they cry, "Mama, mama."

Long is El's "hand" as the sea,
The "hand" of El as the flood.

Long is El's "hand" as the sea,
The "hand" of El as the flood.

Repetitive parallelism is manifestly an archaic literary feature which is also found in Sumerian poetry, e.g.,

He met me, he met me, The lord Kulianna met me, etc.

The feature could of course be very late since it continues in use to the present day as a catchy lyrical device.

I dropped it, I dropped it, I dropped my yellow basket.

O. Loretz also considered the problem of the refrains of the Canticle in connection with the history of redaction of the work and the question whether they were bound with the individual songs before the collection or were inserted by the redactor for breaking up (Auflockering) or knitting together (Verknüpfung) of the Songs (1971, 60). Loretz listed eight refrains and showed their distribution within the Canticle in tabular form.

The refrains, Loretz observed, could be varied or combined with others and are not bound to any rigid scheme. The similar situation with Ugaritic clichés, refrains, or parallels was noted. In no case did it seem to Loretz that the redactor attempted by means of the refrain to give any special interpretation to a poem or to the collection as a whole; this element of the Songs was apparently taken over by the redactor as found.

Some of the glosses which Loretz detected in the Canticle could be regarded as cross references to other passages, e.g.

1:15 [=4:1]	6:4 [=6:10]
2:9 [=2:17, 8:14]	6:5c–7b [=4:1c–2,3c–d]
3:2 [=3:1]	

Other supposed glosses Loretz took as supplementations and explanations, as well as references to other passages:

2:12,13	6:9
3:1,7,11	7:4,8,9,10
4:5,8,12	8:5,11,12
5:11	

The references to the "king" in 1:4,12, 3:7,9,11, 6:6 Loretz regarded as glosses by a later hand intended to supply a direct connection with Solomon named in the superscription 1:1. From the same hand, according to Loretz, may have come the two supposed inserts 1:3c,4e which recall the harem maidens of 6:8–9. In 1:4, however, Loretz took "the king," *hammelek̲,* to be a gloss and he read the verb as imperative and changed the possessive suffix of the word for "chambers" to the second person: "Bring mich[, König,] in dein Schlafzimmer! Bring me[, O king,] to your bedroom!" The second person suffixes of the rest of the verse, however, Loretz altered in various ways on the assumption that they had been introduced to support the allegorical identification of the king as Yahweh. Similarly in 3:6 and 8:5 Loretz would delete the references to the desert, while in 3:9, 6:12 (?), and 8:10 he would also alter the possessive suffixes on the assumption that they had previously been tampered with in the interest of allegorical reinterpretation. These changes, in Loretz's view, are to be considered in connection with the history of interpretation rather than of the development of the text. The notion that the allegorical exegesis was decisive for the reception of the book into the Canon seemed dubious to Loretz who perceived several indications that the

Canticle came into the Canon before the allegorical exegesis came into vogue.

Demonstrations of diversity of views on the literary integrity and structure of the Song of Songs could be extended, but the few samples cited should suffice. The present writer agrees with Haupt in appreciation of the charming confusion in the Canticles and has not been convinced by any of the efforts to demonstrate or restore order or logical sequence and progression.

FORM CRITICISM AND CANTICLES; PRAISE OF PULCHRITUDE AND PARALLEL LOVE POETRY

Human beauty, and especially that of women, is not infrequently noticed in the Old Testament, as a matter of general interest and as having special relevance to the context; cf. Gen 6:2, 12:11,14, 24:16, 29:17; Deut 21:11; Judg 15:2; II Sam 11:2, 13:1, 14:27; I Kings 1:3*f;* Esther 1:11, 2:7; Job 42:15; Ps 45:12[11E]. The reference in Ezek 16:7 to Jerusalem's attainment to puberty is not an individual description but merely notice of normal physical development:

You grew and became tall,
And came into full flower;
(Your) breasts developed,
Your hair sprouted,
But you were stark naked.

Apart from the Song of Songs, there is not a great deal of detailed attention to feminine pulchritude in the Bible, although there are occasional expressions of appreciation for it. In the famous alphabetic acrostic on the virtues of the good wife in Prov 31:10–31, the emphasis is on home economics and the only reference to physical beauty is an admonition as to its deceptive and transient character in the next to the last verse:

Charm is deception, beauty a breath,
A god-fearing woman, she's to be praised.

LXX reads here, instead of the clumsy "woman of the fear of YHWH" of MT, "a woman of intelligence" which is surely the original sense, the MT reflecting a pietistic movement which equated reverence with wisdom. While a woman could scarcely be blamed for being beautiful, it was no intrinsic moral merit and intelligence and piety were more important. Beauty without intellect was an incongruity, as the ancient aphorist put it, Prov 11:22:

A gold ring in a swine's snout, (Is) a fair woman devoid of sense.

A good wife was also the pious man's reward and her modesty and self-control a particular blessing, Sir 26:2–3,14–15; her beauty, too, merited mention, 16:18:

The sun rising over the mighty peaks
Is the beauty of a good woman keeping house.

A lamp shining on a holy lampstand
Is a beautiful face on a good figure.
Gold pillars on silver pedestals
Are beautiful feet and shapely heels.

No virtue was more appreciated in the woman than sparing speech and prudent silence, Sir 25:20,

As gravel to an old man's feet, So is a talkative woman to a quiet man;

and Sir 26:14,

A gift from the Lord is a silent woman,
Priceless she who disciplines her impulses.

The dangers of chance encounters with women are signaled in Sir 9:5–9 and a man is further warned against the beautiful and wealthy woman in 25:21*f*.

Don't fall for a woman's beauty, Nor yearn, for what she has.
It is anger, insult, and shame When a woman supports her husband.

The Canaanites were allegedly given to lust and infatuation with feminine charm, but Jews were not supposed to succumb to such temptation, as the young hero Daniel reminded one of the reprobate judges who had tried to seduce the beautiful Susanna (vs. 56):

"You descendant of Canaan and not of Judah, beauty has beguiled you, and lust has corrupted your heart!"

The story of Judith and Holofernes naturally lays great stress on the surpassing beauty of the heroine who used her charms to save her people. Her beauty was so wondrous that Holofernes' men exclaimed:

"Who can despise these people, when they have such women among them? It is not right to leave one man of them alive, for if we let them go they will be able to beguile the whole earth" (Judith 10:19).

Unfortunately, the narrator did not favor us with a description of Judith's wondrous beauty and charm.

The only detailed description of feminine pulchritude from post-biblical Jewish sources comes from the sectarian community at Qumran, the description of Sarah's beauty in the Genesis Midrash 20:1–8. As pointed out by M. H. Goshen-Gottstein (1959–60), this appears to be the only residue of a Jewish *waṣf*-tradition. There is in the Talmud (TB Ketubot 17a) allusion to the custom of singing about "the beautiful and desirable bride," *kallāh nā'āh waḥăsûḏāh,* which traditionally included description of bodily traits. The sources, however, do not specify which physical charms of the bride were described. Such a custom, ordinarily repugnant to feminine modesty, was intended to increase the groom's desire for the bride. And this is precisely the purpose in the Genesis Midrash, as the quasi-bride (Sarah) is made to appear desirable in the eyes of a quasi-consort:

How . . . and (how) beautiful the look of her face . . . and how fine the hair of her head, how fair indeed are her eyes and how pleasing her nose and all the radiance of her face . . . how beautiful her breast and how lovely all her whiteness. Her arms goodly to look upon, and her hands how perfect . . . all the appearance of her hands. How fair her palms and how long and fine all the fingers of her hands. Her legs how beautiful and how without blemish her thighs. And all maidens and all brides that go beneath the wedding canopy are not more fair than she. And above all women is she lovely and higher is her beauty than that of them all, and with all her beauty there is much wisdom in her. And the tip of her hands is comely (N. Avigad and Y. Yadin, 1956, English section, p. 43).

This detailing of Sarah's charms is a midrashic elaboration of Gen 12:14–15, a passage which, quite naturally, piqued the interest of the rabbis (cf. L. Ginzberg, I, 222*f*). In answer to the question why the *waṣf*-tradition found expression only in this particular midrash, Goshen-Gottstein suggested that it was perhaps excluded from "official" or "higher" literature and allowed to remain only in such an extracanonical document. It is of interest to note that special assurance is given that Sarah had wisdom as well as beauty, and this wisdom, presumably, included discretion and discipline in speech and silence, as the ancient Egyptian encomium specified:

Sweet her lips when she converses,
She says not a word too much. (W. K. Simpson, 1973, 316)

Wetzstein's comparison of the lovers' praises of each other's beauty in the Song of Songs to the *waṣf* in praise of the bride and groom in village weddings of Syria was elaborated by Budde as the key to the understanding of the Canticles, a view which gained wide acceptance in the first half of the present century. The *waṣf,* or description, understandably, is a staple of Arabic love songs and has analogues in other love poetry. While praise of feminine pulchritude predominates in love poetry generally, description and praise of the male lover is less common. The following samples are among those cited in English translation by Jastrow (1921, 245*f*) from G. Dalman's *Palästinischer Diwan* (1901):

(Page 100)

The eyebrows of my beloved
Are like the line of a stylus, drawn with ink,
And the hair of his forehead like the feathers of birds dyed with henna.
His nose is like a handle of an Indian sword glittering,
His teeth like pebbles of hail and more beautiful,
His cheeks like apples of Damascus,
His breasts beautiful pomegranates,
His neck like the neck of the antelope,
His arms staffs of pure silver,
His finger golden pencils.

Her teeth are like pearls,
Her neck like the neck of the antelope,
Her shoulders are firm,
The work of a master;
Her navel is like a box of perfumes,
With all spices streaming therefrom,
Her body like strains of silk,
Her limbs like firm pillars, etc.

(Page 193)

The bridegroom is the light of the moon,
With the sun adjoining,
His bride is the light of the morning,
Passing all in beauty.

(Page 308)

Thy black eyes wound me,
All the beauty of the world is gathered to thee,
The maidens of the city come to compare themselves with thee,
None are there like thee,
None is equal to thee.

An anthology of "Modern Palestinian Parallels to the Song of Songs" has been presented by S. H. Stephan (1922) based on Dalman's *Palästinischer Diwan* and on Stephan's own collection of Palestinian folk songs. Comparison of these early Palestinian songs (i.e. the biblical Song of Songs) and those in use some twenty-five hundred years later, "shows a striking resemblance between the old and the new, both in the expression of ideas and in the grouping of words," according to Stephan (p. 199). Stephan disavowed the defense of any theory and professed to "let each word speak with its own force, unchained and unchanged"; he hoped that no one would be offended by the breadth of treatment in his paper. The following observations and conclusions were drawn by Stephan from his comparison of Canticles with the folk songs of his day (footnotes and citations of Arabic omitted):

There is no doubt whatever about the general idea of these poems, which is the same as that treated of in Canticles—the mutual love of the sexes. In monologues and dialogues are described the reciprocal love and longing of the male and female for each other.

To him "she" is altogether a charming and beautiful maiden. She is of *good family* (7 2) for he calls her the *prince's daughter*. Her *stature* (7 7; 2 14) is like a *palm tree*. She is *beautiful, sweet* and yet *terrible* (6 3), *fair as the moon, bright as the sun* (6 9). Her *feet* (7 1) are beautiful. Her *face* (2 14) is comely, "pars pro toto": Her *speech* and *voice* (2 14; 4 3) are sweet. Her *odours* (3 16; 4 10,12–14) are aromatic, full of the fragrance of all spices and sundry powders of the perfumer. Although her *complexion* (1 5) has been bronzed by the sun, which has burnt her *face* (1 6), she is none the less fair, attractive and beautiful. Our contemporary songster is so much absorbed by her charms that he calls her *his life*. The ravenblack *hair* with its attractive *curls* and *locks* (4 3; 6 6) is coloured with henna for the wedding night and appears to him like purple (7 5; 6 4).

The *hair* and the dark *eyes*, with which she has ravished his heart (4 9), so that he cannot but cry out, calling her the *fairest amongst women* (1 8; 4 9; 5 9 and 1 7; 6 4), are her most striking features. Both Canticles and the folk-songs praise her *dove-like eyes* (4 1; 1 15b); yet we in our turn go a little farther, and ascribe to her doe-like or gazelle-like eyes.

Her lovely *cheeks* seemed to the old bard to be a slice of pomegranate (4 3; 6 6), yet we consider them nowadays like apples, white and red, or like roses.

When Canticles compares her *teeth* (6 6) to a flock of white sheep coming up from the washing, our present songsters are inclined to liken them to hail-stones or to silver. Her *lips* are considered nowadays not so much as a thread of scarlet (4 3), but more as delightful roses in full blossom, as sweet as honey or sugar (4 11). Her *mouth* is like the best wine (7 9); and her *throat* has the same attribute of beauty, though it may be compared now and then to amber.

Her *breasts,* seemingly the most attractive part of her graceful person, are to the old singer like wine (1 2; 4 10), even far better (4 10; 1 2). We consider them as pomegranates and rarely as clusters of grapes (7 8). But in common parlance "the groom may take one breast for a cushion and the other as an eider-down quilt." . . . His love for her inspires him to describe her with a variety of pretty appellatives, common to both periods, such as *dove* (2 14), *roe* (3 6) an *enclosed garden,* a *spring shut up,* a *fountain sealed* (4 12); a *garden fountain,* a *well of living water* (4 15). He is captured by her beauty; first he considers her fair, and then as spotless (4 7). Yes, to him she is at the same time a *rose in a flower garden* (2 1) and a *proud horse* (1 9).

It is not usual to enumerate the attractions and charms of the man. So we have in our contemporary songs comparatively few ditties which deal comprehensively with the beauty of the male.

The bride describes him as "white and ruddy, chosen out of thousands" (5 10). His *form* and *countenance* are excellent (5 15) and therefore the virgins love him (1 2). His flowing *locks* are bushy and black as a raven (5 11). His *cheeks* are as a bed of spices (5 13). His *mouth* is very sweet, altogether lovely (5 16). His *hands* are gold rings set with beryls (5 14). And last, but not least, his *stature* is like the cedars—nowadays like a palm tree (5 15)–and his *belly* is like ivory overlaid or set with sapphires (5 14). Such is her friend and her beloved (5 16), a handsome youth, who is sure of the sincere love of maidens (1 2). To him she said in olden times: "Draw me and I will run after thee" (1 4). She may hear today just the same words from his lips.

He calls her *sister, bride* (4 9) and *friend* (2 10). She in her turn calls him her *beloved* (5 4; 1 7; 2 3; 5 8), and her *friend* (5 1; 2 9). The words "friend, beloved, graceful, fair" and half a dozen synonyms are used equally for both sexes. All these expressions are taken over into the mystical and spiritual terminology of the Sufis.

While in the Canticles the man is compared to a deer or a hart, in our days it is the wife to whom these attributes are solely applied. The palm tree and the bird are common to both parties.

The *erotic motives* in all songs, old and new, are numerous. We shall dwell on them only enough to show the common ideas of both periods. The *tatooing* of hands and arms is common to both sexes. But the fairer sex, especially the *fellahat* and *badawiyat* permit themselves to be tattooed even on their belly (5 14b) as far as the *mons*. There are two colours, red and blue, used expressly for this purpose. The use of the *mandrake* (7 13) as an *aphrodisiac* is still known in Palestine, but it serves more for that purpose in Upper Mesopotamia. The nuptial couch (1 16) is often mentioned in our songs.

She pretends to be love-sick during his absence: neither of them can sleep for longing to be with the other. Yet he asks her acquaintances not to wake her up before she wishes (2 7). What is said in Cant. 8 6, that love is fire, is in full agreement with our ideas.

Nature, with her unrivaled beauty, has made a deep impression on our poets. The moonlit *night,* the *stars, flower gardens* and *orchards, wells* and *springs, flora* and *fauna,* and even *minerals* have their place in our folk-songs. The beloved girl is likely to be compared with them all: the proud *horse,* the graceful *doe* or *gazelle,* the lovely *dove* or *birds* in general. Even the *sun,* the *full moon, Orion* with *Pleiades* are not as strange metaphors as they would seem at first sight. *Flora's daughters* are almost all numbered among the similes applied to the female charms. The *mountains* and the *valleys* have their roles; nor are even the *earth* and the *stones* forgotten. *Wind* and *weather,* as well as the *seasons,* must do their utmost to please the beloved one. And *Nature* as a loving mother will surely deign to help her on all occasions required. . . .

Such is our idea of the charms of Nature. We love her in our own way; now and then we fear her; but all her beauty we ascribe to our own sweethearts.

In the following samples of Stephan's translations it seemed best for several reasons to omit the transliteration of the Arabic original of the songs as well as the numerous footnotes. Parallels with Canticles suggested by Stephan are summarily noted at the end of each sample. Other parallels proposed by Stephan are cited in the NOTES on specific verses in the commentary.

III

(Page 231)

1 Your swaying stature, O my life,
O willow bough, is like a palm branch.
    You are the most beautiful one to me!
    (May) your creator and maker (be exalted), O my life!
2 He knocked at the door and I opened to him
And welcomed him.
    I poured him a glass of sweet wine,
    Saying: "Please take it, O my life."
3 He knocked at the door with grace;
I opened it for him gently,
    And served him a dish with "knafe,"
    The dessert being from his rosy cheek.
4 The coquette passed by me,
On her head a bunch of flowers and shrubby stock.

O God, mayest thou keep her (stature) safe.
He is my beloved and I am his.
5 My beloved and I in the flower garden—
Roses overshadowed us.
I asked for a kiss from her forehead,
O God, mayest thou guard our secret!
6 My beloved and I in the cab
His eyes are black and guarded.
O God, may a kiss be saved for me!
"You are quite welcome to it!"

Verses 1, 4, 5 are recited by the male lover, 2, 3, and 6 by the female beloved. On vs. 1 Stephan cited for comparison 2:14, 7:8, 5:9–10, 1:6, 6:1. On vs. 2 he cited 5:2,6, 8:2, 5:1b. The "knafe" of vs. 3 is a cheese pastry with almonds or pine nuts. On the last line of vs. 4, cf. the refrain of 2:16, 6:3, 7:11. On vs. 5, cf. 5:1, 2:3. On vs. 6, cf. 5:12, 8:1.

XIII

(Page 251)

1 On the little uncle; on the uncles:—(she is) white and ruddy, what joy!
2 On the little uncle:—with the club—she turned her cheek and told me: "Kiss!"
I stretched out my hand to the guarded thing: beat your wings, O dove!
3 On the little uncle:—she told me—she unbuttoned her petticoat—
I want a youth like myself, in whose bosom I may spread my couch and sleep.
4 On the little uncle: at the pool she threw a green gage at me,
She is d-d dexterous, for she distracted me so quickly!
5 On the little uncle:—O Asma, under the fig tree we exchanged kisses,
The procurer came and took from me one hundred mejidis.
6 On the little uncle:—O my god-father, you blossom of the gardens,
I'll stab myself with a dagger and forget that life exists.
7 On the little uncle:—O my uncle, take a kiss from my mouth.
Father has divorced mother, and brother has gone to Damascus.
8 On the little uncle:—O Mansur, there is a bird under the navel,
There is also a landau and a phaeton, a hotel as well.
9 On the little uncle:—take and give—under the navel is a wondrous thing.

There is a captain and a ship, on board of which is Abdulhamid . . . (p. 250). The "club" (*dabbūs*) in the second verse refers to the *membrum virile*, as noted by Stephan. The "hand" may also have the same sense here, as in the Song of Songs 5:4. The "guarded thing" (*al-maḥrūs*), Stephan explained, refers to the *mons mulieris*. This song, according to Stephan, deals with a girl of doubtful virtue. On vss. 3 and 5, cf. 2:3,13. On vs. 6, cf. 4:13. The "bird" under the navel in vs. 8 stands for *pudendum muliebre,* although elsewhere "bird" is used of the *membrum virile*. (In a torrid seduction scene in the Ugaritic myth and ritual text called "The Birth of the Beautiful Gods" (23[52]:41,44,47*f*) there is the pregnant refrain:

Lo, the bird roasts over the fire, Bakes over the coals.

In vs. 9, the "take and give" means mutual response in coitus. The rider of this pleasure craft, Abdulhamid, plays in the popular mind a role like Harun ar-Rashid of the Arabian Nights.

XIV

(Page 251)

1 The blushing myrtle is on his cheek,—
He is white, O—the burning of my heart for him.
I cannot more forget the cruelty,
O, my desire, it is not right of you (sc. to let me suffer)
2 Visit me, O, you with the radiant face
And heal my heart from its miseries.
Then I shall uncover your breast and see
a garden—what a fine one too!
3 Visit me, O you with the tender heart,
And heal my heart from sorrows.
All this love (making) is a farce,
Which my beloved imposed upon me.
4 For long I have loved you;
My soul and heart is a ransom for you;
There is a garden planted on your breast
Written above it: *mâšalla* (i.e. it is a beautiful one).

On vs. 1, cf. 5:10 and on vs. 4, 4:12,13, 5:14. This song, known to Stephan since 1906, appears to be of Egyptian origin. The language is semiclassical. The term *mâšalla* of the last line is from the classical *mâ ša'a llâhu,* "what hath God wrought!" an expression of surprise and admiration which is also inscribed on amulets and on doors as protection against the evil eye.

XXI

(Page 260)

1 As I was descending to the valley At two o'clock,
There met me the beloved, kissed me, And let me kiss his cheeks.
2 As I was descending to the valley In the rain,
My beloved met me (oh my eye!) And wrapped me in his mantle . . .

"Two o'clock" here means two hours after sunrise. On the wrapping in the mantle, Stephan appropriately cited Ruth 3:9 and Ezek 16:8. Stephan suggested that since Ezekiel was a captive in Mesopotamia, he may have taken over this allegory from daily life there. Stephan related how in 1915 he was "unwillingly witness of an incident which illustrates this passage" when he saw a man in broad daylight, between 8 and 9 A.M., some twenty yards off the road between Baghdad and Mo'azzam, *expandit amiculum suum super puellam* (i.e. he spread his cloak [*'abaye*] over a girl). There is no need to go to Mesopotamia for precedent or parallel to uninhibited, public sexual activity, matinee or vesper; cf. I Sam 2:22, II Sam 16:22.

XXII

(Page 261)

1 My beloved went away—haven't you seen him, O eye?
May God bless the days which passed (sc. in his company).
2 I saw him wearing fine linen; his beauty is like amber.
He is like the gazelle in form, eyes painted with kohl (stibium).
3 I saw him wearing new coloured linen; his beauty sparkles.
He gleams like the moon between two stars.
4 I saw him resting with his cheek on his hand—how sweet is his cheek!
How sweet is sleep on his cheek for a year and two months! . . .

Stephan cited as parallel with vs. 1, 3:3. For vs. 2, 4:13*f,* 1:9, 1:17. For vs. 3, 6:9.

XXVI

(Page 264)

1 Lo, the moon has risen from your side and is getting high, my friend!
2 How wonderful are your brows and pair of eyes, my friend!
3 May my dear soul be sacrificed on your behalf, if you so order me, my friend!
4 You have no equal among the lovers, no, you have none!
5 O slender palm tree with a bough, moved by every breeze,
6 I am not covetous, nor have I cast my eye on your riches;
7 I only wish you to be my brother for ever and ever, my friend!

On vss. 2 and 3, cf. 5:9, 8:7, 5:12, 1:15. On vs. 4, cf. 1:4, 5:1, 6:1. On vs. 7, cf. 8:1.

XXVII

(Page 264)

1 Look, O mother at the canary—How the honey flows from his mouth!
2 O, mother, look at his tall stature—And (so) the virgins have sung him.

Cf. 4:11, 7:8, 1:3.

XXVIII

(Page 264)

1 O fair one, like a poplar tree, Your cheek is like crystal;
2 Your love has probed in my heart And made (there) a pit . . .

Cf. 7:8, 4:15.

XXIX

(Page 265)

1 Between the brown and the white (sc. girls) I wasted my life.
2 The white ones are twice refined sugar, wrapped in silk,
3 And the brown ones are perfume of crystal vases, prescribed for the sick.

This song is one of many dealing with the complexion of girls.

XXXIX

(Page 270)

1 God and the Prophet loved you, O coffee-bean,
2 Even in Yemen they do not plant a bean like you.
3 I'll become a dervish and lead an ascetic life for your love's sake—
4 Confound the one who saw you and did not love you.

The roasted coffee-bean is brown and thus Stephan cited 1:5.

XL

(Page 271)

1 O wanderer northwards, only tell him,
2 Greet the beloved and only tell him:
3 "Your playmate lies awake the whole night,
4 He watches with the setting moon."
5 Though I sleep at night my eye is awake;
6 Can the promised one not sleep?
7 We spread the couch and prepared the bed,
8 The cock crowed, yet we have not seen our beloved.

Cf. 3:1, 5:2.

XLI

(Page 272)

1 I spent the night counting the stars alone,
2 And embracing the white breasts beside me.
3 O my cousins—each one of them
4 Strikes a bird from the ninth heaven (with her glance)!
5 To the clear spring Halime went for water.
6 Her black locks—she let them hang loose.
7 Away with you, O white ones, for you are not worth getting!
8 Come, you brown ones, O best of friends!

9 The fairest of white ones flattered me with vain hopes.
10 Their face is as the full moon, which shines at night.
11 When they left my body withered away,
12 Confined to bed—by my great love for my friends.

Cf. 6:4, 1:5, 6:10, 5:8, 2:5.

XLII

(Page 273*f*)

1 The dove cried and said:—"They have not come;
2 Those, who have promised me to-day, have not come.
3 I adjure you by the prophet, O well, did they not come?
4 Did not the cattle of my friends come to water?"
5 The dove cried out and said: "I come to you,
6 At midnight I came to you, O my beloved.
7 I thought there were torches at the door of your house,
8 But lo, your cheeks were turned toward me." . . .

On vs. 4, Stephan cited 3:3b and 4:1,2. On vs. 6, he adduced 5:2.

XLIV

(Page 274)

1 I crossed mountains, where there were no paths,
2 I wandered all the night and my relatives did not know where I was.
3 If I had known that death was in my path,
4 Before departing, I would have bidden farewell to the beloved ones.

Cf. 2:8, 4:8.

XLV

(Page 275)

1 I'll cry out: "Great is God,"
2 For her whose breasts are pomegranates and larger.
3 But I fear that old age will befall me,
4 Then she of the beautiful fillet will hate the sight of me.

In vs. 3, "old age" is personified as "the grey and great (one)." The senescent Lothario may still praise God who provides buxom beauties, if only for viewing.

XLVI

(Page 275)

1 He passed by me, turning his head on all sides;
2 He is worth the house and everything around it.
3 I uncovered his breast and there appeared around it
4 The moon and the stars in the height of heaven.

Cf. 6:9,10.

L

(Page 277)

1 I sleep at night and dream of you, in peace,
2 O light of foot, whose walk is graceful.
3 They told me of the healing taste of his palate;—
4 The patient drank of it and recovered . . .

Cf. 3:1 (Ps 63:6), 7:1,9.

LI

(Page 277)

1 Sing an *'atâba* to the first of the fair;
2 Put civet and ambergris on your braid.
3 Your eyes are a river, from whose source I drew,
4 And your breast is a garden, with herbs underneath . . .

A variant of vs. 4 is "And your breast is a garden, a grazing place for youth." Cf. 5:9, 3:6, 5:12, 7:9, 6:11. A variant of lines 3 and 4 is:

My eyes are springs for you, if you come to drink,
And my breast is a garden, with herbs sprouting for you.

Cf. 8:2.

LIII

(Page 277)

1 I never admired anything like her form with a slender hip;
2 She, who is chary of her charms, is slender as a bough.
3 I'll ride on noble relay horses
4 To search for my playmate in the desert . . .

Cf. 7:7, 5:6, 3:6.

LIV

(Page 279)

1 My beloved is away
And my heart has melted.—
For a long while
He has sent no message.
2 Examine me
Oh physician,
As to what I suffered
On behalf of the beloved one.
3 By God, Oh Lord!
This is a wondrous thing;
Yet my heart melted
For the beloved ones.

Cf. 3:1, 1:7, 5:6, 2:5, 7:11, 5:8, 2:5, 8:6. This song is known all over Palestine and Syria, according to Stephan who heard it in Aleppo in 1912.

These popular Palestinian songs express in provincial terms the universal pleasures and pains of love. The parallels with the Song of Songs are sometimes rather remarkable and it seems not unlikely that these folk ditties preserve elements of an ancient and rich poetic tradition which the modern lyricists were free to adapt. The variants of some of the lines show the fluidity and mutability to which folk songs are susceptible. The fact that these songs cited by Stephan are distinctly secular, dealing often with premarital or extramarital love, does not militate against the possibility that the more ancient versions were sacral and cultic in character.

The application of form criticism to the Song of Songs has been attempted only rarely and without spectacular results. F. Horst (1935) distinguished in the Canticle eight different poetic forms, including the *waṣf,* or Beschreibungslied (descriptive song).

1. The Song of Admiration (Bewunderungslied) represented in 1,9–11,15, 2:1–3, 4:9–11, 6:10+(4b)+5a, 7:7–10. All these are in the form of direct address (Address-schema): the groom addressing the bride. The reverse, with the bride addressing the groom, is not attested in the Song of Songs, but this Horst regarded as accidental. Twice, however, in 1:15–17 and 2:1–3, there are reciprocal Songs of Admiration. The peculiarity of the Song of Admiration is best seen in 7:7–10. The song begins with an introduction which expresses admiration in the form of a rhetorical question, adds a comparison with respect to the figure and breasts, and ends with the wish for union with the loved one. The second part of the Admiration Song depicts the effects (Wirkungen) of such beauty, the wish or longing for union with the loved one, or the joy of such a union (1:16b, 2:3b, 7:9*f*); this can also be the avowal of the enchanting effect of the glance and the necklace of the loved one (4:9), or a request to avert her bewitching glance (6:5a), or the promise to prepare for her still more splendid adornment (1:11).

The Song of Admiration is also attested in Arabic poetry, especially in the songs of the Thousand and One Nights, and in the folk poetry.

2. Comparisons and Allegories. The basic form of the independent Comparison, according to Horst, is the short sententious line with a pregnantly sketched comparison, such as 1:13*f* and 4:12–15. The latter example, however, is no longer a pure Comparison Song (Vergleichslied) but is developed into a larger song approximating the type of the Admiration Song (Bewunderungslied).

As an example of the Allegory, Horst cited 6:2; the allegorical character is now obscured by the choral introduction of the preceding verse, but 4:16–6:2 and the concluding vs. 6:3 make it clear that the garden with the balsam beds represents the maiden and her charms, the pasturing and plucking of lilies the enjoyment of her love. As an independent allegorical song, Horst offered the little foxes of 2:15 which, in accordance with G. Jacob's interpretation (1902, 12), refers to the warding off of paramours. Another brief, isolated allegory is 1:12, the king being the bridegroom, the table by which he reclines the young wife, and the nard her charms. One could also adduce 2:16*f* as an allegory, the erotic sense being missed through failure to understand the similar passage in 8:14.

Comparisons and Allegories, Horst noted, have their place in wedding riddles, as in Judg 14:14,18.

3. The Descriptive Song (Beschreibungslied, Arabic *waṣf*) Horst saw in 4:1–7, 6:4a,5b–7, 5:10–16, 7:1–6. The Thousand and One Nights also employs the *waṣf*. The content of the Descriptive Songs of the Canticle, Horst noted, is a series of more or less detailed descriptions of the bodily features of the bride, or, more rarely, also of the bridegroom. The parts of the body are treated in order, either beginning with the head (eyes, hair, teeth, etc., as in 4:1*ff*, 6:4a,5b–7, 5:10*ff*), or, as in 7:1*ff*, from admiration of the dance steps to the description of hips, vulva, breasts, neck, eyes, nose, head, and hair. Horst conceded that one might regard the Descriptive Song as a special kind of Song of Admiration, but, because of the lack of the "exclamation" peculiar to the Song of Admiration and the special "Sitz im Leben" of the Descriptive Song, it seemed justified to regard the latter as a distinct form.

The Descriptive Song regularly has a brief introduction, either an affirmation (4:1), or a comparison (6:4a), or a rhetorical question (7:2a), or a general admiration of the beauty of the person praised, corresponding to the introduction which occurs in the Song of Admiration. It may, however, as in the case of 5:10*ff*, impose the detailed description on a general description. A concluding line may be lacking (as in 7:1*ff*), or may be based on the introduction (4:7, 5:16b).

The two choral introductions of 7:1 and 5:9, according to Horst, point to antecedents in wedding celebrations. According to 7:1, the Descriptive Song is sung about the bride as she performs her dance. The Descriptive Song, according to Horst, has been combined with other pieces which sing of the search for the missing lover, his rediscovery, and union with him. Here one may think of a marriage custom which echoes the cult drama of the myth of Tammuz and Ishtar.

The Descriptive Song, in Horst's view, may have had its origin in such wedding customs as the song during the bride's dance, but in the course of time was used separately and applied to other things, such as the bride's ornaments, or even in a modern example (cited by Dalman, 1901, 112) for the description of a lost knife. Horst cited 3:6–11 as an example of a mixed form of Descriptive Song and Song of Admiration. A song fragment with a beginning similar to that of 3:6*ff* is 8:5a.

4. Self-Description Horst found in two charming examples, 1:5*f* and 8:8–10. Both exhibit a dichotomy: the description of the present appearance and the justification of such exposition from past conduct of the brothers (as guardians of the maiden). In 1:5*f* the description proceeds from the present appearance and the justification follows. (On the dark color of the maiden

Horst compares the contest between the "brown" [bedouin] and the "white" [city] girl of neo-Arabic folk poetry.) In 8:8–10 the order is reversed; the restraint of the brothers becomes broader and is vividly brought out by use of direct discourse; the self-description is then short, taking up one of the figures previously used and ending with the assertion that now all is well. (The sense of this song, according to Horst, is not as Budde explained it: that the brothers were anxious lest her nascent beauty bring danger to their sister. Rather they were afraid that their sister would remain with them, either because she was flat as a wall, unattractive, and unapproachable, or because she was too liberal and gave entry to anyone.)

5. The Vaunt Song (Prahllied) is exemplified, according to Horst, in 6:8*f* and 8:11*f*.

6. The Jest (Das Scherzgespräch) was seen in 1:7*f* where a maiden in longing love and desire for a rendezvous with her beloved asks where he rests with his animals at noon; she is too shy to ask his fellow shepherds. The answer which the shepherd gives the fairest of women is that if people do not know the way to one another, they should follow animal instinct. Young goats in the ancient Near East were especially connected with love and therefore could be a particularly reliable guide.

7. The Description of an Experience (Erlebnisschilderung) is a poetic narrative in the first person (Ichform), as in 3:1–4, 5:2–7, 6:11*f*.

8. Songs of Desire (Sehnsuchtslieder) are scarce in the Song of Songs and this, Horst observed, is remarkable in view of the number of such songs in the Thousand and One Nights. In Arabic poetry the lament for disappointed or lost love, lost by separation or death, is often connected with the Song of Desire, but this is not the case in the Song of Songs. The explanation suggested by Horst was that such songs were deliberately omitted in collections of love songs to be sung at weddings.

The preponderant form of the Song of Desire expresses in a series of imperatives the content of the desire and closes with a shorter or longer statement of cause (Begründung) connected with *kî*, "for," as in 2:4*f*. In 8:6 there is only one imperative followed by an expanded portrayal of the power of love. In 1:2–4 there is an imperatival (jussive) expression of the desire with a statement of cause and then the resumption of the imperative. The statement of cause thus takes on the style of the Song of Admiration. The song 2:14 (related to 8:13) sets before the regular schema an address. The song in 2:10–13 comprises a summons and an address with the statement of cause in between. The song 4:8, which has been influenced by Phoenician-Canaanite myth, as first perceived by Bertholet, 1918, presents only the imperatives and omits the statement of cause.

A stylistic variant of this type of song is found in 8:1 with substitution of the wish-formula for the imperative and a series of apodoses as the statement cause.

Horst concluded that ancient Hebrew poetry had impressed a series of forms for the love song through which the mood and feelings of lovers are expressed, but that not all the forms have been preserved; the love-lament, in particular, is absent in the Song of Songs. Also lacking, in contrast with the richness of the Thousand and One Nights, are Parting-Songs, Consolation Songs, Vows, etc. Happily, in Horst's view, the rimed indecencies and praises of pederasty are also missing.

The quest for parallels to the descriptive songs of the Canticle has moved from the *waṣf* of neo-Arabic folk poetry to the love songs of ancient Egypt, to the Sumerian and Akkadian hymns of ancient Mesopotamia, and recently has been brought closer to the Syro-Palestinian setting with the Ugaritic texts from North Syria dating to the middle of the second millennium B.C. and closer still in the description of Sarah's beauty in the Genesis Apocryphon among the texts from the caves by the Dead Sea from the last pre-Christian century.

W. Herrmann (1963) has treated some of the more striking examples of descriptive songs in the literatures of the ancient Near East. The present brief survey includes some of the samples cited by Herrmann and adds a few items from earlier and later studies.

In a Sumerian love song dedicated to Shu-Sin, fourth ruler of the Third Dynasty of Ur, ca. 2000 B.C., written in the Emesal dialect, or "woman language," probably composed by the *lukur*-priestess (Akkadian *nadîtu*) who evidently played the role of the goddess Inanna in the Sacred Marriage Rite, the lady addresses the king as her god and speaks of herself in the third person as "the wine-maid," praising her charms in order to arouse the passion of the god-king preparatory to their sacral sexual union:

> My god, sweet is the drink of the wine-maid,
> Like her drink sweet is her vulva, sweet is her drink,
> Like her lips sweet is her vulva, sweet is her drink,
> Sweet is her mixed drink, her drink.
>
> (*SMR*, 94)

(For an earlier translation by Kramer, cf. *ANET*, 496. Cf. further Herrmann, 1963, 177n8.)

An Old Babylonian hymn to Ishtar praises her as the "most awesome of goddesses," "queen of women," "greatest of the Igigi (i.e. the great gods of heaven)" and stresses her sex appeal. Since the document is not a sacred marriage text, the divine lady's charms are described in general terms:

> She is clothed with pleasure and love.
> She is laden with vitality, charm, and voluptuousness.
> Ishtar is clothed with pleasure and love.
> She is laden with vitality, charm, and voluptuousness.

In lips she is sweet; life is in her mouth.
At her appearance rejoicing becomes full.
She is glorious; veils are thrown over her head.
Her figure is beautiful; her eyes are brilliant.
(Translation by F. J. Stephens, *ANET*, 383)

Herrmann (178) regarded it as obvious that the description here applies to the statue of the deity and saw in this the "Sitz im Leben" of the Mesopotamian descriptive song.

J. B. Trotti (1964, 124*f*) adduced a passage from a hymn to Ninurta as the only instance of "a form related to the song of description." The text was cited in German (from A. Falkenstein and W. von Soden, 1953, 258*ff*), but an English rendering of the German may be given here for purposes of illustration:

Lord, your face is the Sun,
Your crown. . . .
Your two eyes, Lord, are Enlil and Ninlil
. . . .
Your teeth the Seven-deity
Your two ears Ea and Damkina . . .
Your head is Adad . . .
Your neck is Marduk . . .
Your breast is Shullat . . .

This text, as Falkenstein and von Soden noted, is of significance as reflecting a movement toward monotheism in the late Babylonian period. It is clear that the form is similar to that of the descriptive song, but the purpose is quite different and related rather to the Egyptian hymns which likewise equate bodily members of a great god with lesser gods.

Among the Mesopotamian materials relevant to the Song of Songs, the Sumerian composition called "The Message of Lu-dingir-ra to His Mother" has striking similarities both in structure and phraseology with the descriptive hymn of Song of Songs 5:10–16. A fragment of the text in Akkadian had been taken as part of a collection of proverbs, but with the recovery of the Sumerian text, M. Civil (1964) recognized the supposed proverbs as translated from the Sumerian composition in question. The text is now known from four tablets of the Old Babylonian Period and a couple of trilingual (Sumerian-Akkadian-Hittite) fragments, one of which was found at Ugarit (where it must have been imported from the Hittite capital in antiquity). The composition was manifestly of considerable interest and import which could not be explained by a mere letter to mother with the message "your beloved son greets you." The context of the composition consists largely of instructions by Lu-dingir-ra to the courier detailing characteristics by which his "mother" may be recognized. The courier apparently did not inquire, as did the Jerusalem girls (Song of Songs 5:9) as to what was so unusual or distinctive about the figure to be sought, but Lu-dingir-ra presupposes such a question and gives the courier an elaborate and detailed description with five separate "signs." The instructions to the messenger at the beginning bear some similarities to the stereotype pattern of the Ugaritic mythological texts, but also with notable differences; the Ugaritic messengers regularly deliver their communiqués orally. Lu-dingir-ra says (translation of Civil, 3),

Royal courier, start on (your) way,
As a *special envoy,* give this message to Nippur,
Start the long journey!
No matter if my mother is up or if she is sleeping,
Take the straight path to her dwelling.
Messenger, without inspecting my greetings,
Put into her hands the letter of greeting.
My mother is a very cheerful person, she is covered with ornaments.
If you do not know my mother, I shall give you some signs:
The name is Šāt-Ištar, go to (her) with these instructions.

The first sign (not numbered like the following tokens) is seen by J. S. Cooper (1971, 158) as a condensed version of the "Woman of Valor" in Prov 31:10*ff*. There are, however, items which do not comport with the concern for home economics:

(Her) body, face (and) limbs are *smooth.*
The gracious goddess of her (city) quarter,
Since her childhood, had decreed her fate.
She went directly (and) *with reverence* to the house of her father-in-law.
She stands humbly before the goddess, her lady,
Knows how to look after Inanna's place,
Does not disobey the orders of (her) lord,
She is energetic (and) makes her affairs prosper.
Is loving, gentle (and) lively.
(She is) a lamb, good cream (and) sweet butter flow from her.
(Civil, 3)

It appears that the comely Šāt-Ištar (Lady of Ishtar) had been decreed by the goddess Inanna/Ishtar to be some sort of functionary in the cult, perhaps a hierodule or even a priestess who represented the divine lady in sacred marriage rites.

The second sign supplies further interesting details. Here the translation is that of Cooper (160) rather than of Civil; there is no need here to enter into discussion of minor differences in text and translation:

My mother is brilliant in the heavens, a doe in the mountains,
A morning star abroad at noon,
Precious carnelian, a topaz from Marḫaši.
A prize for the king's daughter, full of charm,
A *nir*-stone seal, an ornament like the sun,
A bracelet of tin, a ring of *antasura,*
A shining piece of gold and silver.
. . . .
An alabaster statuette set on a lapis pedestal,
A living rod of ivory, whose limbs are filled with charm.

In a recent study of Sumerian imagery, W. Heimpel (1968, 60*ff*) interpreted details of Lu-dingir-ra's letter as descriptive of concrete activities and objects worn or possessed by the mother, rather than as lyric metaphor. Since the messenger is supposed to recognize the mother, specific and concrete signs would be needed rather than poetic description. It would be rather difficult to find a mortal conforming in any concrete fashion to the description given by Lu-dingir-ra, but, if found, the messenger should have no trouble recognizing her. Cooper (159*ff*) pointed out that the lyric description of the Song of Songs 5:10–16, also presented ostensibly for purposes of identification like that of Lu-dingir-ra, can hardly be considered a concrete description of a man. In both instances much of the description evokes an exquisite statuette—explicitly mentioned by Lu-dingir-ra and obviously implicit in the figures of the Canticle—of precious metals and stones. Cooper noted that the specific references to pieces of jewelry in Lu-dingir-ra's description can be taken either as parallels to the statuette—that is, the mother is compared to finely wrought jewelry—or as adornments of the statuette, but not as jewelry actually worn by the mother. (An exception to this point appears to be the statement in line 8, "she is covered with ornaments," but it is not clear whether this applies to clothing, costume jewelry, or possibly to an inlaid statue.) This is a significant point and the same observation applies to the description in the Canticle; the male figure is likewise composed of or compared to precious metals and stones and the jewels are inlaid in the materials and are not represented as costume jewelry. Some scholars have vigorously opposed the notion that the present passage has reference to a statue or statuette, but this seems to be an overreaction to early efforts to see it as a description of the god's statue in a fertility rite, as Cooper (160n16) observed. Apart from any theories about the "Sitz im Leben" of either or both of the texts, Lu-dingir-ra's Letter and the present passage, the explicit reference to a statuette in the Sumerian text, line 30, coupled with the other similarities, tends to support the view that the language of 5:10–15 suggests an image composed of several materials, such as described in Dan 2:32*ff* and illustrated by archaeological finds. The poet, of course, could express more with words than an artisan might be able to illustrate either because of material, technical, or artistic deficiency.

The form-critical analysis of ancient Egyptian love poetry by A. Hermann (1955; 1959) has bearing and influence on the study of the Song of Songs. Hermann found three major forms in the Egyptian love poems: the *Tagelied,* the *Beschreibungslied,* and the *Paraklausithyron.* The Tagelied, "day song," deals with the parting of lovers at daybreak in fulfilled love. The Paraklausithyron is the song of the lover at his mistress' door. The Song of Songs 5:2 affords an excellent example of the Paraklausithyron. The Beschreibungslied, or descriptive song, Hermann found to be a set form of love poetry in which, however, the poet has considerable freedom in drawing on a "fund of images" in making comparisons. The distant origin of this form of description is in ancient cultic texts, but the use in the later love lyrics is patently secular. The cultic texts listing and describing members of the body are magic spells for healing and ritual litanies equating the members of the body of the deceased king with various gods. Three of these descriptive catalogs were treated by Hermann Ranke (1924) who saw the lists as falling into multiples of nine and argued that the number nine was a fixed canon set in Heliopolis where it was believed that all the gods were parts of the one god Ptah as divided into enneads. Hermann Grapow (1924, 108) noted that even in the oldest texts the gods attending the sun god formed a body, or corporation, of nine gods, "die Körperschaft der neun Götter." W. R. Dawson (1931) found that the lists of the parts of the body, both internal and external, each part being assigned to the protection of a god or goddess, are, with a single exception, arranged more or less in order from head to foot, but there is no uniform number of parts listed. (See NOTES on 5:10–16.)

A magical text on the base of a statue treated by A. Klasens (1953) offers in two of the spells (VIII and X) lists of members of the body to be healed with the help of the magical statue. The ritual involved the identification of the various members of the patient with the corresponding parts of a diety. Spell VIII gives assurance that Ptah is able to extinguish the patient's fever. Ptah declares: "Your flame is not, your glow is not in any limb (of the patient). For he (the patient) is Horus, the son of Osiris, the lord of protection, who puts his magical power into action, effective in salvation, great of protection." Then begins the list of members of the body:

His head is the head of Re-Harachte
His crown is the crown of Khepri
His face is the face of Nefertem,
etc. (Klasens, 60)

Spell X identifies the members of the patient with Horus and with other gods and asserts their vigor. "Your head belongs to you, Horus, it will be stable, wearing the white crown and the *wrrt*-crown. Your eyes belong to you, Horus, etc." (p. 62). Trotti suggested (1964, 137*f*) that the descriptive cult hymns and the lists of bodily parts in healing magic show strong structural similarity to the song of description, but he saw no evidence to indicate that the love poetry involves magical incantation or cultic usage. Trotti did, however, affirm that the general literary pattern of the song of description was influenced by the venerable and ubiquitous cultic and magical form, the schema of which the love poets adapted.

The Egyptian sources, as one would expect, also offer examples of praise of womanly beauty and charm. The oldest example, significantly, is found in a hymn to the goddess Hathor on a stela of King Waḥ-Ankh-Antef of the Eleventh Dynasty (cf. Hermann, 1959, 25n73). Queen Hatshepsut of the Eleventh Dynasty in an inscription in her temple is described as "fairer than all the women in the entire land" (cf. S. Schott, 1950, 89). The beauty of Mut-Nefertari, wife of Ramses II, is also accorded poetic praise (cf. Schott, 95 and Herrmann, 1963, 178n20).

The Egyptian love songs of the New Kingdom offer examples of physical descriptions comparable to those of the Song of Songs. A song from the obverse of Papyrus Harris 500, Nineteenth Dynasty, ca. 1300 B.C., provides the earliest preserved description and comparison of bodily beauty in Egyptian love poetry.

Distracting is the [foliage] of my
  [pasture]:
[the mouth] of my girl is a lotus bud,
her breasts are mandrake apples,
her arms are [vines],
[her eyes] are fixed like berries,
her brow a snare of willow,
and I the wild goose!
My [beak] snips [her hair] for bait,
as worms for bait in the trap.
(Tr. Simpson, 1972, 299)

As noted by Herrmann (1963, 179), five parts of the body are mentioned, the mouth and breasts being equated with plants, the arms, forehead, and hair with parts of the bird trap. The physical features selected for emphasis are those having special erotic charm.

The Turin Papyrus Love Songs presents in "Songs of the Orchard" three ditties in which different trees of the garden speak of themselves in relation to their mistress. The first tree praises itself in terms of the lady's charms:

[The pomegranate] says:
Like her teeth my seeds,
Like her breasts my fruit,
[foremost am I] of the orchard
since in every season I'm around.
(Tr. Simpson, 312; cf. Hermann (1955), 128, and Herrmann, 180n29)

The first stanza of The Chester Beatty Love Songs, a cycle of seven songs called "The Songs of Extreme Happiness," details the lady's exceptional charms:

One, the lady love without a duplicate,
  more perfect than the world,
  see, she is like the star rising
  at the start of an auspicious year.

She whose excellence shines, whose
    body glistens,
  glorious her eyes when she stares,
  sweet her lips when she converses,
  she says not a word too much.

High her neck and glistening her
    nipples,
  of true lapis her hair,
  her arms finer than gold,
  her fingers like lotus flowers unfolding.

Her buttocks droop when her waist is
    girt,
her legs reveal her perfection;
her steps are pleasing when she walks
    the earth,
she takes my heart in her embrace.

She turns the head of every man,
all captivated at the sight of her;
everyone who embraces her rejoices,
for he has become the most successful
    of lovers.

When she comes forth, anyone can see
that there is none like that One.
(Tr. Simpson, 315*f*)

Note that the figure is surveyed from the top downward, from eyes to soles, more or less in order, except that the hair is slightly out of place as mentioned between the breasts and the arms.

In the Ugaritic texts there are occasional references to feminine beauty and charm. Baal's sister-consort, the violent and volatile Virgin Anat, is called "fairest among the sisters of Baal," *n'mt bn aḫt b'l* (10[76].2.16), and "fair(est) sister of [Baal], *n'mt aḫt* [*b'l*] (10[76].3.11). The goddess Anat in her threat against the young hero Aqht for refusal to give up his bow, addressed the stubborn youth contemptuously as "handsome one, strongest of men," *n'mn 'mq nšm* (17[2 AQHT].6.45). The lips of El's eager but patient wives, when, after repeated preliminary potency rites, he finally kissed them, were sweet:

He bent, their lips he kissed.
Lo, their lips were sweet,
Sweet as grapes. (23[52].49–50)

The paragon of feminine pulchritude was quite naturally the love goddess herself and King Keret thus saw the beauty of his predestined bride, his dream girl, in terms of the divine ideal, the goddess(es) Anat and Ashtart (14[KRT].143–155):

Give me the girl Hurray,
Your beauteous firstborn progeny,
Whose charm is like Anat's charm,
Whose beauty like Ashtart's beauty,
Whose pupils are azurite gems,
Whose eyeballs alabaster bowls.
Let me bask in the beauty of her eyes
Whom in my dream El has given,
In my vision the Father of Mankind.
Let her bear progeny to Keret,
A boy to El's servant.
Keret awoke and it was a dream,
El's servant, and it was a vision.

Among the recently published mythological and ritual texts from Ugarit, there is one (UG 5.3) which presents a description of Baal at his enthronement, as he sits high, wide, and handsome on his holy mountain. The text is fragmentary and incomplete, but parallels with the only extended description of the male protagonist of the Song of Songs, 5:10–16, are notable. Both descriptions, as observed by L. R. Fisher and F. B. Knutson (1969, 163), begin with the head, proceed to the legs and feet, and return to the mouth. The descriptive portion of the text Fisher and Knutson rendered (p. 159) as follows:

His head is wonderful.
Dew is between his eyes.
Of hostility speak his legs
(even) [his] horns which are upon him.
His head is descending from the heave[ns],
[from the ten]t of the bull.
There is his mouth like two cloud[s].

This text is replete with difficulties and uncertainties and a treatment differing in detail from that of Fisher and Knutson has been offered by M. Pope and J. Tigay, 1971. The following translation is offered for comparative purposes with omission of philogical argumentation, for which cf. the aforementioned treatments by Fisher and Knutson, Pope and Tigay:

Baal sat as a mountain sits,
Hadd *w*[*ide*] as the ocean,
Amid his mount, Divine Sapon,
On [the beauteous] mount of dominion.

Seven lightning bolts [ ],
Eight storehouses of thunder,
A lightning shaft he [holds].
On his head a *phylactery,*
Between his eyes an *ornament.*
His feet stamp on the *wicked,*
His horns [*ris*]*e* above him.

His head is in the *snow* (?) in
heaven,
At his feet is *moisture.*
His mouth like two *clouds* (?)
[ ] like wine love
[His] heart [ ]

The description of Baal above, apart from the uncertain words which may characterize the material of which the head is made, or perhaps ornaments or phylacteries worn on the head, or forehead (between the eyes), gives no hint of statuesque traits or precious metals, stones, and gems. Nevertheless, the text bears resemblances to the Akkadian texts which describe divine images from head to foot and gives the identification, the "Göttertypentext," or god-type-text. The storm god Ninurta is thus described (cf. Pope and Tigay, 119*f*):

The head has a horn and a *polos*(?)
-headdress
(He has) a hum[an] face.
There is a cheek.
He has a *pursasu*-coiffure.
His hand(s) are those of a hum[an].
[His right hand?] is rais[ed] high.
The divine-wea[po]n [ ]
in hi[s] left (hand) [ ]
the guide rope of a [ ]
and he carries a . . . [ ]

(with) a sash [of] lamb[skin?]
[h]is [chest] is covered.
He [w]ears a [waistband].
He wears a b[e]lt.
The [b]od[y] is (that of a) man.
The garme[nt]
His r[ight] foot f[ro]m his [on]
is exposed [a]nd stands firm.
His left foot is exposed [ ]
His foot/feet tread(s) on the
a[*nz*]*u*-bird
His name: Ninurta.

Descriptions of a series of infernal gods seen by Prince Kumma in his "Vision of the Nether World" (cf. *ANET*², 109*f*) mention for run-of-the-mill deities only the head, hands, and feet, e.g.:

[Ma]mitu (had) the head (of) a goat, human hands (and) feet. Nedu, the gatekeeper of the nether world, (had) the head (of) a lion, human hands, feet (of) a bird. 'All that is Evil' (had) two heads; one head was (that of) a lion, the other head [. . .].

[. . .]. (had) three feet; the two in front were (those of) a bird, the hind one was (that of) an ox; he was possessed of an awesome brilliance. Two gods—I know not their names—one (had) the head, hands (and) feet (of) the Zu-bird; in his left [. . .];

The other was provided with a human head; the headgear was a crown; in his right he carried a Mace; in his left [. . .]. *In all,* fifteen gods were present. When I saw them, I prayed [*to them*].

The prince of the infernal realm, Nergal, is given somewhat fuller treatment:

A man (also), his body was black as pitch; his face was like that of Zu; he was clad in a red cloak; in his left he carried a bow, in his right he[ld] a sword; *with* the left fo[ot] he *trod* on a *serp[ent]*.

When I moved mine eyes, valiant Nergal was seated on a royal throne; his head-gear was the crown of royalty; in his two hands he held two wrathful *Maces;* two heads [. . .].

[. . .] they were cast down; *from* [. . .] of his *arms* lightning was flashing; the Anunnaki, the great gods, stood bowed to the right (and) to the left [. . .].

The nether world was filled with terror; before the prince lay utter *st[ill]ness*. [. . .] took me by the locks of my forehead and dre[w me] before him.

When [I] saw him, my legs trembled as his wrathful brilliance overwhelmed me; I kissed the feet of his [great] godhead as I bowed down; when I stood up, he looked at me, shaking his [head].

The *waṣf* devoted to the Mesopotamian infernal prince is, *mutatis mutandis,* similar to the descriptions of the supernal Ancient of Days of Dan 7:9 and the "one like a son of man," i.e., anthropoid, in Enoch 106 and Rev 1:13–16. The image which Nebuchadnezzar saw in his dream, Dan 2:31*ff*, was explicitly a gigantic statue made of materials decreasing in value from head to feet, from gold to brittle clay, unlike the figure of Canticles 5:10–16 which is composed of gold and precious stone and jewels throughout, and unlike the statuettes of Baal found at Minet I Beida and Ras Shamra, one with gold-plated head and silver-plated body, and the other executed in no less than five materials, electrum, gold, silver, bronze, and steatite (cf. Pope and Tigay, 120, 127). See Plate VII and NOTE on 5:11a.

The reverse of the text giving the description of Baal is also fragmentary, but it ends with what may reasonably be taken as preliminary to a nuptial affair between Baal and Anat:

[ ] poured oil of peace in a bow[l]
[She washed] her hands, did Virgin Anat,
Her fingers, the Progenitress of Peoples.
She took her lyre in [her] hand.
She put the harp on her breast.
She sang the love of Mighty Baal
The love of <the Prince, Lord of Earth>
(On the restoration of the last line, cf. Pope and Tigay, 130)

Fisher and Knutson (1969, 164) appropriately cite a parallel Sumerian account of Inanna's preparation for union with Dumuzi. Kramer (*SMR,* 77) rendered the passage thus:

Inanna, at her mother's command,
Bathed herself, anointed herself with goodly oil,
Covered her body with the noble *pala*-garment,
Took along the . . . her dowry,
Arranged the lapis lazuli about her neck,
Grasped the seal in her hand.
The Lordly Queen waited expectantly,
Dumuzi pressed open the door,

Came forth into the house like the
moonlight,
Gazed at her joyously,
Embraced her, kissed her . . .

The music is missing in the passage above, but figures in another lyric in which the goddess speaks as the Venus-star:

Last night, as I, the queen, was
shining bright,
Last night, as I, the queen of heaven,
was shining bright,
Was shining bright, was dancing about,
Was uttering a chant at the
brightening of the oncoming light,
Het met me, he met me,
The lord Kulianna met me,
The lord put his hand into my hand,
Ushumgalanna embraced me.
(*SMR*, 72)

An Old Babylonian dialogue between a man and a woman concerning love, first taken to be a discussion of Hammurabi with a young woman whom he wished to persuade to marry his son (W. von Soden, 1950) has been treated by M. Held (1961, 1962) as a dialogue between a young man and a young woman about love. The text, according to Held, has nothing to do with Hammurabi who is mentioned once in an oath formula. "The young woman is not a *nadītum* priestess, nor is she the bride-to-be of Hammurabi's son, but rather a young woman (any young woman) arguing the case of a faithful lover. Her rival is not a *kinītum* concubine, but another young lady in whom her lover apparently has a deep interest. In short, our composition belongs to the category of love lyrics" (1961, 2). The faithful lover, in Held's view, is the young lady who has been deserted by her heart's choice for another woman who is variously referred to as "slanderer," "rival," and "the other woman." The constant maiden refuses to be discouraged by the harsh words of her beloved and believes that true love will triumph in the end and that, with the help of the goddess of love, she will rewin the affection of him whom she loves. She invokes the goddess as witness and challenges her rival:

May my faithfulness endure!
Ishtar the Queen being witness;
May my love remain in honor, (but)
may she
Who slanders me come to shame!
Gr[an]t me to revere (him), to charm
(him),
Always to find favor with (my)
darling,
At the command of (the goddess)
Nanâ . . . forever;
Where is my rival?
(1961, 6, lines 9–16)

To the young man's reply referring to her tricks and ordering her to go, she again affirms her constancy:

I cling to you, and this very day
I shall reconcile your love with mine.
By praying and praying to Nanâ,
I shall win your reconciliation, my
"master,"
As a gift forever.
(1961, 6, lines 22–26)

Each time she is rebuffed with assertions that he no longer loves her and bluntly ordered to go away, she persists:

I sense my beauty spots;
My upper lip becomes mo[ist],
While the lower one trem[bles].
I shall embrace him, I shall kiss him,
I shall look and look [at him];
I shall attain victory . . .
Over my go[ssipy women],
And I shall [return] happily to my lo[ver].
(1961, 7, lines 20–27)

Again and again she importunes him:

I seek your sweetness;
My "master," I long for your love! (1961, 8, lines 11–12)

She speaks of his having absconded:

My eyes are very tired,
I am weary of looking out for him;
To me, it is as if he were passing by my quarter;
The day has gone by, (but) where is [my darling]?
(1961, 8, lines 20–23)

The obdurate male chauvinist says:

I swear to you by Nanâ and King Hammurabi:
I am telling you how I really feel;
Your love means no more to me than
Trouble and vexation.
(1961, 9, lines 6–9)

The importunate lady's final effort includes an incantation against gossipers and detractors:

They come down to me because I (still) trust my lover,
My gossipy women,
More numerous than the stars of heaven.
Let them hide! Let them be scarce!
At this moment let 3600 (of them) go into hiding!
I stay and
Keep listening to the words of my "master."
(1961, 9, lines 10–16)

This last outburst proved effective, and, for reasons not immediately obvious, caused a change of heart in her lover, restored the broken relationship, and turned him from the other woman:

My one and only, your features are not unlovely;
They are as before,
(When) I stood by you,
And you leaned your [hea]d (against me);
"[Agr]eeable-One" is your name,
"[La]dy-of-Good-Sense" is your title;
May the other woman be our enemy,
Ishtar being witness!
(1961, 9, lines 17–24)

The compliment paid to the charms of "my one and only" (*et-ti*) is not lavish. Held's rendering "your features are not unlovely" may give the impression of greater eloquence than the terse original *lā masku,* "not ugly." This appears, however, in keeping with the gentleman's character and temperament which Held has aptly appraised.

The young man . . . is boastful and has no regard for true love; he believes that a man's place is in pursuits other than love. His philosophy is crystal clear: "Whoever lies (idle) for a woman('s company) is (like) one who hoards the wind" (1:6–7)—quite a remarkable forerunner of Qoheleth and his attitude toward women! Throughout the poem he never admits that another woman has had a hand in shaping his views, but this fact makes the climax even more impressive, since it is only at the very end that he not only capitulates but also admits that his wisdom has been gained in the company of a rival woman . . . (1961, 5).

A remarkable feature of this composition was noted and emphasized by Held. "There are never any allusions to sex or sexual relations, no reference to the bedchamber, no description of the human body." The expression in 1:6 *ša ana šinništim ipparaqqadu,* "who for a woman lies supine," in Held's view, has "no sexual implications whatever" and "can only mean: 'Whoever lies (idle) for a woman('s company).'"

Any allusion to sex would be against the style and tone of our poem. At any rate, there is a vast gap between the tone of this composition and that of the so-called "Divine Love Lyrics" published by Lambert [1959]. The latter are quite "anatomical"; any such realism is singularly absent from our poem, which never goes beyond an embrace and a kiss, and this despite the fact that it is a secular composition throughout, without any cultic or religious implications. True, the goddesses of love are invoked, and the young lady prays to them and seeks their support; yet this hardly makes the poem a cultic composition of any sort. Our poem is as secular as the love poems in the Song of Songs, with which it has much in common (1961, 4).

The points at which Held perceived parallels to the Song of Songs were at 1:14 in the use of *mārum,* "son," as the designation of the male lover, as with *dōḏ* in the Song of Songs, and rendered by Held as "darling" in 1:21. "That we are wide awake," *ki-ma e-re-nu,* was taken to mean that the dream of love was broken and was compared to the motif of sleep and wakefulness in the Song of Songs 5:2*ff;* in 3:11 the use of *inbum,* "fruit," in the sense of sweetness, was compared to *pĕrî* in the Song of Songs 2:3, 4:13,16; in 3:18,21 the waiting by the window or door in expectation of the lover's appearance was compared to Song of Songs 2:9 and 5:2*ff*. Finally Held noted what the poet of the Song of Songs says in 8:7 of the power of love and concluded: "We can hardly hope for a better and earlier corroboration of his statement than the case of the faithful lover in our dialogue—truly a human and universal document" (1961, 5).

The "so-called Divine Love Lyrics," as Held (1961, 4) termed them, which were treated by W. G. Lambert (1959) must be noticed here. There can be no doubt that the designation "divine" is appropriate, since it is clear, in spite of their meager content and damaged condition, that the documents deal with sacral sexual rites involving the divine consorts Marduk and Ishtar of Babylon. The occasion, Lambert suggested, was the New Year festival, since it is common knowledge that a sacred marriage took place between the god and his spouse at this festival, with Marduk in Babylon and elsewhere with other gods (p. 6).

> A matter which can hardly escape notice is the similarity of the problems presented by our text to those of the Song of Songs. Both are love poetry with no apparent sequence or development. In both there is a frequent change of speaker, and at times narrative or monologue occurs. In both the scene changes, and the lovers appear to have left their metropolitan environment. Let it be stated at once that there are no grounds for assuming any direct connection between the Babylonian and Hebrew works. Yet the similarity stands out. Only when more of the Babylonian text has been recovered will it be possible to make a serious comparison (p. 7).

Lambert has since 1959 identified a dozen additional fragments and two more pieces of a related Ritual Tablet which proves that the pieces which he had previously connected on purely internal evidence really belong to a single corpus and that the paragraphs were for recitation in rituals of Ishtar of Babylon.

Most intriguing is a series of lines featuring female genitalia and a canine:

> "Into your genitals in which you trust I
> will make a dog enter and will tie shut the door."
> "Into your genitals in which you trust, like
> your precious stone before you."
> "Genitals of my girl-friend, why do
> you constantly so do?"
> "Genitals of my girl-friend, the district of
> Babylon is seeking a rag."
> "Genitals with two finger(s?), why do
> you constantly provoke quarrels?"
> (Lambert, 1975, 105)

The dog in this context is especially provocative in view of the dog in the divine banquet (*mrzḥ*) at Ugarit and in orgies alleged to have been carried on by early Christians (cf. pp. 211–215).

In the second new text called "Ritual of Zarpanitum and Games of Marduk," there are further suggestive statements:

> By night there is not a good
> housewife,
> By night there is not a good
> housewife,
> By night a married woman creates
> no difficulty.
>
> I am a . . . for Zarpanitum,
> My hair is flowing and my hands
> *hang loose*.
> (Lambert, 1975, 109)

It appears that during these rites married women were permitted or required to be promiscuous and non-resistant, to let their hair down, and, so to speak, "let it all hang out." Again in a fragmentary line (p. 111), there is mention of a dog:

A dog is like . . . With the pluckings of a bird will I pluck you.

The bird-plucking recalls a similar activity in the Ugaritic sacred marriage text (23[52].37–39):

He raised and shot skyward.
He shot a bird in the sky.
He plucked and put it on the coals.

The translations of the texts given by Lambert in his first study were slightly revised in the subsequent treatment and the citations are from the later version:

Bring down and place . . .
Of the Lord of Babylon . . . . . .
Where the wild doves nest,
The pigeons fill the trees,
And the fledglings of the . . . . bird
Surround Bel like a crown,
The needles of cypress and fir
Pour down upon the Lord of Babylon.
(1975, 119)

On the cypress and fir, cf. Song of Songs 1:17.

There are some bizarre items and actions mentioned, as witness the following:

Before her a dormouse [. . .]
Behind her a rat.
He girded his garments:
He is a shrew mouse, born of a mouse.
I sent [you(?)], my girl-friend, to Kār-bēl-mātāti.
Why did you break wind and become embarrassed?
Why did you make the wagon of her lord a . [.] smell?
(1975, 121)

As for the rodents, there may be something of relevance in the doom pronounced in Isa 66:17 on those

Who sanctify and purify themselves
For the gardens,
Following one in the middle,
Eating swine flesh,
Vermin and rats . . .

The embarrassment of the divine lady at making a stink in her lord's carriage conveys to the modern reader a note of levity and Rabelaisian humor reminiscent of Ben Franklin's essay on sentimental windbreaking. It is hard to imagine a serious reason for mention of this episode in the ancient ritual myth. Whether the wagon (*sabarra,* on which cf. A. Salonen, 1951, 61) has any connection with the mysterious chariot of Song of Songs 6:12 is provocative of speculation.

The sight of the consort (*tappatu,* rendered "concubine" by Lambert,

1959, and in the 1975 article as "girl-friend") made a strong impression on the divine lover and he burst into direct address in praise of her beauty:

At the river crossing of Kār-bēl-mātāti
I saw my girl-friend and was
completely overwhelmed.
You are white like a gecko,
Your skin is dusky like a pot,
You are exuberant, you are made
[happy].
(1975, 121)

The "anatomical" realism which Held (1975, 121) perceived in these lyrics in contrast to the chaste dialogue with which he dealt (1961, 4b) is obvious in the following lines:

[Genitals of] my girl-friend, the
district of Babylon is seeking a rag,
[To] wipe your vulva, to wipe your vagina.
[Now] let him/her say to the women of
Babylon, "The women will not give
her a rag
To wipe her vulva, to wipe her vagina."

[Into] your genitals in which you trust,
like your precious stone before you,
Set your [. . .] before you, sniff the
smell of the cattle,
Like something not mended by the
tailor, like something not soaked by
the laundryman.

Into your genitals in which you trust I
will make a dog enter and will tie
shut the door;
I will make a dog enter and will tie shut
the door; I will make a ḫabḫuru-
bird enter and it will nest.

Whenever I leave or enter
I will give orders to my (fem.) ḫabḫuru-birds
"Please, my dear ḫabḫuru-bird,
Do not approach the mushrooms."
Ditto. The smell of the armpits.

You are the mother, Ištar of Babylon,
The beautiful one, the queen of the Babylonians.
You are the mother, a palm of carnelian,
The beautiful one, who is beautiful
to a superlative degree,
Whose figure is red to a superlative degree,
is beautiful to a superlative degree.
(Lambert, 1975, 123)

The lines above make it clear, in spite of the puzzling and disconcerting references to rags for wiping the vulva, dogs and birds shut up inside the lady's genitals, smell of cattle, armpits, dirty clothing, etc., that the ritual is in honor of the beautiful queen of Love, Ishtar.

Among the new fragments treated by Lambert is a provocative dialogue between the divine lovers:

As for me, my boy-friend scares me,
As for me, my boy-friend scares me:
(he says).
"I will lift you up like a wall, I will
bring you down like a ditch.
I will break you like a . . . . . .
I will roll you over like a rotating
harrow from the shed . . [. .]
I will plaster you over like beauty . . [. ."]
Come, my lord of beauty, I will . . [. . .]
Should you lift me up like a wall
people [will . . .] in my shade.
Should you bring me down like [. . .]
Should you break me . . [. .]
Should you roll me over like . [. .]
Should you plaster me over like . . [. .]"
(1975, 125)

This enigmatic exchange is vaguely reminiscent of a puzzling passage of the Song of Songs, 8:8–10, wherein the "little sister" is conditionally equated with a wall and a door and there is an anonymous threat to build a silver buttress over her and close her with a cedar panel, to which she gives a defiant retort.

An additional cuneiform text has been cautiously added to the comparative materials relevant to the Song of Songs by Jack M. Sasson (1973a, 359–360). This text, published by I. J. Gelb (1970) dated to the late third millennium, is an incantation invoking love-magic for help against a girl. Because of the many uncertainties connected with the text, Sasson deemed it unprofitable, if not audacious, to elaborate comments into overdeveloped speculations. Sasson's rendering follows essentially that of the tentative translation offered by Gelb and his colleagues:

Enki loves the 'lover' [lit. 'love-magic']. The 'lover,' son of (the goddess) Inanna enters(?) the sanctuary(?). By the exudation of the *(kanaktu)-tree* he drives(?) . . . God is the sweet . . . Send into the orchard, Send into the orchard the exudation of the *(kanaktu)*-tree, Make your (m.) lover happy. I seized your (f.) mouth of far-away. I seized your (f.) variegated eyes. seized your vulva of evil/teeth/urine(?). I leaped into the orchard of (the god) Sin. I cut off a poplar-tree. Daily (?) . . . among my box-wood-trees, as the shepherd protects (??) the flock, (as) the she-goat her kid, (as) the ewe her lamb, (as) the she-ass her foal. (like) two strings are his arms, (like) a . . . and a seal-ing-ring(?) are his lips; a pitcher of . . . is in his hand; a pitcher of cedar is on his shoulder. The 'lover' has bewitched her and made her into an ecstatic. I seized your (f.) mouth of love. I adjure you, by Inanna and Išḫara, as long as his *zawarum* and your (f.) *zawarum* are not joined together, may you (f.) not have peace.

At first glance Sasson saw little in this text to compare with the Canticle. But closer inspection led to the recognition of "many of the Biblical elements in capsule form." The fact that the cuneiform text is apparently an incantation presents no difficulty since it has been suggested that segments of the Song of Songs may have been quoted to stimulate conjugal bliss, if not male potency (cf. R. Gordis, 1971, 375–388). Both texts are developed in a loose style, with vignettes on scenery, injunction to lovers, first person accounts, and description of the beloved's physical attributes, with little apparent logical order. Both texts dwell on the swain's physical characteristics. The allusion to his arms and lips and the odoriferous materials on his shoulder reminded Sasson of Canticles 5:14–15, while the equation of his lips with a sealing ring suggested 8:6. The lover is described as bewitching, driving the woman to ecstatic frenzy, and this Sasson compared to 5:6–7 where the lover's absence drives the lovesick lady to desperate search for him. Again the lover is depicted as a shepherd, as in Canticles 1:7–8. The entrance into a sanctuary(?) was conjecturally related to 2:4 and 3:4. The fragrant incense in the orchard reminded Sasson of 4:16. The leap into the orchard to cut down a poplar-tree raised the question whether this is to be understood in terms of 7:9 where it is clear that the tree climbing refers to pleasure "taken on a metaphorically described inamorata." The final adjuration in the name of the goddesses Inanna and Išḫara, patronesses of sexual activity, may well be euphemistic and Sasson suggested reference to 5:8. It would help if we knew the meaning of the term *zawarum*. W. von Soden suggested that the word is to be identified with Hebrew *ṣaww'ār*, "neck (area)." It seems more likely that the connection envisioned entails organs located considerably lower than the neck or chest.

It must be admitted that Sasson has found striking parallels to the Song of Songs in this brief Akkadian text.

GITA-GOVINDA, THE SO-CALLED "INDIAN SONG OF SONGS"

The elaborate Sanskrit lyrical composition called the Gita-Govinda, or Song of Govind, by the poet Jayadeva, who flourished in the middle of the twelfth century, has been dubbed "The Indian Song of Songs." Adam Clarke in his notes on the Song of Songs, composed in 1798, illustrated many of its passages from the Gita-Govinda and was pleased to learn later that Dr. Mason Good had done likewise in his translation and notes published in 1803 (cf. Adam Clarke, 1855, 847). Edwin Arnold (1875) provided an English version of the Gita-Govinda based on the edition of the Sanskrit text and

Latin translation of Christian Lassen. The poem consists of twelve cantos, each containing twenty-four songs of eight verses. The scriptural authority and inspiration for these songs is the Bhāgavata Purāna which relates the miraculous birth of Krishna, his escapades, and his amorous exploits which endeared him to the common folk. Krishna had a predilection for the *gopīs* or milkmaidens and he loved to do the round dance with them by moonlight. By divine illusion he could make himself into as many Krishnas as there were *gopīs*. Krishna married numerous *gopīs,* but he had a favorite later known as the fair Rādhā, daughter of his foster-father Nanda. The tenth chapter of the Bhāgavata Purāna is permeated with the erotic emotions of the *gopīs* and the longing of Rādhā in her separation from Krishna, and this Jayadeva took as the subject matter of his song. The mystical interpretation of this Sanskrit idyl or pastoral drama has been that Krishna represents the human soul drawn alternately between earthly and celestial beauty. Krishna, at once human and divine, is attracted by the sensual pleasures represented by the *gopīs* and wastes his affections upon the delights of their illusory world. Rādhā, the spirit of intellectual and moral beauty, wishes to free him from this error by enkindling in him a desire for her own surpassing loveliness. As Lassen explained in his Latin *prolegomena,* Krishna is

> the divinely-given soul manifested in humanity. . . . The recollection of this celestial origin abides deep in the mind, and even when it seems to slumber—drugged as it were by the fair shows of the world—it now and again awakes, . . . full of yearning to recover the sweet serenity of its pristine condition. Then the soul begins to discriminate and to perceive that the love, which was its inmost principle, has been lavished on empty and futile objects; it grows a-wearied of things sensual, false, and unenduring: it longs to fix its affections on that which shall be stable, the source of true and eternal delight. Krishna—to use the imagery of this poem—thrones Rādhā in his heart, as the sole and only one who can really satisfy his aspirations. . . . (Arnold, vi*ff*).

This parable of passion purported to portray the soul's emancipation from sensual distraction to the joys of the higher spiritual plane is so markedly sensuous that Western minds have had some difficulty in appreciating the mystical meaning. Passages deemed too bold and florid for European tastes have been generally deleted or bowdlerized and the last canto which celebrates the consummation of the love of Krishna and Rādhā is so luxuriantly physical in its descriptions that verecund translators have either omitted it or cast over it the veil of Latin so that the mystic beauties may be perceived only by the initiated.

The Gita-Govinda of Jayadeva was sung as accompaniment to dances in the temples and at religious festivals as late as the end of the eighteenth century, as witnessed by Sir William Jones (cf. John A. Ramsaran, 1973, 54n15). That the poem had religious character is certain whether or not one accepts the mystical meanings attributed to the erotic verses. On this point Ramsaran (53*f*) cites A. Berriedale Keith (1953, 194):

Efforts have been made to establish that the poem has a mystical significance and to interpret it in this sense. The desire, in part at least has been prompted by the feeling that the loves of Kṛṣṇa and Rādhā are too essentially of the body rather than of the mind, and that to ascribe them to the divinity is unworthy. But this is to misunderstand Indian feeling. The classical poets one and all see no harm in the love-adventures of the greatest deities, and what Kālidāsa did in the Kumārasambhava was repeated by all his successors in one form or another. But, on the other hand, it must not be forgotten that the religion of Jayadeva was the fervent Kṛṣṇa worship which found in the god the power which is even concerned with all the wishes, the hopes and fears of men, which, if in essence infinite and ineffable, yet expresses itself in the form of Kṛṣṇa, and which sanctions in his amours the loves of mankind.

Unlike the biblical Song of Songs, the poet Jayadeva injects himself into his song repeatedly to prevent the carnal-minded reader from misconception of the true meaning of the erotic symbolism. Edwin Arnold in his translation set off the poet's intrusions in red letters or in italics, e.g., in the seventh sarga (pp. 72*f*) he prays:

O great Hari, purge from wrong
The soul of him who writes this song;
Purge the souls of those that read
From every fault of thought and deed;
With thy blessed light assuage
The darkness of this evil age!
Jayadev the bard of love,
Servant of the Gods above,
Prays it for himself and you—
Gentle hearts who listen! too.

At the end of the eleventh sarga, he says (p. 102):

What skill may be in singing;
What sound in song,
What lore be taught in loving,
What right divined from wrong:
Such things hath Jayadeva—
In this his Hymn of Love,
Which lauds Govinda ever,—
Displayed; may all approve!

The mention above of what Kālidāsa (fl. fifth century A.D.) did in the Kumārasambhava provides pretext for a sample of the same. The following description of the Indian love-goddess Pārvatī by the Hindu poet Kālidāsa was translated by Prof. Stanley Insler (Canto I, vss. 31–50):

31. After her childhood, adolescence became a natural adornment to her statuesque body. That body! It was a cause of drunkenness one could not call brandy. A weapon of Cupid, but entirely distinct from his flower-arrows.
32. Like a painting unfolding under the artist's brush, like a lotus opening under the rays of the sun, her body, sharing in this fresh youthfulness, became beautiful in all aspects.
33. As she delicately walked upon the ground and the lustre of the nails of her rounded toes emitted their reddish radiance, her feet assumed the uncanny beauty of the crimson lotus.

34. One could say that the royal swans instructed her in her gait, for it was both graceful and sportive. They were certainly eager to imitate the jingling of her silver anklets!
35. After shaping her beautiful legs, so perfectly curved and not excessively long, the Creator had to make a special effort at the loveliness to be achieved in forming the rest of her body.
36. Her thighs were beyond comparison, even though other plump and voluptuous things are known in the world. One could not compare the trunks of the royal elephants because of their roughness, nor certain plantain stalks because of their inherent coolness.
37. Can we not simply describe the beauty of the faultless girl's lap by saying that it was later enjoyed by Śiva, a distinction not shared by any other woman?
38. A fine line of pubic hair shone above the knot of her skirt, as it plunged into her dimpled navel. Black and brilliant it was, like the sapphire set in the middle of her girdle.
39. Her middle was nipped, and bore three charming folds of flesh, employed, we might say, as a ladder for Cupid to climb across her tender youthfulness,
40. To the very full breasts of the lotus-eyed damsel. Such breasts! Pale yet black-nippled, pressing against one another so fully that there was not even room for a lotus filament between them.
41. In my opinion her arms were even softer than those most delicate Śirīṣa flowers. For Cupid, even though he was destroyed, had been able to make them into slings to entrap Śiva's neck.
42. Her hands, with their lovely nails, set to shame the delicate leaves of the Aśoka tree and rendered fruitless the somber radiance of the newly risen moon in the evening sky.
43. Curving above her breasts, her neck was perfectly round like the string of pearls adorning it. Each beautified the other so, that who could say which of the two was really the ornament?
44. When the fickle goddess of fortune resides in the moon, she enjoys not the benefits of the lotus; nor the advantage of the moon, when she reposes in the lotus. But once she reached Pārvatī's mouth, she found the pleasures of both united there.
45. Cover a flower with a tender leaf, and place a pearl upon scintillating coral. Thus you might imitate the brilliant smile cast from her copper colored lips.
46. Her voice flowed with ambrosia when she spoke with noble voice. In comparison, the cuckoo's call was grating to the hearer, like a discordant lute being played.
47. The long-eyed girl's darting glance was indistinct from the movement of a blue lotus in a windy place. Did she steal it from the female antelopes, or did they from her?

48. Long and fine-lined were her brows, whose beauty seemed
to be formed with cosmetic paste. Even Cupid, noticing their
sportive assault, lost all fascination with his own bow.
49. If lower animals could perceive a sense of shame,
certainly the yaks would lose the affection for their own tails,
once they had seen the mane of hair of the daughter of the
mountain king.
50. By accumulating all objects of comparison and setting
them in their proper place, she was fashioned with especial
effort by the Creator of everything, with the desire to see
total beauty existing in a single place, let us say.

INTERPRETATIONS OF THE SUBLIME SONG

"Know, my brother, that you will find great differences in interpretation of the Song of Songs. In truth they differ because the Song of Songs resembles locks to which the keys have been lost." Thus the great Jewish savant Saadia began his commentary on the Song of Songs. In proportion to its size, no book of the Bible has received so much attention and certainly none has had so many divergent interpretations imposed upon its every word. A thorough survey of the history of interpretation of the Canticle would require the lifelong labors of teams of scholars. All that can be offered here is a brief sketch based on previous surveys with some attention to more recent developments.

Interpretations of the Song of Songs fall first of all into either allegorical or literal mode. The allegorical approach is the older and prevailed both in the Synagogue and the Church. The Jewish interpretation saw the Song as depicting the relation of Yahweh and the Chosen People, Israel, as his bride. This interpretation is reflected in the Talmud spreading over the first half of the first millennium of the common era, and was fully developed a little later in the Targum as a historical allegory covering the highlights of Israel's experiences from the Exodus to the impending Advent of the Messiah. Essentially the same interpretation is offered by the Midrash Rabbah and by the great medieval commentators Saadia, Rashi, and Ibn Ezra. A mystical mode was also developed in Jewish intellectual circles of the Middle Ages which presented the love affair of the Song as the union of the active and passive aspects of the intellect. In Christian circles the Song was related to the mutual love of Christ and the Church as his bride and allegories were developed with great imagination and ingenuity. Origen conceded that the Song might be an epithalamium for Solomon's marriage with Pharaoh's daughter, but in the higher sense it applied to Christ and the Church, or to Christ and the individual believer. The Marian interpretation which identified the Lady of the Canticle as the Virgin Mary developed as a concomitant of Mariolatry and the veneration and virtual apotheosis of Mary as Virgin Mother of God and Queen of Heaven. The Marian interpretations are of particular interest for the comparativist as reflecting the survival and revival of the ancient and widespread cult of the great goddess of life and fortune, love and war, who was worshiped under many names and with varying emphases throughout the ancient world and whose cult survives most strikingly in the worship of Kali in India as the black and beautiful virgin-mother, creative, beneficent, terrible, destructive Time who takes all in toll. Medieval Christian scholastics, like their Jewish counterparts, found in the Canticle a treasure-trove of insights into the mysteries of the mind and the marriage of the active and passive intellects, which helped to distract them from the prurient interest of the Song. The approach of the Targum, which may have been developed in reaction to Christian exploitation of the Canticle, was adapted by Brightman to include the history of the evangelical church up to the second coming of Christ. Other Christian interpreters, such as Keil, Joüon, and most recently Robert, interpreted the Canticle throughout, after the fashion of the Targum, with reference to Israel's history. The identification of the bride with Wisdom, proposed already by Don Isaac Abravanel (d. 1508), found a modern advocate in G. Kuhn.

The flexibility and adaptability of the allegorical method, the ingenuity and the imagination with which it could be, and was, applied, the difficulty and virtual impossibility of imposing objective controls, the astounding and bewildering results of almost two millennia of application to the Canticle, have all contributed to its progressive discredit and almost complete desertion. Literal modes of interpretation which take the language of physical, sexual love to mean more or less what it seems to say have developed and gained wide acceptance in the last century.

Chief among the literal modes of interpretation are the Dramatic Theory, with a variety of differing analyses from simple two-character dialogue to the love-triangle and on to a production with several characters; the Wedding Cycle theory sparked by Wetzstein's description of Syrian wedding celebrations; the Secular Love Song interpretation, suggested by Theodore of Mopsuestia in the fifth century and developed by Herder and many others in the last two centuries; and Cultic or Liturgical interpretations which see the Song(s) as originating in the sacred marriage rite of fertility worship.

One would expect to find in the earliest translation of the Song of Songs, in the Septuagint (LXX), some intimations of the mystical or allegorical interpretation. The evidence, however, is surprisingly meager. The only passage which can be adduced in support of mystical or allegorical exegesis is 4:8 where MT *mērōʾš ʾămānāh,* "from the top of (Mount) Amana," is rendered *apo arxē pisteōs,* "from the beginning of faith." Very little can be made of this as support for any specific mode of interpretation, since the translators of the LXX occasionally mistook proper names for common nouns or adjectives, and vice versa. (This sort of error is commonplace and in recent times produced a short-lived theory of interpretation of the Ugaritic mythological texts known as the Negebite Hypothesis.) The proper name Tirzah in 6:4 is taken as a common noun, *eudokia,* "delight," and in 7:1[2H] *baṯ nāḏîḇ,* "daughter of nobility," or "noble maiden," is rendered "daughter of Nadab." LXX's rendering of the Song of Songs is for the most part quite literal and straightforward and offers little that can be taken as evidence that the translator understood it in any other than the literal sense.

It has been supposed that Jesus ben Sira's apostrophe to Solomon (Sir 47:14–17) contains an allusion to the Song of Songs:

How wise you were in your youth,
Like a flood filled with understanding.
Your mind covered the earth,
And you filled it with enigmatic
parables.

Your fame reached to distant isles,
And you were beloved for your peace.
Countries admired you for songs,
Proverbs, parables, and
interpretations.

This last verse was taken to refer to the books attributed to Solomon—Proverbs, Ecclesiastes, and the Song of Songs—and, since the "enigmatic parables" (*parabolai ainigmatōn*) mentioned in vs. 15 appear to be distinct from Proverbs (*paroimia*) mentioned separately in vs. 17, it was argued that the "enigmatic parables" characterize the Song of Songs as allegory. It is clear, however, that Sir 47:17 simply echoes I Kings 10:23–24 and supplies no specific information on the Song of Songs and its interpretation or literary classification.

The Wisdom of Solomon 8:2 has also been alleged to contain a clue to interpretation of the Song of Songs. Solomon speaks of his wooing of Wisdom:

Her I loved and wooed from my youth.
I sought to bring her home as my bride.
I was a lover of her beauty.

On Solomon's love affair with Wisdom, see below, pp. 110*f*.

Josephus in his arrangement of the biblical books (*Against Apion* 1.8) has been supposed to impute allegorical interpretation to the Song of Songs. Josephus mentioned twenty-two books justly deemed divine, five attributed to Moses, thirteen to the prophets, and four described as containing hymns to God and precepts for human life (presumably referring to Psalms, Job, Proverbs, and Ecclesiastes). Thus no place would be left for the Song of Songs except among the Prophets, and Josephus must have understood it allegorically in order to have placed it there. This argument, as Ginsburg noted, collapses on consideration that Ruth and Esther also fall among the Prophets and by the same token would have to be interpreted allegorically. Moreover, it is rather improbable that Josephus intended to place the Song of Songs among the Prophets; it is more likely that the Song was somehow included among the four books described as consisting of hymns to God and precepts for men (cf. Ginsburg, 24).

Classical Jewish exegesis of the Song of Songs is represented in the Talmud, the Targum, and Midrash, covering roughly the first half of the first millennium of the common (or Christian) era. Three Midrashim on Canticles have come down to us (cf. E. E. Urbach, 1971), Midrash Rabba, Aggadat Shir Ha-Shirim, and Midrash Shir Ha-Shirim (cf. Urbach, 247n1), in which allegorical, mystical, historical, and eschatological interpretations commingle in confusion.

The period between the destruction of the Temple, A.D. 70, and the revolt of Bar Kokhba, A.D. 132, apparently saw the development of the normative Jewish interpretation of the Canticles as an allegorical account of the history of the relationship between the Divine Presence of God, the Shekinah, and the Community of Israel from the Exodus from Egypt onward. This is reflected in II Esd 5:24,26 where the author uses the symbolic names for Israel derived from the Canticles, "from all the flowers of the world Thou hast chosen for Thyself one lily" and "from all the birds that have been created Thou hast named for Thyself one dove." It was Rabbi Aqiba in particular who pioneered in the development and promotion of this line of interpretation which made the Song of Songs the Holy of Holies. For Aqiba, "the whole world was not worth the day the Song of Songs was given to Israel" (Mishnah Yadayim III 5). A dictum attributed to Aqiba in Aggadat Shir Ha-Shirim (ed. S. Schechter, 1896, 5) was slightly and convincingly emended by Urbach (250n10) to read: "Had not the Torah been given, Canticles would have sufficed to guide the world."

The tribulations and martyrdom during the Hadrianic persecutions gave rise to interpretations of the Canticles as alluding to Jewish martyrology and Israel's uniqueness among the nations of the world, as in Aqiba's interpretation of 5:9–10, 6:1, 2:16. When Aqiba himself died a martyr's death, the verse 1:4e was applied to him (cf. Urbach, 251n11).

By comparing the homilies of the rabbis on various verses of the Song of Songs with Origen's interpretations of the same verses, Urbach (257) shows how it is possible to recover parts of "a Judaeo-Christian dialogue" that began in the third century and continued in the fourth.

> At times Origen had need only to transcribe the homilies of the Sages and change a few of their concepts in order to find in them what he wanted, but such is his pleasure upon discovering an exposition of this nature that he does not lightly let it go; short dicta and brief comments become in his hands long homilies and entire wordy dissertations. It is the Rabbis who furnish the ideas and the sparkling homiletical interpretations, but his tiresome treatment of them and his tendency to drown them in a sea of words cause their charm and flavour to grow insipid at times. Yet, notwithstanding, his words are imbued with the enthusiasm of one who has found a sphere in which to display his talents (p. 258).

In the fourth century when Christianity became dominant in the Roman empire, the tone of the Jewish-Christian debate became more strident. Chrysostom's words are not like Origen's and the reactions from the Jewish side differ from those of the preceding century (cf. Urbach, 270n70). Christianity was no longer a sect or just another religion, but had become identical with the wicked kingdom. This point Urbach illustrates with Rabbi Azariah's homiletical exposition on 2:11–12 which related the winter to the wicked kingdom who entices the world and misleads it with lies, the flowers to the illustrious men who would reappear to lead Israel in the messianic war, and the pruning (*zāmîr*) to the lopping off of the wicked kingdom like a foreskin—"the time has come for Israel to be redeemed; the time has come for the wicked kingdom to come to an end. The time has come for the kingdom of Heaven to be revealed" (cf. Urbach, 271).

As the kingdom tarried, competition continued and intensified between Jews and Christians in the interpretation of the Canticles for reciprocal edification and polemic.

The Targum and Subsequent Jewish Interpretations

The date and provenance of the Targum to the Song of Songs are crucial to its evaluation and the understanding of its place in the history of exegesis. It appears likely that this Targum stems from Palestine, as suggested by the use of the specifically Palestinian title *'āḇ bêṯ dîn* (7:5) and eulogy of the Sanhedrin (7:3). Whether it is referred to in the 'Aruk as the Jerusalem Targum is disputed (cf. R. Loewe, 1966, 163n18). The last verse of the Targum alludes to "this polluted land," presumably Palestine, defiled by the continued occupation by gentiles which is the reason for God's refusal to resume occupancy. It is likely that the word *'ar'ā'* here means "the Land" rather than "the (whole) earth" and the demonstrative "this" suggests that the writer was a resident rather than an exile.

The redaction of the Targum to the Hagiographa in general has been referred to the period between the fifth and the eighth centuries A.D. and the Targum to the Song of Songs to the latter part of that period, on the grounds of the use of Arabic terms for the jewels of the high priest's breastplate in 5:14. This argument, as Loewe (1966, 164) noted, is not in itself very substantial, since it is not unusual where no questions of textual sacrosanctity are involved for strange terms to be replaced by more familiar ones. Such a process is particularly likely in the case of jewels and Loewe pointed out that in some of the Yemenite manuscripts the Biblical Hebrew names are restored (from Exod 28:17–21, 39:10–14). The assignment of the redaction of the Targum of the Song of Songs to the early Islamic period may be supported on other grounds. The Aramaic presents a generous mixture of Palestinian and Babylonian forms. At first sight, the references in 1:7 to "the sons of Esau and Ishmael who associate their errors with you as companions" seems promising. In view of the monotheistic emphasis of Islam, it could be argued that the attribution of a theology that compromises absolute monotheism to Ishmael (the Arabs) no less than to Esau (Rome) must be placed in the *jâhiliyyat,* the (time of) Ignorance, the pre-Islamic period before A.D. 622. Loewe, however, suggested (p. 165) that it is more circumspect to conclude that this formulation implies a situation in which Jewry had not yet come to appreciate the monotheistic emphasis of Islam, as well as one in which the Targum was as yet unlikely to come to the notice of Islam's own apologists and propagandists. There is, however, a passage which Loewe regarded as well-nigh conclusive evidence that this Targum is to be dated after the beginning of the expansion of Islam, or, more precisely, after the conquest of Palestine in 636–638. The passage in question is 8:8–10 and the crucial clause is *wĕyāhĕḇā kaspā lĕmiqnēy yiḥûḏ šĕmēh de mārēy ʻālĕmā,* "and she gives money for acquisition of the Unity of the Name of the Master of the world." The paying of a poll tax by Jews to non-Jewish governments has a long history, but it was never a license to practice Judaism until expanding Islam imposed the *jizya* on the People of the Book (*'ahl 'al-kitāb*), Jews and Christians, and certain others, as exemption from the choice between Islam and the sword. Loewe settled on this development following the Islamic conquest of Palestine, beginning with the battle of the Yarmuk in 636, as the historical context to which the Targumist adapted R. Berekiah's exegesis of Song of Songs 8:9 (cf. Loewe, 166n35). The suggestion by J. Neusner of an alternative Sassanid background in the payment of the *haraj* was rejected by Loewe (167n39) chiefly in view of the Palestinian origin of this Targum.

The assignment of this Targum to the seventh century, Loewe noted, is merely to postulate a date by which it had, so to speak, crystallized. It contains exegesis for which there are midrashic parallels going back to Tannaitic sources. Moreover, the esoteric, mystical interpretation also developed in Jewish circles in the late Tannaitic period and with it the sort of reaction reflected in the Targum.

The Targum to the Song of Songs announces itself as a History of Salvation in an excursus on the Ten Songs which mark milestones of human and Jewish experience, from the first song composed by Adam (Psalm 92) when his sin was pardoned through the intervention of the Sabbath, through Solomon's Song itself, number nine in the series, to the tenth and last song which paraphrases and elaborates Isa 30:29 as the marching song of the final redemption. This climax, though expressed in conventionally Jewish messianic idiom, seemed to Loewe strangely out of character in construction and design and recalled the majestic architecture of Milton's proem to "Paradise Lost." Loewe (1966, 169n54) suggested that although the beginning of "Paradise Lost" is modeled on that of the *Iliad,* it is not inconceivable that Milton may have known the motif of the Ten Songs of Jewish history, with their messianic climax, from the Targum to the Song of Songs itself which would have been available to him both in Latin translation and in Brian Walton's *Polyglot.* Origen, in his introduction to the Song of Songs, rehearses a history of progressive revelation in a series of six songs of the Old Testament (Exodus 15, Deuteronomy 32, Judges 5, II Samuel 22=Psalm 18, Isa 5:1*ff,* and the Song of Songs) climaxing in intimacy with Christ in Solomon's Song. Loewe (170), while not claiming any specific connection between the Targum's Ten Songs and Origen's scheme of six, suggested that the whole *Tendenz* of the Targum, which evinces a marked emphasis on Israel's potential perfection, combined with emphasis on the inhibiting effects of her proclivity to sin, owes something to a stimulus originating outside of Judaism.

The Targum to the Song of Songs was seen by Loewe (1966, 170–173) as consisting of five movements:

First Movement, 1:2 – 3:6. (a) (1:2–17) The Exodus and Sinaitic revelation, the sin of the golden calf, atonement effected by Moses' intervention, the merits of the patriarchs, and the construction of the tabernacle prefiguring the Temple. (b) (2:1 – 3:6) The theme repeated, with Israel's triumphant entry into Canaan as the climax. "Contrapuntal" hints taken up in subsequent movements: God's choice of Israel evinced through gift of Torah, particularly the Oral Torah (1:2). Exile as a necessary testing experience for Israel. Solomon's Temple a shadowy prefigurement of the Temple to be built in messianic times. *Second Movement,* 3:7 – 5:1. Solomon's Temple and its dedication (3:7 – 4:1); the devotion of the priests (4:2–5) and the physical protection that the cult affords Israel as long as she remains steadfast in piety and devotion to ancestral institutions (4:6–7). God invites Israel to share occupancy of the Temple, comparing her chastity to that of a bride; he accepts sacrifices and confirms the right of the priesthood to perquisite portions (4:8 – 5:1). *Third Movement,* 5:2 – 6:1. Israel's sin, loss of two and a half tribes, half-hearted and futile remorse followed by true repentance, but too late to stave off punishment of the exile (5:2–7). Israel confides to the prophets her lovesickness for God. Scriptural phrases regarding the lover's physical charms are converted into a panegyric of the Deity's expertise as a Jewish scholar, an assertion of the cosmic significance of Torah, God's concern for the welfare of Jerusalem and Israel's sages (5:8–16). Israel confesses that her own refractoriness has alienated God from her, and the prophets offer to aid her in recovering his love through repentance (6:1). *Fourth Movement,* 6:2 – 7:11. (a) (6:2–12) God accepts her prayer, effects rebuilding of Temple, and reoccupies it in a spirit of reconciliation. He praises Israel's devotion to the cult and to rabbinic scholarship which finds recompense in prosperity that impresses the gentiles. The climax is the divine guarantee of Israel's future well-being. (b) (7:1–11) Theme repeated with variations. *Fifth Movement,* 7:12 – 8:14. (a) Exiled throughout the Roman empire, Israel entreats God to remain accessible to her prayers. She attempts to calculate the date of the future redemption, but abandons prognostication in favor of description of the messianic program (7:14*f*). The Messiah, commissioned to take up his kingdom and reveal himself to Israel, is invited to join Israel in procession to Jerusalem to attend a Talmudic discourse—the anonymous guest lecturer being presumably the Deity Himself (cf. 5:10). The Messiah teaches Israel the fear of God (8:2) and restrains her from haste to return to Jerusalem before the eschatological war is ended (8:4). The resurrected righteous issue from beneath the Mount of Olives into a Land of Israel now purged of defilement of the wicked who had died and been buried there, and earth's inhabitants marvel at Israel's merits and recall the appearance at Sinai to receive the Law

(8:5). Israel requests renewed intimacy with God in perpetuity (8:6). God replies that gentile hostility cannot dissolve his love and that Israel's devotion to Torah in exile will be compensated with a double portion of spoils of the camp of Gog (7:7). (b) The picture reverts to the situation preceding the outbreak of the eschatological war and the angels declare their willingness to support Israel (8:8), if she has been willing to pay (to the Moslems, according to Loewe) money for the Unity of the Name (8:9). Israel affirms her zeal for the Law and finds favor with God and the inhabitants of earth (8:10). (c) A second flashback (8:11–14) concerns the fortunes of the Davidic dynasty to whom God's vineyard Israel had been entrusted for safekeeping. Israel still in exile receives divine assurance (8:13). But the Land is still polluted and unfit for God's occupancy, so he is bidden to retire temporarily to heaven to regard Israel's tribulations with sympathy and wait till such time as he sees fit to restore her to Jerusalem and reestablish the temple cult (8:14).

Four features of the Targumic scenario seemed to Loewe to call for explanation. First, the prominence accorded Torah, or rather the Oral Torah, as the symbol of God's love for Israel and the means by which rabbinic leadership retains God's providential interest even while they are in exile. Secondly, the emphasis on Israel's sin, thirdly, on the atoning value of the temple cultus, and finally, the very restricted role accorded the Messiah. The explanations of these features Loewe found in analysis of the Targum of the Song of Songs as anti-Christian apologetic, on the one hand, and as polemic against Jewish esotericism on the other hand.

The Church inherited from the Synagogue the allegorical approach to the Song of Songs and replaced God and Israel by Christ and the Church as the two main characters of the dialogue. Origen, although not the first to adopt this line, became its classical exponent and his work influenced subsequent Christian commentators. Loewe presents some striking and convincing arguments that the exegesis of the Targum to the Song of Songs is apologetically motivated in reaction to Christian interpretation. It is axiomatic, in Loewe's view, that wherever a piece of rabbinic exegesis implicitly emphasizes Jewish repudiation of a notion or belief so prominently associated with Christianity that any Jew might be expected to have heard about it, that anti-Christian apologetics is to be assumed as the main motivation, though not necessarily the sole motivation, of the Jewish exegete. The same applies when a Jewish exegete takes pains to enunciate some Jewish notion capable of acting as a counterpart to a well-known Christian idea.

Loewe offered two cases of possible or probable interaction between the exegetical ancestry of the Targum and that of Origen and his successors. In 1:5 the basic elements of the Targum's exegesis are *black* in sin, fair in penitence, the reconciliation being effected by the making of the curtains of the tabernacle and by Moses who went up to heaven and made peace between them and their King ("Solomon"). A similar scheme is presented by Origen: *black* in sin, but after penitence, the equivalent of conversion, blackness is no longer a defect but a mark of beauty. Origen pictures the Gentile Christians as chiding Jewish Christians for reproaching them with their ignoble, pagan antecedents. The Gentile Christians claim that they have a beauty all their own achieved through conversion. The comparison with Solomon's curtain, far from being a reproach, is in fact a compliment, the curtains being none other than those of the tabernacle, and "Solomon" standing for Christ the peacemaker. Although the argument is directed against Jewish Christians and not (except perhaps obliquely) against Jews, it is not improbable, according to Loewe, that the Targum here formulates a rejoinder to what was taken as a rebuke by the Church to the Synagogue, countering the implicit Christian claim to have been wholly transmuted through conversion with the assertion of complete reconciliation between God and penitent Israel after their own most spectacular act of apostasy.

In the second instance, 7:5[4E], the Targum presents a eulogy on the scholars of the Sanhedrin who possess the near-esoteric knowledge of astronomy required for calculation (*ḥešbôn*) of calendar intercalation. Aquila's rendering of the place name Heshbon as *epilogismos* presumably reflects an interpretation congruent with that of the Targum since the term is used of calculation of dates (cf. Loewe, 1966, 176n77). Theodoret took note of the Aquilan *epilogismos* and gave it a Christian exegetical twist. "From the many gates (Hebrew *ša'ar baṯ rabbîm*) of the Old and New Testaments, the Apostles, and the patristic writers, the Church has drawn manifold waters of sound teaching and the 'eyes' of pious souls are the pools in which these waters are collected." The text therefore means, according to Theodoret, that "the contemplative activity (*theōriai*) of your soul, and the multitude of your pious reckonings (*logismoi*) resemble pools that gather water from many directions, since you receive from many mouths the flowings of doctrine." According to Loewe, the Church here got hold of the wrong end of the rabbinic stick and whittled it down to a peg on which it crammed most of its own exegetical wardrobe.

Other passages are adduced by Loewe in which the Targumist launches elaborate discussion of the Torah and its significance in order to oppose patristic treatment of the same texts. In 1:2, e.g., the patristic citations merely rehearse and allude to the conventional Pauline view of the Law as a dispensation rendered obsolete by the revelation in Christ. Theodoret put it succinctly: "I have heard of your speech through the medium of the written word, but desire to hear your very voice as well. I would fain receive the holy doctrine by immediate word of mouth, and kiss it with the lips of my own mind." The Targum here insists on the significance of Torah in the theology of election, including the full apparatus of the Oral Torah, the six orders of the Mishnah and the Talmud, and employs markedly particularistic language to enunciate Israel's unique privilege as the recipient of the revelation of Torah. Such emphasis, in Loewe's view, is most satisfactorily accounted for by the assumption that it is a deliberate counterattack.

In 1:3, as one would expect, the ointment was identified by Origen and

Theodoret with the world-wide diffusion of the Christian message. Origen stressed that it was the preaching of Christ's gospel which brought the biblical history of salvation to the world.

Now at last is the name of Moses heard about abroad, having been previously confined to the narrow borders of Judea; for none of the Greeks mention him, nor do we find any written reference to him, or to the rest of the Biblical story in any historical treatise of non-Jewish composition. But as soon as Jesus shone forth in the world, he carried the Law and the Prophets out into it with him, and in very truth our text—*thy name is oil poured out*—so found its fulfillment.

Loewe (1966, 178) suggested that Origen's negative statement that Moses was not a figure of world history before the spread of Christianity is not sufficiently explicit to be intended to controvert the Targum's exegesis. The Targum, however, reflects the midrashic tradition (cf. Loewe, 178nn89,90) that the miracles at the crossing of the Sea won proselytes for Judaism. Allusion to this legend in the Targum's exegesis of 1:4, according to Loewe (179), could well have been motivated by a desire to refute Origen's assertion that the true message of Israel had to wait for Christ not merely for its fulfillment, but for its effectual publication as well.

In 1:4 Loewe thought to have caught the Targumist picking up an actual word from the patristic tradition and turning it to his own account. Origen interpreted the verse to mean that Christ had brought the soul to an understanding of his mind, introducing it thereby into his own royal chamber and this in turn led to Paul's reference (Col 2:3) to Christ in whom all treasures (*thēsauroi*) of wisdom and knowledge are hid. The Targum here uses *ganza,* the exact equivalent of the Greek term *thēsauroi,* as the heavenly source of the Torah, which Loewe (1966, 180) suspected as a deliberate counterassertion of the enduring validity of the Torah and the adequacy of the Sinaitic revelation against the patristic exegetical claims of a new and superior revelation through Christ. The Targumist, Loewe suggested, subtly insinuated his apologia by adopting or reclaiming Paul's reference to the treasures hidden in Christ. Conceivably, also, in Loewe's opinion, the Targumist intended an allusion to the well-known words of Jesus (Matt 5:19) about laying up treasures in heaven as a reminder that this doctrine of supererogatory treasure in heaven had been anticipated in rabbinic thinking. Cf. AB 15[3] on Job 22:28–30.

The treatments of the last two verses of the Canticle by Theodoret and the Targumist exhibit no obviously apologetic matter, but illustrate how the Church and the Synagogue integrated the Song into its own variety of messianism. The exegetical results of Theodoret's lengthy exposition, as summarized by Loewe, are that participation in the kingdom, which ultimately belongs to all Christians as of right through their faith, is not achieved for the present except by the departed righteous who have been placed on the same footing as the incorporeal angels, relieved of corporeal obstacles to that concentration on Christ which is necessary to achieve the kingdom. Christians in this life are frustrated by corporeal obstacles, but possess Christ as an antidote. Having at their disposal only the physical senses for the comprehension of Christ, they pray that the waiting period for Christ's second coming be foreshortened as much as possible.

The Targumist, like Theodoret, acknowledges that the messianic climax of history must be set in motion by a force outside humanity. This, however, is not to be done by a Messiah, but by God Himself. The time for the climax is not yet; but the Targumist neither importunes God to foreshorten the interval nor regards the waiting period as spiritually barren. Israel's function in history is to implement Torah. Reconciled now with God after the cycle of sin, punishment, and true repentance, Israel is conscious that if history is not yet mature enough for its messianic climax, the impediment no longer lies with them. The bones of the wicked continue to defile the Land and their presence symbolizes the unfitness of an unregenerate world for the presence of God. It is not the Messiah, but God who is addressed in the last verse. Whereas the Christian exegesis, dominated by apprehension lest the believer fall prey to the forces of temptation, desires that the period of harrowing waiting be arbitrarily foreclosed, the Targumist bids Israel get quietly on with its job. The difference, in Loewe's view (1966, 184), lies in the doctrine of original sin which Christianity maintains and Judaism rejects.

The rescue of the Song from the clutches of the Church was not the only concern of the Targumist. It was also his purpose, in Loewe's view, to combat Jewish esotericism. Within Jewry itself, the Song had become involved in a complex of esoteric theology which threatened to compromise some of the fundamental principles of Judaism and the Targumist felt obliged to formulate his paraphrase in terms which would convey his rejection of the interpretation developed by Jewish gnostics no less than the patristic Christ-Church exposition. The sort of Jewish gnostic interpretation opposed by the Targumist is represented in the midrashic text called Shi'ur Qōmah (printed, from *sēp̄er rāzî'ēl* and other sources, in Solomon Musajoff, 1921, 30*ff;* cf. G. Scholem, 1965a, 36n1) which gives descriptions and dimensions of God's body based on the catalogue of her lover's physical charms recited by the Lady of the Canticle in 5:10–16. Scholem (61*f*) has pointed to a connection between the Shi'ur Qōmah and one of the hymns preserved in the *hêḵālôṯ rabbāṯî*—a literary genre some of which at least, according to Scholem, ascends to the second or third century of the common era. This hymn links up with a midrashic passage (Genesis Rabbah 3,4) with esoteric affinities regarding the alleged creation of light from the divine garment which Scholem regarded (60) as part of the Shi'ur Qōmah traditions. This, Loewe suggested (1966, 185), must be the background of the Targumist's introduction of reference to the divine garment in the beginning of his own paraphrase of the passage from which, according to Saul Lieberman (cf. Scholem, 1965a, Appendix D, pp. 118*ff*), the Shi'ur Qōmah had grown. The snowy white robe in which God is clothed when occupied with the twenty-four books of Scripture (5:10) Loewe saw as a convention so well-established that the Targumist was unable to bypass it. Consequently, he reinterpreted it in terms appropriate to the meanings which he saw in the passage and repudiated by exclusion the esoteric doctrine of the divine garment as the material from which light was created—a doctrine perhaps the more reprehensible because of its non-esoteric prominence in the history of Greek religious symbolism (1966, 186).

Loewe's detailed comparison of the treatments of 5:10–16 by the Targumist and Theodoret in relation to the mystical dimensions of the Deity presented by the Shi'ur Qōmah (pp. 187–193) is too complex to be summarized here, and it must suffice to note some of his conclusions and generalizations with respect to the Targumist's purposes and methods (pp. 193–195). Some of the sources for the Targumist's exegesis of the Song of Songs can be identified in the midrashic literature, in the Talmuds, and in part from Tannaitic sources. Although the validity of the Song of Songs as an allegory of the relationship of God and Israel was established by Rabbi Aqiba, and may have antedated him, the surviving midrashic sources do not reveal an over-all picture of how the Song is to be interpreted so as to illustrate that relationship. The Targum introduced detailed interpretation along these lines through its marked emphasis on Torah, and particularly on the Oral Torah, as the discourse between God and Israel, a theme round which is constructed a "history of salvation" from the creation of the world to its future eschatological climax. The climax God is anxious to implement, but realism compels the Targumist to recognize that the time is not yet ripe. The history is marked by Israel's love for God and longing for communion with Him, but also marred by Israel's penchant for sinning and the frustrations of Gentile hostility. Atonement is effected by the practical institutions which derive from the Torah—the Temple and sacrificial cult, rabbinic learning and the direction of the Sanhedrin—contingent always upon true repentance in response to God's constant demand.

The Targum's emphasis on the abiding value of these institutions Loewe saw as constituting mute repudiation of Christian notions of original sin, atonement, and salvation through Christ to whose relation with the Church Christian exegetes had reapplied the allegorical interpretation of the Song of Songs inherited from the Synagogue. The Targumist's reaction against the Christian tradition of exegesis, according to Loewe, affords adequate explanation of the de-emphasis of the role of the Messiah in the eschatological climax. Loewe's postulation of anti-Christian apologetic as the Targumist's motivation need not stand or fall on the possibility of indicating actual points of contact with Christian exegesis of the Canticle, although there are a number of likely instances of this. Paul's idea of the Church as the true Israel was "in the air" and sufficient cause for a counterattack from Judaism. It would have been strange indeed if the Synagogue had failed to react to the notion of the

Church as the Bride of Christ being identified with the maiden of the Song. The refutation was essayed by means of the theme of the Oral Torah discovered as implicit in the very document on which the Church staked its own claim.

At the time the Targum to the Songs took shape, after A.D. 636, the conventional rabbinic circles to which the author-redactor belonged were also viewing with misgivings the extravagances in Jewish esoteric circles which read the maiden's praise of her lover's physical charms as a description of the mystical body of God. This exegetical endeavor Scholem has shown to go back to Tannaitic times and has characterized it as a Gnostic movement which nevertheless remained, paradoxically, within the orthodox (or orthopractic) orbit of Toranic observance. The Targumist's exegesis of the crucial passage in the Song (5:10–16) was geared to an interpretation of the physical description as an allegory of the metaphysical significance of Torah and in particular of the functional significance of Oral Torah, according to Loewe. The Targumist was fighting a war on two fronts, "Zweifrontenkrieg," but on ground which he himself had carefully chosen. His weapon was the theme of Torah and Israel's unique possession of the Oral Torah. The weapon, however, was wielded more against one front than the other. The Christian interpretation had to be completely repudiated, while the Jewish esoteric extravagance had merely to be checked and kept in place, out of the reach of the immature whose stable fare should always be the Oral Torah in its practical halakic aspect. The question of the Targum's influence on later Jewish exegesis, in particular its relation to the Zohar, go beyond the scope of Loewe's investigation, and certainly also beyond the scope of this attempt at summary. The Targum's abiding influence, however, is reflected in various Jewish vernacular folk-versions of the Song of Songs, in Spanish, Italian, Arabic, and Hebrew, some of which were still being printed in the nineteenth century and may occasionally be heard chanted in Sephardi communities to this day.

Because of the importance of the Targum for the history of interpretation, a translation is given in the NOTES with each verse, along with other samples of Jewish and Christian interpretation.

Following the development of the Targum to the Song of Songs, there is a gap in our information on Jewish exegesis of the Song until the time of the great savant Saadia who was born in Egypt about 892 and died in the year 942. He was Gaon, or spiritual and intellectual leader, of the Jewish community in Babylon and among his many philosophical and exegetical works, including a translation of the Bible into Arabic, is a commentary on the Song of Songs which was originally composed in Arabic and later translated into Hebrew. His observation that the Song of Songs is like a lock to which the key has been lost was cited above and bears repeating since it applies to the key which he fashioned and to subsequent efforts as well.

In his introductory summary Saadia agrees in essence with the interpretation of the Targum, that in the Song of Songs Solomon relates the history of the Jews, beginning with the Exodus and extending to the advent of the Messiah. His stress on the Oral Law also accords with the Targumist's emphasis. When, however, he comes to the exegesis of the text, verse by verse, his exposition bears little relationship to that of the Targum. According to Saadia's analysis, in 1:2–3:5 is described Israel's servitude in Egypt, the emancipation, the giving of the Law, the battles with Sihon and Og, and God's displeasure at Israel's reaction to the report of the spies. In 3:6–4:7 the erection of the Tabernacle, the wilderness wanderings, and the status of Moses and Aaron are described. The entry into Canaan, the building of the Temple, the separation of Israel and Judah, the move of the Shekinah to abide with Judah, and the people's pilgrimage to Jerusalem at the three great festivals are the subjects treated in 4:8–5:1. Verses 5:2–6:3 take the history through the destruction of the Temple, the Babylonian Exile and Return, the Second Temple and renewed covenant with the penitent people. The spiritual welfare of the returnees was seen as treated in 6:4–9. Some were faithful and godly, but others married foreign women and forgot the holy tongue. The ongoing dispersion is the concern of 6:10–7:9, in which the people remain many days without king or priest, but still belong to God. The sufferings of the Messiah son of Joseph and the manifestation of the Messiah son of David, an obedient Israel, and God's joy with them as a bridegroom with his bride, are the subjects of 7:12–8:4. From 8:5 to the end are described Israel's restoration, the building of the Third Temple, and a grateful people acting in accord with the divine will.

Rabbi Solomon (son of) Isaac, known by his initials as Rashi, was born at Troyes in 1040 and died there about 1105. His commentaries, especially on the Pentateuch, continue to hold first place in Jewish scriptural study. Rashi at the beginning of the introduction to his commentary on the Song of Songs alludes briefly to other interpretations, some offering exposition of the entire book, and others of separate passages, but all incompatible both with the context and with the language of Scripture. He, therefore, resolved to understand the implications of the text, explaining it in order, and including the interpretations of the rabbis.

"My view," said Rashi,

> is that Solomon (fore)saw by the Holy Spirit, that Israel would be carried into one exile after another and would suffer one calamity after another; that in exile they would lament their former glory and remember the former love which God had shown them above all other nations; that they would say, "I will go and return to my first husband, for it was better with me than now" (Hosea 2:9[7E]); that they would remember God's kindnesses and their evil sin and the benefits God promised them at the end of days. Hence Solomon produced this book by divine inspiration in the language of a woman saddened by a living widowhood, longing for her love. She recalls their love in youth and confesses her guilt. Her lover is saddened by her sorrow and remembers the loyalty of her youth, the charms of

her beauty, and her good works which had bound him to her with an everlasting love. The intent was to show Israel that God did not afflict her willingly, that though He did put her away, He has not cast her off, for she is still His wife, and He her husband, and ultimately will return to her.

Rashi's grandson Rabbi Samuel ben Meir, or Rashbam, also produced a commentary along the lines laid out by his grandfather. The Song, according to Rashbam, represents exiled Israel as a virgin sighing and mourning for her love who left her and went far away, as describing his eternal love for her, declaring in a Song, "Such ardent love my love did show when with me," and telling her friends and companions in colloquial manner, "Thus did my love speak to me and thus I answered him."

While the commentaries of Rashi and Rashbam were giving comfort and hope to depressed Jewish communities in France and Germany, the celebrated Ibn Ezra, Rabbi Abraham Ibn Ezra ben Meir, or Raba, composed a commentary for the help of his coreligionists in Spain. The commentary was presented in three different glosses, as he explained at the beginning:

Says Abraham the Spaniard:
I will interpret this book with all my ability,
As far as my power extends,
If YHWH God be with me.
So that in his ways I may be perfect,
I have explained it three times:
The first time I will disclose
Every hidden word.
The second time I will declare its explicity
In accordance with its simplicity.
In the third it will be interpreted
Along the lines of the Midrash.

The first exposition dealing with lexical and grammatical matters shows a keen philological sense. The second is introduced apologetically:

This book surpasses all the songs which Solomon composed and perish utterly perish its being (understood as) erotic literature. Rather it is by way of allegory (*māšāl*), like the prophecy of Ezekiel concerning Israel, "And behold your time was a time of love," "your breasts were formed," "and I covered your nakedness," "and you became mine" (Ezek 16:7,8); and when it is said with reference to the captivity, "where is the bill of your mother's divorce?" (Isa 50:1) and, again, of future time, "as the groom rejoices over the bride, so shall your God rejoice over you" (Isa 62:5). Were it not a book of high import, as spoken by the Holy Spirit, it would not have defiled the hands (i.e. have been admitted to the canon of sacred Scripture). This is the simple sense. In the Third Exposition I will interpret and allegorize it (1:2–3). A girl outside the city in the vineyards saw a shepherd passing by and became enamoured of him and longed for him in her heart and said, "O that he would kiss me many times." And, as if he were hearing her, she spoke to him thus: "For better is your love than wine. Your love gladdens more than wine, because of the odor of your ointments, for your name is like ointment which is poured out, the odor of which is diffused, therefore the girls love you" (1:4). Each one says to him, "Draw me! And even were the king to bring me to his chambers, we would rejoice more in you. The subject of the second 'they love you' is again damsels (*'ălāmôṯ*)."

Ginsburg (46) stressed that "it has generally been overlooked that Ibn Ezra distinctly states in the second gloss in which he professes to give the literal meaning of the narrative, that "the lovers are a *shepherd* and a *shepherdess* and that the *king* is a *separate* and *distinct* person from the beloved shepherd." This Ginsburg hailed as "an important step to the right understanding of the Book."

Actually Ibn Ezra was not so explicit on this point as Ginsburg alleged. At the beginning of 1:2 he identifies the lover as a shepherd, but said nothing about Solomon: "A damsel outside the city in the vineyards sees a shepherd passing by and falls in love with him, and longs for him in her heart and says, 'O that he would kiss me many times.'" Solomon is several times mentioned in the second exposition, in connection with 1:5, 3:7, 6:8, 8:11. In 3:7 the implication is that Solomon is an outsider distinct from the (shepherd) lover who speaks, but this is not explicitly stated.

In the Third Exposition, interpreted along the line of the Midrash, Ibn Ezra explained that

> Some say that the "daughters of Jerusalem" signify the nations of the world, as "I will give them to you as daughters, but not of your covenant" (Ezek 16:61). Others say that the daughters of Jerusalem mean literally daughters, the mother being the assembly of Israel represented as talking to her daughters as a man talks with his own thoughts, as will be clear to you from "where is the bill of your mother's divorce?" (Isa 50:1) and likewise "And Jerusalem shall dwell again in her place, in Jerusalem" (Zech 12:6), and it says "Make Jerusalem know" (Ezek 16:2). He began with their being in Egypt and Solomon began from the days of Abraham who was the head.

In the opinion of Graetz (1871, 119), cited by H. J. Matthews in the Preface to his Translation of the Commentary of Ibn Ezra on the Canticle (1874, x),

> Ibn Ezra was fully conscious that the Canticles in their simple literal meaning contain a love-story, but he had not the independence and not sufficient boldness to follow up this knowledge, and, consequently, in the exposition of this book as of other books of Holy Scripture, especially the Pentateuch, he employed all sorts of devices as a blind, so as not to be charged with heresy as being a rationalist. He explained the Canticles in a simple sense as a love-song, at the same time applying them in an allegorical sense to the synagogue. But he was only serious with the First Exposition (called by him "the second time" [*happa'am haššēnîṯ*] because the First puts together the grammatical and lexicographical matter), in which he conceives the Canticles as a song of the love that existed between a young girl and a shepherd. As Ibn Ezra possessed a fine exegetical tact, his "Second" Exposition contains much that is right, and had it been made use of by the later commentators, it might have led to the just interpretation of the Canticles. In truth it is his own fault that the sober side of his commentary was overlooked; he has played at hide and seek.

In Graetz's words, "er hat Verstecken gespielt."

Ibn Ezra mentioned in the introduction to his commentary that philosophers explain the book as referring to the mysterious harmony of the universe and to the union of the divine soul with the earthly body. The philosophical interpretation had considerable vogue in Jewish intellectual circles in the Middle Ages. Joseph Ibn Caspi early in the thirteenth century composed a brief commentary explaining the Song of Songs as representing the union between the active intellect and the receptive material intellect. The discovery of the general design of the book was credited to a suggestion of the luminary Maimonides in his *Guide to the Perplexed* (part III, ch. 51). With all the particulars of this book, Solomon intended merely to hint at the subject in general, according to Ibn Caspi. It is most certain that he calls here the highest order of the human intellect "the fairest of women," and the active intellect (*haśśēḵel happô'ēl*) "the handsome lover"; frequently the latter term designates the whole intellectual mind, for this is the meaning required in several places in the book. It is known that the active intellect stirs up or brings the receptive intellect from rest to action, as is known to the philosophers; that the intellect requires that you should seek it, as it is written, "If you seek it, it will be found by you."

After having explained the general design, it is not necessary to explain particulars; the design is indicated in only a few passages, while the whole is treated in accordance with the train of a poetical composition and logical science; and this Solomon declares in the beginning of the book by saying "The Song of Songs." (For more of Ibn Caspi's commentary, with the Hebrew text in the footnote, cf. Ginsburg, 47–49.)

A similar and more elaborate commentary explaining the Song of Songs as representing the union of the receptive and active intellects was composed by Moses Ibn Tibbon about the same time as Joseph Ibn Caspi. A few generations later Immanuel ben Solomon, spiritual leader of the Jewish community in Rome, known as "the Prince of Knowledge in Rome" (*'allûp̄ hadda'aṯ bĕmaḡdî'ēl*), produced a commentary elaborating the intellectual interpretation. The following samples are based on the translation of Immanuel's exposition of the first verse given by Ginsburg (49–55 with the Hebrew text in the footnote): Immanuel agreed with the opinion of the Rabbins

> . . . that this book is the most sublime of all the Books given by inspiration. Expositors, however, differ in its interpretation, and their opinions are divided, according to the diversity of their knowledge. There are some—but these are such as go no further than the material world, and that which their eye sees, looking forward to the good of this world and its glory, to the great reward of their labors and a recompense from God, desiring to be restored to their greatness, and to the land flowing with milk and honey, and to have their stomachs filled with the flesh of the Leviathan, and the best of wines preserved in its grapes—such men interpret this sublime song as having reference to the history of the Patriarchs, their going down to Egypt, their Exodus from thence with a mighty hand and out-

stretched arm, the giving of the Law, the entry into the land of Canaan, the settlement of Israel in it, their captivity, restoration, the building of the second Temple, the present dispersion, and their final ingathering which is to take place. Such interpreters regard this book, which is holy of holies, as some common book, or historical record of any of the kings, which is of very little use, and the reading of which is only a loss of time. But there are other sages and divines, who have attained to know the value of true wisdom; they are separated from the material world, despise the mere temporal things, heartily desire to know the courts of the Lord, and have a footing in the Jerusalem which is above, and with heart and flesh sing to the living God; these have put off the garments of folly, and clothed themselves in the robes of wisdom, and while searching after the mysteries of this precious book through the openings of the figures of silver, glanced at golden apples of the allegory concealed in it. They in the vessel of their understanding, traversed its sea, and brought to light from the depth, the reality of the book. Thus they have declared that the book was composed to explain the possibility of a reunion with the incorporeal mind, which forms *the perceptive faculty,* and influences it with abundant goodness.

The female-companion (*r'yh*) corresponds to the corporeal intellect (*haśśēḵel haḥomrî*) which longs for the influence of the active intellect (*haśśēḵel happô'ēl*) and desires to be like it as much as possible, to cleave to it and to come up to its standing, which is its ultimate end and purpose. (Ginsburg here rendered *hr'yh* as "The shepherds," presumably an error for "shepherdess," which meaning he wished to read into the term in the interest of his own theory of interpretation.)

The learned divines mentioned above expounded the design of the book in general, but did not explain it in regular order from beginning to end, until the celebrated sage, Moses Ibn Tibbon, explained the book according to wisdom. But even Ibn Tibbon overlooked several particulars and failed to notice their design and perceptive contemporaries, wishing to know more of the book, insisted with a command of love that Immanuel himself write a complete commentary following the path marked out by the learned Ibn Tibbon.

The book, as all truly wise men who commented on it have seen, according to Immanuel, is divisible into three main sections, viz. 1:2–2:17, 3:1–5:1, and 5:2 to the end. The three sections refer to three different kinds of men. The first section (1:2–2:17) represents man in the garden of Eden before he sinned and brought into activity his choice for good and evil. "Turn, my love, and be like a gazelle," etc. (2:17) represents one who endeavors to learn wisdom, but is afraid lest he should be terrified when looking up to God, seeing that his fruit is not yet ripe. Again, "Catch us the foxes," etc. teaches that the fruit is not yet ripe. In the first section there is no mention that the female-companion (*hr'yh*) actually ate the fruit (Ginsburg here rendered *hr'yh* as "the shepherdess," in the interest of his own theory). When she said, "I desired to sit under its shade, and its fruit is sweet to my taste" (2:3) merely declares her desire. The term fruit is here used in the sense of *words, wisdom,* and *instruction.* The entire first section of the Song, therefore, refers to the mind of man when still young, before it develops to the purpose for which its existence was designed, and when the powers of the body still control because he has not pursued his studies beyond mathematics and physics. The first section is subdivided into two parts. The first part (1:2–2:7) represents one who fears God and shuns evil, but his knowledge of God is derived from tradition and he has no wisdom of his own. The second part of the first section (2:8–17) represents one who has studied mathematics and physics.

The second section (3:1–5:1) represents one who has found the virtuous woman whose desire is to her husband, and who seeks her beloved while upon her couch, and in whom her husband may safely trust; that is, a mind which has developed its potential to reality and has, as it were, stretched forth its hand and taken of the tree of life, eaten, and lives forever. This is the meaning of 3:4. In 3:9 he is called King Solomon, but elsewhere Solomon, or Shulamite, the feminine form. The beloved came to his garden, ate and drank, and with his friends indulged in a sumptuous feast (5:1). This means, according to Immanuel, that he took from the tree of life, ate, and lived forever, without trouble or hindrance, having passed through all three (degrees) in proper order, he finished the course without committing mischief or error. His carnal powers, which are the watchmen who walk the city, and especially his intellectual powers, which are those that guard the walls, are all profitable, pointing the right way to the mind, and never misleading, hindering, or delaying its course. When she asked the watchmen, "Have you seen him whom my soul loves?" (3:3), they did not answer her, because it is not in their nature to teach. But when she had passed them, she found her beloved and was united with him (3:4) and they made a couch and a palanquin, rejoicing and feasting.

The second section is also subdivided into two parts (3:1–5 and 3:6–5:1) and the second part is epexegetical of the first.

The third section (from 5:2 on) represents a man who has a sinful wife beguiled by carnal appetites and she has eaten of the tree of knowledge of good and evil and has given also to her husband with her and he has eaten. The expression *with her* is stressed because man cannot eat of it except *with her*. Man, indeed, has no access to it, except through the woman; she finds it and takes it up; she is the one who pursues pleasure, and is drawn after sensual lust. But she when retiring to bed does not seek for him or wait for him, but undresses, washes her feet, perfumes her fingers with myrrh, which is temporal instead of eternal ointment, falls asleep, and is even too lazy to open when her beloved knocks at the door (5:2–4). Her husband, however, influences her, and she repents and opens to him in spite of her great laziness, as she was not in a deep sleep, her heart being awake. But her beloved had gone away. She sought him and could not find him. The guards found her and beat her and stripped off her cloak. They misdirected and hindered her from getting to her beloved. Sin once tasted is hard to forsake. It is not stated in Scripture that Adam after the fall ever ate of the tree of life. This may be a hint, according to Immanuel, that it is almost impossible for one who has once eaten of the tree of knowledge of good and evil to eat of the tree of life. "For the difficulty of uniting a couple a second time is as great as dividing the Reed Sea," which was supernatural, but it is not really impossible. Thus Solomon left the matter hidden (*sāṯûm*). He recounted how they longed for each other afterward and praised one another like lovers, but they are no more found united and have no more a nuptial couch, a palanquin (*'appîryôn*), feast or joy in the way of man and wife. At the end we find him cautioning her and saying, "neighbors hear your voice," since it is not proper for a woman to make her voice heard by young men, "for a woman's voice is nakedness" (i.e. sexually exciting). He requests her to let her voice be heard by him and no other. But she brazenly said to him, "Flee, my love" etc. (8:14), as if the neighbors were husbands and her love a paramour who must hide and flee from them lest they accost him.

This section also is subdivided into two parts, the first 5:2–8:5 and the second 8:5 to the end of the book. The second part is epexegetical of the first. This, according to Immanuel, is the division of the Book in accordance with the consensus of sages who spoke in exposition of this book.

Ginsburg (56) felt it important to assert that the distinguished poet Immanuel took the hero and heroine of the plot to be a shepherd and a shepherdess, and regarded Solomon as a *separate* person whom the rustic maiden adduced in illustration of her deep and sincere love to her shepherd, affirming that if this great king were to bring her into his court and offer her all its grandeur and luxuries, she would still rejoice in her humble lover. It is difficult to find either in the Hebrew text which Ginsburg cites, or even in his own translation of it, adequate grounds for this assertion. No reference to 1:4 is cited and the references to King Solomon, Solomon, and Shulamite suggest that all these are designations of the husband. The literal history of the sincere and ardent attachment formed between a humble shepherd and shepherdess which Ginsburg found beautifully explained by Immanuel before attempting to palm upon it his philosophical theory appears to have been read into Immanuel's treatment.

Immanuel's contemporary, Rabbi Levi ben Gershon, or Ralbag, presented the same philosophical theory in a lengthy commentary which was printed in the Amsterdam Rabbinical Bible of 1724.

Ginsburg found in the Bodleian Library at Oxford an anonymous manuscript commentary on the Song of Songs which he judged, from appearance and style and use of French words, to have been written by a French Jew in the twelfth or thirteenth century. This commentary, Ginsburg reported (p. 56),

interprets *this Song as celebrating the virtuous love contracted between a humble shepherd and shepherdess;* and likewise regards Solomon *as a distinct person,* whom the shepherdess adduces in illustration of her deep and sincere attachment to her beloved, affirming, that if this great king were to offer her all the splendour and luxury of his court, she would spurn all, and remain faithful to her humble shepherd.

Although the handwriting was bad and much effaced, Ginsburg considered the manuscript valuable for its remarks on the verbal difficulties and poetic figures of the Song and suggested that its publication would amply repay any Hebrew scholar and would be a boon to Biblical and Hebrew literature. Ginsburg's esteem for this manuscript was doubtless influenced in part by the purported agreement with his own interpretation.

The manuscript (Bodleian MS. Oppenheim 625) has since been edited by H. J. Matthews, 1896. S. Salfeld (1879b, 76*f*) gave a brief description of this commentary on the basis of Duke's citations (Jeschurun) and classed it among four anonymous commentaries in the sense of Kimchi, many of its explanations being taken from Ibn Ezra and David Kimchi. Matthews concurred with Ginsburg in ascribing the composition to a French rabbi of the thirteenth century. More than thirty interesting French words in Hebrew transliteration are sprinkled throughout the commentary. The author quotes by name Parchon, Ibn Ezra, and Yefet (ben 'Ali) and he must have been familiar with Rashi, although he is not cited. Matthews flatly declared that "Ginsburg is wrong in his statement that the anonymous commentator regards the lover and Solomon as distinct persons" and this judgment is confirmed by the present writer's perusal of the text. The commentary is of interest in the history of medieval Jewish exposition of the Song by reason of its explanation as an erotic poem without reference to allegorical interpretation.

In the middle of the fourteenth century Rabbi Isaac Sehula, urged by his friends to produce a commentary on the Song of Songs, surveyed the existing expositions and was bewildered by the conflicting theories. Some, he found, explained it literally, others related it to the union of the body with the soul, still others expounded it according to the Midrash, and others again held that it represents the union of the active and passive intellect. All these he felt compelled to reject in favor of the theory that it represents the love of the people of Israel to their God. (Cf. Ginsburg, 57 for citation of a portion of the Hebrew text from a manuscript in the Bodleian Library.)

From the mid-fourteenth to the mid-eighteenth centuries a number of Jewish commentaries were produced, repeating and elaborating previous views with little novelty. Among those that merit mention but need not be given a great deal of attention are: Meir Arma of Saragossa who was born about 1475 and whose commentary espousing the philosophical interpretation was printed in the Amsterdam Rabbinical Bible of 1724, and Obadiah Sforno who died in 1550 and whose commentary, also published in the Amsterdam Rabbinical Bible, presented the traditional interpretation stressing the mutual bonds of love between God and His most favored people. The composer of the Song, according to Sforno, set forth the kindness of God and His mercy on all His creatures and how from these He chose a lineage who love Him and know His name. His kindness overcame His people and thus it is fitting that their love for Him be great and strong. The whole book presents the words of the congregation of Israel to God while they were in the agony of the exile and God's response. Others—Moses of Cordovero, Abraham Levi, Ibn Shoeb, Elisha Galico, Moses Alshech—produced commentaries on the Song toward the end of the sixteenth century.

In the late sixteenth century a new idea was proposed by the celebrated Don Isaac Abravanel who saw the protagonists of the Song of Songs as Solomon and Wisdom rather than God and Israel. Thus it was necessary to regard only the Bride as an allegorical figure, with Solomon speaking for himself as the Bridegroom and lover of Wisdom. This view was followed and developed by Abravanel's son, Leo Hebraeus (cf. *Dialogi di Amore,* 1564, ch. iii. See Rowley, 199n4, for bibliography to which may be added Delitzsch in Literaturblatt des Orients, no. 6, 1840, cited by Ginsburg, 58n7). This line of interpretation was followed by few subsequent scholars, notably E. F. K. Rosenmüller and was adopted and adapted in the present century by Gottfried Kuhn (1926), who identified the Bride with Wisdom but saw the Bridegroom as a type of the seeker after wisdom rather than as the historical Solomon. Kuhn also gave the book its plain meaning, since every pure marriage to a degree can find its image (*Spiegelbild*) in the Sublime Song (p. 60, cited by Rowley, 199n4). This interpretation takes on new interest in light of the Qumran text of the acrostic poem of Sir 51:13–30.

The following translation is based on the Hebrew text as reconstructed by J. A. Sanders (1971) and is, perforce, strongly influenced by this, Sanders' most recent rendering (pp. 432*f*), as well as by his previous efforts (1965, 84, and 1967, 117). The present writer is in agreement with Sanders and M. Delcor (1968), in discerning in the poem deliberate ambiguity, *mots à double entente,* both erotic and pious, despite denials of erotic intent by A. Di Lella (1966, 92–95) and I. Rabinowitz (1971, 174) and P. W. Skehan's evasion of the issue (1971). The translation here offered is quite literal, and philological commentary is unnecessary for present purposes. The perceptive reader need hardly be informed that "hand" and "foot" are elsewhere euphemisms for genitalia in order to appreciate that Solomon's affair with Wisdom is related in terms most intimate and non-Platonic.

The line numbers correspond to those of Sanders' reconstructed text and translation (1971, 431–433).

1 I was a lad, ere I had erred,
Then did I seek her.
2 She came to me in her beauty
And to the end I explored her.
3 Blossoms drop in ripening;
Grapes rejoice the heart.

4 My foot trod in the plain,
For from my youth I knew her.
5 I inclined my ear a little,
And much instruction I got.
6 A nurse she became to me,
And for my tutelage I give praise.

7 I was eager to sport with her,
I was zealous for good,
I would not turn back.
8 I kindled my desire for her,
And my face I did not avert.
9 I stirred my desire for her,
And on her heights I was not lax.
10 My hand open[ed her gates],
[And] her secrets I contemplated.
11 My palms I cleansed for [her,
And in her purity I found her].
12 [A mind I got for her from the start;
Therefore I will not forsake her.
13 My loins burned like an oven to look at her,
So I bought her, a good buy.
14 Yahweh made my reward eloquence
And with my tongue I praise him.
15 Turn aside to me, O fools,
And lodge in my house of study.
16 How long will you lack all this,
And your throat thirst for her wealth?
17 My mouth I opened and spoke with her.
Buy for yourselves Wisdom without money;
18 Your necks bring to her yoke,
And her burden let your soul bear.
19 Near is she to all who seek her;
He who sets his soul finds her.
20 See with your eyes that I was young,
But I toiled for her and found her.
21 Hear fully what I learned in my youth,
Silver and gold acquire with me.
22 My soul will delight in my school,
And not be ashamed of my song.
23 Your works perform in righteousness,
And he will grant] your reward in its time.

In the mid-eighteenth century a new era began in Jewish study of the Bible and in Hebrew literature in general with the movement for enlightenment launched by the philosopher Moses Mendelssohn. Mendelssohn's translation of the Song of Songs was published in Berlin in 1788 with introduction and commentary by his colleagues Löwe and Wolfssohn who pointed to the conflicting views of the Rabbins which obviously could not all be right and they questioned whether any were right. The commentary considered only the literal sense, with philological notes, and referred those fond of mazes to the traditional treatments. The book was divided into a series of separate songs, some celebrating the love between a shepherd and shepherdess, others between a king and a princess. (Ginberg's survey has here [p. 59] a prize misprint "between the king and his princes.")

On the Jewish side of the scale, the credit or blame for the invention of what was for a while regarded as the true design of the Song goes to S. Löwisohn, who first elaborated the view that the Song of Songs celebrates the victory of true and virtuous love in humble life over the temptations of royalty; that this book records the virtuous liaison of a shepherdess and a shepherd, the rustic maid being tempted by the celebrated savant and bon vivant Solomon to transfer her affections, spurned every allurement and enticement and remained faithful to her humble lover (1816, 32–41). In this Löwisohn was anticipated in part by the Christian exegete J. F/T. C. Jacobi (on the confusion with respect to the second initial, cf. Rowley, 203n3), who some forty-five years before had thought to rescue the Sublime Song from reproach by an easy and unaffected explanation (Jacobi, 1772; cf. Ginsburg, 87*f* and Rowley, 203n3). Löwisohn's explanation was not followed by the learned Leopold Zunz (1832, 334, nor in his introduction to A. Bernstein's commentary of 1834; cf. Ginsburg, 59n3 and Rowley, 208n5) who regarded the Song as an *epithalamium,* but it was adopted by Dr. S. Herxheimer, chief rabbi of Anhalt, and by Christian David Ginsburg, who was born in Warsaw, versed in Jewish learning, converted to Christianity before he was fifteen, and spent some time as a missionary to Jews before he composed his Commentary to the Song of Songs in 1857 at the age of twenty-six. Ginsburg will be considered below among Christian exegetes, although his interpretation is equally valid or invalid for either faction of the People of the Book.

Ginsburg at the end (p. 60n3) of his survey of Jewish exegesis of the Song of Songs up to his day, the middle of the nineteenth century, gives a list of the names of some of the Jewish commentators and the Hebrew titles of their works, selected from a large number of authors of the seventeenth to the nineteenth centuries, which he was not able to analyze in his historical sketch. The present writer spent a part of the summer of 1967 scanning the catalogue of works on the Song of Songs in the Library of the Hebrew University in Jerusalem, including a considerable number in Yiddish, but hurried perusal of a few of the more provocative items sufficed to confirm the impression that such gleanings were unlikely to repay the effort. A listing of titles would considerably enlarge without enhancing this sketch.

Christian Interpretations

Christian exposition of Solomon's Sublime Song may be conveniently surveyed more or less in chronological order up to the last century when modern criticism and the recovery of some of the religious literatures of ancient Egypt, Mesopotamia, Syria, and Anatolia added new and provocative data and sparked novel and revised views of the Song, allegorical and otherwise.

Allegorical interpretation of sacred poetry was by no means a Jewish or Christian invention. Early Greek intellectuals who were repelled by the plain meaning of some of the cherished poetry of their culture found ways to attribute to the offending passages explanations quite at variance with the simple sense. The gross behavior of the Homeric gods was transformed by means of allegory by such early philosophers as Xenophanes, Pythagoras, and Plato.

J. Tate (1927, 214*f*) traced the reading of new meaning into Homeric myth back as far as Pherecydes of Syros who was born ca. 600 B.C. Origen

(*Contra Celsum* VI 42) quoted Celsus to the effect that Zeus' words to Hera (*Iliad* XV 18) are the words of God to matter which hint darkly that God took matter in its originally confused state and bound it by certain proportions and ordered it. Celsus said that Pherecydes thus understood the verses of Homer and similarly with reference to the netherworld (*Iliad* I 590). Thus two offending passages of Homer were given new and more acceptable meaning by conforming them to the new cosmology. Pherecydes was credited with reading doctrine into the myths and like the later philosophers remolding and extending the myths in the interest of philosophy. Accordingly the origins of allegorical interpretation may be sought among the early philosophers who expressed their doctrines in mythical language and attempted to interpret mythical and poetic traditions as though they were conscious allegories. Maximus of Tyre (IV 4, ed. Hobein) mentions Pherecydes and Heraclitus as having used mythology to express philosophic truth, thus proving, in Maximus' view, that Homer and Hesiod did the same. What it may rather prove, Tate suggested (p. 215), is that Pherecydes and Heraclitus thought (like Maximus) that this is what Homer and Hesiod had done. Whether Heraclitus and Empedocles actually did regard the mythical traditions as explicitly allegorical, and did so interpret them, remains uncertain. In any case, it is probable that allegorical interpretation did not spring full-blown from the brain of the grammarian Theagenes of Rhegium, whom Tatian assigned to the time of Cambyses, as historians of Greek allegorical interpretation have assumed. It is more likely that it started even earlier and grew gradually with the conscious and deliberate use of mythical and poetic language to express religious and philosophical thought. In the Hellenistic era the Stoics especially resorted to allegory to relieve the embarrassment occasioned by the bad examples set for mortals by the gods. In the mythology the gods were all too human and emotionally involved in conflict and intrigue and thus were unacceptable models for the Stoic ideal of dispassionate equanimity. Thus the carnal passions of the gods had to be sublimated and transformed by allegory into indifferent and dispassionate spirituality.

When Christianity moved from Palestine westward into the Hellenistic-Roman world, the ideals of the Church were progressively influenced by and conformed to those of the Gentile rather than the Jewish world. In the Hellenistic-Roman cults of the Levant, holiness and purity were associated with sexual renunciation. The Roman Vestal Virgins were paragons of virtue. The frank sexuality of the Song of Songs may thus have presented special problems for the Western Gentile Christians and provoked objections to its inclusion in the sacred Scriptures. Marcion argued that all the Hebrew Scriptures ought to be rejected by Christianity because they falsely asserted that the good God had created nature and the natural impulses. The Song of Songs in particular was deemed unworthy of acceptance as Holy Writ because of its sensual anti-ascetic character. Marcion's view was rejected by the

Church which elected to accept the entire Hebrew canon rather than throw it all away or prolong controversy over the merits of individual books. Thus from the early days of the Church, Solomon's salacious Song, which at first blush tended to appeal to the pernicious pruriency of men, women, and children, had to be interpreted in a way that would eliminate the evil impulse and transform and spiritualize carnal desire into praise of virginity and celibacy and sexless passion of the human soul and/or the Church for God, and of God's response in kind. This was accomplished by means of allegorical interpretation in much the same way that the Greek philosophers had managed to change the lusty gods of Homer and Hesiod into spiritual ideals. Celibate Christian theologians were thus able by allegory to unsex the Sublime Song and make it a hymn of spiritual and mystical love without carnal taint. *Canticum Canticorum* thus became the favorite book of ascetics and monastics who found in it, and in expansive sermons and commentaries on it, the means to rise above earthly and fleshly desire to the pure platonic love of the virgin soul for God. In the medieval cloisters, as among the Jews of the ghettos, no other book of sacred Scripture received more attention than the Song of Songs.

The first Christian known to have allegorized the Song of Songs was the Roman Hippolytus who lived around A.D. 200. Only fragments of Hippolytus' commentary have survived, but enough remains to show how the sensual language was taken to mean something quite different from the plain and simple sense. The one introduced into the chamber(s) in 1:4 was explained as those whom Christ had wedded and brought into his Church. The breasts in 4:5 meant the Old and New Covenants. The "hill of frankincense" in 4:6 was the eminence to which those who crucify fleshly desire are exalted. (Cf. P. C. Hanson, 1959, 116*f.*)

A pioneer Christian commentator on the Song of Songs was Origen, who flourished in the middle of the third century and produced extensive commentaries on the Bible. Most of the original Greek of Origen's ten-volume commentary on the Song of Songs has been lost, but four books were translated into Latin by Rufinus, as far as "the little foxes" of 2:15, and two of Origen's homilies on the Canticle were translated by Jerome himself. Jerome, in the prologue to his translation of the two homilies, addressed to the Most Blessed Pope Damasus (Damasus I, 366–384), gave this appraisal:

> While Origen surpassed all writers in his other books, in his *Song of Songs* he surpassed himself. In ten full volumes, containing nearly twenty thousand lines, he expounded first the version of the Seventy, then those of Aquila, Symmachus, and Theodotion, and finally a fifth, which he tells us that he found on the coast near Actium. And this exposition of his is so splendid and so clear, that it seems to me that the words, *The King brought me into His chamber,* have found their fulfilment in him. I have passed over that work, for it would require far too much time and labor and expense worthily to render into Latin such a mighty theme. It is not strong meat that I offer here; instead of that, with greater faithfulness than

elegance I have translated these two treatises which he composed for babes and sucklings into the speech of every day, to give you just a sample of his thinking, so that you may reflect how highly his great thoughts should be esteemed, when even his little ones can so commend themselves (R. P. Lawson, 1957, 265).

Origen was probably influenced in his interpretation of the Song of Songs by his elder contemporary Hippolytus. Origen tended toward thoroughness in all that he did. He took seriously and literally Jesus' saying about the removal of bodily members that offend and lead to sin and proceeded to castrate himself. He was fully convinced also that the literal sense of the Song of Songs was likewise something to be eliminated. Origen fully espoused Plato's interpretation of love as distinguished by two opposing types, the earthly and physical versus the heavenly and spiritual. "There is," he said, a propos of Canticles 1:4, "a love of the flesh which comes from Satan, and there is also another love, belonging to the Spirit, which has its origin in God; and nobody can be possessed by the two loves. . . . If you have despised all bodily things . . . then you can acquire spiritual love." The sacred marriage mystery of the Hellenistic Gnostic cults also influenced Origen, as Adolf Harnack pointed out (1961, II, 295; cf. W. E. Phipps, 1974, 88). The Gnostics regarded the divine Spirit as the exclusive bridegroom of the devoted soul and the influence of this idea is vividly illustrated in the Acts of Thomas which reflects Gnostic notions current in Origen's day. An earthly wedding was made the occasion for a renunciation of human sexuality in favor of mystical marriage with the divine. Jesus appeared to the newlyweds and declared: "If you abandon this filthy intercourse you become holy temples, pure and free from afflictions and pains both manifest and hidden, and you will not be girt about with cares for life and for children, the end of which is destruction." The startled couple refrained from sexual intercourse and the bride later declared: "I have set at naught this man and this marriage which passes away before my eyes, because I am bound in another marriage. I have had no intercourse with a short-lived husband . . . because I am yoked with the true man." In a similar story the true bridegroom is explicitly identified. The apostle Thomas urged another wife to forsake horrid intercourse because it leads to eternal damnation. The woman accordingly rejected the advances of her spouse and said to him: "He whom I love is better than you and your possessions. . . . Jesus himself will set me free from the shameful deeds which I did with you. You are a bridegroom who passes away and is destroyed, but Jesus is a true bridegroom, abiding immortal forever." (Cf. Schneemelcher, 1969, Acts of Thomas 12–14, pp. 83,98,117,124; cf. Phipps, 1974, 89.) Origen combined the Platonic and Gnostic attitudes toward sexuality to denature the Canticle and transform it into a spiritual drama free from all carnality. The reader was admonished to mortify the flesh and to take nothing predicated of the Song with reference to bodily functions, but rather to apply everything toward the apprehension of the divine senses of the inner man. (See commentary on 1:4.)

Origen's influence on later commentators on the Song was considerable. Although there is some disagreement as to how much of Theodoret's commentary can be used as testimony to the original Greek of Origen's lost work, it is obvious that Theodoret borrowed liberally from Origen, as from other predecessors (cf. Loewe, 1966, 174n69).

The question of the degree of Jewish influence on Origen's interpretation of the Song of Songs is disputed. According to Ginsburg (61), Origen's instruction in Hebrew by R. Hillel "imbued him with Hagadic interpretations of the sacred text." Littledale (xxiii*f*) protested the allegation of some modern critics that

> the dazzling powers of Origen which gave the tone to the traditional interpretation which has held its ground ever since his day drew from Talmudic sources. . . . Considering how embittered the opposition to Origen became even in his own life-time, this is not very probable in itself, but it is refuted by the contemporaneous language of S. Cyprian who was not influenced by Origen's works, and also by Theodoret's incidental mention of an earlier and consentaneous tradition ascending much nearer to primitive times. Of this tradition but one written fragment has come down to us, a solitary note on Cant. iii 9 by Theophilus of Antioch, who died between [*sic*] A.D. 178 and 179, a few years before Origen was born. But the fragment is decisive as to the method followed in the second century, and materially lessens the probability of Talmudic influence. . . .

Raphael Loewe's presentation of parallels between Origen/Theodoret and the Targum to the Song of Songs (1957) supplies convincing proof of the correctness of Ginsburg's brief statement and refutation of Littledale's objection. Further proof is provided by Urbach's study which demonstrates that Origen was familiar with the Jewish exegesis of his day, especially in the historical exegesis whereby he set the Church in the place of Israel as the Bride, and in the mystical interpretation which he developed into a spiritual love song between the soul and the Logos. According to Urbach (1971, 252), "In his historical exegesis Origen follows entirely in the footsteps of Jewish interpretation, and it is easy to point to parallels; but even in the mystic-spiritual exposition Jewish elements are to be found." Origen knew of the Jewish custom not to teach boys the Creation stories of Genesis, the Work of the Chariot in the beginning of Ezekiel, the rebuilding of the Temple at the end of Ezekiel, or the Song of Songs. These things, Origen explained, were called by the Hebrews *deuterōseis* (translating the plural of the term *mišnāh, mišnāyôṯ*):

> But it behooves us primarily to understand that, just as in childhood we are not affected by the passion of love, so also to those who are at the stage of infancy and childhood in their interior life—to those, that is to say, who are being nourished with milk in Christ, not with strong meat, and are only beginning *to desire the rational milk without guile*—it is not given to grasp the meaning of these sayings. For in the words of the Song of Songs there is that food, of which the Apostle says that *strong meat is for the perfect;* and that food calls for hearers *who by ability have their senses exercised to the discerning of good and evil.* And indeed,

if those whom we have called children were to come on these passages, it may be that they would derive neither profit nor much harm, either from reading the text itself, or from going through the necessary explanations. But if any man who lives only after the flesh should approach it, to such a one the reading of this Scripture will be the occasion of no small hazard and danger. For he, not knowing how to hear love's language in purity and with chaste ears, will twist the whole manner of his hearing of it away from the inner spiritual man and on to the outward and carnal; and he will be turned away from the spirit to the flesh, and will foster carnal desires in himself, and it will seem to be the Divine Scriptures that are thus urging and egging him on to fleshly lust!

For this reason, therefore, I advise and counsel everyone who is not yet rid of the vexations of flesh and blood and has not ceased to feel the passion of his bodily nature, to refrain completely from reading this little book and the things that will be said about it. For they say that with the Hebrews also care is taken to allow no one even to hold this book in his hands, who has not reached a full and ripe age. And there is another practice too that we have received from them—namely, that all the Scriptures should be delivered to boys by teachers and wise men, while at the same time the four that they call *deuterōseis*—that is to say, the beginning of Genesis, in which the creation of the world is described; the first chapters of Ezechiel, which tell about the cherubim: the end of that same, which contains the building of the Temple; and this book of the Song of Songs—should be reserved for study till the last. (Lawson translation, 1957, 22*f*, 313n7.)

This tradition is alleged in another version by Gregory Nazianzen. The Hebrew sages, Gregory asserted, had an ancient and praiseworthy rule according to which

. . . it is not permitted to people of all ages to study every book of the Bible. Since not every book is comprehensible to every person, it is also not of benefit to every person. On the other hand, they held that things whose meaning was hidden from an inexperienced person on account of their strange form, can do him harm; while certain books were permitted to all from the outset and had become the common heritage of all, other books were made available only to those of twenty-five years and upward—they are the books under whose simple surface a mystic grace lies hidden (cf. Urbach, 1971, 252n14).

This alleged restriction on the reading of the Canticles is not confirmed by explicit pronouncement by the Jewish Sages in the classical sources. In the Yemenite Midrash to Canticles, however, Rabbi Isaac Nappaḥa (a Palestinian Amora of the third generation [fourth century]) is cited as saying that "Any one who reads the Song of Songs nowadays is as one who bore false testimony." The same Midrash also asserts that "The Sages say that the Song of Songs may be read according to its simple sense, but no profundity may be taught therein except to a judge or the head of a city" (cf. Urbach, 275). The profundity here obviously has reference to esoteric doctrine and not to the simple allegory of God's love for Israel.

Athanasius, archbishop of Alexandria, who died in 373, regarded the Song of Songs as a Jubilee song of the church at the incarnation of the Son of God.

The whole book is an allegory to be understood enigmatically from beginning to end. Only those well versed in allegory ought to study it because it is certain to be corrupted by others. It is called the Song of Songs because it is the greatest and the last song, celebrating in the present the coming of Christ which other songs regard as in the future. It is an Epithalamium celebrating the marriage of Him who is the loved of God with human flesh. Here are no threats or woes, as in other books, but the Bridegroom is present and all is turned to joy. The book is replete with dialogues between the Son of God and the human race; sometimes between Christ and man in general, and sometimes between Him and his ancient people; sometimes between Him and the Gentile Church, sometimes between the Gentiles and Jerusalem; and sometimes between ministering angels and men.

Gregory, bishop of Nyssa in Cappadocia, late in the fourth century wrote an extensive commentary on the Canticles, carrying the exposition as far as 6:9. The Bride throughout was seen as representing the soul of man and little attention was given to the usual identification with the Church. The soul enters into spiritual union with God as the perfect and blessed way to salvation. "Let him kiss me," etc. e.g., was explained as the language of the soul to God, the soul having become worthy to speak to God face to face. A spiritual meaning was found for each verse with confirmation in other verses of Scripture. The vehement strictures against those who adhered to the literal meaning are witness that the allegorical and mystical interpretations were not wholly satisfactory or convincing to some of the faithful.

Philo, Bishop of Carpasia in Cyprus, who died ca. 374, a pupil and friend of Epiphanius who was influential in his advancement to the bishopric, wrote one of the early commentaries on Canticles, enshrining many of the ideas of Origen and probably also of his own teacher Epiphanius. It is apparent that there is considerable interdependency between the commentary of Philo of Carpasia and that of Gregory the Great. Cornelius à Lapide supposed that Philo's work must have been heavily interpolated with that of Gregory which was some two centuries later, but Littledale suggested that Cornelius was driven to this unlikely explanation by reluctance to admit that the great Western Doctor would stoop to borrow material from the East. Littledale regarded Philo's commentary as one of the most valuable and frequently cited his expositions.

Jerome, who was born in Dalmatia in 331 and died near Bethlehem in 420, introduced the allegorical interpretation into the Western churches. He was, like Origen, instructed in Hebrew by Jews (but was not especially grateful or charitable and Ginsburg [64n1] ascribes much of the blame for subsequent sufferings inflicted on Jews by so-called Christians to Jerome's vituperations). Jerome's admiration for Origen's work on the Song has been noted and in his own commentary Jerome embraced Origen's views almost entirely, regarding it as a nuptial and dramatic song celebrating the union of

Christ with His Church and/or the human soul. The interlocutors are the bride and her companions and the groom and his companions.

Jerome, like Origen, regarded the Canticle as suitable only for advanced students of the sacred Scriptures. In a letter to Laetia, daughter-in-law of his old friend Paula, in response to a request for advice on how to bring up her infant daughter (also called Paula) as a virgin consecrated to Christ, Jerome—after discussing sundry matters, such as bathing (not recommended because of the danger of exciting sexual desire)—gave the following directions for the maiden's education in biblical studies:

> Let her treasures be not silk or gems but manuscripts of the holy scriptures; and in these let her think less of gilding, and Babylonian parchment, and arabesque patterns, than of correctness and accurate punctuation. Let her begin by learning the psalter, and then let her gather rules of life out of the Proverbs of Solomon. From the Preacher let her gain the habit of despising the world and its vanities. Let her follow the example set in Job of virtue and of patience. Then let her pass on to the gospels never to be laid aside once they have been taken in hand. Let her also drink in with a willing heart the Acts of the Apostles and the Epistles. As soon as she has enriched the storehouse of her mind with these treasures, let her commit to memory the prophets, the heptateuch, the Books of Kings and of Chronicles, the rolls also of Ezra and Esther. When she has done all these she may safely read the Song of Songs but not before: for, were she to read it at the beginning, she would fail to perceive that, though it is written in fleshly words, it is a marriage song of a spiritual bridal. And not understanding this she would suffer from it (*The Nicene and Post-Nicene Fathers*, VI, Letter cvii, p. 194).

Theodore, bishop of Mopsuestia, at the end of the fourth century wrote a commentary on the Song of Songs in which he rejected allegorical meaning and read it in its literal and plain sense, as an erotic song. Theodore theorized that Solomon's subjects had criticized his marriage with an Egyptian princess and that the king responded to the protest by boldly singing of his love in this Song. Unfortunately, Theodore's commentary did not survive and is known only from the attacks on it. His great learning, no doubt, discouraged debate during his lifetime. In little more than a century after Theodore's death, at the Council of Constantinople in 550, his views were condemned as unfit for Christian ears.

It is of interest that Theodore's brother, Polychronius, Bishop of Apamea, who died about 427, is credited with a commentary on Canticles, a few fragments of which have survived. The traditional interpretation was espoused: "The Bridegroom is our Lord; the Bride is the Church; the friends of the Bridegroom are angels and saints; the maidens are the followers of the Church." The authenticity of this commentary, however, is questionable (cf. Rowley, 1952, 206n2).

About the same time that Theodore of Mopsuestia was disquieting the Eastern church with his assertion of a literal interpretation of the Canticle, another bold cleric shocked the Western church with a similar view. A

Roman monk named Jovinian went about barefoot, poorly dressed, living on bread and water, and remaining celibate, but he jarred ecclesiastics with attacks on the dominant ascetic tendencies of the day. Jovinian had a good knowledge of Scripture which he employed effectively in support of his argument that there was no moral difference between fasting or eating, virginity, widowhood, or marriage. He protested especially against the prevailing hierarchy of virtues with its corresponding scale of blessedness and asserted that the divine element in human life is the same in all circumstances; all who are baptized and born anew in Christ have equal dignity, grace, and blessedness. He cited Scripture as proof that marriage was in no way inferior to virginity and celibacy in the divine scale of values. The Song of Songs taken literally in praise and sanctification of marital sex was invoked in the attack on asceticism.

Jovinian's views incensed the ecclesiastical establishment and in 390 Pope Siricius convened a synod in Rome to have him condemned. Jovinian and his adherents took refuge in Milan, but in 395 Ambrose convened a synod in Milan to endorse Rome's condemnation. Augustine wrote against Jovinian and especially against his denial of the perpetual virginity of Mary and the egalitarian notions of sin. Jerome in particular attacked Jovinian's defense of marriage with intense animosity in a treatise *Adversus Jovinianum*. The heretical notion that sexual expression could be as holy as repression was most reprehensible to Jerome. Unfortunately, most of what is known of Jovinian comes from the extreme reactions to his attacks on asceticism. He has received recognition from some church historians as a pioneer of Protestant ideology.

Theodoret, Bishop of Cyrus in Syria, who died around the middle of the fifth century, was distressed by the skepticism in some circles with regard to the traditional allegorical interpretation of the Canticle and vehemently berated the dissenters and reasserted the traditional allegorical view. In the preface to his commentary, Theodoret made his view perfectly clear:

> Since the majority of those who slander the Song of Songs and deny it to be a spiritual book, weave fables unworthy of crazy old women, some of them saying that Solomon the Wise wrote it concerning himself and Pharaoh's daughter; while others, taking a somewhat more philosophical view, call it the Royal Speech, so as to understand the people by the Bride and the King by the Bridegroom; we think that we shall be well employed in refuting at the outset of our exposition these false and mischievous theories, and then will proceed to set forth the true and clear meaning of the author. And yet these men ought to know that the holy Fathers, much their superiors in wisdom and spiritual insight, were they who placed this Book amongst the divine Scriptures, and approving it as full of the Spirit, pronounced it worthy of the Church. For had they thought otherwise, they would never have included a work whose subject was passion and desire in the number of Holy Writ. . . . Seeing that this is so, let us consider whether it be reasonable for us to follow our own theories, paying no attention to so many eminent men, and despising the Holy Spirit Himself, by not listening to him who says so well: "The

thoughts of mortal men are miserable, and our devices are but uncertain", (Wisd. ix. 14) and blessed Paul saying of certain persons, "They became vain in their imaginations, and their foolish heart was darkened" (Rom. i. 21). But let us cry thus with Blessed Peter, "We ought to obey God rather than man" (Acts v. 29). Let us also say to them, "Whether it be right in the sight of God to hearken unto you more than unto God, judge ye: for we cannot but speak the things which we have seen and heard by the Holy Ghost." . . . Coming then from the old to the new Bride, let us in this wise interpret the Song of Songs, and rejecting false and mischievous theories, let us follow the holy Fathers, and recognize one Bride conversing with one Bridegroom; and learn from the holy Apostles who that Bridegroom and Bride may be. For the inspired Paul teaches us that, writing thus, "I have espoused you to one husband, that I may present you as a chaste virgin to Christ," (2 Cor xi 2). He calls her a Bride who is made up of many. For he does not say, "I have betrothed *thee*", but *you,* that is, holy souls, perfected in virtue. For Divine Scripture understands the Church by the Bride, and calls Christ the Bridegroom. (Littledale, p. xxii.)

Theodoret's commentary followed and elaborated on Origen's work. Littledale in his anthology of devotional exposition of the Canticle frequently cited Theodoret and some of his interpretations were chosen for illustration of traditional Christian exposition in the present work, often without identifying it as Theodoret's idea. (For a comparison of Theodoret with the Targum, cf. R. Loewe, 1966, esp. 187–90 on 5:10–16.)

Ambrose, who died near the end of the fourth century, did not write a formal commentary on Canticles, but in his other writings drew numerous illustrations from the Canticles which were gathered in a single volume by William of St. Thierry at Rheims in the middle of the twelfth century.

Cyril of Alexandria, who flourished in the first half of the fifth century, contributed to the allegorical exposition of Canticles such items as the identification of Solomon's palanquin as the Cross of Christ, its silver supports as the thirty pieces paid to Judas, its purple cushion as the purple garment in which the soldiers robed Christ, and the nuptial crown as the crown of thorns.

Justus of Urgel who flourished in the first half of the sixth century was one of the earliest of the Latin commentators on the Canticles whose work is extant. He followed the line of his Eastern predecessors, but frequently added a remark of his own with the germ of the sort of mystical exposition which developed in the twelfth century. Littledale cited Justus occasionally.

A commentary ascribed to Cassiodorus, who died about 562, was cited not infrequently by Littledale who considered the work marked by great good sense, in spite of its disputed authenticity.

The seventh and eighth centuries saw little development in the production of commentaries on the Canticles. Gregory the Great, who died near the beginning of the seventh century, composed a commentary occasionally cited by Littledale for its devout and beautiful passages, apart from the materials cribbed from Philo of Carpasia. Isidore of Seville compiled a brief gloss on the Canticles, containing, in the estimation of Littledale, no fresh matter, and thus to be passed over lightly. Late in the seventh century Aponius wrote one of the better early Latin commentaries from which Littledale chose a number of citations. The work is incomplete, but an epitome of the missing portion by Lucas, Abbot of Mount St. Cornelius, is extant and in part fills the gap (cf. Littledale, xxxiv).

The ninth century was also relatively sterile. Littledale listed Angelomus of Luxeuil who compiled at the behest of the Emperor Hlothar I a commentary based mainly on Aponius and Gregory the Great. A contemporary, Haymo, Bishop of Halberstadt, compiled a terse gloss judiciously selected, but with little original material. Strabo of Fulda also compiled a gloss on the Canticles which Littledale cited only rarely.

The tenth century had little or nothing to add to the history of exposition of the Canticles. From the eleventh century there is likewise little worthy of note. Radulphus of Fontenelle, first Abbot of S. Vandrille, brought forth an epitome of the work of Gregory the Great, itself apparently derivative in part from Philo of Carpasia (cf. Littledale, xxxiv*f*). Michael Psellus, a Greek physician, around the middle of the century composed a metrical paraphrase based on the commentary of Gregory of Nyssa, with occasional introduction of new material.

The twelfth century witnessed a great upsurge of interest and literary activity devoted to the Canticles by celibate scholastics and mystics who found it a fertile field, an endless sea, and unfathomable abyss, a perennial spring, an inexhaustible mine, for mystical endeavor. Near the turn of the century, the "Scholastic Doctor," Anselm of Laon, was probably the actual author of a commentary later printed under the name of his more eminent namesake and contemporary, Anselm of Canterbury. The work, which has also been attributed to Hervé of Dol, is frequently cited by Littledale. Among twelfth-century writers on the Canticles listed by Littledale were Marbod of Rennes who composed a metrical paraphrase of the Canticles in neat hexameters closely following the Vulgate with little exegetical augmentation; Honorius of Autun who left two independent commentaries, both containing many beautiful passages which even Littledale regarded as fanciful; Richard of St. Victor commented on parts of the Canticles which Littledale regarded as worthy of his great reputation as a mystical divine. Rupert, Abbot of Deutz, produced a lengthy gloss on the Canticles, presenting the Bride as the Blessed Virgin throughout the work and departing from this rule only occasionally, and that, as Littledale commented (p. xxxvi), under great stress; similarly Philip Harveng, Abbot of Bona Spes, in Hainault, glossed the Canticles with application to the Blessed Virgin, but judged by Littledale as much inferior to that of Rupert and thus rarely cited; Irimbert, Abbot of Ambden, commented at length on detached portions of the Canticles and his work, first published in a

Thesaurus Anecdotorum by the learned Bernard Pez, is occasionally cited by Littledale.

Bernard of Clairvaux takes the prize in his own and in any century for devout and prolific prolixity on the Canticles. In eighty-six sermons of surpassing and extended eloquence, he progressed almost to the end of the second chapter of the Song. Littledale cited Bernard frequently and perforce extensively and in his introduction (p. xxxv) lamented that the wonderful sermons were all too few, but conceded that "their eloquence and fervour are far more conspicuous than the actual amount of direct illustration which they yield, though it is by no means scanty, and they not merely deserve, but compel perusal." Bernard saw the action in three stages: first the groom leads the bride to the garden, then to the cellar, and finally takes her to his apartments; this is admittedly a logical progression, even though it does not accord with the order of reference in the Song. A few samples of Bernard's eloquence are cited below in connection with specific verses.

An episode in Bernard's youth, related by his contemporary and biographer William of St. Thierry, throws light on the saint's zeal for asceticism and his contempt for the flesh, especially female flesh. Young Bernard once exchanged admiring glances with a girl and experienced an erection which so perturbed him that he dunked himself in an icy pond till the tumescence subsided and there and then he resolved to become a monk. This experience helps one understand Bernard's obsessive elaboration of allegorical interpretations of the Canticle in order to purge it of any suggestion of carnal lust and make it show forth the life of the spirit unstained by sex and sin. The reader of the Song was admonished to bring chaste ears to this discourse of love and never to imagine that it is a man or woman to be thought of, but rather the Word of God and a Soul (Sermon 61).

Bernard's vindictiveness toward Abelard was probably motivated as much by the latter's love-life as by his criticism of the Augustinian doctrine of original sin. Bernard brought formal charges of heresy against Abelard in 1141, requesting Pope Innocent III to exterminate the "fox destroying the Lord's vineyard" (2:15; cf. Letters 239 and Sermon 64). Abelard was forbidden to write or teach and his books were burned. Peter the Venerable interceded on behalf of Abelard and gained permission for him to spend the rest of his days at Cluny where he read, prayed, and kept silent. Bernard believed that heretics should be killed (Sermons 66, 12). Enemies of God he regarded as nonentities (Sermons 50, 7) and so he could hardly have been completely satisfied with Abelard's punishment. The Venerable Peter reproved heresy-hunter Bernard thus: "You perform all the difficult religious duties; you fast, you watch, you suffer; but you will not endure the easy ones—you do not love." (Quoted in Henry Adams, *Mont-Saint-Michel and Chartres* [1904], Boston, 1933, 313*f,* cited after W. E. Phipps, 1974, 92n58.)

Bernard's concern for the spiritual, asexual interpretation of the Canticle and extirpation of heresy was matched by his zeal for holy war against Muslim infidels. His fiery rhetoric rallied thousands for the Second Crusade:

> The Living God has charged me to proclaim that he will take vengeance upon such as refuse to defend him against his foes. To arms, then! Let a holy indignation animate you to combat, and let the cry of Jeremiah reverberate through Christendom: Cursed be he that withholdeth his sword from blood. (Letter to the Bavarians, quoted in A. J. Luddy, *Life and Teaching of St. Bernard,* Dublin, 1927, 528; cited after Phipps, 92n60.)

Phipps reflecting on the fact that Bernard was hailed by Dante (*Paradiso* 31–33) as the supreme guide to the heavenly realm, and by historians and theologians as a shining example of the power of faith, concluded: "If Bernard exemplified what has been recently called the golden age of Western spirituality, it is indeed a sad commentary on the course of Christianity." He was, for all his praise of love, a vehement hater.

Bernard's disciple, Gilbert of Hoyland, or Gilbert Parretanus, took up where Bernard left off and in forty-eight additional sermons advanced beyond the middle of the Book, halfway through the fourth chapter. Gilbert, in Littledale's estimation, approached more nearly than any others to the beauty and fervor of Bernard's style and many paragraphs of Littledale's devotional commentary were supplied by Gilbert.

For the thirteenth century, Littledale listed and occasionally cited from commentaries by Alanus de Insulis, the Universal Doctor, who followed Rupert of Deutz in relating the Canticle to the Blessed Virgin; William Little of Newbury, or Guilielmus Parvus, whose commentary, since lost, was cited secondhand on the basis of Delrio who ca. 1600 saw a manuscript of it at Louvain; Thomas of St. Victor's mystical and mostly incomprehensible comments based on the Hierarchies of Pseudo-Dionysius; John Hailgrin, Archbishop of Besancon and Cardinal of St. Sabina, composed a gloss on the Canticles along the same line as Rupert and Alan, not remarkable in merit, in Littledale's opinion; Cardinal Hugo of St. Cher included the Canticles in his great work on the Bible, condensing, systematizing, and supplementing the earlier patristic comments; and lastly a Catena of dubious authenticity ascribed to Thomas Aquinas, which Littledale regarded as of such meager value as to be altogether pretermitted.

In the fourteenth century Nicolaus of Lyra, reputedly a convert from Judaism, who became the ornament of erudition in the Franciscan Order by virtue of his proficiency in Hebrew and the ability to use it constructively in exegesis, composed a treatise on the Canticles in which he revived the long-neglected notion of the spiritual kinship and identity between the Jewish and Christian communions. This Littledale hailed as striking at the root of the charge by modern literalists that the mystical exposition was severed from all relations to the Old Testament. Actually, Nicolaus' interpretation of the Canticles had little to do with mystical exposition, since he adapted the mode of the Targum as adopted by Aponius, taking the first six chapters as recounting the history of Israel from the Exodus to the birth of Christ and the last two chapters as dealing with the Christian Church and her progress and peace achieved in the days of Constantine. The little sister of 8:8 he identified as the Church humble and abject among the worldly enemies, for so she was till the time of Constantine (*Ecclesia humilis et hoc fuit usque ad tempas Constantine*). Lyra's influence on Luther has been recognized and epitomized in the jingle, *Si Lyra non lyrasset, Luther non saltasset,* "If Lyra had not peeped, Luther had not leaped." Nicolaus' surname lent itself to other plays, such as *Nisi Lyra lyrasset, totus mundus delyrasset,* "Had Lyra not chanted, the whole world had ranted."

Apart from Nicolaus of Lyra, Littledale mentioned only one other commentator on the Canticles in the fifteenth century, namely the Emperor Matthew Cantacuzene, who, after a year of sharing the Byzantine throne with his father John V, retired to a monastery on Mount Athos and wrote a commentary on the Canticles which was regarded by Littledale as worthy of notice as being the only Greek commentary which depicts the Blessed Virgin as the Bride.

In the fifteenth century, the "Most Christian Doctor," John Gerson, treated the Canticles in his *Sympsalma in Canticum,* and indirectly also in a treatise on the Magnificat. His writings, though full of piety and fervor, Littledale dismissed as contributing little to the exposition of the Song. Dionysius Leewis à Rykel, better known as Dionysius the Carthusian, the Ecstatic Doctor, was the first to treat each chapter under three rubrics, the Church as *Sponsa universalis,* the holy soul as *Sponsa particularis,* and the Blessed Virgin as *Sponsa singularis,* a method which was adopted by several later commentators. Contemporary with Dionysius the Carthusian was Nicolas Kempf of Strasburg, known as Nicolaus de Argentina, who was Prior of the Carthusians at Gaming in Austria, and who composed a commentary on the Canticles drawn mainly from Gregory the Great and Bernard, but with many passages contributed by the compiler himself. Henry Harphius in his treatise on the mystical life, *Theologia Mystica,* offered extended meditations on detached verses of Canticles which Littledale found replete with beauties.

For the sixteenth century Littledale found slim pickings among allegorical and mystical expositors and adduced only three. Jacob Parez de Valentia, Bishop of Christopolis, treated the Canticles in a gloss exhibiting little originality or power, but with a few suggestive passages. Francis Teitelmann, a Franciscan of learning and considerable critical skill, wrote on the Song without adding greatly to the thesaurus of mystical exposition. Thomas of Villanova, Archbishop of Valencia, outlined an intended commentary on the Canticles and sketched three chapters before death interrupted his work. The patristic spirit shone through the fragment and Littledale lamented the failure to complete the work.

Martin Luther was passed over in Littledale's anthology of mystical expositors, but in his introduction Littledale paid his respects to Luther and Lutheran biblical scholarship. In offering moral argument against literalism in the exegesis of the Canticles, Hengstenberg's remark that "The literal interpretation of this Book gained its honors in the age of Rationalism, when the Church was degraded to its lowest level, and when it was bare and void of sound ecclesiastical judgement, and of holy taste and tact," Littledale applied to Luther. Hengstenberg might have gone further, Littledale averred, had his position allowed it, and have pointed out that

> . . . the Lutheran body, true to the animal and earthly instincts of its celebrated founder, has always been nearer to the ground than any other large Christian community, and less capable of lofty spiritual views. The whole sect, in its three centuries of existence, though prolific in respectability, has not given birth to one man in whom the common consent of other men recognized the marks of a saintly character. . . . In the field of the outer letter of Biblical study, in textual and grammatical criticism, in historical elucidation, it has laboured in a spirit of diligence and zeal beyond all praise, yet as
>
> the least erected spirit that fell
> From heaven; for even in heaven his looks and thoughts
> Were always downward bent, admiring more
> The riches of heaven's pavement, trodden gold,
> Than aught divine or holy else, enjoyed
> In vision beatific.
>
> Consequently, from being thus always engaged with the outer shell, the inner sense and the religious aroma have always escaped it. It has expended much care and science on Holy Writ, but its spiritual chemistry has invariably been of the kind which turns the most lustrous diamonds into black and worthless lumps of carbon, never of that higher constructive type which makes the light of jewels flash on our eyes from the dark places of the Bible (Littledale, xxvi*f*).

This jaundiced judgment on Luther and later Lutheran scholarship appears to have been motivated mainly by Littledale's reaction to Luther's rejection of the allegorical interpretation of Solomon's Song. Luther, unable to accept the allegorical fancies of the Fathers, or to go all the way in admission of the literal erotic sense, propounded the theory that the Bride of the Song is the happy and peaceful State under Solomon's rule and that the Song is a hymn in which Solomon thanks God for the divine gift of obedience.

The Swabian reformer John Brentius concurred in Luther's interpretation of the Canticles. In Geneva, however, Sebastian Castellio revived the accursed view espoused by Theodore of Mopsuestia that the Song has no allegorical meaning whatever, but is a colloquy of Solomon with his lady friend (*colloquium Salomonis cum amica quadam Sulamitha*) and as such unworthy of a place in the sacred canon since it dealt merely with earthly affections. Calvin was distressed by the radical view of his fellow reformer and it was this tension, combined with a disagreement on the question of

Christ's Descent to Hell, which made Geneva too small for the two of them so that Castellio felt it prudent to get out of Calvin's town. Calvin issued a statement on Castellio's departure: "Our principal dispute concerned the Song of Songs. He considers that it is a lascivious and obscene poem, in which Solomon has described his shameless love affairs" (cf. Rowley, 1952, 207nn1,2).

Edmund Spenser, "the prince of poets in his time," appears to have espoused Calvin's position that the Canticle deals with human love but is also inspired. Among the works ascribed to Spenser is *"Canticum canticorum* translated," but this translation has not survived. (Cf. Israel Beroway, 1934, 23–45; on the authenticity of the ascription, pp. 23*f*.) In spite of the loss of Spenser's translation, a good deal of the Canticle echoes in his own poems, e.g., "The Faerie Queen," "Amoretti," and especially "Epithalamion," which he composed for his own wedding after some forty years as a bachelor. The most notable passage there is lines 171–180 wherein are several reverberations of the Canticle:

Her goodly eyes lyke saphyres shining bright,
Her forehead yvory white,
Her cheekes lyke apples which the sun hath rudded,
Her lips lyke cherryes charming men to byte,
Her brest like to a bowle of creme uncrudded,
Her paps lyke lyllies budded,
Her snowie necke lyke to a marble towre,
And all her body like a pallace fayre,
Ascending uppe with many a stately stayre,
To honors seat and chastities sweet bowre.

For discussion of this passage and others, cf. Beroway. He concluded (p. 45) that the influence of *Canticum canticorum* on Spenser's poetry was "far greater than uninvestigated or conditional supposition would have it be" and that "Spenser's *'Canticum canticorum* translated' is veritably translated into a new, a highly fragmentary and shadowy, but discernible form in the pages of his extant poetry."

In England the traditional Christian view continued unchallenged. Thomas Wilcocks in *An Exposition upon the Book of Canticles,* 1624, affirmed that the book celebrates the marriage between Christ and his Church and "the great love of the bridegroom to his spouse, which is never removed, but always abideth constant, how oft soever she fall away, and seem, as a man would say, to forsake her husband" (cf. Ginsburg, 69,70n1).

For the seventeenth century, Littledale found worthy of inclusion in his anthology of mystical exposition of the Canticles: the learned Jesuit Martin Delrio who offered a twofold treatment, first literal and textual comment, then a catena of earlier expositions; Michael Ghislerius who bequeathed to posterity a mammoth folio of nearly a thousand pages in double column and small type, discussing every verse in five different ways, the text, then application to the Church, the holy soul, and the Blessed Virgin as the Bride, followed by a long catena of ancient expositors; the English Nonconformist Henry Ainsworth adjudged worthy of consultation for rabbinical learning and apt parallelisms from other books of Scripture; Luis de la Puente, or De Ponte, for his large volume of Sermons on the Canticles, regarded by Littledale as heavy and lifeless, and below De Ponte's reputation; Cornelius à Lapide whose commentary was so well known (and respected) that it need only be mentioned; finally the German Protestant theologian John Cocceius, deemed enormously learned and diligent, and of great piety, of whom it was said that "Grotius sees Christ nowhere, but Cocceius sees Him everywhere," and who recalled "the spirit of the best medievalists by his remarkable gift of mystical appreciation" (Littledale, xxxix).

Among expositors of the seventeenth century ignored or passed over too lightly by Littledale Thomas Brightman merits special notice. Brightman adopted the view of Aponius and de Lyra that the Song describes historically and prophetically the condition of the Church and "agrees well-nigh in all things with the Revelation of St. John." Brightman divided the Song into two parts: 1–4:6 describing the condition of the Legal Church from the time of David to the death of Christ, and 4:7–8:14 which describes the state of the Evangelical Church, from A.D. 34 to the second coming of Christ. Ginsburg (pp. 70–74) presented a full outline of Brightman's curious commentary and some specimens of his mode of exposition aptly characterized as the fullest development of the Chaldee (Targumic) intrepretation Christianized. The beginnings of Protestantism appear in 5:8 which was applied to the multitudes who flocked to Peter Waldo to seek the Beloved in 1160. In 5:9–10 Christ appears at the battle of the Albigenses against the anti-Christian bands of Innocent the Third. The faithful teachings of Michael Cesenas, Peter de Corbaria, and John de Poliaco, condemned by Pope John in 1277, are the subject of 5:12. The preaching of Robert Trench in 1290 is referred to in 5:13. The next verse, 5:14, refers to the eventful year 1300, which was the first resurrection mentioned in Rev 1:20 and to the activities of such notables as Dante, William of Ockam, John of Gaunt, King Philip of France, King Edward of England, and John Wycliffe. John Huss, Jerome of Prague, and the shaking off of the Romish yoke by the Bohemians are the subject of 5:15–17. Chapters 6–8 describe the restored Church, from Luther to the coming of Christ, ending with the care which the Bridegroom will exercise over the Church, His Bride, and her desire to be carried with Him to eternal mansions.

Johannes Cocceius' interpretation, not unlike that of Brightman, presented the Song as a prophetical narrative of the transactions and events that are to happen in the Church. The divisions of the book correspond to the periods of the history of the Church and to the seven trumpets and the seven seals of the Apocalypse of John. Chapters 1–2 cover the period of the preaching of the Gospel to Jews and Gentiles; 3–4 the period of the increase of the Church and persecution from without; 5–6:8 the period of peace without, but danger within. The period of the Reformation is covered in 6:9–7:10; 7:11–8:3 the unsettled post Reformation period. The persecution is covered in 8:4–6 and the rest after the sufferings and longing for the spread of the Gospel in 8:7–14. The exposition becomes particularly full and detailed with the Reformation and culminates with the future triumph of Protestantism. John Wycliffe is the bannered host of 6:10, the Shulamite of 6:13[E] is that part of Bohemia which made peace with the Roman Church, while 7:5 refers to Martin Luther (Cocceius, 1665, or 1701.)

In the last decade of the seventeenth century, the Roman Catholic Bishop Jacques Bénigne Bossuet, rejecting the traditional allegory, assumed that the object of the Song is the marriage of Solomon with the daughter of Pharaoh. Since the nuptial feast among the Jews was carried on for seven days, Bossuet divided the poem into seven parts to correspond to the festal days.

For early eighteenth-century England the commentary of J. Durham may be cited as representative. As the key to the Canticle, *clavis cantici,* Durham explained the purpose and scope as the portrayal of the love between Christ and the Church in all times and circumstances.

> The great scope of this Song is to set out that mutual love and carriage that is between Christ and the Church in five different branches. It holdeth out the Church's case, and Christ's care of her, in all her several conditions, and under all dispensations. . . . And in all these, her various conditions, in all ages, are painted forth, before Christ's incarnation, as well as now, without respect to any particular time or age; besides the Church then and now is one. . . .
>
> This book, in its matter, is a comprehensive sum of all those particulars formed in a song, put together, and drawn on as a board, for the believer's edification, to show, 1. What should be, and will be their carriage, when it is right with them as to their frame. 2. What are their infirmities, and what they use often to fall into, even they who are believers, that they may be the more watchful. 3. To shew what they meet with, that they may make for sufferings, and not stumble at them when they come. 4. That the care and love of Christ to them, in reference to all them, may appear, that they may know upon what grounds to comfort themselves in every condition, and may have this Song as a little magazine, for direction and consolation in every condition (1723, 11*f*).

An oft-cited sample of Durham's exposition is his interpretation of 2:15, "Take us the foxes," etc. as giving clear guidance to the secular authorities to support the Church in stamping out every heresy and schism, great or small (cf. Ginsburg, 81*f;* Rowley, 195).

The rationalism of the eighteenth century was strongly reflected in the essay of Wm. Whiston (1723) who boldly asserted that the Song of Songs "exhibits from the beginning to the end marks of folly, vanity, and looseness," and that "it was written by Solomon when He was become Wicked and Foolish, and Lascivious, and Idolatrous." With respect to the allegorical and mystical view, Whiston wrote:

I venture to affirm, as to the internal Composition and Contents of this Book itself; that so far as the common Meaning of Words and critical Judgment of the Nature of the Book can guide us, this Evidence is wholly on the other Side; and this so certainly and plainly, that 'tis next to a Demonstration against its allegorical Meaning, and consequent Authority.

Such a book, in Whiston's view, had no place in the Canon of Sacred Scripture.

The learned Bishop Robert Lowth, who discovered the key to the appreciation of the poetry of the Bible (i.e. parallelism), devoted two of his "Lectures on the Sacred Poetry of the Hebrews" to the Song of Songs. The subject of the Canticles, Lowth concluded, "appears to be the marriage feast of Solomon (who was, both in name and reality the Prince of Peace)." As for the identity of Solomon's bride, Lowth deemed the conjecture to have an appearance of probability that she was the daughter of Pharaoh, to whom Solomon was known to be particularly attached. "May we not, therefore," he asked, "with some shadow of reason, suspect that, under the allegory of Solomon choosing a wife from the Egyptians, might be darkly typified that other Prince of Peace, who was to espouse a church chosen from among the Gentiles?" Lowth, however, advised caution in carrying the figurative application too far, and of entering into precise explication of every particular, since these minute investigations "are seldom conducted with sufficient prudence not to offend the serious part of mankind, learned as well as unlearned" (cf. Lecture xxx, the Gregory translation, p. 345).

Similarly, Thomas Percy, Bishop of Dromore, condemned commentators so busily engaged in opening and unfolding the allegorical meaning of the book as wholly to neglect the literal sense which ought to be the basis of their discoveries. If a sacred allegory may be defined as a figurative discourse, which, under a lower and more obvious meaning, delivers the most sublime and important truths, it is the first duty of an expositor, according to Percy, to ascertain the lower and more obvious meaning. Till this is done, it is impossible to discover what truths are couched under it; without this all is vague and idle conjecture. It is erecting an edifice without a foundation (cf. Ginsburg, 85n1).

John Wesley's verecundity appears to have dictated the espousal of the traditional allegorical view of the Song. The description of the bridegroom and bride, Wesley felt, was such as could not with decency be used or meant concerning Solomon and Pharaoh's daughter; many of the expressions and descriptions would be absurd and monstrous as applied to them. Accordingly, it followed that the book is to be understood allegorically, "as concerning that spiritual love and marriage which is between Christ and his Church" (III, 1926).

In 1768 a new theory was introduced by Thomas Harmer who agreed with Grotius, Bossuet, Lowth, Percy, et al., that the Song celebrated the nuptials of Solomon and Pharaoh's daughter, but added another wife to the mix. The

Shulamite was not the Egyptian wife, but the previous principal wife, a Jewish queen who was displeased at Solomon's marrying a Gentile wife and giving her equal honor and privilege. The situation resembles the conduct of the Messiah toward the Gentile and the Jewish Churches, but more than that Harmer did not seek in the way of mystical meaning. The Song was presented as a threeway colloquy between Solomon and his rival wives (cf. Ginsburg, 86, for an analysis of the confused plot). The affair ends in a standoff. The Jewish queen is admonished by Solomon to keep her distance, but there is no dissolution of either of the marriages. Such is the state of affairs with respect to the relation of the Jewish and Gentile churches to the Messiah. The Jewish Church persists in refusal to accept the Gentiles as fellow-heirs, but does not renounce the relationship to the Messiah, nor has the Messiah rejected them. This fractured state continues, awaiting the reconciliation promised in the New Testament.

The theory of Harmer was adopted and defended by Ann Francis who also presented a poetic version of the Song (1781).

In Germany Johann David Michaelis (d. 1791) of Göttingen (in Notes to Bishop Lowth's *Praelectiones*) emphasized a consideration generally ignored, that there is nowhere in the poem mention of a marriage ceremony nor of circumstances attendant on such. Accordingly, Michaelis concluded that the Song describes the chaste passion of conjugal and domestic love, the attachment of two delicate persons who have been long united in the sacred bond. "Can we suppose," he asked, "such happiness unworthy of being recommended as a pattern to mankind, and of being celebrated as a subject of gratitude to the great Author of happiness?"

In Germany also a certain Herr von Puffendorff propounded a new theory and mode of analysis which must rank high on the list of competitors for the prize for bizarre schemes of interpretation. According to Puffendorff (1776), Solomon, who was versed in Egyptian mysteries, composed the Song in hieroglyphics. The decipherment by Puffendorff revealed that the Song treats almost exclusively of the sepulcher of the Savior, his death, and the communion of believers who long for his Advent. Ginsburg (p. 89) gives a sample of Puffendorff's exposition on 1:3, the virgins being the pure and chaste souls locked up in the dark sepulcher and waiting for the light (playing on *'lm* in the sense of darkness).

> The Egyptian Neitha, or Minerva, tutelary deity of pious souls, was covered with a veil which none was allowed to uncover. The virgins, concealed in the same manner, have to expect that through marriage they will emerge into light. Thus the souls are here represented, which in the dominion of darkness wait for salvation and light.

The allegorical and mystical interpretation of the Canticles was severely shaken in the late eighteenth century by the work of the devout and gifted German poet and critic J. G. von Herder whose sensitive appreciation of

Hebrew poetry opened new vistas for lovers of literary beauty. Herder (1778) failed to find in the Song any sense other than the obvious, literal meaning. Herder denounced the allegorizers as violating common sense and established rules of literary and linguistic analysis. The theme of the Song, in Herder's view, is true and chaste love in its various stages and in this there is beauty and worth to justify its place in the Bible. Herder acknowledged a marked unity throughout the poem as it described love from its first germs to full maturity, its ripened fruit and first regermination. He did not, however, regard the book as a single composition but as a collection of detached songs, or amorets. J. F. Kleuker (1780) elaborated on Herder's interpretation and subsequent commentators, notably J. C. C. Döpke (1829) and A. Bernstein (1834) have influenced later students of the Song, especially Protestants of both liberal and conservative bent.

The nineteenth century saw few new ideas in the interpretation of Solomon's Sublime Song, but a growing dissatisfaction with allegorical interpretations and continuing efforts to find the lost key of which Saadia spoke.

The marriage of Solomon with Pharaoh's daughter continued to have its advocates. Mason Good, however, argued that Solomon's liaison with the Egyptian princess was a purely political move, without antecedent personal intimacy or exchange of affection, out of keeping with the reciprocal affection, gentleness, modesty, and delicacy of mind uniformly and perpetually attributed to the beautiful and accomplished fair one of the Canticles. Accordingly, Solomon's lady fair was not an Egyptian princess, but a native of the district of Sharon. The Song, composed of separate amorets, also conveyed a spiritual allegory (cf. Ginsburg, p. 92).

Dream Theories, Melodrama

In 1813 and 1816 the Roman Catholic priest and scholar Johann Leonhard von Hug published two pamphlets (1813 and 1816) propounding and defending a novel interpretation of the Song of Songs as a dream. The pamphlets comprised notes for a doctoral examination and response to criticism. Taking his cue from 5:2, "I sleep, but my heart wakes," Hug saw the entire Song as a dream. Hug found the Song to be composed of thirty-eight disordered fragments, the disarray being a major argument in support of the dream sequence. The dreaming shepherdess represented the people of the ten Northern tribes, the people of Israel, and the burden of the dream is her longing to be reunited with the King of Judah in the formation of a new Solomonic state. The Song, in Hug's view, was probably composed in the time of Hezekiah (seventh century B.C.) who would thus be the groom and the ten tribes his bride. This view of the political plot failed to receive wide acceptance, but the notion that the Songs are dream sequences has continued to find advocates.

Solomon B. Freehof has similarly suggested that the whole book is a series of dream experiences (1948–49). "The book is not the story of two lovers seeking each other in actual places, but in imaginary. 'On my bed at night I sought my beloved' (3:1). In other words, the book is a sequence of dreams. . . . Once the book is read thus," according to Freehof, "its very disorder makes sense" (p. 401). This explanation, it was alleged, throws light on the motive of the rabbis who gave the book its symbolic interpretation. The rabbis did not take dreams lightly, but regarded them as a vehicle of communication between God and man. To interpret a dream was not merely therapy, but also a religious duty. The only way a dream can be interpreted is symbolically or allegorically and to the rabbis the symbolism seemed clear. The love-language was seen as descriptive of the eternal love between God and Israel. As in a dream, the lovers are parted. God seeks Israel, but Israel seems lost. Israel seeks God, and God seems far away. Eventually they find each other and Israel is forever united with God. Freehof suggested that modern efforts to seek a logical sequence from scene to scene are unrealistic, since dreams are not logical and cannot be explained by the categories of waking life. "The dream is the outcome of longing desire expressed in symbolic scenes and actions. Therefore, whether the specific interpretation given by tradition is correct or not, the *approach* of tradition, namely to explain this sequence of dreams symbolically, is essentially sound" (p. 402; see NOTE on 5:2a).

Dr. Max N. Pusin, a psychiatrist practicing in New Jersey, has in recent years made use of the Song of Songs in teaching a course for physicians and psychologists on the interpretation of symbols and dreams at the New Jersey College of Medicine. Dr. Pusin explained his work to the writer in a letter of 19 November 1971 and granted permission to cite portions of the letter.

Dr. Pusin gave two reasons for his choice of the Song as a text: "(1) It contained two dreams, and (2) it was full of similes, metaphors, symbols, and other figures of speech. . . . The Song proves to be a veritable Dream Book." Dr. Pusin has drawn up a table of symbols taken from the Song, and compared it to the list of Typical Symbols given by Freud in his *Traumdeutung* (*The Interpretation of Dreams*, 1900) and elsewhere.

It can be seen that the Song contains nearly every category of Freudian symbol and that the *meanings* of the symbols are nearly identical, as far as one can determine, with those of Freud. Some of the techniques used by the mind in forming dreams, too, are utilized by the author of the Song. The results can only be called striking, indicative of the fact that, as analysts put it, the composer had an easy and direct access to the unconscious. This is the mark of great artistic genius. . . . The dreams of the Song are . . . remarkable. Except for the opening lines in the second dream (5:2–6c), and the ending lines of the first dream (3:4c) the two dreams are identical. They consist basically of the dreamer's anxious search for her Beloved in which she must elude "the Keepers of the Walls." In the first dream, she does elude them and finds her Beloved. It is, therefore, a happy, wish-fulfilling dream. In the second dream she is caught by the same "Keepers of the Walls," and is beaten, wounded, and stripped of her mantle. That is an anxiety dream, a depressive nightmare, if you wish, in which there is frustration and punishment of forbidden desires. One must note in this regard that the *Wall* of the dreams is clearly a symbol of chastity as can be seen from the lovely, playful, and meaningful little "virginity"-dialogue between the Shulamite and her brothers in 8:8–10—as was clearly recognized by the Talmudic rabbis (I am, of course, referring to the contrasting symbols of the wall and the door). A sexually wayward woman was commonly punished by stripping her of her clothes (cf. Ezek 16:37–39).

The most fascinating aspect of the dreams to me was the resemblance to modern-day (real) dreams obtained from my patients. The patients are invariably female, and the circumstances such that they are forcibly kept from their beloved either by parental figures or by the dictates of conscience. Such resemblance strongly favors the "dramatic" theory of a woman kept by force from her Beloved; it also gives a significant boost to those few who have suggested that the work was written by a woman. Is it likely that a man, no matter how great an artist, could know of, and present so vividly a woman's dreams? This new fact must be added to the other facts: (1) that more than 85 per cent of the lines are for women; (2) that the central, pivotal figure whose vicissitudes we follow is a woman; (3) that Solomon's lines (especially his stylized, monotonous *wasfs*) are constantly interrupted by the spirited Shulamite; (4) that Solomon and her brothers are cast as "mild" villains; (5) that she has no father, but her mother (and *his* mother, 8:5) is referred to frequently (to the exclusion of men); (6) that the theme is romantic love versus marriages arranged by considerations of money (8:7) or by power of the king (8:11–12) as seen from a woman's standpoint.

As you can gather, I favor the theory that the song is a unit, a brief musical playlet. It was probably written in Persian times for the purpose of entertaining the bride and groom and the wedding guests on one of the seven days of the wedding feast. It uses material and themes from popular sources and from older times just as all poets do to this very day.

Although the present writer is not convinced by Dr. Pusin's arguments, his views as a psychiatrist are of general and particular interest and must be admitted among the more intriguing interpretations that have been suggested.

From the digression on recent dream theories we return to interpretations of the early nineteenth century.

A novel variation of the political allegory was put forth in 1823 by G. Ph. C. Kaiser who identified the Bride as a new colony near the Jordan River and the bridegroom as the triumvirate Zerubbabel-Ezra-Nehemiah. The Song allegedly celebrated the restoration of the Jewish State (Verfassung). As with many such efforts, the title tells the tale: *Das Hohelied, ein Collectiv-Gesang auf Serubabel, Esra, und Nehemia, als die Wiederhersteller einer jüdischen Verfassung in der Provinz Juda* 1825 (The Exalted Song, a collective-song about Zerubbabel, Ezra and Nehemiah as the Restorers of a Jewish State in the Province of Judah).

In England a disputation between two learned divines, Dr. J. Pye Smith and Dr. James Bennett, carried on in the *Congregational Magazine* during the years 1837 and 1838, helped to sharpen the issues in the controversy over literal versus allegorical interpretation of the Canticles. Dr. Smith denounced the allegorical method as contrary to all the laws of language and reason and detrimental to real religion. The Song Dr. Smith regarded as a pastoral ecologue, or a series of ecologues, representing the honorable loves of newlyweds, with some other interlocutors. Dr. Bennett in rejoinder argued for the necessity of the allegorical interpretation on the ground that the language of the Song in its literal sense is contrary to the nature and modesty of women. Dr. Bennett's eloquence is exceptional, but his argument appears to be based on limited acquaintance with women, and that presumably within a narrow segment of Victorian society:

That this is *not* a song of human loves is clear from the beginning to the end. It opens with the language of a female: "Let him kiss me;" it is full of her solicitous seeking after him; it abounds with praises of his person, and her dispraises of herself, of her person and her conduct; it invites other females to love him, and it speaks of him as her brother, and of her as his sister. Let any one examine the Song, and then muse over these facts, recollecting that Solomon is, in the opening of the poem itself, said to be the writer. Was ever such a human love-song composed by mortal, since man either loved or wrote verses? What writer, with the feelings, or the reason, of a man, would begin a poem on his fair one by describing her as courting him? Let it not be said, "We must not transfer our modern and northern ideas to the ancient Orientals, who had not our delicate notions of the female character;" for this would only make my case stronger. It would be more abhorrent from the secluded, submissive character of Eastern brides to ask the gentlemen to come and kiss them, than it would be from the dignified confidence of British women. It is not a question of climate or age, but of *nature*. The bridegroom, who is supposed to love this fairest of women, himself puts into her lips this speech: "Let him kiss me!" Never would human love speak thus. Though men like to court, they do not like to be courted; and while they think it cruel to be rejected when they court, they without mercy reject her that courts them; as the forward female has usually found, from the days of Sappho to this hour. Women were endowed with the form and qualities intended to attract courtship, and they feel it; and when they do not feel it, men despise them. No man, therefore, in his senses, would think to compliment his fair one by writing of her, to her, as if she had lost her retiring modesty, her female dignity, and degraded herself by doing that for which every man would despise her. The very first word of this Song, then, stands a witness against the notion of its being a human love-song; for it would better suit Solomon's strange woman, that with an impudent face caught and kissed the young simpleton, than Solomon's princess-bride, or Dr. Smith's supposed chaste monogamist. Till fishes mount to sing with larks on the shady boughs, and nightingales dive to ocean's depths to court the whales, no man, of any age, of any clime, of any rank, can be supposed to write ordinary love-songs in such a style. We are told, by the first word, that a greater than Solomon is here, one who must be courted, and that loves more than human are the theme. This is the Bridegroom of whom the Psalmist says, "He is thy Lord, and worship thou him:" "Kiss the

Son, lest he be angry, and ye perish from the way." Such a spouse may exhibit his Bride as *asking* for his love; every other must present *himself* as asking for hers, and begging this acceptance of his (*Congregational Magazine* 21 [1838], 148*f*).

Christian D. Ginsburg in his valuable sketch of the history of interpretation of the Canticles accorded J. T. Jacobi the honor of first elucidating the true design of the Song of Songs. Jacobi alleged that the purpose is not to describe the chaste passion of conjugal love, but to celebrate fidelity. The heroine of the book was a humble woman who was wedded to a shepherd. King Solomon was smitten with her beauty and tried to persuade her to forsake her husband and enter the royal harem, tempting her with all the luxuries and splendors of his court. She, however, resisted every temptation and remained true to her humble husband. This hypothesis, despite the imperfections of Jacobi's pioneer effort to develop it, was espoused by Ginsburg as the key to the long lost treasure and the climax of the quest. Each commentator who followed and developed this line was hailed by Ginsburg as contributing to the final solution of the long-standing puzzle.

Rabbis Ibn Ezra (pp. 46,88), Immanuel ben Solomon (pp. 49–56), and an anonymous French savant (pp. 56*f*) were featured for their recognition of the alleged truth that the lovers are a shepherd and a shepherdess and that the king is a separate and distinct person from the beloved shepherd, an important step to the right understanding of the Book. Von Herder was included among those who admitted that the book describes the love of a shepherd and a shepherdess. C. F. von Ammon's interpretation (*Salomon's verschmähte Liebe, oder die belohnte Treue,* i.e. Solomon's spurned Love, or Fidelity rewarded) was welcomed (p. 91) as a glimpse of light amid the dense darkness surrounding this book. Ammon not only vindicated the unity of the book, but showed that "it celebrates the victory of true and chaste love in humble life over the allurements of courtly grandeur." Similarly, F. W. K. Umbreit (1820) and the celebrated H. Ewald (1826) showed that the poem celebrates the victory of virtuous and sincere love, which no splendor can dazzle or flattery seduce (cf. Ginsburg, 92*f*), followed by L. Hirzel (1840), E. Meier (1854), F. Hitzig (1855), and F. Friedrich (1885) (cf. Ginsburg, 93–95,100*f*).

The year 1856 was hailed by Ginsburg (101) as the beginning of the union of Jew and Christian, Englishman and German in the opinion that the book presents the victory of virtuous love over all the temptations of royalty. Dr. Samuel Davidson (1856, 806) affirmed that the poem

> warns against impure love, encourages chastity, fidelity, and virtue, by depicting the successful issue of sincere affection amid powerful temptations. The innocent and virtuous maiden, true to her shepherd lover, resists the flatteries of a monarch, and is allowed to return to her home.

In the same year, Umbreit affirmed that he still held to the view propounded in his commentary.

The following year, 1857, Ginsburg published his own commentary which presented and elaborated this interpretation with great zeal and learning and in full confidence that it was the only reasonable and satisfactory solution to the enigma of the Song. Ginsburg (4–6) maintained that the book,

. . . upon careful examination, will be found to record an example of virtue in a young woman who encountered and conquered the greatest temptations, and was, eventually, rewarded; the simple narrative of which, divested of its poetic form, is as follows. There was a family living at Shulem, consisting of a widowed mother, several sons, and one daughter, who maintained themselves by farming and pasturage. The brothers were particularly partial to their sister, and took her under their special care, promising that her prudence and virtue should be greatly rewarded by them. In the course of time, while tending the flock, and, according to the custom of the shepherds, resorting at noon beneath a tree for shelter against the meridian sun, she met with a graceful shepherd youth, to whom she afterwards became espoused. One morning, in the spring, this youth invited her to accompany him into the field; but the brothers, overhearing the invitation, and anxious for the reputation of their sister, in order to prevent their meeting, sent her to take care of the vineyards. The damsel, however, consoled her beloved and herself with the assurance that, though separated bodily, insoluble ties subsisted between them, over which her brothers had no control. She requested him to meet her in the evening, and as he did not come, she feared that some accident had befallen him on the way, and went in search of him, and found him. The evening now was the only time in which they could enjoy each other's company, as, during the day, the damsel was occupied in the vineyards. On one occasion, when entering a garden, she accidentally came in the presence of King Solomon, who happened to be on a summer visit to that neighbourhood. Struck with the beauty of the damsel, the King conducted her into his royal tent, and there, assisted by his court-ladies, endeavoured with alluring flatteries and promises, to gain her affections; but without effect. Released from the King's presence, the damsel soon sought an interview with her beloved shepherd.

The King, however, took her with him to his capital in great pomp, in the hope of dazzling her with his splendour; but neither did this prevail: for while even there, she told her beloved shepherd, who had followed her into the capital, and obtained an interview with her, that she was anxious to quit the gaudy scene for her own home. The shepherd, on hearing this, praised her constancy, and such a manifestation of their mutual attachment took place, that several of the court-ladies were greatly affected by it.

The King, still determined, if possible, to win her affections, watched for another favourable opportunity, and with flatteries and allurements, surpassing all that he had used before, tried to obtain his purpose. He promised to elevate her to the highest rank, and to raise her above all his concubines and queens, if she would comply with his wishes; but, faithful to her espousals, she refused all his overtures, on the plea that her affections were pledged to another. The King, convinced at last that he could not possibly prevail, was obliged to dismiss her; and the shepherdess, in company with her beloved shepherd, returned to her native place. On their way home, they visited the tree under which they had first met, and there renewed their vows of fidelity to each other. On her arrival in safety at her home, her brothers, according to their promise, rewarded her greatly for her virtuous conduct.

Ginsburg divided the narrative into five sections. The statements of the various speakers on these five sections admittedly were not recorded in the order stated, but "may be easily deduced from it" (p. 7). A detailed outline and summary of the developments in each of the five sections was presented (pp. 7–11) and Ginsburg concluded:

Thus this Song records the real history of a humble but virtuous woman, who, after having been espoused to a man of like humble circumstances, had been tempted in a most alluring manner to abandon him, and to transfer her affections to one of the wisest, and richest of men, but who successfully resisted all temptations, remained faithful to her espousals, and was ultimately rewarded for her virtue.

Few, Ginsburg presumed, would question the importance of a Book in the sacred canon which thus records an example of virtue, since "the avowed object of Holy Writ is to teach all that is good and conducive to human happiness." The significant point is that "the individual who passes through the extraordinary temptations recorded in this Song, and remains faithful, is *a woman.*" Here Ginsburg found the reply to Solomon's oft-reiterated query, "A virtuous woman, who can find?" "He has found one at least of spotless integrity, and her virtue is recorded in Scripture, for the defence of women against a prevalent but unjust suspicion." Ginsburg then presented eloquent argument for the equality of women and an appeal for their liberation which is of particular interest in the light of the contemporary movement.

The main points of Ginsburg's argument were, first, that the biblical account clearly states that man and woman were created with the same intellectual and moral powers, *exactly like one another* (Gen 2:20), with no intimation of subserviency of the woman to the man, or of her being weaker or less virtuous than he.

The fact that the Tempter assailed the woman, and not the man, so far from showing that the woman was weaker, would rather prove that she was stronger; that the cunning serpent knew this, and was persuaded, if he could only prevail over the woman, she, with her superior influence, would be sure to succeed with the man, as the sad result showed.

Further,

the curse which God pronounced upon the guilty pair, proves that the woman was created with the same intellectual and moral capacities as the man. Had the woman been weaker in these respects than the man, she would not have been accountable in an equal degree for her sin, and would not have been punished with the same severity.

Moreover, no change has taken place in the relative position of men and women, with respect to intellectual and moral equality, since the Fall.

The curse upon the woman in relation to the man does not refer to any *intellectual* or *moral,* but to a *physical,* inferiority. . . . The man, with his superior strength and boldness, was henceforth to be the protector; the woman, suffering and mild, the protected.

The notion that the woman is intellectually or morally weaker than man is, therefore, not the teaching of the word of God.

While man, through his superior out-of-door qualities, or physical strength and courage, is the supporter, protector, and ruler of the woman; she, through her superior in-door qualities, her endurance and her charms, ameliorates his government, and sways his inmost heart. Their different characteristics, arising from their different destinations, were designed to blend together so as to produce a happy harmony, and *to make both one.*

How vilely and treacherously man has employed his superior strength and audacity to crush and degrade women is related at length and with great depth and intensity of emotion by Ginsburg (14*ff*).

As the human race became more and more alienated from their creator, intrinsic merit and moral character were despised, and physical force became rampant; the stronger, as among animals, oppressed and preyed upon the weaker, and thus woman became the slave of man, and was absolutely sold in the capacity of daughter or wife, as cattle and other property.

Beginning with the Bible, Ginsburg offered ample samples from history of man's degradation of woman, stressing particularly the disgrace of polygamy and slavery, the subjugation of women for the gratification of man's carnal appetites and a plaything for his leisure hours. Quotations from heathen sources in loud execration of the natural infidelity, immorality, and depravity of women, and in derogation of their judgment and good sense are matched with similar sentiments from representatives of people of the book. The Prophet of Islam, e.g., said:

I stood at the gate of Paradise, and lo, most of its inmates were the poor; and I stood at the gate of hell, and lo, most of its inmates were women.

The Caliph Omar's advice about women, "consult them, and do the contrary of what they advise," is matched with Moore's paraphrase:

Whene'er you're in doubt, said a sage I once knew,
'Twixt two lines of conduct, which course to pursue,
Ask a woman's advice, and whate'er she advise,
Do the very reverse, and you're sure to be wise.

While Jewish women were supposedly treated more leniently and enjoyed greater privileges than their sex in other nations, still it is evident from the Old Testament that they were not wholly emancipated. Polygamy was practiced. Weakness of moral character was imputed to women and their infidelity and incontinency were dilated upon (Num 5:12; Prov 31:10; Eccles 7:28). Women were not admitted as legal witnesses because of their natural levity (Josephus *Antiquities* iv 8,15), and Maimonides (*hilkôṯ 'ēḏûṯ* ix 1) listed women along with slaves, children, idiots, the deaf, the blind, the wicked, the despised, relatives, and those interested in their own testimony, among the ten categories of persons disqualified as legal witnesses. Small wonder then that the pious Jew in his morning devotions says, "Blessed art thou, O Lord our God, King of the Universe, who has not made me a woman."

The significance of the Song of Songs in the history of Women's Liberation, as interpreted by Ginsburg, is such that one would wish that this interpretation could be sustained. His eloquent exposition makes it a pioneer manifesto on the emancipation of women (pp. 18–20):

Now, if one sex of the human family has been so degraded by the other; if she whom God created to be a help-mate and counterpart has been reduced by man to the slave of his carnal lusts; if such slavish and inhuman treatment has been justified on the false plea of the natural unfaithfulness and incontinency of the sex; if exclusion from society and imprisonment have been deemed necessary for the preservation of her morals, how greatly has woman been alienated from the original design of her creation how unjustly has her character been aspersed how inhumanly has she been treated and how great is the importance of a book which celebrates the virtuous example of a woman, and thus strikes at the root of all her reproaches and her wrongs!

The importance of this view of the book may be further seen from the fact, that, in proportion to the degradation of women, men themselves have become degraded; for, deprived of the meliorating influences which the delicacy and tenderness of women were designed to have over them, and never more needed than in their fallen state, they have abandoned themselves to their worst passions and desires, and thus their whole civil and social condition has been proportionally undignified and unblest. Look, on the other hand, at the state of society where woman is restored to her rightful position, there we shall find refinement of manners, purity of conversation, mutual confidence and affection, domestic happiness, intellectual enjoyment, freedom of thought and action, sympathetic repose, and whatever, in fact, tends to mitigate the unavoidable evils of the present life; all referable, in a greater or less degree, to the unrestricted influence of woman upon the child and upon the man. In religion, her influence is still more potent. If first in the transgression, she is first in the restoration; and were man as ready to follow her in doing good as he has been in doing evil, the world would long ago have been in a holier and happier state than it is at present. Who constitute the principal part of our worshipping assemblies? Women. Who are the main support of our various benevolent and evangelical institutions? Women. Let it not be said, then, that a Book which celebrates the ascendency of a virtuous woman in humble life over all the blandishments of wealth and royalty, is unworthy of a place in Holy Writ.

The importance of this book is, moreover, enhanced by the circumstances more immediately connected with the time in which it was written.

The conduct of Bath-sheba with David was calculated to confirm man in his opinion that woman was naturally unfaithful and incontinent, and that it was requisite to exclude her from society, in order to preserve her morals. But the narrative here recorded forms a contrast to the conduct of Bath-sheba. It shows the power of virtue in a woman, even of humble life. As the wife of an officer of rank, accustomed to luxury and wealth, the temptations of Bath-sheba were not so great, and yet she surrendered to them. Whereas the Shulamite, a humble shepherdess, to whom the promise of costly apparel and of elevation from a low and toilsome occupation to the highest rank, must have been an extraordinary allurement, triumphed over them all. If one woman yielded to small incitements, this book shows that another overcame unparalleled temptations, and thus checked the clamour against woman which might have arisen from the conduct of Bath-sheba with David. (See below *The Song of Songs and Women's Liberation*, pp. 205–210.)

The year 1852 witnessed a novel hypothesis propounded by Heinrich Augustus Hahn who denied that Solomon represents the Messiah, because at that early period the idea of a personal Messiah had not yet developed. The bridegroom of the Song, according to Hahn, is the kingdom of Israel and the bride represents "Japhetic heathenism." The allegorical meaning is that Israel in God's service is destined eventually to overcome heathenism with the weapons of justice and love, and bring the heathen into fellowship with Israel and with God. The Song, Hahn regarded as a dramatico-didactic poem in six parts.

The traditional allegorical view was quickly reasserted by W. Hengstenberg who insisted that Solomon represents the Messiah and the bride is the people of God, Israel, rather than Japhetic heathenism as alleged by Hahn. The poem, according to Hengstenberg (1853), celebrates the Prince of Peace and all the mercies which through him flow to the people of God. The poem Hengstenberg divided in two parts, the first (1–5:1) describing the advent of the Messiah and the tribulations which will precede his coming, and the second (5:2–8:14) describing Israel's punishment, repentance, and reunion with God through the mediation of the daughters of Jerusalem, i.e., the heathen, whose salvation the daughter of Zion (Israel) had first helped to accomplish. The restored Israel again becomes the center of the kingdom of God in a new covenant of immutable love.

In 1853 in America, the Reverend Professor George Burrowes of Lafayette College published an exposition of the Song as "illustrating by imagery drawn from the court of Solomon, the mutual love of Christ and the Church, as exercised in the case of individual believers."

The Wedding Week Theory

The hebdomadal division of the Canticles, corresponding to the Hebrew wedding week, proposed by Bossuet in 1693, was taken up again by Ernest Renan who noted (1860, 86) the similarity of the Song to modern Syrian wedding poetry and the custom of seven-day wedding festivals among Arabs at Damietta in Egypt and in certain localities in Syria. In 1873 a scholarly

German consul in Damascus, J. G. Wetzstein, published a study of contemporary marriage customs in Syria (1873), describing the seven-day festivities during which the spouses were enthroned on the threshing sledge, crowned as king and queen, and descriptive poems (*waṣf*, plural *awṣaf*) praising their beauty were sung in their honor. War songs were also sung and the bride performed a sword dance (cf. J. G. Wetzstein, 1868, 105*f*,*n*45). See below pp. 143*f*.

Delitzsch in his commentary of 1875 included an appendix of remarks by Wetzstein who cited an example of a *waṣf* composed in the early part of the nineteenth century for the wedding of the daughter of the sheik of Nawā. The poem was produced on very short notice by a noted poet of the Hauran during a horseback ride of about a mile en route to the wedding and thus may be assumed to consist of typical and traditional material. The author himself recited his poem in praise of the bride as she performed the sword dance. A young man of Nawā reproduced the poem from memory for Wetzstein in 1860:

Here hast thou thy ornament, O beautiful one! put it on, let nothing be forgotten!
Put it on, and live when the coward and the liar are long dead.
She said: Now shalt thou celebrate me in song, describe me in verse from head to foot!
I say: O fair one, thine attractions I am never able to relate,
And only the few will I describe which my eyes permit me to see:
Her head is like the crystal goblet, her hair like the black night,
Her black hair like the seven nights, the like are not in the whole year;
In waves it moves hither and thither, like the rope of her who draws water,
And her side locks breathe all manner of fragrance, which kills me.
The new moon beams on her brow, and dimly illuminated are the balances,
And her eyebrows like the arch of the *Nûn* drawn by an artist's hand.
The witchery of her eyes makes me groan as if they were the eyes of a Kufic lady;
Her nose is like the date of Irak, the edge of the Indian sword;
Her face like the full moon, and heart-breaking are her cheeks.
Her mouth is a little crystal ring, and her teeth rows of pearls,

And her tongue scatters pearls; and, ah me, how beautiful
her lips!
Her spittle pure virgin honey, and healing for the bite of
a viper.
Comparable to elegant writing, the *Seijal* waves downwards
on her chin,
Thus black seeds of the fragrant *Kezḥa* show themselves
on white bread.
The *Mânî* draws the neck down to itself with the spell
written in Syrian letters;
Her neck is like the neck of the roe which drinks out of
the fountain of *Ḳanawât.*
Her breast like polished marble tables, as ships bring
them to *Ṣêdâ* (Sidon),
Thereon like apples of the pomegranate two glittering piles
of jewels.
Her arms are drawn swords, peeled cucumbers—oh that I had
such!
And incomparably beautiful her hands in the rose-red of the
Hinnâ-leaf;
Her smooth, fine fingers are like the writing reed not yet cut;
The glance of her nails like the Dura-seeds which have lain
overnight in milk;
Her body is a mass of cotton wool which a master's hand
has shaken into down,
And her legs marble pillars in the sacred house of the
Omajads. . . .

The *Nûn* is the name of the letter *n* which in its independent form resembles a half circle open at the top; the poet presumably had in mind the inverted letter. The *Seijal* and the *Mânî* are tattoo designs, the former an arabesque of the final form of the letter *Mim,* and the latter a talisman containing an angel's name ending in *'l* worn above the windpipe. (For further detail on these and other obscure terms in the poem, cf. "Remarks by Dr. J. G. Wetzstein" in Delitzsch's commentary, 1885, 174*f*.)

In 1888 B. Stade (II, 197) remarked that J. G. Wetzstein had supplied the most conducive contribution to the understanding of this peculiar book in our time.

Two decades after the publication of Wetzstein's articles, K. Budde applied the material to support the theory that the Song is a collection of poems sung at peasant weddings (1894a, 1894b, and in his commentary, 1898). The crux of the argument is that customs are tenacious and that the peasant weddings of Syria described by Wetzstein may be presumed to have persisted for centuries, even millennia, and thus they throw light on the origin and purpose of the Canticles as folk wedding songs. The descriptions of the bride and groom in the Song resemble the Syrian wedding *waṣf* and the Shulamite's Manhanaim Dance (7:1*ff*) was related to the sword dance performed by the bride (although there is no mention of any sword wielded by the Shulamite). This explanation of the Canticles, as reflecting ancient Syro-Palestinian village wedding songs in which the groom and bride were king and queen for a week, was widely acclaimed and accepted as solving the riddle of the book, and it dominated discussions of the problem for more than a quarter of a century (cf. Rowley, 210n4).

Criticism and reservations with regard to this peasant wedding hypothesis were many and varied. W. W. Cannon, e.g., commented (1913, 29): "It is an enormous assumption that these wedding ceremonies described by Wetzstein as taking place in Syrian villages near Damascus in 1861 were necessarily the same in weddings in Judea more than 2000 years earlier, or at any time." It was pointed out by several critics (cf. Rowley, 211n5) that the bride of the Canticles is never called "queen," as would be expected in accord with Budde's hypothesis. C. Gebhardt (1931, 12) likewise disputed the relevance of Budde's assumptions and denied that the wedding customs of Syrian peasants, being of hybrid origins as the result of numerous invasions, could have any bearing on Jewish poetry.

Hilma Granqvist in her study (II, 137n) found no evidence of a "king's week" in local weddings and little to suggest the existence of such a custom in other writings on Palestinian wedding customs. It has also been objected that the war songs of the Syrian weddings are missing among the Canticles and that the extent of the collection is insufficient for a seven-day songfest. Answer to the latter objection has been that the Canticles are only sample selections. It could also be observed that in folk singing a few words can be dragged out and repeated for a long time. The Arabic *waṣf,* or descriptive song, was not limited to marriage celebrations and Dalman (1901, xi*ff*) adduced some prenuptial examples. Accordingly, a number of critics have concluded, following Herder, that the Canticles are simply a collection of love lyrics rather than wedding songs. Rowley (212nn1–7) cited several distinguished representatives of this view and expressed his own inclination to agree. "I am not persuaded that the marriage-week theory is soundly based, or that the songs had anything to do with a wedding occasion. They appear rather to be a series of poems in which a lover enshrined the love he gave and the love he received."

The centennial issue of *Theologische Quartalschrift* (*TQ*) was distinguished by an article of Paul Riessler (1919) which presented yet another novel theory of interpretation of the Song of Songs with application of the nuptial allegory to the Essenes. The sequence of events in the nuptials of the Canticles differs in several respects from regular Israelite marriage procedures and these deviations Riessler took to be deliberate and the key to the understanding of the Song as an Essene manifesto. The strange climax with the call to flee shows that the poet did not intend to lead forth an ordinary couple. The figure of the swift young gazelle at the end along with the reference to the bridegroom as a gazelle or young stag standing behind the wall and peering in the window Riessler connected with the suitor of Wisdom as a Peeping Tom in Sir 14:22–24 and related the figure to the devout seekers for righteousness and justice who resorted to the desert (I Macc 2:29). Thus the Song of Songs may represent an invitation to enter a religious community such as the Essenes and Therapeutae (p. 16). Various details were related to the Essenes, their practices, and their tribulations. The watchmen of 5:7 who struck and injured the bride may refer to the Pharisees, and the nobles of 7:1 to the Sadducees, neither of which was especially friendly toward the Essenes (p. 18). The summons to flee to solitude at the end suggested to Riessler the segregated regimen for novices in the Essene order. Riessler admitted that the Song still contained many allusions and figures no longer understood, and that supposition was still required (p. 19). His suppositions, not surprisingly, have not won wide acceptance.

Cultic Interpretation

The view that the Song of Songs derives from pagan fertility worship was developed in the present century and, in spite of resistance, has continued to gain ground with the accelerating recovery and progress in interpretation of documents of religious literature of the civilizations of the ancient Near East, especially of Mesopotamia, and more recently the Ugaritic mythological and religious texts. Already in 1906, Wilhelm Erbt (pp. 196–202) suggested that the Song of Songs is a collection of paschal poems of Canaanitish origin, describing the love of the sun-god Tammuz, called Dod or Shelem, and the moon-goddess Ishtar under the name of Shalmith. This view was accorded scant notice and even less favor, partly no doubt, because of its reliance on the astral theories of Hugo Winckler and the Pan-Babylonian school. Erbt's view was criticized briefly by V. Zapletal (1907, 52–56), and appears to have been largely ignored thereafter. Less than a decade later, O. Neuschotz de Jassy devoted a volume to a radically different cultic interpretation, explaining the Canticles as a Hebrew translation of certain Osirian litanies made in Alexandria during the Ptolemaic period. Solomon, in de Jassy's scheme, represented Osiris, Jerusalem, city of peace, was the abode of the dead, and the Shulamite was the goddess Isis. The Song deals with the resurrection of Osiris, rather than with love, and the kisses of 1:2 are not those of lovers, but the resurrection kiss of the priest of Osiris. Again little attention was paid to de Jassy, as to Erbt. Joseph Halévy in a scornful review (1914) declined to respond to the gratuitous crudities of the author and wished for him a larger dose of good sense and modesty.

The cultic interpretation of the Song of Songs received new impetus from a catalog of Akkadian hymn titles edited near the end of the First World War by E. Ebeling (1923). The text, *Keilschrifttexte aus Assur religiösen Inhalts,* Heft IV, no. 158, presents series of sentences which are called *irâtu,* the plural of *irtu,* "breast," a designation of a type of love song. Line 6 of the text reads *napḫar* 23 *i-ra-a-tu ša e-šir-té,* "total 23 *irtu*-songs for the decachord," and seventeen lines later line 24 reads "total 17 *irtu*-songs for the *kitmu*-instrument." In line 38 the goddess Nanā, a cognomen of Ishtar, is mentioned. Accordingly, Ebeling concluded that we have here a series of titles or first lines of hymns to Ishtar. G. A. Barton (1920, 464*f*) attempted to link the lines together and translated the whole as a single hymn to Tammuz as the ideal lover. S. Langdon (1921) regarded the text in question as a collection of musical compositions, some sacred and some profane (pp. 183,190). Although some Tammuz liturgies were already known (cf. e.g. S. Langdon, 1913), they had not been related to the Song of Songs.

T. J. Meek was impressed by the similarities between Canticles and the hymn list edited by Ebeling and presented the first formulation of his view in a paper before the Society of Biblical Literature in 1920 (later published in 1922–23), and developed in subsequent articles (1924a and b). Meek's translation of the hymn list is given below with omission of the Akkadian transliteration and textual and philological notes (cf. 1924a, 246–252):

KAR, IV, No. 158, Rev., Col. II.

1. I beheld thee (masc.) and . . .
2. Shine out like a star of the sky!
3. In a dirge over thy (masc.) death.
4. This is the desire that rejoiceth my heart (lit. liver).
5. The utterance of thy (masc.) mouth is the word of my life; prosper thou me!
6. A total of 23 *irtu*-songs for the decachord.
7. How I do long for the bountiful one!
8. The day that the lord of my right hand embraced me.
9. Come, take me! I give welcome to the son.
10. At any time, O lord, thou mayest enter now.
11. I am pressed to thy (masc.) breast.
12. With the fates of night.
13. By the name of the son I revive (?) the vegetation.
14. Ah, I behold the fat of the land.
15. The day bringeth gladness, even joy of the heart.
16. Upon me may the son beam; come thou in!
17. Not a rival (fem.) equalled me.
18. My Nippurite is a jar of sweetness.
19. Be joyous, be happy!
20. Thou hast caressed me; be thou my lord!
21. The fragrance of cedar is thy love, O lord.
22. To the door of the lord she did come.
23. For this night, for these evenings.
24. A total of 17 *irtu*-songs for the *kitmu*-instrument.

25. How gorgeous she is; how resplendent she is!
26. She seeketh out the beautiful garden of thy (masc.) abundance.
27. Today my heart is joy (and) gladness.
28. O, come down to the garden of the king (which) reeks with cedar.
29. Thou, O son, art a lover of my bosom.
30. On the other side of the river is the city of lamentation.
31. To the place of sorrow thou (masc.) didst go in the month of lamentation.
32. Joyously come, O son!
33. Like the pavilion of the maidens.
34. O bird of child-bearing, harbinger of light, honey is thy (fem.) voice.
35. O watchman of the garden of lamentation.
36,37. Every day in Larsa lamentation abounds.
38. Rejoice, O Nana, in the garden of Ebabbara, which thou lovest.
39. The maiden whose heart bore lamentation.
40. How can I always keep silent!
41. O, I long for the couch of the sons.
42. My eye-lids are full of sleep.
43,44. Thy (masc.) love is indeed a jewel; thy longing is indeed gold.
45. My love is a light, illuminating the shadows.
46. By night I thought of thee (masc.).
47. The utterance of thy (masc.) mouth.
48. After I lay in the bosom of the son.
49. Thy (masc.) passion is of the lapis-luzuli of the mountain.
50. Joyfully hasten, O king.
51. Welcome is the lover.
52. In thy (fem.) abundance flourish!
53. I possess thy (masc.) love.
54. In the breath of . . .

Meek saw parallels to the Song of Songs particularly in line 9 for which he cited 1:2*ff*, 2:6, 4:16, 7:12*ff*, and 8:1*ff* with alleged reference to the union of Tammuz and Ishtar for the purpose of reviving life in nature. In line 14 "the fat of the land" was related to Isa 5:1 and "the fat of *tûraq*" in Canticles 1:3. In line 15 the "joy of the heart" was referred to the joy occasioned by the revival of the life and vegetation of the world, overlooking the striking parallel in Song of Songs 3:11 with reference to connubial joy. For line 19, Meek cited Canticles 1:4 and 2:12 and referred to his discussions of these verses in his previous articles. On line 21 it was noted that "cedar is everywhere connected with the fertility cult and appears in Cant. 1:17." The "door of the lord" in line 22 Meek related to the netherworld as the house of Tammuz and cited as parallel Canticles 2:4 which he rendered, "Bring me to the house of wine and look upon me with love." Canticles 4:16 was cited as parallel to line 28. For line 32 the parallels proposed were 2:17, 7:12, 8:14 and 2:10,13, 4:8. For line 34, 2:14, 4:11, 5:1. For line 35, the "watchman of the garden of lamentation," was compared to 3:3, 5:7, and 8:11 as referring also to the netherworld and its guards. In line 41, "the sons" was explained as "A euphemistic name for the male votaries of the fertility cult" and related to the "youths" of Canticles 2:3. Line 46 was compared to Canticles 3:1.

Meek concluded his brief survey of the parallels thus:

> Even a casual perusal of the lines of the hymns listed above must convince the most skeptical of two things: (1) that these hymns were taken from the liturgy of the Tammuz-Ishtar cult, and (2) that the similarity between them and the songs in the book of Canticles is so close that both must belong together. The structure of the songs is the same (two lovers representing god and goddess wooing each other and alternating in the praise of each other's charms); the general theme is the same (love); many of the phrases are quite identical; the figures are introduced in similar fashion; the lines breathe the same delight in love; and the intent of all is manifestly to bring about the awakening of life in nature. Both are liturgies of the fertility cult. The only difference is that one group has come from Babylonia and the other from Palestine, where numerous influences tended to obscure and efface its original character (1924, 252; cf. 1922–23, 13).

Thus in Meek's view the Song of Songs was from the beginning a religious composition, but connected with the cult of Tammuz-Adonis rather than the worship of the God of Israel. The Song, however, was no longer in its original and offensive form as a Tammuz liturgy, but had been revised to render it innocuous and to harmonize it with the Yahweh cultus. In the course of time the original liturgy came to be reinterpreted and adapted to meet changing conditions, beliefs, and practices, and parts of it were doubtless lost and others added, while around the residuum gathered other songs of like nature. The original character of the poem was forgotten and it came to be thought of as a song of love, with its two chief characters as types of the ideal lovers. Its use as a religious song in connection with the rites of spring continued in certain circles. Finally the name of Solomon got attached to it and the allegorical method of interpretation combined with the prestige of Solomon's name helped smooth the way to its general acceptance. The panegyric on love (8:6) "crept into the text, and lo, in a generation or two the book had become canonical, 'The Song of Songs'!"

The editor of the symposium *SSS,* W. H. Schoff, contributed an article on "The Offering Lists in the Song of Songs and their Political Significance" (pp. 80*ff*) in which it was suggested that the ingredients of the anointing oil and the incense in the descriptions of the temple and the tabernacle were derived from the Tammuz cult. Some of the spices, such as spikenard, saffron, aloes, and henna, Schoff supposed, were introduced in a later revision of the text, since they are not likely to have been known in Israel in pre-exilic times. The alleged political purpose was to legitimize certain elements of the popular Tammuz cult in the official state worship.

The transfer of the features of the Tammuz cult to the worship of Yahweh, Schoff suggested, occurred in the following way. When Jerusalem was captured by David, the worship of Tammuz and Astarte continued and Solomon for political reasons installed it in the Temple. Its influence is seen in the description of the Temple structure, vessels, and ceremonies in I King 4*ff* and of the tabernacle in Exodus 25. Spices peculiar to the Tammuz cult were used in the sacred oil and incense, Exodus 30. A strong party, including many Judeans, was devoted to these divinities and their interests had to be considered and conciliated, especially in view of the prophetic opposition. At the spring festival the king and queen represented the god and goddess in a sacred marriage. When, under foreign domination, there was no longer a king and queen, the rites were probably carried on by elected functionaries. Yahweh was gradually substituted for Tammuz and the Daughter of Jerusalem for Astarte, but the ritual remained essentially the same. New spices, not known in pre-exilic times, spikenard, saffron, aloes, and henna, were introduced, just as such additions were made in the Talmudic descriptions of the oil and incense. (The supposition that certain spices were unknown because they are not mentioned in Scripture is precarious, since henna or camphor [*kōp̄er*] is now mentioned in Ugaritic.) The Canticles, originally a Tammuz liturgy, were preserved among other sacred scriptures in the temple archive "because they referred in some way to the services and ceremonies of the temple."

Reactions to Meek's views were slow and those who remained unconvinced were, for the most part, content to voice reservations or outright rejections rather than replies (cf. Rowley, 220). N. Schmidt (1926), however, offered criticisms in some detail. Schmidt admitted at the outset that the assumption of pagan survivals in the festivals of Israel and in its sanctuaries is perfectly legitimate and he conceded foreign origins for Purim, Hanukkah, Mazzoth, Shabuoth, and Sukkot. Most of the sanctuaries were taken over from the former inhabitants, and in all of them, including the royal temple in Jerusalem, heathen cults were carried on. It is thus natural that the effort should be made to find in Canticles the remains of an Adonis litany. Nevertheless, the arguments in favor of this view were not convincing to Schmidt. Ezek 8:14 shows that Tammuz was worshiped in the temple in Jerusalem and that his home was supposed to be in the north. There was mourning for Hadad-Rimmon in the valley of Megiddo (Zech 12:11). While the lamentation "Alas, Adon" over Jehoiakim and Zedekiah (Jer 22:18, 34:5) is not necessarily connected with the Adonis cult, Isa 17:10*f*, which refers to the planting of gardens of Na'man (a cognomen of Tammuz-Adonis), was admitted as a possible allusion to Adonis. In view of what was known about the Adonis cult, it would naturally be assumed that there was also rejoicing over the resurrection of the god; but of this no direct evidence had been adduced. Astarte was worshiped in Israel from early times and the "queen of heaven" for whom the women made cakes (Jer 7:18, 44:17) was undoubtedly Ishtar-Venus. But whether she was thought of in Israel as having descended to the netherworld to bring back Tammuz, Schmidt rightly emphasized (p. 157), we do not know. (These gaps in the evidence stressed by Schmidt have since been largely filled by the Ugaritic myths which present Mighty Baal and Virgin Anat in the full cycle of the fertility myth, as consorts, with Baal's death at the hands of Mot, the infernal god of death and sterility, Anat's mourning and search for the body of her brother-consort, Baal's resurrection, the rejoicing, the sacred marriage, and passages descriptive of the beauty of both of the consorts.) The similarities of the *irtu*-song which Meek regarded as sufficiently marked to convince the most skeptical that both are liturgies of the fertility cult did not so convince Schmidt.

Meek's assertion that "many of the phrases are quite identical" was rebutted by Schmidt who admitted that "there is a general resemblance in the woman's frank invitation to come and taste love," but correctly affirmed that "the most careful search does not reveal a single phrase that is quite identical." The features which Meek stressed are characteristic of love poetry generally. "But there is no hint in Canticles of either a god or a goddess, and lovers are wont to praise each other's charms." The numerous references to lamentation in the Babylonian songs have no counterpart in Canticles. "It certainly seems fanciful to discover in the woman's allusion to her sun-burnt complexion (1:6) a reference to the drying-up of vegetation." To Meek's assertion that "the intent of all is manifestly to bring about the awakening of life in nature" Schmidt retorted: "This is so far from being manifest that there is not the slightest hint of such an intent in the Canticles. . . . The 'blessings of the womb' were dear to the Hebrews. But there is not the slightest trace in Canticles of this kind of fertility."

Meek's opinion that the many hapax legomena in Canticles as well as certain peculiarities of language "bespeak a non-Hebraic origin" was judiciously criticized by Schmidt. Meek had listed a large number of alleged Babylonian loanwords to show that Canticles "in its early form came more or less directly from the Canaanites" whose language was "essentially the same as the Akkadian." (Here Meek was doubtless influenced by B. Landsberger's and Theo Bauer's designation of the Amorites as East Canaanites.) Schmidt listed the twenty-three alleged loanwords, discussed several of them, and concluded that "There is no evidence that any of them is an Assyrian loanword." Schmidt's generalizations about loanwords and the relations of various Semitic dialects were especially judicious.

The motif of the goddess' descent to the netherworld to rescue her consort, seen by Erbt and Meek in the search in the city streets, was not admitted as such by Schmidt whose summary complaint was that

> Almost everything that a couple of lovers would be likely to notice under the Syrian sky is brought into connection with the Tammuz cult: sun, moon, and stars, mountains, rivers, fountains, fields, and gardens; houses, tents, huts, rafters, pillars, and panels; cedars, cypresses, vines, lilies, apples, olives, and pomegranates; wine, honey, milk, and perfumes; doves, gazelles, foxes, and horses. By the allegorical method it is all turned into veiled allusions to the infernal regions and the practices of sacred prostitution. Verily, what has been described as "die Leidengeschichte des Hohenliedes" still continues (pp. 161*f*).

Although admitting that there is much evidence that Shemesh, Tammuz, Astarte and other divinities were worshiped in the royal temple at Jerusalem before the Exile, Schmidt denied that there is the slightest indication that the kings and queens of Judah, or of Israel, represented Tammuz and Astarte at the paschal feast, or any trace of a protest against such a custom in the Deuteronomic law or in the prophets. It was scarcely conceivable to Schmidt that when the high priest became the head of the state, that kings and queens were elected *pro tempore* to impersonate divinities whose worship was no longer tolerated in the presence of Yahweh. "Any custom, symbol, or offering characteristic of the proscribed cults would naturally be removed." (Such assumptions, though commonplace, are nevertheless highly questionable in view of the vitality and persistence of religious traditions, especially those related to the vital concern of life, death, and love.)

Meek's theory thus did not commend itself to Schmidt who rather regarded the Canticles as secular love songs, the divan of a poet who derived some of his conceits and imagery from popular festivities. In his translation and commentary (1911, 241) Schmidt had suggested that the dance of the Xylophoria furnished the occasion for the first canticle. The poet may have elsewhere contributed his share to the merry ballads of marriage feasts. "It is not impossible that he also drew upon ideas and expressions that had grown up in connection with the customs at the agrarian festivals and in the once popular cults." The analogy of erotic poetry does not favor the assumption that he confined himself to wedded love, and many passages become quite incomprehensible on this view. "Experience and observation, a passion for beauty in nature, rare in the ancient world, a joy in the life of the senses as spontaneous as the warbling of a bird in the mating season, and an admirable mastery of form molded these precious lyrics." Thus Schmidt (p. 164) preferred to take the Canticles as secular love songs, even of extramarital love, rather than admit more than casual influence of popular agrarian festivities.

Meek's articles stirred renewed interest in the possibilities of cultic interpretation of the Canticles and a number of eminent scholars adopted and adapted his views (cf. Rowley, 217*f*). L. Waterman (1925) suggested that the Song as an old Tammuz liturgy had been reduced to the level of folk poetry, rather than revised to accord with Yahwism, and then made into an allegory of the political relations between Israel and Judah following the Disruption. A complete commentary on the Canticles as Tammuz cult songs was presented by W. Wittekindt (1926) who expounded the book as a Jerusalem liturgy for celebration of the wedding of Ishtar and Tammuz. H. G. May contributed to the development of the cultic interpretation of the Canticles with an important article on "The Fertility Cult in Hosea" (1931–32) and again in collaboration with W. C. Graham (1936, 122*ff*). N. H. Snaith (1933–34) related the Song to the stories of the rape of the maidens of Shiloh (Judg 21:19–21) and the sacrifice of Jephthah's daughter (Judg 11:37–40). Snaith divided the Song into two groups of alternating passages, one associated with the rites of autumn and the other with the spring. "The autumn passages naturally precede the spring passages, since the pre-Exilic times the year began in the autumn and not in the spring" (p. 132). The origin of the Song, Snaith believed, is to be found in the Tammuz-Adonis ritual of North Syria since the topographical background is also the area to which the Syrian Adonis ritual primarily belongs, and the references which Meek, Wittekindt, and others had found showed that these early traces of its origins still remain, although overlaid during the centuries and reinterpreted and interpolated through the generations. Snaith's division of the Song into alternating autumn and spring litanies was in the interest of combining the seemingly conflicting indications that the Tammuz-Adonis rites took place at different times of the year. W. O. E. Oesterley (1936, 15) expressed the opinion that

> there is much justification for the interpretation of the Song as being a survival of a number of early liturgies of the fertility cult. What has been said is far from exhausting all that can be urged in favour of this interpretation. It is not to be denied that there is a good deal in the Song which admits of a different interpretation: that there are wedding-songs pure and simple in which there is not necessarily any reference to the Tammuz-myth seems certain; but it is probable that they are based, all unconsciously, on early traditional liturgies of the cult whose meaning had been entirely lost.

The case for connection of Canticles with the Tammuz cult was deemed to be greatly weakened, or, as some supposed, destroyed, by the absence of clear evidence from the cuneiform sources for the resurrection of Tammuz. In 1960 at the International Congress of Orientalists in Moscow, S. N. Kramer emphasized the absence of such evidence and in his treatment of "Mythologies of Sumer and Akkad" (1961, 10), Kramer sought to correct and rectify some of the current misconceptions and misstatements relating to the myths of the ancients, on the basis of a hitherto largely unknown Sumerian myth concerned with the death of Dumuzi, or Tammuz. The content of the new text, taken together with the myth "Inanna's Descent to the Nether World," according to Kramer,

> demonstrates beyond reasonable doubt that Dumuzi dies and "stays dead"; indeed he must not "under any circumstances" leave the Nether World and return to the upper regions, since in that case Inanna would have no substitute and would therefore be forced to return to the Nether World. It is for this reason, too, that we find only laments for Dumuzi's death; there are no songs of rejoicing to celebrate his resurrection. But for more than half a century now, students of mythology . . . have taken Dumuzi to be the original prototype of the dying god who rises annually from the dead, the very archetype of the deity who dies every summer and is revived every spring. In an effort to get at the reasons for this erroneous but well-nigh universal view of the Dumuzi myth, I combed the relevant cuneiform literature patiently and carefully, but could find no supporting evidence whatever from the texts; it is based on nothing but inference and surmise, guess and conjecture.

E. M. Yamauchi (1965) combined Kramer's view with the study of Pierre Lambrecht (1955) indicating that belief in the resurrection of Adonis was a late development and concluded:

In the first place, it is clear that the identification of Tammuz, Adonis, Attis, Osiris, and Baal as expressions of the same type of a rising and dying fertility god must be abandoned. . . . In the second place, biblical studies which assumed the traditional view of Tammuz's resurrection—such as Theophile Meek's interpretation of Canticles—will need to be drastically revised. . . . Finally, Tammuz can no longer be considered a prototype of Christ. Moreover, the resurrection of Inanna-Ishtar offers a contrast and not a comparison. Whereas, according to Christian theology, Christ died as a substitute for man so that he could take him to heaven, Ishtar died and needed a substitute so that she herself could get back to heaven. Inanna, instead of rescuing Tammuz from hell, sent him there (p. 290).

Within a few years, however, there was a significant shift in Kramer's view of Dumuzi's death and resurrection. As a result of the discovery of the end of the Sumerian myth and a brilliant insight by A. Falkenstein, "we actually have textual evidence for Dumuzi's return to life after a six-month sojourn in the land of the dead" (cf. S. N. Kramer [1966]; *SMR*, 107*ff* and 155n4).

Thus Kramer could write in 1969:

From Mesopotamia the theme of the dead Dumuzi and his resurrection spread to Palestine, and it is not surprising to find the women of Jerusalem bewailing Tammuz in one of the gates of the Jerusalem temple. Nor is it at all improbable that the myth of Dumuzi's death and resurrection left its mark on the Christ story, in spite of the profound spiritual gulf between them. Several motifs in the Christ story may go back to Sumerian prototypes. . . . Above all, as we now know, Dumuzi, not unlike Christ, played the role of vicarious substitute for mankind; had he not taken the place of Inanna, the goddess of love, procreation, and fertility, in the Nether World, all life on earth would have come to an end. Admittedly the differences between the two were more marked and significant than the resemblances—Dumuzi was no Messiah preaching the Kingdom of God on earth. But the Christ story certainly did not originate and evolve in a vacuum; it must have had its forerunners and prototypes, and one of the most venerable and influential of these was no doubt the mournful tale of the shepherd-god Dumuzi and his melancholy fate, a myth that had been current throughout the ancient Near East for over two millennia (*SMR*, 133).

Jewish Mysticism

Jewish mystical speculation developed a line of interpretation of the Song of Songs which relates it willy-nilly to the modern cultic interpretation involving the union of male and female deities. The boldest exposition of this Jewish mystical approach, based largely on Gershon Scholem's studies of medieval Jewish Mysticism, has been presented by Raphael Patai in a book entitled

The Hebrew Goddess, 1967, from which most of the following sketch is drawn.

The absence of feminine companionship for the God of Israel was not absolute, at least not in Jewish mysticism. Philo of Alexandria in his treatise *On the Cherubim* offered three interpretations, the last of which is of relevance to the present concern with the bisexual and heterosexual aspect of deity.

While God is indeed one, His highest and chiefest powers are two, even goodness and sovereignty. Through His goodness He begot all that is, through His sovereignty He rules what He has begotten. And in the midst of the two is a third which united them, Reason, for it is through reason that God is both ruler and good. Of these two potencies, sovereignty and goodness, the Cherubim are symbols, as the fiery sword is the symbol of reason . . . these unmixed potencies are mingled and united . . . when God is good, yet the glory of His sovereignty is seen amid the beneficence . . . where He is sovereign, through the sovereignty the beneficence still appears. (Philo *De Cherubim* vii 21–24, lx 27–30; LCL, II, 21–27; cf. also *De Vita Mosis* ii 98–99, LCL, VI, after Patai, 113 and 302n36.)

In the passage just quoted bisexual symbolism is implicit, although Philo here stopped short of saying anything about a female aspect of God. This highly significant step Philo takes elsewhere in speaking of the creation of the world apropos of Prov 8:22:

. . . The Architect who made this universe was at the same time the father of what was thus born, whilst its mother was the knowledge God had union, not as men have it, and begot created things. And Knowledge, having received the divine seed, when her travail was consummated, bore the only beloved son who is apprehended by the senses, the world which we see. Thus in the pages of one of the inspired company, wisdom is represented as speaking of herself after this manner: "God obtained me first of all his works and founded me before the ages" (Prov viii 22). True, for it was necessary that all that came to the birth of creation should be younger than the mother and nurse of the All. . . . I suggest then, that the father is reason, masculine, perfect, right reason, and the mother the lower learning of the schools, with its regular course or round of instruction. (Philo *De Ebrietato* viii 30 and ix 33, LCL, III, 333–335.)

Patai observed that the process of *creation* in this passage is represented unequivocally as *procreation.* Elsewhere (*De Cherubim* xiv 49, LCL, II, 39) Philo calls God "the husband of Wisdom" who drops the seed of happiness for the race of mortals into good and virgin soil." Philo's language and metaphor is mythological, as in the Ugaritic myths where creative activity by the gods is presented in terms of sexual procreation.

In speaking of the Cherubim of the Sanctuary, Philo says that they symbolized "the two most ancient and supreme powers (or 'virtues') of the divine God": his creative power, called "God" which is a "peaceable, gentle and beneficent virtue," and his kingly power, called "Lord," which is "a legislative, chastising and correcting virtue." (Philo *De Vita Mosis* iii; *Quaest. in Gen.* 57.) On this basis, Patai applied the masculine traits to Cherub A representing God (Elohim) and the feminine traits to Cherub B representing Lord (Yahweh) in the following dichotomy:

God (Elohim)	*Lord* (Yahweh)	*God* (Elohim)	*Lord* (Yahweh)
Father	Mother	Goodness	Sovereignty
Husband	Wife	Peaceable	Legislative
Begetter	Bearer	Gentle	Chastising
Creator	Nurturer	Beneficent	Correcting
Reason	Wisdom		

Each of these two series of divine attributes is symbolized by one of the Cherubim, according to Philo, and this, in Patai's view (p. 115), is the earliest indication that one of the Cherubim in the Temple represented a male, and the other a female figure.

Josephus is the only witness who has left a detailed description of the Jerusalem Temple as it was in its last years before the destruction by Titus in A.D. 70. Concerning the Cherubim and the Ark, Josephus tells us: "On its cover were two images which the Hebrews call Cherubim; they are flying creatures, but their form is not like that of any of the creatures which men have seen, though Moses said he had seen such things near the throne of God." (*Antiquities* III 6.5). Here Josephus has apparently mixed Moses and Ezekiel (cf. Ezek 9:3, 10:1–22). Josephus tells us no more about the Cherubim, but is at pains to insist that apart from the altar, the table, the censer, and the candlestick, which are all written in the Law, "there is nothing further there, nor are there any mysteries performed that may not be spoken of; nor is there any feasting within the place" (*Against Apion* II 7,8). This insistence that there were no unspeakable mysteries or any feasting in the Temple is to be connected with the statements that when Antiochus (Epiphanes) ravaged the Temple he did not find anything there that was ridiculous, although what was found cannot be revealed to other nations (*Wars* V 5.5). Josephus' curious vacillation between the assertion that there was nothing at all in the Holy of Holies, and the admission that there was something there, but nothing ridiculous, and that what was there could not be revealed, Patai plausibly related to the figures of the two Cherubim and the embarrassment occasioned by their representation in sexual embrace. The representation of the Cherubim in sexual embrace is attested in Talmudic tradition by Rab Qetina who flourished in the late third or early fourth century:

When Israel used to make the pilgrimage, they (the priests) would roll up for them the *pārōḵeṯ* (the curtain between the Holy and the Holy of Holies in the Second Temple) and show them the Cherubim which were entwined with one another, and say to them: "Behold! your love before God is like the love of male and female" (TB Yoma 54a).

Rab Hisda objected to Qetina's assertion on the grounds that such a procedure would have violated the injunction of Num 4:20 that the priests should not go in to see the holy (things) and die. Rab Nahman, however, answered

Hisda's objection with the explanation that a bride who still lives in her father's house is bashful toward her groom, but once she lives in her husband's house is no longer bashful toward him. Thus the Israelites while they were in the desert were bashful and would not look at the Shekinah, but once they settled in their land, they could feast their eyes on her (Patai, 304n57).

There is a Talmudic tradition that the Cherubim, although they were golden statues, had mobility: "As long as Israel fulfilled the will of God, the faces of the Cherubim were turned toward each other; however, when Israel sinned, they turned their faces away from each other." (TB Baba Bathra 99a). Whether the Cherubim spent more time vis à vis or dos à dos, their ideal and proper position was face to face. The sexual embrace of the Cherubim is confirmed by the testimony of the distinguished Palestinian sage Rabbi Simeon ben Laqish (ca. 200–275) with reference to the sacking of the Temple: When strangers entered the Sanctuary, they saw the Cherubim intertwined with each other; they took them out into the marketplace and said: "Israel, whose blessing is a blessing and whose curse a curse, should occupy themselves with such things! And they despised them, as it is written, 'All who honored her despise her, because they have seen her nakedness'" (Lam 1:8; TB Yoma 54b). This same tradition, that the heathen saw the Cherubim in sexual embrace and ridiculed the Jews for their hypocrisy, is preserved in other Midrashim:

> When (Israel's) sins caused the Gentiles to enter Jerusalem, Ammonites and Moabites came together with them, and they entered the House of the Holy of Holies, and they found there the two Cherubim, and they took them and put them in a cage and went around with them in all the streets of Jerusalem and said: "You used to say that this nation was not serving idols. Now see what we found and what they were worshiping." (Cf. Patai, 305–308, for references and an extended discussion of the historical setting of this incident.)

The occasion(s) on which the Cherubim were shown to the people was said by Rab Qetina to be when Israel made the pilgrimage. Every male Israelite was required to make the pilgrimage to the Temple in Jerusalem three times a year, at Passover in the spring, at the Feast of Weeks (a week of weeks later), and at the Feast of Booths (Sukkot) in the autumn, two weeks after the New Year (cf. Exod 23:14–17, 34:23–24; Deut 16:16). The latter festival was especially noted for enthusiasm and conviviality and the fact that both men and women participated in it and on the seventh day the sexes used to mingle freely and indulge in what was euphemistically termed "lightheadedness" (*qallûṯ rō'š*) (cf. TB Moed Qatan 27b; Sukkot 51b; on the sexual sense of this lightheadedness" cf. Jastrow's *Dictionary,* p. 1373b, s.v. *qallûṯ*). Such ritual license is a regular feature of fertility religions to which the Israelites succumbed on occasion, notably in the episode of the Golden Calf (Exod 32:6) and in the notorious incident at Shittim (Num 25:1–9).

Medieval Jewish savants who were inclined to rationalism tended to ignore the Talmudic tradition of the Cherubim represented in marital embrace and concentrated on attributing to them symbolic meanings which emphasized the unity and uniqueness of God as distinct from the Cherubim. Maimonides (d. 1204), e.g., explained that the two angels over the ark (i.e. the Cherubim) were made to consolidate the popular belief in the existence of angels and to refute idolatry. If there had been one image, this might have been misleading, since it might have been thought that that was the image of the deity who was to be worshiped, as done by idolaters. Since there were two Cherubim and the explicit statement that "the Lord is One," the validity of the belief in the existence of angels and the fact that they are many is confirmed, and the error that they are the deity confuted—the deity being one and having created the multiplicity (cf. Maimonides, *Guide to the Perplexed* III 45. Translated from the Arabic by S. Pines, 1963, 577). Mystics, on the other hand, seized on the embrace of the Cherubim for the reinforcement of the basic doctrine of the sanctity of sex and the cosmic necessity of sexual intercourse between man and wife. The Qabbalah found in the clasping Cherubim basis for two of its central doctrines, that union of male and female is the prime state of blessedness and that when man sins he causes a separation in the male and female aspects of deity which in turn leads to transcendental and universal disaster.

> Three times a day a miracle took place with the wings of the Cherubim. When the holiness of the King revealed itself over them, the Cherubim, of themselves, stretched out their wings and covered their bodies with them. . . . A cloud descended and when it settled upon the Lid, the wings of the Cherubim intertwined and they beat them and sang a song . . . and the Priest in the Temple heard their voices as he was putting the incense in its place. . . . The two Cherubim, one male and one female, both sang . . . "And he heard the Voice speaking to him from between the two Cherubim and He spoke to him" (Num. vii 59). Rabbi Yiṣḥaq said: "From this we learn that God is just and right (Deut. xxxii 4) that is male and female, and likewise the Cherubim were male and female" (Zohar iii 59a, after Patai, 134).

This passage from the Zohar reflects Philo's view that the male and female Cherubim represented the male and female elements in God.

Hugo Gressmann (1920, 64–65) suggested that originally there must have been two images in the Ark, one representing Yahweh and the other his wife 'Anatyahu or Astarte. Similarly Julian Morgenstern (1940, 121n98) conjectured that the two sacred stones in the Ark originally "represented Yahweh and, in all likelihood, His female companion." Patai's findings tend to agree with these conjectures. As Patai recapitulated the development (p. 136), the Ark originally contained two images or slabs of stone representing Yahweh and his consort. At a later stage, when it was forbidden to represent God in visual form, his erstwhile female companion was reduced to the position of a female guardian, represented in the two female Cherubim whose wings covered the Ark which also served as the seat of Yahweh. After the destruction of the first Temple, the idea slowly gained ground that the one and only God comprised two aspects, a male and a female one, and that the Cherubim in the Holy of Holies of the second Temple were the symbolic representation of these two divine virtues or powers. In Talmudic times the male Cherub was considered a symbol of God and the female Cherub, held in embrace by Him, represented the personified community of Israel. Finally the Qabbalah developed its mystical theory of the Sephiroth and especially the two major divine entities, the King and the Matronit, and considered the Cherubim as their visual representation.

The Shekinah

The "Shekinah" is a post-biblical term frequently used in rabbinic literature to denote the divine presence on earth. In its fullest development in late midrashic literature, the Shekinah represented an independent entity, God's feminine alter ego, who could, and did, confront her male counterpart and argue with him on behalf of man. She was thus by function and position tantamount to a goddess, as Patai aptly indicated in the title of his study, the fourth chapter of which (pp. 137–156) deals with the origin and development of the concept. The present summary is, perforce, limited to essential points.

The concept of the Shekinah developed as a part of the process of hypostatisation or personification of divine qualities or aspects, a subject which has been treated at length by H. Ringgren (1947).

The hypostatisation of Wisdom appears in Proverbs 8, where Wisdom is presented as a primordial creation; she was from the beginning a playmate of God. Similarly in Job (28:13–28) Wisdom is described as a personage whose dwelling and nature is known to God but not accessible to man. In the Apocrypha the personification of Wisdom is even more explicit. Wisd Sol 8:3 affirms that "she (Wisdom) proclaims her noble birth in that it is given to her to live with God, and the Sovereign Lord of all loved her. . . ." The term used here of God's cohabitation is *symbiosis,* which term is used in the same chapter with reference to marital connubium and thus it is clear that Wisdom is here regarded as God's wife, as observed by G. Scholem (1952, 48–49). Philo also affirmed that God is Wisdom's husband (*On the Cherubim* xiv 49, LCL, II, 39). The elaborate Gnostic myth which developed around Wisdom as a sort of female deity need not detain us here (cf. Patai, 139*f* and 311n18). While Wisdom had all the prerequisites for developing into a female deity, this did not take place within normative Judaism. Rather it was the figure of the Shekinah which developed into the Hebrew Goddess.

The term *šĕḵînāh* first appears in the so-called Targum Onkelos, somewhere between the first and fourth centuries. It serves to put some distance between God and man. Where the Hebrew text speaks of a direct connection or manifestation of God, the Targum Onkelos interposes the Shekinah, as in Exod 25:8 where "Let them make Me a sanctuary that I may dwell among them" becomes "Let them make before Me a sanctuary, that I may let My Shekinah dwell among them." The earlier use of the term was thus in the sense of an abstract hypostasis introduced wherever anthropomorphic and anthropopathic implications were to be avoided.

Since our concern is with the idea of the Shekinah as a divine entity separate and distinct from God, we pass over the complexities of development of the intermediate stages in the process of personification (cf. Patai, pp. 144–147). First, it must be emphasized that the concepts of the Shekinah and the Holy Spirit are virtually synonymous, as has been demonstrated for the Talmudic period by A. Marmorstein (1950, 130*f*). Thus when a Talmudic teacher spoke of the Holy Spirit, he may as well have used the term Shekinah. According to Rabbi Aha,

> The Holy Spirit comes to the defense (of sinful Israel) saying first to Israel: "Do not be a witness against your neighbor without cause," and afterward saying to God: "Do not say, 'I will do to him as he did to me' " (Midrash Leviticus Rabbah 6.1).

Here it is clear that the Holy Spirit and God are treated as two separate and discrete divine entities, since she is alleged to have admonished God to refrain from punitive action against Israel. The function of the Holy Spirit here is clearly related to the Christian concept of the Spirit as Paraclete. The Shekinah is depicted in a similar role in later time in Midrash Mishle:

> When the Sanhedrin wanted to add King Solomon to the three kings (i.e. Jeroboam, Ahab, and Manasseh) and four commoners (Balaam, Doeg, Ahitophel, and Gehazi) who had no share in the World to Come, Shekinah rose up before the Holy One, blessed be He, and said: "Master of the World! seest Thou a man diligent" (Prov. xxii 29). . . . They want to count him among mean men. In that hour, a divine voice was heard saying to them: "Let him stand before Kings; let him not stand before mean men" (Midrash Mishle, ed. Buber, 47, cited after Patai, 149, 313n71).

This is the first and only midrashic reference to a differentiation between God and the Shekinah, according to the expert par excellence in this field, G. Scholem, (1952, 59). Patai, however, averred (p. 313n70) that while Scholem is technically correct on this point, he is in substance wrong because the differentiation between God and the Holy Spirit in the passage cited from Midrash Leviticus Rabbah is essentially identical with the differentiation between God and the Shekinah. Patai cited another eleventh-century passage from Moses of Narbonne who said, in the name of Rabbi Aqiba, that

> when the Holy One, blessed be He, considered the deeds of the generation of Enoch and that they were spoiled and evil, He removed Himself and His Shekinah

from their midst and ascended into the heights with blasts of trumpets . . . (*Bereshit Rabbati,* ed. Albeck, 27, after Patai, 149, 313n72).

It could be argued that this passage does not unequivocally distinguish between God and His Shekinah, since they could be construed as synonymous in this instance. Patai, while admitting that three passages are rather meager evidence, still regarded them as sufficient to establish that the idea of two separate divine entities did exist in Talmudic times and that there were some teachers at least who saw nothing objectionable in this. Others, however, strictly opposed any implication of plurality and by so doing gave indirect testimony to the vitality of the notion combatted.

The female persuasion of the Shekinah, as well as that of the Holy Spirit, is indicated by grammatical gender in Hebrew and Aramaic and thus her sex is suggested by verb, pronoun, or adjective in every statement about her. The Talmudic sages in their midrashic homilies were not averse to comparing God with either or both sexes (cf. Patai, 151*f*). The Shekinah, however, in Talmudic sources comes close to being regarded as the feminine manifestation of deity. The tender and compassionate side of the divine nature, especially the penchant for weeping, was often related to the Shekinah. The love-aspect of God was also related to the Shekinah which filled the Temple like Solomon's palanquin inlaid with love (*Pesiqta di Rab Kahana,* ed. Mandelbaum, 4; cf. Patai, 152 and 313n81). The Shekinah also represented the divine punitive power, as indicated by a Tannaitic passage which mentioned ten occasions on which the Shekinah descended for punitive purposes, and predicted another descent in the future in the days of the battle of Gog and Magog. (*Aboth di Rabbi Nathan,* ed. Schechter, 102. J. Goldin [1955], 140*f*.) The mixture of vengeful and compassionate traits of the Shekinah, Patai (153) discerned in the legends in which she took the souls of six exceptional individuals whom the Angel of Death could not overcome, Abraham, Isaac, Jacob, Moses, Aaron, and Miriam, who died only through a kiss of the Shekinah (TB Baba Bathra 17a; cf. *Midrash Canticles Rabbah* i 2[5]).

Moses, after his death, whether by a kiss of God or a kiss of the Shekinah, was carried on the wings of the Shekinah a distance of four miles to his burial spot (TB Sota 13; Sifre Deut 355). Since in the Zohar Moses is said to have given up carnal contact with his wife in order to be always ready to communicate with the Shekinah (cf. Patai, 153,194), Patai suggested that a notion clearly stated in the Zohar was already present in rudimentary form in Talmudic times, that Moses and the Shekinah were like husband and wife. An interesting parallel was suggested by Patai between the Shekinah carrying her dead husband, Moses, to his burial place, and Anat carrying the body of her brother-consort, Baal, to his burial place on Mount Zaphon (Patai, 153). A possible parallel to this motif may be adduced from another source: An oenochoe (jug) of the Bibliothèque National of Paris shows a winged and armed goddess, no doubt Athena who was identified with Anat, carrying the body of a defunct male over undulations which may be either waves or hills (cf. Denyse Le Lasseur, 1919, fig. 126, p. 336). Although there is nothing in the *Iliad* about such an episode, Le Lasseur opined (p. 337) that there is no ground to reject apriori the hypothesis of Athena carrying the body of one of her favorite warriors. The identification of Athena and Anat suggests that the scene depicts Anat with the corpse of her brother-consort Baal, rather than that of an earthly hero. See Plate XIII.

In the conclusion of his chapter on the Shekinah (pp. 154–156), Patai suggested that the concept seems first to have served merely as a convenient means of solving the problem presented by anthropomorphism. By interpolating the Shekinah, it was no longer God who was said to have acted in a human way, but his "presence." This "presence," Patai supposed, was conceived as something akin to a "presence" at a spiritualists' seance, "a barely visible indication of what is acknowledged to be pure spirit and therefore not apprehensible by the senses." This spiritual "presence," however, began to take on substance and became more closely joined to the fate of Israel, accompanying the people into their exiles and sharing their hopes and despairs. In this capacity, the Shekinah came near to being identified with the personified "Community of Israel," *kĕneseṯ yiśrā'ēl.*

As the distance between God and his Shekinah grew, the latter took on increasingly pronounced physical attributes. "The more impossible it became to think of God himself in anthropomorphic terms, the more the Shekinah became humanized." There was nothing strange or heretical in biblical times about a plural concept of the godhead, according to Patai, who cited the example of Yahweh's appearances to Abraham in the shape of three men (Gen 18:2). Philo's theosophic discernment of the two aspects of deity, as well as the Talmudic postulation of God and the Shekinah as two divine entities, Patai regarded as not too far removed from the biblical indeterminacy as to the number of persons in the godhead. The assignment of masculinity to one and femininity to the other aspect, however, was a step never taken, or at least not clearly formulated or expressed in Talmudic Judaism, until the days of the Qabbalah. The fact that all the names of God (Yahweh, Elohim, the Holy One) were masculine, while the term Shekinah (as well as other manifestations such as the Holy Spirit, the Word, Wisdom) was feminine, pointed inevitably in the direction of the sexual differentiation which developed in the medieval mystical movement of the Qabbalah.

Shekinah-Matronit in Qabbalah

The latency of the feminine element in the Jewish concept of God for a millennium and a half, from ca. 400 B.C. to A.D. 1100, was, in Patai's view, a remarkable psychological phenomenon. In spite of the masculine predominance at the highest level, popular belief was peopled with and haunted by a wide range of feminine numina, from she-demons to exalted hypostases of divinity.

The term Qabbalah, meaning "reception," that is, what has been received, was a great Jewish religious movement which reached its literary peak in the thirteenth century and enjoyed great popularity for a few centuries thereafter. Its roots reach back beyond the Talmud to Philo of Alexandria, and doubtless beyond that to survivals of ancient mythological motifs in folk religion. The foundations of Qabbalism were laid in Babylonia and Byzantium in the seventh and eighth centuries in midrashic works dealing with the mysteries of Creation, the structure of the universe, the seven heavens, and the divine chariot (*merkāḇāh*) on which the throne of God was transported. These cosmological and theosophical works were transmitted to Italy and Germany, and finally to Spain where their ideology developed apace. The chief work of the Qabbalistic movement, appropriately titled the Zohar, i.e. Splendor, was written by Moses de Leon in Castile ca. 1286, but attributed to Simeon ben Yohai, the Palestinian mystic of the second century. Written in the form of a mystical commentary on the Five Books of Moses, in an artificial sort of Aramaic, this opus of nearly a million words is a veritable sea. The expulsion of Jews from Spain in 1492 brought leading Qabbalists to Safed in Galilee which became the great center of Qabbalah in the sixteenth century. From Safed the Qabbalah spread to the major Jewish communities of Asia, Africa, and Europe in a kind of mass movement mixed with an upsurge of Messianic expectations which prepared the way for Sabbatai Zevi in the seventeenth century and for the Hasidic movement in Eastern Europe.

In Qabbalistic doctrine the feminine divine entity, the Shekinah, or the Matronit, "the Matron," played a major role. This development, in spite of the obvious difficulty of reconciling it with normative Jewish emphasis on the absolute unity of God, is an indication of its popular appeal in response to a deep-seated religious need corresponding to Christian devotion to the Virgin Mary tantamount to apotheosis. The issue of polytheism versus monotheism which exercised the intellectuals did not greatly concern the masses to whom the simple idea of a motherly mediator was comprehensible and convenient. Lip service could be paid to the Unity of God with recitation of the Shema, and logicians could explain how the Shekinah was merely a symbol which helped to comprehend the mystery of His nature without compromising His fundamental unity. Cf. Patai, 161*f*.

The godhead in Qabbalistic doctrine was the ideal family composed of Father, Mother, Son, and Daughter. The blessed tetrad was deduced from the Tetragrammaton, the ineffable Name (*šēm hammĕp̄ōrāš*), YHWH, the consonants of which symbolized the four divine elements Wisdom, Understanding, Beauty, and Kingship.

Wisdom spread out and brought forth Understanding, and they were found to be male and female, Wisdom the Father, and Understanding the Mother. . . . Then these two united, and lighted up each other, and the H (i.e. the Mother) conceived and gave birth to a Son. Through the birth of the Son the Father and the Mother found their perfection, and this led to the inclusion of everything: Father, Mother, Son and Daughter (Zohar iii 290a, after Patai, 163).

Patai suspected, with good reason, that the Qabbalistic myths about the tetrad reflect outside, non-Jewish influence, and to substantiate this assumption he assayed a rapid survey of polytheistic tetrad myths. Among ancient triads and tetrads considered were the Egyptian Shu, Tefnut, Geb, and Nut; the Sumerian An, Ninhursag, Enki; the Canaanite El, Asherah, Baal and Anat; the Greek Cronus, Rhea, Zeus and Hera; the Roman Saturn, Ops, Jove and Juno. Juno in her capacity as goddess of marriage was also known as Matrona, whence the Matronit of the Qabbalah. The Iranian triad of Zurvan, Ohrmazd, and Ahriman was also a tetrad in that Zurvan (Time) was hermaphrodite.

The divine triad in Hindu mythology is of particular interest. Shiva, the great lord of procreation, lives in marital bliss with Parvati, the Great Mother, symbolized by the female organ, known by a variety of names, especially as Devi (Goddess), that is, *the* goddess, par excellence. Under the name Kali, the Goddess assumes terrifying forms, wields an array of weapons, engages in horrendous slaughter, demands massive sacrifices, animal and human, to allay her insatiable thirst for blood. She is Shakti, Female Energy, Woman Power and her wan consort is able to function only through her. Shiva, if united with Shakti, is able to exert his powers as lord; without her, he is not able to stir. Whoever grasps the goddess' nature and becomes one with her masters the universe. All love and power reside in her. She creates, nourishes, comforts, disciplines, and destroys. Her worshipers address her as mother and she takes them to herself as children.

Common features distilled by Patai from these various tetrad myths are: the divine tetrad consists of parents and two children, usually a son and a daughter, but sometimes two sons. The four deities stand for, or are in control of, the major components of the world, such as air, moisture, earth, and sky, or they represent a combination of such major components of nature. Another recurrent characteristic is that the daughter in several of the tetrads is a goddess of both love and war (p. 170). This latter feature is particularly significant for the understanding of the martial traits of the Lady of the Canticle derived ultimately from the figure of the great goddess of Love and War.

Qabbalistic literature offers accounts of episodes in the life of the divine family, Father, Mother, Son, and Daughter, which amount to veritable biographies. According to Patai (170*f*)

so many of these episodes are clearly mythological that in the face of their cumulative evidence the contention that all is merely mystical symbolism and speculation about the "aspects," or "emanations," or even "elements" of a one and only God, must appear as a pious fiction. The four entities of the godhead in these passages function as independent persons who address, converse with, act upon and react to, each other, Moreover, the deeds they perform, the experiences they undergo and the feelings they display are well couched in unmistakably mythological terms, strikingly similar to the tetrad myths sketched above.

The sexual symbolism of the Qabbalah is pervasive and the language is fairly explicit. The relation between Father and Mother is a perpetual honeymoon: "Never does the inclination of the Father and the Mother toward each other cease. They always go out together and dwell together. They never separate and never leave each other. They are together in complete union" (Zohar iii 290b, after Patai, 171). Another passage in the Zohar describes the instant and constant readiness of the Female for coition and the perfect coincidence of orgasms in the partners:

> When the seed of the Righteous One (*ṣaddîq*) is about to be ejaculated, he does not have to seek the Female, for she abides with him, never leaves him, and is always in readiness for him. His seed flows not save when the Female is ready, and when they both as one desire each other; and they unite in a single embrace, and never separate. . . . Thus the Righteous is never forsaken (Zohar i 162 a–b; Patai, 172).

Here Ps 37:25, "I have never seen the righteous forsaken," is given a bizarre twist. The marital embrace of the Father and the Mother was so tight and so permanent that the two become one, androgynous. The pair were termed "companions" (*rē'îm*), and the Mother was called *ra'ăyāh,* "Female Companion," the term applied to the Lady of the Canticle in 1:9,15, 2:2,10,13, 4:1,7, 5:2, 6:4.

> The Female (component of the godhead) spread out from her place and adhered to the Male side, until he moved away from his side, and she came to unite with him face to face. And when they united, they appeared as veritably one body. From this we learn that the male alone appears as half a body . . . and the female likewise, but when they join in union they seem as veritably one body . . . (On the Sabbath) all is found in one body, complete, for the Matronit clings to the King and they become one body, and this is why blessings are found on that day (Zohar iii 296a; Patai, 173).

The details of the Qabbalistic theogonies and cosmogonies need not detain us here, since the present interest is only in features possibly relevant to the interpretation of the Song of Songs. The divine family was not without its tensions. The parents loved the children, but the father's inordinate attachment to the daughter and the mother's affection for the son bordered on incest. The Midrash Rabbah on the Song of Songs 3:11 served as the basis for the development of this motif in the Zohar. The meaning of "the crown with which his mother crowned him" was explained by Rabbi Yoḥanan with a parable about a king who had an only daughter of whom he was exceedingly fond. At first he called her "daughter," till not satisfied with that he called her "sister," and still not satisfied with that he called her "mother." Thus the Holy One loved Israel. The passages cited as proof were Ps 45:11, Song of

Songs 5:2, and Isa 51:4, the latter derived by reading *ūl'ūmî,* "and my people," as *ūl'immî,* "and to my mother." This parable so pleased Simeon ben Yoḥai that he up and kissed Yoḥanan on the mouth (Midrash Rabba Song of Songs iii 11 2). Moses de Leon (Zohar i 156b) added to this Midrash the natural jealousy of the Mother who reproached the Daughter and demanded that she cease beguiling her husband. The Mother reacted with excessive attachment to the Son and continued to hold him on her lap, press him to her breast, and to suckle him even after he was grown (Zohar iii 17a, 88b; cf. Patai, 176). The motifs of incest and jealousy are mythologems which occur frequently in accounts of divine tetrads (cf. Patai, 176 and 315nn40a,41).

In many mythologies the older couple of the divine tetrad withdraws into virtual retirement, so in the Qabbalistic tetrad the action centers on the younger pair. Patai (177) overlooked the parallel presented by the Ugaritic myths in which the younger brother and sister consorts, Mighty Baal and Virgin Anat, dominate the scene while the father and mother, El and Asherah, recede into the background. In the Qabbalistic tetrad it is the tempestuous love affair between the Son and the Daughter which is the major subject of the narration, especially the tragic separation occasioned by the destruction of the Jerusalem Temple and the exile of Israel. The marriage of the Son and Daughter, or the King and the Matronit, was apparently consummated with Solomon's building of the Temple which served as their wedding chamber and bedroom.

The question of incest did not bother the Qabbalists any more than it vexed the ancient mythographers, since among the gods there were no impediments to any kind of liaison. Jesus' assertion (Matt 22:30) that after the resurrection there is no marrying, but rather they (the risen ones) "are like the angels of God" appreciates in interest when set between pagan accounts of free love among the gods and the Qabbalistic doctrine that "Above on high there is neither incest, nor cutting off, nor separation, nor keeping apart; therefore, above on high there is union between brother and sister, and son and daughter" (*Tiqqune Hazohar* 34, p. 77, cited by Patai, 178, after J. Tishby [1961, II, 623]; cf. Patai, 316n46). The troubles which beset the union of the King and the Matronit were the result of the virtual identification of the latter with the "community of Israel." When Israel as the bride of God, the King, sinned, as she was inclined to do, the result was alienation and separation. In Qabbalistic theosophy, as in the Indian myth of Shiva and Shakti, the god has power only when united with the goddess, and thus the King separated from the Matronit was no king (Zohar iii 5a, 69a). Human marriages were intended to be like the divine ideal and failure to imitate the divine example diminished the image of God. "When is a man called complete in his resemblance to the Supernal?" the Zohar asked and gave answer:

When he couples with his spouse in oneness, joy and pleasure, and a son and daughter issue from him and his female. This is the complete man resembling the Above: he is complete below after the pattern of the Supernal Holy Name, and the Supernal Holy Name is applied to him. . . . A man who does not want to complete the Holy Name below in this manner, it were better for him that he were not created, because he has no part at all in the Holy Name. And when he dies and his soul leaves him, it does not unite at all with him because he diminished the image of his Master (Zohar iii 7a, after Patai, 179*ff*).

Adultery similarly was damaging to the divine union as well as to the wronged husband, and to social order:

The groom and the bride, as soon as they receive the seven blessings under the wedding canopy, become united following the Supernal example. And therefore, he who commits adultery with another man's wife damages the union, and, as it were, causes a separation on high into two authorities. Because the union of the Community of Israel (i.e. the Matronit) is only with the Holy One, blessed be He (i.e. the King), such an adulterer "Robs his father and his mother" (Prov. xxviii 24)—"his father," this is the Holy One, blessed be He; "his mother," this is the Community of Israel (Zohar iii 44b, after Patai, 179).

Patai explained the development of the Zoharic doctrine thus:

Man everywhere fashions his gods in his own image, and familism was, and has remained until quite recently, a most important factor, if not the central one, in the socio-psychological image of the Jew. The Jew could not imagine a Jewish life without the family, nor one not centered around the family. The lone, aloof God, adored by the Jews up to the time of the Kabbalistic upsurge, could not satisfy the emotional craving which sought a reflection of earthly life in the heavenly realm. The lone, aloof God, even if cast in the image of the father, even if surrounded by all his heavenly hosts, the angels and archangels, functioning as the heavenly patrons of the elements of which nature and mankind were composed, could not be recognized as a reflection in God of the human condition. And vice versa, human existence, always appearing to Jewish consciousness in multiple form of man, wife and children, could not be recognized as the true reflection of God, in whose image man was said to have been created, as long as that God was alone.

"The removal of this barrier of non-correspondence was a stroke of genius of Jewish mysticism," according to Patai. The similarity of God and man was thus established down to small details.

By uniting with his wife, begetting children, and maintaining his family, the Jew acted—now he knew—exactly as God did, because He too lived on high in a family circle of His own, with His Wife, His Son and His Daughter. And more than that: by marrying and begetting children, man directly contributed to the well-being of the Divine Family, promoted the happiness and the completeness of the Supernal Couple and their Children. The emotional satisfaction derived by the mystic from this belief, however much or little of it was allowed to rise over the threshold of conscious knowledge, contributed in no small measure to the popular appeal of the Zoharic doctrine (Patai, 181*f*).

The usual assumption that Qabbalistic theosophy was simply the result of mystical speculation was questioned by Patai, although he had just characterized it as "a stroke of genius of Jewish mysticism." The Spanish Qabbalists must have been familiar with non-Jewish religious systems beyond those that flourished around the Mediterranean basin. The foremost authority on Jewish mysticism has affirmed that the teachings of Abraham Abulafia, a contemporary of Moses de Leon, "represent but a Judaized version of that ancient spiritual technique which has found its classical expression in the practices of the Indian mystics who follow the system known as *Yoga*" (G. Scholem, 1961, 139). If Yoga could influence Abulafia, one may assume, Patai suggested, that Indian mythology may also have been known to Moses de Leon and reflected in his thinking. Knowledge of Indian theosophy could have reached Spain through the intermediacy of the Arabs. The Zohar's tetrad, according to Patai (p. 183), shows greater similarity to the Indian than to any other. Most striking is the idea that the God is powerless if not united with the goddess, found in both the Zohar and in Indian mythology. To these considerations suggested by Patai, we would add the similarities noted between the Tantric hymns to the black and beautiful goddess and certain passages of the Song of Songs, especially 1:5. In addition to the possibility of mediation of Indian theosophy to Spain by means of the Arabs, there is also likelihood that such ideology may have developed earlier from the welter of fertility cults of Syria-Palestine, Anatolia, Egypt, and the Hellenistic-Roman world and that they continued to evolve, spread, and interact in all directions.

Our primary interest is in the fourth person of the Qabbalistic tetrad, the Daughter, who in addition to the old Talmudic term Shekinah and a profusion of other epithets, is most frequently designated "the Matronit."

> Of the four persons of the Kabbalistic tetrad it is she who plays the greatest role as the central figure in both divine happenings and relationships, and the occurrences through which human fate, and in particular the fate of Israel, is propelled forward. She is the central link between the Above and the Below. She is the person through whom man can most easily grasp the ineffable mystery of deity, and who most fully identifies herself with the interests, the joys and woes, of Israel. She is unquestionably the most poignant, and at the same time the most Jewish, expression of the idea of a goddess (Patai, 186).

The detailed similarity between the life history, character, deeds, and feelings attributed to the Matronit by Jewish mysticism and ancient Near Eastern goddesses who occupied central positions in their respective pantheons was aptly characterized by Patai (186) as "perhaps the most fascinating facet of the history of religious and mythical ideas." We pass over Patai's brief sketch of some of the major goddesses of love and war, Inanna in Sumer, Ishtar in Akkad, Anat in Canaan, Anahita in Persia. All of these goddesses exhibit the same traits of chastity and promiscuity, motherliness and bloodthirstiness which characterize the Matronit, the daughter-goddess of Qabbalistic literature.

Although the Matronit in Qabbalistic theory was the lowest of the ten Sephirot (aspects or emanations of the godhead, corresponding roughly to

Gnostic *aeons*), she was built up in Qabbalistic literature "into a palpable individuum whose acts, words and feelings only make sense if she is considered a true mythological deity" (p. 191). The *popular-mythical* view of the Matronit, in contrast with the *scholarly-mystical* view, had, according to Patai,

a marked resemblance to the popular Mariolatry of the Latin countries, where the Virgin is not the Jewish woman whose womb God chose to reincarnate Himself in human form—as the official Catholic doctrine has it—but as Mother of God, herself a goddess, who through the ages never ceased to perform miracles and to whom, therefore, direct and personal adoration is due. . . . She thus supplied the psychologically so important female divine figure in Judaism, a religion in which the element had been submerged for many centuries prior to the emergence of Kabbalism (p. 191).

The relatively late reappearance of the goddess Patai regarded as a remarkable feat of religious resurgence. "Reappearance" Patai stressed because goddesses did figure prominently in popular Hebrew religion in biblical times, as shown in the first two chapters of his book. In Patai's view,

Even more remarkable, however, is the reappearance in the figure of the Matronit of the four basic traits of chastity, promiscuity, motherliness and bloodthirstiness, which place her right alongside the great ancient Near Eastern love-goddesses (p. 192).

The example of the Virgin Mary was adduced by Patai to facilitate the understanding of the paradoxical virginity of the Matronit.

Mary bore Jesus to God, and several other sons and daughters to her earthly husband Joseph, yet she nevertheless remained *The* Virgin and is adored as such to this day. Similarly with the Matronit, who paradoxically retained her virginity while being the lover of gods and men. Her virginity is spoken of in the Zohar in both figurative expressions and direct statements.

The "red heifer, perfect, with no blemish in her, and on which yoke never came" (Num 19:2) was applied to the Matronit whom "neither Satan, nor the Destroyer, nor the Angel of Death" could overcome (Zohar iii 180b; Patai, 193). A striking parallel to the paradoxical virginity of Mary and the Matronit is found in the Virgin Anat of the Ugaritic myths who is still called "Virgin Anat" in the midst of a text (11[132]) which though fragmentary, relates her thousandfold copulation with Mighty Baal, her pregnancy and parturition.

The Matronit, like other love-goddesses, did not limit her choice of partners to her peers, but also had liaisons with mortals. Her Mesopotamian prototype, Ishtar, in addition to human paramours, included a stallion among her lovers. The Ugaritic goddess Anat offered her love to the young hero Aqhat, as did Ishtar to Gilgamesh, only to be spurned. The Matronit, for her part, first attached herself to the patriarch Jacob, but, because of his relations with his two wives and two concubines, their union was not consummated till after Jacob's death (Zohar i 21b–22a). Her second husband was none other than Moses who separated from his earthly wife, Zipporah, and copulated with the Matronit while still in the flesh (Zohar i 21b–22a).

When Solomon built the Temple, the Matronit entered into marriage with her Twin, the King. Patai presents a detailed account of the wedding, and variant versions of their sexual routine, nightly, weekly, and yearly. The weekly union was consummated on Friday nights, the divine coition serving as the mythical validation of the traditional weekly union of devout husbands and wives on the night of the Sabbath (Zohar iii 296a). The act was performed as a pious duty in emulation of the union of the Supernal Couple. If conception occurred, it was assured that the child thus conceived would receive a pure soul procreated in the divine copulation of the King and the Matronit (Zohar ii 89a–b). When the devout earthly couple thus copulated, they stimulated by example the cosmic generative forces. The human sexual act stimulated the King, who ejaculated his seminal fluid and fertilized the Matronit who gave birth to human souls and to angels (Zohar i 12b; cf. Patai, 196 on the bizarre terminology for the divine phallus, semen, and other sexual symbolism).

With the destruction of the Temple, the bedchamber of the King and the Matronit was destroyed and their cohabitation disrupted. Since blessings are found only where male and female are united, the King was thus deprived of his potency. The Matronit, banished from her place and driven into exile, was forced into liaisons with other gods and suckled their children, the Gentiles (Zohar i 84b). The King, deprived of his true queen, took to himself the demoness Lilith who thus assumed rule over the Holy Land (Zohar iii 69a).

Even in exile the Matronit continued to be drawn to the pious men of Israel, particularly when they engaged in the study of the Law and the performance of good works. The pious mystics thus made it a rule to copulate with their wives only on Friday night, spending the other six days in celibate devotion to study and holy deeds. The objection that the scholars thus risked misfortune, since "blessings are found only where male and female are together," was countered with the assurance that when they were away from their wives, the Shekinah coupled with them. Similarly when sages were separated from their wives during menstrual periods, or while on a journey, the Shekinah joined them and thus they were never bereft of the blessed state of bisexual togetherness (Zohar i 49b–50a; Moses Cordovero, *Pardes Rimmonim,* Gate 16, § 6; cf. Patai, 198 and 317n30). Consolation of the neglected housewife was not provided for in this scheme.

The maternal instincts of the Shekinah-Matronit, like her insatiable sexual appetites, were strong. As the spiritual mother of Israel, she suckled her children. True to her maternal nature, she was not able to reject the bastards fathered on her by the heathen gods during her exile from Jerusalem, but nourished them as she had suckled Israel (Zohar i 84b, iii 17a–b, 186b).

The violent side of the divine Virgin-Mother, so vividly portrayed in the

Ugaritic myths, is seen also in the Shekinah-Matronit of the Zohar. The King entrusted to her the ministry of war and placed under her control all forces and weapons, myriads of supernatural soldiers and all kinds of weapons, with which she wrought vengeance on sinners (Zohar ii 29a) such as the Egyptians at the Sea (Zohar ii 50b) and the Canaanites under Sisera (Zohar ii 51a–b). Even in the long exile the Shekinah was always ready to defend Israel against her enemies, but again Israel's sins hampered her. When Israel sinned, the Shekinah's hands were weakened, but when they repented she regained her strength and shattered Israel's foes (Zohar iii 75a–b).

The monstrous, horrendous character of the Shekinah-Matronit as destroyer rivaled that of her prototypes, Inanna, Ishtar, Anat, and Atargatis, and her contemporary Kali-Durga in India. The Shekinah-Matronit surpassed the monster bull Behemoth who devoured the grass of a thousand mountains each day and gulped all the waters of the Jordan in a single draught. The Shekinah-Matronit swallowed in one bite as much as Behemoth could eat in a day and gulped a thousand rivers at a time. Her arms stretched out in twenty-four thousand directions, her claws ready to rip and kill. Her hair was more terrible than that of Medusa, spangled with thousands of shields, streaming with hosts of fearsome warriors arranged in groups under such names as "lords of severity," "lords of insolence," from whom escape was impossible. Between her legs issued her terrifying son Metatron who reached from one end of the world to the other, and two daughters, Lilith and Naamah, infamous queens of she-demons (cf. Patai, 201,317n40).

The martial aspect of the Matronit has a parallel in a function of the Virgin Mary which is not well known. Cyril of Alexandria at the opening of the Council of Ephesus in 431 delivered a sermon in which he praised Mary as the mother and virgin "through whom the Trinity is glorified and worshiped, the cross of the Savior exalted and honored, through whom heaven triumphs, the angels are made glad, devils driven forth, the tempter overcome, and the fallen creature raised up even to heaven" (cf. *Encyclopaedia Britannica,* 11th ed., s.v. "Mary"). A portrait of the Virgin attributed to St. Luke accompanied the Byzantine emperors in battle until the fall of Constantinople (cf. Hastings *Dictionary of the Bible,* s.v. "Mary"). The Emperor Justinian's general Narses looked to Mary for direction on the field of battle and expected her to reveal the time for the attack (cf. Evagrius [d. 600] *Ecclesiastical History* iv). The Emperor Heraclius bore the image of the Virgin on his banner (*Encyclopaedia Britannica,* 11th ed., s.v. "Mary"). The German Knights (*Deutscher Ritterorden*) chose the Virgin as their patroness (cf. *Realenzyklopädie für protestantische Theologie und Kirche,* XII, s.v. "Marie").

The Virgin Mary as war goddess and the use of her representation as a palladium and battle standard developed early from the identification with the goddess Athena-Victoria. The Emperor Constantine worshiped Athena and Apollo who appeared to him at Autun before the Battle of Milvian Bridge. Constantine's *labarum,* under which sign Christianity became a religion of conquest, had as its base the saltire or cross chest bands of the soldier and the war goddess which continue to this day as the symbol of the Queen of Battles on flags and military uniforms (cf. M. H. Pope, 1970, 192*ff*).

Only a few points may be noted here from Patai's chapter on Lilith (pp. 207–245). The crucial consideration is that Lilith, despite all the representations of her as a separate entity, is merely a hypostasis of the evil side of the great goddess. A passage of Zoharic literature quoted by Patai makes this quite clear: "Come and see: The Shekhina is at times called the Mother, at times the Slave-Woman (i.e. Lilith), and at times the King's Daughter" (*Zohar Hadash* Tiqqunim, Warsaw: Levin-Epstein, n.d., 117a top; cited after Patai, 239 and 322n96). The Zohar explained that Lilith is the "nakedness" of the Shekinah, the evil aspect of the goddess which predominated in the period of the exile: "When Israel was exiled, the Shekhina too went into exile, and this is the nakedness of the Shekhina. And this nakedness is Lilith, the mother of a mixed multitude" (Zohar i 27b; cited after Patai, 239).

The contrasting characterizations of Lilith and the Matronit mask opposite aspects of the same thing. As Patai put it: "behind the evil mask of Lilith and the good one of the Matronit, the numen, embodying man's fears and desires is disconcertingly, yet reassuringly, the same" (p. 243). The identity of opposites in Lilith and the Matronit was explained by Patai in terms of the ambivalence of the (male) religio-sexual experience.

The final stage in the development of goddess-figures in Judaism was the personification and deification of the Sabbath as the Bride of God and the devotion of the Sabbath night to sexual intercourse in her honor. The effort to prohibit sexual intercourse on the Sabbath, along with nearly every other type of activity, is reflected in Jub 50:8 which banned the act on the Sabbath under pain of death. The Samaritans, Qaraites, and Falashas prohibited sexual intercourse on the Sabbath, but in normative rabbinic Judaism it became a sacred duty (*miṣwāh*) to engage in marital intercourse on Friday night (TB Ketubot 62b; Baba Qamma 88a). Garlic was eaten on the Sabbath eve for its supposed euphoric and aphrodisiac effects. Even the study of sacred texts was no excuse for neglect of the marital obligation. Rabbi Yehudah ben Hiyya used to spend all his time in study, returning home only on the Sabbath eve to do his duty. When he went home on Fridays a pillar of fire preceded him. One Friday he forgot the time and continued engrossed in study. His father-in-law, Rabbi Yannai, said: "Turn over his bed, for Yehudah must be dead. Were he alive, he would never have neglected his marital duty." The words were self-fulfilling and Yehudah died at that moment (TB Ketubot 62b).

The personification and deification of the Sabbath and the devotion of Friday night to sacral sexual intercourse has connections with the great virgin goddess. Philo of Alexandria in his allegorical explanation of the sanctity of the Sabbath related it to virgin goddess Athena by way of Pythagorean numerology, the number seven being the only one in the first decade (digits 1–10) which is not a product of any other two numbers in the decade and which does not itself produce a number in the decade when multiplied by another number in the decade. The Pythagoreans, according to Philo, "liken seven to the motherless and ever-virgin Maiden (i.e. Athena), because neither was she born of the womb nor shall she ever bear" (cf. Patai, 248 and 323n8). Again Philo explained that since

> it is in the nature of seven alone . . . neither to beget nor to be begotten . . . other philosophers liken this number to the motherless virgin Nike, who is said to have appeared out of the head of Zeus, while the Pythagoreans liken it to the Sovereign of the Universe: for that which neither begets nor is begotten remains motionless . . . (and) there is only one thing that neither causes motion nor experiences it, the original Ruler and Sovereign. Of Him seven may be fitly said to be a symbol . . . (cf. Patai, 248*f* and 323n9).

The fullest exposition of the nature of the Sabbath, as sprung from the Father like Athena from the head of Zeus or immaculately conceived like Mary, was presented by Philo as an insight of Moses:

> The prophet (Moses) magnified the holy seventh day, seeing with his keener vision its marvelous beauty stamped upon heaven and the whole world, and enshrined in nature itself. For he found that she (the Sabbath) was in the first place motherless, exempt from female parentage, begotten by the Father (God) alone, without begetting, brought to birth, yet not carried in the womb. Secondly, he (Moses) saw not only these, that she was all lovely and motherless, but that she was also ever virgin, neither born of a mother nor a mother herself, neither bred from corruption nor doomed to suffer corruption. Thirdly, as he scanned her, he recognized in her the birthday of the world, a feast celebrated by heaven, celebrated by earth and things on earth as they rejoice and exult in the full harmony of the sacred number (Philo *Vita Mosis* ii 210, LCL, VI, 553).

The festive character of the Sabbath is emphasized in the Talmud: "He who celebrates the Sabbath with enjoyments will be given an inheritance without bound. . . . The Sabbath is like the spice which endows the Sabbath-meals with a delicious scent." Rabbi Yose ben Yehudah mentioned the meal and the ready bed as the things that make the Sabbath night good:

> Two ministering angels accompany a man on Sabbath eve from the synagogue to his house. One is the good angel, the other an evil one. As the man arrives in his house, if he finds the candle burning, the table set and his bed made, the good angel says: Be it the will (of God) that it be like this on the next Sabbath!

A single passage mentions the reception of the Sabbath as Queen and Bride:

> Rabbi Hanina used to wrap himself (in festive clothes) towards evening on Friday and say: "Come, let us go to receive Sabbath the Queen." Rabbi Yannai used to put on (festive) clothes on the eve of the Sabbath and say: "Come, O bride, come, O bride!" (The passages above occur in TB Shabbat 119a.)

A midrashic passage presents the Sabbath as personified and complaining to God about her lack of a mate:

> Rabbi Simeon ben Yohai said: "The Sabbath said before God, 'Master of the Worlds! Each day has its mate, but I have none! Why?' The Holy One, blessed be He, answered her: 'The community of Israel is your mate.' And when Israel stood before Mount Sinai, the Holy One, blessed be He, said to them: 'Remember what I told the Sabbath: "The community of Israel is your mate." Therefore, remember the Sabbath day to keep it holy' " (Genesis Rabbah 11:8).

The Sabbath here as number seven is odd one out after three pairs. It is of interest that here the community of Israel figures as the male partner in mating with the female Sabbath, whereas in the allegorical interpretation of the Song of Songs Israel is the bride.

The personification and deification of the Sabbath was fully developed by the Falashas, the black Jews of Ethiopia. This community, attested since the twelfth century, was cut off from the mainstream of Rabbinic Judaism and had no knowledge of the Mishnah and Talmud. The Falasha book *Teezaza Sanbat,* or commandments of the Sabbath, written in Geez (classical Ethiopic) dates from the fourteenth century but contains much older materials. The book deals with the story of Creation and the prime role of the Sabbath as daughter of God, pre-existent with Him before Creation, like Wisdom in Proverbs 8. It is of particular interest that the Sabbath begins with dawn of Friday, Venus' Day:

> The Sabbath will rise from her seat on Friday at dawn. . . . The Sabbath will look upon the souls of the just in the garden, and they will rejoice on Friday. . . . When the Sabbath rises from the right hand of God, Friday at dawn, the angels rise immediately with the Sabbath and crown her. . . . When the Sabbath rose from her seat on Friday morning, 640,000 angels followed her, and she worshiped the Creator.

The deification of the Sabbath is explicit in the *Teezaza Sanbat:* "Sabbath means: I am God. It is not the day but I (who say it), says God . . ." (cf. W. Leslau, 1951, 3,9,10,16,17,21,23–24,36,37–38 and other citations by Patai, 253–258). Another Falasha document, the *Abba Elijah,* explains that the name Sabbath itself means "I am God alone" (Leslau, 42,45; cf. Patai, 323n30 on the expression "God's Sabbath").

The Ethiopian Christians regard Mary in much the same way as the Falashas view the Sabbath. A Falasha is cited as explaining (Leslau, 147n95): "The mediatrix of the Christians is Mary; ours is the Sabbath."

The personification and adoration of the Sabbath which reached its peak in the sixteenth century among the Qabbalists of Safed was evidenced earlier by the great luminary of learning Abraham Ibn Ezra who lived and traveled in Spain, Italy, and France. On the night of the 14th of Tebeth, 4919 (7 December 1158), while sojourning in England, Ibn Ezra dreamed that a man handed him a letter scented with myrrh and said, "Take this letter which the

Sabbath sent you." Opening the letter, he found in it a poem in which the Sabbath sang her own praises as "the crown of the religion of the precious ones," and extolled her merits in lines like these:

> I am the delight of males and females. In me rejoice the old and the young.
> (Cf. I. L. Baruch, 1936, 333–335. Cited after Patai, 258 and 324n33)

A poem composed by one Menahem ben Jacob in the thirteenth century, and printed in prayer books of the nineteenth century, addressed the Sabbath as Queen and Bride:

> How sweet is your rest, O you Queen Sabbath,
> Let us hasten toward you, O anointed bride.
> (Cf. Patai, 258 and 324n34)

These lines are strikingly similar to the opening refrain of the famous sixteenth-century Sabbath song, "Come, my love" (*leḵāh dôḏi*) which eclipsed all other hymns to the Sabbath!

The reception of the Sabbath as queen and bride was designed to induce her to come in her beneficent form as the Matronit to the exclusion of her evil alter ego Lilith. The Zohar prescribed the preparation thus:

> One must prepare a comfortable seat with several cushions and embroidered covers, from all that is found in the house, like one prepares a *ḥuppa* (canopy) for a bride. For the Sabbath is a queen and a bride. This is why the masters of the Mishna used to go out on the eve of the Sabbath to receive her on the road, and used to say: "Come, O bride, come, O bride!" And one must sing and rejoice at the table in her honor. And more than this; there is yet another mystery. One must receive the Lady (i.e. the Sabbath) with many lighted candles, many enjoyments, beautiful clothes, and a house embellished with many fine appointments, for through this rejoicing and these arrangements one causes the Evil Handmaid (i.e. Lilith) to remain in the dark, hungry, crying and wailing, wrapped in mourning clothes like a widow. For when one is fulfilled, the other is destroyed. The Good Inclination is the Holy Matronit, the Holy Kingdom which descends on the Sabbath . . . and the King proceeds to receive her with many hosts. And the Evil Inclination, the Evil Handmaid, remains in the darkness like a widow without her husband, without a chariot. Those about whom it is said that they offered sacrifices and burnt incense to the Queen of Heaven and the stars, which I (God) have not commanded them to do, they worshipped the Evil Maid who rules on the eve of Sabbaths and Wednesdays. What did they do? They took dark clothes, and darkened the lights and made a mourning on the Sabbath eves . . . (Zohar iii 272b).

Patai (260) commented on the above passage from the Zohar:

> It is a peculiar, yet again almost inevitable, coincidence that the same night on which the pious prepare to receive Queen Sabbath, and on which God Himself proceeds to unite with her, should also be the time when Lilith roams and seduces man. It is up to man, the passage above seems to say, to make his choice between the holy bride, the Sabbath, and the unholy one, Lilith.

The passage, however, by implication, says even more than this. Patai in his chapter on Lilith makes it clear that she is none other than the evil aspect of the same Goddess whose good side is the Matronit. The mention of the worship of the Queen of Heaven, with allusion to Jer 7:18, 44:17–19, makes it clear that the reference is to the persistence of the old-time religion, the cult of the great Goddess, older by millennia than the revelation of the name of the God of Israel. The issue here is whether one performed similar rites in the name of the Queen of Heaven, Inanna-Ishtar, Anat, Atargatis, Venus, or in the name of Yahweh and his Sabbath Bride.

The Qabbalists of Safed, according to Patai (261), "developed the custom of leaving the town on Friday toward dusk, and proceeding to the adjacent hills and fields in order to receive the Sabbath in the open." It seems more likely that they followed, rather than developed, an ancient custom of devoting the evening of Friday (Frī[g]day, Frīg being the old Teutonic love-goddess corresponding to Venus) to venereal activity. "The festive procession going to receive the Sabbath outside the town resembled in both form and spirit the processional fetching of the bride by the entourage dispatched in traditional Middle Eastern Jewish weddings by the bridegroom's family to escort her to the wedding canopy" (Patai, 263). The emphasis on the open country and the fields outside of town suggests alfresco amour under the benign glow of the Venus star (which helps one to understand the French expression for "out-of-doors," à la belle étoile, the beautiful star being Venus). The Bride and Queen greeted at dusk in the open country around Safed, we may plausibly surmise, was the epiphany of the Evening Star, Ishtar-Venus, Queen of Heaven. The question of the Canticle (8:5a): "Who is this ascending from the steppe?" is thus answered. The vesper sortie into the field recalls the invitation of the Canticle (7:12–13) "Come, my love, let us hie to the field . . . there will I give you my love." The euphoria of the procession as they marched to the field singing the hymn composed by Solomon Alqabeṣ "Come my love to meet the Bride / The presence (face) of Sabbath let us receive," could lead to "lightheaded" activities if both sexes were present.

Just what was done by the devout mystics after they got to the field, is not entirely clear, but one may imagine that in the popular observances there were those who tarried to indulge in the kind of celebration congenial to the Love Queen. According to Patai (p. 263),

> The fields in which all this took place were, through the arrival of the Sabbath-Shekhina, turned into the "sacred apple orchard," which in itself is a mystical manifestation or aspect of the Shekhina, a sacred grove sanctified by the union of God with His bride and producing the souls of the just.

The concept of the Shekinah as the Sacred Apple Orchard, based on a Talmudic passage (TB Ta'anit 29b), Patai noted (p. 324n47),

> is closely paralleled by the Catholic view of Mary as the Olive Tree, expressed, e.g. by St. Alfonso di Liguori (1696–1787) as follows: ". . . Mary was called the

olive tree, like a fair olive in the plains (Sir 24:19), for as the olive tree produces nothing but oil, the symbol of mercy, thus from the hands of Mary nothing but graces and mercies proceed." See *The Way of St. Alphonsus Liguori,* ed. Barry Ulanov, 1960, 87.

A closer parallel, however, would seem to be presented by the apple tree of Canticles 8:5c as the scene of the arousal of the Lady's lover and the place where his mother also had conceived him. From of old the sacred grove had been the scene of the worship of Asherah, mother of the gods, and reformers in Israel had repeatedly to chop and burn arbor shrines; cf. Exod 34:13; Deut 7:5; Judg 6:25–30; Isa 17:8, 27:9; Jer 17:2.

Whatever the nature of the alfresco greetings of Queen Sabbath, the pious Jew returned from the synagogue on Sabbath eve to be received by his wife who became the earthly representative of the Sabbath Queen, the Shekinah-Matronit, with whom he would perform the sacred rite of copulation in mystical and sympathetic imitation of the Supernal union of the divine King and Queen, God and His spouse, the Sabbath. At the Sabbath meal the husband circumambulated the table with two bunches of myrtle (the tree sacred to Ishtar and symbolic of wedding rites) and sang the welcome song to the messengers of peace who accompanied him from the synagogue. Prov 31:10–31, in praise of woman-power, was chanted in honor both of the earthly wife and the divine Sabbath-Shekinah-Matronit, the Bride of God, whose image now mystically merged with that of the man's wife. Both God and His Bride were invited to join in the sacred meal, as the husband chanted an Aramaic poem composed by Isaac Luria describing the sexual union of God and His Bride. Patai rendered the first six stanzas thus:

Let me sing the praises of Him who enters the gates
Of the orchard of apple trees, holy are they.

Let us invite her now, with a freshly set table,
With a goodly lamp which sheds light on the heads.

Right and left, and the bride in between
Comes forth in her jewels and sumptuous raiments.

Her husband embraces her, and with her *Yesod,*
Which gives her pleasure, he presses her mightily.

Cries and sighs have stopped and ceased,
New faces come, spirits and souls.

He brings her great joy, in a double measure,
Light pours upon her, and blessings on end.

The *Yesod,* or "Foundation," one of the ten Sephirot of the divine physique, corresponds to the penis. It is "hers" because with it God unites with his Bride. The verb (*ktš*) rendered by Patai "presses" has also the sense "penetrate" and "deflower" (cf. Patai, 325n52). Following the singing of the hymn, the Hasidic Jew pronounced a prayer in Aramaic:

Be it the will before the Ancient One, the Most Holy One, and the Most Hidden of All, that the Supernal Dew be drawn from Him to fill the head of the Small Face and to fall upon the Orchard of Holy Apples, in radiance of face, in pleasure and in joy for all. (Cf. Patai, 265 and 325n53.)

The festal meal, with wine, song, and words of Torah, lasted till near midnight, because the proper time for the mystical marital intercourse was just after midnight. The Mishna (Ketubot 5:6) gives the approved schedules for sexual intercourse for people of various occupations designed to meet the biblical injunction (Exod 21:10) that a man may not diminish a wife's food, clothing, or conjugal rights. The frequency varied from daily intercourse for men of leisure to six-month intervals for sailors. For scholars the proper time was Friday just after midnight. The Shulhan 'Aruk, the codification of religious law by Joseph Caro, a leader among the Qabbalists of Safed, prescribes (No. 240; cf. Patai, 325n56) that the act should be performed "neither in the beginning of the night nor towards its end, lest the husband hear the voices of people and be brought to thinking of another woman, but in the middle of the night." The deeper reason for the choice of the time was that this was precisely when the King and the Matronit were believed to engage in the act and it was of great importance for the earthly pair to join them in mystical union. The Zohar explained this with reference to Isa 56:4–5, "the eunuchs who keep My sabbaths, and choose what pleases Me, and hold fast to My covenant" were the scholars who study the Law all week long and

castrate themselves for the duration of the six days of the week, tiring themselves out with the study of the Law, and on Friday night they spur themselves to copulation because they know the supernal mystery of the hour in which the Matronit couples with the King. . . . Happy is the lot of him who sanctifies himself in this holiness and knows this mystery (Zohar ii 89a, cited after Patai, 266*f* and 325n59).

The explication of the precise timing of the sacral sexual intercourse was given by Isaac Luria, "the Holy Lion." The Matronit, it seems, has two aspects, a lower one called Leah, and a higher one called Rachel. The King, who is called "the Small Face" in this connection copulates all day and up till midnight with the inferior Leah who reaches only to His chest. During the day and the night up to midnight the Small Face engages in copulation with Leah, which is, mystically speaking, of a low degree. After midnight on weekdays, and up to midnight on Fridays, a higher type of copulation takes place with Leah. But on Friday after midnight the highest and best copulation is carried on with Rachel in a face-to-face position. This is the time of grace in which the scholar should unite with his wife, after pronouncing the proper formula: "I fulfil the commandment of copulation for the unification of the Holy One, blessed be He, and the Shekhina" (cf. Patai, 267 and 325n60). Thus, as Patai put it (p. 268):

When midnight came, and the fulfilment of the commandment to rejoice on the Sabbath found its most intense expression in the consummation of the marital act, this was done with the full awareness, not only of obeying a divine injunction, but also of aiding thereby the divinity himself in achieving a state of male and female togetherness which God is just as much in need of as man.

One may agree with Patai (268*f*) that

It is certainly a very far cry from the ancient Canaanite orgiastic mass festivals performed in honor of Astarte, the goddess of sexual love and fertility, to the mystically oriented and privately observed celebration of marital sex in honor of the Sabbath, the divine queen and consort of God. Yet, quite apart from the historic development which led from the first to the second in the course of nearly three millennia, one can discover in both at least one common feature which indicates their generic relatedness. Both observances are culturally conditioned and traditionally formulated responses to the basic human psychological need to elevate and sanctify the sexual impulse by attributing to the sex act a higher, a religious, a divine significance. In both, the act becomes more than the end-in-itself that in physiological reality it actually is; it becomes a sacrosanct observance directed at a loftier and greater aim: the exertion of beneficial influence upon the great ultimate realities of the metaphysical world. And in both it is a female deity whose invisible yet omnipresent countenance is supposed to light up into a benign and pleasurable smile when she observes the fervid performance of her favorite rite.

In the conclusion to his study of "The Hebrew Goddess," Patai attempted to put in proper perspective the persistent sexual imagery of the Qabbalah with the observation that, from the viewpoint of the Qabbalists,

there was nothing unusual in resorting to the symbolism of coitus in speaking of certain cosmic and divine events. Thus, for instance, in the cosmic realm, the conjunction of the sun and moon—that is the appearance of these two luminaries close to each other in the sky—was described verbally and visually as a man and a woman in sexual embrace, with an explicitness which today would be considered pornographic, but which in those days was taken for what it was intended: symbolic representations of an otherwise hard-to-imagine event.

In the realm of the divine, Patai recalled the view of the eleventh-century Roman Catholic divine Peter Damiani who held that the Virgin Mary when she matured possessed such charm and beauty that God was filled with passion for her and sang the Canticles in praise of her and later took her as the golden couch on which He, worn out by the doings of men and angels, lay down to rest (cf. Patai, 273).

Patai's study *The Hebrew Goddess* has been quoted and summarized extensively because of its obvious relevance for the understanding of the Song of Songs. There can be little doubt that the personified Sabbath greeted as the divine Bride by the Qabbalists of Safed was originally none other than the great Love-goddess who had been worshiped in that region for millennia. The goddess' special day was the last of the week, the same day consecrated to the Virgin Mary as Queen of Heaven. The Sabbath Bride was greeted at sundown, the time when Venus appears as the evening star, and the welcome was an alfresco affair, à la belle étoile. The rites in her honor featured marital union which was in essence and intent a weekly sacred marriage. The scriptural libretto for these proceedings in which earthlings emulated and stimulated the divine bride and groom in this vital function was, and continues to be, most appropriately, the Sublime Song of Love ascribed to Solomon who is renowned for his zeal and devotion in this way of worship. This weekly use of the sacred love songs is certainly more original and appropriate to their nature, content, and universal appeal than the application to the annual celebration of the once-upon-a-time salvation of the elect at the Reed Sea.

Historical Allegory

The work of three European Roman Catholic scholars, Joüon, Ricciotti and Robert, may be treated summarily with special emphasis on Robert as the latest in a line of interpretation which began with the Targum. Each of these endeavored to find within the Old Testament the basis for treating the Canticle as a historical allegory. Using similar methods, they nevertheless came out with interpretations that differed widely in detail.

Paul Joüon, distinguished Jesuit Semitist, in his commentary on *Canticum Canticorum* (1909), interpreted it as an allegory composed for the encouragement of the exiles on return to their homeland. It was written by Jews and for Jews and the applications of the Song to Christ and the Church, or the soul, or the Virgin Mary, though legitimate from the Christian point of view as typologically related to Israel, are secondary, the primary and literal sense being in terms of Yahweh and Israel (pp. 15–20). Viewed in its Jewish context, the Song has to be explained by parallels from within the Bible, not from foreign literature (pp. 3–4). It was primarily in the Prophets that Joüon found the parallels to the Song. The occurrence of doublets within the Song provided the basis for division into two sections or covenants. The first covenant, 1:5 – 5:1, covers the period from the Exodus to the installation of the Ark in the city of David. The second, 5:2 – 8:14, begins with the Exile and extends to the rebuilding of the Temple, with an appeal for fidelity to the new covenant. Three appendices, 8:8–14, refer to the construction of the walls of Jerusalem, 8–10; Israel as the Vineyard of Yahweh, 11–12; and a final messianic appeal, 13–14. Thus Joüon's interpretation parallels that of the Targum, though with less emphasis than the Targum on the messianic era. In contrast to the Targum, Joüon read history into the Song in strictly chronological order. A philosophy of history is also supplied. The first covenant was broken by Israel's infidelity (5:2–9); repentance evoked a new covenant which, hopefully, will endure (8:6–7).

Giuseppe Ricciotti (*Il Cantico dei Cantici,* 1928) also read history into the Canticle, seeing it as an allegory in protest for the early simple, pastoral life of the Israelites and against the urban life and the elaborate Temple. Ricciotti assigned the composition of the Canticle to the period of Ezra and Nehemiah and did not read into it historical events beyond that period. He did, however, see in 1:2–4 and 8:1–4 references to the messianic era and thus in these aspirations a philosophy of history, but with no time limits set for the advent of the Messiah and hence no apocalyptic urgency.

The work of André Robert (1883–1955) is of special interest as the latest and most elaborate exposition of the Canticle as a historical allegory or midrash in this century. Robert's views were set forth in a series of articles by him and his pupils André Feuillet and Raymond Tournay. An extensive commentary written largely by Robert with the assistance of Feuillet, was edited and considerably augmented by Tournay, RTF, 1963. The works of Robert on Canticles are listed separately, pp. 31*f*. The following summary of Robert's view and method is based on Tournay's preface (pp. 10–17).

The method which Joüon had applied in the attempt to explain the Canticle by parallels from within the Bible was further developed by Robert who defined the Canticle as a "midrash." The vocabulary of the poem is biblical, utilizing classical themes of king, shepherd, flock, vine, garden, Lebanon, the flowering of spring, night awaking, all with an eschatological meaning, grouped around the central theme developed already by Hosea, Jeremiah, and Trito-Isaiah: the unfaithful spouse (Israel) taken back by her husband (Yahweh) as if it were the first nuptials. The constant reference to biblical data, the dramatization and reinterpretation of the events and aspirations of the epoch which followed Nehemiah, show that we are confronted with a pure midrash. Throughout his commentary Robert applied the principle that one cannot discover the thought of a sacred author without going back to the tradition that inspired it. The tableau in 3:6–8 is not a description of a wedding cortège but expresses eschatological and messianic hopes. The day of Solomon's espousals, 3:11, is the messianic future assimilated to a marriage.

Apropos of 4:5 Robert saw in the image of the two breasts no symbolic value (p. 166), but in 7:4[3E] he suggested that the allusion may be to the twin mountains Ebal and Gerizim (p. 261). The comparison of the nose of the beloved to a tower, 7:5[4E], is an example of the freedom of the poet who uses hyperbole to translate an intense feeling.

In the dispute about the allegorical character of the Song of Songs, Robert conceded that while decisive argument is rare in the realm of exegesis, one has the right to require a positive likelihood based on sufficient convergence of objective data. Robert, having noted the alleged mention of Yah(weh) in 8:6, asks how a book which is wholly occupied with God and the love of God could envelop its thesis in a continual mystery, and only lift the veil in its conclusion (p. 302). One would expect that the author of the Song of Songs would make allusion in his work to the major facts of the holy history, such as the covenant of Abraham, the miracles of Exodus, the installation of the ark, the return from exile. According to Robert and Tournay (p. 14), such allusions are made precisely in those passages which are judged unintelligible by the partisans of naturalistic interpretation. The mountains of Beter in 2:17 could thus recall the conclusion of the covenant with Abraham (p. 129; cf. Feuillet, 1961a, 30). The horse of Yahweh among Pharaoh's chariotry, 1:9, and the columns of smoke, 3:6, take us back to the time of the Exodus. The chariots of Ammi-nadib, "my people is noble," 6:12, recall the translation of the Ark from Philistine country to Jerusalem (cf. Tournay, 1959a, 289*f*). Even the name Ammi-nadib, followed by the appellation *bat-nāḏîb,* "daughter of a noble," 7:2[1E], is alleged to allude to the nobility of Israel, the chosen people. The return of the ark to Zion prefigures the great return of Israel in eschatological times.

The foxes of 2:15 represent Israel's neighboring enemies that spoil the chosen vine, Israel. Texts such as Ezek 34:23–30, Ps 80:2,9,14[1,8,13E], unite the classical theme of the wild beasts with the shepherd and the flock, as it is alleged to be in 2:15–17. As for the symbol of the dove to represent Israel, it was used already by Hosea and remains classic in Judaism (RTF, 121; cf. Tournay, 1959b, 363). Thus, if the beloved is at the same time the chosen people and its habitat, the Holy Land, it is easy to account for the numerous references in the Canticle to flowers, gardens, perfume, in the passages where the young girl is on the scene as in 1:16. Palestine in messianic times will be the Garden of the Lord, paradise. One ascends from the desert of Judah or any other area to go to Mount Zion, 3:6, and descends from the Temple hill toward any point of Palestine, 6:2,11 (cf. RTF, 141,227). The "mountain of myrrh" and "the hill of incense," 4:6, thus designate the site of the Temple, the word *mōr,* "myrrh," having been deliberately chosen to evoke Mount Moriah; cf. II Chron 3:1 (p. 168). The eschatological finale of Hosea 14:6 mentions the lily of the Canticles' refrain 2:16, 6:3 (cf. pp. 96,139). We could not understand how in 4:5 the Beloved seeks his nourishment among the lilies except as he leads his flock to pasture there. The refrain "my love is mine and I am his" merely transposes the covenant formula "I will be your God and you will be my people" (cf. Feuillet, 1961a, 22*ff*). From such perspective comes the explanation of the expressions "our bed," "our house" (1:16–17), "our wall" (2:9), "our land" (2:12), "our doors" (7:14[13E]), as the common property of Yahweh and his bride, the chosen people. The same figures could be applied to one or to the other to denote the reciprocity of their love (Feuillet, 1961a, 15).

In the formula of conjuration, 2:7, 3:5, 8:4 (cf. RTF, 108,128,437 and Tournay, 1959a, 306), it is suggested that the divine name is evoked by paronomasia. The author of the Canticle did not wish to mix the ineffable name with the language of love and only hinted at it. The Hebrew texts of Esther and I Maccabees do not mention the divine name and in later Judaism there is a multiplication of substitutes for the Name. The Canticle is alleged to be already on the way to that development.

The Canticle is further alleged to contain numerous unequivocal indices to prevent the attentive reader from interpreting it "à contresens." It is a didactic and learned work. The author is a specialist in Scripture and not a popular poet. The profusion of geographical names makes no sense in a "duo d'amour," but fits very well if the Beloved is Israel and the nation and its territory are inseparably united as in the prophetic writings; cf. Hosea 2, Jeremiah 3 (cf. Tournay, 1959a, 303). The abundance of symbols should not be surprising, following a century and a half after Ezekiel, the first great biblical allegorist, and a century after Zechariah. In this perspective it is not astonishing, in Tournay's view, that Robert saw in the description of 7:16 an evocation of the Temple of Solomon (RTF, 16).

If marriage as such had been the perspective of the Canticle, the poet, it is argued (RTF, 17), would have made allusion to the fecundity of the wife and the arrival of children, as in Ruth 4:11, and silence on this point would be inexplicable. The female initiative in the search is also improper. In the Egyptian and Arabic love songs it is the young man who goes after the girl. Admittedly, Ishtar seeks her lover Tammuz, as Isis seeks Osiris, but that is in a context frankly cultic and mythological—which is categorically rejected for the Canticle. The male of the Canticle remains mysterious, almost imperceptible, appearing and disappearing suddenly, while the exigencies are formulated with respect to the female partner (cf. Feuillet, 1961a, 34). The author of the Canticle, in spite of the love language, maintains the mystery of the transcendent God whose name he avoids pronouncing. In exploiting the literary genre which he has chosen, the author, according to Tournay, remains on this side of the excesses of Ezekiel 16 and 23 to say nothing of Jer 31:22 which describes the renewal of relations between Israel and her divine husband (as the female wooing the male).

If the message of the Canticle does not directly deal with matrimony, it does not follow that it has no teaching relative to the union of man and woman. In 8:6–7 Robert recognized a full tableau of conditions which should endue ideal conjugal love: the husband requires of the wife a love without reserve and she vows to him an unshakable fidelity (RTF, 17,300). This passage speaks of love in generic terms and calls for strength and exclusiveness. But the message of the Canticle is more, surpassing the simple perspective of marriage (p. 204).

So many positive indications exist which oblige us to treat the Canticle as an allegorical midrash, that their remarkable convergence could not well be an accident, in the view of Tournay who cited A. Lefèvre's endorsement of Robert's view (1954, 133) to the effect that accord ought to be realized not only on the basis of the departure which sees the Canticle as the love song of Yahweh and his people, but also on the point which Robert has elucidated: that the love of the wife with its hesitations and resumptions describes the stages of the conversion of Israel in anticipation of her final salvation.

Richard Tuttle Loring in a dissertation (1967) examined thirty-six Christian works which follow more or less the line of the Targum. Special attention was given to the three twentieth-century commentators mentioned above, and in particular to Robert, because Loring considered it "curious" that this interpretation "should still be advocated by scholars with all the modern linguistic tools at their disposal." It seems unlikely that this line will be followed further.

Robert's commentary is frequently cited at length in the notes of the present commentary because of its excellent summaries of the issues, although it is rare that Robert's answers are found convincing.

Mystical Marriage

The intimate connection of the Canticle of Canticles with Roman Catholic Mystical Theology is a topic too vast to be covered in depth, but a brief consideration is necessary in view of its importance in the history of interpretation. Since a carnal mind is apt to offend in thus dealing with such a delicate topic, it seems best to base this exposition, as far as possible, on the explanation of a sympathetic expert. The following points are taken from an article by the Rev. Paschal P. Parente (1944).

> Mystical Theology in its most sublime form is commonly called the *spiritual marriage* or the transforming union. The union of the soul with God through charity and sanctifying grace, known in this life by faith only, is fully enjoyed and made manifest in the light of glory. Some privileged souls, however, receive from God even in this life a perception or awareness of this union, of the supernatural, of God Himself. It is a kind of experimental knowledge of God, the true form of *theognosia* or mystical knowledge. . . . When the loving awareness of God becomes most transcendent and permanent we have the mystical marriage. The analogy of this supreme mystical union with marriage is based on the fact that, like marriage, it is the fusion of two lives in one. It is, like marriage, the most intimate and the most permanent union in this life . . . the exalted spirituality, the ardent love of God, the divine condescension and familiarity confer upon the soul a certain liberty of expression, a freedom in using a love-language which reminds one of the Canticle of Canticles (p. 142).

Parente ventured to call the Canticle of Canticles

> an allegorical dramatization of the various mystical states. It suffices to call to mind the prayer of quiet in all its manifestations of mystical sleep and mystical inebriation, the ecstatic union with the raptures, the flight of the spirit and the mystical espousals, and finally the mystical marriage. Man's spirit in an animal body is capable, with the help of divine grace, of emancipating itself from sensual love and affections to such an extent that it can love God with a purity and ardour that resembles the love of the heavenly spirits. When the human soul has reached such perfection it discovers the insufficiency of human language in expressing spiritual concepts and ideas without resorting to images taken from the senses. Every idea of a tender, intimate, ardent love that man possesses is taken

ultimately from natural love and is symbolised by conjugal union. Herein is to be found that cause of all misapprehension and misunderstanding of both the mystical states and the Canticle of Canticles. They are both little understood because they use human words and expressions in speaking of divine love. What other words would man understand better here below? . . . Mortal must be taught the mysteries of divine love in his own language and with his own earthly ideas of love. It is obvious that when words and expressions of human love are employed to express divine or spiritual love, such words must be understood allegorically and not literally. Should we take the language of the Canticle and many expressions of Mystical Theology in the obvious literal sense, we would discredit and debase them to such a degree that the Canticle could no longer be considered a sacred book nor could Mystical Theology be deemed a sacred science (p. 143).

It is exactly its spiritual and allegorical interpretation that has vindicated to the Canticle of Canticles a divine origin and a place among the *canonical* books in both Jewish and Christian tradition. Otherwise, how could a book be considered as divinely inspired for our instruction and edification in which the name of God is never mentioned and no religious or supernatural idea ever seems to occur? How could the Canticle of Canticles be numbered among the sacred books of both the Synagogue and the Christian Church if it were to be understood simply in its literal sense as an epithalamium, a melodramatic interpretation of the delights and anxieties of the wedded love of Solomon and Pharaoh's daughter or, perhaps, a country maiden? (p. 144).

Rationalists of the modern age generally deny the divine origin of the Canticle, because they cannot understand anything supernatural, nor can they see any allegory of the spiritual, veiled by the literal sense of the text. Reviving more or less the views of Theodore of Mopsuestia, of Abraham Ibn Ezra of Grotius, Clericus, etc., they hold that the subject of the book is one of a purely natural love, reciprocal affection and admiration, offending sometimes against decency. Their opinion about the nature of the mystical states and mystical phenomena is of the same kind: mere illusions, morbid conditions, forms of hysteria! Thus, Mystical Theology and the Canticle find themselves associated in the condemnation of the rationalists and unbelievers. We find the Canticle and Mystical Theology also associated in Jewish and Christian tradition, where they have been the subject of profound studies and an object of singular esteem and admiration (p. 144).

It is under this positive aspect that Parente considered the relation between the Canticle of Canticles and Mystical Theology. Only the high points of the correlation can be cited here.

The allegory or metaphor of marriage in expressing the love of God for his own people is not limited to the Canticle of Solomon. Among the biblical passages that present this marriage metaphor are Hosea 1:19–20; Ps 45:11–12; Matt 9:15, 25:1–13; John 3:28–29; Eph 5:23–25; Rev 19:7,9.

Christian tradition took over the allegorical interpretation of the Canticle from the Jews seeing in it the most sublime expression of the love of God for his people. In the process of adaptation of this allegory to Christian ideas the Word, or Christ, took the place of Yahweh; the Church, that of the Synagogue.

This is the *Christological* interpretation first introduced by Hippolytus of Rome and by Origen, and continuing to this day.

In the course of time a few variations of a mystical and ascetical nature were introduced. The Christian soul took the place of the Church as the mystical bride of Christ. This is the interpretation of the Canticle that was most favoured by such great mystics as St. Bernard, Gerson, Richard of St. Laurence, St. Teresa, St. John of the Cross. With them the Canticle offers an allegory or dramatization of mystical states and especially of the mystical nuptials of the perfect Christian soul with the Son of God. Along with the Christological interpretation, a *Mariological* interpretation was introduced very early by St. Ephrem, St. Ambrose, St. Epiphanius, St. Peter Chrysologus. They understood the Virgin Mary to be the real, mystical bride of the Canticle. Their interpretation is encouraged by the liturgy of the Church. In several feasts of the Virgin Mary both the Divine Office and the Mass adopt with preference verses and lessons from the book of the Canticle. And, indeed, what other soul was there that could claim in all truth to have celebrated the mystical nuptials with God except Mary Immaculate, the true Mother of God? The Fathers used to interpret occasionally one or more parts of the Canticle in a Mariological sense. Since the twelfth century, however, the entire Canticle of Canticles has been applied to the Virgin Mary by such authors as Rupert de Deutz, Denis the Carthusian, Cornelius à Lapide, Nigidius and others (p. 146).

The first place in allegorical interpretation of the mystical bride is given to the people of God (the Church and the Virgin Mary), the second place to the individual Christian soul. Neither excludes the other. As Origen put it in his first Homily on the Canticles,

This book must be understood in the spiritual sense, namely, in the sense of the union of the Church with Jesus Christ, under the names of bride and groom, and of the union of the soul with the Divine Word.

Or as St. Gregory of Nyssa put it,

What is written here makes one think of nuptials, but what is meant is the union of the human soul with God.

St. Augustine (*City of God* XVII 20) explained that

The Canticle of Canticles is the spiritual joy of saintly souls at the nuptials of the King and Queen of the City, of Christ and His Church. This joy, however, is hidden under the veil of an allegory in order to render the desire more ardent and the discovery more delightful at the apparition of the bridegroom and his bride.

St. Bernard in his first sermon on the Canticles declared that

Solomon, inspired by God, sang the praises of Christ and his Church, the grace of sacred love, and the mysteries of the eternal nuptials. (Cf. Parente, 147.)

A new trend in the mystical application of the Canticle signaled by Parente involves the mystical union of the soul with Christ in Holy Communion. This mystical application was not unknown to the great mystics of former days, according to Parente, but more has been written on the subject in the present generation which is styled the Eucharistic era.

The common complaint about the lack of logical order in the Canticle is made by those who

> forget the fact that a mystical book of that form is based on the logic of the heart rather than that of the mind, and that love little cares about logical order. Still a certain order and unity prevails through the entire book; there is unity of purpose, and a unity of style and persons (p. 149).

A division which has been admitted in principle by several authors separates the Song into seven parts according to the days of the week, each day marking progress in love, from imperfect love, through seven stages, to complete surrender and love at rest in its transforming union of spiritual marriage.

> After the Gospel of St. John no other sacred book has enjoyed the predilection of the mystics as the Canticle of Canticles. Only a mystic can easily discover the divine beauty hidden under the veil of idyllic poetry so rich in oriental color and imagery. The language of mystics is not for everybody to use. It is pure sentimentality in the mouth of the uninitiated. For this reason, the reading of the Canticles of Solomon was not permitted indiscriminately for many centuries in the past. As we have remarked repeatedly, the only sense of the Canticle intended by God is the spiritual or allegorical sense. Those who stop at the literal sense of the text and perceive nothing of the spiritual meaning read something that refers to natural love only and find anything but edification. A carnal man should not read this book. It is the book of perfect souls, purified by a life of endless trials and mortifications whose conversation is in heaven (pp. 149*f*).

By way of examples of the predilection of mystics for the Canticle of Canticles Parente presented the cases of two of the most eminent mystics of the modern age, St. Teresa of Avila and St. John of the Cross.

St. Teresa knew only the parts of the Canticle read in the Divine Office, but it was on that basis that she wrote her book "Conceptions of Divine Love on some Words of the Canticles" (*Conceptos del Amor de Dios sobre algunas Palabras de los Cantares*), ca. 1577. What was saved of her *Conceptos* was first published in 1612 by Father Gratian. Teresa was so moved by the Canticles that one of her confessors directed her to write her thoughts. Another confessor, alarmed at the presumption of a woman writing on such a difficult and delicate subject, ordered her to burn the manuscript at once. Teresa obediently consigned her manuscript to the fire. It happened, however, that another nun had previously copied for herself the first seven chapters of the manuscript and thus the work was saved in part. The name of the male chauvinist confessor St. Teresa did not divulge.

At the end of the seventh chapter of the *Conceptos* Teresa noted:

> My purpose, when I began, was to let you understand, daughters, how you might delight yourselves when you hear any words of the Canticles, and that you might

meditate on the great mysteries contained in them, although in your own opinion they may seem obscure (Parente, 151).

Speaking of herself, it seems, Teresa wrote:

I know a person who for many years lived in great fears, and nothing could comfort her, till our Lord was pleased she should hear certain words from the Canticles, and by them she understood her soul as well (*Conceptos* I, after Parente, 151 n9).

Again she reminisced:

I remember well I once heard a religious man give a very excellent sermon, the greater part of which was about these caresses of the Spouse with God; but the sermon caused great laughing among the audience; and everything that he said was taken in such bad part (for he spoke on love, the subject being the *Mandatum,* he preached on certain words of the Canticles) that I was astonished. I see clearly that it is owing to our having too little practice in the love of God, which makes us think a soul cannot speak with God in such expressions (ibid.).

The application of the Canticle to the sacramental union of the soul with Jesus in the Eucharist was most vividly made with reference to the osculation mentioned in the first verse of the Canticle, "Let him kiss me with the kisses of his mouth":

O my Lord and my God, what words are these for a worm to utter to its Maker! I acknowledge these words may have many meanings; but the soul that is so inflamed with love as to make her a fool desires nothing else but to utter these words, that God would not take away His love from her. O Lord, what are we astonished at? Is not the deed more astonishing? Do we not unite ourselves with the Most Holy Sacrament? I was thinking also whether the Bride here requested the favour which Christ bestowed upon us later when He became our food . . . O my Lord, if a kiss implies peace and friendship, why do not souls beg of you to ratify it with them? What better thing can we ask of you? That which I request of you, my Lord, is to grant me this peace with a kiss of your mouth (ibid.).

One more quotation from Teresa's *Conceptos* will serve to illustrate the effect of the Canticles on her:

O Lord of Heaven and earth! How is it possible that, though living in this mortal life, one may enjoy you with such particular friendship and that the Holy Ghost should so plainly express it in these words; and yet we will not understand what are the caresses wherewith His Majesty regales souls in these Canticles? What courtings, what sweet attractions! Only one word would be sufficient to dissolve us into you. . . . By how many ways and means do you express love for us! . . . By certain words which wound the soul who loves you, words which you scatter in the Canticles, and which you teach her to say to you! . . . Now, my Lord, I ask you nothing else in this life but "to kiss me with the kiss of Your mouth," and this in such a way that I should not be able even though I wished, to withdraw myself from this union and friendship (*Conceptos* III, after Parente, 152).

The mystical initiation into the love of God takes place in stages. God begins by taking the heart without letting the soul understand why and how. The first mystical experience proves too much for the soul in a mortal body and produces a kind of mystical sleep, swooning, or inebriation, which St. Teresa called the *prayer of quiet.* When the soul's faculties are completely absorbed, we have the *ecstatic union,* a state which no earthly interest, noise, pain, or joy can disturb. In order to further purify the soul from any vestiges of self love, the second *dark night* falls upon the soul bringing consternation and spiritual agony. This passive purgation purifies the soul for the supreme mystical union, the spiritual marriage, a permanent union which nothing can disturb or interrupt (cf. Parente, 155–158). See Plate XIV.

The predilection of St. John of the Cross for the Canticle is manifest in his *Cantico Espiritual,* an imitation and almost a paraphrase of the Canticle of Canticles, of which an editor said,

It is an incomparable canticle, perhaps the most sublime that was ever intoned here on earth to divine love after the great Canticle of the wise king Solomon, a canticle that inebriates every mystical soul. (P. Silverio de S. Teresa, III, Introducción, after Parente, p. 152. An English translation by K. Kavanaugh and O. Rodriquez is available in *The Collected Works of St. John of the Cross* [1964], 393–565.)

It is of interest to note that St. Teresa of Avila and St. John of the Cross were born just twenty-four miles apart and the two first met when he was twenty-five and she fifty-two and together they went on to found the order of Discalced Carmelites (cf. K. Kavanaugh, 1964, 17*f*). The Spiritual Canticle was written while Brother John was in the prison of his order in Toledo. Even on his deathbed his esteem and predilection for the Canticle was manifest when a few hours before his death he requested a reading from the Canticle and on hearing the tender expressions of love kept repeating them to himself and saying, "Oh! what precious pearls" (P. Gerardo [1912], I, 9; cited after Parente, 153n13).

Mariology and the Lady of the Canticle

The validity of the identification of the Lady of the Canticle with the Virgin Mary featured in Roman Catholic treatments through the centuries has in recent decades been questioned and rejected by some Catholic scholars (cf. Roland E. Murphy, 1954a). P. Alfonso Rivera has set forth the grounds for the Marian interpretation of the Canticle in a comprehensive article entitled "Sentido mariologica del Cantar de los Cantares?" (1951; 1952): the arguments for the literal sense and the fuller sense (*sensus plenior*) with a conspectus of the history of the Marian interpretation from patristic times. This article is not presently accessible to the writer and resort is made to the discussion and critique by Murphy who regarded it as the best exposition of the Marian interpretation presented up to that time (1952) (cf. Murphy, 1954a, 23).

Rivera applied the Canticle to the Virgin Mary by individualizing the collective object to which the poem refers, urging that what is true of the Church is true in a very special way of her who had such a privileged relationship to Christ and thus the Canticle is to be understood of the Blessed Virgin both in the literal sense and in the fuller sense. To Joüon's objection that individualization "volatilizes" the literal sense of the Canticle, Rivera replied that the Semitic mentality frequently binds together the individual and the universal. This Murphy acknowledged to be true but questioned whether it is applicable to the Canticle or to such figures as the Servant of the Lord in Isaiah and the Son of Man in Daniel where "the hagiographer's descriptions fluctuate between the collectivity and the characteristics of an individual ascribed to the collectivity." According to Murphy,

> there is no such fluctuation in the Canticle; in fact everything is individual. Never for a minute can there be a doubt that the author is conveying his ideas through the symbols of an individual man and woman and is within the world of those symbols. So true is this that the naturalistic interpretation absolutely excludes, mistakenly, the ulterior reference to the collectivity, the Israel of God. It must be admitted that the collective interpretation finds its justification only in the marriage theme which appears so consistently throughout the Old Testament. Indeed, without this literary tradition one would be hard pressed to understand the Canticle other than as the description of the love of two individual characters (p. 24).

Rivera distinguished between the case of the Virgin Mary and any other individual soul, since it would be readily granted that the words of the Canticle do not refer to St. Teresa of Avila and her mystical union with God. Mary, Rivera contended, is not just a member of the Church, but one whom the description of the bride in the Canticle fits in a special and singular way, not as distinct from reference to the Church, but as part of it in view of her intimate relation to the Church. This Marian meaning, Rivera argued, is admirably suited to the Christological sense of the Canticle, since the fidelity and beauty of the bride in the Canticle is eminently true of Mary through whom the Word was made flesh. To this Murphy replied that "Mary's intimate relationship to both Christ and the Church is not a necessary part of the literal sense of the Canticle." Murphy conceded that,

> in the concrete order of things, the Church is unthinkable without Mary. But this is no argument that there is an express divine intention to describe her union with God in the Canticle. Because it refers to the Church, it does not thereby refer necessarily to every aspect of the Church, including Mary's role. Unless there is something within the Canticle which necessarily refers to what we may call the Marian aspect of the Church, we must refrain from referring the Canticle to her in the literal sense. Otherwise there will be no limit to the "inclusiveness" of the symbol of the bride.

Buzy, e.g., following the process of individualization within the literal sense, included all the faithful under the figure of the bride (Murphy, 26n18). Murphy pointed out the weakness of applying individual verses such as 4:7,12 to the Blessed Virgin, for the sake of convenience, and neglecting others. Further, Murphy regarded it as

> impossible for the verses to refer in the literal sense now to the collectivity, now to the individual soul of Mary. This veritable impasse suggests that the Canticle is not to be applied in a literal sense to Mary in such fashion as to refer individual words to her. To do so is to disregard the parabolic nature of the poem. The individual verses are not to be taken singly. From this point of view, the Canticle can be compared to the parable of the Prodigal Son. We accept, for example, that here Almighty God is symbolized under the figure of the father; but we do not apply each pertinent verse to Him. Rather, the whole story is an imaginative description whose sole purpose is to convey the mercy and forgiveness of God. Similarly, the purpose of the Canticle is to express the beauty and fidelity which will characterize the People of God in its Messianic betrothal. The individual scenes are described solely to highlight this aspect; we are not dealing with a theological treatise which progresses logically and gives weight to each detail. To forget this is to go contrary to the proper literary genre in which the Canticle has been written (p. 27).

Rivera concluded that the Canticle refers to Mary in the fuller sense which he defined as the literal sense which restricts to the noblest individual what is said of the collectivity in general. Murphy, however, argued that one may not go so far. All that one may be permitted to understand by the literal sense is that the Canticle has messianic reference and that spiritual Israel which is the Church is symbolized by the figure of the bride. The individualization which Murphy saw as a logical process of deduction on the part of the reader, and as perfectly natural, should nevertheless be recognized as an accommodated sense. The various texts of the Canticle can then in the accommodated sense be applied to the Blessed Virgin who more than any other single creature merits the recognition given to the fidelity of the spouse. The application to an individual member of the Church, according to Murphy, is likewise thus justified (p. 27).

Murphy cited the Bull, *Munificentissimus Deus,* in which the Holy Father himself took note of a certain liberty in the application of Canticles 3:6 to the exaltation of Mary in heaven:

> Often there are theologians and preachers who, following in the footsteps of the holy Fathers, have been free in their use of events and expressions taken from Sacred Scripture to explain their belief in the Assumption . . . (Ps. 131:8; Ps. 44) Likewise they mention the Spouse of the Canticles "that goeth up by the desert, as a pillar of smoke of aromatical spices, of myrrh and frankincense" to be crowned. These are proposed as depicting that heavenly Queen and heavenly Spouse who has been lifted up to the courts of heaven with the divine Bridegroom.

From this passage Murphy was unable to draw any certain conclusion for or against the Marian interpretation of the Canticle, although it seemed to him that the liberty consisted precisely in the individualization of the verse, 3:6, along the lines of the Marian interpretation of 4:7,12 mentioned above.

As the Marian exegesis of the Canticle has declined, along with other modes of allegorical treatment, and the literal interpretation as human love songs has found increasing favor with leading Roman Catholic exegetes, there have been parallel developments in the recovery and study of documents from ancient Mesopotamia and Syria which tend to strengthen the cultic interpretation relating the Lady of the Canticle to the love goddesses and fertility rites of the ancient Near East, to Ishtar and her congeners. Martial traits of the Bride of the Canticle reflecting an Ishtar-Gestalt were signaled by the Jesuit Assyriologist F. X. Kugler in 1927, but possible implications of this insight were not pursued by Kugler or taken up and developed by other Catholic scholars. The reluctance of Roman Catholics to exploit pagan parallels in support of Mariology and Marian interpretation of the Canticle is readily understandable, even though for the historian and comparativist the pagan antecedents, parallels, survivals, and revivals are of great interest and relevance. With growing movements for liberation within the Roman Catholic Church, as in other areas and arenas, it is likely that more attention will be accorded the evidences for pagan origin of the Canticles, not only by Roman Catholic scholars, but by Protestant and Jewish scholars as well.

The Marian interpretation of the Song of Songs takes on renewed interest in the light of the affinities of the Black Beauty of 1:5 with Kali of India and in view of the veneration of black representations of the Virgin Mary in numerous shrines across Europe. The several black goddesses of the ancient Near East, the anonymous black goddess of the Hittites, the black Aphrodite, the black Demeter of Phigalia, Artemis or Diana of the Ephesians, Isis of Egypt whose cult enjoyed great popularity in the Roman world, Athena and other goddesses represented by black stones, including the black stone of Mecca, viewed together suggest that the swart Lady of the Canticle may indeed be related to the black madonnas of Europe and to the great black goddess of India, the violent, venereal virgin, Mother Kali. The extent of the worship of black goddesses, both in space and time, from India to Europe, and from the second millennium to the present, suggests a continuum and historical connections which may be eventually clarified as new data accumulates. There are random bits and pieces of evidence which hint at connections or common traditions between Western Asia and India, such as the possible use of the Indo-European word for "fire" (Sanskrit *agni*) in a Ugaritic sacred marriage text (23[52].15), or the provocative suggestion of J. T. Milik that the element *soma* attested at Dura-Europus designates the sacred drink in the Vedic form of the word, rather than in the Avestan form *haoma* which would be expected; cf. 2:15. The Tantric traditions of India, especially the left-handed (*vāmācāra*) erotic rites, are of particular interest for the appreciation of some of the myths and rituals presented by the Ugaritic texts and for the parallels to the orgiastic activities alleged to have persisted in Western funeral feasts into Christian times. The quest for occult success in the left-handed way required of the aspiring adept a regimen of wine, meat, and women. "They drink constantly and enjoy beautiful women." "With red eyes they are always exhilarated and replete with flesh and wine" (cf. A. Bharati, 1965, 68,72,79,292*ff*). The elements of Tantric worship, wine, meat, fish, parched grain, and sexual union, had their counterparts in the ancient love feasts of the West; on the victuals and menus of the sacral meals at Dura (cf. J. T. Milik, 1972, 202*ff*). The Tantric hymns to the Goddess offer some of the most provocative parallels to the Song of Songs.

Humanizing the Sublime Song

In the past two decades there has been a notable trend toward the interpretation of the Song of Songs as human love poetry. At the end of his résumé of the history of the exegesis of the Song in 1952 Rowley remarked that

> it will be clearly observed that there is as yet no generally accepted view of the interpretation it should be given. . . . The view I adopt finds in it nothing but what it appears to be, lovers' songs, expressing their delight in one another and the warm emotions of their hearts. All of the other views find in the Song what they bring to it (p. 232).

In adopting this view which has so much in common with that of Theodore of Mopsuestia rejected by the Church, the question again arises whether one is not proposing something which is "unfit for Christian ears" and in accord with Castellio and Whiston who boldly pronounced the Song as unworthy of a place in the canon. Ibn Ezra had also pronounced this notion repugnant:

> Abhorred, abhorred be the idea that the Song of Songs is in the category of love songs, but rather has it the character of a parable; and were it not for the greatness of its excellence it would not have been incorporated in the corpus of sacred writings.

The Westminster Assembly in its annotations on the Song of Solomon had paid its respects to this view:

> Both among them (i.e. the Jews) as well as other Readers, there were some that had lower conceptions of it, and received it as an hot carnall pamphlet, formed by some loose Apollo or Cupid, rather than the holy inspiration of the true God. But this blasphemy hath perished with the father of it (cf. Rowley, 233nn3,4).

Rowley, however, took exception to the position that the allegedly defunct view is blasphemous or that the Song thus interpreted would be unfit for inclusion in holy writ.

The view that the Song was written for use in connection with fertility rites did, however, seem to Rowley to make it unworthy of a place in the canon. Rowley cited Graham and May (1936, 230) who related the aesthetics of the Canticle to those of the pagan cult: "The same appreciation of sheer beauty and the power of love comes to classic expression in the Song of Songs, which has been designated, and rightly so for the pure in heart, as the 'Holy of Holies' of the Old Testament." On this Rowley commented in a tone somewhat Pecksniffian: "This endorsement of an extreme judgment comes indeed somewhat strangely from authors who hold that the Song is a survival from a fertility cult liturgy (p. 123)" (Rowley, 234n1). "But," according to Rowley,

> if we have songs that express pure human love, and the mutual loyalty of lovers to one another, even though the physical side of their love is expressed with a frankness we should not emulate, I do not think the Song is undeserving of inclusion in the Canon. For there is no incongruity in such a recognition of the essential sacredness of pure human love. The Church has always consecrated the union of man and woman in matrimony, and taught that marriage is a divine ordinance, and it is not unfitting that a book which expresses the spiritual and physical emotions on which matrimony rests should be given a place in the Canon of Scripture (p. 234).

A similar view was expressed by the conservative Protestant scholar E. J. Young (1949, 327) and cited by Rowley:

> The Song does celebrate the dignity and purity of human love. This is a fact which has not always been sufficiently stressed. The Song, therefore, is didactic and moral in its purpose. It comes to us in this world of sin, where lust and passion are on every hand, where fierce temptations assail us and try to turn us aside from the God-given standard of marriage. And it reminds us, in particularly beautiful fashion, how pure and noble true love is. This, however, does not exhaust the purpose of the book. Not only does it speak of the purity of human love, but by its very inclusion in the Canon, it reminds us of a love that is purer than our own.

It is of general humane interest that the appreciation of the Song of Songs as glorifying human love has grown especially in conservative Protestant scholarly circles. An article by R. B. Laurin (1962, 1062–1063) will serve to illustrate the tendency and progression. All are agreed that "The Song of Songs is a poem, or a series of poems, in which love is exalted. The theme throughout is pure, passionate, sexual, hungry love. Even the allegorical approach cannot disguise this." "The Wholesomeness of Sex" is the heading of the section following that entitled "The Exaltation of Love" which ends with the question, "What, then, is the modern message of the book?"

> It is a strange paradox that among those most vociferous about their belief in the Bible "from cover to cover" is often found an attitude that sex is "nasty." The Victorian embarrassment with sexual matters has not disappeared from the contemporary scene. The Bible should have given the lie to this kind of attitude. It is,

to be sure, fully aware of lust and the misuse of sex; but at the same time it is forthright in approving the wholesomeness of sex. The passionate, physical attraction between man and woman, who find in this the fulfillment of their deepest longings, is seen as a healthy, natural thing. . . . But in the Song of Songs, we find a whole book taken up with the most detailed appreciation of the physical world and its beauty. A man and a woman's love for each other, and it is certainly not "platonic love," is set in the midst of expressions about the smell of perfume, the singing of birds, the beauty of flowers, and the physical attributes of each other. . . . So the Song of Songs has an important emphasis here. There is a basic, God-ordained wholesomeness to sex, to the use of our bodies in this manner. We are to remember that God established a physical attraction between the sexes; this is not wrong. And in the marriage relationship, as the Song stresses, sex is to have its normal, healthy role in providing fulfillment and joy for both partners. It is not something to be shunned, but to be praised.

But sex is not necessarily love, Laurin admonished in a paragraph on "The Ingredients of Love."

Important as sex is, it may become a degrading thing, practised as an animal might. Sex must be joined with other motives and feelings. Here is where the Song of Songs also contributes a modern message. The book is not simply a Kinsey report on the sexual behavior of the ancient male and female. It speaks of other elements in the love relationship that make it full and meaningful.

The meaningful ingredients are "Exclusiveness" and "Steadfastness."

The contemporary world has popularized infidelity to the marriage bond, has televised comedies on the theme of adultery, and has left the impression that love is where you find it in the satisfaction of lust. Not so the Song of Songs. It speaks of the exclusive love of two people, each wrapped up in the other, each pure, each faithful to the other, each innocent of any involvement with others. So the maiden tells her lover that she has reserved the fruits of love exclusively for him (7:13).

The element of exclusiveness, be it noted, is nowhere explicit in the Canticle, in this verse or elsewhere, but is a presumption generally read into the text. The figure of the tower used to describe the lady's neck and nose (4:4, 7:4,5) is given a bizarre explanation.

Here the metaphor of the "tower" signifies inaccessibility, insurmountability, purity, virginity, faithfulness an apt figure to express the exclusiveness of a lover. It is the picture of a maiden with head held high, standing aloof from all advances.

The neck in biblical metaphor is indeed connected with stubbornness and pride, or with servility, but there is nowhere any indication of a relation to defense of virginity or sexual exclusiveness. Leroy Waterman (1925, 180) remarked that "Her neck is described in a manner to suggest the earliest recorded case of goitre." A nose like the tower of Lebanon (7:5d) seems even more difficult to understand as denoting sexual exclusiveness. The seeming hyperbole is readily explicable if the Lady in question is superhuman with her other features in proportion to the head like Carmel (7:6a). As for the alleged aloofness of the heroine of the Canticle, she gets out of bed at night and roams the streets and squares in search of her elusive lover.

Other parts of the Song, according to Laurin, speak of the maiden's "moral purity." "The fierce eyes (6:5) and the formidable army (6:4) are expressive of protected virginity." The qualification "moral" is an additive to whatever purities are ascribed to the black beauty (1:5) who is without blemish (4:7). The Ugaritic Goddess Anat is termed "Virgin" even as she is depicted in thousandfold coupling with her consort Mighty Baal, and further when she becomes pregnant. "The 'dove' hidden in the clefts of the mountains is an image of innocence and purity (1:15, 2:14, 5:2)." But beside being a symbol of innocence, harmlessness, and stupidity, the dove is notable for its lechery and thus was the attribute of the love goddess.

The element of steadfastness in love is illustrated by 8:6–7 which Laurin appropriately hailed as perhaps the climax of the book. Love is thus the Power of Life.

There are other lessons about love in the Song of Songs—the joy that it brings to the one loved, how it lays hold of one's whole life, so that separation can never be a permanent situation, how it cannot be taken for granted (cf. 2:5–6, 3:1–5, 5:2–8, 8:14). But there is something else which cannot be forgotten. The Song of Songs is in the canon; the Old Testament is Christian Scripture. The difference that Christ has made must be integral to our use of the book. The Christian faith has brought a new power, a new force into the love relationship. It can transform the commonplace and help us to achieve the true use of sex and real fulfillment in love that mere biological and romantic love cannot. And something more. It can help us to understand that our love for one another is an imperfect example of God's love for us. The maiden said that "love is strong as death"; Paul tells us that God's love in Christ has overcome death (Rom 8:35–39) (Laurin, 1063).

The fact that the Song of Songs is in the Canon of Sacred Scripture and yet has tended in recent times to be ignored, particularly in Protestant circles, has sparked an interest in rescue and rehabilitation, rediscovery and reemphasis of its modern message. A doctoral dissertation by R. B. Dempsey (1963) devoted the final chapter to the effort to set forth possible uses of Canticles today which will be consistent with good scholarship, sound exegesis, and the Christian message. This chapter involved a poll to determine some of the uses being made of the Song of Songs in church, synagogue, and seminary and attempted "to offer some creative examples of actual and possible uses to be made of Canticles today" (p. 13). A questionnaire was mailed to one hundred priests, rabbis, and ministers and to several seminary instructors of Old Testament. Fifty per cent were returned. While this is too small a sample to represent an accurate opinion poll, the author felt that it did reflect what some were currently thinking and doing, and some interesting suggestions were offered in the returns. The questionnaire (Appendix B, pp. 169–172) inquired in some detail about the use made of the Song of

Solomon in preaching, teaching, counseling, personal devotions, corporate worship, hymnody, and type of interpretation employed.

The suggested uses were treated under the rubrics of Literary Appreciation, Devotions, Worship, Teaching, Research, Theological Study, Marriage Counseling (ch. 7, "Modern Use of Canticles," pp. 126–153). While each of these sections contain much of interest, it is section "7. Use in Marriage Counseling" (pp. 147–153) which is most intriguing. The questions on counseling use had been: "A. Have you ever made use of the Song of Solomon in premarital counseling? In counseling in marital problems? B. Do you feel that the Song of Solomon has possibilities in this field?" Of the respondents, thirty-one had never made use of Canticles in premarital counseling, while five had. Twenty-three felt it had possibilities and another five thought it might. Nine thought it had no possibilities and one of the nine considered such use an imposition while another regarded it as a joke (p. 147n1). The author exhibited an awareness of the complexities of family, premarital, and marital counseling and suggested that when occasion warrants there should be referral to trained specialists or even to a psychiatrist. The deficiencies in sex education in the home, however, challenge the church and synagogue to help prepare the homemakers of tomorrow. Since

> the idea that sex is evil is very often connected with a religious point of view . . . in overcoming such perverted religious ideas, it is important to give an adequate religious foundation to a healthy view of sex. . . . The Song of Solomon offers to the one engaged in premarital counseling a wonderful religious source for presenting the sexual aspect of marriage as a thing of beauty and enjoyment (pp. 149, 150).

Dempsey closed his section on marital counseling with a quotation from Raymond Calkins (1935, 79):

> If this book [the Song of Solomon] were read in its literal significance and its lessons laid to heart, today there would be fewer unhappy marriages contracted purely from lust of money or of body. The remedy for the licentiousness of much of modern society can be found only in such ideal concepts of the nature of love and human relations as this book enshrines. It is an atmosphere so pure, so sweet, so true that we must recover it if we would recover the stability of the home and of family life. The book reminds us that true romance is not dead in the world; that the ideal of human love remains a reality; that the highest forms of human happiness lie . . . in the simpler, truer, and more satisfying forms of human affection and devotion (Dempsey, 153).

In the final chapter of his dissertation, Dempsey offered a number of conclusions of which a few may be noted here.

> The rise of modern criticism, the study of comparative cultures, and a rising tendency to let the poem speak for itself have driven the allegorical approach into retreat. The allegorizing of Canticles is simply inconsistent with good hermeneutical principles (p. 154).

In corporate worship, Dempsey recommended that Canticles

be used only with extreme care in a mystical sense in hymnody, prayers or sermons. So to use the book is to distort its meaning. Whatever use in worship to which the Song of Solomon is put, it must be consistent with its content concerning the love between a man and a woman.

The recommendation of use of materials from the Canticles in prayers and in wedding services of synagogue and church (p. 157) is bolstered with a sample prayer (pp. 136*f*) replete with phrases from Canticles and a wedding ceremony consisting largely of verses from the same source (pp. 138*ff*).

The didactic possibilities of Canticles were deemed good. "It provides the religious teacher with excellent material with which to teach the biblical views of romance, sex and marriage." The book also has "some secondary teaching aspects, e.g. Jewish custom, Hebrew poetic style and biblical flora," but "the basic teaching thrust is related to married love" (p. 141).

The modern use of Canticles ought to include premarital counseling and in some cases marital adjustment counseling. . . . Canticles is an exquisite presentation of the total involvement of both partners, each for the other, according to the divine plan for human happiness. . . . In dispelling wrong conceptions of sex, or in helping to rekindle the romance of a marriage, this poem can frequently be used by the parish minister in dealing with troubled marriages.

During the last century the traditional allegorical approach to Canticles has been for the most part abandoned because of the discoveries of scholarship, the spread of a more natural view of love and sex, and a realization that in the final analysis Canticles is love poetry. It is the firm conclusion of this paper that this does not mean that Canticles has no use today, but that it means that new uses of the book are in order. It is a tragic mistake to neglect or misuse the most beautiful and most instructive poetry on love and marriage in the Judeo-Christian Canon (p. 158).

Similar sentiments find expressions on the liberal side of contemporary Protestantism. B. Davie Napier stated his view of the Song with striking eloquence:

It has on occasion been carelessly said that the Song has no religious-theological value. I must take emphatic personal exception. If it informs and nourishes and enriches the category of joyful, rapturous, sexual love; and if it has the power to restore something of tenderness and freshness to the marriage relationship, then surely in the sense to which we have consistently held in these pages, the Song of Solomon has even theological justification. As one who continues to delight in the poems, I cheer the ingenuity and inspiration of the allegorical interpretation which preserved the Song of Solomon. The Song properly belongs in a canon of sacred literature from a people who were able to look at *all* the gifts of a rich creation with gratitude to the Giver and joy in the gift (1962, 356).

The traditional Jewish allegorical interpretation is still maintained in orthodox circles, but the general trend among conservative and reform Jewish scholars is toward the literal understanding as human love songs. S. M. Lehrmann, e.g. (1946, p. xii), adopted Ewald's three-character theory. The story describes the trials of a beautiful maiden from Shunem or Shulem who was a shepherdess. She was in love with a shepherd of the village, but her brothers did not approve and they transferred her to work in the vineyards in the hope of keeping her away from her lover. One day she was seen by Solomon's servants as the king was en route to his summer resort in Lebanon. She was taken against her will to Solomon who falls in love with her at first sight, sings of her beauty, and tries to induce her to abandon her shepherd and accept the love and luxury he offers. The court ladies also try to persuade her, but her heart belongs to her shepherd. She yearns for her true love and is taunted by the court ladies that he has rejected her. She speaks with her love as if he were present and dreams that he has come to rescue her. She awakes and rushes into the street to seek him, but she is maltreated by the watchmen who take her as a woman of the street. The king, finally convinced of the constancy of her love for the shepherd, allows her to return home. She is joined by her true lover and leaning on his arm, returns to her village. They pass the scenes so dear to them while she recounts her recent misfortunes. The story ends on a note of triumph. Her love could not be overcome by the lures of luxury. She assures her brothers that their concerns for her virtue were unwarranted. She has proved that love can endure.

The tale she tells to their assembled friends makes a strong protest against the luxury and vice of the court, and pays testimony to the beauty and dignity of pure love and fidelity . . . (p. xi).

The main moral of the Book, is that love, besides being the strongest emotion in the human heart, can also be the holiest. . . . This book pictures love as a reward enjoyed only by the pure and simple, a joy not experienced by the pleasure-seeking monarch and the indolent ladies in the court. It is a joy reserved for the loyal and the constant, and is denied to the sensual and dissolute. . . .

This moral doubtless preserved a Book otherwise devoid of religious character, in which the name of God does not appear unless it is included in the word *shalhebeth-yah* (viii 6). . . .

The best moral of the story, however, is that the Book portrays the guardianship of God over His people and the loyalty which Israel has displayed throughout the ages towards his faith. Like the Shulammite in the story, Israel has been forcibly taken away from his homeland. Many suitors clamoured for Israel's hand—Rome, the Church, Islam, who called with siren voices that he exchange his God for another, but the reply has always been that *many waters cannot quench the love* for his ancestral faith. Like the Shulammite, Israel suffered because of his refusal to be unfaithful, but in the end love and fidelity always emerge triumphant. *Amor omnia vincit* (pp. xii–xiii).

The commentary of Israel Bettan (1950), from the side of Reform Judaism, takes the view that Canticles is an anthology of love songs.

A recent word from the side of Reform Judaism comes from Sheldon H. Blank in the Prolegomenon to the reissue of the Christian David Ginsburg's Commentary:

For whatever reason, but probably because our times no longer insist on a moralizing, political, or "religious" tendency in every biblical book, this Tammuz cult theory, along with the edifying tale interpretation, along with allegorical and all other such by-ways, today appears less convincing than the "hot carnall pamphlet" approach once favored by some blaspheming readers (p. xliv).

Similarly, Robert Gordis, in the camp of Conservative Judaism (1954), saw the Song of Songs as

unique among the books of the Bible in spirit, content and form, . . . the only book in the canon lacking a religious or national theme, . . . the only complete work which is entirely secular, indeed, sensuous, in character (p. 1). The only justifiable conclusion is that the Song of Songs, like the Psalter, is an anthology, running a wide gamut of its emotions. . . . It contains songs of love's yearning and its consummation, of coquetry and passion, of separation and union, of courtship and marriage (pp. 17*f*).

In the *JPSV The Five Megilloth and Jonah* (1969), in the Introduction to the Song of Songs, p. 3, H. L. Ginsberg characterized the Canticles as

a collection of love songs which bears considerable resemblance to both ancient and modern love songs of the Near East. The lovers dwell on each other's physical beauty, which they describe (as popular Arab love songs still do) by means of far-fetched similes, and on their sexual enjoyment of each other, which is likened to delightful sensations of taste and smell; but this is done with a naive, natural candor and without grossness. There is also an appreciation of the sights, sounds, and smells of the Eretz Israel spring which we should not have suspected from the other books of the Bible. No doubt Israel always had such songs, but they were handed down orally and were modified, and old verses or whole songs were replaced by new, as the language changed. . . .

The book is entirely profane. God is never invoked or alluded to. Yet, because it was attributed to Solomon, and because it was possible to understand all of the songs as wedding songs (though some of them were surely not that originally), the book was accepted as canonical without reinterpretation. For marriage was ordained by God (Gen. 2.18,24), and it is gratifying to note that its sexual basis was never regarded as shameful by either the Bible or the Rabbis.

Catholic Views of Canticles as Songs of Human Love

In recent decades some Roman Catholic scholars have written in favor of understanding the Canticle as a divinely inspired treatment of the sanctity of married love. In Europe A. M. Dubarle (1954, 67–86) and M. A. van den Oudenrijn (1953), while allowing of a higher meaning, admit that in the literal sense the poem describes human love. The description of faithful and happy human love points to the corresponding characteristics of divine love, in Dubarle's view, while van den Oudenrijn sees the divine love as the antitype of the typical sense in the revelation of Eph 5:23*ff*. In the United States

Roland E. Murphy has been most forthright in criticism of the allegorical, mystical, messianic, and Mariological treatments of the Canticle and outspoken in support of the literal sense so long renounced and denounced by Roman Catholic exegetes. In a review of Cardinal Bea's commentary, Murphy (1953) addressed himself to Bea's argument for the "interpretatio figurata (allegorica)," that there is one literal sense, the metaphorical, in which the Canticle as a whole treats only of the higher union of God and His people. Bea stressed that the Canticle is a parable rather than an allegory in which each detail has a higher meaning. Even the individual units within the poem, in Bea's view, have no significance independent of the general theme of mutual love. The characters in the poem are not simply Yahweh and Israel but also Christ and the Church, i.e., the Canticle is messianic. The ascetico-mystical and the Marian interpretations Bea judged to be more than mere accommodations: because of tradition and liturgy, these interpretations "pertain to the complete meaning intended by the Holy Spirit Himself" (Bea, 1953, 8). The "merely naturalistic" interpretation which construes the Canticle as a nuptial or love song depicting human love, was condemned by Bea on the basis of the Fifth Ecumenical Council's condemnation of the view of Theodore of Mopsuestia. Murphy, however, invited Catholic exegetes to look at the implications of the condemnation of Theodore which was aimed at his disdainful attitude toward the Canticle. According to Theodore, Solomon wrote the Song to please his Egyptian consort and justify his marriage. The Song, in Theodore's view, was neither to be contemned as though it were an exhortation to impurity, nor praised as if it were a prophecy relative to the Church. Murphy questioned, first, whether the condemnation of Theodore's view of the Canticle could be generalized into a condemnation of the interpretation of the Canticle as a poem dealing with merely human love. Secondly, Murphy raised the question whether the argument that the so-called naturalistic interpretation is contrary to the tradition of the Church is not on a par with the rejection of Solomonic authorship which could with equal ease be alleged as contrary to the tradition of the Church. Thirdly, Murphy averred,

> one cannot ascertain the precise historical reason why the Canticle was accepted into the canon, outside of the fact that it was ranked with the other writings as a book of God. But surely a poem of love (not to be called "profane") which exalts pure love between husband and wife, is not below the dignity of divine inspiration. There seems to be no reason why a Catholic cannot hold the Canticle is such a poem. Nor does the term "naturalistic" do justice to such a view which recognizes a sacred feature in human life, instituted and blessed by God.

Of particular interest is Murphy's rejoinder to Bea's argument that 5:2, relating a night visit by the lover, cannot be a "factum naturale," but must have a deeper meaning. Certain things described in the text were judged by Bea to be so improbable in the daily life of Orientals that this is of itself a sufficient sign that the author did not intend to describe love between two human beings. The incredible features for Bea were that the girl wanders alone at night searching for her lover (3:2, 5:6), that she wants to bring him to her mother's house (3:4), that she seeks him in the fields (1:7). Murphy questioned whether "these specific points indicate that the inspired writer was describing a higher and greater reality than merely human love." Bea's reasons Murphy found unconvincing.

If there is a departure from the usual conduct of an Oriental woman, could not the author have allowed this to indicate the intensity of her love, which impelled her to go beyond the conventions of her sex? . . . Perhaps the point need not be raised at all since the canons we establish for Oriental women are necessarily colored by the effect of Islam in the Orient; it is quite conceivable, even if unprovable, that conditions were different in the land of Deborah, Hulda, and Ruth (who did go out at night!) (p. 504).

In a paper read at a General Meeting of the Catholic Biblical Association in 1953 Father Murphy asserted that

it is a mistake to state, as some Catholic exegetes do, that the work would never have entered the canon had it been a poem about merely human love. Human love is certainly worthy of divine inspiration since it is of divine creation (p. 11).

In a review of "The Canticle of Canticles in the Confraternity Version" (1955), Murphy affirmed that

In the literal sense the poem describes human love. Accordingly, the divine purpose in inspiring such a work would be to inculcate that the love He has created in mankind is a sacred thing, and fidelity its prime characteristic. There is a great deal to be said in favor of this interpretation. There can be no objection against it from the point of view of inspiration; such a topic is surely worthy of divine authorship because "male and female He created them." Indeed, one could point to various passages in the Bible which exemplify this theme (e.g. Prov 5 and 6). Moreover, this seems to be the more obvious meaning of the poem and is, therefore, in line with the directive of Leo XIII that one should not depart from the obvious sense except for a reason of necessity (p. 98).

A French Protestant View: Sacred and Sexual

An interesting interpretation of the Canticle as dealing with human love has been presented by Daniel Lys, Professor of the Free Faculty of Protestant Theology at Montpellier, in a commentary with the striking title *Le plus beau chant de la création* (1968).

The two opposing theses which confront each other with respect to the interpretation of the Canticle are mutually unacceptable to Lys. In the first thesis the original sense of the Canticle is held to be sexual and profane and the allegorical interpretation was developed to sacralize it. Since it is unlikely that a purely profane song could have become holy, the allegorists try to prove that the Canticle is already an allegory in the intention of the author and that this is visible in the text. In the second thesis the original sense of the Canticle is seen as allegorical and profane and it is the forgetting of this sense which led to the conserving of only a sexual and profane sense for the Canticle. To this Lys objected that, if the allegorical sense is original, it is not likely that it could have been forgotten to the point of being sung in the banquet halls to the displeasure of Aqiba. Against this sort of alleged accidental character of the Canticle, Lys proposed to take the Canticle for what it says and to assume that the author was conscious of what he was doing in writing it. Of all the amorous literature which must have flourished among the Israelites, as among all people, the Canticle is the only text chosen for canonization, and for what reason, Lys asked, if not because the natural sense of the text has theological import? The literal sense of the Canticle, according to Lys, is not necessarily obscene and there is no need to moralize or allegorize it. Lys opposes the naturalist explication which makes the canonical character of the Canticle accidental and ignores the grounds for other theses, but he favors the naturalist explication on condition that it show the purpose of the Canticle fairly with respect to the elements on which other theses are based. As a working hypothesis, in opposition to the unacceptable theses mentioned, Lys would say that the original (and peculiar) sense of the Canticle is *sexual* and *sacred:* the fact that the second element of the definition is not understood leads to seeing only a profane sexual song; inversely if the first element is not understood, one falls into allegory. These two elements can only be understood together. As to the theological import of the love song, the liturgical hypothesis sees the love as sexual and sacred, but only when the hierogamy transposes it to the divine plane and thus forces an allegorical interpretation of its sexual character.

For the pagans the union of the god and goddess, represented by the sacred marriage of the king and priestess, had as its purpose the magical fertilization of the earth and the renewal of the seasonal cycle. Thus love is *utilitarian.* In Israel this notion underwent a double demythicization. The divine marriage gave way to a new type of conjugal relation: the marriage between God and his people, in which salvation comes not from an agrarian rite of sacred marriage but from the intervention of YHWH in the history of his people and of the world, for the purpose of making history and not to fecundate the earth. For the pagans it was necessary that the archetype be copied in order that human life be authentic. But for Israel it was not a matter of escaping history through the mythical cycle, but of living in history where God intervenes. If the Canticle describes human love on the divine model, it is not a question of copying a primordial archetype, but to experience in sex the relationship of covenant or marriage (alliance). Human love is not a religious system to mount up to God, to cease to be human and become divine, to act upon God in the fertilization of the Earth. At a stroke sex and eros are liberated from this religious care and role: in this the second demythicization consists; the sexual relation between man and woman has no longer the import of sacred marriage for the purpose of fertility, and from this fact it rediscovers its true role in creation. Thus if the demythicization by the prophets leads us to speak of the creature who has to live in history, then the Canticle is none other than a commentary on Genesis 2. One understands then why this human love song has taken up the vocabulary of sacred marriage. It is not simply a matter of accidental influence of ambient language, . . . but it is a question of conscious decision to transform the sense to show the true meaning of love, that it is not a simple instrument in a magical operation with a view to the fecundation of the universe (nor even simply with a view of procreation of descendants, differing, it seems, with the rest of the Old Testament) but love, according to Lys, has its end in itself (*fin en soi*). This is the revelation which is also a veritable revolution.

To accomplish this demythicization, the author of Canticles used the language of "alliance." The best way to demythicize pagan eros, according to Lys, is to describe human love not only in the fashion of profane Egyptian songs but also on the model of the love of God for his people, since that "alliance" itself constitutes the fundamental demythicization of the hierogamy. This love of God is not subordinate to any result but has its end in itself (it is free; and this is why God loves in spite of everything). It is not a matter of surpassing human love to describe divine love, nor of sublimating eros in agape, nor of limiting eros by agape, but rather, according to Lys, of living eros fully in the fashion which God teaches us to love, in a free and reciprocal face-to-face relation. This is what Paul said to the Ephesians (Eph 5:25)—Husbands, love your wives, as Christ loved the church and gave himself up for her—which the allegorists unconsciously take in the opposite sense, seeing in the Canticle a description of mystical love in the language of sexuality (all the Bible rejects sexuality in God!). It is a matter of loving one's wife as Christ loved the Church, and this is just what Hosea experienced. It is not a matter of description of God's love for Israel on the model of Hosea's love for Gomer, but for the sake of what God wished to make of Israel he led Hosea into his relation with Gomer, to love her not according to the juridical code (with right of divorce) but according to God's love. Thus love finds its own value. This is not to say that every sexual union is sacred as such: it is so in the measure where, as in the Canticle, it demythicizes pagan love and reflects "Alliance." "C'est l'Alliance qui fond l'alliance," according to Lys (and not the inverse).

If his hypothesis is correct, it ought, Lys claims, to be able to account for the diverse arguments used by the different theses and to explain the particularities and difficulties of the text. This essential intention does not prevent the author from borrowing from folklore, from the learned poetry of Egypt, from the documents of Israel's past, and at the same time from sacred marriage hymns and the vocabulary of marriage: this could explain a certain diversity without excluding unity, in Lys' view. This also is alleged to explain the geographic symbolism as describing the lovers not as allusions to events of history but as recalling the concrete way God loves his people. This explains the absence of the divine name, the presence of which would have been equivocal of the fact of his role in pagan love now demythicized. Love is never personified nor divinized in the Old Testament. This also explains the absence of allusion to procreation, since love has its end in itself, so that sexuality should no more be reduced to its function of reproduction than to that of excitation, since the child is not the end of marriage but the result showing the accomplishment of the unity of the couple. Conjugal love, according to Lys, is not the cause but the consequence of the Liberation; it is no longer subordinated to an end pursued (such as the fecundation of the earth and the salvation thus realized) so that the value of the union would be subordinated to this end and could make place for a better relation with another partner; the one who chose and loves Israel in spite of everything, at the same time that he has liberated eros from its utilitarianism, has reclothed eros with gratuity and liberty. It is thus, according to Lys, that the love of man for his neighbor and above all for his mate is none other than the love by which man responds to God's love: it is not a matter of comprehending that the Canticle, a sexual poem, testifies of the divine love because it is not a matter of a fictitious narrative speaking of something else or of two senses of which the one goes back typologically to the other. There is in the Canticle only one sense, according to Lys, and it is in the reality of this human love that the reality of the divine love is shown (cf. in this sense John 13:35, Matt 22:37–40, uniting Deut 6:5 and Lev 19:18; and the double reading of the variants of I John 4:19).

Lys defends his explication against the charge that it is an allegory in reverse, which would consist of taking a text relating to the love of God for Israel (e.g. the covenant [alliance] of Sinai) and saying that it is only an image of the love of a boy for a girl. The love of God for his people is indeed real, a result of the history of salvation, and it is this which serves as the model here as in Hosea 1–3 and Esther 5. Lys denies making a typology in reverse, since there are not two senses, but a single one, human love in the language of divine love. It is necessary, Lys felt, to note that when divine love is described on the model of human love, as in Ezek 23, the author utilizes the sociological reality as it is, and this means in fact bigamy! (cf. also Jer 3:1–10), while in the Canticle on the contrary the divine love models human love in monogamy. (The text cited by Lys in support of this affirmation of monogamy is 6:8–9 which speaks of the unique perfection of the lady in relation to a retinue of queens, concubines, and maidens, hardly an assertion of monogamy!) This alleged monogamy is, Lys conceded, extraordinary in a society in which polygamy was usual and posed no problem. Thus, according to Lys, if the Canticle hymns the sexual relation, it is not toward a greater lust but because of a greater love, in order that it be understood and lived as such in the authentic sense in which God the Creator gave it. Thus it is not a matter of opposing the literal sense and the spiritual sense, but of affirming the spiritual sense. This explication Lys endeavored to set in evidence in the exegesis of his commentary. Thus, says Lys, is the word of L.-F. Céline true: "L'amour, c'est l'infini mis à la portée des caniches" (*Voyage au bout de la nuit,* 1932, 12–13). One may not even say that the Canticle pretends to have a didactic character (it draws no moral, it does not speak of marriage, it is content to praise physical beauty and sexual attraction): it is content—but this is essential—to take love seriously. In this measure, according to Lys, the Canticle could and ought to be classed among the Wisdom writings.

The Song of Songs and Women's Liberation

Leaders of the contemporary Women's Liberation Movement appear to have overlooked C. D. Ginsburg's interpretation (1857) of the Song of Songs as a melodramatic manifesto for the emancipation of women. (See above, pp. 137–141.) Quite understandably, the modern Movement has had little use for the Bible except as a provocation for protest, to be indicted as the primary document of patriarchalism. The androcentric Creation myth of Genesis 2–3 has been understood as laying the blame for the human predicament on the female of the species and this attitude has persisted through the centuries. The Apostle Paul paid his respects to the sisters thus: "Let a woman learn in silence and in total submission. I let no woman teach or usurp authority over a man. She is to be quiet, because Adam was made first, then Eve. Adam was not deceived; rather it was the woman who was deceived and fell into sin. They, however, will be saved by childbearing, if they continue in faith, love, and sanctity, with modesty" (I Tim 2:11–15). Attempts to acquit Holy Writ of male chauvinism by appealing to the stories of heroines like Deborah or the tender tales of Ruth, or Mary and Martha, serve only to reinforce the general indictment. The God of the Fathers has scant appeal to the sisterhood.

It has recently been argued by a partisan of both the biblical faith and of Women's Liberation (Phyllis Trible, 1973) that there is neither war nor neutrality between the two movements and that it is possible to depatriarchalize the biblical faith. Professor Trible does not deny that the Bible comes from a male dominated society and that biblical religion is patriarchal, yet she asserts that the more she participates in "the Movement," the more she discovers freedom through the appropriation of biblical symbols. Thus she is able to

> affirm that the intentionality of biblical faith, as distinguished from a general description of biblical religion, is neither to create nor to perpetuate patriarchy but rather to function as salvation for both men and women. The Women's Movement errs when it dismisses the Bible as inconsequential or condemns it as enslaving. In

rejecting Scripture women ironically accept male chauvinist interpretations and thereby capitulate to the very view they are protesting. But there is another way: to reread (not rewrite) the Bible without the blinders of Israelite men or of Paul, Barth, Bonhoeffer, and a host of others. The hermeneutical challenge is to translate biblical faith without sexism (p. 31).

In the interest of disavowing sexism in translation of the biblical faith, Trible stresses both the asexual and effeminate traits of the biblical deity. The gynomorphic imagery, activity, and speech applied to Yahweh, especially by Second Isaiah, make him midwife, seamstress, housekeeper, nurse, and mother. Accordingly, Trible concludes that Yahweh is neither male nor female.

Consequently, modern assertions that God is masculine, even when they are qualified, are misleading and detrimental, if not altogether inaccurate. Cultural and grammatical limitations (the use of masculine pronouns for God) need not limit theological understanding. As Creator and Lord, Yahweh embraces and transcends both sexes. To translate for our immediate concern: the nature of the God of Israel defies sexism (p. 34).

Trible finds encouragement for Women's Liberation in the Exodus theme, but she corrects a tendentious distortion of the tale by an overweening liberatrix. "So compelling is this theme of freedom from oppression that our enthusiasm may become unfaithfulness to it." The Exodus theme, Trible noted (p. 34n25) is not a paradigm for "leaving home" and developing a community without models, as alleged (by Mary Daly, March 1972, 172*f*). The Exodus, Trible points out, is rather a return home and its models are drawn from the patriarchal traditions. Nevertheless the story does teach that God hates slavery and acts through human agents for liberation. Women especially nurtured the Exodus revolution. The Hebrew midwives disobeyed Pharaoh, and his own daughter thwarted him and adopted a Hebrew child. Women alone in the Exodus story were first to defy the oppressor and took the initiative that led to deliverance. Thus, if Pharaoh had realized the power of these women, he might have reversed his decree and had the females killed rather than the males. A patriarchal religion which creates and preserves such feminist traditions contains resources for overcoming patriarchy, according to Trible.

A third theme negating sexism Trible found in the concept of corporate personality by which all are embraced in the fluidity of transmission from the one to the many and vice versa. Even though Israel did not apply this principle specifically to women, Trible regards it as a profound insight to be appropriated by the Women's Liberation Movement in view of the solidarity of the sexes.

A brief investigation of the Yahwist Creation story in Genesis 2–3 in the interest of depatriarchialization leads Trible to some very interesting results at odds with the traditional interpretation which approaches the story with the presupposition that it affirms male dominance and female subordination. Only the main points of her argument may be noted here.

The ambiguity of the term *'āḏām* in Genesis 2–3 is of crucial import. On the one hand it designates the first man as male and on the other it is a generic term for humankind, including both male and female. In commanding *'āḏām* not to eat of the tree of the knowledge of good and evil, God spoke to both the man and the woman, Gen 2:16–17. Before the differentiation of the sexes, Gen 2:21–23, *'āḏām* is basically androgynous, one creature incorporating both sexes. Trible rebuts the common view that female subordination is implicit in the order of events in the two Creation stories, that in contrast to the Priestly account in which *'āḏām* is created male and female, the woman in the Yahwist account was an afterthought, a second, subordinate, inferior sex. The reverse, however, is the case, according to Trible. The Yahwist account moves to a climax in the creation of woman. The woman as man's helper is his counterpart. "God is the helper superior to man; the animals are helpers inferior to man; woman is the helper equal to man" (p. 36). The creation of man from dust and woman from man's rib is no ground for male superiority, since both required divine processing to be made human.

To call woman "Adam's rib" is to misread the text which states carefully and clearly that the extracted bone required divine labor to become female, a datum scarcely designed to bolster the male ego (p. 37).

As for the charge that the woman bears the primary blame for the fall, Trible denies any basis for this judgment in the narrative itself.

If there be moral frailty in one, it is moral frailty in two. Further, they are equal in responsibility and in judgment, in shame and in guilt, in redemption and in grace. What the narrative says about the nature of the woman it also says about the nature of the man (p. 40).

Comparison and contrast of the roles of the man and the woman in the temptation and fall do not enhance the male image. The woman acts independently, without seeking her husband's advice or consent. The man, by contrast, is passive and receptive.

His one act is belly-oriented, and it is an act of acquiescence, not of initiative. The man is not dominant; he is not aggressive; he is not a decision-maker. . . . He follows his wife without question or comment, thereby denying his own individuality. If the woman be intelligent, sensitive, and ingenious, the man is passive, brutish, and inept. These character portrayals are truly extraordinary in a culture dominated by man. I stress their contrast not to promote female chauvinism but to undercut patriarchal interpretations alien to the text (p. 40).

The contrast between the woman and the man fades after the fall. Both are judged for their shared disobedience, but the judgments describe rather than prescribe. The statement that the man will dominate the woman is not a license for male supremacy, but rather a condemnation of the pattern which is a perversion of the creation. Sin now vitiates all relationships and the subordination of the female to the male signifies the shared sin. "Whereas in creation man and woman know harmony and equality, in sin they know alienation and discord. Grace makes possible a new beginning" (p. 41).

Trible made a fresh approach to the Yahwist Creation story in the interest of undermining the traditional male chauvinist interpretation and she regarded the effort as fruitful. As a result of her rereading, the patriarchal patterns pale and the Yahwist is set in opposition to his male dominated culture. The vision of a trans-sexual God shapes the understanding of human sexuality.

On this issue Trible found company for the Yahwist in the male and female who celebrate the joys of erotic love in the Song of Songs. The Paradise of Genesis 2 which was lost in Genesis 3 is seen as regained and even improved in the Song of Songs. The sensuality of Eden is broadened and deepened in the Song. In Eden the woman presumably worked as well as the man, but in the Song she definitely works, keeping a vineyard and pasturing flocks, 1:6,8. There is a strong matriarchal coloring in the Song. The lovers speak seven times of mother, but father is totally ignored. There is mutuality of the sexes, without male dominance, female subordination, or stereotyping of either sex. Unlike the first woman, the lady of the Canticle is not a wife and her love does not entail procreation. She actively seeks the man, desires him on her bed, rises and searches for him in the streets and squares, openly without secrecy or shame. When she finds her lover, she grabs and holds him. The theme of alternating initiative of the lovers runs throughout the Song. Whereas in the story of loss of Paradise, the divine judgment decreed the woman's desire for her husband and subjugation to him, this in the context of sin and perversion, the Song of Songs reverses the male-female relationship.

> Here desire is joy, not judgment. Moreover, the possessive reference has switched from the wife's desire for her husband to the desire of the male lover for the female. Has one mark of sin in Eden been overcome here in another garden with the recovery of mutuality in love? Male dominance is totally alien to Canticles. Can it be that grace is present? (p. 46).

The lovers of the Canticle, in Trible's understanding, are not the primeval couple living before the advent of disobedience, nor are they an eschatological couple, as Karl Barth supposed. They are seen as living in the "terror of history," but their love is unterrified. Though the Song hints at threats —of winter, of foxes that spoil the vineyards, of the anger of brothers, jealousy, anxiety, abuse at the hands of watchmen—the discordant notes blend into the total harmony of love. As death did not swallow the primeval couple, neither does it overwhelm the historical couple. "For love is strong as death" (8:6).

Thus the Song of Songs is seen as a sort of midrash on Genesis 2–3, by variations and reversals creatively actualizing the major motifs and themes of the primeval myth.

Female and male are born to mutuality and love. They are naked without shame; they are equal without duplication. They live in gardens where nature joins in celebrating their oneness. Animals remind these couples of their shared superiority in creation as well as their affinity and responsibility for lesser creatures. Fruits pleasing to the eye and to the tongue are theirs to enjoy. Living waters replenish their gardens. Both couples are involved in naming; both couples work. If the first pair pursue the traditional occupations for women and men, the second eschews stereotyping. Neither couple fits the rhetoric of a male dominated culture. As equals they confront life and death. But the first couple lose their oneness through disobedience. Consequently, the woman's desire becomes the man's dominion. The second couple affirm their oneness through eroticism. Consequently, the man's desire becomes the woman's delight. Whatever else it may be, Canticles is a commentary on Genesis 2–3. Paradise Lost is Paradise Regained (p. 47).

Yet the midrash and commentary is admittedly incomplete.

Even though Song of Songs is the poetry of history, it speaks not at all of sin and disobedience. Life knows no prohibitions. And most strikingly, no Deity acts in that history. God is not explicitly acknowledged as either present or absent (though eroticism itself may be an act of worship in the context of grace). Some may conclude that these omissions make the setting of Canticles a more desirable paradise than Eden. But the silences portend the limits. If we cannot return to the primeval garden (Gen 3:23–24), we cannot live solely in the garden of eroticism. Juxtaposing the two passages, we can appropriate them both for our present concern (p. 47).

Trible concluded that, contrary to Kate Millet's *Sexual Politics,* the biblical God is not on the side of patriarchy and the myth of the Fall does not "blame all this world's ills on the female." Rather the myth negates patriarchy and does not legitimate the oppression of women. It explores the meaning of human existence for male and female, revealing the goodness and frailty of both, their intended equality under God and with one another, solidarity in sin and suffering, and common need of redemption. The symbols of the Yahwist myth illuminate a present issue, and at the same time exercise a sobering check on it. Neither male nor female chauvinism is warranted and both are perversions of creation. The Song of Songs, however, counterbalances the "undertone of melancholy" of the Yahwist myth and shows man and woman in mutual harmony.

Love is the meaning of their life, and this love excludes oppression and exploitation. It knows the goodness of sex and hence it knows not sexism. Sexual love expands existence beyond the stereotypes of society. It draws unto itself the public and the private, the historical and the natural. It transforms all life even as life enhances it. Grace returns to the female and male (p. 48).

Placing the Yahwist myth of Genesis 2–3 alongside the Song of Songs, the trans-sexual nature of Yahweh, the female role in the Exodus, and the concept of corporate personality, Trible believes to have demonstrated a depatriarchalizing principle at work in the Hebrew Bible. Depatriarchalizing, she maintains, is not an operation which the exegete performs on the text, but a hermeneutic operating within Scripture itself, to be exposed rather than imposed. The history of tradition and interpretation shows that the meaning and function of biblical materials is fluid and that diverse traditions appear, disappear, and reappear. The task of recovering the depatriarchalizing principle in Scripture has only begun, according to Trible.

> For our day we need to perceive the depatriarchalizing principle, to recover it in those texts and themes where it is present, and to accent it in our translations. Therein we shall be explorers who embrace both old and new in the pilgrimage of faith (p. 48).

Whether Trible's effort at depatriarchalizing the Hebrew Scriptures will find favor with either conservative biblical scholars or anti-biblicists in the Women's Liberation Movement, remains to be seen. With regard to the Song of Songs she is certainly correct in recognizing the equal and even dominant role of the female and the absence of male chauvinism or patriarchalism.

Love and Death

It has been recognized by many commentators that the setting of Love and Passion in opposition to the power of Death and Hell in 8:6c,d is the climax of the Canticle and the burden of its message: that Love is the only power that can cope with Death. Throughout the Song the joys of physical love are asserted, but this singular mention of Death and his domain, Sheol, suggests that this fear may be the covert concern of the Canticle, the response to inexorable human fate with the assertion of Love as the only power that frustrates the complete victory of Death. The sacred marriage was a celebration and affirmation of this vital force. The inevitable circumstance in which Life and Love come into stark confrontation with Death is in mortuary observances, not only in the wake and burial but in the ongoing concern to commune with the departed and provide for their needs in the infernal realm with offerings of food and drink.

The sacral meal with ritual drinking of intoxicating beverage, music, song, dance, and sexual license was a feature of religious praxis in the Near East from early times. Glyptic art of ancient Mesopotamia presents vivid scenes of such festivities. Seals from the Royal Cemetery at Ur depict banquet scenes with celebrants imbibing from large jars through drinking tubes while a bed with cross bands is presented by an attendant. The cross bands, or saltire, are the symbol and attribute of the great goddess of love and war (cf. M. Pope, 1970). The saltire of the love goddess adorning the couch (perhaps also serving to brace it) suggests the use to which it will shortly be put and this is graphically confirmed in other scenes which show the bed occupied by a copulating couple. Beneath the love couch is sometimes depicted the scorpion, symbol of the goddess Išḫara, or the dog related to the goddess Gula.

Both these goddesses, Išḫara and Gula, are, according to H. Frankfort (1955, 38), "aspects of that great goddess of fertility whose union with a male god, consummated at the New Year's festival, insured the prosperity of the community; for the fertility of nature depended upon this act." The dog under the love couch depicted on a Mesopotamian seal of the Early Dynastic III period (ca. 2500 B.C.), see Figure *1,* recalls the canine beneath the couch which is common on Hellenistic funerary sculptures but which has not been plausibly explained. A recently published Ugaritic text, however, when correlated with observations by a couple of Fathers of the Church concerning accusations against the early Christians, throws light on the persistent canine at the connubium and the funeral feast. The Ugaritic text UG 5.1) describes a banquet given by El, the father of the gods, in which a dog has an important but unspecified role. The highlights of the affair are given here in translation without notes (for details cf. M. Pope, 1972).

El offered game in his house,
Venison in the midst of his palace.
He invited the gods to mess.
The gods ate and drank,
Drank wine till sated,
Must till inebriated.
. . . .
. . . .
'Astarte and Anat arrived
'Astarte prepared a *brisket* for him,
And Anat a shoulder.
The Porter of El's house chided them:
"Lo, for the dog prepare a *brisket*.
For the cur prepare a shoulder."
El his father he chided.
El sat (in) (his pl)ace,
El sat in his *mrzḥ*.
He drank wine till sated,
Must till inebriated.
. . . .
. . . .
An apparition accosted him,
With horns and a tail.
He floundered in his excrement and
urine.
El collapsed, El like those who
descend into Earth.
Anat and 'Astarte went roaming.

There is a gap of a couple of lines on the obverse of the tablet and the text continues for several lines on the reverse, with mention of the return of the goddesses and the administration of various medicines, including juice of green olives, to relieve the deity's crapulence.

The mention of special pieces of meat for the dog, the same cuts prepared by the goddesses for their father, recalls the allegations against the early Christians regarding the role of the dog in their festal meals. Tertullian in chs. 7 and 8 of his *Apology* (ca. 197) in rebutting the charges that Christians in their reprobate feasts murdered and ate infants and climaxed the celebration with an incestuous sexual orgy, mentions dogs as "the pimps of darkness" procuring license for these impious lusts by putting out the lights in a rather bizarre fashion. Tertullian ridiculed the charges simply by recounting the alleged proceedings:

Yet, I suppose, it is customary for those who wish to be initiated to approach first the father of the sacred rites to arrange what must be prepared. . . . Now, you need a baby, still tender, one who does not know what death means, and who will

Love, death, and dogs

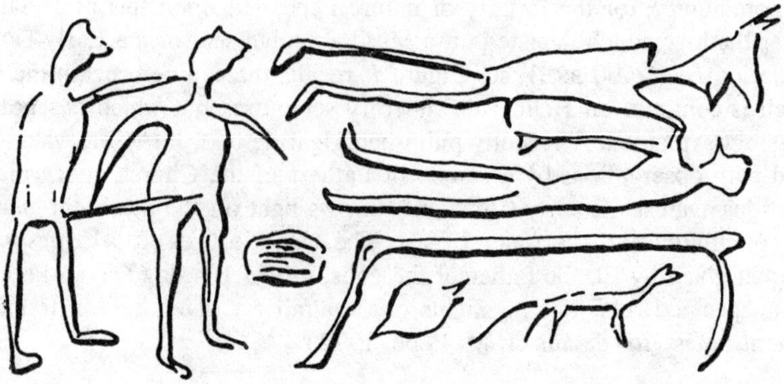

1. Early Mesopotamian "sacred marriage" scene with dog under the couch

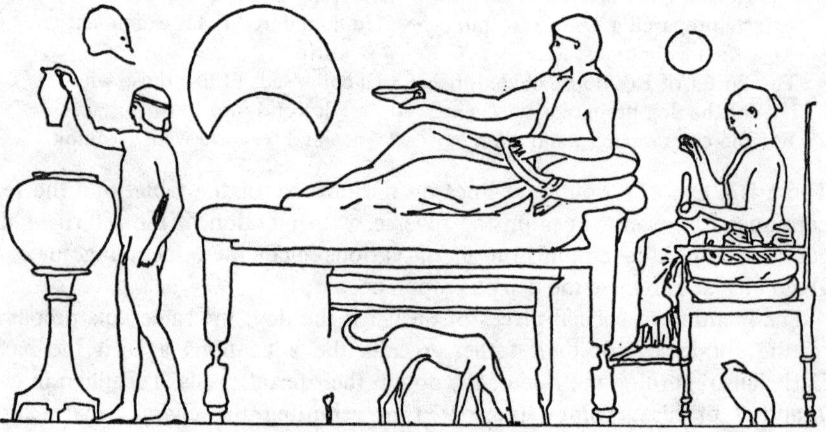

2. Anatolian tomb relief

smile under your knife. You need bread, too, with which to gather up his juicy blood; besides that, candlesticks, lamps, some dogs and bits of meat which will draw them on to overturn the lamps. Most important of all, you must come with your mother and sister.

These rites were alleged to have been performed for the purpose of gaining eternal life, to which charge Tertullian retorted:

For the time being, believe it! On this point I have a question to ask: If you believed it, would you consider the acquisition of eternal life worth attaining with such a (troubled) conscience? Come, bury your sword in this baby, enemy though he be of no one, guilty of no crime, everybody's son; or, if that is the other fellow's job, stand here beside this (bit of) humanity, dying before he has lived; wait for the young soul to take flight; receive his fresh blood; saturate your bread with it; partake freely! Meanwhile, as you recline at table, note the place where your mother is, and your sister; note it carefully, so that, when the dogs cause the darkness to fall, you may make no mistake—for you will be guilty of a crime unless you commit incest. (The E. J. Daly translation, 1950, 25–29.)

Marcus Minucius Felix (fl. 200–240) tells us a bit more about these alleged initiation rites for Christian novices:

An infant covered with a dough crust to deceive the unsuspecting is placed beside the person to be initiated into the sacred rites. This infant is killed at the hands of the novice by wounds inflicted unintentionally and hidden from his eyes, since he has been urged on as if to harmless blows on the surface of the dough. The infant's blood—oh, horrible—they sip up eagerly; its limbs they tear to pieces, trying to outdo each other; by this victim they are leagued together; by being privy to this crime they pledge themselves to mutual silence. These sacred rites are more shocking than any sacrilege.

Minucius Felix continues:

On the appointed day, they assemble for their banquets with all their children, sisters, and mothers—people of both sexes and every age. After many sumptuous dishes, when the company at the table has grown warm and the passion of incestuous lust has been fired by drunkenness, a dog which has been tied to a lampstand is tempted by throwing a morsel beyond length of the leash by which it is bound. It makes a dash, and jumps for the catch. Thus, when the witnessing light has been overturned and extinguished, in the ensuing darkness which favors shamelessness, they unite in whatever revolting lustful embraces the hazard of chance will permit. Thus, they are all equally guilty of incest, if not indeed, yet by privity, since whatever can happen in the actions of individuals is sought for by the general desire of all. (*Octavius,* the Rudolph Arbesmann translation, 1950, 337–338.)

Dogs figure in cultic symbolism and funerary rites of many cultures and there is no warrant to consider the topic in detail here since dogs play no part in the Song of Songs. The practice of putting pieces of meat on or around a corpse, as among the Parsees (cf. J. Modi, 1922, 56–58) is easily understood as intended to distract the dogs from attacking the corpse. There is a rabbinic story (Midrash Rabbah Qohelet 5:10) about the death of King David and the cutting of an animal's carcass to keep the hungry dogs from attacking the corpse. Other references to food for dogs at funerals and weddings occur in rabbinic literature (cf. TB Moed Qatan 28b, Erubin 81a, Midrash Rabbah on Lev 28:6). An Anatolian funerary relief from Thasos, dating to the fifth century B.C., shows a dog under the banquet couch with muzzle to the ground, as if eating (Figure *2;* cf. A. Kurgal, 1961, 272*f* and fig. 240), while a stela from Piraeus, also of the fifth century B.C., shows the dog reclining under the banquet couch and gnawing at a hefty hunk of meat (Figure *3;* cf. E. R. Goodenough, 1953–68, XI, fig. 224). The meat in this instance could be explained as a sop. An early Corinthian crater, however, shows leashed dogs underneath the couches of the celebrants which suggests that the details related by Tertullian and Minucius Felix as to the function of the dogs as "the pimps of darkness" in sacral sexual orgies, for all its similarities to a Rube Goldberg mechanism, may have been an ancient artifice (Figure *4;* cf. H. Payne, 1931, pl. 27 and p. 302, no. 780).

It is of interest to observe that the earliest representation of the dog under the couch, ca. 2500 B.C., is in a scene with two couples copulating in different positions and suggestive at least of the sort of group activity of which the later Christians were accused. Scenes of group sex involving three or more participants are not uncommon in the glyptic art of ancient Mesopotamia. The dog continued on funeral reliefs down to late antiquity, as on the urn of Iulia Eleutheris in the Thermen Museum in Rome showing mourners engaged in *conclamtio mortis* while beneath the bier reposes the persistent canine (cf. A. C. Rush, 1941, pl. III and pp. 108*f*).

The dog played an important role in the funerary cults at Palmyra and Hatra (cf. Milik, 1972, 164–168). At Hatra there appears to have been a sanctuary dedicated to the infernal deity Nergol as a dog (*nrgwl klb'*) (p. 166).

The term *mrzḥ* applied in the Ugaritic text to the place where El imbibed to the point of delirium, diarrhea, and enuresis, and finally to a state resembling death, is of particular interest and importance for the understanding of the nature and purpose of the bacchanalian banquet. This word occurs twice in the Old Testament, Amos 6:7 and Jer 16:5, and the *RSV* renderings "revelry" in the first instance and "mourning" in the second, reflect the long standing puzzlement as to the precise meaning of the term. In Amos 6:4–7 the dissolute luxury of the proceedings is explicit:

They lie on ivory beds,
Sprawled on their couches,
Eating rams from the flock,
Bullocks from the stall.
They chant to the tune of the lyre,
Like David they improvise song.
They drink wine from bowls,
Choicest oils they smear,
But are not sickened at Joseph's ruin.
Therefore they will go at the head of
the exiles,
And the sprawlers' banquet cease.

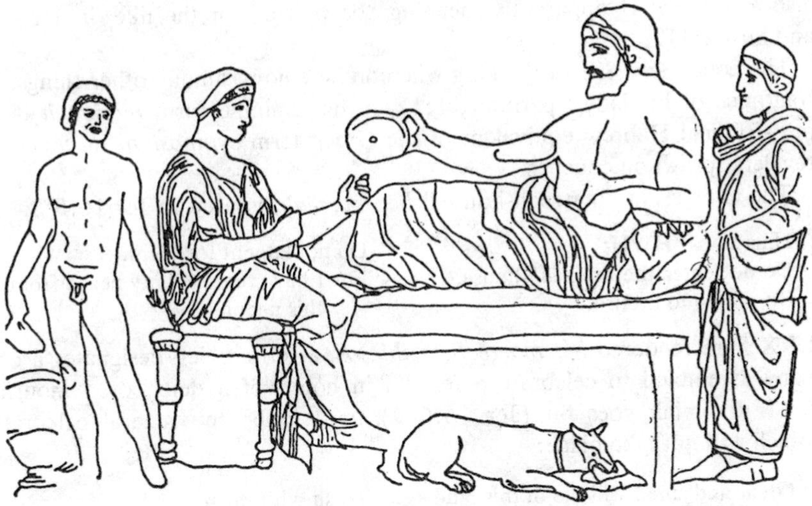

3. Funerary relief from Piraeus

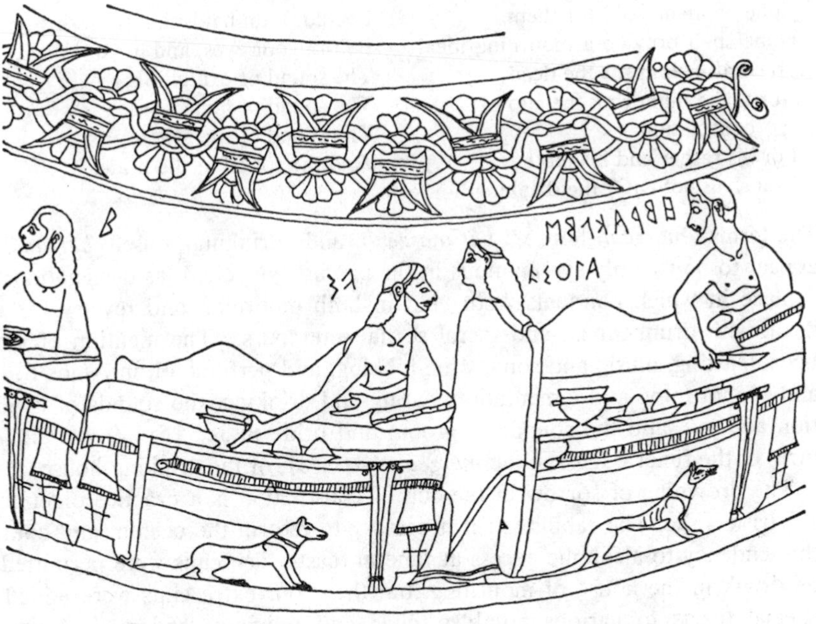

4. Corinthian crater (mixing bowl) showing leashed dogs under banquet couches.

The "sprawlers' banquet," *marzēaḥ sĕrûḥîm,* is ambiguous. The root *srḥ* I is applied to an overhanging curtain in Exod 26:12 and to a spreading vine in Ezek 17:6, and possibly to a flowing headdress in Ezek 23:15. There is also a root *srḥ* II apparently meaning "be putrid," or the like, in Jer 49:7 and Sir 42:11.

The couch (*mēsiḇ*) of the king whereon he enjoys, among other things, the fragrance of his lady's perfume, 1:12, in its feminine form *mĕsibbah* is the post-Biblical Hebrew equivalent of the Greek term *symposion,* in which the revelers sprawl on couches.

The expression "marzēaḥ-house," *bêṯ marzēaḥ,* is used in Jer 16:5:

Thus says YHWH:
Do not enter the *marzēaḥ*-house,
Do not go to mourn,
Do not lament for them.
For I have removed my peace from
    this people.

LXX here rendered *bêṯ marzēaḥ* as *thiasos,* a term which designates a company assembled to celebrate a festival in honor of a deity, or a mourning feast. Jeremiah goes on (Jer 16:6–9) to describe the funeral celebration which will not take place:

Great and small will die in this land
And they will not be buried.
None shall mourn or lament;
None shall gash himself,
None be made bald for them.
None shall provide a mourning meal
To comfort him for the dead,
Nor make him drink the cup of
    consolation
For his father and his mother.
You shall not enter the drinking-house
To sit with them,
To eat and to drink.
For thus says YHWH of Hosts,
The God of Israel:
Behold, I am banishing from this place
Before your eyes, and in your days,
The sound of exultation,
The sound of joy,
The sound of the groom,
And the sound of the bride.

The terms "*marzēaḥ*-house," *bêṯ marzēaḥ,* and "drinking-house," *beṯ mišteh,* appear to be roughly synonymous in the passage just cited, as designations of a place in which banquets were held in both mourning and revelry for the dead, with drunkenness and sacral sexual intercourse. The mention of ivory beds, feasting, music and song, wine bibbing, and perfume oil in Amos 6:4–7 and of mourning and lamentation, eating and drinking, the sounds of exultation and joy, and the sounds of groom and bride in Jer 16:6–9 are all features of the funeral feast in the *marzēaḥ* (-house), or the drinking-house.

The drowning of sorrow in the cup of consolation is a practice older than the Irish wake. The rabbis felt it necessary to reform the custom and control the tendency to alcoholic excess at funeral feasts. Ten cups were permitted to be drunk in the house of mourning, but then four extra cups were added as special toasts to various notables, civic and religious leaders, and one in honor of Rabban Gamaliel, so that some became intoxicated and the limit of ten cups was restored (cf. TB Ketubot 8b; Sotah 14a). At the festival of Purim, however, it was permissible to drink until one could not tell the difference between Haman and Mordecai (TB, Megillah 7b; Shulhan Aruk 695:2). The example of the father of the gods of Ugarit, reeling in drunken delirium, wallowing in excrement and urine, and collapsing as if dead, was on occasion emulated by the Israelites, to judge from the prophet's animadversion, Isa 28:7–9:

These, too, reel with wine,
With drink they stagger;
Priest and prophet stagger with drink,
Dazed with wine,
Reeling with drink.
They stagger in ———,
Totter in ————;
All the tables full of vomit,
Excrement without place.

The mention of tables full of vomit and excrement in the last couplet suggests that similar terms may have originally stood in lines f and g where MT has the bizarre readings *br'h,* vocalized as *bārô'eh,* "in the seer," and *pĕlîliyyāh,* "judicial decision," as the setting of their staggering. With very slight change of *br'h* one may restore *bḥr',* "in excrement." The word *ḥere'* was considered obscene and the less offensive term *ṣo'āh,* "excretion," was imposed in Isa 36:23=II Kings 18:27. It is harder to guess what term may have been changed to *pĕlîliyyāh,* but the context suggests the common connection and parallel of solid and liquid excreta, as in Isa 36:12 and Ugaritic *ḥr'* and *ṯnt,* "excrement" and "urine." Isaiah's allusion to priests and prophets reeling among tables strewn with vomit and excrement, and the appalling picture of the drunken father of the gods wallowing in his own filth recall the rabbinic derision of the coprophilia ascribed to the cult of Baal Peor whose worship was alleged to include ceremonial defecation (TB Abodah Zarah 44b). A Jew was forbidden to relieve himself before the idol, even with the intention of degrading it, since this was the alleged mode of worshiping Baal Peor (TB Sanhedrin 60b, Mishnah Sanhedrin vii 6). A story is told of a certain Jew who entered the shrine of Baal Peor, defecated and wiped himself on the idol's nose and the acolytes praised his devotion saying, "no man ever served this idol thus" (TB Sanhedrin 64a). It is difficult to know whether this story is based on direct knowledge of such worship or was suggested by one of the meanings of the verb *p'r* in Jewish Aramaic.

While the coprological aspects of the cult of Baal Peor were not especially attractive, there were other features which had potent appeal and to which the Israelites succumbed at the first encounter with the Moabites at Shittim, Num 25:1–2,6–8, and frequently thereafter. The "sacrifices" to which the Moabite women invited their Israelite cousins featured a contact sport which made it possible for Phinehas to skewer an Israelite man and a Moabite woman with a single thrust of the spear, Num 25:7–8. Now these festivities are explicitly identified as funeral feasts in Ps 106:28:

They yoked themselves to Baal Peor,
And ate the sacrifices of the dead.

These sacrifices of the dead characterized by sacral sexual intercourse are identified by the rabbis as *marzĕḥîm* in the Sifre (Numbers 131), the same term applied to the setting of El's potation and self-pollution. Midrashic comment further related the *marzēaḥ* to the Mayumas festival (cf. Midrash Leviticus Rabbah 5:3, Numbers Rabbah 10:3), a celebration which featured wife-swapping. Mayumas festivals were observed along the Mediterranean, especially in port cities like Alexandria, Gaza, Ashkelon and Antioch, with such licentiousness that the Roman rulers felt constrained to ban them. Rabbi Hanan apparently alluded to such rites in his comment that "it was done in the cities of the Sea what was not done in the generation of the Flood" (Midrash Genesis Rabbah 20:8). The equation of Marzēaḥ and Mayumas is also made in the mosaic map of the sixth-century church at Madeba which labels the Transjordanian area in which the Baal-Peor apostasy occurred as "*Betomarseas* (i.e. Beth Marzēaḥ) alias (*ho kai*) Maioumas." Several scholars have recently treated the term *marzēaḥ* in detail (cf. E. Y. Kutscher, 1965, 167–171; O. Eissfeldt, 1966, 167–171, and 1969; B. Porten, 1968), and only a brief summary with a few supplementary observations need be given for the present concern to understand the nature of the *marzēaḥ* and suggest a relationship to the Song of Songs.

Considerable information on the *marzēaḥ* comes to us from Palmyra in the form of dedicatory inscriptions and tessarae decorated with banquet scenes and bearing inscriptions mentioning the term *mrzḥ*. J. T. Milik has brought together the Semitic and Greek epigraphic materials dealing with these celebrations by gods and mortals with chapters on the vocabulary of the Palmyrene tessarae and inscriptions, and other data on the religious associations at Palmyra, Dura, Hatra, Syria, Phoenicia, and among the Nabateans. This work is a veritable treasure-trove of information on the funeral feasts, with data which may be correlated with the Ugaritic materials to provide new and provocative insights which may have relevance for the understanding of the Song of Songs. Some data from Milik's study will be briefly noticed in supplements to the commentary which had been completed before Milik's work appeared. There is much in Milik's study which will stimulate further research and discussion (J. T. Milik, 1972).

The members of the association were termed in Aramaic *bny mrzḥ'*, "children of the *mrzḥ*," and specific deities were sometimes designated, e.g., *bny mrzḥ nbw*, "members of the mrzḥ of Nabu." The most popular association at Palmyra was apparently associated with Bel (Baal), to judge from the numerous tessarae which mention the priests of Bel. Each *mrzḥ* had a chief, Phoenician *rb mrzḥ*, Aramaic *rb mrzḥ'*, Greek *symposiarchēs*. The priests of Bel at Palmyra were organized in a college headed by the chief priest, *archiereus kai symposiarchēs* (cf. Milik, 109*f*), who served also as eponym for dating the acts of the association. The symposiarch of the priests of Bel was also chief of all other symposia of the city and had charge of the "house of distribution, *bt qsm'* (cf. Milik, 110; not "house of divination" as suggested by H. Ingholt, 1926, 132*f*,141). An inscription erected in recognition of the services of a certain Yarḥai Agrippa in the year A.D. 243 notes that in his leadership of the symposia he "served the gods and presided over the distribution (*qsm'*) a whole year and supplied old wine for the priests a whole year from his house."

The Akkadian documents from Ugarit which mention the *marzēaḥ* suggest that it was an important institution. The king Niqmepa bequeathed "a house of the *marzēaḥ*-men" to the *marzēaḥ*-men and their children. A house of the *marzēaḥ*-men of (the god) Šatran was taken over for official use, but another house was given in its place. A vineyard of Ištar was divided between the *marzēaḥ*-men of the city of Ari and those of the city of Siyanni (cf. Eissfeldt, 1966, 167–171; 1969, 187–195). In a fragmentary Ugaritic alphabetic text (2032) there are five or six occurrences of the phrase *mrzḥ'n*[. . .] and in line 2 occur the words *šd kr*[. . .], "field vineya[rd]." Eissfeldt proposed the restoration *mrzḥ 'n*[*t*] and suggested that the text may deal with the bequest of several vineyards to the *marzēaḥ* (Kultverein) of Anat.

The connection between the *marzēaḥ* and the funeral feast, attested in both biblical and rabbinic references, is confirmed by Ugarit data. Although there are no explicit references to the funeral character of the sacrificial banquet in which all the gods become drunk but El sits in his *mrzḥ* and topes till he sinks down as if dead, and although there are no hints of sexual activities in connection with this occasion which centers on El's hangover and its medicinal relief, there are elsewhere hints of sexual activity in connection with funeral feasts at Ugarit. The so-called Rephaim Texts (20–22[121–124]), thus designated because of the frequent occurrence of the term (*rpum* in the nominative case and *rpim* in the oblique cases), which in biblical usage is connected with the departed dead, denizens of the netherworld (cf. Isa 14:9, 26:14,19; Ps 88:11; Prov 2:18, 9:18, 21:16; Job 26:5), supply all the elements of a *marzēaḥ*, a funeral feast to which the gods and the deified dead are invited to join with the mourners in a seven-day celebration with flesh and wine and with hints, at least, of sexual activity. The Rephaim Texts apparently belong to the Aqht Epic and fit into the action following the murder of Danel's son Aqht. In spite of the fragmentary state of the texts and numerous lexical and grammatical uncertainties, it is apparent that Danel invites the Rephaim to a *mrz'* (122:1), a variant form of *mrzḥ*, in a shrine (*aṯr*, "place") in his house.

From the various strands of evidence, we gather that the *marzēaḥ* was a religious institution which included families and owned houses for meetings and vineyards for supply of wine, that the groups met periodically to celebrate seven-day feasts with rich food and drink and sometimes with sexual orgies. The biblical and rabbinic identification of these revels as funeral feasts is illustrated by a wealth of sepulchural sculpture depicting the deceased as participating in the banquet. The charge that the early Christians in their initiation rites immolated infants and ate their flesh and drank their blood is of interest in light of the cannibalistic language of the Eucharist in which the bread and wine are Christ's flesh and blood. The eating of the flesh and drinking of the juices of deceased loved ones is a primitive practice and is attested also at Ugarit. In a brief vignette inscribed on the back of a lexical text, the goddess Anat is depicted as consuming the flesh and blood of her brother consort (Baal):

Anat went and waxed mad (?)
At the beauty of her brother,
And at the handsomeness of her
brother,
For he was fair.
She ate his flesh without a knife,
She drank his blood without a cup.

While we are not informed whether Anat's beauteous brother was alive or dead when she thus consumed him, we may reasonably assume that he was defunct and that this was a mourning rite motivated by what anthropologists have termed "morbid affection." M. Astour (1965, 180) related Anat's cannibalism to the raw flesh feasts of the Dionysiac and Orphic orgies. It is apparent that the Christian Eucharist and Love-Feast, as well as the Jewish Qiddush, represent radical reformations of the ancient funeral feasts with elimination of such gross features as cannibalism, drunkenness, and sexual license. Paul's rebuke of unseemly behavior at the sacred meals (I Cor 11:21, Rom 13:13) and the charges ridiculed by Tertullian and Minucius Felix suggest that there were those who resisted reform and persisted in the old ways and this is confirmed by the repeated condemnations of other fathers of the Church.

In his first letter to the Christians at Corinth the Apostle Paul was distressed about licentious conduct in the festal meals when they partook of "spiritual" (pneumatic) food and drink, I Corinthians 10–11. Paul cited in censure of the Christian misbehavior the example of the Israelites' mode of worship of the Golden Calf: "The people sat down to eat and drink and rose up to sport (*paizein*)," I Cor 10:7. The kind of sport implied by the Hebrew term in Exod 32:6 (*lĕṣaḥēq*) is clear from Isaac's uxorious play in Gen 26:8. Paul explicitly inveighed against fornication in these pneumatic feasts and cited as a warning the fate of the twenty-three thousand (give or take a thousand; cf. Num 25:9) who fell in a single day, with obvious reference to the affair at the shrine at Baal Peor, Numbers 25. We are told in Ps 106:28 that the cult of Baal Peor involved the eating of sacrifices for the dead. The rabbis further identify the festivities of Baal Peor as *marzĕḥîm* and relate them to the infamous Mayumas festivals, a correlation supported by the Madeba Map which labels the area in which the scandal occurred as Marzeah-House, alias Mayumas (cf. C. S. Clermont-Ganneau, 1901, 339–345).

The etymology of the term *marzēaḥ* remains unclear. Joseph Qimḥi, followed by his son David, connected the word with Arabic *mirziḥ* alleged to signify a vehement voice or loud cry as in mourning or revelry. Eissfeldt posited a meaning "unite" for the root *rzḥ* and took the word to designate a cultic union, "Kultverein" (cf. 1966b, 45*f*, and 1966a, 176). B. Porten

(1968, 186n147) regarded Eissfeldt's distinction between two supposed homonyms *rzḥ*, "shout," and *rzḥ*, "unite," to be arbitrary. The basic meaning of *rzḥ* in Arabic is to fall down from fatigue or other weakness and remain prostrate without power to rise; it may be used of a man, a camel, or a grapevine. A *marzaḥ* is a place where a camel collapses from fatigue and a *mirzaḥ* is a prop for a fallen grapevine. The collapse of El in his *mrzḥ* and the *mirzāḥ* of sprawled ones Amos 6:7 comport with this sense of the term. The celebrants at a *marziḥ, thiasos,* or symposium recline on couches and after several rounds of drink would, no doubt, be aptly described as sprawling, or perhaps even more relaxed to the state of comatose stupor.

Whatever the etymology, it is apparent that the **marziḥ* designated a bacchanalian celebration roughly synonymous with the Greek *thiasos* and *symposion.* The "Marzeāḥ House" is thus virtually synonymous with the "Banquet House," *bêṯ mišteh* literally "house of drinking." Rabbi Aqiba anathematized those who trilled verses of the Song of Songs in "drinking houses" and this has been understood to mean that the good rabbi objected to the singing of snatches of the most holy song in the wine shops or taverns. The banquet house, or drinking house, however, was not a tavern or pub, but rather a place for sacral feasting and drinking, as evidenced by Belshazzar's feast in the *bêṯ mištěyā',* Dan 5:10, with the appropriation of the holy vessels taken from the Jerusalem Temple for sacral drinking in praise of the heathen gods by the king and his nobles and courtesans, Dan 5:1–4,10. The more explicit term "house of the drinking of wine," *bêṯ mišteh hayyayin,* is used in Esther 7:8 when the king returned to the wine-fest and found Haman prostrate on the couch with Esther, Haman apparently being in a drunken stupor and unaware of his predicament. In the festival of Purim which is supposed to celebrate and commemorate the deliverance of the Jews through the elimination of their enemy Haman by the counterplot of Mordecai and Esther, it is nevertheless permissible and even obligatory to become more than moderately inebriated. It has been suggested that Purim is in reality a disguised "feast of the dead," related to the Persian All Souls' Day, *Farvardigan,* and that the feasting and gift-giving are survivals of offerings to the dead. The avoidance of the name of the God of Israel in the Book of Esther was explained as due to this original connection with the cult of the dead. It is of interest in this connection that Esther and the Canticle are the only biblical books which make no mention of the ineffable name (cf. L. B. Paton, *Esther,* ICC, 1908, 85–87,91, and 1921, 146n62).

The unique term "house of wine" in Song of Songs 2:4 is manifestly an elliptical expression for "house of the drinking of wine," as in Esther 7:8, since a musty wine cellar would hardly be an appropriate setting for the activity envisaged:

He brought me into the wine house,
His intent toward me Love.

Other details of the Canticle also are suggestive of orgiastic revelry. The lady requests stimulants to renew her jaded desire, 2:5,

> Sustain me with raisin cakes,
> Brace me with apples,
> For faint from love am I.

These raisin cakes (cf. Hosea 3:1) survive today in Purim pastries called Hamantaschen (corrupted from German *Mohntaschen,* "poppy pockets," from the practice of stuffing them with poppy seeds). These cuneiform tarts have nothing to do with Haman's three-cornered hat or his ears, but probably originally represented the pubes of Queen Esther=Ishtar, Queen of Heaven. The mandrakes mentioned in 7:14[13E] give further hint of interest in stimulation. The repeated adjuration, 2:7, 3:5, 8:4, relating to the arousal of love when it is willing, suggests protracted and repeated amative activity. The reference in 7:10[9E] to the fine wine gliding over the lips of sleepers (if one follows MT against the versions) is understandable on the supposition that one could continue to imbibe even in sleep, or while unconscious, by means of a drinking tube or with an attendant to dribble the wine through the lips. In competitive drinking, contestants may recline and drink through tubes for maximum intake and effect. The dead too were provided with drink through tubes leading into the tombs. Thus the "sleepers" over whose lips the wine drips may refer to the funerary libation. It is striking, and perhaps no accident, that this verse evoked for the rabbis the image of deceased scholars whose lips move in the grave whenever a saying is cited in their name.

The references to myrrh, spice, honey, wine, and milk in a single verse of the Canticle, 5:1, are suggestive of the funeral feast since all these elements are associated with funerary rites and sacrifices. Myrrh and spices were used in anointing the corpse for burial (cf. Mark 16:1, Luke 24:1, John 19:39–40). Spices were also used as condiments in the savory stew for the funeral meal. Ezek 24:10 mentions the mixing of spices in the preparation of the pottage symbolic of Babylon's evil:

> Heap the wood, Mix the spices,
> Kindle the fire, Let the bones cook.
> Prepare the meat,

(The emendation of *weharqaḥ hammerqāḥāh,* "mix the spices," on the basis of LXX *kai elattōthē ho zōmos,* "and let the liquor be boiled away," is a dubious procedure.) Libations for the dead in Homeric times included honey, wine, and milk, as when Ulysses poured to the congregation of the dead libations of honey and milk and sweet wine (*Odyssey* xi 28*f*) and Achilles laid beside Patroclus' bier jars of honey and oil (*Iliad* xxiii 172). In all parts of the Aryan world honey was a food sacred to the dead. In India the *pitaras,* "fathers," were supplied rice soup mixed with honey, similar to the mead of barley water and honey served by the peasants of White Russia to their ancestors. In Greece honey cakes, *melitoutta,* were given to the dead and were believed also to appease the infernal watchdog Cerberus. Honey cakes continue as an essential part of the commemorative funeral meal among Lithuanian and Russian peasants (cf. Paton, 1921, 13,97,132,137*f*,165,199, 225). Herodotus reported (i 198) that the Babylonians buried their dead in honey. The Spartans reportedly brought home the body of King Agesipolis preserved in honey and that of King Agesilaus in wax (cf. D. C. Kurtz and J. Boardman, 1971, 191). A first-century epitaph from Crete (W. Peek, 1955, no. 1157; Kurtz and Boardman, 299) bids the parents of three defunct brothers bring offerings of honeycomb and incense.

The open invitation of 5:1ef,

Eat, friends, drink, Be drunk with love!

suggests the sort of climax to be expected in a thoroughly inebriated mixed group. Similar invitations are given in the Ugaritic texts, as when El says to his erstwhile spouse Asherah:

Eat, yea drink!
Eat from the tables meat,
Drink from the jars wine;
From a gold cup the blood of the vine.
Lo, the affection of King El will
arouse you,
The Bull's love will excite you.
(4[51].4:35–39)

Or the invitation to the votaries in the ritual portion of the "Birth of the Beautiful Gods"

Eat of the food, Ay!
Drink of the foaming wine, Ay!
Peace, O King,
Peace, O Queen,
O entrants and archers.
(23[52].6–7)

These invitations recall the frescoes of the catacombs and some of the uninhibited scenes which create the impression of a cosy drinking party, as described by F. van der Meer (1961, ch. 18, "The Feasts of the Dead," p. 503):

> Above the heads of the serving girls, who are hastening to supply the guests, stand the words: 'Agape, mix my wine! Eirene, give me some warm water!—phrases which certainly do not elevate the ladies Love and Peace to the status of heavenly allegories; incidentally these ladies make their appearance no less than four times —the painter was obviously repeating a stereotype.

Among the slogans in these scenes of Christian love feasts for the dead were the cry *Refrigera bene* which van der Meer rendered "Take good refreshment, eat and drink!" and *eis agapēn,* "To the heavenly feast" (literally "to love") and above all *In pace.* According to van der Meer (p. 506),

> The people who chiselled these mystical allusions did their work in the midst of pagans and in the midst of persecution; but that reverent atmosphere is now definitely a thing of the past. The food upon the tables, once a thing so full of meaning, has achieved vestigial survival, but those at the table now have manners

more suited to a pothouse, while the crude decorations represent nothing more than the husks of an ancient symbolism which now garnish the wine jugs of an ordinary, and distinctly convivial, wake!

Sepulchural gardens were common in the Graeco-Roman world, adjacent to the tombs, hence the technical term "garden tomb," *kēpotafion, cepotafium.* Strabo (XVII 1,10) described the district west of Alexandria as containing many gardens (*kēpoi*) and tombs (*tafai*). Jocelyn M. C. Toynbee (1971, 95*ff*) cites several inscriptions and documents referring to funerary gardens. Of particular interest is an inscription found near Rome, dating probably to the second century, set up by the parents in memory of their ten-year-old son. The text includes a prayer to Osiris to give the dead lad cool water. The parents made for the boy "an eternal bridal chamber" (*aiōnion nymphōna*) and for themselves in expectation of their death a garden tomb (*kēpotafion*). Toynbee wondered (p. 96) whether the "eternal bridal chamber" was "for mystic marriage with the god." Extensive evidence associating sacral sexual rites with mortuary celebrations should relieve somewhat the puzzlement at the designation of a tomb as an "eternal bridal chamber." Toynbee goes on to cite some of the very interesting Latinized versions of Greek funerary terminology. In addition to *cepotafium* and the diminutive *cepotafiolum,* there are the Latin terms *hortus, horti,* and *hortulus.* These sepulchural plots are frequently described as surrounded by an enclosure-wall (*murus, maceria*). The enclosed garden is reminiscent of the *gan/l nā'ûl,* the *hortus conclusus,* of Canticles 4:12.

In addition to the general words for buildings used in the funerary inscriptions in association with the gardens, such as edifice (*aedificia*) and monument (*monumenta*), there are words that refer specifically to the places where the funerary feasts were celebrated. There are references to dining rooms (*cenacula*), eating houses (*tabernae*), summer houses (*tricliae*), bars or lounges (*diaetae*), sun terraces (*solaria*), storehouses (*horrea*), and even, in one case, apparently, rooms to let(?) or brothels(?) (*stabula* and *meritoria*). In the sepulchural gardens were paths (*itinera*). Water was supplied by cisterns (*cisternae*), basins (*piscinae*), channels (*canales*), wells (*putei*), and pools (*lacus*). The funerary garden is variously described as a small estate (*praedolium*), a field (*ager*), or as orchards (*pomaria* or *pomariola*). One tomb was adorned with vines, fruit trees, flowers, and plants of all kinds (p. 97), another with trees, vines and roses, and yet another with a vineyard and enclosure-walls. The funerary terminology is strikingly similar to certain expressions of the Canticle.

The garden-tomb setting and terminology of the Graeco-Roman mortuary cult recalls the reprimand of Second (or Third?) Isaiah, Isa 65:1–7, depicting Israel's God as constantly waiting and making overtures to an unresponsive people addicted to abominable rites in the funerary gardens:

I was available to those who did not
ask,
Accessible to those who did not seek.
I said, "Here I am! Here I am!"
To a nation that did not call on my
name.
I spread my hands all day
To a rebellious people
Who walk in a no-good way,
Following their own devices,
A people who provoke me
To my face, constantly,
Sacrificing in the gardens,
Burning incense on bricks,
Sitting in the tombs,
Spending the night in crypts,
Eating pig meat,
Carrion broth in their vessels.
They say, "Stand back;
Don't touch me, I'm holy to you."
These are smoke in my nose,
A fire that burns all day.
Lo, it is written before me:
"I will not be quiet, I will requite
I will requite in the bosom
Your crimes and your fathers' crimes
Together," says the Lord.
"Because they burned incense on the
mountains,
Disgraced me on the hills,
I will measure out their wage
Promptly on their lap."

The Qumran Isaiah Scroll offers in 65:3d a reading radically different from MT. In place of MT's "and burning incense on the bricks," the Qumran text presents the provocative reading *wynqw ydym 'l h'bnym*, "and they suck/cleanse hands upon/as well as the stones." In view of the well-attested euphemistic use of "hand" for phallus (cf. 5:4a) and the possibility that *'l h'bnym* in Exod 1:16 refers to genitalia in general or testicles in particular, the verb *ynqw*, could be connected either with *ynq*, "suck," or *nqy*, meaning "cleanse" in the factitive or D stem. Fellatio would inevitably be suggested by *ynq*. It is hard to imagine how cleansing hands could be bad.

An Old Babylonian text published by J. J. Finkelstein (1966) has a bearing on the present concern with mortuary meals. Finkelstein's masterly treatment of the document established its "Sitz im Leben," that is, the reason it was written and the manner in which it was used. The text lists the ancestors of Ammiṣaduqa, last king of the First Dynasty of Babylon, and includes collectively "the dynasties of the Amorites, the Haneans, the Gutium, the dynasty not recorded on this tablet, and the soldier(s) who fell while on *perilous campaigns* for their (his) lord, princes, princesses, all persons from East to West who have neither caretaker (*pāqidum*) nor attendant (*sāḫirum*). All these are invited (lines 39–43):

Come ye, e(a)t this, (drin)k this, (and)
Ammiṣaduqa, son of Ammiditana, the king of Babylon, bless ye.

The restorations of the imperatives *aklā*, "eat ye," and *šityā*, "drink ye," in lines 39–40 are suggested by the traces of the poorly preserved signs as well as by the unmistakable context of the whole as a *kispu* offering which consisted of food and drink for the dead.

The nature and function of the text as a whole is hardly open to doubt: it is the invocation to an actual memorial service to the dead, the central action of which was the offering to the *etemmū*—ghosts or spirits of the dead—of the *kispu,* which consisted of food and drink (p. 115).

It is no ordinary *kispu* ceremony, however, of the standard sort held semi-monthly on the first and sixteenth day.

The inclusion of the spirits of other than the dead ancestors, including even the ghosts of anyone and everyone "from East to West" who otherwise has none to offer them the *kispum,* suggests that the occasion was an extraordinary one, but the text itself offers no clue as to what it might have been. The performance might still have been scheduled for the first or sixteenth day of the month, but this would have been coincidental with some other momentous occasion which called for a more inclusive mortuary "feast." One might think of the coronation of the new king as an occasion suitable for such an expression of royal "largesse"—when perhaps even the living population received something above their normally miserable fare. What could be more appropriate for Ammiṣaduqa, as the newly crowned *šar mīšarim,* than to demonstrate his concern for his people's welfare by a special food distribution to all—to the dead as well as the living? (p. 116).

The present writer ventures to suggest that the occasion in question was a sort of Hallowmas, a feast for All Saints and Souls.

The affirmation 8:6c,d "For Love is strong as Death, / Passion fierce as Hell" has been generally recognized as the theme and message of the Song of Songs. This is also the assurance of Paul's praise of love in I Cor 13:8: "Love never quits" (*hē agapē oudepote ekpiptei*). "There are three things that last, Faith, Hope, Love—and Love is the greatest." The nature of the Love (*hē agapē*) which Paul commended to the Corinthians had little in common with the sort of love feasts which they were wont to celebrate. Nevertheless, these pagan love feasts were also a response to death with the assertion of life in its most basic modes of expression, eating, drinking, and copulation, all requisite for the continuation of life. Mother Earth, from whom man comes and to whom he returns, she who creates, nourishes, destroys, and takes man back into her ample womb, was worshiped at the ancestral graves with love feasts and commemorative rites to ensure the continuation of life. It is no accident that tombstones and memorial stelae are sometimes distinctly phallic in form, as often with the Greek *herma,* and that the term *yāḏ,* "hand," in Ugaritic and Hebrew is applied to the phallus and in Hebrew to a memorial stela (I Sam 15:12; II Sam 18:18; Isa 56:5), while the terms for "memory" and "phallus" appear to be related to the same root, **ḏkr, zkr.* (On phallic tomb monuments in Greece, cf. Kurtz and Boardman, 1971, pp. 241–244, figs. 50, 51, 52.)

The Epistle of Jude inveighs against impious persons who had sneaked into the Christian community and had perverted the grace of God to an excuse for fornication and unnatural lust. These people are described, Jude 12, as "reefs (*spilades*) in your love feasts (*en tais agapais humōn*)." In a parallel passage, II Peter 2:13, they are called "blots (*spiloi*) and blemishes (*mōmoi*) who revel in their love feasts" (choosing the variant *agapais* over *apatais,* "dissipations"). The charges and invectives laid on these subversives, Jude 8–16; II Peter 2:4–22, stress sexual licentiousness. The point of interest here is the explicit connection of this sort of conduct with the love feasts. Passing over the question of the relation of the Agape and the Eucharist (on which see the excellent treatment by A. J. Maclean in *ERE,* s.v. Agape), it will suffice to stress the original and essential character of these celebrations as mortuary meals, continuing the ancient and well-nigh universal practice of providing refreshment for the dead and sharing it with them in a communal and commemorative meal. Such celebrations from time immemorial had not infrequently featured orgiastic revelry, drunkenness, gluttony, cannibalism, incest, and sundry other excesses. In the early church the cult of the martyrs evolved quite naturally from the need to offer a tolerable substitute for these irrepressible practices (cf. van der Meer, *Augustine the Bishop,* 1961, ch. 17, "The Cult of the Martyrs," pp. 471–497). As long as the offerings, whether to ancestors or martyrs, remained moderately decent affairs, there was no need to prohibit them. The charge that Christians offered food and wine to appease the shades of the martyrs Augustine rebutted with the argument that the altars were built to God in honor of the martyrs and not to the martyrs as if they were gods; honor was paid to the martyrs merely to encourage others to emulate them and share in their merits (cf. Sister Mary Daniel Madden, 1930, 109–111). It was doubtless difficult for newcomers to Christianity to appreciate the subtle difference between outwardly similar procedures in offerings to the ancestors and the martyrs. The toleration of the memorials for the martyrs was probably a concession to recent converts who were reluctant to relinquish the pleasures of the old-time revels. The trouble came when the grosser features of the pagan celebrations were carried over into the Christian love feasts, as the protests of early Christian writers attest. Augustine was tolerant toward the harmless sort of devotion to the saints and martyrs which his mother practiced, but not toward the drunken carousals carried on in some circles. When his mother Monica first came to Milan, she went to church with a basket of food and wine for the graves of the saints, as she had been accustomed to do in Africa, but was informed by the porter that this practice had been banned by the bishop. Augustine well understood the reasons for this ban imposed by Ambrose, since these meals for the saints were too much like pagan *parentalia* and served as an excuse for drunkenness. There were those who worshiped at the tombs, set food before the dead, drank to excess, and then attributed gluttony and drunkenness to religion. One should not judge Christianity, Augustine argued, by the behavior of the masses, who remained superstitious or were so enslaved to sensual pleasures that they forgot their promises to God. In his sermons Augustine tried to persuade the people that such excesses were pagan and did not derive from the stock and vine of justice of our patriarchs. Sir 30:18, which compares the placing of food on graves to putting dainties before a mouth that is closed, was explained as referring to a sick person who refuses food, since the Patriarchs kept no *parentalia*. Tobit 4:7, however, commands the deposit of food and pouring of wine on the graves of the just, but not on those of the wicked, and from this Augustine deduced that the faithful may perform this sort of *memorial* for their relatives provided it is done with pious intention (*Sermones* 361, 6; cf. Madden, 110, and van der Meer, 525). Those who persisted in heathen revelry, however, were blasted by Augustine: "The martyrs hate your wine jugs and cooking pots and your gluttony" (*Sermones* 273, 8).

There they bring bread and wine to the grave and call the dead by name. How often after his death they must have called out the name of the wealthy glutton when they got drunk in his mausoleum, and yet not a drop fell on his parched tongue (*Enarrationes in Psalmos,* 48, 1, 15, cited after van der Meer, 520).

Similarly Zeno of Verona inveighed in the style of the prophet Amos:

God is displeased by those who run along to the gravesides, offer their lunch to stinking corpses and then in their desire to eat and drink suddenly, with pot and glass, conjure up martyrs at the most unfitting places (*PL* 11, 366, cited after van der Meer, 520).

The Donatists, in particular, were charged with utter wantonness, as

those gangs of vagabonds who bury their own selves upon their graves in loathesome promiscuity, seducing one another into all manner of vice (cf. van der Meer, 520n89).

Madden (111) in her summation modestly concluded that

out of the pagan customs in honor of the dead, abuses developed in the festivals held to honor the memory of the martyrs. It became necessary to take measures against these abuses. The allusions to the traces of these customs relating to the honoring of the dead show that this phase of paganism had a strong hold on the hearts of the people, even after they had become Christians.

It is beyond the scope of this present effort to attempt any systematic treatment of funeral cults in the ancient world. The preceding discussion was intended merely to suggest that certain features of the Song of Songs may be understood in the light of the considerable and growing evidences that funeral feasts in the ancient Near East were love feasts celebrated with wine, women, and song. The Greek term *agapē,* LOVE, attached to these feasts certainly included *eros* as well as *philia,* to judge from the condemnations of drunkenness, fornication, and other excesses in the New Testament and the Church Fathers. The appearance of some of the characteristic terms of the Canticle in the Ugaritic mythological and ritual texts, especially in connection with the term **marziḥ,* and in the inscriptions from Palmyra which confirm and elucidate the connection of the *marziḥ/thiasos/symposion* with the funeral feast, opens new possibilities, yet to be fully tested and exploited, for the understanding of the cultic origins of the Canticles. This approach seems capable of explaining the Canticles better than any other and is able to subsume aspects of other modes of interpretation as enfolding elements of truth. The connection of the Canticle with the funeral feast as expressive of the deepest and most constant human concern for Life and Love in the ever present face of Death adds new insight and appreciation of our pagan predecessors who responded to Death with affirmations and even gross demonstrations of the power and persistence of Life and Love:

Kî 'azzāh kammawet̠ 'ahăb̠āh
Hoti krataia hōs thanatos agapē
Quia fortis est ut mors dilectio

For Love is strong as Death.

See Plate XII

BIBLIOGRAPHIES

BIBLIOGRAPHY I

TEXTS AND VERSIONS

Hebrew

M(asoretic) T(ext): *Biblia Hebraica.* Eds. R. Kittel, P. Kahle, A. Alt, O Eissfeldt, 7th ed. Stuttgart, 1951. Cited as *BHK.*

Canticum Canticorum prepared by F. Horst, 1935.

Qumran texts: from Cave 4 two fragments offering no significant readings; cf. *RB* 63 (1956), 57 (communication of F. M. Cross), from Cave 6 a leather fragment of 1:1–7 with a few variants; cf. M. Billet, J. T. Milik, R. de Vaux, *Les 'Petites Grottes' de Qumrân,* pp. 112–114. Oxford, 1962.

Greek

The Septuagint, or LXX

Swete, H. B. *The Old Testament in Greek,* II, 506–518. Cambridge, 1922.

Rahlfs, A. *Septuaginta,* 3d ed. Stuttgart, 1940.

Field, F. *Origenis Hexaplorum quae supersunt Veterum Interpretum Graecorum in totum VT Fragmenta.* Aquila, Symmachus, Theodotion. Oxford, 1875.

Latin

Old Latin

Sabatier, P. *Bibliorum sacrorum latinae versiones antiquae sen Vetus italica, II,* 375–388. Reims, 1743. Cf. C. de Bruyne, "Les anciennes versions latines du Cantique des Cantiques," *RBén* 38 (1926), 91–122.

Wilmart, A., "L'ancienne version latine du Cantique I–III," *RBén* 23 (1911), 11–36.

Vulgate

Biblia Sacra iuxta Latinam Vulgatam Versionem, XI, *Proverbia, Ecclesiastes, Canticum Canticorum,* 173–197. Rome, 1957.

van den Oudenrijn, M. A., "Scholia in locos quosdam cantici canticorum," *Biblica* 35 (1954), 268–270.

Vaccari, A., "Latini Cantici canticorum versio S. Hieronymo ad Graecam Hexaplarem emendata," *Biblica* 36 (1955), 258–260.

Syriac

The Peshitta

Lee, S. *Vetus Testamentum Syriace.* London, 1823.

Ceriani, A. M. *Translatio syra Pescitto Veteris Testamenti ex codice Ambrosiano.* Milan, 1876.

The Old Testament in Syriac according to the Peshitta Version. Edited in behalf of the International Organization for the Study of the Old Testament by the Peshitta Institute of the University of Leiden. Sample edition: Song of Songs —Tobit—4 Ezra. The Song of Songs edited by J. A. Emerton. Leiden, 1966.

Euringer, A., "Die Bedeutung der Peschitto für die Textkritik des Hohen Liedes," in Biblische Studien Freiburg, 1901, pp. 115–128.

Salkind, J. M., *Die Peschitta zu Schir-Haschirim* textkritisch und in ihrem Ver hältniss zu MT und LXX untersucht. Dissertation, Bern, 1905.

Bloch, J., "A Critical Examination of the Text of the Syriac Version of the Song of Songs," *AJSL* 38 (1921), 103–139.

Haefli, L. *Die Peschitta des Alten Testaments,* Altestamentliche Abhandlungen, XI, 17. Münster, 1927.

Köbert, Raimund, "Syrische Fragmente eines griechischen Kommentars zum Hohen Lied," *Biblica* 48 (1967), 111–114.

The Syro-hexaplar

Ceriani, A. M. *Codex syro-hexaplaris Ambrosianus,* in Monumenta sacra et profana, VII. Milan, 1874.

Paraphrasis Caldayca, en los Cantaras de Selomoh, con el texts Hebrayco, y Ladino traduizida en langua Espanola. Edited and translated by M. Belmont(e). Amsterdam 5424/1664. A work often reprinted, containing a Spanish translation of the Targum to the Song of Songs.

Targum Canticles in *Mikraoth Gedoloth.* Warsaw, 1874. *Hamesh Megilloth,* ed. J. Kapah. Jerusalem, 1961.

de Lagarde, P. A. *Hagiographa chaldaica.* Leipzig, 1873.

Silber, E. *Sedeh Jerusalem, ein Kommentar zu Targum Chamesh Megilloth.* Kritisch bearbeitet. Czernowitz, 1883.

Riedel, J. W. *Die Auslegung des Hohenlieder in der jüdischen Gemeinde und der griechischen Kirche.* Leipzig, 1898. German translation of the Targum of the Song of Songs, pp. 9–41.

Gollanez, H. *The Targum to the Song of Songs.* London, 1908.

Melamed, R. H., "The Targum to Canticles according to Six Yemen MSS. Compared with the 'Textus Receptus' (Ed. de Lagarde)," *JQR* 10 (1919–20), 377–410; 11 (1920–21), 1–20; 12 (1921–22), 57–117.

Schwarz, M. *Az Enekek Enekenek Targuma.* Dissertation, Budapest, 1928. Hungarian translation of the Targum of the Song of Songs, pp. 51–79.

Vulliard, P. *Le Cantique des Cantiques d'après la tradition juive.* Paris, 1925. French translation of the Targum to the Song of Songs, pp. 67–103.

Liebreich, L. J., "The Benedictory Formula in the Targum to Song of Songs," *HUCA* 18 (1944), 177–197.

———"Midrash Lekah Tob's Dependence upon Targum to the Song of Songs 8.11–12," *JQR* 38 (1947), 63–66.

Churgin, P. *The Targum to the Hagiographa* (targum ketubim). Modern Hebrew. New York, 1945. Targum on Canticles, pp. 117–139.

———"Targum Shir Hashirim," in *Gibeath Saul, Essays Contributed in Honor of Rabbi Saul Silber,* ed. C. D. Regensburg. Chicago, 1935. Hebrew part, pp. 82–102.

Sperben, A. *The Bible in Aramaic, Based on Old Manuscripts and Printed Texts,* 4 vols. Leiden, 1959–67.

Heinemann, J., "Targum Canticles and its Sources" (modern Hebrew), *Tarbiz* 41 (1971), 126–129. English summary, p. ix.

Melamed, E. Z., "Rejoinder" (to J. Heinemann), *Tarbiz* 41 (1971), 130.

———"Targum of Canticles," *Tarbiz* 40 (1971), 201–215.

Coptic

Ciasca, A. *Sacrorum Bibliorum Fragmenta Copt-sahidica Musei Borgiani,* II. Rome, 1889. Canticles iv 14 – v 13, p. 215.

Maspero, G. *Fragmenta de la Version thabaine de l'Ancien Testament,* Mémoires de la Mission archeologique française du Caire, VI, 197–207. Paris, 1892.

Thomson, H. *The Coptic (Sahidic) Version of Certain Books of the Old Testament, From a Papyrus in the British Museum.* London, 1908.

Vaschalde, A. (Inventory of Coptic texts.) *RB* 29 (1920), 94*f*.

Worrell, W. H. *Coptic Texts in the University of Michigan Collection,* Humanistic Series, vol. 46. Ann Arbor, 1942. (MS dated to A.D. 600, pp. 25*ff*.)

Armenian

Zohrab, J. *Armenian Bible.* Venice, 1805.

Euringer, S., "Ein unkanonische Text des Hohenliedes (Ct VIII 15–20) in der armenischen Bibel," *ZAW* 33 (1913), 272–294.

Oskian, H., "Première et deuxième traduction du Cantique des Cantiques," *Handes Amsorya* 38 (Vienna, 1924), cols. 215–234, 297–312, 409–419.

Lyonnet, S. *Les origines de la version arménienne de la Bible et le Diatessaron,* Biblica et orientalia, XIII, 10 and 114. Rome, 1950.

Georgian

Euringer, S., "Bemerkungen zur georgischen Uebersetzung des Hohenliedes," *BZ* 14 (1916), 97–116.

Ethiopic

Euringer, S. *Die Auffassung des Hohenlieder bei den Abessiniern.* Leipzig, 1900.

———"Schöpferische Exegese im athiopisches Hohen Liede," *Biblica* 17 (1936), 327–344, 479–500; 20 (1939), 27–37.

Gleave, H. C. *The Ethiopic Version of the Song of Songs.* London, 1951.

Ullendorff, E. *Catalogue of Ethiopian Manuscripts in the Bodleian Library,* II. Oxford, 1951.

Leslau, W. "The Gafat Text of the Song of Songs," in *Gafat Documents, Records of a South-Ethiopic Language* (New Haven: American Oriental Society, 1945), pp. 101–138.

Arabic

Arabic Bible, editions of Mosul, 1875, Jesuit Fathers, Beirut, 1885. British Foreign Bible Society, Cambridge, 1932.

Bacher, W., "Die Saadjanische Uebersetzung des Hohenliedes by Abulwalid Merwan Ibn Ganah, nebst einigen Bemerkungen zu Merx's Ausgabe derselben," *ZAW* 3 (1883), 201–211.

BIBLIOGRAPHY II

CHRONOLOGICAL, PRE-1800

SECOND–THIRD CENTURIES

Tertullian

Apology, tr. Sister Emily Joseph Daly, in *The Fathers of the Church, A New Translation*, X, 25–29. New York, 1950.

Hippolytus

Fragmenta in Canticum Canticorum, PG 23, 767.

Bonwetsch, G. N., and H. Achelis, eds. *Hippolytus Werke*, erste Band: exegetische und homiletische Schriften ("Die griechischen christlichen Schrifsteller der ersten drei Jahrhunderte": Hippolytus, I Bd.; Leipzig, 1897), pp. 341–374, Greek text and German translation.

Kommentar zum Hohenlied, Texte und Untersuchungen, 23, NF 8, 1902.

Richard, M., "Une paraphrase grecque résumée du commentaire d'Hippolyte sur le Cantique des Cantiques," *Muséon* 77 (1964), 137–154.

Origen

Duae homiliae in cantica interprete Hieronyma, PG 13, 37–58, *PL* 23, 1175–1196.

Fragmenta interprete Rufino, PG 13, 61–216.

Scholia ex Catena Procopii, PG 17, 253–278.

Baehrens, W. A., ed. *Origenis Homiliae in Canticum canticorum*, GGS, Origen VII, 1925.

de Brouwer, A. *Origène* "L'étape de la Sagesse," *BVC* 58 (1964), 13–18.

Chênevert, J(acques). *L'église dans le commentaire d'Origène sur le Cantique des Cantiques*, Studia; travaux de recherche, 24, 1969.

Lawson, R. P. *Origen. The Song of Songs. Commentary and Homilies. Ancient Christian Writers*, vol. 26. Westminster, Md., 1957.

Rousseau, O. *Origène, Homélies sur le Cantique des Cantiques*, Sources chrétiennes, 37. Paris, 1953.

Snowden, F. M., Jr. (See Bibliography III.)

Pseudo Athanasius

Homilia in Canticum Canticorum, PG 27, 349–1361.

Minucius Felix

Octavius, tr. Rudolph Arbesmann, in *The Fathers of the Church, A New Translation,* X, 337–338. New York, 1950.

Augustine

Madden, Sister Mary Daniel. *The Pagan Divinities and Their Worship as Depicted in the Works of Saint Augustine,* Patristic Studies, XXIV, 1930. The Catholic University of America.

Simon, P., "Die Kirche als Braut des Hohenlieder nach dem heiligen Augustinus," in *Festgabe J. Kardinal Frings,* pp. 24–41. Köln, 1960.

van der Meer, F. (See Bibliography III).

Gregory of Nyssa

Commentarium in Canticum Canticorum, PG 44, 775–1120.

From Glory to Glory: Texts from Gregory of Nyssa's Mystical Writings, translated by H. Musurillo, S.J., selected and with an introduction by J. Daniélou, S.J., pp. 152–288. New York, 1951.

Dörries, H., "Griechentum und Christentum bei Gregor von Nyssa," *TLZ* 88 (1963), 569–582.

van den Eynde, C. *La version syriaque du commentaire de Grégoire de Nysse sur le Cantique des Cantiques; ses origines, ses témoins, son influence.* Louvain, Bureaux du Muséon, 1939.

Langerbeck, H. *Gregorii Nysseni in Canticum Canticorum,* Gregorii Nysseni Opera, VI. Leiden, 1960.

Musurillo, H. A., "A Note on Gregory of Nyssa's *Commentary on the Song of Solomon.*" Hom. IV: Didascaliae A. M. Albareda (B. M. Rosenthal), pp. 321–326. New York, 1961.

Wistrand, A., "The New Edition of Gregory of Nyssa," *JTS* 12 (1961), 291–298.

Philo of Carpasia

Commentarium in Canticum Canticorum, PG 40, 27–151.

Theodore of Mopsuestia

PG 87, 27–214.

Vosté, J. M., "L'oeuvre exégétique de Théodore de Mopsueste au iie concile de Constantinople," *RB* 38 (1929), 382–395, 542–549.

Ambrose of Milan

Commentarius in Canticum Canticorum, PL 15, 1851–1962 (collected by Guillelmus, Abbas Sancti Theodorici).

Jerome

Interpretatio Homiliarum duarum Originis in Canticum. PL 23, 1117–1144.

Gregory of Elvira

Tractatus de Epithalamis seu Explanatio beati Gregorii Eliberritani in Cantica canticorum, PL Supplement I, 1958, cols. 473–514.

Buckley, F. J. *The Church and Christ according to Gregory of Elvira.* Rome, 1964.

Vaccari, A., "Hieronymi in Ct curae hexaplaris, Notulae Patristicae 2," *Gregorianum* 42 (1961), 728*f.*

Theodoret of Cyrrhus

Explanatio in canticum canticorum, PG 81, 27–214.

Ashby, G. W. *Theodoret of Cyrrhus as Exegete of the Old Testament: A modern Fifth Century Commentary on Scripture.* Publications Department, Rhodes University, Grahamstown, South Africa, 1972.

Nilus

Sovic, A., "De Nili Monachi Commentario in Canticum canticorum reconstruendo," *Biblica* 2 (1921), 45–52.

Procopius of Gaza

Canticum in Canticorum, PG 87, 1545–1754, 1755–1780.

Cassiodorus, Senator Flavius Magnus Aurelius

Expositio in Canticum Canticorum, PL 70, 1055–1106.

Justus of Urgul

In Canticum Salominis Explicatio mystica, PL 67, 963–994.

Isidore of Seville

Expositio in Cantica Canticorum Salomonis, PL 83, 1119–1132.

Gregory the Great

Commentarium in Canticum Canticorum, PL 180, 441–474.

Expositio super Canticum, PL 79, 471–548.

Testimonia in Canticum, PL 79, 905–916.

Capelle, B., "Les homilies de Saint Grégoire sur le Cantique," *RBén* (1929), 204–217.

Verbraken, P., ed. *Expositiones in Canticum canticorum,* Corpus christianorum, Series latina 144, 1963.

Paterius

Liber de testimoniis, PL 79, 905–910.

Bede, the Venerable

In Cantica canticorum allegorica expositio, PL 91, 1065–1236.

Aponius

In Canticum canticorum explanatio, PL Supplement I, 1958, cols. 800–1031.

Aponii, scriptoris vetustissimi, In Canticum canticorum explanationis libri duodecim, Quorum alia editi emandati et aucti, inediti vero hactenus desiderate e codice Sessoriano monachorum cisterciesium S. Crucis in Jerusalem urbis nunc primum vulgantur, eds. H. Bottino and J. Martini. Rome, 1843.

Witte, J. *Der Kommentar des Aponius zum Hohenliede. Untersuchung über die Zeit und den Ort seiner Abfassung, über die Persönlichkeit des Verfassers und über die Stellung des Kommentars in der Geschichte des Auslegung des Hohenliedes, unter Zugrundelegung der ersten Ausgabe des gazen Kommentars von Jahre 1843.* Inaugural dissertation, Erlangen. 1903.

Alcuin of York

Compendium in Canticum Canticorum, PL 100, 641–664.

Walafrid Strabo

Glossa in Canticum Canticorum, PL 113, 1125–1168.

Angelome of Luxeuil

Enarrationes in Cantica Canticorum, PL 115, 555–628.

Haimo or Aimo of Auxerre (formerly known as or confused with Haimo of Halberstadt)

Commentarium in Cantica Canticorum, PL 117, 295–358.

Saadia, Ben Joseph

Commentary on the Song of Songs, ed. J. Kapah, *Hamesh Megilloth.* Jerusalem, 1961.

Commentary on the Song of Songs, ed. S. A. Wertheimer, *Sefer Geon-ha-Geonim.* Jerusalem, 1925.

Yepheth, Ben 'Ali (the Qaraite, tenth century)

In Canticum canticorum commentarium arabicum, quod ex unico Bibliothecae nationalis parisiensis manuscripto codice in lucem edidit atque in linguam latinam transtulit J. J. L. Barges . . . Lutetiae Parisiorum, prostat apud Ernestum Leroux, 1884.

Gregory of Narek

Kibarian, C., "Gregory of Narek and the Exegesis of the Song of Songs" (Armenian), *Pazmaveb* 119/1–2 (1962), 110.

Tobia ben Elieser

The Commentary of Rabbi Tobia ben Elieser on Canticles. Edited for the first time from the MSS in Cambridge and Munich by A. W. Greenup, 1909.

Williram

Hoffmann, H. *Williram's Uebersetzung und Auslegung des Hohenliedes in doppelten Texten aus den Breslauer und Leidener Handschrift heraus-*

gegeben und mit einem vollständige Wörterbuche versehen. Breslau, 1827.

(Double translation of the Song of Songs into Latin Hexameters and Old High German accompanied with commentaries extracted from the Fathers. The Latin translation was published by Merula, Liege, 1598, the German by Hoffmann, as cited above.)

Haupt, J., ed. *Das Hohelied übersetzt von Williram, erklärt von Rilindis und Herrat, Äbtissiner zu Hohenburg in Elsars* (1147–1196), 1864.

Seemuller, J. *Willirams deutsche Paraphrase des Hohenliedes mit Einleitung und Glossar.* Strassburg, 1878.

Robert of Tumbalena

Commentarium in Cantica Canticorum, PL 150, 1364–1370.

Kehrer, Bartholmäus. *Zum geistesgeschichtlichen Aussagewert des Hohelied-Kommentars Roberts von Tumbalenia im Vergleich mit Willirams von Ebersberg.* Marburg, 1966.

Rashi (Rabbi Solomon ben Isaac)

Rashi's Commentary on the Song of Songs.

Judah Rosenthal, ed. *Samuel K. Mirsky Jubilee Volume.* New York, 1958.

Peter Damian

Collectanea in Vetus Testamentum Testimonia De Canticis Canticorum, PL 145, 1143–1154.

Anselm of Laon

Enarratio in Canticum Canticorum, PL 162, 1187–1228.

Leclerq, J., "De Commentaire du Cantique des Cantiques attribué à Anselme de Laon," *Recherches de théologie ancienne et médiévale* 16 (1949), 29–39.

Bruno of Asti

Expositio in Cantica canticorum, PL 164, 1233–1288.

Wolbero (Abbot of S. Pantaleonis, Cologne)

Commentaria Vetustissima et Profundissima super Canticum Canticorum Salomonis, PL 195, 1001–1278.

Bernard of Clairvaux

Sermones in Canticum, PL 183, 799–1198.

Otto Baltzer, ed. *Bernard of Clairvaux, Ausgewählte sermone des heiligen Bernhard über das Hohelied.* Freiburg, i.B. und Leipzig, 1893.

Delfgaauw, P. "An Approach to St. Bernard's *Sermons on the Song of Songs,*" *Coll. Ord. Cist. Reg.* 23 (1961), 148–161.

Deroy, J. P. T. *Bernardus en Origenes. Enkele opmerkingen over de invlo von Origenes op St. Bernardus super Cantica.* Haarlem, 1963.

"*Cantica Canticorum:* Eighty-Six Sermons on the Song of Solomon," translated by S. J. Eales in *Life and Works of Saint Bernard, Abbot of Clairvaux,* ed. Dom J. Mabillon. Four volumes, Catholic Standard Library, London, 1889. Volume IV, 2d ed., 1895.

Leclercq, J. "Recherches sur les Sermons sur le ct de St. Bernard," *RBén* 66 (1956), 63–91; 70 (1960), 562–270.

———*Receuil d'études sur S. Bernard et ses écrits.* Rome, 1962.

Sancti Bernardi Opera, Editio Critica, I Sermones super Cantica 1–35. Recensuerunt J. Leclercq, C. H. Talbot, H. M. Rochers, Editiones Cistercenses. Rome, 1957.

Rupert of Deutz

In Cantica canticorum de incarnatione Domini commentarii, PL 168, 837–962.

Honorius Augustoduniensis (formerly known as Honorius of Autun)

Expositio in Cantica canticorum, PL 172, 347–495.

Sigillum Beatae Mariae ubi exponuntur Cantica Canticorum, PL 172, 496–518.

Philipp of Harveng

Commentarii in Canticum canticorum, PL 203, 181–490.

Moralitates in Canticum, PL 203, 490–584.

Gilbert de la Porree

Sermones de Cantica Canticorum. Strasbourg, 1497.

Samuel Ben Meir (Rashbam)

Commentar zu Kohelet und dem Hohen Liede von R. Samuel ben Meir, ed. A. Jellinek. 1885.

William of St. Thierry

Expositio super Cantica canticorum, PL 180, 473–546.

Davy, M. M. *Guillaume de Saint-Thierry: Commentaire sur le Cantique des Cantiques. Teste, notes critiques, traduction.* Paris, 1958.

Déchanet, J. M., and M. Dumontier. *Guillaume de Saint-Thierry, Expositio super Cantica Canticorum, Exposé sur le Cantique des Cantiques,* Sources Chrétiennes 82. Les Editions du Cerf, 1962.

Haurlier, J., "Guillaume de Saint-Thierry et la Brevis Commentario in Cantica," *Anal. O. S. Cist.* 12 (1956), 105–114.

Pellegrino, M., "Tracce di sant Agostino nel De Contemplando Deo e nell' Expositio super Cantica canticorum di Guglielmo di Saint Thierry," *REA* 9 (1963), 103–110.

Ibn Ezra, Abraham ben Meir

Commentary on the Canticles after the First Recension, ed. H. J. Matthews. 1874.

Commentary on the Song of Songs, Mikraoth Gedoloth. 1874.

Richard of St. Victor

In Cantica canticorum explicatio, PL 196, 405–524.

Gilbert of Hoyland

Sermones in Canticum Salomonis, PL 184, 11–252.

Gilbert Foliot (Benedictine Abbot of Gloucester, Bishop of Hereford)

Expositio in Cantica Canticorum, PL 202, 1147–1304.

William of Newburgh

Gorman, J. C., ed. *William of Newburgh's Explanation Sacri Epithalamis in Matrem Sponsi: A Commentary on the Canticle of Canticles (Twelfth Century).* Spicilegium Friburgense, eds. G. Meerseman and A. Hänggi, No. 6. Fribourg, 1960.

Ibn Aknin, Joseph ben Judah

Divulgatio Mysteriorum Commentarius in Canticum Canticorum, ed. A. S. Halkin. 1964.

Jean Halgrin (Regent of University of Paris)

Expositio in Cantica Canticorum (Paris, 1520), *PL* 206, 21–859. (Also attributed to Thomas the Cistercian.)

Thomas the Cistercian

In Cantica canticorum commentarii, PL 206, 21–859.

Azriel (Ezra) Ben Menahem

Vajda, G., *Le commentaire d'Ezra de Gérone sur le Cantique des Cantiques, Traduction et notes annexes,* Pardes, Etudes et Textes de mystique juive). Paris, 1969.

Alain de Lille (Alanus de Insulii)

In Cantica canticorum ad laudem Deiparae Virginis Mariae elucidatio, PL 210, 51–110.

Gallus, Thomas

Commentaires du Cantiques des Cantiques, Texte critique avec introduction, notes et tables par Jeanne Barbet. Préface de Msgr André Combes, Textes philosophiques du Moyen Age, 14. Paris, 1967. (Commentary in French, text in Latin . . . bibliographical footnotes.)

Thomas Aquinas, Sancti Thomae Aquinatis, Doctoris Angelici Ordinis praedicatorum

"In Canticum Canticorum expositio altera," in Thomas Aquinas, *opera Omnia ad fidem optimarum editionum accurate recognita,* twenty-five volumes, Parma, 1852–73. Volume XIV, 387–426. 1863.

Vrede, W. *Die beiden dem hl. Thomas von Aquin zugeschreibenen Kommentare zum Hohenliede*. Inaugural dissertation, Münster. Berlin, 1903.

Weisheipl, J. A. *Friar Thomas D'Aquino,* pp. 326*f,* 369. New York, 1974.

(The two commentaries attributed to Aquinas printed in the Parma Vulgate are now recognized as spurious; the first belongs to Haymo of Auxerre, and the second to Gilles of Rome.)

Moses Ben Nahman, Nachmanides (Ramban)

Commentary on the Song of Songs, ed. C. B. Chavel, in *The Writings of R. Moshe B. Nachman*. Jerusalem, 1964.

Moses Ibn Tibbon

Commentary on the Song of Songs. Lyck, 1874.

Peter Olivi, O.F.M. *Saint Bonaventure, Postilla in Canticum* (Apocryphal). Cf. Bonelli, *S. Bonaventurae Opera,* Supplementum I, 51–281.

Gilles of Rome

In Cantica Canticorum Continuatio. (See Spicq, *Esquisse d'Ure Histoire de L'Exégèse Latine au Moyen Age,* p. 320, Bibliography III, and Weisheipl, above, under Thomas Aquinas). Edit. Rome, 1555.

Shemariah b. Elijah Ikriti of Negropont

Commentary on the Song of Songs, ed. J. Kapah, in *Hamesh Megilloth.* Jerusalem, 1961.

Immanuel b. Solomon

Der Kommentar zum Hohen Liede, ed. S. B. Eschwege. Frankfurt am Main, 1908.

Nicolaus of Lyra

"Postilla venerabilis Patris, Fratris Nicolai de Lyra super Canticum canticorum," in *Biblia Sacra cum glossa interlineari, ordinaria et Nicolai Lyrani Postilla* . . . six volumes, Venice, 1588. Volume III, folios 355 recto, 368 verso.

Adinolfi, M. "Maria et Ecclesia in Cantica canticorum penes Lyranum," *Christianity Today* 62 (1959), 565–569.

Robert Holcoth, O.P.

In Cantica canticorum. Venice, 1509.

Tamak Abraham ben Isaac ha-Levi (of Barcelona)

Megillat Šir haš Širim. Sabbioneta, 1558.

Commentary on the Song of Songs, with the text; with additional comments by Joel ibn Shu'aib.

Commentary on the Song of Songs, based on MSS and early printings with an introduction, variants and comments by Leon A. Feldman, 1970.

Dionysius the Carthusian
Enarrationes in Canticum, in *Dionysii Opera Omnia,* VII. Monstrolu, 1898.

Perez, Jacobus
Expositio in Cantica Canticorum Salomonis. Valencia, 1486.
In Canticum Canticorum. Lugduni (Lyon), 1512, 1514.

Lambert, F.
In Cantica canticorum Salomonis . . . commentarii. Wittenberg, 1524.

Luther, Martin
Vorlesung über des Hohelied, 1530–31: in Cantica Canticorum brevis, sed admodum dilucida enarratio. D. Martini Lutheri, edited by G. Buchwald and O. Brenner, in D. *Martin Luther's Werke: Kritische Gesamtausgabe Erste Abteilung,* edited by J. K. F. Knaake and others (58 volumes in 72; Weimar, 1883–1963). Volume XXXI, 2, 586–769. 1914.
Luther's Works, ed. J. Pelikan. Volume XV, St. Louis, 1972.

Leo Hebraeus
Dialogi di amore, The Philosophy of Love, trs. F. Friedeberg-Seeley and J. H. Barnes, 1937.

Clarius
Isidore. Canticum Canticorum Salomonis. Venice, 1544.

Castellio, Sebastian
Notae in Canticum Canticorum in Biblia latina. Geneva, 1547.

Tittelmans, Franciscus
Doctis commentarii in Cantica canticorum Salomonis, . . . Antwerp, 1547.

Ponce de León, Luis
La perfecta casada. Traduccion literal y declaracion del Libro de los cantares de Salomon. Respuesta que desde su prisión da á sus emulos el maestro fray Luis de León, año de 1573, Biblioteca clásica española. Barcelona, 1884.
La perfecta casada; exposición del cantar de cantares de Salomon. Edicion y preambolos del Padre Félix Garcia y Frederico Carlos Sainz de Robles; nota biográfica de Francisco Pacheco, 10th ed. Madrid: Aguilar, 1970.

Teresa of Avila
Conceptos del Amor de Dios sobre algunas Palabras de los Cantares, ca. 1577.

John of the Cross
Cantico Espiritual, 1578–91.
P. Gerardo, *Vida del Mistico Doctor San Juan de la Cruz,* Toledo, 1912.

Kieran Kavanaugh and Otilio Rodriguez, trs. *The Collected Works of St. John of the Cross,* New York, 1964.

P. Silverio de S. Teresa, *Obras de S. Juan de la Cruz.*

J. L. Morales, *El cantico espiritual de San Juan de la Cruz: su relacion con el cantar de los cantares y otras fuentes escrituristicas y literarias,* 1971.

Bartimaeus, Andreas

Certaine verie Worthie, godly and profitable sermones upon the fifth chapter of the Songs of Solomon. Dedicated to Henrie, Earle of Huntington, Lord of Hastings, Hungerford, Botreaux, Mullens & Moyles, etc. London: Robert Waldengrave for Thomas Man, 1583. (Moral, allegorical, anti-Romish.) The Folger Shakespeare Library, Washington, D.C.

Genebrard, G.

Canticum Canticorum Salomonis versibus et commentariis illustratum, Gilb, Genebrardo, Theologi Parisiensi, Professore Regio Auctore, Adversus Trochaichum Theodori Bezae paraphrasim. Subjuncti sunt trium Rabbinorum Salomonis Iarhij, Abrahami Abben Ezrae, & innominati cuiusdem commentarii eodem interprete. Paris, 1570, 1585.

Cornelius Gandavensis

Paraphasis et Adnot, in Libros Sapientales, Gandavi, 1570.

The Song of Songs. . . . Translated out of the Hebrew into Englishe meeter, with as little libertie in departing from the words as any plaine translation in prose can use. Middleburgh: Richard Schilders, 1587. The Folger Shakespeare Library, Washington, D.C.

Gallico, Elisha ben Gabriel

Pērūsh Shīr ha-Shīrīm. Venice, 1587.

Theodor de Beze

Sermons sur les trois premiers chapitres du Cantique des cantiques de Salomon. 1586.

Ba'al Shem, Elijah ben Moses Loanz

Sēfer Rinnat dōdīm. Basel, 1600.

Laniado, Abraham ben Isaac

Sēfer nequddōt ha-kesef. Venice, 1619. (Commentary on the Song of Songs, with text, including the Targum, with Judaeo-Spanish translation).

Dove, J.

The Conversion of Solomon. A Direction to Holinesse of Life, Handled by way of commentary upon the Whole Booke of Canticles. 1613.

Gouge, Wm.

An exposition of the Song of Solomon, called Canticles. Together with profitable observations, collected out of the same. . . . London. Printed by Iohn Beale dwelling in Aldersgate streete and there to be solde. 1615. (Written by an anonymous author who gave the manuscript to William Gouge as "a free donation.")

Sanctius (Sanchez)
In Canticum canticorum commentarii. Cum expositione Ps. LXVII *quem in Canticis respexisse videtur Solomon.* 1616.

Ghislerius, M.
Commentarii Michaelis Ghiserlii Romani Ex Clericis Regular, quos Theatinos nuncupant, in Canticum Canticorum Salomonis iuxta lectiones vulgatam, hebraeam, et graecas. Editio quinta, Venetiis, 1617.

S. François de Sales
Le Cantique des Cantiques, écologue de Salomon, mistiquement déclaré. In Oeuvres Complètes, III, Paris, 1862.

Ainsworth, Henry
Solomon's Song of Songs: in English metre with Annotations and References to other Scriptures for the Easier Understanding of it. 1623.

Heiland, G. L.
Historische überauströstliche Erklärung des Hohenliedes Solomonis. 1624.

Wilcocks, Thomas
An Exposition upon the Book of Canticles. 1624.

Thalman, J(ohannes)
Amor crucifixus; kurze einfältige Erklärung, des Hohenliedes Salomonis. . . . Leipzig, M. Wachsmans Erben, 1629.

Cornelius à Lapide
Commentarii in Canticum Canticorum, auctore R. P. Cornelio Cornelii A Lapide E Societate Iesu, S. Scripturae olim Louanij postea Romae Professore. Indicibus necessariis Illustrati, nunc primum prodeunt, Commentaria in Scripturam Sacram, IV, part II. Antverpiae, 1657; Paris, 1875.

Cotton, John
A Brief Exposition of the whole Book of Canticles, or, Song of Solomon, Lively describing the Estate of the Church in all the Ages thereof, both Jewish and Christian, in this day: And Modestly pointing at the Gloriousnesse of the restored Estate of the Church of the Jewes, and the happy accesse of the Gentiles, in the approaching daies of Reformation, when the Wall of Partition shall bee taken away. A Work very usefull and seasonable to every Christian; but especially such as endeavor and thirst after the settling of Church and State, according to the Rule and Pattern of the Word of God. Written by that Learned and Godly Divine John Cotton, Batchelor of Divinity, and now Pastor of the Congregation at Boston, in New England. London, 1642. Second Printing, 1648.

Grotius, Hugo
"Annotations to Canticum Canticorum," in *Annotations in Vetus Testamentum,* 1644.

Brightman, T.
The Workes of that Famous Reverend, and Learned Divine, Mr. THO. BRIGHTMAN: viz. A Revelation of the Apocalyps: Containing an Exposition of the whole Book of the Revelation of Saint John, Illustrated with Analysis and Scholions. Wherein the sense is opened by the Scripture, and the event of things foretold, shewed by History. Whereunto is added, A most comfortable exposition of the last and most difficult part of the Prophesie of Daniel, wherein the restoring of the Jews and their calling to the Faith of Christ, after the utter overthrow of their last three enemies, is set forth in lively colours. Together with a Commentary on the whole Book of Canticles, or Song of Salomon. London, 1644.
(The commentary on the Song of Songs is presented on pages 971–1078 with a title page: A Commentary on the Canticles, or the Song of Salomon. Wherein the Text is Analised, the Native signification of the Words Declared, The Allegories Explained, and the Order of times whereunto they relate Observed. Unto which is added brief notes out of several Expositors of the Revelation, touching the rising and fall, Progresse and finall destruction, of the Enemies of the Church; with some other Observations out of divers Writers.)
An abridgement of the original Latin work on the Song issued in Basel in 1614.

Sib(be)s, Richard
Bovvels opened: or, A discovery of the near and dear love, union and communion betwixt Christ and the church, and consequently betwixt Him and every believing-soul. Delivered in divers sermons on the fourth, fifth, and sixth chapters of the Canticles. By . . . Dr. Sibs. . . . being in part finished by his own pen in his life-time, and the rest of them perused and corrected by those whom he intrusted with the publishing of his works. 3rd ed. London, Printed by R. Cotes for J. Clark, 1648. (Copies in Rare Book Room, Beinecke Library and Medical Library of Yale University. The card for the copy in the Medical Library classifies it as "Historical." The cataloguer apparently assumed that it deals with relief from constipation.)

Robotham, John
An exposition of the whole book of Solomon's song, commonly called the Canticles, wherein the text is explained and usefull observations raised thereupon. . . . 1651. London, Printed by M. Simmons, 1651.

Guild, Wm.
Loves entercovrs between the Lamb & His bride, Christ and His church. Or, A clear explication and application of the Song of Solomon. London, 1658.

De Salazar, F. Q.

Expositio in Canticum Canticorum, 2 vols. Lyon, 1642.

Cocceius, Johannes

Cogitationes de Cantico Canticorum Salomonis ut Icone regni Christi. Lugduni Batavorum, 1665. Or *Opera omnia theologica, exegetica, didactica, polemica,* 3d ed., 1701, II, 553*ff.*

C. S. McCoy, "The Covenant Theology of Johannes Cocceius," Ph.D. dissertation, Yale University, 1956.

Groenewegen, H.

Het hoogh-liedt Salomons, uytgelyt als een voorsegginge van die dingen, die in het Coninckrijcke Christi Jesu: dat is, in de kerke des nieuwen Testaments souden geschieden: in seven verscheyden tijden. Delff, 1670.

de la Place, Josue

Exposition et Paraphrase du Cantique des Cantiques. Saumur, 1670.

Ferguson, David

Epithalamium mysticum Salomonis regis; sive, Analysis criticopractica antici canticorum. . . . Insuper harmonia Hebrai textus cum paraphrasi Chaldaea & versione Graeca LXXII. . . . Cui praengitur textus Hebraus, ad calcem vero additur Appendex de Dagesh Leni, & sceleton grammaticae Hebrea. . . . Edinburgi. Typis T. Brown, prostat apud I Cairns, 1677.

Trotti de la Chetardie, J.

Explication de l'Apocalypse par l'histoire ecclésiastique, pour prémunir les catholiques et les nouveaux convertis contre les fausses interpretations des ministres. Bourges, 1692.

Oeuvres complètes de M. de la Chétardie, curé de Saint Sulpice, réunies pour la première fois en collection et classés selon l'ordre logique, publiées par M. l'Abbé Migne, two volumes, Paris, 1857. (Material on the Song of Songs in volume I, cols. 665–1046: "L'Apocalypse expliquée par l'histoire ecclésiastique.")

Bossuet, J. B.

Libri Salomonis, Canticum Canticorum, Paris, 1693.

Oeuvres Completes, thirty-one volumes, Paris, 1875. "Cantiques des Cantiques," I, 609–678.

Simson, P.

The Song of Solomon, called the Song of Songs. Fitter to be sung with any of the common tunes of the Psalms. Very necessary to be taught children at school. In the Gorbals (Glasgow), 1701. (This work is also ascribed to P. Symson or A. Simson; cf. W. J. Cowper, "A Gorbals Imprint of 1701, with notes on Patrick Simson's 'Spiritual Songs,'" *Records of the Glasgow Bibliographical Society,* VI, 1920, 1–13.)

Guyon, Jeanne Marie (Bouvier de la Motte)
The Song of Songs of Solomon. With explanations and reflections having reference to the interior life. Translated from the French by James W. Metcalf, 1865.

van Marck, J.
In Canticum Shalomonis commentarius seu analysis exegetica, qua Hebraeus textus, cum versionibus veteribus confertur, vocum & phrasium vis indagatur, rerum nexus monstratur, & in sensum genuinam cum ex anime variarum interpretationum inquiretur. Annexa est etiam analysis exegetica Psalm XLV. Amstelaedami, 1703.

Hamon, J(ean)
Explication du Cantique des cantiques. Ouvrage singulier ou l'on trouvera les plus importantes instructions de le religion pour les divers états du Christianisme. Four volumes. Revûe & corrigée par Monsieur Nicole. Paris, J. Estienne, 1708.

de la Bonnodiere, J. R. Allaneau
Le Cantique des cantiques, pastorale sainte. A monseigneur, et madame, le duc et la duchesse de Bourgogne. A Caen, Chez Guillaume Richard Poisson, 1708. (Latin and French on opposite pages.)

de Carrieres, R. P.
Commentare litteral sur les Proverbes de Salomon, l'Ecclesiaste de Salomon, le cantique des cantique de Salomon, la cantique des cantique de Salomon, la Sagesse, l'Ecclesiastique insere dans la traduction françoise avec le texte latin à la marge. Paris, 1714.

Durham, J.
Clavis Cantici, or an Exposition of the Song of Solomon. Edinburgh, 1723.

Whiston, W.
A supplement to Mr. Whiston's late Essay, towards restoring the true text of the Old Testament, proving that the Canticles is not a sacred book of the Old Testament; nor was originally esteemed as such either by the Jewish or the Christian Church. London, 1723.

Calmet, Dom
Commentaire littéral sur tous les livres de l'Ancien et du Nouveau Testament. Eight volumes, 2nd edition, Paris, 1724–1726. (Material on Song of Songs in vol. 5, pp. 67–120. 1726.)

Croxall, S.
The Fair Circassian, A Dramatic Performance Done from the Original by a gentleman-commoner of Oxford (Samuel Croxall). London, J. Walts, 1729.
"He has all along kept the sense of the vulgar translation in view, and

. . . what he was oblig'd, by the Nature of his Design, to add, has given no true Illustration to the Sublime Meaning of the Allegorical writing." The Folger Shakespeare Library, Washington, D.C.

Jablonski, D. E.
Hohes Lied Salomonis aus andern Sprüchen der H. Schrift deutlich erklärt und mit einer neuen Vorrede versehen, 1733.

Tans'ur, W.
Heaven on Earth: or, The Beauty of Holiness. In two books, containing, I. The whole book of the Proverbs of King Solomon, composed in English verse and set to musick, II. The Song of Songs, which is the Song of Solomon. Together with various hymns, anthems, and canons: with instructions to the musick; and expositional notes on the whole. Composed in two, three and four musical parts according to the most authentic rules, and set down in score for voices or musick. London, 1738.

Bland, J.
A grammatical version, from the original Hebrew, of the Song of Solomon, into English blank verse. The whole being a drama in seven scenes. To which is added a supplement from the forty-fifth Psalm, the Song of Moses from Deut. xxxii, and the Lamentation of David over Saul and Jonathan from 2 Sam. Chap. I. Likewise grammatically translated by J. Bland, 1750.

Gifford, A.
A Dissertation on the Song of Solomon; with the Original Text, divided according to the Metre; and a Poetical Version. London, 1751.

Gill, J.
An Exposition of the Book of Solomon's Song, Commonly called Canticles, wherein the Authority of it is Established and Vindicated, against Objections bothe Ancient and Modern; several Versions compared with the Original Text; the different Senses, bothe of Jewish and Christian Interpreters considered; and the Whole opened and explained in proper and useful Observations. To which is added the Targum, or Chaldee Paraphrase upon the Whole Book, faithfully translated out of the Original Chaldee; together with some Explanatory Notes upon it. 2nd edition, 1751.

Lowth, Bishop Robert
De Sacra Poesi Hebraeorum Praelectiones, 1753. Translated into English, 1793.

Romaine, Wm.
Twelve discourses upon some practical parts of Solomon's song. Preached at St. Dunstan's church in the West, London, 2nd ed. London, J. Worrall, 1759.

Voltaire (François Marie Arouet)
Précis de l'Ecclésiaste, et du Cantique des cantiques. A Genève, Chez les frères Crammer, 1759.

Wesley, John
Explanatory Notes upon the Old Testament, III. 1765.

Harmer, Thomas
The outlines of a new commentary on Solomon's song, drawn by the help of instructions from the East . . . by the author with observations on divers passages of Scripture. Corrected with care. London, Printed for J. Buckland, 1768.

Jacobi, J. F.
Das durch eine leichte und ungekünstelte Erklärung von seinen Vorwürfen gerettete Hohe Lied. Celle, 1772.

von Goethe, J. W.
Das Hohelied Salomonis. 1775.

von Puffendorff, S.
Umschreibung des Hohenliedes, oder die Gemeinde mit Christo und den Engeln im Grabe, nebst andern biblischen Eklärungen, ed. D. C. H. Runge. Bremen, 1776.

von Herder, J. G.
Salomon's Lieder der Liebe, die ältesten und schönsten aus den Morgenlande. Leipzig, 1778. Ed. J. C. Muller, Stuttgart and Tübingen, 1827, Band 4.

Kleuker, J. F.
Sammlung der Gedichte Salomonos. . . . Hamm, 1780.

Francis, Ann
A Poetical Translation of the Song of Solomon. London, 1781.

von Ammon, C. F.
Salomon's verschmähte Liebe, oder die belohnte Treue. (Solomon's spurned Love, or Fidelity rewarded). Leipzig, 1790.

Patristic catenas on the Canticle:
Devreesse, R., "Chaines grecques exegetiques," in *Supplement au Dictionnaire de la Bible*, I, 1928 (Pirot-Robert-Cazelles), cols. 1158–1161.

Patristic commentaries:
Cavallera, F., "Cantique des Cantiques," in *Dictionnaire de Spiritualite*, IIA, 1953, cols. 93–101.

Ohly, F., *Hohelied Studien. Grundzüge einer Geschichte der Hohenliedauslegung des Abendlandes bis um 1200*. Wiesbaden, 1958.

BIBLIOGRAPHY III

ALPHABETICAL, POST-1800

Aalders, G. C.
1948 *Het Hooglied.*
Adeney, W. E.
1895 *The Song of Solomon and the Lamentations of Jeremiah,* Expositors Bible.
Adinolfi, Marco
1959 "Maria et Ecclesia in Cantico Canticorum penes Lyranum," *DT* 62: 559–565.
Aḥitub, S.
1975 "The Meaning of Sĕmadar," *Lĕšonénu* 89: 37–40.
Albright, W. F.
1931–32 "The Syro-Mesopotamian God Šulman-Ešmun and Related Figures," *AFO* 7: 164–169.
1942 *Archaeology and the Religion of Israel.*
1949 *The Archaeology of Palestine.*
1956 Review of M. Pope, *El in the Ugaritic Texts,* in *JBL* 75: 255–257.
1963 "Archaic Survivals in the Text of Canticles," in *Hebrew and Semitic Studies Presented to Godfrey Rolles Driver,* eds. D. Winton Thomas and W. D. McHardy, pp. 1–7.
Altmann, Alexander
1967 "Moses Narboni's 'Epistle on Shi'ur Qoma': A Critical Edition of the Hebrew Text with an Introduction and an Annotated English Translation," in *Jewish Medieval and Renaissance Studies,* ed. A. Altmann, pp. 225–228.
Altschul, J.
1874 *Der Geist des Hohenliedes: Geschichte, Kritik und Uebersetzung.*
de Ambroggi, P.
1948 "Il cantico dei cantici: Struttura e genere letterario," *La Scuola Cattolica:* 113–130.
1952 *Il Cantico. Dramma d'amore sacro.*
Amiet, P.
1961 *La glyptique mésopotamienne archaique.*
Andrae, Tor
1935 *Mohammed: the Man and His Faith,* tr. T. Menzel.
Anema, S.
1950 *Het Hooglied: Metrische bewerking met nieuwe verklaring.*

Angénieux, J.

1965 "Structure du Cantique des Cantiques," *ETL* 41: 96–142.

1966 "Les trois portraits du Cantique des Cantiques," *ETL* 42: 582–596.

1968 "Le Cantique des Cantiques en huit chants à refrains alternants," *ETL* 44: 87–140.

Arintero, J. G.

1958 *Exposicion mistica del Cantar de los Cantares.*

Arnold, E.

1875 *The Indian Song of Songs, From the Sanskrit of the Gita Govinda of Jayadeva. With other Oriental Poems.* London.

Astour, Michael

1965 *Hellenosemitica.*

1966 "Some New Divine Names from Ugarit," *JAOS* 86: 227–284.

1968 "Two Ugaritic Serpent Charms," *JNES* 27: 13–36.

Audet, J. P.

1955 "Le sens du Cantique des Cantiques," *RB* 62: 197–221.

1957 "The Meaning of the Canticle of Canticles," *TD* 5: 88–92.

1958 "Love and Marriage in the Old Testament," *Scripture* 10: 65–83.

Avalon, Arthur

1953 *Wave of Bliss.* Ganesh, Madras.

———and Evelyn Avalon

1952 *Hymns to the Goddess Translated from the Sanskrit.* Madras.

Avigad, N., and Y. Yadin

1956 *A Genesis Apocryphon.*

Balkan, K.

1954 Kassitenstudien, I, *Die Sprache der Kassiten.*

Bardy, G.

1954 "Marie et le Cantique chez les Pères," *BVC* 7: 32–41.

Barnett, R. D.

1973 "Monkey Business," *JANES* 5 (The T. H. Gaster Festschrift): 1–5.

Barr, James

1973 "Ugaritic and Hebrew *'ŠBM'?*" *JSS* 18: 17–39.

Barre, H.

1951 "Marie et l'Église du Venerable Bede à Saint Albert le Grand: Marie et l'Église, I," Bulletin de la Société Française d'Études Mariales, IX, 59–125.

Barth, Karl

1961 "Labor et Fides, On the Song of Songs and Genesis 2:23," in *Church Dogmatics,* pp. 316–325.

Barton, G. A.

1920 *Archaeology and the Bible,* 3d ed.

1925 "A New Inscription of Libit-Ishtar," *JAOS* 45: 154–155.

Baruch, I. L.

1936 *Sepher HaShabbat.* Tel Aviv.

Bauer, Hans

1912 "Zu Simsons Rätsel in Richter Kapitel 14," *ZDMG* 66: 473–474.

Bea, Augustinus

1953 *Canticum Canticorum Salomonis,* Scripta Pontificii Istituti Biblici, 104.

Bentzen, A.

1953 "Remarks on the Canonisation of the Song of Solomon," *StOr* 1: 41–47.

Ben-Yehudah, Eliezer

1917 "Three Notes in Hebrew Lexicography," *JAOS* 37: 324–327.

Benz, E.

1965 "Ich bin schwarz und schön: Ein Beitrag des Origines zur Theologie der negritudo" in *Wort und Religion, Ernst Damman zum 65 Geburtstag,* eds. H. J. Greschat and H. Jungreithmayr, pp. 225–241. Stuttgart.

Berlin, N. Z. Y.

1967 *Rinah Shel Torah Megillat Shir ha-Shirim 'im Perush Rashi* (Song of the Torah. Song of Songs with Rashi's Interpretation).

Bernstein, A. (pseudonym A. Rebenstein)

1834 *Das Lied der Lieder, oder das hohelied Salomo's.*

Beroway, Israel

1934 "The Imagery of Spenser and the Song of Songs," *JEGP* 33: 23–45.

Bertholet, Alfred

1918 "Zur Stelle Hoheslied 4:8," Baudissin Festschrift, BZAW 33: 47–53.

Bettan, Israel

1950 *The Five Scrolls: a Commentary on the Song of Songs, Ruth, Lamentations, Ecclesiastes and Esther.* Cincinnati.

Beumer, B. J.

1954 "Die marianische Deutung des Hohen Liedes in der Frühscholastik," *ZKT* 76: 411–439.

Bewer, J. A.

1922 *The Literature of the Old Testament.*

Bharati, Agehananda

1965 *The Tantric Tradition.* Anchor ed., 1970.

Bishop, E. F. F.

1967 "Palestiniana in Canticulis," *CBQ* 29: 20–30.

Blackman, A. M.

1925 "Philological Notes," *JEA* 11: 210–215.

Blank, S. H.

1970 "Christian David Ginsburg and His Times," in Ginsburg, C. D., *The Song of Songs* [1857, reprint] and *Coheleth* (*Commonly Called the Book of Ecclesiastes*) [1861, reprint]. Translated from the Original Hebrew with a Commentary, Historical and Critical. Prolegomenon by S. H. Blank, pp. ix–xliv. Library of Biblical Studies, Ktav, New York.

Blochet, E., tr.

1897 Kamal ad-Dīn's *History of Aleppo,* in *Revue de l'Orient Latin 5.*

Blommerde, A. C. M.

1969 *Northwest Semitic Grammar and Job.*

Boehmer, Julius

1936 "Welchen Sinn hat Hohes Lied 4.8?" *MGWJ* 44: 449–453.

Bogaert, M.

1964 "Les suffixes verbaux non accusatifs dans le sémitique nord-occidental et particulièrement en hébreu," *Biblica* 45: 220–247.

Böhl, F. M. Th.
1923 "Älteste keilinschriftliche Erwähnungen der Stadt Jerusalem und ihrer Göttin?" *AcOr* 1: 76–80.

La Bonnardière, A. M.
1955 "Le Cantique des Cantiques dans l'oeuvre de saint Augustin," *RÉA* 1: 225–2370.

Bonsirven, J.
1934 "Exégèse allégoriques chez les rabbins Tannaites," *RSR* 24: 35–46.

Boyd, B.
1947 " 'A Song about Dodai,' a lyrico-dramatic poem topically Interpreted, being a Literary Study of the Song of Songs." Dissertation, Union Theological Seminary, Richmond, Va.

Breasted, J. H.
1906 *Ancient Records of Egypt,* II.

Brekelmans, C. H. W.
1969 "Some Considerations on the Translation of the Psalms by M. Dahood: I. The Preposition *b*=from in the Psalms According to M. Dahood," *UF* 1: 5–14.

Breuer, R.
1923 *Lied der Lieder, übersetzt und erläutert.*

Broadribb, D.
1961–62 "Thoughts on the Song of Solomon," *Abr-Nahrain* 3: 10–36.

Brock, Y. I.
1968 *The Song of Songs, as echoed in its Midrash; an insight into the traditional conception of Jewish nationhood.*

Brotz, Howard
1964 *The Black Jews of Harlem.*

Brown, J. P.
1965 "Kothar, Kinyras, and Kythereia," *JSS* 10: 197–219.
1969 "The Mediterranean Vocabulary of the Vine," *VT* 19: 146–170.

Bruno, Arvid
1956 *Das Hohe Lied: Das Buch Hiob Eine rhythmische und textkritische Untersuchung nebst einer Einführung in das Hohe Lied.*

Bruston, Charles
1891 *La Sulammite; melodrame en cinque actes et en vers: Traduit de l'hébreu avec des notes explicatives et une introduction sur le sens et la date du Cantique des cantiques.*

Buber, Solomon
1894 *Midrasch Suta. Hagadische Handlung über Schir ha-Schirim, Ruth, Echah und Koheleth, nebst Jalkut zum Buche Echah. Wilna.*

Buchanan, B.
1967 "A Dated Seal Impression Connecting Babylonia and Ancient India," *Archaeology* 20: 104–107.

Budde, Karl
1894a "The Song of Solomon," in *The New World,* III, 56–77.
1894b "Was ist das Hohelied?" *Preussische Jahrbücher* 78: 92–117.
1898 *Das Hohelied erklärt,* Karl Marti's kürzer Handkommentar zum Alten Testament, XVII.

du Buisson, Le Comte de Mesnil
1962 *Tesseres et monnaies de Palmyre.*

Burney, C. F.
1908–09 "Old Testament Notes," on "Rhyme in the Song of Songs," *JTS* 10: 584–587.

Burrowes, George
1853 *A Commentary on the Song of Solomon,* 1st ed.

Burrows, Millar
1958 *More Light on the Dead Sea Scrolls.*

Butte, A.
1947 *Le Cantique des Cantiques.*

Buzy, T. R. Denis
1940a "Un chef-d'oeuvre de poésie pure: le Cantique des Cantiques," in *Mémorial Lagrange,* pp. 147–162.
1940b "La composition littéraire du Cantique des Cantiques," *RB* 49: 169–194.
1944 "L'allégorie matrimoniale de Jahvé et d'Israël et le Cantique des Cantiques," *RB* 52: 77–90.
1946 "Le Cantique des Cantiques," in *La Sainte Bible.*
1947 "Le Cantique des Cantiques," *ATh* 8: 1–17.
1951–52 "Le Cantique des Cantiques, Exégèse allégorique ou parabolique?" in *Mélanges J. Lebreton,* I, *RSR* 39: 99–114.

Cabaniss, Allen
1967 "The Song of Songs in the New Testament," *Studies in English* 8: 53–56.

Cabassut, A., and M. Olphe-Gaillard
1953 "Cantique des Cantiques," in *Dictionnaire de Spiritualité,* IIA, cols. 101–109.

Calkins, Raymond
1935 *Religion and Life.*

Cambe, M.
1962 "L'influence du Cantique des Cantiques sur le Nouveau Testament," *RThom* 62: 5–26.

Cannon, W. W.
1913 *The Song of Songs edited as a Dramatic Poem.*

Cantwell, L.
1964 "The Allegory of the Canticle of Canticles," *Scripture* 16: 76–93.

Capdevila, A.
1919 *El Cantar de los Cantares.*

Carlebach, J.
1923 "Das Hohelied," *Jeschurun* 10: 97–109, 196–206, 291–295, 355–364, 435–444.
1931 *Das Hohelied, übertragen und gedeutet.*

Cassuto, Umberto
1925 "Il significato originario del Cantico dei Cantici," *Giornale della Societa Asiatica Italiana* 1: 23–52.

Castelli, D.
1892 *Il Cantico dei Cantici, studio esegetico, traduzione e note.*
Catarivas, D.
1950 *Une nouvelle interpretation du Cantique des Cantiques.*
Charlier, C.
1953–54 "Pensée et amour chez le sémite," *BVC* 4: 100–108.
Cheyne, T. K.
1889 "Canticles," in *Encyclopaedia Biblica,* I, cols. 681–695.
Chouraqui, A., and Lucien-Marie de Saint-Joseph
1953 *Le Cantique des Cantiques.*
Christian, S. L.
1926 *The Song of Mystery. A Devotional Study of the Canticle of Canticles.*
Civil, M.
1964 " 'The Message of Lu-dingir-ra to His Mother' and a Group of Akkado-Hittite 'Proverbs'," *JNES* 23: 1–11.
1968 "Išme-Dagan and Enlil's Chariot," *JAOS* 88: 3–14.
Clarke, A. G.
1855 *The Holy Bible, Containing the Old and New Testaments . . . with a Commentary and Critical Notes,* III, Job to Solomon's Song.
Claudel, Paul
1948 *Paul Claudel interroge le Cantique des Cantiques.*
Clermont-Ganneau, C. S.
1901 "Maioumas et les fêtes orgiaques de B'el-Peor," in *Recueil d'Archéologie Orientale,* IV, 339–345.
Cohen, G. D.
1966 *The Song of Songs and the Jewish Religious Mentality,* the Samuel Friedland Lectures.
Conrad, D.
1971 "Der Gott Reschef," *ZAW* 83: 157–183.
Constant, A. L.
1841 *L'assomption de la femme; ou, Le livre de l'amour.*
Cook, A. S.
1968 *The Root of the Thing: a Study of Job and the Song of Songs.*
Cooper, J. S.
1971 "New Cuneiform Parallels to the Song of Songs," *JBL* 90: 157–162.
Copley, F. O.
1956 *Exclusus Amator: A Study in Latin Love Poetry,* American Philological Monographs, XVII.
Cowles, H.
1876 *Proverbs, Ecclesiastes, and the Song of Solomon, with notes critical, explanatory, and practical, designed for both pastors and people.*
Crawford, O. G. S.
1956 *The Eye Goddess.*
Crawley, A. E.
1929 *Studies of Savages and Sex,* ch. IV, "The Nature and History of the Kiss."

Crim, K. R.

1971 "'Your neck is like the Tower of David' (The Meaning of a Simile in the Song of Solomon 4:4)," *BT* 22: 70–74.

Cross, Frank Moore

1973 *Canaanite Myth and Hebrew Epic.*

Cumont, Franz

1905 *Religions orientales dans la paganisme romain.*

Cunitz, A. E.

1834 "Histoire Critique de l'interprétation du Cantique des Cantiques." B.Th. thesis, Strasbourg.

Curley, F. X.

1955 "The Lady of the Canticle," *AER* 133: 289–299.

Dahood, M. J.

1962 "Ugaritic Studies and the Bible," *Gregorianum* 43: 55–79.

1963 "Hebrew-Ugaritic Lexicography I," *Biblica* 44: 289–303.

1964a "Hebrew-Ugaritic Lexicography II," *Biblica* 45: 393–412.

1964b "Ugaritic Lexicography," in *Mélanges Eugène Tisserant,* I, Studi et Testi 231, Citta del Vaticano, 81–104.

Dales, G.

1960 "Mesopotamian and Related Female Figurines." Dissertation, University of Pennsylvania.

1963 "Necklaces, Bands and Belts on Mesopotamian Figurines," *RA* 57: 21–40.

Dalman, G. H.

1901 *Palästinischer Diwan.*

1925 "Die Blume *ḥabaṣṣelet* der Bibel," in *Vom Alten Testament: Karl Marti zum siebstigen Geburtstage gewidmet,* pp. 62–68.

1928–42 *Arbeit und Sitte in Palästina,* 7 vols.

Daly, Mary

March 1972 "The Spiritual Revolution: Women's Liberation as Theological Re-education," *Andover-Newton Quarterly:* 172*f*.

Davidson, Samuel

1856 *The Text of the Old Testament Considered.* London. See p. 806.

Davidson, W.

1817 *A Brief Outline of an Examination of the Song of Solomon: in which many beautiful prophecies contained in that inspired book of Holy Scripture are considered and Explained; with remarks, Critical and Expository.*

Dawson, W. R.

1931 "Notes on Egyptian Magic," *Aegyptus* 2: 23–28.

von Deines, H.

1953 "Die Nachrichten über Pferd und Wagen in den ägyptischen Texten," MIOF, I, 1–15.

Delcor, Matthias

1967 "Two Special Meanings of the Word *yād* in Biblical Hebrew," *JSS* 12: 230–240.

1968 "Le texte hébreu du Cantique de Siracide L1 et SS et les anciennes versions," *Textus* 6: 27–47.

Delitzsch, Franz
1885 *Commentary on the Song of Songs and Ecclesiastes,* tr. from the German by M. G. Easton. Clark's Foreign Theological Library, LIV.
Dempsey, Robert Brinkerhoff
1963 "The Interpretation and Use of the Song of Songs." Dissertation, Boston University School of Theology.
Deutschlaender, S.
1847 *Sefer Mar'eh Lebanon:* Commentary on the Song of Solomon, in two parallel parts, one literal, the second allegorical; the biblical text in Hebrew and in German in Hebrew letters.
Dhorme, É.
1923a "A propos du mot *ŠLḤ,*" *JPOS* 3: 45–48.
1923b *L'emploi métaphorique der noms de parties du corps en hébreu et en akkadien.* Paris.
Dicken, E. W. T.
1963. *The Crucible of Love.*
Dijkema, F.
1927 "Het Hooglied," *Nieuw theologisch tijdschrift* 16: 223–245.
Di Lella, A.
1966 "Review of J. A. Sanders, *The Psalms Scroll* of Qumran Cave 11," *CBQ* 28: 92–95.
Dimmler, E.
1921 *Das Hohelied Salomos.*
Döpke, J. C. C.
1829 *Philologisch-kritischer kommentar zum Hohenliede Salomos.*
Dornseiff, Franz
1936 "Ägyptische Liebeslieder, Hohes Lied, Sappho, Theokrit," *ZDMG* 90: 589–601.
Doughty, C. M.
1888 *Travels in Arabia Deserta.*
Driver, G. R.
1933 "Studies in the Vocabulary of the Old Testament," *JTS* 34: 33–44, 375–385.
1936 "Supposed Arabisms in the Old Testament," *JBL* 55: 101–120.
1947 "On *TPŠY HMLḤMH* (Num. 31:27)," *JQR* 37: 85.
1950 "Hebrew Notes on 'Song of Songs' and 'Lamentations'," in *Festschrift Alfred Bertholet,* pp. 134–156.
1957 "Problems of Interpretation in the Heptateuch," in *Mélanges bibliques rédigés en l'honneur de André Robert,* pp. 70–71.
1974 "Lice in the Old Testament," *PEQ* 106: 159–160.
Drubbel, Adrien
1947 "Het Hooglied in de Katholieke schriftverklaring von de laaste jaren," in *Bijdragen der Philosophische en Theologische faculteiten der Noord-en Zuid-Nederlandse Jezuiten,* pp. 113–150.
Dubarle, A. M.
1954 "L'amour humain dans le Cantique des Cantiques," *RB* 61: 67–90.
Duprat, A. J. B.
1891 *Les Harmonies entre le Cantique des Cantiques et l'Apocalypse.*

Durand-Lefèbvre, M.
1937 *Étude sur l'origine des vierges noires.*
Dussaud, René
1919 *Cantique des Cantiques: Essai de reconstruction des sources du poème attribué a Solomon.*
Ebeling, Erich
1917 *Ein Hymnen-Katalog aus Assur,* in the *Berliner Beiträge zur Keilschriftforschung,* 1/3.
1925 *Liebeszauber im Alten Orient.*
1931 "Aus dem Tagewerk eines assyrischen Zauberpriesters," *MAOG,* V, Heft 3.
Edgerton, Franklin
1924 "The Hindu Song of Songs," in *SSS,* pp. 43–47.
Edmonds, J. M., ed.
1912 *The Greek Bucolic Poets,* LCL.
Edwardes, A.
1959 *The Jewel in the Lotus.*
———and R. E. L. Masters
1962 *The Cradle of Erotica.*
Eisenstein, J. D.
1928 *Oşar Midrashim.*
Eisler, Robert
1910 *Weltenmantel und Himmelszelt.*
Eissfeldt, Otto
1965 *The Old Testament: An Introduction,* tr. from 3d German ed. by Peter R. Ackroyd.
1966a "Etymologische und archäeologische Erklärung alttestamentlicher Wörter," *OrAnt* 5: 165–176.
1966b "Sohnespflichten in alten Orient" *Syria* 43: 39–47.
1969 "Kultvereine in Ugarit," in *Ugaritica,* VI, ed. C. F. A. Schaeffer, pp. 187–195. Paris.
Eitan, Israel
1925 "The Crux in Prov. 27.16," *JQR* 15: 420–422.
Erbt, Wilhelm
1906 *Die Hebräer: Kanaan im Zeitalter der hebräischer Wanderung und hebräischer Staatengrundungen.*
Erman, Adolf
1925 "Hebräische *GLŠ* 'springen'," *OLZ* 28: 6.
Euringer, S.
1913 "Ein unkanonischer Text des Hohenliedes (Cnt. 8:15–20) in der armenischen Bibel," *ZAW* 33: 272–294.
1936 "Schöpferische Exegese im Äthiopischen Hohenliede," *Biblica* 17: 327–344, 479–500.
1937 "Ein Äthiopisches Scholienkommentar zum Hohenliede," *Biblica* 18: 257–276.
1939 "Schöpferische Exegese im "Äthiopischen Hohenliede," *Biblica* 19: 27–37.

Ewald, H. G. A.
1826 *Das Hohe Lied Salomos, übersetzt mit Einleitung, Anmerkungen und linem Anhang über den Prediger.*

Exum, J. Cheryl
1973 *A Literary and Structural Analysis of the Song of Songs, ZAW* 85: 47–79.

Falconer, H.
1904 *The Maid of Shulam.*

Falkenstein, Adam
1963 "Sumerische religiöse Texte," *ZA* 55: 11–67.

———and Wolfram von Soden
1953 *Sumerische und Akkadische Hymnen und Gebete.*

Farnell, L. R.
1896–1909 *Cults of the Greek States,* 5 vols.

Fein, H. H.
1943 *The Vineyard Keeper, a lyric drama in five scenes, based on the Song of Songs of Solomon.*

Feliks, J.
1974 *The Song of Songs: Nature, Epic, and Allegory* (in Hebrew). Includes Rashi's Commentary.

Feuillet, André
1952 "Le Cantique des Cantiques et la tradition biblique," *NRT* 74: 706–733.
1953 *Le Cantique des Cantiques,* Lectio Divina, X.
1961a "La formule d'appurtenance mutuelle (11,16) et les interprétations divergentes du Cantique des Cantiques," *RB* 68: 5–38.
1961b "Le Cantique des Cantiques et l'Apocalypse," *RSR* 49: 321–353.
1961c "Le Cantique des Cantiques et le mystère pascal," *La Vie Spirituelle:* 394–408.
1963 "La recherche du Christ dans la Nouvelle Alliance d'apres la Christ-anophie de Jo. 20,11–18. Comparison avec Cant. 3,1–4 et l'episode des pélerins d'Emmaüs" in *L'Homme devant Dieu. Mélanges H. de Lubac,* I, *Théologie* 56: 99–112.
1964 "Einige scheinbare Widersprüche des Hohenliedes,' *BZ* 8: 216–239.

Finkelstein, J. J.
1966 "The Genealogy of the Hammurapi Dynasty," *JCS* 20: 95–118.
1968 "An Old Babylonian Herding Contract and Genesis 31:38f.," *JAOS* 88: 30–36.

Fischer, Johann
1950 *Das Hohelied,* Echter Bibel.

Fisher, L. R., and F. B. Knutson
1969 "An Enthronement Ritual at Ugarit," *JNES* 28: 157–167.

Forbes, R. J.
1955 *Studies in Ancient Technology,* 9 vols.

Forrest, W. M.
1928 *King or Shepherd? The Song of Solomon Newly Rendered and for the First Time Given as a Complete Drama.*

Fraenkel, S.
1878 *Beiträge zur Erklärung der mehrläutigen Bildungen im Arabischen.*
Fraisse, E. A.
1903 *Essais de Critique: La clé du Cantique des Cantiques.*
1904 *Appendice à ma clé du Cantique.*
Frankfort, Henri
1949 "Ishtar at Troy," *JNES* 8: 195–200.
1955 *Stratified Cylinder Seals from the Diyala Region.*
Frazer, Sir James George
1922 *The Golden Bough,* IV/1.
Freedman, D.
1970 "A New Approach to the Nuzi Sistership Contract," *JANES* 2: 77–85.
Freehof, S. B.
1948–49 "The Song of Songs. A General Suggestion," *JQR* 39: 397–402.
Friedländer, Moritz
1894 "The Plot of the Song of Songs," *JQR* 6: 648–655.
Fulco, W. J.
1971 "The God Rešep." Dissertation, Yale University.
Gadd, C. J.
1932 "Seals of Ancient Indian Style Found at Ur," *PBA* 18: 1–22.
Gaiani, V.
1951 De argumento Cantici canticorum ceteris in libiris Veteris Testamenti illustrato.
von Gall, A. F.
1904 "Jeremiah 43,12 und das Zeitwort 'ṬH," *ZAW* 24: 105–121.
Gaster, M.
1893 "Das Schiur Komah," *MGWJ* 37: 179–230.
Gaster, T. H.
1952 "What the Song of Songs Means," *Commentary* 13: 316–322.
1961 "Canticles 1.4," *ExpT* 72: 195.
1969 "The Song of Songs," in *Myth, Legend, and Custom in the Old Testament: A Comparative Study with Chapters from Sir James G. Frazer's Folklore in the Old Testament,* pp. 808–814.
Gawilkowski, M.
1971 "Inscriptions de Palmyre. Belḥamôn et Manawat au dieu anonyme." *Syria* 48: 407–412.
Gebhardt, Carl
1930 "Das Lied der Lieder," in *Der Morgen,* pp. 447–457.
1931 *Das Lied der Lieder übertragen mit Einführung und Kommentar.*
Geitmann, C.
1908 "Canticle of Canticles," in *The Catholic Encyclopaedia,* II, 303–305.
Gelb, I. J.
1970 "No. 8. Incantation invoking love magic," in MAD, no. 5, pp. 7–12.
Gerleman, Gillis
1962 "Die Bildsprache des Hohenliedes und die altägyptische Kunst," *ASTI* 1: 24–30
1965 *Ruth Das Hohelied,* Biblischer Kommentar Altes Testament, XVIII.

Gesenius, Wilhelm
1815 *Geschichte der hebräischen Sprache und Schrift.* Leipzig.
Geslin, C.
1939 *L'amour selon la nature et dans le monde de la grace: Le Cantique des Cantiques.*
Gessner, T.
1881 *Das Hohe Lied Salomonis erklärt und übersetzt.*
Gifford, E. S., Jr.
1962 *The Charms of Love.*
Gilbert, G. H.
1909 "How Men Have Read the Song of Songs," *Biblical World* 33: 171–181.
Gilbert, P.
1948 "La composition des receuils de poèmes amoureux égyptiens et celles du Cantiques des Cantiques," *Chronique d'Égypte* 23: 22–23.
Ginsberg, H. L.
1969 "Introduction to the Song of Songs," in *JPSV*, pp. 3–4.
1970 "The Northwest Semitic Languages," in *The World History of the Jewish People, II. Patriarchs and Judges,* ed. B. Mazar, pp. 102–124. On the particle *še,* p. 69.
Ginzberg, Louis
1909–28 *The Legends of the Jews,* 6 vols.
Gladden, W.
1897 *Seven Puzzling Bible Books: A Supplement to "Who Wrote the Bible,"* ch. VI, "The Song of Songs."
Glueck, Nelson
1939 *Explorations in Eastern Palestine,* III, AASOR, XVIII–XIX.
1968 *The River Jordan.*
Goebel, Maximilian
1914 *Die Bearbeitungen des hohen Liedes im 17 Jahrhundert.*
Goedicke, Hans, and J. J. M. Roberts, eds.
1975 *Unity and Diversity: Essays on the History, Literature, and Religion of the Ancient Near East.*
von Goethe, J. W.
1923 *Das Hohelied* [1775] mit sieben Radierungen von W. Jaeckel.
Goetze, Albrecht
1933 *Kleinasien,* Kulturgeschichte des alten Orients—Handbuch der Altertumswissenschaft, ed. W. Otto, 1.T 3 Bd, 3 Abschritt 1 Lfg.
1941 "The Nikkal Poem from Ras Shamra," *JBL* 60: 353–374.
Goitein, S. D.
1965 "*AYUMMA KANNIDGALOT* (Song of Songs VI.10)," *JSS* 10: 220–221.
Goldin, J.
1955 *Sayings of the Fathers According to Rabbi Nathan,* Yale Judaica Series, X.
1971 *The Song at the Sea.*

Golding, W.

1942 "The Song of Songs, Newly Interpreted and Rendered as a Masque," *The Menorah Journal* 30: 161–185.

Goltz, G. F. G.

1850 *Das Hohe Lied Salomonis, eine Weissagung von den letzten Zeiten der Kirche Jesu Christi.*

Good, E. M.

1970 "Ezekiel's Ship: Some Extended Metaphors in the Old Testament," *Semitics* 1: 79–103.

Goodenough, E. R.

1953–68 *Jewish Symbols in the Greco-Roman Period,* 13 vols.

Goodspeed, E. J.

1933–34 "The Sulamite," *AJSL* 50: 102–104

Goodwin, T. A.

1895 *Lovers three thousand years ago as indicated by the Song of Solomon.*

Goodyear, W. H.

1891 *The Grammar of the Lotus.*

Gordis, Robert

1943 "The Asseverative *kaph* in Ugaritic and Hebrew," *JAOS* 63: 176–178.

1949 "A Wedding Song for Solomon," *JBL* 63: 263–270.

1954 *The Song of Songs: A Study, Modern Translation, and Commentary.* Jewish Theological Seminary.

1969 "The Root *DGL* in the Song of Songs," *JBL* 88: 203–204.

1971 *Poets, Prophets, and Sages.*

1974 *The Song of Songs and Lamentations: a study, modern translation and commentary*. Revised and augmented edition, includes bibliographies.

Goshen-Gottstein, M. H.

1959–60 "Philologische Miscellen zu den Qumrantexten. Die Schönheit Saras (1 Q Genesis Midrasch) und der *wasf* im Hohenliede," *RQ* 2: 46–48.

Gottwald, N. K.

1962 "Song of Songs," in *IDB, IV,* 420–426.

Grad, A. D.

1970 *Le véritable Cantique de Salomon: Introduction traditionelle et kabbalistique au Cantique des cantiques avec commentaires verset par verset précédés du texte hébreu et du sa traduction.*

Gradenwitz, P.

1949 *The Music of Israel.*

Graetz, H.

1871 *Schir Ha-Schirim oder das Salmonische Hohelied.*

Graham, W. C.

1929 "Notes on the Interpretation of Isaiah 5:1–14," *AJSL* 45: 167–178.

———and H. G. May

1936 *Culture and Conscience.*

Granqvist, Hilma

1931–35 *Marriage Conditions in a Palestinian Village,* 2 vols., Societas Scientarum Fennica, Commentationes Humanarum Litterarum, III, 8, and VI, 8.

Grapow, Hermann
1924 *Die bildlicher Ausdrücke der Aegyptischen.* Leipzig.
Graves, Robert
1955 *The Greek Myths,* 2 vols., Penguin ed.
1960 *Food for Centaurs.*
1965 *Mammon and the Black Goddess.*
Gray, J. C., and G. M. Adams
1903 "The Song of Solomon," in *Biblical Encyclopaedia,* III, 55–78.
Greenfield, J. C.
1964 "Ugaritic *mdl* and its Cognates," *Biblica* 45: 527–534.
1965 Review of *Hebrew and Semitic Studies Presented to Godfrey Rolles Driver,* eds. D. W. Thomas and W. D. McHardy, *JAOS* 85: 256–258.
1967 "Amurrite, Ugaritic and Canaanite," in *Proceedings of the International Conference on Semitic Studies, Jerusalem, 1965,* pp. 92–101. On Ugaritic *gl̲t,* p. 99, n. 36.
Greengus, S.
1975 "Sisterhood Adoption at Nuzi and the 'Wife-Sister' in Genesis," *HUCA* 46: 5–31.
Grelot, Pierre
1962 *Le couple humain dans l'Écriture.*
1964a *Man and Wife in Scripture,* tr. Rosaleen Brennan.
1964b "Le sens du Cantique des Cantiques d'apres deux commentaires recents." A review of RTF, *RB* 71: 42–56.
Gressmann, Hugo
1920 *Die Lade Yahve's.*
Griffis, W. E.
1900 *The Lily among Thorns: A Study of the Biblical Drama Entitled The Song of Songs.*
Grill, Severin
1962 "Die allegorische Auslegung des Hohenliedes als christlich-judisches Gemeingut," *Freiburger Rundbrief* 14/53–56: 15–16.
Grimme, Hubert
1914 "Semitische P-Laute," *ZDMG* 68: 259–269.
Grintz, J. M.
1971 "Do Not Eat on the Blood," ASTI, VIII, 78–105.
Grünhut, Ladislaus
1931 *Eros and Agape. Eine metaphysisch-religionsphilosophische Untersuchung.*
Grünhut, Lazar
1891 *Midrasch Schir ha-Schirim.*
Gurney, O. R.
1962 "Tammuz Reconsidered: Some Recent Developments," *JSS* 7: 147–160.
Güterbock, H. G.
1956 "Periodicals Germany," *Oriens* 9: 311–316.
Habersaat, K.
1934 *Das Hohelied bei den Kirchenvätern und anderen christlichen Erklärern vom 2–13 Jahrhundert.*

1936a "Glossare und Paraphrasen zum Hohenlied. Ein Beitrag zur Geschichte der jüdische-deutschen Hohelied-Uebersetzungen," *Biblica* 17: 348–358.

1936b *Das Hohelied Salomonis bei Goethe* (1775).

1945 *Materialen zur Bibliographie des Hohen Liedes.*

Hahn, H. A.

1852 *Das Hohe Lied von Salomo, übersetzt und erklärt.* Breslau.

Halévy, Joseph

1922 "Le Cantique des Cantiques et le Mythe d'Osiris-Hetep," *RevSém* 14: 248–255.

Haller, M.

1940 *Das Hohe Lied,* in *Die Fünf Megilloth,* Handbuch zum Alten Testament, ed. O. Eissfeldt.

Hallo, W. W.

1969 "Black is Beautiful," *Bulletin of the Congregation Mishkan Israel,* Series 55, no. 14, Hamden, Conn.

1970 "The Cultic Setting of Sumerian Poetry," in *Actes de la 17e Rencontre Assyriologique Internationale,* pp. 116–134.

———and J. J. A. van Dijk

1968 *The Exaltation of Inanna.* Yale Near Eastern Researches, no. 3.

Hamp, Vinzenz

1957 "Zur Textkritik am Hohenlied," *BZ* 1: 197–214.

Hanauer, J.

1907 *Folklore of the Holy Land.* London.

Hanson, P. C.

1959 *Allegory and Event.*

Harbsmeier, Götz

1952 *Das Hohelied der Liebe,* Biblische Studien, no. 3.

Harnack, Adolf

1961 *History of Dogma.* Translated from the 3d German ed. by Neil Buchanan. 7 vols.

Harper, A.

1902 *The Song of Solomon,* Cambridge Bible for Schools and Colleges.

1907 *The Song of Solomon, with Introduction and Notes,* Cambridge Bible for Schools and Colleges.

Harrington, W. J.

1965 *Record of the Promise: The Old Testament;* on the Canticle of Canticles, pp. 271–280.

Harris, Rendel

1916 *The Origin of the Cult of Aphrodite.*

Hartmann, M.

1899 *Lieder der libyschen Wüste.*

Hatto, A. T.

1965 *An Enquiry into the Theme of Lovers' Meetings and Partings at Dawn in Poetry.*

Haupt, Paul

1902a "Biblical Love-Ditties: A Critical Interpretation and Translation of the Song of Songs," in *Open Court,* pp. 1–11.

1902b "The Book of Canticles," *AJSL* 18: 193–241.

1903 "The Book of Canticles," *AJSL* 19: 1–32.
1907 *Biblische Liebeslieder, das sogenannte Hohelied Salomons.*

Hazan, A.
1936 Le Cantique des Cantiques enfin expliqué, suivi de La Belle et le Pâtre. Version française pour la scène.

Heimpel, W.
1968 *Tierbilder in der sumerischen Literatur,* Studia Pohl, 2.

Held, M.
1961 "A Faithful Lover in Old Babylonian Dialogue," *JCS* 15: 1–26.
1962 "(Title as above): Addenda and Corrigenda," *JCS* 16: 37–39.

Hengstenberg, E. W.
1853 *Das Hohe Lied ausgelegt.* Berlin.
1855 *Das Hohelied Salomonis.*

Herde, R.
1968 *Das Hohelied in der lateinischen Literature des Mittelalters bis zum 12. Jahrhundert,* Münchener Beiträge zur Mediavistik und Renaissance-Forschung, 3.

Hermann, Alfred
1955 "Beiträge zur Erklärung der ägyptischen Liebesdichtung," *Ägyptologische Studien* 29: 118–139.
1959 *Altägyptische Liebesdichtung.* Wiesbaden.

Herrmann, Wolfram
1963 "Gedanken zur Geschichte des altorientalischen Beschreibungslieder," *ZAW* 75: 176–197.
1968 *Yariḫ und Nikkal und der Preis der Kūṯarāt-Göttinen.* BZAW 106.

Hess, J. J.
1924 "Über das präfigierte und infigierte ʿim Arabischen," *ZS* 2: 219–223.

Hill, W. D. P.
1959 *The Idylls of Theocritus in English Verse.*

Hir-Grandvaux, L.
1882 *Le Cantique des Cantiques,* in *La Sainte Bible.*

Hirschberg, H. H.
1961 "Some additional Arabic Etymologies in OT Lexicography" *VT* 11: 373–385.

Hirzel, L.
1840 *Das Lied der Lieder, oder Sieg der Treue* (Song of Songs or Victory of Virtue).

Hitzig, Ferdinand
1855 *Das Hohe Lied.* Kurgefasste exegetische Handbuch zum Alten Testament, XVI.

Holeman, H. G.
1856 *Die Krone des Hohen Liedes; einheitliches Erklärung seines Schlussactes.*

Hölscher, Gustav
1920 "Elemente arabischer, syrischer and hebräischer Metrik," in BZAW 34, Festschrift Karl Budde: 93–101.

Honeyman, A. M.
1939 "The Pottery Vessels of the Old Testament" *PEQ* 80: 76–90.
1949 "Two Contributions to Canaanite Toponymy" *JTS* 50: 50–52.

Hontheim, J.
1908 *Das Hohelied.*
Horst, Friedrich
1935 "Die Formen des althebräischen Liebesliedes," in *Orientalische Studien Enno Littmann zu seinem 60 Geburtstag,* pp. 43–54.
1953 "Die Kennzeichen der hebräischen Poesie," *TRu* 21: 97–121.
Houghton, W.
1865 *An essay on the Canticles, or the Song of Songs: With a translation of the poem, and short explanatory notes.*
von Hug, J. L.
1813 *Das Hohe Lied in einer noch unversuchten Deutung.* Freyburg and Constanz.
1816 *Schutzschrift für seine Deutung des Hohen Liedes, und derselben weitere Erläuterungen.* Freyburg.
Hulst, A. R., and David Lerch
1959 "Hoheslied," *RGG,* 3d ed., III, cols. 428–431.
Hurvitz, A.
1968 " 'Aramaisms' in Biblical Hebrew," *IEJ* 18: 234–240; on the Song of Songs, pp. 236*f.*
Hutton, James
1857 *A Popular Account of the Thugs and Dacoits, the hereditary garotters and gang-robbers of India.* London.
Huxley, Francis
1974 *The Way of the Sacred.*
Hyde, W. W.
1924 "Greek Analogies to the Song of Songs," in *SSS,* pp. 31–42.
Ibbotson, J. D., Jr.
1913 "The Song of Songs, A Secular Poem," *BW* 41: 314–321.
Ingalls, D. H. H.
1971 "Remarks on Mr. Wasson's SOMA," *JAOS* 91: 188–191.
Ingholt, Harald
1926 "Un nouveau thiase à Palmyre," *Syria* 7: 128–141.
Isserlin, B. S. J.
1958 "Song of Songs IV,4: An Archaeological Note," *PEQ* 90: 59–60.
Jacob, Georg
1902 *Das Hohelied auf Grund arabischer und anderer Parallelen untersucht.*
Jacobsen, Th.
1961 "Toward the Image of Tammuz," *HR* 1: 189–213.
Jameson, A. (Mrs. Anna Brownell Murphy)
1848 *Sacred and Legendary Art,* 2 vols.
Jastrow, Morris, Jr.
1921 *The Songs of Songs, Being a Collection of Love Lyrics of Ancient Palestine: A New Translation Based on a Revised Text, together with the Origin, Growth, and Interpretation of the Songs.*
Jaussen, A. J.
1908 *Coutumes des Arabes.*

Jellinek, Adolph
1853–77 *Beth ha-Midrash.*
Jochims, Uwe
1960 "Thirza und die Ausgrabungen auf dem tell el-*fār'a,*" *ZDPV* 76: 73–96.
Johansen, H.
1927 "Die palästinisch-arabische Dichtkunst und die weltliche hebräische Poesie," in *Festschrift für Adolf Schlatter,* pp. 53–72.
Joüon, Paul
1909 *Le Cantique des Cantiques: Commentaire philogique et exégétique.*
Kaempf, S. J.
1875 "Die runden Zahlen im Hohenliede," *ZDMG* 29: 629–632.
1877 *Das Hohelied.*
Kaiser, G. P. C.
1825 *Das Hohelied, ein Collectiv-Gesang auf Serubbabel, Esra, und Nehemia, als die Wiederhersteller einer jüdischen Verfassung in der Provinz Juda.* Erlangen.
Kakati, Bani Kanta
1948 *The Mother Goddess Kāmākhyā.*
Kaske, R. E.
1962 "The *Canticum Canticorum* in the Miller's Tale," *Studies in Philology* 59: 479–500.
Keith, A. B.
1953 *A History of Sanskrit Literature.*
Kelley, C. R.
1960 "Conservative View of the Song of Solomon." Dissertation, Dallas Theological Seminary.
Kessler, R.
1957 *Some Poetical and Structural Features of the Song of Songs,* ed. John Macdonald. Leeds University Oriental Society Monograph Series, no. 8.
al-Khalesi, Y. M.
1966 "Unpublished Figurines in the Iraq Museum." Dissertation, University of Baghdad.
King, C. W.
1887 *The Gnostics and Their Remains.*
Kingsbury, T. L.
1903 *Commentary and Notes on the Song of Songs,* The Bible Commentary —The Speaker's Commentary, IV.
Kinlaw, D.
1968 *The Song of Solomon,* The Wesleyan Bible Commentary.
Klasens, A.
1952 A magical statue base in the Museum of Antiquities at Leiden, *Oudheidkundige medelingen uit het Rijksmuseum van Oudheiden,* 33.
Kline, M. G.
1959 "Bible Book of the Month. The Song of Songs," *Christianity Today* 4: 22–23, 39.

Klostermann, Erich
1899 "Eine alte Rollenverteilung zum Hohenlied," *ZAW* 19: 158–162.
Knight, G. A. F.
1955 *Esther. Song of Songs. Lamentations.* Torch Bible Commentaries.
Kohler, K.
1878 *Das Hohe Lied übersetzt und kritisch neubearbeitet.*
Koldewey, R.
1911 *Die Tempel von Babylon und Borsippa.*
Kopf, L.
1956 "Das arabische Wörterbuch als Hilfsmittel für die hebräische Lexikographie: *VT* 6: 286–302." On Songs of Songs 7:3, pp. 293*f*.
Kortleitner, F. X.
1902 *Canticum Canticorum explicatum.*
Kramer, S. N.
1955 "Love Song to a King," in *ANET*, p. 496.
1956 "To the Royal Bridegroom. The First Love Song," ch. 23 in *From the Tablets of Sumer*, pp. 249–253.
1961 "Mythologies of Sumer and Akkad," in *Mythologies of the Ancient World*, ed. S. N. Kramer.
1962 "The Biblical 'Song of Songs' and the Sumerian Love Songs," *Expedition* 5: 25–31.
1963 "Cuneiform Studies and the History of Literature: The Sumerian Sacred Marriage Texts," *PAPS* 107: 485–527.
1966 "Dumuzi's Annual Resurrection: An Important Correction to 'Inanna's Descent'," *BASOR* 183: 31.
1969a "Inanna and Šulgi: A Sumerian Fertility Song," *Iraq* 31: 20–22.
1969b "The Sacred Marriage and Solomon's Song of Songs," in *SMR*, pp. 85–106.
Krauss, Samuel
1934 "Die 'Landschaft' in biblischen Hohenliede," *MGWJ* 78: 81–97.
1936a "Der richtige Sinn von 'Schrecken in der Nacht', HL III 8" in *Occident and Orient*, Moses Gaster Eightieth Anniversary Volume, pp. 323–330.
1936b "Die Rechtslage im biblischen Hohenliede," *MGWJ* 44: 330–339.
1941–42 "The Archaeological Background of Some Passages in the Song of Songs," *JQR* 32: 115–137.
1942–43 (Title as above), *JQR* 33: 17–27.
1944–45 (Title as above), *JQR* 35: 59–78.
Krinetzki, Leo
1962 "Die Macht der Liebe. Eine ästhetisch–exegetische Untersuchung zu Hl 8, 6–7," *Münchener Theologische Zeitschrift* 13: 256–279.
1964 *Das Hohe Lied: Kommentar zu Gestalt und Kerygma eines alttestamentlichen Liebesliedes.*
1970 "Die erotische Psychologie des Hohen Liedes," *TQ* 150: 404–416.
Kronasser, Heinz
1963 *Die Umsiedlung der schwarzen Gottheit. Das hethitische Ritual, KUB,* XX, 4. Vienna.

Kugler, F. X.
1927 "Vom Hohen Liede und seiner kriegerischen Braut," *Scholastik* 2: 38–52.

Kuhl, Curt
1937 "Das Hohelied und seine Deutung," *TRu* 9: 137–167.

Kuhn, Gottfried
1926 "Erklärung des Hohenliedes," *NKZ* 37: 501–510, 521–572.

Kurgal, A.
1961 *Die Kunst Anatoliens.* Berlin.

Kurtz, D. C., and John Boardman
1971 *Greek Burial Customs.*

Kutscher, E. Y.
1965 *Words and Their Histories* (in Hebrew).

LaBotz, Paul
1965 *The Romance of the Ages; An exposition of the Song of Solomon.*

Lachs, S. T.
1960 "An Egyptian Festival in Canticles Rabba," *JQR* 51: 47–54.
1964–65 "Prolegomena to Canticles Rabba," *JQR* 55: 47–54.
1965–66 "The Proems of Canticles Rabba," *JQR* 56: 225–239.

Lambert, Maurice
1961 "La littérature Sumérienne à propos d'ouvrages récents," *RA* 55: 177–196.

Lambert, W. G.
1959 "Divine Love Lyrics from Babylon," *JSS* 4: 1–15.
1969 "An Eye Stone of Esarhaddon's Queen and Other Similar Gems," *RA* 63: 65–71.
1975 "The Problem of the Love Lyrics," in *Unity and Diversity: Essays in the History, Literature and Religion of the Ancient Near East,* eds. H. Goedicke and J. J. M. Roberts, pp. 98–135.

Lambrecht, Pierre
1955 "La résurrection d'Adonis,' in *Mélanges Isidore Levy,* pp. 207–240.

Landsberger, Benno
1960 "Einige unerkannt gebliebene oder verkannte Nomina des Akkadischen," *WZKM* 56: 109–129.
1961 (Title as above), *WZKM* 57: 1–23.

Landsberger, Franz
1955 "Poetic Units within the Song of Songs," *JBL* 73: 203–216.

Langdon, S.
1913 *Babylonian Liturgies.*
1921 "Babylonian and Hebrew Musical Terms," *JRAS*: 169–191.

Laroche, Emmanuel
1947 "Recherches sur les noms des dieux hittites," *RHA,* tome VII, fasc. 46, 7–139.

LaSor, W. S.
1952(?) "Isaiah 7:14—'Young Woman' or 'Virgin'?" Privately published pamphlet.

Laurin, R. B.
1962 "The Life of True Love: The Song of Songs and Its Modern Message," *Christianity Today* 6: 10/1062 – 11/1063.
Leahy, F. S.
1955 "The Song of Solomon in Pastoral Teaching," *EvQ* 27: 205–213.
Leemans, W. F.
1960 *Foreign Trade in the Old Babylonian Period.*
Lefèvre, A.
1954 "Review of A. Feuillet, *Le Cantique des Cantiques,*" *RSR* 42: 131–135.
Lehrmann, S. M.
1946 Introduction and Commentary to the Song of Songs, in *The Five Megilloth,* ed. A. Cohen, Soncino Press. pp, x–xii, 1–32.
Le Lasseur, D.
1919 *Les déesses armées dans l'art classique grec et leurs origines orientales.*
Lemaire, A.
1975 "*Zāmîr* dans la tablette de Gezer et le Cantique des Cantiques," *VT* 25: 15–26.
Lerch, David
1957 "Zur Geschichte der Auslegung des Hohenliedes," *ZTK* 54: 257–277.
Leslau, W.
1951 *Falasha Anthology.*
Lesetre, H.
1889 "Cantique des Cantiques" in *Dictionnaire de la Bible,* II, cols. 194–195.
Le Strange, Guy
1890 *Palestine under the Moslems.*
Lethbridge, J. W.
1878 *The Idylls of Solomon: The Hebrew Marriage Week.*
Levias, C.
1934 "Enallage in the Bible," *AJSL* 50: 104–108.
Lewy, Julius
1938 "Lexicographical Notes," *HUCA* 12–13: 97–101.
Lichtenstädter, Ilse
1931–32 "Das *NASĪB* der altarabischen *QAṢĪDE,*" *Islamica* 5: 17–96.
Linder, Sven
1952 *Palästinische Volkgesange.* Aufgezeichnet und gesammelt. Aus dem Nachlass herausgegeben und mit Anmerkungen versehen von H. Ringgren, I, UUÅ 5.
Littlewood, A. R.
1967 "The Symbolism of the Apple in Greek and Roman Literature," *Harvard Studies in Classical Philology,* 72: 147–181.
Loewe, Raphael
1965 "The Divine Garment and the Shi'ur Qomah," *HTR* 58: 153–160.
1966 "Apologetic Motifs in the Targum to the Song of Songs," in *Biblical Motifs: Origins and Transformations,* ed. A. Altmann, Philip W. Lown Institute of Advanced Judaic Studies, Brandeis University, Studies and Texts, III, 159–196.

Loretz, Oswald
1963 *Gotteswort und menschliche Erfahrung.*
1964 "Zum Problem des Eros im Hohenlied," *BZ* 8: 191–216.
1966 "Die theologische Bedeutung des Hohenliedes," *BZ* 10: 29–43.
1971 *Das althebräische Liebeslied: Untersuchungen zur Stichometrie und Redaktionsgeschichte des Hohenliedes und des 45 Psalms.* AOAT 14/1.

Loring, R. T.
1967 "The Christian Historical Exegesis of the Song of Songs and Its Possible Jewish Antecedents: A Chapter in the History of Interpretation." Dissertation, General Theological Seminary, New York.

Loveless, W. P.
1945 *Christ and the Believer in the Song of Songs.*

Löw, Immanuel
1936 "Marmor. Ein Kapitel aus meinem: Mineralien der Juden," in *Occident and Orient,* Moses Gaster Anniversary Volume, pp. 374–379.

Löwisohn, S.
1816 *Melizat Jeschurun.* Vienna.

Lund, Eimar
1892 *The Song of Songs.*

Lurssen, Johanna
1917 *Eine mittelniederdeutsche Paraphrase des Hohenliedes.*

Lys, Daniel
1958 "Le plus beau chant de la création. Préliminaire à une exégèse du Cantique des Cantiques," *ÉTR* 33: 87–117.
1968 *Le plus beau chant de la création. Commentaire du Cantique des Cantiques,* Lectio Divina, LI. Les Éditions du Cerf.

Magnus, E. I.
1842 *Kritische Bearbeitung und Erklärung des Hohen Liedes Salomo's.*

Maiworm, J.
1955 *Das Hohelied. Ct nach dem hebr Urtext übersetzt und erklärt,* Bibelstudien 3.

Malamat, Abraham
1971 "Mari," *BA* 34: 1–22.

Malin, J. S.
1947 *The Song of Songs with the Targum translated from the Aramaic into [modern] Hebrew.*

Margolis, M. L.
1924 "How the Song of Songs Entered the Canon," in *SSS,* pp. 9–17.

Marmorstein, Arthur
1948 "The Jewish 'Blessing of Virginity'," *JJS* 1: 33–34.
1950 *Studies in Jewish Theology,* eds. J. J. Rabinowitz and M. S. Lew.

Martin, G. C.
1908 *The Song of Songs.* The Century Bible, VII.

Martineau, R.
1892 "The Song of Songs," *American Journal of Philology* 13: 307–328.

Marx, L.
1964 *Canticum Canticorum.* In deutsche Verse übertragen und erläutert. Vorwort von Albrecht Goes.

Matthews, H. J.

1896 "Interpretation of the Song of Songs" (in Hebrew), in *Festschrift zum 80en Geburtstag Moritz Steinschneider's,* pp. 238–240; Hebrew section, pp. 164–185.

May, H. G.

1931–32 "The Fertility Cult in Hosea," *AJSL* 48: 73–98.

1955 "Some Cosmic Connotations of Mayim Rabbim, 'Many Waters'," *JBL* 74: 9–21.

Mazar, Benjamin

13 April 1963 "The 'Perfume Factory' of King Josiah; and a Canaanite 'High Place' of 5000 Years Ago—Recent Discoveries at Engedi, by the Dead Sea." *The Illustrated London News,* 242, 546*f*.

Meek, T. J.

1922–23 "Canticles and the Tammuz Cult," *AJSL* 39: 1–14.

1924a "Babylonian Parallels to the Song of Songs," *JBL* 43: 245–252.

1924b "The Song of Songs and the Fertility Cult," in *SSS,* pp. 48–79.

1956 *The Song of Songs: Introduction and Exegesis, IB,* V, 98–148.

Meeks, W. A.

1974 "The Image of the Androgyne: Some Uses of a Symbol in Earliest Christianity," *HR* 13: 165–208.

Meer, F. van der

1961 *Augustine the Bishop,* translated by B. Battershaw and G. R. Lamb.

Melamed, E. Z.

1961 "Break-up of Stereotype Phrases," *SH* 8; on Song of Songs 1:9, 128*f*.

Menhardt, H.

1934 *Das St. Trudperter Hohelied; kritische Ausgabe von Hermann Menhardt. Mit Schriftbildern.*

Milik, J. T.

1972 *Dédicaces faites par des dieux (Palmyre, Hatra, Tyr) et des thiases sémitiques à l'époque romaine,* Recherches d'épigraphie proche-Orientale, I. Institut français d'archéologie de Beyrouth. Bibliothèque archéologique et historique, XCII. Paris.

Miller, Athanasius.

1927 *Das Hohe Lied, übersetzt und erklärt,* Die Heilige Schriften des Alten Testaments, eds. F. Feldmann and H. Herkenne, Band VI, Abteilung 3.

Miller, J. L.

1957 The Interpretation of the Song of Songs: The Ancient Versions. Dissertation, Harvard Divinity School.

Miller, P. D., Jr.

1970 "Apotropaic Imagery in Proverbs 6:20–22," *JNES* 29: 129–130.

Minocchi, S.

1898 *Il Cantico dei Cantici di Salomone tradotto e commentato con uno studio sulla donna e l'amore nell'antico oriente.*

Modi, J. J.

1922 *The Religious Ceremonies and Customs of the Parsees.*

Montefiore, M.
1874 *Interpretation of the Song of Songs* (in Hebrew).

Montgomery, J. A.
1924 "The Song of Songs in Early and Medieval Christian Use," in *SSS*, pp. 18–30.

Moody-Stuart, A.
1857 *The Song of Songs: An Exposition of the Song of Solomon*, 2d ed. 1860.
1869 *The Song of Songs: An Exposition of the Song of Solomon with a Metrical Version of the Song of Solomon by William Skinner Rentoul.*

de Moor, J. C.
1968 "Murices in Ugaritic Mythology," *Orientalia* 37: 212–215.
1969 "Studies in the New Alphabetic Texts from Ras Shamra I," *UF* 1: 167–188.

Moret, A.
1917 "Le lotus et la naissance des dieux en Egypte," *JA* 10: 499–513.

Morgenstern, Julian
1939 "The Mythological Background of Psalm 82," *HUCA* 14: 29–126.
1940 "Amos Studies III," *HUCA* 15: 59–304.

Moulton, R. G.
1930 *Biblical Idyls.* The Modern Reader's Bible.

Movers, T. C.
1841–56 *Die Phönizier*, 4 volumes.

Mowinckel, Sigmund
1961 *Salomos høysang. Gammelhebraiske kjaerlighetsdikte.*

Muller, H. P.
1965 "Mann und Frau im Wandel der Wirklichkeitserfahrung Israels," *ZRGG* 17: 1–19.

Murphy, R. E.
1949 "The Structure of the Canticle of Canticles," *CBQ* 11: 381–391.
1953 Review of A. Bea, *Canticum Canticorum Salomonis*, *CBQ* 15: 501–505.
1954a "The Canticle of Canticles and the Virgin Mary," *Carmelus* 1: 18–28.
1954b "Recent Literature on the Canticle of Canticles," *CBQ* 16: 1–11.
1955 "The Canticle of Canticles in the Confraternity Version," *AER* 133: 87–98.
1961 *The Book of Eccelsiastes and the Canticle of Canticles*, Paulist Fathers, Pamphlet Bible Series, 38.
1968 "Canticle of Canticles," in *JBC.*
1973 "Form-critical Studies in the Song of Songs," *Interpretation* 27: 413–422.

Musajoff, S.
1921 *Sēper merkāḇāh šĕlēmāh;* on Shi'ur Qomah, pp. 30a–43b. Jerusalem.

Napier, B. D.
1962 *Song of the Vineyard.*

Neher, André
1954 "Le symbolisme conjugal, expression de l'histoire dans l'Ancien Testament," *RHPR* 34: 30–49.

Neil, J.
1885 *Kissing: Its Curious Bible Mentions.* London.

Neuschotz de Jassy, O.
1914 *Le Cantique des Cantiques et le mythe d'Osiris-Hetep.*

Newton, A. L.
1907 *The Song of Solomon compared with Other Parts of Scripture.*

Nicoll, W. R.
1905 *The Garden of Nuts: Mystical Expositions with an Essay on Christian Mysticism.*

Nivedita (The Sister Nivedita of Ramakrishna-Vivekanada, Margaret E. Noble)
1950 *Kali the Mother.*
1963 *An Indian Study of Love and Death,* 2d ed.

Nöldeke, Theodor
1904 *Beiträge zur semitischen Sprachwissenschaft.*
1910 *Neue Beiträge zur semitischen Sprachwissenschaft.*

Nygren, Anders
1932 *Agape and Eros; a study of the Christian idea of love,* tr. A. G. Herbert. 2 vols.

Oesterley, W. O. E.
1936 *The Song of Songs: The Authorized Version together with a New Translation, an Introduction and Notes, with Engravings on Copper by L. Sandford.*

Oettli, S.
1889 *Das Hohelied,* in Streck, Zickler, *Kurzgefasste Kommentar zum Alten Testament,* VII.

Ogara, F.
1936 "Novi in 'Canticum' commentarii rescensio et brevis de sensu litterali et typico disceptatio," *Gregorianum* 17: 132–142.

Ohly, F.
1958 *Hohelied-Studien: Grundzüge einer Geschichte der Hohenliedauslegung des Abendlandes bis zum 1200.* Schriften der wissenschaftlichen Gesellschaft an der Johann Wolfgang Goethe-Universitat, Frankfurt am Main, Geisteswissenschaftliche Reihe, no. 1, Wiesbaden.

Ohnefalsch-Richter, M.
1893 *Kypros, die Bibel und Homer.* 2 vols.

Oppel, A.
1911 *Das Hohelied Salomonis und die deutsche religiöse Liebeslyrik.*

von Orelli, Conrad
1900 "Hohes Lied," *Realencyklopädie für protestantische Theologie und Kirche* 8: 256–263. (Gotha.)
1911 "Song of Solomon," *The New Schaff-Herzog Encyclopaedia of Religious Knowledge,* XI, 1–4.

van den Oudenrijn, M. A.
1953 "Vom Sinne des Hohen Liedes," *DT* 31: 257–280.
1962 *Het Hooglied.*

Parente, P. P.
1944 "The Canticle of Canticles in Mystical Theology," *CBQ* 6: 142–158.

Parker, B.
1961 "Administrative Tablets from the Northwest Palace, Nimrud," *Iraq* 23: 15–67.
Parrot, André
1959 *Mission archéologique de Mari II: Le palais-documents et monuments.*
Patai, Raphael
1967 *Man and Temple in Ancient Jewish Myth and Ritual,* 2d ed.
Paton, L. B.
1921 *Spiritism and the Cult of the Dead in Antiquity.*
1926 "The Song of Songs," *A New Standard Bible Dictionary,* eds. Jacobus, Nourse, and Zenos, pp. 860*f.*
Patterson, D.
1958 Review of S. D. Goitein, *The Art of Narrative in the Bible,* in *JSS* 3: 90–93.
Payne, Humfry
1931 *Necrocorinthia: A Study of Corinthian Art in the Archaic Period.* Oxford.
Peek, W.
1955 *Griechische Versinschriften,* I, *Grab-Epigramme.*
Perella, N. J.
1969 *The Kiss, Sacred and Profane. An Interpretative History of Kiss Symbolism and Related Religio-Erotic Themes.*
Perles, Felix
1895 *Analekten zur Textkritik des Alten Testaments,* NF 1922.
Pflaum, Heinz
1926 *Die Idee der Liebe; Leone Ebreo*
Phipps, W. E.
1970 *Was Jesus Married? The Distortion of Sex in the Christian Tradition.*
February 1972 "The Kiss of Love," *Pastoral Psychology* 23, no. 221.
January 1973 "The Sensuousness of Agape," *Theology Today* 29/4.
1974 "The Plight of the Song of Songs," *JAAR* 42: 82–100.
1975 *Recovering Bible Sensuousness.*
Piatti, D.
1953 "Il Cantico dei Cantici alla luce del libro di Geremia. Una enigma biblico svelato?" *DT* 56: 18–38, 179–210.
1958 *Il Cantico dei Cantici.*
Picard, Charles
1922 *Ephèse et Claros.*
Plessis, J.
1914 *Étude sur les textes concernant Ištar-Astarte.*
Pope, M. H.
1964 "The Word *šaḥaṯ* in Job 9:31" *JBL* 83: 269–278.
1966 "Marginalia to Dahood's 'Ugaritic-Hebrew Philology'," *JBL* 85: 455–466.
1970a "The Saltier of Atargatis Reconsidered," in *Near Eastern Archaeology in the Twentieth Century: Essays in Honor of Nelson Glueck,* ed. J. A. Sanders, pp. 178–196.
1970b "A Mare in Pharoah's Chariotry," *BASOR* 200: 56–61.

1972 "A Divine Banquet of Ugarit," in *The Use of the Old Testament in the New and Other Essays: Studies in Honor of William Franklin Stinespring,* ed. J. M. Efird, pp. 170–203.

———and W. Röllig

1962 "Syrien: Die Mythologie der Ugariter und Phönizer," in *WbM,* pp. 219–312.

———and J. H. Tigay

1971 "A Description of Baal," *UF* 3: 117–130.

Porten, Bezalel

1968 "The Marzēaḥ Association," in *The Archives from Elephantine,* pp. 177–186.

Porter, J. R.

1962 "Samson's Riddle: Judges xiv 14,18," *JTS* 13: 106–109.

Pouget, G. S., and J. Guitton

1948 *Le Cantique des Cantiques,* 2d ed.

Rabin, Chaim

1973 "The Song of Songs and Tamil Poetry," SR 3: 205–219.

Rabinovitch, I.

1952 "The Biblical Melody of the Canticum Canticorum," in *Of Jewish Music, Ancient and Modern,* tr. A. M. Klein, pp. 105–110.

Rabinowitz, Isaac

1971 "The Qumran Hebrew Original of Ben Sira's Concluding Acrostic on Wisdom," *HUCA* 42: 173–184.

Radet, C.

1927 "Artemis d'Ephèse," *JS* 112: 14–22.

Ramlot, M. L.

1964 "Le Cantique des Cantiques, 'une flamme de Yahve'," *RThom* 64: 239–259.

Ramsaran, J. A.

1973 *English and Hindi Religious Poetry*. Leiden.

Randolph, C. B.

1905 "The Mandragora of the Ancients in Folklore and Medicine," *PAAAS* 12: 487–537.

Ranke, Hermann

1924 "Die Vergottung der Glieder des menschlichen Körpers bei den Ägyptern," *OLZ* 27: 558–563.

Ravetch, I. S.

1934 "Shir Hashirim: Some Aspects of Interpretation." Thesis, Jewish Institute of Religion, New York.

Reider, Joseph

1925 "Studies in Hebrew Roots and Their Etymologies," *HUCA* 11: 87–97.

Reisman, D.

1973 "Iddin-Dagan's Sacred Marriage Hymn," *JCS* 25: 185–202.

Renan, Ernest

1860 *Le Cantique des Cantiques. Traduit de l'Hébreu avec une étude sur le plan, l'âge, et le caractère du poème.*

Reuss, Eduard

1895 *Das Alte Testament übersetzt, eingeleitet und erläutert.*

Rexroth, Kenneth

26 April 1969 "Classics Revisited—LXXXV. The Song of Songs," *Saturday Review of Literature*: 16.

Ricciotti, Guiseppe

1928 *Il Cantico dei Cantici. Versione critica dal Testo Ebraico con Introduzione e Commento.*

Richter, Georg

1938 "Zur Enstehungsgeschichte der altarabischen Qaṣīde," *ZDMG* 92: 552–569.

Riedlinger, H.

1958 *Die Makellosigkeit der Kirche in den lateinischen Hoheliedkommentaren des Mittelalters.*

Riessler, Paul

1919 "Zum Hohen Lied," *TQ* 100: 5–37.

Ringgren, Helmer

1947 *Word and Wisdom: The Hypostatisation of Divine Qualities and Functions in the Ancient Near East.* Lund.

1952 "Die Volksdichtung und das Hohe Lied," UUÅ 5: 82–118.

1953 "Hohes Lied und hieros gamos," *ZAW* 65: 300–302.

1958 *Das Hohe Lied,* in Das Alte Testament Deutsch, XVI/2.

Rivera, P. Alfonso

1951 "Sentido mariologico del Cantar de los Cantos," EM 1: 437–468.

1952 (Title as above), EM 2: 25–42.

Robert, André

1939 "Le Psaume CXIX et les Sapientiaux," *RB* 48: 5–20.

1944 "Le genre litteraire du Cantique des Cantiques," *RB* 52: 192–213.

1945 "La description de l'Époux et de l'Épouse dans Cant v, 11–15 et VII, 2–6," in *Mélanges E. Podechard,* pp. 211–223.

1948 "Les appendices du Cantique des Cantiques (VIII, 8–14)," *RB* 55: 161–183.

1954 "La paix eschatologique dans le Cantique des Cantiques," in *Actas del XXXV Congresso Eucaristico Internacional,* Sessiones de Estudii, I, 335–337. Extract excursus in RTF, pp. 333–335.

Robson, J. P.

1860 *The Song of Solomon, versified from the English translation of James of England, into the dialect of the colliers of Northumberland, by principally those dwelling on the banks of the Tyne.*

Rosenmüller, E. F. K.

1813 "Über des Hohenliedes Sinn und Auslegung," *Analekten,* eds. C. A. G. Keil and H. G. Tzschirner, I/3, 138–162.

Rosenthal, Franz

1939 "Die Parallelstellen in den Texten von Ugarit," *Orientalia* 8: 213–237.

Rosenthal, J. M.

1958 "Rashi's Interpretation of the Song of Songs" (in Hebrew), in *Samuel K. Mirsky Jubilee Volume,* eds. S. Bernstein and G. A. Churgin, pp. 130–188.

Rosenzweig, F.

1970 *The Star of Redemption,* tr. W. W. Hallo; on Song of Songs, pp. 199–204.

Roth, R., and W. D. Whitney

1856 *Atharva Veda Sanhitā*, I. Berlin.

Rothstein, J. W.

1893 *Das Hohelied.*

1902 "Song of Songs," in *Hastings Dictionary of the Bible*, pp. 595–597.

Rowe, Alan

1940 *The Four Canaanite Temples of Beth Shan.*

Rowley, H. H.

1938 "The Song of Songs. An Examination of Recent Theory," *JRAS*: 251–276.

1939 "The Meaning of 'the Shulammite'," *AJSL* 56: 84–91.

Rozelaar, Marc

1954 "The Song of Songs on the Basis of Greek-Hellenistic Erotic Poetry" (in Hebrew), *Eshkoloth* 1: 33–48.

Rubinstein, Arie

1953 "Notes on the Use of the Tenses in the Variant Readings of the Isaiah Scroll," *VT* 3: 92–95.

Rudolph, Wilhelm

1942–43 "Das Hohe Lied im Kanon," *ZAW* 59: 189–199.

1962 *Das Buch Ruth. Das Hohelied. Die Klagelieder,* Kommentar zum Alten Testament, XVII/1–3.

Rundgren, Frithiof

1962 "*'appirjon,* Tragsessel, Sanfte," *ZAW* 74: 70–72.

Rush, A. C.

1941 *Death and Burial in Christian Antiquity.*

Sabar, Yona

1970 "A Neo-Aramaic Homily on *Bešellaḥ.*" Dissertation, Yale University.

Salfeld, S.

1878 "Das Hohelied Salomo's bei den jüdischen Erklären des Mittelalters," *Magazin für die Wissenschaft des Judenthums,* 5: 110–178.

1879a (Title as above), *Magazin für die Wissenschaft des Judenthums,* 6: 20–48, 129–209.

1879b *Das Hohelied Salomo's bei den jüdischen Erklärern des Mittelalters. Nebst einem Anhange: Erklärungs problems aus Handschriften.*

Salonen, Armas

1951 *Die Landfahrzeuge des alten Mesopotamien.*

1961 "Die Türen des alten Mesopotamien; eine lexikalische und kulturgeschichtliche Untersuchung," Annales Acadamiae Scientiarum Fennicae, Ser. B, t. 124. (Helsinki.)

1963 *Die Möbel des alten Mesopotamien.*

Salters, E.

1923 *Historia Amoris: A History of Love Ancient and Modern;* on the Song of Songs, pp. 14*f*.

Sanders, J. A.

1965 *The Psalms Scroll of Qumran Cave 11,* Discoveries in the Judaean Desert of Jordan, IV; on Sirach 51:13*ff*, pp. 79–85.

1967 *The Dead Sea Psalms Scroll;* on Sirach 51:13*ff*, pp. 113–117.

1971 "The Sirach 51 Acrostic," in *Hommages à André Dupont-Sommer,* pp. 429–438.

Sarna, N. M.

1959 "The Interchange of the Prepositions *Beth* and *Min* in Biblical Hebrew," *JBL* 78: 310–316.

Sasson, J. M.

1973a "A Further Cuneiform Parallel to the Song of Songs?" *ZAW* 85: 359–360.

1973b "The Worship of the Golden Calf," in *Orient and Occident: Essays Presented to Cyrus H. Gordon,* AOAT 22, pp. 151–159.

Sbinga, J. S.

1966 "Une citation du Cantique dans la Secunda Petri," *RB* 73: 107–118.

Schechter, Solomon

1896 *Aggadat Shir Ha-Shirim.*

Schlottmann, K.

1867 "Der Brautzug des Hohenliedes (3,6–11)," *Theologische Studien und Kritiken* 40: 209–243. (Hamburg.)

Schmidt, Nathaniel

1911 *The Message of the Poets.*

1926 "Is Canticles an Adonis Liturgy?" *JAOS* 46: 154–164.

Schmökel, Hartmut

1952 "Zur kultischen Deutung des Hoheliedes," *ZAW* 64: 148–155.

1953 "Hoheslied und altorientalische Götterhochzeit," *FuF* 27: 110–113.

1956 *Heilige Hochzeit und Hoheslied.* Abhandlungen für die Kunde des Morgenlandes, XXXII/1.

Schneemelcher, W., ed.

1964 *New Testament Apocrypha,* II. Philadelphia.

Schoff, W. H.

1924 "The Offering Lists in the Song and Their Political Significance," in *SSS,* pp. 80–120.

Scholem, Gershon

1952 "Zur Entwicklungsgeschichte der kabbalistischen Konzeption der Shechinah," *ErJb* 21: 45–107.

1961 *Major Trends in Jewish Mysticism.*

1965a *Jewish Gnosticism, Merkabah Mysticism, and Talmudic Tradition.*

1965b *On the Kabbalah and Its Symbolism.*

Schonfield, H.

1960 *The Song of Songs, Translated and Annotated.*

Schott, Siegfried

1950 *Altägyptische Liebeslieder. Mit Märchen und Liebesgeschichten.*

1957 "Wörter für Rollsiegel und Ring," *WZKM* 54: 177–185.

Schoville, K. N.

1969 "The Impact of the Ras Shamra Texts on the Study of the Song of Songs." Dissertation, University of Wisconsin.

Schwarz, L. W.

1964 "On Translating the Song of Songs," *Judaism* 13: 64–76.

Scott, D. R.

1915 *Pessimism and Love—A Study of Ecclesiastes and the Song of Songs.*

Seerveld, C.
1967 *The Greatest Song. In Critique of Solomon freshly and literally translated from the Hebrew and arranged for oratorio performance.* Trinity Pennyasheet Press.
Segal, M. H.
1962 "The Song of Songs," *VT* 12: 470–490.
Segal, M. Z.
1957 "The Scroll of the Song of Songs, Its Unity and Date" (in Hebrew), *Mahanayim* 32: 133–138.
Segar, M. F.
1918 "Echoes of Canticles in Mediaeval Literature," *The Catholic World* 106: 782–789.
Segert, Stanislav
1953 "Vorarbeiten zur hebräischen Metrik," *ArOr* 21: 481–542.
1956 "Die Versform des Hohenliedes," in *Charisteria Johann Rypka,* pp. 285–299. Prague.
Seiple, W. G.
1902 "Theocritean Parallels to the Song of Songs," *AJSL* 19: 108–115.
Shuraydi, H. A.
1971 "The Medieval Muslim Attitude toward Youth." Dissertation, Yale University.
Siegel, H.
1955 *The Sublime Songs of Love: A New Commentary on the Song of Songs and Related Essays.*
Siegfried, C.
1898 "Prediger und Hoheslied," in *Handkommentar zum Alten Testament,* ed. W. Nowack.
Sigwalt, Ch.
1911 "Das Lied der Lieder in seiner ursprünglichen Textordnung," *BZ* 9: 27–53.
Simke, Heinz
1962 "Cant. 1,7f in altchristlicher Auslegung," *TZ* 18: 256–267.
Simon, Maurice
1951 "Song of Songs," *Midrash Rabbah,* trs. H. Freedman and Maurice Simon.
Simon, P.
1951 "Sponsa Cantici. Die Deutung der Braut des Hohenliedes in der vornizanischen griechischen Theologie und in der lateinischen Theologie des 3 und 4 Jahrhunderts." Dissertation, Bonn University.
Simpson, W. K., ed.
1972 *The Literature of Ancient Egypt,* Part 4: Songs, Poetry and Hymns, The Love Songs and the Song of the Harper, tr. W. K. Simpson.
Skaist, A.
1969 "The Authority of the Brother at Arrapḫa and Nuz (Nuzi)," *JAOS* 89: 10–17.
Skehan, P. W.
1965 "The Biblical Scrolls from Qumran and the Text of the Old Testament," *BA* 28: 87–100.
1971 "The Acrostic Poem in Sirach 51:13–30," *HTR* 64: 387–400.

Smalley, Beryl
1950 "Some thirteenth century commentaries on the sapiential books," *Dominican studies* 3: 236–274.

Smith, J. M. P.
1927–28 "The Syntax and Meaning of Gen 1:1–3," *AJSL* 44: 108–115.
1928–29 "The Use of Divine Names as Superlatives," *AJSL* 45: 212–213.

Smither, P.
1948 "Prince Meḥy of the Love Songs," *JEA* 34: 116.

Snaith, N. H.
1933–34 "The Song of Songs, The Dances of the Virgins," *AJSL* 50: 129–142.
1949 "Solomon and the Rose of Sharon: a Springtime Idyll," in *The Story of the Bible*, II.

Snowden, F. M., Jr.
1970 *Blacks in Antiquity: Ethiopians in the Greco-Roman Experience;* on Origen and the Song of Songs 1:5, pp. 198–205.

von Soden, Wolfram
1950 "Ein Zweigespräch Hammurabis mit einer Frau," *ZA* 49: 151–194.
1973 "Ergänzende Bemerkunden zum 'Lieberzauber' Text," MAD 5, no. 8, *ZA* 62: 273*f*.

Sparks, H. F. D.
1959 "The Symbolical Interpretation of Lebanon in the Fathers," *JTS* 10: 264–279.

Speiser, E. A.
1954 "Authority and Law in Mesopotamia," *JAOS* Suppl. 17, pp. 8–15. Reprint 1967 in *Oriental and Biblical Studies,* eds. J. J. Finkelstein and Moshe Greenberg, pp. 313–321.
1965 "Palil and Its Congeners: A Sampling of Apotropaic Symbols," in *Studies in Honor of Benno Landsberger,* Assyriological Studies no. 16, pp. 389–393. Chicago.

Spicq, C.
1944 *Esquisse de l'exégèse latin au Moyen Âge;* on Song of Songs, see pp. 58, 104, 115, 151.

Spoer, H. H.
1906 "Some Contributions to the Interpretation of the Song of Songs, Suggested by Travel in Palestine," *AJSL* 22: 292–301.

Stade, Bernhard
Geschichte des Volkes Israel, II, 197.

Staerk, Willi/y
1920 *Lyrik, Psalmen, Hoheslied und Verwandtes,* in Schriften des Alten Testaments in Auswahl, 2d ed., III/1.
1937 "Warum steht das Hohe Lied im Kanon?" *Theologische Blätter* 16: 289–291. (Leipzig.)

Staton, J. T.
1859 *The Song of Solomon in the Lancashire dialect, as spoken at Bolton. From the authorized English version.* Translated for Prince Louis Lucien Bonaparte.

Steindorff, G.
1942 *When Egypt Ruled the East.*

Steinmann, Jean
1961 *Poésie Biblique. Isaie, Jeremie, Job, Cantique des Cantiques.*

Stephan, S. H.
1922 "Modern Palestinian Parallels to the Song of Songs," *JPOS* 2:1–80// 198–278 (double pagination).

Stickel, J. G.
1888 *Das Hohelied.*

Stowe, C. E.
1847 "Solomon's Song," *The Biblical Repository and Classical Review,* 3d series, 3: 255–272. Reprint, *The Journal of Sacred Literature,* NS 1 (1852), 320–329. (London.)

Stuiber, Alfred
1959 "Die Wachhutte im Weingarten," JAC 2: 86–89.

Suarès, C.
1972 *The Song of Songs: The canonical 'Song of Solomon' deciphered according to the original code of the Qabala.*

Sudermann, Hermann
1908 *Das hohe Lied* (*The Song of Songs*), tr. by Thomas Saltzer, 1916.

Suys, Émile
1932 "Les Chants d'Amour du papyrus Chester Beatty I," *Biblica* 13: 209–227.

Szczygiel, Paul
1922 "Zum Aufbau und Gedankengang des Hohen Liedes," *TGl* 14: 35–47.

Taoussi, A.
1924 *Le Cantique des Cantiques de Salomon.*

Tarn, W. W., and G. T. Griffith
1959 *Hellenistic Civilization,* 3d ed.

Tate, J.
1927 "The Beginnings of Greek Allegory," *Classical Review* 41: 214–215.

Terry, M. S.
1893 *The Song of Songs: An Inspired Melodrama.*

Thilo, Martin
1921 *Das Hohelied neu übersetzt und ästhetische-sittlich beurteilt.*

Thomas, D. W.
1953 "A Consideration of Some Unusual Ways of Expressing the Superlative in Hebrew," *VT* 3: 209–224.

Thomson, W. M.
1865 *The Land and the Book.*

Thrupp, J. F.
1862 *The Song of Songs: A Revised Translation with Introduction and Commentary.*

Tietz, H.
1870 *Das Hohelied, metrisch übersetzt und mit Anmerkungen nach dem Midrash versehen.*

Tishby, J.
1961 *Mishnat haZohar*

Tobac, E.
1926 *Les cinq livres de Salomon.*

Torcyzner, N. *See* Tur-Sinai, N. H.

Torelli, Achille

1892 *Sul Cantico dei Cantici: congetture,* Opere di Archille Torelli, volume primo.

Tournay, R.

1953 "Bulletin bibliographique," *RB* 60: 414–417.

1955 "Notes on commentaries on SoS," *RB* 62: 284–286.

1959a "Les chariots d'Aminadab (Cant. VI 12): Israel, peuple théophore," *VT* 9: 288–309.

1959b "Le Psaume LXVIII et le Livre des Juges," *RB* 66: 358–368.

1963 "Les affinités du Ps. XLV avec le Cantique des Cantiques et leur interprétation messianique," VTS, IX, 168–212.

———and M. Nicolay

1967 *Le Cantique des Cantiques, commentaire abrégé,* Lire la Bible, IX.

Toutain, J. F.

1907–20 *Cultes païens dans l'empire romain.* Vol. II.

Toynbee, J. M. C.

1971 *Death and Burial in the Roman World.*

Treves, D. B.

1969 *Sefer Shir ḥadash.*

Trible, Phyllis

1973 "Depatriarchalizing in Biblical Interpretation," *JAAR* 41: 30–48.

Tristram, H. B.

1873 *The Natural History of the Bible.*

Tromp, N. J.

1969 *Primitive Conceptions of Death and the Netherworld in the Old Testament.*

Trotti, J. B.

1964 *Beauty in the Old Testament.* Dissertation, Yale University.

Tur-Sinai, N. H.

1948–55 *The Tongue and the Book* (*Ha-Lashon weha-Sepher*), 3 vols.; on the Song of Songs, see Vol. II.

Ulanov, Barry, ed.

1961 *The Way of St. Alphonsus Liguori.*

1962 "The Song of Songs: The Rhetoric of Love," in *The Bridge. A Yearbook,* 4: 89–118.

Umbreit, F. W. K.

1820 *Lied der Liebe, das älteste und schönste aus dem Morgenlande.*

1856 Herzog's *Real-Enzyklopädie für protestantische Theologie und Kirche,* VI, 220.

Urbach, E. E.

1960–61 "Rabbinic Exegesis and Origen's Commentary on the Song of Songs and Jewish-Christian Polemics" (in Hebrew), *Tarbiz* 30: 148–170.

1971 "The Homiletical Interpretation of the Sages and the Expositions of Origin on Canticles, and the Jewish-Christian Disputation," *SH* 22: 247–275. (Translated from the Hebrew article, above.)

Vaccari, Alberto

1938 "Il Cantico dei Cantici nelli recenti publicazioni," *Biblica* 9: 443–457.

1955 "Latina Cantici Canticorum Versio a S. Hieronymo ad graecam hexaplarem emendata," *Biblica* 36: 258–260; cf. *RivB* 4 (1956), 359–373; 5 (1957), 209–304.

1963 "Cantici Canticorum latine a s. Hieronymo recensiti emendatio," *Biblica* 44: 74–75.

Vajda, G.

1957 *L'amour de Dieu dans la théologie juive de moyen âge,* Études de philosophie médiévale, no. 46.

de Vaux, Roland

1947 "La première campagne de fouilles a Tell el-Fā'ah, près Naplouse," *RB* 54: 394–433.

Vermès, Géza

1958 "The Symbolical Interpretation of Lebanon in the Targums: The Origin and Development of an Exegetical Tradition," *JTS* 9: 1–12.

Virolleaud, Charles

1933 "La Naissance des Dieux Gracieux et Beaux, Poème Phénicienne de Ras-Shamra," *Syria* 14: 128–151.

Vogel, E. K.

1971 "Bibliography of Holy Land Sites," *HUCA* 42: 1–96.

de Vries, C. E.

1969 "A Ritual Ball Game?" in *Studies in Honor of John A. Wilson,* SAOC, 35, pp. 25–35.

Waldman, N. M.

1970 "A Note on Canticles 4, 9," *JBL* 89: 215–217.

Wasson, R. G.

1971 "The Soma of the Rig Veda: What Was It?" *JAOS* 91: 169–187.

Waterman, Leroy

1919 "*DWD* in the Song of Songs," *AJSL* 35: 101–110.

1925 "The Role of Solomon in the Song of Songs," *JBL* 44: 171–187.

1948 *The Song of Songs Translated and Interpreted as a Dramatic Poem.*

Weber, D., and J. A. Knudtzon

1908–15 *Die El-Amarna Tafeln.*

Weiner, Herbert

1961 *The Wild Goats of En Gedi.*

Weiss, B.

1859 *The Song of Songs Unveiled: A New Translation and Exposition of the Song of Solomon.*

Weissbach, F.

1858 *Das Hohe Lied Salomos erklärt, übersetzt und in seiner kunstreichen poetischen Form dargestellt.*

Weiss-Rosmarin, T.

1946 "Passover and the Song of Songs," *The National Jewish Monthly* 274: 297–299.

Weitzner, E.

1961 *The Song of Songs: A Paraphrase.*

Wellhausen, Julius
1897 *Reste arabischen Heidentums.*
1905 *Prolegomena zur Geschichte Israels,* 6th ed.
Welsersheimb, L.
1948 "Das Kirchenbild der griechischen Vaterkommentare zum Hohen Lied," *ZKT* 70: 393–449.
Wetzstein, J. G.
1868 "Sprachliches aus den Zeltlagern der syrische Wüste," *ZDMG* 22: 69–194.
1873 "Die syrische Dreschtafel," *ZE* 5: 270–302.
White, E. F.
1969 "Hathor at the Jubilee," in *Studies in Honor of John A. Wilson,* SAOC, 35, pp. 83–91.
Widengren, Geo.
1955 *Sacrales Königtum im Alten Testament und im Judentum.*
Wiéner, Claude
1957 "Recherches sur l'amour pour Dieu dans l'Ancien Testament," in *Étude d'une racine.*
Williams, T.
1801 *The Song of Songs, which is by Solomon. A new translation with commentary and notes.*
Wilson, C. T.
1906 *Peasant Life in the Holy Land.*
Winandy, Jacques
1960 *Le Cantique des Cantiques, poème d'amour mué en écrit de sagesse.*
Winckler, Hugo
1897,1905,1906 *Altorientalische Forschungen,* 3 vols.
1901 "Kulturgeschichtlich-mythologisce Untersuchung," *MVAG* 6: 151–230.
1903 *Die Keilinschriften und das Alte Testament.*
Witt, R. E.
1971 *Isis in the Graeco-Roman World.*
Wittekindt, Wilhelm
1926 *Das Hohelied und seine Beziehungen zum Ištarkult.*
Woods, T. E. P.
1940 *Shulamith—A Love Story which is an Interpretation of the Song of Songs, which is Solomon's.*
Wordsworth, C.
1868 *The Books of Proverbs, Ecclesiastes, and Song of Solomon, with Notes and Introductions.*
Würthwein, Ernst
1967 "Zum Verständniss des Hohenliedes," *ThR* 32: 177–212.
Wutz, F. X.
1940 *Das Hohelied.*
Yadin, Yigael
1962 *The Scroll of the War of the Sons of Light against the Sons of Darkness.*
1963 *The Art of Warfare in Bible Lands.*

Yamauchi, E. M.
1965 "Tammuz and the Bible," *JBL* 84: 283–290.

Young, E. J.
1949 *An Introduction to the Old Testament.*

Zapletal, Vincenz
1907 *Das Hohelied kritisch und metrisch untersucht.*

Zimmern, Heinrich
1915 *Akkadische Fremdwörter als Beweiss für babylonischen Kultureinfluss.*

Zöckler, Otto
1868–1870 *The Song of Solomon.* Translated from the German with additions by W. H. Green. A Commentary on the Holy Scriptures, Critical, Doctrinal, and Homiletical, with Special Reference to Ministers and Students, ed. J. P. Lange. Translation of Lange's *Theologische-homiletische Bibelwerk,* 13.

Zolli, Eugenio
1940 "In Margine al Cantico dei Cantici," *Biblica* 21: 273–282.
1948 "Visionen der Liebe im Hohelied," *WZKM* 51: 34–37.

Zuenz, A. L.
1964 *Sefer Melo ha-'omer* (romanized title).

Zunz, Leopold
1832 *Die gottesdienstlichen Vorträge der Juden, historisch entwickelt.*

TRANSLATION and NOTES

I
(1:1–17)

1 The Sublime Song of Solomon
2 a Let him kiss me with his mouth's kisses!
b Truly, sweeter is your love than wine,
3 a Than the smell of your precious oil.
b Turaq oil is your name.
c Therefore girls love you.
4 a Draw me after you, let us run!
b The king brought me to his chambers.
c We will exult and joy in you.
d We will savor your love above wine.
e Rightly do they love you.
5 a Black am I and beautiful,
b O Jerusalem girls,
c Like the tents of Qedar,
d Like the pavilions of Salmah.
6 a Stare not at me that I am swart,
b That the sun has blackened me.
c My mother's sons were incensed at me,
d They made me a vineyard guard;
e My own vineyard I did not guard.
7 a Tell me, my true love,
b Where do you pasture?
c Where do you fold at noon?
d Lest I be as one veiled
e Among your comrades' flocks.
8 a If you do not know,
b O fairest of women,
c Follow the sheep tracks,
d And graze your kids
e Close to the shepherds' huts.
9 a To a mare among Pharaoh's cavalry
b Would I compare you, my darling.
10 a Your cheeks adorned with bangles,

b Your neck with beads.
11 a Bangles of gold we will make you,
b With spangles of silver.
12 a While the king was on his couch,
b My nard yielded its scent.
13 a A bundle of myrrh is my love to me,
b Between my breasts he lodges.
14 a A cluster of cypress is my love to me,
b From the gardens of En Gedi.
15 a Indeed you are fair, my darling,
b Indeed you are fair.
c Your eyes are doves.
16 a Indeed you are fair my love,
b Yea pleasant.
c Our couch is luxuriant.
17 a Our bower's beams are cedars,
b Our rafters cypresses.

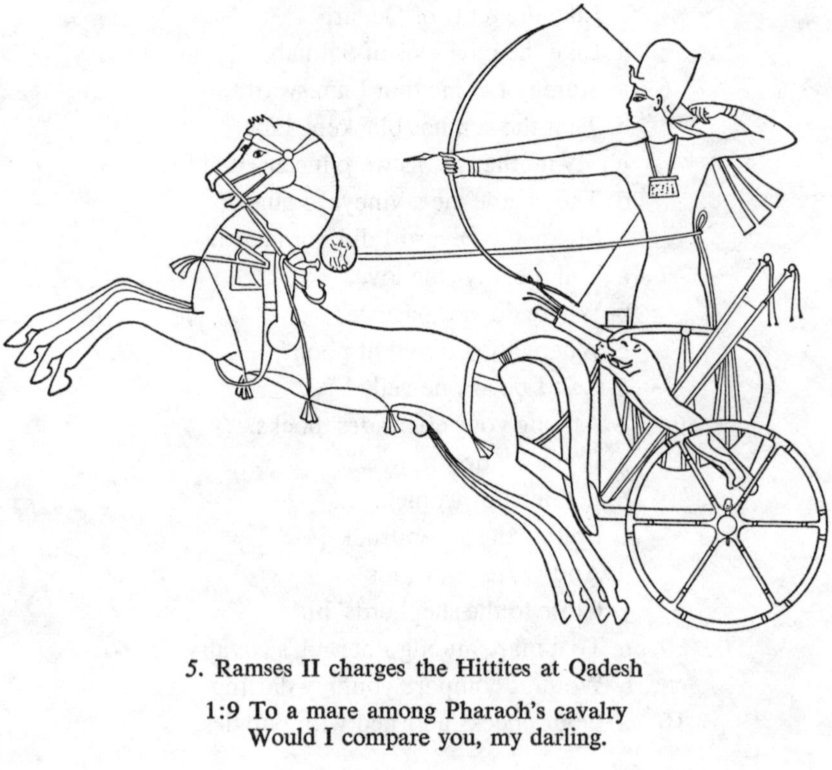

5. Ramses II charges the Hittites at Qadesh

1:9 To a mare among Pharaoh's cavalry
Would I compare you, my darling.

NOTES

1:1. *Song.* The word *šîr* is the generic term for "song," usually of glad song, there being special terms for sad song, elegy, dirge, and lament; cf. Gen 31:27; Isa 30:29; Prov 25:20; Judg 5:12. The term is frequently applied to Israelite cultic worship, e.g. Pss 42:9[8E], 69:31[30E], is used in the titles of several Psalms, and applied to the Levitical choirs and instrumental accompaniment. It is also applied to pagan cultic song, in connection with wine drinking, Isa 24:9; Amos 6:5; and even a whore's song, Isa 23:15. The instruments mentioned for the accompaniment are the harp (*nēḇel*), lyre (*kinnôr*), trumpets (*ḥăṣôṣĕrôṯ*), and cymbals (*mĕṣiltayim*), Amos 6:5; I Chron 15:16, 16:42.

In Ugaritic the verb is used in the Nikkal Hymn which celebrates the marriage of the lunar goddess Nikkal (Sumerian *NIN.GAL* Great Lady) to the lunar god Yar(i)ḫ. In other instances the word is used in connection with festivities at the court of the great weather and fertility god Baal-Hadd. The goddess Anat, when she tried to get the marvelous composite bow from the hero Aqhat, offered him love and immortality in return and gave the youth an enticing word picture of the divine dolce vita (17[2AQHT].6.26–31):

Ask life, O Hero Aqhat,
Ask life and I will give it,
Immortality and I will bestow it.
I will make you count years with Baal,
With El's sons you shall count months
Like Baal whom they hail and serve,
Hail, serve, and give drink,
Singing and chanting before him.

The Anat poem opens with a description of a feast honoring Baal (3[ʿNT].1.3–25):

He served Mighty Baal,
Honored the Prince Lord of Earth.
He rose, prepared and fed him,
Proffered a breast before him,
With keen knife a fatling-slice.
He stood, prepared, and gave him drink,
Put a cup in his hand,
A flagon in both his hands.
A great vessel, mighty to view,
A jar reaching to heaven,
A holy cup woman sees not,
A goblet Asherah eyes not.
A thousand jars it holds of wine,
A myriad is mixed in its mixture.
He rose, chanted and sang
To cymbals a pleasant song.
Sang the hero sweet of voice
Before Baal on the heights of Ṣapan.
Baal looked at his daughters,
Eyed Pidray, Miss Light,
Then Ṭallay, Miss Rain
Pidray he experienced . . .

(As often, the text becomes fragmentary just at the point of crucial interest.)

The Ugaritic text RS 24.245, recently published in *Ugaritica, V,* contains on the obverse a portrayal of Baal's physique with some striking parallels to Canticles 5:10–16 and on the reverse a fragmentary description of Anat's serenade to her brother and lover, Baal:

She poured the oil of peace in a bo[wl],
Washed her hands, did Virgin Anat,
Her fingers, the Progenitress of Peoples.
She took her harp in hand,
Put the lyre to her breast,
Sang the love of Mi[ghty] Baal,
The love of [The Prince Lord of Earth].
(UG 5.3.2.4–8)

The word *rimt* here conjecturally rendered "lyre" has been generally equated with a similar term in Hebrew (cf. Ezek 27:16; Job 28:18) designating some gem usually taken to be "coral." The putting of this object to the breast has been supposed to refer to pectoral ornamentation. The parallelism with *kinnor,* "harp," and the reference to a love song favor a musical instrument. J. Greenfield suggested (orally) that the word might be connected with *rim,* "bull" or "buffalo," and compared Mesopotamian harps or lyres in the form of a bull's head. The lyre was perforce held on or near the chest in playing, whether standing or sitting. If *rimt* designates a musical instrument, the problematic *mšr* in the broken parallel passage 3['NT].3.1–2 is a mistake for *tšr,* "she sings."

The construct connection of the same noun in the singular and plural, *šîr haššîrîm,* "song of (all) the songs," as with "slave of slaves" (Gen 9:25), "king of kings" (Dan 2:37; Ezra 7:12), "prince of princes" (Num 3:32), "God of gods" (Deut 10:17), "heaven of heavens" (I Kings 8:27), "beauty of beauties" (Jer 3:19), "vanity of vanities" (Eccles 1:2 and *passim*), "ornament of ornaments" (Ezek 16:7, applied to the development of the breasts and pubic hair of a female) always indicates some sort of superlative sense. This is most clear in Exod 26:33, "and the veil shall make a separation for you between the holy (place) and the holy of holies." Thus *šîr haššîrîm* designates the absolutely superlative song, the very best, the sublime song. Similar usage is attested in Ugaritic, e.g. Keret's army is designated *ṣbu ṣbi* "army of (an) army" (14[KRT].2.86), which has been taken to mean an elite corps. The context, however, stresses multitude, or innumerable troops, superlative in quantity, if not in quality.

Efforts to construe the expression as partitive rather than superlative, "a song of the songs of Solomon," i.e. one of Solomon's songs (so Ibn Ezra and David Qimḥi) have not carried conviction since there are other ways of making this clear if it were the meaning intended. Similarly, the suggestion (Kleuker) that *šîr* be read *šēr,* "chain," hence a catena or series of songs, is unlikely. The word *šîr* has nothing to do with the Greek *seira,* "chain," since the verb *š(y)r* is attested in Ugaritic of singing with musical accompaniment (3['NT].1.18–20). The rabbinic playing with the phrase for homiletic purposes is not to be taken seriously. Rabbi Simeon, e.g. said in the name of Ḥanin from Sepphoris that the expression means "a double song," and Rabbi

Simon said "double and reduplicated," i.e. composed of two strands, Israel's praise of God and God's praise of Israel, and reduplicated in its beauty and holiness (cf. Midrash Rabbah, Soncino ed., 19n4). It was also suggested that "song" and "songs" add up to at least three songs and these three were then related to the three biblical books ascribed to Solomon: Proverbs, Ecclesiastes, and the Song of Songs (cf. Midrash Rabbah i 1,10).

LXX and Vulgate render MT literally, *Aisma Aismatōn* and *Canticum Canticorum.* The designation Canticles, or Canticle of Canticles, from the Latin diminutive *canticulum* is appropriate to the brevity of the whole, and especially to the extreme brevity of the individual units. This usage is attested in an anonymous work of the sixteenth century, "The Pilgrim of Perfection," which refers to "the Canticles of Solomon." Daniel Lys' commentary (1968) has dubbed the Song, "Le Plus Beau Chant de la Création." We will from time to time refer to it here as "sublime" or "superlative."

The relative particle *'ăšer* here employed, but omitted in translation, is the regular one in Biblical Hebrew, but it does not recur in the rest of the book which uses only the proclitic particle *še-*. Admittedly a single deviation of this sort cannot be taken as proof, but it does render the superscription suspect as being an editorial addition and not part of the original composition.

Haller, following Kuhn, emended *'ăšer* to *'ăšîrāh,* "I would fain sing," "I will sing to Solomon," thus eliminating the single discrepant use of the particle. *NEB* adopts this emendation and renders, "I will sing the song of all songs to Solomon, that he may smother me with kisses." This reading could be supported by Ugaritic usage, *ašr nkl,* "I will hymn Nikkal," *ašr ilht kṯrt,* "I will hymn the skilled goddesses," but there is nothing in the context to encourage resort to the emendation. There is scant material in the Canticles which would be suitable as a hymn to Solomon, apart from his notoriety as a lover, unless some of his liaisons with foreign women were sacred marriages after the manner of Mesopotamian kings. The entire superscription, along with its singular use of the particle *'ăšer,* may be dismissed as secondary.

of Solomon. The preposition *lĕ* before the name is generally construed as *lamed auctoris,* attributing authorship to Solomon, as certain Psalms, e.g. 3 and 4, are ascribed to David, *mizmôr lĕḏāwîḏ*. These two expressions, however, are not perfectly analogous since *mizmôr* is indefinite and receives its determination from the proper name David, while "the Song of Songs" is already determined by the article quite apart from its connection with Solomon. However, we should not put too much stress on the article in this case since the article is often absent in poetry and poetic expressions and a measure of determination is already implicit in the superlative sense of the terms "king of kings," "holy of holies," etc. The superscriptions of Ugaritic texts consisting of *l* plus a proper name, *lb'l, lkrt, laqht* show us that the *l* need not be *lamed auctoris* since the authorship of these texts can hardly be attributed to the god Baal or the heroes Keret, or Aqhat; the meaning is rather that the composition deals with or concerns the god or hero named. So also "the Song of Songs" might relate in some way to Solomon without implication of authorship. It is, nevertheless, most likely that the intent of the superscription was to attribute the authorship to Solomon.

The Targum introduced the Song thus:

> Songs and praises which Solomon, the prophet, king of Israel, spoke by the spirit of prophecy before the Lord of all the World, YHWH.
>
> Ten songs were uttered in this world. This song was best of them all. The first song Adam uttered at the time his guilt was pardoned and the Sabbath Day came and shielded him. He opened his mouth and said, "A Psalm, a Song for the Sabbath Day" (Psalm 92).
>
> The second song Moses uttered with the Israelites at the time the Lord of the World divided for them the Reed Sea. They all began and spoke in unison, as it is written (Exod 15:1): "Then sang Moses and the Israelites."
>
> The third song the Israelites uttered at the time the well of water was given to them, as it is written (Num 21:17), "Then sang Israel."
>
> The fourth song Moses, the prophet, uttered, when his time had come to depart from the world. Then he reproved the people thereby, as it is written (Deuteronomy 32), "Give ear, O heavens, and I will speak."
>
> The fifth song Joshua, son of Nun, uttered when he waged war on Gibeon and the sun and moon stood for him thirty-six hours and they ceased to utter the song. He opened his mouth and sang the song, as it is written (cf. Josh 10:12): "Thus sang Joshua before YHWH."
>
> The sixth song Barak and Deborah uttered on the day YHWH delivered Sisera into the hands of the Israelites, as it is written (Judg 5:1): "Then sang Deborah and Barak, son of Abinoam."
>
> The seventh song Hannah uttered when she was granted a son from YHWH, as it is written (I Sam 2:1): "And Hannah prayed (in prophecy) and said."
>
> The eighth song David, king of Israel, uttered for all the miracles YHWH did for him. He opened his mouth and uttered the song, as it is written (cf. II Sam 22:1): "David sang in prophecy before YHWH."
>
> The ninth song Solomon, king of Israel, uttered by the Holy Spirit before the Lord of all the World.
>
> And the tenth song the exiles will utter at the time they come forth from exile, as clearly written by the hand of Isaiah the prophet (cf. Isa 20:29): "This song you shall have for joy on the night the festival of Passover is hallowed, and gladness of heart, as the people who go to appear before YHWH three times a year, with varieties of song and the sound of music(?) (*ṭab̲lā'*) to enter the mountain of YHWH and to worship before YHWH, the Strong One of Israel." (This paraphrase differs both from MT and Targum of Isa 20:29).

Midrash Rabbah on this verse is extensive and discursive. Only a few samples may be noted. The assumption that "Song of Songs" refers to three songs—(cf. p. 295) Proverbs, Ecclesiastes, and the Song of Songs—provoked discussion as to the order in which they were composed. Rabbi Jonathan argued from the way of the world that when a man is young he composes songs; when he grows older he makes sententious remarks; and when he becomes an old man he speaks of the vanity of things. The excellence of the Song of Songs is affirmed as the fine flour of Solomon's literary output. Even the numerical value of the word *šîr,* "song," is significant as corresponding to the years of the Patriarchs plus the Ten Commandments (*š*=300, *y*=10, *r*=200). The discrepancy between 510 and the 502 years of the Patriarchs (Abraham 175, Isaac 180, Jacob 147) is rectified by knocking off the years of famine. The references to Solomon, King Solomon (3:9,11) and simply to "the king" were diversely explained as referring to Solomon, to God, and the Community of Israel.

Origen enumerated six other songs in Scripture, with Solomon's sublime song as the climactic seventh. The six songs preceding the Song of Songs were: the Song of the Sea, Exodus 15; the Song of the Wall, Num 21:17*f;* the Song of Moses, Deuteronomy 32; the Song of Deborah, Judges 5; David's Song of Deliverance, II Sam 22=Psalm 18; the Song of Asaph, I Chron 16:8*ff.* (Cf. R. P. Lawson, *Origen,* 46–50; Littledale.)

2a,b. *me . . . his . . . your.* The shift from third person to second has evoked various emendations to mitigate or eliminate the incongruity. Many moderns read *yašqēnî,* "let him make me drink," or the imperative *hašqēnî,* "make me drink." But these changes also necessitate alteration of "his mouth" to "your mouth." The assumption of more than two speakers is fanciful. It seems best to leave the text unaltered, since enallage (shift in person) is common in poetry; cf. Deut 32:15; Isa 1:29; Jer 22:24; Micah 7:19; Psalm 23.

2a. *kiss.* The root *nšq* has all the range of meanings of our word "kiss." There is in Ezek 3:13 the application to wings of the cherubim touching each other, but elsewhere it is a matter of at least one mouth applied to a variety of objects—mouth, lips, hands, feet, an idol, a calf; cf. James Neil, 1885; A. E. Crawley, 1929, ch. IV, and N. J. Perella, 1969. H. H. Hirschberg (1961, 377) argues that the noun *nĕšîqôṯ* here means not "kisses" but "odors," related to Arabic *našaqa,* "to smell (a scent or odor)" and thus is an excellent parallel to *rēaḥ* in the following verse. The verb then cannot be related to *nšq,* "kiss," but must be connected with the root *š*(*w*)*q,* Arabic *šāqa,* "fill someone with desire, excite him." The word *pîhû,* "his mouth," is then an error for *pyḥyk,* related to Arabic *fāḥa* "to give forth scent," and thus Hirschberg attains the sense he wishes, "The scents of your perfumes excite me."

There can be no doubt that the kisses here are lovers' kisses. The cognate word in Ugaritic is used of the lovemaking of the Father of the Gods with a couple of females (it is disputed whether the female partners are divine or human):

He bent, their lips he kissed
Lo, their lips were sweet,
Sweet as grapes

As he kissed, they conceived.
As he embraced, they became pregnant.
(23[52].49–51)

Similarly, the hero Danel, after seeking, and receiving divine aid for his impotence, embraced, kissed, and impregnated his wife. In another passage Danel hugs and kisses a stalk of grain in some sort of (fertility?) ritual (19[1AQHT].2.63*ff*); cf. 7:8.

with. The preposition *m* before the word *nĕšîqôṯ,* "kisses," is generally taken as partitive, "some kisses," but in spite of this, the translation is usually "with kisses." Considerable discussion has been devoted to the question whether the female wished just a few kisses or even a single one. Ginsburg e.g. opined that the singular "is preferable, for the Shulamite does not so much wish for a *number* of kisses as for the presence of her beloved; *one* would be sufficient if he could only come." The problem vanishes with the realization that both the prepositions *m* and *b* can mean either "to," "from," or "with," as the context requires. Thus the common rendering "with" is fully justified.

2b. *Truly.* Construing the kî as asseverative, with W. F. Albright (1963, 2n3).

sweeter. Again with Albright in the light of Ugaritic *yn ṭb,* "good wine," and *yn lṭb,* "wine not good/sweet." Certainly pleasant taste was the quality most prized in wine, but other qualities than sweetness may also have been valued and cultivated. It would be interesting if *yn lṭb* could be shown to designate "dry wine." M. Dahood (1964, 90) cites the Vulgate of PS 34:9[8E], *gustate et videte quoniam suavis est Dominus* in support of the rendering "sweet" for *ṭb* as applied to taste. (The interest of the expression in Ps 34:9 is not in the choice of "sweet" or "good" to describe the taste of God, but in the possibility that the figure of speech reflects the primitive notion of eating divinity in a communal meal.)

your love. The reading "your breasts" by LXX (*mastoi sou*) and Vulgate (*ubera tua*) appears mistaken, although there are grounds for the choice, since the words *dôḏîm,* "love(s)," and *daddayim,* "breasts," "teats," appeared the same in the ancient consonantal orthography, *ddm.* The figure in Isa 60:16, of Zion sucking the milk of the nations and the breast of kings relates to economic nourishment and exploitation and it would be preposterous, as Ginsburg remarked, to appeal to this catachresis in support of the LXX and Vulgate rendering "breasts" in the present passage. In Prov 5:19 the word is given the vowels for "breasts" although it stands in parallelism with *'ahăḇāh,* "love," whereas in Prov 7:18 where it is likewise parallel to *'ahăḇāh,* "love," and associated with the same verb *rwy,* "be sated," the Masoretic vocalization is *dôḏîm,* "love(s)." In the present passage, the vocalization *dôḏêḵā,* "your love(s)," is certainly preferable to the reading *daddêḵā,* "your (masc.) breasts," or *daddayiḵ,* "your (fem.) breasts," since the female is speaking about and to the male. (The argument that *dad*(*d*) in Hebrew designates the female breast only, whereas for the male breast a different word (*ḥāzēh*) is used, is not compelling in view of the history of the latter word whose Akkadian cognate, *iztu*>*irtu,* is applied in Ugaritic to the female breast.)

In Ugaritic *dd* occurs in parallelism and synonymy with other words for "love," *yd* and *ahbt*. Baal sends his divine errand boys to his sister-consort Anat with a message of love, using all three words (3['NT].3.1–5), and the goddess in another text serenades Baal in virtually identical terms: cf. p. 293. In the Nikkal Hymn (24[77].23) the West Semitic lunar god Yar(i)ḫ says of his intended bride, the Sumero-Akkadian lunar goddess Nikkal

I will make her field a vineyard, The field of her love (*dd*) an orchard.

Akkadian *dādu* which is cognate with Hebrew *dôḏ* and Ugaritic *dd* designates both love as lovemaking and the object of love. In the meaning "lovemaking" it is always used in the plural, as in Hebrew, while as a designation of the object of love, "darling," or the like, it may be either singular or plural. The term is also applied to the younger or youngest son as one especially favored. A homophone, *dādu*, referring to some sort of aquatic animal with a shell, a foot, a part of the human body, does not appear to have anything to do with love (cf. *CAD*, III, 20), unless there was an Akkadian analogue to the widespread use of words for bivalve shellfish such as the clam as a designation of the vulva.

2. The Targum related the kissing to the giving of the Law:

> Said Solomon, the prophet: Blessed be the name of YHWH who gave us the Law by the hand of Moses, the Scribe, a Law inscribed on two tablets of stone, and six orders of the Mishnah and the Talmud by oral tradition (*girsā'*), and spoke to us face to face as a man kisses his companion, from the abundance of the love with which He loved us, more than the seventy nations.

This verse and the following one are cited in the Talmud (Abodah Zarah 35a) in a sudden change of subject during a discussion between Rabbis Ishmael and Joshua on the prohibition of cheese from pagan sources because it was curdled with rennet from calves sacrificed to idols. Rabbi Joshua suddenly switched the topic with the question as to whether the reading in 1:2 should be *dôḏeḵā*, "your (masc.) love," or *dôḏayiḵ*, "your (fem.) love." Rabbi Ishmael opted for the latter and Joshua contradicted him by citing 1:3 which is obviously addressed to a male. "Your love is better than wine" was explained by Rabbi Dimi: "The Congregation of Israel said to the Holy One (blessed be He), 'Master of the World, the words of your friends are more pleasant to me than the wine of the Law' " (meaning that the oral expositions of the rabbis are of more value than the written Law). "A scholar is like a flask of perfume which diffuses its fragrance when open."

The Midrash Rabbah offers numerous wordplays and associations of ideas on the kissing, the love, and the wine, applying them in a variety of ways to the words of the Law, the patriarchs, and Israel. "Better your loved ones than wine" means that God loves Israel more than the seventy nations (seventy being the numerical value of *yyn*, "wine").

3a. *Than*. The preposition *lĕ* before the word *rēaḥ*, "odor," has long occasioned difficulty. LXX read simply the conjunction *wĕ*, "and." Syriac, Ibn Ezra, *KJ* took the *lĕ* in the sense of *lĕma'an*, "because," connecting it with *'al-kēn*, "therefore," of the next colon. Luther's rendering is strange, "dass man deine gute Salbe rieche." Some modern scholars translate "to the smell," but the word *rēaḥ* never refers to the olfactory sense as such but always to the odor emitted or sensed. The *lĕ* has been taken as the *lamed* of reference, "as regards"; thus Hengstenberg, *ad odorem unguentorum tuorum quod attinet bonus est.* Recent translations tend to ignore the problem. Albright on the basis of Ugaritic solves the difficulty simply by connecting this line with the preceding and construing *lĕrēaḥ* as parallel to the preceding *miyyayin:*

Truly thy love is sweeter than wine, It is sweeter than the scent of thy perfume.

precious oil. Lit. "good oil," *šemen ṭôḇ,* Akkadian *šamnu ṭâbu.* Perfumed oil and aromatic spices were a necessity in the warm climate of the Near East and were used by males as well as females; cf. Ps 133:2, "like the precious oil on the head, running down the beard." For occasions at which one wished to avoid offense, or find favor, as for worship, II Sam 12:20, weddings and other feasts, Ps 45:8; lovers' trysts, Prov 7:17; Ruth 3:3, perfumed oil was indicated. The best quality *(rē'šîṯ šĕmānîm,* Amos 6:6) was expensive, because of the rare spices and other aromatic agents used, and thus available only to the wealthy. Among the treasures which Hezekiah showed the Babylonian emissaries, along with his gold, silver, and armaments, was the royal supply of precious perfume oil, II Kings 20:13.

3b. *Turaq oil.* The word *tûraq* remains obscure. In keeping with LXX *ekkenōṯen* and Vulgate *effusum,* it has been construed as a *hof'al* (causative-passive) form of the hollow root *r(y)q,* "empty," hence "emptied" or "poured out." Perfume oil thus spilled would diffuse its delightful fragrance. Accordingly, Gordis renders "oil wafted about." The fact that the noun *šemen* is regularly construed as masculine and thus incongruent with the feminine form of the verb is, as Gordis notes, not necessarily fatal to this interpretation since a number of nouns are ambivalent in gender. The usual emendation, on the basis of Esther 2:3,9,12; Prov 20:30, to *tamrûq* (applied to the purification of girls with a year's application of various perfume oils after [first] menses before they were presented to the king) is extremely dubious in spite of Krinetzki's explanation that the scribe mistakenly wrote *tmwrq* instead of *tmrwq* and then the meaningless form was mistakenly corrected to *twrq.* The word may be attested in Ugaritic in a text listing various items of silver, oil, wine, clothing, vessels, and implements. Line 20 of the text (*UT* 145) lists *w.ṯn.irpm.w.ṯn.trqm,* "two (measures) of *irpm* and two of *trqm.*" Gordon (*UT* 19.371) suggests the connection of *irpm* with Egyptian *irp* "wine." Since the text mentions oil and wine more than once, it seems likely that *trq* is a term for some type of high grade cosmetic oil, as suggested also by the context of its occurrence in the Song of Songs. Syriac rendered *tûraq* as "myrrh."

your name. In Semitic usage the name represents the essence of a person or thing, (cf. I Sam 25:25) hence the justifiable renderings of AT, "your very self," and Gordis "thy presence," Jastrow "thou art." Ginsburg rendered,

> Sweet is the odour of thy perfumes, Which perfume thou art, by thy name diffused abroad,

taking the second clause as explanatory of the preceding one, "Sweet is the odour of thy perfumes, because thou art that perfume."

3c. *girls*. The basic sense of the root *'lm* (Ugaritic and Arabic *ǵlm*) has reference to sexual ripeness without presumption one way or the other as to virginity or sexual experience; thus the masculine form *'elem* designates a young man and the feminine form *'almāh* a nubile girl or young woman (in spite of the exceptional rendering of the LXX in Isa 7:14 as *parthénos*, "virgin"); *'almāh* is synonymous with *na'ărāh*, "girl," cf. Gen 24:16,28,43 (the girl's virginity has to be specified by the technical term *bĕṯûlāh*). Prov 30:19, "the way of a man with a girl (*'almāh*)" does not necessarily imply virginity before, and certainly not after, the act or fact. In an Aramaic-Greek bilingual inscription from Palmyra the cognate of the word in question is rendered by the Greek as *hetairai*, "courtesans"; cf. W. S. LaSor (1952?). LXX *neánides* and Vulgate *adolescentulae* are proper renderings here.

The Targum understood the fragrance as the mighty works of God and the damsels as the righteous who follow the good path:

> At the sound of your miracles and mighty works which you performed for the people, the House of Israel, all the peoples who heard the report of your mighty works and goodly signs trembled; and your Holy Name was heard in all the earth, more choice than the copious oil applied abundantly to the heads of kings and priests. Therefore the righteous love to follow your goodly path in order that they may possess this world and the world to come.

Midrash Rabbah related the fragrant ointments to the hymns chanted by the patriarchs and the precepts performed by them, which were mere fragrances as compared to God's name which is like ointment poured forth. Another explanation identified the oils as the two oils of anointment, the oil of priesthood and the oil of kingship, or the two Laws, the written and the oral. Again, as oil is improved by pounding, so Israel had to be brought to repentance by chastisement. As oil will not mix with other liquids, Israel does not mix the other nations of the world (Deut 7:3). As oil brings light to the world, so does Israel (Isa 60:3). As oil floats above all liquids, so Israel is above the nations (Deut 28:1). As oil is noiseless when poured, so Israel makes no noise in this world, but will in the future (Isa 29:4).

This verse was also applied to Father Abraham. As a vial of perfume gives no scent when stored away, but only when moved, so God ordered Abraham to become a wanderer on earth in order that his name might become great (Gen 12:1–2). The word *'ălāmôt*, "girls," was given several interpretations, reading *'ôlāmôṯ*, "worlds," or relating it to the root *'lm*, "hide," or to *'almûṯ*, "youthful vigor," or taking it as *'al-mûṯ*, "upon death." The maidens were variously identified as proselytes, as the generation of destruction (i.e. those of the time of Bar Kochba's revolt and the repression under Hadrian), or as Israel.

The Church Fathers similarly saw the damsels as the saints, and the suggestion of youth and vigor evoked Christian souls reborn in baptism who, having put off the old man and the wrinkles of sin, renewed their youth like eagles (Gregory, Ambrose), or those who, conscious of their weakness, loved Christ their strength (Cassiodorus). Weak and imperfect souls, of course, as Rupert noted, could never have dared to love God had not his Word been made flesh and poured forth as ointment. The purity and vigor of youth characterized the young churches, or the souls of the martyrs (Origen, Philo Carpathius, Gregory of Nyssa). The supposition that *'ălāmôṯ* means "virgins" reminded Cornelius à Lapide of the Church as the pure bride of Christ (II Cor 11:2) and Dionysius the Carthusian thought of those who in virginity of soul and body served and loved God, some even to death, and of the numberless ones who in their youth forsake the evil and deceitful world and enter convents and holy retreats to give themselves in spirit to the pure embraces of the divine. (Cf. Littledale.)

Moderns who take the Song as descriptive of human love have some difficulty with the bride's statement that all the girls love her mate. Ginsburg commented, "How natural for a woman, greatly admiring, and dotingly attached to her beloved, to think that every damsel must be enamoured of him!" Natural as this conceit may be, it is questionable whether a doting damsel with discernment would wish to suggest to the swain of her choice that all the other girls were in love with him.

This line is assigned by proponents of the dramatic three-character interpretation not to the Shulamite but to the women of Solomon's harem, or the chorus of Jerusalem girls. In cultic interpretation the damsels are the votaries of the fertility god, supposedly Tammuz. Ezekiel is witness to the solicitude of Jerusalem's women for Tammuz, Ezek 8:14. Dan 11:37 mentions among the ancestral deities of the tyrant (Antiochus Epiphanes) one called "the Delight of Woman," usually taken to be Tammuz-Adonis, but it might refer to Baal-Hadad, or even to a goddess, such as Baal's sister-consort Anat, or the later blending of Ishtar and Anat as Atargatis.

4a. *Draw me after you.* LXX reflects the reading "they drew you" and connects this to what precedes these words, "Therefore the damsels loved you, they drew you. After you for the odor of your ointment we will run." Similarly Vulgate with slight variation. Most modern interpreters follow Targum and Luther (Zieh mich dir nach, so laufen wir), against the punctuation of MT. Job 21:33, where the prepositional phrase "after you" precedes the verb *mšk*, "draw," appears to support Targum, Luther et al. But the verb *mšk* does not need a preposition to indicate direction and thus the question whether "after you" relates to the drawing or the running remains moot and is of little consequence. The verb *mšk* is used of the drawing power of divine love in Hosea 11:4, "I drew them (Israel) with bands of love," and Jer 31:3, "I loved you (Israel) with an eternal love, therefore I drew you (with) constancy." Cf. John 6:44, 12:32 which use the same verb as the LXX in the present passage.

4b. *The king.* For allegorists the king is either YHWH or Christ; for proponents of dramatic theories, it is Solomon; in the Syrian wedding festival the bridegroom is "king"; and "king" is a common title of the male deity in fertility liturgies throughout the ancient Near East.

his chambers. Whether applied to a tent or to a more substantial structure, *ḥeḏer, ḥăḏārîm* refers to the *interiora domus.* Arabic *ḫadara* means to withdraw and the *ḫidr* of the tent is the section closed off with a curtain for privacy. In Ugaritic, King Krt goes into his *ḥdr* to weep (14[KRT].1.26), as did Joseph, Gen 43:30, and El, the father of the gods, resides in a complex of seven chambers, or eight enclosures (*bšb't ḥdrm / bṯmmt ap sgrt* 3['NT].5.19–20, 34–35), cf. *ḥeḏer bĕḥeḏer,* "a chamber within a chamber," as a hiding place, I Kings 20:30, 22:25, or a secret place, II Kings 9:2. Delilah hid the Philistines in her *ḥeḏer* so they could pounce on Samson, Judg 16:9,12, and Amnon enticed his sister Tamar into his *ḥeḏer* and raped her, II Sam 13:10. In II Sam 4:7 the word is modified by *miškāḇ,* "bed." The word can also designate other sorts of rooms, such as storerooms, Prov 24:4. In spite of LXX *tameion autou* and Vulgate *cellaria sua,* there is no reason to suppose that the chamber in the present context is a storeroom, as Dahood (*PNWSP,* 50n2) seems to suggest. The damaged reading of Ugaritic text 23[52].76, *wḥbrḫ.mla yn,* "and his storehouses full of wine," may be relevant to Prov 24:4, but not to the present verse where the concern is not with the storage of wine but with its use in the enhancement of love which simulates and stimulates the divine fertility which sustains life.

4c. *We will.* Note the enallage (cf. 2a.). Here we have one of the chief proof passages for those who see more than two actors in the drama. Ginsburg asserted that

> few readers of the original Hebrew, whose minds are not biased by a preconceived theory, can carefully peruse the three preceding verses without observing that two persons are here introduced—viz. *the beloved to whom* and *the king of whom,* the damsel speaks.

The king, in Ginsburg's view, brought the Shulamite into his apartments and thus separated her from her beloved, in whom, however, she still delights. She begins by invoking her absent lover in the *third* person; but no sooner had she expressed her desire to be with him, than he is, as it were, present to her mind, and she forthwith, dropping the third person, addresses him in the *second,* and so continues to speak to him throughout the third verse. In the fourth verse she tells her absent lover what the king has just done and then continues to address him (the absent lover who is present in her mind's eye) in the second person. Similarly, Ibn Ezra understood that the maid assured her true love, "Even if the king were to bring me into his chambers, I would still rejoice and be glad in you." Delitzsch explained the changes in person thus, "Those who are singing are not at present in the innermost chamber. But if the king brings one of them in, . . . then—they all say—we will rejoice and be glad in thee." Virtually any difficulty, real or supposed, may be obviated by invoking additional characters to whom the troublesome words may be assigned.

Various dodges and devices are employed to eliminate or obscure the incongruities, in person and number. Graetz, e.g., changed the first singular suffixes "me," to "us" (*-nî* to *-nû*), "draw us, we will run," "the king led us"; *JPSV* (1969) eliminated *'aḥărêḵā,* "after thee," without note or comment, while *NEB* rendered it simply "together," without comment.

The same sort of switch from first person singular to plural occurs in the Sumerian sacred marriage songs. S. N. Kramer (*SMR,* 92) notes the parallel between the ecstatic words of King Shu-Sin's bride in the sacred rite and those of the beloved in the present verse:

Bridegroom, let me give you my caresses,	In the bedchamber, honey-filled,
My precious sweet, I would be laved[?] by honey,	Let *us* enjoy your goodly beauty;

Here Kramer did not comment on the enallage, but in another instance he noted the sudden switch to the plural for which he could offer no explanation. The bride, in transports over her lover's multilayered mane, begs him to press it to *our* bosom:

My bridegroom, fit for [his] six-layer mane,	My lion, heavy with [his] four-layer mane,
My sweet, press it to our bosom,	My brother of fairest face, press it close to our bosom.

In spite of the differences in the two languages, there appears to be a common tradition of enallage in the sacred marriage songs, whatever the explanation, and it is the bride who refers to herself with plural pronouns in begging the love of the groom. Since the female in the sacred rite represented the great goddess, it may be that the shift to the plural was intended to suggest the excellence of divinity. Or, perhaps, the priestess as surrogate both for the goddess and for mortal females speaks for those who vicariously share her joy in the love of the king who represents the god.

4d. *savor.* LXX reads "we will *love* your breasts more than wine." This unusual rendering of *zkr,* "remember," reflects the difficulty the translator sensed with regard to the usual meaning of the causative conjugation of this verb, mention, recite, extol, celebrate, or the like. Gordis, following Ibn Janaḥ, rendered, "We shall inhale thy love rather than wine," citing Lev 24:7; Isa 66:3; Hosea 14:8[7E]; Ps 20:4[3E] where the root is used of olfactory appreciation of incense and burnt offerings, and he compares further I Sam 26:19 where *yrḥ,* "smelling," is used for accepting an offering. This judgment appears correct and the sense is accepted in *JPSV,* with more appropriate choice of wording, since "savor" combines the senses of smell and taste involved in the appreciation of fine wine:

Let us delight and rejoice in your love, Savoring it more than wine—

(Note, however, the slight departure from the wording of MT, reading "in your love" instead of "in you" in 4b and omitting "your love" in 4c.)

4e. *Rightly*. The word *mêšārîm* has been considered difficult in the present context. LXX rendered *euṯutēs egapēsen se,* "right loves you." Vulgate *recti,* "the (up)right," and similarly Syriac, Targum, and Luther. The connection of the word with wine drinking here and in 7:10[9E] and Prov 23:31 suggested to Ibn Ezra that the term in these passages is a designation for a sort of wine. T. H. Gaster, on the basis of Ugaritic *mrṯ* and Aramaic *mērāṯ,* presumably related to Hebrew *tîrôš,* "new wine" (now attested in Ugaritic as *trṯ*) proposed (1961) emendation to *mimmērāš,* "more than new wine," as parallel to *miyyayin,* "more than wine," in the preceding hemistich. With the change of the last word from verb, "they love you," to noun, "your love," a striking balance is attained with parallel words for wine and love. *JPSV* (1969) adopts the first part of this proposal, with slight adaptation, "Like new wine they love you." *NEB* renders, without explanation, "more than any song," leaving the reader to divine that the latter part of the word is taken as *šîrîm,* "songs."

N. H. Tur-Sinai (1950, 369) on the basis of Akkadian *mušartu,* which he took to mean "paramour," and *mušaru,* "membrum virile," interpreted *mêšārîm* as "sexual potency." Eliezer Ben-Yehudah (B-Y, VI, 2980*f*) also ascribed sexual connotation to the term, but both these interpretations are dubious, as noted by Gordis who, however, went on to suggest that in the light of the common rabbinic phrase *yîšar kōaḥ,* "may (your) strength be firm," and *sēper hayyāšār,* probably "The Book of Heroes" (Josh 10:13; II Sam 1:18) the stich may mean, "For thy manliness do they love thee." In his translation, however, Gordis opted for "fine wine." M. Dahood (*PS I,* AB 16, fourth NOTE on Ps 49:15) has posited for *mêšārîm* the meaning "throat" in Song of Sol 7:10 and Prov 23:31 and revised accordingly Ps 49:15[14E], reading *bĕmêšārîm* for MT *bām yĕšārîm,* and translating "When they descend into his gullet like a calf." The gullet is admittedly the natural channel for beverages and comestibles but this meaning for *mêšārîm* cannot be established on the basis of the two or three passages where such a meaning is conceivable.

There is no warrant for assuming a sense for *mêšārîm* other than the well-attested meaning "equity," or the like, a synonym of *ṣeḏeq,* "righteousness," and *mišpāṭ,* "justice," with which it is commonly associated; cf. Prov 1:3, 2:9, 8:6; Pss 9:9, 58:2, 75:3, 96:10, 98:9, 99:4; Isa 33:15, 45:19. Rashi was right in taking the word as adverbial in the present passage. The claim

(Hengstenberg) that the word never occurs as an adverb is nullified by a glance at Ps 58:2[1E] and 75:3[2E]. The omission of the preposition *b*- before words beginning with a labial has been supposed to be common, but the fact is that adverbial accusatives, omitting any preposition, regardless of the initial consonant of the noun, are more frequent than has been appreciated.

The Akkadian cognate *mīšarum* is relevant for understanding of biblical uses of *mêšārîm*. This term is frequently associated with *kittum*, "truth," in both legal and religious contexts. The source of *kittum* was divine, not human. The sun god, representing divine justice, was "Lord of Truth and Equity," *bēl killi(m) umīšari(m)*. It was the purpose of man-made law (*dīnāti*) to bring the operation of human society into harmony with the Cosmic Law or Truth, *kittum*. When this was achieved the result was the quality *mīšarum*, "equity." It was the prime duty of the king to achieve and maintain this balance and thus royal decrees and edicts were sometimes referred to as *mīšarum* acts. A king, usually early in his reign, in order to remedy inequities, especially economic imbalances and to assure his subjects that he was truly a just ruler, *šar mēšarim*, would issue a *mīšarum* edict in order to bring the human condition closer to the divine ideal. Cf. E. A. Speiser, 1967, 318–321.

4. The Targum, taking its cue from *mêšārîm* as designating the upright, related this verse to the Exodus and the giving of the Law:

> When the people of the House of Israel went out from Egypt, the Presence (Shekinah) of the Lord of the World led the way before them as a pillar of cloud by day and a pillar of fire by night. The righteous of that generation exclaimed: "Lord of all the World, we will be drawn after you and we will run after your goodly way. So draw us near to the base of Mount Sinai and give us your Law from your treasure house of the firmament. And we will rejoice and be glad with the twenty-two letters with which they are written and we will be mindful of them and will love your divinity and will remove ourselves far from the idols of the peoples. And all the righteous who do right before you will revere you and love your commands."

The line "draw me after you we will run" is applied in the Talmud (TB Hagigah 15b) to Rabbi Aqiba who "went up unharmed and came down unharmed" (i.e. he followed God into Paradise on the deepest mysteries of theosophy) and when the ministering angels sought to thrust him away, God said, "Let this elder be, for he is worthy to avail himself of my glory."

Midrash Rabbah presented several wordplays on *mšk*, "draw." For example the remotely similar word *maškěnûṯā'*, "dwelling place," suggested the divine presence, the Shekinah, and the further play with the root *škn* to invoke *šěkēnîm*, "neighbors," and Israel's wicked neighbors. The chambers suggested to some the mystical interpretation of Scripture. The wine was related to the Law and also to the patriarch, taking *miyyayin* to mean "through wine," instead of "more than wine," through the wine of the patriarch whose merits and love of God are memorable.

Some Christians saw a distinction between the Synagogue which expressed longing for Christ in the preceding verses and the Gentile Church in the present verse which is eager to come to him. St. Bernard wondered why the Bride needed to be drawn and found the answer in the giant steps of Christ mentioned in 2:8 and the swift pace of the divine Word, Ps 147:15. The reference to running and the fragrance of ointment, especially the extra words of LXX and Vulgate, "Draw me after you, we will run for the odor of your ointments," provoked a variety of comments relating the running to the quest for Christ, like gallant hounds after the scent of game (Cardinal Hugo). St. Basil mentioned pigeon fanciers who captured the birds by sending out one smeared with perfume to lure others to the cote.

The LXX and Vulgate rendering of "chambers," *tamieion* and *cellaria,* suggested storerooms for treasure. St. Bernard and Cardinal Hugo saw the treasure rooms as representing the four senses of Scripture: the Historical which holds only rough food fit for slaves and cattle; the Topological (with three compartments supplying oil and wine for refreshment, balms and spices for delight, and ointments for healing); Allegory which stores the weapons and the golden shields of Solomon, i.e. of Christ and the Church Militant; and finally Anagogue (Spiritual Sense) containing only pure gold, precious stones, the life eternal. (Cf. Littledale.)

5a. *Black . . . and.* LXX rendered precisely "Black am I and beautiful," *melaina eimi* (*egō*) *kai kalē*. Effort was made to mitigate the blackness with the rendering *fusca,* "dark," rather than *nigra,* "black," as reflected in citations by early Christian expositors which waver between *nigra* and *fusca,* between "and" and "but" (*et/sed*), and in the terms for beauty, *pulchra/speciosa/formosa.* Vulgate *Nigra sum sed formosa,* "Black I am, but comely," has been generally followed in the vernacular versions, with emphasis on the adversative relation between the blackness and the beauty. Luther rendered "Ich bin schwarz, aber gar lieblich," and similarly *KJ,* "I am black but comely." *RSV* changed *KJ*'s "black" to "very dark" and in the succeeding verse further softened "black" to "swarthy." Some commentators seek to modify the blackness with the explanation that the Hebrew *šḥr* denotes a ruddy hue in connection with sunburn. Lexicographers generally separate *šḥr* I related to blackness from *šḥr* II which is connected with the "dawn" and as a verb means "to seek." As a verb, *šḥr* I occurs only once in the canonical Old Testament, in Job 30:30 as applied to Job's skin blackened by heat. In the Hebrew of the Wisdom of Jesus Ben Sira (Sir 25:17) it is applied to the effect of wickedness on a woman's appearance and stands in parallelism with the verb *qdr.* The adjective *šāḥôr* clearly means "black" and is so rendered by *RSV* in all places except here in Song of Songs, 1:5. It is applied to healthy black hair in Lev 13:31,37, as opposed to yellowish, diseased hair, in the diagnosis of skin ailments. In Song of Songs 5:11 the locks of the male lover are "black as a raven." The horses of the second chariot in Zech 6:2,6 are *šĕḥôrîm,* "black," in contrast to the red, white, and dappled grey steeds of the other three chariots.

The notion that the blackness of necessity implies the antithesis of beauty has some support in biblical usage, since bodily health and beauty are described as white and ruddy in 5:10 and in Lam 4:7*f:*

Her princes were purer than snow,
Whiter than milk.
In body ruddier than coral,
Their limbs fairer than sapphire.

Their visage is now blacker than soot,
Not recognized in the streets.
Skin tight over their bones,
Grown dry as wood.

The equation of beauty and health with whiteness or ruddiness and the opposite with blackness can apply only where ruddy/white is the normal skin color; it has no meaning with respect to innate blackness which has its own beauty. Stephan (1923, 7) cited in connection with the present verse a portion of an Arabic ditty on the charm of a dusky damsel:

O darkest one, how often was I blamed for (loving) you!
But the more they blamed me, the more my passion for you increased.

(The epithet here rendered "darkest one" is more literally "brownest of brown" [*asmar is-sumri*].)

Rashi apparently had difficulty conceiving that our lady could be both black and beautiful and thus he supposed that the beauty applied to her limbs, which would retain their shapeliness despite the blackening. (This same logic was presumably operative in Jerome's choice of the *formosa.*) Rashi explained that the blackness in this case is not innate, but will revert to white if she stays for a while in the shade, as the tents of Qedar similarly blackened by exposure in the desert may be washed to become like the curtains of Solomon. (Apparently Rashi did not appreciate the synonymous poetic parallelism and, being a Provençal Frenchman, perhaps had no acquaintance with Bedouin tents and apparently did not know that the black goat hair would not wash white). In another connection, however, Rashi overcomes his melainophobia and goes to some trouble to demonstrate that black *is* beautiful. In Num 12:1 Miriam and Aaron rebuked Moses for marrying a negroid (Cushite) woman. (The term Cushite is still used in modern Israeli Hebrew with derogatory and racist overtones.) YHWH himself came to Moses' defense and his wrath was kindled against Miriam and Aaron so that Miriam was punished with seven days of leprosy. The divine displeasure rested not on Moses, but on his accusers (as Malcolm X correctly stressed in his autobiography [p. 298] though he misunderstood in part and referred erroneously to "Moses' adultery with Ethiopian women"). The divine reaction to Moses' choice seemed sufficient endorsement and Rashi concluded that "this teaches us that everyone acknowledged her beauty, just as everyone acknowledges the blackness of Cushites." Rashi then adds the proof that Black *is* Beautiful by noting "'Cushitess' equals 'good-looking' by Gematria" (i.e. the numerical value of the letters in *kwšyt* [20+6+300+10+400=736], "Cushitess," and *ypt mr'h* [10+80+400+40+200+1+5=736], "good-looking," are the same).

The unprejudiced rendering "black and beautiful" is understandably favored by persons who value their own blackness, real or imagined. The Black Jews of Harlem, the Commandment Keepers, under the leadership of Rabbi

Wentworth A. Matthew who claims descent from Solomon and the Queen of Sheba, maintain that Ham and Shem were black, and only Japheth, ancestor of the Gentiles, was white. Jacob also was black because he had smooth skin. Solomon was black because he says so in Song of Songs 1:5, "I am black and comely," ignoring the clear indication of the Hebrew that the speaker is feminine (cf. Howard Brotz, [1964], 18*f*). The Rev. Jacob A. Dyer of Jamaica, New York, in an unpublished paper on "The Biblical Attitudes toward Race and Color" has correctly stressed that Solomon is not the speaker in the Song of Songs 1:5. Dyer goes on to argue cogently for the propriety of the Greek rendering "Black *and* Beautiful."

Origen's interpretation of the present passage is of particular interest in view of the melainophobia evident in the traditional exegesis, both Jewish and Christian. Origen's exegesis has been treated at some length by Ernst Benz (1965) and only a few relevant items need be noted here. The Bride for Origen represented the Church gathered from among the Gentiles, and the daughters of Jerusalem whom she addresses represent the Synagogue, dear because of the election of the Fathers, but nevertheless enemies of the Gospel (Rom 11:28). The Synagogue vilifies the Church of the Gentiles for her ignoble birth, calling her black. The Church replies:

I am indeed black, O daughters of Jerusalem, in that I cannot claim descent from famous men, nor have I received the enlightenment of Moses' Law. But I have my own beauty. For in me too is that primal thing, the Image of God in which I was created. You compare me to the tents of Qedar and the curtains of Solomon because of my dark coloring; but even Qedar was descended from Ishmael, as his second son, and Ishmael was not without his share in the divine blessing (cf. Gen 25:13 and 16:11). You liken me to Solomon's curtains which are none other than the curtains of the Tabernacle of God (Exod 25:2*ff*). I am indeed surprised, O daughters of Jerusalem, that you should want to reproach me with the blackness of my hue. How could you forget what is written in your Law as to what Mary (Miriam) suffered who spoke against Moses because he had taken a black Ethiopian to wife? (Numbers 12). How is it that you do not recognize the true fulfilment of that type in me? I am that Ethiopian. I am indeed black by reason of my lowly origin; but I am beautiful through penitence and faith.

(Note that Origen's attitude toward negritude is not wholly positive here.)

Origen then, while on the subject of the Church that comes from the Gentiles and calls herself black yet beautiful, proceeded to collect and elucidate other passages from Scripture which present types foreshadowing this mystery. Other passages treated by Origen in this connection are the story of Solomon and the Queen of Sheba (in which he confused Saba with the royal city of Ethiopia which Cambyses later renamed Meroe), and the allusions to Ethiopia in Ps 68:31; Zeph 3:10; and the story of Ebed-Melek, the Ethiopian eunuch (Jeremiah 38–39). Of particular interest is Origen's exegesis of the story of Moses' Ethiopian wife. The episode, according to

Origen, lacks coherence and he supplied coherence by explaining Moses' marriage in mystical terms. Moses, representing the spiritual law, entered into union with the Ethiopian woman, the Church gathered from among the Gentiles. Mary (Miriam) typifies the forsaken Synagogue, and Aaron represents the priesthood according to the flesh; both object to seeing their domain taken away from them and given to another nation. It was the marriage with the Ethiopian woman, in Origen's view, which made Moses worthy of the endorsement which he received from the Lord. For all the great and splendid achievements of faith and patience that are recorded of Moses, he was never so highly praised, and that by the highest authority, as on the occasion when he took the Ethiopian wife.

Benz stressed Origen's positive evaluation of blackness as a contribution to the theology of negritude. Origen's attitude was doubtless influenced by conditions in the early Church in Alexandria where Greeks, Romans, Jewish-Christians, Indians, Arabs, and Ethiopians lived in fraternal harmony. Unfortunately, Origen goes on to plaster his supposed positive attitude toward negritude with a whitewash of highly questionable quality. With application to the individual soul that returns to repentance after many sins, Origen explained that this means that she is black by reason of sins, but beautiful through her repentance. And finally, because she who now says "I am black and beautiful" has not remained in her blackness to the end, the daughters of Jerusalem say later on concerning her: "Who is this that comes up, having been made white . . . ?" The reference is to 8:5 where LXX instead of "from the desert," read *leleukanthismenē,* "made white" and Rufinus rendered *dealbata* (*Quae est ista quae ascendit dealbata, incumbens super fraternum suum?*). In the following verse, Origen explained that the black and beautiful one gives good reason for her blackness which is not a natural condition, but something suffered through force of circumstance, "because," as she says, "the sun looked down on me." This shows, according to Origen, that she is not speaking of bodily blackness, because the sun tans or blackens when it looks *at,* and not when it looks down *on* anyone. Origen then refers to the theory that the natural blackness of the Ethiopian was caused by inherited sunburn. But this is not the case with the Gentile Church. The Sun of Justice did not look (directly) at the Gentile Church, but looked askance (Rufinus makes a play on *despicere* and *adspicere*). The blackness then for which she is reproached resulted from the sun having looked at her askance because of her unbelief and disobedience. But when she repents and He looks at her directly, then her light will be restored and her blackness completely banished. Thus, by dint of some fancy exegetical footwork, Origen outdid himself again and undermined his own positive approach to the theology of negritude.

The mitigation of the blackness to sunburnt brown may be bolstered by numerous poetic parallels in praise of the beauty of dark damsels and nutbrown maidens. Theocritus (*Idyl* x 26–29) praises the dark Levantine beauty:

Bambyca fair, to other folk you may a Gipsy be;
Sunburnt and lean they call you; you're honey-brown to me.
(J. M. Edmonds, 1912, LCL)

Or in a more recent rendering:

All things ye touch are lovely; all decry
Thy beauty, call thee Syrian, sunburnt,
spare,
And only I,
I call thee golden, honey hued.

Dark is the purple violet, dark as thou
The lettered hyacinth, yet there adorn,
First of all flowers, the garland;
(W. D. P. Hill, 1959, 45)

Dark beauties vied with lighter hues in appeal to Arab lovers, as seen from samples of Palestinian folk songs:

Between the brown and the white (sc. girls) I wasted my life.
The white ones are twice refined sugar, wrapped in silk,
And the brown ones are perfume of crystal vases, prescribed for the sick.
(Stephan, 1922, 66)

And if you are brown, you are like honey hidden in pots,
And if you are white, you are like a princess honoring our house (sc. with a visit),
(p. 68)

The fascination exercised by blackness is best captured in a poem of Lord Herbert of Cherbourg:

"Sonnet of Black Beauty"

Black beauty, which above that common light,
Whose Power can no colours here renew
But those which darkness can again subdue,
Dost still remain unvary'd to the light?
And like an object equal to the view,
And neither chang'd with day nor hid with night,
When all these colours which the world call bright,
And which old Poetry doth so pursue,
Are with the night so perished and gone,
That of their being there remains no mark,
Thou still abidest so entirely one,
That we may know thy blackness is a spark
Of light inaccessible, and alone
Our darkness which can make us think it dark.

The cultic interpretation of the Canticle which identified the female protagonist as originally the great goddess of Love and War provided also a new slant on her negritude. In 1914 Oswald Neuschotz de Jassy argued that the Black Beauty of the Canticle is none other than Isis and that the Solomonic Song is a lamentation on the death of Osiris. The influence of the cult of Isis on Christianity had long been appreciated, as witness the comment of C. W. King (1887, 173),

The Black Virgins so highly venerated in certain French Cathedrals during the long night of the Middle Ages, proved when at last examined by antiquarian eyes to be the basalt statues of the Egyptian goddess, which having merely changed the name, continued to receive more than pristine adoration. Her devotees carried into the new priesthood the ancient badges of their profession; "the obligation to celibacy, the tonsure, the bell and the surplice."

In 1926, Wittekindt equated the black and burnt one (reading with Rothstein *nik̲wāh* for MT *nā'wāh*) with Ishtar as a supposed lunar goddess. He explained the blackness by the widespread notion that the waning moon, when she disappears and becomes dark, is at that moment wedded to the sun; and when she reappears, she is pregnant and waxing. As for other black goddesses, Wittekindt cited the Black Demeter, the many-breasted Artemis of Ephesus, the Black Aphrodite of Corinth, the black representations of the Virgin Mary (*madonna nera*), the black Balti (=Ishtar) in Harran, and the various black stones representing goddesses, including the Black Stone of the Ka'ba-t at Mecca.

A special study of the numerous black madonnas in the churches and monasteries of Europe (some 275 examples) was made by Marie Durand-Lefèbvre (1937). Various hypotheses to account for the blackness were considered in detail. (1) Natural causes of discoloration in materials. (2) Choice of an "ethnic type" as a model. The portraits attributed to Saint Luke were presumed to represent a Judean type of Virgin darkened by exposure to the sun during the flight into Egypt. (3) Oriental origin, propagation of a model derived from Asia. (4) Symbolic sense based on the passages from Canticles used in the Office of the Virgin: Canticles 1:5, *Nigra sum sed formosa,* and 1:6, *Nolite me considerare quod fusca sim,* and Luke 1:35, *Spiritus, Sanctus superveniet in te et virtus Altissimi obumbrabit tibi.* (5) Survival of ancient cults.

In discussing these theories, Durand-Lefèbvre admitted that in some instances the dark coloration of the effigies might be fortuitous, e.g. blackened by smoke or fire, or made of black wood or stone—ebony or basalt, chosen because of easy availability or by reason of some quality other than its blackness. The use of black paint, however, suggested strongly that the negritude was not accidental, but an intrinsic and necessary attribute of the Virgin. As for the notion that the intention may have been to depict an "ethnic type," Durand-Lefèbvre found nothing to suggest this other than the blackness; the hair was straight, the face elongated, the nose long and straight. Thus it seems clear that the intention of the artist was not to portray an African physical type. The portraits attributed to St. Luke are generally of Greek workmanship, and of a dark complexion. The date of these representations, according to Durand-Lefèbvre, ranges from the eighth to the twelfth centuries. They are usually painted on wood with brown to black tint. Among the representations attributed to St. Luke are the famous black madonna of Częstochowa in Poland, Ste. Marie Majeure, and Notre-Dame d'Oropa, each having its own cult legends and miracles. For further discussion of portraits of the Virgin attributed to St. Luke, see A. Jameson, 1848, I, 155.

The oriental origin of the Black Virgin seemed to Durand-Lefèbvre highly probable and she suggested that the clergy of the Eastern Churches might have brought the black statues and paintings to Rome between the sixth and twelfth centuries, during the iconoclastic quarrels, or at the capture of Constantinople by the Turks, or they could have been brought back by pilgrims or Crusaders. On the other hand, there may have been no cause to bring Black Virgins from the East to Rome, since it is likely that they were already there as survivals of ancient pagan cults. Aphrodite was worshiped in a black form as *Aphrodite melainis* and Pausanias, hard-pressed to explain her blackness, suggested that it was because mankind usually made love at night (cf. Robert Graves, 1955, I, 72). Black effigies were consecrated particularly to Diane, Demeter, Cybele, Venus, and Isis. Athena who shared with Diana the title "White Virgin" was also adored in the form of a black stone (cf. Durand-Lefèbvre, 153).

Worship of the Great Goddess of Phrygia was the first oriental cult borrowed by the Romans, and her sacred image, a black aerolith, was sent to the Romans by Attalus in 204 B.C. and carried into the Temple of Victory (F. Cumont, 1905, 43; Durand-Lefèbvre, p. 148).

The Black Demeter was worshiped in Pausanias' day in Arcadia, and it was mainly to see her that Pausanias went to Phigalia. Her shrine was in a grove of oaks around a cave where a cold spring rose from the earth. Her wooden image seated on a rock was like a woman in all respects except the head; she had the head and hair of a horse, and out of her head there grew images of serpents and other beasts. Her tunic reached to her feet and on one of her hands was a dolphin, on the other a dove. (The dolphin and dove were also attributes of Atargatis.) The Phigalians called her "Black" because she had black apparel. Her ancient wooden image had been destroyed by fire and the Phigalians had not replaced the image and had neglected the goddess' festivals and sacrifices, until barrenness fell on the land. They went to the Pythian priestess who gave them the oracle that the famine was due to the anger of the goddess at the neglect of her worship. The Phigalians then restored Demeter to even greater honor than before and commissioned Onatas of Aegina to make a new image. Onatas then, about two generations after the Persian invasion of Greece, made the Phigalians a bronze image of Demeter, guided partly by a copy of the ancient wooden image which he had discovered, but mostly by a vision in dreams (Pausanias, *Description of Greece,* xli–xliii).

The grotto of Demeter in time became a Christian shrine dedicated to

Panagia and a fecund black goddess was thus succeeded by the Virgin Mary (cf. Durand-Lefèbvre, 148). Diana, protectress of women in childbirth, generatrix of fruits and fountains, was virginal, and both peaceful and warlike. Her cult was most famous at Ephesus where her first image was said to have been erected by the Amazons. Her torso with numerous breasts bespeaks fertility and on the sheath which clothes the lower part of the body are depicted rams, bulls and bees. According to Pliny (*Historia Naturalis* xvi 213) the image was made of ebony. It has been supposed that the original symbol of Diana was an aerolith, or black stone, like that of Cybele. (Cf. C. Picard, 1922, 274). Confused with Cybele and Mother Earth, Diana-Artemis prepared the way and contributed to the popularity of the cult of the Mother of Christ in the area of Ephesus where St. Paul had encountered the cult (cf. C. Radet, 1927, 22).

Isis, to whom the Christian Virgin was often compared, was transported to the Greco-Roman world and her cult had considerable vogue, as attested by numerous inscriptions. Her image was sometimes black, as was the clothing of her devotees (cf. J. Toutain, II, 7). She appears to be a blend of all goddesses (cf. Apuleius *Metamorphoses* XI 4).

> Because the transition from paganism for which the name of Isis stood was a stealthy and insensibly prolonged blending rather than a sudden disruption, statues like the one in Paris might stay inside Christian churches without arousing comment. Images of Isis could become "black Madonnas" (R. E. Witt, 1971, 274).

From an eleventh-century Jewish source, Midrash Leqaḥ Ṭôḇ of Tobiah Ben Eliezer, we receive apropos of Num 21:29, the interesting piece of intelligence that Chemosh, the chief god of the Moabites, was worshiped as a Black Goddess:

> This is Chemosh, the Abomination which is in the desert (*miḏbār*). It is a black stone, its form like that of a black woman. It was in the midst of the high place (*bāmāh*) and Moab and her environs used to go to it to worship her. Thus it says (Judg 11:24): "Will you not possess what Chemosh your god gives you to possess?" That is, in the tongue of Ishmael (i.e. Arabic), Makkah (i.e. Mecca), . . . (For the text, cf. Solomon Buber, 1894, 250; cf. L. Ginzberg, 1909–28, III, 352; VI, 120n715).

The confusion between Moabites and Muslims and Chemosh and the Ka'ba-t of Mecca need not detain us here. The point of interest is the allegation that Chemosh was worshiped as a black stone with female form.

Chemosh has been generally assumed to be a male deity, but the compound Ashtar-Chemosh of the Mesha stela (line 17) provoked speculation as to whether the first element in the compound represents a male or female deity. The South Arabic Ashtar was male and at Ugarit there was a male *'ṯtr* and female *'ṯtrt*. But on the other hand, among the Eastern Semites the goddess had the masculine form of the name, Ishtar. As the Venus Star, the deity was androgynous. In some divine compounds the name of the goddess takes precedence, as we see from Anat-Yahu at Elephantine. (For the wife's name preceding the husband's in Greek inscriptions from Phrygia, cf. W. Tarn and G. T. Griffith, 1959, 138.) The deity Chemosh is attested now at Ugarit in the compound *ṯṯ wkmṯ,* a common pattern in Ugaritic which seems to apply to male deities exclusively, although this is uncertain. The analysis of Ashtar-Chemosh remains moot, although some savants have inclined to identify the first element as the goddess Ashtart, Astarte. Although scant weight may be attached to a medieval midrash which identifies Chemosh as a black goddess and confuses Moab and Mecca, still the tradition is provocative and highly interesting when viewed in the context of Song of Songs 1:5 and related to other black goddesses attested with greater certainty. Solomon built a "high place" (*bāmāh*) for Chemosh on a mountain facing Jerusalem (I Kings 11:7) and it survived till destroyed by Josiah along with a shrine to Ashtart in the same locale (II Kings 23:13).

That the sacred black stone of Mecca, like other black aeroliths, originally represented the great goddess worshiped by the pagan Arabs in the time of Ignorance [i.e. before Muhammad] seems altogether likely. According to Isaac of Antioch, the pagan Arabs worshiped the Venus Star under the title Al-'Uzza, "The Strong (Female)," and Syrian women ascended the roof tops to pray to the star to make them beautiful (Isaac observed that it didn't seem to make much difference, since there were both beautiful and ugly women among the Arabs as among all other peoples). Captives were sacrificed to her, her favorite being adolescent boys, as related by the Church Father Nilus (cf. J. Wellhausen, 1897, 40–44). The goddess Al-'Uzza had one of her chief shrines in Nakhla a few miles north of Mecca. In the eighth year after the flight to Mecca, Muhammad sent the valiant warrior Khalid to destroy this sanctuary. While Khalid was chopping down the last of the three acacia trees which were sacred to the goddess, a naked black woman with flowing hair confronted him. She was accompanied by a priest who cried out: "Be courageous, Al-'Uzza, and protect yourself." Khalid shook with terror, but he took courage and with a single stroke split her head and she then turned into a black cinder (from Wakidi, cited by Wellhausen, *Muhammad in Medina,* 351; cf. Tor Andrae, 1935, 18). It is clear from the words of the priest that the black woman represented the goddess and that her apparition was calculated to put Khalid and his cohorts to flight.

It seems altogether likely, as suggested by J. M. Grintz (1971, 103n57) that the Aza'el or Uza of Enoch 8:1 is none other than the goddess Al-'Uzza. Enoch tells us that Aza'el

> taught men to make swords, and knives, and shields, and breastplates, and made known to them the metals (of the earth) and the arts of working them, and bracelets, and ornaments, and the use of antimony, and the beautifying of eyelids, and all kinds of costly stones, and all colouring tinctures. (R. H. Charles, *APOT* II, 192.)

Grintz further cites the midrash (A. Jellinek, IV, 127) that "Aza'el did not repent and still remains in his perverted state, corrupting the people by means of the multi-coloured dress (attire) of women." The use of the masculine pronoun here could be accounted for on the ground that the Venus Star is both masculine and feminine and by reference to the male Ishtar of Akkadian (*Ishtar* ^{d}*UŠ*) and the *'ṯr* and *'ṯrt* of Ugaritic. The same midrash, Grintz noted, mentions that *"Shemḥazai* (an alternate form of *'Uzza*) had conversed with Estahar (the Venus-Star=Ishtar). The alternate forms *'Uzza, 'Aza'el* most probably stem from the desire to "naturalize" the strange god(dess)'s name by giving it a form similar to that of the other angels found in Jewish tradition such as Gabriel, Michael, etc. (This would also explain the form *Shemḥazai* or *Shem'azza=Shem-'Uzza* as equivalent to *YHWH-'Uzza.* This bringing of the ineffable name of the God of Israel into association with a cognomen of the pagan goddess of love and war is especially provocative in the light of the compound *'nt yhw* at Elephantine; cf. B. Porten, 1968, 177*ff*.) The ritual of the two goats, chosen by lot, one for Yahweh and one for Azazel, Lev 16:8, takes on new interest in this connection. It has long been appreciated that Azazel is no ordinary demon, but a deity to be propitiated on equal footing with Yahweh. The sending of the goat for Azazel (=*'Uzza,* "Strong Lady," i.e. 'Aštart-Anat) to the wilderness or steppe-land (*miḏbār*) is appropriate for the goddess whose Akkadian title was *bēlit ṣēri,* "Lady of the Steppe." The place to which the goat was dispatched, *Bêṯ Ḥidûdô,* "sharp place" (Mishnah Yoma 6:8) was not far from Jerusalem and it is surmised that this cliff overlooked the valley of the Qidron, Gehinnom, the entrance to the netherworld; cf. NOTE on 6:11.

The ancient Hittites worshiped a Black Goddess of some importance, as we learn from a royal directive regarding the proper ritual for reinstallation of the goddess after she had been removed from her temple in Kizzuwatna:

> Thus says Muršiliš, the Great King, son of Šuppiluliumaš, the Great King, the Hero: When my father Tudḫaliyaš, the Great King, carried away the Black Goddess from the Temple of the Black Goddess in Kizzuwatna, he let it stand anew in Samuḫa in a temple. The cultic activities and prescriptions which were deposited in the Temple of the Black Goddess—the wood-tablet scribes and the people of the Temple came and falsified them—now these (prescriptions) I Muršiliš, the Great King, on clay tablets restore. And when in the future a king, or queen, or king's son, or king's daughter comes into the Temple of the Black Goddess of Samuḫa, then the following cultic actions should take place.

Detailed directions and regulations follow, prescribed by Ulippi, Priest of the Black Goddess. The name of the goddess, unfortunately, is not given and she is referred to only by the Sumerogram *DINGIR GE*$_6$, "Black Deity." The female sex of the deity is suggested, however, by the headdress of the divine image, called *kureššar* (4:30; cf. 3:39) which applies to feminine headgear; moreover, in the mixed Sumerogram and Akkadogram *URU-LIM ŠA*

TA-RA-AM-MI, "the city which thou lovest" (3:45), the verb is Akkadian *tarammī,* present-future second person feminine singular of *rāmu,* "love," "thou (feminine) lovest." The Black Goddess appears as the theophorous element in Hittite female proper names, written *SAL* (i.e. female) *DINGIR* GE_6*-wiyaš,* still without giving a clue to her proper name. (Cf. E. Laroche, 1947, 57*f*).

Another deity, Pirinkar, mentioned in the Hittite text (1:13) is also feminine. This Hurrian goddess is associated with Šaušga and both Pirinkar and Šaušga are related to Ištar. Pirinkar or Pirwa has been viewed as bisexual and related to Ištar (cf. H. G. Güterbock, 1956, 312).

The character of the Hittite Black Goddess is not fully revealed in the ritual for her reinstallation, but there are some intimations. Special attention is paid to the goddess' jewelry and ornamentation, and in particular to her breast ornaments. A violent and bloodthirsty side of her nature is suggested by the ritual which prescribes that the new image of the goddess, the wall of the temple, the utensils, and everything that belongs to the Black Goddess be smeared with blood. (For text, translation and commentary, cf. H. Kronasser, 1963).

Most notorious of all black goddesses is Kali of India whose worship under many different names and aspects is endemic and especially developed in Bengal and in her chief cult center Kāli-ghat (i.e. Calcutta) where daily animal sacrifices are still offered in her temple. One of the meanings of her primary name Kali is "Black." She is beautiful, ever young and virginal, and at the same time horrendous, violent, destructive and insatiable in her thirst for blood and flesh, wine and sexual intercourse. The color of the Devī (Goddess) may vary with the form under which she is contemplated: in conferring liberation she is white; as controller of women, men, and kings she is red; she is saffron as controller of wealth and tawny as creatrix of enmity; in the thrill of love and passion she is rose-colored; in the action of slaying she becomes black (cf. A. and E. Avalon, 1952, 7*f*). As Kali, the Black, the color of her representations in art comport with her name, but with variations from soot black to purplish, bluish and even greenish hues. In hymns to the Goddess her swart beauty is frequently emphasized, as illustrated by the following samples from the translations of Sir John Woodroffe and spouse (Arthur and Evelyn Avalon):

> I remember again and again the dark primeval Devi swayed with passion,
> Her beauteous face heated and moist with the sweat (of amorous play)
> (p. 35, st. 15)

> May (thy) glory, dark as collyrium cloud, Be ever in my heart.
> (p. 60, st. 8)

> Salutation to thee, O giver of blessings,
> Dark Virgin, observant of the vow of chastity,
> Whose form is beauteous as that of the rising sun,
> And thy face as that of the full moon;

Thy form and chastity are of the purest.
Dark art Thou like the blue-black cloud,
Whose face is beauteous as that of Samkarshaṇa.
(p. 142. Samkarshaṇa is a name of her consort Shiva.)

Ever are we protected by Her whose abode is the Kadambra forest,
The weight of whose breasts are garlanded with glittering gems,
Whose breasts are rising,
And excel the mountains in greatness;
Whose cheeks are flushed with wine,
Ever singing sweet songs; the playful one, dark as a cloud,
Ever compassionate to all.

(pp. 162*f*, st. 3)

5b. *Jerusalem girls*. These girls, daughters of Jerusalem/Zion, are often addressed in the course of the Canticle, 2:7, 3:5,10,11, 5:8,16, 8:4. Explanations of their role vary according to the theories of interpretation. For proponents of the "naturalist" hypothesis, they are the female wedding guests. The name of the town might be changed to suit the locale (Budde, Rothstein), or Jerusalem retained under pretense that all weddings take place there (Siegfried). In the dramatic theory, they are the women of the royal harem. Dussaud would see the appellation not as an indication of origin but of distinction, as one would speak of a Parisienne. Joüon regarded the term as a symbolic designation of the pagan nations desirous of coming under the law of Zion. Robert took his cue from the fact that the city, region, or nation is considered as the mother of its inhabitants. The city could be personified and to a degree distinguished from the elements which compose it (cf. Isa 4:4, 49:20–21, 51:22, 60:4; Ezek 19:2,10, 23:2). In Hosea 2:4–7[2–5E], the fiction is pressed to the point that Israel's children are invited to plead against their mother. Throughout the Book of Deuteronomy, the thought oscillates between personification and concrete reality, whence the alternative use of *thou* and *you* in addressing the nation. Accordingly, Robert felt there is a strong presumption that the Canticle uses the expression in its classical sense. The daughters of Jerusalem are the population of the city, the feminine form being used because the city is personified and plays the role of the bride; they are imperfectly distinguished from the city itself, since in 3:11 the daughters of Zion are invited to come out (of the city?) and see King Solomon crowned for his wedding day. Their evocation in the poem is seen by Robert as a dramatic trait: a little earlier the bride was alone and engaged in a monologue; now, thanks to the presence of this group, a sort of dialogue is sketched, which gives to the principal personage occasion to express his sentiments more completely. The process recalls that of the chorus in ancient tragedy, a simple literary process which in no way authorizes us to assume the existence of a nuptial procession. It appears that Robert was on the right track and was suddenly startled by the realization that 3:11 lends itself to the cultic interpretation, hence the disclaimer.

In the cultic interpretation, the Jerusalem girls are naturally and literally understood as the local lasses who participated in and witnessed the sacred marriage rite, including cult personnel, singers, dancers, and presumably the spectators.

5c. *tents.* The word is similar to the term for the odoriferous aloe tree which is mentioned along with myrrh and other spices in 4:14; Ps 45:9[8E]; Prov 7:17, which caused some to mistake tents for aloes here.

Qedar. A tribe of northern Arabia, connected with one of Ishmael's sons, cf. Gen 25:13; Isa 21:16, 42:11; Jer 2:10, 49:28; Ezek 27:21; Ps 120:5. Assurbanipal mentions a king of *qi-id-ri* or *qi-da-ri,* i.e. Qedar (*ANET,* 298*ff*), in connection with his campaign against the Arabs. Pliny (*Historia Naturalis* v 11) relates the Cedrae to the Nabateans. In rabbinic usage the term is applied to Arabs collectively, the Arabic language being designated as "the tongue of Qedar." The Qaraite commentator Yefet ben Ali substituted for Qedar the name of the prophet Muhammad's tribe, the Quraish, "She compares the color of her skin to the blackness of the hair tents of the Quraish." The root *qdr* itself carries the idea of darkness (being used of an eclipse of the sun and/or moon, Joel 2:10, 4[3E]:15; Micah 3:6; of darkening storm clouds, Jer 4:28; of a turbid stream, Job 6:16; of mourning (garb) Jer 8:21, 14:2; Job 5:11, 30:28; Pss 35:14, 38:7[6E], 42:10[9E], 43:2) and Symmachus accordingly translated the name as *skotasmos,* but the prime implication of blackness relates to the typical Bedouin tent, the hair house (*bēt šaʿr*) woven from wool of black goats.

5d. *pavilions.* It has been generally assumed that the reference here is to decorative hangings, curtains, tapestries, or the like. Gordis, for example, suggested that "Solomon's curtains" is a generic term like Aaron's beard, a Vandyke beard, or Louis Quatorze furniture. Magnus, however, perceived correctly from the poetic parallelism that the term *yĕrîʿôṯ* is here a metonym for *'ōhel,* "tent," and this is confirmed by other instances of parallelism, Isa 54:2; Jer 10:20, 49:29; and in particular by Jer 4:20:

Suddenly devastated are my tents, Instantly my pavilions.

The word is related to the root *wrʿ/yrʿ,* "tremble" and is applied to curtains and such because of their tremulous motion in the breeze. The term is applied to the curtains or sections of Yahweh's wilderness dwelling, the "tabernacle," in Exodus 26. The "curtains" constituting the roof over the dwelling were to be made of goats' (hair), Exod 26:7. LXX and Vulgate mistakenly render *yĕrîʿôṯ* as "skins." Cassiodorus explained that as tabernacles are made from the skin of dead animals, God's tabernacle, the Church, is framed of those who have mortified themselves with regard to affections and lusts. Again the verse speaks of the seeming hardship and repulsiveness of the Christian life, as seen by the world, whereas those who view it from the inside see not the black goats' hair tents of warfare, but the purple, bejeweled, golden tapestry of the Prince of Peace. (Cf. Littledale, ad loc.).

Aversion to black (cf. NOTE on 5a.) extends even to the curtains.

Schmökel, for example, explains that the black goat hair tents of Qedar (like those of the present-day Bedouin) stand as a figure of the "black" bride in contrast to the white or light colored wall hangings in the king's palace, which represent the "light" side of the appearance and manner of the goddess. Solomon's name is invoked as the richest and most luxurious King of Israel (Schmökel, 1956, 51n3). Similarly, E. F. F. Bishop explains that constant rough wear and exposure to all weather means that the black sackcloth of the tent soon comes to have a very poor, dark, dirty appearance. So the bride's low estate is in contrast to the daughters of Jerusalem, as different as the tents of Qedar from the curtains of Solomon (1967, 21). The notion that there is implied contrast between the blackness of the bride and the paler hue of the "daughters" of Jerusalem, or the black tents of Qedar and the lighter colored wall drapes of Solomon, is purely fanciful. The bride is both black *and* beautiful, like a Bedouin tent. W. M. Thomson appropriately noted that "Even black tents, when new and pitched among bushes of liveliest green, have a very comely appearance, especially when both are bathed in a flood of evening's golden light" (p. 171).

Salmah. MT volcalizes *šĕlōmōh,* i.e. Solomon. Winckler (1903, 152) and Wellhausen (1905, 213) proposed the reading Salmah, the name of an ancient Arabian tribe mentioned in Assyrian and South Arabic sources and in the Targumim (cf. Targum Onqelos Gen 15:19; Num 24:21; Judg 4:17) and the Jerusalem Talmud. This tribe preceded the Nabateans in the region of Petra. In I Chron 2:11 *Śalmā'* is given as the father of Boaz, and so also in Ruth 4:20 although the following verse reads *śalmôn.* The parallelism of *šlmh* with Qedar confirms the interpretation as a tribal name and this view has been widely adopted, e.g. by Zapletal, Miller, Ricciotti, Guitton, Bea, T. H. Gaster (1952, 322) and RTF.

5. The Targum took the blackness to refer to Israel when they made the calf:

> When the House of Israel made the Calf, their faces grew dark like the Ethiopians who dwell in the tents of Qedar. And when they turned in penitence, and their guilt was pardoned them, the precious radiance of their faces increased like the angels, because they made the curtains for the Tabernacle. And the Presence of YHWH dwelt among them and Moses, their master, went up to the firmament and made peace between them and their King.

Midrash Rabbah offered multiple choice: the individual black through his own deeds, but comely through the works of his ancestors; the Community of Israel black in its own sight, but comely to the Creator (citing Amos 9:7 with the inference that the Cushites or Ethiopians were not beautiful); Israel in Egypt black in rebellion, but comely with the blood of the Passover and the circumcision; at Horeb, black with rebellion and comely with obedience (Ps 106:19 and Exod 24:7) and similarly in the wilderness (Ps 78:40 and Num 9:15); the evil report of the spies black in contrast to the bravery of Joshua and Caleb (Num 13:32 and 32:12); Israel black with whoredom at Shittim (Num 25:1) but comely through the action of Phinehas (Ps 106:30); the sin of Achan black and the zeal of Joshua comely (Josh 7:1 and 19); the kings of Israel black in contrast with those of Judah, and both black compared with the prophets. The blackness is applied to Ahab who did momentarily alter his dark image by austerities at the death of Jezebel (I Kings 21:27), even though one rabbi supposed that the period of Ahab's fasting was three hours. Finally R. Levi ben Ḥaytha applied this verse in three ways. "I am black on the days of the week and comely on the Sabbath; black all the days of the year and comely on the Day of Atonement; black in this world and comely in the world to come." The tents of Qedar, on the outside ugly, dingy, and ragged, yet inside containing precious stones, were likened to the disciples of the wise whose external appearance was repulsive to the world, but inside they were beautiful with the knowledge of Scripture, Midrash, Talmud, and other religious lore.

The doctors of the Church, seeking to explain the representations of Mary as black, resorted to the biblical data to sum up her mystical qualities, her moral beauty, the divine love which embraces her, her election and position above all other women, her mystic espousal with divinity, her sadness and the persecutions which she endured; the flora named in the Solomonic poetry are precisely those from which her statues were carved—the incorruptible ebony symbolizes her indestructible purity and holiness; the cedar and cypress with their eternal green express the source of life and the bed pure and immaculate; the apple tree "under which her mother conceived," the tree of Paradise. Mary has the beauty of the moon, the purity of dawn, the intrepid force of an army. The names of the places of the Orient where the man of the twelfth century saw the images of the Mother of God, are also named in Solomon's Song: Lebanon, Damascus, Carmel (cf. Durand-Lefèbvre, 1937, 178*f*). Such devotional explanations do little to illuminate the blackness.

The Greek Fathers, applying this verse to the whole Church, related the blackness to the Gentile element and the comeliness to the Hebrew. The black and the beautiful was also applied to the mixture of saints and sinners which comprise the Church. The Virgin Mary also had her dark days and her beautiful moments, as when her reputation was blackened by slander because of her premarital pregnancy, though she was full of grace; and black too, as Mother of Sorrows, when she stood by the Cross and was despised with her Son, but beautiful in the joy of His Resurrection. (Cf. Littledale.)

6a. *Stare not.* The rendering is intended to be non-committal, in keeping with the ambiguity of the original. The common interpretation presumes an implication of scorn or disdain because of the blackness. *NEB* makes this explicit with "Do not look down on me." *RSV*'s "gaze" and *JPSV*'s "stare" are more appropriate as indicating interest and fascination without hint of disdain or revulsion. M. Dahood suggests (AB 16, first NOTE on Ps 49:17[16E]) "Do not envy me in that I am black," (reading *tēre'* for MT *tīrā'*) and cites the analogous use of *'yn,* "to eye," in I Sam 18:9 where *NEB* renders "Saul kept a jealous eye on David." There is in the present context no more hint of envy at the bride's blackness than there is of disdain. The blackness is striking and beautiful, but not necessarily enviable.

With slight alteration of the vocalization, one could read "do not fear me." Schmökel (1956, 53), on the basis of this reading, raises the question, "Why is the community afraid?" He then suggests that the allusion may be to the cultic clothing of the goddess or her priestess who wore the dark mantle in mourning and longing for the dead god Tammuz.

swart. This hapax form *šĕḥarḥōreṯ* is often taken as diminutive of *šāḥôr,* "black," hence *NEB*'s rendering "a little dark I may be." Delitzsch explained it as "blackish" (*subnigra*). *RSV and JPSV* chose "swarthy," possibly to lighten the darkness. The choice of "swart" here is for poetic reasons, rather than for its possible suggestion of diminution of the darkness.

6b. *blackened.* It is uncertain here whether the root of the verbal form *šĕzāp̄aṯnî* is *šzp* which occurs elsewhere in Job 20:9 and 28:7 in the sense of "see, look at." There is also a similar root *šdp* used of blasting or scorching of grain by the hot east wind (Gen 41:6,23,27; the noun is used in Deut 28:22; I Kings 8:37; Amos 4:9, Haggai 2:17; II Chron 6:28). *KJ* rendered "the sun hath looked upon me," but *RSV* "the sun has scorched me," the former agreeing with LXX and the latter resembling the Vulgate *quia decoloravit me sol.* The tropical sense of scorching or sunburn is conveyed by the sun's gaze. Dahood proposed (1964a, 406) derivation of the form from the noun *zep̄eṯ,* "pitch," as a *šap̄'ēl* causative, "make black as pitch," which would, Dahood suggested, create the needed balance to *šĕḥarḥōreṯ*. This would intensify the very blackness which many critics have sought to mitigate.

6c. *mother's sons.* Here there is no corresponding line, as one would expect, putting "brothers" in parallelism with "mother's sons," as in Gen 27:29 and Ps 50:20. In Deut 13:7[6E] the two terms are in apposition. This use as a poetic synonym for "brother" has nothing to do with the technical uses distinguishing between stepfathers and mothers and half sisters (half brothers are not mentioned) in prohibitions of incest in Lev 18:6–18. Since the bride's father is nowhere mentioned in the Canticle, but only the mother, 3:4, 6:9, 8:2, Delitzsch conjectured that the father was dead, that the mother had remarried, and that the sons of the second marriage ruled in the house of the mother. There is an indirect allusion to brothers who speak of their concern for a little sister with no breasts (8:8) and Delitzsch surmised that the stepbrothers were rigorous guardians of their sister's honor and in their zeal perhaps a trifle harsh betimes. This is a plausible but fanciful construction. It is likely that a line or part of a line has been lost in which there was reference to "my brothers" as the parallel antecedent to "my mother's sons," as in the poetic passages noted above and also in Ugaritic:

> My brothers Baal made my destroyers, My mother's sons my annihilators.
> (6[49].6.10–11)

It is fruitless to speculate about the role of the bride's brothers. It appears to be an allusion to some mythological motif otherwise unknown. There are in the Mesopotamian and Ugaritic myths many such allusions which remain enigmatic although the language is clear.

Siegfried saw in the reference to the mother only an indication of primitive matriarchy. Others (Dussaud, Guitton, Buzy) noted that Israelite society gave brothers the right of surveillance of their sisters. Joüon, taking Israel as one of the daughters of the human race, saw the brothers as the other nations, and particularly the Egyptians who enslaved their sister. Robert, taking the cue from Joüon that the sister and brothers represent nations, reasoned that if the sister is Israel and the brothers other nations, then the mother must be an older nation. Ezek 16:3,44–45 ascribed Israelite origins to the Amorites and Hittites of the land of Canaan. But the perspective here, according to Robert, goes beyond Ezekiel's horizon to the older tradition that the ancestral home of Abraham was Ur of the Chaldees (Gen 11:28,31, 15:7). Moreover, Jacob is called an Aramaean in Deut 26:5 and Isaac and Jacob go back to their relatives in Harran to get wives (Gen 24, 25:20, 28:1*ff*, 31:20,24). This reminiscence of origin was not lost after the Exile, and Robert accordingly understood the allusion to the brothers as the Chaldeans of Nebuchadnezzar who destroyed Jerusalem and took Judah captive. Thus the uterine brothers of the bride gave her miserable treatment, expressed by her somber color (cf. Judith 5:6*ff*,18).

The anger of "my mother's sons" was applied in Jewish allegory to Dathan and Abiram who informed against Moses when he slew the Egyptian (cf. J. Goldin, 1955, 95). Christians related it to the persecution of the Primitive Church by the Church's mother, the Synagogue, or to the Judaizing party within the Church. The reading of the LXX and Vulgate "they fought against me" was applied to various conflicts against and within the Church and within the individual soul.

incensed. LXX and Vulgate "fought against me." The form *niḥērû* is apparently a *nip̄'al* of *ḥry,* "burn, be angry." The participle of this conjugation is used in the same sense in Isa 41:11 and 45:24. Why the brothers were incensed is a matter of conjecture and a stimulus to speculation. Schmökel regards the statement "the sons of my mother were angry with me" as difficult to understand and proposes to read *ben 'immî ḥar bî* which he renders "Meiner Mutter Sohn hat mich heiss gemacht." Gerleman, following G. R. Driver (1933, 380*f*), construes the word as a *pi'ēl* of *nḫr* which in Akkadian and Arabic means "snort" (cf. KB, 609b).

Wittekindt, following Erbt (1906), connected the verb with the root *ḫrr,* "pierce," and the noun *ḥōr,* "hole," mentioned in 5:4. The stich 6d Wittekindt regarded as an addition; thus the distich would read:

My mother's son perforated me. My vineyard I did not guard.

6d,e. *vineyard.* The sexual symbolism of terms like "vineyard," "orchard," "field" is well established. The plowing and cultivation of a field is a natural figure for sexual intercourse and doubtless has some association with the custom of ritual copulation on freshly plowed fields in order to ensure or encourage fertility. The prophet of Islam (Quoran 2:223) rephrased an ancient proverb:

Your women are your tillage; So come to your tillage as you wish.

Amarna letters 75:15, 85:37, 90:42 refer to an earlier version of the proverb to the effect that a woman without a husband is like an untilled field. (Cf. D. Weber and J. Knudtzon, 1908–15, 1159*f*, and A. Goetze, 1941, 367.) The Nikkal Hymn from Ugarit which relates the marriage of two lunar deities makes the groom say of his prospective bride (24[77].22–23):

I will make her field vineyards (*krmm*), The field of her love orchards.

The neo-Hebrew term *pî hakkerem,* "mouth of the vineyard," as a designation of the navel suggests that the "vineyard" itself is nearby.

An Egyptian text of the Ramesside period depicts an amorous adventure of a military official who encountered a girl "who guards a vineyard" (cf. A. Hermann, 1959, 165). A similar expression occurs in an Old Egyptian song wherein the girl refers to herself as a piece of ground in which the youth dug a "canal" (S. Schott, 1950, 56,2; Hermann, 153). The parallels above are cited by Gerleman who stressed the Egyptian influence on the Canticle. Gerleman noted also the classical uses of *kēpos* and *hortus* as metaphors for feminine pudenda.

More striking are the uses of field in the Sumerian Sacred Marriage songs:

Lordly Queen, your breast is your field, Your broad field that pours out plants,
Inanna, your breast is your field, Your broad field that pours out grain,
(Kramer, *SMR*, 81)

Kramer noted (p. 100) that a favorite motif of the Song of Songs is the "going down" of lovers to garden, orchard, and field and that this is also the theme central to several Sumerian poems of the kind that might have been chanted during the Sacred Marriage celebration:

My sister, I would go with you to my field, My sister, I would go with you to my garden,
My fair sister, I would go with you to my field, My fair sister, I would go with you to my garden.

The field, garden, and orchard is here said to belong to the male, King Shulgi, who is speaking to his "fair sister," the goddess Inanna, but it is clear that the reference is to the bride's charms which are to be enjoyed by the groom.

In other instances, the bride's pudenda are referred to directly as she sings a song about her vulva which she calls "the boat of heaven," the new crescent moon, fallow land, a high field, a hillock which she wishes to have plowed:

As for me, my vulva,
For me the piled-high hillock,
Me—the maid, who will plow it for me?

The answer comes:

Oh Lordly Lady, the king will plow it for you,
Dumuzi, the king, will plow it for you

And joyfully she responds:

Plow my vulva, man of my heart! (Kramer, *SMR*, 59)

In addition to the Ugaritic reference to the cultivation of the bride's field, vineyard, orchard cited above, there is in the enigmatic ritual portion of the poem called "The Birth of the Beautiful Gods" mention of the field(s) of the goddess(es) Asherah and perhaps Anat (23[52].13):

wšd.šd.ilm	And the field is the field of the gods,
šd.aṯrt.wrḥm	The field is of Asherah—and—Virgin
	(Cf. 23[52].28)

The term *rḥm* here rendered "Virgin" has the primary meaning *uterus* and the derived meanings "girl" (cf. Judg 5:30) and "compassion" (similar to our use of "hysteria") and is applied to Anat as *rḥm ʿnt* as a variant of the regular epithet *btlt ʿnt,* "Virgin Anat."

6d. *vineyard guard.* Cf. 8:1–12 on vineyard guarding or keeping. The expression here *nôṭērāh ʾeṯ-hakkĕrāmîm,* "a (female) guardian of the vineyards," has an exact parallel in Ugaritic in the masculine form *nġr krm* which occurs in a roster of royal personnel classified according to occupation (2011.12) and in a mythological fragment (2000.2.1). A similar expression *nġr mdrʿ,* "guardian of the sown," also occurs in "The Birth of the Beautiful Gods" (23[52].68,69,73). The "Guardian of the Sown" is encountered at the edge of the steppe or desert by the newborn gods whose mouths stretch from heaven to earth as they gulp down the birds of the air and the fish in the sea:

A lip to earth, a lip to heaven,
And there enter their mouths
The birds of the air and the fish in the sea. (23[52].61–63)

The voracious godlings demand that the Guardian of the Sown open to them whatever supplies of food and wine there are. The role of the Vineyard Guard, *nġr krm,* in the mythological text (2001) is difficult to determine because the text is too fragmentary to arrange in parallel lines and it is impossible to be assured of the sense except where it is confirmed by the poetic parallelism. It is clear that the text involves the goddess Aštart and the gods El and Baal, and there are at least a couple of words which are provocative and suggestive. The form *arbḫ* of 2.10 appears to be a noun; in Arabic the root *rbḫ* means to faint or swoon during coition. The vocable *rbd* of 2.13

is applied in Prov 7:16 to the covering of the adulteress' couch and in Arabic the root is used of darkening coloration, inclining to blackness. In the present state of affairs it is impossible to prove the point, but it is possible that this Ugaritic mythological fragment which mentions vineyard keeping in connection with Aštart (Ishtar), El, and Baal, and offers words suggestive of sexual involvement and/or turning black, may be the mythological key to the understanding of the motif of the Black Beauty of the Canticle. It is to be hoped that parallel passages may be recovered to clarify this provocative fragment.

There is indirect reference to the God of Israel as a vineyard guard in Isa 27:2*f*. The vineyard represents Israel, as in the famous Vineyard Song of Isa 5:1–7. The burden of both songs is similar, that the vineyard, in spite of every care, was unproductive:

A wine-vineyard, sing of it!	Lest anyone should harm it,
I, Yahweh, its keeper.	Night and day I guarded it.
Momently I watered it.	*Wine* I get none.

The emendation of *ḥēmāh,* "wrath," to *ḥemer,* "wine," in the last line seems justified by the context, just as *ḥemer* is to be preferred over the variant *ḥemeḏ* in the first line of the ditty. The figure of the vineyard gets lost in the succeeding lines, Isa 27:4b–11, in a mixture of threats and promises, but the verdict is clear in the end:

Therefore his Maker will not pity him,	His Creator will show him no favor.

6e. *My own vineyard.* The double determination, *karmî šellî,* "my vineyard which is mine," is unusual and must be emphatic, "my very own vineyard," cf. 8:12. The reference presumably is to the maiden's body and specifically to her sexual parts. If the brothers made her a guardian of chastity, she did not protect her own.

Some commentators would expunge the line "my own vineyard I did not guard" on the ground that the stich is overloaded and isolated, uncoordinated with the distichs which precede and follow, and that it interrupts the thought-sequence of the poetry (Buzy). This would apply to greater or lesser degree to many of the lines of the Canticle, e.g. 6c, which is missing a parallel line which should have preceded it with "my brothers" to match "my mother's sons."

A number of commentators identify the vineyard with the bride, or her face, which reflects innocence and beauty, or her physical charms. If the physical charms include all parts, the bride would scarcely announce that she neglected intimate feminine hygiene. The well-attested sexual symbolism of vineyard and field strongly suggest that the purport of her statement is that she had not preserved her own virginity. Such an announcement might occasion little or no stir at a wedding in modern avant-garde liberated circles, but self-proclaimed premarital promiscuity by the bride at a rustic Palestinian wedding might be disconcerting to the guests, as it would be to those who interpret the Songs as praise of monogamy. For the cultic interpretation, however, the bride's liberality with regard to her charms comports with the character and activity of the love goddess who retains her honorific title Virgin despite her many amours.

For Robert the key to the problem of the vineyard is supplied by traditional biblical data, the allegory of the vine being a classical theme developed in Isa 5:1–7; Jer 12:10; Psalm 80, and always with reference to misfortunes caused by Israel's sins, especially at the Exile. Hosea 2 Robert sees as related to this theme. The vineyard of the bride is Palestine and when she says that she has not guarded her vineyard, she alludes to the faults for which God had to punish her. When she contrasts her vineyard with the other domains which her mother's sons obliged her to guard, she alludes to the Exile and to Babylonia where she had to submit to forced labor imposed by the conqueror, and where, after so many years, the great majority of Israel still lived.

6. The Targum related this verse to the sin of idolatry:

> Said the Assembly of Israel to the peoples: "Do not despise me because I am darker than you, because I have done according to your deeds and have bowed down to the sun and the moon, since false prophets caused the powerful fury of YHWH to be drawn down upon me. They taught me to worship idols and walk according to your laws, but the Lord of the World, my God, I did not serve and did not follow after His laws, nor keep His commands and His Law."

Midrash Rabbah also related the blackness to the sin of idolatry, with citation of numerous biblical passages. The reference to the sun suggested the horses which the kings of Judah had given to the solar deity (II Kings 23:11). The blackening interestingly enough evoked the sin of the Israelites with the Midianite women at Baal Peor (Numbers 25). Rabbi Isaac suggested that when the Israelites went in to each woman, they went in pairs and one of them would blacken the woman's face while the other stripped her of her ornaments. The women would say to them: "Are we not also God's creatures, that you do so to us?" And the Israelites would answer: "Is it not enough for you that we were punished through you?"; Num 25:3 is then cited. A parable is adduced of a prince who went out and got sunburned, but with bathing became white again and his good looks were restored. So Israel was tanned with the sun of idolatry, but the other nations served idols from their mother's womb; for when a pregnant woman bows in an idolatrous temple, the unborn child bows with her. The expression "sons of my mother" was applied to Dathan and Abiram, Jeroboam son of Nebat, Ahab, Zedekiah, and even Jezebel. The vineyard keeper also received a variety of explanations, e.g., the prophets of Baal and Asherah who were kept, fed and pampered by Jezebel, and Pashhur son of Malkiah who was kept in luxury by Zedekiah. The neglect of the vineyard was applied to Israel's derelictions and lapses in religious duties.

Christian expositors found a great variety of allegory in this verse. The sun could represent the heat of temptation and suffering or the warmth of Christ. The sufferings which the Church endured were for Christ's sake, the Sun of Righteousness. Or the Saints may be looked on by men as burning and shining lights, but when compared with the perfect righteousness of Christ, they feel themselves to be utter blackness. The mother's angry children designated the sons of the Synagogue, the Church's mother, who persecuted the Primitive Church. The attempt to crush the infant Church was the cause of its moving out among the gentiles to become keeper of the vineyards, thus forced to abandon its own vineyard, the parent religion (cf. Acts 13:46). Reference was also seen here to Adam's failure to keep the vineyard of the Garden of Eden, or his own vineyard, Eve, against the wiles of the Serpent. Or the verse could be applied to the perils of high office in the Church, when those set to guard the Vineyard neglect their own souls and, after preaching to others, become derelict. Christ as Vineyard Keeper gave up all self-concern and became keeper of all others. The vineyard also was seen as the state of consecrated virginity, and Saint Ambrose warned against the Ahabs and Jezebels who would turn the garden of sweet fruits into a patch of pot-herbs, the secular life, like the vineyard of the man void of understanding (Prov 24:30). (Cf. Littledale.)

7a. *my true love.* Lit. "the one (whom) my soul loves," i.e. "the one whom I love." "Soul," *nep̄eš,* designates the person or self including all its appetites and desires, physical and spiritual.

7b,c. *Where.* Elsewhere the form *'êḵāh* means "how." It is commonly used as the opening of a lamentation or dirge, as in Lam 1:1, 2:1, 4:1,2; Isa 1:21; Jer 48:17. The apparent meaning "where" in this passage agrees with its cognate *ēkā* in Akkadian, somewhat like the reversal of meaning in English and German who/where and *wo/wer.*

7b. *pasture.* The verb *r'y* has in the simple stem the double sense like English "feed": to eat, or cause to eat. The object, the flock, is understood and need not be expressed. The line, however, is short, with only four syllables, and would have been bolstered by the addition of the object.

The sexual suggestiveness of pastoral and bucolic terminology is patent and the use of terms for eating with sexual sense is commonplace. Wittekindt cited (17n2) from Arabic folksong (M. Hartmann, 1899, 202, vs. 134):

Come, a spring pasture I will show thee, Which no man has yet trodden.

The oft-cited parallel in Gen 37:16 in which Joseph inquires where his brothers are pasturing (their flock) is not especially noteworthy and it may be doubted whether the similarity in wording implies that the author of either passage must have been familiar with the other. The question is natural for anyone trying to locate a shepherd. In the Joseph story the reason for the quest and the question is clear, but not so in the present instance.

7c. *fold.* The verb *rbṣ,* applied to the lying down of four-footed animals, either wild or domestic, is here used in the causative stem, as in Ps 23:2. It is difficult to find a single English word for this action. We choose the somewhat archaic usage of "fold," "confine (sheep)," as in John Fletcher's patent paraphrase of the present verse in description of pastoral lovers' tryst:

These happy pair of lovers meet straightway,
Soon as they *fold* their flocks up with the day.
("Faithful Shepherdess" ii 3)

at noon. Midday is the usual siesta time in warm climates. Ginsburg quotes Virgil (*Georgics* iii 331):

When noon-tide flames, down cool sequester'd glades,
Lead where some giant oak the dell o'ershades,
Or where the gloom of many an ilex throws
The sacred darkness that invites repose.

Littledale also cited another pastoral vignette by Virgil (*Culex* 103):

The roaming she-goats, at their herdsman's will,
Besought the low fords of the whispering stream,
Which rested blue beneath the verdant moss,
And now the sun had reached his midmost toils,
When to the thick shade drove the swain his flock.

E. F. F. Bishop (1967, 20*f*) cites C. T. Wilson (1906, 173):

In the deep valleys which descend from the Tableland of Moab . . . I have often seen the shepherds bring their flock at noon to drink and then rest in the cool shade of the bushes by the waterside."

The siesta of Palestinian shepherds, according to Stephen (1923, 204) extends from the fourth to the ninth hour of the day, affording ample time for a love tryst.

The usual answer to the query as to the significance of the noon hour, viz. that it is the time for repose and amorous colloquy, misses the point, according to Robert, since the rest is for the flock and not for the shepherd. The latter is idle all day and alone in the field and thus always accessible for a love tryst. Joüon, haunted with the idea of the enslavement in Egypt, saw the hour as signifying the crushing labor, in opposition to the night which is the time of repose. But this symbolism, according to Robert, does not accord with either custom or the mode of thought of the sacred writers for whom darkness signifies trial and suffering. These images have for the most part eschatological import, as in Amos 5:18,20; Isa 5:30. The texts which speak of midday present it several times in the sense of happiness (Isa 58:10; Ps 37:6; Job 11:17) while trial is represented by the image of darkness (Deut 28:29; Isa 59:10; Job 5:14). Thus the time when Yahweh will lead his flock back to Palestine will be midday, that is to say the full day of salvation and unclouded happiness. The bride, to wit the nation Israel, figured as the flock, is still in exile: she languishes for the day, beseeching Yahweh to let her know it. Thus Robert managed to apply this passage to the Exile and Return.

The mention of noon inspired St. Bernard's rambling eloquence:

O true noonday, fulness of glow and light, abiding of the sun, dispeller of shades, drier up of marshes, ejector of evil odors! O perennial solstice, when the day shall no more go down! O noontide glory! O vernal mildness! O summer beauty! O autumnal plenty, and lest aught should be lacking to my tale, O rest and festival of winter! Or, if thou wouldst rather have it so, winter alone is over and gone. Show me, says the Bride, the place of such love and peace, and fulness, that as Jacob, yet abiding in the flesh, saw God face to face, and his life was spared, so I too may look on Thee in Thy light and glory, by contemplation in trance of soul, as Thou feedest more abundantly, and restest more securely. For here too Thou feedest, but not in security, nor canst Thou rest, but Thou must needs stand and watch, because of the terrors of the night. Alas! here is no clear light, nor full refreshment, nor safe dwelling, and therefore tell me where Thou feedest, where Thou restest at noon. Thou called me blessed when I hunger and thirst after righteousness. What is that to their happiness who are filled with the good things of Thy house, who feast and rejoice before God, and are merry and joyful? When wilt Thou fill me with joy with Thy countenance? Thy Face, Lord, will I seek. Thy Face is the noon. Tell me where thou feedest, where thou restest at noon. I know well where Thou feedest, but restest not, tell me where Thou dost both rest and feed. (Littledale's rendering.)

7d. *Lest.* With LXX and Vulgate taking *šallāmāh* as negative equivalent to Aramaic *dilmā'*, against *KJ, RSV, AT* which construe the compound as interrogative. Gordis correctly equated the form *šallāmāh* with the Aramaic *dilmā'*, "lest," but then proceeded to translate and analyze it as the interrogative, "for why?" comparing it with the expression *'ăšer lāmmāh* in Dan 1:10, which, however, does not mean "for why," but "lest," as many modern translators have realized. The *māh* of *šallamāh* and of Aramaic *dilmā'* has nothing to do with the interrogative *mā(h)*, but is a negative particle; cf. AB 15 on Job 16:6b and 31:1b.

as. The particle *k-* was construed by Gordis as asseverative, "Why, indeed" on the basis of his study, 1943. Similar usage Gordis would find in 8:1 and probably in 7:1[6:13E]. A point commonly overlooked with respect to the Ugaritic usage is that in every case the asseverative particle *k-* stands before a verb at the end of a line, and not before nominal forms as in the allegedly asseverative biblical examples.

veiled. The participle *'ôṭěyāh* here has occasioned some difficulty. Many modern exegetes adopt the reading of the Syriac, Vulgate, and Symmachus, reflecting *ṭô'ăyāh,* "a wanderer," with metathesis of the first two consonants of the MT. *JPSV* renders, accordingly, "as one who strays," and adds the misleading note "Meaning of Heb uncertain." It is not that the meaning of *'ṭy* is uncertain, but that the implications of the well-attested sense of the word are here incompatible with certain theories of interpretation. The word has cognates in Akkadian, Syriac, and Arabic and is used more than a score of times in the Bible, always of a person wrapping or concealing oneself in a garment. In I Sam 28:14 the active participle is used, as above, to describe Samuel rising from the grave wrapped in a mantle, *'ôṭeh mě'îl.* LXX rendered "as one wrapped," or "veiled," *hos periballomenē.* Rashi explained the veiling as indicating mourning. The aversion to the natural interpretation of the word derives from the connection of the veil or envelopment in a robe with sacred prostitution, as when Tamar veiled and wrapped herself so as to be taken for a cult prostitute and thus waylaid her father-in-law on the way to a sheep-shearing, Gen 38:14. Although the root *'ṭy* is not used of Tamar's action, it appears that what she did is just what our lady in the Canticle does not wish to do. She wishes to know where she can find her lover, so that she will not have to resort to the device which Tamar used.

Ginsburg rejected the meaning "veiled" on the ground that wherever the word is used of covering the body in mourning or disguise, the part covered is mentioned. He also rejected the association with harlotry on the ground that Tamar covered her face, not as a sign that she was a prostitute but in order to disguise herself so that her father-in-law would not recognize her. Judah took her for a harlot, not because of the veil, but because she sat by the wayside. It is explicitly stated, however, that he thought she was a harlot, because she had covered her face. Since harlots both covered their face and sat by the wayside, Judah had double cause to take her as she intended to be taken.

There is another root, *'ṭy* II, used in Jer 43:12 of a shepherd delousing his garment. The two words which have become identical in Hebrew remain distinct in Arabic, the initial consonant of the first being *ǵ* and of the second '. *NEB* follows the suggestion of A. F. von Gall, 1904, that the root meaning "to delouse" is indicated in the present passage and thus renders "that I may not be left picking lice." For defense of this rendering, see Driver, 1974.

Ginsburg was amazed that anyone could read this verse and yet believe that the king was the object of the damsel's attachment, since this verse shows so clearly that it was a shepherd. Delitzsch, on the other hand, thought the country damsel so simple that she had no idea of the occupation of a king and could not imagine a higher and fairer calling than that of a shepherd. Moreover, Scripture also describes governing as "tending of sheep"; and the Messiah, of whom Solomon is a type, is specially represented as the future Good Shepherd. One must go further, however, and note that shepherd is a common epithet for both kings and deities.

Robert, unable to accept the MT and its possible implications, adopted the reading reflected by Vulgate *vagari* and again found a way to relate the verse to the Exile and Return. The passage he took to be inspired by Jer 31:21–22 in which Virgin Israel is exhorted to return to her cities. The sense was clear to Robert; the nation Israel which is outside of Palestine and apparently abandoned by Yahweh, is errant like a woman away from home. Robert cites Jer 33:12 and Ezek 34:14–15 which refer to Yahweh as shepherd restoring the scattered people to their former good pasture on the mountains of Israel. This he thinks answers the question of the bride, as to where the shepherd, who is Yahweh, will lead his flock, Israel. To Palestine, for there alone is the place of green pastures, of security and repose.

The Targum related this verse to Moses' misgivings about Israel's fidelity and future:

> When the prophet Moses' time came to depart from the world, he said before YHWH: It has been revealed to me that this people will sin and be carried into exile. Now tell me how they will sustain themselves and live among the nations whose decrees are strong as the heat of the noonday sun in the summer solstice, and how they will be carried away among the flocks of the children of Esau and Ishmael who associate their idolatries as companions to you.

Midrashic interpretation of this verse was applied mostly to Moses' concern for the Israelites as his flock, but it was also related to the covering of the upper lip by lepers (Lev 13:45).

Christian interpreters were able to find many meanings in the reference to "rest at high noon" and "the feeding of the flock." Noon, the time of light and heat, was variously explained as persecution of the Church, sin's fiery assaults the Church in her brilliance as the light of the world, or Christ the Sun of Righteousness as the Church's head who gives light and warmth to His Church. (Cf. Littledale.)

8a. This verse is variously ascribed to a chorus of harem ladies, Jerusalem girls, or even the companions of the shepherd lover, depending on the type of interpretation espoused. LXX mistook the "ethical dative," "if you do not know for yourself," and rendered the suffix as accusative rather than dative, "if you do not know yourself."

Graetz paid his respects to the LXX translation and to others still more extravagant, such as that of Renan, "si tu es simple à ce point," with the stricture that such could only be produced by Hebraists who had not Hebrew imbued in their sap and blood. According to Graetz, the words *'im lô'*, "if not," are to be taken as energic affirmative, rather than negative, and the dative, "for thyself," shows that the verb "thou knowest" is used as a sort of imperative, like Job 5:27. Graetz rendered accordingly, "O nein, merke es dir," "O no, mark it (for) thee." Robert's objection that this sense exists only as the apodosis of propositions of imprecation or oath is both specious and confused; the part of the sentence containing *'im lô'*, "if not," would be the protasis, and the apodosis of an oath or imprecation is often suppressed or unexpressed. In such incomplete conditional sentences, "if" introduces a negative asseveration and "if not" the positive. It is not clear in the present instance whether the clause introduced by *'im lô'* is to be taken as affirmative, with Graetz, or as the protasis of a negative condition. The latter appears more likely, but it makes little difference in the sense. More important is the second point made by Graetz, that the answer given in vs. 8 to the question posed by the bride in the preceding verse is delivered by the groom since it would be absurd to suppose that others would answer for him.

Gordis, following Tur-Sinai, understood these lines as a quotation of the speech of the shepherd's comrades used without a formula of citation which he ventured to supply:

Why, indeed, should I be a wanderer
Among the flocks of thy comrades,
Who would say to me:
"If thou knowest not, . . ."

8b. *fairest of women.* Cf. 5:9b and 6:1b. The use of the term "women" here does not rule out application to a goddess, since there is little else to which a goddess could be compared for beauty. In a Sumerian sacred marriage poem, Dumuzi addresses the goddess Inanna:

Let me inform you, let me inform you,
Inanna, most deceitful of women, let me inform you.
(*SMR,* 78)

The goddess Durgā is addressed as a woman in one of the Tantric hymns:

Purest woman art thou on earth.
Thy well-formed ears are decked with beautiful earrings.
Thy face challenges the moon in beauty.
(Avalon, 143)

8c. *the sheep tracks.* These references to following, in the companions' flocks are strikingly similar to the words of the *galla* demons of the netherworld in pursuit of Dumuzi:

Let us follow him among the head sheep,
Let us be with him by the "head" sheep of his friend.
Let us follow him among the "rear" sheep,
Let us be with him among the "mounting" sheep of his friend,
Let us follow him among the . . . sheep,
Let us be with him among the . . . sheep of his friend.
(*SMR,* 129*f*)

8d. *kids.* Delitzsch considered this assignment of kids rather than sheep "an involuntary fine delicate thought." He added a suggestion which probably comes much nearer to the truth: that kids are named because the kid is "a near-lying erotic emblem"; cf. Gen 38:17, apropos of which it has been fittingly remarked that the he-goat was the proper courtesan-offering in the worship of Aphrodite (Movers, 1841, I, 680).

JPSV supplies an explanatory footnote to its rendering: "As a pretext." The intent, presumably, is to suggest that the lady resorts to the pastoral ploy in order to tryst with her beloved at siesta time.

8e. *huts.* Robert made his interpretation of the verse depend on the alleged singular sense of the plural noun *miškĕnôṯ,* "près de la demeure des pasteurs." Elsewhere in nine of the nineteen occurrences of the plural form of the word in poetic passages, the sense is singular. Except for the Targum, all ancient interpreters construe the word as plural. Robert summarizes the various explications proposed and finds them incoherent or arbitrary. All becomes clear, according to Robert, when one gives the singular sense to *miškĕnôṯ* and sees the shepherds as the kings of the pre-exilic period.

This latter interpretation is classic; cf. Jer 23:1–8; Ezekiel 34; Zech 10:3, 13:7–9. In these allegories Yahweh has rejected the ancient kings in order to take upon himself the conduct of the flock. The dwelling of the shepherds is Zion, according to Robert, and it is to this goal that our verse orients the steps of the bride. When she is told to follow the tracks of the flock, this alludes to the first repatriates who were reinstalled in Palestine after the decree of Cyrus in 538 B.C. The mass of the nation, personified under the figure of the bride, should imitate them and make the return trip along the route which she had followed in going to Babylon (cf. Jer 31:21). By a literary fiction similar to the poet's usage of "the daughters of Jerusalem" (cf. NOTE on 5b), the bride is here distinct from the flock of repatriates, according to Robert.

8. Ginsburg hailed this verse as incontrovertible proof that the damsel is a *shepherdess* and the beloved a *shepherd,* a "fact" which those who maintain the theory that the Song celebrates the marriage of Solomon with the daughter of Pharaoh, or some other prince's daughter, have to get over. There is now a good deal of pastoral data which Ginsburg would have found difficult to integrate with his view of the Canticle.

The association of the love goddess with the flocks is well established. The term "Aštart of the flock" is used of the fertility and increase of the flock in Deut 7:13, 28:4,18.

In a Sumerian sacred marriage poem, Inanna's presence blesses the garden, the stall, and the sheepfold and she is called a hierodule, or sacred prostitute, as she brings her fecund presence to bear on the animals:

> Lordly Queen, when you enter the stall,
> Inanna, the stall rejoices with you,
> Hierodule, when you enter the sheepfold,
> The stall rejoices with you . . .
>
> (*SMR,* 101)

Dumuzi the shepherd also liked to frequent the sheepfold:

> In those days, the shepherd, to make the heart rejoice,
> To go to the stall, to brighten its spirit,
> To light up the holy sheepfold like the sun,
> The shepherd Dumuzi took it into his holy heart.

Dumuzi informed the goddess of his intent:

> My spouse, I would go to the desert land,
> Would look after my holy stall,
> Would learn the ways of my holy sheepfold,
> Would provide food for my sheep,
> Would give them fresh water to drink.
>
> (*SMR,* 102)

Dumuzi entertained his sister Geshtinanna in the sheepfold. After they had eaten and drunk holy fare, honey, butter, beer, and wine, he showed her how sheep copulate with mother or sister. Kramer comments on the difficulty of translating the passage because of missing key words and obscurities in meaning, but he renders it thus:

> He lined up [?] [sheep], brought them into the stall,
> The lamb, having jumped [on the back] of its mother,
> Mounted her . . . , copulated with her.
>
> The shepherd says to his sister:
> My sister, look! What is the lamb doing to its mother?
>
> His sister answers him:
> He having [jumped] on his mother's back, she[?] let out [?] a shout of joy.
> If, he having jumped on his mother's back, she[?] let out [?] a shout of joy,
> Come now [?], this is because . . . he has filled her with his semen.
> The kid having jumped [on the back] of his sister,
> Mounted her . . . , copulated with her.
> The shepherd says to his sister:
> My sister, look! What is the kid doing to his sister?
> His sister answers him innocently[?]:
> He having jumped on his sister's back, she[?] let out a shout of joy.
> If, he having jumped on his sister's back, she [?] let out a shout of joy,
> Come here now[?], [this is because he has flooded her with his fecundating semen . . ."

This text breaks off after a few more obscure lines and Kramer does not comment beyond expressing the hope that additional tablets may be excavated one day (*SMR,* 103, 153n40). The interest and relevance of this episode for the pastoral and bucolic symbolism of the Song of Songs, and for the present passage in particular, is obvious. Just what Dumuzi's motive was in showing his sister Geshtinanna the incestuous intercourse of the flocks is not explicit, but one can imagine that it was not entirely innocent curiosity.

The sacred sheep stall was especially connected with the fertility goddesses Inanna, Ishtar, Astarte. W. W. Hallo and J. J. A. Van Dijk (1968, 53n22) suggest that the sacred stall may even have served as a kind of "lying-in hospital," citing as evidence a text (VAT, 8381) which says "to his wife whom he had impregnated in the stall, the holy sheepfold, whom he had impregnated in the birth house, the stall, the holy sheepfold, in her lap he deposited the life-giving seed of mankind."

The Targum ascribes this verse to God in admonition of Moses:

> The Holy One, blessed be He, said to Moses the prophet: "If the Assembly of Israel, which is compared to a beautiful maiden whom my soul loves, wishes to wipe out the Exile, let her walk in the ways of the righteous, let her present her prayers by the mouth of the pastors and leaders of her generation; let her teach (or lead) her children, compared to the kids of goats, to go to the Assembly House and to the House of Learning; then by that merit, they will be sustained in the Exile until the time when I send the King, the Messiah, who will lead them to rest in their Dwelling, the Sanctuary which David and Solomon, the shepherds of Israel, will build for them."

This verse is cited in the Talmud (TB Shabbat 33b) in support of Rabbi Gorion's view that when there are righteous men in a generation, they are seized for the sins of the generation; when there are no righteous men in a generation, school children are seized for the sins of the generation.

The meaning of this verse dawned on Johanan ben Zakkai when once he was walking in the market place and saw a girl picking grain from under the feet of Arab cattle. On inquiring of her, he discovered that she was the daughter of Nakdimon ben Gorion and he remembered that he had signed her marriage deed for the sum of a million gold pieces. In the days of her father's prosperity, woolen carpets were laid for her to walk to the Temple. Johanan ben Zakkai said to his disciples, "All my life I've read this verse, (quoting the passage) and not understood it, and now I come along and learn what the meaning is: That Israel has been surrendered to the meanest of peoples, and not merely to a mean people but to their cattle dung!" (Cf. Goldin, 1955, 88, and E. E. Urbach, 1971, 249n5).

The LXX and Vulgate reading, "if you do not know yourself," led early commentators to relate the verse to self knowledge, of the Church or the faithful individual. Jerome, addressing the Abbess Eustochium, made this verse divine admonition: "Unless thou know thyself, and keep thy heart with all watchfulness, unless thou fly from the glances of youth, thou shalt go forth from My chamber to feed the goats, which are to stand on My left." Bernard of Clairvaux took the words as the Bridegroom's rebuke to the Bride who, ignorant that she is still in the body and among worldly and carnal souls, yet dares to ask God to show her the place of His glory.

Theodoret related the tracks of the flock to the Saints of the Old Covenant who by faith belonged to the New; the kids are the weak and sinful members, and the shepherds' tents the Churches of the Apostles. Aponius attributed the words to Christ who urges the Synagogue to come to the knowledge of the truth. Jesus' post-resurrection charge to Peter, "Feed my sheep" (John 21:16) was also correlated with the present verse. The kids are the weak and errant servants entrusted to the care of wise and holy pastors. The petulant kids need to be restrained, guided, and fed in spiritual tabernacles. (Cf. Littledale, 30*ff*).

9a. *mare*. The comparison of the female protagonist to a mare in the chariotry of Pharaoh seems at first blush simple and straightforward, but it has, nevertheless, exercised exegetes through the centuries and no consensus has been achieved with regard to certain details. The comparison of one's beloved to a mare is not the problem, since the comparison is quite explicit and there are parallels in other literatures. The parade example generally cited by commentators is Theocritus' characterization of Helen of Troy's graceful movement (*Idyl* xviii 30,31):

As towers the cypress mid the garden's bloom,
As in the chariot proud Thessalian steed,
Thus graceful rose-complexion'd Helen moves.

Horace (*Odes* III xi 9) likened Lyde to a three-year-old filly which gambols over the spreading plains and shrinks from touch, to wedlock still a stranger, not yet ripe for eager mate. Arabic poetry also presents striking comparisons of a damsel to a filly (Dalman, 1901, 319,317). Henry VIII compared Anne of Cleves to a Flander's mare, but his intent was reproach rather than compliment.

The supposed difficulties of the verse are concerned with the numerical incongruity between the mare and the chariotry, the hapax legomenon *sûsāṯî* being vocalized as a singular while the noun designating the chariotry is plural in form. The Vulgate construed the reference to the horse as collective, *equitatus,* and similarly Rashi, Rashbam, and the *KJ,* "a company of horses," to match the collective chariotry. An imaginative exegete, of course, need not be frustrated by mere grammatical detail, real or imaginary, and this apparent difficulty has been dismissed with the observation that a single horse could be hitched to different chariots successively. Some modern interpreters adjust the numerical imbalance between horse and chariots by the expedient of changing the singular designations of the horse to plural. It seems likely, however, that Ibn Ezra was correct in the opinion that the controverted word denotes a mere mare, a female horse, *nĕqēḇaṯ sûs,* and not a company of horses.

To reconcile the supposed numerical incongruity between horse and chariotry, some interpreters accept the single mare and adjust the chariotry accordingly. Since the singular *reḵeḇ* is regularly used as the collective, it has been supposed that the unique plural form is *nomen unitatis,* a plural of indetermination or generalization referring to any chariot and none in particular (Joüon, 136j). Since there is a common term, *merkāḇāh,* for a single chariot, used in both poetry and prose, one may wonder why this term was not used if that were really the intended sense. The term *reḵeḇ* can refer both to the vehicles and the horses, or to the horses alone, without regard to the vehicles, as shown by the statement that David hamstrung the *reḵeḇ* captured from Hadadezer, except for a hundred (II Sam 8:4). As will be seen, the term in the present instance is concerned with the horses and not the chariots and there is no need to resort to the dubious argument that the plural form is intended as *nomen unitatis* for a vehicle.

The vocalic ending of *lĕsûsāṯî* was construed by the versions as the possessive suffix first common singular, "my." Midrashic interpretations related the suffix to YHWH and developed the concept of the heavenly mare employed instead of the regular cherubic transport by the God of Israel in the episode at the Reed Sea. Origen also applied the suffix to the Lord's chivalry which surpassed and excelled that of Pharaoh and related the figure to the excellence of the Church. Origen further developed the theme of God's chivalry by citing the vision of Elisha's servant at Dothan who was allowed a glimpse of the celestial cavalry of fiery horses and chariots, II Kings 6:17 (cf. Littledale, 32*f*).

Robert similarly saw Yahweh as speaking of his horse which represents the nation Israel. The author is not concerned whether the horse in question is hitched alone or with other horses since the comparison would retain its force in either case. It is, according to Robert, not a question of comparison of physical charms or of ornaments; what is made parallel are two analogous situations of the nation personified, her current state of humiliation in exile and the servitude in Egypt at the beginning of her history. This is a classical theme of Second Isaiah (43:16*ff*, 48:21, 51:9–10, 52:4) which is also used in the post-exilic literature (Isa 11:11–16; Zech 10:8–12) as an implicit exhortation to confidence that the one who formerly liberated his people with great miracles is well able to snatch them from the hands of their enemies and lead them to Palestine. The passage Isa 43:13, "Like a horse in the desert, they did not stumble," refers to Israel's passage through the Sea, and Robert took it as the inspiration for both the present passage, and the reference to horses in Wis 19:9.

Some interpreters understood the horse or horses to belong to Pharaoh, as well as the chariot or chariots, but to others the mention of horse(s), chariot(s), and Pharaoh together recalled Solomon's trade in horses and chariots from Egypt, I Kings 10:26–29. Renan's rendering made the presumed relation explicit, "à ma cavalle quand elle est attelée aux chars que m'envoie Pharaon." Ginsburg likewise took the horse to be a highly prized mare of Solomon's which he always put to one of Pharaoh's chariots. The latest development in exegesis of the passage is Gordon's rendering, "I liken thee, O my darling, to my mare from the stud of Pharaoh" (*UT* 10.1), taking the vocalic ending of *lĕsûsāṯî* as the possessive suffix, "my," the preposition *b-* as meaning "from," and the plural of *reḵeḇ* as designating a stud. This might be defended if the context required it, which is not the case.

The *î* ending of *lĕsûsātî* has nothing to do with the possessive suffix, but is, as many commentators have recognized, the survival of the old genitive case ending (cf. GKC, 9*l–o*) dubbed *ḥireq compaginis* by early grammarians who were wont to attach learned Latin labels to enigmatic grammatical features.

A crucial consideration overlooked by commentators is the well-attested fact that Pharaoh's chariots, like other chariotry in antiquity, were not drawn by a mare or mares but by stallions hitched in pairs. This bit of intelligence radically alters the usual understanding of the verse and dispels the notion that there is a grammatical incongruity which needs harmonizing. The juxtaposition is between a single mare and a plurality of stallions and it requires only a modicum of what is called "horse sense" to appreciate the thrust of the comparison. The situation envisaged is illustrated by the famous incident in one of the campaigns of Thutmose III against Qadesh. On his tomb at Thebes, the Egyptian soldier Amenemheb relates how the Prince of Qadesh sent forth a swift mare which entered among the army. But Amenemheb ran after her on foot and with his dagger ripped open her belly, cut off her tail, and presented it to the king, thus preventing a debacle before the excited stallions could take out after the mare (cf. J. H. Breasted, 1906, no. 589, p. 233; G. Steindorff, 1942, 58). This, incidentally, is one of the few cases in

Egyptian literature where the word for horse is identifiable as a grammatically feminine form. The only other case which has been adduced is the account of Amenhotep II's affection for a mare (cf. H. von Deines, 1953, 4*ff*).

When he was yet a boy, he loved his horse, rejoiced over her, was constant in her care, while he learned to know her way, was clever in her control, and penetrated her nature. His majesty said to his company: "Request for him a very beautiful mare (*śśm.t nfr.t wr.t*) from the stall of my majesty in Memphis and say to him: 'Protect her, let her become strong, let her trot, handle her well, otherwise one will quarrel with you' " Thereupon the king's son was commissioned: "Protect the mare of the royal stall." And he did what was bidden.

This passage has been cited (Gerleman, 1965, 107) to illustrate the present verse but it has scant relevance. The mare of Solomon's Song is not in Pharaoh's stall but among the stallions of the chariotry where her presence would occasion no little stir.

Rabbinic Midrash on our passage reveals familiarity with the *ruse de guerre* employed by the Prince of Qadesh which almost spelled disaster for Thutmose III and attributes to it success on the occasion of the confrontation of YHWH and His people with Pharaoh's army at the Reed Sea. Midrash Rabbah informs us that the Israelites appeared like mares and the wicked Egyptians who pursued them were like stallions eager with desire, and they ran after them till they sank in the sea" (M. Simon, 1951, I, 9, no. 6, p. 71).

Rabbi Joshua ben Qorḥah credited the God of Israel with the use of this stratagem:

When Pharaoh came into the sea, he came on a stallion, and the Holy One, blessed be He, revealed himself to it (i.e. the stallion) on a mare, as it is said, "To My mare among Pharaoh's chariots." But (someone may object) did He not rather ride on a cherub, as it is said (Ps 18:11[10E]), "He rode upon a cherub etc."? In that event say: The cherub appeared to the horses of Pharaoh like a mare, and they all came into the sea. (Goldin, 1955, ch. 27, pp. 113*f.*)

This motif, with minor variations, is found also in Pirqe Rabbi Eleazar (Lemberg ed., 1874, ch. 42, p. 46a) and in a seventeenth-century manuscript in the Aramaic dialect of the Kurdish Jews of northern Iraq; cf. Yona Sabar (1970, 22,68,123,254*f*. For other versions, e.g., that the mare was Pharaoh's mount, cf. Ginzberg, VI, 9n44). It is thus clear that some of the rabbis were aware that the Egyptians, like other peoples, used male horses for war and were familiar with the excitement that could be caused by the scent or presence of an estrual mare. Herodotus III 85 relates how Darius became king through the ruse of his clever groom Oebares who used the scent of a mare to excite Darius' stallion to neigh.

The use of male horses in warfare is more fully documented in ancient Near Eastern art than in literature. One need only look at the numerous representations of cavalry and chariotry to verify this. (A handy collection is found in Y. Yadin, 1963; cf. pp. 186*ff*,192*f*,196,200,210,212,214–217,232*ff*, 240*f*,300,334,336*ff*,382–387,402*f*,450,452). In the rules of the Qumran Sectaries relating to holy war, the prescribed cavalry are male horses (*sûsîm zĕkārîm*), fleet of foot, tender of mouth, and long of wind. In view of the sectaries' aversion to sexual impurity, one might suppose that the specification of male horses may have been motivated by a concern to avoid bestiality. That possibility was considered by Yadin in his commentary on the War Scroll, but he inclined to the view that this was only a side issue and that the primary reason was the suitability of stallions for battle. (Yadin, 1962, 182).

Ginsburg cited an anonymous medieval Hebrew commentary which related the Black Beauty of 1:5 to the mare mentioned in 1:9, but with both the blackness and the equine character regarded figuratively. Wittekindt (21*ff*, 28*ff*) emphasized the manifold connections of the Love Goddess with a horse, especially the stallion in the list of her abused lovers in the Gilgamesh Epic (vi 53). But it was the cult of the Black Demeter which in particular supplied the parallels for a mare-goddess, black and beautiful. According to Pausanias (*Description of Greece* viii 42.4) Black Demeter's cult image in Phigalia was like a woman in all respects except the head and hair which was that of a horse, and from the head grew images of serpents and other beasts. On one of her hands was a dolphin and on the other a dove (which were also attributes of Atargatis). Demeter, according to Pausanias (viii 25.4), in the form of a Fury (*Erinus*) mated with Poseidon and gave birth to the horse Areion. In ancient Indian myth, Saryanu turned herself into a mare and Visavat changed himself to a stallion and pursued and mated with her. She gave birth to the two Asvins who correspond somewhat to Castor and Pollux. It has been suggested that the Sanskrit *Saryanu* is cognate with Greek *Erinus* and that the Greek and Hindu myths are inherited from a common source. (Cf. J. G. Frazer, *Pausanias' Description of Greece,* vol. 5, 1898, 291).

From Ugarit we have a recently published mythological text (UG 5.7) which introduces an unnamed Mare-Goddess. The text begins thus: "The Stallion's Mother, the Mare / Daughter of the Fountain, Daughter of Stone / Daughter of Sky and Deep / called to Špš her mother . . ." The Mare-Goddess asked her mother, the Sun-Goddess, to summon various deities who are mentioned according to rank (El, Baal, Dagan, Anat and/or Aštart, Yariḫ, Rešep, Ṯṯ and/or Kemoṯ, Mlk, Kṯr and/or Ḫss, Šḥr, and/or Šlm, and Ḥoron). The text, a strange combination of narrative and incantation, deals with serpent charms, presumably cosmic. The text has been thrice treated by M. C. Astour (1965, 265); (1966); (1968), who cited the data from Pausanias relative to *Dēmētēr Melaina* ("Black Demeter") or *Dēō Hippolechos,* "Deo who bore a horse." The cave of Demeter was located near a spring recalling the Ugaritic epithet "Daughter of the Fountain." She sat on a rock which comports with the epithet "Daughter of Stone," and her symbols the dove and dolphin relating to sky and sea, as Astour suggested, suit the Ugaritic epithet "Daughter of Sky and Deep."

The suggestion that the female protagonist of the Song of Songs may be related to a goddess with sometime equine form is nothing new. The appearance of a mare-goddess at Ugarit provides possibly relevant data older and less remote than Pausanias' account of the Phigalian Demeter. There is no inclination at present to press for an identification of the Black Beauty of Canticles with the mare-goddess. Whatever may be the ultimate decision in this regard, the point of the comparison of the Lady Love with a mare in Pharaoh's chariotry in the Song of Songs 1:9 is that she is the ultimate in sex appeal, as appreciated already by some sensitive rabbinic interpreters.

9b. *compare*. *JPSV*'s "I have made you look, my darling, / Like a mare in Pharaoh's chariots" provides an introduction to the following quatrain supposedly descriptive of the ornamentation of an Egyptian war horse. There is, however, no warrant for the rendering "I have made you look like," rather than "I have compared you." The verb *dmy* in the simple stem means "resemble" and in the factitive stem, as here, it means "to compare." It is used only of the thought process, of imagination and planning, and never of the physical action of making one thing look like another.

my darling. This form, *ra'yāṯî,* the regular designation of the bride by the groom (1:15, 2:2,10,13, 4:1,7, 5:2, 6:4), with the first person possessive suffix, is not found elsewhere. The form could be read in the Kētib of Judg 11:37, but would make sense there only as vocalized to correspond with the form in the succeeding verse, with reference to the companions of Jephthah's daughter who take to the hills with her to beweep her virginity. In Ps 45:15, the form *rē'ôṯêhā,* "her companions," is applied to the virgin attendants of the bride. Wittekindt's effort to relate the term in the Jephthah story and in Ps 45:15 to Ishtar's title as shepherdess is unconvincing and unnecessary to his general thesis, since there is ample evidence in the Canticle to characterize the bride as a shepherdess, as do even the most resolute opponents of the cultic interpretation. Delitzsch explained the term as related to a root *r'y* meaning "guard," "care for," "tend," "delight in something," "take pleasure in intercourse with one." The word is formed on the same pattern as *na'ărāh,* and *'almāh,* "girl." The masculine form *rē'eh* appears to have the same meaning as the commoner form *rēa'* with no sign of a third radical *y*. This shorter masculine form is used only once in the Canticle, 5:16, where it is parallel to the dominant designation (twenty-six times) of the male lover, *dôḏî,* "my love." The general sense of both the masculine and feminine forms appears to be "fellow," "friend," "companion." The simplicity of Vulgate's *amica mea* and *amicus meus,* "my friend," is attractive. Contemporary use of "friend" includes the sense "lover," but not in direct address. The Greek term *hetaira* corresponds exactly.

The Targum connected vs. 9 with Pharaoh's debacle at the Reed Sea, but failed to mention the *ruse de guerre* involving the mare among stallions:

> When Israel went out from Egypt, Pharaoh and his army pursued after them with chariots and horsemen, and the way was closed for them on four sides. On the right and left was the wilderness full of fiery serpents. Behind them was the wicked Pharaoh with his army and before them was the Reed Sea. What did the Holy One (Blessed be He) do? He revealed himself in His mighty strength at the sea, dried up the sea, but the mud he did not dry up. Said the wicked ones, the mixed multitude of foreigners who were among them: The sea He is able to dry up, but the mud He is not able to dry up. At that moment the anger of YHWH waxed against them and He would have drowned them in the waters of the sea as Pharaoh and his armies, his chariots and his horsemen and horses were drowned, had it not been for Moses, the prophet, who spread his hands in prayer before YHWH and turned back the anger of YHWH from them. And he and the righteous of that generation opened their mouths and sang songs. And they passed in the midst of the Reed Sea on dry land by virtue of the merits of Abraham, Isaac, and Jacob, the beloved ones of YHWH.

The most interesting and valid insight of the Midrash Rabbah in this verse has already been noted. There are, of course, the inevitable wordplays. Rabbi Pappus, for example, suggested reading for *lĕsûsātî,* "to my mare," *lĕśîśātî,* "at my rejoicing," to arrive at the explanation that God said, "I rejoiced over the Egyptians to destroy them in the sea." Rabbi Aqiba rejected this suggestion. "Enough of that, Pappus. The word *śîśāh* is always written with *ś* and here we have *s*." Pappus asked Aqiba, "How then do you explain the words?" Aqiba replied, "God appeared on a male steed, as it says (Ps 18:11[10E]) *And He rode upon a cherub and flew*. Pharaoh then said, 'Surely this male steed kills its rider in battle; I will therefore ride on a female steed.' Pharaoh then changed to a white horse, a red horse, a black horse, and, if one may say so, God appeared on a red, a white, or a black horse, hence it says (Hab 3:15), *You trod the sea with your horses*." Following this bit of horseplay, involving, if one may say so, changing horses in midstream, Aqiba went on to cite other biblical passages descriptive of the divine prowess and resourcefulness in battle. The wicked Pharaoh came out with breastplate and armor, so God put on righteousness as a coat of mail (Isa 59:17). Pharaoh brought naphtha, and so did the Holy One (Ps 18:13[12E]). Pharaoh brought up catapult stones, and God did the same (Exod 9:23). Pharaoh took swords and lances, and so did God; Pharaoh brought arrows and so did God (Ps 18:15[14E]). Here Midrash Rabbah let Rabbi Levi and others continue Aqiba's line of interpretation, with more citations of scriptural references to God as a warrior.

Christian interpreters made the Church, or the faithful soul, the object of comparison to the gallant mare, because of her swiftness in running after Christ, her obedience and submission to His yoke, her drawing of the Gospel chariot into all lands, her fruitfulness in bringing forth young abundantly by preaching. Mention has already been made of Origen's exegesis of this passage and other expositors developed the chivalrous theme. St. Bernard (Sermon 39) emphasized that the comparison of one soul here is to a company of horses rather than to a single horse because of the armies of virtue in a single soul that is holy, an orderly array of affections, discipline in habits, equipment in prayer, vigor in action, dreadfulness in resolution, and steadiness in battle. The fight against Pharaoh is no light struggle. "There Israel is brought out of Egypt, here man out of the world; there Pharaoh is routed, here the Evil One; there Pharaoh's chariots are overwhelmed, here the carnal and secular desires which war against the soul; those went down in waves, these in weepings. And I believe that now the demons, if they encounter such a soul, cry out, 'Let us flee from the face of Israel, for the Lord fighteth for him.' " (Cf. Littledale.)

10a. LXX *ti* reflects the exclamatory *māh*, "how beautiful," which is not in MT.

with bangles. LXX, followed by Vulgate, reflects *kattôrîm* instead of MT *battôrîm* and takes the word *tôrîm* as the plural of *tôr*, "turtledove," "like turtledoves." Delitzsch exclaimed, "What absurdity. Birds have no cheeks; and on the side of its neck the turtle-dove has black and white variegated feathers, which also furnishes no comparison for the color of the cheeks." Wittekindt, however, welcomed the turtledoves as connected with the dove as a symbol of Ishtar. Most commentators have recognized that the word designates some sort of ornamentation on horse harnesses and trappings. Connection of the word with the root *t(w)r*, "turn," "go around" (*circumire*), suggests a round object or perhaps a row or series. *JPSV* renders "plaited wreaths." Others have thought of tassels and fringes. The occurrences of the word in Ugaritic in connection with chariots do not clarify the nature of the item. In a price list of commodities, including oil, wood, a pair of mares, mantles(?), reeds, and some uncertain items, the term is listed between the mares and the mantles(?):

s̀stm.b.šb'm	a pair of mares at seventy
t̠lt̠.mat.trm.b.'šrt	three-hundred *trm* at ten
mit.adrm.b.'šrt	a hundred mantles at ten
	(1127.6–8)

Another text records delivery of eight chariots to the palace along with their wheels, their arrows, and *trhn*, "their *tr*" (1121.1–5). A third text (1122.1–7) lists three chariots coated with gold (*t̠lt̠ mrkb*[*t*].*ṣpyt bḫrṣ*), and a set(?) of coated *trm* (*w.trm.aḥdm.ṣpym*); three royal chariots which are not coated [. . .] their [*t̠*]*r* (*t̠lt̠ mrkbt.mlk.d.l.ṣpy* [. . . *t*]*rhm*); on the lower edge of the text *tr* occurs in a broken line along with the word *šsb* which might be a causative verbal form of the root *sbb*, "turn." Again on the upper edge we have *ṣmdm trm.d*[*ṣ*]*py*, "pairs(?) of *trm* which are[?] coat[ed?]." Gordon suggests that the root of the word is *t(w)r*, "turn," because of the applicability of the verb *šsb*, and that therefore *tr* is the device that turns the chariot (cf. *UT* 19.2539,2594). The expression *arb'.ṣmdm.apnt*, "four pairs (of) wheels" (1123.7) compared with *kṣmdm trm*, "like pairs of *trm*," suggests that the object is something made in pairs. The suggestion that the term designates the device that turns a chariot seems dubious since the chariot pole was a single shaft and the chariot turned with the pole according to the movement of the attached horses. Whether the Ugaritic word *trm* associated with chariots has anything to do with the *tôrîm* in the present line is uncertain. It is clear from the context and the parallelism that *tôrîm* are ornaments worn on the cheeks of a horse or a woman, while *ḥărûzîm* are beads or necklaces of some sort. Here we may resort to representations in ancient Near Eastern art to get some idea of the kind of ornamentation which the poet envisaged, whether on a horse, a woman, or a goddess.

10b. *beads.* This word (*ḥărûzîm*) does not occur elsewhere in the Bible, but in post-Biblical Hebrew it is used of stringing pearls or fish. In Arabic the verb is used of sewing or stitching and the noun *ḫaraz* designates a neck ornament of beads strung together; a shoemaker's awl is *miḫraz,* suggesting that the basic sense is "pierce." The *ḫaraz* was usually made up of more than a single strand, generally three.

10. The Targum applied this verse to the Law as the bridle which kept Israel in the right way:

> When they went forth to the wilderness, YHWH said to Moses: "How fit is this people to be given the words of the Law to be as bridles in their jaws that they might not depart from the good path; as the horse does not depart which has the bridle in its jaw. And how fit is their neck to bear the yoke of of my precepts which would be on them like the yoke on the neck of the ox that plows in the field and supports himself and his master."

Midrashic exegesis found in the ornamentation of the cheeks and neck a catena of allegorical meanings. The cheeks were said to refer to Moses and Aaron, the *tôrîm* suggested the two *Tôrôt,* the Written Law and the Oral Law, or the teachers of Scripture and Mishnah. The neck with beads was seen as the Sanhedrin with its seventy members like pearls on a string. Rabbi Abba ben Mimi and his associates explained the necklace as the Rabbis linking up the words of the Pentateuch with those of the Prophets, and the Prophets with the Writings while the fire flashed around the words and they rejoiced as on the day of their delivery on Mount Sinai (Deut 4:11). The linking of perforated beads suggested the analogies of scholars who could connect but not penetrate texts, those who could penetrate but not connect, and those who were expert both in linking and penetrating texts.

Christian expositors were no less imaginative. Origen understood these words as spoken by the Bridegroom to comfort the Bride who blushed at the rebuke she had received. The cheeks, as the seat of modesty, are the members of the Church eminent for purity and modesty. The dove, because of its conjugal fidelity, suggested the Church which remains faithful to her Beloved and mourns for Him when he is absent from Her. For Aponius the dove was Christ and her cheeks the Doctors of the Church eminent in holiness and thus like Him. St. Bernard stressed the solitary, retiring habits of the dove and exhorted the faithful to sit solitary like the turtle(dove) and have nothing to do with the crowds. The Greek

Fathers thought of the unvarying note of the turtledove and the grave and steadfast discourse of true Christians in contrast to the frivolous loquacity of pagans. To others the mournful sound of the turtledove bespoke the tears of pity and intercession of the saints who are the cheeks of the Church.

The neck and necklace received their share of allegorical and typical attention. The flexibility of the neck suggested obedience, as also the pliability of the necklace. Ambrose observed that the law of God is not a yoke to the obedient neck, but a collar which even dumb animals are proud to wear. The neck, as the channel for the passage of food and of speech, was seen as representing the Doctors of the Church who communicate the doctrine of Christ to the people; they are the link between the Head, which is Christ, and His Body, which is the faithful laity. The necklace which surrounds the neck suggested the true obedience of the Religious which embraces every action. The jewels of the necklace are the good works of the saints. The separate parts of the necklace united by one flexible band bespeak the many virtues twined with humility which adorn the Bride of Christ. (Cf. Littledale.)

11a. *we.* This plural has commonly been taken as the *plurale majestatis,* God speaking of Himself, which Christian expositors understood as including Father, Son, and Holy Ghost. On the plural of majesty in the Psalter, cf. Dahood, *PS I, II, III,* subject indexes. In the Canticle, of course, plural subjects are handled according to the theories of interpretation. Delitzsch, for example, understood that Solomon was the speaker and included himself along with others, especially the women of the palace.

11b. *With.* The use of the preposition *'im,* "with," may suggest that the silver spangles are added to the gold *tôrîm,* but *JPSV* took it the other way,

We will add wreaths of gold To your spangles of silver.

In Ugaritic the preposition *'m* is used of direction toward a person or place, usually in the cliché "Then did he/she set face toward (*'m*) So-and-So"; but this use does not seem appropriate to the adding of one thing to another. Actually, the text does not say "we will add," but "we will make for you."

spangles. The exact nature of these *nĕquddôṯ,* "points," can only be guessed. LXX rendered *stigmatōn,* Symmachus *poiklimatōn,* Vulgate *vermiculatas.* This particular form is unique in the Bible, but other forms of the root *nqd* are used, in Gen 30:32 and 31:12 of spotted sheep and goats, and in Josh 9:5 and I Kings 14:3 of some sort of dry (crumbly?) food. Whether this word has anything to do with the root *nqd* connected with sheep and shepherding is not certain; lexicographers usually separate the two roots, connecting *nqd* I with Arabic *nqṭ* applied to the diacritical points used to distinguish similar letters. In post-Biblical Hebrew, *nĕquddôṯ* is the term for the signs used in the Tiberian system of vocalization. (Arabic *nqṭ* and Hebrew *nqd* may be reflexes of a common root differently affected by Geer's Law concerning assimilation and dissimilation of so-called emphatic consonants.) The choice of the term "spangles" here is intended to suggest the use of small bright bits of metal or other glittering material for decoration. But if "spangles" is used in its usual contemporary sense as designating small glittering dots or points, like sequins, then it seems unlikely that they would be adorned with wreaths. It is not clear in what sense *JPSV* uses "spangles." If in the original meaning "clasp," "buckle," "brooch," "bracelet," "stud" (German "Spange"), then wreaths of gold might be added as decoration. The relative values of the precious metals presumably influenced *JPSV*'s decision to make the gold accessory to the silver. In view of the uncertainty as to the nature of *tôrîm,* the translation should perhaps be as vague as the original.

The Targum related the gold and silver ornaments to the Law:

> Thus it was said to Moses: "Go up to the firmament and I will give you the two tablets of stone hewn from the sapphire of my glorious throne, bright as pure gold, arranged in lines, written by my finger, graved on them the Ten Words, refined more than silver purified seven times seven (which is the sum corresponding to forty-nine, the methods by which the matters therein are interpreted), and I will give them by your hand to the people of the House of Israel."

Midrash Rabbah related the ornaments here to the spoil taken from the Egyptians at the Reed Sea, to the Torah learned by Onqelos, to the letters and ruled lines of the Torah, the tabernacle, the ark and its staves, etc. Judah ben Rabbi interpreted vss. 10–11 as referring to the Law, the Prophets, and the Writings, with the final reference to the silver studs meaning the Song of Songs itself which completes Scripture.

Several early Christian expositors took lines of interpretation similar to that of the Targum, relating the golden ornaments to the knowledge of Scripture intertwined with silver threads of types, prophecies, counsels, and eloquent preaching. Origen, following the LXX rendering of *tôrîm* as *homoiōmata,* "similitudes," took the speakers to be the Angels who ordained the Law, and the Prophets who expound it. They have as yet no gold, because the Law, as only the shadow of the good things to come, can offer only similitudes of gold, such as the ark, the altar, the shew-bread, etc., which are mere types of the future mysteries. The silver was seen as moral precepts and counsels, in small quantity, mere spots (*stigmata*), unlike the true Solomon who made silver and gold as plentiful as stones (II Chron 1:15). The golden ornaments were seen as signifying the purification of the Church by means of the fiery persecutions, the Martyrs being the golden jewels of the Church and the silver spots their suffering (cf. Gal 6:17). The Vulgate rendering of *tôrîm* as *murenulas,* "little eels," suggested to Gregory the Great the Church's preaching: "The eel is a fish which, when taken, twists itself into a circle, in imitation of which an ear-ring is made, called *murenula,* by which is denoted preaching which hangs to the ears and enters them." The tortuous twinings of the little eels suggested also the involved and difficult doctrines of the Scriptures. Again the gold was seen as the contemplation of the divine mysteries and the silver as the channels through which the contemplation must be made. Or the gold is Christ's love and the silver the good works and wisdom by which its benefits are effected. For Saint Jerome the gold denoted the Virgin life. Before Christ there was the silver of chaste marriage and widowhood, but with Him came the more precious golden gift of virginity. (Cf. Littledale.)

A. Robert, RTF, again saw the Exile as the focal point. The general idea of the verse is that the bride, in Babylon as in Egypt, retains her beauty in the midst of abasement and servitude, and that she remains capable of seducing the heart of the groom. The thought, according to Robert, is exactly the same as in vss. 5 and 6: it is repeated with insistence, as the fundamental affirmation which authorizes hope (cf. Ezek 16:11–13).

12a. *While.* The element *'aḏ* regularly means "until" and *'aḏ-še* here might seem to be equivalent to *'aḏ 'ăšer,* "until that," as is the case in 2:7d,17a, where the verbs are imperfect or present-future. Here, however, with the verb in the perfect, or preterite, the meaning is manifestly "while," as all translators and commentators have recognized. The meaning of *'aḏ* here thus appears to be the same as *'ôḏ*. This use of *'aḏ* in the sense "while" is also attested in II Kings 9:22; I Sam 14:19; Ps 141:10; Prov 8:26; Neh 7:3. Ugaritic *'d* regularly means "until," but in the cliché *'d lḥm šty ilm* the meaning appears to be "while" rather than "until," "while the gods ate and drank."

the king. The change from pastoral terminology in vss. 7–8 to royal terminology is very important for those who see two male protagonists, the shepherd whom the maiden truly loves, and King Solomon who tries to win her for himself. For Ginsburg this was Solomon's first futile attempt to gain the girl's affections. Frequent and sudden change of image occurs throughout the Canticle and the efforts to identify the changes with different speakers are fanciful to the point of absurdity. Robert observed that Yahweh is the King of Israel and it was proper to recall this title in a passage which makes allusion to his sojourn in the Temple! Shepherd and king are also royal and divine titles and are used especially of fertility gods.

couch. The masculine form of the noun here used, *mēsaḇ* (<*mēsibb*), designates a low couch or divan on which participants in a banquet reclined. The feminine form, *mĕsibbāh,* in post-Biblical Hebrew is applied to a banqueting party on the order of the Greek symposium. The root of these words, *sbb,* "go around," "surround," is appropriate to the disposition of the celebrants around the table. The present occurrence is the only one in the Bible to which the meaning "couch" is applied, but there may be a couple of other passages where this sense has not been recognized. In the phrase *habbayiṯ mēsaḇ* of I Kings 6:29, *mēsaḇ* is construed adverbially as equivalent to the regular expression *missāḇîḇ,* "round about." The context however, which deals with the cherubim, has associations with sexual symbolism and may refer to the house or chamber where symposia were held. Again the word occurs in the masculine plural in II Kings 23:5, in construct with Jerusalem, and is likewise interpreted adverbially, "round about Jerusalem." L. Waterman in *AT* apparently felt the need for a word to parallel the preceding term for pagan shrines, "high places (*bāmôṯ*), and rendered "in the sanctuaries around Jerusalem." A few lines later (vs. 11), there is reference to the *liškāh,* a chamber for banqueting (cf. I Sam 9:22) and ceremonial wine-bibbing (cf. Jer 35:2–5). The variation *liškāh/niškah* (cf.

Neh 3:30, 12:44) suggests a foreign word. The term occurs in Greek as *leschē* or *lescha* and is also associated with drinking. The maid Melántho asked Odysseus (*Odyssey* xviii 328–332):

> Why don't you go off and sleep at the bronzesmith's house—or off to the *leschē*, instead of saying many insolent things here with many people? Aren't you frightened at all? Either wine has your *phrenes*, or you are always in this frame of mind.

The association of *leschē* with the bronzesmith's house is also mentioned by Hesiod (*Works and Days* 493*f*):

> Leave to one side the bronzesmith's seat and the warm (?) *leschē* in winter time.

Perhaps the *leschē* was located near the smithy for warmth in winter. Plutarch suggests (*Lycurgus* xxv 1–2) that the *leschē* was the setting for symposia. The eastern connection of the *leschē* is indicated by Pausanias (iii 15.8) who mentions that there was at Sparta a painted *leschē* with adjacent shrines of the hero Cadmus son of Agenor. The *liškôṯ* destroyed by Josiah in the Temple precincts, along with other elements of the cult of the fertility deities Baal and Asherah, were chambers for sacral feasting, drinking, and sexual orgies in communion with and emulation of the gods. The symposia carried on in the *liškāh* are probably what is designated by the terms *mēsaḇ* and *mĕsibbāh* and it seems likely that the house *mēsaḇ* of I Kings 6:29 and *messibê* (of) Jerusalem mentioned in II Kings 23:5 were places where the banquets were held, otherwise known as *marzēaḥ* houses. (Cf. Pope, 1972, 190*ff*.)

The suggestive sexual entendre of *mēsēḇ*, "couch," is affirmed by Rab Judah who reported in Rab's name (TB Sabbath 62b, 63a) that the men of Jerusalem were vulgar. "One would say to his neighbor, 'On what did you dine today? On well-kneaded bread or bread not well-kneaded; on white wine or [63a] on dark wine; on a broad couch or on a narrow couch; with a good companion or with a poor companion?'" R. Ḥisda observed: "And all these are in reference to immorality."

12b. *nard*. The word is derived from Sanskrit *naladas*, through Persian. The substance is an aromatic oil extracted from the valerian *Nardostachys jatamansi* which grows in northern and eastern India. The hairy part of the plant immediately above the root yields the perfume. In the Apocalypse of Peter 3:10 the hair of the angels is a wreath of nard blossoms. Originally the term denoted only the Indian nard, but later also other related valerians. In its original home, nard was used as a love charm, as indicated by a passage in the Atharva Veda (6.102.5–6; R. Roth and W. D. Whitney, 1856, 132): "Of ointment, of *madugha* (licorice?), of costus, and of nard, by the hands of Bhaga, I bring up quick a means of subjection." (Cf. J. P. Brown, 1969, 161.)

The use of nard and other perfumes in the classical symposium is well documented. The participants bathed and anointed themselves with perfumed unguents, and put on wreaths of flowers. (Cf. Brown, 160n9). Nard was rather expensive. The alabaster box/flask, or pound of ointment of pure nard which the woman poured on Jesus' head was estimated to be worth three hundred dinars (Mark 14:5; John 12:5). In Luke's version of the episode, the woman was a sinner (Luke 7:37): the nard was presumably part of her professional paraphernalia. The setting of the incident was a banquet, and wine was doubtless part of the menu, but the usual implication of the association of wine, women, and perfume, is sublimated into a messianic anointing and funerary preparation. Luke turns the episode into one of the great lessons of forgiveness.

The expensiveness of nard presented a difficulty for those interpreters who insisted that the female protagonist of the Canticle was a rustic shepherd girl.

yielded. Literally "gave," *nāṯan*. In Arabic *natana* has the specific meaning, to give an evil odor. Rabbinic exegesis played on the meanings "give" and "be foul" in relation to this verse. Israel's sin with the golden calf at Sinai was like a bride playing the harlot while still under the bridal canopy. And yet the divine love did not even then forsake them, as the sacred author indicated in this verse by writing "gave" and not "made foul" (cf. TB Shabbat 88b, Gittin 36b).

The Targum turned the nard to the evil odor of idolatry:

> And while Moses, their master, was still in the firmament to receive the two tablets of stone, the Law and the Ordinance, the wicked of that generation and the mixed multitude with them rose and made the golden calf, and they corrupted their deeds. And there went forth against them an evil name in the world, while heretofore their odor had gone forth as fragrance in the world. After this they became stinking as nard, the odor of which is altogether bad, and the plague of leprosy came down upon their flesh.

Midrash Rabbah cited an interesting difference between Rabbis Meir and Judah on the interpretation of this verse. Meir took it that while God was still at table, Israel gave forth an evil smell and said to the calf, "This is your god, O Israel." Rabbi Judah rebuked him: "Enough of this, Meir; the Song of Songs is not expounded in a bad sense, but only in a good sense, for the Song of Songs was revealed only for the praise of Israel." Meir then went on to connect the verse with the construction of the tabernacle rather than the sin with the calf.

The Church Fathers assigned four principal meanings to the King's repose on his couch. First, it was related to the repose of Christ's Godhead in heaven. As St. Bernard put it in his forty-second sermon, "The lying-down of the King is in the bosom of the Father." Others saw reference to the Incarnation. Again it was applied to the Passion and Death of Christ. And lastly the repose was equated with the indwelling of Christ in the holy soul. Naturally, application to the Virgin was not overlooked. Philip Harveng put the words in the mouth of the Mother of God: "The King himself, Son of the Most High King, Himself no lesser dignity, from His equal throne with the Father, from His Royal seat, from the secret dwelling of His unapproachable Majesty, where the Angels see and desire His Face evermore, vouchsafed to come hither to earth for the salvation of perishing souls, and rested in my chamber. In my womb, I say, that King gladly laid Himself down, and found nought in me to make His dwelling displeasing to Him. And there lying, He filled me marvelously with His grace. While preserving my virginity, He took away my maiden barrenness, and His forceful fire consumed me as a whole burnt-offering and filled the entire house with the most fragrant perfume of ointment." The nard was generally taken to represent Christ or the Church. It was only after Christ came in the flesh that the sweet odor of the Church ascended to God, filling His house, the whole earth, and no longer shut up in the narrow casket of Judea. Again the nard symbolized repentance as typified by that Mary who anointed Christ's feet with nard; she is the type of all truly penitent souls. The nard could be broken out on all occasions, at the Eucharist, the Resurrection, the Ascension, and at Pentecost. "When the fires of Pentecost came down after Christ went up and entered His chamber once more, then the words of salvation and the holy examples of the Saints of God sent their fragrance over all the earth, because the incense was kindled by the flame of the Spirit." (St. Gregory; cf. Littledale.)

13a. *bundle.* The word *ṣĕrôr* denotes a bundle or pouch, such as a money-bag (Gen 42:35; Prov 7:20) which could be closed (Job 14:17), presumably tied with a string or a drawstring; cf. AB 15 on Job 14:17.

myrrh. This substance (cf. 3:6, 4:6, 5:5,13), Hebrew *môr,* Greek *smurna, murra,* is an aromatic gum which exudes from cracks in the bark of the *Balsamodendron myrrha* which grows in Arabia, Abyssinia, and India. The Arabian myrrh was superior and often adulterated with that from India. It was highly prized and from earliest times was an article of international trade. It was used for incense (cf. Exod 30:23); for perfuming the garments (Ps 45:9[8E]), a lovers' couch (Prov 7:17); purifying girls for the king's bed (six months' application of oil of myrrh and six months with other perfumes, Esth 2:13[12E]); for embalming a corpse (John 19:39).

my love. This is the first of more than a score of uses of the term *dôḏî* applied to the male lover by the female. Theorists who wish to see two lovers, Solomon and the Shepherd, apply this term to the latter, the maiden's only true love. For Renan this is the capital point and key to the whole poem. The term cannot refer to the king who is in his divan, but to the girl's beloved shepherd. What was dimly glimpsed in vs. 7 is now an absolute certainty, namely that it is the shepherd who is the object of the maiden's desires. Similarly, A. Miller remarked that the damsel in vs. 7 said "whom my soul loves," but now is emboldened to use this tender term. Joüon explained the term as designating one who gives rather than receives affection, and thus applies to God. Robert saw no basis in the Canticle for the nuance stressed by Joüon, but asserted that it is a matter of conjugal love as the passionate effusions of the bride indicate. With this there could be little disagreement, except for the implications of the term "conjugal." Waterman attempted to prove that the translation, "my beloved," Vulgate *dilectus meus* (LXX here has "my brother"), is wrong and that the word is to be interpreted as a proper name, to be vocalized *Dodai.* An unpublished dissertation, by Bernard Boyd (1947) takes its cue from Waterman's thesis. There is, however, no firm philological ground for this view. As in many languages, a word for love is virtually personified as the term of reference for one's beloved.

13b. *Between my breasts.* The wearing of a sachet of some perfumed substance between the breasts was common in the Near East, at least until more convenient ways of applying perfume became available. One may still find in antique shops necklaces with a little hollow pod for holding the aromatic material. Whether the term *bāttê hannep̄eš* mentioned among other items of feminine finery in Isa 3:18–23 designates such perfume receptacles is uncertain, but seems the best guess. Delitzsch scouted the notion that our lady might have worn such a sachet of myrrh, since he assumes that the exotic and expensive material would be unattainable for a rustic maid. Graetz assumed that the reading "between my breasts" could not be correct because vss. 13 and 14 should correspond, therefore he emended to *bên śeḏê,* "in den Gefilden von . . . ," but offered no substitute for the deleted word *yālîn.*

Robert asked whether the image of the breasts may not symbolize the tribes of the North and the South. As Jerusalem occupies a median position between the one and the other (still in Benjamin, but touching the southern limit of Judah), the beloved could be said to repose between the breasts of the bride. But this interpretation has its difficulties, Robert admitted; cf. 4:5. One could, he suggested, understand simply: on my breasts=on my heart=at the center of Israel. A symbolic sense, according to Robert, may be hidden under this expression. One might note that it contrasts with the description of Hosea 2:4*f* and Ezek 23:3,21, which brand the prostitutions of the bride. If our author thought of these references, he wished, according to Robert, to make it understood that the time of infidelities was past, and that the nation intends now to belong only to her legitimate spouse.

lodges. The verb *l*(*y*)*n* regularly means "spend the night." The *nomen loci mālôn* designates a place where one passes the night. The form *mĕlûnāh* is applied to the lodge in which the watchman stays to guard the crops as harvest nears, Isa 1:8, 24:20. Some commentators on the basis of Job 19:4; Ps 49:13[12E]; Prov 15:31, opt for the meaning rest, remain, repose. Robert, for example, renders "repose" and remarks that, in spite of the realism of the description, it does not appear that the primary meaning of the verb is intended. Rather the author wishes simply to put in relief the constant presence of the groom and the intimacy of the relation which unites him to the bride.

The bundle of myrrh and the breasts are lost in the Targum:

> At that time YHWH commanded Moses: "Go; descend, for the people have done wrong. Get away from me and I will execute them." Then Moses turned and begged mercy before YHWH and YHWH remembered for them the binding of Isaac, whose father bound him on Mount Moriah on the altar, and YHWH turned from His anger and made His Presence dwell among them as formerly.

This verse is cited in the Talmud (TB Yoma 54a) to settle an argument about the structure of the tabernacle, whether its staves protruded through the curtain. Rabbi Judah maintained that the staves did protrude like a woman's breasts and adduced this verse as proof. Elsewhere (TB Shabbat 88b) this verse is ascribed to Israel addressing God: "Lord of the World, though my life be distressed and embittered, yet my love for you lies between my breasts" (with wordplays on *ṣĕrôr*, "bundle" as *mēṣar*, "distressed"; and *mōr*, "myrrh," as *mēmar*, "embittered").

Midrash Rabbah did not dwell at length on the bag of myrrh. It was applied simply to Abraham who was chief of all righteous men, as myrrh is most excellent of all spices. The position between the breasts was explained by Gen 18:2, to mean that Abraham was clasped between the Divine Presence and an angel.

Christian expositors referred to the myrrh as Christ's Passion. The bundle suggested that Christ came bound in human form, that he binds Himself to us with cords of love, or that all His sayings, doctrines, and miracles are bound together with the cord of truth and cannot be taken separately. The bitter myrrh typifies the suffering and death of Christ and must be the lot of all his followers. The use of myrrh in burial of the dead, to preserve the body from corruption, as when Nicodemus brought myrrh and aloes for the burial of Christ (John 19:39), reminds the Church of her own preservation from the rottenness of sin through His death.

The breasts were seen as the Old and New Testaments, the one containing prophecies and types of the Passion, the other the history of its results, with the scarred form of the Man of Sorrows lying between the two. The breasts belong to the holy soul who carries Christ between the two great commandments, love of God and love of neighbor. The breasts are those of Christ's dear Mother preserved pure from all taint in His Incarnation. In the hour of his Passion the sword passed through her bosom and she tasted with Him the bitterness of death, thus it has been the delight of Christians through the centuries, especially of virgin souls, to wear the crucifix on their breasts. (Cf. Littledale.)

14a. *cluster*. The word *'eškôl* regularly denotes the cluster of grapes, as in 7:9[8E]. Here and in 7:8[7E] it is applied to clusters other than grapes.

cypress. The term is part of the international Mediterranean vocabulary, Ugaritic *kpr*, Hebrew *kōper*, Arabic *kāfūr*, Greek *kypros*, Latin *cyprus*. *KJ* rendered "camphor." The plant, *lawsonia alba/inermis*, a shrub eight to ten feet in height, grows in profusion in the Levant and in Asia. It was cultivated in Egypt, Cyprus, and Palestine, especially at Ascalon, and still grows on the coastal plain and around Jericho. Its bluish-yellow flowers grow so thick that they resemble a bunch of grapes. The dried leaves are used for making a reddish-orange cosmetic dye with which Muslim women stain their hair, hands, feet, and nails. Its modern use as a hair dye is common. In the present passage, the interest is olfactory, as in the case of the nard and myrrh just mentioned. The manufacture of *kypros*, according to Forbes (1955, III, 32, Table v) was like the process for rose perfume, except that unless one removes the flowers and squeezes them out, decay sets in and ruins the perfume.

The term *kpr* occurs in Ugaritic. At the broken beginning of the episode in which the goddess Anat goes on a rampage of wanton slaughter of mankind, there is mention of cypress and perhaps musk:

kpr.šbʿ.bnt.	cypress which gratifies girls,
rḥ.gdm wanhbm	smell of musk and ambergris(?)
	(3[ʿNT].2–3)

The goddess' penchant for perfume is exhibited even when she engages in carnage, for she perfumes herself both before and after the slaughter. The Indian goddess Kali, like Anat/Ishtar, also indulges in perfumery and is particularly partial to cypress or camphor. In the hymn to the primordial Kali, Ādyakāli, which contains a hundred of her names beginning with the letter "K," several lines begin with epithets compounded with the element *karpūra*, "camphor." She is also partial to musk and the musk deer:

Who art attached to those who worship Thee with musk,
Who lovest those who worship Thee with musk,
Who art a mother to those who burn musk as incense,
Who art fond of the musk-deer,
And who art pleased to eat its musk,
Whom the scent of camphor gladdens,
Who art adorned with garlands of camphor,
And whose body is besmeared with camphor and sandal paste,
Who art pleased with purified wine flavoured with camphor,
Who drinkest purified wine flavoured with camphor,
Who art bathed in the ocean of camphor,
Whose abode is the ocean of camphor . . .

(Avalon, 1952, 46, lines 67–77)

Such as worship Thee with fragrant flowers and sandal paste,
Ground with cool water and powdered camphor,
Gain the sovereignty of the whole world.

(p. 31)

Her lotus feet glitter with beautiful anklets,
Crowned, adorned, and gracious,
Holding two white fly-whisks, a mirror, jewel case, and a box filled with camphor.

(p. 88, no. 10)

At time of recitation I remember the Mother,
Lustrous as the scarlet hibiscus,
Her body pasted with saffron and sandal,
Her hair kissed by musk;

(p. 165, no. 7)

The most appropriate note on this verse is the citation by Gerleman of the Nubian Samuēl Alī Hissein (b. 1863) who tells us that apart from its cosmetic quality which makes the ugly beautiful, and its countless yellow and thick blossoms, what makes henna more valuable and attractive is its fragrance. Women often stick it in their braids and put it in their armpits. This suggests that the cluster of cypress was used like the bundle of myrrh, as a sachet tucked in one or more of the convenient interstices of our lady's form.

14b. *From the gardens.* Delitzsch and Meek (in *AT* and the commentary of *IB*, V) recognized that the preposition *b-* here is better rendered "from" than "in," and thus also *JPSV, NEB, NAB* (the *JB*'s "among the vines of En Gedí" presents an example of translation error arising from dependence on the French original without reference to the Hebrew. French "vigne" means both "vine" and "vineyard," but English "vines" is not normally used in the sense of "vineyard").

En Gedi. Literally, "Kid-Fountain," an impressive oasis on the western shore of the Dead Sea set in an amphitheatre of inaccessible cliffs which still today are the haunt of the mountain goat. Josh 15:62 lists En Gedi among six cities in the area. The strong spring and the warm climate supply the conditions for the extraordinary fertility, like that at Jericho, to which Ben Sira alludes (24:14):

> I was exalted like a palm tree in En Gedi   Like the rose bushes in Jericho.

Pliny also speaks of the rich growth of the palm (*Hist. nat.* v 17) and Jerome mentions the balsam and viticulture (*Onomastica sacra,* ed. P. de Lagarde, 1887, 119, 14*f*).

Excavations at En Gedi (Tell el-Jurn) by Israeli archaeologists revealed five occupational levels from the Roman Byzantine period, third–fifth centuries A.D., back to the latter days of the Kingdom of Judah, ca. 625–580 B.C. In the courtyards of level V were discovered a series of large barrels, up to a meter in height, standing in close groups, and beside these barrels an abundance of pottery, various basalt utensils and implements of bronze, iron and bone, as well as clods of asphalt from the Dead Sea. Among the pottery characteristic of the latest stage of the Judean Kingdom were decanters and perfume juglets. According to Professor Benjamin Mazar (1963, 546) the findings in the courtyards, uncovered *in situ* under a layer of ashes, appear to have served the needs of the perfume industry. The arrangement of the vessels and tools appear to fit the preparation of perfume, which requires only simple operations. It appears that from the time of Josiah to the end of the Judean Kingdom En Gedi was a royal estate and its inhabitants employed in the production of perfume balm. For bibliography of excavation reports on Tell el-Jurn, see E. K. Vogel, (1971), 28*f*.

For the Targum, the vineyards of En Gedi supplied sacrificial wine rather than perfume:

> Lo, then Moses came down with the two tablets of stone in his hands. But because of the sins of Israel his hands were heavy, and (the tablets) fell and were broken. Then Moses went and crushed the calf, and scattered its dust in the brook and made the Israelites drink, and he killed all who deserved killing. He ascended a second time to the firmament and prayed before YHWH and made atonement for the Israelites. Then he was commanded to make the Tabernacle and the Ark. At that time he [God] instructed Moses and he [Moses] made the Tabernacle and all its vessels, and the Ark. He put

in the Ark two other tablets and appointed Aaron's sons as priests to offer the sacrifice on the altar and to pour the wine on the sacrifice. Whence did they have wine to pour? Were they not in the desert, no proper place for agriculture; they had no figs, vines, or pomegranates. But they went to the vineyards of En Gedi and took from there clusters of grapes and pressed wine from them and poured it on the altar, a quart (quarter of a hin) for each lamb.

Midrash Rabbah referred the cluster of *kōp̄er* to the binding of Isaac, because he was bound like a cluster and he atones (*mĕkappēr*) for Israel's sins. A triple play on "the vineyards of En Gedi" related it to Jacob's deception: he entered his father's presence with face *kĕrûm,* "covered" or "painted" (a play on the noun *kerem,* "vineyard," and the verb *krm*); he put on goatskin (playing on *gĕdî*); and he took the blessings which are the eye (*'ên*) of the world. The cluster *'eškōl,* also suggested the pun, *'îš še-hakkōl,* "the man who has everything," i.e. Scripture, Mishnah, Talmud, etc. Ben Nazirah, however, referred the cluster to God. Rabbi Johanan applied this verse and the preceding to the incense of the House of Abtinus (the family which preserved the hereditary secret of preparation of incense for the altar) and this called forth discussion of the eleven ingredients of the secret formula, deduced from citations of Scripture.

The word *kōp̄er* called forth some interesting Christian interpretations. The identity of the form with the Hebrew word for ransom suggested reference to the fragrance of the Redemption wrought by Christ. The Greek and Latin transcriptions of the word are identical with the name of the island of Cyprus, famous for wine, and with the mistaking of the preceding word *'eškôl* as designating a cluster of grapes, the way was opened for more exercise of the imagination, since the vine and the grape are richer religious symbols than a bunch of henna. The grape of Cyprus reminded some of the Latin Fathers of the grapes carried on a pole by the spies, and thus of the Crucifixion. En-Gedi also allowed for some wordplay. LXX misunderstanding of the play on the name of Gad in Gen 49:19, reading, "Gad, a temptation shall tempt him," became the basis for the analysis of *Engaddi* as "the eye of my temptation," opening new vistas for the allegorists. (Cf. Littledale, 44*f.*)

15a,b. *fair.* The feminine form of the adjective, *yāp̄āh,* is used eight times of the bride, five times in the absolute form, as here, (4:1,7, 6:4,10) and three times in the superlative expression, "the fair(est) of women," *hayyāp̄āh bannāšîm* (1:8, 5:9, 6:1). The masculine form of the adjective is only once applied to the male lover, in vs. 16. The verbal form *yāp̄û* is applied to the bride's love, or her breasts, in 4:10, and to her feet in 7:2[1E]. This word has been treated by Trotti, 1964, along with other words relating to beauty. There is no need to consider the seventy occurrences treated by Trotti, but a few summary comments may be in order. The word has cognates in Ugaritic, Aramaic, and Arabic and occurs in one of the Amarna letters (no. 138, 126) as *ya-pu* glossed by *ḫa-mu-du,* "desirable." The term is used in the Old Testament primarily in physical description of men and women, but also occasionally of animals and inanimate objects. It is not used of God. The term is occasionally applied to males (e.g. Joseph, Gen 39:6; David's eyes, I Sam

16:12, and his general appearance, I Sam 17:42; Absalom, II Sam 14:25), but more often to women (Sarah, Gen 12:14; Tamar, II Sam 13:1; Abishag, I Kings 1:3,4; virgins, Amos 8:13; Job's daughters, Job 42:15). Of the features that especially contribute to human beauty, the eyes are most often mentioned. The beautiful Rachel is contrasted with Leah with the weak (sore?) eyes, Gen 29:17. The "light that lies in woman's eyes" has been many a man's undoing, and the sages warn the simple against this hazard, Prov 6:25. According to Ben Sira (Sir 26:9), "A woman's wantonness is revealed by roving looks, And by her eyelids." The natural seductive power of the feminine eyes was enhanced by the liberal use of eyepaint. One of the common objects found in excavations in Syria-Palestine is the palette used for grinding kohl (stibium or antimony) for eyepaint. Jer 4:30 compares ruined Zion to a jaded vamp who vainly enlarges her eyes with paint. The artifice appears to be associated with women of dubious virtue; cf. II Kings 9:30; Ezek 23:40, but Job named one of his beautiful daughters *Qeren happûḵ,* "Horn of Kohl" (Job 42:14).

15c. *doves.* Syriac, Vulgate, Ibn Ezra, Luther, *KJ,* and others take this so-called *comparatio decurtata* as elliptical for "your eyes are dove eyes," i.e. like dove eyes. (Gerleman's note that Vulgate and Syriac appear to have read or conjectured *dĕyônāh,* "thine eyes are those of a dove," seems to forget for the moment that the Canticle uses *še* instead of *dĕ* for the relative particle.) Resort to 5:2, where the bride is addressed as "my dove," has no relevance to the interpretation of the present passage and does not of itself prove that the doves themselves, and not just the eyes, are the point of comparison with the bride's eyes, as Ginsburg argued. More appropriate is the appeal to the analogy of 4:1,2 where the bride's eyes are again doves, her hair *like* a flock of goats, her teeth *like* a shorn and washed flock; and similarly 7:3,5[2–4E], where her belly is a mound of wheat, her eyes the pools of Heshbon. This should be ample indication that LXX, Targum, Rashi, and many moderns were right in rendering and interpreting literally. What aspect of the dove is envisaged in relation to the bride's eyes is not clear and commentators have made divergent suggestions: the feathers of the dove, its lively motion, its purity, gentleness, and innocence. The most likely guess is the glistening color of the dove and its quick movements:

> In the Spring a livelier iris changes on the burnish'd dove,
> In the Spring a young man's fancy lightly turns to thoughts of love.
> (Tennyson, "Locksley Hall")

A twelfth-century bestiary, according to E. S. Gifford, Jr. (1962, p. 45) assures us that doves have a sweet disposition and ask for love with their eyes.

15. Haupt suppressed the entire verse as a doublet of 4:1; others delete only the last line as supposedly added to call attention to the parallel and complete it. The assertion (Jastrow) that the last line is clearly out of place and spoils the rhythm is a subjective judgment that would be difficult to dem-

onstrate. The same applies to the elimination of the middle line (Zapletal and Dussaud). Robert pointed out that this procedure forgets that repetition is characteristic of the Canticle. Gerleman offered a novel explanation of the characterization of the bride's eyes as doves. The human portraits which confront us in sculpture, on tomb reliefs and palace murals present a richness of individual traits and recurring features which amount to artistic convention. The representation of the eye, according to Gerleman, belongs to these conventionally shaped features and is constructed throughout in a form which reminds one strongly of the body of a bird. The figurative language of the Song of Songs, especially in the so-called descriptive songs, presents many features which Gerleman believed become understandable if we reckon pictorial art as their source of inspiration. Thus the characterization of the bride's eyes becomes explicable with the help of the linear illustration of Egyptian art.

The Targum interpreted the doves as Israel's sacrificial and praiseworthy obedience to the divine will:

> When the Israelites did the will of their King, He, by His Word, praised them in the family of the holy angels. He said: "How lovely are your deeds, My beloved daughter, Assembly of Israel, in the hour when you do my will, working at the words of My Law. And how proper are your deeds and purposes, like pigeons, or young doves, fit to be offered on the altar."

Midrash Rabbah referred the dove eyes to the Sanhedrin, citing Num 15:24, "If it be hid from the eyes of the Congregation." As there are two hundred and forty-eight parts of the human body which move only by the direction of the eyes, so Israel can do nothing without the Sanhedrin. Characteristics of the dove were ascribed to Israel. The dove is innocent and graceful in step, so is Israel innocent and graceful in gait when going up to celebrate the festivals. The dove is distinctive and so is Israel, with respect to shaving, circumcision, and fringes. The dove is chaste, and so is Israel. The dove sticks out its neck for slaughter, and so also does Israel (Ps 44:23[22E]). The dove atones for iniquities, and Israel atones for the nations, the seventy bullocks offered at the Feast of Tabernacles being for the sake of the seventy nations (cf. TB Sukkah 55b), in order that the world be not desolated by them. Ps 109:4 is cited in this connection. The dove, once she recognizes her mate, never changes him for another, and so Israel, after she learned to know the Holy One, blessed be He, never exchanged Him for another. As the dove, when it enters the cote, knows its own niche and nest, and fledglings, so when the three rows of scholars sit before the Sanhedrin, each knows his place. As a dove, even if its young are taken away, never abandons its cote, so Israel, although the Temple was destroyed, did not cease to celebrate the three festivals every year. As the dove produces a new brood every month, so Israel produces every month fresh learning and good deeds. As the dove goes away, but always returns to its cote, so will the Tribes return (Hosea 11:11). Rabbi noted that when a certain species of dove is being fed, others smell the food and flock to her cote, and thus proselytes are attracted to Israel.

The bride's beauty and her dove eyes receive a fair share of allegorical treatment by the Fathers of the Church. The double affirmation of her beauty suggested to Origen that she is fair not only when near the Groom, but even when He is absent. Gregory the Great saw the dual affirmation, like the two breasts, as the double beauty of the Church in her love of God and love of neighbor. Bernard elaborated the duality: the Church is fair in soul and chaste in body, fair by gifts of nature and fairer still by blessings of grace, fair within and fair without, in the beauty of the sacraments, the manifold ranks of the hierarchy, in supernatural gifts of grace.

The dove eyes were allegorically apprehended as the enlightening graces of the Holy Ghost, the inner vision of the soul, the type of meekness and purity, and conjugal fidelity. The Venerable Bede contrasted doves and hawks. Not surprisingly, the verse was also applied to the Virgin par excellence, as in the hymn *Regina misericordae:*

Mary, thou art bridal dove,
  Thou art turtle dowered,
Ivory abode of love,
  City strongly towered;

Thou, inviolate by stain,
  Name of violet bearest,
Rose-bud, lily flower, plain,
  Child, spouse, mother fairest.
(Cf. Littledale, ad loc.)

16a. *Indeed.* The particle here has affirmative force, like its Arabic cognate *'innā,* "verily."

16a,b. It is clear from the use of masculine forms of the adjectives, as well as the designation *dôḏî,* that the bride now reciprocates with praises of the groom's beauty in terms similar to those he had just used of her. The same sequence of synonyms, *ypy* and *n'm,* are addressed to the female in 7:7[6E], although elsewhere in biblical usage *n'm* appears to be confined to male persons, except in the names of Tubal-Cain's sister Naamah (Gen 4:22) and Ruth's mother-in-law Naomi. The same sequence of terms occurs in Ugaritic with reference to the beauty of Baal:

Anat went wild
At the beauty (*tp*) of her brother
And the handsomeness (*n'm*) of her
  brother

For he was beautiful (*ysmsm*)
She ate his flesh without a knife
And drank his blood without a cup
(RS 22.225, 1–5)

(The word *tp,* because of the association with other terms for beauty, *n'm* and *ysmsm,* is to be derived from the root *ypy*[*wpy*], with a *t-* preformative [*tōpī*], since *tuppu,* "drum," in this connection [the drum of her brother and the handsomeness of her brother] would scarcely be appropriate or apposite.)

Interpreters who envisaged a love triangle between Solomon, the Shulamite shepherdess, and her beloved shepherd swain, were forced to incredible devices to make and maintain the distinction between the two males. Hitzig here suggested that the first two words, up to but not including *dôḏî,* are terms of mutual politeness and that the term *nā'îm,* "charming," is added at once to distinguish her beloved from the king who is to her insufferable. To this Delitzsch rightly objected that the second person suffixes, feminine and masculine, with the particle, *hinnāk* and *hinnekā,* indicate an interchange between two persons and not three.

16c. *couch.* The word, *'ereś,* is one of the common terms for bed or couch, used for the usual purposes, sleep, illness, and lovemaking, the later use obviously intended in the present instance, as in Prov 7:16. The bed in the Sumerian sacred marriage rite receives considerable attention. It is characterized as "ornate," reminiscent of the ivory beds on which the wealthy of Samaria lolled and sang and toped, Amos 6:4–6, and the carved ivory decorations of the bed of the King of Ugarit. The king's craving for the nuptial bed and the preparation and sweetening of the bed is ecstatically hymned by the Sumerian poet:

He craves it, he craves it, he craves the bed,
He craves the bed, that rejoices the heart, he craves the bed,
He craves the bed that sweetens the lap, he craves the bed,
He craves the bed of kingship, he craves the bed,
That she make it sweet, that she make it sweet, that she make the bed sweet,
That she make sweet the bed of kingship, that she make sweet the bed,
That she make sweet the bed of queenship, that she make sweet the bed,
The [lord] covers the bed for her, covers the bed for her,
The [king] covers the bed for her, covers the bed for her . . .
(*SMR,* 82)

luxuriant. LXX *syskios,* Vulgate *floridus.* The rendering "verdant," or "green," is misleading since the term does not refer to color as such, but to the lush and luxuriant foliage of trees in general. Meek (*IB,* V) was reminded of the sacred tree that was a feature of the Baal cult, the scene of alfresco sacral amours (cf. Jer 3:6,13), and also of the bower of "fresh new grass, dewy lotus, crocus, and hyacinth, thick and soft" which the "divine earth" prepared as the nuptial couch of Zeus and Hera (Homer *Iliad* xiv 347–351). In the Sumerian sacred marriage the nuptial bed in the *gipar*-house (the part of the temple where the high priestess who represented the goddess in the holy rites resided) was similarly strewn with luxurious plants:

My house, my house, he will make it "long" for me,
I the queen—my house, my house, he will make it "long" for me,
My *gipar*-house, he will make it long for me,
The people will set up my fruitful bed,
They will cover it with plants of *duru*—lapis lazuli,
I will bring there the man of my heart.
(*SMR,* 76)

The Targum allowed the fertility motif and the love couch to come through, as grounds for gratitude:

The Assembly of Israel replied before the Lord of the World and thus she said: "How lovely is your Holy Presence at the time You dwell among us and receive with favor our prayer; at the time You cause love to dwell in the bed (*puryānā*) and many children upon the earth, and we increasing and growing like the tree planted by the spring of water, its branches fair and fruit plentiful."

Midrash Rabbah offered different explanations of this verse. It was understood as God praising Israel and as Israel praising God. The couch was taken to mean the Temple. The luxuriant nature of the bed suggested the parable of a king who went to the desert and suffered in a short bed which cramped his limbs, but when he got to the city he was given a longer and more comfortable bed. Thus until the Temple was built the Divine Presence was confined between the poles of the Ark, but when the Temple was built the poles were lengthened (I Kings 8:8). Before the Temple was built the Divine Presence was moved from place to place (II Sam 7:6), but now had a permanent dwelling. The fertility motif was also admitted with respect to the Temple as a couch. As the couch is used for propagation, so David could say before the Temple was built, "Go, number Israel" (I Chron 21:2), but afterward they were innumerable like the sand of the sea (I Kings 4:20).

Christian expositors applied this verse to the disputed question of the physical aspect of Christ, whether he was as described in Isa 53:2 or in Ps 45:3[2E]. The "shady bed," according to the wording of LXX, was seen as protective. Origen explained that the Bride says "*our* bed" because her members belong to Christ and the bed is shady because of the promise of Ps 121:6. Theodoret took the bed to represent the Holy Scriptures, shaded and guarded by the grace of the Holy Spirit and sheltered from the heat of wickedness. The "flowery bed" of the Latin reading was applied to the tranquility of the Church, flowery with the many virtues of the saints. For St. Bernard the Church's bed meant the cloisters and convents where one lives free from the cares and anxieties of life. The diminutive term *lectulus,* "little bed," of Vulgate, suggested to Nicolaus de Argentina the hard and narrow bed of the Cross which was the bridal couch of Christ and His Church. Rupert saw in the flowery bed the hallowed womb where the Incarnate Lord rested for nine months. To these and other interpretations Littledale added the suggestion that the green or flowery bed may be taken as the pastures of heaven.

17a. *Our bower's.* Lit. "our houses," *bāttênû.* As in Ugaritic, the plural is used in the sense of singular, perhaps as suggested by C. H. Gordon (*UT* 19.463) because the home consisted of several buildings.

beams. This word, *qôrôṯ,* is used in Gen 19:8, in the idiom "enter the shade of one's roof." In I Kings 6:15,16 MT reads *qîrôṯ,* "walls," but LXX's reading reflects *qôrôt,* "rafters," which better suits the context. In II Chron 3:7 the word is written defectively. The etymology is unclear, but the word may be related to Akkadian *qarītu* and Arabic *qariyyat,* "beam," "pole," etc., with a development much like English "yard."

cedars. The use of the word in the plural, *'ărāzîm,* apparently suggests the poetic and romantic theme of alfresco amour as a clean, healthy pursuit with a minimum of overhead, as reflected in Moffatt's paraphrase:

Our bed of love is the green sward,
Our roof-beams are your cedar boughs,
Our rafters are the firs.

PLATE I
2:5 Sustain me with raisin cakes

Mold from palace kitchen at Mari, for making cakes in form of the Love-Goddess, Ishtar, Queen of Heaven

PLATE II
3:10 Its sides love inlaid

Ivory inlay of love scene from bed of king of Ugarit

PLATE III
4:4 Like David's tower your neck,
built in courses

Terracotta figurine in the Babylonian Collection, Yale University

PLATE IV
2:4 He brought me into the wine house,
His intent toward me Love

Terracotta figurine from Iraq Museum.

PLATE V
5:4 My love thrust his "hand" into the hole

Terracotta plaque from Nippur described as "female figure with a necklace."

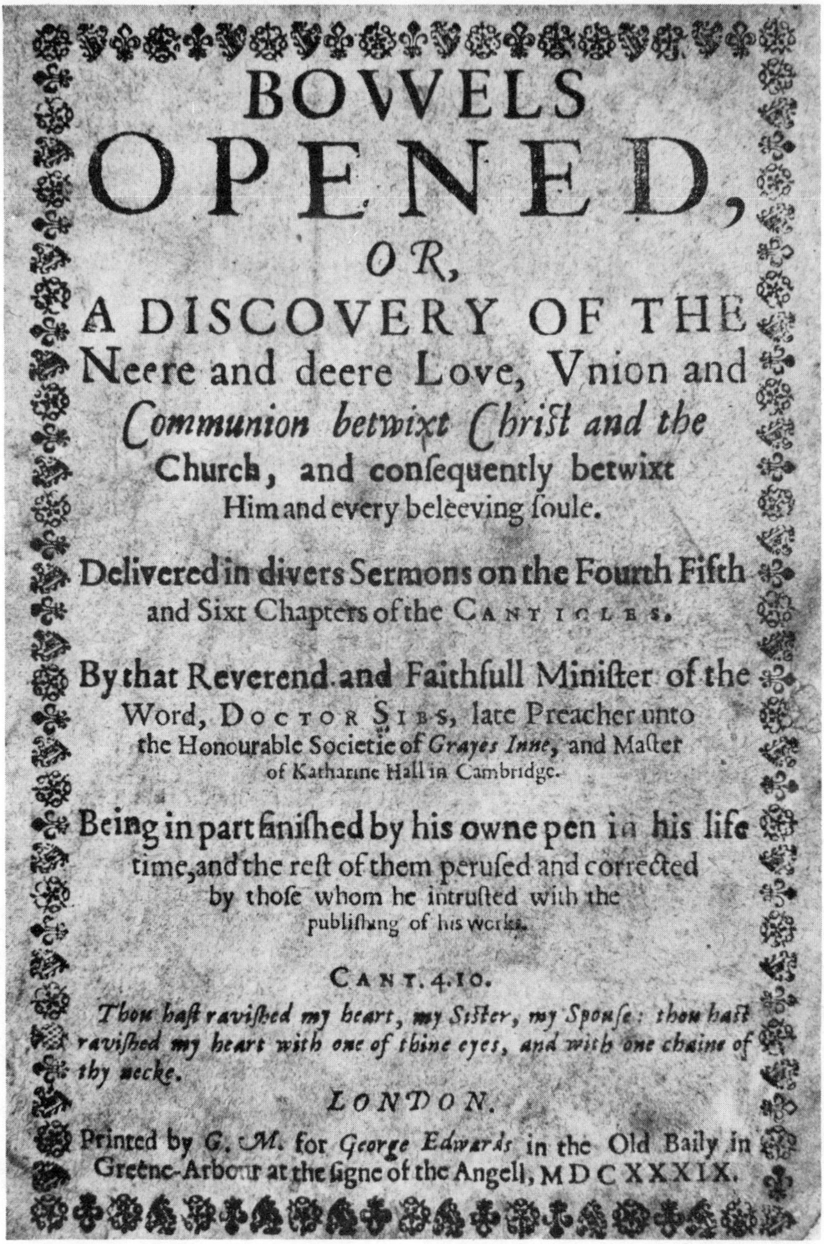
BOVVELS
OPENED,
OR,
A DISCOVERY OF THE
Neere and deere Love, Vnion and
Communion betwixt Christ and the
Church, and conſequently betwixt
Him and every beleeving ſoule.

Delivered in divers Sermons on the Fourth Fifth
and Sixt Chapters of the CANTICLES.

By that Reverend and Faithfull Miniſter of the
Word, DOCTOR SIBS, late Preacher unto
the Honourable Societie of *Grayes Inne*, and Maſter
of Katharine Hall in Cambridge.

Being in part finiſhed by his owne pen in his life
time, and the reſt of them peruſed and corrected
by thoſe whom he intruſted with the
publiſhing of his workes.

CANT. 4. 10.
Thou haſt raviſhed my heart, my Siſter, my Spouſe: thou haſt raviſhed my heart with one of thine eyes, and with one chaine of thy necke.

LONDON.
Printed by G. M. for *George Edwards* in the Old Baily in Greene-Arbour at the ſigne of the Angell, MDCXXXIX.

PLATE VI
5:4 And my bowels were moved for him (*KJ*)

Title page of Dr. Sibs sermons on Canticles. Copy in Medical Library of Yale University classified as "historical," apparently on the assumption that the concern is relief of constipation.

PLATE VII
5:11a His head finest gold

Statuette of Baal from Ugarit composed of five materials. The original gold overlay on the copper core is only partially preserved. The helmet with crest and hauberk is of steatite doweled to the head with horns of electrum. The left arm is attached with a silver dowel.

PLATE VIII
7:5 Your neck like an ivory tower

Ivory head from the palace of Ugarit.

PLATE IX
6:10 Awesome as with trophies

The Goddess as Destroyer in union with her husband, the two aspects of Shiva, in the cremation-ground. Painting of the Bengal School, twentieth century.

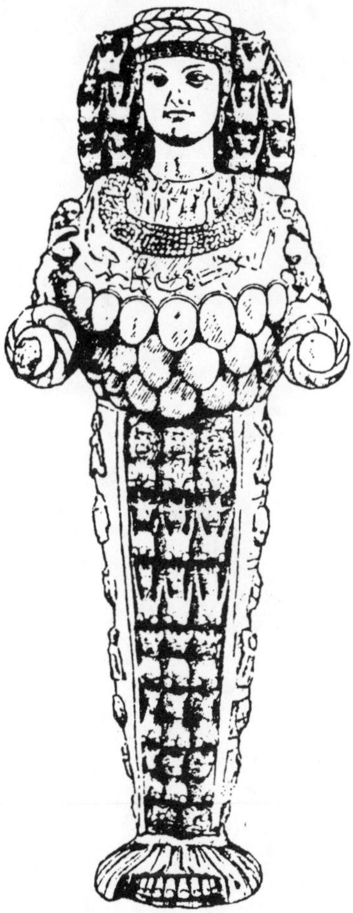

PLATE X

7:8 Your stature resembles the palm,
your breasts like clusters

The goddess Artemis/Diana of Ephesus with protuberances of uncertain character usually taken to represent breasts.

PLATE XI

8:1 O that you were as my brother
who sucked the breasts of my mother

Goddess suckling two godlings or princelings. Ivory panel from the bed of the king of Ugarit.

PLATE XII
8:6 For Love is Strong as Death
Etruscan sarcophagus lid of alabaster, 4th century B.C.

PLATE XIII
Winged Athena carrying corpse (human or divine?)

PLATE XIV
St. Theresa receives the shaft of love.
Sculpture of Giovanni Bernini, S. Maria della Vittoria, Rome.

The exposition in *IB* by H. T. Kerr (III, 146 apropos of 8:6–7,) quotes Moffatt's rendering and explains:

A house, as we say, is not a home, but love can transfigure and exalt the meanest abode. So too the lovers' experience the thrill of the great outdoors which love captures and transforms for their own enjoyment.

The cedars constitute the beams of the bridal chamber, as in the Mesopotamian cult structure for the sacred marriage (cf. Schmökel, 1956, 9,113). The bed of the sacred marriage rite of Mesopotamia is characterized as fruitful and ornate in the epic tale of Enmerkar of Erech. The ruler of Aratta suggested that Enmerkar should accept his rule and then both rulers could perform the sacred marriage rite with the goddess, but with Enmerkar slightly inferior:

Let him [Enmerkar] bend the neck before me, carry the basket before me,
When he has bent the neck before me, has indeed bent the neck before me,
Then he and I———
He will lie with Inanna by a wall,
But I will lie with Inanna in the lapis lazuli house of Aratta;
He will lie by her side in a fruitful bed,
But I will lie in sweet slumber on an ornate bed;
He will gaze upon Inanna only in a dream,
But I will converse with Inanna by her feet, the all-white."

(*SMR*, 58)

The place of the sacred rite is described as flourishing with vegetation, as the goddess bathes her holy lap and cohabits with Dumuzi:

At the king's lap stood the rising cedar,
Plants rose high by his side,
Grains rose high by his side,
. . . [and] gardens flourished luxuriantly by his side.

(*SMR*, 65)

17b. *rafters*. The Kethib *rāḥîṭēnû* is a hapax legomenon. The Qere changes the laryngeal *ḥ* to *h*. The reading *rhṭ* suggests "runners" of some sort, as connected with the Aramaic *rěhaṭ*, "run." The anonymous Hebrew manuscript used by Ginsburg explained the word as meaning "bolt," because it runs backward and forward. Ginsburg, however, leaned on Rashbam, who explained the word as denoting one of the apartments of the house. Ginsburg rendered, "retreat," although his note suggests a preference for "arbor" as parallel to his translation "bower" for "houses" in the preceding line. The plural noun *rěhāṭîm* is used thrice of the gutters of a watering trough, rendered "runnels" by *RSV* in Gen 30:38,41 and "troughs" in Exod 2:16. The Samaritan version in Exod 2:16 is *rḥtym* which suggests that the change of *ḥ* and *h* is merely dialectal. The parallelism with *qôrôṯ*, "beams," and the use of cedar and cypress hardly suggests gutters. Robert appealed to Arabic *rhṭ* in the sense of "be assembled," "reunited," and rendered "lambris," ceiling or wainscoting, as composed of boards joined together. LXX *phatnōmata* and

Vulgate *laquearia* similarly suggest the hollows or panels of a wainscoted ceiling or wall.

cypresses. Not to be confused with the cypress or henna of vs. 14a. The form *bĕrôṯim,* with *ṯ* instead of the usual Hebrew spelling with *š,* Akkadian *burāšu,* is a feature of Aramaic or northern dialect. As with the parallel word for cedar, the form is used predicatively in the plural as designating the material of the structure in question, not the living trees of the forest. The name of the tree was taken over into Greek and Latin with the *ṯ* or *t, brathy* and *bratus*. The tree is particularly associated with Lebanon, cf. Isa 60:13, and Wetzstein was inclined to derive the name of Beirut from this tree. Philo of Byblos gives "Brathy" as a name of Mount Hermon. Pliny compared the *bratus* to the cypress, *arbor bratus cupresso similis,* and LXX and Vulgate respectively so render *kuparissoi* and *cypressina*. Meek thought the description of the hut or booth suggestive of the green bowers of Sukkoth or the Festival of Booths and as further evidence in favor of the liturgical interpretation, he noted, too, that in the Adonis festival, booths were erected containing images of Adonis and Astarte in representation of their marriage.

In the Sumerian sacred marriage, oil of cypress is mentioned as sprinkled on the ground in connection with Dumuzi's marriage to Inanna, as she says:

To my mother he will say the word,
He will sprinkle cypress oil on the
ground,
To my mother Ningal he will say the
word,
He will sprinkle cypress oil on the
ground,
He whose dwelling is fragrant,
Whose word brings deep joy.
(*SMR*, 78)

17. The Targum referred the structure to the Temple of the messianic future:

> Said Solomon, the prophet: "How lovely is the Temple of YHWH, built by my hands, with cedar wood. But more lovely will be the Temple which is to be built in the days of the King, the Messiah, the beams of which will be cedars from the Garden of Eden, and its pillars will be of fir, juniper, and cypress.

Midrash Rabbah related the cedar beams to Jacob's pillow at Bethel which became like a feather bed beneath him. Another explanation was that the cedar beams refer to the righteous men and women, prophets and prophetesses who issued from Jacob. The cypresses were alleged by Rabbi Johanan to be useless because they bend and he cited Hosea 14:9[8E] which he interpreted as Ephraim's assertion, "I am he who bowed himself to uproot the idolatrous impulse." The cypress runners were assigned to the floor on which the priests ran (I Kings 6:15). From this Rabbi Johanan deduced the practical advice to house builders to make the ceiling of cedar and the floor of cypress.

The Talmud (TB Yoma 38a) related this verse to the miracle story about the doors which Nicanor brought from Alexandria for the Temple.

The house or houses were variously interpreted by Christian exegetes: as the local churches on earth which are the joint dwelling of Christ and the elect soul; as the Holy Scriptures, incorrupt as cedar, perfumed as cypress; as the individual soul itself. As applied to the Church, the beams, the most important part of a structure, are its prelates and great preachers who are cedar because of their incorruption; the rafters represent either the clergy or the faithful laity, or the great dogmas of the Church. The cedar shrine, unblemished and repelling all evil, was further seen as the pure womb of the immaculate Mother of Christ. (Cf. Littledale.)

II
(2:1–17)

1 a I am the crocus of the plain,
b The lotus of the valley.
2 a Like a lotus among brambles,
b So is my darling among girls.
3 a Like the apple in the wild wood,
b So is my love among boys.
c In his shade I love to sit,
d And his fruit is sweet to my palate.
4 a He brought me into the wine house,
b His intent toward me Love.
5 a Sustain me with raisin cakes,
b Brace me with apples,
c For faint from love am I.
6 a His left hand under my head,
b His right hand clasps me
7 a I adjure you, Jerusalem girls,
b By the gazelles or hinds of the steppe
c That you neither incite nor excite
d Love until it is eager.
8 a Hark my love,
b There he comes,
c Leaping over mountains,
d Bounding o'er hills.
9 a My love resembles a buck,
b Or a young stag.
c Lo, there he stands at our wall,
d Peeking in the window,
e Peering through the lattice.
10 a My love spoke and said to me,
b Arise, my darling,
c My fair one, come.

11 a For, lo, the winter is past,
b The rain is over, gone.
12 a Blossoms appear in the land,
b Pruning time has come.
c The voice of the turtledove
d Is heard in our land.
13 a The fig ripens her fruits,
b The vines in bloom give scent.
c Arise, come, my darling,
d My fair one, come away.
14 a My dove in the cliff crannies,
b In the covert steep,
c Show me your form,
d Let me hear your voice;
e For your voice is pleasant,
f Your form fair.
15 a Catch us foxes,
b Little foxes,
c Vineyard spoilers,
d Our vineyards in bloom.
16 a My love is mine
b And I am his
c Who browses on the lotus.
17 a Until the day breathes,
b And the shadows flee,
c Turn and be, my love,
d Like a buck, or young stag,
e On the cleft mountains.

6. Ashurbanipal and consort in ceremonial wine-bibbing

2:4 He brought me into the wine house,
His intent toward me love.

NOTES

2:1a. *crocus.* The exact nature of the flower is unknown. The word *ḥăḇaṣṣeleṯ* is used elsewhere only in Isa 35:1. The term occurs in Akkadian as *ḫabaṣillatu,* perhaps the *Asphodelus microcorpus,* but not much information is supplied about the plant. LXX and Vulgate are quite noncommittal, using only generic terms, *anthos* and *flos.* Luther similarly rendered, "eine Blume." Targum uses *narqīs,* "narcissus," and similarly Saadia. LXX, Vulgate, and Targum, however, take the word as meaning "lily" in Isa 35:1. Attempts to get a clue from analysis of the word have not been especially productive, e.g. the suggestion that the word is derived from *ḥbṣ* or *ḥmṣ,* "shine," with an *-l* afformative, or compounded from *ḥbṣ* and *baṣal,* "bulb." Löw (*FJ,* II, 156) considered the word "halbe Zwiebel," a compound of *ḥăṣî,* "half," and *bṣl,* "onion," and identified the plant as a kind of lily. Aquila's rendering *kalykōsis,* "rosebud," and Codex Venetus *rodon,* "rose," gave rise to the traditional "rose of Sharon," which is hardly correct since the rose apparently was brought in at a later period from Armenia and Persia. Many writers have taken the word to designate the meadow-saffron, *Colchium autumnale,* a pale, flesh-colored flower with leafless stem which covers the fields of warm regions after the mowing. The rustic maid is supposed to compare herself to this simple and common flower, as one who has grown up in the quiet simplicity of rural life and has no interest in the splendor of the city and the palace. Apart from the rose fanciers, the consensus is that the plant is some sort of common bulb, such as the asphodel, crocus, hyacinth, or narcissus. The crocus or daffodil is taken as a fair guess. Cf. G. Dalman, 1925.

plain. LXX and Vulgate here take the word, *šārôn,* in the generic sense and not as a proper name. The word is plausibly connected with the root *yšr,* "straight," "even," as with another word for "plain," "tableland," *mîšôr.* The word is regularly provided with the article as designating "*the* plain," par excellence, the coastal area from Jaffa northward to Athlit, noted for its fertility. In I Chron 5:16 it is used without the article with reference to the pasture lands of Sharon, following the mention of Gilead and Bashan. According to Eusebius and Jerome, there was also another district by this name between Mount Tabor and the Lake of Tiberias, and Delitzsch supposed that this was the Sharon here intended because the Shulamite, in his view, was a Galilean and she thus calls herself a flower from the neighborhood of Nazareth.

1b. *lotus*. LXX *krinon,* "lily," Vulgate *lilium*. The word *šôšannāh,* variant forms *šôšān* and *šûšan,* Akkadian *šešanu,* is derived from Egyptian *sššn* or *sšn,* Coptic *šošen,* "the sacred lotus," or "water lily," *Nymphae lotus*. The climate and conditions of the upper Jordan Valley seem suitable for the lotus, but there is no evidence that it flourished there. The word might have been adopted to apply to some flower or flowers similar to the Egyptian lotus, but, if so, the identity of the plant or plants is uncertain. The word *ṣe'ĕlîm* in Job 40:21 is sometimes rendered "lotus" (cf. AB 15, ad loc.), but the reference is not to the *Nymphae lotus* but to the thorny shrub *Zizyphus lotus*. It has been supposed that *šôšannāh* is related to the numeral *šēš,* "six," as designating the number of its petals. Delitzsch proposed a connection with *šēš,* "linen," and *šayiš,* "alabaster," as designating a white lily. In 5:13, however, the characterization of the male lover's lips as *šôšannîm* suggests a red flower, although it could be argued that the reference is to the shape rather than to the color of the lips. On the assumption that the reference is to color, proponents of the cultic interpretation have taken the flower to be the scarlet anemone associated with the death, resurrection and marriage of Tammuz or Adonis (cf. Wittekindt, 94*f*). The term anemone is derived from Adonis' epithet *na'man,* "beautiful." The fields of Syria-Palestine from mid-February to April are carpeted with deep red anemones suggesting royal robes, and this is probably the picture envisaged in the famous exhortation, "consider the lilies of the field," Matt 6:28=Luke 12:27, which surpass even the regal splendor of a Solomon. While the traditional rendering "lily" is certainly to be preferred to the anemone, there is no reason to scout the established meaning of the Egyptian term as designating the lotus. According to John Trever (*IDB,* s.v. "Lily"), the only lily of Palestine which could possibly have been intended is the *Lilium candidum* and this does not fit any of the passages in which the terms *šûšan, šôšān, šôšannāh* are used. The prominence of the lotus on Canaanite Astarte plaques and other representations of Syrian deities (*ANEP,* 469–70,472–475,566; cf. 314–316) "would suggest a wider Egyptian influence of the flower than previously thought, and may indicate an original meaning 'lotus' for *šûšan*" in Trever's view. The ramifications of the lotus symbolism are not confined to Egypt, but take us over the entire Mediterranean area and eastward to India, China, and Japan. The association of the lotus with the mother-goddess as a symbol of life, fecundity, and perfection persists in the Christian representations of the Madonna with her lily symbolizing a sort of perfection diametrically opposite its primitive meaning. In Indian erotology, the lotus woman, *padminī,* is the ideal female and her proportions and charms are described in detail, including her smooth and tiny vulva which is like the lotus bud and her love-water perfumed like the newly burst lily.

valley. The term *'ēmeq,* here used in the plural and with the article, *hā'ămāqîm,* may designate either a deep valley or simply a plain, as applied for example to the plain or valley of Jezreel, Josh 17:16. The terms for the flowers and the terrain are here loosely used in synonymous parallelism. In Sir 50:8 *šôšān* stands in parallelism with *peraḥ,* "bud," and the *šôšān,* "lotus," is set by the water streams, *yiḇlê mayim,* which would be in the valleys:

Like the lotus by the water streams, Like the bud of Lebanon in summertime.

Robert rightly appraised the mistaken notions of the commentators who attempt to make an apposition between 2:1 and 1:17. There is, Robert (RTF) asserted, not the least indication that the bride intends to abase herself. The identification of the bride with the vernal vegetation, and indirectly with the country which it characterizes, signifies salvation after trial, wth the prosperity it procures. Our verse, to Robert's ear, gives an eschatological sound. Similarly Robert interpreted 2:11–15 and 7:12–14[11–13E], in accordance with his hypothesis that the Canticle throughout has reference to the Exile and the Return.

The Targum ascribed this and the following verses to the assembly of Israel:

> Said the Assembly of Israel: "During the time that the Lord of the World makes His Presence dwell in my midst, I am like the narcissus (*narqîs*) fresh from the Garden of Eden and my actions are comely like the rose (*wardā'*) which is in the plain of the Garden of Eden."

Midrash Rabbah made a play on the first part of *ḥăḇaṣṣelet,* connecting it with the root *ḥbb,* "love." (Said the Community of Israel: "I am the one, and beloved (*ḥăḇîḇāh*) am I. I am she whom the Holy One, blessed be He, loved more than the seventy nations.") And on the second part, connecting it with *ṣēl,* "shade," and the name of the artisan Bezalel (because I made Him a shade (*ṣēl*) by the hand of Bezalel). The name Sharon suggested a play on *šîrāh,* "song," and recalled the Song of the Sea, Exodus 15. Other explanations made plays on *ḥabûyāh,* "hidden," and *bĕṣēl,* "in the shadow of" (hidden in the shadow of Egypt/the Sea/Mount Sinai/the ruling powers). Rabbi Berekiah made the wilderness the speaker. Said the wilderness: "I am the wilderness, and beloved am I, for all the good things of the world are hidden in me." Citations are then made of Isa 41:19 and 35:1. The rabbis also ascribed this verse to the Land (of Israel) which says: "I am it, and I am beloved, since all the dead are hidden in me (Isa 26:19). When God shall require them, I shall return them to Him and I shall blossom forth with good deeds like the *ḥăḇaṣṣeleṯ* and chant a song before Him (Isa 24:16)." Additional interpretations are given with the Community of Israel identified as the speaker.

Christian commentators vary in their attribution of the verse, but the majority of the Western Fathers, and some from the Eastern Churches as well, inclined to credit the speech to the Groom. For Origen, the plain was the level, cultivated ground, and the valleys, the rocky untilled soil: the former the people who cultivated the Law and the Prophets, the latter the untilled dwelling of the Gentiles.

The Bridegroom was thus the Flower among the Jews, but because the Law brought no man to perfection, the Word of God could not go on beyond the flowering to the fruition. The Bridegroom accordingly was made a Lily in the valleys of the Gentiles, a Lily such as even Solomon in all his glory did not match, for Solomon's flesh was not born spotless, without man's desire or woman's intercourse with man. When He became the Lily in the valleys, His beloved became a lily too, and so too His neighbor, that is, every soul who follows His example.

Aponius understood the flower of the field to refer to Christ before His Incarnation, but afterward He became the Lily of the valleys when he descended to this vale of tears to remove sin and falsehood and cool desire, as the lily has the qualities of whiteness, fragrance, and after it has been parched by fire, medicinal properties. For Ambrose, Christ was the Flower of Mary sprung from the Virgin's womb to shed the sweet perfume of faith throughout the world. A flower, though cut down, retains its fragrance, and does not lose it even when torn and pulverized. So Christ bloomed ever more beauteously with the shedding of His precious blood, breathing forth the gift of eternal life to those who were dead. The plain and valleys were seen as the perfect humility in Mary and in Christ's human nature, or the order of virgins in the Church as untilled soil whose flower and reward is Christ.

As applied to the Bride, the flower of the plain was understood as the Jewish Church, believing Israel under the Law and the Prophets, and the Lily as the Church after she had heard the Gospel of Christ. The lily, too, was applied to any holy soul, but above all to the Blessed Virgin as the fairest and most fragrant flower in the world, the peerless Virgin Mother of God. (Cf. Littledale.)

2a. *brambles.* Since the term *ḥôaḥ* regularly denotes a spiniferous plant (II Kings 14:9; Isa 34:13; Hosea 9:6; Job 31:40), it is likely that the reference is to the plants surrounding the *šôšannāh,* and not to the *šôšannāh* itself.

These words are clearly spoken by the Groom in praise of the Bride's beauty which surpasses that of the girls about her as a beautiful flower stands out among thistles. In the Fable of Jehoash mocking Amaziah, II Kings 14:9, the thorn or thistle is contrasted with the mighty cedar of Lebanon. In Job 31:40 wheat and barley are contrasted with thistles and weeds regarded as a useless nuisance.

2b. *girls.* Literally "daughters," meaning women in general, as in Gen 30:13; Isa 32:9; Prov 31:29, where *RSV* renders "women" instead of *KJ*'s "daughters."

The Targum made a contrast between this and the preceding verse:

> But when I turn from the path which is straight before me, and He removes His Holy Presence from me, I am like the rose that blooms among thorns which pierce and tear her petals, even as I am pierced and torn by the evil decrees in the exile among the nations.

In Midrash Rabbah this verse was applied to Rebecca (Gen 25:20) by virtue of plays on words that have one or two consonants in common (*ra'yāṯî* "my darling," suggested *ram'ay* "trickster," and that in turn *'ărammî,* "Aramaean"). Laban the Aramaean suggested Laban the Trickster and thus Rebecca was a flower among tricksters. Other interpretations applied the verse to the redemption from Egypt, the performance of acts of piety, and oppression by the secular powers. Rabbi Abun said: "This *šôšannāh* when the sun beats on it withers, but when the dew falls it revives. So Israel, while the shadow of Esau is ascendant, seems to be withered in this world, but when the shadow of Esau passes away Israel will blossom" (Hosea 14:6). (Esau here means Rome.)

Christian expositors related the lily among thorns to the Church against the Synagogue, the schools of philosophy, or political parties. The words were also applied to the inner Church of the elect surrounded by the outer Church of the called wherein were many reprobates who showed no grace or beauty in their lives. The Virgin Mary in particular was identified as the rose among thorns, the thorns being variously interpreted as slanderous tongues, her sufferings through the Crucifixion, and even her kinship with the unbelieving Jews (Peter Damiani). Littledale cited the Latin of the Christian poet Sedulius and translated:

As from the sharp thorns springs the gentle rose,
Stingless, and hides its mother with its bloom;
So blessèd Mary, come of Eva's stem,
A new Maid, purged that elder Maiden's sin.
Thorns bear the rose, Judea Mary bore.

3a. *apple*. The word *tappûaḥ,* Arabic *tuffāḥ,* is assumed to be derived from the root *npḥ,* "breathe, pant," with reference to its scent. In 7:9[8E] the smell of the bride's nostril's, or breath, is compared to this fruit. The nature of the tree and the fruit is uncertain and there has been no lack of suggestions: apricot, orange, lemon, quince, apple. LXX *mēlon* and Vulgate *malus* favor the apple, but Targum speaks of the *'eṯrôḡ,* "citron." The apricot, orange, and lemon(?), are recent importations in the area and the quince is unsuitable to the context of 7:9[8E] since its fruit is odorless though sharp to the taste. The occurrence of the word in place names (Josh 12:17, 15:53, 16:8, 17:8) tells us nothing of the nature of the tree. The apple tree figures again in 8:5.

The apple tree has special significance in the Sumerian sacred marriage mythology. King Shulgi invites his "sister," the goddess, or the priestess representing the goddess, into his garden or orchard:

I would go with you to my orchard[?]
My sister I would go with you to my
apple tree,
May the . . . of the apple tree be in my
hand.
(*SMR*, 100)

In another poem the goddess Inanna sings,

He has brought me into it, he has brought me into it.
My brother has brought me into the garden.
Dumuzi has brought me into the garden,
I strolled[?] with him among the standing trees.
I stood with him by its lying trees,
By an apple tree I kneeled as is proper.
(*SMR*, 101)

The bride also refers to the groom as "My apple tree that bears fruit up to its crown" (*SMR*, 96).

The pleasures and dangers of dalliance under the apple tree are proverbial and even enter into modern song, as "In the Shade of the Old Apple Tree" and "Don't Sit Under the Apple Tree." Scant wonder then that some interpreters have "accentuated the sensual note," as Robert put it, and even the frankly erotic. Robert felt that Joüon abused the symbolism in seeing the apple tree as the figure of the Tabernacle in the wilderness; rather, Robert suggested, God and his dwelling are in a way identified here as in 5:15 and the fruits symbolize the sacrificial meal, the same thought recurring in 2:4, 5:1, 8:5.

wild wood. Literally "trees of the forest." The *tappûaḥ,* whatever its nature, compared to the other trees of the forest is as far superior as the lotus compared to the thistle. The bride responds in kind to the praise she has just received.

3b. *boys.* Literally "sons," used like "daughters" above, to designate male youth in general; cf. Prov 7:7, "I saw . . . among the boys, a lad lacking a mind." Meek here notes that "the sons" is used in the Tammuz liturgies as a designation of the male votaries of the cult, and Ishtar is called "daughter." There is no need to appeal to cultic terminology here, since in both cases "the daughters" and "the sons" are common non-cultic terms for girls and boys.

3c. *In his shade.* This metaphor is often used of political protection (Judg 9:15; Ezek 17:23, 31:6,12–17; Hosea 14:8[7E]; Lam 4:20; cf. Dan 4:12) and of divine protection (Pss 17:8, 36:8[7E], 57:2[1E], 121:5; Isa 49:2, 51:16). It has been supposed that the sense of protection is here intended, but Rabbi Jose ben Zimra observed that the apple tree is shunned by all people when the sun beats down, because it provides no shadow (Midrash Rabbah, Song of Songs, Soncino ed., p. 99). There is, moreover, as Robert remarked, no hint of external peril from which the bride needs protection. In this context one could hardly miss the sexual sense of the metaphor, and Dom Calmet and Cornelius à Lapide saw here an allusion to spreading the skirt over a woman as signifying marriage; cf. Ruth 3:9; Ezek 16:8.

3d. *fruit.* The term *pĕrî* is often used metaphorically of the result or recompense of an action. In Prov 8:19 the word stands in parallelism with *teḇû'āh,* "income," and *NEB* renders "harvest/revenue."

sweet. The root *mtq* in the primitive sense applies to taste, the opposite of "bitter," and then figuratively to any pleasant activity, and especially erotic pleasure. In an episode in Ugaritic myth, the senescent father of the gods, El, after considerable preliminary effort, and remarkable patience on the part of the recipients of his amorous attention, succeeded in his purpose:

He bent, their lips he kissed
Lo, their lips were sweet,
Sweet as grapes.

As he kissed, they conceived,
As he embraced, they became pregnant.
(23[52].49–51)

Sweetness is especially emphasized in the Sumerian sacred marriage poems. The nuptial bed which the king craves sweetens the lap and the queen makes sweet the bed, cf. 1:16c.

The bride also speaks sweetly to the groom:

> Bridegroom, dear to my heart,
> Goodly is your pleasure, honey-sweet,
> Lion, dear to my heart,
> Goodly is your pleasure, honey-sweet.
> (*SMR*, 92)

Again she speaks to the king of her own sweet charms:

> My god, sweet is the drink of the wine-maid,
> Like her drink sweet is her vulva, sweet is her drink,
> Like her lips sweet is her vulva, sweet is her drink,
> Sweet is her mixed drink, her drink.
> (p. 94)

The groom is the "honey-man" of the gods who sweetens the bride:

> The honey-man, the honey-man sweetens me ever,
> My lord, the honey-man of the gods, my favorite of his mother,
> Whose hand is honey, whose foot is honey, sweetens me ever,
> My sweetener of the . . . navel[?], my favorite of his mother.
> (p. 96)

palate. The gums, palate, roof of the mouth, as the organ of taste, and perhaps also of sensation in osculation; cf. 5:16, 7:10[9E]. Meek suggested that *lĕḥikkî,* "to my palate," be shortened to *lî,* "to me," on metrical grounds. It is true, as Meek noted here, that ancient writers were no more infallible than their modern counterparts and metrical slips are found in all literatures. Until we know more about biblical prosody, the assumption of error on the basis of two syllables, more or less, is dubious.

3. The Targum related this verse to the giving of the Law:

> As the citron is lovely and praised among ornamental trees and all the world acknowledges it, so was the Lord of the World praised among the angels at the time He revealed Himself on Mount Sinai, at the time He gave the Law to His people. At that time, I longed to dwell under the shadow of His Presence and the words of His Law were as spice on my palate and the reward for my observances stored up in the world to come.

This verse is applied in the Talmud (TB Shabbat 88b) to Israel's zeal to do the Law even before hearing it (Exod 24:7). "Why were the Israelites compared to an apple tree? To teach that as the fruit of the apple tree precedes its leaves, so the Israelites give precedence to 'we will do' over 'we will hear.'" (The change of *tappûaḥ,* "apple," to *'eṯrôg,* "citron," in the Targum was apparently dictated by the consideration that the fruit of the apple does not precede its leaves, while that of the citron stays on the tree from year to year and thus may be said to precede its leaves.)

Among the multiple choices offered by Midrash Rabbah there is the identification of the apple tree with God on the day of the giving of the Law. The nations refused to sit in His shade, but Israel rejoiced to do so. Other comparisons between Israel and the apple tree related its times of blossoming and emission of fragrance to the giving of the Law and the departure from Egypt. The longing for the shade was applied to Israel's hopes by the [Reed] Sea, the anticipation of receipt of the Torah. The sweet taste of the fruit was referred to the twelve months the Israelites spent before Mount Sinai regaling themselves with the words of the Law, the taste sweet to Israel but bitter to the nations.

Christian interpreters found a host of allegories in the tree, the sons, the shade and the fruit. Gregory of Nyssan explained that when Christ took on the nature of man, He became one of the trees in the forest of this life, a fruitful one able to make even the wild trees of man fruitful. (Dante used this figure in the opening of the Divine Comedy). As an apple tree Christ shared the nature of the other trees in the wood of humanity and was tempted, like us, but remained sinless. The fruit of the apple tree as beautiful, fragrant, delicious, and juicy was compared to the Holy Eucharist. Aponius and Psellus identified the tree as the pomegranate (in agreement with the Arabic version), relating its ruddy and watery fruit to the bleeding side of Christ on the Cross, and the seeds to the members of One Church united in His body, crimson with His blood. The sons were explained as the Angels, or Angels who taste and see that God is good (Ps 34:8). (Cf. Littledale.)

4a. *brought me into*. Following MT and Vulgate *introduxit me*. LXX, Syriac took this and the first word of the following line as imperative, and some modern interpreters adopt this reading on the supposition that the damsel asks the friends of her loved one, or the chorus of young women, or some hearers not specified, to arrange to get her close to her beloved. With Robert, it seems preferable to accept the MT and assume that the versions were influenced by the imperatives of the following verse.

the wine house. This wine house has been a challenge to interpreters. Ginsburg rendered "that bower of delight," explaining that, wine being frequently used in this book for delight, the words are but a designation of the manifestations of love denoted in the preceding verse by the delicious apple tree. Delitzsch, however, conceded flatly, in a footnote, that in Hebrew "house of wine" means the house in which wine is drunk. Other critics proposed other meanings: cabaret, a hut in the vineyards where the watchmen rested and refreshed themselves, a banquet hall, a wine cellar, a vineyard, or a village near Shunem called Bet-hay Yayin.

One must agree with Robert that most of these interpretations are strange or unjustified, but his own explanation is no more convincing. The figure of the banquet, according to Robert, proceeds from the false hypothesis that the Canticle speaks of a marriage; moreover, one cannot invoke vs. 5 where it is certainly not a matter of a meal. The most likely sense is that of a wine cellar, a place where wine is stored and drunk. But what is this cellar? The naturalist schools sees it as an allusion to the nuptial chamber, and Wittekindt to the sanctuary of Ishtar, a place of sacred prostitution. But the safest way to arrive at the meaning, Robert suggested, is to ask the biblical texts. They gave answer to Robert that Palestine was always considered a country of vineyards, and that wine is always listed among the agricultural products, along with grain (Deut 33:28; Isa 62:8; Hosea 7:14, 9:2; Zech 9:17; Prov 3:10), or with grain and oil (Deut 7:13, 11:14, 12:17; Jer 31:12; Joel 1:10, 2:19,24; Ps 4:8[7E]; Neh 5:11, 10:40, 13:5,12, etc.). Moreover, it is doubtful that wine is only mentioned by the Canticle as a symbol of love. The thought expressed here is in full accord with that of 1:4,12,16,17. Thus Robert makes the "wine house" refer to the land of Palestine.

Robert's appeal to the biblical texts for the clue to the meaning of the wine house ignored a wealth of data relative to the uses of wine, especially in association with women and song in worship of the powers of fertility, which cult persisted for millennia in Syria-Palestine; cf. Isa 5:11–12,22, 28:1–3, 7–8; Jer 35:5; Hosea 4:10–14, 7:4–5,14,16, 9:1–2,4,10. The present verse recalls the royal chamber(s) of 1:4 to which the bride is brought and about which there is exultation and joy. The term "wine house," *bêṯ hayyayin,* is not found elsewhere in Scripture, but a similar term, *bêṯ mišteh hayyayin,* "house of the drinking of wine," occurs in Esther 7:8 as the designation of the place where the "wine feast," *mišteh hayyayin,* was held, Esth 5:6, 7:2,7. The usual term is *bêṯ mišteh,* generally rendered "house of feasting," but literally "house of drinking"; cf. Jer 16:8; Eccles 7:2. At Belshazzar's feast in the *bêṯ mištĕyā'* (Dan 5:10), the king and his nobles and the concubines and courtesans drank wine and praised the gods. This use of the sacred vessels taken from the Temple in Jerusalem may not have been unprecedented since they may have seen similar use in the drinking chambers (cf. 1:12a) in the Temple court (Ezek 40:17, 42:13) where an attempt was made to seduce the Rechabites into joining the holy toping in violation of their vow of abstinence (Jer 35:2). The attempt was unsuccessful (Jer 35:6,14). On the *bêṯ marzēaḥ* as a place for sacral feasting, drinking, and copulation, cf. p. 210–229.

4b. *intent.* This word (*deḡel*) in the present context has occasioned no little difficulty and discussion. LXX rendered as an imperative, "set love upon me," to correspond with the reading of the verb of the preceding line which was likewise construed as an imperative. Vulgate rendered *ordinavit in me caritatem.* Symmachus apparently read *diḡrû,* "heap upon me love." Graetz achieved similar sense by emending to *gaddĕlû:*

Führet mich doch in die Weinkeller, haufet auf mich Liebeszeichen.

The root *dgl* is used three more times in the Canticle, 5:10, 6:4,10, which suggests at least that the consonants ought not to be changed, but this has no bearing on the question whether in the present instance the word should be read as noun or verb. Ginsburg took *dgl* as a verb in the perfect or preterit tense, conforming to the perfect used in the preceding line, and attributed to it the meaning "cover," "shade":

He led me into the bower of delight, And overshaded me with love.

Many interpreters retain the MT reading *diglô,* but are hard put to find a convincing explanation of the line according to the presumed sense of the term *degel,* as "banner," "ensign," "standard." In Num 1:52, 2:2–3,10,17–18,25,34, 10:18,22,25, the term is repeatedly used in connection with the military units of the various tribes during their marches through the desert. They encamped and decamped each man according to his *degel.* The rabbis and the ancient versions always took *degel* to designate a military unit; LXX usually renders *tagma,* "unit drawn up in military order," and Vulgate uses various terms with this general meaning. Midrash Rabbah on Numbers 15 informs us that "*dĕgālîm* is nothing but armies," and the Midrash on Psalm 20 explains that one recognizes his *degel* by the *signum* or banner. In the Elephantine Papyri and in the Qumran War Scroll, the term is similarly applied to military units which are named after their commanders. The evidence for taking the primary sense of *degel* as banner or standard appears tenuous. The standard explanation has been that the supposedly secondary meaning "military unit" developed by metonymy from the original sense "banner" by which the unit was identified. The military metaphor in the present verse, however, remains troublesome.

Gerleman suggested a non-military sense, analogous to the term *ġāya* used in old Arabic drinking and love songs to designate an emblem hung on a house to indicate that a drinking fest was being held there. The wine house, however, in Gerleman's view, was in this instance not a place for drinking but for a love tryst. (One wonders why the two activities need to be separated.) Yadin considered this line in connection with the use of *degel* in the War Scroll and concluded that the word could not be taken either in the sense of military unit or flag, and proposed the emendation to *raglô,* "his leg," to correspond to the left and right hand mentioned in vs. 6. Transposing 4b after vs. 6, Yadin (1962, 62n2) proposed the rendering:

He brought me to the banqueting house
  He stayed me with flagons
He comforted me with apples
  For I was sick of love.

His left hand *was* under my head,
  While his right hand embraced me
And his leg was over me *in* love.

R. Gordis is on the right track (1969) in connecting *degel* with Akkadian *dagālu,* "see," "look." The meaning of the present passage, according to Gordis, is: "And his glance upon me is loving." Further pursuit of the Akkadian uses of the root *dgl* would have led Gordis to what appears to be the exact sense desiderated here. The noun *diglu* is used in Akkadian in the sense of "wish," i.e. desire or intent, e.g. in an Old Babylonian letter we have *šumma di-gi-il-ki alkimma UD.5.KAM maḫria tašbi,* "If (it is) your wish, come and stay with me for five days"; cf. *CAD,* III, 136a. Thus, a sense appropriate to the context is obtained: "His intention toward me (was) love." This sense was approximated by Ben-Yehudah (B-Y, II, 889) who posited the sense "admiration," based on Akkadian *diglu,* "cynosure" (*Bezold,*

Augenziel). If further elucidation seems called for, we have in ancient Mesopotamian art illustrations of the execution of the intent in question in the form of clay molds for mass production of these items of sacral pornography. The female bends over a jar and sips the beverage through a drinking tube while the male couples with her from the rear. No banners are in view in such scenes, but in one representation the male hoists a flagon. See Plate IV.

A striking parallel to this verse is supplied by one of the Sumerian *balbale* songs

> My beloved met me,
> Took his pleasure of me, rejoiced as one with me,
> The brother brought me into his house,
> Laid me down on a fragrant honey-bed.
> (*SMR*, 104)

4. The Targum made the Wine House the Academy and the banner of love the regimen of study of the Law:

> The Assembly of Israel said: YHWH brought me into the Academy of Research on Sinai to learn the Law from the mouth of Moses, the great Scribe, and the regimen (*ṭēqas*) of His Commandments I received in love and I said: "All that YHWH has commanded I will do and I will obey."

Midrash Rabbah did not devote a great deal of attention to this verse. The numerical value of the letters of *wdglw*, "and his banner," being forty-nine, was referred to the number of reasons for declaring a thing clean and the same number for declaring a thing unclean. There follows a juggling of the letters *dglw* to get the meanings "his babbling," "his thumb," "his omission," "his deceit."

Christian expositors found multiple meanings in the wine house and the banner of love. The introduction to the wine cellar, in accordance with the wording of Vulgate, was taken to mean admission into the Catholic Church where alone the wine of the Spirit is found. It was understood to refer to Holy Scripture, similar to the interpretation of the Targum. Some explained it with reference to the upper room in Jerusalem where the disciples were gathered on the Day of Pentecost (Acts 2:2). The wine house was also explained as the Altar of God where the Cup of Salvation, the Wine that makes glad the heart of man, is given by the Bridegroom to His love. Again it was understood to refer to the mystery of the Incarnation because Christ's body housed the Divine Word, the true Wine of the soul; and again to the contemplation of eternity in which the holy Angels, inebriated with the wine of wisdom, behold God face to face. Further, the wine house was interpreted as the heavenly mansion where the marriage feast of the Lamb is prepared.

The banner of love was generally referred to Christ's love. The rendering of LXX, "Bring me, etc." was interpreted as the Jewish Church asking the Prophets to lead her to Christ, and of the Christian Church appealing to the Apostles and Doctors for further instruction in the divine mysteries and guidance for their affections, or of postulants for the Religious Life requesting admission from Superiors and seeking instruction in the rule and order which they propose to follow. The wording of Vulgate "He set love in array over me," suggested the leader in the battle of love teaching that in all things love is the more excellent way, or as attacking the fortress of the heart with the invincible and irresistible power of love. (Cf. Littledale.)

5a. *Sustain.* The verb *smk,* "lean, prop, support," is used in Gen 27:37 of providing someone with food and drink and in Ps 51:14[12E] of the spirit. The use of the *Piel* here is unique, but the meaning appears to be the same as with the simple stem. To whom the masculine plural imperative is addressed is a matter of speculation. It could refer to the Jerusalem girls of vs. 7, since the masculine plural form is often used instead of the feminine in the imperative and the imperfect. It is possible, as a number of commentators have supposed, that the words are addressed to no one in particular, but are an outcry under the pressure of extreme emotion. As Delitzsch put it,

Like a pennon, the love of the king hovers over her; and so powerful, so surpassing, is the delight of this love which pervades and transports her, that she cries out:

> Support me with grape-cakes,
> Refresh me with apples:
> For I am sick with love.

Hirschberg asserted that all the familiar interpretations of this line miss the mark. Even if *sammĕḵûnî* could be understood in the sense of "strengthening by food," which he considered doubtful, raisin cakes and apples, he alleged, are not known as remedies for the alleviation of love-sickness or satisfaction of erotic passion. Accordingly, Hirschberg proposed to read *sm kwny k'ššyšwt,* "the perfume of my clitoris (or vagina)is like raisin cakes." Starkly but realistically the passage describes, according to Hirschberg, a familiar physiological fact connected with the arousal of feminine passion. This is unwarranted abuse of philology in the interest of eroticism.

The verb *smk* is not used in the Palmyrene and Nabatean funerary inscriptions, but the noun *smk'* is several times used as a designation of the meal, and the probable meaning of the term *gnt smk'* is given in *DISO* as "jardin de banquet funèbre."

raisin cakes. This word, *'ăšîšôṯ,* has been a vexation to translators and commentators. LXX *en murois,* "with perfumes," may reflect *bĕśāmîm,* "spices." Rahlfs emends to *amorais,* "sweet cakes." Symmachus' *oinanthē* appears to reflect the *sĕmāḏār* of 2:13,15, 7:13. Vulgate *floribus,* "with flowers," suggests the reading *ṣîṣôṯ*. *KJ*'s "Stay me with flagons" is based on the rabbinical explanation of the term *'ăšîšāh* in II Sam 6:19 as meaning "a jug of wine," *garbā' ḏĕḥamrā;* cf. Jastrow, *Dictionary,* 128a. Dom Calmet explained that the bride felt ill in the wine cellar and requested that they make her a bed of apples and a pillow of wine bottles! The singular form *'ăšîšāh* is used in II Sam 6:19 and I Chron 16:3 among the sacral foods which David distributed to the people at the conclusion of the celebration for the installation of the Ark of YHWH in Jerusalem, at which celebration David's wife Michal charged him with indecent exposure (II Sam 6:20). The word is connected with the term *'ešpār* which occurs only in these two passages, apparently cognate with the Arabic term *sufrat* which designates a sort of hardtack or biscuit of dates and cereal.

These *'ăšîšîm* are mentioned in Isa 16:7 in a taunting lament over Moab's imminent downfall. The taunt continues, Isa 16:12:

It will happen when he appears,
When Moab exerts himself upon the height,
When he enters the sanctuary to worship,
That he will not be able.

We know from the incident at Shittim, Numbers 25, the sort of worship for which Moab was notorious. The point of the gibe is that despite the vaunted *'ăšîšîm* which were supposed to give venereal vigor, Moab will be impotent when he attempts to worship the goddess. These "raisin cakes" were loved by the Israelites in connection with their pursuit of other gods; cf. Hosea 3:1. Jer 7:18 describes the making of cakes (*kawwānîm*) for the Queen of Heaven. "The children gather wood, the fathers kindle the fire, the women knead the dough to make cakes for the Queen of Heaven and pour libations to other gods." From Jer 44:19 we gather that these cakes were not only for the Celestial Queen but were apparently also made in her likeness. "When we were offering incense to the Queen of Heaven and pouring libations to her, was it without (approval of) our men that we made for her cakes to represent her (*lĕha'ăṣîḇāh,* to fashion her, i.e. to make an image of her) and poured libations to her?" Hirschberg, following a suggestion of Tur-Sinai (1948, I, 103n1) supposed that these cakes were in the form of the female organ, relating the term *kwn* to Arabic *kayn* (plural *kuyun*), clitoris, used *pars pro toto,* like Latin *cunnus,* for the entire organ. The custom of baking cakes in the shape of genitalia was widespread in antiquity. In the Greek Thesmophoria sweet cakes of sesame and honey in the form of the female organ, called *mulloi,* were carried about and offered to the goddesses (cf. L. R. Farnell, III, 99). It is likely that the common form of the cakes for the Queen of Heaven was the triangle or wedge, *cunnus,* representing the *mons veneris,* the oldest and simplest symbol for woman, as seen in the Sumerian ideogram. The passage in Jer 44:19 which suggests that the cakes for the Queen of Heaven were made in the form of the goddess is illustrated by a mold representing the nude goddess which was found in the palace at Mari; cf. A. Parrot, 1959, 1044, pl. XIX. The locus of the find, in the royal kitchen, suggests that it was used as a mold for the notorious cakes for the Celestial Virgin Queen which the Israelites also loved; cf. A. Malamat, 1971, 21, fig. 9). See Plate I.

The earliest attestation of worship of the Virgin Mary in Christian history involved the use of these persistent pastries for the Celestial Virgin. Epiphanius protested that women in Thrace, Scythia, and Arabia were worshiping the Virgin as a goddess and offering a kind of cake (*kollyrida tina*) whence they were dubbed Collyridians and reckoned heretical (*Haeres* 78).

Etymological approaches to the meaning of *'ăšîšîm/'ăšîšôṯ* have not achieved certainty, but are not without interest. The verb *'šš* is used just once in Isa 46:8 in the imperative of the reflexive stem in tandem with the imperative of *zkr,* "remember." Qimḥi suggested relating the form *hiṯ'ôšāšû* to the noun *'îs,* "man," in the sense of "make yourselves men." Connection with *'ēš,* "fire," has also been proposed, with the meaning "become incensed." Following Rashi's conjecture of the sense "become firm," Gesenius suggested connection with roots meaning "to cram, press together, make compact," either by treading, or stamping, or in any other way, comparing Arabic *'aṯaṯa* "tread," "stamp," "subdue," and *'assa* meaning in the factitive stem "to make firm." Thus *'ăšîšāh* would be a pressed cake of dried grapes.

The use of raisins in the cakes used in worship of the love goddess suggests a belief in their effectiveness as aphrodisiacs, apparently good for both sexes, as with the apples. On the notion that raisins and other dried fruits are efficacious energizers and preventative of enervation and debility, T. H. Gaster cited the testimony of Sir William Gull, M.D., before the Committee of the House of Lords on Intemperance in 1881, that he had always found raisins helpful. (Gaster, 1969, n. 333, p. 812.)

In Akkadian *ašišu* means "wise, sage" and apparently also something like overpowering" or "engulfing" as applied to *abūbu,* "deluge." A warrior, or the war goddess Ishtar, is characterized as *abūbu ašišu,* "an engulfing deluge"; cf. *CAD,* I, part II, 441a, and H. Zimmern (1915, 31). In Isa 46:8, in a taunt of the impotent heathen idols which cannot move but have to be carried, the root *'šš* is used in juxtaposition with *zkr* which has associations with male sexual potency.

5b. *Brace.* The basic meaning of this root, *rpd,* appears to be "spread," "underlay," "support." Arabic and Old South Arabic *rpd* have this sense. In Akkadian *rapādu* means "roam about." A noun of this root is used in 3:10 of a part of the structure called *'appîryôn* which Solomon built for himself. This form *rĕp̄îḏāh* appears to have a meaning similar to Arabic *rifādah,* "saddle blanket." The masculine plural noun *rĕp̄îḏîm* is applied to resting places in the wilderness, Exod 17:1,8, 19:2; Num 33:14. The verb is used outside the present passage only in Job 17:13, of spreading a bed, and in Job 41:22[30E], of the ventral scales of Leviathan spreading the mud. The term *byt hrpd* is used in Lachish Letter IV, line 5 and Torczyner (Tur-Sinai) interpreted it as "the bedding house," or "sleepinghouse." In this connection Torczyner proposed what he regarded as the correct translation of the passage under discussion: "Lead me to the vines, bed me at the trees."

Ugaritic *rbd* is perhaps cognate with Hebrew and Arabic *rpd, b* and *p* frequently interchanging in Ugaritic. The form *lrbd* occurs in broken context in text 2001.2.13. It is clear that this text, in spite of its fragmentary state, involves a banquet and perhaps sexual activity in which the principles are El, Baal, and Aštart. The hapax form *marḇaddîm* in Prov 7:16, used with the cognate verb, "with spreads I have spread my bed," has parallels in Ugaritic *mrbd/mrbdt* which occur in lists of cloth and clothing (1111:11; 2050:9).

Hirschberg (1961, 373*f*), in keeping with his interpretation of the preceding line, proposed to change *rpd* to *dpr* and emend the line to read: *dpr nyby ktpwḥym*. Arabic *dufr* signifies a pungent odor. The word *nîḇ*, or *nûb*, "hollow," would designate the vagina. (This word Hirschberg would also restore in Prov 5:20a as apposite to *ḥēq*, "lap," which would make a striking parallelism:

Why get carried away with an alien *cunnus*, And embrace the lap of a stranger?)

Thus Hirschberg produced the meaning "The scent of my vagina is like apples"; cf. 7:9d. Again, Hirschberg tampers with an impeccable text. The sense which he seeks to impose here is indeed found in 7:9d[8dE], but that is no warrant for the textual mayhem exerted to produce that sense here.

apples. Apples and apple juice were used in Mesopotamian incantations and rituals against impotency:

> [Incan]tation. The beautiful woman has brought forth love.
> Inanna, who loves apples and pomegranates,
> Has brought forth potency.
> Rise! Fall! Love-stone, prove effective for me. Rise!
> . . . Inanna . . .
> She has presided over love.
> Incantation. If a woman looks upon the penis of a man.
> Its ritual: either <to> an apple or to a pomegranate
> You recite the incantation three times.
> You give (the fruit) to the woman (and) you have her suck the juices.
> That woman will come to you; you can make love to her.
> (Biggs, 70 [*KAR* 61, lines 1–10] similarly, p. 74 [*KAR* 69, lines 4–5)

Stephan (p. 209) cited from the Palestinian lore collected by the indefatigable Dr. Tewfik Canaan a couple of proverbs on the effect of apples: "Apples do not satisfy hunger; they only console one (occupy one)," and the more significant variant, "Apples only stimulate the appetite." The "appetite" (*nafs*=Heb. *nepeš*) can refer to all sorts of desires, including the sexual, as M. Dahood has pointed out (1962, 71) in elucidation of Prov 19:2:

Without knowledge, desire (*nepeš*) is no good; The fast one with the "feet" sins.

"Feet" is a standard biblical euphemism for genitalia.

5c. *faint from love*. Robert rightly explained the construct "sick of love" as the genitive of cause, "malade par (le fait de) l'amour." His next remark, "Le cas est plutôt rare," applies to the grammatical point and not the malady, as indicated by the Joüon citation (129i). The verb *ḥly* does not mean "be wounded," as LXX *tetrōmenē* suggests. One may, of course, be sick as the result of a wound, cf. II Kings 8:29. Vulgate *quia amore langueo* seems to come closest to the sense. Jastrow attributed this line to a commentator who took it over bodily from 5:8, but then Jastrow added the comment, "There is only one cure for such a disease—the one set forth so naively in the following two lines" (His left hand under my head, His right hand embraces me). This presumes the mention of sickness which Jastrow would, nevertheless, delete. Again Jastrow's comment on the raisin cakes and apples of the preceding lines takes a cue from the mention of love-sickness: "The raisin is again, because of its sweetness, an erotic symbol, like the apple in the following line, to suggest that the love-sick maiden can be rescued from her languishing condition only by the caresses and embraces of her lover." The love sickness in question might involve a sort of nymphomania combining surfeit and insatiable desire, hence the appeal for the stimulants. In one of the *balbale* songs of Inanna the goddess speaks of fifty performances by her lover and it is he who reaches the point of surfeit and calls for release:

My precious sweet, lying by my "heart,"
One by one "tongue making," one by one,
My brother of fairest face, did so fifty
    times . . .
My brother, with staying [?] [his] hands
    on his hips[?]

My precious sweet is sated:
"Set me free, my sister, set me free,
Come, my beloved sister, I would go to
    the palace . . ."

(*SMR,* 104)

In a Ugaritic Baal myth, just before the god had to descend to the netherworld, he engaged in marathon copulation with a heifer (perhaps his sister Anat in the form of a heifer, a motif anticipating the Passiphae myth):

He lay with her seventy-seven times
She made him mount eighty-eight.
And she conceived and bore a male. (5[67].5.19–22)

In another episode, unfortunately fragmentary, Baal and the Virgin Anat are glimpsed *in flagrante* in a torrid love scene in which Baal performs thousandfold:

He waxed hot and grabbed [her] vulva
She waxed hot and grabbed [his] testicles
[Mighty] Baal copulated by the thousand. (11[132].1.1–3)

The text becomes increasingly fragmentary in the succeeding lines, but there is mention of Virgin Anat, pregnancy and birth, Virgin Anat and again Mighty Baal before the text peters out completely. Even Robert remarked that the perfume of the apple in 2:3 and 7:9[8E] excites love and symbolizes it, and that here it is given as a strengthener or refresher (*reconfortant*). The Syrian practice of breathing the perfume of an apple, especially in cases of sickness, was noted by Joüon. The sickness here is identified as connected with love and we are left to our own imagination as to the exact nature of the infirmity for which raisin cakes and apples are requested.

Recourse to stimulants to promote prolonged or repeated coitus, sacral or profane, has been long and widely employed, with resort to such things as alcohol, special foods, and drugs. The left-handed tantric ritual in India added to the five M's (*mada,* wine; *matsya,* fish; *mamṣa,* meat; *mudrā,* parched grain; *maithuna,* ritualistic copulation), as elements of the secret worship, one that does not begin with M, *bhāng, Cannabis indica;* cf. Agehananda Bharati, 1965, 70, 253, 301. On the use of opium and hashish in marathon sexual bouts, cf. A. Edwardes and R. E. L. Masters, 1962, 96*f,* 100–111.

The Targum made the sustenance, the stimulus, and the cure for this love-sickness the study of the Law:

> At the time I heard His voice speaking from the midst of the flame of fire, I trembled and shook. At last, with trembling, I approached Moses and Aaron and I said to them: "Receive you the voice of the Words of YHWH from the midst of the fire, and bring me to the House of Study, and sustain me with the Words of the Law, upon which the world is based, and put chains upon my neck, explaining the holy words which are sweet on my palate like apples of the Garden of Eden. And I will be occupied with them, if perchance I may be healed by them, since I am sick with love."

Midrash Rabbah on this verse begins with a series of plays on the word, *'ăšîšôṯ,* connecting it with *'ēš,* "fire," and relating it to two fires, the heavenly and the earthly, or the fires of the Written Law and the Oral Law, or the fires of Abraham, and Moriah, Moses and the bush, the fire of Elijah, and of Hananiah, Mishael, and Azariah. Another play related the words to laws (*hălāḵôṯ*) as "well-founded" (*mĕ'uššāšôṯ*). The apples were taken to refer to *haggāḏôt* which have a fragrance and taste like apples. The love sickness was applied to the Community of Israel and followed by a series of parables illustrating, or illustrated by, other biblical references, apparently losing sight of the point of departure.

Christian interpretations based on the LXX's "strengthen me with ointments, strew me with apples, for I am wounded with love," explained the ointments and apples in a variety of ways, the ointments as that poured forth by Christ, or as the graces of the Holy Spirit, the apples as the fruit of the Tree under which the Bride sat, or the apples that hung on the Tree (the Cross), or as discourses on divine matters, sweet to the palate of the Bride. The Vulgate, "Prop me with flowers, surround me with apples," suggested to Gregory the Great a mother calling her children around her bed to see their beauty and be comforted; the flowers are the younger and weaker offspring, beginners in the spiritual life; the apples are those who have progressed toward perfection. Similarly, Origen saw in the flowers and the apples the catechumens and the faithful, while Aponius saw them as all pure souls, and the Apostles. The flagons of *KJ* naturally suggested the chalice of the Holy Eucharist, and the apples the bread, the true medicine of the soul which longs for Christ. But one difficulty in accepting this meaning, apart from the fact that there is nothing to suggest that *'ăšîšôṯ* means flagons," was that the Bride speaks not to the Groom but addresses the friends with plural verbs. The love wounds or sickness were seen as a happy fever, not a consuming, but a perfecting fire, a happy disorder in which the soul relishes no earthly things, but only the taste of heavenly things, the love of God. The wound, according to Augustine, hastened the Bride's true healthfulness, for whoever is not so wounded (i.e. with the Divine Love) can never attain true health. (For these and more examples, cf. Littledale.)

St. Gregory saw the Bride's love-sickness as her wounding by Christ with "Love's Arrow." The subsequent verse was then taken to refer to Christ as the "Archer." At first it was the Bride herself who was wounded by the arrow, but then the bride becomes the arrow, as the purified soul seized with heavenly love. "Therefore she says: 'His left hand is under my head,' whereby the arrow is directed to the mark. But 'his right hand embraces me,' and draws me to Him and makes me light for the ascent." In this verse Gregory saw the true meaning of the philosophy of divine ascent. The human soul is the arrow which is set on the bowstring by Christ the Archer who shoots it toward the heavenly target and the force which carries it aloft is love's longing. (Cf. A. Nygen, 1932 , II, 229, on the Ascent and the Arrow.)

6. This verse, which is repeated in 8:3, needs little explication. There is no reason to take the nominal sentence as optative rather than indicative, "Let his left hand be under my head," unless one espouses the view that the reference is to the absent shepherd lover. It should be fairly obvious that the lovers are together and that the female is not addressing herself to a distant lover. The verb *ḥbq,* "embrace," "clasp," is used both of affectionate greeting (Gen 29:13) and of sexual embrace (Prov 5:20). In Ugaritic it is once used of hugging and kissing a stalk of grain, and of helping a goddess mount her ass, but all other occurrences apply to sexual embrace.

Robert remarked that the naturalist school gave this verse an erotic sense. Apart from an allegorical interpretation, it is hard to see how this could be avoided. Joüon thought that the embrace signified Yahweh's presence in the Temple. Robert agreed with Ricciotti that the situation is depicted in the preceding verse; the bride became faint and her beloved, standing (*debout*), receives her in his arms. There is nothing more to see in this scene, according to Robert, than reciprocal demonstrations of a passionate love. It is not clear how one can divine from the wording of this verse that the lovers are standing.

A rather striking parallel to this verse occurs in a Sumerian sacred marriage song:

Your right hand you have placed on my
vulva,
Your left hand stroked my head,
You have touched your mouth to mine,
You have pressed my lips to your head,
(*SMR,* 105)

Graphic illustration of this position, with details not mentioned in the texts, were mass produced from clay molds for the inspiration and edification of the faithful worshipers of the fertility deities in Mesopotamia.

The Targum made the two hands four miraculous clouds to protect Israel in the wilderness:

> While the people of the House of Israel were wandering in the wilderness, they were surrounded by four clouds of glory from four directions (winds of the earth), so that the Evil Eye had no power over them: one above them, so that neither heat of the sun, nor rain, nor hail could overwhelm them; and

> one from below carrying them as the male nurse carries the infant in his bosom; one ran before them three days' journey to flatten mountains and set up camps; it killed all the poisonous serpents and scorpions of the desert and spied out for them a proper place so that they could be occupied with the study of the Law which had been given to them by the right hand of YHWH.

Midrash Rabbah related the hands to the two tablets of the Law, the left to the first tablet and the right to the second. Other explanations applied the two hands to the fringes and the phylacteries, the *Shema'* and the *'Amidah* (or Eighteen Benedictions), the *sukkāh* and the cloud of the Divine Presence to come (Isa 60:19) and the *mězûzăh* (Deut 6:9). Rabbi Johanan derived from this verse the rule of Deut 11:22. "to love YHWH your God . . . and to stick to Him." How is this adhesion effected? With *His left hand under my head.*

Christian expositors were likewise creative in interpretation of the two hands. The left hand was seen as representing the divine support in the temporal needs, the right as the promise of eternal life; the pledge of the Holy Spirit and the blessedness of the Heavenly Country; the old Law and the new Gospel; in mystical contemplation the left represented the highest grade of intellectual meditation and the right denoted close union with God; the left represented the Manhood of the Eternal Word, the right the Godhead of the Crucified One, etc. (Cf. Littledale.)

7a. *adjure.* The causative stem of the verb *šb'* is used for adjuration or imposition of an oath, as against the use of the reciprocal stem for the act of swearing; cf. Gen 24:3,37. Jonathan made David swear a separate oath of love, I Sam 20:17, in connection with their covenant. The perfect is used in the sense of a present, as with *verba dicendi* (GKC, 106i). There is disagreement among interpreters as to the speaker, since the grammar here does not make clear whether the speaker is male or female. This adjuration recurs at 3:5 and 8:4, in the latter instance preceded by the same couplet as here,

> His left hand is under my head, His right clasps me,

but with omission of the reference to the gazelles and hinds.

Jerusalem girls. Some interpreters would expunge "Jerusalem" here, *metri causa,* but Robert rightly objected that this phrase is constant in the Canticle and would be incomprehensible thus truncated. The notions that the Jerusalem girls are the women invited to the marriage, or the ladies of Solomon's harem, or the heathen nations, or the tribes of Israel, were all scouted by Robert who would rather see here, if there is any historical import, the group of the first repatriates, as opposed to the bulk of the nation still in exile. It may be however, Robert admitted, a simple literary evocation giving the two principal personages a way to express their sentiments, and similarly Gerleman; cf. 1:5a.

7b. *gazelles or hinds.* LXX "by the powers and forces of the field," and similarly Targum, "by the Lord of Hosts and by the Strength of the land of Israel." Traces of polytheism were detected here by some of the "naturalist" critics, but Joüon considered it an allusion to the armies of angels and their chiefs. Codex Alexandrinus omitted "or the hinds" in 8:4, which suggests the possibility that the phrase may be a gloss here to ensure that *ṣĕḇā'ôṯ* not be misunderstood as part of the common title, "the Lord of Hosts." Modern critics are generally agreed in taking the words to designate cervine creatures. Proponents of the cultic interpretation found here no little support since these animals were sacred to Astarte. The reason for the goddess' special connection with these animals is not far to seek, since their beauty and amative propensities are part of the imagery of the world's love poetry. In Mesopotamian incantations to restore sexual potency, the stag is one of the amorous examples used to encourage the impotent. In a fragmentary incantation, a female urges the ailing male:

> With the love-[making of a mountain goat(?)] six times,
> With the love-making of a stag seven times,
> With the love-making of a partridge(?) twelve times,
> Make love to me! Make love to me because I am young! [(. . .)]
> And the love-making of a stag . . . Make love to me! [Incantation formula].
> (Biggs, text no. 9, p. 26, lines 4–8)

7c,d. in accordance with the adjuration and the regular use of oath formulae, the positive condition introduces a negative oath, the sanction or curse attendant on the violation of the condition being usually suppressed. (Cf. Pope, "Oaths," *IDB*, III, 575–577.) The Jerusalem girls are adjured not to arouse or excite love until it (love) is willing. In the light of the preceding appeal for the application of stimulants, the suggestion of Meek that the women were engaged in some rite of sympathetic magic which was intended to arouse love between the god and goddess at the proper season, viz. at the time when the growing season should begin, is highly provocative. Rituals and incantations for stirring up love are known in all times and places, and some of the ancient Mesopotamian incantations have already been cited.

7c. *incite . . . excite.* The root *'(w/y)r* in the simple and passival stems is used of being aroused or excited to some activity, and in the factitive and causative stems of arousing or stirring someone to action. The state of inactivity from which one is aroused need not be sleep; actually sleep is rarely mentioned, as in Zech 4:1; Job 14:12; Ps 73:20. The activities to which one is aroused are usually those that require extra effort, especially strenuous endeavors like war, work, and love. The common interpretation, that one of the lovers is asleep and the other cautions against disturbing his/her slumber, makes a tender scene but misses the point. The object of the excitation is love which has its whims. In Ugaritic the verb *'(w/y)r* is once used with the noun *ahbt*, "love," as the subject. El greets his erstwhile spouse Asherah, who has come to intercede on behalf of the up-and-coming young god Baal, offers her food and drink, and then mentions his love:

> Yea, the affection of King El will stir you,
> The love of the Bull excite you (*t'rrk*). (4[51].4.38–39)

Van Selms suggested that the days of active sexual intercourse between the divine pair were past and that El gallantly reminds his spouse of the good old days. It seems more likely, however, that the two are now estranged and that El attempts to revive the old feeling.

7d. *Love.* The word *'ahăḇāh* is here prefixed by the article, as in 3:5, 8:4,7. Elsewhere in the Canticle it is used without the article, 2:4,5, 3:10, 5:8, 7:7, 8:6. Some authors think that here it has the usual abstract sense, but others wish to see concrete application, *abstractum pro concreto,* with reference to one or the other of the two chief protagonists. Robert espoused this view and also considered this nuance indubitable in 7:7[6E]. The verb at the end of the present verse, Robert noted correctly, postulates a subject capable of will. It does not necessarily follow, however, that the subject must be a person. Words for love are virtually personified in many poetic uses and love certainly has a will of its own, fickle as it may be. Some interpreters ascribe the words to the bride and suppose that she speaks of the groom, as reflected in *KJ,* "nor awake *my* love, till he please." Others ascribe the words to the groom, "awake not my beloved until it pleases her" (Renan); Delitzsch rendered the adjuration: "That you arouse not and disturb not love / Till she please." The term *hā'ahăḇāh,* Delitzsch asserted, is not abstract for concrete, but love itself in the giving and receiving. In this he must be deemed correct, but for the rest his interpretation here, as throughout the Canticle, is bound to a preconceived theory of interpretation.

eager. The root *ḥpṣ* denotes pleasure, desire. The Arabic cognate means "to strive hard" for something. There is a second root *hpṣ* (**ḥpḍ*), used of bending wood in Arabic, and applied to the arched tail of Behomoth in Job 40:17, but it does not seem to have any likely application in the present instance. The emendation by Dussaud of *teḥpaṣ* to *'eṯ'appēq,* "je me ressaisisse," is quite unnecessary.

The adjuration Bettan took to mean that the maiden opposed the arousal of love by artificial means, preferring gentle, natural love. Gordis, however, regarded this as unlikely on the ground that there is no reference to these artificial means in the text, but the context implies that she is already experiencing passionate love in all its fullness. Accordingly, Gordis interpreted the verbs which he admitted most naturally mean "arouse, stir up," in the sense of "disturb," i.e. "interfere with" and "until she wishes" he explained as meaning "until love wishes (*scilicet*) to be disturbed, because it has been satisfied." Gordis rendered:

> That you disturb not, nor interrupt our love   Until it be satiated.

Both Bettan and Gordis missed the point. The love-sick lady's call for raisin cakes and apples is not a rejection of stimulants but a request for them. The adjuration can scarcely be an appeal not to be disturbed or interrupted in the course of love-making before satisfaction has been achieved. The root *'w/yr* never has the sense of interrupt, but always refers to excitement. The appeal for aphrodisiacs in one verse and the request not to excite love till it is willing are not necessarily contradictory. The stimulants are requested by the lady herself and there is no indication that she is ever averse to love.

7. The Targum transformed the adjuration by altering cervine fertility symbols to divine titles:

> Thereafter it was commanded of Moses by prophecy, and from YHWH's presence, to send couriers to spy out the land. And when they returned from spying they put out an evil report about the land of Israel and they were delayed forty years in the wilderness. Moses opened (with) his mouth and said: "I adjure you, O Assembly of Israel, by YHWH of Armies, by the Strong One of the land of Israel, that you do not presume to go up to the land of Canaan until it be the will of YHWH and all the men of war shall have finally died from the camp; as your brothers, the Ephraimites, presumed who went out thirty years before from Egypt, before the end had come, and they fell by the hand of the Philistines who dwell in Gath, and they killed them. But wait until the time of the forty years and thereafter your children will go up and take it."

Midrash Rabbah, similar to LXX and Targum, took the *ṣĕḇā'ôṯ* as referring to armies rather than gazelles and made the adjuration to be by the hosts of heaven and earth. The word *ṣĕḇā'ôṯ* also provoked plays on the word *ṣiḇyôn,* "will," with reference to the patriarchs who carried out the divine will, and also to the generation of the great persecution. The word was also divided into *ṣĕbā' 'ôṯ,* "army of a sign," the sign being that of the circumcision. The hinds of the field evoked Job 5:23 and were also identified with the tribes on the basis of Gen 49:21. Rabbi Ḥelbo noted that four adjurations are mentioned (here and in 3:4, 5:8, and 8:4) and explained that God adjured Israel not to rebel against the governments, not to try to hasten the end, not to reveal their mysteries to the nations, and not to go up from the diaspora by force. Other explanations were offered for the four adjurations. The burden of the adjuration, not to arouse or excite love till it please, was briefly but diversely explained, as referring to Isaac's love for Esau (Gen 25:28) and God's love for Israel (Mal 1:2). *Till it please* was referred to the heavenly kingdom and the deliverance which God will bring when it pleases Him.

This verse figures in a rabbinic discussion about leaving Babylon for Israel (TB Ketubot 111a). Samples of interpretation of this verse by churchmen, reflect the imagination and ingenuity of expositors and lack of reliable method or theory. On the basis of LXX, the field was taken to be the Church with each soul having its own plot to cultivate; the powers of the field were seen as the angels whom the elect souls are enjoined to imitate. The adjuration is that of one saint urging others to beseech God not to call Love to Himself by death before His own good time, to allow her to work in His service. Littledale, after reviewing various interpretations, suggested that the true mystical import is that the Bride urges all devout souls to be patient and not try to hasten God's good time.

After citing several modern efforts, from Dom Calmet's to Joüon's, Robert proposed that the exiled nation is in torpor, and that she should be aroused spontaneously by the free return of her heart to Yahweh (cf. Isa 51:17,

52:1). Robert further noted that God does not pardon sins without preliminary repentance (Jer 3:12–13, 4:14; Ezek 18:23–32, 33:11). Moreover, that repentance needs be perfect (cf. Hosea 14:4[5E]; Jer 3:21–22; Ezek 11:17–20, 36:24–29,31–32; Jer 31:33–34). Robert adduced ample evidence, however, of imperfect conversion in the post-exilic period. Thus the Canticle's author could say that the bride loves and sleeps—loves in the person of the few who remained faithful, sleeps because of the indifference and faults of the masses. Yet salvation cannot come without sincere, heartfelt, conversion. The freedom for, and the sincerity of the return to God constitute, for Robert, the teaching of this verse, whose fundamental importance is indicated by its position at the end of this section in 3:5 and 8:14. It is difficult to find anything new in the method or the result in this typical attempt by Robert to put the exegesis of the Canticle on a firm critical, historical basis.

8a. *Hark*. The argument that *qôl* must be rendered as an interjection, "hark" because the sound of the groom's feet could not be heard from the distant mountains, nor could he very well sing while running at such a speed as described here (Ginsburg, ad loc.), is patently absurd. The use of *qôl,* here, as in Isa 40:3, like English "hark," implies an auditory response. It is quite legitimate to render *qôl* as an interjection, "hark," or to paraphrase with Robert, "J'entends mon Bien-aimé" (cf. Joüon, 162e), but this has no real bearing on the interpretation. The assertion (Gerleman) that LXX and Vulgate did not understand the word *qôl* as an outcry is questionable. The same objection could be raised to *KJ* and *RSV,* "The voice of my beloved!" were it not for the exclamation point. It is by no means clear whether the sound which the bride hears is the lover's voice or the commotion raised by his speed. It could be either. Robert's argument that the groom does not begin to speak till vs. 10, is not compelling. The lover could have come running or flying and shouting or roaring at the same time. In the light of the subsequent characterization of his locomotion, it seems more likely that the reference is to the sound and movement of his speedy approach.

8b. *There*. The element *zeh* has here its original deictic force and is used virtually as an adverb (cf. GKC, 136d; Joüon, 143a). The same usage, "there he stands," occurs below in 9c.

8c. *Leaping*. This verb *dlg* is used in Isa 35:6 of the lame man leaping as a hart; in II Sam 22:30=Ps 18:30 of leaping a wall, or, more likely, reading *šôr* for *šûr,* leaping (like) a bullock. In Zeph 1:9 it is used of jumping over the doorstep.

8d. *Bounding*. The usual meaning of *qpṣ* is "draw together," "shut," e.g. "shut the mouth," Isa 52:15; Job 5:16; or the hand, Deut 15:7. The meaning "jump" is not met elsewhere in the Bible, but is attested in Aramaic *qpṣ* and Arabic *qfz* (with shift of *ṣ/z,* according to Geers Law).

8c,d. *mountains . . . hills*. These are standard poetic parallels, both in the Bible and in Ugaritic. Robert objected to Dom Calmet's explanation that the groom leaps over the mountains, although admitting that the obscure passage in Zeph 1:9 could be invoked in favor of this. It is useless, Robert remarked, to add to the hyperbole already evident in the description which represents the frantic running of the loved one in mountainous country.

The Targum applied the skipping and jumping to time off from servitude by virtue of the supererogatory merit of the Patriarchs and the Matriarchs:

> Said Solomon, the king: "While the people of the House of Israel were serving in Egypt, their complaint went up to high(est) heaven. Then, behold, the glory of YHWH was revealed to Moses on Mount Horeb and He sent him to Egypt to release them and to bring them out from the bitter oppression of Egypt. And they leaped over the terminal date by virtue of the merit of their fathers and skipped over the time of servitude a hundred and ninety years for the righteousness of their mothers, who are likened to the hills."

In the Talmud (TB Rosh ha-Shanah 11b) the mountains are also identified with the Patriarchs and the hills with the Matriarchs in connection with proof that the Patriarchs were born in the month of Tishri, since I Kings 8:2 identifies the seventh month as Ethanim and in Micah 6:2 *'ēṯānîm* stands in parallelism with mountains.

Midrash Rabbah referred this verse to Moses in different ways, and the leaping over the mountains to the passing over of calculated time periods in order to speed the promised deliverance. Similar application was made to the Messiah.

Christian expositors took some considerable exegetical and allegorical leaps with this verse. The voice of the Beloved was that of Christ and the present verse was seen as representing the last few moments before His Advent (cf. Isa 40:3; Heb 1:1). Another view made the voice the call to resurrection before the second Coming. His leaping and skipping was on Church, Synagogue, Gentiles and Jews, from heaven into the Virgin's womb, from the womb to the manger, from the manger to the Jordan, from the Jordan to the Cross, from the Cross to the grave, from the grave to heaven. Again Christ comes leaping to us as we study Holy Scripture, in passage after passage on the hills of the Old Testament, and on the higher and more conspicuous mountains of the New Testament. (Cf. Littledale.)

9a. *buck.* Two different words have fallen together as non-homologous homophones in Hebrew *ṣĕḇî,* one meaning "gazelle" (**ẓaby*) and the other "beauty" (*ṣb'* or *ṣby*). In II Sam 1:19 the play on the two words makes it difficult to decide whether to translate "buck" or "beauty." The parallelism here with *'ayyāl,* "stag," as in Deut 12:15,22, 14:5, 15:22; I Kings 5:3 [4.23E], makes it clear that the animal is intended. The swiftness and agility of the gazelle, and its beauty are all intended in the present passage.

9b. *young stag.* The word *'ōp̄er* occurs only in the Canticle, here and in 2:17, 4:5, 7:4[3E], 8:14. In post-Biblical Hebrew the term designates the young of an animal; in Arabic it is applied to the young of the chamois or ibex. (The semi-Bedouin in the area of Khirbet Qumran and En Gedi still take their domestic female goats to the vicinity of the cliffs in order to have them interbreed with the wild goats to improve the stock.) The word *'ayyālîm* is here used in the plural to indicate indetermination. LXX adds after this verse, "on the mountains of Bethel."

9c. *there.* Cf. 8b.

our wall. This word, *kōṯel,* occurs only here in the Hebrew portion of the Bible, but the Aramaic form is found in Dan 5:5 and Ezra 5:8. It is apparently a loanword from Akkadian *kutallu,* "backside," "back of the head." The word in Arabic, *kawṯal* or *kawṯall,* is applied to the stern of a ship. In Josh 2:15 Targum uses this word to translate Hebrew *qîr,* "wall."

9d. *Peeking.* This verb *šgḥ,* used only in the causative stem, is rare in the Bible. In Isa 14:16 it is used in a context which makes clear that the meaning is "to stare, look intently,"

> Those who see you will stare at you (and) ponder.

In Ps 33:14 it is used of God's surveillance of earth's inhabitants from the vantage point of the heavens. It is used also in the Hebrew of Sir 40:29 and 50:5, and in post-Biblical Hebrew and Aramaic. It does not appear to have cognates in other Semitic dialects.

9d,e. *in . . . through.* LXX renders the preposition *min* here as *dia* and Vulgate as *per,* and similarly most moderns, "through." Since the lover is outside the house, he looks in or through the window. The emendation of the masculine singular participles *mašgîaḥ* and *mēṣîṣ* to first person singular imperfects, *'ašgîaḥ* and *āṣîṣ,* in order to make the bride the subject who looks out the window from inside the house (Budde, Haupt, Dussaud, Staerk), is quite mistaken; the regular preposition used for looking out a window is *ba'aḏ* and *min* is never used in that sense. The preposition *b-* may also be applied to looking out a window, as in Prov 7:6.

9d. *window.* The word is determined with the article *ha-* and is plural, *haḥallônôṯ,* "the windows," as is also the parallel word *haḥărakkîm,* "the lattices." Delitzsch suggested that the plurals are to be understood as *synechdoche totius pro parte,* which is the same as the plural of categories; "but with equal correctness," Delitzsch asserted, "we conceive of him [i.e. the groom] as changing his standing place." The former explanation seems more likely, i.e. that the plurals are plurals of indetermination, than that the amorous voyeur runs from window to window. The word *ḥallôn,* apparently related to the root *ḥll,* "perforate," is the usual word for an opening in the wall for ventilation and light, a wind-eye or window. The meaning is sufficiently broad so as to apply to a window of a hut or a palace. In Ugaritic it is one of the terms used for the window in Baal's palace or temple which was the subject of protracted disagreement between the architect-god Koshar who wished to install a window and Baal who objected (the architect-god eventually prevailed). The biblical uses of the term apply to the windows in Noah's ark, in royal residences, temples, fortresses and private houses.

9e. *Peering.* This verb *ṣwṣ* is hapax legomenon, having apparently nothing to do with *ṣ(w/y)ṣ,* "blossom." There is a similar verb in Arabic *waṣwaṣ,* used of women peeping from behind the veil. The synonymous parallelism, window//lattice, peeping//peering, establishes the general sense.

lattice. This word, *ḥărakkîm,* is also hapax legomenon in the Bible, but is used in post-Biblical Hebrew. A verb *ḥrk* of uncertain meaning occurs once in Prov 12:27. Arabic *ḥaruka* means "move, be agitated," and apparently has no connection with this noun. The root is more likely *ḫrk;* cf. Arabic *ḫark,* "fissure." The word is simply a poetic synonym for window, like Ugaritic *ḥln//urbt,* or *'ešnāḇ,* "lattice," in Judg 5:28 and Prov 7:6. Perhaps the word designates window-lattice, like the *śĕḇāḵāh* through which Ahaziah fell, II Kings 1:2, Arabic *šibāk,* "lattice," "window."

That the bride is in some sort of house, is clear. Robert is probably right, but for the wrong reasons, that the house is in a city and that the city could only be Jerusalem.

Why is the lover outside the house playing the peeping Tom? In a Sumerian sacred marriage scenario there is an episode which may throw light on the situation for those who do not rule out in advance the possibility of relevance to the biblical song. The lover stands outside the beloved's house and inquires:

> My sister, why have you shut yourself in the house?
> My little one, why have you shut yourself in the house?
> (*SMR,* 97)

The lover here, although not mentioned by name, is the shepherd Dumuzi (cf. *SMR,* 98).

Exclusion of the groom from the house while the bride is preparing her toilet and undergoing various processes of beautification, just as the Sumerian goddess kept her lover waiting outside until she was properly prettified, is still a feature of peasant nuptials.

9. The Targum related the peering and peeping through the window to the inspection for the prophylactic blood of Passover and Circumcision:

> Said the Assembly of Israel: "At the time when the glory of YHWH was revealed in Egypt on the night of Passover, and He killed every firstborn, He rode upon the swift thunder-cloud and ran like a gazelle or a young antelope, and shielded the houses where we were. He stationed himself behind our wall and looked through the window, peered through the lattice, and saw the blood of the Passover slaughter and the blood of the circumcision which was marked on our doors, and He hastened from high(est) heaven and saw His people eating the festal-sacrifice, roasted with fire, along with bitter herbs and endives and unleavened bread, and He had pity on them and did not allow the Destroying Angel to destroy me."

Midrash Rabbah, recalling the leaping of the preceding verse, related the leaping to God's leaping from Egypt to the Reed Sea, from the Reed Sea to Sinai, and from Sinai to the future redemption. Another explanation was that the Holy One leaps from synagogue to synagogue or from one house of study to another, in order to bless Israel because of the merit of Abraham. The young stag behind the wall was related to God at Sinai (Exod 19:11) and the peering through the window to the speaking (Exod 20:1). The elusive gazelle was applied to the sporadic appearance and disappearance of Moses as (future) deliverer. The wall was explained as the western wall of the Temple (the only wall left standing after the destruction, the present-day Wailing Wall) which God swore would never be destroyed.

Among Christian explanations of the furtive gazelle, Gregory the Great saw it as Christ during the period when He was working miracles and enduring insults because He was hiding Himself in one way, but showing who He was in another. The wall was seen as human sin and weakness which prevent us from seeing Christ constantly, and yet He gives glimpses of Himself by making openings in the wall. This was seen as the same wall to which Hezekiah turned his face and wept (II Kings 20:2) because he could not yet behold his Savior. The wall was also seen as the partition separating Jew and Gentile, the Law which hid Christ. The window and lattice were given a variety of explanations, identified with the Prophets and the Apostles. Epiphanius saw the windows as the chief Messianic Prophets, Isaiah, Jeremiah, and Daniel. St. Bernard applied the apertures to our human weaknesses; he also saw the gaps and crevices in the wall as those in Christ's own body through which he looked out on suffering mortals to share and pity their sorrows. Again the wall was seen as the Holy Eucharist in which Christ shows Himself in part to those who feed on Him in faith. (For these and other examples, cf. Littledale.)

10a. This formula does not recur in the Canticle and some critics suppress it, on metrical or other dubious grounds. The use of the perfects *'ānāh . . . 'āmar,* also trouble some critics, as also do those in 3:1–4. Robert suggested that here it is not necessarily a matter of past actions, rather the bride recounts under the form of historical narrative a scene which is of itself outside of time and which localizes itself rather in the future; it expressed, for Robert, who was prepossessed with the notion of exilic reference, the ardent hope for a complete restoration of the nation. How this could be seen in a simple cliché, "he spoke and said to me," passes understanding. The two verbs are frequently used coordinately in Job and Daniel. The stereotyped formula is reflected in the cliché of the Gospels, "Jesus answered and said."

10b. *Arise.* (Vulgate and some MSS of LXX add *hasten.*) The so-called ethical dative, or *dativus commodi,* is difficult to render into idiomatic English; "arise thou for thyself" is neither good prose nor poetry. Reconstructions of the situation vary according to theories of interpretation. Delitzsch supposed that Solomon again passes, perhaps on a hunting expedition into the northern mountains after the winter rains, which made them inaccessible, are over; and after long waiting, the maiden again sees him, and he invites her to enjoy with him the spring season. With *qûmî,* "arise," he calls upon her to raise herself from her stupor and follow him. Joüon explained that Yahweh invites Israel to come to the desert and supported this with appeal to Jer 2:2. For Robert, however, the situation was quite different. The nation Israel is like a captive, asleep in its own land, and Yahweh makes a joyous appeal which seems to presage immediate salvation. The true sense of the appeal is revealed by the parallels in Isa 51:17 and 52:2. Again, for Robert it is a matter of the collapsed and humiliated bride, the nation, shaking off her torpor.

10. The Targum interpreted this verse as the divine call to Israel, God's beloved, to flee from slavery in Egypt:

> And at morning time my Beloved answered and said to me: "Get you up, O Assembly of Israel, my beloved from of old, beautiful in deeds; depart, go forth from the servitude of the Egyptians.

Midrash Rabbah understood the redundant use of the two verbs of speaking thus: "He spoke to me by the agency (hand) of Moses and said to me by the agency of Aaron." The feminine imperative "arise" was addressed to the daughter of Abraham (Gen 12:1). "My fair one" means the daughter of Isaac who drew close to Me and glorified Me on the altar. "And come away" was addressed to the daughter of Jacob who listened to his father and his mother (Gen 18:7).

The call to rise and come away provided Christian interpreters ground for exhortation of the faithful to rise from worldly pleasures and earthly things and come away from this world to Him who had overcome it. Rupert of Deutz ascribed the summons to the Archangel Gabriel addressing Mary: "Thou, the Heavenly Sender of the message would say, 'My love for thy lowliness, My dove for thy gentleness, My fair one for thy purity, come. Come, Mary, come, for Eve hath fled to a hiding-place. Come, and believe the Angel bringing thee glad tidings; for Eve believed the whispering serpent. Come, and crush the serpent's head, for Eve was deluded with the head, and tempted with the belly, and tangled in the tail of the serpent. Come, and say, Behold the handmaid of the Lord. For Eve hid and excused herself alike. The serpent, said she, deceived me, and I did eat. This is the Voice of My Beloved, and He saith this to me, Rise up by faith; hasten by hope, come by charity.'" (Cf. Littledale.)

11a. *winter.* The word *sĕṯaw* (Qere *sĕṯāyw*) is hapax legomenon in the Bible, but occurs in Old Aramaic, Judeo-Aramaic, and Syriac. Its Arabic cognate *šitā'* in the dialect of Jerusalem is the common word for rain as well as winter, a matter easily understandable to those who have experienced Jerusalem winters.

11b. *rain.* The word *gešem* always designates heavy rain, as in Gen 7:12, and is occasionally accompanied by words to emphasize the point, I Kings 18:41,45; Ezek 13:11,13.

over, gone. The two asyndetic verbs, *ḥālap̄ hālaḵ,* the latter followed by the *dativus commodi, hālaḵ lô,* "it has gone for itself," are similar in orthography and sound. Zapletal suppressed *hālaḵ lô* as dittography for *ḥālap̄,* while Meek suggested that *ḥālap* be deleted on metrical grounds as a gloss to *hālaḵ.* There is no warrant for deleting either word; the two verbs together emphasize the point that the rainy season is completely past, over, and gone.

11. The Targum identified the winter with its incessant rain as the misery

of the servitude in Egypt, mentioned in the covenant with Abraham (Gen 15:13):

> For, lo, the time of servitude, which is like the winter, has ceased, and the years of which I spoke to Abraham between the parts have been cut short, and the bitterness of the Egyptians which is compared to constant rain is over and gone and you will not again see them forever.

Midrash Rabbah related the winter to the four hundred years which Israel had been sentenced to sojourn in Egypt, and the rain was related to the two hundred and ten years that they were actually there. The question was raised, "Are not 'rain' and 'winter' the same thing?" Rabbi Tanḥuma said: "The real hardship (of winter) is its rain. So the real bondage of Israel in Egypt was eighty-six years, from the birth of Miriam." The name Miriam is then explained (erroneously) as meaning "bitterness," with reference to Exod 1:14.

Early Christian expositors generally applied this verse to the Gospel revelation which ended the rigor and harshness of the Jewish Law on the one hand and the Gentile idolatry on the other. The Sun of Righteousness having dispelled the rain of sin and error, the Saints, Apostles, and Martyrs spring up like flowers in the new field of the Church. The winter and rain were also understood as the time of Christ's passion and the flowering of Spring as His Resurrection. (Cf. Littledale.)

12a. *Blossoms*. This form, *niṣṣānîm,* is unique in Scripture. The usual forms are *nēṣ* (<*niṣṣ*) and *niṣṣah;* cf. Gen 40:10; Isa 18:5; Job 15:33. The present form is simply the basic pattern *niṣṣ* with the *-an* afformative. The root meaning of the word is related to brightness; cf. Ezek 1:7 where the participle *nōṣēṣ* is used of the glistening or sparkling hooves of the creatures which formed Yahweh's hybrid vehicle. The spring flowers of Palestine are a striking spectacle. From the end of the winter rains until May, the uncultivated land is spread with tapestries of wild flowers in brilliant and varied hues.

12b. *Pruning time*. Or "singing time." It is difficult to decide here between the two meanings of *zāmîr,* "pruning" or "singing." The ancient versions and authorities, LXX, Aquila, Symmachus, Vulgate, Targum, Rashbam opted for "pruning"; Rashi, Qimḥi, Ibn Ezra, and most moderns favor "singing." Luther rendered simply "spring" (der Lenz). The objection to pruning is that it supposedly comes too late in the year, around July–August, to suit the present vernal setting. The Gezer Calendar places the two months of pruning, *yrḥw zmr,* between harvest and ingathering. The present passage suggests that pruning or singing time came in the spring not long after the end of the rains and the appearance of the flowers. Isa 18:5, cited below, appears to confirm this impression. On pruning, cf. G. Dalman, IV, 330*f*. Whether taken as pruning or singing, the term *zāmîr* gives aid and comfort to the proponents of the liturgical or cultic interpretation, since all applications of the term to singing refer to cultic song, as Ehrlich pointed out (VII, 7); Meek inclined to the meaning "singing," noting that this same word in Akkadian appears in the title of Tammuz ritual songs.

KJ interprets in italics "the time of the singing *of birds* is come." Delitzsch noted as regards bird-song that beside this passage the use of *zmr* for the singing of birds is not demonstrable; Arabic *zamar* is used only of the shrill cry of the ostrich, and particularly the female ostrich.

The rendering "blossoms" for *niṣṣānîm* above was influenced by the observation that all occurrences of its cognate form *niṣṣāh* are connected with the budding of the vine and the development of the green grape clusters, and, in one crucial instance, with the process of pruning. In Gen 40:10, Joseph in his dream saw the vine bud blossom and ripen instantly. In Job 15:33, the picture is of the vine shaking off its green grapes and the olive tree tossing its buds or blossoms. The most instructive passage, however, is Isa 18:4–6:

Thus said Yahweh to me:
"I will look calmly from my dwelling
As the heat glistens from the sun,
Like the dew cloud in the heat of
harvest."
For before the harvest,
When the budding is done,
And the blossom becomes grapes,
He will lop the shoots with pruning
hooks,
The suckers he will strip away.
They will be left together
For the birds of prey of the mountains
And the beasts of the earth.
The mountain birds will summer,
And all the earth beasts winter there.

The mention of *niṣṣāh,* "blossom," here in connection with pruning before summertime appears to strengthen the choice of pruning over singing in the present passage. It is possible, even likely, that the poet was aware of the possible ambiguity of the *zmr* in the present passage and used it deliberately for the provocative double entendre.

In the Ugaritic poem called "The Birth of the Beautiful Gods" which is a sort of sacred marriage myth and ritual, there is in the ritual portion which precedes the detailed account of the ups and downs of the senescent El, before he is able to consummate union, mention of a vine-pruning ritual:

Death and Evil sits.
In his hand the scepter of sterility,
In his hand the scepter of widowhood.
Let the vine pruners prune him,
Let the vine binders bind him.
Let them lop his tendrils like a vine.
(23[52].8–11)

12c. *turtledove.* The *tôr,* Latin *turtur,* is mentioned in Jer 8:7 along with other migratory birds that know and keep to their proper times. The return of the turtledoves to Palestine-Syria in early April is a notable event for bird watchers. The sound of their cooing, a subdued and sorrowful sound, is a sure sign of spring; cf. E. F. F. Bishop, 1967, 26.

12d. *in our land.* A number of critics would delete *bĕ'arṣēnû,* "in our land," as unnecessary repetition after the occurrence of "in the land" at the end of vs. 12a. The line is considerably overweighted by the prosaic and useless element and it seems best to eliminate it. Zapletal attempted to rectify the matter by inserting *sĕmāḏār* from the following verse. Robert, naturally, preferred to retain "in our land" in keeping with his fixation on the Return. The suffix "our," for Robert, here and in 1:16–17 and 2:9 refers to the groom and the bride, Yahweh and Israel.

12. The Targum continued to relate this verse, as the preceding, to Gen 15:13–14, with a precise translation of Gen 15:14:

> And Moses and Aaron, who are likened to palm branches, appeared to perform miracles in the land of Egypt. The time of the extirpation of the firstborn arrived and the voice of the Holy Spirit of Redemption of which I spoke to your father (already you have heard what I said to him): "The nation which they shall serve I will judge, and afterwards they will go out with much property." Now I wish to do what I swore to him by my Word.

Midrash Rabbah with a pun on *niṣṣānîm,* "flowers," and *nāṣôḥôṯ* "victors," related the verse to the appearance of Moses and Aaron in Egypt (Exod 12:1). Taking *zmr* in the sense of "pruning," wordplays were made on cutting off the uncircumcised or pruning the Egyptians and their idolatry. The root *zmr* was also taken in the sense of "sing" and connected with the Song at the Sea (cf. Exod 15:1–2) and the Law (Ps 119:54). The voice of the turtle (*tôr*) was applied to Moses as a good spy or explorer (*tayyār*), with reference to Exod 11:4.

In the Talmud (TB Ta'anit 25b, Yoma 21a) the word *tôr,* "turtledove," was taken as the Aramaic form of the word for "bull" and applied to the mythical rain-bull Ridyā seen as a three-year-old calf standing between the upper and lower deeps; cf. Ps 42:8[7E].

Among Christian interpretations of this verse, the blossoms were seen as the Saints, Apostles and Martyrs springing up like flowers in the new field of the Church. The pruning time was related to John 15 where the Father as vinedresser removes the useless branches from the True Vine. The individual soul also needs to prune itself to remove faults and offenses so that the beautiful fruit may be ripened by the Sun of grace. The sense of singing, rather than of pruning, was referred to the Blessed Virgin's chanting of the glory of the Incarnation, the Baptist crying in the wilderness, and the preaching of the Apostles. The voice of the turtledove reminded Nicolaus de Argentina of the Seven Words from the Cross. (Cf. Littledale.)

13a. *ripens.* The verb *ḥnṭ* is used elsewhere in Scripture only in Gen 50:2,26 where it is applied to the embalming of Jacob and Joseph in Egypt. No suitable sense is suggested by this usage, since figs are not particularly noted for a balmy or spicy smell. The most likely explanation appears to be the connection with the Arabic factitive stem *ḥannaṭa,* applied to the ripening of fruits. The fig begins to ripen with reddish and yellowish streaks from the base of the fruit upwards. The term for wheat, *ḥiṭṭāh* (<*ḥinṭat*) may be related to this root by reason of its coloration in ripening.

The rabbis applied terms for the various stages of the fig's development to that of a woman (TB Niddah 47a), an unripe fig, a fig in the early ripening stage, and a ripe fig. She is like an unripe fig while yet a child, and in maidenhood like a fig in its early ripening.

fruits. The word *pag*(*g*) is hapax legomenon. Aramaic *paggāh* and Arabic *fagg*, or *figg* designate the green, unripe fruit of the fig or date. English does not appear to have a specific single term for young figs.

The budding of the fig tree is a sign of spring and harbinger of summer, as we are told in Mark 13:28: "From the fig tree learn its lesson: as soon as its branch becomes tender and puts forth its leaves, you know that summer is near." This is the primary point of the present line. The sacral sexual associations of the fig, however, suggest further possible implications. On the basis of Gen. 3:7, the Tree of the Knowledge of Good and Evil whose fruit awakened sexual awareness in our first parents has been supposed to be the fig. (Cf. TB Berakot 40a, Midrash Gen Rabbah 15:7.) The fig was sacred over a vast area of Asia, from India to the Mediterranean. The *Ficus religiosa* of India is venerated by both Brahmins and Buddhists. It was under a fig tree that Gautama Buddha was endued with divine power. The venerable tree in Anarjapoora, Sri Lanka, said to have been planted in 288 B.C., is believed to be descended from a branch of the Buddha's tree. The fig was featured in the cult of Dionysus/Bacchus and Demeter/Artemis. Statues of Priapus were made of fig wood and maidens of Athens wore garlands of figs and carried fig cakes in the procession of Athena. The twin founders of Rome were suckled under the *Ficus ruminalis*. Figs were a favorite food of the poor, and esteemed by Roman epicures as well. The remains of offerings at the Isis temple in Pompeii indicates that figs were a major item. (Cf. PW, s.v. Feige, xviii Aberglaube and xix Sakrales.) The fig persists as a potent symbol in the obscene gesture called "making a fig" (*far la fica*) and in amulets in the form of a hand making the fig sign (*mano in fica*) worn to ward off the evil eye. The fig gesture and the amulet have been compared to the *sheila na gig* (nude female with exposed vulva) carved on some old Irish churches to affront evil thoughts (cf. F. Huxley, 1974, 56, 63).

The similarity of the word for the figs' young fruit, *pag(g)*, Arabic *fajj, fijj*, to Latin *fic(us)* and Old English *fygge* is striking. The Arabic word, however, is applied to the young fruit of a variety of plants, including melons.

13b. *in bloom. The term sěmāḏār*, used here as attributive accusative, "the vines (being) in bloom," occurs in the Bible only here, in 2:15c, and 7:13c. The word is also found in Judaic-Aramaic, Syriac, Mandean, and neo-Hebraic. It has been suggested (cf. KB, 661a) that it is composed of prefix *s*- and *mdr*, "turn around," in neo-Syriac. W. F. Albright has suggested that Aramaic *smāḏrā* may stand for older **summaddar* and be derived from *sumaktar*, attested in the meaning "slave born in the house," Latin *verna*. An original sense like "blossom" would thus be quite possible, according to Albright. On the proposed Cossean origin of the term, cf. K. Balkan, 1954, 138*ff*. In Albright's view, there is no proof of Cossean origin and alternatively he suggests that the word may be Indo-Aryan, or from some Anatolian tongue; cf. Albright, 1963, 2*fn*3.

The term has been variously translated. LXX rendered *kyprizousin* as parallel to the following clause, "they gave a smell." Vulgate rendered *florentes*.

In rabbinic usage the term designates "bud." Luther, accordingly, rendered "die Weinstocke haben Augen gewonnen"; *KJ* "and the vines *with* the tender grapes give a *good* smell"; *RSV* "and the vines are in blossom; they give forth fragrance." It has been supposed that the term designates a kind of wine flavored with vine blossoms. The term in the form *samadir* was found on two labels excavated at Nimrud in 1952 and published by Barbara Parker (1961, 19 — ND 2303, 2304). The context indicates that *samadir* is a plant or blossom from which an (aromatic?) oil is pressed; cf. J. Greenfield, 1965, 257a). An inscription on a jar found by Y. Yadin at Hazor has been read *lpqḥ smdr*, "(belonging) to Peqah semadar," the first word perhaps referring to the usurper king of II Kings 15:25 and the latter to the content of the jar.

13d. LXX adds here, as in vs. 10 above, "my dove" after "my fair one."

13. The Targum applied the ripening figs to the youth and infants of Israel who sang the Song at the Sea:

> The Assembly of Israel, likened to the first fruits of the figs, opened her mouth and sang the Song (*šîrĕṭā'*) by the Reed Sea. Even youths and sucklings praised the Lord of the World with their tongue. Immediately, the Lord of the World said to them: "Get you up, O Assembly of Israel, My beloved, My beautiful one, go hence to the land which I promised to your fathers."

Midrash Rabbah applied the green figs to the sinners of Israel who perished in the three days of darkness (Exod 10:22*f*) and the vines in bloom to those who repented and were delivered. The call to rise up and come away was related to Israel's leaving the wilderness, to God's message to Israel through the word of Daniel and Ezra, and through Elijah and the Messiah.

The green figs were seen by some Christian interpreters as representing the Synagogue which was unable to produce mature fruit. As applied to the Church, the young fruit might designate the early Martyrs and Saints, and Bernard of Clairvaux applied the sweet figs to the gentle and meek and the produce of the vine to the zealous and fervent. Others saw the green figs as the first fruits of the devout soul, immature, but with the prospect of better fruit to come. (Cf. Littledale.)

14a. *My dove.* The term *yônāṯî*, is augmented in 5:2, "my sister, my darling, my dove, my perfect one," and again in 6:9, "my dove, my perfect one." The gentleness and amativeness of the dove make it a fitting universal symbol of love and peace. "My dove" is also attested as a term of endearment in classical writings (cf. PW, IV. 2R [1932]. Sp. 2495). John Gay in his *Fables* put it epigrammatically:

> In constancy and nuptial love I learn my duty from the dove.

The dove is the lovebird *par excellence* and the symbol and attribute of the love goddesses, Ishtar, Atargatis, Aphrodite. At Babylon in the doorway of the Temple of Ninmaḫ (Exalted Lady) R. Koldewey found a terracotta model of a dove in a brick box (Koldewey, 1911, p. 7, fig. 4; cf. p. 19, fig. 20). At Beth-shan in the older strata of the Astarte Temple were found small shrines with figures of doves; cf. A. Rowe, 1940, II, 28. Doves and sparrows accompanied Aphrodite (Hesiod *Theogony* 188–200). The dove's prodigious erotic propensities made it powerful medicine in love magic, from ancient to recent times. The Mesopotamian prescriptions for sexual potency make use of a number of birds, some of which may be doves. The medieval faith in a dove's tongue concealed in the mouth for effective kissing, or the Pennsylvania "Dutch" prescription of a dove heart (neither of which is large enough to interfere with osculation) at least gave added confidence (cf. E. S. Gifford, Jr., 1962, 44–47, on doves and other birds, sparrows, swallows, even chickens, in love magic).

cliff crannies. Doves make their nests in cliff-side clefts and caves; when frightened they are reluctant to emerge. Jer 48:28 applies this figure to the stricken Moabites:

Leave your cities and dwell in the cliff,
O inhabitants of Moab!
Be like the dove that nests
In the sides of the cavern's mouth.

There are two localities known as "Valley of Doves" (Wadi Ḥamām) in Palestine, one near Jericho and the other near the northwest corner of the Sea of Galilee, north of Majdal. Tristram saw immense flocks of doves breeding in the ravines near Jericho, and in the precipitous cliffs of Wadi Ḥamām thousands of doves appeared with a rush and a whir that could be felt like a gust of wind. The Galilean Valley of the Doves is "a wild pass closed in between two perpendicular rocky walls perforated with numerous caves" (W. M. Thomson, 1865, 269; cf. Bishop, 1967, 25). This is the picture we get in Isa 40:8:

Who are these that fly up like a cloud,
Like doves to their crannies?

The same picture of the frightened dove is applied in the *Iliad* (xxi 493) to the huntress-goddess,

Artemis ran off in tears, as a wild dove,
attacked by a diving hawk,
will fly to a hollow rock,
A narrow cleft where she
cannot be taken.
(Tr. Robert Fitzgerald)

In Ps 74:19a the persecuted community may be represented by the turtledove:

Deliver not to the beasts
The life of your turtledove.

Dahood, however, interpreted *twrk* as "those taught by you," and *NEB*, connecting the root with *wdy* rather than *wry*, rendered, "Cast not to the beasts the soul that confesses thee."

cliff. The term *sela'* is applied to craggy cliffs as inaccessible refuge and dwelling for both man and beast. Arabic *sil'* denotes a cleft in rock. The *sela'* par excellence was the stronghold of the Edomites, the formidable rock castle Umm el-Biyārā in Petra, II Kings 14:7. The cliffs serve also as the abode of the eagle, Job 39:28, and the rock badger or cony, Ps 104:18; Prov 30:26. God is also a *sela'* and a fortress, II Sam 22:2.

14b. *covert steep.* LXX "near the rampart," Vulgate *in caverna maceriae.* The term *sēṯer,* "covert," usually designates a hiding place. A parallel to the present phrase is found in I Sam 25:20 when David accosted Abigail as she was riding *bĕsēter hāhār,* in a mountain defile. The word *maḏrēḡāh* occurs elsewhere only in Ezek 38:20, in the plural, in parallelism with mountains and walls. The Arabic cognate *madrajā* designates the rugged pass or defile between mountains. In post-Biblical Hebrew the term is applied to stairs.

Robert rightly remarked that the result of these expressions is that the bride is in an inaccessible place and that the groom cannot get to her. The sequel shows that he cannot even see her. Renan imagined that the lover is regarded as being outside the seraglio, at the foot of a terraced tower. Delitzsch supposed that this verse showed that the girl lived in the mountains, remote and inaccessible, far removed from intercourse with the world. Joüon thought that the rocks and cliffs might allude to the regions last occupied by the Israelites before they crossed the Jordan (Num 33:41–50). Robert, however, pointed out that many places in Palestine would suit the description here. According to Robert, it is not a question of a house or a town, but it is clear that the bride does not make herself available to the groom; he cannot approach, see, or hear her. The separation is not his doing, since he entreats her earnestly. Thus Robert is reminded of the psychological situation allegedly presupposed in 2:7 and 5:2; as deeply as she may be attached to Yahweh, the nation has not fully returned and he presses her to decide.

14f. *form.* The rendering "countenance" or "face" (*KJ, RSV, NEB, JPSV*) is hardly adequate for the term *mar'eh,* "appearance," which includes the total visual impression. Luther rendered "Gestalt," and *AT* "form."

14. The Targum equated the dove in the clefts of the rock with Israel's predicament at the Reed Sea:

> And as the wicked Pharaoh pursued after the people of Israel, the Assembly of Israel was likened to the dove shut up in the clefts of the rock, with the snake threatening it from within, and the hawk threatening it from without. Thus was the Assembly of Israel shut in on four sides of the world: in front of them was the sea, behind them the enemy pursued, and on two sides the deserts full of fiery serpents which wound and kill men with their sting. Then immediately Israel opened her mouth in prayer before YHWH and the Voice came forth from the high(est) heaven and thus it spoke: "You, O Assembly of Israel resembling the dove, clean and hiding in the covert of the clefts of the rocks, and in the hidden places of the stairs, show me your countenance and your worthy deeds, and let me hear your voice, for sweet is your voice in prayer in the small sanctuary and your countenance is beautiful with good deeds."

Midrash Rabbah identified the dove with Israel (cf. Hosea 7:11) in a variety of ways. When Israel went out of Egypt, they were like a dove fleeing from a hawk.

The dove flew into a crevice and encountered a serpent. Caught between the hawk and the serpent, the dove began to cry and beat its wings until the master of the cote came to the rescue. Such was Israel's predicament at the Reed Sea. Aqiba interpreted the verse as applying to Israel when they stood before Mount Sinai. The dove in the cleft of the rock meant Israel hidden in the shadow of the mountain. Jose the Galilean interpreted the verse with reference to the alien powers, but others, following Rabbi Meir, referred the verse to Israel hiding in the tent of meeting, and others to the Temple. The sweet voice was referred to the singing of the Levites in the Temple. Rabbi Elijah interpreted the verse as referring to the festival pilgrims (Deut 16:16) and the melodious recitation of the Hallel (Psalms 113–118).

This verse figures in a rabbinic discussion on the difference between man and woman (TB Niddah 31b). Man searches for woman as his lost rib. In lying together the man faces downward towards the earth from which he was created ("missionary position") while the woman faces him from whom she was created. A man is easily sated sexually, but not so a woman, because he was made from soft earth and she from a hard rib. A woman's voice is sweet because she was created from the resonant rib and the man from (dull) earth. Again (TB Ketubot 75a) a harsh voice in a woman was considered a bodily defect, as a dog bite turned to a scar would be a defect. In another connection (TB Berakot 24a), when reciting the *Shema'* in bed, a man should not be in a state of sexual excitement, and a woman's voice, like her hair (cf. 4:2) and her legs (Isa 47:2) may excite a man.

The LXX rendering "rampart" suggested to some Christian expositors of this verse the Old Law from which they are commanded to flee in order to pass on to the safe refuge of the Gospel Rock. The identification of Christ as the Rock (I Cor 10:4) made the dove's refuge the sure doctrines of the Faith and the mysteries of the Gospel. The Vulgate reading "in the caverns of the wall" was applied to the doctrines of the Apostles, the examples of the Saints, the wounds of Christ, the hidden mysteries of God's glory. The suggestion of secret retirement and meditation was applied to the Blessed Virgin. The face and the voice were seen as the works and the prayers of the Church or of the holy soul. Aponius saw here Christ calling on the Jewish Church to turn back to Him whom they had crucified. Several Greek Fathers understood the latter part of the verse as the words of the Bride longing to see and hear Christ in the flesh, and no longer in prophetic mystery. (Cf. Littledale.)

15a. *Catch.* The imperative is masculine plural and the question to whom it is addressed is a vexed one. Delitzsch suggested that if the king is now engaged in hunting he might thus address his followers, but immediately countered this supposition with the assertion that the song is a vinedresser's ditty, in accord with the Shulamite's experience as a vineyard keeper, a figure which aims at her love relation.

(for) *us.* Presumably the reference is to the pair of lovers, whose bed and bower were mentioned in 1:16–17. In 2:9c the suffix refers to the wall of the house of the bride and her parents from which the groom is temporarily excluded, while in 2:12d the reference is again to the lovers.

Hitzig supposed that the Shulamite addresses the foxes, "hold for us," i.e. "wait, you little rascals!" but the sense "wait," "hold off," is not attested for *'ḥz*, "grasp," "seize," "hold fast."

foxes. The term *šûʻāl* may designate either foxes or jackals. These were the animals caught by Samson and made incendiary torchbearers, Judg 15:4. *NEB* renders "jackals" and suggests in a note the alternative "fruit bats."

Robert Graves (1960, 272*ff*) stimulated by the monumental study of the mushroom by Valentina and Gordon Wasson, has proposed that the little foxes of the Canticle represent hallucinogenic mushrooms. Cf. R. G. Wasson, 1971, and D. H. Ingalls, 1971.

15c. *Vineyard spoilers*. Reynard's partiality to grapes is affirmed by the ancient fable about Sour Grapes; cf. James Hanauer, 1907, 2, for the fox and the grapes motif. The depredations of the foxes in the vineyards are signaled by Theocritus:

> I hate the brush-tail foxes, that soon as day declines
> Come creeping to their vintaging mid goodman Micon's vines.
> (J. M. Edmonds, LCL, 1912, v 112–113)

Or in the more recent poetic rendering,

> A plague on the foxes, bushy tailed vermin that creep
> To plunder the vines in the evening when Micon's asleep!
> (W. Douglas P. Hill, 1959, 26)

The challenge of this enigmatic verse has never daunted the allegorists. Targum took the marauding foxes to refer to the Amalekites who held a grudge because Jacob had deprived Esau of the birthright and blessing:

> After they had crossed the sea, they murmured about the water and the wicked Amalek came upon them, he who kept a grudge against them on account of the birthright and the blessing which Jacob our father, took from Esau. And he came to wage war against Israel because of neglect of the words of the Law. And the wicked Amalek stole from beneath the wings of the cloud of glory souls from the tribe of Dan to kill them because the image of Micah was in their hands. At that time the House of Israel was doomed, likened to a vineyard about to be destroyed, had it not been for the righteous ones of that generation who are likened to the good perfume.

Midrash Rabbah similarly interpreted the foxes as various enemies of Israel, the Egyptians, the Assyrians, the Amorites, the Edomites: the righteous who made the vineyard bud were Noah, Daniel, and Job.

This verse is applied by the Talmud to the situation related in Exod 2:3 (TB Soṭah 12a). When the Egyptians learned that an Israelite child was born, they would take other children there so that it would hear them crying and cry with them, as it is written, "catch for us, etc."

The Church has never lacked foxy foes, within and without, to spoil the vineyard and to whom this verse could be applied. The command is not to kill them, or even to drive them out, but to *take* them, i.e. convince them of their error and convert them. They are little foxes, not formidable foes like lions, tigers, or bears, but skulking rascals whose only resource is slyness and the only defense needed against them vigilance. The fox and the grapes were especially adaptable to the concerns of the monastic and celibate vocation; the little foxes, for example, may be the petty relaxations and violations of the rules which, unchecked, could ruin the whole order; thus there has to be a wall, tall or strong enough to keep out the foxes (Neh 4:3). The flowering vineyard, naturally, suggested the harvest to come, when the Lord of the Vineyard will gather the mature grapes and remove the worthless materials. (Cf. Littledale.)

Among modern interpretations, Dom Calmet explained that the groom, coming home and finding his vineyards plundered, gives the order to hunt the foxes that caused the damage. For Delitzsch the vineyards, beautiful with fragrant blossoms, refer to the Shulamite's covenant with love, and the little foxes are the enemies, great and small, the adverse circumstances that threaten to gnaw and destroy love in bloom before it has reached the ripeness of full enjoyment. Von Herder and the others took the verse as a couplet from popular nuptial songs alluding to the unhappy consequences of illicit love. Wittekindt and Haller regarded the verse as a fragment of an Orphic cult song to the accompaniment of dances in which the youths were clothed in fox pelts. Similarly, Meek felt that the verse reads like a snatch from a rustic dance song which seems to have no point beyond being reminiscent of some ancient fertility rite like the Roman Cerialia or Robigalia, with foxes figuring in the former and puppies in the latter. Ginsburg imagined that the Shulamite here quotes the words of her brothers who had overheard her lover's invitation to come out for a bit of vernal venery, and to prevent the rendevous, set their sister to tending the vineyard and catching or chasing foxes. She referred to this episode in 1:6 as she repelled the disdainful looks of the court ladies and explained her brown complexion as caused by her brothers' maltreatment. Harper and Guitton understood that the maiden imprisoned in the harem sang a rustic song in reply to her true lover who was outside. The vine in bloom is none other than her own ripe charms in danger of being ravished by her foxy captor, Solomon. Joüon and Ricciotti saw in the vine the nation Israel and in the foxes the Canaanites.

Robert took his cue from this point, having already shown, to his satisfaction, that in 1:6 the vine, the bride, and the nation are at least identified. Hosea 2 and Jer 12:7*ff* were cited as authorizing this conclusion. The little foxes (not young, but of minor importance, and yet malicious) represented, to Robert's mind, the neighboring small nations that settled in the Holy Land. They were a constant obstacle to the complete restoration and a cause of trouble and scandal. One understands thus that their disappearance would be in the foreground of the preoccupations of the Israelites; it would constitute the first act of Yahweh's intervention at the time of salvation (cf. Isa 11:4–5; Ps 72:4,12–14). Thus understood, the verse is not isolated from its context as would seem at first sight. If the vine in bloom symbolizes the new times, it is normal that one would wish first the removal of the trouble-makers. Such a wish, according to Robert, is better understood on the lips of the bride than on those of the groom.

16a,b. This phrase is repeated in reverse in 6:3 and partly in 7:11[10E]. A. Feuillet has aptly termed it "the formula of mutual belonging" (1961a). Because of its importance, as expressing the fundamental theme of the Canticle: the intense desire which the lovers have of meeting at last and of enjoying one another, Feuillet chose this formula as a point of departure for his study of the divergent interpretations of the Canticle. The interpretation favored and elaborated by Feuillet was, not surprisingly, the allegorical, essentially identical with that presented by Robert. As Robert succinctly put it, the phrase "My love is mine and I am his" is based on the well-known prophetic formula: Israel is the people of Yahweh, and Yahweh the God of Israel (Deut 26:17–18, 29:12[13E]; Hosea 2:24; Jer 7:23, 11:4, 24:7, 31:33; Ezek 34:30–31, 36:28, 37:23; cf. Pss 95:7, 100:3). In these texts the order is not always the same; Yahweh is named first in Deut 26:17–18; Hosea 2:24; Jer 7:23, 31:33; elsewhere it is Israel. Robert had the impression that in some cases the order was chosen to indicate to whom the initiative falls; thus in Deut 26:17–18 it is God who assumes the duty of concluding the covenant; in Hosea 2:24 he reestablished the relations in pity after the bride repents; Jer 31:33 shows him creating a new covenant. In the three passages of the Canticle, the order also varies; in 6:3 and 7:11[10E] the bride is named first; here it is the groom that comes at the head. According to Robert, in the former instances it is only a matter of the eagerness of the groom.

16c. *browses.* The ambiguities of this line present some delicate problems. The crux of the issue is whether the participle of *rʿy,* "pasture," "feed," is here used in the sense of eat, or cause to eat, and whether the flowers in question, the *šôšannîm,* indicate what is eaten or the locale of the feeding; whether the lover feeds on the flowers, or (on something else) among the flowers, or pastures (his flock) among the flowers. LXX rendered *ho poimainōn en tois krinois,* construing the participle as transitive and presumably assuming the unexpressed object as the flock, *pascit* (*gregem*). Vulgate, however, rendered *qui pascitur inter lilia,* "who feeds himself among the lilies."

A. Feuillet has taken this issue as crucial for the interpretation of the Canticle and has championed the interpretation of LXX as the only plausible translation of 2:16c, in opposition to Vulgate. Most modern interpreters, however, side with Vulgate, not only literalists and those whom Robert dubbed "l'école voluptueuse," but also some authors who incline to the allegorical interpretation. (The allegorist need not vex himself unduly over such detail.) Following the lead of Vulgate, the meaning would be that the lover finds his pleasure in a beautiful young girl whose charms are symbolized by the flowers. *NEB* reflects this interpretation, "he delights in the lilies." According to Budde (1898, 12), the lilies should be considered the complement of the object of the verb, that is the lover feeds on the lilies, which in accordance with the designation of his lip as lilies in 5:13, would be none other than her lips, i.e. he lets himself graze on her lips. Haupt and Wittekindt are here, as Robert put it, "frankly obscene." Haupt rendered:

My dearest is mine, and his am I, who feeds on the (dark purple) lilies
Till the breeze (of the morning) arises, and away the shadows are fleeing.

To feed on the dark purple lilies (that is the hair on the *mons Veneris*), according to Haupt, is synonymous with "to uncover the nakedness" (Lev 18:6*ff*), the Homeric *zōnēn luein* (*Odyssey* xi 245), and the Shakespearean "break her virgin-knot" (*Tempest* IV i 7). Kuhn supposed that the lover is here compared to an animal that grazes, as he is elsewhere compared to a stag or a roebuck, these animals chosen by the poet as terms of comparison by reason of the freedom of their sexual relations which are liable to no constraint. Such interpretations are vigorously opposed by Feuillet who defends the rendering of LXX and of É. Dhorme in the *Bible de la Pléiade:*

Mon bien aimé est à moi, et moi à lui, lui qui mène paître parmis les lis.

A survey of the uses of the verb *r'y*, which is too much to offer here, shows that a strong case can be made for either line of interpretation and that, in the final analysis, the choice is determined by predilection. The expression *r'y b-* is often ambiguous. Gen 41:2,18 will serve to illustrate: *KJ* rendered "and they fed in a meadow": *RSV* "and they fed in the reed grass"; *AT* "and browsed in the sedge"; *NEB* "and they grazed on the reeds." The verb *r'y* may be used in either sense of "feed," with or without prepositions or the *nota objecti;* e.g. Micah 5:3[4E], "he shall stand and feed (himself or his flock?) in/on the strength of Yahweh." One may eat ashes, *r'y 'pr* (Isa 44:20), or wind (Hosea 12:2[1E]), as the mouth of fools eats folly, Prov 15:4, without use of the *nota objecti.* Or the preposition *b-* may refer to the area in which the feeding takes place, e.g. Gen 37:13, "in Shechem"; Num 14:33, "in the wilderness"; I Chron 27:29, "in Sharon"; cf. Ezek 34:13. Since *r'y* is in some instances a synonym of *'kl* "eat" (e.g. in Isa 5:17 where it stands in parallelism with *'kl,* and in Jonah 3:7 with *šty,* "drink"), the preposition *b-* could presumably be used with the object of the eating in either of the senses of *r'y,* "eat, or cause to eat, of something," as with *'kl b-* in Exod 12:43. There seems to be no way to decide the matter on grammatical grounds.

The references here and in 4:5 to browsing on/among the lotus, and the expression "to pluck lotus" in 6:12, recall the *lotophagi* of the *Odyssey.* It seems unlikely that the interest here is in the alleged narcotic effects of lotophagy, indolence, abulia, and amnesia. In 4:5 the figure is used of the lady's breasts as twin gazelles feeding on/among the lotus. It is probable that the meaning is to be sought in the rich sexual symbolism of the sacred lotus which was the attribute of the great goddess of fertility. In Indian Tantrism the lotus is laden with sexual symbolism and represents the female organ as a whole and in all its parts and functions and is attributive to every feature of the great goddess in her venereal aspect. Lotophagy in these circles, Sanskrit *padmachāṭī,* "lotus licking," and *padmakōmpalachāṭī,* "licking a lotus stamen," is applied to *cunnilingus;* cf. Edwardes and Masters, 1962, 312.

16. The Targum continued from the preceding verse the relation to Amalek:

> At that moment, they turned in repentance; and Moses, the prophet, was ready and he prayed before YHWH. Joshua, his servant, was equipped and went forth from beneath the cloud of glory of YHWH and with him heroes, the righteous, who resemble in their deeds the rose. They waged war against Amalek and shattered Amalek and his people by the anathema of YHWH which kills and shatters as the decree of the sword.

Midrash Rabbah made this refrain Israel's affirmation of her belonging to God, correlating it with other passages of Scripture such as Exod 4:22, 20:2; Isa 5:7, 51:4, 63:16; Jer 31:9; Deut 14:1; Pss 80:2, 121:4; Ezek 34:31. It was also interpreted as a mutual aid agreement: He fights for me against those who challenge me, and I fight for Him against those who provoke Him. The latter part of the refrain, "that feeds among the lilies," was quoted by Rabbi Johanan who suffered with gallstones to Rabbi Hanina who used to come and utter an incantation to relieve the pain. When Hanina fell ill, Johanan attempted to encourage him with the assurance that the rod of the Holy One, blessed be He, lights only upon those whose heart is pliant like lilies.

The nominal sentence, "My love to me and I to him," invited a variety of elaborations on the nature of the mutuality by the Christian Fathers: My Beloved is careful for me, and anxious for my salvation; I am careful for Him, to obey Him in all things, etc. St. Bernard took the brevity and incoherence of the Bride's words as an indication of her emotion. She is too fervent and eager to be altogether silent, but too deeply and inexpressibly happy to say much. The sparse speech is thus a mark of the one to whom Isa 7:14 refers, whom all generations will call blessed (Luke 1:48). The lilies were understood as pure souls who retain the whiteness of chastity and impart a fragrance to all who are near. The hymn *Jesu Corona Virginum* alludes to the present verse:

> Who feedest where the lilies spring,
> Surrounded by the Virgin ring,
> With glory decking them, Thy brides,
> And granting spousal gifts besides.

St. Bernard (Sermons 70, 71) related the lilies to Christ's own truth, meekness, and righteousness. Again the feeding on the lilies suggested to Bernard (Sermon 72) that sinners have to be masticated with Christ's teeth of suffering and trial in order to be incorporated into His mystical body. The Hebrew participle *rô'eh,* "feeder," "pastor," evoked the figure of the Good Shepherd who feeds us in the pleasant pastures of the divine Mysteries. The books of Holy Writ were also commended as good pastures where one may feed and ruminate. The word *šôšannîm* recalled the gathering of maidens into the palace Shushan, Esther 2:8. (Cf. Littledale.)

17a. *Until.* The choice between "while" and "until" for *'ad še* is difficult here. In 1:12a the association with a verb in the perfect commended the sense "while"; here one verb is in the imperfect and the other perfect and the time setting may be either future or present. *KJ, RSV* and *AT* render "until," *NEB* has "while" and *JPSV* "when." Haupt connected this verse with what precedes, but most interpreters make a new departure here and in 4:6.

breathes. This verb occurs here and in 4:6, and the imperative of the causative stem in 4:16. The meaning is apparently "breathe," "exhale," related to Ar. *p(w)ḥ,* "give forth scent." KB places other occurrences in Ezek 21:36[31E]; Ps 10:5; Prov 6:19, 14:5,25, 19:5,9, etc. with a different root. *JPSV* here renders "blows gently" but adds a note that emendation yields "declines" with reference to Jer 6:4. In Jer 6:4*f* it is clear that the reference is to the passing of the day and the approach of night:

> Sanctify war against her;
> Up and let us attack at noon!
> Woe to us, for the day has passed (*pānāh*)
> The evening shadows lengthen.
> Up, let us attack by night,
> And destroy her strongholds.

The context here and in 4:6 favors nocturnal setting for the exercise in question, thus the breathing of the day, as with the flight of darkness, means the end of night and the break of day when the amative activity ends.

17c. *Turn.* Most interpreters explain the imperative *sōḇ* here as "turn" and supply "to me," but others take it in the sense of "return" as with Vulgate *revertere.* Haupt, as a pioneer of "l'école voluptueuse," here rendered "(Do thou spring to the) feast" and he explained in his notes that he meant "Accumb," i.e. recline at the meal with reference to the accumbation at the dining couch, or bridal bed. In the Hebrew text, according to Haupt, this imperative, "Feast" (or "Regale") forms the conclusion of the preceding stanza. Budde related the word to the play of young animals. *AT* similarly rendered "gambol." Robert was unable to see how the naturalist school could arrive at the belief that the author intended to designate here voluptuous pleasure, but he also found equally fantastic some of the attempts to avoid coarseness, e.g. Graetz's and Dussaud's understanding that the bride asks her lover to flee, or Harper's view that she begs him to leave the environs of the harem because she fears for his life. Robert held that the choice has to be either "come," or "return." Joüon preferred "come" because after vs. 16 the groom is with the bride. But if the groom is present in vs. 16, he is certainly absent in 3:1*ff*, and there must have been a rapid change of perspective. The uses of the imperative of *sbb* in I Sam 22:17–18 and II Sam 18:30, according to Robert, indicate that the meaning is "return" rather than "turn." The groom, accordingly, is absent; the Shulamite had thought to possess him (vss. 8–16), but this was an illusion, or a reality that did not last (cf. 3:1); she calls him and goes to search for him (3:2–4). St. Bernard is invoked in support of this understanding: "Doubtless he had only stolen away to be recalled more ardently, to be retained more strongly." Robert's preference for "return" is again influenced by his theory of interpretation. In I Sam 22:17–18 and II Sam 18:30 the imperatives of *sbb* are not properly rendered "return," but "turn," and "turn aside." The parallel passage 8:14 has *bĕraḥ,* "flee," and thus Delitzsch argued that consequently the meaning of *sōḇ* here is "turn thyself from here away." Nevertheless, Delitzsch supposed that she (the Shulamite) holds him (Solomon) in her embrace, inseparable from him, and will wander with him upon the mountains. If, however, the hills of spices are, as Gordis remarked on 4:6, "obvious symbols for the body of the beloved," then a different understanding of the turning and swift movement of the young stag is indicated, especially in light of the use of the stag as a model of sexual prowess in Mesopotamian potency rituals. Schmökel (1956) rendered, "Tafele, tue es gleich, Liebster, der Gazelle" (i.e. Dine, Dearest, do it like the gazelle), citing Budde and the use of the noun *mēsaḇ,* "table," in 1:12.

17d. This verse repeats 2:9a,b, but here in the form of an exhortation rather than a simple declaration. Budde's explanation that the gazelle and fawn represent love-play is rejected by Robert on the ground that in Scripture these animals are noted for agility. Outside of Scripture, however, these animals are known for their beauty and their sexuality, as illustrated by their role in Mesopotamian potency charms and incantations.

17e. *cleft.* Many interpreters have taken *beṯer* as a proper name, e.g. Aquila, Symmachus, Vulgate and *KJ*. LXX took the word as characterizing the mountains, and similarly many moderns, e.g. *AT* "upon the craggy mountains," *RSV* "rugged mountains." The rugged mountains were seen by some as the separation of the lovers, or the pass the male had to cross. Luther's "Scheideberge," according to Delitzsch, are "mountain peaks, from one of which to the other one must spring." The Canticle ends in 8:14 with a variant of this expression, using *bĕśāmîm,* "spices," instead of *beṯer;* accordingly some translators either emend *beṯer* or take it as a synonym of *bĕśāmîm.* Some savants have seen the word *beṯer* as a contraction of Greek and Latin *malabathron,* which is a plant of uncertain sort. Some would relate *malabathron* to Sanskrit *tamalapatra* which designates betel nut. This seems highly unlikely since the betel palm which bears the nut grows in South India, Sri Lanka, Thailand, the Malay Archipelago, the Philippines, Micronesia, and Melanesia where it is widely used as a masticatory, chewed with lime. It has no special aromatic qualities. However, there appears to have been another *malabathron* from which unguents were made; cf. Harper ad loc. for references.

JPSV strikingly rendered 2:17:

When the day blows gently
And the shadows flee
Set out, my beloved,
Swift as a gazelle
Or a young stag,
For the hills of spices!

Similarly *NEB,*

> While the day is cool and the shadows are dispersing, turn, my beloved, and show yourself a gazelle or a young wild goat on the hills where cinnamon grows.

but with alternatives in the note, "on the rugged hills," or "on the hills of Bether."

Haupt's interpretation will serve as a sample from "l'école voluptueuse":

> (Do thou spring to the) feast, O my dearest, like a buck of gazelles or a pricket,
> (To the feast) on the mountains of myrrh, (to the feast) on the hillocks of incense!

In his notes Haupt explained the mountains of myrrh and the hillocks of incense as the *pudendum* or *mons Veneris,* hyperbolical expressions for the sweet body of the bride.

If the cleft mountains or the spice mountains refer to the breasts, *mons Veneris,* or other bifurcated charms of the bride, the exhortation to the lover to be like a gazelle or stag on the said hills resembles the word of the goddess to King Shulgi,

> To prance on my holy bosom like a 'lapis lazuli' calf, you are fit

On the use of such terms as cleft, slit, and the like for the rift in the *mons Veneris,* see Edwardes and Masters, 1962, 62–65.

A locale east of the Jordan designated "the Bithron" in II Sam 2:29, and Bar Kochba's Bethar are not to be considered, according to Delitzsch, who further notes that an Assyrian list of animal names mentions *bitru,* along with *ṣabi,* gazelle, and *apparu,* the young of the gazelle or of the hind, and suggest that it may be the name of the *rupicapra.*

Khirbet Beitar, Hebrew *Ḥorvat Beter,* a late Chalcolithic site near Beersheba, was excavated by I. Ben Dor in 1952–54 and later by M. Dothan (cf. *'Atiqot* II [1959], pp. 1–7), but there is hardly anything that could be related to this verse except the consonants *btr.*

For Gerleman the "Bether-Berge" alias "Balsamberge," seemed to have a half-legendary character of a poetic wonderland like the land of Punt in Egyptian love lyrics. The summoning of a gazelle or stag to the "Bether-Berge" Gerleman recognized as veiled speech for an invitation to a love-tryst.

Robert rendered "sur les montagnes de l'alliance" and appealed to Genesis 15 for the explication. The author of the Canticle has, according to Robert, recalled the memory of God's covenant with Abraham. The Babylonian Captivity in the post-exilic literature was like a second bondage in Egypt, so, to comfort the small band of repatriates in Palestine, the covenant promise of Genesis 15 is recalled, evoked by the mountains of *beṯer,* the mountains of the division of the victim, or more clearly, by metonymy, the mountains of the Covenant. Toward these mountains the groom, returning at last to his normal dwelling place, should haste like a gazelle or fawn. In the mention of the word *beṯer* the author of the Canticle recalled to God, and to Robert, the ancient promise which must be realized because it was formulated by Israel's husband. One must emphasize, Robert noted, the fact that the vision of Genesis 15 promises above all the possession of Palestine (vss. 7,16,18–21). Here, through Robert's effort to put the interpretation of the Canticle on solid critical, historical basis, we have come full circle back to the Targum.

The Targum related the mountains of cleavage (*beṯer*) to Mount Moriah, the sacrifice of Isaac, and the division of the animal when Abraham cut a covenant with Yahweh (Gen 15:10):

> And in a few days the Israelites made the calf of gold, and the cloud of glory which had sheltered them was lifted and they were left exposed and deprived of the use of their weapons on which was inscribed the great name interpreted with seventy names. And YHWH wished to destroy them from the earth, except that He called to mind the covenant He had established by His promise to Abraham, Isaac, and Jacob who were swift in worshiping Him as a gazelle or a young antelope, and the sacrifice when Abraham offered Isaac, his son, on Mount Moriah and before this he had offered there his sacrifice and divided it equally.

Midrash Rabbah cited the divergent views of Rabbis Judah and Berekiah on the meaning of this verse. The former explained "Until the day breathes" as meaning "until I insert a breathing space in the night of foreign domination" and he applied it to the domination by Egypt which God reduced from four hundred to two hundred years. The turning like a gazelle or hart Judah explained as referring to the eventual change of the divine attitude from judgment to mercy, to hasten the deliverance of Israel. The mountains of Bether Judah related to the pieces *bĕṯārîm* (cf. Gen 15:10,17). Berekiah took the first part of the verse to mean "Till I make the day blaze," citing Ezek 21:36. The shadows, according to Berekiah, signify distress and mourning. There was agreement with Judah on the meaning of the turning like a gazelle or hart. Bether was related to the city Bethar where Hadrian crushed the Bar Cochba revolt with great slaughter.

A few samples of Christian allegorical exposition of this verse may serve to edify or astound. The "day" was referred to the Resurrection, the day of the revelation of eternal glory, when the shadows of this world's night flees away. "Turn" was applied to the conversion of the heathen, or by several divines as a prayer to have Christ visit our souls, even if only fleetingly like the sudden and rare appearances of the stag on the hilltops. The "mountains of Bether" were taken to refer to the proud and haughty, humbled by Christ, or conversely His visits to lofty and contemplative souls. Cocceius saw it as a prayer to break down the divisions between Jew and Gentile, believers and idolaters. Nicholas of Lyra explained the mountains as Sinai where Israel's sin with the golden calf almost caused God to abandon and destroy them, just as all occasions of sin are gulfs opened between the soul and God. In the figure of overcoming mountains, Honorius saw the Bridegroom leaping over the nine divisions of the Angelic hierarchy in order to come to His bride who is of his own nature, bone of His bone and flesh of His flesh. (Cf. Littledale.)

III
(3:1–11)

1 a On my bed at night
b I sought him whom I love.
c I sought, but did not find him.
2 a I will rise and roam the city,
b In the streets and squares.
c I will seek him whom I love.
d I sought, but did not find him.
3 a The guards found me
b They who patrol the city.
c Have you seen the one I love?
4 a Scarce had I passed them by
b When I found the one I love.
c I grasped and would not loose him
d Till I brought him to my mother's house,
e To the chamber of her who conceived me.
5 a I adjure you, Jerusalem girls,
b By the gazelles or hinds of the steppe,
c That you neither incite or excite
d Love until it is eager.
6 a Who is this ascending from the steppe,
b Like columns of smoke,
c Redolent with myrrh and incense,
d All the pedlar's powders?
7 a Behold Solomon's bed,
b Sixty heroes round it,
c Valiants of Israel,
8 a All of them war-skilled,
b Battle-taught,
c Each with sword at his side
d Against night terror.
9 a A litter he made for himself,
b Did King Solomon,

c From wood of Lebanon.
10 a He made its posts silver,
b Its bolster gold,
c Its cushion purple wool,
d Its sides love inlaid.
11 a Jerusalem girls come out
b Look, O Zion's girls,
c At King Solomon,
d At the crown his mother gave him
e On his wedding day,
f On the day of his heart's delight.

NOTES

3:1a. *On my bed.* The implication of premarital sexual activity on the part of the lovers which some interpreters have seen in the ambiguous reference to seeking the lover in bed is, in the case of the Sumerian goddess' love affairs, quite explicit. There is no conflict between mother and daughter such as Graetz imagined in the biblical Canticle, but the goddess does feel it necessary to deceive her mother as to her whereabouts and her activities. The goddess as the Venus-star was scintillating and cavorting when she encountered Dumuzi who made love to her.

> Last night, as I, the queen, was shining bright,
> Last night, as I, the queen of heaven, was shining bright,
> Was shining bright, was dancing about,
> Was uttering a chant at the lengthening of the oncoming light,
> He met me, he met me,
> The lord Kulianna met me,
> The lord put his hand into my hand,
> Ushumgalanna embraced me.

After a while the goddess tries to break away and begins to worry about what she will tell her mother.

> Come now, wild bull, set me free, I must go home,
> Kuli-Enlil, set me free, I must go home,
> What can I say to deceive my mother,
> What can I say to deceive my mother, Ningal.

Her lover advises the expedient of prevarication, an art in which the goddess has considerable aptitude and experience.

> Let me inform you, let me inform you,
> Inanna, most deceitful of women, let me inform you,
> Say my girl friend took me with her to the public square,
> There she entertained me with music and dancing,
> Her chant the sweet she sang for me,
> In sweet rejoicing I whiled away the time there.
> Thus deceitfully stand up to your mother,
> While we by the moonlight indulge our passion,
> I will prepare for you a bed pure, sweet, and noble,
> Will while away sweet time with you in plenty joy.
> (*SMR*, 77*f*)

at night. The plural here does not indicate that the bride's solitary anguish lasted for several successive nights; it is rather a plural of composition designating nighttime (cf. Joüon, 136b).

1c. *I sought*. Schmökel would delete the second *biqqaštîw*, "I sought him," as dittography, on the basis of mistaken notions about meter.

1–2. Although these verses present no philological problems or difficulties in translation, there are many variant interpretations. The seemingly clear statement that the bride looked for her lover in bed at night and could not find him, some interpreters find impossible to accept as relating an external reality. "She does not mean to say," according to Delitzsch, "that she sought him beside herself on her couch; for how could that be of the modest one. . . . How could this night-search, with all the strength of love, be consistent with the modesty of a maiden? It is thus a dream which she relates." Delitzsch further argued that if her beloved were a shepherd, she would not seek him in the city, but in the field or in some village, hence the beloved of her soul is none other than Solomon who in her dream is transported to the mountain of her native home. *JPSV* added an explanatory footnote to "at night": "I.e. in a dream." Ginsburg, however, did not resort to dreamland to defend the maiden's honor from Harmer's slur that there can be no reasonable doubt that these are the words of one to whose bed the beloved was no stranger. As Ginsburg imagined it, the beloved for some reason did not come in the evening as requested, and she, unable to wait, retired; but her thoughts kept her awake. Thus the words at which unnecessary umbrage has been taken do not mean, "I sought him in my bed," but, "Even when I reclined upon my nocturnal couch, I could not give him up; I still sought to find him."

For Robert (RTF), as the fleeing shadows of 2:17 mean the coming of salvation after trial, so, reciprocally, the night and the shadows are the classical image of the long wait of the soul oppressed by suffering (Isa 5:30, 8:22, 9:1[2E], 21:11, 26:9, 49:9, 59:9, 60:1–2; Amos 5:18–20; Joel 2:2; Zeph 1:15; Ps 112:4). The motif of searching and not finding is met several times in the prophets (Isa 51:1, 65:1; Zech 8:21–22), but the closest parallels, in Robert's view, are Jer 29:13 and Hosea 3:5, 5:6,15. These texts, especially Hosea 3:5, allow Robert to comprehend the underlying intent of the present passage: the bride thought she had the groom; suddenly he disappeared; thence it is to be understood that the dispositions of the one who is searching are not yet perfect. Thus, for Robert, it is unnecessary to see in our passage either an allusion to events of the period of the Judges (Joüon, Ricciotti), nor a real scene (Miller), nor an account of a dream (Budde, Siegfried, Harper, Guitton). Still less is it a matter of erotic poetry celebrating free love (Staerk) or of a cult chant in honor of the dead and resurrected Tammuz (Wittekindt, Haller).

In the Ugaritic myths, the motif of the goddess seeking her missing consort is poignantly presented. With the death of Baal and the subsequent lack of fertility, the cultic cry is:

Where is Mighty Baal, Where is the Prince Lord of Earth?
(6[49].4.28–29, 39–40)

The solar goddess Shapsh volunteers to assist in the search for Baal, using the same verb as here:

I will seek Mighty Baal *abqṯ aliyn b'l*
(6[49].4.44)

Anat's search for her missing brother and consort is thus described:

Anat went and roamed
Every mountain inside the Earth (i.e. the netherworld),
Every hill inside the Steppe.

1–4. Feuillet (1963), has drawn a parallel between the present passage and the Christophany in John 20:11–18 and the episode of the pilgrims on the road to Emmaus, Luke 24:13 (99–112). A. Cabaniss (1967) has also treated the present passage in connection with II Tim 1:17, "but when he arrived in Rome he searched for me eagerly and found me." The parallel between the search for the dead Christ and the present passage is indeed striking and has an ancient background. The case of Onesiphorus' seeking and finding Paul in Rome has little relevance apart from the phraseological parallel.

1. The Targum turned the quest of the missing bedmate to the search for the cloud and crown taken from Israel because of the sin with the golden calf:

> When the people of the House of Israel saw that the clouds of glory were lifted up from over them, and that the crown of holiness which had been given them at Sinai was removed from them, and that they were left in darkness like the night, they sought the crown of holiness which had been lifted from them and could not find it—

Midrash Rabbah offered differing explanations of the night and the bed. Abba ben Kahana took it as referring to sickness, citing Exod 21:18. Rabbi Levi applied the nights to Israel's bondage to Egypt, Babylon, Media, Greece, and Edom (i.e. Rome). Rabbi Alexander read *ballêlôṯ,* "in the nights," as *bā'û lêlôṯ,* "nights have come," and explained that as Israel slept neglectful of the Law, one night followed another. Another explanation referred the night to Egypt, with Moses as the object of the quest (cf. 2:9).

Christian expositors generally understood the object of the quest to be Christ. St. Ambrose saw here the Synagogue on the bed of the Mosaic Law, searching in vain for her Lord in the dark shadows of the ceremonial types and hidden prophecies. Cornelius à Lapide saw the Church in the early days after Pentecost preaching in Jerusalem, unable to find Christ in the hard hearts of the Jews, and thus compelled to rise and begin the mission to the heathen. As applied to the individual soul, rather than the Church at large, it was taken to indicate the impossibility of finding Christ while reclining in carnal pleasures and in the darkness of sin. Those who seek Christ the easy way do not find Him, but those who seek Him in persecution find Him quickly. One may fail in the search, not for lack of diligence, but because He dwells in inaccessible light which is as night to man's eyes. Mary Magdalene failed in her quest because she sought Him in the bed of the sepulcher, looking for the living among the dead, yet she was blessed in the search. St. Bernard (Sermon 75) cited John 7:34 and Isa 55:6 and urged that the search be launched before it is too late, not in a half-hearted and leisurely manner, not after the flesh in tomb, manger, or womb, but in His dwelling-place in Heaven. (Cf. Littledale.)

2a. *the city.* Some critics, following Haller, would delete "in the city" as a doublet taken from the following verse. As to the identity of the city, Harper rightly argued that it need not be Jerusalem, but could be any city which had defenses, as distinct from a mere village. The indication of the article, as in Prov. 1:21, is scarcely ground for suspecting that the reference is to the capital Jerusalem. The frequent mention of the daughters of Jerusalem would indeed suggest this, but the alleged allusions to the Temple (1:4,17, 3:4, 5:10–16), claimed by Robert to show that the Holy City is the center of the author's perspective, are his own construction.

The term "city" is also a regular designation of the netherworld. Cf. Tromp, 1969, 152–154.

2. Budde removed this line as a superfluous gloss. Schmökel also relegated it to a footnote with the bizarre suggestion that perhaps older words were built into this transformation and that the original reading might have been:

'ăqûmāh-nnā wĕ'arḥîḇennû	I will arise and rescue him,
ḇaššôqîm 'ăsôḇĕḇāh	On the knees I will go around.

The otherwise unattested plural of *šûq, šĕwāqîm,* Schmökel would read as *šôqîm,* "knees," and interpret the going around on the knees as an expression for prolonged seeking, perhaps to be connected with the representations of (probably cultic) knee-ambulation, "Knielauf," on seal cylinders. The suggestion seems dubious in the extreme. Plural formations like *šûq, šĕwāqîm* are attested for other words of this sort, e.g. *šôr, šĕwārîm* (Hosea 12:12[11E]), *dûd, dĕwāḏîm* (II Chron 35:13); cf. Joüon, 96A 1.

2d. LXX adds "I called him, but he didn't hear/answer me," from 5:6.

2. The Targum identified the object of the quest for the lost lover as the Holy Presence which had forsaken Israel:

> Said the Israelites one to the other: "Let us rise and go and surround the Appointment-Tent which Moses spread outside the camp, and let us request instruction from YHWH and the Holy Presence which has been removed from us." Then they went around in the towns, in the streets and squares, but could not find (the Holy Presence).

Midrash Rabbah gave short shrift to this verse, simply identifying the object of the quest as Moses.

Early Christian interpreters generally understood the city here as meaning the Church. It was also taken as the earthly Jerusalem where the Apostles preached, but found Moses rather than Christ in the hearts of the people. The quest in the earthly city where he had taught (Luke 13:26) was now vain because He had gone up to the Heavenly Jerusalem, but He could still be sought in the Church militant on earth. The streets and squares were seen as representing two types of life within the Church, the secular and the religious, each with its Saints, but the former narrower and more spiritual and the latter broader and more carnal. The Holy Scriptures were also taken as the streets of the Church through which the soul seeks her Lord, but fails to find Him so long as she looks to the letter rather than the spirit. As there are two cities, Jerusalem above and Babylon below, some understood the latter to be meant here, as signifying the whole world. The streets and squares suggested to Cassiodorus the weary pilgrimage of the Gentiles in search of the Lord, in the sects of philosophy, in the mystery cults, and in cloudy speculation. St. Ambrose stressed that Christ is not found in the market place where there is strife, inequity, fraud, deceit, idleness, thieves, idolatry. (Cf. Littledale.)

Many critics have felt that the scene cannot be real. The main objection is to the picture of the maiden scouring the streets at night in search of her lover. Graetz supposed that she waited till daylight to begin the search. A number of interpreters have supposed that it was all a dream. For Robert the tableau is purely allegorical, the author wishing to signify that the nation having reentered Palestine has not experienced the benefits which she had expected. She is in Palestine, but it is still night, a time of uncertainty and suffering; she searches for her beloved throughout the city of Jerusalem, where he ought to be found, since this is the place which he had chosen as his dwelling from of old. These data, according to Robert, correspond to the state of mind of the post-exilic period which is manifest in a number of texts, especially Isaiah 58, 59, 60, 62, 63:15–64:12, 66:1.

3a. *The guards.* Graetz took this reference to city street patrol here and in 5:7 as an indication of late date for the Canticle. According to Graetz, there is no trace of this sort of patrol in ancient Israelite history because Israel had no standing militia. Even among the Greeks night patrols were rare and became common only in the Macedonian period (Graetz, 63). Epstein cited, against Graetz, Ps 127:1; Isa 62:6; cf. Isa 21:11.

On your walls, O Jerusalem,
I have posted guards;
All day and night
They are never silent.
(Isa 62:6)

Graetz dismissed this as only an apparent parallel having nothing to do with the present case, since there they are guards of Jerusalem's newly rebuilt walls who are continually to remind God of his promise to restore the city. In 5:7e Graetz passed over without comment the reference to guards of the walls.

found. The verb *mṣ'*, "find," "come upon," is also used in this sense in Ugaritic where in one instance *mġy,* "arrive," "come," is parallel with *mẓ'*, "find," both used in the sense of "encounter."

wn(?) ymġy aklm	*wymẓa ʿqqm*
He came upon the Eaters	He encountered the Rippers
	(12[75].1.36–37)

JPSV rendered, "I met the watchmen," and put in a note the literal rendition, "The watchmen met me."

3b. *patrol.* Lit. "who go around in the city," and so LXX rendered woodenly. Vulgate *qui custodiunt civitatem.* The Greek term *peripoloi,* as Graetz noted, is a fairly exact equivalent of the Hebrew. Behind both apparently stands the Akkadian term *sāhir dūri,* "one who goes around the wall," which is given in a lexical text as the equivalent of *ma-ṣar muši,* "night watchman"; thus our text seems almost to echo the Akkadian equation, "(night) watchman"="one who goes around the wall" (cf. *CAD,* D, 192a). *JPSV*'s "patrol" is adopted as the best designation of the watchman's rounds.

The "profane" view that these are human love ditties or peasant wedding songs encounters some difficulty here. A maiden(?) who misses her lover in bed, rises to roam the streets in search of him, encounters the town guards (who in the parallel passage 5:7 beat her and take off her clothes) seems a dubious candidate for a village bride and the whole episode a questionable theme for a wedding song. The search is reminiscent of the whore's vain quest in Hosea 2:7. For the dramatic interpretation which regards all this as a dream, there are no problems since anything can happen in a dream and even the most chaste of maidens may have erotic escapades in dreamland.

Exponents of the cultic hypothesis have seen in the theme of searching and finding, or not finding, and the encounter with the city patrol, a parallel with the myth of Ishtar's Descent to the Netherworld in which the goddess parleys with the guards of the seven gates of the infernal city, supposedly rescues her lover, all of which ends in a sacred marriage. H. Schmökel took note of the problems attendant on the attempted correlation of this search episode with Inanna's descent to the netherworld. Kramer has shown that the general assumption that the goddess' descent was for the purpose of rescuing Dumuzi, who, for some unknown reason, was being held captive there, is erroneous, since, according to the earliest version, Dumuzi was not even in the netherworld when Inanna arrived there. Rather in the earliest form of the myth it was the goddess who later delivered over her mate as a substitute for herself in order to escape the infernal region (cf. *SMR,* 155). As for Dumuzi's resurrection, Kramer has emphasized that this was only a surmise on the part of scholars before the recently discovered ending of the Sumerian myth supplied actual textual evidence for Dumuzi's annual return to life after a six-month sojourn in the netherworld; cf. Kramer, 1966. Apart from the Mesopotamian myths, it should be stressed that we can now adduce parallels to the search motif from sources much closer in space and time to the biblical Canticle, viz. from the Ugaritic myths.

In the search for her revived consort Anat is advised by El to enlist the aid of the sun goddess Shapsh, just as she had done in the location of his body for burial.

Aloud El cried to Virgin Anat,
"Hear, O Virgin Ana[t],
Say to the Lamp of the Gods, Shapsh,
'Parched are the furrows of the field, O
Shapsh,
Parched are the furrows of El's fields.
Baal neglects his plow land.
Where is Mighty Baal,
Where is the Prince Lord of Earth?'"
Virgin Anat departed,
Then did she set face
Toward the Lamp of the Gods Shapsh.
She lifted her voice and cried,
"Message of Bull El thy father
Word of the Beneficent, your sire,
'Parched are the furrows of the fields, O
Shapsh,
Parched the furrows of El's fields.
Baal neglects his plow land.
Where is Mighty Baal,
Where the Prince Lord of Earth?'"
Then answered the lamp of the Gods,
Shapsh,
(The next two lines defy sensible
translation)
"And I will seek Mighty Baal."
Then answered Virgin Anat,
"Whither, Whither, O Shapsh,
Whither, Whither . . ."
(6[49].3.22 – 4.47)

3. The Targum identified the city patrol as composed of Moses, Aaron, and the Levites:

> Said the Assembly of Israel: Moses and Aaron and the Levites, who keep watch of the Word of the Appointment-Tent and who surround it round about, met me, and I asked them about the Glorious Presence of YHWH which had been removed from me. Moses, the great Scribe of Israel, answered and said: I will ascend to the high(est) heaven and pray before YHWH; perhaps He will forgive your guilt and make His Presence dwell among you as before.

Midrash Rabbah identified the city patrol as the tribe of Levi, on the basis of Exod. 33:27, and the loved one as Moses.

The usual Christian explanation of the watchmen is similar to that of the Targum which applied the words to Moses and Aaron as watching over Israel. The Church's watchmen were the teachers raised up by God at various times—Patriarchs, Prophets, Apostles, Doctors; cf. Isa 62:6; Jer 6:17. St. Bernard (Sermon 76) praised the good watchmen who keep long vigil while we are sleeping, who pass the night in prayers, detect the ambushes of the enemy, forestall the counsels and frustrate schemings of the malignant. Others identified the watchmen as the holy Angels who guard the Church and the faithful. The whole verse was also applied to the Gentile Church which asked the pagan philosophers and idol priests the one question they could not answer, "Have you seen Him?" Similarly the Jewish Church seeking Him in the City of Holy Writ is asked, "Have you seen Him?" Neither can answer, for unless the Lord guards the city, the watchman keeps vain vigil, Ps 127:1. (Cf. Littledale.)

4c. *loose him.* The verb *rpy,* meaning in the simple stem "be loose," is here used in the causative stem as an antonym to *'ḥz,* "grasp," "hold." The sequence of tenses, perfect followed by imperfect, attracted the attention of some critics who would see it as an inversion like the prose usage with *wāw* consecutive. This was convenient for those who wished to apply the allusion to some past event in Israel's history. Graetz, however, in keeping with his theory that the mother was violently opposed to the liaison and that the girl could not therefore bring her lover home, took the verb as future, "I will not let him go until I (shall have) brought him into my mother's house." Robert likewise, in keeping with his theory of eschatological concern, supposed that the heroine had in view a future event, one ardently awaited, the object of an anxious hope: hence the torment which she carries in her soul and imparts to us. Accordingly, Robert rendered, "Je l'ai saisi et ne le lâcherai point," in keeping with LXX *kai ouk aphēsō auton.* It seems preferable to take the imperfect here as describing the durative aspect of her hold; she would not and did not release him till she got him into the room where she wanted him.

4d,e. The term *hôrāh* is used in Hosea 2:7[5E] in parallelism with "mother,"

For their mother whored, She who bore them debauched.

In Gen 49:26 the masculine plural form *hôrai,* which might conceivably mean "my progenitors" (so *KJ*), is usually emended both on the grounds of poetic parallelism and the eminently logical assumption that the root meaning "conceive," "be pregnant," is inapplicable to the male.

The mother's house or chamber has been understood in a variety of ways. Dom Calmet supposed that the reference is to the women's quarters which were separate. The mother, he assumed, must be dead. In this connection, one is reminded of the statement, Gen. 24:67, that Isaac brought his bride into the tent of Sarah his (deceased) mother. The words "Sarah his mother" are usually expunged as an error. Graetz imagined that the mother was hostile to the liaison and that therefore the daughter could not yet bring her lover home. Harper commented that bringing him to her mother's house must signify that he was to be her acknowledged lover. Joüon held that the loss and return of the groom alludes to the Ark of the Covenant which was captured by the Philistines and eventually returned first to David's Tabernacle, then to Solomon's Temple, "the house of my mother." With this latter item Robert agreed, since he had already identified the chamber of 1:4 with the Temple and related it to the coming eschatological reign of Yahweh. For Robert "my mother's house" means the Temple. Israel, having refound her God and King (1:4) who is now enthroned in the sanctuary, has no other desire.

The cultic school related the lost and found lover to Ishtar's search for Tammuz and her descent into the netherworld to rescue him. The guards who patrol the city were seen as wardens of the seven gates of the infernal realm where at each stage Ishtar had to negotiate her admission. In the Sumerian Sacred Marriage myths, the mother of Inanna is Ningal (Great

Lady), spouse of the moon god Nanna, and her role in the marriage rite is similar to that of the mother of the bride in the Song of Songs. It is to her mother's abode that Inanna brings her spouse Dumuzi and he has to "say the word" to the mother and sprinkle cypress oil on the ground before the official union. The goddess sings ecstatically as she brings her lover home.

I have come to our mother's gate,
I, in joy I walk,
I have come to Ningal's gate,
I, in joy I walk.
To my mother he will say the word,
He will sprinkle cypress oil on the ground,
To my mother Ningal he will say the word,
He will sprinkle cypress oil on the ground,
He whose dwelling is fragrant,
Whose word brings deep joy.
My lord is seemly for the holy lap,
Amaushumgalanna, the son-in-law of Sin,
The lord Dumuzi is seemly for the holy lap,
Amaushumgalanna, the son-in-law of Sin.
(*SMR*, 78)

Dumuzi's enigmatic cognomen "Amaushumgalanna" seems to mean, according to Kramer, "The Mother, dragon of Heaven." Perhaps it reflects a Semitic type theophorous name in the form of a nominal sentence, "The Mother (is) the dragon of Heaven." Sin is the Semitic name for Nanna, the moon god of Ur.

4. The Targum made the mother's house the Tent of Meeting and turned the chamber to classrooms for instruction in the Law, with Moses and Joshua as the teachers:

> Then after a little time, YHWH turned from His fierce anger and He commanded Moses, the prophet, to make the Appointment-Tent and the Ark and He caused His Presence to dwell in the midst of it. And the people of the House of Israel offered their sacrifices and were occupied with the words of the Law in the chamber of the House of Study of Moses, their Master, and in the classroom of Joshua, son of Nun, his assistant.

Midrash Rabbah identified the loved one here as Daniel and devoted considerable attention to the handwriting on the wall, and other details of Belshazzar's feast.

Christian interpreters found in this verse a variety of hidden meanings. The opening word, *kim'aṭ*, "scarcely," "just a little," was loaded with meanings. It is only a little that one has to wait for Christ, since He comes the moment one forsakes self and sin. The knowledge of God is granted with little toil, since He gives himself freely and instantly the moment He perceives the affection of the seeker. The creed which sums up the mysteries of salvation is quickly learned. Momentarily affliction prepares an eternal, incomparable load of glory (II Cor 4:17). The time between the utterance of the Canticle and the coming of Christ was nine centuries, yet it seemed only a little while because of the Church's love for Him. The "passing" was applied to learning and completion of the course of instruction. "Holding fast" could be and was related to devotion and persistence in prayer. "Mother's house" was understood by some expositors as referring to the Synagogue as parent of the Church which resolved never to release her hold on her Lord by zealous prayer until He turn and have mercy on the Synagogue and enter into the hearts of the Jews and dwell there. The mother's house was also applied to the Church and to the individual soul in a variety of ways. Theodoret related the verse to Gal. 4:26, explaining that the Bride with the holy boldness of love declares that she will not let her Bridegroom go until she bring Him into her true mother's house, "the Jerusalem above which is free and the mother of us all." And this is because Christ Himself dwells in holy souls (II Cor. 6:16). The Venerable Bede related 3:1–4 to Mary Magdalene who sought her Lord during the night of His absence from His Church, came with spices to His tomb, was found there by the Angels, questioned them about Him, passed them, found Him whom her soul loved, and did not let Him go till He sent tidings of His Resurrection back to Jerusalem by her. This passage, accordingly, forms the first Lesson in the Breviary at St. Mary Magdalene's Day. (Cf. Littledale.)

5. The Targum again, as in 2:7, made Moses adjure the Israelites:

> When the seven nations heard that the Israelites were about to seize their land, they rose at once and cut the trees, stopped up the water springs, laid waste their towns and fled. Said the Holy One, blessed be He, to Moses, the prophet: "I promised the fathers of these to bring up their children to seize the land producing milk and honey. But I am bringing their children into a land waste and empty. I will now detain them forty years in the wilderness, that My Law may be blended into their bodies and meanwhile these wicked peoples will build up what they have destroyed." Thus Moses spoke to the Israelites: "I adjure you, O Assembly of Israel, by YHWH of Hosts, and by the Strong One of the Land of Israel, that you do not presume to go up to the land of the Canaanites until the completion of the forty years and it be the will of YHWH to deliver the inhabitants of the land into your hands, and you will cross the Jordan and the land will be subdued before you."

6a. *Who.* The interrogative pronoun *mî* regularly means "who?" in Hebrew, but in Akkadian it has the meaning "what?" Such changes in meaning are not uncommon in closely related languages; compare, e.g. the reverse of meaning in English and German who/where and *wo/wer*. The basis for the assumption of the change of meaning is the presumption that the answer to the question "who/what is this?" is given in the succeeding verse, "Behold the bed of Solomon." One would expect the answer to be given immediately to the question, as it is in Isa 63:1:

Who is this coming from Edom,
Garment stained from Bozrah?
The one glorious in apparel,
Striding in his great strength?
"(It is) I who speak vindication,
Mighty to save,"

Or in Jer 46:7,8:

Who is this that rises like the Nile,
Like floods whose waters surge?
Egypt rises like the Nile,
Like floods whose waters surge.

But the answer need not be given at all, on the assumption that it is obvious or well known, e.g. in Isa 60:8,

Who are these that fly up like a cloud, Like doves to their crannies?

The answer is understood from the context to be the Israelites in the Diaspora stirred up to return to the Land of Promise. To judge from the use of the same rhetorical device elsewhere in the Canticle, 6:10, no answer need be given, since the succeeding verse cannot very well be taken as an answer. Either there is no connection between 6:10 and 6:11, or else the answer must be obvious. The key to the understanding of the present verse has to be seen in the identical line in 8:5a, and there it is clear from the succeeding line that the one who comes up from the desert is none other than the Bride.

ascending. Robert noted that this detail embarrasses most commentators who forget that often in the Bible *'ly* is a consecrated term meaning "aller à Jérusalem," used not only in speaking of a traveler who goes to the Holy City from any point of Palestine or Egypt, but even from such distant regions as the Tigris and Euphrates (Ezra 1:3,11, 2:1,59, 4:2, 7:6,7,28, 8:1; Neh 7:5,6,61, 12:1). Accordingly, Robert declared that this is undoubtedly the sense here, given the author's preoccupations and the texts which he utilizes as a base (Isaiah 58, 59, 60, 62, 63:15–64:12, 66:1), and that one is justified in assuming that the thought is of the return of the captives. What the author allegedly sees going up to Jerusalem is a caravan of repatriates.

steppe. The term *miḏbār* designates the unsettled and unsown steppe-land where vegetation grows spontaneously, in spite of sparse rainfall, and where cattle and sheep browse and various wild animals roam (cf. Jer 2:2; Hosea 2:5[3E]; Joel 2:22; Ps 65:13[12E]; Job 38:26). The term is applied to specific areas, such as Edom, Beer-sheba, Damascus, Gibeon, Ziph, Judea, Moab, Sinai, En Gedi, Paran, Qadesh, Tekoa, etc. The desert par excellence is the Syrian and Arabian desert to the east of Palestine (cf. Judg 11:22). Ginsburg rendered the term here as "country," Haupt as "meadows" (explained as "the pasture-land"). Budde and others, following Wetzstein, took the term to refer to the open area outside the city gate, the threshing floor, where weddings were celebrated. Siegfried saw the reference to the desert as a purely poetic trait. Robert divined a spectator posted on the heights around Jerusalem who sees in reality, or is supposed to see hyperbolically, the caravan of repatriates coming from the northeast.

In Mesopotamian and Ugaritic myth the desert or steppe-land was a term for the netherworld. Both Dumuzi and Baal took to the steppe-land in anticipation of their approaching doom. Dumuzi in premonition of his fate took to the steppe:

His heart was filled with tears, he went forth to the steppe,
The shepherd—his heart filled with tears, he went forth to the steppe,
He fastened his flute (?) about his neck, uttered a lament:
"Set up a lament, set up a lament, O steppe, set up a lament,
O steppe, set up a lament, set up a wail . . ."

(*SMR,* 121*f*)

In order to "sweeten the place where her husband lies," the desertlike steppe, Inanna killed another deity, Old Bilulu and turned her into a water skin to supply fresh cool water for her love (*SMR*, 130*ff*).

In Ugaritic myth Baal also met his doom in the desert or steppe-land. In anticipation of his impending demise at the hands of Mot (Death), Baal is told to take his meteorological paraphernalia and entourage and descend to the netherworld:

And thou take thy clouds,
Thy wind, thy buckets(?), thy rain,
With thee thy seven lads,
Thy eight swine(?)
With thee Pidray, girl of light,
With thee Ṭallay, girl of rain,
Then set face toward Mount Knkny;
Lift the mountain on the hands,
The hill on the top of the palms;
Descend to the infernal charnel house
Be counted among those who descend
into Earth.

———

Mighty Baal hearkened.
He loved a heifer in the pasture,
A cow in the steppe of Šḥlmmt.
He lay with her seventy-seven (times),
She made (him) mount eighty-eight
And she conceived and bore a male.
(5[67].5.6–22)

It was in the same place that Mot met and mangled Baal, as he boasted to Baal's sister-consort, Anat, who sought her missing lover. In response to Anat's plea, "Thou, Mot (Death), give (me) my brother!" Mot replied:

What do you wish, O Virgin Anat?
I went and I roamed
Every mountain to the inwards of Earth.
Every hill to the inwards of the fields/
steppes.
Soul was lacking among men,
Soul (among) earth's multitudes.
I came to the pleasant pasture land,
To the beautiful fields/steppes of Šḥlmmt.
I met Mighty Baal;
I put him like a lamb in my mouth,
Like a kid in my jaws was he crushed.
(6[49].2.12–23)

Sparing philological commentary on the Ugaritic passages rendered above, it will suffice to note that the terms rendered "pasture" (*dbr*) and "pasture-land" (*arṣ dbr*) are manifestly approximate synonyms for the cognate term *mdbr*, "desert." Both terms *dbr* and *mdbr* are used in poetic parallelism with *šd*, "field," "steppe"; in the passages above *dbr* or *arṣ dbr* is parallel to *šd šḥlmmt*. The analysis of *šḥlmmt* is uncertain, but the connection with the netherworld is indicated by the context, and the consonants *mt* or *mmt* may refer to death. Some connect *šḥl* with Arabic *sāḥil*, "shore," thus *šḥlmmt* would mean "shore of death." Others would take *šḥl* as meaning lion and thus *šḥlmmt* would mean "lion that kills" or "Lion of Mametu," as a title of Nergal (cf. *UT* 19.2396). Elsewhere in Ugaritic *mdbr* is used in parallelism with *šd*, "field," "steppe." In the poem called The Birth of the Beautiful Gods which relates a sexual liaison between El and a pair of females, the voracious offspring of the union, whose mouths stretch from heaven to earth and who gulp the birds of the air and the fish in the sea, are sent away with their mothers to forage in the desert or steppe. El addresses them thus:

"O wives (whom) I espoused,
O sons (whom) I begot,
Up, forage in the Desert of Qadesh;
There sojourn with stones and trees
Seven full years, eight cycles."
While the beautiful gods walked the steppe,
Roamed the edge of the desert,
There met them the Guard of the Sown,
And they cried to the Guard of the Sown,
"O Guard, Guard, ope[n]."
And he opened a breach for them and they entered.
(23[52].64–71)

The parallelism of *mdbr* and *šd* here and of (*arṣ*) *dbr* and *šd* in the passages preceding suggest that the terms *dbr* and *mdbr* are virtually synonymous.

The goddess Ishtar has a significant relationship of some sort with the desert or steppe, since one of her epithets is "Lady of the Steppe," *bēlit ṣēri*. A similar title is applied to Ashtart in Ugaritic, *'ṯtrt šd,* "Ashtart of the Steppe."

6b. *columns*. This word occurs elsewhere only in Joel 3:3[2:30E] among evil portents in the heavens and on the earth, blood and fire, and columns of smoke, presaging the terrible day of Yahweh. The term *tîmĕrāh* is apparently a synonym for *'ammûḏ,* "pillar," "column," applied to the pillars of fire and cloud symbolizing the presence of Yahweh preceding the Israelites in the desert, Exod 13:21,22, 14:19,24; Neh 9:12,19. In Judg 20:40 a column of smoke, *'ammûd 'āšān,* rose from the burning of Gibeah. In the present passage LXX and Vulgate rendered "like a pillar of smoke," but Aquila read *kiṯmûnaṯ, hōs homoiōsis,* "like the likeness," instead of *kĕṯîmĕrôṯ*. LXX and Vulgate appear to be correct in construing the form as plural of generalization and rendering it as singular. There is no need to emend the prefix *k-* to *b-,* or to change the plural form to singular, as do several errant critics. The column of cloud by day and fire by night as the sign of the divine presence during Israel's wilderness wanderings suggest that here the smoke column may also be the sign of a theophany.

6c. *Redolent*. With MT and LXX reading *mequṭṭereṯ,* against the reading of Aquila and Vulgate which reflect the reading *miqqĕṭōreṯ, ex aromatibus*. Although the factitive stem of *qṭr* is used numerous times of offering sacrifice, i.e. of making the animal or the incense go up in smoke, the passival form of the factitive stem here used is unique. Nevertheless, in view of the manifest denominative origin of this verb, the meaning "perfumed," or "censed" is eminently appropriate here, with *KJ* and *RSV,* against Luther, "von Myrrhen," and similar renderings that take the *m-* prefix as the partitive use of the preposition *min,* "from," e.g. *NEB,* "from burning myrrh." In accordance with the common usage of the active factitive stem in the sense of sacrifice, some interpreters have supposed that clouds of smoke and incense ascended from the multitude of offerings, such as were offered when David brought the ark to Jerusalem (II Sam 6:13) and Solomon installed it in the Temple.

incense. The term *lĕḇônāh* means literally "white (stuff)," since the best grade, or frank-incense, was whitish when crushed into flakes or powder. In Exod 30:34 the recipe for making pure and holy perfume of sweet spices included pure *lĕḇônāh*. The stuff was burned along with other sacrificial materials; cf. Lev 2:1–2,15–16.

6d. *pedlar's*. The participle *rôḵēl,* "merchant," like our term "trader" (treader) is related to the itinerant aspect of commercial activity. The Arabic verb *rkl* means "kick a horse in order to make him go." Ezek 27:12–25 lists some of the international commerce that moved by sea and land through the port city of Tyre, including the best of all kinds of spices. The pedlar's powders are thus imports and there is nothing to suggest that the reference is to tribute paid to Solomon.

powders. The feminine noun *'ăḇāqāh,* here used in the construct state, is not found elsewhere in the Bible, but the masculine form *'āḇāq* is used in Deut 28:24 as a synonym of *'āpār,* "dust"; in Exod 9:9 it is applied to the ashes or soot from the kiln sprinkled on the Egyptians to produce the plague of boils; in Ezek 26:10 it is used of the dust raised by horses and chariots; and in Nahum 1:3 of the whirlwind as the dust cloud at Yahweh's feet. The meaning "powder" is appropriate to the present context. The word is of special interest as the source of the term *abacus* which in its primitive form was a tray of sand, rather than a frame of beads, used for arithmetical computation.

6. As for the meaning of this verse, Dom Calmet saw the bride coming from her quarters, welcomed by her companions with a cry of admiration. They compare her to a column of aromatic smoke. Although this comparison is somewhat unusual, it fittingly emphasizes the tall stature of the Shulamite, her majestic bearing, her straight and confident gait. According to Delitzsch, the bride comes from a great distance, from Galilee; because of the difference in rank, Solomon does not go to meet her, as was the custom (cf. I Macc 9:39), but had her brought to him. She comes, not on a camel like Rebecca, but carried on a litter surrounded by an escort for protection and as a mark of honor. The lavish expenditure of spices, the smoke and fragrance of which signaled the approach of the procession from afar, are part of the royal honors. For Budde, the perfume is from the bridal bed (cf. Prov 7:17). Haupt took the references to rising from the desert to mean that the village of the bridegroom was probably situated on a hill so that the procession came up from the meadows between the two villages. The pillars of smoke he explained as the beacon fire carried in a cresset on a long pole at the head of the caravan to serve as a guiding light at night, while the smoke signaled the direction during the day. This is the origin of the legend of Exod 13:21; cf. Exod 14:19; Num 14:14; Deut 1:33; Isa 4:5; Neh 9:12,19; Ps 78:14. (Alexander the Great on his march through Babylonia and Susiana reportedly had a long beacon pole over the royal tent which could be seen everywhere as fire by night and smoke by day.) The bride is so perfumed that the sweet smell may be noticed at a distance. (In Ps 45:9[8E] the garments of the bridegroom are all fragrant with myrrh and powder of aloes.) Harper supposed that King Solomon comes from Jerusalem to the royal residence in the north, in special splendor in order to overawe the Shulamite. She notices the approaching train and asks what it may be. Joüon saw a description of the taking of the ark to the sanctuary in Jerusalem.

Robert perceived eschatological concerns. The mass of returning captives cross the great Syrian desert, or are seen as they advance in the desert of Judea; Yahweh is in their midst. This is a classical datum, Yahweh leading his people in Palestine (Jer 31:7–10, 32:37; Ezek 34:11–16, 36:24, 37:21, 39:27–28; especially Isa 40:3–5,9–11, 43:5–6, 46:3–4, 49:9b–10, 52:7–9,12 53:10–12; finally Zech 10:8,10). Among these texts Robert called special attention to Isa 52:12 which makes manifest allusion to the column of fire and smoke guiding and protecting the Israelites during the exodus from Egypt. Such is exactly the point of view of our author, according to Robert; the column of smoke is a sign of the divine presence and protection, at the same time giving to the return from exile the character of a second exodus. There is nothing in the description, according to Robert, which makes one think of a wedding procession, nor even anything which announces the presence of the bride.

A fatal flaw in all previous interpretations is alleged by Gerleman to be the failure to offer a satisfactory answer to the question "Who is that coming up from the desert?" A sensible interpretation of this verse, according to Gerleman, can only be achieved by regarding it as an independent piece freed from all connection with a wedding. The Old Testament knows nothing of a nocturnal procession coming out of the desert with myrrh and incense and protected by a weapon-wielding escort, and Gerleman proposes a radically new interpretation drawn from the Egyptian sphere. The parallel he finds in the two great processional festivals at Luxor, the Opet festival when the God Amun was carried from Karnak to join his consort Mut at Luxor, and the "Valley Festival" when Amun was taken across the Nile to visit the mortuary temples on the west bank. Both festivals are described in numerous songs and hymns and depicted in more or less complete pictorial sequence. Each begins with a festive procession and ends with a recession along the same route. In the procession of the god to his house, the people, accompanied by the king who leads the procession, go to the graves which for the holiday are turned into "the House of the Heart's Joy." Priests dispensing incense, and numerous armed soldiers, accompany the procession which takes place in the night. The nucleus around which the procession is formed is the portable boats, the great bark of Amun and three smaller barks, one of which was for the king. The events with which these annual festivals are connected are obviously a very significant part of ancient Egyptian social life in which everyone took part and which gradually took on secular character. The Opet festival continued into the New Kingdom, being mentioned by Ramses II and III, and is attested at least as late as Pianchi. The common features of the Egyptian festivals, and the portrayal of the procession in the Canticle—the desert, the incense, the palanquin, the escort, the night—are indeed striking and Gerleman finds it tempting to assume, in view of these correspondences, that an Israelite poet, probably in the court circles, formed his portrayal of a royal procession after the manner of the Egyptian festival which was well known to him. That does not mean, however, that the cultic character of the Egyptian festival is to be found in the Canticle, that an Israelite king was thought of as a participant in an Egyptian festival. The similarity relates only to the artistic representational matters. The portrayal of the procession is enriched with traits borrowed from the pompous festal culture of Egypt.

The defect which Gerleman saw in previous interpretations, namely the failure to account for the female who is the central figure in the procession, also applies to Gerleman's interpretation. The poem which follows, 3:9–11, and the present passage are regarded as independent poems having originally nothing to do with one another, but brought together by a collector as a connected poem the theme of which is a royal wedding, the festal arrival of a princess and the waiting king. All this is for Gerleman a "Royal Travesty"; the loving couple are set in a "wish-situation" in the royal sphere of life. The procession here depicted is reminiscent of the representation of Yahweh's descent from Sinai to his sanctuary, as recognized by Kuhn (1926, 528). The desert, the pillar of smoke and the ark of the covenant are matched in the Canticle by the desert, the fumes of incense and myrrh, and the royal litter.

Schmökel looked to Mesopotamia rather than Egypt for light on this procession. The colors for the representation here are borrowed from the Sumero-Akkadian procession as best known from the New Year's festival in Babylon. All the gods presumably had, like Marduk, their procession, and Schmökel suggested that Dumuzi was festally received on his return from the netherworld, and that a syncretized form of Yahweh, garbed in the raiment of the returning Tammuz, was hymned at the Spring Festival. The sixty warriors as companions of the bride, Schmökel suggested, are related to the sacred number of Ishtar, as in 6:8, and their function may be to protect the newly risen Tammuz from the pursuing hostile powers of the netherworld, the "Terror of the Night." The sword bearers surround the throne on which the chosen representative of Tammuz sits in splendor; smoke rises from the brazier before him and the choir assembled in the sanctuary sings an introit. This is the beginning of the third and final scene of the cult-drama of the Song of Songs as understood by Schmökel. A further point is made by Schmökel in connection with this passage, namely that the peasant wedding festival of Lebanon in the time of Wetzstein, might be an echo of the ancient Ishtar-Tammuz rites, but could not itself explain the text of the Song of Songs.

Renan's understanding of this scene may serve as representative of the dramatic school. The scene has a character peculiar to itself. The interlocutors are the bourgeois of Jerusalem, who form a male chorus. They assist, and we make them assist, at a solemn entry of Solomon into Jerusalem. We see first the cortège in the distance, which announces itself by a cloud of perfumes. Then the palanquin of Solomon defiles past, its guard composed of sixty men; its litter contains a new dazzling beauty whom he is taking to his seraglio, and the king himself, with his crown on his head, ready for the ceremony of marriage.

The Targum ascribed the exclamation to the peoples of the land on the appearance of Israel approaching from the desert:

> When Israel came up from the wilderness and crossed the Jordan with Joshua, son of Nun, the peoples of the land exclaimed: What chosen people is this coming up from the wilderness, perfumed with incense of spices, supported by the merit of Abraham who worshiped and prayed before YHWH on Mount Moriah, anointed with the oil of grandees, with the righteousness of Isaac who was bound in the shrine of the Holy Temple, called the Mountain of Incense, and for whom miracles were wrought, through the persistence of Jacob who wrestled with him till the break of dawn and overcame him; and he was delivered, he and the twelve tribes.

Midrash Rabbah expatiated on this verse at considerable length. The wilderness was the source of Israel's elevation and decline (cf. Num 14:35). From the wilderness came the Law, the tabernacle, the Sanhedrin, the priesthood, the service of the Levites, royalty, and prophecy. The pillars of smoke were related to the pillars of fire and cloud in the wilderness wandering. The myrrh was referred to Abraham, the frankincense to Isaac, and the pedlar's powders to Jacob. Rabbi Johanan related the aromatics to the incense of the house of Abṭinas, a priestly family which had the secret formula for preparing frankincense for the Temple. The question, "Who is this, etc.," clearly relates to a female whom the Midrash identified as Elisheba, daughter of Amminadab and wife of Aaron. This estimable lady experienced five joys in a single day; her brother-in-law (Moses) became king, her brother (Nahshon) a prince, her husband (Aaron) high priest, her two sons deputy high priests, and her grandson (Phineas) the priest anointed for war. But her joy turned to mourning when her sons were destroyed and she became like pillars of smoke.

Christian writers ascribed the question to the patriarchs of the Jewish Church watching in wonder at the Gentile Church rising from the wilderness of heathenism, or to the Angels marveling at the progress of the soul that clings to Christ. The Church, or the holy soul, dwells in the wilderness of the world, in exile from the kingdom, but not deserted by her Spouse. She always strives to come up to reach Him whom she loves. The pillar of smoke represents those who strip themselves of evil habits and worldly wealth and rise in the perfume of fair fame and buoyancy of spirit. Myrrh denotes mortification of the flesh, and frankincense the purity of prayer; the former is applied to the dead body of sinful pleasures of the world and the latter is burned in the censer of the heart, on the coals of virtue, with the fires of God's love. The powders are other virtues, good works of the faithful soul, not in lumps, but uniformly distributed, as ground by contrition. The word for pillars, *tîmĕrôṯ*, was connected with *tāmār*, "palm tree," which, slender and straight below, spreads out a wide crown of perennially green foliage, amid which hang luscious fruits; and because the palm never bends before the winds, it is a symbol of victory. Thus the Church, from small beginnings, shot up to stately height and spread its perpetual youthfulness and fecundity through the world, and, unshaken by persecutions, now stands as the memorial of Christ's triumph over the grave.

The application to the Assumption of the Blessed Virgin was made in the pseudepigraphic letter to Paula and Eustochia attributed to St. Jerome. The Holy Ghost speaks of her ascension: Who is this that ascends through the wilderness as a slender wand of smoke from spices? Like a slender wand of smoke (*sicut virgula fumi*) because she was slight and delicate, worn with holy discipline, but kindled within, as a burnt offering, by the fire of devout love and longing charity. Of smoke from spices (*ex aromatibus*) because she was filled with the perfumes of many virtues, so that the sweetest fragrance flowed from her, pleasing even to angelic spirits. The Mother of God once ascended from the desert of this world as a Rod sprung from the root of Jesse and now the souls of the elect marvel in gladness that she surpasses the dignity of angels in the sanctity of her merits. (Cf. Littledale.)

7a. *bed.* The term *miṭṭāh* is one of the two common words for bed, couch, litter, used for sleep, rest, recuperation from illness, for feasting and revelry (Ezek 23:41; Esther 1:6) and presumably for love-making, although the term *miškāḇ* is commonly used when sexual activity is specifically mentioned. It may be portable (I Sam 19:15) and serve as a litter or bier (II Sam 3:31). Royalty and the wealthy had beds ornamented with ivory (Amos 6:4) and gold and silver (Esther 1:6).

6–7. The answer to the question, "Who is this ascending from the steppe?" appears to be given in the following verse, "Behold the bed of Solomon." Solomon's "bed" would thus be or include his intended bride. In Lu-dingirra's description of the remarkable "mother," who, as J. S. Cooper suggested (1971, 162) may not be a natural mother at all, but the goddess Inanna in motherly guise, the lady is equated, among other seemingly bizarre things, with a chariot (see Introduction, pp. 70–72) and a litter, both aromatic:

I shall give you a fifth sign about my mother:
My mother is a palm tree, with a very sweet smell.
A chariot of pine wood, a litter of boxwood.
A good . . . giving perfumed oil.

We have rabbinic witness that the word for "couch" in 1:12a, *mēsaḇ,* was used by vulgar Jerusalemites with reference to one's partner in sexual intercourse. The Arabic *'irs,* "husband" or "wife," dual *'arsān,* "husband and wife," may be related to the word *'arš,* "couch," Hebrew *'ereś,* in spite of the irregularity of the sibilants. It should occasion no surprise to find terms for "bed" used with sexual entendre. If the bed or the litter here contains the bride, or is used in 3:7a as a surrogate for the bride, we can then understand the personal interrogative "who?" rather than "what?" in 3:6a.

Solomon. Solomon's bed is here designated, pleonastically, "his bed which is to Solomon," *miṭṭāṭō šellišlōmōh,* as with "my vineyard which is to me" for "my vineyard" 1:6, 8:12 (cf. GKC, 129h). This pleonasm has become the regular mode for indicating the possessive in modern Hebrew.

A number of critics delete or otherwise tamper with this line. Budde, e.g., augmented it to read, "Behold the bed of the king, king Solomon." There is no valid cause for altering the line.

The reference to Solomon here and elsewhere in the Canticle gives critics no little difficulty. Outside the Canticle, with the possible exception of the superscription of Ps 72, references to Solomon are generally taken as historical, but few except ultra-conservative interpreters consider the Canticle to have close connection with Solomon. The suggestion that the Canticle was composed on the occasion of Solomon's marriage to an Egyptian princess has few proponents. For most critics, of whatever school, Solomon is invoked as a literary fiction. Kuhn distinguished two different Solomons in the Canticle, one the historical figure and the other Wisdom incarnate, desirous of intimacy with the nation Israel. In allegorical interpretations, Solomon represents either God or the Messiah. Ricciotti took the references 3:7–9 and 8:11–12 to mean Solomon son of David, but here and elsewhere in the Canticle to represent Yahweh.

Robert regarded it as incredible that the pompous monarch of the tenth century would be presented in the Canticle. The eschatological sense which Robert read in the Canticle has no place for the figure of Solomon. Further, it is repugnant to apply the name of Solomon to Yahweh. And what of Solomon's mother mentioned in vs. 11? To attribute a mother to Yahweh would be anathema to post-exilic orthodoxy. The hypothesis favored by Robert is that the name of Solomon in the Canticle is a messianic title. The superscription to Psalm 72 and its content, which describes the messianic reign as an epoch of peace and prosperity, suggested to Robert that the author designated the Messiah under the title Solomon. This induction finds confirmation, in Robert's view, in the title Shulamite applied to the bride in 7:1[6:13E]. The word *šālôm,* Robert explained, expresses a state of being in which nothing is lacking and which has no fear of being troubled in its quietude. It is euphoria with security. Nothing better could be desired for oneself and for others, above all, naturally, in times of suffering. The hope for peace is part of the eschatological expectation (Isa 26:3,12, 32:17–18, 48:18; Pss 29:11, 85:9–14[8–13E], 125:5=128:6); it is tied to the hope of the return of the captives (Isa 52:17, 60:17, 66:12; Jer 33:6; Ezek 37:26; Zech 9:10–12; cf. Pss 22:6–9, 147:14). It has finally a purely messianic character (Isa 9:5–6; Ezek 34:25; Micah 5:4; Zech 9:10; Ps 72:7–8). Thus the title of Solomon awarded by our author to the mysterious personage whom he makes enter the scene at this point is, in Robert's view, the echo of the intense desire for peace which animates the souls of his contemporaries. The connections which this Messiah of the Canticle sustains with Yahweh is further elaborated by Robert in connection with 8:1.

A number of modern critics sought to solve the difficulties by removing the name of Solomon. Meek observed, however, that if Solomon in this passage is not playing the role of the god in a festal procession, it is difficult to see how his name got into the text, and to delete it, with Jastrow and others, is too easy a way out. Moreover, there is no indication anywhere that the bridegroom in secular weddings was ever carried in procession, whereas the god was. Solomon's name, according to Meek, is manifestly derived from Shelem, the name of a fertility god; the name appears also in the word Jerusalem, abbreviated Salem in Gen 14:18; Ps 76:3[2E]. If our book is a liturgy, the name that stood here originally must have been Shelem, and it was changed to Solomon when the liturgy came to be adapted to the Jerusalem cultus. This suggestion by Meek seems plausible, and a god Shalim is now known from the Ugaritic myth, The Birth of the Beautiful Gods. This god, however, has a very minor role in the myth and it seems quite unlikely that such an insignificant deity could be the male protagonist of the Canticle. Moreover, though the bed is designated as Solomon's, there is nothing to suggest that he is the incumbent. It may rather be that the occupant is the bride, as suggested by the personal interrogative "who?" and the feminine demonstrative and verb.

According to Hirschberg (1961, 380) there has been a total misunderstanding of *šlmh* in the Song of Songs. The beloved is one whose physical charms are already intimately known to her lover and, since it is hardly possible to assume that an illicit relationship would give rise to songs of praise publicly recited, we have to accept the theory that the Canticle deals with a wedding. But it is, Hirschberg maintains, a wedding song of a peculiar character—namely in honor of a bride whose marriage has already been consummated. The root *šlm* has the sense of "perfecting" or "concluding" (an action) and in certain Arabic tribes it was customary to give the bride a gratuity (*taslīmat*) before the first cohabitation after defloration. While the root *šlm* may also mean "to pay," the particular character of this present makes its understanding as "consummation-gift" more likely.

7b,c. *heroes/valiants*. The same word, *gibbôr,* is used in both lines. This is the term applied to David's elite guard; cf. II Sam 10:7, 23:9,16,17,22; I Kings 1:8. Some critics would delete 7c, *miggibbôrê yiśrāʾēl* "of the heroes of Israel," as metrically superfluous and as an explanatory gloss to the preceding line which needs no explanation. There is no valid reason to reject the line. In connection with the preceding line it may be understood in the sense of a superlative, "heroes . . . of the heroes of Israel," i.e. the elite of an elite. Following Wetzstein and Budde, the military motif finds an explanation in Syrian weddings. In certain times and places in Syria, an armed escort may have been necessary and afterward became ceremonial. Weddings were celebrated with martial display in the cities as well as in the villages.

Joüon noted that the ark was associated with war and was a pledge of victory and that the priesthood was always quite military. The sixty warriors in Joüon's view were the priests who surround the ark. Ricciotti referred to the priests and elders mentioned in I Kings 8:3–4. Thilo assumed that the sixty were composed of five from each of the twelve tribes of Israel. Robert was content to note that Solomon was a king and it was normal that he would have his guards. The warriors surround the litter. There is no indication that Solomon occupied the litter. Joüon supposed that Yahweh's invisible presence was in the litter. Siegfried supposed that the king was in the litter, but not visible; the author of the Canticle puts himself in the place of the spectator who sees the litter, but not the king inside.

The Targum made of Solomon's bed the Temple, and of the sixty heroes, the letters of the priestly blessing (Num 6:24–26):

> When Solomon, the king of Israel, built the Temple of YHWH in Jerusalem, YHWH spoke through His Word: How lovely is this Temple, built for Me by the hands of King Solomon, son of David. And how comely are the priests at the time they spread their hands standing on their dais and blessing the people of the House of Israel with the sixty letters which were transmitted to Moses their Master, and with that blessing surrounding them like a high and strong wall and with which all the valiants of Israel are strengthened and prospered.

Midrash Rabbah, in addition to relating the sixty men to the letters of the priestly blessing (Num 6:24–26), referred the number also to the divisions of the priests and Levites (twenty-four each) and the divisions of the people of Israel (twelve); cf. I Chronicles 24, 25, 27. Rabbi Johanan interpreted the verse as referring to the Sanhedrin, but the Rabbis generally related the verse to the sixty myriads over twenty years of age who went forth from Egypt (cf. Num 1:44).

Christian interpreters understood Solomon's bed to represent the Church, because therein the Saints delight in the embrace of the true Prince of Peace. The sixty valiant men were seen as the Doctors who defend the Church with their preaching or seek heavenly bliss through contemplation. Sixty, as made up of six and ten, suggested the six days within which God finished his work and the wages (a denarius) to be paid the faithful laborers in the vineyard. David's elite guard consisted of thirty warriors and his kingdom denotes only the Jewish Church. But this Solomon rules both Jews and Gentiles and therefore his guard is doubled. Or the sixty valiant ones are holy thoughts and resolutions which guard the soul, armed with the sword of the Spirit. They are sixty because the five senses, ruled and guided by reason, become a sixth supreme sense and these are trained in obedience to the Ten Commandments to resist the snares and terrors of the Evil One. Again the bed on which the King lay down was the Cross, the bridal bed of the Church, wherein is the true repose of the Saints, which is also the battle standard round which the valiant are ranged. The bed of Solomon was also referred to the hallowed womb of the Virgin Mother, fenced about by the Patriarchs, Kings, and Prophets, or by the special guard of Angels around the manger of His birth. Other interpretations held the bed to represent Holy Writ, or prayer, or the tomb around which the Jews posted a guard, or the final repose of the faithful in the bliss of heaven. (Cf. Littledale.)

8a,b. *war-skilled/battle-taught*. The passive participle in the expression *'ăḥûzê ḥereḇ* has been generally taken in the active sense, as, e.g. *KJ* "They all hold swords." *AT* and *RSV* rendered with passive participles, "armed," and "girt." Delitzsch almost divined the sense of the expression in his commentary but did not indicate it in translation; he explained that the expression properly means "held fast by the sword so that it does not let them free, which, according to the sense=holding fast (=practised in the use of the sword)." F. Perles (1922, 52*f*) noted the exact parallel between the two passive participles and, on the basis of Akkadian *aḫāzu,* "learn," suggested that the meaning is "skilled with the sword." J. Greenfield (1964, 532*f*) called attention to the similar use of the Ugaritic cognate in the expression *aḫd ḥrṯh,* "skilled in plowing," as applied to oxen (1129.8–9). In this light, M. Dahood read in Ps 77:5 *'ăḥûzôṯ* instead of MT *'āḥaztā* and rendered, "My eyes are accustomed to vigils" (cf. *PS II,* first NOTE on Ps 77:5). The synonymy of the verbal forms suggests the same for the nouns, and the choice may fall with either of the meanings "war" or "weapons," since *ḥereḇ,* "sword," may be taken in the sense of Arabic *ḥarb,* "war," and similarly *milḥāmāh* may designate not only war but also weapons; cf. Lewy, 1938, 98*f;* Driver, 1947, and 1950, 145*f.* It seems best to take both nouns in the broader sense of war or battle, with *JPSV,*

All of them trained in warfare, Skilled in battle.

8d. In agreement with the line of interpretation based on Wetzstein's study of Syrian peasant weddings, S. Krauss (1936, 323–330) sought to explain the night terror on comparative anthropological grounds. Krauss took his cue from G. Dalman's observation (1928, I, 639) that the nocturnal terrors may be the demons threatening the marriage procession and that the pillars of incense mentioned in 3:6 were intended to disperse these evil epirits. Krauss, however, correctly emphasized that the sixty guards protect Solomon's bed and not the wedding procession. Demons were believed to be especially dangerous at nuptial affairs and to lie in wait for newlyweds. Krauss suggested that the present passage relates to the motif of the Tobias-Nights, the story in the Book of Tobit (3:7*ff*) about the unlucky Sarah who had lost seven husbands to the wicked demon Asmodeus before any of them could consummate the marriage. The same motif is found in II Esd 10:1. The Jewish custom of continence for a three-day period after marriage has been supposed to be based on the fear of demons. Similarly the marriage canopy (*ḥuppāh*) has been thought to be originally a shelter against the demons. In Vedic religion the demons were believed to threaten the bride, and arrows were shot into the air to repel them (cf. *EUT,* 40n70). In Armenia the bride and groom were guarded by a man armed with a sword. The accompaniment of the bride and groom by a number of men and women, the paranymphs of the Greeks, the *šwšbyn* of the rabbis, and the bridesmen and bridesmaids of the English wedding, may go back to this belief, as Krauss suggested.

Interesting material was cited by Krauss from rabbinic sources illustrative of the terrors connected with nuptials. In view of the reported deaths of one or both of the newlyweds, usually the groom, in the bridal chamber, Krauss suggested a new understanding of Ps 19:6[5E], "like the bridegroom coming out of the *ḥuppāh*." Similarly the Baptist's words in John 3:29 become intelligible: "It is the bridegroom who has the bride; but the bridegroom's friend who stands outside and listens for his voice is very glad when he hears the bridegroom speak. So this joy of mine is now complete." The allusion is to the *šwšybnym* who wait at the entrance of the *ḥuppāh* for the consummation of the marriage; they are called in Pirqe Rabbi Eleazar c 12, "those who guard the *ḥuppāh*." This service of the friend of the bridegroom explains in the simplest way why Solomon's bed is surrounded by sixty valiants.

Krauss cites an obscure but intriguing reference to sixty personnel connected with the *ḥuppāh* in one of the many rabbinic versions of the Story of Judith (*Sefer Halakot waAgadot,* ed. Hegger, p. 136) which reads *w byn kl ḥwph wḥph ššym prgzw šl ʿnny,* "and between each *ḥuppāh* sixty *prgz* of *ʿnny.*" Krauss suggested that the copyist of Hegger's text mistakenly wrote *pargoz* for *pagoz,* a word which occurs in a *piyyut,* "poem," on the Judith Story recited in the Ashkenazi rite on the first Sabbath of Hanukkah. Krauss supposed this word to have the meaning "rider," citing the references to the clouds as a vehicle in Isa 19:1 and Ps 68:5[4E]. In the light of Baal's epithet "Cloud Rider" in Ugaritic myth, it may be that the messianic title *ʿnny* derives ultimately from a designation of the Weather god. In any case, the mention of sixty personnel, presumably militant, in association with the marriage canopy is provocative. The thirty companions of Samson (Judg 14:11) are doubled for the king.

The explanation of the "correct" sense of the night terror offered by Krauss carries conviction. His supposition that the explanation is especially suited to the peasant wedding interpretation is questionable. In Ugaritic we have a text recounting a marriage between two lunar deities and the ceremony follows the custom of mortals, with the weighing of the bride price and the blessing of the bride in terms reminiscent of Isa 7:14. This should suffice to show that features of human marriage ceremony may be expected in divine nuptials as well.

8d. *night terror.* T. H. Gaster (1969, no. 335, p. 813) cites as an exact parallel the description of Zaqar, god of dreams, in a Mesopotamian incantation as *puluḫtu ša lilâti,* "the terror of the nights." According to Gaster, this verse combines two ideas. The "terror by night" denotes on the one hand simply the dangers which may beset the wedding procession, since weddings are usually celebrated in the East at nightfall. On the other hand, Gaster suggests that the expression alludes to untoward happenings during the bridal night, with reference to Krauss' article, and to nightmare in general.

M. Dahood connects the term *paḥad̠,* traditionally rendered "dread," with Ugaritic *pḫd,* "flock," and understands it to refer to a pack of wild dogs. The present line he would render, "Each man has his sword at his side against packs marauding at night." Similarly in Ps 91:5, "You need not fear the pack of night," and Isa 24:18, "He who escapes the howling pack will fall into the pit" (cf. *PS I,* second NOTE on Ps 14:5; *PS II,* first NOTE on Ps 91:5). Fearsome as a pack of wild dogs may be, it does not seem likely that this alleged meaning is appropriate or adequate to the degree of dread suggested by the context of most of the occurrences of the term, especially the references to the divine dread, Gen 31:42,53; I Sam 11:7; Isa 2:10,19,21; Job 31:23. The use of *pḥd* as a verb is not easily understood as derived from a noun designating an aggregation of anything, whether sheep or dogs, even the hounds of heaven.

Joüon and Ricciotti took vss. 7–8 as resuming the theme of vs. 4; Israel keeps guard around the ark and the reference to nocturnal surprises may be applied to the guard maintained by the Levites in the Temple. Robert regarded it as more normal to think, with Budde and others, of the insecurity which reigns in the Near East, even during the day (cf. Judg 21:19–23; Neh 4:3–17; I Macc 9:37–42). But the evocation of warriors does not suppose a time in which it was necessary to guard wedding festivals; it is rather, according to Robert, a case of a king surrounded by his guard, the function of which is both to honor and protect him.

7–8. The significance of the sixty sword-wielding warriors surrounding the royal bed or litter to guard against night terror may perhaps at last be elucidated by the parallel role of the Mesopotamian *kurgarrû* in celebrations in honor of the goddess Inanna/Ishtar. The *kurgarrû* and the *assinnu* are specifically connected with the cult of Ishtar and they are said to have been changed by her from men to women in order to show the people piety, *kurgarrî LÚ i-sin-ni ša ana šupluḫ nišī Ištar zikrūssunu utēru ana* [*SAL*]-*ti* (Era IV 55). B. Landsberger (1960, 120n31), accordingly, took the *kurgarrû* to be eunuchs and translated [*LÚ*] *KUR.GAR.RA*^{meš} *ša tušāri ma-li-lu* as "die (kastrierten) Tempelgaukler die Krieg spielen," "the (castrated) Temple-clowns who play war." *CAD,* however, denies that there is any specific evidence that either the *assinnu* or *kurgarrû* were eunuchs or homosexuals (*CAD,* I, Part II, 341, s.v. *assinnu;* VIII, 559, s.v. *kurgarrû*). The mention of change from men to women, it was suggested, may mean simply that Ishtar turned their interest from the masculine role to the feminine. Reference to the *kurgarrû* in the Descent of Ishtar as neither male nor female may mean that they were transvestites performing in female apparel. The *kurgarrû* were especially connected with swordplay and with dancing and it seems likely that they performed martial exercises in the cultic celebrations of the great goddess of Love and War. There is reference to the teaching of *kugarrûtu,* the art of the *kurgarrû,* and to a chief of the *kurgarrûs,* which suggest a highly skilled and prestigious art. Females were apparently admitted to the profession, since there is mention of *SAL.KUR.GAR.RA* (cf. *CAD,* VIII, 559a).

The performance of the *kurgarrû* priests and their associates is most graphically portrayed in Iddin-Dagan's hymn to his divine bride Inanna, in the second through the fifth *kirugu,* lines 34–85. The translation below is that of D. Reisman, 1973, 186*ff*.

34 Second kirugu.

35 They play the silver algar instrument before her,
36 They walk before the pure Inanna.
37 To the great lady of heaven, Inanna, I would say: "Hail!"
38 The holy drum, the holy timpany, they beat before her,
39 They walk before the pure Inanna.
40 To the great lady of heaven, Inanna, I would say: "Hail!"
41 The holy harp, the holy timpany, they play before her,
42 They walk before the pure Inanna.
43 To the eldest daughter of Su'en, Inanna, I would say: "Hail!"

44 Third kirugu.

45 The male prostitutes comb their hair (?) before her,
46 They walk before the pure Inanna.
47 They decorate the napes of their necks with colored bands (?)
48 They walk before the pure Inanna.
49 They place upon their bodies the "cloak of divinity,"
50 They walk before the pure Inanna.
51 The righteous man and the first lady, the woman of the great wise women,
52 They walk before the pure Inanna.
53 The soothing harp which they had held, they place at their side,
54 They walk before the pure Inanna.
55 They gird themselves with the sword belt, the "arm of battle,"
56 They walk before the pure Inanna.
57 The spear, the "arm of battle," they grasp in their hands,
58 They walk before the pure Inanna.

59 Fourth kirugu.

60 Their right side they adorn with women's clothing,
61 They walk before the pure Inanna.
62 To the great lady of heaven, Inanna, I would say: "Hail!"
63 Their left side they cover (?) with men's clothing,
63a They walk before the pure Inanna.
63b To the great lady of heaven, Inanna, I would say: "Hail!"
64 With jump ropes and colored cords they compete before her,
65 They walk before the pure Inanna.
66 To the eldest daughter of Su'en, Inanna, I would say: "Hail!"

67 Fifth kirugu.

68 The young men, carrying hoops, sing to her,
69 They walk before the pure Inanna.
70 The maidens, the šugia priestesses, coiffured,
71 They [walk] before the pure Inanna.

72 The sword, the double-edged axe, before her. . . .
73 They walk before the pure Inanna.
74 The ascending k u r g a r r a priests grasped the sword,
75 They walk before the pure Inanna.
76 The one who covers the sword with blood, he sprinkles blood,
77 They walk before the pure Inanna.
78 He pours out blood on the dais of the throne room.
79 The t i g i drum, the š e m drum, the a l a instrument, they make loud noise.
80 The hierodule truly stands alone in the pure heaven.
81 All the lands, the black-headed people, the people numerous as sheep,
82 Upon them my lady looks in a friendly way from the midst of heaven,
82a They walk before the pure Inanna.
83 The lady of the evening, Inanna, is lofty.
84 The maiden Inanna I will praise.
85 The lady of the evening [is] as lofty as the horizon

The sexual orientation and bilateral transvestitism of the performers need not distract us here, since our interest at the moment is in the references to the sword in lines 55, 57, 72, 74, 76. In line 72 Reisman's translation of the Sumerian *gír ba-da-ra* as "The sword, the double-edged axe," is questionable. Hallo rendered *gíri-ba-da-ra,* Akkadian *paṭru* and *paṭarru,* as "dagger and sword," noting the normal association of these weapons with the "androgynous dervishes" (*kur-gar-ra*); (cf. Hallo and Van Dijk, 1968, 59, 75). Reisman's translation of line 74, "The ascending priests, etc.," is provocative. The Sumerian complex is *kur-gar-ra-e-da,* and it is the element e_{11} which Reisman rendered "ascending." Römer (1965, 166) was baffled by the item: "Was das Verbum e_{11} hier besagt, verstehe ich nicht." As a verb of motion e_{11} has several meanings, and one can only guess that it may denote here the acrobatics or gyrations of the sword dancers. The references to blood in lines 76 and 78 recall the predilection of the goddess for bloodshed and blood bibbing. Among the functions which the *kurgarrû*s performed for the pleasure of the divine lady was fumigation with incense of the fragrant reed: "The expert singers sit before her on the ground, those (who) play the lyre, the small harp and the clappers, the (players) of the flute, of the *sinnatu* instruments, and of the 'long (pipes)' the *kurgarrû*s<who carry>the spindle, the . . . and the whip, ease her mind with (incense of) 'sweet reeds,'" (*CAD,* VIII, 558a). The "sweet reed" (*GI.MEŠ DÙG.GA.MEŠ*) with which the goddess' inwards are soothed, is presumably the same as the aromatic cane of Exod 30:23 and the "sweet cane" of Jer 6:20; Isa 43:24; Ezek 27:19; and simply "cane" in Canticles 4:14a, q.v. The mention of incense as soothing the goddess recalls the columns of smoke and clouds of myrrh and frankincense which accompany Solomon's litter as it rises from the desert or steppe-land surrounded by the sixty skilled swordsmen, like the *kurgarrû*s who accompany Inanna/Ishtar. Among the functions ascribed to the *kurgarrû*s is protection by means of countercharms (Maqlu vii 96; cf. *CAD,* VIII, 558b).

The mysterious night terror against which the swordsmen guard has been plausibly explained as meaning the pesky demons who threaten to spoil brides at weddings. The armed *kurgarrûs* in the wedding procession of Iddin-Dagan and Inanna may serve the same purposes as the sixty warriors around Solomon's perfumed nuptial litter which presumably transported his intended bride, a priestess representing the goddess.

8. The Targum made the sword the Law and the skilled warriors those adept in the Law, with the sign of circumcision, like a sword, the defense against terrors of the night:

> And the priests and the Levites, and all the tribes of Israel, all of them grasp the words of the Law, which is likened to the sword, and they swing it and turn it, as valiants learned in warfare; and each and every one of them has the seal of circumcision on their flesh, just as the flesh of Abraham their father was sealed, and by it they are strengthened like a hero with the sword girt on his thigh, and on this account they are not afraid of dangers or the shades that prowl by night.

Midrash Rabbah explained the skill with the sword as referring to Exod 12:48. When it was decreed that no uncircumcised male could eat the Paschal meal, each man allegedly took his sword from his thigh and had himself circumcised, Moses performing the surgery while Aaron pulled back the flesh and Joshua administered the drink (as pain killer). The reference to the night terror evoked the observation that before a man sins, he inspires fear in all creatures, but once he has sinned, he is afraid of others. A number of illustrations are offered, ending with the example of Solomon who, before he sinned, ruled over male and female singers (*šārîm* and *šārôṯ,* Eccles 2:8), but after he sinned he had male and female demons (*šēḏîm* and *šēḏôṯ,* playing on the interchange of the similar letters *r* and *d*) who used to heat the baths for him. After Solomon sinned, he appointed sixty mighty men to guard his couch because he was afraid of demons.

In the Talmud (TB Yebamot 109b) this verse is made a judicial admonition. A judge should always imagine himself as wearing a sword between his thighs and with Gehenna open beneath him, to prevent perversion of justice.

The night terror evoked the tale of Solomon replaced as king by the demon Ashmodai and forced to beg (TB Gittin 68b). Ashmodai, when communing with the queens, wore stockings to hide his legs, which were spindly like those of a cock; he visited the women during their periods of menstrual uncleanness and always asked for Solomon's mother, Bathsheba. Solomon dispelled the demon by means of a ring inscribed with the divine name. Nevertheless the experience left Solomon in fear of the demon, as the verse attests.

Christian interpreters generally related the sword to Holy Scripture. Gregory the Great observed that it is not said that they all *have* swords, rather that they all *hold* swords. Thus it is no very wonderful thing to know God's Word, but it is so to do it. He who is familiar with the Divine Scripture has a sword, but if he neglects to live in accordance with it, he does not *hold* the sword, and is therefore not *expert in war,* because he does not know how to wield his weapon or resist temptation.

Other references to the sword or to the weapons of spiritual warfare were brought to bear on the present passage, especially the two swords of Luke 22:38. The sword in the hand was taken to denote the active strife of the soul against evil spirits, or zeal for martyrdom, and the sword on the thigh the passive restraint of carnal passions. The only effective weapon against the assaults of the flesh, according to Richard of St. Victor, is the love of God. Thus wearing the sword, the valiant men are conformed to their Leader of Whom Ps 45:4[3E] speaks. Psellus took the swords to denote the sign of the Cross and in this connection Littledale was reminded of the cross-handled sword of the Crusaders. The *fear in the night* was quite naturally related to the snares of the devil and all the terrors of adversity, and ignorance of this dark world, where attack may come from any quarter. (Cf. Littledale.)

9a. The word *'appiryôn* is hapax legomenon and has been the subject of much discussion. LXX rendered *phoreion* and Vulgate *ferculum.* Jerome, in his commentary to Isa 7:14, explained the word as a borrowing from Greek *phoreion.* It has been related to Sanskrit *paryanka, palki,* "palanquin." G. Widengren proposed derivation from Persian **aparyān* (<*upari-yāna*) (1955, 122n80). The Mishnah (Sotah ix 14) uses *'appiryôn* in the sense of Greek *phoreion:* "in the last war it was decreed that a bride should not pass through the town in an *'appiryôn,* but our Rabbis later sanctioned it" (The war was that against Hadrian, the ban was on grounds of security, and the reversal for the sake of modesty). The idea that the word may be borrowed from Greek has been opposed on the ground that Greek *phoreion* is used only in late *koinē* by such writers as Plutarch, Polybius, and Herodian the grammarian. However, Rundgren (1962), argued that the word is not to be derived from Iranian *upari-yāna,* but from Greek *phoreion,* first used by the rhetorician Deinarchos, ca. 300 B.C. Delitzsch made a determined effort to find a Semitic etymology and considered that he had succeeded in proving it to be a Hebrew word, derived from *pry,* "to cut," "make," "frame," with the meaning "bed," here "bed of state."

Budde thought that the present passage alludes to I Kings 10:18–20 which describes Solomon's magnificent throne. The throne was set in a Throne Hall (I Kings 7:7), a reception room where the king dispensed justice, received dignitaries and tribute, and carried on various affairs of state. Joüon supposed that the author had in mind the luxurious edicule constructed for newlyweds. It had sometimes the form of a bed of foliage, such as alluded to in 1:16. Joüon related the term *'appiryôn* to the *ḥuppāh* or marriage canopy, Isa 4:5; Joel 2:16; Ps 19:6[5E]. Robert, denying all relation to nuptials in 3:6–11, seized on this suggestion of Budde to bolster his view that the author of the Canticle wished to recall this souvenir of Solomonic splendor and majesty apropos of the Messianic King. The author's choice of the word *'appiryôn,* according to Robert, is not impossible, yet he prefers the emendation proposed by Winckler (1905, II, 236) to *'appeḏen,* a Persian loanword in Akkadian meaning "palace" (Old Persian *apadāna,* Akkadian *appadān*), used in Dan 11:45 of the pavilion of the King of the North (Antiochus

Epiphanes). Ricciotti gave to the word *'appeḏen* here the sense of "palace," but Robert, because of the description of vs. 10, and above all because of the presumed allusion to I Kings 10:18–20, believed that the author had in mind the platform of the audience hall with the royal throne. Thus is evoked for Robert at once a souvenir of the golden age of Israel and the most characteristic trait of the pomp and power of the Persian empire at its apogee; implicitly the author compares the Messiah not only to Solomon, but also to the "Great King," "King of Kings," Darius or Xerxes, whose empire then comprised all the Orient and threatened to stretch to Europe.

Gerleman argues that the description of the structure in vss. 9–10, with pillars and an inside, suggests a building rather than a portable contraption. He suggests a palace room, a throne room where the king seated on his throne holds audience. This opens up new possibilities for an etymology, and Gerleman suggests Egyptian *pr,* "house," with *'a-* preformative and *-yôn* afformative. Although the majority of interpreters understood the term as designating some sort of litter or portable throne, a number opted for a fixed structure. The Zohar (i 15a) speaks of a palace and Ibn Ezra of a superb edifice.

made. The same verb is used in the accounts of Solomon's various building operations (I Kings 6:31,33, 7:6,7,51, 10:18), as if the king did the work himself. Some critics would delete "the king, Solomon" as metrically superfluous. Others would expunge only Solomon. Haupt, e.g. rendered:

> It was made for the King, this conveyance,   of Lebanon's wood (it is fashioned),

and explained that Solomon seems to be a subsequent insertion, while "King" is merely a name for the King of the Wedding Feast, i.e. the bridegroom, just as they speak in England of the May Lord and the May Queen, or as a lady may be referred to on the Continent as Queen of the Ball. (The first seven days after a wedding [cf. Gen 29:27; Judg 14:12; Tobit 11:19] were called in the neighborhood of Damascus "the King's Week"; during this time the young pair played king and queen and the best man was styled vizier of the king. In some districts west of the Jordan the names King and Queen were also applied to the groom and the bride.) Against the deletion of either or both of the words "king" and "Solomon," Robert adduced the consideration that the full formula, "the king, Solomon made/built/sent," etc., is characteristic of the accounts in I Kings (6:2, 7:13–14,51, 9:11,15,26,28, 10:13, 16,21,23). This emphatic form is, in Robert's view, all the more requisite for the Solomon of the future.

9. As in vs. 7, the Targum equated Solomon's litter with the Temple:

> A holy Temple Solomon the King built for himself from fir(?), box, and cedar which he brought from Lebanon, and overlaid it with pure gold.

Midrash Rabbah on 3:10 explained *'appiryôn* as referring to the Ark (of the Covenant) and equated the word with *pûryômā,* "litter." In the Jerusalem Talmud,

Ketubot 26b, in a discussion of the term *hênûmā'* (adapted from Greek *humenaios*), designating a curtained litter on which a virgin bride was carried in procession, it is said that "there (i.e. in Babylon) they call it (i.e. *hênûmā*) *namnûmā'* while here (i.e. in Palestine) the Rabbis call it *pûryômā'*." The term *namnûmā'* may be plausibly related to the Semitic root *n*(*w*)*m*, "sleep." The terms *pûryômā'* and *piryôn* in Midrash Rabbah on Canticles 3:10 are strikingly similar to Greek *phorēma*, "that which is carried," and *phoreion*, "litter, sedan chair," from *phoreo*, "bear, carry." Jastrow (1921, 1147) suggests that *phoreion* is "a phonetic coincidence" with *piryôn*. The word *'appiryôn* looks like a variant of *piryôn*, with prosthetic *'alep̄* and secondary doubling of the *p*, but there is no need for the addition of prosthetic *'alep̄* to a form like *piryôn*. The origin of the term *'appiryôn* thus remains obscure.

As Jewish interpretation related this verse to the Tabernacle or the Temple, Christian expositors similarly applied it to the Church. Philo of Carpasia explained that as Christ made His own human body first to be the litter in which the Godhead is borne, so He made the Church the vehicle in which He, the Man-God, would be caried in procession among the people to whom He comes as King and Conqueror. The wood of Lebanon, the incorruptible cedar of the White Mountain, was variously explained as denoting holiness, truth, and perseverance of the Saints. But Lebanon also stands in Scripture as the symbol of pride, as it is written, "The Lord shatters the cedars of Lebanon," Ps 29:5b. Thus we may understand that the very framework of the Church is composed of sinners and idolaters whom God has converted. One of the earliest of Christian comments on the Song, by Theophilus of Antioch (ca. A.D. 190), made the wood of Lebanon to typify Ruth the Moabitess; as Lebanon lies outside the Holy Land, so Christ took His flesh from Gentiles as well as from Judah. The tree of Lebanon was also related to the Cross made of wood of a Gentile mountain because Christ elected to die by a Roman punishment rather than a Jewish one. The litter was also understood as representing the glorious Virgin, royal seat of Solomon the Savior, uncorrupt in body and soul. (Cf. Littledale.)

10a. *posts.* The function of the pillars or posts depends on the understanding of the nature of the structure in question. A litter or palanquin as well as a fixed structure could have pillars or posts. These could serve either as legs on which to set it down or as supports for a canopy, or both.

10b. *bolster.* This nominal form *rĕp̄îḏāh* is unique, but see 2:5 on the root and its uses. LXX rendered *anakliton* and Vulgate *reclinatorium,* the latter being the vulgar name for the *fulchra,* the prop or support at the head or foot of the bedstead. In view of the uses of the verb in Hebrew and Arabic in the sense of "spread underneath," and "support," the term "bolster," which may designate a long pillow for a bed, or a supporting piece in a structure or apparatus, seems appropriate. Taking the cue from the meaning "stretch" or "spread," Robert saw two possibilities: something on which one stretches, i.e. a bed, or that which stretches over something else, as a roof, dais, or baldaquin; his choice was the last.

10c. *cushion.* The word *merkāḇ* occurs twice elsewhere, in Lev 15:9 designating a seat or saddle which may be polluted by one who has a discharge, and in I Kings 5:6[4:26E] with reference to chariotry. It is here manifestly a seat of some sort. LXX rendered *epibasis,* Vulgate *adscensum.*

purple. The term *'argāmān* is of Anatolian origin, having in Hittite the sense of "tribute." It designates cloth dyed with the reddish purple dye extracted from the murex shellfish. The dye was very expensive and became at an early period the emblem of royalty (cf. *Odyssey* xix 225). Heathen idols were also clothed with purple, as mentioned in Jer 10:9 and Baruch 6:72 (AB 44; in *RSV,* The Letter of Jeremiah). Purple was lavishly used in decoration of the tabernacle, Exod 26:1,36, 27:16; and the vestments of the high priest, Exod 28:5,6,8,15,33. The veil of Solomon's Temple was made of violet, purple, crimson, and fine linen, embroidered with cherubim, II Chron 3:14. Thus purple symbolized both royalty and divinity. This point is stressed by Robert who saw in the Solomon of the Canticle a messianic figure.

The *'appiryôn* here with silver pillars and purple seat compares with the descriptions of *phoreia* given by Athenaeus who tells of the appearance of the tyrant Athenion "on a silverlegged phoreion with purple coverlet" (Athenaeus v 13, ed. Schweigh, II, 317). The same author (v 5, ed. Schweigh, II, 253) describes Antiochus Epiphanes in a festal procession preceded by two hundred women sprinkling perfume-ointments from golden urns, behind them eighty women sitting in pomp on golden-legged *phoreia* and five hundred on silver-legged *phoreia.*

Nothing is said in the present passage about the mode of carrying the *'appiryôn,* assuming that it was a portable apparatus. The Greek *phoreia* were carried by six or eight porters and designated by the numbers as *hexaphoron,* or *octaphoron.* We have in Ugaritic myth a remarkable description of the fabrication of some sort of furniture for Baal by the artisan god Koshar (*kṯr wḫss*), in anticipation of the splendiferous house which Baal hopes to build. There are many obscurities in the description of the items, but it includes, besides throne and footstool, carrying-apparatus of gold:

Hayyan went up to the forge,
In the hands of Ḫassis were the tongs.
He poured silver, cast gold;
Poured silver by the thousand,
Gold he poured by the myriad.
He poured *ḫym* and *tbṯḫ:*
A divine dais of two myriads,
A divine dais silver plated,
Coated with red gold.
A divine throne with head-support,
A divine footstool overspread(?),
A divine litter(?) with straps(?)
On carriers of gold.
(4[51].1.24–38)

10d. *sides.* The element *tawk>tôḵ* is regularly used as a preposition, usually compounded with *bĕ-,* "in the midst of." The use as a noun, as here, in the sense of "interior," "middle," "halfway point," is not uncommon; cf. Deut 3:16; Josh 12:2; I Kings 8:64. The form here used, *tōḵō,* "its interior," occurs also in Ezek 15:4, applied to the charring of the interior of vine wood. In the present instance the word may be a technical term for a specific part of the 'appiryôn, as with the other terms, *'ammûḏ, rĕpîdāh,* and *merkāḇ,* but this seems unlikely in view of the sense of the word. Since the reference is to inlaid decoration, the "interior" applies, presumably, to the recess in which the ornamentation is set.

love. Interpreters have been troubled with the use here of the word "love," *'ahăḇāh,* in connection with the ornamentation of a piece of furniture. LXX rendered the word in the accusative case, *agapēn,* "a love (act/mark/gift)," "the middle of it a mosaic, a love (gift) from daughters of Jerusalem." Vulgate *charitate constravit* is ambiguous, and similarly *KJ*'s "paved *with* love." The adverbial interpretation may be related to the beauty of the work or the motivation and feeling with which it was executed, e.g. Luther, "lieblich gepflastert"; Ginsburg, "tesselated most lovely"; or *RSV* "lovingly wrought." Renan supposed that "love" was intended as *abstractum pro concreto* and rendered, "In the center sparkles a beauty chosen among the daughters of Jerusalem (Au centre brille une belle choisie entre les filles de Jérusalem)." A number of critics (Graetz, Budde, Haupt, Dussaud, Ricciotti, Wittekindt, Miller, Haller) emend *'ahăḇāh* to *hoḇnîm,* "ebony," mentioned in Ezek 27:15.

The suggestion of G. R. Driver (1936), that the word *'hbh* here designates "leather" rather than "love," cognate with Arabic *'ihāb* which designates (human) skin and (raw) leather, has found acceptance with Meek (*IB*) and Hirschberg (1961, 373*f*). Similarly, in Hosea 11:4, "bands of love," Driver suggested should be rendered "bands of leather." Barr (*CP,* 154) thinks that in the Song of Songs 3:10, since the parallels are substances like "silver," "gold," and "purple," there seems to be strong reason for accepting the rendering "leather." *NEB* in the present passage renders "and its lining was of leather," without a note, but in Hosea 11:4 *ḥaḇlê 'āḏām* is rendered "leading strings" and *'ăḇôṯôṯ 'ahăḇāh,* "bonds of love," but with notes that the alternatives are "cords of leather" and "reins of hide." Dahood (*PNWSP,* 54) proposed that the final consonant of the word *rāṣûp̄* represents the particle *p* of Ugaritic, Arabic *fa,* and corrected the text to read *tôḵô rāṣô p̄ĕ 'ahăḇāh,* "Within it there is pleasure and love." Gerleman emended *'ahăḇāh* to *'ăḇānîm,* "stones," "ihr Inneres ist mit Steinen belegt," and cited the article "Mosaik" in PW, XVI (1935), 328*ff*.

Ginsburg, although he translated "Its interior tesselated most lovely," came near to divining the sense of the line in his final remark: "The interior of these couches is generally painted with baskets of flowers and nosegays, intermixed with short sentences or mottoes, expressing the power of love." Love scenes are appropriate decoration for a love couch. The ivory beds on which the luxurious and uxorious inhabitants of Zion and Samaria lolled, feasted, drank, and sang, Amos 6:4–7, were probably decorated with carved ivory inlay like the bed of the king of Ugarit which was ornamented with inlaid ivory carvings of a war scene, the great goddess suckling two youths, and the king embracing his wife. This seems to explain the heretofore baffling reference to the love inlay of Solomon's bed. See Plates II and XI.

inlaid. The passive participle *rāṣûp̄* is hapax legomenon but the meaning of the noun *riṣpāh*, "pavement" (Ezek 40:17*f*, 42:3; II Chron 7:3), and the use of the cognate verb in Akkadian and Arabic with reference to fitting stones together, support the rendering of LXX *lithostrōton*, "stone pavement." In II Kings 16:17 *marṣep̄eṯ 'ăḇānîm*, "a pavement of stones," replaced the brazen bulls that had supported the Sea. In Esther 1:6 the beds (*miṭṭôṯ*) which Ahasuerus supplied for the people, great and small, during the seven-day drink-fest (*mišteh*) were furnished with white curtains(?) and blue hangings fastened with cords of linen and purple (wool) on silver rings and marble pillars, beds of gold and silver on inlay (*riṣpaṯ*) of porphyry(?) and alabaster, mother-of-pearl and turquoise(?). The text appears a bit garbled and it is generally assumed that the beds were set on mosaic pavement, but it may be that the mosaic work was decoration on the bed frames.

Although ivory is not mentioned in the present context, one is reminded of Solomon's great ivory throne which was plated with the finest gold, I Kings 10:18. This ivory throne presumably was so-called because of the use of carved ivory inlay for decoration. Certainly this was the case with regard to the ivory houses of Amos 3:15, since ivory is hardly suitable for the construction of even a small house.

11a. The preposition *min* here has occasioned no little difficulty. LXX rendered *apo,* Vulgate *propter, KJ* "for," *RSV* and *JPSV* "by." Either "by" or "for" is possible, both grammatically and logically, although it is hard to see why Solomon's bed would be decorated *for* Jerusalem girls unless they shared its pleasures in actuality or vicariously. *JB* deleted the line and *NEB* ignored the preposition and connected the line with what follows:

> Come out, daughters of Jerusalem; you daughters of Zion come out. . . .

This seems to be the best way to deal with the problem. The troublesome element *m-* can be left with the preceding line as enclitic, emphatic *-m* attached to the word *'ahăḇāh,* "love."

The Targum identified the pillars of the palanquin with the Ark of the Testimony, and the seat inlaid with love as the cover of the Ark:

> After he had completed it, he placed therein the Ark of the Testimony, which is the Pillar of the world. Inside it the two tablets of stone which Moses had hidden there in Horeb, which were more precious than refined silver, more beautiful than pure gold. And he spread out and covered above it the curtain of blue and purple. And between the cherubim, above which was the lid, dwelt the Presence of YHWH who caused His name to dwell in Jerusalem out of all the cities of the land of Israel.

Midrash Rabbah offered multiple choice for the meanings of the parts and materials of the apparatus. The inside inlaid with love was referred to the merit of the Law and of the righteous who study and practise it. It was also taken to mean the Divine Presence, the Temple, and the World. The gold plating provoked discussion of techniques for working and refining gold, including such unusual methods as feeding it to ostriches in olive size chunks which they excreted refined, or burying it in excrement for seven years.

Christian expositors were not less resourceful and imaginative than the rabbis in finding meanings for the parts and materials of the litter. The silver pillars were seen as the gifts of the Holy Ghost with which Christ was endued (cf. Prov 9:1). The golden *reclinatorium* was taken to denote His most pure and holy soul. The purple typified His Passion. The inside paved with love was understood as His love-filled heart. Applied to the Virgin Mary as the bearer of Christ, the golden slope of the litter was the ardent love which prepared her for the conception of the Divine Son, or her holy breast on which the Infant Savior reclined. The purple ascent was her sorrowful participation in the Passion of her Son. Her heart in her midst was strewn with love for all weak and suffering souls, the daughters of Jerusalem in Babylonian exile below.

The Vulgate rendering of *'appiryôn* as *ferculum* led to an interesting interpretation based on the classical use of the word as denoting a dinner tray or a dish of meat. Thus the tray became Holy Writ, the woodwork frame the inspired Seers, Apostles, and Evangelists, the silver the outer form of their words, the gold their inner meaning, while the purple was seen as the royal cloth of Christ's Passion which covers the whole and on which the food is served. The food is mingled of rare and costly ingredients, the fruits of the Spirit, peace, patience, joy, and the name of the dainty dish is Love. The inlay or tesselation of love was related in a variety of ways to the Love of Christ. Gregory Nyssen applied it to dedicated virginity which is the special offering of the daughters of Jerusalem to the Bridegroom. Similarly, Gillebert, preaching to Cistercian nuns, related the whole verse to the cloistered life. (Cf. Littledale.)

come out. The form *ṣĕ'eynāh* is unique and abnormal, apparently influenced improperly by the parallel imperative from *rĕ'eynāh*. The two feminine plural imperatives taken together furnished the title for the medieval Yiddish commentary on the Pentateuch intended for women, *Ṣĕ'enāh ūR'eynāh,* "Come out (females) and see."

11b. *Zion's girls*. This phrase, *bĕnôṯ ṣiyyôn,* is unique in the Canticle and does not occur elsewhere in canonical Scripture. "Zion's sons," however, are mentioned in Lam 4:2, "Zion's precious sons." The common term *baṯ ṣiyyôn,* regularly rendered erroneously "Daughter of Zion," properly "Miss Zion" (genitive of apposition), represents Jerusalem personified, whereas the plural, "daughters of Zion/Jerusalem," refers simply to the female inhabitants of the metropolis. Although the expression "daughters of Zion" is not elsewhere attested, there is no reason to expunge it since it forms a perfect poetic parallel to "daughters of Jerusalem."

11b,c. *Look . . . At*. The verb *r'y,* "see," with the preposition *b-* attached to its object, has a variety of meanings, depending on the context; in general the *b-* after verbs of perception conveys the nuance of intensity, "to gaze," with either pain or pleasure (cf. Joüon, 133c). Cf. NOTE on 1:6a.

11d. *crown*. A crown may be an emblem or symbol of happiness, as in Job 19:9, or Wis 2:8, "Let us crown ourselves with rosebuds ere they wither." In

Jewish weddings crowns were worn by both the groom and the bride until the time of the war with Rome in A.D. 70, when the custom was abandoned as a sign of mourning (cf. TB Sotah 49a). There is a rabbinic proverb, "a bridegroom resembles a king," *ḥāṯān dômeh lĕmeleḵ* (Pirqe de Rabbi Eliezer, ch. 16). In the Greek Church in Egypt, the bride and groom stood before the priest with the two crowns of flowers, cloth, or tinsel placed on the book of the Gospels; following the prayers and benedictions, the priest placed one crown on the head of the groom and the other on the bride, covering both with a veil (cf. Ginsburg, 153).

his mother. The mention of Solomon's mother, according to Delitzsch, points to the beginning of Solomon's reign. The seduction fable is shattered, since the marriage takes place with the joyful consent of the queen mother who wreathed a fresh garland around the head of her youthful son, not an old crown that had already been used.

11e. *wedding day.* The form *ḥăṯunnāh,* denominative of *ḥāṯan,* "marry," is not found elsewhere in Scripture. In Ugaritic the cognate *ḫtn* is used with reference to the marriage of the lunar deities Yariḫ and Nikkal.

11f. Literally, "and on the day of the joy of his heart." Bickell and Horst would suppress this line, but without cause; it forms an excellent parallel to the preceding line. Ehrlich would delete the conjunction *wāw,* "and," at the beginning of the line, but this also is quite mistaken. Gordis properly points to this use of the *wāw* in parallel cola "with no sense of addition," i.e. simply as repetitive, and cites Zech 9:9:

Humble and riding on an ass, And on a he-ass, son of a she-ass,

which was mistaken in the NT echo (Matt. 21:2,7) to refer to two beasts, an ass and her colt; cf. AB 15 on Job 11:12. The same usage of *w-* is common in Ugaritic, e.g.

No house has Baal like the gods And a court like Asherah's children.
(4[51].4.50–51)

Budde held that this verse proves that Solomon here means merely "bridegroom," since an actual king was not crowned on his wedding day, or by his mother. Harper objected that Budde failed to cite any evidence in support of this opinion. The queen mother, according to Harper, may have played an important part in her son's wedding and she may quite well have placed the crown on his head. Harper, missing the synonymous parallelism, was bothered by the two supposedly different days and commented: "Either this day, or another, so that the meaning may be either that he was married on this day, or that he had been married formerly, and now was wearing the crown his mother then gave him. The latter is more probable." This sample may serve to illustrate the need for some literary instincts when dealing with poetry.

Robert rightly emphasized that it is all important to understand what kind of espousals are here meant. One can discover the thought of the author, Robert stressed, only by going back to the biblical tradition which inspired it. Two texts were adduced as prime inspiration of the present passage. The first is Isa 61:10:

I will joy greatly in Yahweh,
My soul will exult in my God;
For he has clothed me with garments of salvation,
Wrapped me in the robe of righteousness,
As the bridegroom puts on a garland,
As the bride decks herself with jewels.

Here, the community of repatriates, speaking by the mouth of the prophet, thanks God for salvation, that is reestablishment in Palestine which is supposedly realized in a complete fashion, the splendor of which is compared to wedding finery. The advent of the new times, which is simply a resumption of the ancient relations, is thus compared to nuptials. More explicit, according to Robert, is the second text, Isa 62:3–5. The prophet, addressing Jerusalem declares,

You shall be a glorious crown in the hand of Yahweh,
A royal diadem in your God's hand.
You shall no more be called "Forsaken,"
Your land no more called "Desolate,"
But you shall be called "My delight is in her (Hephzibah),"
Your land, "Married" (Beulah);
For Yahweh delights in you,
And your land shall be married.
For as a young man marries a virgin,
Your sons/builders will marry you,
As the bridegroom rejoices over the bride,
Your God will rejoice over you.

One sees clearly, according to Robert, that the eschatological restoration is compared to the return to favor of an unfaithful wife, but the originality of this text is to show that by an incomprehensible outpouring of the divine mercy, the former miseries are as if they had never existed, and the unfaithful one is taken again without afterthought or reservation, with the spontaneous and overflowing joy of a first love. All this goes along as if it had been the absolute beginning of a first union.

Such, according to Robert, is the doctrinal current to which the Canticle 3:11 is connected by means of the intermediary of its two textual bases, Isa 61:10 and 62:3–5. In this light, Robert held, it becomes very clear that the day of the espousals of King Solomon, the day of the joy of his heart, is the day of eschatological messianic future, assimilated to a marriage, inasmuch as it renews and consecrates forever the covenant of Sinai, carried to its ultimate perfection. The crown is the symbol of royal power, and, if one wishes, but secondarily, the traditional ornament of the bridegroom. The mother of the king is the nation; this image, which would have been unacceptable in the hypothesis where Yahweh would have been put on the scene, raises no objection if it concerns the Messiah; he is a son of the nation Israel; he could also be called the bridegroom inasmuch as he represents Yahweh. The mother of the king, that is, the nation, crowns him on the day of his espousals. It seems that we have here an allusion to a constant practice in Israel. The kings, even if they succeeded their predecessor legally, even if they had been first designated by God and consecrated by a prophet, did not begin to function until they had received the assent of the people.

Thus, according to Robert, the tableau of Canticles 3:6–8, instead of being the vulgar description of a wedding procession, is the expression of eschatological and messianic hopes. It is a simple sketch the elements of which do not join materially, but harmonize to evoke a powerful thought. At vs. 6 Robert sees the captives returning in an assemblage which recalls the exodus; vss. 7 and 8 describe the king in his litter surrounded by his guard; no doubt, he mounts to Zion for the scene of the coronation; 9 and 10 describe the throne of the audience hall, where he goes to present himself to the people. One could suppose that at vs. 11 he is installed. He sits with majesty, wearing the royal crown, in token of his supreme authority, which his people ratify. At this spectacle the author lets escape an exclamation of admiration and invites the girls of Zion to come and see the one whose advent marks the end of the trials of the nation. It is in fact the hour of the complete and definitive restoration, that of the new covenant predicted by the prophets.

11. The wedding day coronation of King Solomon the Targum identified as the dedication of the Temple with a fortnight of celebration:

> When Solomon the King came to make the dedication of the Temple, a herald went forth with vociferation and thus he said: Come out, O inhabitants of the districts of the land of Israel, and people of Zion, and look at the crown and diadem with which the people of the House of Israel have crowned King Solomon on the day of dedication of the Temple. And rejoice with the joy of the Feast of Booths which Solomon celebrated at that time for fourteen days.

Midrash Rabbah seized upon the daughters of *Zion* to make a wordplay about those who are distinguished (*měṣuyyānîm*) by hair style, circumcision, and fringes. King Solomon was taken to mean the King (God) who produced all creatures in their full perfection (*šělēmôṯ*) and created the sun, moon, stars, and constellations in their fullness. (Bar Kappara judged from this that Adam and Eve were created as at twenty years of age.) The reference to creation and perfection led to an extended discussion of cosmology before return to consideration of the latter part of the verse. Rabbi Hanina ben Isaac observed that there is no reference in Scripture to Bathsheba making a crown for her son Solomon. The meaning is, therefore, that as a crown is set with jewels, so the Tent of Meeting was conspicuous with blue, purple, scarlet, and fine linen. The day of espousals was related to the time at Sinai when Israel was like a bridegroom. The gladness of heart was referred to the joy of receiving the Law (Ps 19:9), or to (the day of consecration of) the Temple.

In the Talmud (TB Ta'anit 26b) the day of espousal is related to the giving of the Law, and the day of joy of heart to the building and eagerly awaited rebuilding of the Temple. R. Simeon ben Gamliel commented that there were never in Israel greater days of joy than the fifteenth of Ab and the Day of Atonement. On these days the girls of Jerusalem used to go out in white garments which they borrowed in order not to shame any who had none. All these garments required ritual immersion. The Jerusalem girls came out and danced in the vineyards and exclaimed, "Young man, lift your eyes and see what you choose for yourself."

Christian interpreters saw in the daughters of Zion the children of the Church, holy souls, citizens of the heavenly city who with the angels enjoy perpetual peace in contemplating the glory of God. The command to go out meant to leave the troubles of this world, so as to look on the Beloved with unburdened soul. King Solomon, the truly Peaceful One, represented Christ, and the crown with which His Mother crowned Him was the flesh received from His Virgin Mother. The day of his espousals was understood as the time of the Incarnation, and the gladness of heart as His joy in the redemption of mankind. Again the entire verse was referred to Christ's Passion. Solomon, foreseeing that Passion, warned the daughters of Zion, the people of Israel, to go out and see the crown of thorns with which His mother, the Synagogue, had crowned Him on the day he espoused the Church and redeemed mankind from the power of the devil. Go forth thus means to pass from unbelief and recognize that He who suffered as Man was Very God. The hymn *Exite, Sion filiae* gave the summons:

Daughters of Sion, see your King!
  Go forth, go forth to meet Him!
Your Solomon is hastening
  Where that dear flock shall greet Him!
The sceptre and the crown by right
He wears, in robe of purple dight.

It glitters fair, His diadem,
  But thorns are there entwining,
And from the Red Sea comes each gem
  That in its wreath is shining:
Their radiance glows like stars at night,
With precious blood-drops are they
    bright.

(For this and more, cf. Littledale.)

IV
(4:1–16)

1 a Behold you are fair, my darling,
b Behold you are fair.
c Your eyes are doves
d Behind your veil.
e Your hair like a flock of shorn goats
f Streaming down Mount Gilead.
2 a Your teeth like a flock of ewes
b Coming up from washing,
c All of them twinning,
d None bereft among them.
3 a Like a scarlet fillet your lips,
b Your mouth comely.
c Like a pomegranate slice your brow
d Behind your veil.
4 a Like David's tower your neck,
b Built in courses.
c A thousand shields hung on it,
d All bucklers of heroes.
5 a Your breasts like two fawns,
b Twins of a gazelle,
c Browsing on the lotus.
6 a While the day breathes
b And the shadows flee,
c I will hie me to the myrrh mountain,
d To the frankincense hill,
7 a You are all fair, my darling.
b No blemish is in you.
8 a Come from Lebanon, bride,
b Come from Lebanon, come.
c Come from the peak of Amana,
d From the peak of Senir and Hermon,

e From the lions' dens,
f From the panthers' lairs.
9 a You ravish my mind, my sister, bride,
b You ravish my mind with one of your eyes,
c With a single gem of your necklace.
10 a How fair your love,
b My sister, bride.
c Sweeter your love than wine,
d The scent of your perfume than any spice.
11 a Your lips drip honey, bride,
b Honey and milk under your tongue,
c And the scent of your robes
d Is like the scent of Lebanon.
12 a A garden locked is my sister bride,
b A pool locked, a fountain sealed.
13 a Your groove a pomegranate grove
b With fruits delectable,
c Cypress with nard,
14 a Nard and saffron,
b Cane and cinnamon,
c With all fragrant woods,
d Myrrh and aloes,
e With all prime perfumes.
15 a A garden fountain,
b A well of living water,
c Cascading from Lebanon.
16 a Stir, O North-wind,
b Come, O South-wind!
c Breathe on my garden.
d Let its spices flow.
e Let my love enter his garden.
f Let him eat its delectable fruits.

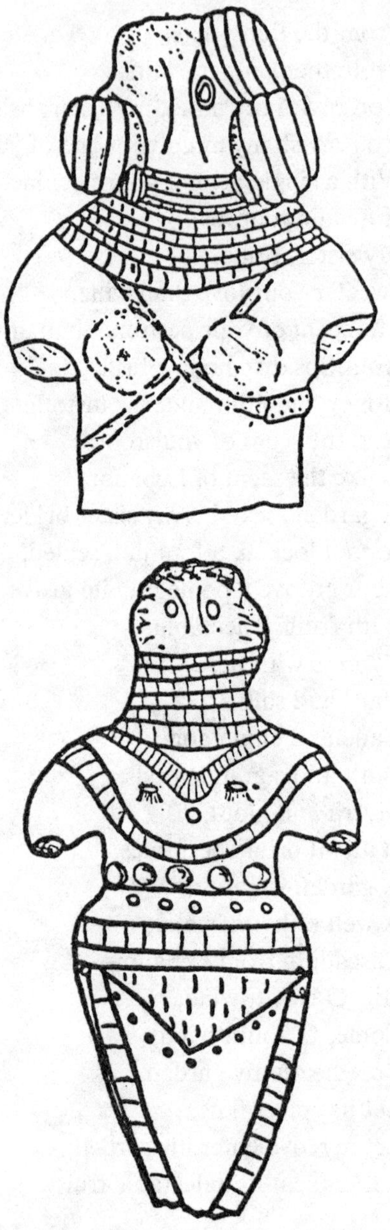

7. Terracotta figurines of goddess with layered necklace

4:4 Like David's tower your neck,
Built in courses.

8. Gazelles feeding among lotus

4:5 Your breasts like two fawns,
Twins of a gazelle,
Browsing on the lotus.

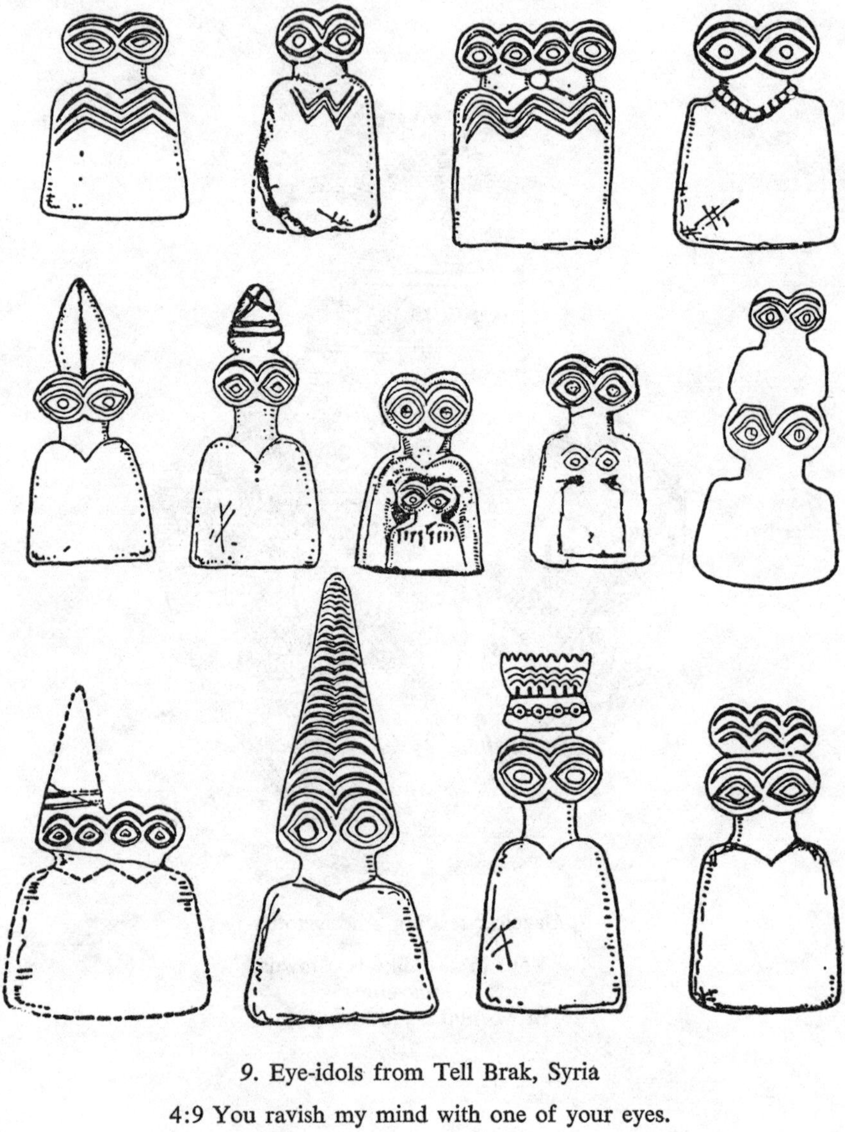

9. Eye-idols from Tell Brak, Syria

4:9 You ravish my mind with one of your eyes.

NOTES

4:1a–c. Identical with 1:15. Some critics would eliminate the repetition "behold you are fair" in 1b and others would insert the comparative particle *kĕ,* "like," before "doves" in 1c, on the basis of 5:12 and Origen's fifth column (Quinta) *hōs peristerai.* The use of the comparative particle in the succeeding verses, 4:3–5, is cited in support of this suggestion. Note the variation in 4:4a.

1d. *veil.* The word *ṣammāh* which occurs also in 4:3, 6:7 and in Isa 47:2, in each instance with the possessive suffix, *ṣammāṯēḵ,* was troublesome to early translators and interpreters. LXX took the word to mean "silence," "without thy silence," and the Arabic version similarly rendered "besides the beauty of thy silence." Vulgate *abusque eo quod intrinsecus latet,* "without that which lies hid within," veils the meaning. Qimḥi and Rashi understood the word to refer to locks of hair, hence *KJ* "thou hast doves' eyes within thy locks." LXX Codex Venetus elaborated, "looking out from behind thy hair flowing down from thy head like a mane." Hengstenberg cited I Tim 2:9 and I Peter 3:3 with reference to the braiding or plaiting of hair. Graetz took the word to refer to a filet or band holding the hair. Dahood finds the word *ṣammāh* in Ps 69:5[4E] in the sense of "locks" by reading *miṣṣammāṯî,* "(more) than my locks," instead of MT *maṣmîṯay,* "my destroyers." In spite of the parallelism thus achieved between "the hairs of my head" of the preceding verse and the restored "locks," this hardly suffices to establish the meaning "locks" for *ṣammāh.* The hairs of the head are practically innumerable (cf. Ps 40:13[12E]), but the same would scarcely be said of locks or bunches of hair. Symmachus was certainly correct in changing LXX's "silence" to "veil," *kalumma.* In Aramaic the verbs *ṣĕmam* and *ṣamṣēm* are used of veiling the face, e.g. Targ Gen 24:65 and Midrash Genesis Rabbah.

Several critics (e.g. Haupt, Zapletal, Staerk, Wittekindt, Haller, and Schmökel) would delete the phrase *mibba'aḏ lĕṣammāṯēḵ,* "from behind your veil," as metrically superfluous and/or mistakenly borrowed from vs. 3 below. Neither argument is convincing.

The veil is supposedly intended to conceal or detract from the beauty of the female to impede and discourage unauthorized ocular enjoyment of the subject. Often, however, the effect is quite opposite the alleged intent, because of "the light that lies in woman's eyes." The concealing of the other features enhances the beauty of the eyes which are often the most attractive natural feature.

On the veil of the sacred prostitute and the love-goddess, cf. 1:7.

1e. *shorn.* It has been suggested (e.g. Ehrlich, Gordis, Meek) that the passive participle, *haqqĕṣûḇôṯ,* here expresses imminent action, not yet completed. Gordis rendered "ready to be sheared," and Meek suggested "about to be shorn." Sheep, according to Meek, are washed before shearing, not afterward. Shorn ewes Meek regarded as anything but beautiful, whereas Graetz considered the unshorn ugly and scraggly and in need of tonsorial care for beautification. Midrash Rabbah, Qimḥi and Ibn Ezra took the word to denote uniformity of size and shape. The notion of shearing suggested in Midrash Rabbah the spoliation of Egypt at the Reed Sea. Sheep are normally washed before the shearing to cleanse the wool. Delitzsch cited Columella (*De re rustica* VII) to the effect that sheep were also bathed a few days after shearing. In the present instance, however, the ewes are just coming up from the washing and the concern is for their cleanliness and beauty; the shearing would be done before the animals had an opportunity to get soiled again. The appearance and especially the whiteness of a shorn sheep would not be greatly improved by washing. Wool, especially clean wool (Dan 7:9), and snow are the poetic and proverbial parallel comparisons for whiteness, Isa 1:18; Rev 1:14; Enoch 46:1.

goats. The goats of Syria-Palestine are for the most part coal black. Cf. 1:5c,d on the black tents of goat hair. The hair of the groom was also black; cf. 5:11c.

1f. *Streaming.* The exact meaning of the verb *glš* remains uncertain. It is used in Scripture only here and in 6:5 in the same expression. LXX may have read *šeggālû* (from *gly,* "uncover, reveal") instead of *šeggālĕšû,* while Syriac and Vulgate possibly reflect *še'ālû* (from *'ly,* "ascend"). Rabbinic exegetes also had some difficulty with the word in the present context. The connection of the word with water in extra-biblical usage evoked in Midrash Rabbah the image of the piling up of the waters at the Reed Sea and the equation of Mount Gilead with Mount Sinai. Rabbi Joshua of Siknin, however, explained that the word relates to the thinning of a woman's hair when it grows too thick, or of pumpkins when they sprout too profusely and have to be thinned. Following this line, Rashi supposed that the word means "make bald," i.e. quit or descend the mountain. Ibn Ezra, however, rejected the connection with baldness and proposed that the word here means "look forth," like *šqp* used in 6:10. Similarly Rashbam suggested the meaning "which are seen." Luther, apparently influenced by rabbinic exegesis, rendered "die beschoren sind" (which are shorn). Graetz also took his cue from the Syriac and neo-Hebrew use of the word in connection with removal of hair or feathers and accordingly rendered the word here as "geglattet" (made smooth). Graetz was concerned with improving the lady's appearance since comparison of her hair with a flock of black goats, unshorn and scraggly or bristly (*struppig*) seemed to him unpretty and thus he supposed that the poet gave assurance that the goats had been smoothed. The figure of the goats on the mountain may suggest either a verb of motion or repose. The preposition *m(in)* here employed could indicate either movement or position.

Appeal to Arabic *jalasa,* "sit," as a possible cognate of *glš* provides the options that the meaning here might be "ascend," "descend," or "repose," since *jalasa* belongs to the class of Arabic words with opposite senses (*aḍdād*); cf. Theodor Nöldeke, 1910, 9n2. Delitzsch rendered accordingly, "Which repose downwards on Mount Gilead" (note the translation of the preposition *min*). Delitzsch noted that Arabic *jls* differs from its synonym *q'd* in that the former indicates direction from beneath to above and the latter the opposite. (His translation, however, reflects the sense of *q'd* rather than *jls.*) A flock of goats encamped on a mountain, Delitzsch pointed out, would appear to one viewing from a distance as if rising up almost perpendicularly and, at the same time, as if hanging down lengthwise.

Light on the meaning of *glš* in the present instance has been seen in an Egyptian text. In Papyrus Lansing, verso 1,9, a young scribe wishes his tutor to possess an estate with livestock, "many goats, capering kids, and many lowing oxen." Adolf Erman pointed out (1925, 5) that the determinative  after the word *k'-r'-św* suggests that it must mean "skip," "dance," or the like, and that the orthography shows the word to be foreign. Erman, therefore, suggested that the word corresponds to the *glš* used of goats here and in 6:5. Thus the line should be rendered, "Thy hair is a herd of goats that skip from Mount Gilead"; cf. Blackman, 1925, 210.

To roil the lexical muddle or puddle still more, Ugaritic now offers both nominal and verbal uses of a root *gl<u>t</u>* which could be equated with Hebrew *glš.* The noun *gl<u>t</u>* occurs in the Baal Epic in reference to the services which the great weather god may be expected to render when and if a proper house is provided for him. Asherah, the mother of the gods, having extracted from her erstwhile consort, the sire of the gods, what she takes to be a building permit for Baal's house, praises her senescent spouse's wisdom because now the rains will come in due course:

The season of his rain (*mṭr*) Baal will set,
The season of watering (*<u>t</u>rt*) with *gl<u>t</u>*

He will utter his voice in the clouds,
Flash to earth with lightning.
(4[51].5.68–71)

A number of savant Semitists have suggested that *gl<u>t</u>* here is equivalent to Arabic *<u>t</u>alj,* Hebrew *šeleḡ,* "snow"; cf. de Moor, 1969, 181n105. The noun again occurs with the same preposition in a recently published text (UG 5.3.1.7) describing the grandeur of Baal as he sits enthroned on his holy mountain. His head is in/with *gl<u>t</u>* in the heavens (*rišh bgl<u>t</u> bšmm;* cf. Fisher and Knutson, 1969, and de Moor, 180). This passage will be considered again in connection with 5:11. The nominal use of *gl<u>t</u>* in Ugaritic contributes little or nothing to the clarification of the verb *glš* in the Canticle. There is yet to be considered the single occurrence of *gl<u>t</u>* as a verb in Ugaritic. In a fragment published in *PRU,* V (2001.1.5), there is the phrase *wtgl<u>t</u> thmt.* Since the subject of the verb is the cosmic ocean, the *tĕhôm* of the biblical account of Creation, Gen 1:2, the word manifestly designates a motion applicable to water. J. C. Greenfield (1967, 99n36) proposed the translation "and the abyss was roiled." The Ugaritic usage in connection with water suggests for the present passage with reference to the lady's tresses and a flock of goats on a mountain some such meaning as "surge" or "stream."

1. The Targum related this verse to Solomon's sacrifices at the dedication of the Temple. The hair like a flock is lost in concern for the leaders and sages of the Assembly, but the gentry are represented as doves. The mention of Gilead recalled the heap of stones which Jacob called *Gal'ēd.* (Gen 31:47):

> On that day King Solomon offered a thousand burnt offerings on the altar and his sacrifice was accepted with favor before YHWH. A Voice came forth from heaven and said: "How lovely you are, O Assembly of Israel, and how comely are those leaders of the Assembly and the Sages sitting in the Sanhedrin, they who enlighten for ever and ever the people of the House of Israel, resembling the young of a dove; and even the rest of the members of your Assembly the people of the land, they are righteous as the sons of Jacob who gathered stones and made a heap in the mountain of Gilead."

Midrash Rabbah referred the beauty to Israel's devotion to the Law, both the positive and the negative precepts, in the religious duties of the household, *ḥallāh, tĕrûmāh,* and tithes, and the religious duties of the field, gleaning, the forgotten sheaf, the corner, the second tithe, and the renunciation of ownership, etc., including among other duties circumcision, prayer, the Shema', *mĕzûzāh,* phylacteries, *sukkāh, lulab,* citron, repentance and good deeds; and finally fair both in this world and in the world to come. The eyes as doves were referred to the Sanhedrin, as in 1:15, with detailed comparison of Israel's good qualities with characteristics of the dove. Israel is further likened to the dove as bringing light into the world, with citation of Gen 8:11 for the dove and Isa 60:3 for Israel. Rabbi Levi expressed appreciation for the light that lies in woman's eyes with the observation that, "If a bride's eyes are unattractive, one must survey her whole body, but if her eyes are beautiful, one need not look at the rest of her body." "Thy veil," *ṣammāṯēḵ,* coupled with *mibba'aḏ,* "from behind," evoked an observation on the charm of the upsweep coiffure; "When a woman binds up (*mĕṣammeṯeṯ*) her hair behind, this is a great ornament to her. So when the great Sanhedrin sat behind the Temple that was an ornament to the Temple." The problematic verb *glš* was interpreted by Rabbi Levi as meaning "stream away," "the mountain from which you streamed away." The use of *glš* for thinning out thick hair or profuse pumpkins was cited in support of the view that the line means "the mountain from which I tore away [spoil], I made a mound of witness (*gal'ēḏ*) to other nations."

Christian expositors found edifying suggestions both in the LXX which speaks of silence and in the Vulgate reference to veiling. The holy soul knows when to speak and when to keep silent, to utter discourse in season and avoid risk of sin by importunate speech. The divine mysteries are unspeakable and silent prayer goes up from every contemplative soul kindled with longing for God. The veiling suggested modesty and moderation and a host of other homely virtues. Tertullian related the veil to the modesty and reserve of Christian maidens and to the Bride's submission to her Husband and her duty to keep herself for and to Him alone. The veil is bestowed on consecrated nuns at the profession: "Receive, Virgin of Christ, the veil, a token of virginity and chastity, whereby may the Holy Ghost come upon thee, and the power of the Highest overshadow thee against the heat of evil temptations, through the help of your Lord Jesus Christ."

As the eyes were sometimes taken to denote the Church's teachers who give light to the rest of the body, the hair was explained as the more perfect members of the Church who are closest to Christ their Head. As hair is insensate and dead, so those who have come closest to Christ, by adopting the Religious Life, are dead to the world and its desires. The Saints are compared to a flock of goats because of their love for lofty heights. Again the hair of the Bride is compared to a flock of goats because the peoples of the Church chew the cud of the Law, contemplate heavenly things in faith, are clean animals, and feed on high. Gilead taken as "Heap of Witness" (*gal'ēḏ*), was related to the Martyrs and extended to all the Prophets and Apostles who, by word and deed, bore faithful witness to Christ. Another view stressed the multitude of the hairs rather than their height as applied to the whole body of professing Christians rather than the more eminent Saints. Again the superfluous and non-essential character of hair suggested the human cares and occupations which are no vital part of the Church's life, but can be made a grace and a beauty. Aponius applied the figure to wealthy Christians, surrounded by luxury, unwilling to adopt Apostolic simplicity, yet useful and ornamental to the Church by reason of their faith and almsgiving. Another explanation saw in the hair springing out of the head a type of the holy thoughts and words of the devout soul, dead to the world and the flesh, brought out of the darkness of sin, ignorance, and ungodliness, to truth, knowledge, and piety, by means of the Gospel, revealed from Mount Gilead, the hill of Divine testimony. (Cf. Littledale.)

2a. *ewes.* Interpreters have confused matters by focusing on one or the other of the features of the lady's dental beauty, the symmetry or the whiteness, both of which are integral to the picture. The passive participle feminine plural *qĕṣûḇôṯ,* is here taken as the poetic equivalent of the common term *rĕḥēlîm* used in the otherwise identical parallel in 6:6.

2b. *washing.* The washing suggested to Delitzsch the *saliva dentium* which heightens the gleam of white teeth and is mentioned frequently in the love songs of Arab poets (and seen nowadays on television advertisements of the sex appeal bestowed by dentifrices). The sheep of Syria-Palestine are yellowish and usually dingy and a bath greatly enhances their appearance.

2c. *twinning.* The term *maṯ'îmôṯ* would seem to mean "producers of twins," or the like, as the causative participle denominative from *tĕ'ōm* or *tō'em,* "twin"; cf. 4:5, 7:4[3E] where the word is used of matching breasts like twins of a gazelle. Multiple births among sheep were allegedly extremely infrequent in the ancient Near East; cf. Finkelstein, 1968, 35n20. Modern sheepmen, however, reportedly resort to special feeding of ewes at breeding time in order to increase the number of twins produced and it is claimed that the value of this practice, called "flushing," has been proved experimentally; cf. *Encyclopaedia Britannica,* s.v. "Sheep." The understanding of the present metaphor is not dependent on the relative frequency of twin births among sheep. Multiple births were apparently rare enough to be regarded as a special manifestation of divine favor. Ishtar attempted to seduce the hero Gilgamesh with the promise, among other enticements, that:

> Your nanny-goats will bear triplets, Your ewes twins.
> (Gilgamesh VI 18)

Theocritus (*Idyls* i 25) speaks of "nannies with twins at teat" (*didumatokos*). If twinning among sheep was rare, perfectly matched teeth may also have been unusual and thus all the more appreciated. The interest in twinning here is not fecundity but symmetry and perfection. Rashi understood the term to refer to the regular and orderly character of a flock of ewes under the care of an experienced shepherd who looks after them so that the wool will not be damaged and washes them from day to day. Teeth like well-groomed ewes would thus be fine and white and arranged in rows like wool. The lady's teeth are white and flawless, perfectly aligned and without gap or break.

1,2. Robert Burns, describing the lass that lived "On Cessnock banks," mixed the Canticle's metaphors of hair and goats on the mountain and teeth and clean sheep:

> Her teeth were like a flock of sheep, That slowly mount the rising steep;
> With fleeces newly washen clean, And she's twa glancin', sparklin' een.

2. The damsel's dentition suggested to the Targumist the Priests and Levites who ate the sacrifices and the matching clean sheep recalled Jacob's fleecing of Laban:

> And how comely are the Priests and Levites who bring your sacrifices and eat the holy flesh and the tithe, and the offering, pure from any compulsion or robbery, just as the flocks of Jacob's sheep were clean at the time they were shorn and came up from the brook of the Jabbok; for there was not among them any distrained or stolen and all of them resembled one another and bore twins every time and there was not a barren or aborting one among them.

Midrash Rabbah related the ewes (*qĕṣûḇôt*) to the spoil of Egypt at the Reed Sea. The expression "which came up from the washing" elicited from Abba ben Kahana, in the name of Judah ben Il'ai, the observation that before the song [of Deborah], it is written of the Israelites that they *again* did evil in the sight of the Lord (Judg 4:1), but after the song (Judg 6:1) *again* is omitted. Were they now doing it for the first time? The truth is that the song had wiped out all that went before. The pairing or matching of the teeth was connected with Exod 14:19, with Israel placed between the angel and the Divine Presence, so that none suffered injury.

Several early Christian interpreters, following Gregory of Nyssa, took the teeth to mean the Doctors of the Church who grind down the hard sayings and dogmas of the Faith to make them suitable for reception by the body of Christians who are shorn and free of encumbrance. The washing denoted the cleansing of the conscience from all pollution, and the twinning that calmness of soul and purity of life which is never barren of virtues. Augustine saw the teeth as the teachers cutting away the converts from their former superstitions, the washing as Holy Baptism, and the twins as the love of God and of one's neighbor. Aponius related the upper and lower rows of teeth to the books of the Old and New Testament. St. Bernard (Sermon 63) accommodated the metaphor of the teeth to the Religious Life. As the teeth are whiter than the rest of the body, so the Religious are the purest members of the Church. Teeth have no flesh and the Religious have renounced the flesh (Rom 8:9). Teeth have no skin, and true monks allow no scandal or obstacle to remain among them. As the teeth are cloistered by the lips, so are the Religious cloistered by the walls of the convent. They are seldom seen, and so the Religious should appear only when doing some deed of charity. The teeth have to masticate food for the whole body and the Religious are bound to pray for the whole estate of the Church. The teeth do not taste the dainties they chew, and so the Religious take no credit for the good they do. Teeth do not easily decay and perseverance is a quality of the cloistered life. They are ranked in fixed and even order, and nowhere is there such orderliness as in the convent. There are upper and lower teeth, so the monasteries have dignitaries and ordinary members united in harmonious toil. When the lower teeth move, the uppers remain still, denoting the calmness with which Superiors should rule, even when there is commotion in the lower ranks of the community. The teeth were further exercised to denote the operations of the soul in the assimilation of divine truth. The devout mind ponders and discusses all matters, crushes and grinds with the teeth of discernment. The teeth of the Bride are compared to shorn sheep, the shearings being innocent meditations, which cut away the outer things, such as love of earth and desire for wordly wisdom. They come up from the washing of compunction and penitential tears. They are even, not because all Christians are equally given to the practice of virtue, but because all virtues spring from one common source, which is love, so that each merit is love under one form or another. They produce twins because they develop both contemplation and action, or teach by precept and example. (Cf. Littledale.)

3a. *lips.* This word here and in vs. 11 and 5:13 is plural rather than the usual dual form. A scarlet or crimson thread, by reason of its conspicuous brightness, served as a convenient marker; cf. Gen 38:28,30; Josh 2:18,21. Decorative drapes for the tabernacle (Exod 26:1,31,36, 27:16, 36:35; Num 4:8), priestly vestments (Exod 28:5,8,33) and female finery (II Sam 1:24; Jer 4:30) were made of crimson cloth. Egyptian women painted their lips (cf. *ANEP,* 23, fig. 78) and it is likely that women in other ancient societies did likewise.

3b. *mouth.* Not "speech" as LXX (*lalia*), Vulgate (*eloquium*), Rashi, Ibn Ezra, Luther, and others, understood it. Poetic parallelism suggests that *miḏbar* here designates the instrument and organ of speech rather than the action or content of speech. Delitzsch cited the analogy of the Syrian Arabic use of *minhar,* "breather," in place of *'anf,* "nose."

3c. *pomegranate.* Gerleman suggested that the comparison of the damsel's temples with a slit pomegranate reflects an old Egyptian artistic convention.

The pomegranate is frequently employed as a decorative element in Egyptian art and is one of the favorite motifs of Egyptian painters. Pomegranates of faience, glass and gold are common adornments. Egyptian painters often represented the pomegranate fruit as sliced so that the inner fruit was depicted alongside the outer part. Sometimes the cut divides into one red and one bright yellow half, and in representations of the late period the fruit was divided into one dark and one bright red half. The figure, as Gerleman understood it, is that the veil divides the damsel's temples into a visible bright colored half and a dark half only faintly visible behind the semitransparent veil. Rashi similarly explained that the reference here is to the outer half of the pomegranate which is red. Near Eastern poets frequently compare the color of cheeks with pomegranates or apples. Ginsburg cites a Persian ode quoted by Sir William Jones: "The pomegranate brings to my mind the blushes of my beloved when her cheeks are covered with a modest resentment." An Egyptian love poem likens the beloved damsel's teeth to pomegranate seeds and her breasts to its fruit (Schott 58).

slice. Ibn Ezra conjectured that the noun *pelaḥ* here designates the red flower of the pomegranate. The verb, however, is used of slicing wild gourds into a cooking pot, II Kings 4:39, and in I Sam 30:12 the term is applied to a slice of fig cake. The word may designate either of two parts of a divided object as seen from its application to millstones, both upper and lower, Judg 9:53; II Sam 11:21; Job 41:16[24E]. Whether the reference is to temples or cheeks, the aspects both of unity and duality are implicit.

brow. The term *raqqāh,* apart from the identical passage in 6:7, occurs only in Judg 4:21,22, 5:26 with reference to the temple or thin part of the skull alongside the eye sockets through which Jael drove the tent peg into Sisera's brain. It is difficult to understand why temple(s) would be regarded as meriting special mention for beauty. A more general term seems indicated. Graetz suggested that the word is a synonym for *mēṣaḥ,* "brow." Robert observed that in Aramaic *rummānā'* means both pomegranate and cheek and suggested that this perhaps influenced the LXX rendering *mēlon sou. JPSV*'s choice of "brow" seems most suitable here.

3. The Targumist took his cue from the mention of scarlet and lips to connect the verse with Isa 1:18 and the High Priest's prayer of the Day of Atonement:

> And the lips of the High Priest were uttering prayers on the Day of Atonement before YHWH and his words changed the sins of Israel which resembled a scarlet thread and made them white like clean wool. And the king who was at their head was full of precepts like the pomegranate, as well as the Overseers and Archons who were near the king, who were righteous and in whom there was no evil.

Midrash Rabbah applied this verse to the Song at the Sea, Exodus 15. At that time Moses began to extol Israel, saying, "Your temples are like a split pomegranate," as if to say, even the emptiest among you is full of pious deeds as a pomegranate with seeds; how much more then those behind the veil, the modest and restrained (*mĕzummāṯîm,* playing on *ṣammā*[*t*], "veil").

The scarlet thread reminded some Christian expositors of Rahab the harlot (Josh 2:18,21) who was seen as a type of the Bride. The scarlet color was referred to the preaching of the Passion, but the thread itself was love. The scarlet also suggested the tongues of flame that came down at Pentecost, as well as the blood of Martyrs and Christ's own blood. Vulgate *vitta,* fillet or headband, suggested to some Latin commentators the Doctors of the Church who by their eloquent preaching bound the multitude of the faithful, like the tresses of the head, into one orderly body in the Church. The holy soul likewise binds itself with the discipline and fear of God. The speech of the Bride is comely, pleasant and edifying, because it springs from love and flows from the fountain of grace. The words are sweet because the conscience is cleansed from the bitterness of sin, and the dregs of fleshliness, with no taste of rancor, wrath, envy, or any hurtful thing, but only kindliness, meekness, patience and humility. The cheeks like a piece of pomegranate reflect the modesty of the Bride and denote the virgins of the Church who imitate the ruddy Passion of the Virgin-born Christ, white like the seeds of that fruit in purity, and with a life as hard and austere as the pomegranate rind. John Chrysostom, on the basis of the LXX reading, related the whole passage to secret almsgiving. (Cf. Littledale.)

4a. *David's tower.* The erect and bold carriage of the lady's bespangled neck is likened to a commanding tower adorned with trophies of war. No clue is offered as to the identification of the tower in question apart from the association with David. The implication is that the tower was famous and especially distinguished for the features which make a tower notable, namely size, strength, and symmetry. Delitzsch assumed that the tower in question was that mentioned in Neh 3:25*f,* "the tower projecting from the upper house of the king at the court of the guard." The lady's neck is formidable indeed. Gordis asserted that a large neck, like a prominent nose (cf. 7:5[4E]), was a mark of beauty to the ancients. One may be forgiven for skepticism on this point. The representations of the female form in the art of the ancient Near East do not support this assertion. To R. B. Laurin (1962, 1063) "the metaphor of the 'tower' signifies inaccessibility, insurmountability, purity, virginity, faithfulness—an apt figure to express the exclusiveness of a lover. It is the picture of a maiden with head held high, standing aloof from all advances." To this it will suffice simply to note that throughout the Song the female is the aggressor and, far from holding herself aloof, she goes on a nocturnal prowl to seek her lover (3:1–4). The size of the damsel's neck stretches poetic hyperbole a bit as applied to a peasant lass or any earthly creature. Waterman remarked that this is "the first recorded case of goitre!" If the lady is divine, her proportions would not be abnormal.

4b. *courses.* The unique term *talpiyyôṯ* has puzzled translators and commentators. LXX simply transliterated the word, taking it apparently as a proper name. No such locality was known in antiquity; the suburb of modern

Jerusalem was so named only recently. Versions independent of LXX rendered variously; Aquila *eis epaelxeis,* Symmachus *eis hupse,* Vulgate *cum propugnaculis.* The Talmuds explained the word as referring to Jerusalem as the hill (*tēl*) to which all mouths (*piyyôt*) turn (TB Berakot 30a), and similarly Saadia. Dom Calmet likewise discerned in the word the two elements *tēl,* "hill," and *piyyôt,* "mouths," in the sense of valleys, supposing that the reference is to a tower built by David on a height in the valleys of Lebanon.

The assumption that the clue to the meaning of *talpiyyôṯ* is furnished by the reference to suspension of weapons in the succeeding lines has hindered proper understanding of the term. Ibn Ezra apparently inclined to the view that the term is equivalent to *lĕ tālôṯ piyyôṯ,* "for suspending weapons," even though there is no evidence that *piyyôṯ,* "mouths," is applied to weaponry, apart from the use of "mouth(s)" for the edge(s) of a sword. *KJ*'s rendering "armoury" and *RSV*'s "arsenal" reflect Ibn Ezra's conjecture. Gesenius appealed to Arabic *talafa,* "destroy," to form a *nisbah, talpî,* "destructive," as a poetic term for weapons. The Targum, Rashi, and Rashbam construed *talpiyyôṯ* as equivalent to *tĕ'al(le)piyyôṯ,* from the root *'lp,* "teach," with elision of the *'ālep̄.* The sense thus would be "instruction" or the like. The Targum seized on the didactic concern for the exegesis of the line: "And the Head of the college (*rēš mĕṯiḇtā'*) was full of merit and great in performance of good works, like David, King of Israel, for upon the speech of his mouth the world was built and on the Teaching of the Law (*'ulpān 'ôrāyṯā*) with which he was occupied." Ginsburg likewise connected the troublesome term with the didactic sense of *'lp* and rendered:

Thy neck is like the tower of David, Reared for the builder's model.

Dussaud, Dalman, and Horst on the basis of the use of *tĕlî* as a term for weapon in Gen 27:3 proposed alteration of *lĕṯalpiyyôṯ* to *liṯliyyôṯ.* Perles (83*f*) appealed to Akkadian *tilpanu,* "bow." Graetz confidently asserted that the word can only be Gr. *tēlōpis* and he rendered accordingly, "gebaut zur Fernschau." On this Haupt remarked, "If *talpîyôth* had been a Greek word the Septuagintal translators would probably have recognized it." Haupt later (*Polychrome Bible,* Kings, p. 95) proposed connection of the word with Akkadian *šulbū* (*Šafel* of *labū*), "fortify."

The meaning "trophies" was proposed by several scholars, but with differing derivations; even the emendation to *tĕluyyôṯ,* "suspended things," i.e. trophies. Kuhn and Haller proposed emendation to *lappĕṯîlôṯ,* i.e. "by line(s)" in the sense of "according to exact measure," on the basis of Ezek 40:3 where a flaxen line is mentioned along with the reed measuring stick. Delitzsch came close to the proper understanding of the picture. After considerable discussion, he opted for the sense "built in terraces," with the explanation that the damsel's neck was surrounded by ornaments so that it did not appear as a uniform whole, but as composed of terraces. These terraces,

Delitzsch supposed, were built one above the other like the Babylonian ziggurat.

A. M. Honeyman (1949, 51*f*) dispelled the "ghost" place name and offered the only plausible explanation of the term *talpiyyôṯ*. In form the word is a feminine plural of the *taqtilat* nominal pattern from the root *lpy* meaning "to arrange in courses." The sense appropriate to a tower is "built of coursed masonry." It is, of course, the repeated layers of structural material which increase a tower's strength. The mention of the thousand shields in the succeeding line Honeyman related also to the exterior appearance of the tower; the picture is not of the interior stocked as an arsenal, rather the courses of masonry with drafted margins and bosses on the outer faces of the stones resembled rows of warriors' shields, the usual shield (*māḡēn*) being a round targe of leather. The comparison of our Lady's neck adorned with a multiple layered necklace, to a formidable tower decked with shields, while seemingly outré by western standards, was not inept or strange. Her neck is again compared to an ivory tower in 7:5[4E]. A further parallel was noted by Honeyman in the apocryphal NT work Acts of Thomas 8:8. The verse was rendered as follows by Honeyman.

> Like David's tower is thy neck, laid in course,
> On which the thousand shields are hung, all the warriors' targes.

Honeyman's suggestion was further developed by B. S. J. Isserlin (1958) who saw two kinds of elements on the tower: on top a series of beads resembling round shields; and below something resembling either the short or the long side of building stones (according to whether the masonry is laid in headers or stretchers). In the quest for neckwear of this type in the ancient Near East, Isserlin settled on the necklace represented on the well-known sculpture from Arsos in Cyprus, the upper beads of which looked to him like a row of round shields such as represented on the relief depicting Sennacherib's siege of Lachish, while the lower elements evoked roughly bossed headers, as found in ancient Palestinian defense works.

The statue from Arsos is dated by Dikaios to the beginning of the sixth century B.C. and Isserlin considers this a possible clue to the dating of the Song of Songs, since the necklace "belongs to an Iron Age family" and is quite different from Hellenistic necklaces. The possibility of survivals of older styles (such as the multiple necklace of Phoenician derivation worn by the "Lady of Elche" in Spain, perhaps as late as the Hellenistic era) Isserlin took as a warning not to depress unduly the date of composition of this passage; a date during the seventh/sixth or at latest the fifth century might deserve consideration. He noted, however, that we cannot assume that all passages of the Song of Songs as we now have it must date from the same period and opted for the sixth century as a compromise period that could accommodate other chronological indications contained in the Song.

Illustration of our Lady's layered neckwear more striking than the necklace on the sculpture from Arsos is supplied by the elaborate multiple necklaces on Mesopotamian clay figurines which have been the object of special study by George F. Dales (1960; 1963). Some of the necklaces represented are prodigies of extravagance with multiple layers remarkably resembling courses of masonry. The multiple layers of ornamentation on the front of the neck are represented by incised strips of clay which resemble masonry layers of brick or stone. The heavy neckwear was apparently held close and high by a counterweight attached to bands hanging down the back, represented on the terracottas by incised lines. Of the line drawings (after Dales, 1963, figs. 8 and 34) on p. 454, our Figure 7, the top one is probably from the Larsa Period and the bottom from Mohenjo-Daro.

4c. *A thousand shields.* The word *māḡen* is here determined by the definite article, *'elep̄ hammāḡēn.* Delitzsch regarded the determination as significant and recalled the two hundred golden (large) shields (*ṣinnāh*) and the three hundred golden (small?) shields which Solomon put in the House of the Forest of Lebanon, I Kings 10:16–17. These golden shields were taken away by the Pharaoh Shishak, and Rehoboam replaced them with brass shields. The guards carried these shields when they accompanied the king to the temple (I Kings 14:26–28; cf. II Chron 12:9–11). Shields said to have belonged to King David and which were in the temple were issued to the captains of the guard on the occasion of Joash's accession to the throne (II Kings 11:10; cf. II Chron 23:9). It is not reported that these shields were hung on a tower. The figure of five hundred is here doubled. A display of even five hundred golden shields seems very improbable, as Delitzsch remarked.

The hanging of warrior's shields on tower walls is attested in Ezek 27:11. In I Macc 4:57, however, gold crowns and small shields are mentioned as decoration for the front of the rededicated temple. I Macc 13:29 mentions trophies of arms and carved prows of the ships which Simon Maccabeus placed on the monument over the grave of his father and brothers as an everlasting memorial.

hung. Haupt, Zapletal, Dussaud, and Horst would delete *tālûy* as confused dittography of *'ālāyw* influenced by the paronomasia of *bānûy* and *tālûy,* thus recovering the desiderated *qînāh* metre. Robert in defense of the retention of *tālûy* points to the two occurrences of *tly* in Ezek 27:10,11, the second with the preposition *'al.* The fact that *tālûy* is singular although referring to the thousand shields suggested to Robert that such was intentional.

4d. *bucklers.* The exact meaning of the term *šeleṭ* is uncertain. LXX here rendered *bolides,* "darts," Vulgate *armatura.* Among the terms for weapons in the Old Testament none is so variously rendered by LXX as this one. Most puzzling is Jer 51:11 where it is taken by LXX to mean "quivers" because it is the object of the verb *ml',* "fill"; it may be, however, that the verb here has the meaning "prepare." Similarly in Ezek 27:11 LXX chose "quiver," although the usual view is that the reference is to shields. In II Sam 8:7 and I Chron 18:7 the renderings are *chlidonas,* "bracelets," and *kloious,* "ornaments," and in II Chron 23:9 *ta hopla,* "arms." The use of the term in the Qumran War Scroll apparently in the sense of "dart" led Yadin to reexamine the seven passages which use the word in the Old Testament and the use of an Aramaic cognate in Genesis Rabbah 93:7 where the commentary ascribed to Rashi explains it as a synonym of *šēḇeṭ,* "staff," which is also used in the sense of "dart," as in II Sam 18:14. Yadin's analysis indicates that the term either included several types of weapons, or else there were different opinions as to its meaning. The opinion of Tur-Sinai (in B-Y, XIV, 7154n2) is that *šeleṭ,* in keeping with the root-meaning, basically means "prowess," and came to be used of tools of prowess, be these shields or other arms (Yadin, 1962, 133–135).

The armor attached to the walls gives an impression of force at rest and represents an austere beauty made of prosperity and power, according to Robert, and this he would apply to the New Jerusalem, citing Ps 122:7.

4. The Targum applied the tower to the Head of the Academy and the weaponry to the learning of the Law:

> And the Head of the Academy, he who is Master to you, is mighty in merit and great in performance of good deeds, like David the King of Israel, and upon the word of his mouth the world was built and he was occupied with teaching the Law. The people of the House of Israel were confident and victorious in war as though they were holding in their hands all kinds of weapons of warriors.

Midrash Rabbah mixed with the treatment of this verse a number of references to the verses immediately preceding. The term *talpiyyôṯ* was applied to the book of Psalms as uttered by many mouths (*piyyôṯ*), among whom were Adam, Abraham, Moses, David, and Solomon. The thousand shields was referred to the thousands and myriads whom God shielded by the Sea, for the sake of him who came for a thousand generations (i.e. Moses; cf. Ps 105:8).

Christian commentators generally related the neck to the Prelates and Doctors of the Church, with a variety of reasons for the connection. The neck is just below the head, so the Prelates occupy the highest position under the Head in the body of the Church. The neck also is the channel which transmits food to the body, so the preachers are the Channels of the Word. They are like David's tower because of their strength, their soaring upward toward heavenly things, and because they are foremost in the brunt of battle. The Vulgate rendering of *talpiyyôṯ* as *propugnaculis,* was applied to the mysteries of Holy Scripture, the gift of miracles, and the examples of love, mercy, patience and other virtues in the life of Christ. The shields were taken by Gregory of Nyssa to denote the angelic guardians of the Church against all darts (LXX *bolides*) of the mighty ones. A common view was that shields represent the defenses of the soul against the assaults of sin. (Cf. Littledale.)

5a. *two*. Some critics (e.g. Dalman, Zapletal, Dussaud, Wittekindt, Miller, Horst, Haller, Jastrow) would delete the word "two" as unnecessary before the dual form "breasts," and as overloading the metre. Gordis suggests that the presence of the numeral emphasizes that both breasts are alike. Kuhn, instead of *šĕnê,* "two," suggested reading *šinnê,* "teeth of," as a designation of the extremities of the breasts, a rather bizarre way to refer to nipples. To Joüon's observation that the breasts naturally represent fecundity, Robert objected that this is not so in biblical language, except, perhaps, in Gen 49:25. This is scarcely an adequate appraisal of biblical references to breasts. Although there is not the obsession with breasts as symbols of female sexuality which characterize contemporary western culture, there are, in addition to allusions to the maternal nutritive function of breasts, e.g. Isa 28:9; Joel 2:16; Ps 22:10[9E]; Job 3:12, several references outside the Song of Songs to female breasts as objects of sexual attraction for the male, Ezek 16:7, 23:3,21; Hosea 2:4[3E]; cf. 1:13, 7:4,8[3,7E], 8:8,10.

5a,b. The gazelle is celebrated in Arab poetry for its perfection in form and beauty. The use of the numeral, the dual noun, and the term "twins" emphasize the perfect symmetry of the breasts. The youth of the fawns bespeak the youthful freshness and small size of the mammary orbs. According to the Arab ideal of feminine pulchritude, the breasts were among the attributes that should be small. The breasts of the numerous figurines of the love-goddess are regularly represented as small, often abnormally small, perhaps indicating their virginal character. (Cf. Albright, *YGC,* 133.)

5c. The lady's breasts are again compared to two fawns, twins of a gazelle, in 7:4[3E], but there the lotus-eating motif is not repeated; it is rather her "belly" that is lotus-hedged. Gerleman notes that the gazelle appears three times elsewhere as a poetic image for the youth, the male lover—2:9,17, 8:14—and he has the impression that these gazelle-comparisons have a formalistic stamp, a charming decoration in nature stiffened to pure ornament. Given this impression, it is surprising that the common motif of the gazelle and the lotus in Near Eastern art was overlooked; cf. Goodyear, 1891, pls. xxxvi, xxxvii, xxxviii, and the notes on the deer, gazelle, oryx, ibex, wild goat and lotus in connection with these illustrations, pp. 243–250.

There is, however, something wrong with the picture of the two breasts as fawns browsing on or among lotuses. Following Bochart, several commentators have imagined the twin gazelles as the nipples of the breasts. "The two *paps* rise upon the breast like lilies from the ground; among which, if we conceive two red kids feeding, that were twins and perfectly alike, they appeared like the *nipples* or *teats* upon the paps, to those that behold them afar off." This conceit Ginsburg rightly regarded as extravagant. Elsewhere, in 2:9,17, it is clearly the male lover who is depicted as the gazelle or stag and the feeding on or among the lotus presumably refers to his partaking of the charms of his lady fair. In 7:4[3E] where the breasts are again compared to two fawns, twins of a gazelle, there is no reference to their feeding on or among lotuses. It seems likely, therefore, that the allusion to lotus-eating should be deleted here, as mistakenly introduced from the cliché referring to the male lover.

5. The Targum related the two breasts to the two Messiahs and to Moses and Aaron:

> Your two commanders who will save you, Messiah Son of David, and Messiah Son of Ephraim, resemble Moses and Aaron, sons of Jochebed, who are likened to two young antelopes, twins of a gazelle. By their merit the people of the House of Israel were fed for forty years in the wilderness on manna and plump fowl, and water of Miriam's well.

Midrash Rabbah also identified the two breasts as Moses and Aaron. As the breasts are the beauty and ornament, the charm, glory, and pride of a woman, so were Moses and Aaron the beauty and ornament, the charm, glory, and pride of Israel. As the breasts are full of milk, so Moses and Aaron filled Israel with Torah. As whatever a woman eats helps to feed the child at the breast, so Moses taught Aaron all the Torah which he had learned (Exod 4:28). As one breast is not greater than the other, so it was with Moses and Aaron (Exod 6:26,27). Other proposals for the identification of the two breasts, such as Moses and Phinehas, or Joshua and Eleazar, appear somewhat disparate.

Christian expositors devoted more attention to the two breasts than did the Rabbis, and offered greater variety of explanations. The breasts of the Church at which her children are nourished were identified as the two Testaments, twins because of the perfect accord between them, the Old rich in type, and the New in fulfillment. Another view saw the breasts as the twin precepts, love of God and love of neighbor. Gregory of Nyssa insisted that they represented the outer and inner man united in one sentient being, visible and invisible, whether applied to the whole Church or the individual soul, but none of the Fathers followed him in this interpretation. Psellus also stood alone in explaining the two breasts as denoting the Blood and Water which flowed from the side of the crucified Savior. The Doctors of the Church who teach the faithful were identified with the breasts; they are compared to young roes because of the clarity of their insight into divine mysteries, and their speed in hastening to reach their Lord; they feed among the lilies of a pure conscience and a holy life, until the day breaks and the shadows flee and they attain the prize which He has prepared for them. The teachers of the church are like breasts in their maternal tenderness and the twin mounds of contemplation and action both yield the same spiritual nutriment. Again the breasts denote the edification of faith and training in holiness, or the shunning of evil and the practice of good. They are twins because born at one time of grace, of the same Father, Christ; and Mother, the Church, they feed among the lilies of the Scriptures, until the dawn of the day that has no evening. (For these and other explanations, cf. Littledale.)

6a,b. Identical with 2:17a,b. Several critics would delete the verse as disruptive. Graetz placed it after vs. 7. It is absent from the Hexapla of LXX and replaced by the text of Aquila, but it is found in the Syro-hexaplar (cf. Field, 417n17).

6c. *I will hie me to . . .* Syriac here has the feminine imperative instead of the first person verb. Graetz made the whole of 6c,d interrogative and exclamatory on the assumption that "with me" of the succeeding verse is supplementary to the verb of 6c so the meaning is, "I go not alone, but you shall and will accompany me." If this were the intent, the verb presumably would have been plural, *nēlēḵ lānû*. The sentiment here is like that expressed in 7:8–10[7–9E] where the lady's form is compared to a palm tree and her breasts to fruit clusters and the lover feels the urge to climb the palm, grasp its branches, and taste the fruit clusters, as here he wishes to betake himself to her charms figured as a mount of myrrh or a hill of incense.

6c,d. The effort to localize the myrrh mountain(s) and frankincense hill(s) in the north of Palestine on the basis of the statement of Florus (*Epitome Rerum Rom* iii 6) that Pompey the Great passed over Lebanon, through that scented grove, through that frankincense and balsam forest (*per nemora illa odorata, per thuris et balsami sylvas*), is vain since neither myrrh nor frankincense is indigenous to any part of Palestine. Delitzsch thought that Florus' reference to Pompey's journey alluded to the gardens of Damascus.

In Gerleman's view, this verse leads us wholly into the realm of poetic unreality. The question of the geographical localization of the myrrh mountains and frankincense hills has little sense. Likewise it is wrong, he felt, to relate the words to the maiden's breasts. For Gerleman the mention of gazelle twins pasturing among lilies necessarily evoked thoughts of a distant wonderland, similar to the Egyptian notions about Punt which in Egyptian art and literature are radiant with the lustre of legend, especially in love poetry. Gerleman, apropos of 2:17, cites as samples of the legendary charm of Punt two bits of Egyptian love songs. A maiden, depicted as a birdcatcher, says:

Many birds from Punt alight in Egypt,
salved with myrrh.
The first one grabs my bait.
His fragrance is brought from Punt,
His claws are full of balsam.
(Schott 50,1)

A young man says:

When I embrace her
and her arms spread round me,
it is like (being) in Punt.
It is like [anointing with] oil.
(Schott 66,4)

The lady's breasts as mounds of myrrh and spices could also be a wonderland where her consort may cavort like a stag.

6. The Targum took the fleeing shadows to mean the demons dispelled by the incense of the Temple:

> And all the time that the House of Israel held fast to the methods of their righteous fathers, the demons and shades that roam morning and noon fled from among them, for the Glorious Presence of YHWH dwelt in the Temple which was built on Mount Moriah, and all the demons and harmful agents would flee at the smell of the spice incense.

Early Christian interpreters related this verse to Christ's Passion as the mystery hidden under the types of the mountain of myrrh and the hill of frankincense. The myrrh denoted death and the frankincense the Divine nature. He speaks of a mountain when referring to His death, and of a hill with reference to His Divinity, because it was such a great, unspeakable and unsearchable thing that He, who was in the form of God and thought it no robbery to be equal with God, should humble Himself, take the form of a servant, and submit to death on the Cross (Philip 2:6). Similarly, the mountain of myrrh was understood as the human body of the Bridegroom voluntarily offered to death, a stone cut out without hands which become a great mountain (Dan 2:34,35). The myrrh recalled the anointing in the tomb by Joseph of Arimathea. The mountain and the hill were seen as the souls of the Saints, lofty in contemplation. The Bridegroom promises to come to this mountain and hill to bless with His visitation those souls which mortify their members, feelings and lusts and offer themselves as a sacrifice acceptable to God. The ethical dative, "I will go for myself," was taken to mean that the Bridegroom speaks to Himself rather than to the Bride. He will go for Himself because His love admits no partner and His journey no companion. The mountain of myrrh again was seen as the bitterness of repentance and the hill as devotion of prayer; because penitential sorrow surpasses prayer as a mountain does a hill (cf. Luke 15:7). Another interpretation related the calling of the peoples to Christ, the Gentiles as the mountain of bitter myrrh, and the hill of frankincense as the Jews. (Cf. Littledale.)

7b. *blemish.* LXX rendered the Hebrew *mûm* with the similar sounding word *mōmos,* "blame, reproach." Many interpreters have seized upon this point in order to moralize. In vss. 1–5, according to Delitzsch, Solomon has praised the Shulamite's external beauty, but in vs. 6 her soul has disclosed itself and now the fame of her spotless beauty is extended to her soul no less than to her external appearance. While the word *mûm* may sometimes refer to moral as well as physical blemish (cf. Prov 9:7; Job 11:15, 31:7; Deut 32:5), there is no hint here of interest other than in corporeal beauty. Robert, in accordance with preconceived theory, sees allusion to Israel's purification by the Exile, as in Isa 40:2.

7. The Targum applied the praise to Israel, conditional on performance of the divine will:

> And at the time that your people, the House of Israel, did the will of the Lord of the World, He would praise them in high(est) heaven, and thus He said: "You are all beautiful, O Assembly of Israel, and no blemish is in you!"

Midrash Rabbah referred this verse to Jacob because his couch was blameless before God and no flaw was found therein. Simeon ben Yohai related it to the time that Israel stood before Mount Sinai (Exod 24:7). At that time there was none among them with flux, no lepers, lame, blind, dumb, deaf, lunatics, imbeciles, dullards or doubters. But after they had sinned, it was not many days before they had all these (Num 5:2).

This verse was made the scriptural basis for the requirement that members of a court must be clean in respect to righteousness and also from physical defects (TB Yebamot 101b). Freedom from genealogical blemish was also included in this requirement (TB Qiddushin 76b, Sanhedrin 36b).

As applied to the Church Militant here on earth, beset with weakness and stained with the sins of her children, this verse required qualifications which were unnecessary with reference to the Church Triumphant which will be without spot, wrinkle, or blemish of any sort (Eph 5:27). Even the Church Militant, in spite of her blemishes, was all fair in the sight of her Bridegroom, fair in the ranks and orders of Saints, great and small, in her Martyrs and Virgins, in her members temperate, almsgiving, and penitent. Daily penitence keeps her free of mortal sins and removes the stains of venial guilt. She is fair with the beauty of the Gospel Law, the knowledge of God, of true faith and worship, fair in the outward beauty of her Sacraments and stately rites, in the grace and righteousness of her members, and in the holy deeds of her Saints.

With reference to the holy soul, the words of this verse could not have full application in this world. Nevertheless, like the Church Militant, she could still be fair on earth, in mind, soul, and flesh, purged of all passions, adorned with holiness, free from all evil concupiscence, and in mind set free from frivolous thoughts and made glorious and godlike by the grace of the Holy Ghost. Those consecrated to virginity were presumed to approximate this ideal more nearly than others, but above all this verse was deemed appropriate to the Virgin of Virgins. (Cf. Littledale.)

8a. *Come.* Reading with LXX, Vulgate, Syriac as imperative feminine singular, *'ĕṯî,* rather than MT *'ittî,* "with me."

from Lebanon. The rendering "to Lebanon" (Haller, Zapletal) is possible, but there is no clear warrant here to choose that sense. Lebanon here refers to the range of mountains on the north of Palestine, consisting of two parallel chains running southwest to northeast. In the Bible Lebanon is used of both ranges, but in modern usage that term is applied to the western range while the eastern is called Anti-Lebanon.

bride. Syriac here prefixes "my sister," as in vss. 9,10,12. Possibly the second occurrence of *'ty,* "come," or "with me," was corrupted from *'ḥty,* "my sister," as Graetz supposed. Wittekindt, on the other hand, deleted the word for "bride."

8c. *Come.* Vulgate has here *coronaberis,* apparently having read *ta'ăṭĕrî* instead of MT *tāšûrî.* There are two possibilities for the sense of the verb *tāšûrî,* one meaning "to look" and the other cognate with Arabic *sāra* (medial y), "travel." In view of the preceding verb(s) of locomotion, it seems preferable to choose that sense for *tāšûrî,* although "look" also offers acceptable sense. *JPSV* renders "trip down," but the word "down" is hardly necessary and "trip" suggests the sense of skip, dance, or stumble. Blommerde (1969, 119) takes the verb in the sense "appear," "Appear from the top of Amana." This would be appropriate to a theophany, but a mountain peak seems an unlikely place for a human bride to reside.

Amana. LXX rendered "from the beginning of faith," taking *'ămānāh* as a common noun in a sense similar to its use in Neh 10:1[9:38E], 11:23. Although this name is not used elsewhere in the Bible, it is generally assumed to be the same as the river name Abanah (*Qere* Amanah), II Kings 5:12, which issues at the foot of the Anti-Lebanon and flows through Damascus under the modern name Baradā. The modern name of the mountain at the source of the Baradā is Jebel Zebedāni. Akkadian inscriptions mention the mountain in variant forms of the name *Umānum, Ammana,* and *Ammun.* Sargon II obtained alabaster from there.

8d. *Senir and Hermon.* According to Deut 3:9, Senir is the Amorite designation of Mount Hermon which the Sidonians called Sirion. Syriac of Deut 4:48 also identifies Hermon and Sirion where MT has garbled the name. In I Chron 5:23 Senir and Mount Hermon are again juxtaposed. It is not clear whether the two terms are completely synonymous or whether Senir properly designates only part of the Hermon range, the southern section north of Damascus which the Arab geographer Abulfeda termed Sanīr.

8e,f. *lions' . . . panthers'.* Panthers may still survive in the wilds of the Anti-Lebanons, but lions have disappeared. According to Tristram (1873, 116) lions lingered in Palestine till the time of the Crusades and are mentioned by historians of the twelfth century as living near Samaria. Panthers or leopards preyed on flocks in Gilead in recent times (Tristram, 113). Commentators have been sore vexed to explain the interest here in lions and leopards, or panthers. Delitzsch pictured Solomon as inviting the Shulamite to accompany him to the heights of the Anti-Lebanon where the two alone could look down on the lions and panthers, near to them but inaccessible, and there she could enjoy the prospect of the extensive pleasant land which was subject to the sceptre of him who held her safe on these cliffs, and accompanied her over these giddy heights. There on Amana, which signifies fidelity and the faithful covenant, Solomon would betroth the Shulamite in faithfulness; cf. Hosea 2:20[22E]. Such would certainly be an exciting honeymoon befitting an impressario like Solomon. Graetz waxed ecstatic over the groom who courted danger and whose beloved gave him courage. Ginsburg opined that no one would invite his beloved to go with him to dangerous mountain tops to take a view of the country!

Already in 1918 Bertholet saw the present passage as a remnant of the Adonis cult. Bertholet took his departure from a passage by Theodor Bar Koni relating the story of the shepherd Tammuz who loved a famous beauty and fled with her to the mountains of Lebanon where her husband Hephaistos pursued (thus we learn that the fair one was none other than Aphrodite) and was slain by Tammuz who in turn was killed by a boar. A sculpture from Ghineh near Byblos depicts Adonis or Tammuz being attacked by a bear, while Philo of Byblos attributes the death to unspecified wild beasts. The lion motif Bertholet supposed to have come from contamination from related myths. At Amathus on Cyprus, where Melqart was worshiped along with Adonis, a statue represents the former god fighting a lion. Eshmun was apparently conceived as a lion-fighter and Attis, in his amours with a nymph, was discovered by the lion of the Corybantes. The death of Hyas was also occasioned either by a boar or a lion. Bertholet stressed the fluid character of such details, citing the Shiite legend of Husain whose opponent Shimer has a canine muzzle and swine bristles. The lion along with leopards in the Canticle Bertholet would explain simply on the basis of poetic parallelism, as in Jer 5:6.

The conception of the divine shepherd, Bertholet pointed out, reaches back beyond Theodor Bar Koni to the ancient Tammuz hymns of Mesopotamia. The Idylls of Theocritus also present Adonis as a shepherd and the affinities with the Song of Songs have long been noted. The connection of Adonis with Lebanon is further attested by Lucian *de dea Syria* § 8.

The correspondence of these features with Song of Songs 4:8, in the view of Bertholet, is not accidental. The Adonis myth was known on Israelite and Jewish soil, as witnessed by the allusions to Adonis gardens in Isa 17:10, the Tammuz cult in the temple in Ezek 8:14, and Jerome's references to Tammuz-Adonis worship in Bethlehem. Bertholet, taking his cue from Baudissin, ascribed the impact of the Adonis myth on Song of Songs to the influence of mimed representations of the Adonis mysteries which were colored by profane erotic poetry.

Schmökel (pp. 72–75), though championing the sacred marriage cultic interpretation, was not satisfied with Bertholet's interpretation. Schmökel would delete the word *kallāh,* "bride," in order to have the words addressed not to the female but to the distant male consort, since the seeker and finder in the Canticle is always the female. The one to whom the call applies, in Schmökel's view, is Tammuz the Shepherd. He it was who was destroyed by lions, or other predators, such as leopards, which endanger the sacred flocks. The mountains here represent the death-place of the god, as in the Sumerian Tammuz hymns "mountain" and "steppe" are designations of the netherworld, the death of the god being described as departure to the mountain, or imprisonment or overpowering by the mountain.

As Schmökel understood the cultic framework, we have here the beginning of Scene II in which the priestess who represents the goddess, accompanied by her female chorus, raises her voice in the "Seduction Call" (Lockruf) that precedes the entrance of the divine couple. The moment is at hand, and the assembled community shares in the cultic experience of it; the longed-for Beloved who was thought to be lost reappears.

Schmökel mentioned in passing the associations of the goddess Ishtar with Lebanon, as the Consort of Baal Lebanon and later as *oreia mētēr,* "Mountain Mother," as well as her relation to lions, but these considerations, he asserted, do not come into play here. This is simply because Schmökel's preconceived theories force him to tamper with the text and rule out obviously relevant evidence.

A number of critics have found the verse incomprehensible and entirely disconcerting. Budde excised the verse as incompatible with his hypothesis. It remained also unintelligible to Robert who noted that lions are mentioned as inhabiting the thickets of the Jordan, Jer 49:19=50:44; Zech 11:3, but there is no other mention that the mountains of Lebanon were a special haunt of these ferocious beasts. Thus he felt compelled to understand the verse in a figurative sense. Harper hinted that the lions and leopards may be intended to represent the hostility toward the Shulamite in Solomon's royal residence in the Lebanon and her rustic lover calls her to leave Solomon and come back home to him. Joüon thought that the beasts designated Israel's neighbors, while Ricciotti understood them as the perils of idolatry in the Persian and Greek periods. Robert, eschewing such speculation, sought to establish the symbolism in consultation with the biblical tradition. Robert arrived at the understanding that the lions and leopards of Canticles 4:8 refer to the peoples who were the instruments of the divine wrath toward Israel. But why should these be located in the Anti-Lebanon? Robert offered two reasons. These mountains which close the north-northeast horizon of Israel determined the classical route of invasions. Again Scripture also compares the enemies of Yahweh with high, wooded mountains and forests, particularly with the cedars of Lebanon (Isa 2:12–14, 32:19; Jer 21:14, 46:22–23; Ezek 21:2–3[20:46–47E]). In particular Isa 10:33–34, 32:16–19; Ezek 31; Zech 11:1–2; Ps 29:5–6 are cited by Robert as explicit or implicit references to the Assyrians or the heirs of their empire. Thus there is no doubt that the country which the Assyrians once ruled is designated by the figures of Amana, Senir and Hermon and also by the lions and leopards, according to Robert. The author of the Canticle thinks of the Israelites, descendants of the captives of Sargon and Nebuchadnezzar, who on the banks of the Tigris and Euphrates comprise the bulk of the nation. These are solicited to return to Palestine where Yahweh has taken possession of his temple. As they come from the great Syrian desert across the Beqa', they are invited to contemplate the summits of the Anti-Lebanon, the country of their fathers, which appears for the first time to their eyes, as the Israelites of the time of the Exodus, coming out of the desert to Nebo and Pisgah, saw at their feet the Land of Promise (Deut 32:48–52, 34:1–4).

The difficulties commentators have found in this passage disappear when we see the lady as the goddess, Lady of the Steppe (*bēlit ṣēri*), Mountain Mother, and Mistress of the Beasts (*potnia thērōn*). The goddess of love and war, Inanna, Ishtar, Anat, Atargatis, is regularly associated with the lion which served as her attribute and her vehicle.

8. The Targum took the bride as Israel and the reference to mountain tops, lions and leopards, as cities of Syria and Lebanon that will be tributary to Israel:

> Said YHWH by His Word: "With Me shall dwell the Assembly of Israel, resembling a modest bride. And with Me they shall ascend to the Temple and shall bring gifts to you, O heads of the people who dwell by the river Amana and who dwell on top of Snow Mountain, and the peoples who are in Hermon. And they shall bring tribute to you O inhabitants of strong cities, mighty as lions, offerings from cities of the mountains which are stronger than leopards."

Midrash Rabbah opened discussion of this verse with reference to the twelve months allowed a bride to prepare for the wedding (cf. TB Ketubot 57a). Allusion to the sensual Ahasuerus' program for beautifying candidates for his harem (Esther 2:12) with six months' oil of myrrh and six months' spices and ointments occasioned a remark by Rabbi Jannai on oil of unripe olives as a depilatory and skin softener. Citation of Exod 24:10 led to a connection with Israel's return from Babylon, Isa 43:14. R. Levi proposed that the reading should be "to Lebanon" rather than "from Lebanon," but this was countered by the assertion that the text means that God first leaps forth *from* the Sanctuary and then he punishes the nations of the world. The verb *tāšûrî,* "look," suggested the noun *tĕšûrāh,* "gift," (I Sam 9:7) and, associated with Amana taken as the name of the river Abanah (cf. II Kings 5:12), recalled II Kings 8:9 in support of the explanation that the nations will bring the Israelites themselves as a gift to the Messiah (Isa 66:20). Another explanation of Amanah connected it with the root *'mn* (similar to LXX, "from the beginning of faith") and referred it to Abraham and his belief in God (Gen 15:6). Senir, taken as *śônē' nîr,* "one who hates a furrow," was applied to Isaac who was tried only once. Mount Hermon was referred to Jacob because all the good of Hermon is on its lower slopes, so from Jacob (the last of the patriarchs) issued the priesthood, the Levites, and royalty. The lions' dens were referred to Sihon and Og who were proud and mighty but did not come to aid one another. The mountains of the leopards referred to the Canaanites who were bold as leopards (cf. Josh 8:17 where they left Ai and Bethel open and all the men went out after Israel).

Christian interpreters found in this verse a wealth of edifying allegory. Christ in the person of Solomon was here heard calling the Gentiles, drawing the Church in betrothal to Himself away from idolatry. Lebanon which to the Greeks denoted incense further typified Gentile idolatry as lying outside the Land of Promise. Shenir and Hermon were taken to denote the Law. Theodoret explained Shenir as meaning "path of lanterns" with reference to that light which illuminated the night before the Sun of Righteousness arose. Hermon's dew which fell on Zion hill (Ps 133:3) denoted the precepts of the Law. From these, and from the lions' dens of fierce and persecuting Jews and the leopards' mountains of subtle and deceitful sophists of the Gentiles, the Bride is urged to come away. Lebanon in the sense of whiteness was related to Baptism. The triple repetition of the summons was given trinities of meanings. The Bride must be perfect in thought, word, and deed; she should come by faith (Amanah), freed from the body, to receive a heavenly reward; come at the Resurrection to be crowned with double glory; come in faith, hope, and charity; come from merit to reward, from faith to sight, from peril to safety, from misery to salvation; come renouncing the devil, world, and self; come in the name of Father, Son, and Holy Ghost. The summons was especially addressed to virgin souls and above all to the Assumption of the Blessed Virgin. (Cf. Littledale for further samples of fervent dilation on this verse.)

9a,b. *ravish.* The verb *libbaḇtînî* has been construed as denominative from **libb* or **libab,* "heart," but has been understood in opposite senses of "hearten" or "give courage," and "dishearten" or "deprive of sense." LXX *ekardiōsas hēmas,* "thou hast heartened us," is ambiguous and could be understood as *e(k)kardiōsas,* "thou hast unheartened." Most of the Greek Fathers, according to Littledale, understood it in the sense of wounding. Vulgate *vulnerasti cor meum* clearly interpreted the force of the verb as privative. Contrariwise, Syriac interpreted it in the factitive, causative sense, "you have given me courage"; similarly Symmachus, *etharsunas*. The only other OT occurrence of *lbb* as a verb is in Job 11:12 in an obscure proverbial saying where it apparently means "get sense," "be made intelligent," or the like; cf. AB 15, ad loc. Commentators who picture Solomon and the Shulamite among the lions and panthers in the mountains choose naturally the factitive sense "embolden, encourage." Ginsburg explained, "The beloved here accounts for his extraordinary strength and courage, which would enable him to rescue his beloved one from her critical position; and to say: 'Thou has deprived me of all heart' would be a positive contradiction." This interpretation depends, of course, on the highly improbable situation envisaged. Most translators and commentators have taken the verb in the privative sense "take away, ravish, capture the heart."

N. M. Waldman has recently proposed (1970, 215) that the verb is not to be derived from *lb, lbb,* "heart," but is identical with Akkadian *labābu,* Late Hebrew *lbb,* and that a semantic development has taken place in the Hebrew from a sense of "rage" or "be aroused to fury" to one of "be aroused sexually." This semantic development is not, however, apparent in Akkadian, according to Waldman, who finds the analogy in comparing Greek *orgē,* "passion," "wrath" and *orgaō,* "swell with lust." The equation of *nalbubu=šigū,* both verbs meaning "to rage" in the commentary on Ludlul Bēl Nēmeqi (cf. *BWL* 34:86 commentary) Waldman related to Hebrew *šṭy* by way of the Akkadian expression *kalbu šegû,* "mad dog," which in Hebrew is *keleḇ šôṭeh.* In addition to the use of *šṭy* for madness or insanity, it is also used of sexual excitement in Midrash Rabbah on Num 25:1*ff*. On the analogy of *šṭy,* "rave," "rage," and "be sexually aroused," Waldman suggested that a similar development took place in the case of *lbb*. Thus *libbaḇtînî* might be rendered, according to Waldman, "You have passionately aroused me." Support for this interpretation is adduced from Mandaic *mlakia mlabia rhamta,* "Angels instigating love," and the use of *rhb* in 6:5 below with reference to the effect of the lady's eyes.

Overlooked by Waldman is the sexual sense of "heart" in Mesopotamian usage. The Sumerian term *ŠÀ.ZI.GA,* translated into Akkadian as *nīš libbi,* "rising of the heart," is used of male sexual passion and potency in Mesopotamian sexual sorcery (cf. Biggs, 2–10). The "rising of the heart" is not simply a term for male interest in sexual relations or his wish for sexual intercourse, but for the ability to get and maintain an erection sufficient for sexual intercourse, hence the meaning "potency" defined by Biggs (3n13) as "capacity to function adequately in the sexual act." The Sumero-Akkadian use of "heart" in an explicit sexual sense suggests at least the possibility that it might have sexual connotations in West Semitic usage. Whether in the factitive, causative sense of "embolden, encourage, excite," or in the privative sense of "capture, rapture or ravishment of the heart or mind," the possible sexual implications of the term can be missed only by dint of studious evasion or gross insensitivity to prurient interests.

The ravishing effect of beauty, especially the effect of the eyes and the effect of a single glance is a common feature of love poetry.

Where is any author in the world
Teaches such beauty as a woman's eye?
(Shakespeare, *Love's Labour Lost* IV iii 312)

There's language in her eye, . . .
(*Troilus and Cressida* IV v 55)

Wine comes in at the mouth
And love comes in at the eye;
That's all we shall know for truth
Before we grow old and die.
I lift the glass to my mouth,
I look at you and I sigh.
(W. B. Yeats, "A Drinking Song")

"The alleged power to charm down insanity, or ferocity in beasts, is a power behind the eye," according to Emerson, and, conversely, also, as the Canticle testifies, to effect the reverse.

Stephan (13*f*) cited several samples from modern Palestinian love songs:

She stood opposite me and deprived me of reason—(lit. "and took my heart [mind]," *w-aḫditli bâli*)
Your dark eyes slew me while I was singing (i.e. being without a care),
And your eyebrows drove shame from me . . .
The darkness of your eyes have slain (lit. slaughtered) me
O one clad in purple clothes, it is worth while falling in love with you,
For your eyes are black and sparkle, and have slain (me) indeed.

9a. *my sister. JPSV* rendered here and in the succeeding vss. 4:10,12, 5:1, "my own" and put the literal sense "sister" in a footnote, presumably to avoid the suggestion of incest. The Billy Graham Crusade edition paraphrased variously, "my lovely one," "my darling," "my darling bride."

The terms "brother" and "sister" are commonplace in many languages with reference to friendly relations without implication of consanguinity, incest, or homosexuality, though by no means limited to purely Platonic relationships. The Semitic usage goes back at least to the Old Babylonian period; (cf. M. Held, 1961, 13, note to I.14). In Ugaritic, the goddess Anat, when she tried to seduce Aqhat in order to obtain his wonderful bow, addressed the youth thus:

Hear, O hero Aqhat
You are (my) brother,
And I [(your) sis]ter.
[. . .] satiety of your flesh.
(18[3 AQHT]1.24)

When Abraham passed off Sarah as his sister, Gen 12:13, 20:2, he was only half a liar since she was his half-sister, though not a uterine sister, Gen 20:12. In the Additions to Esther, 15:9, the king comforted Esther with the words, "I am thy brother, be of good cheer." Tobit and Raguel addressed their wives Anna and Edna as "sister," Tobit 5:20, 7:16. In I Cor 9:5 the combination "sister-wife" has dismayed interpreters and translators concerned with apostolic and priestly celibacy: "Have we not a right to take along a sister-wife (*adelphēn gunaika*) like the other apostles, and the Lord's brothers, and Cephas?"

On the wife-sister motif in the patriarchal narratives, cf. Speiser, *Genesis*, AB 1, 91–94, 150*ff*, 203*ff*; A. Skaist, 1969. D. Freedman, 1970, rebuts Speiser's arguments about the relation of the patriarchal marriages to the Nuzi sistership (*aḫātūti*) contracts, and regrets (p. 85) "that the popularity of the Anchor Bible Series will result in the canonization of Speiser's thesis among laymen and scholars not adequately equipped to question his arguments." See now, S. Greengus, 1975. Thus the discussion continues and there is no need to be unduly worried about canonization of the views of any scholar, however great his erudition and prestige.

9b. *one of your eyes*. The numeral is masculine, although eyes are normally feminine, as are other parts of the body occurring in pairs, with the notable exception of breasts. The usual expedient is to gloss over the difficulty by rendering "one" as "glance" or to supply a supposedly missing word for "glance." Thus *JPSV*, "with one [glance] of your eyes." The true solution, according to Ginsburg, lies in the fact that members of the human body, although usually feminine, are most of them employed occasionally as masculine. Job 21:20 and Zech 4:10 are cited as examples for eyes as masculine, along with the present passage and 6:5. In Zech 4:10 the number of the divine eyes is seven. On these "eyes" as roving secret service agents, like the private "eyes" of the Persian king, cf. AB 15[3] on Job 1:6. In Job 21:20 the reference is clearly to normal human eyes, but the verb precedes the noun and therefore need not agree with it in gender or number. It may be that the eyes in question here are not ordinary human eyes, but the multiple eyes of the goddess. O. G. S. Crawford (1956) has found the eye motif, which he interprets as the symbol of the Goddess, scattered over a large part of the world, from Mesopotamia to Spain. Most striking are the figurines exhumed in the temple of Ishtar at Tell Brak in Syria. The multiple eyes one on top of the other, either singly or in pairs, diminish in size as they rise and thus give the impression that the top of the head is all eyes trailing off to infinity; cf. H. Frankfort, 1949. See Figure *9*, p. 456.

The black goddess Kali of India has three eyes and her peculiar sword (which is manifestly related to the so-called sickle-sword of Western Asia) is also frequently provided with a single eye. The power of the goddess' eye for good or ill is prodigious. Bani Kanta Kakati (1948, 44) relates a legend apropos the fickleness of the amorous goddess, that the Koch king heard report that at the time of evening prayer the goddess danced within closed doors in the temple. The king wished to see the dancing goddess and asked the chief priest to provide him this opportunity. The priest advised the king to peep through a hole in the wall. As he did so his eyes met those of the goddess and she became incensed and tore off the head of the priest. The king and his descendants were forbidden on dire penalty ever to cast even a glance at her hill and this is the reason given for the contemporary practice of descendants of the Koch kings to pass by the goddess' hill under cover of umbrellas.

The power of the goddess' eye to excite amorous passion and to make either male or female sexually irresistible and seductive is prodigious and a favorable glance from her is a consummation devoutly wished:

> If but a glance from Thine eye falls on a blind old man incapable (through his years) of love, then hundreds of youthful women with loosened hair will follow him, their upper cloths slipping from their breasts rounded like jars and their girdles and lower cloth falling from about them.
>
> (A. Avalon, 1953, 18, vs. 13)

Avalon in the commentary of the verse above says, "So great is She the Desirable One (Kamanīya) that but a side glance from Her upon any person or thing makes him or it the object of desire. This is a classic Sanskrit description of the state of women under the influence of passion."

9c. *a single gem*. The singular form of the noun *'ănāq* is unique, but the masculine plural occurs in Prov 1:9 with reference to some form of women's neck ornamentation, and in Judg 8:26 the feminine plural is applied to camel's neck decor. The singular noun here emphasized by the numeral "one" explicitly designates a single unit of the lady's neckwear, either a single bead, gem, jewel, chain, or coil, depending on the type of ornament envisaged. We have seen evidence for a rather complex form of neckwear on terracotta figurines of goddesses. In the light of the parallelism of *'ănāq* with "eye," it seems best to take the work in the sense of "gem." Joüon rendered "pierre précieuse," citing the Ethiopic cognate in a similar sense.

necklace. The unique form *ṣawwārôn,* here written and vocalized as plural, *ṣawwĕrônāyiḵ,* is of uncertain meaning. Ginsburg construed the *ôn* afformative as diminutive expressive of affection and rendered "thy neck," explaining that plural forms are sometimes used for certain members of the body, e.g. the face. Other interpreters take the word as designating the necklace rather than the neck. It makes no real difference here since the reference is to a unit of the neckwear which is on the neck.

Of particular interest here is the Sumero-Akkadian use of "eye" as a designation of a variety of jewelry. This topic has been recently treated by W. G. Lambert (1969), but without recognition of the possible import of some of the data for the present passage of the Canticle. An agate eye-stone of Esarhaddon's wife *Ešarra-hamât* acquired by the Ashmolean Museum, Oxford, moved Lambert to a consideration of similar gems. These objects were doubtless intended to represent eyes since trouble was always taken to secure a piece of agate with a white band and to cut it so that the white appeared around the brown or black, which represented the pupil. The earliest examples noted are Old Babylonian. Inscriptions on the objects sometimes give only the king's names and titles, but many are votive to a named god or goddess, among whom are Nanna, Ningal, Enlil, Ninlil, Ninurta, Adad, Nusku, Marduk, Nabu, Sarpanitum, and Nergal. One of three eye-stones offered by Kurigalzu states a reason:

[To] Adad
his [lord]
[Kuriga]lzu
[son of Burna]buriyaš

for his good health
(*a-na ba-la-ṭi-šu*)
gave (this).

Nevertheless, the function of these objects is disputed. It has been suggested tentatively that they served as dress ornament and it has been thought one could see them on the garment of a statue of Adad. It has been generally assumed that these eyes were set in the eye sockets of divine statues suggested by G. A. Barton (1925), but Lambert notes that none so far have been found *in situ.* It could be argued, Lambert observed, that the eye-stones served an unknown function, or that beyond being votives they had no function and the eye form had no special significance. The latter possibility seems rather unlikely and for the time being we should rather say that the function is unknown or uncertain.

Two other important passages are cited by Lambert. One, from a *Lamaštu* ritual, requires the use of eyes in groups of three, four, and seven. One will recall the three eyes of Kali noted above and the seven eyes of Yahweh mentioned in Zech 4:10. The other passage, the obscure ending of the Akkadian Descent of Ishtar, twice mentions eye-stones in connection with the goddess:

Her lap was full of eye-stones.

Again,

She filled [. . .] with her eye-stones.
(Cf. Lambert, 1969, 71 for the Akkadian text and references.)

Lambert noted that Unger thought that he could detect eyes on the garment of a statue of Adad (*RLV* 4, 415). If this is so, one may think of the sapphire-studded ivory loins of the male lover in 5:14. The gem-filled "lap" (literally "knees," a standard euphemism for the genital area) of the goddess may be what was intended by the elaborate decorations on the girdles of some of the terracotta figurines treated by G. Dales (1963). A detail not discussed by Dales is what appears to be two (or perhaps three) eyes on the chest of an elaborate Larsa period figurine (fig. 34, p. 37). Although they are in the position where breasts might be expected, they are too small for breasts and appear to be circumscribed by eyelashes (cf. Figure 7, p. 454).

9. The Targum paraphrased the verb as meaning "fixed upon the tablet of the heart" and applied the verse to Israel and her scholars, even the least of which was beloved of God:

> Fixed upon the tablet of My heart is your love, My sister, Assembly of Israel, likened to a bride who is modest. Fixed upon the tablet of My heart is the love of the least of your scholars righteous like one of the scholars of the Sanhedrin, and like one of the kings of the House of Judah, upon whose neck was placed the crown of kingship.

Midrash Rabbah offered several explanations of the first part of this verse. The two hearts, for example, were the blood of the Passover and of the Circumcision in Egypt. The single bead of the necklace was identified as Moses.

This verse is cited in the Talmud (TB Shabbat 52b) in connection with the question of animals going out on the Sabbath as proof that the verb *lbb* indicates proximity, since rams may go out *lĕḇûḇîn,* i.e. coupled. The one eye is applied to Israel's spiritual perception of the greatness of the Torah at its reception and both eyes to the material perception of its greatness, having observed it (TB Shabbat 88b).

Some Christian expositors took the LXX *ekardiōsas* in the sense of "hearten," and the repetition of the verb as the giving of a double heart, denoting the trust and confidence Christ has in the fidelity of the Church. The Vulgate's suggestion of wounding was applied to Christ's love for the Church and to the proof of that love which He gave in suffering on the Cross. It is said twice of the Jewish Church because she wounded him with nails while living, and with spear when He was dead. It applies to evil Christians because they wound Him daily with their sins and to the faithful for whom He was wounded in Passion and Compassion. Each wound and blow was double, since hate smote Him in His Body, and love in His Heart. The double address, "my sister, my bride," occasioned no little comment. She was called "sister" in order to show that it is no carnal bridechamber of which the marriage-song sings. He calls her "bride" because the Word has wedded to Himself the human soul; in calling her sister, He witnesses that He also has worn our flesh. Sister denotes also the royal station of the Bride, as kings and queens address one another as brother and sister. The eye which so struck the Bridegroom was seen as the faculty of Divine contemplation. The right eye is the one that looks at heavenly things, the sinister eye is fixed on earth. If the eye is single, the whole body is full of light (Matt 6:22). Jerome took the eyes to mean the virgin life and married life. The left eye, married, was given because of weakness of those who do not see aright; the right eye of virginity is dearer to God. The eye was also seen as denoting the Doctors of the Church, a single eye because of the unity of doctrine. The neck which joins the head to the body was taken to represent the joining of souls to Christ by conversion. (Cf. Littledale.)

10a. This line is missing in LXX B. LXX, Vulgate, Syriac, Arabic, and Luther took *ddyk* as "thy breasts" rather than "thy love"; cf. 1:2.

10b. Several critics (Haupt, Staerk, Dussaud, Wittekindt) would expunge *kallāh,* "bride," on metrical grounds.

10c. Except for the initial particle, identical with 1:2b.

10d. LXX B has "the odor of your garments," rather than "your perfumes," reading *śimlôṯayiḵ* for *šĕmānayiḵ*, apparently under the influence of the following verse.

10. The Targum applied this verse to the divine love for Israel and her saints:

> How beautiful to Me is your love, My sister, Assembly of Israel, which is likened to a modest bride. How good to me is your love, more than the seventy nations, and the good name of your saints more fragrant than all spices.

Midrash Rabbah offered the observation that there are ten places in Scripture where Israel is called "bride," six in the Song of Songs, and four in the prophets. The passages in the Song are 4:8,9,10,11,12 and 5:1. In the prophets the alleged instances are Jer 7:34; Isa 61:10, 49:18, 62:5. This datum evoked another interesting but quite irrelevant statistic that there are likewise ten places in Scripture where God is said to put on clothes. The comment of Rabbi Samuel ben Naḥman on the smell of the oil is abundantly confirmed in the exposition of every verse and word of the Canticle: Just as oil of itself is odorless, but if scented it gives off all kinds of odors, so when a verse is expounded you can find in it all manner of excellent thoughts.

The LXX and Vulgate reading of "breasts" instead of "love" led to some interesting expositions by early Christian interpreters. LXX's wooden wording "Your breasts are fair from wine" was taken to refer to the doctrine of the Church and the breasts no longer give milk for babes and weaklings in faith, but the immortal wine of the Saints, the fuller teachings reserved for the full-grown. Another explanation was that the wine is the blood of Christ inbibed by the Bride which makes her breasts fair and ample, filled with the milk of love of God and man. The breasts were also taken to mean the active and contemplative states in the Church, again with the wine as the efficient cause of their loveliness. On the basis of Vulgate, the breasts were taken to denote the Doctors of the Church who supply spiritual nourishment in the form of milk which they had received in the form of heavenly Bread. This milk is better than the wine of the ceremonial Law which failed at the mystical marriage of the Church and was replaced by Christ with a more generous vintage. As applied to the faithful soul, the breasts were taken to be spiritual and corporal compassion by which the true follower of Christ shared all suffering. The Vulgate use of two different words for breast, *mammae* and *ubera,* suggested a distinction, *mammae* being the blessing of fertility, *ubera* the glory of virginity. With these two breasts the Church daily conceives, daily gives birth, daily gives suck, and yet remains virgin, God thus doing through the Church what He did by the Virgin Mary.

LXX's reading of "garments" instead of "oil" was taken to denote the works of mercy done by the Church, or the graces with which she is endued through the Gospel. Expositors of the Vulgate similarly understood the scent of the ointment as the virtues and good deeds of the Church spread over the world by preaching, a superior mode of diffusion to observance of the Law, the lore of philosophy, and worldly vanities. They are called unguents as derived from the unction of the Holy Ghost, typified by the sacred anointing oil of Exod 30:25. (Cf. Littledale.)

11a. *honey*. The word *nōpeṯ* designates liquid honey. Its sweetness is noted in Prov 24:13, 27:7. The Ugaritic cognate *nbt* is used in parallelism with oil as signs of plenty confirming the resurrection of Baal, and in parallelism with wine in sacrificial libation. The closest parallel to the present line is in the description of the allurements of the exotic female in Prov 5:3, whose lips drip honey and her palate is smoother than oil. Similarly Theocritus *Idyl* xx 26,

> More sweet my lips than milk in luscious rills,
> Lips, whence pure honey, as I speak, distils.

In Prov 16:24 pleasant words are honey comb, sweet to the throat or appetite and therapeutic to the body. Slanderous words are poisonous, Ps 140:4[3E]. Commentators generally have understood 11a,b, to refer to sweet talk and have scouted the notion that the allusion is to *saliva oris osculantis* and the pleasures of deep and wet kissing. Cornelius à Lapide, cited by Robert, noted that some refer this to kissing, others to the breath of the mouth of an eager female, but the preferred reference is to friendly and sweet conversation. This seems plausible in the light of Prov 5:3 and the use of the verb *nṭp* elsewhere for speech, Amos 7:16; Ezek 21:2[20:46E],7[2E]; Micah 2:6,11, but possible implication of osculation can hardly be excluded since it is clear that the expression of love in the Canticle goes beyond conversation or osculation.

Robert suggested that the apparent dependence of 11a,b on Prov 5:3 furnishes a clue to the date of the Canticle. Since Prov 1–9 refer exclusively to Deuteronomy, Isaiah, and Jeremiah, there is no probability that this collection had been affected by a composition so peculiar and so foreign to its purpose as the Canticle. If this hypothesis is correct, Robert regarded it as a datum which determines the upper limits beyond which the composition of the Canticle cannot go. In view of the Sumerian parallels, there is no reason to pause over this proposition which was certainly influenced by Robert's preconceived view of the exilic setting of the composition.

11b. *Honey and milk*. Perhaps a reverse echo of the characterization of the Land of Promise as flowing milk and honey, Exod 3:8,17; Lev 20:24; Num 13:27; Deut 6:3.

under your tongue. In Ps 10:7 this expression is used of storing curses in the mouth and mischief under the tongue; in Job 20:12 the evil man is pictured as savoring his wickedness in his mouth and hiding it under the tongue in order to prolong enjoyment of the flavor. Here, as in the preceding line, the reference may be to the sweets to be tasted by the partner.

In the Sumerian sacred marriage songs the sweetness and honey clearly refer to sexual pleasure; cf. *SMR*, 92,94,96.

Stephan (1923, 16) cited among other Palestinian parallels the following item on honey lips and the sweetness of wet kisses:

> There comes the queen of girls;
> Her saliva is like crystal sugar (or sugar candy).
> O, how sweet is the sucking of her lips, sweeter than sugar or honey.

11c. The parallelism with Gen 27:27 is usually remarked by commentators, but it seems unlikely that the odor which Isaac took to be that of Esau's garments, the smell of the field, was similar to the spicy scent of our lady's raiment. More to the point is Ps 45 9[8E] which speaks of the perfumed robes of the royal bridegroom. Hosea 14:6, speaking of the nation's return to God, predicts that his fragrance shall be like Lebanon. Vulgate in the present line, read instead of Lebanon *lĕḇônāh,* "incense," *sicut odōr thuris.*

11. Targum made the sweet lips the prayers of Israel's priests and the fragrant garments their robes:

> And at the time when the priests pray in the court of the Temple, their lips drip liquid honey and your tongue, O modest bride, with your utterances of songs and praises sweet as milk and honey and the scent of the garments of the priests is like the scent of frankincense.

Midrash Rabbah took the verb "drip" as its point of departure in consideration of this verse and applied it to sixty myriad prophets and sixty myriad towns in Israel. The honey drip was further applied to the scriptural knowledge and expository skill of the scholar. Honey and milk under the tongue was referred to the grasp of legal principles (*hălāḵôṯ*) and even to the ability to read Scripture with proper modulation and intonation. The scent of the garments provoked some discussion of body odors and sanitation of garments, including the technique of rolling in the grass, as it is written, "He makes me lie down in green pastures." This verse was applied to the study of the work of the Chariot (TB Hagigah 13a) to stress the confidential nature of such mystical lore. Things sweeter than honey and milk should be kept under the tongue.

Christian expositors found in the honey lips and tongue and fragrant garments a treasury of allegories. The Doctors of the Church bring forth her holy teaching like honey; they also supply milk for the infants. The honey comb represents the Scriptures containing both wax and honey, the letter and the hidden meaning; it drips because it is too plentiful to be contained in the cells and it has manifold senses, literal, allegorical, moral, and anagogical. The preachers too are like honey combs because the sweet doctrines of the Gospel come from men weak and frail as the wax cells (cf. II Cor 4:7). They drip, not pour, because of the need to apportion the output to the capacity of the bearers (cf. Prov 25:16). The devout soul also draws honey from the flowers of Scripture, a figure elaborated eloquently by Richard of St. Victor. The honey dripping from the lips of the Church was also taken to refer to Him whose most pure Body, taken from the Blessed Mary, stored the golden honey of the Godhead, ever pouring forth grace for each, according to receptive capacity.

The garments smelling like Lebanon, or incense, were referred to the holy acts of the Church in the devout soul which partake of the divine blessedness. As the garment is made of many threads, crossing and recrossing each other, so the holy life does not consist of a single virtue or good deed, but of a multitude woven into a fabric; such is the fine linen of the righteousness of the Saints (Rev 19:8; cf. Job 29:14). Good works are termed garments because they cover sins, give spiritual warmth, and are marks of distinction, as one learns from numerous passages of

Scripture (cf. Prov 10:12; I Peter 4:8; Ps 132:9; Rev 16:15; I Kings 1:1; Lev 21:10). The seemly garment of abstinence and virginal purity especially gives forth a pleasant odor. (Cf. Littledale.)

12a. *garden.* A common term in the Canticle, 4:15,16, 5:1, 6:2,11, always applied to the lady. In 8:13 she is addressed not as a garden but as "one dwelling in the gardens." The verb to which the noun *gan(n)*, "garden," is related has the root meaning "cover, enclose, defend, protect." Robert remarked that the cloture is an affirmation of proprietary right and at the same time a protection. There is also the possibility for erotic interpretation of the garden (advocated by "l'école naturaliste) as with other horticultural terms, field, furrow, grove, branches, fruit, etc. Lu-dingir-ra, in the message to his mother, in the third "sign," describes her as "A garden of delight, full of joy"; cf. Civil, 1964, 3, line 35). Stephan (16) quoted a modern Arabic line:

The garden of your beauty in its bloom
is fairer and more resplendent than a flower garden.

locked. The verb *n'l* is used of bolting or locking a door from the inside, as when Ehud after stabbing Eglon bolted the door from inside and sneaked out another way, Judg 3:23, and Amnon had his servant put Tamar out and bolt the door after her, II Sam 13:17. A garden or vineyard would be hedged or walled for its protection, cf. Isa 5:5. The locked garden denotes virginity, as in colloquial Arabic a deflowered virgin is termed "opened," *maftûḥa(t)*. Stephan (16) cited a modern Palestinean parallel to 4:12–15:

Your breast, O you, is like a pomegranate fruit,
And your eyes have captured us, by God and (by) the Merciful One.
Your cheek shines as it were a Damascene apple;
How sweet to pluck it in the morning and to open the garden.

12b. *pool.* Some fifty Hebrew MSS, as well as LXX, Vulgate, Syriac, read here *gan* instead of *gal,* and many modern translators and commentators accept this as repetition of the preceding line. Gordis, Meek, Ringgren, *JPSV* take the word to mean "fountain" or "spring," parallel to *ma'yān* in the following line. E. M. Good (1970, 94n44) renders "pool," taking his cue from Ugaritic *gl,* "cup." He suggests a cup or bowl-shaped pool. There is a similar word *gullôṯ* used as a designation of some sort of water supply in Josh 15:19 and Judg 1:15. In I Kings 7:41 the term is used of the capitals of pillars constructed by Hiram of Tyre for the temple of Solomon. In support of his interpretation of the word as designating a bowl-shaped pool, Good should have cited the confirmation from Eccles 12:6 where the word *gullāh* is used in parallelism with *kaḏ,* "pitcher,"

Ere the silver strand is loosed,	Smashed the pitcher by the fountain,
The golden bowl shattered,	Shattered the bowl at the cistern.

J. P. Brown (1969, no. 7, pp. 158–160) has convincingly connected Hebrew *gullāh,* Ugaritic *gl,* Akkadian *gullatu* with Greek *gaulos,* "bowl." The parallelism of Eccles 12:6 is reflected and clarified by a citation from Antiphanes, "Everybody gives the name *gauloi* to *kadoi* if they are potbellied," or "see potbellied drinkers give the name *gauloi* to *kadoi*" (reading with the MSS *hoi progastores*); in either case the rounded character of the *gaulos* is implied, which fits its Semitic etymology, from *gll*. Brown goes on to relate the loanword to a variety of vessels and receptacles, for wine, milk, or honey, a well-bucket, and (roundish) cargo ships. Brown did not perceive the relevance of his treatment for the present passage of the Canticle, but it tends to confirm Good's proposed rendering "pool."

fountain. Prov 5:15*ff* uses *ma'yān* and other terms for water supply as a figure for the female sexual partner, to stress the point that a man should have and keep to his own private supply:

Drink water from your cistern,
Flowing from your well.
Should your springs scatter abroad,
Water channels in the streets?
Let them be for you alone,
No strangers with you.

Let your fountain be blessed,
Get joy from the wife of your youth,
A lovely hind, a graceful doe.
Let her love sate you at all times,
With her love be constantly excited.
Why, my son, be excited by an exotic,
Embrace the bosom of a stranger?

In contrast to the sealed fountain, Lu-dingir-ra's mother was characterized as "A canal which brings luxuriant waters to the irrigation ditches."

sealed. The verb *ḥtm* is used of sealing a document for purposes of authentication, I Kings 21:8, or blocking something from view, Job 9:7, or access, Deut 32:34. The latter purpose is envisaged here.

12. The Targum related the closed garden and sealed fountain to the modesty of Israel's women, both married and virgin, and compared the pent-up flood to the spring of Paradise:

> And your women who are taken by men are modest as the modest bride and like the Garden of Eden which no man is permitted to enter except the saints whose souls are sent into it by the hand of the angels. And your virgins are concealed and hidden in chambers and sealed thus like the spring of living water which issued from beneath the Tree and was divided into four heads of rivers. And if it had not been sealed by the Great and Holy Name, it would have come gushing forth and overflowed all the world.

Midrash Rabbah related the sealed garden and spring to propriety in sexual relations. The repetition was explained as recognition that sexual intercourse can be in two ways—natural and unnatural. From Lev 24:10*f* it is deduced that Israelite women were exemplary because only one woman was singled out for blame and the text identified her by name. Sarah's avoidance of immorality was noted, as was Joseph's. The present verse was taken to signify that the avoidance of immorality itself was sufficient merit to procure Israel's deliverance from Egypt.

This verse figured in a rabbinic controversy as to whether the fish the Israelites remembered having eaten in Egypt (Num 11:5) referred to real fish or was a euphemism for illicit sexual intercourse. (TB Yoma 75a). It was agreed, after discussion, that both (fish and illicit sexual activity) were implied.

The navel, or some other navel-like cavity (*nābhi*), of the Great Goddess of India is similarly characterized as secure, inviolate pool (*pallalama-pradhrlshyam*), i.e. from all except her consort Shiva to whom alone the beauty of her thighs is known:

O Devī! may I never forget thy navel, As it were a secure inviolate pool . . .
(Avalon, 1952, 37, st. 20 and n3,4)

Robert related this verse to the classical theme of the divine jealousy as in 8:6. Traditionally the closed garden and sealed fountain has been related to the Church as the Bride of Christ, to the holy soul, but especially to the Virgin Mary. The virginity of the Virgin of virgins was naturally commended to lesser aspirants. Saint Ambrose, who ruled the convents of Milan, admonished the inmates: "Thou, O virgin, art a garden inclosed, preserve thy fruits, let no thorns arise in thee, but let thy grapes flourish, let not any take from thee the fence of thy modesty . . . Thou art a sealed fountain, O virgin, let no one defile or trouble thy waters." St. Jerome warned the Abbess Eustochium that consecrated virgins ought to be shut up and sealed, not given to leave their home and wander, not even to seek their Bridegroom in the streets, lest they fall like Dinah, though she had patriarchs for her brothers and Israel himself for her father. Cf. Littledale, ad loc., who further cites Catullus a poet not of an ascetic turn:

As a hid flower within closed garden grows,
By plough uninjured, and by herds unknown,
And fed by winds, sun, rain, in beauty blows,
Till youths and damsels wish it for their own:
And yet if it be lightly plucked, and fade,
No youths or damsels wish for it again;
So dear and honoured is a spotless maid.
But if she lose her virgin bloom through stain,
On her no youths are bent, for her no damsels fain.

13a. *groove*. The word *šělāḥayiḵ* has continued as a stumbling block to translators and commentators. LXX rendered *apostolai sou,* Vulgate *emissiones tuae*. Graetz changed the vocalization to *šillûḥayiḵ*, "thy gifts"; others (Dalman, Perles, Rothstein) would read *lěḥāyaiḵ,* and thus *NEB,* "your two cheeks; cf. 4:3. The verb *šlḥ* is used of trees sending forth roots (Jer 17:8), and branches (Ps 80:12[11E]), and the noun *šělûḥāh* is used of branches, Isa 16:8. Accordingly, the word has often been taken in the sense of "plants" (*KJ*), "shoots" (*RSV, JB*), "products" (*AT*). *NAB* paraphrases, "you are a park that puts forth pomegranates." Some translators and interpreters, however, have recognized that the reference is to a part of the lady's body. *JPSV* rendered "your limbs." O. Loretz (1963, 93) proposed the meaning "javelin" as metaphorical for the beloved's breasts, KB, s.v. *šělāḥîm,* suggest "skin." A more intimate portion of the anatomy has been imagined by members of "1'école naturaliste." Haupt (1902b, 203,237) rendered "thy supply," but in the note gave the literal meaning as "conduit," citing Neh 3:15 with the explanation that the name *šelaḥ* denoted originally not the pool but the conduit leading the water of the Virgin's Spring (just outside Jerusalem) to the reservoir cut in the rock. This tunnel is called in the Siloam inscription *nqbh,* "perforation," similar to the word *nĕqēḇāh, perforata,* the Hebrew term for female. Joüon took *šelaḥ* here as designating a canal, but supposed that the poet meant the spring Gihon and the royal garden. Dhorme (1923) adjudged the alleged vaginal allusion as too realistic and proposed the meaning "canal" as metaphorical for womb. On *šelaḥ* as a designation of the channel to the netherworld, cf. AB 15 on Job 23:18. (The expression *'āḇar bĕšelaḥ* does not mean "fall by the sword" but to cross over [to the netherworld] by way of the channel.) Hirschberg (1961, 380) cites Arabic *šalḫ* in the sense of vagina.

pomegranate. The word for "pomegranate(s)," *rimmônîm,* is missing in some MSS of the LXX, but this is scarcely ground for deleting it. The pomegranate was among the fruits brought by the spies from the fertile land of Canaan, Num 13:23; in Deut 8:8 it is mentioned along with wheat, barley, grapes, figs, olives, and honey as a prize product of the land; in Joel 1:12 with the vine, fig tree, palm and apple. The pomegranate also figures in the sexual symbolism of the Sumerian sacred marriage songs:

> My sister, I would go with you to my pomegranate tree,
> I would plant there the sweet [?] honeycovered [?] . . . (*SMR,* 100)

grove. The word *pardēs* is an Old Persian, Avestan, loanword *pairi-daēza,* "enclosure," "park," which occurs also in Eccles 2:5 and Neh 2:8 as a designation of royal parks and forests. Cf. Loretz, 1964, 23.

J. P. Brown (1965) has suggested that the pomegranate paradise of 4:13, which was near to the "flowing streams from Lebanon," 4:15, and the doves (of Aphrodite) "upon the springs of water," 5:12, refer to the River of Abraham, Adonis, or Kawṯar, and its source at Khirbet Afqā in Lebanon. The identification of the Nahr Ibrahim or River (of) Adonis is based on the reference to Kawṯar in the Quran, Sura 108, and on the explanation of the commentators that "Kawṯar is a river in the Garden [of Paradise] whose banks are of gold, whose flowing is upon pearls and rubies, whose water surpasses snow in whiteness and surpasses honey in sweetness, and whose land is better than the smell of musk" (al-Tabarī, *Tafsir* XXX, 189, cited after Brown, 200).

What was known or believed of the fragrant Adonis, flowing from its great spring in the middle of the Lebanese "paradise" at Afqā, could have led, in Brown's view (201), to the idea of Kawṯar recorded by the Quranic commentators.

The connection of Kawṯar/Tammuz/Adonis with Afqā is explained in a Syriac text purporting to be a sermon of Melito of Sardes:

> The people of Phoenicia worshipped Balthi, queen of Cyprus, because she fell in love with Tammuz, son of Kuthar, king of the Phoenicians, and she left her own kingdom, and came and dwelt in Gebal [Byblos], a fortress of the Phoenicians, and at the same time she made all the Cypriotes subject to the king Kuthar, for before Tammuz she had been in love with Ares, and committed adultery with him,

and Hephaistos her husband caught her, and was jealous over her, and came and slew Tammuz in Mount Lebanon, while he was hunting wild boars; and from that time Balthi remained in Gebal, and she died in Aphaqa, where Tammuz was buried. (Cf. Brown, 198.)

On Afqā as a possible location of the abode of El in the Ugaritic myth, cf. M. Pope, *EUT*, 72–81, and Albright, 1956, 255*f*.

13b. *With*. Hirschberg (1961, 380) questions whether the word *'m* here and in 14c,e represents the preposition "with," since the articles named are not "with" the woods of frankincense or "with" all the chief spices, but are themselves the wood or the spices. Accordingly, he takes the word as a noun in the sense of Arabic *'amm* which mostly denotes a multitude of people, but may also occasionally stand for "all the plants or herbs." The point is somewhat forced since prepositions are nominal forms and Arabic *'amm,* "be common to all, concern all, comprise all, cover entirely, involve," gives ample scope to the rendering "with." As Delitzsch put it, the concluding phrase amounts to a poetic *et cetera.*

delectable. Beside the three occurrences in the Canticle, here and in 4:16, 7:14[13E], the word *meged, mĕgādîm,* occurs in the Old Testament only in Deut 33:13–16 where it is applied four times to the choicest fruits of the earth.

13c. *Cypress*. Cf. 1:14. Hirschberg (1961, 380) interprets *kĕpārîm* here as corresponding to Arabic *'al-kafirān* which designates "the groin next to the genitals."

nard cf. 1:12.

13. The Targum applied the verse to Israel's young men:

> And your young men are full of precepts like pomegranates, and love their wives and beget children righteous as themselves; their odor therefore is like the pleasant spices of the Garden of Eden, cypress and spikenard.

Midrash Rabbah rang the changes on the key word *šlḥyk,* relating it to *šlḥ,* "send," in the sense of present gifts. Thus Israel presented thirteen things to God (Exod 25:3–7) and God presented thirteen things to Israel (Ezek 16:10–12). Another explanation made it thirteen and twenty-six, since it was the custom for the groom to double the gift of the bride. With the vocalization *šĕlûḥayik,* the explanation is that "Your God will one day make you like a park of pomegranates in the messianic age." The term is also applied to the miraculous well of Miriam which during the forty years in the wilderness produced for the wandering Israelites various kinds of herbs, vegetables, and trees (including vines). When Miriam died, the well ceased to produce (Num 20:5). Another explanation related the word to the fertile and medicinal stream of Ezek 47:12. (These connections with well and stream are especially interesting in view of the explanation offered above, that the term here designates the vulva or vagina.) Yet another explanation related the verse to the sending of Elijah the Prophet before the great and terrible day (Mal 3:23[4:5E]).

This verse figured in a rabbinic controversy whether yellow menstrual discharges are unclean (TB Niddah 19b). It was adduced also in a consideration of the Nazirite vow (Num 6:5) with respect to long hair (TB Nazir 3a). In both instances Job 5:10b, "He sends (*šôlēaḥ*) water on the face of the fields," is cited in elucidation of the noun *šelaḥ* in the present verse. Again in a discussion whether certain things are sold when a town is sold (TB Baba Batra 68a,b) the suggestion that *šělāḥîm* is equivalent to *bêt haššělāḥîm,* "fields which need irrigation," is scouted in favor of equation with Aramaic *gěnûnyātā',* "gardens."

Christian interpreters, on the basis of LXX *apostolai* and Vulgate *emissiones,* related the apostolates and emissions of the Bride to the Church's arguments for the faith and its spread through preaching and planting local churches throughout the world, each of which is a paradise and replica of the original. The *apostolai* were also seen as the Apostles themselves, ruddy like pomegranates with the blood of martyrdom and producing many spiritual offspring like the grains inside the fruit. Another view took the emissions to denote the flow of irrigating water, typifying the devout souls baptized, and another saw the sendings as the Bride's gifts to her Spouse at the time of betrothal, in token of her love and faith, as especially the Saints presented to Him.

As applied to the holy soul, the emissions were generally seen as the words uttered for God's glory. The term was also related to the virtues of the Virgin who was the Paradise in which God placed the Man, Christ as the second Adam, to dress and keep it.

The pomegranates as applied to the Church denoted the martyred Apostles. Again the thorny branches and the hard bitter rind of the fruit represented the austere and mortified life, ruddy with suffering and white with purity and good works. The many seeds represented acts of charity, or fraternal unity within a religious order or house.

The choice fruits were seen as devout souls guarded by rigid external discipline (on the basis of LXX *akrodruōn,* applied to fruits or nuts with shells), or as Saints and their good works or spiritual graces (on the basis of Vulgate "apples").

The *kōper,* was connected with anointing, and taken to represent anointed Saints or Prelates. The henna plant, with white clustering blossoms, denoted purity in the Religious life. The nard suggested the anointing of Christ before His Passion (John 12:3), the unction of God's love, or hope as the links between faith and love. (Cf. Littledale.)

14a. *saffron.* The word *karkôm,* hapax in the Old Testament, but used in the post-biblical literature, comes from Sanskrit *kurkuma,* cognate with Greek *krokus,* and designates the *crocus sativus* which in Arabic is called *za'farān,* hence saffron. The *crocus sativus* and other species yielding saffron are found in Syria-Palestine. Women and children gather the pistil and stigma which are sun dried and pulverized for a condiment. The traditional connection of saffron with Akkadian *azupīru* and *azupirānû* (R. C. Thompson, Dictionary of Assyrian Botany, 160*f*) is questioned in *CAD,* I, 531a.

14b. *Cane.* The "cane," *qānēh* is the aromatic spice cane, *qěnēh-bōśem,* mentioned in Exod 30:23 among the ingredients of the holy anointing oil. Jer 6:20 mentions good or sweet cane from a far country, parallel to incense from Sheba; Isa 43:23–24 mentions the burdensome expense of the incense and cane in the sacrifices; Ezek 27:19,22 mentions cassia and cane among the precious items Tyre imported from South Arabia. According to Pliny

(*Hist. nat.* xii 48) the best aromatic calamus grew in Arabia. Polybius (v 46) and Strabo (xvi 4) mention it as found also in the valley of Lebanon.

cinnamon. Cinnamon, *qinnāmôn,* is also mentioned in Exod 30:23 as an ingredient of the holy perfumed oil for the priests. It is among the spices with which the adulteress perfumed her bed in Prov 7:17. The cinnamon tree, *laurus cinnamomum,* was indigenous to Ceylon (Sri Lanka) in the East Indies and later cultivated on the Malabar coast, Sumatra, Borneo, and Cochin China (Vietnam).

14c,e. *With.* Cf. 4:13b.

14c. *fragrant.* All varieties of incense trees grow in the lady's grove. The term *lĕḇônāh* is appropriate to the white color of the aromatic resin. The Greeks took the term *libanos, libanōtos* from the Phoenicians. The precious frankincense was imported from Arabia, cf. Isa 60:6; Jer 6:20.

14d. *Myrrh.* Cf. 1:16.

aloes. Not the medicinal aloes, the leaves of which are non-aromatic and used as a drastic purgative. The aloes mentioned in Num 24:6 as planted by YHWH, parallel to cedars, are problematic and perhaps an error, *'hlym* for *'ylym,* "oaks." Ps 45:9[8E] mentions aloes along with myrrh and cassia as the fragrant perfume of the royal, nuptial robes; the adulteress' couch, Prov 7:17, is spiced with myrrh, aloes, and cinnamon. Aromatic aloes (*aloëxylon agallochum*) come from the East Indies' tree *Aquilaria agallocha.*

14e. *prime.* Cf. Ezek 27:22 for the use of *rō'š* to designate the finest quality of spices, precious stones, and gold, as in rabbinic use of *'alpā'* for grade "A" materials.

As with 14c, this line provides a poetic *et cetera,* reminiscent of the style of Dan 2:2, 3:3,7,10 which mentions every sort of sorcerer, official, or musical instrument which the author could think of at the moment and then adds an all inclusive *et cetera.*

13,14. It is notable that most, if not all, of the trees and spices of this groovy grove are exotics. Harper suggested that the listing of the rare plants was probably intended to hint that the bride's charms are similarly rare and much to be admired. The rare and foreign character of these objects to which the bride is compared was deemed by Harper entirely incompatible with the supposition that the book is a collection of popular songs (Volkslieder), since in them the comparisons are always with homely well-known objects. Robert noted Siegfried's insinuation that each of the essences just mentioned had an erotic signification well known to contemporaries. This seems altogether likely, particularly in view of similar figures in erotic literature generally.

14. The Targum simply translated the list of spices continued from the preceding verse, with no attempt to allegorize:

> Spikenard and saffron, fragrant calamus, and cinnamon, all the woods of incense, pure myrrh, aloes, with all kinds of spices.

Midrash Rabbah gave little attention to the spices. One interesting item is the assertion that cinnamon used to grow in the Land of Israel and the goats and deer used to eat it. The spices were referred to those which the modest and blameless women of Israel used to gladden their husbands' hearts during the forty years in the wilderness. To the question as to how they could obtain such spices in the wilderness, Rabbi Johanan answered, "From the well" (i.e. from Miriam's miraculous well; cf. preceding verses).

Christian expositors found many meanings in the different spices. The golden hue of saffron suggested love as the most precious of virtues. The quality of elasticity when trampled under foot was given as the cause for relating the saffron to humility. The three golden stamens of the plant were related to the threefold love of the devout soul for the Persons of the Blessed Trinity, and fulfillment of the triple duty to love God, neighbor, and self. The ancient custom of sprinkling the bridal couch with saffron, wine and flowers and the saffron hue of the bridal veil in ancient Rome, suggested the mutual love of the Bride and Groom. The supposed effects of saffron as a febrifuge suggested justice or the Divine grace which cools carnal desires.

The cane, or *calamus,* as the reed pen, and sweet cane suggested the Doctors of the Church and their writings full of sweet instruction. The slenderness and loftiness of the reed suggested temperance and its straightness, justice. The hard sheath and inner sweetness of the *calamus* applied to the religious life of poverty and cloistered contemplation.

Cinnamon, with its outer gray bark and inner brown spice, was taken to denote the Saints lowly and penitential in their external appearance and behavior, but inwardly warm with the heat of Divine love. The ashy gray bark also suggested obedience, the turning of self-will to ashes.

The incense trees were referred to saintly obedience to God or to the more eminent Saints towering like the cedars of Lebanon. The connection of whiteness with the name Lebanon and the term for frankincense, *lĕḇōnāh,* gave cause for referring the word to Virgins, snow white in chastity and rising boldly toward heaven.

Myrrh and aloes suggested the preparation of Christ's body for burial (John 19:39) and the necessity of sharing His death before one can share in His Resurrection.

The chief spices were explained as the spiritual gifts of the Holy Ghost, or the great doctrines of the Church. Gillebert put it all together in application to Christ who suffered as our propitiation in the camphor, was burned in the nard, rose in golden beauty like the crocus, or saffron, ascended like the reed, and like the cinnamon gives forth a burst of fragrance when broken, as in the Eucharist. (Cf. Littledale.)

15a. *garden fountain.* Lit. "a fountain of gardens." LXX B read "A fountain of a garden and . . .". The "and" of the LXX B has been thought to derive from a misreading of *y* for *w* at the end of the word for "garden," i.e. *gannî,* "my garden." The letters *w* and *y* are often difficult or impossible to distinguish. Thus Budde rendered "The fountain of my garden is a well of living waters." It seems more likely that two phrases simply continue the series of appositions.

15b. Verbatim with the second half of Gen 26:19. In Jer 2:13, 17:13, with substitution of *mĕqôr,* "fountain," for *bĕ'ēr,* "well," the expression is applied to Yahweh whom Israel had forsaken. "Living water" for fresh or running water is commonplace, Lev 14:5–6,50–52, 15:13; Num 19:17.

15c. *Cascading.* It is possible that *nôzĕlîm* here modifies waters along with *ḥayyîm,* "waters fresh and flowing." More likely *nôzĕlîm* is a poetic synonym for water, as in Isa 44:3; Prov 5:15; Ps 78:16. In Ps 78:44 it is used as a parallel to *yĕ'ôrîm,* "streams," or "rivers." It is difficult to find a suitable poetic term. *JPSV*'s rendering "rill" has poetic sound, but the connotation of smallness may not be suitable. The streams that flow down the forested mountains of Lebanon when the snows are melting in the spring are an impressive sight and the valleys roar with the sound of the tumbling waters. Jer 18:14 has this scene in view although the text is apparently in disarray.

12–15. J. S. Cooper (1971, 161–162) has drawn merited attention to the parallels between this passage and Lu-dingir-ra's description of his "mother." In the third sign by which the courier may recognize the illustrious lady, Lu-dingir-ra says:

My mother is rain from heaven, water for the finest seed.
A harvest of plenty . . . . . . ,
A garden of delight, full of joy,
A watered pine, adorned with pine cones,
A spring flower, a first fruit,
An irrigation ditch carrying luxuriant waters to the garden plots,
A sweet date from Dilmun, a date chosen for the best.

Were it not for the word "mother" in the Lu-dingir-ra text and "sister, bride" in Song of Songs 4:12, it would be difficult to detect any difference in the tenor of the two passages, according to Cooper, and this tenor is decidedly erotic. Cooper noted a contrast between the Lu-dingir-ra text and the Song of Songs in that the references to bodily parts in the latter makes the imagery far more explicit. The reason for the reticence in Lu-dingir-ra's description, Cooper suggested, was that it would be very unseemly to describe one's mother in such specific terms. The erotic language of the Song of Songs is to be expected, according to Cooper, but is very problematic in the description of Lu-dingir-ra's mother, and he suggested that the author may have used the only vocabulary he knew for describing a woman, vocabulary drawn from the erotic literature, where most descriptions of women would naturally be found. Cooper's alternative suggestion seems more likely, that the "mother" is not a natural mother at all, but the goddess Inanna in motherly guise. The epithet "mother" is used of Inanna/Ishtar in erotic contexts (cf. Lambert, 1959, 11, lines 18,20).

You, the mother, Ištar of Babylon,
The beautiful, the queen, Ištar of Babylon.
You, the mother, palm .[. . . .]. . (Lambert, 13)

In a Sumerian sacred marriage text the goddess is also addressed as "mother" (cf. Kramer, 1963, 503, lines 56*f;* 504, lines 56*f*). Cooper remarked (162n22) that in the Dumuzi laments, a genre which has not yet been the subject of modern scientific study, the figure of Dumuzi as son, brother, and husband, in relation to Inanna as mother, sister, and wife, cannot always be interpreted in terms of conventional family relationships. The possibility that Lu-dingir-ra's mother may be the goddess seemed to Cooper incompatible with the first "sign" which appeared to him to be a condensed version of the description of the "Woman of Valor" in Prov 31:10*ff*. On this misgiving cf. the notes on 5:10–16 below where it is remarked that the first "sign" also presents features which have little to do with home economics and suggest that Šāt-Ištar, "Lady of Ishtar," was perhaps a hierodule or priestess who represented and was identified with the goddess in sacred marriage rites.

15. The Targum saw the purpose of the waters from Lebanon to supply Israel for the sake of those who study the Law, and for the sake of the Temple called here Lebanon:

> And the waters of Siloah flow gently with the rest of the waters that proceed from Lebanon to water the land of Israel for the sake of those occupied with the words of the Law, who are likened to the well of living waters, and by the virtue of the oblation of water poured on the altar of the Temple which is built in Jerusalem, which is called Lebanon.

Midrash Rabbah, apropos this verse, credited Rabbi Johanan with the observation that the word "well" (*bĕʾēr*) is found forty-eight times in the Torah, corresponding to the number of qualities by which knowledge of the Torah is acquired (cf. Pirqe Abot VI 6). The streams flowing from Lebanon Rabbi Azariah related to the development of a legal principle (*hălāḵāh*); one student contributes a trickle and another a trickle, until the *hălāḵāh* issues forth.

This verse was recommended for recitation to make a dream about a well auspicious. If one sees a well in a dream, he should rise early and say, "a well of living waters" before another (inauspicious) verse comes to mind, viz. Jer 6:7. For these and other verses to recite or avoid after dreaming of rivers, birds, pots, grapes, mountains, horns, dogs, etc., cf. TB Berakot 56b.

Christian expositors explained the fountain as Holy Scripture or the Church as the expounder of Scripture. As a fountain of gardens it irrigates the local churches and all holy souls. It is also a well because of its depth and hidden mysteries. The living waters flow from the perennial source of Divine wisdom, unlike the teaching of heretics stored in broken cisterns hewn by human hand (Jer 2:13), and the waters are virtually identical with the source (Ps 36:8; John 4:14). He is Lebanon, the stone cut by no human hand, the mountain which fills the whole earth (Dan 2:34–36), its whiteness representing His absolute holiness and purity, and the incense His atoning sacrifice and constant intercession. His Bride also is Lebanon washed white with His own Blood, and from her stream the waters of Baptismal grace and Apostolic teaching, as the river whose streams make glad the city of God (Ps 46:4). It was noted that the fountain deepens to a well and the well turns to streams, denoting the continual increase and advance of God's grace in the Church and in the soul, as Wisdom's canal grew to a river and the river to a sea (Sir 24:30–31), or as the stream from the Temple (Ezek 47:1–12). The devout soul is also a perennial fountain, ever renewed by God, ever bubbling forth with love for Him and expanding in love for its neighbor; it is also a well containing the deep grace and knowledge of the Holy Spirit, sufficient to supply itself and pour forth for others. The Religious Life was also seen as the fountain, watering the gardens of the various Orders and in turn the devout souls therein. The verse was also applied to the Blessed Virgin as the fountain whence came forth the Divine River of Mercy to water the earth, parting into four sacramental channels, Incarnation, Passion, Resurrection, and Ascension, flowing from Lebanon as the mysterious height of Godhead. (Cf. Littledale.)

16a. *Stir.* The verb *'(w)r* is used for arousal or excitation from inactivity, lethargy, or somnolence to various activities usually zealous or violent, most often to war. Jer 25:32 employs the term of a wind storm, Ps 57:9[8E] of music, Zech 13:7 of a sword, and Hab 2:19 of stirring dumb stone (an idol) to speech. The possibilities of the word for suggestion of sexual excitement are patent and most obvious in the noun *'ayr,* or *'îr,* as a designation of the stud ass whose sexual propensities are prodigious and scandalous. On the equine sexual exploits of the angelic "Watchers" or "Aroused Ones," *'îrîm,* in the Book of Enoch, cf. J. Morgenstern, 1939. On the Ugaritic use of the verb with reference to love or sexual excitement, cf. note on 2:7.

North-wind. This is the only instance of use of the term *ṣāpôn* as the name of the wind; the usual application is to the direction north where lies the fabled mountain of the gods. The names of the directions as well as the winds therefrom are feminine, cf. Isa 43:6. The north-wind is cold, Sir 43:20; cf. Job 37:9b on the cold "scatter-winds."

16b. *Come.* The use of the verb *b(w)'* in the sexual sense, as in Gen 16:2, 38:16, suggested to Siegfried that the wind is here a figure for the groom. One may think of Eduard Mörike's "Jung Volkers Lied"

Da kam der Wind, da nahm der Wind Als Buhle sie gefangen

But this seems rather unlikely since it is the male lover himself here who invokes the wind.

16b. *South-wind.* Delitzsch supposed that the east wind was purposely not mentioned because of its adverse and destructive effect; cf. Job 1:19, 27:21; Jer 13:24. The interchange of cold and heat Delitzsch thought would promote the growth of the garden, but he recognized that the main concern is the stirring up the fragrance of the garden so that it becomes like a sea of incense. The change of winds is merely for poetic parallelism and has no special significance. Robert rightly stressed that the intent was not to spread the odor afar since this would be contrary to the fundamental idea of the Canticle, the charms of the bride being for the groom alone.

16c. *my garden.* The uncertainty here as to the speaker is not serious. Whether the bride or groom speaks, the scented garden clearly represents the lady's charms which are meant for her lover's enjoyment.

16e,f. This is clearly an invitation by the lady to her lover to enjoy to the utmost all her charms which are his preserve. Kramer remarks apropos of 4:10,16 that "it is not impossible that the 'garden' is a euphemism for the vulva" (*SMR,* 152n17). Harper, supposing that the Shulamite is held by Solomon against her will, remarked: "This last clause of the verse is spoken, it should be remembered, by a loving woman shut up in a royal dwelling away from her lover, and expresses her longing for the time when she shall be wholly his."

16. The Targum related the north and south winds to the corresponding sides of the Temple and the invitation of the beloved to enter and eat was addressed to God:

> And on the north side was a table and on it twelve (loaves) of show-bread; on the south side was the Candlestick to give light; and on the altar the priests offered the sacrifice and sent up on it the spice incense. The Assembly of Israel said, "Let God, my beloved, enter the Temple and receive with favor the sacrifices of His people."

For reasons obscure the Midrash Rabbah used this verse to introduce a Rabbinic disputation on the types of sacrifices offered, or not offered, by the children of Noah (i.e. by those who lived before the Revelation at Sinai). After considerable discussion of the sacrifices, the verse was applied to the Messianic Age, when the Messiah who is in the north shall awake and come and build the Temple which is in the south (Isa 41:25). In this world the north and south winds do not blow at the same time, but in the time to come God will drive the two winds together (Isa 43:6). Rabbi Johanan derived from this verse a lesson in good manners, that the bridegroom should not enter the bridal chamber until the bride gives him permission.

This verse was cited in connection with a rabbinic disputation on peace offerings (TB Zebaḥim 116a) and explained as meaning, "Awake, O people whose rites were performed in the North and come, O people, whose rites will henceforth be performed in the North and the South." "Awake" was taken to refer to the ingathering of exiles.

The north as the region of darkness and cold was taken as typical of the powers of evil (cf. Isa 14:13; Jer 1:14, 4:6), thus this verse was understood by some Christian expositors as an order to Satan to quit the garden, and a prayer to the Holy Spirit as the warm south wind, to enter. God came from the south (Teman), Hab 3:3. Others took the two winds as diverse operations of the same Holy Spirit, the north cooling and the south warming. Again the winds were taken to denote the nations of different parts of the earth, invited to awake and enter the garden. The winds also were seen as the troubles and persecutions afflicting the Church, the north wind representing terrors and threats, the south guileful flatteries. Again the north wind was seen as the bane of sorrow and trial and the south as the antidote of grace and comfort. Satan, as the north wind, is challenged to come out of secret ambush and face the Holy Spirit, the south wind, in battle for possession of the garden.

As applied to the Blessed Virgin, the hymn *Imperatrix gloriosa* put it thus (in Littledale's paraphrase):

That soft south-wind, through thee going,
And thus fruitfulness bestowing,
Put to flight the north-wind's blowing,
With his breath of greater might;

Therefore thou hast borne the Flower,
Yielding fruit within thy bower,
When to Gabriel in that hour,
Thou didst hearken with delight.

LXX and Vulgate place the latter part of this verse with the following chapter, but some of the Greek and Latin Fathers treated it with what precedes. A few sample explanations will suffice. The Church was seen here as inviting Christ to see the children she has raised up for Him, the newly baptized converts. The fruits were also applied to the virginal life. The Bride invites Christ to hallow the produce of the fruits of virginity, that He, Who proceeded from a Virgin, may taste thereof. He who said, "My food is to do the will of Him who sent me" (John 4:34) tastes His pleasant fruits whenever He visits and enters any holy soul to assay its progress in sanctity. The Vulgate rendering "apples" evoked comparison with Eve who offered her spouse an apple which was not hers to give nor his to accept, but Mary here calls to her God to eat His own fruit. Again the Virgin Mother was seen here as desiring her Son to call her out of this world to Himself, or the soul longing to flee away and be at rest with Christ. (Cf. Littledale.)

V
(5:1–16)

1 a I entered my garden, my sister, bride;
b I plucked my myrrh with my spice;
c I ate my honeycomb with my honey;
d I drank my wine with my milk.
e Eat, friends, drink,
f Be drunk with love!
2 a I slept, but my mind was alert.
b Hark, my love knocks.
c Open to me, my sister,
d My darling, my dove, my perfect one!
e For my head is drenched with dew,
f My locks with the night mist.
3 a I have removed my tunic
b How shall I put it on?
c I have washed my feet
d How shall I soil them?
4 a My love thrust his "hand" into the hole,
b And my inwards seethed for him.
5 a I rose to open for my love,
b And my hands dripped myrrh,
c My fingers liquid myrrh,
d On the handles of the bolt.
6 a I opened to my love,
b But my love had turned and gone.
c My soul sank at his flight.
d I sought, but could not find him.
e I called him, but he did not answer me.
7 a The guards found me,
b They who patrol the city;
c They struck me, they wounded me,
d Took my veil from me,
e They who guard the wall.

8 a I adjure you, Jerusalem girls,
b If you find my love,
c What will you tell him?
d That I am sick with love.
9 a What is your beloved above another,
b O fairest of women,
c What is your beloved above another,
d That you thus adjure us?
10 a My love is radiant and ruddy,
b Conspicuous above a myriad.
11 a His head finest gold,
b His locks luxuriant,
c Black as the raven.
12 a His eyes like doves by waterducts,
b Splashing in milky spray,
c Sitting by brimming pools.
13 a His cheeks like spice beds,
b Burgeoning aromatics.
c His lips lotuses,
d Dripping liquid myrrh.
14 a His arms rods of gold,
b Studded with gems;
c His loins smoothest ivory,
d Encrusted with sapphires.
15 a His legs marble pillars,
b Based on sockets of gold.
c His aspect like the Lebanon,
d Choice as the cedars.
16 a His mouth is sweet,
b And all of him desirable.
c This is my love, this my mate,
d O Jerusalem girls.

10. Festal scenes from ancient Mesopotamian glyptic featuring feasting, music, dance, and sexual congress

5:1 Eat, friends, drink,
Be drunk with love!

NOTES

5:1. The series of four verbs in the so-called perfect have been variously understood by translators and commentators and rendered as preterit, present, or future, depending on preconceptions with regard to the nature and timing of the nuptials. Delitzsch supposed that the marriage had already taken place, and accordingly rendered, "I am come"; Budde and others who regarded the song as sung during the week after the celebration of the marriage rendered "I come"; while those who think the complete consummation to be still in the future tend to render the verbs as present and explain them as future. Cannon, e.g. rendered "I come," but explained in the note that the preterities in this verse are the so-called *perfect confidentiae,* "to indicate actions the accomplishment of which lies in the future, but is regarded as dependent upon such an unalterable determination of the will, that it may be spoken of as having actually taken place." (*Tenses,* § 13.) Similarly Robert, RTF, rendered "je viens" in accordance with his view that it is not a question of marriage, but that the perspective is eschatological, announcing the proximate coming of Yahweh and is therefore a perfect of certitude, or a present announcing a fact of which the accomplishment is imminent. Robert's detection of a certain solemnity in the response of the groom to the invitation of his beloved is certainly a highly subjective judgment.

1b. *plucked.* The verb *'ry* occurs in Scripture only here and in Ps 80:13[12E] and is usually taken to mean "gather, pluck," or the like on the basis of the Ethiopic cognate and its use in Mishnaic Hebrew for plucking figs. In Arabic the noun *'ary* is used of honey and *'iry, 'ariy* designates a manger, while the verb may apply to making honey, driving clouds and bringing rain, or eating at the same manger (with another animal). This latter usage explains the Ugaritic noun *ary* in the sense of "siblings" to designate the gods as children of Asherah in the cliché:

aṯrt wbnh̠	Asherah and her children,
ilt wṣbrt aryh	The Goddess and the band of her sibs.

The series of verbs, "I came," "I gathered," "I ate," "I drank" here seems a logical sequence, but in the light of the Arabic use of *'ry* with reference to eating there is a lingering suspicion that the parallelism here between *'ry* and *'kl* may be synonymous. In Ps 80:13[12E] the word also occurs in tandem with two verbs meaning to eat. Israel, figured as a vine transplanted from Egypt, is despoiled and devoured by enemies figured as wild beasts:

Why have you broken her walls,
That all passers-by *'ry* her?

The boar from the bush rips her,
The wild creatures feed on her.

It is clear that *'ry* is not in synonymous parallelism with *prṣ,* "break," but rather with the two following verbs *krsm* and *r'y* since all three have the same object, *viz.* "her." The meaning "pluck, gather" would be appropriate for both occurrences of the verb *'ry,* but the sense "eat" is also possible.

The association here with honey recalls Samson's riddle, Judg 14:14, and its solution. H. Bauer (1912) recognized the nominal play on *'ry* in the senses of "honey" and "lion," but overlooked the verbal play on *'ry* in the sense of "eat." In the solution to the riddle a thoughtless scribe, not understanding the play substituted another word for "honey," *dĕbaš* (Arabic *dibs,* Akkadian *dišpu*), according to Bauer. J. R. Porter (1962) supposed that the pun depended on the fact that the old word for "honey," *'ary,* was no longer in use when Samson posed his riddle. Samson at least knew three meanings for the root *'ry* and packed them all into a triple play:

From the eater issued eats,
From the strong issued sweets.

myrrh . . . spice. On myrrh and spices in perfumery, cf. 1:12b,13c,14a, 3:6c, 4:6c,d. In the present context, however, the reference is to eating and drinking. Myrrh is bitter and there is no evidence that it was eaten, at least not as a food. It was however, mixed with wine. The drinking of spiced wine, *yayin hāreqaḥ,* is mentioned in 8:2 as part of the nuptial procedure. The wine mingled with myrrh offered to Jesus on the cross (Mark 15:23) was apparently intended as an analgesic or anesthetic. Pliny (*Hist. nat.* xiv 92) mentions *vinum murrinam* but its purpose is not clear. J. P. Brown (1969, 150) notes that in Canticles 4:10–14 wine appears in connection with nine spices, including *lĕḇônāh* (4:14c), and that *libanos,* "frankincense," mixed with wine was given to elephants to enrage them for battle (III Macc 5:[2],45).

1b,c,d. *with.* The preposition *'im,* "with," here joins each pair of items plucked(?), eaten, and drunk, myrrh with spice, honey with honeycomb, wine with milk. Only in the last instance do the paired items differ in kind.

1c. *honeycomb.* The two words for honey are puzzling here, as are the two terms for similar materials in the preceding line. LXX and Latin here read "with my bread" apparently to avoid too much honey. The word *ya'ar* is used twice in I Sam 14:25–26, first apparently in the usual sense of "forest" and in the following verse it is not clear whether the word means "forest" or "honey"; in vs. 27, however, *ya'ăraṯ haddĕḇāš* into which Jonathan dipped the tip of his staff was clearly the honeycomb. On the basis of I Sam 14:27, it appears that *ya'ar* designates the comb of wild honey.

honey. The common word for honey with slightly differing forms in several Semitic dialects, Akkadian *dišpu,* Arabic *dibs,* Hebrew-Aramaic *dĕḇāš* <**dibš.*

1d. *wine with . . . milk.* Greek *oinogala* which Chloe presents to Daphnis

(Longus I 23). Milk and honey, oil and wine were the gifts of a fertile land and among the elements of fertility worship. When Baal returns to life, after his demise at the hands of Mot,

The skies rain oil, The wadies run honey.
(6[49].3.6–7)

When Dionysos appears in the land, the characteristic effects, according to Euripides (*Bacchae* 136*ff*) are that "The ground flows with milk, flows with wine, flows with the nectar of bees"; cf. Brown (1969, 149*f*).

1a–d. Going to the garden, the field, the vineyard or orchard is a favorite motif of the Song of Songs and also a central theme in several Sumerian sacred marriage songs. In a poorly preserved composition representing a conversation between King Shulgi and his "fair sister," the goddess Inanna, the goddess complains of a scarcity of vegetation. No one, it seems, is bringing her the offerings of date clusters which were her due, and there is no grain in the silos. (The situation is reminiscent of a fragmentary passage in the Ugaritic Epic of King Keret, 16[12G].3.12–16, which speaks of the lack of food due to the absence of the sweet rain of Baal:

The plowmen lift their heads,
Upward the grain [sto]wers.
Spent is the food [from] their jars.
Spent the wine in their bottles,
Sp[e]nt the oil in [their vats]).

King Shulgi invites "his fair sister" to accompany him to the field and to do something to the grain.

My sister, I would go with you to my field,
My fair sister, I would go with you to my field,
I would go with you to my large field,
I would go with you to my small field,
To my "early" grain irrigated with its "early" water,
To my "late" grain irrigated by its "late" water,
Do you [fructify?] its grain,
Do you [fructify?] its sheaves.

After a break of some lines there is a passage in which the goddess commands a farmer to plow Shulgi's barren fields. Next Shulgi invites her to his garden and orchard:

My sister, I would go with you to my garden,
My fair sister, I would go with you to my garden,
My sister, I would go with you to my garden,
Do you [fructify?] the *ildag*-tree.
I would go with you to my orchard[?],
My sister I would go with you to my apple-tree,
May the . . . of the apple-tree be in my hand.
My sister, I would go with you to my pomegranate-tree,
I would plant there the sweet[?] honey-covered[?] . . .
My sister I would go with you to my garden,
Fair sister, I would go with you to my garden,
Like the plants of the orchard[?] . . .
(*SMR*, 100 and 153n5)

The poem, according to Kramer, continues for another eight fragmentary lines which mention plants and date clusters. Kramer has given a text edition and translation (1969a). Another unpublished Inanna composition in the British Museum gives, according to Kramer, a song of the goddess which is still closer in content and mood to the biblical book:

> He has brought me into it, he has brought me into it,
> My brother has brought me into the garden.
> Dumuzi has brought me into the garden,
> I strolled[?] with him among the standing trees.
> I stood with him by its lying trees,
> By an apple-tree I kneeled as in prayer.
>
> Before my brother coming in song,
> Before the lord Dumuzi who came toward me,
> Who from the . . . of the tamarisk, came toward me,
> Who from the . . . of the date clusters, came toward me,
> I poured out plants from my womb,
> I placed plants before him, I poured out plants before him,
> I placed grain before him, I poured out grain before him . . .
> (*SMR,* 101)

1f. *Be drunk.* Various means are used to mitigate the effect of the imperative of *škr,* the basic sense of which is to be or become intoxicated with alcohol, and only figuratively with blood or love. Critics who assume that the groom addresses the male guests, suppose that he invites them not to get drunk, but to drink moderately. Harper explained that it appears to have been the custom for the bridegroom to invite the guests to show sympathy at such a feast by departing from the habitual abstemiousness of the East in regard to wine; cf. John 2:10. But then he went on to argue that *škr* may merely mean to drink to satiety, not to drunkenness, citing as proof Haggai 1:6 where "to satiety," *lĕśoḇʻāh,* is parallel to *lĕšoḵrāh.* Here Harper completely missed the whole negative point of this context, that it is scarcity of food and drink and not abstemiousness that prevents satiety or drunkenness.

The terms "to satiety," *ʻd šbʻ,* and "to drunkenness," *ʻd škr,* occur in poetic parallelism in a description of a divine banquet tendered by El, father of the gods and sometime head of the pantheon:

> The gods ate and drank, Drank wine till sated, Must till inebriated.
> (UG 5.1.1.3–4)

Any question about the degree of inebriation and intoxication is removed later in the text (lines 16–17) when El drank to satiety and inebriation and beyond to the point of *locomotor ataxia,* hallucinations, diarrhea, enuresis, and loss of consciousness. The definition of satiety and drunkenness is, of course, relative to a number of variables. According to a popular jingle:

> He is not drunk who from the floor
> Can rise again and drink some more.
> But he is drunk who prostrate lies
> And cannot drink and cannot rise.

The gods of Ugarit eat and drink at almost every occasion, as a matter of hospitality, and drunkenness is not otherwise mentioned. The invitation to eat and drink is commonplace in the Ugaritic myths. At the beginning of a text which later describes in considerable detail the efforts and eventual success of the aged father of the gods to consummate sexual union with a couple of females, there occurs a few lines after the invocation of the gracious and beautiful gods, an invitation to the communicants:

Eat of the bread, ho! Drink of the wine, ho!
(23[52].6)

Delitzsch recognized that the consummation of marriage was implicit in the present passage and he noted that Solomon and his Bride here "hover on the pinnacle of full enjoyment." The words of Solomon here, in Delitzsch's view, cannot be thought of as spoken to the guests. Between 4:16 and 5:1 the bridal night intervenes and the words of 1a are "Solomon's morning salutation to her who has now wholly become his own." Contrariwise, Siegfried understood the invitation to be addressed to the wedding guests. "Eat you too, O companions, and intoxicate yourselves, O friends." This would mean in prose, according to Siegfried, "do ye marry also." Hitzig understood the invitation to be addressed by the poet to the young pair, while Ginsburg ascribed the words to the daughters of Jerusalem. To be drunk with love may be a mere figure of speech, as love is sweeter than wine, but certainly the wine and the drunkenness are not excluded but are preliminary to the love. Food, drink and sexual gratification, usually after the meal, are traditional hospitality even for the wayfaring stranger in some societies. In an episode in one of the Ugaritic myths, El offers his erstwhile spouse Asherah (who has just come on a long journey to ask a favor of him) food, drink, and love:

Eat, yea, drink,
Eat from the tables food;
Drink from the jars wine,
From a gold cu[p] blood of the vine.
Let the love of King El excite you,
The affection of the Bull arouse you.
(4[51].4.35–39)

In the Christian love feasts, drunkenness was not unheard of and, indeed, appears to have been customary for some who were devoted to the old-time religion. Cf. pp. 211*ff*.

with love. The versions, LXX, Vulgate, Syriac, and the savants Rashbam, Ibn Ezra, Rashi, and many moderns take *dôdîm* to be in synonymous parallelism with *rēʿîm,* "friends." Thus *RSV* rendered:

Eat, O friends, and drink: drink deeply, O lovers!

The plural of this word, however, regularly means "love," as in Ezek 16:8, 23:17; Prov 7:18, and elsewhere in the Canticle, 1:2,4, 4:10, 6:1, 7:13[12E]. Accordingly, we follow *AT*'s "and be drunk with love," and similar recent renderings: *JPSV,* "Drink deep of love!"; *NEB,* "until you are drunk with love"; *NAB,* "Drink freely of love!" Stephan (1923, 17) quoted a couplet from a song describing a symposium with hetaerae:

Well then, let us be drunk in the garden of caressing (lit. take and give);
Let us pluck the roses "from her mother" while the critical are asleep.

A modern Egyptian line cited by Stephan in this connection runs as follows:

I entered your garden and plucked your pomegranates . . .

1. The Targum ascribed this verse to the deity at the sacrificial meal and applied the invitation to the friends as the priests who share the meal and eat what is left over:

> Then said the Holy One, blessed be He, to His people of the House of Israel: "I have come into the Temple which you built for Me, O My Sister, Assembly of Israel, who is likened to the chaste bride, and I caused My Presence to dwell among you. I received with favor your spice incense which you prepared for My name. I sent fire from heaven and it devoured the burnt offerings; and the holy oblations were received with favor, red wine and white wine, which the priests poured out on My altar. Now, you priests who love My precepts, come and eat what is left of the offerings and delight yourselves with the bounty prepared for you."

Midrash Rabbah cited the suggestion that "my garden" here means "my bridal chamber" (*ginnûnî*), with reference to the original home of the Divine Presence in the lower realm from which it ascended by stages to the seventh firmament at the sins of Adam, Cain, Enosh, the generations of the Flood and the Tower, the men of Sodom, and the Egyptians in the days of Abraham. Seven righteous men brought the Divine Presence down by stages—Abraham, Isaac, Jacob, Levi, Kohath and Amram. Each brought it down one stage. Then came Moses and brought it down to earth. The latter part of the verse was taken to mean the sacrifices and drink offerings. The friends invited to eat were identified as Moses and Aaron, while those invited to drink are Nadab and Abihu who became drunk to their hurt. Another explanation identified the friends as the princes and those invited to drink as the nobles.

Christian expositors exploited the key words of this verse with amazing versatility and variety. The Bride gave the invitation in the preceding verse and the Groom here responds and complies with alacrity (Isa 58:9). God came into His garden in the Incarnation. The myrrh denotes the suffering (John 19:30,41). He gathered the myrrh and spices in the tomb, or the myrrh in death and the spices on return. The myrrh was seen as the martyrs, the spices as the saints. The myrrh denotes Baptism by which we are buried with Him, the spice the graces of the Holy Spirit which he breathes and His disciples. The honey, wine and milk were given a variety of interpretations. The honey was seen as the sweetness of the Godhead stored in Christ's human Body. The wine and the milk were understood as the hypostatic union of the two Natures in Christ. The honeycomb and wine figured holy preachers, the honey and milk devout hearers. The preachers are wine because they declare the mighty Sacraments of the Scriptures, the hearers are milk because they are weaker and need to have the mysteries explained and simplified. Again the honey and honeycomb denote the Saints who delight in the study of Holy Writ and make their hearts and memories the cells in which they store like bees the sweets drawn from the flowers of the Law, the Prophets, the Psalms, and the Gospels. LXX rendering "bread" instead of "honeycomb" suggested a prophecy of the Holy Eucharist and the invitation to friends was seen as a call to the faithful, no longer servants, but friends (John 15:15), "Come, eat of My Bread, and drink of the wine I have mixed" (Prov 9:5). The invitation to be drunk evoked the assurance that the Lord's Chalice does not inebriate, but makes sober with spiritual wisdom and knowledge of God. As ordinary wine relaxes the mind and relieves sorrow, the Blood of the Lord and the Cup of Salvation casts out the memory of the former self and the oppression of sins with the joy of pardon. The invitation to the friends was further explained as the call to the faithful to imitate the example of the Saints. The friends were also seen as the angelic spirits invited to rejoice at seeing the elect translated from this life to eternal blessed rest (Luke 15:6). (For these and other examples, cf. Littledale.)

2a. *slept . . . alert.* The verbal forms here are stative participles designating action begun in the past and lasting to the present. The choice of tense by translators is determined by the theory of interpretation. Budde, e.g. supposed that the Shulamite relates a dream she had prior to her marriage. Harper's view was that the alleged dream occurred in the night which he supposed intervened between vss. 1 and 2. The Shulamite had a very trying day, after an interview both with Solomon and with her ever loving shepherd swain, night came and she had one of those troubled dreams which so often follow a frustrating and agitated day. The following morning she narrates her dream to the ladies of Solomon's court. She has just awakened and is still under the influence of the dream.

This supposed dream is of crucial importance for the dramatic school of interpretation. The dramatic element, according to Harper, is here very pronounced and is evidently intended to give unity and movement to the whole poem. The Shulamite relates her dream to the ladies of the Court in vss. 2–7. Verse 8 is her request to the court ladies and vs. 9 is their reply. Verses 10–16 are a description of her lover as he dwells in her brooding imagination. The court ladies ask the whereabouts of this model of manly beauty and the Shulamite replies evasively, wishing to keep her lover for herself alone. All this, Harper argued, would be in place in a love tale presented in a series of songs, but in a collection of verses to be sung at weddings in general it is impossible that the bride could be made to speak thus. Such references to prenuptial love would be not only unbecoming, but impossible. Further, Harper noted that in Budde's view of the Canticles as a collection of wedding songs, there is no connection between the various lyrics.

S. B. Freehof (1948–49) has taken this verse as the key to the entire book. As a description of an actual occurrence, the scene makes little sense, but as a dream it is typical, almost classic, according to Freehof. Further the dream characteristics are allegedly found not only in ch. 5 but throughout the book. The classic dream experience of running through the city and over the fields appears constantly, 1:4, 6:1, 7:1[6:13E], 8:5. The book is full of strange flights and sudden movements, the characteristic activities in dreams.

The rapid succession of scenes have defied all attempts by modern scholars to arrange a logical sequence of localities. In a dream, however, one scene follows rapidly and vividly, the dreamer being suddenly transported from scene to scene, moving along almost magically from place to place. The descriptions are also curiously overdrawn, e.g. Solomon's pavilion with its pillars of silver and vault of gold, hair like a flock of goats, head of fine gold, etc. It is not sufficient, Freehof claimed, to say that these descriptions are typical Oriental exaggeration. Even such must be understandable and have some logic. But many of the descriptions in this book cannot, Freehof asserted, be seen at all with the open eye, but have the wild improbability and strange exaggeration of dream pictures. In addition, many of the images have to do with dreams and sleeping. The book frequently speaks of lying in bed at night, and of events that will last until the day dawns and the shadows flee. And over all this mysterious and improbable landscape the plea is heard: "I beg you, O daughters of Jerusalem, do not awaken love till it desireth." This means in other words, according to Freehof, "Do not awaken me. Let me continue to dream." Once the book is read as a dream sequence, its very disorder makes sense, to Freehof at least.

According to Freehof, the rabbis, especially Akiba, sensed the true nature of the book and thus gave it symbolic interpretation because they did not take dreams lightly but regarded them as the vehicle of communication between God and man. The love language of the dream suggested the eternal love between Israel and God. As in a dream lovers are parted and seek and eventually find each other, so Israel is finally forever united with God. Modern interpretations, Freehof suggested, may not be at all realistic in the vain search for logical sequence from scene to scene. In dreams there is no logic except perhaps some deeper hidden logic. A dream cannot be explained, but must be interpreted according to its own strange laws. Thus Freehof argued that the traditional approach to the interpretation of the Song of Songs, to explain this sequence of dreams symbolically, is essentially sound.

Gordis took 5:2 to 6:3, the longest and most elaborate song in the collection, as a dream-song. In a dream everything is possible.

With regard to the oneirological interpretation of this passage, or of the whole book, it should be noted that neither the verb nor noun of the common West-Semitic word for dreaming or dream is found anywhere in the book. If the rabbis understood the whole book as a dream, we would expect that somewhere they would have at least given a hint. See above pp. 132*ff*.

The state concisely characterized as somnolence with an alert mind does not necessarily refer to dreaming. It seems very appropriate to the sort of sleep in which one is not wholly unconscious but can respond immediately to a real or imagined sound. This would suit very well the condition of one expecting or hoping for a tryst with a lover. Cf. 3:1.

The view of Joüon and Ricciotti that the sleep of the Shulamite represents her infidelities which kept her heart from being at peace was partly approved by Robert who, however, took exception to Joüon's notion that the infidelities were anterior to the Exile. The horizon of the Canticle, according to Robert, is uniquely post-exilic (cf. Isaiah 56–59, 63–66) and its thesis is that the nation, imperfectly converted, is in a sort of sleep from which she will emerge only by a decision of the free will (2:7, 3:5, 8:4). Nevertheless her heart is awake, that is to say it remains attached to Yahweh, despite appearances. Robert noted a certain analogy of thought and expression in the present passage to Isa 26:9a, "My soul yearns for thee in the night, my spirit within me earnestly seeks thee."

2b. *Hark*. The word *qôl* here, as in 2:8, does not mean "voice," but "noise" or "sound" and is often used as exclamation, as in Isa 40:3 where "the voice of him that crieth in the wilderness" means: "Hark! one cries: 'In the wilderness etc.' "

knocks. LXX and Latin supply "on the door." The verb *dpq* in Gen 33:13 is used of driving sheep, as in Arabic. In Judg 19:22 it is used in the reflexive stem of the Gibeonite riffraff who were pushing themselves and one another against the door. Here, presumably, the night caller is less boisterous. A gentle rap would suffice to arouse the alert sleeper.

A. Feuillet (1961b) develops the idea that Rev 3:20 is a reminiscence of the present passage.

2d. *my dove, my perfect one*. Cf. 6:9a, and 1:15, 1:14, 4:1. *JPSV* rendered the expression as a hendiadys here "my faultless dove," but in 6:9a as separate, "my dove," "my perfect one."

2e. *drenched* [lit. filled] *with dew*. Stephan (1923, 17) asserted, apparently on the basis of Palestinian folklore, that the dew is believed to be harmful to the eyes, and he cited Dan 4:22,30[25,33E], 5:21. The heavy Palestinian dew is bone-chilling before the sun comes up to warm and dispel it; cf. Hosea 13:3. In a Ugaritic description of Baal (UG 5.3.1.5) it is said:

rišh . tply ṭly . bn ʿn[h]

Fisher and Knutson (1969, 159) rendered:

His head is wonderful, Dew is between his eyes.

Unfortunately, this translation is fraught with difficulties and other possibilities have been suggested; cf. Pope and Tigay, 1971, and NOTES on 5:11.

2f. *locks*. The exact meaning of the term *qĕwuṣṣôṯ* is uncertain; it occurs elsewhere in the Old Testament only in vs. 11 below. The root of the form is problematic, since it appears to be a blend of a "hollow" root *q(w)ṣ* and a geminated one *qṣṣ*. The original quality of the sibilant is also uncertain and it may be that Geers Law involving the assimilation or dissimilation of "emphatic" consonants is involved. The lexicons usually relate the word to Arabic *quṣṣat* which designates the hair over the forehead. The post-biblical use of the word suits the context here. In TB Nedarim 9a it is used of the hair of a beautiful young man who proposed to become a Nazarite and in TJ Horayot

III 4 of a man who was a prostitute in Rome: the hair was arranged in separate masses, heap on heap. In Midrash Rabbah on Gen 28:11 *qawwāṣ*, "bushy haired," is an antonym of *qērēaḥ*, "bald." In Syriac *qawṣāṯā* designates locks of hair and is used in the Syro-hexaplar of Job 16:12.

mist, or "droplets." This nominal form occurs elsewhere only in Amos 6:11 in a quite different context. There it is applied to the smashing of a house to *rĕsîsîm*, "bits" or "pieces," the parallel synonym being *bĕqî'îm*, "splinters." In Ezek 46:14 the infinitive of the verb is used of oil combined with flour to "temper" (*KJ*) or "moisten" it (*RSV*). Arabic *rašša*, "sprinkle," "strew," "sow," "rain lightly," and the noun *rašš*, plural *rišāš*, "sprinkling," "light rain," "dew," gives the meaning desiderated here, which is already clear from the parallelism with *ṭal*, "dew."

2e,f. The dew of Palestine-Syria is sometimes so heavy as to soak the clothes, like Gideon's fleece, Judg 6:38. A similar passage is found in Pseudo-Anacreon iii 10 where love is depicted as a hapless dew-soaked swain begging entrance:

"Fear not," said he, with piteous din,
'Pray ope the door and let me in.
A poor unsheltered boy am I,
For help who knows not where to fly.
Lost in the dark, and with the dews,
All cold and wet, that midnight brews.' "

(After Ginsburg, ad loc.)

2. The Targum applied the sleeping and waking to Israel's sin and exile, repentance and return, and the wet hair as that of the deity soaked by the tears of the penitent people:

> After all these words, the people of the House of Israel sinned, and He delivered them into the hand of Nebuchadnezzar, King of Babylon, and he led them into exile and in the exile they resembled a man who slumbers and cannot be aroused from his sleep. Then the voice of the Holy Spirit enlightened them by means of the prophets and It (or She) aroused them from the slumber of their mind. The Lord of All the World answered and thus He said: "Return in repentance, open your mouth, pray and praise Me, My sister, My beloved, Assembly of Israel, likened to the dove in the perfection of your works, for the hair of My head is filled with your tears, like a man the hair of whose head is soaked with the dew of heaven, and the locks of My hair are filled with the drops from your eyes like the man whose locks of hair are filled with drops of rain that fell in the night."

Midrash Rabbah related the contrasting lethargy and alertness to Israel's ambivalent attitude toward such matters as religious observance and charity, sacrifice and prayer, ritual and study. "My heart" was related to God on the basis of Ps 73:26 read as "God is the rock, my heart." The knocking was attributed to Moses, with citation of Exod 11:4. The command "open to me" was applied to the small opening, like the eye of a needle, which Israel presents for repentance to come through, but which God will enlarge wide enough for a wagon to pass through. "My sister" evoked a far-fetched pun on the knitting of Israel to God by the blood of the Passover and the circumcision. "My love" was related to Israel's love of

God at the Reed Sea (Exod 15:2); "my dove" to the distinction of receiving the commandment; "my perfect one" to Israel's devotion at Sinai. The reading *tĕ'ûmāṯî*, "my twin," for *tammāṯî*, "my perfect one," suggested the case of twins who feel each other's pains, with God as Israel's twin sharing the pain in times of trouble (Ps 91:15). The head filled with dew was related to the theophany of Ps 68:9[8E] and the locks with the drops of the night with the theophany of Judg 5:4.

Christian expositors related the sleep, taken in an unfavorable sense, to the Church's relaxation of zeal following the end of pagan persecution, or to the soul's relapse into spiritual sloth after conversion. Taken in a favorable sense, the sleep denoted the Bride's slumber after her Lord has given her a draught from His inebriating chalice which closes her eyes to all earthly cares. She slumbers now in perfect repose and trust, but her heart is awake in eager love for Him. St. Ambrose in his Exhortation to Virgins gave this admonition: "Let thy flesh sleep, let thy faith wake, let the allurements of the body slumber, let the prudence of the heart keep watch, let thy members breathe the odor of Christ's Cross and grave, that slumber bring no heat, and arouse no passions." Ascribed to the Bridegroom, the words were taken to refer to His sleep in the grave, where His Body slept, but His divine nature was awake, even as a reminder that the Church may rise from contemplation to action and understand that it is her duty to go out and compel the heathen to come in. The words were taken as expressive of Christ's anxiety for the negligent and erring. Christ knocks at the door of the Church, addressing her as sister because she is through Him co-heir to the kingdom; as friend (Vulgate *amica*) because she is versed in heavenly mysteries; as dove because she is filled with the Holy Ghost; undefiled because she is cleansed by Him from sin.

The head filled with dew and the locks with drops of the night were given a variety of meanings. The night was seen as denoting iniquity and its dew and drops as those who grow cold and chill the Head of Christ by failing to love God. The wet locks were taken to denote those who give only partial obedience to Christ, or to careless and ignorant bishops and clergy who do not preach with sincerity. Again the wet tresses adorning the Head were taken to be the Saints persecuted by cold and unloving and unbelieving souls. The locks and dew drops were also given auspicious meanings, the locks interpreted as Saints, Angels, Apostles, or Prophets, and the dew drops as the holy doctrines they possess and impart. The dew was also explained as the heavenly grace which moistens the dry heart during the darkness of this world and makes it glad. Again the dew drops glittering in the clear night were seen as the starry virtues with which the Saints were decked when the full moon of the Church shone on the conversion of the Gentiles. The dew filled head was also seen as typifying the Resurrection in the early morn, and the drops of night as the souls redeemed and the nations won over to the faith, still cold in their sins and the darkness of imperfect knowledge, but soon to be lightened and warmed by the life and teachings of their pastors. (Cf. Littledale.)

3. Commentators generally remark that the lady's reasons for not opening the door are of a very trifling sort such as are insurmountable only in dreams. It seems likely that a door is assumed in the present context and the LXX and Old Latin versions supply the door as the object of the knocking in the preceding verse. But the word "door" is recognized even by the most modest

of commentators as a figure for a female unusually open and receptive to sexual overtures. The request to "open" in the preceding verse could in certain circumstances have sexual connotations. The reference to taking off the robe and putting it on again would admittedly apply most naturally to the usual practice of dressing before answering the door. The reluctance to soil her clean feet is understandable, especially if she had no slippers handy. But in view of the well-known use of "feet" as a euphemism for genitals, the language here is at least suggestive. The "feet" here are construed as masculine as indicated by the object suffix "them" in the verb of 3d; cf. 4:9d. When David, anxious to conceal the fact that he was responsible for Bathsheba's pregnancy, urged her husband to go home and wash his feet, he intended to suggest something more and Uriah caught at least part of the intent, "and I, shall I go to my house to eat and drink and lie with my wife?" II Sam 11:11a. The language of the lady may represent a bit of coy pretense intended to tease the eager male.

3b,d. *How*. The form *'êḵāḵāh* is found elsewhere in the Old Testament only in Esther 8:6.

3d. *soil*. The word *ṭnp* is hapax in the Old Testament. It is, however, attested in Aramaic and Akkadian in the same sense as here. In Arabic the meaning in the simple stem is "be suspect" or be "corrupted." The *pi'ēl* has here, as normally, factitive force.

2–3. In a Sumerian sacred marriage song which Kramer saw as a form of playlet (*SMR*, 97, 152n27) there is a parallel to the present situation which was overlooked by Kramer. There are no stage directions in the playlet which adds to the usual difficulties of translating and interpreting a Sumerian text; but, as Kramer understands the scenario, the lover is standing outside the beloved's house and asks:

My sister, why have you shut yourself in the house?
My little one, why have you shut yourself in the house?

The sister answers:

I washed myself, soaped myself,
Washed myself in the holy kettle,
Soaped myself in the white basin,
Dressed myself in the garments of queenship, of the queenship of heaven,
That is why I shut myself in the house.
I painted my eyes with kohl,
I fixed my hairdo, the . . . ,
Tested the weapon that will make triumphant his reign,
Set straight my twisted lips,
Piled up my loosened locks,
Let them fall to the "border" of my nape,
Put a silver bracelet on my hand,
Fastened small beads about my neck,
Fixed their . . . about my neck sinews.

Although she is now fully dressed, bejeweled, and "made-up," she still does not open the door. To induce her to admit him, he reminds her that he has brought gifts of honey and bread. On hearing this, the goddess turns to her attendants and gives orders to let her lover in with fanfare of music. Although the lover is not mentioned by name, he is evidently the shepherd Dumuzi and he wishes to bring with him into the house his lambs and kids. The text, according to Kramer, becomes obscure because of the shift of speakers without indication of their identity. Some females, whom Kramer takes to be companions of the goddess, chant:

> Lo, high [?] is our bosom,
> Lo, hair has grown on our vulva,
> At the lap of the bridegroom
> let us rejoice . . .

And the goddess seems to encourage them:

> Dance ye, dance ye,
> O Bau, let us rejoice because
> of my vulva,
> Dance ye, dance ye,
> Thus [?] will he be pleased,
> will he be pleased.

Following the rubric designating the song as a *balbale* of Inanna, the refrain is repeated:

> Let him come, let him come, . . . pray [?] let him come.

Kramer (*SMR,* 99) finds in this particular poem "little that is reminiscent of the Song of Songs, at least as we have it now in our undoubtedly expurgated form, except for such stylistic features as the brother-sister designation of the lovers and the presence of a chorus of maidens." Despite the differences in detail, there is a striking parallel in the delay of the two ladies to admit the lover and in the explanations for the delay or reluctance. The feminine penchant to keep her suitor waiting while she goes on beautifying herself is an old and ever-new stratagem to tease and tantalize, which usually works but may be overplayed.

3. The Targum attributed the first half of this verse to Israel and the second to God:

> The Assembly of Israel answered before the prophets: "Lo, already, I have removed the yoke of His commandments from me and have worshipped the idols of the nations. How can I have the face to return to Him?"
>
> The Lord of the World replied to them through the prophets: "Moreover, I Myself have already lifted My Presence from among you, how then can I return since you have done evil? I have cleansed my feet from your filth, and how can I soil them among you with your evil deeds?"

In the Midrash Rabbah on this verse Rabbi Johanan remarked: "There is no one so simple but knows how to take off and put on her clothes." He then proceeded to explain that the reference is to Nebuchadnezzar's attack on Israel and stripping of the vestments of priesthood and royalty. Another explanation related the situation to the time of Pentecost (when Israel was given the Law at Sinai) when sleep was sweet and the night short (yet Israel rose to receive the Law). The foot washing was explained as removal of the filth of idolatry.

Christian expositors of this verse presented considerable diversity. The Bride, previously eager for the company of her Beloved, now offers trifling excuses for her unwillingness to get up and open the door. Augustine applied this verse to the lull in missionary zeal which the Church experienced following its establishment under Constantine. Others applied it to the undue exaltation of the contemplative over the active life, when the Church pleaded its own spiritual advantage as an excuse for not exercising itself to convert others. A favorable sense was obtained by taking the refusal as resolve against relapse into sin. The Church, having put off the old man (Col 3:9) and washed herself in the Blood of the Lamb, determines that nothing will lure her back to her former ways. Again, the words were interpreted as the vow of voluntary poverty. Philo of Carpasia applied the verse to the Bridegroom, Christ, who stripped off the mortality of His Flesh and passed in His Ascension from the narrow limits of earth to the region where death had no more hold on Him. (Cf. Littledale.)

4a. *thrust*. The verb *šlḥ* designates motion toward something and its use here with the preposition *min*, "from," has been somewhat disconcerting to translators. Horst's emendation to *šlp* "take out/off," seems to be implicit in some translations. *JPSV* rendered "My beloved took his hand off the latch" and added a note "Meaning of Heb[rew] uncertain." Some choose a verb with minimum motion such as "put." *NEB* has "slipped," but *JB* resolutely renders "thrust."

"hand." The use of *yāḏ*, "hand," as a euphemism for phallus was recognized in the last century by some commentators on Isa 57:8–10 where the term is twice used in that sense. Ugaritic now shows this usage to be pre-Israelite. In the poem called "The Birth of the Beautiful Gods," the venerable father of the gods is engaged in an effort to tup two eager females. His "hand" is said to be as long as the sea, but he appears to have some difficulty achieving or maintaining an erection since the eager females observe:

O man, man, your rod is down, Your love-staff droops
(23[52].46–47)

There is repeated reference to roasting a bird which may be a ritual to remedy the condition lamented by the ladies. At length El succeeds in consummating the union and the birth of the beautiful gods is the result. (Cf. *EUT*, 35–42.) In another passage apparently descriptive of a sexual liaison, since there is reference to kissing lips, a "hand" is mentioned followed by a word *sǵr* of uncertain meaning (22.2[124].4–5).

The term is used quite unmistakably in the Manual of Discipline (1QS 7:13) of the Essene sect at Qumran. Among punishable indecencies such as walking naked, or spitting in the midst of the assembly, there is a thirty-day penalty for the man who puts out his "hand" from beneath his clothing or whose clothing is torn so as to reveal his nakedness. For a detailed discussion, cf. Delcor (1967). Whether the word "hand" in the present passage refers to the membrum virile depends on the nature of the hole into which it is inserted.

On "hands" in Isa 65:3 of the Qumran Isaiah scroll, see above p. 225.

into. In spite of the fact that the preposition *min* regularly means "from," the difficulty of that meaning with the verb *šlḥ* was appreciated by a number of translators and interpreters. Vulgate rendered *per,* and similarly several modern translations, *AT, JB, NEB, NAB,* "through," while *KJ* rendered "by the hole," In numerous instances prepositions have to be translated in unusual ways, but it was the Ugaritic uses of *b* and *l* both in the sense of "to" and "from" which moved some scholars to reconsider the uses of *b, l,* and *m(in)* in a number of OT passages; cf. Sarna, 1959; Dahood, 1963, 300*f,* and *PS I,* on Ps 18:7; C. Brekelmans, 1969. While not all the examples of alleged interchange of *b-* and *mi(n)* which have been adduced are convincing, it is hard to see how some scholars can continue to deny the phenomenon or seek to explain it away. There is no warrant here for reviewing and appraising the numerous alleged instances of interchange of the two prepositions. Suffice it here to offer one more which ought to convince the most stubborn skeptic. In Prov 17:23 and 21:14 there are the variant expressions *šōḥaḏ mēḥēq* and *šōḥaḏ baḥēq,* "a bribe from/in (the) bosom," which is obviously the same idiom no matter what the force of the prepositions. While bribery necessarily involves a transaction from the briber to the bribed, the time-honored method is for the briber to slip the bribe into the bosom or pocket of the recipient.

the hole. A number of translators and critics (Haupt, Dalman, Zapletal, Dussaud, Horst, Buzy) after *haḥōr,* "the hole," add *baddeleṯ,* "in the door." Such an asyndetic relative construction is quite possible, but would be a bit awkward here. *RSV* and *JPSV* simply render the word as "latch," but it is hard to see how a hole can be a latch. This is the word for any kind of a hole, a cave where men or animals may hide or dwell, I Sam 14:11; Job 30:6, Nahum 2:13[12E]; an eye socket, Zech 14:12; a hole bored in a box lid II Kings 12:10[9E]; or a hole in a wall, Ezek 8:8[7E]. The assumption that the hole in question was a latch-hole in the door is reflected in Midrash Rabbah. Rabbi Abba ben Kahana said: "How comes the hole of the door to be mentioned here, seeing that it is a place where vermin swarm?" (The answer is a *non sequitur* dealing with the problem of the choice of Cyrus for his historic role rather than some righteous man like Daniel.) The hole has been supposed to be a window in the front wall of the house (Siegfried) or a peephole in the front door (Budde).

Most translators and commentators have understood the aperture to be the keyhole of the front door. In Near Eastern villages old-fashioned door locks (how old is uncertain) and keys were made of wood. The key was often of considerable size, usually over a foot in length, and the keyhole large enough for a man's hand. The lover could thus put his hand through the hole, but could not open the door without the key. The door, of course, could be opened from the inside by lifting the bolt which was provided with handles for that purpose. The lovesick lady could have made it easy for her lover by simply leaving the door unlocked. This was the stratagem in a Sumerian sacred marriage song in which the accommodating parents of the bride address the lover:

> Our son-in-law, when the day has passed,
> Our son-in-law, when night has come,
> When moonlight has entered this house,
> When moonlight has dimmed[?] [the light] in this house,
> We[?] will remove for you the lock from the door.
>
> (*SMR*, 99)

Given the attested use of "hand" as a surrogate for phallus, there can be no question that, whatever the context, the statement "my love thrust his 'hand' into the hole" would be suggestive of coital intromission, even without the succeeding line descriptive of the emotional reaction of the female.

4b. *my inwards.* The word designates primarily the inward parts of the body, the intestines, bowels, guts, and is used of the source of procreative powers male and female, of the seat of the emotions, pity, compassion, distress, and here of erotic emotion. In 5:14c, it is used of the external area above the thighs and presumably below the waist. In Gen 25:23; Isa 49:1; Ps 71:6 the word stands in poetic parallelism with *beṭen* in the sense of womb. The Akkadian cognate is used in similar senses; cf. É. Dhorme, 1923b, 135*f*.

seethed. The verb *hmy* denotes commotion and stir, with particular reference to noises, growling of dogs or bears, murmur of doves, groans of distress, murmuring in prayer, the sounds of lyre or flute, the roar of the sea, the noise of the city streets, the boisterous behavior of an inebriated man or woman. As applied to the insides, the guts, or bowels, as the seat of the emotions, biblical expression is literally very near to the current locution "to get or have one's bowels in an uproar." The classic passage is Jer 4:19, which in the earthy language of the *KJ* is:

> My bowels, my bowels! I am pained at my very heart; my heart maketh a noise in me; I cannot hold my peace, . . .

In Jer 31:20 the expression is used of Yahweh's concern for Ephraim:

> Is Ephraim my dear son,
> Is he my darling child?
> Often I speak of him,
> I cherish his memory still.
> Therefore my guts stir for him;
> I will surely pity him.

In Isa 16:11 the poet's bowels sound like a harp or lyre in anguish over the impending woes of Moab. In Ps 22:15[14E] the heart of the complainant melts like wax in the midst of his insides.

In the present passage *KJ* rendered "and my bowels were moved for him" which would not now be considered felicitous, although the Rev. Dr. Sibs in 1648, for his sermons on chs. 4–6 of the Canticle, took his title from this passage: *Bowels Opened.* (See Plate VI.)

for him. Lit. "upon him," in the sense of "because of him," or "for him." Vulgate here takes the meaning to be "at his touch," *et venter meus intremuit ad tactum ejus,* presumably at his touching her body rather than the door hole. This provided opportunity for a type of interpretation which Cornelius à Lapide (*apud* Robert) adjudged scarcely chaste. A number of Hebrew MSS read here *'ālay,* "upon me," which is preferred by a number of critics (Ewald, Graetz, Dalman, Zapletal, Rothstein, Joüon, Staerk, Horst, Buzy) and is interpreted in the sense of a *dativus commodi,* "for me." *RSV* adopted this reading, "and my heart was thrilled within me." It does not seem to make a great deal of difference which reading is chosen; her thrill is occasioned by his action, whatever it was.

With the notable exception of *KJ,* translators tend to resort to paraphrase and circumlocution to bowdlerize the wording of the original:

and my heart yearned for him. (*AT*)
and my heart was thrilled within me. (*RSV*)
I trembled to the core of my being. (*JB*)
my heart trembled within me. (*NAB*)
And my heart was stirred for him. (*JPSV*)

The bowel movement, however, is retained by *NEB:*

my bowels stirred within me.

The Targum applied this verse to the exile of the northern tribes by Sennacherib and the divine distress at Jeroboam's worship of the molten calf:

> When it was clear before YHWH that the people of the House of Israel did not wish to repent and return to Him, He stretched forth His mighty blow against the tribe of Reuben and Gad and the half-tribe of Manasseh on the other side of the Jordan and delivered them into the hand of Sennacherib, King of Assyria, and he exiled them to Laḥlaḥ and Ḥabur, rivers of Gozan, and to the cities of Media. And he took from their hand the molten calf which sinful Jeroboam had put in Leshem Dan, which is called Pamios, in the days of Peqaḥ, son of Remaliah. When I heard, My bowels were in turmoil on account of them.

The Christian exposition of the hand and the hole was not pressed as avidly as with some other passages, but there were remarkable efforts. The hand was seen as the symbol of power in operation, and the hole was taken to denote the partial and imperfect glimpse which the soul gets when any barrier is placed between it and God. The hand symbolizes the Eternal and Incarnate Word seen through a peephole, as in a glass darkly. Among other things, the hand through the hole was interpreted as Christ making his Bride, the Church, pass through trouble and persecution. If she will not open when He knocks, He will punish. Philo of Carpasia reminded the faithful how Christ drew the doubters to Himself through the hole which he showed to Thomas, John 20:27.

The gastric commotion was generally understood to describe the mingled awe and delight of the Bride and especially the rejoicing of the hallowed womb of the Virgin Mother when the Right Hand of God came to her secretly and mysteriously at the Annunciation, and found her pure and free from every sin in her spotless maidenhood. (Cf. Littledale.)

5a. *I rose*. The verb *qamtî,* "I rose," is followed by the independent personal pronoun, but without hint of emphasis. This usage is frequent in Qohelet (cf. Eccles 1:16, 2:1,11,15, 3:17,18) and has been taken as a characteristic of late Hebrew. It may be, however, that it is a matter of dialectology rather than chronology. The independent personal pronoun is frequent in Ugaritic both before and after first person finite verbal forms and after the infinitive absolute.

5b,c. *hands . . . fingers*. A standard pair in poetic parallelism in Ugaritic and Hebrew; cf. Isa 2:8, 17:8, 59:3; Ps 144:1. In Ugaritic there are several examples, such as

It (a weapon) darted from Baal's hand(s)
Like an eagle from his fingers.
(2.4[68].20–21)

He washed his hands to the elbow,
His fingers up to the shoulder.
(14[KRT].3.157–158)

Vir[g]in Anat washed her hands,
The Progenitress of the Peoples her fingers.
(3[ʿNT].2.33)

5b. *dripped*. There is ambiguity in the situation which is not clarified by the verb. The question is whether the myrrh drips from the hands onto the bolt or whether the myrrh is on the bolt in such quantity as to smear the hands that grasp the bolt.

5c. The force of the verb *nṭp,* "drip," in the preceding stich extends to the present line. Omission of a synonymous verb in the second parallel stich is the commonest pattern in Ugaritic poetry.

liquid myrrh. Or "flowing myrrh," *mōr ʿôḇēr,* called in Exod 30:23 *mōr dĕrôr*. This is the liquid which flows out of the bark, or out of an incision in the bark of the *Balsamodendron myrrha* and was especially valued. LXX here reads *smyrnan plērē* (abundant myrrh?) and Vulgate *pleni myrrha probatissima*. Syriac repeats the verb "dripped."

5d. Vulgate ends the sentence with the second mention of myrrh and begins a new sentence, "I opened the bolt of the door for my Beloved." LXX, Syriac, and Arabic agree with the wording and arrangement of MT here.

It is not clear which of the lovers deposited the myrrh on the handles of the door bolt. It has been supposed that the Bride had anointed herself rather profusely and dripped on the handles, or that she had a box of unguent ready to anoint the dark tresses of her lover and accidentally broke or spilled it in her haste to open the door. Delitzsch supposed that Solomon (not the imaginary shepherd) had come perfumed as for a festival and had dropped the costly ointment on the bolt handles. (Thus there is no worry about the extravagance; Solomon could afford it.) An apparent parallel from Lucretius (*De rerum natura* IV 1173) is cited in support of this understanding—a lover shut out weeps, piles flowers at the threshold, and smears unguent on the doorposts:

At lacrymans exclusus amator limina saepe	The tearful lover, shut without, oft clothes
Floribus et sertis operit, potesque superbor	With flowers and wreaths the threshold, and anoints
Unguent amarcino.	The door jambs with marjoram.

Evidence has been adduced from Mesopotamia for pouring precious, perfumed oil on thresholds, doors, and door bolts; cf. A. Salonen, 1961, 120*f*. Unfortunately, the reasons for this practice are not elaborated and we have only statements such as "twenty (measures) of pure oil to embellish his door he dedicated," or "I poured lavishly oil over threshold, locks, bar and doors." There is, however, nothing to connect this with a lover smearing his lady's door bolt with such.

The preceding verses present a number of striking parallels to the classical *paraclausithyron* (weeping outside the door), or the song of the locked-out lover, a motif which has been treated in detail by Frank O. Copley, 1956. This literary form Copley saw as an outgrowth of the *kômos,* the revelry following the symposium when the inebriated youths took to the streets in search of further diversion. Coming to a brothel, they might noisily demand entry and threaten to break the door, or, if in a mellow mood, they might simply sing a song. The Greeks developed the boisterous street ballad into the *paraclausithyron* expressive of lovers' sufferings and sorrows and the Romans further elaborated and enriched the form with psychological and erotic interest, making it a key element in love literature before it finally fell into limbo. (The motif lives on in popular song, in such lines as "Who's that knocking at my door?" or "Open the door, Richard.") Throughout its classical history the *paraclausithyron* maintained, with slight variation, its basic characteristics. The love-affair could be either heterosexual or homosexual, but the excluded lover pleads to be let in, begs, cajoles, complains, threatens, falls asleep outside the door, or he despairs and departs leaving his garland, or having scribbled some verses on the door, or having smeared it with unguents.

Several parallels between common features of the *paraclausithyron* and Canticles 5:1–5 may be briefly noted. The reference to the eating of honey, with suggestion of sexual entendre, and the drinking of wine, resembles a fragment by Anacreon which Copley (14n30) rendered: "I have dined on a bit I broke from a dainty honeycake; I have drunk off a flagon of wine: now I pluck my lute and sing to a graceful, lovely maid, as I go on my revel. . . ." The lady's state of somnolence with mind awake has a parallel in a passage of Aristanetus (2.19):

"My dear, either I've been seeing things in my sleep—as one does, of course—or else I really did hear a band of young men in front of my house, revelling and battling over me in the dead of night. I must have seen it: it can't have been a dream . . ." (Copley, 25).

The excluded lover's complaint about the inclement weather is common in the *paraclausithyron:*

"Rain there was, and night—and third blow to love—wine. Boreas blew cold, and I was alone. But Moschus the beautiful had greater might than these. 'Would that you might wander like me, and at no single door find peace!' Thus much to the boy I cried, drenched to the skin" (Copley, 2).

The lady's excuse for not opening the door—that she had taken off her robe and washed her feet—does not appear to have been used by the coy mistresses of the classical songs. An opposite response is depicted in Ovid's *Amores* (3:1) where Elegeia boasts (Copley, 83):

It was I who taught Corinna to deceive her guard and tempt the stern doorway from its duty, to slip from bed, to wrap herself in her loosened robe, and to move through the night in (*sic*) feet that stumbled not.

The Sumerian stratagem, noted above, was simply to remove the lock in anticipation of the tryst.

The liquid myrrh on the door bolt has its parallels in various tokens left by disappointed lovers, flowers, wine, verses, or perfume. Copley (26) cites a passage in the romance of Chariton *Chaereas and Callirrhoe* (1:3.2) in which the disappointed suitors of Callirrhoe "scattered about the signs of a revel—left garlands at the door, poured unguent on it, made mud-puddles of wine, and threw down half-burned torches." The pouring of perfumed oils on the thresholds, doors, and door bolts in ancient Mesopotamia, mentioned above, shows that the practice long antedated the Greek and Roman usage and that both the myrrh-dripping door bolt of the Canticle and the unguent-smeared door of the classical *paraclausithyron* had ancient Near Eastern antecedents and prototypes.

The reversal of the roles of pursuer and pursued, following the departure of the locked-out lover, has a partial parallel in the *Alexandrian Erotic Fragment* which Copley (20) regarded as one of the anonymous masterpieces of ancient love poetry. In this instance, the lovesick girl, passing through the streets toward the house of her beloved, complains to herself about the betrayal by him whose talk had been so bold and vaunting (p. 21). "This is no common wrong he has done me now. I shall go mad, for passion grips me, and I am all aflame. Deserted, deserted am I." The fate of this frustrated female is hidden by the fragmentary state of the text, but it is likely that she remained rejected, in keeping with the standard plot of such poems (cf. Copley, p. 22). It is a curious coincidence, as Copley noted (150n59), that

Plutarch in the passage (*Amatorius* 753B) which has given the song its name (*Tò paraklausithyron*), speaks of the singer as a woman.

It is apparent that there is a connection between the classical *paraclausithyron* and Song of Songs 5:2–5, but there is nothing to suggest direct dependence.

5. The Targum took the reference to the door bolt to mean the closing of the door in the face of belatedly penitent Israel:

> When the mighty stroke of YHWH was strong upon me, I was appalled at my actions and the priests brought the sacrifice and offered up spice incense but it was not received with favor, because the Lord of the World shut the doors of repentance in my face.

Midrash Rabbah stressed that "It was I who rose and not the other nations" which has been understood by the commentaries to refer to Israel's rising to build the Second Temple. The myrrh was taken in the sense of bitterness with reference to the supposition that Cyrus decreed that whoever had crossed the Euphrates should remain, but those who had not yet crossed should not do so (these being the ones who were permitted to return to Israel). The opening to the Beloved was also explained as signifying repentance and the myrrh, or bitterness, as referring to the sin of worshiping the calf (Exod 32:4). The myrrh was also interpreted as meaning the Master (*mar*) who forgave (Exod 32:14). The handles of the bolt referred to those who were debarred from returning.

Christian interpreters of this verse applied the rising and opening to the Church's preaching. Cassiodorus explained that one who wishes to open the hearts of others to Christ by preaching must himself first rise up and be alert in zeal for good works and fulfill in deed what he preaches, lest he having preached to others should himself become a castaway (I Cor 9:27).

The dripping myrrh was variously explained. The supposition that the Bride had anointed herself for the reception of the Bridegroom encountered the objection that she would not then have refused to open the door. (Such ambivalent behavior, however, is not uncommon.) Others assumed that the myrrh on the door bolt was left by the Bridegroom when He put His hand through the hole and tried the lock. The myrrh was usually taken to mean repentance and voluntary mortification. As coming from the Groom, the myrrh thus recalled His Passion. The mention of the fingers did not escape attention and these were interpreted as the virtues of the holy life, liberality, frugality, humility, frankness. The fingers are said to be full of myrrh because mortification of carnality is essential in all our actions. The myrrh is most choice (*probatissima*) when every prompting of the Enemy, all carnal pleasure, is excluded. Inferior myrrh is the penitence that comes from fear of punishment, or from actual punishment. The best myrrh is that which flows from a softened heart, melted by the love of God. It was noted that it is the Bride's hands, rather than her mouth, which drop the myrrh, thereby teaching us that an austere life of self-denial is more important than eloquent preaching in the effort to influence sinners. The myrrh dropping on the handles of the bolt was explained as repentance directed toward a single barrier or besetting sin, a particular act, habit or temper of mind. The myrrh of repentance on the stiff or rusted bolt makes it easier to move. Littledale concluded his summary of expositions of this verse with a sample from Cocceius:

The *lock,* whereby our heart is opened to Christ, or by which Christ is shut up within the heart, is faith. Its bolt is withdrawn when our heart is expanded, so that Christ can always come to us, with all His retinue, and in every array. The bolt of this lock is shot by fulness and pleasure. And it is very properly shot against other desires, but not against the kingdom of Christ, to prevent it from flowing into us wholly. The fulness which shuts out everything save Christ, is from the Holy Ghost, but that which checks any desire for Him is of the flesh. Besides, the Bride hints that she found the myrrh on the lock, that is, the effectual working of the Holy Ghost when she desired to open her heart. And if we desire to press the parable further, she finds this fragrant ointment on her hands and fingers, that is in her toil and action, which she has begun in the fear of God.

6b. *had turned.* The passive participle of *ḥmq* is used in 7:2[1E] of the contours or curves of the dancer's hips or thighs. As a verb of motion it occurs elsewhere in the Old Testament only in Jer 31:22, in the reflexive stem, applied to Israel pictured as a perverse girl. *KJ* there translated, "How long will you go about, O thou backsliding daughter?"; *AT* rendered "hesitate" and *RSV* "waver." As a verb of motion it apparently designates a half turn. In Arabic the word is not used as a verb of motion, but in the sense "be stupid," or "be foolish," which might develop from an original sense of "turn away (from good)."

and gone. The verb *'br* has the primary sense of "cross over," but also simply to pass on, leave a place; cf. Isa 29:5; Micah 1:11; Ps 144:4; Job 6:15. The two verbs are asyndetic, *ḥāmaq 'āḇar,* forming a single expression which LXX apparently recognized and translated with a single verb *parēlthen,* while Vulgate rendered with two *at ille declinaverat atque transierat.*

6c. *My soul sank.* Lit. "My soul (*nep̄eš*) went out." This expression is used of Rachel's dying in Gen 35:18. In Jer 15:9 an experienced childbearer who has had seven children is described as failing, as languishing and exhaling (*npḥ*) her soul (*nep̄eš*). The word *nep̄eš,* from a primitive meaning "throat," developed a wide range of meanings involving breathing as a sign of life and liveliness, including all the instincts, drives, and appetites of life. In Ps 146:4 the word *rûaḥ* is used instead of *nep̄eš* for expiration. Dispiritment may be occasioned by a variety of causes and may be serious, chronic, or terminal, or merely temporary or trivial, as when the Queen of Sheba saw all of Solomon's wealth and splendor, I Kings 10:5, there was no spirit (*rûaḥ*) in her. In a Ugaritic myth relating to the death of Baal, the demise occasioned loss or lack of spirit among mankind. The god Mot (Death), in boasting of his victory over Baal, says to Baal's solicitous sister Anat:

I went and roamed
Every mountain to the inwards of Earth,
Every hill to the inwards of the Fields.
Spirit (*npš*) was absent among men,
Spirit (among) earth's multitudes.
(6[49].2.15–19)

at his flight. The form *bědabběrô* is ambiguous. It may mean "at his speaking," i.e. "when he spoke," or "at what he said." *JPSV* rendered "I was faint at what he said," but added a note that "Change of vocalization yields 'because of him.'" It seems more likely that *dbr* here is the verb of motion which includes among its various meanings the sense of "turn back," "turn aside," "flee," "desist." Akkadian *duppuru,* with interchange of *b* and *p,* offers the sense "go away," "absent oneself," which seems preferable here; cf. *CAD,* III, 186*ff.*

6d,e. Some critics expunge 6d as borrowed from 3:2. Robert, however, regarded it as replete with significance if one admits that the Canticle has a purpose other than the description of human love.

6. The Targum interpreted the lover's withdrawal as the removal of the Divine Presence from Israel:

> Said the Assembly of Israel: "I wished to request instruction from YHWH but He lifted His Presence from me. My soul longed for the sound of His Words and I sought the Presence of His Glory, but I did not find it. I prayed before Him, but He covered the heavens with clouds and would not accept my prayer."

This verse was ascribed by R. Joshua ben Levi (TB Shabbat 88b) to Israel at every word that went forth from the mouth of God. Since their souls departed at the first word, how could they receive the second? God brought down the dew which revives the dead and revived them (Ps 68:10[9E]).

The bolt of the door was taken by the Vulgate as the beginning of this verse rather than the end of the preceding, *Pessulum ostii mei aperui dilecto meo,* "the bolt of the door I opened for my beloved." This bolt or bar was taken to denote worldly pleasure which shuts God from the heart, or ignorance and blindness removed by the preaching of the Gospel. As a small lock can close a large door, so in the spiritual life small neglects and defects are the surest barriers to grace, and these must be removed before the Beloved can enter the soul. Parez explained the bolt as the ceremonial Law which barred access of the Gentiles and hid the sanctuary of Christ; this bar was removed by the Incarnation. The door here recalled the little doors (*ostiola*) of olive wood at the entrance to the sanctum sanctorum (I Kings 6:31) and the olive, as the source of anointing oil, evoked the thought that one may slip easily through the narrow entrance with the help of the oil of grace (a similar thought is echoed in a bit of contemporary folk doggerel of the genre called "talking blues": "If you want to get to heaven, let me tell you how to do it. Just grease yourself with a little mutton suet. Then jump right into the Devil's hand and slide straight into the Promised Land. Take it easy. Go greasy."). The door led to a great variety of edifying exposition, since there is a great diversity of doors, the door of natural religion, the door of the Sacraments, the door of experimental grace, etc.; above all, Christ as the Door (John 10:9). The withdrawal was taken to refer to Christ's sudden and brief appearances after the Resurrection, and to His departure from the world.

The passing out, or liquefaction of the soul (Vulgate *Anima mea liquefacta est*) was seen as passing from sin to holiness, or as melting with heavenly love. The Bride fainted at the speech of the Bridegroom, because she could not, while still in the body, long endure the power of Christ's love, because the perishable body weighs down the soul (Wis 9:15). The fruitless search was difficult to explain. It is the old mystery: Why does God seek when not sought, come when not called, but withdraw when sought and flee when called? The words were easily taken as a warning to the Church or soul that neglects to hear and obey the call of the Lord; they will seek and not find Him (John 7:34). (Cf. Littledale.)

7. Cf. 3:1–3. The watchmen who impede the maiden's search and strip off her mantle reminded T. J. Meek of the watchmen who impeded Ishtar in her descent to the netherworld and stripped her of her garments.

7d. *veil.* This word, *rĕḏîḏ* is rendered here by LXX as *theristron* which designates a light mantle worn in summer. The word occurs elsewhere in the Old Testament only in Isa 3:23 in a list of items of female finery. LXX also uses *theristron* to translate *ṣāʿîp,* "veil," in Gen 24:65, 38:14,19 (a disguise and an identifying mark of a holy woman, or sacred prostitute, *qĕḏēšāh*). On the veil as associated with Ishtar and sacred prostitution, cf. 4:1,3 on *ṣammāh.* Robert, following the usual rendering, "mantle," appealed to archaeological illustration on the relief depicting Sennacherib's capture of *Lachish* in which the women wear a kind of veil covering the head and the shoulders and reaching down almost to the ankles. Robert cited Arabic *ridāt,* mantle, or cloak. (Note, however, that Arabic *rd'* may also be used of letting down the veil, and the noun *ridā'* may designate a jeweled girdle.) The long mantle meets the exigencies of the situation as Robert understood it; she put it on to protect her from the cold of the night. The supposition that she left her robe behind in fleeing from the guards (Delitzsch, Budde, Siegfried), like Joseph from Potiphar's wife, Gen 39:12–13, or the young man at the arrest of Jesus, Mark 14:51–52, Robert rightly rejected, supposing that the guards in their brutality tore it off her shoulders.

In the descent of Inanna/Ishtar to the netherworld, there are seven items of the goddess' dress and ornamentation which are removed one by one at each of the seven gates of the infernal city. In both the Sumerian and Akkadian versions, one of the items removed is the *dudittu* or *tudittu* which is some sort of ornament worn on the breast of females, both human and divine. It was one of the essential pieces of jewelry given to the bride at her wedding and it could be made of silver, gold, bronze, copper, ivory or semi-precious stones. Dales (1963, 31–33) concludes from his study of necklaces, bands and belts on Mesopotamian figurines that the *dudittu* can best be thought of as an ornament or pendant, probably suspended from a necklace, such as appear frequently on Mesopotamian figurines of the goddess. The *dudittu* apparently had talismanic powers. The removal of a lady's *dudittu* was not approved treatment and there is mention of a curse for rending a (woman's) cloak, breaking her *tudittu* and snipping off her *dīdu* (garment); cf. CAD, *IV,* 135b–136a. (On the *dīdu* as a hip band, cf. Dales, 39.) The word *rĕḏîḏ* in the present passage may have arisen from a scribe's mistaking the similar letters *r* and *d* to produce *rdd*(*t*) from an original *ddd*(*t*) (*dudittu* having developed from *dudidtu*).

Robert took his cue from the mention of watchmen here and in 3:2–3 and accordingly envisioned the cadre of the scene to be Jerusalem as mentioned in Isa 52:8 and 62:6 with its walls rebuilt and watchmen stationed on them. Thus the date is some time after the first mission of Nehemiah, ca. 445 B.C., and the hostility of the guards may figure the evil disposition of the civil powers mentioned in Neh 5:13.

7. The Targum identified the city patrol as the Chaldeans who besieged Jerusalem:

> The Chaldeans, those who guard the roads, seized me and pressed me round about the city of Jerusalem, part of me they killed by the sword and part of me they carried into captivity. They lifted the royal crown off the neck of Zedekiah, King of Judah, and they brought Him to Riblah and they put out his eyes, the people of Babylon who harassed the city and watched the walls.

Midrash Rabbah here referred the city patrol to Tattenai and his associates (Ezra 5) and the wounding to the accusation they wrote against Judah and Jerusalem (Ezra 4:7). The previous explanation, that the watchmen are the Tribe of Levi (3:3), was repeated. The *rĕḏîḏ* taken from the Bride was explained as weapons inscribed with the Ineffable Name which God had given the Israelites at Horeb. After Israel sinned, the Name was removed. The keepers of the wall were explained as those who keep the walls of the Torah (i.e. who expound and administer it).

Christian expositors took the city watchmen to be the pagan Roman rulers who persecuted the Church and stripped the Martyrs of that outer veil of flesh which covered their souls. Again the veil was explained as the external aids of religion taken away when the priests were imprisoned, altars torn down, and Scriptures burned. With the city taken to mean the whole world, the watchmen were explained as the evil spirits who prowl the earth wounding souls, stripping them of their faith. The depredations suffered by the Bride led St. Jerome to advise Christian virgins that it is prudent to remain sheltered and not to venture forth even in search of Christ. The watchmen, taken in a favorable sense, were explained as the Guardian Angels, or as the Saints. The Guardian Angels entrusted with the care of souls smite them with the sword of the Word of God and with tribulations and wound them with love, taking away the veil of carnal thoughts and habits which obscure the vision of the mind. Or the watchmen as the Apostles and Evangelists found the Jewish Church vainly seeking Christ and they wounded them with words and took away the veil of the ceremonial Law which lay on their hearts and hid from them the light of God's face. This is the veil of which the Apostle spoke, II Cor 3:13. As applied to the individual soul, it is found by the Church's watchmen who smite and wound her with the arrows of divine love, with counsels of mortification, and injunctions to repentance, taking from her the veil of ignorance and showing her how to abandon evil habits and serve God truly. (Cf. Littledale.)

8c. *What*. LXX, Syriac, and Vulgate ignore the interrogative *māh,* apparently missing the rhetorical intention to emphasize the message, as in Hosea 9:14,

Give them, O Yahweh!
What will you give them?
Aborting womb and dry breasts.

Like *KJ*, several modern versions omit the interrogative, e.g. *AT, RSV, JPSV; JB* and *NAB*, however, give it expression. *NEB* interestingly takes the *māh* as negative,

if you find my beloved, will you not tell him that I am faint with love?

8d. The expression here is the same as in 2:5c except for the introductory particles; here *še*, "that," and there, *kî*, "because, for." The versions, ancient and modern, generally render the same in both instances although the contexts are different; in the first instance the lovesickness is presumably caused by surfeit and the request is for stimulants, whereas the sickness in the present is occasioned by the lover's absence.

The first part of the charge, "I adjure you, Jerusalem girls," is repeated in 2:7, 3:5, 8:4 where the adjuration is by the gazelles and hinds of the field not to arouse or excite love until it is willing. Here the Jerusalem girls are adjured, without mention of gazelles or hinds (which LXX, however, supplies), that if they find the missing lover they should inform him of his lady's lovesickness. Robert apparently took this to mean that the unaroused, unready love previously mentioned is now "chose faite." The progress of the action, according to Robert, is evident. Harper was troubled by the apparent difficulty that the Shulamite's loss was only in a dream and now the author seems to represent her as carrying over her dream into real life. To critics who think that this verse and the following contain material inserted only to introduce some subsequent description of the Shulamite's beloved, Harper protested that, even if this is so, we should look for some rational and intelligible transition. But the only suggestion Harper could offer was that the dream is being related by the Shulamite while she is still not quite awake and she is represented as not distinguishing between dreams and reality. Robert noted that a number of authors, including Harper, had failed to understand that we are in the realm of fiction and he quoted Buzy to the effect that the actors are always at the mercy of the poet who calls on them and makes them speak at the whim of his poem or of his fantasy.

8. The Targum equated the Jerusalem girls with the prophets who are adjured to tell the deity of Israel's lovesickness:

> The Assembly of Israel replied: "I adjure you, O prophets, by the decree of the Word of YHWH, if our love should appear to you, tell Him that I am sick from love of Him."

Midrash Rabbah explained here that Israel in Egypt yearned for deliverance as a sick person yearns for healing.

Some Christian interpreters applied this verse to the yearning of the Blessed Virgin for the presence of her Divine Son after His Ascension to Heaven. Others saw here set forth the Communion of Saints in the bond of intercessory prayer. The Church boldly declares her love for Christ her Spouse and calls in the Apostles, Prophets, and Martyrs as her defenders, guardians, and perfectors of her hope, who intercede for the Bride, the Church militant, still veiled in mortal flesh, but eagerly longing to reach her divine Bridegroom. Thus, burning with love and devotion, she asks her faithful patrons for their prayers on her behalf, binds them with an oath. The Bride is sick of the love of worldly things, dead and crucified to earthly concerns, and they to her (Col 3:3; Gal 6:14). (Cf. Littledale.)

9a,c. MT *māh dôḏēḵ middôḏ* seems to say, literally, "What is your love(r) from a love(r)?" Since neither the LXX nor any modern translation makes grammatical sense of the MT, Albright proposed a minor emendation with a radical effect on the meaning. With the addition of another *k* following the *dôḏēḵ* the reading *māh dôḏēḵ kĕmô dôḏ* is achieved, and this, according to Albright, would mean: "What is wrong with thy lover as a lover?" (1963, 4). The sense thus achieved is difficult to reconcile with the immediate or larger context. One gets the distinct impression from our lady's exuberant praises that there is nothing wrong with her lover as a lover. The trouble is that he has absconded, leaving his consort lovesick. It does not seem likely that the lover's prowess would be thus impugned. The Jerusalem girls who are adjured to deliver the message to the absconded lover inquire as to the nature of this lover; they wish to know what he is like, how they will recognize him, and above all what makes him so special that his lady is so infatuated and lovesick? Vulgate brings out this concern for quality with *qualis est dilectus tuus ex dilecto*. The question gives cause for the glowing descriptive hymn.

A similar literary device is used in the Sumerian composition called "The Message of Lu-dingir-ra to His Mother," cf. below on vss. 10–15. Lu-dingir-ra's expressed concern that the courier might not know or recognize the "mother" serves as the provocation for the following hymn of praise in five parts or "signs." Approximately fifty lines are devoted to description of the remarkable lady in order that the courier may recognize her so that he may stand in her radiant presence and deliver the momentous message: "Your beloved son Lu-dingir-ra greets you." The message which the Jerusalem girls are pledged to deliver in case they find the absconded lover—that his lady is lovesick—is not mentioned again and is forgotten in the course of the impressive description of the intended recipient of the message.

9. The Targum attributed this verse to the prophets in querying Israel's intention and choice with respect to worship:

> The prophets answered and said to the House of Israel: "Which God do you wish to serve, O Assembly of Israel, fairest of all the peoples, and whom do you wish to fear that thus you adjure us?"

Midrash Rabbah attributed the queries to the other nations addressed to Israel, meaning to say, "What is your God more than other gods? What is your defender more than other defenders?"

Some Christian interpreters took the questions to be those asked by one believer of another whenever they desire to increase their affection for heavenly things. Some supposed that the questions are addressed to the Bride merely to give her the opportunity to dwell on the graces of her Beloved, while others assumed that the queries are made in earnest by weak and untried believers desiring to be instructed as to the identification marks of the true Christ in order to recognize Him among the welter of false pretenders. Again, the questions were attributed to the Angels who ask the Bride to tell what she has been able to learn of her Spouse, so as to love Him so, since even they who see Him face to face are not able to understand Him fully since He is not of their nature. They are eager to learn from her who suffers with and for Him the mystery of sorrow which is one of the "things into which angels long to look" (I Peter 1:12). (Cf. Littledale.)

10a. *radiant*. The adjective *ṣaḥ* is used of clear, warm or hot air or wind, Isa 18:4; Jer 4:11, and in Isa 32:4 of lucid words. In Lam 4:7 the verb (*ṣḥḥ*) is applied to Israel's princes as compared to milk. In Arabic *ṣḥḥ* is used primarily of health and the clear glowing complexion of radiant health, like the use of the word for "color," *laun,* in Iraqi Arabic with reference to one's state of health. In view of the following references to gold and precious stones, and the indications that the poet had in mind representation in the form of a statue made of precious materials, the word seems best rendered as "radiant."

ruddy. This is the regular adjective for the color "red," as applied to blood, II Kings 3:22; the juice of grapes, Isa 63:2; pottage, Gen 25:30; a cow, Num 19:2; a horse, Zech 1:8, 6:2. The verb is used of the bodies of Zion's princes, ruddier than coral, Lam 4:7. Commentators tend to refrain from remarking on the red coloration here, except to allegorize. The problem is whether the redness is intended to designate the normal color of a healthy body, or cosmetic artifice. In the Ugaritic epic and mythological texts there are references to redness in connection with toiletry. In the Keret Epic, the Father of the Gods appears in a dream to the suppliant king and orders him to cease weeping, to bathe and become red, and offer sacrifice (14 [KRT].2.60*ff*). Compliance with the divine command is related in terms almost identical with those of the imperative (14[KRT]3.154*ff*):

Krt awoke and it was a dream,
The servant of El, and t'was a vision.
He bathed and ruddled himself,
Washed his hands to the elbow,
His fingers to the shoulder.
He entered the shade of the tent.
He took a lamb of sacrifice in his hand,
etc.

In the Aqhat Epic, the murdered hero's sister Puġat performed her toilet, bathed and ruddled herself and put on a warrior's garments with sword in scabbard over this woman's apparel when she visited the camp of her brother's murderer. There is a significant item added to the description of Puġat's toilet, viz. mentioned of the substance used for the ruddling (19[1 AQHT].4.204*ff*):

She washed and ruddled herself,
Ruddled herself with *ġlp* . . .

J. C. de Moor (1968) has plausibly identified *ġlp* with the murex purple snail which, in addition to the principal use as a dye for textiles, was employed by the Romans as a cosmetic for face and hair. The cognate *'lp* is used in Gen 38:14 of Tamar's toilet in preparation for impersonating a sacred prostitute. G. R. Driver (1957) took the verb *tiṯ'allāp̄* to mean "she scented herself" although the ancient versions as well as the cognates suggest a cosmetic application rather than perfume. According to de Moor (214n2), there is no need to avoid a rendering like "to purple oneself, to make oneself up." There is, however, no indication that the present passage has to do with either the rosy glow of health, or its simulation with cosmetic art. Gerleman's citation of the description of the splendor of the high priest Simon when he emerged from the sanctuary, Sir 50:5*ff*, seems most apt. The appearance of the priest rivals a theophany:

> How glorious he was when the people gathered round him as he came out of the inner sanctuary!
> Like the morning star among the clouds, like the moon when it is full;
> like the sun shining upon the temple of the Most High, and like the rainbow gleaming in glorious clouds;
> like roses in the days of the first fruits, like lilies by a spring of water,
> like a green shoot on Lebanon on a summer day; like fire and incense in the censer,
> like a vessel of hammered gold adorned with all kinds of precious stones;
> like an olive tree putting forth its fruit, and like a cypress towering in the clouds.

The "strange mingling of colors," as Gilbert of Hoyland termed it, called forth its share of allegorizing on white and red, in connection with Isa 1:18, 63:2; Rev 1:13,16, 7:14, 19:13; Mark 9:3; Luke 23:11; cf. Littledale, ad loc. who cites among other hermeneutical gems an old Eucharistic hymn:

Ave Christi corpus verum,	Hail, O Flesh of Christ divine,
Ave dulce rubens merum,	Hail, O sweet and ruddy wine,
Caro cibus, sanguis potus,	Blood the cup, and Flesh the meat,
Et ubique Christus totus.	And in each is Christ complete.
Hic est Sponsus candidatus,	This is He, the Bridegroom, dight
Dilectus et rubricatus,	In His vesture red and white:
Castus ortus hunc albavit,	White, for Him a Virgin bore,
Sanguis fluens rubricavit.	Red, for He His Blood did pour.

10b. *Conspicuous.* LXX rendered *dāḡûl* as related to *deḡel* as a designation of a military unit, *eklelochismenos,* chosen from a *lochos.* Vulgate *electus, KJ* "chiefest," *AT, RSV* "distinguished," *JB* "to be known," *NEB* "a paragon," *JPSV* "pre-eminent," *NAB* "he stands out." In view of Gordis' connection of *deḡel* in 2:4, *dāḡûl* here, and *nidḡālôṯ* in 6:4,10 with Akkadian *dagālu,* "see," the rendering "conspicuous" appears to offer greater perspicuity than "distinguished."

a myriad. A myriad myriads, apart from the indefinite "innumerable," is the largest number offered by the Bible, cf. Dan 7:10. A myriad itself is a considerable quantity and is used occasionally in expressions designating a superlative quantity or quality; cf. Micah 6:7; Ps 3:7[6E], 91:7, Sir 47:6. The largest number so far attested in Ugaritic is three hundred myriad, i.e. three million, applied to Keret's army which figures in parallel to "innumerable," (14[KRT].2.88–90):

Your army, people aplenty, Three hundred myriads, Freemen innumerable.

A mere myriad is also used in Ugaritic as a superlative. The divine bowl of Baal is enigmatically characterized by the relative phrase "in which are buffalo by the myriad(s)" (4[51].1.44).

10. The Targum applied the white and ruddy appearance of the lover to God who spends day and night in the study of Scripture and Mishnah. The term *dāḡûl* was taken to refer to God's banner over the army of angels:

> Then the Assembly of Israel began to reflect on the praise of the Lord of the World, and she said: "That God do I desire to serve who is enveloped by day in a robe white as snow, and occupied with the twenty-four books of the Law and the words of the Prophets and the Writings, and by night with the six Orders of the Mishnah; and the glorious splendor of YHWH whose face shines like fire, from the magnitude of the wisdom and the judgment which He renews every day and will in the future publish for His people on the Great Day; and His banner is over a myriad myriads of angels who minister before Him.

Midrash Rabbah saw an antithesis between the white and the ruddy. God was white to Israel in Egypt, at the Reed Sea (Exod 12:12,29) and ruddy to the Egyptians (Exod 14:27). Again He is white to Israel on the Sabbath and on New Year, but ruddy on other days of the week, or year; or ruddy in this life and white in the world to come.

Christian expositors were able to find great variety of explanations for the whitish and ruddy hue of the Beloved. He is both white and ruddy because He gives the prizes of peace as well as war. He is white in love and gentleness to His Saints and penitents, but ruddy in anger against the ungodly and reprobate. The Hebrew word for "ruddy," *'āḏôm,* suggested Adam and Christ as the Second Adam who came to repair the loss incurred through the First Adam. His brightness reflects the glory of God (Heb 1:3). His garments are whiter than any earthly fuller can bleach (Mark 9:3). His head and hair white as wool or snow, eyes like a flame of fire, face like the sun shining in full strength (Rev 1:16). The word *'āḏôm* also evoked the epiphany from Edom of the crimson robed Treader of the Grapes of Wrath (Isa 63:1–6) and that firstborn who bartered his birthright for a bit of red pottage (Gen 25:29–30) and earned the name Edom. The white and the red further evoked the contrast presented in Isa 1:18, and the application to Christ's apparel, white and shining with the purity of His Virgin birth and ruddy with the Blood of His voluntary Passion. Again the white and the red were taken as types of His twofold character, as when He let Himself be arrayed by Herod in a white robe and by Pilate in purple (Luke 23:11), or when there issued from His side both blood and water (John 19:34). The blood-spattered vesture (Rev 19:13) pertains to His victorious royalty, while the white alb signifies

His everlasting priesthood. The white and the red were seen also as showing Christ under the Sacramental veil of the white bread and ruddy wine of the Eucharist. (Cf. Littledale.)

The term *dāḡûl,* as a passive participle related to the noun *deḡel,* "banner," "standard," is taken by LXX and Vulgate to mean "elect," *electus ex millibus.* The mention of a banner or standard recalled the root of Jesse destined to be raised as an ensign of the people whom the nations will seek (Isa 11:10). LXX rendered "elect from ten thousand," Vulgate "elect from thousands." Philo of Carpasia offered mystical explanations of the ten thousand; the thousand denotes perfection and He who is perfect came after the ten precepts of the Law, and, coming into the world from the Virgin's womb, passed over nine choirs of the Angelic hierarchy. The only begotten Son of the Father excels the thousand thousands who serve Him and the myriad myriads who stand before Him (Dan 7:10).

Rabbi Aqiba's exegesis of this verse as presented in Shirta is of particular interest and import:

Before all the Nations of the World I shall hold forth on the beauties and splendor of Him Who Spake and the World Came to Be! For, lo, the Nations of the World keep asking Israel, "What is thy Beloved more than another beloved, that thou dost so adjure us" (Cant 5:9), that for His sake you let yourselves be slain, as it is said, "Therefore do the maidens (*'lmwt*) love Thee" (Cant 1:3)—they love Thee to the point of death (*'d mwt*)!—and it is written, "Nay, but for Thy sake are we killed," etc. (Ps 44:23). Look you! you're attractive, look you! you're brave. Come, merge with us! But Israel replies to the Nations of the World: "Have you any notion of Him? Let us tell you a little bit of His Glory: My Beloved is white and ruddy," etc. (Cant 5:10*ff*).

And when the Nations of the World hear but a little bit of the Glory of Him Who Spake and the World Came to Be, they say to Israel, "Let us go along with you, as it is said, 'Whither is thy Beloved gone, O thou fairest among women? Whither hath thy Beloved turned Him, that we may seek Him with Thee?'" (Cant 6:1). But Israel replies to the Nations of the World: "You have no part of Him"; on the contrary, "My Beloved is mine, and I am His" (Cant 2:16), "I am my Beloved's and my Beloved is mine," etc. (Cant 6:3).

11a. A number of critics eliminate this bothersome line. Budde regarded it as debris from several stichoi now lost; Zapletal considered it as an explicative gloss to *'āḏôm,* "ruddy," of the preceding verse. Some of the Greek versions (Aquila, Symmachus) and Syriac appear to have read *'eḇen,* "stone," instead of *keṯem.* LXX apparently read *kĕp̄āz* and took it as a proper name, "gold of Kaiphaz." The term *keṯem,* whether of Egyptian or Sumerian origin, is a designation for some special kind of gold; so also is *pāz,* likewise of uncertain origin. The combination *keṯem pāz* is not attested elsewhere, but in Dan 10:5 the loins of the anthropoid apparition are girt with *keṯem 'ûp̄āz* and since *'ûp̄az* is otherwise unknown it seems likely that *'û* should be read *'ô,* "or," or corrected to *û,* "and," with *pāz* regarded as a gloss to *keṯem.* In

I Kings 10:18 the expression *zāhāb mûpāz* is interpreted by the Chronicler as *zāhāb ṭāhôr,* "pure gold," II Chron 9:17. The Targum took the expression as equivalent to *dĕhaḇ ṭāḇ,* "fine gold," and so also Vulgate, *aurum optimum.* Ibn Ezra understood *keṯem* as meaning "diadem" and *pāz* as "precious stones." Rashi was unusually vague with his rendering *sĕḡûlôṯ mĕlāḵîm,* "royal hoards," taking *ktm* in the sense of "hide," "conceal." The syntax of *keṯem pāz* is not a construct, or bound-form, like *keṯem 'ôpîr,* "gold of Ophir," but the two words are in apposition, like *na'ărāh bĕṯûlāh,* "a girl," "a virgin," Deut 22:28, or *zĕḇāḥîm šĕlāmîm,* "sacrifices, peace offerings," Exod 24:5.

The closest biblical parallel to this line is frequently ignored by commentators, apparently because it suggests an unwelcome line of interpretation. The vision of the great and shining image which Nebuchadnezzar saw in his troubled dream had a head of fine gold, Dan 2:32, whereas in Daniel's own vision of a similar image composed of various shiny metals and precious stones, Dan 10:5, the loins are golden. Friedrich Horst in a study of the forms of the ancient Hebrew love song (1935) mentioned the present passage in discussion of the "Beschreibungslied" (Arabic *waṣf*), but took no interest in the golden head. Wolfram Herrmann, however (1963) starting with the description of Sara's beauty in the Genesis Apocryphon from Qumran, concentrated on descriptions of feminine beauty because the evidences from Mesopotamia, in the main, are concerned with goddesses. The Egyptian descriptive song during the Eighteenth Dynasty becomes detached from religion and the court and passed over into the sphere of the love song. Here again Herrmann dealt only with descriptions of feminine pulchritude, and so too with respect to the Ugaritic and OT materials, returning finally to the starting point of Sara's beauty. For the present passage two features stressed by Herrmann with respect to the Mesopotamian materials are of crucial interest. First, the oldest examples belong in cultic connection to the sacred marriage, and secondly, Herrmann noted, the Sitz im Leben of the Sumero-Babylonian Descriptive Song is obviously the description of the representation of gods (Götterbild). Hallo has recently stressed that in many Sumerian and Akkadian hymns "the deity is apostrophized precisely in terms of the characteristics associated with the statue . . ." (1970, 120). The Akkadian "Göttertypentext" (*ANET,* 515) describes several statues, each following a standard pattern descending from head to foot. Similar is the description of gods seen by the Prince Kumma in his "Vision of the Netherworld" (*ANET,* 109*f*). The image or statue described in Nebuchadnezzar's vision, Dan 2:32*ff* had, like our present figure, a head of gold and a torso of various other materials; cf. below 5:14–15. At Minet el Beida a statuette of Baal was found with gold-plated head and silver-plated body, and at Ras Shamra another remarkable effigy executed in no less than five materials, electrum, gold, silver, bronze, and steatite.

Among recently published mythological texts from Ugarit there is one, unfortunately fragmentary and containing some obscure terms, which describes the god Baal as he takes his seat in his sanctuary and is later serenaded by his ever loving sister, the goddess Anat:

Baal sat as a mountain sits,
Hadd as [widely?] as the ocean;
In the midst of his mount, Divine Ṣapon,
In [the sanctuary], the mount of his
dominion.
Seven lightning bolts [ ],
Eight storehouses of thunder.
A lightning shaft he h[olds].
On (?) his head *tply*,
Ṭly between his eyes.
(UG 5.3.1.1–5)

The description continues with references to the god's feet, horns, head, and mouth. The parallels with the present passage were noted in a study by Fisher and Knutson (1969); for differing views with regard to certain details, cf. Pope and Tigay (1971), in which Tigay suggested that the enigmatic word *tply* possibly represents *tĕp̄illîn* or phylacteries, while the present writer proposed a possible relation to Akkadian *pelû,* "red." The difficulties presented by the parallel word *ṭly* are even more formidable and need not be discussed here. The point of interest here is the correspondence in order of the descriptions, from head to feet and back to the mouth, and the similarities with the order in the Mesopotamian Göttertypentext.

11b. *luxuriant*. The term *taltallîm* is hapax legomenon in the Old Testament, but occurs in rabbinic literature in the sense of "curls," in connection with *qĕwûṣṣôṯ,* "locks"; cf. 5:2*f*. The word has also in rabbinic usage the meaning "hillock(s)." Delitzsch, accordingly, rendered "His locks hill upon hill," similar to the Targum's interpretation *dĕḡûrîn dĕḡûrîn, cumuli cumuli.* Delitzsch explained that "Seen from the neck upwards, his hair forms in undulating lines, hill upon hill." LXX rendered *elatai* which term is applied to palm buds, or the spathe or sheath of the palm bud, and Vulgate supplied the word for palm, *sicut elatae palmarum.* Akkadian *taltallū* is applied to the pollen of the date panicle and Arabic *taltalat* is used of the envelope or spadix of the date palm as well as of a drinking vessel made of this envelope. The word **taltall* is similar in pattern to three other hapax legomena which designate plant shoots or branches, *zalzallîm* (Isa 18:5), *salsillôṯ* (Jer 6:9), and *sansinnîm;* cf. 7:9. The long black hair of the maiden in Arabic poetry is also likened to date clusters and to vines; cf. Ilse Lichtenstädter (1931–32, 43).

11c. *black*. The word here is the same as in 1:5,6 and is the usual term for blackness. Among dark-haired peoples, black hair is naturally associated with youth and health. The priest in examining for skin diseases checked whether the hairs were (healthy) black or (morbid) white, Lev 13:31,37. In Eccles 11:10 the term *šaḥărûṯ* used in apposition to *yalḏûṯ,* "childhood," or "youth," probably refers to "blackness" (of the hair) rather than to "dawn," i.e. to the prime of life rather than "the beginning of life" (*RSV*). Medieval Muslim literature is replete with allusions to black hair as the sign of youth and grey of advancing age; cf. Hasan Ali Shuraydi, 1971, ch. II, "The Physical Qualities of Youth."

raven. The raven or crow, *'ôrēḇ* (Akkadian *āribu,* Arabic *ġurâb*) is mentioned in the Old Testament as unclean (Lev 11:15; Deut 14:14) and as a scavenger (Prov 30:17; Job 38:41), but for its blackness only in the present passage. In Arabic poetry it is a common comparison for blackness and especially black hair.

11. The Targum applied this verse to the excellence and the riches of the Law:

> As for His Law, it is more desirable than pure gold; and the interpretation of the Words in which are heaps (and) heaps of meanings and precepts for those who keep them they are white as snow, and those who do not keep them are like the face of the raven.

Midrash Rabbah explained the head as the Torah (Prov 8:22) and the fine gold as the words of the Torah (Ps 19:11[10E]). The curly locks were referred to the ruled lines (required for writing sacred texts). The blackness was applied to the letters. The words for "locks," "curls," and "black," suggested a series of word plays. His locks (*qĕwûṣôṯāyw*) suggested the ornamental strokes or thorns (*qôṣîm*) on the letters and the curls (*taltallîm*) "heaps of heaps" (*tillê tillîm*), thus even details of the Torah which appear to be mere strokes are thorns upon thorns and heaps upon heaps. (Cf. TB Erubin 21–23). The word for "raven," (*'ôrēḇ*) suggested the evening (*ma'ărîḇ*) and observations that the full crop of the Torah is garnered by night (Prov 31:15; Lam 2:19) or both day and night (Josh 1:8). Simeon ben Laqish remarked that often after he had labored at the Torah by day, it became clear to him at night. Several parallels and puns are offered on the learning of masses and details of Torah. The smallest letter, *yôḏ,* (the Greek *iota*) cannot be removed from the Torah (cf. Matt 5:18). The raven locks were also applied to the students of the Torah who look black and repulsive in this world, but in the time to come their appearance will be like torches and lightning (Nahum 2:5[4E]v.4]). Again the blackness suggested those texts of the Torah regarded as too repulsive to be recited in public, but which are especially pleasant (*'ārēḇôṯ*) to God (Mal 3:4). The proof of this is that the sections dealing with flux in males and females are separated (Lev 15). The blackness was also explained as writing of black fire on a white fire scroll given by God to Moses (Deut 33:2).

The Talmud (TB Hagigah 14a) explains that there is no contradiction between the representation of God with snow white hair in Dan 7:9 and with raven black locks in the present verse, since God assumes whatever appearance suits the occasion. In Canticles, He is portrayed as fighting against the Egyptians on Passover and in Dan 7:9 as judge. The white head is appropriate to the judicial role and black headed youth to the martial role.

The Church Fathers for the most part took their cue from the Apostle's affirmation that "the Head of Christ is God," I Cor 11:3, and related the pure gold to the Godhead, but also to the Head of the Man Christ Jesus in whom shone the brightness of deity, or to Christ as the sinless Head of the Church. The LXX reading "gold of Kaiphaz" was taken by Philo of Carpasia to refer to Cephas or

St. Peter as the head of Christ's mystical Body, the Church. Some of contemplative turn saw in the gold head the emblem of the inexhaustible treasures of divine illumination bestowed on the Saints who seek the perfect knowledge of God. The bushy or curly locks were taken to denote the Saints, Angels, Apostles and Martyrs who are closest to the Head. Other possibilities suggested by the word *elatai* were exploited; taken to mean "pines," application was made to the stately height attained by the Apostles, or to the Saints or the Church as pine-built ship sailing over the world as a life-boat for mankind. Some supposed that the *elatai* were aromatic and evergreen which afforded new resources for edifying allegory. The blackness of the locks was taken to denote the humility of the Saints, or their sinfulness as compared to the golden glory of the Head. As applied to Christ, the blackness stands in contradiction to the snow white hair of the visions in Dan 7:9 and Rev 1:14, but this was reconciled by relating the white to the holiness of His virgin life and the black to His passion when he was scorched with the fire of suffering. The blackness also related to the Divine attributes as well as to the mysteries of Holy Scripture which are alike hidden from us by impenetrable darkness (Ps 18:11). (Cf. Littledale.)

By way of modern allegory, Robert cited Joüon's application of this verse to the costume of the high priest and the following verses to the Temple of Jerusalem and suggested that the latter direction is the one in which the explication of verse is to be sought. A priori no hypothesis is more likely, according to Robert. The bride being identified by the Canticle with the land of Palestine (8:2–6 is offered as special proof-text for this allegation), it is normal that, by analogy, Yahweh should be identified with the Temple. The inspiration of 5:11–15, according to Robert, is the account of the construction of the Temple by Solomon in I Kings 6–7. Gold is several times mentioned, I Kings 6:21b,22,32,35, and especially vss. 20 and 21a which mention pure gold, *zāhāḇ, sāgûr*. In Robert's view, the gold head of the groom is assimilated to the gold-plated Holy of Holies of the Temple.

12a. *like doves.* Cf. 1:15, 4:1, where the eyes are equated with, rather than compared to, doves. The question whether the eyes are compared to doves' eyes or to the whole doves seems answered by what follows. The eyes are like doves by the watercourses or pools.

12b. MT "bathing in milk," LXX "bathed in milk," Vulgate *quae lacte sunt lotae*. Doves are fond of bathing and choose their abodes in regions with abundant water, but they rarely have the opportunity to bathe in milk. The bright eyes of the lover, the dark pupils encircled by milky white eyeballs, remind the poet of doves bathing in pellucid streams. The Gita-Govinda, sometimes termed the Indian Song of Songs, offers a similar description of eyes: "The glances of her eyes played like a pair of water birds of azure plumage that sport near a full-blown lotus pool in the season of dew."

12c. The meaning of this unique expression *yôšeḇôṯ 'al-millē'ṯ* is uncertain. LXX rendered "sitting by the fulness of water" and similarly Vulgate *et residént juxta fluenta plenissima*. Luther preserved the enigma with "und stehen in der Fülle," "and stand in the fullness." The use of *millū'* with reference to the setting of jewels and inlay of precious stones, as in Exod 25:7, 28:17, 35:9,27, 39:13 and I Chron 29:2, suggested similar sense here and thus *KJ* and *RSV* rendered "fitly set." The practice of making statues with eyes of jewel inlay would seem to support this interpretation. *NAB,* however, applied the milk bath and jewel inlay to the lover's dentition:

> His eyes are like doves beside running waters,
> His teeth would seem bathed in milk, and set like jewels.

Delitzsch opined that *millē't̠* could not refer to water without the expression of the word and Harper suggested the emendation *millē't̠* to *mĕlô' hammayim,* "sitting upon full streams." Kuhn emended *millē't̠* to *mik̠lā'ôt̠,* "enclosures," on the assumption that the doves needed to be near sheep pens in order to bathe in milk. Meek (*IB,* V) cited Akkadian *milû,* "flood," in support of *AT*'s rendering "sitting by a pool." The context appears to favor the dove bath over the jewel inlay, as with recent renderings, *JB* "at rest on a pool," *JPSV* "Set by a brimming pool," and *NEB* "as they sit where water is drawn."

12. The Targum applied the dove eyes to the divine surveillance of Jerusalem in appreciation of those who study the Law:

> His eyes are looking constantly toward Jerusalem to do good to her and to bless her, from the beginning of the year to the end of the year, like doves that stand and look toward the streams of water, on account of the merit of those who sit in the Sanhedrin, occupied with the study of the Law, making justice stream smoothly like milk, and those who sit in the House of Study circumspect in judgment until they determine to acquit or to condemn.

Midrash Rabbah identified the eyes with the Sanhedrin, citing Num 15:24 with reference to the eyes of the congregation. As the two hundred and forty-eight members of the body are all directed by the eyes, Israel can do nothing without the Sanhedrin. The Midrash further related *ml't* to the fulness of the Torah. The similar form *ml'ty* in Isa 1:21 has the numerical value of four hundred and eighty-two which was taken as the number of synagogues in Jerusalem.

Christian expositors saw the eyes as the Prophets and Seers of the Old Testament and the Overseers of the Church. The contemplative Saints who ever look to God were compared to doves in their innocence and the water represented either the baptismal font or the Holy Scriptures from which they ever drink and saw themselves mirrored as well as the hawk or other enemy that may approach. The milk represented sincerity. Gregory of Nyssa saw in the rivers of waters the holy virtues which wash away contrary vices. For Philo of Carpasia the Saints were like doves' eyes by reason of the gifts of the Holy Spirit. Or, as in the Targum, the eyes were those of God which are over the righteous, Ps 34:15, and brighter than the sun, beholding the conduct and secrets of men, Sir 23:19. Again the eyes are the inner eyes of Christ's Humanity, His wisdom and knowledge shining with dovelike simplicity and attested also by the clear and candid aspect of His bodily eyes. (Cf. Littledale.)

Robert, in keeping with his view that the preceding and following verses relate to the Temple, found here, as in vs. 13, an allusion to the bronze sea of Solomon's Temple (I Kings 7:23–26; II Chron 4:2–5). The expression *'ăp̄îqê mayim,* he asserted, applies perfectly to a basin of such ample dimension, as does the word *millē't;* the two thousand *bat* capacity amounting to some four hundred and fifty hectoliters (ca. twelve thousand gallons). Doves bathing in milk evoked for Robert the idea of extreme whiteness and from that he moved to the assumption that the poet had in mind the purification of the priests which was the purpose of the bronze laver, the great reservoir of lustral water (Exod 30:18–21, 38:8, 40:32; cf. II Chron 4:6).

13a. *cheeks.* The word *lĕḥî* (**liḥy*) does not of itself denote the beard, but the cheek or jaw where the beard, if there is any, grows. In 1:10 the beauty of the bride's cheeks is noted.

beds. Reading the plural *'ărûḡôṯ* instead of the singular (*'ărûḡaṯ*), with LXX and some Hebrew MSS, as in 6:2 where the same expression is used of the lady's charms parallel with "garden." In Ezek 17:7,10 the term is also used in the plural of garden beds. In Arabic the word is said to designate a piece of sandy ground good for producing plants. The verb in Hebrew is twice used of animals longing for water, Ps 42:2[1E]; Joel 1:20. The Arabic use of the verb in the factitive stem in the sense of "build in a sloping line," or "in steps," suggests the meaning "terraces." LXX here read *phialai,* "vials," but Symmachus rendered *prasiai* and Vulgate *areolae.* Modern English versions generally follow *KJ*'s "bed," but read the plural, "beds of spices." The reference may be to the use of perfume oil on the beard; cf. Ps 133:2.

13b. *Burgeoning.* Reading *mĕḡaddĕlôṯ* rather than MT *migdĕlôṯ,* "towers," as with LXX *phuousai.* The *pi'el* or factitive stem of *gdl* is used of growing plants and children, Ps 144:12, and hair, Num 6:5.

Gerleman retains the reading "towers" and thinks to have found the explanation of the "towers of ointment" (Salbtürme) from Egyptian illustrations of festal affairs in the New Kingdom in which the heads of distinguished guests are decorated with a peculiar cone-shaped top which Erman has explained as an "ointment cone" (Salbkegel) which gives the head of the wearer a precious odor. The difference between head and cheeks did not deter Gerleman who noted the description of the cheeks is dominated by a single idea, leaving aside all accidental and subordinate details, that of fragrance, which in ancient oriental love poetry had the function of an erotic topos immediately comprehensible, the force of which conception does not need to be confirmed by particular realism.

aromatics. This form, *merqāḥîm,* is hapax legomenon in the Old Testament, but it is clear from the context that the reference is to aromatic herbs or spices. Various forms of the root *rqḥ* are used in the Old Testament of perfume ointment and the perfume apothecary. Both this word and the preceding one are absent from the Syriac. Vulgate *consitae a pigmentariis* may or may not reflect the reading *nĕṭû'ôṯ mērôqĕḥîm.*

13c. Syriac supplies the comparative particle here which is quite unnecessary since the force of the particle *k-* in 13a can extend to this line and no particle is required in the first place, since the equation of two very different items amounts to a comparison.

lotuses. Cf. 2:1,16, 4:5, 6:2, 7:3[2E]. In imitation of 4:3a Rothstein altered *šôšannîm* to *šānî,* "crimson," on the ground that comparison with the pale lily could not be applied to the lips of a healthy and vigorous man. The flower in question, whether lily, anemone, or lotus, must be reddish or purplish.

13d. Cf. 4:11, 5:5b. Syriac reads "myrrh and nard," which Graetz accepted. Robert, like Delitzsch, understood the figure to apply to sweetness of speech rather than to kisses (Siegfried) or aromatic breath (Rosenmüller, Budde, Harper, Fillion). The Canticle begins with explicit reference to kisses and it seems likely that the several references to mouth, lips, and tongue are intended to include amative oral activities other than sweet-talk. The suggestion that "lips" here refer to the mustache (Haupt, Staerk, Miller) is unlikely since there is a special term for this, *śāp̄ām.*

Robert managed to discover in the poet's admiration of the cheeks and beard of the Beloved and the celebration of the charm of his discourse an evocation of items relating to the Temple. Solomon, according to I Kings 6:29 decorated the walls of the sanctuary, inside and out, with carved figures of cherubim, palm trees, and open flowers. The imagination of the poet, according to Robert, sees in the walls of the edifice the cheeks of the Bridegroom: the vegetal motifs become the flower beds of aromatic plants figuring his beard anointed with perfumed oil. Moreover, the allusion to the bronze sea divined in 5:12 seemed to Robert to return here, since its brim (lip) was like that of a cup (and like[?]) a lily (lotus?) flower (*peraḥ šôšān*). Here again the allegory was transparent to Robert.

Targum based its interpretation on the reading *lûaḥ,* "tablet," rather than *lĕḥî,* "cheek," and related the line to the giving of the Ten Words.

> The two stone tablets which He gave to His people were written in ten lines resembling the lines of the spice garden, multiplying details and meanings as the garden multiplies spices; and the lips of His sages who are occupied with the Law distil sense (taste) on every side and the word of their mouth is like choice myrrh.

Midrash Rabbah referred the lily lips to the scholar fluent in Mishnah and the myrrh-dripping lips to one not so fluent, but who reviews (*'ôḇēr*) and repeats what he has learned and masters it.

This verse was taken by R. Joshua ben Levi (TB Shabbat 88b) to mean that with every word that went forth from God's mouth the whole world was filled with spices. But since the world was thus filled from the first word, where did the spice of the second word go? God brought forth the wind from His store-chambers and made each fragrance pass in order, as it says, "His lips are *šôšannîm,* dropping myrrh that passes on" (taking *'ôḇēr* here in its usual sense) and reading *šeššônîm,* "which repeat in succession," instead of *šôšannîm,* "lilies" (lotuses). Other word plays were made on *mōr,* "myrrh," as *mar,* "bitterness," and *šôšannîm* as *šeššônîm,* "repetitions," i.e. study (TB Shabbat 30b, Pesaḥim 117a).

R. Eleazar (TB Erubin 54a) expounded the text "His cheeks are a bed of spices" thus: "If a man allows himself to be treated as a bed on which everybody treads and as a spice with which everyone perfumes himself, his learning will be preserved. Otherwise it will not."

Christian expositors also followed this line, applying it to the preachers of the Gospel, the Martyrs, and even the Confessors who bind the impenitent and loose the penitent. Theodoret applied the lines to the teachings of the Master, as in Luke 14:26 and Matt 19:21, rather than to the servants. The lips, whether ruddy or pale, reminded some of the Master's counsels, the pale lips especially, of His dying hour and their utterance of the Seven Words. (Cf. Littledale.)

14a. *arms.* Lit. "hands," but in biblical usage as in Ugaritic, "hands" and "fingers" can reach as far as the armpit and the shoulder. In Gen 24:30 "hand" as the place where a bracelet is worn is at least as far up as the wrist. In Ezek 13:18 it is not clear what part of the arm is meant by the term *'aṣṣîlê yāḏ* (*KJ* "armholes," *RSV* "wrists"), but in Jer 38:12 it is generally agreed that the term applies to the armpits where the rags were put as pads for the ropes to lift Jeremiah out of the cistern. In Ugaritic the proof passage is in the description of King Keret's lustrations:

He washed his hands to the elbow, His fingers up to the shoulder.
(14[KRT].3.157–158)

rods. LXX *torneutai,* Vulgate *tornatiles,* "turned in a lathe." In I Kings 6:34 the term *gĕlîlîm* is twice used of some part of the doors of the inner sanctuary of Solomon's Temple. The usual guess is that the reference is to "folding" doors which is not incompatible with the basic sense of the "root" *gll,* "roll." The only other occurrence of the word in the Old Testament is in Esther 1:6 where it is used in connection with the fastening of curtains and draperies of the royal palace in Susa and it is not clear whether it refers to silver rings or rods; it is there associated with pillars of marble which seems to favor the meaning "rods." As applied strictly to the hands, neither rings nor rods seem especially appropriate, but with reference to the arms as extensions of the hands the rendering "rods" seems most suitable. The use of the term as a geographical designation in Isa 8:23[9:1E] has no relevance here. The explanation of Cocceius that the hand, when curved to grasp anything, resembles a ring was adopted by Dom Calmet, Fillion, and Renan. Joüon supposed that the description referred to bracelets so large and thick that the whole forearm appeared to be covered with gold. For the reasons noted above, the choice is "arms" rather than "hands," in agreement with *RSV* and *NAB.*

Robert again imagined that our author found his inspiration in the account of the construction of the Temple in I Kings 7:15–22. The word *gĕlîlîm* Robert here rendered "globes," "Ses mains sont des globes d'or." The gold globes are not derived from the account in the Book of Kings (except perhaps from the word *gālîl* in I Kings 6:34), but the imagination of the poet embellished the basic text, according to Robert.

14b. *Studded.* Lit. "filled." Cf. 12c.

gems. The word *taršîš* designates much discussed but still unknown geographical location(s), as well as a precious stone of uncertain nature. The ships of Tarshish were probably a refinery fleet. The jewel *taršîš* is also mentioned in Exod 28:20, 39:13; Ezek 1:16, 10:9, 28:13; Dan 10:6. The variety of renderings by both ancient and modern versions reveal the utter uncertainty as to the identity of the jewel. LXX here merely transliterated the word, Vulgate rendered *hyacinthus* which anciently designated a bluish gem and in modern use a reddish-orange variety of zircon. Modern versions variously render "beryl," "chrysolite," "rubies," "topaz," "jewels," or "jewels/stones of Tarshish." We have no means at present to identify the gem.

Again the wording is most appropriate to the description of a precious icon of a deity.

14c. *loins.* Cf. 5:4b where the term designates the female's reaction to intromission. Robert was certainly right in asserting, against Dom Calmet, that the term (*mēʿîm*) does not here designate the entrails, and mostly correct in his observation that there is no authority for extending the word to mean reins (Renan), chest, or torso (Joüon, Ricciotti, Buzy), body (Harper, *Bible du Rabbinat,* Dussaud—to which may be added *AT, RSV, NAB*). Robert adduced Dan 2:32 in support of the explanation that term here designates the belly or abdomen, seen from the outside. The description in Dan 2:32 divides the image into head, chest, arms, the present term, then thighs, legs, and feet. The term in this instance obviously designates the area below the chest and above the crotch. The rendering "body" is too general, "waist" is too narrow, and belly is a one-sided term, designating only the ventral to the exclusion of the dorsal side of the area in question. The term "loins" includes the lumbar region, front, back, and sides.

smoothest. The noun *ʿešeṯ* is hapax legomenon and the verb likewise is used only once, Jer 5:28, where it follows *šmn* in the sense of "become fat," and thus apparently means something like "be smooth," or "sleek," "they have grown fat and sleek." LXX rendered *puxion,* "box," or "tablet," but Vulgate ignored the difficult word. Luther took the word in the sense of "pure," "Sein Leib ist wie reines Elfenbein." *KJ* rendered "bright," *AT* "column," *RSV, NAB* "work" (with a note that the meaning of the Hebrew is uncertain); *JB* "a block," *JPSV* "a tablet," *NEB* "a plaque." Delitzsch suggested that the word designates an artistic figure, this sense proceeding from the fundamental idea of smoothing, like Arabic *ḫalaq,* and he rendered

"His body an ivory work of art." In the light of the only clue to the basic meaning of the term in Jer 5:28, the best guess seems to be "smoothness" or the like. The use here is possibly superlative, like *qĕṭan bêṯô,* "the small one of his house," i.e. the smallest.

ivory. Lit. "tooth," *šēn,* i.e. of the elephant. Elsewhere the term for ivory is *šenhabbîm,* the latter element representing the ancient Egyptian and African term reflected in the name Yeb for Elephantine, and in Sanskrit *ibha.* The Akkadian *šinni-pīri,* presumably reflects another word for elephant, later Hebrew *pîl,* Arabic *fīl.* Ivory is noted for its smoothness and sheen and thus comports with the presumed sense of the preceding word *'ešeṯ.* Delitzsch understood that Solomon's own person is praised as being like an artistic figure made of ivory—like it in regard to its glancing (*sic,* and perhaps intentional on the part of the translator) smoothness and its fine symmetrical form, but without reference to a definite admired work of art. Again the variety of materials, gold, jewels, and ivory suggest the sort of stature described in Dan 2:32 and the statuettes from Ugarit executed in several different materials.

14d. *Encrusted.* LXX *epi lithou,* "upon stone," hardly indicates the bizarre reading proposed by Kuhn, *mē'al paṯ sappîrîm,* "auf einem Stück von Saphiren." As Robert noted, *paṯ* is never used of anything in the Old Testament except a piece of bread. It is likely that the LXX translator guessed at the meaning of *mĕ'ullep̄eṯ.* Vulgate did somewhat better with *distinctus sapphiris.* Graetz's emendation to *mĕ'uppeleṯ,* "gehoben durch Saphire," is quite unnecessary. The metaphorical use of the reflexive stem of *'lp* in the sense of "swoon," Amos 8:13; Jonah 4:8, is understandable on the analogy of current expressions like "black out" in the sense of be covered with the darkness of unconsciousness. Whether the usage in Gen 38:14 refers to Tamar's covering herself with a mantle or with perfume (cf. 5:10a, s.v. "ruddy"), the Arabic *ġlp* "cover," "envelope," and the Ugaritic use of the noun with reference to a sheath or husk of grain (apart from its possible application to the envelope of the murex shellfish; cf. NOTE on "ruddy" in vs. 10a above), is sufficient to satisfy the sense required in the present passage.

sapphires. Hebrew *sappîrîm.* The term is supposedly from Sanskrit *çanipriya,* "Darling of Saturn," the name coming with the importation of the stone. The term is thought to designate not the true sapphire, but lapis lazuli, a limestone impregnated with blue grains and auriferous pyrites, called in Akkadian *uqnû* and in Ugaritic *iqnu.* The lapis lazuli of the ancients, according to Haupt, appears to have come from the famous Badakhshan mines in northeastern Afghanistan, near Mazar-i-Ilakh, fifteen hundred feet above the bed of the Kokcha, a tributary of the Oxus.

Joüon argued that the sapphire covering shows that the reference is not to the nude chest or torso but to clothing covering that part of the body. No little concern was evinced over the question whether the groom was pictured as nude or clothed. Buzy was confident that the figure was clothed because his external and distinctive appearance is described so that he can be recognized. The logic of this argument is elusive, since one could also be distinctive without clothing. In Delitzsch's view, "That which is here compared is nothing else than the branching blue veins under the white skin." Haupt saw the blue as referring to tattoo marks. Some have supposed that the reference is to a bejeweled belt or girdle.

Robert admitted with respect to the present lines that there is not a word that sends us back to the account relative to the construction of the Temple in I Kings and yet, he alleged, the context invites us to seek the key to the enigma there. The key, for Robert, was the term *'ûlām* in I Kings 6:3, 7:19 (cf. Ezek 40:48–49), a technical architectural term for the massive construction of the entry gate. This vestibule was twenty cubits long, equal to the width of the Temple, and ten cubits deep. According to Robert, one will willingly concede that to the eyes of our author this vestibule figures the beloved's belly, the word *'ûlām* coming from *'wl,* "be in front, march at the head." Moreover, it was a polished, white mass, constructed like the rest of the Temple, of beautiful, cut stones carefully fitted (I Kings 6:7). The sapphires, according to Robert, may allude to sculptures. An analogous comparison Robert found in Lam 4:7 and Isa 54:11.

14. The Targum related the bejeweled body to the various precious stones on which the names of the Twelve Tribes were engraved:

> The twelve tribes of Jacob his servant were enrolled on the plate, the holy golden ornament, engraved on twelve gems, with the three fathers, Abraham, Isaac, and Jacob. Reuben was engraved on ruby, Simeon was engraved on carnelian, etc. They were like the twelve constellations, shining like a lantern, bright and shining like sapphires.

Midrash Rabbah related the polished ivory body to the priestly law of the Book of Leviticus; as the belly is in the middle of the body, so Leviticus stands midway in the Pentateuch. And as a block of ivory can make many nails or javelins, so the book contains many precepts and minutiae. The sapphire was taken as referring to the hardness of the Law which wears out man's strength, as a sapphire imported from Rome was allegedly tried with hammer or anvil, both of which shattered without breaking the sapphire. A play was made on the reflexive form of *'lp* in the sense of "swoon," "faint." The man who grows faint (*niṯ'ălēp̄*) over study of Torah and Halakah will eventually be able to conjure with them.

The Bridegroom's belly also suggested some interesting ideas to Christian exegetes. Theodoret, taking the cue from the LXX's *pyxion* in the sense of "box" referred it to the storehouse of Divine Wisdom. Philo of Carpasia related the Bridegroom's belly to the Law which contained also oracles, prophecies, and typological allusions to Christ. The belly as the weakest and most delicate part of the human body was taken by Cassiodorus to represent the frailty of Christ's assumed Humanity and the ivory its spotless incorruption. The blue of the sapphires suggested the heavenly graces and powers with which Christ's Manhood was endowed, as it says in Exod 24:10, "and they saw the God of Israel, and there was under his feet, as it were, a pavement of sapphire stone, like the very heaven for clearness." (Cf. Littledale.)

15a. *legs.* The term *šôq* here apparently includes the leg in its entirety, not just the thighs, since no mention is made of other parts of the legs or of the feet. In Sir 26:18 beautiful legs and feet of a woman are likened to gold pillars on silver bases.

marble. The term *šēš* (perhaps derived from Armenian *šiš*) designates alabaster or white marble. In Esther 1:6 marble pillars are mentioned in addition to marble pavement of various hues. In I Chron 29:2 (in the form *šayiš*) it is among the precious stones collected for the building of the Temple. Haupt supposed that the legs are characterized as white marble columns because they are not so much exposed to the sun as the bronzed feet represented by the golden sockets. Harper thought that since the lover is an Oriental, and therefore brown in complexion, alabaster would be a better comparison than marble.

15b. *Based.* The verb *ysd* is used in the basic, factitive and causative stems of the laying of foundations of walls and buildings, the world, and especially the Temple.

sockets. Or, perhaps, pedestals. The term *'eden* designates various sorts of sockets, bases, pedestals, used of the bases for the frames of the Tabernacle (Exod 26:19), and the bases of pillars (Exod 27:11; Num 3:36*f*[4:31*f*E]) and the foundations of the earth (Job 38:6). Gerleman remarked that here the socket is that of a statue, on which the legs rest like pillars. In Egyptian sculpture in the round, the socle was a necessary appurtenance of the statue; cf. Gerleman ad loc. and p. 69. In Lu-dingir-ra's description of his mother, she is characterized as "an alabaster statuette, set on a lapis pedestal" (cf. above, p. 71).

Robert supposed that the author may have had in mind the colonnades around the Temple of Solomon.

15c. *aspect.* Or "appearance." The Syriac reading "his chest" instead of "his appearance" apparently came about by confusion of the letters *z* and *d*. In 2:14c the term *mar'eh* is applied to the whole form and figure of the bride.

Lebanon. The awe-inspiring majesty of Lebanon seems somewhat hyperbolic for a mere man, even a king. Delitzsch, nevertheless, understood it of Solomon rising high above the common man, like the cedars, those kings among trees, which as special witnesses of creative omnipotence are called "cedars of God," Ps 80:11[10E].

15d. *Choice.* Symmachus' *neaniskos,* "young man," interpreted *bāḥûr* as a substantive, and likewise the Targum's *'ûlēm,* "like a youth, a warrior, strong as the cedar." LXX *eklektos* and Vulgate *electus* seem to be the only likely sense. The emendation of *bāḥûr* to *'addîr,* on the basis of Ezek 17:23 (Dalman, Dussaud, Haupt) has little to commend it. In Isa 37:24 the term *mibḥar bĕrôšāyw,* "choicest of its firs," stands in parallelism with *qômaṯ 'ărāzāyw,* "tallest of its cedars." That such parallels are heritages of a long poetic tradition is shown by the Ugaritic parallel:

Lebanon and its trees　　Si[r]yon choicest of its cedars.
(4[51].6.20–21)

The terms *bāḥûr* and *mibḥār* are roughly equivalent to Ugaritic *mḥmd,* "choice(est)." In I Sam 9:2 Saul is characterized as *bāḥûr wāṭôḇ* which is usually rendered "a handsome young man," but may perhaps better be rendered literally, "choice and good." Joüon noted apropos of *bāḥûr* that the word implies superiority in comparison with things of the same order, and Robert, in citing this observation, added that this is precisely the idea affirmed at the beginning of the description and which had been the occasion of it (vss. 9–10) and it is normal that it reappear in the "jugement d'ensemble" at the end.

15c,d. The references to Lebanon and cedars were related by Robert to the Temple, as one would by now expect. Cedars were used in profusion, for the roof, the annexes, the wainscoting; they covered the entire walls, to the point that "all was cedar" (I Kings 6:9,10,15,16,18); the incense altar was covered with it (vs. 20); even the inner court was partly built with cedars (6:36, 7:12). Since the cedar was one of the most notable particularities of Solomon's Temple and one of the most expressive indexes of its splendor, we should not be astonished, according to Robert, to see the author of the Canticle sum up by this evocation the bride's impressions of her beloved.

The description of the male lover in 5:10–16 was recognized by Gordis (1954, 33) as in part highly extravagant and surpassing the limits of mere metaphor. Accordingly, Gordis conjectured that the phrases of 5:11,14,15 may be more than mere poetic hyperbole. The basis for this suggestion was the similarity of the aforementioned outlandish metaphor or hyperbole to an Akkadian adjuration for the recovery of a sick man:

Like lapis lazuli I want to cleanse my body,
Like marble his features should shine,
Like pure silver, like red gold,
I want to make clean what is dull.
(Cf. Ebeling, 1931, 37)

"The Biblical *waṣf,*" Gordis suggested, "may therefore be extolling the health and potency of the lover." It is obvious that the present *waṣf,* vss. 10–16, does extol the health, beauty, and sexual appeal of the male protagonist. It is not so obvious why the poet would use a literary form associated with incantations for healing sexual impotence, since there is no hint that our hero has been so afflicted. A relevant consideration which Gordis did not mention is the use of magical statues in conjunction with incantations for healing. The incantation intended to make the ailing human as clean and healthy and shiny bright as the magical statue of the deity which was composed of gold, silver, lapis lazuli, marble, and other beautiful and bright materials. In a fragmentary passage of the Gilgamesh Epic (VIII rev. ii 26), Gilgamesh had a statue made of his late companion Enkidu:

Then Gilgamesh issued a call to the land: O smith, [. . .],
Coppersmith, goldsmith, lapidary! Make my friend [. . .]!
[Then] he fashioned a statue for his friend,
The friend whose stature [. . .]:
[. . .], of lapis is thy breast, of gold thy body, [. . .].
(Cf. *ANET*², 515)

It is hard to know what sort of ritual Gilgamesh was performing for the defunct Enkidu, unless he was trying to cure him of death or assure him of well-being in the afterlife. In any case, there is nothing in Canticles 5:10–16 to suggest a healing ritual. Moreover, the description of the lover in terms of a statue composed of precious metals, stones and gems, suggests that the hero is none other than the great god of sexual power and fertility, Baal, the consort of Ishtar.

15. The Targum saw the marble pillars as students of the Law and the countenance like Lebanon as the Venerable One who changes Israel's guilt to the whiteness of snow:

> As for the righteous, they are the pillars of the world, resting on bases of pure gold, those words of the Law with which they are occupied and instruct the people of the House of Israel to do His Will. And He is filled with compassion for them, like the Venerable One, and He makes white the sins of the House of Israel like the snow and is ready to make victorious war against the nations who transgress His Will, like a young warrior, strong as cedars.

Midrash Rabbah, playing on *šēš*, "marble," and the numeral six (*šēš, šiššāh*), recalled the creation of the world, as it is written, "For in six days the Lord made, etc." (Exod 31:17), and then proceeded to elaborate on analogies of legal interpretation with pillars, pedestals and capitals, the bringing of sections of the Torah into connection with what follows and precedes a passage.

Rabbi Judah ben Simeon expounded the text "His countenance as the Lebanon excellent as cedars" (TB Sanhedrin 100a): He who blackens his face for the sake of the study of Torah in this world, the Holy One (blessed be He) will make his luster shine in the next.

The pillars here reminded Christian expositors of the title given to Peter, James, and John as pillars, and some included the Apostles in general as the legs of the Church. The marble was especially applicable to Peter the Rock and the bases to the Apostles, as is written: "You are built upon the foundation of the Apostles and Prophets" (Eph 2:20). The two legs were seen also as the precepts of love of God and love of neighbor, based on the golden foundations of God's truth and love. Lebanon and the cedars suggested the purity of Christ, white and towering. Lebanon was also taken by Theodoret and others in the sense of incense. The whiteness of Lebanon was applied to the purity of the Church's Virgins. The stones and cedars of the Temple also came from Lebanon, and Christ compared himself to the Temple so that members of the Church as the Body of Christ are likewise part of Lebanon. The cedars that tower to the sky and sink roots deep into the earth were seen as Christ's Divinity which reachest highest heaven and the humanity of His Incarnation which binds Him to the children of man. (Cf. Littledale.)

16a. *mouth.* LXX *pharugx* and Vulgate *guttur.* The word *ḥēḵ* (**ḥink*) designates the inside of the mouth, the gums and palate, as the organ of taste and speech. (The cognate verb *ḥanaka* in Arabic is used of rubbing an infant's gums with prechewed food in order to promote the process of weaning.) The tongue sticks to the palate when one is dumb, tongue-tied, as it were (Ezek 3:26). The lips of the exotic female drip honey and her palate is smoother than oil (Prov 5:3); it is not certain whether this was intended to suggest only sweet and smooth talk or to include other oral love play. Similarly here and in 13b it is not certain whether kisses may not be included, as many commentators, ancient and modern, have understood. The emendation of *ḥikkô,* "his palate," to *ḥinnô,* "his grace" (Dalman, Horst, Wittekindt), is without justification.

The form *mamtaqqîm* has been taken as the plurale tantum, *LXX glukasmoi,* Vulgate *suavissimum.* This form is found elsewhere in the Old Testament only in Neh 8:10 where it is the object of the imperative "drink": "Eat the fats, drink the sweets." (Modern Hebrew uses the form for "sweets," "confections.") Ugaritic *mtq* is used of the sweetness of lips in kissing:

He bent, their lips he kissed Sweet as pomegranates (or grapes).
Lo, their lips were sweet (*mtqtm*) (23[52].49–50)

The use here as a predicate noun identified with the subject, "His palate is sweets," is an emphatic way of saying "His palate is sweet." In Prov 16:21 it is said:

The wise-minded is called intelligent, And sweetness of lips adds effectiveness.

Ps 19:11[10E] and 119:103 characterize the divine ordinances as sweeter than honey. Syriac adds to the sweetness in the present passage a reference to honey.

16b. *desirable.* The form *maḥămaddîm,* "desirable (things)," corresponds to the pattern of *mamtaqqîm* of the preceding stich and the syntax is the same, "His totality is desirable things," i.e. "He is utterly desirable." In Ugaritic *mḥmd* is used of "choice cedars" and of gold (*lḥmd* is apparently a scribal error for *mḥmd* in the expression *lḥmd ḫrṣ*):

The mountains will bring you much silver, The hills the choicest gold.
(4[51].5.100–101)

In Ezek 24:16 *maḥmaḏ ʿênêḵā,* "the desire of your eyes," is applied to the prophet's wife.

16c. *mate.* The term *rēaʿ* has the sense of "companion," "friend," "neighbor," with varying degrees of intimacy without sexual implication, with reference to the person one may meet casually or temporarily, or one to whom the relation is more or less permanent. It is frequently used in expressions of reciprocity, one to/from/with, etc. the other. For the casual relation, cf. Exod 2:13, 22:9; for more intimate relations cf. Deut 13:7[6E]; Micah 7:5. In Ps 88:19[18E] we have "lover and friend" parallel with "my acquaintances"; in Ps 122:8 "my brothers and my companions." It is the term used of the neighbor in the Commandments about coveting a neighbor's house, wife or other chattel, Exod 20:17, and of the great Commandment to love thy neighbor as oneself, Lev 19:18. The word is also used of a sexual partner, legitimate, Jer 3:20, or otherwise Hosea 3, Jer 3:1.

16. The Targum equated the lover's sweet mouth with the divine Commandments and the Jerusalem girls with the prophets:

> The words of His palate are sweet as honey and all His Commandments are more desirable to His sages than gold and silver. This is the praise of God, my Beloved, and this is the power of His strength, my Lord my Beloved, O you prophets who prophesy in Jerusalem.

Midrash Rabbah made several applications of the sweetness of the Divine Word, but also of the bittersweet, e.g. God was like a king who spoke so harshly to his son that he was terrified and fainted. When the king saw that he had fallen into a faint, he began to embrace him and kiss him, and spoke gently to him, saying "What ails you? Do not fear; you are the children of the Lord your God" (Deut 14:1), etc.

Christian expositors understood the mouth here to refer to Christ as the Word and also to the preachers of that Word, beginning with the Baptist Forerunner. The sweetness as predicated only of the throat (LXX *pharugx*, Vulgate *guttur*) was taken to mean the ineffable and priceless divine inner sweetness which God has prepared for those who love Him. The desirability (Vulgate *et totus desiderabilis*) was applied to the mystery of Christ's Humanity which kindles universal longing in the souls of His elect, to the ignominy of His Passion which invites imitation and, of course, to the glory of the Resurrection. (Cf. Littledale.)

VI
(6:1–12)

1 a Whither has your love gone,
b O fairest among women?
c Whither has your love turned
d That we may seek him with you?
2 a My love has gone down to his garden,
b To the balsam beds,
c To browse in the gardens,
d To pluck lotuses.
3 a I am my love's and my love is mine,
b He who feeds on the lotus.
4 a Fair you are, my darling, verily pleasing,
b Beautiful as Jerusalem,
c Awesome with trophies.
5 a Avert your eyes from me,
b For they drive me wild.
c Your hair is like a flock of goats
d Streaming down Gilead.
6 a Your teeth like a flock of ewes
b Coming up from the washing;
c Each one has its twin,
d None bereft among them.
7 a Like a slice of pomegranate your cheeks
b Behind your veil.
8 a Sixty queens are they,
b Eighty concubines,
c Girls without number.
9 a Unique is my dove, my perfect one,
b Unique she to her mother,
c Favorite of her parent.
d The girls saw and praised her,
e Queens and concubines lauded her.

10 a Who is this that looks forth as the dawn,
b Fair as the moon,
c Bright as the sun,
d Awesome as with trophies?
11 a To the walnut grove I went down
b To view the valley verdure,
c To see if the vines had blossomed,
d If the pomegranates had bloomed.
12 a Unawares I was set
b In the chariot with the prince.

11. Mesopotamian cultic chariot scenes

6:12 Unawares I was set
In the chariot with the prince.

NOTES

6:1a,c. *Whither? . . . Whither?* These lines are reminiscent of the cry in the Ugaritic myth of Baal's resurrection:

Where is Mighty Baal, Where the Prince, Lord of Earth?
(6[49].4.28–29)

The query was addressed by El to Baal's consort, the Virgin Anat, after someone had dreamed of Baal's resurrection:

In a dream of Beneficent El Benign,
In a vision of the Creator of Creatures,
The heavens rained oil,
The brooks ran honey,
And I know that Mighty Baal lives,
That the Prince Lord of Earth exists.
. . .
Beneficent El Benign rejoiced
Stamped his feet on the footstool,
Spread his jaws and laughed,
Lifted his voice and cried:
"I shall again have rest,
My soul be at ease in my bosom,
For Mighty Baal lives
For the Prince Lord of Earth exists."
Aloud El cried to Virgin Anat,
"Hear, O Virgin Anat,
Speak to the Gods' Lamp, Shapsh,
'Parched are the fields' furrows, O Shapsh,
. . .
Where is Mighty Baal,
Where is the Prince Lord of Earth?' "
Virgin Anat departed;
Then she set face
Toward the Gods' Lamp, Shapsh;
She lifted her voice and cried,
"Message of Bull El, thy Father,
Word of the Beneficent, thy Sire,
'Parched are the fields' furrows, O Shapsh,
. . .
Where is Mighty Baal,
Where the Prince Lord of Earth?' "
(6[49].4.4–9, 14–25, 28–36, 39–40)

The reply of Shapsh is obscure at the beginning, but in the last line she says something we can understand:

"And I will seek Mighty Baal."
Virgin Anat replied:
"Where, whither, O Shapsh
Where, whither . . . ?"
(6[49].4.44–47)

The Ugaritic words *an, lan,* "where, whither?" are cognate with *'ānāh* (*'ān* plus the directive ending), "whither?" in the present passage, the preposition *l-* serving the function of the directive ending, although Ugaritic also uses the directive ending in other instances. The point of this extended citation of Ugaritic is to show the context of the possible parallel with the query as to the whereabouts of the lover and the search motif in the present passage. The same verb (*bqṯ) for seeking is used by Shapsh, "And I will seek Mighty Baal," and by the Jerusalem girls, "And we will seek him with you."

Wittekindt, and more recently Schmökel, draw parallels with the Tammuz-Ishtar myth. Schmökel (1956, 55n2) cited the question of the *galla*-demons of the netherworld to Dumuzi's sister Geštinanna:

> Where has your brother gone, the man of lament?
> Where has Dumuzi gone, the man of lamentation?

Since the *galla*-demons were seeking Dumuzi to do him harm, it would be more appropriate to cite Inanna's laments and quest. It is surprising that Schmökel should confine his treatment of the passage to Mesopotamian parallels and pass over completely the Ugaritic which are closer in time and space and no less striking.

The search motif continues to be re-enacted annually in Jerusalem in the Easter pageant of the Ethiopian Church when the priests perform the search for the body of Christ.

1c. *turned.* LXX mistakenly rendered *pānāh* as "looked away," *apeblepsen,* despite the appropriate rendering of the parallel verb *hālak̲* in 1a, *apēlthen,* "went away."

1. The question was explained thus by the Targum:

> When the prophets heard the praise of YHWH from the mouth of the Assembly of Israel, they said: "For what sin was the Presence of YHWH withdrawn from thee, thou whose conduct was more beautiful than that of all nations; and whither has thy Beloved turned at the time He left thy sanctuary?" The Assembly of Israel replied: "For the sins of rebellion and insurrection which were found in me." The prophets said: "Now return in penitence and let us rise, and let us pray before Him and let us beg mercy together."

Midrash Rabbah ascribed the question to the other nations and Israel replied, "What business do you have to ask about Him when you have no share in Him? Once I have attached myself to Him, can I separate from Him? Once He has attached Himself to me, can He separate from me? Wherever He is, He comes to me."

Some Christian expositors ascribed the question to the Angels seeking to penetrate the mystery of the Incarnation. A more general view was that the weaker believers ask to be taught by the wiser and more perfect the history and beauties of the Bridegroom. The Venerable Bede explained that God never leaves those He has once taken to Himself, even though he may turn to gather others to Himself. The verb "gone," *abiit,* was referred to the Ascension, and "turned aside," *declinavit,* to Christ's turning from the Synagogue to the Church. (Cf. Littledale.)

2a. *has gone down.* The verb *yārad̲* was taken by Wittekindt as the motive-word for the *descensus ad inferos.* The answer to the question, "Where has Dôd gone?" is thus, "He is dead," i.e. he has descended to the netherworld. Similarly, Schmökel rejected the "profane-explanation" that the lover in "his garden" means that he is in the embrace of his bride, and placed him in the netherworld.

his garden. It is clear that in 4:12 and 5:1 "garden" refers to the bride and her charms. In the present instance, however, interpreters of the cultic school take the "garden" as a designation of the netherworld. Schmökel noted (p. 56) that the realm of the dead is not usually pictured in such soft colors, but he cited in this connection the incipit of an Ishtar-hymn,

> He who descends to the garden is the King, who breaks off the cedar (branches).
> (21, line 28 of translation)

Perhaps more appropriate to this view would be Inanna's lament for her absent bridegroom:

> Gone has my husband, sweet husband,
> Gone has my son, sweet son,
> My husband has gone among the "head" plants,
> My husband has gone among the "rear" plants,
> My husband has gone to seek food, has been turned over to the plants.
> (*SMR*, 128)

In the notes, p. 157, Kramer remarks that the implication of the lines referring to plants is not clear and that the Sumerian words for "food" and "plant" are here identical and there is therefore a play of words that is missed in the translation. It is, of course, possible that "garden" might be used in differing senses in different contexts, and that identical expressions could have quite different meanings.

2b. *balsam beds.* Wittekindt related the garden to the Adonis gardens which were planted with aromatics and he cited with approval the suggestion of Neuschotz de Jassy that the balm here points to the spices with which the dead were embalmed. Since Adonis is the gardener, his relationship to the garden does not cease during his sojourn in the netherworld. The grave of Jesus also lay in a garden and Mary of Magdala mistook the resurrected Christ for the gardener (John 20:15). Wittekindt (174) further adduced Plessis' rendition of a Tammuz canticle:

> Alas, in his youth he sleeps among the flowers of the garden.
> Among the flowers of the garden he lies outstretched . . .

To this may be added further examples from Kramer's chapter "The Sacred Marriage: Death and Resurrection":

> Among the buds he lay, among the buds he lay,
> The shepherd—among the buds he lay,
> As the shepherd lay among the buds he dreamt a dream.
> (*SMR*, 122)

Again it is among the plants of the netherworld that Dumuzi hides from the *galla*-demons; as he tells his sister Geštinanna:

> My friend, I will hide among the plants, tell not where I am,
> I will hide among the small plants, tell not where I am,
> I will hide among the large plants, tell not where I am,
> I will hide among the ditches of Arali, tell not where I am.
> (*SMR*, 124)

The ditches of Arali (one of the names for the netherworld) are presumably irrigation ditches and thus the symbolism is horticultural. The *galla*-demons search for Dumuzi among the plants and ditches of Arali, but he eludes them for the nonce (*SMR*, 125).

2c. *To browse.* Some critics considered the expression *lir'ôṯ baggannîm* unacceptable and emended to *lir'ôṯ baggĕpānîm,* "to look at the vines." Wittekindt, partly on metrical grounds, supposed that a word had fallen out of this stich and suggested addition of *nēlēḵ,* "let us go." Some modern translations supply "his flock" as the object of *lir'ôt,* e.g. *AT, RSV, JB.* Robert, RTF, explained that the shepherd is Yahweh and the gardens represent the land of Palestine and accordingly he added "son troupeau." The land is referred to as "gardens" because it is so fertile (cf. Deut 8:8). For Robert the idea of the verse is that of renovation, abundance, and happiness of the nation in the latter days after the return from exile (Isa 51:3, 61:11). *NEB* apparently took the verb as an Aramaism, *r'y=rḍy,* and rendered "to delight in the garden."

2d. *To pluck.* The verb *lqṭ* is used of picking or gathering a variety of materials—stones (Gen 31:46), money (Gen 47:14), food (Exod 16:4,16,21,26; Num 11:8; II Kings 4:39), grapes (Lev 19:10), firewood (Jer 7:18), arrows (I Sam 20:38), gleaning (Isa 17:5; Ruth 2 *passim*). In Ps 104:28 it is used of food gathering of animals in general, including marine creatures. The parallel with *lir'ôṯ,* "to pasture," suggests grazing. Wittekindt (174*f*), in the interest of relating the line to the cult of Adonis, supposed that the reference was to lamenting women plucking the anemones, the flower of Adonis, so that they would wither and die like him. The wording of several modern versions seems to suggest that the flower gathering is for bouquets or posies. *NEB* renders "to delight in the garden and to pick lilies."

lotuses. Cf. 2:1b.

2. The Targum offers a remarkable explanation of this verse:

> Then the Lord of the World received their prayer with favor and went down to Babylon to the Sanhedrin of Sages and gave rest to His people and brought them out of exile by the hand of Cyrus, and Ezra, and Nehemiah, and Zerubbabel son of Shealtiel, and the Elders of the Jews. And they built the Temple, and appointed priests over the sacrifices, and the Levites over the guardianship of the Holy Word. And He sent fire from heaven and received favorably the sacrifices and the incense and the spices. And as a man feeds his beloved son with delicacies, thus He indulged them, and as a man gathers roses from the plain, so He gathered them from Babylon.

Midrash Rabbah identified my Love with the Holy One (blessed be He), the garden with the world, and the spice bed with Israel. To feed in the gardens refers to synagogues and houses of study. To gather lilies means to remove the Righteous in Israel (by death) and this called forth a discussion of how God determines the right time to remove a righteous man.

Christian expositors stressed the verb "he went down" with a variety of applications to Christ's Advent, Incarnation, and Descent into Hell. He came down in the flesh when the whole creation was groaning and travailing in pain, looking for the promised Savior. He came down for the sake of that man who went down from Jerusalem to Jericho and fell among thieves (Luke 10:30). He came down from His unspeakable majesty to our lowly nature. He came to His Garden as the True Gardener to plant God's field anew (I Cor 3:9) which the wild boar had ravaged (Ps 80:13). He came to cultivate the garden again by planting virtues there and sending through it, by the channels of His Word, the pure and holy springs of doctrine to nurture the plants, and especially the spice beds as those souls in whom the odors of holiness abound. His Garden was taken as the Church Universal, the gardens as the local churches and the devout souls in them. His gathering of lilies was understood as taking out of this world the holy souls who had attained the perfect whiteness of sanctification in order to reward them with eternal bliss. To do this, He went down to the Garden Tomb (John 19:41) and there He consecrated the first-fruits of the Church in appearing to Mary Magdalene. He went down to Hell, to the spice-beds of the Patriarchs and Saints who awaited His coming. Having pierced Hell, He entered triumphant into Paradise (Luke 23:43). He feeds in the fragrant garden of human souls whence He gathers to deck His bridal chamber the white and perfumed lilies, the Apostles, Prophets, Martyrs, and Saints. Had He not first gone down to overcome the sharpness of death, He could not have delighted in the holy feeding in the gardens, in the many churches of the faithful throughout the world. In going down, He turned aside from the unbelieving Jews to the Gentiles and made for Himself a fruitful garden, and beds of spices from which to gather lilies, Virgins, Martyrs, Confessors, and to be fed with the food of worship and prayer. He came in His Incarnation to His garden, the Church, by way of the choicest of all garden spots or spice beds, the spotless Virgin of Nazareth, from whom He gathered the white lilies of purity and holiness. Yet another garden, besides those of the Church and the soul, where He comes to meet His Bride, is in the reading of the Holy Scriptures from which He gathers for her lilies and divers spices to fill the beds of believing souls. (Cf. Littledale.)

3a. Commentators strained to find significance in this line which is the inverse of 2:16a. Delitzsch saw import in the fact that Shulamite always says, not *'îšî*, "my beloved," but *dôḏî*, "my love," or *rē'î*, "my friend"; "for love, although a passion common to mind and body, is in this Song of Songs viewed as much as possible apart from its basis in the animal nature. Also, that the description hovers between that of the clothed and the unclothed, gives to it an ideality favourable to the mystical interpretation." Harper thought that the Shulamite here expresses her jealous feeling. She fears that she has overshot the mark in praising her beloved and she snatches him back, as it were, lest she should lose him. Robert found the inversion of the expression significant and, apparently by way of explanation, quoted Joüon to the effect that the author thus puts in relief that she henceforth belongs to her beloved and that she condemns her past infidelity. Yahweh, for his part, has returned to her: the Shepherd of Israel pastures his flock anew among the lilies. This seems to be reading a great deal between the lines.

3. The Targum paraphrased thus in connection with the preceding reference to the delivery from Babylon:

> And in that day I worshiped the Lord of the World, my Beloved, and my Beloved made His holy Presence dwell with me and He fed me with delicacies.

Among the several Christian interpretations of this verse cited by Littledale, that of Aquinas seems especially noteworthy. The Bride, irradiated with God's glory in which she sees shadowed His wondrous attributes of beauty, goodness, wisdom, and love, is entranced at the sight and so absorbed in Him that she heeds nothing else and neither sees nor hears anything pertaining to earth. As fire melts two masses of metal into one, so the fervor of this love melts the soul and causes it to flow into God and thus to be united with Him and never ever parted from Him.

4a. *Fair you are.* Cf. 4.1a.

4. The comparison of our lady's beauty to the cities of Tirzah and Jerusalem has long vexed translators and commentators. The ancient versions did not recognize *trṣh* as a proper name in spite of the parallelism with Jerusalem and the comparative particle *k* before both words. LXX rendered *trṣh* as *eudokia,* Syriac *ṣeḇyānā,* Vulgate *suavis,* construing *trṣh* as a nominal form of the root *rṣy,* "be pleasing." It is hard enough to explain the comparison of a beautiful female, human or divine, to a city, even Jerusalem, but the city Tirzah is a tougher problem. Cheyne objected that one does not compare beautiful women to cities and proposed the emendation of Tirzah to *ḥăḇaṣṣeleṯ,* "narcissus," and Jerusalem to "lily of the valley," *šôšannaṯ ʿămāqîm.* In favor of Tirzah, Dussaud cited the principle that the image which seems bizarre or unexpected is more likely to be original. Stephan, however, could find no modern Palestinian parallel. "We may nowadays (especially in Syria) term a town beautiful (*ḥilwe*) but we cannot make a direct comparison between a girl and a town" (p. 18).

Tirzah is mentioned as a Canaanite city (Josh 12:24) and Jeroboam moved his capital there at the time of the schism (I Kings 14:17, 15:21,33, 16:6,8,9,15,17,23) where it remained until Omri built Samaria as the new capital (I Kings 16:24,28). The site of Tirzah has not yet been identified with absolute certainty, but the most likely candidate is Tell el-Fārʿa near Nablus, excavated by Roland de Vaux (1947; Jochims, 1960). Delitzsch thought that it could not be on account of pleasantness (the meaning of the name) that Tirzah is mentioned before Jerusalem which in the eye of the Israelites was "the perfection of beauty" (Ps 50:2; Lam 2:15), nor can there be any gradation from Tirzah to Jerusalem, as Hengstenberg proposed, because the adjectives would be reversed if a climax were intended. The reason, according to Delitzsch, was that Shulamite came from the higher region and was not a Jerusalem girl; therefore a beautiful city situated in the north toward Shunem must serve as comparison of her beauty.

Robert saw in the mention of the two capital cities the personification of "Grand Israel," of the nation reestablished in its primitive unity, the traditional aspiration affirmed, above all, after the Exile (Hosea 2:2[1:11E], 3:5; Isa 11:10–16; Jer 31:1–6,27,28,31; Ezek 16:53–55, 37:15–28; Zech 9:13*ff*, 10:6–10; Ps 80; Sir 36:10). Robert, nevertheless, was puzzled by the choice of Tirzah to symbolize the Northern Kingdom rather than Samaria, and he suggested that the simplest explanation is that the author wished to avoid mentioning Samaria because of the aversion toward the Samaritans in his time. According to Robert, there is nothing to be drawn from the mention of Tirzah as to the period of composition of the Canticle, except that the Solomonic authenticity is belied by the allusion to the Northern Kingdom. It could as well be argued, as indeed it has been, that the juxtaposition of the two cities supports a Solomonic date since in the period after the schism no southern poet would have praised Tirzah and no northern poet Jerusalem.

A common construction in Ugaritic now supplies the clue to a plausible explanation of *ktrṣh* mistaken as the name of the city Tirzah and the addition of Jerusalem to balance it. In Ugaritic the asseverative *k* is always used exactly as in the present instance before the verb at the end of a clause, e.g.:

hlk bʻl aṯrt ktʻn	The coming of Baal Asherah eyed (4[51].2.14)
hlm il kyphnh	When El spied her (4[51].4.27)
il aṯtm kypt	El seduced two women (23[52].39)
gm l aṯth kyṣḥ	Aloud to his wife he cried (17[2 AQHT].5.15)
lktp ʻnt ktšth	On the shoulders of Anat she set him (6[62].1.14)

The *k-* is also used before a word referring to beauty, presumably a verbal form, in one of the most provocative passages (RS 225.1–2) in Ugaritic literature:

ʻnt hlkt wšnwt tp aḫh	Anat went insane at her brother's beauty
wnʻm aḫh kysmsm	And her brother's charm for he was handsome.

The suggestion is herewith offered, albeit without dogmatism, that failure to apprehend the sense of *ktrṣh* as the verb *tirṣeh,* "thou art pleasing," preceded by the asseverative *k-*, led to the mistaken vocalization as the name of the city and the addition of Jerusalem as a parallel and to supply more beauty and prestige. We have only to delete "as Jerusalem" in order to strike a balance:

Yāpāh 'att raʻyāṯî kî-tirṣeh	Fair you are, my darling, verily pleasing,
nā'wāh 'ăyummāh kanniḏgālôṯ	Beautiful, awesome as (with) trophies.

The reading "as (with) trophies" makes sense, but for the proposed interpretation "with (the) trophies" would be much better. The confusion of *b-* and *k-* is commonplace.

As indicated above, the suggestion about *ktrṣh* is offered with diffidence and without expectation of instant acceptance. D. N. Freedman regards as far-fetched the supposition that someone misunderstood the word as the name of a city and then supplied another city to balance it. Freedman would stress the perfect poetic parallelism between Tirzah and Jerusalem. Since cities are identified with tutelary deities, and often with goddesses, why, he asks, shouldn't there be comparison of girls with cities? Some of the difficulties with the comparison were noted. There is no harm in offering a new conjecture based on a syntactic feature of Ugaritic. The suggestion agrees at least with the oldest tradition, both Jewish and Christian, which did not understand *trṣh* as the city name.

4c. *Awesome.* LXX *thambos,* Vulgate *terribilis.* The adjective *'āyōm, 'ăyummāh* is found outside the Canticle only in Hab 1:7 where it is applied to the terrible Chaldeans. The cognate noun (*'ēymāh*), however, is common in the Old Testament and always designates something terrifying, horrifying, or awe-inspiring, a theophany, divine or royal majesty, a monster's teeth, war, etc.; cf. Gen 15:12; Exod 15:16, 23:27; Deut 32:25; Josh 2:9; Isa 33:18; Jer 50:38; Pss 55:5[4E], 88:16; Job 9:34; 13:21, 20:25, 33:7, 39:20, 41:6[14E]; Prov 20:2. Commentators have been sore abashed to explain the collocation of beauty and terror. Delitzsch remarked "that Shulamith is both beautiful and terrible is no contradiction: she is terrible in the irresistible power of the impression of her personality, . . ." S. D. Goitein (1965) has adduced in connection with the present passage a number of impressive examples of the transition of Semitic words meaning "awe-inspiring," "terrible," to "terrific" in the sense of "extraordinary," "of unusual, exquisite quality." In view of this widespread usage, Goitein suggests that we should not hesitate to translate the old crux *'ăyummāh,* Song of Songs 6:4,10, simply with "terrific," "splendid."

trophies. The term *nid̲gālôt̲* occurs only here and in vs. 10 below. LXX rendered *tetagmenai* (sc. *phalagges*), "ranked (phalanxes)." Symmachus' *epiphoros hōs tagmata parembolōn,* "terrifying as ranks of camps," may reflect the addition of *maḥănôt̲,* "camps," and similarly Vulgate *terribilis ut castrorum acies ordinata.* Syriac seems to reflect a reading *kannib̲ḥeret̲,* "like a chosen thing." Graetz read "like towers," *kammiḡdālôt̲.* H. Winckler introduced here the god Nergal, and Dussaud regarded this as appropriate to vs. 10 where Nergal, as the equivalent of Mars, would be associated with dawn, the moon, and the sun. Wittekindt (p. 8) rendered "furchtbar wie Planeten(?)." *KJ*'s "terrible as *an army* with banners" rests on the analysis of *kannid̲gālôt̲* as the *Niph'al* participle of a denominative verb from *deḡel,* "banner," "beflagged things," as explained by Harper; cf. Ps 20:6[5E], "we will set up banners(?)," *nid̲gōl.*

Rudolph, taking his cue from the sense "die Bezeichneten" (marked out), explained the word as a name for constellations. Goitein (1965, 221) similarly suggested that *nidgālôṭ* is a term of popular astronomy designating stars of first magnitude which are always brilliant and easily seen. While conceding that "awe-inspiring as an embattled host" is more fanciful than "splendid as the brilliant stars," Goitein concluded that a sober weighing of the available evidence forces us to accept the second translation. Gerleman questioned the connection of the term with *deḡel,* "banner," since this is a secondary meaning and took his point of departure from the primary sense of the root *dgl,* "see." There is, Gerleman suggested, one celestial phenomenon which can rightly be called "die (nur) Gesehene" (something that is only seen), namely a mirage. This optical phenomenon is perhaps mentioned in Isa 35:7 and 49:10 (*šārāḇ*). Among the Arabs the *Fata Morgana* (*sarāb,* *'āl*) is frequently mentioned in poetry and became an almost proverbial figure for the unattainable and deceptive. Diodorus Siculus (III 50.4) described the terrifying impression which the mirage makes on the spectator. Gerleman translated the expression in 6:4 and 10 as "furchterregend wie die Trugbilder" (terrifying as the mirages).

The root meaning of *dgl* allows for another tack in the quest for a convincing explanation of the term *nidgālôṭ,* here and in vs. 10. Under proper circumstances, which are here surmised, the term might designate visual objects of distinctive, spectacular character, hence the conjectural rendering "trophies." Envisioned here are the grisly trophies of the violent virgin goddess of Love and War depicted so graphically for us in the Ugaritic Anat Text. Before developing this suggestion, a few background notes are in order. Wittekindt (9) in 1926 suggested that the mystery of Cant 6:4,10 was not difficult to unravel when we think of the goddess Ishtar and her opposite qualities of Beauty and Terror. The goddess embodies and dispenses Love and Beauty, but she is also the martial man-slayer, like the German Lady Hell (Frau Hölle). In 1927 the Jesuit savant Assyriologist and astronomer F. X. Kugler noted the celestial and martial traits implicit in the description of the Bride in 6:10 which seem incompatible with an earthly bride and related them to the goddess Ishtar (1927, 50–52). Kugler took pains to explain that he did not regard this as a conscious borrowing or approbation of heathen belief any more than the names Hercules or Isidor in Christian families. He regarded it as unlikely that at the time of the origin of the Canticle it was still remembered in Israel how martial traits came to be imputed to a female beauty, just as the meaning and origin of many folk customs is clarified only by arduous archaeological studies. The significance of Kugler's study lies not in its originality, since Wittekindt had already anticipated him in this connection, but in the fact that a devout son of the Church regarded the evidence as strong enough to warrant explanation. Subsequent to Kugler's note, a great deal of new evidence has been added from Mesopotamian sources but, more significantly, from Syria in the recovery of the Ugaritic mythological texts.

In the second column of the Ugaritic mythological text usually called the "Anat Text" because of that goddess' dominant role, the lady suddenly launched a violent assault on mankind, wading in blood and gore, with heads and hands of her victims piled like locusts or locusts' eggs. She attached heads to her back and girded hands to her waist as she fought on, gloating and exulting in the slaughter. A necklace of severed heads and the girdle of severed hands, worn as trophies, would comport with both the sense of *niḏgālôt,* "things [to be] looked at," and with the adjective *'ăyummāh,* "terrible, horrible, dreadful." Cf. 7:1 for a translation of the text with comments. The combination of beauty and terror which distinguishes the Lady of the Canticle also characterizes the goddess of Love and War throughout the ancient world, from Mesopotamia to Rome, particularly the goddess Inanna or Ishtar of Mesopotamia, Anat of the Western Semites, Athena and Victoria of the Greeks and Romans, Britannia, and, most striking of all, Kali of India. The goddess Anat of the Ugaritic myths is elsewhere in the myths distinguished for her violence, but she is also the ideal of feminine beauty. The Sumerian Inanna, distinguished for her beauty, also had her violent and terrible side which is emphasized in the Hymnal Prayer of Enheduanna, the daughter of Sargon the Great. A few lines will serve to illustrate (translation of S. N. Kramer, *ANET*[3], 581–582):

> You are known by your destruction of rebel-lands,
> You are known by your massacring (their people),
> You are known by your devouring (their) dead like a dog,
> You are known by your fierce countenance.
> (lines 125–128)

At the conclusion of the prayer Enheduanna speaks of the things she has done for the goddess, including setting up a nuptial chamber for her and reciting her praises unceasingly. A pregnant statement is made about the reason for the goddess' wrath:

> It is because of your captive spouse, your captive son,
> That your wrath is so great, your heart so unappeased.
> (lines 141–142)

When the goddess accepted Enheduanna's prayer,

> . . . she was clothed with beauty,
> was filled with joyous allure.
> How she carried (her) beauty—like the rising moonlight!
> (lines 145–147)

The hymn ends with the apostrophe:

> My queen garbed in allure, O Inanna, praise!
> (line 153)

The combination of beauty and terror is nowhere seen more vividly than in the Indian goddess Kali whose affinities with the great goddesses of Western

Asia, Inanna, Ishtar, and Anat, are very striking and deserving of special study. The terrible trophies of Kali, a necklace of severed heads and a girdle of severed hands, are her most notable attributes, and are regularly represented in her iconography and frequently mentioned in the hymns of devotion to her:

Proud Lady, brilliant are thy garments,
Bright with coiling serpents.
Thou art clad in tiger skin.
Thy waist is adorned with tiny tinkling bells.
Thou holdest the heads of two demons
Dripping with blood, just severed by the sword.
Thy waist is girdled with heads of demons,
As it were with a garland.
Thus art Thou beautiful, O formidable One.
(Avalon, 1952, 51*f*)

4. The Targum apparently took *trṣh* as a verb, "thou art pleased."

> Said YHWH in His Words: "How beautiful you are, My Beloved, at the time your desire is to do My Will. Beautiful is the Holy House which you built for Me, like the first Sanctuary which King Solomon built for me in Jerusalem. Thy dread was upon all the peoples in the day that the four regiments marched in the desert.

Midrash Rabbah, after a couple of plays on *trṣh* in the sense of "be acceptable" with reference to sacrifices, goes off on a confused and confusing discussion of the use of wagons and oxen for carrying the Tabernacle. (Num 7:3*ff*)

Some Christian expositors applied this verse to Jewish-Christian relations. Athanasius, taking the Greek rendering of *trṣh* in the sense of "approval," referred to the issue of assimilation. "Those who come from the Gentiles ought not to be unlike Jerusalem, that there may be but one people, for this is so when we honor the Law and believe in Christ. For the God of the Law and the Gospels is One, and whoever is not made like Jerusalem does not become the Bridegroom's friend." Similarly, Gregory the Great applied this verse to the Synagogue which is called by the four terms "beautiful," "love," "sweet," and "comely as Jerusalem," and thus when converted will follow the four Holy Gospels as does the Church.

Champions of the Church Militant appropriated the reference to terror to justify their zeal. Cardinal Hugo (thirteenth century) noted that the Church is terrible to heretics, infidels, and evil spirits.

The Church is beautiful by reason of the devout lives of her Saints, comely in her contemplative hermits, and terrible as an army in array by reason of her religious orders and their discipline. For these and other applications of the beauty and terror of the Church, cf. Littledale (ad loc.), who finally noted the fitness of the application to the Virgin Mary as beautiful in her holiness, sweet in gentle meekness, comely as Jerusalem since through her peace was made between God and man she became the abode of the Prince of Peace, and terrible as an army in array because she was surrounded by ranks of Angels.

Modern exegetes have entertained diverse views of the reason for the terror associated with the beauty. Delitzsch understood it to refer to the irresistible power of the impression of the lady's personality, her whole appearance, although she was unconscious of it—a *veni, vidi, vici.* Solomon was completely vanquished by her. Siegfried saw here an allusion to the sword dance described by Wetzstein (cf. Delitzsch's Appendix, 163n1). A young man accepts the challenge to kneel in the circle with the dancer and tries to touch her; he may come away bleeding with many wounds, or even forfeit his life. Joüon saw in the image of the battalions Israel leaving the place of her exile and on the march to Palestine. Robert asserted that in reality this verse is to be related to 4:4, the thought of the two passages being in effect identical. The nation reestablished in Palestine has remained beautiful, but she is nevertheless formidable to her enemies. Long oppressed by foreigners, exposed to the contempt of small nations round about, and torn by factions, she has regained her independence and the power of the era of David and Solomon, with the abundance and well-being of the eschatological era. This hope is closely linked to the reconstitution of the national unity expressed in the first part of the verse. It is thus normal that martial images blend with those signifying prosperity and beauty. If this interpretation is correct, it is a mistake, according to Robert, to oppose the one condition to the other, beautiful *but* terrible, as some authors do.

5b. *For.* The element *še,* commonly employed as the relative particle, has here causal sense.

they. The independent pronoun is here the masculine form *hēm,* although eyes, as other paired organs of the body, are regularly feminine. If the eyes in question are the multiple eyes of the Eye Goddess, the abnormal gender of the pronoun would be explicable.

drive me wild. The causative stem of the verb *rhb* is used elsewhere in the Old Testament only in Ps 138:3 where it refers to the arousal of strength in the "soul" of the supplicant when answered by God. The simple stem of the verb is used of disturbed and disturbing behavior of youth toward elders in Isa 3:5, and in Prov 6:3 of storming a neighbor in urgent haste to be reconciled with him. Elsewhere the noun *rahab̲* is used as an epithet of the sea, especially in mythological allusions; cf. Isa 30:7, 51:9; Pss 87:4, 89:11[10E]; Job 9:13, 26:12. In Arabic the simple stem is used in the sense of "be afraid," the factitive stem of "inspiring fear," and the causative stem of "frightening into flight." LXX rendered the verb in the present passage as *anepterōsan me,* "they made me fly," and similarly Vulgate *quia ipsi me avolare fecerunt,* and Syriac *'ap̄rĕd̲ān* "they made me flee." Luther took the verb to denote sexual excitement, "denn sie machen mich brünstig," "for they make me (sexually) ardent." A sampling of more recent renderings reveals some uncertainty about the precise meaning of the term: *KJ* and R. Gordis, "overcome," *RSV* "disturb," *AT* and *NEB* "dazzle," *JB* "hold me captive," *JPSV* "overwhelm," *NAB* "torment." Robert rendered "car ils me fascinent," and explained that it is not that the looks of the loved one are importunate to the groom, but the intensity of love which they awake in him is such that he cannot bear it. He thus begs her to turn away the eyes which assault him. It is generally appreciated that this passage has to be considered in connection with 4:9. N. M. Waldman (1970, 215–217) suggested that *rhb* here, like *lbb* in 4:9, refers to sexual excitement. Cf. 4:9 on the power of the eye of the great goddess of India.

5c,d. Cf. 4:1e,f which is identical with the present distich except for the omission of the word for "mountain" (*har*) before Gilead and modification of the form of the preposition.

5. It is difficult to see in the Targum's interpretation of this verse any connection with the Hebrew text other than the play on the verb *glš* in the noun *galšûšîṯā'*, "heap(?)," "monument," and the name Gilead interpreted in accordance with Gen 31:48:

> (God says): "Your rabbis, the sages of the Great Assembly, went round about Me, they who consulted Me during the Exile, and they appointed a school for the teaching (*'ulpān*) of My Law; and the rest of your scholars and the people of the land approved Me by the word of their mouth, like the sons of Jacob who gathered the stones and made them a heap/monument on Mount Gilead."

Midrash Rabbah here likened God to a king who was angry with his queen and expelled her from the palace. The queen pressed her face against a pillar outside the palace and the king passed by, saw her, and said, "Remove her from my sight because I cannot bear to see her (thus)." The verb *hirhîḇûnî*, "they have overcome me," was applied to the effect of a fast in overcoming the divine anger, with allusions to Exod 24:7; Pss 87:4 and 68:19. The hair like a flock of goats was taken in an uncomplimentary sense; as a goat is despicable, so the Israelites were despicable at Shittim (Num 25:1).

Among Christian expositors cited by Littledale on this verse, Theodoret (fifth century) attributed the words to God in admonition of the worshiper: "Gaze not steadfastly on Me beyond measure, lest thou shouldst suffer some harm. For I am past searching out, and incomprehensible, not only by man, but by angels. . . . Therefore . . . search not out things that are too hard, seek not that which is too mighty for thee, but ponder evermore upon that which is enjoined thee." Ambrose saw Christ as speaking to the soul, "If thou be perfect, yet there are other souls waiting for Me to redeem and prop up, wherefore turn away thine eyes from Me, for they lift Me up, but I came to lift all up." Ambrose explained this obscure comment by the illustration of the teacher who wishes to lecture on a difficult subject; no matter how learned he may be, he lowers himself to the standard of those to be instructed and uses simple language so as to be understood. Hence these words are an injunction to Christian preachers to withdraw at times from contemplation and from discussing the darker mysteries of the Faith, that they may teach the babes in Christ, and appeal to them with the simplest language of the Gospels and the plainest object lessons of good works.

Among the interpretations of the reference to goats, Gregory of Nyssa related them to the Saints because goats were offered in sacrifice. Goats prefer the steep, rocky places and are thus types of those who deliberately choose a hard and austere life, and pass their time chiefly in silent ascent of the steep Way of perfection.

6. Cf. 6:2 which is identical with the present verse, except for different words for "ewes"; the usual term *rĕḥēlîm* here replaces the problematic *qĕṣûḇôṯ*. Stephan (19) cited a striking classical Arabic parallel to this verse:

> (The teeth are) white, small like many ewes;
> They laugh like "pouring" hail pellets.

The Targum, as in 4:2, related this verse to Jacob's animal husbandry recounted in Gen 30:

> The priests and the Levites ate of your sacrifices and of the holy tithe and the wave-offering, free from all coercion or robbery, for they were pure as the flocks of Jacob's sheep when they came up from the brook of the Jabbok, all of them resembling one another and bearing twins every time, with none aborting or barren among them.

Midrash Rabbah applied this verse to the chastity and virtue of Israel. Just as the ewe is modest, so was Israel chaste and virtuous in the war of Midian. The execution of the ringleaders in the great sin (Num 25:4) is taken to apply to the Midianites and not the Israelites, none of whom was suspected of sin.

Among Christian interpretations of this verse, Cassiodorus explained the teeth as the words of the Church, pure, clean, firm, and strong. The twins were seen as the utterance of the twofold law of love to God and neighbor. Epiphanius understood the twins to refer to the regenerated soul which goes down alone into the baptismal font and comes up joined by the Holy Ghost. Cocceius, in applying this passage and the parallel in 4:2 to earlier and later stages in the history of the Church, took the omission of the word "shorn" here to imply some inferiority in the latter days as compared to the primitive age, chiefly in the matter of relaxation of discipline permitting irregularities and errors which would have been repressed in the era of martyrdom. (Cf. Littledale.)

7. This verse repeats verbatim 4:3c,d. Vulgate here varies the wording with *cortex* instead of *fragmen* for MT *pelaḥ,* and a different rendering of the enigmatic phrase *mibba'aḏ lĕṣimmāṯēḵ,* here *absque occultis tuis,* instead of *absque eo quod intrinsecus latet,* as in the first instance.

The reason for the repetition of much of 4:1–3 here has been variously surmised. Harper mentioned the view of Oettli that the words are mere stock phrases in Solomon's mouth, but suggested that they are rather stock phrases from the marriage *awṣaf* which must have consisted mainly of just such phrases. Joüon saw here a development in the thought of the author who describes now the return from Exile and repeats on purpose in order to stress the analogy of this event with the Exodus from Egypt and to show that the divine love toward Israel is as strong now as then. The reference to the tower of David is not repeated since that would not suit the situation of the Exile. Robert did not attempt to develop this suggestion of Joüon, but was content to recall that repetitions are in the style of the Canticle and that it is normal for the passionate sentiments of the groom to be expressed several times in the same terms.

The Targum applied this verse to

> The royal house of the Hasmoneans all filled with (performance) of the Commandments like the pomegranate; and as for Mattathias himself, the High Priest, and his sons, they were more righteous than all of them, and they fulfilled the Commandments and Words of the Law with thirsty eagerness.

Midrash Rabbah applied the split pomegranate to Israel after the return from the war of Midian when Moses began to praise them, saying, "Even the emptiest among you is full of religious observances and good deeds as a pomegranate is of seeds." The principle here is that if one has an opportunity to sin and avoids it, it is an act of piety.

This verse did not receive a great deal of attention from Christian expositors, in comparison with some other passages, but it did afford edification to those with insight. Aponius saw the cheeks as belonging to those who fall into post-baptismal sin, and, being washed anew with the tears of repentance, beautify the Church with the ruddy blush of shame. Philo of Carpasia saw in the pomegranate the mingled glow of faith and hope in every holy soul that serves the Lord, and the numerous seeds within he likened to the good works and devout thoughts hidden behind the rough rind, one day to be revealed by the Bridegroom who alone knows them at present. Cardinal Hugo compared the pomegranate to the preachers of the Church because of the firm rind and many seeds; the red and white which vie in the cheeks of the pomegranate representing fervor and purity, and the hidden insides, the precious inner devotions. The repetition of this verse in 4:2 and 6:7 was seen by Justus of Urgel as God's foretelling of his twofold love, the conversion of both Jews and Gentiles, and descriptive of the glory and merits of the martyrs in these two portions of His Church. (Cf. Littledale.)

8. Nothing is predicated of these three classes of women. Some critics supply "Solomon's *lišlōmōh* (Budde, Siegfried, Haupt, Dalman, Horst, Haller); Ginsburg inserted "to me," *lî,* i.e. "I have," and Bickell added "in the king's chambers," *bĕḥaḏrê hammeleḵ*. The pronoun "they" is the masculine form *hēm*. The use of the masculine *genus potius* instead of the feminine is frequent with verb forms, but not common with the independent personal pronouns.

It has been generally assumed that the inspiration of the present passage is the reference to the prodigious harem of King Solomon in I Kings 11:3. But the discrepancy in the numbers and ratios of the wives and concubines, seven hundred and three hundred versus sixty and eighty, is difficult to reconcile. Delitzsch, who held to the Solomonic authorship of the Canticle, supposed that the low numbers here reflect celebration of a love relation at the beginning of Solomon's reign before his luxury reached the enormous heights to which he looked back as *vanitas vanitatum* (Eccles 2:8). Ginsburg explained the discrepancy in the numbers by taking the sixty and eighty as indefinite. Harper suggested that Solomon, being here the speaker, would naturally in the present circumstances (as Harper understood them) minimize the size of his establishment and veil it under the vague last phrase. It is difficult to see how sixty and eighty could pass as indefinite for seven hundred and three hundred or how "without number" could be understood as "the vague last phrase" minimizing the number. Several critics (Haupt, Dalman, Dussaud, Haller, Buzy, Robert) delete the disturbing last stich "and girls without number." Robert noted in support of the omission that it does not figure in I Kings 11:3, is not mentioned in the following verse, and, moreover, that it overloads the thought and the rhythm.

W. F. Albright suggested that since the numerical gradation "seventy–eighty" is common in Ugaritic poetry, with well-attested cases also in Hurro-Hittite literature, with regard to 6:8, "it is reasonably certain that 'sixty' is a later substitute for 'seventy' at a time when the numerical gradations of the second millennium had ceased to be normative" (1963, 1). J. Greenfield, however, pointed out that the seven/eight gradation was still normative in the first millennium B.C., as witnessed by its use in late books of the Hebrew Bible, on the Arslan Tash amulet, on Aramaic magic bowls, and in Mandaic texts. Thus Canticles 6:8 can be approached from two points of view, Greenfield suggested. On the one hand, it may not partake of the pattern "seventy–eighty" since an unlimited number is intended. In that case we must compare the Ugaritic text 4[51].7.9–12 where the numbers 66/77/88/99 are used to indicate an unlimited number, while in Canticles this is indicated by "60/80/unnumbered." On the other hand, if one insists that it does partake of a classical pattern, then with Gordis (1954, 91) Greenfield noted that sixty/eighty is in reality three score/four score, i.e. a multitude of the traditional three/four numerical gradation (1965, 257a; cf. Albright, *YGC* 255n136).

The Targum applied this verse to nations that warred against Israel.

> Then rose the Greeks and gathered sixty kings from the sons of Esau, clothed in armor and riding upon horses, and cavalry, and eighty dukes (*dûḵsîn*) of the sons of Ishmael, riding on elephants, besides the remnant of the peoples and tongues among them without number, and they appointed Alexander the King as chief over them, and they came to wage war against Jerusalem.

In Midrash Rabbah this verse was referred to the nations of the world, sixty and eighty of them making one hundred and forty, forty with their own language but no script, forty with no language of their own, but a script, and the maidens without number representing the nations that have neither language nor script of their own. Again the one hundred and forty was applied to seventy nations that know their fathers, but not their mothers and seventy that know their mothers but not their fathers, while the maidens without number are those that know neither. Neither of the deficiencies could apply to Israel, since language and script are mentioned in Esther 8:9 and pedigrees in Num 1:18.

Christian expositors offered a diversity of explanations for the three classes—

queens, concubines, virgins. Origen saw the queens as the perfect souls, the concubines those who are progressing, and the virgins those who are just beginning on the way to perfection. Gregory of Nyssa took the queens to be those who serve God for love, the concubines those who do so from fear, and the virgins those imperfect believers who nevertheless seek salvation. Philo of Carpasia saw the queens as those who led righteous lives before the Law and under it; the concubines as those Gentiles who lived by the law of nature and fell into idolatry, but were at last united to Christ by conversion; and the virgins as the general mass of Christian believers undistinguished by any remarkable graces. Epiphanius took the queens as the Patriarchs, the concubines as the heretical sects of Christendom, the virgins as the heathen schools of philosophy. (For these and more of the sort, cf. Littledale.)

Exegetes of the "école naturaliste" found the supposed allusion to Solomon quite natural since in the Syrian peasant wedding festival the bride and groom play the role of king and queen. Joüon rejected any connection with the luxurious royal harem and, like the Midrash Rabbah, applied the numbers to the multitude of the nations which, compared to Israel, are of scant value in the eyes of Yahweh, although they are all in a certain sense His brides and will become so when the nations will be united with Israel in the worship of the true God. This interpretation Robert regarded as preferable, the idea here being the choice of Israel in preference to every other people. There is no need to seek precision as to what the groups mentioned in the text correspond; they designate *en bloc* the pagan nations under the image of the oriental harem, according to Robert, and the connection with I Kings 11:3 is purely literary.

The cultic school saw here a reference to the votaries of the love goddess, but specific parallels were not adduced. S. N. Kramer noted that the king "Shu-Sin, not unlike Solomon of a much later day, seemed to have been a high favorite with the 'ladies of the harem,' the hierodules and devotees, that made up the cult personnel of Inanna-Ishtar" (*SMR,* 93). In the Song of Songs the bride herself is never directly designated "queen," as she is in the Mesopotamian Sacred Marriage. In a hymn celebrating a ritual marriage of Shu-Sin and the beauteous Kubatum, the votary sings:

O my [queen] who is favored of limb,
O my [queen] who is . . . of head, my queen Kubatum,
O my [lord] who is . . . of hair, my lord Shu-Sin,
O my [lord] who is . . . of word, my son of Shulgi.
(*SMR,* 94; 152n15)

9a. *Unique.* Delitzsch took *'aḥaṯ* here as subject ("one, who is my dove, my perfect one") and in the following line as predicate ("one is she of her mother"). Similarly Renan rendered, "l'unique, c'est ma colombe; elle est unique de sa mère." Delitzsch explained, however, that this does not mean that Shulamite was her mother's only child; *'aḥaṯ, unica,* is equivalent to *unice dilecta,* as *yāḥîḏ* in Prov 4:3 is equivalent to *unice dilectus*. The citation of Zech 14:7 by Delitzsch is not relevant, since *'eḥaḏ* there designates a single (continuous) day without alternation of day and night, a unique day to be sure, but that goes without saying. The parallel with Prov 4:3, however, is very striking:

For I was my father's son,
Tender and unique/special, dear to my mother.

In Gen 22:2 the emphasis is likewise on the special and unique love and not that Isaac was the only (legitimate?) son.

my dove, my perfect one. The identical expression is used in 5:2 where *JPSV* took it as hendiadys, "my faultless dove," but here separately:

Only one is my dove, My perfect one.

9c. *Favorite.* LXX *eklektē,* Vulgate *electa,* and likewise in 10c below where the identical form *bārāh* occurs in a different context. The masculine form *bar* is used in Job 11:4 of Job's innocence or moral purity. The verb is used in the simple stem in Ezek 20:38 of purging the land of rebels, and in Eccles 3:18 of God's testing of men. The passive participle *bārûr* is applied to polished arrows, Isa 49:2, and to sheep or people as select, choice or chosen, Neh 5:18; I Chron 7:40, 9:22, 16:41. The middle/passive (*nip̄'al*) and the reflexive stems are used in Isa 52:11; II Sam 32:27 and Ps 18:27[26E] of purifying one's self. The factitive (*pi'ēl*) is used of purifying in Dan 11:35 and the reflexive of making one's self pure in Dan 12:10. The causative (*hip̄'îl*) is used of cleansing Jerusalem, Jer 4:11, and of sharpening arrows, Jer 51:11. *AT* rendered here "darling," *RSV* "flawless," *JB* "favourite." Robert's "la préferée" is an excellent choice. There is little to be said in support of *NEB*'s interpretation:

her mother's only child, devoted to the mother who bore her.

The interest here is hardly a matter of filial piety, but rather of parental favoritism. It is no special distinction to be a favorite only child.

8–9. Delitzsch felt that the "typical" interpretation here in particular showed its superiority to the allegorical interpretation which, by reason of its very absurdity or folly, became an easy subject of wanton mockery. To see an allegory of heavenly things in such a herd of women—a kind of thing which the Book of Genesis dates from the degradation of marriage in the line of Cain—is a profanation of that which is holy, according to Delitzsch:

The fact is, that by a violation of the law of God (Deut. xvii. 17), Solomon brings a cloud over the typical representation, which is not at all to be thought of in connection with the Antitype. Solomon . . . is not to be considered by himself, but only in his relation to Shulamith. In Christ, on the contrary, is no imperfection; sin remains in the congregation. In the Song, the bride is purer than the bridegroom; but in the fulfilling of the Song this relation is reversed: the bridegroom is purer than the bride.

9d,e. The "girls," lit. *bānôṯ*, "daughters," correspond to the *'ălāmôṯ* of the preceding verse, and thus there is no basis for Robert's elimination of 8c above on the ground that the *'ălāmôṯ* are not mentioned in the following verse. The girls are clearly the same in these two contiguous verses, whether separate from or inclusive of the queens and concubines. Whether they are the same as the "Jerusalem girls" so frequently mentioned in the Canticle (1:5, 2:7, 3:5, 5:16, 8:4) is uncertain. In 2:2b,3b, "girls" and "boys" (*bānôṯ* and *bānîm*), is used of the entire category in each case to emphasize the superiority of the bride to all other females and the groom to all other males, as the lotus stands out among the brambles or the apple tree among scrub wood.

9. The Targum interpreted the verse thus:

> Now at that time the Assembly of Israel which resembled a perfect dove was serving her Sovereign with a single mind and holding to the Law, busy with the words of the Law with a perfect heart, and her merit was clear as on the day she came out of Egypt. Thus when the Hasmoneans and Mattathias and all the people of Israel came out and joined battle with them, the Lord delivered them into their hand. And when the inhabitants of the districts saw this, they blessed them and the kings of the land and the rulers praised them.

(The concubines are eliminated by the interpretation of the word as meaning "districts," *pilḵayyā'*.)

Midrash Rabbah identified the unique undefiled dove with Abraham, citing Ezek 33:24, "Abraham was one." The "only one of her mother" was taken as Isaac, "the favorite of her that bore her" as Jacob, without concern for gender, grammatical or otherwise. The daughters that saw and felicitated her were the tribes, Joseph's brothers (Gen 45:16). Another explanation related this to Leah's jubilation at the birth of Asher (Gen 30:13) and still another to Joseph (Gen 41:38*f*). The quantities sixty, eighty, and "innumerable" were applied to the Law: the sixty queens being the tractates of *hălāḵôṯ*, eighty concubines the sections of Leviticus, the maidens innumerable the additional *hălāḵôṯ*. Again the sixty queens represent the companies of Saints who sit in the Garden of Eden under the Tree of Life and study Torah. Still other interpretations related the queens and concubines to the Israelites who went out of Egypt, the innumerable maidens to proselytes, and the single dove to the Community of Israel.

For Christian expositors the one undefiled dove was the Church Universal having one Lord, one faith, one baptism; or the spotless Humanity of Christ, the only offspring of His Virgin Mother; or Our Lady the Virgin Mother, herself. The daughters that saw and praised were also explained as the Church, the queens and concubines as types of the external world which does not bless the Church and yet is compelled to praise her. (Cf. Littledale.)

10a. *Who is this?* The query is the same as in 3:6 and again in 8:5 and it is the crucial question for the interpretation of the Canticle as a whole.

looks forth. LXX *ekkuptousa*, Vulgate *progreditur*. The verb *šqp* in both the *nip̄'al* and the *hip̄'îl* stems signifies "to look out from above," as a mountain looks over a plain or valley (Num 21:20, 23:28; I Sam 13:18), as God looks down from heaven (Ps 14:2), or as one looks out a window (Jud 5:28; II Sam 6:16; Prov 7:6), or as evil looms from the north (Jer 6:1, the term for north here being the name of the mountain Ṣaphon which was the abode of Baal in the Ugaritic myths). The Arabic shows clearly the connotation of elevation and superiority, the noun *saqf* designating a roof or ceiling, and the verb in simple stem signifying "to become a bishop" and in the factitive stem "to provide with roof or ceiling" and "to make (someone) a bishop."

as the dawn. LXX *hōsei orthros,* Vulgate *quasi aurora consurgens.* The term *šaḥar* denotes the rosy glow of the dawn which comes up on the horizon before sunrise; cf. Gen 19:15, 32:25,27[24,26E]. Harper quoted in illustration Shakespeare's *Hamlet* I 166–167:

> But, look, the morn, in russet mantle clad,
> Walks o'er the dew of yon high eastward hill.

In Ugaritic myth we have the identical expression *km šḥr,* "like the dawn," parallel with *km qdm,* "like the east" (12[75].1.7), but the context is broken. Elsewhere in Ugaritic myth *šḥr* is the name of the deified dawn, linked with the deified dusk, or sunset, in the compound *šḥr w šlm,* "Dawn and Dusk," in the myth called "The Birth of the Beautiful Gods." In Isa 14:12 the morning star (*hēlēl*) is called Son of Dawn (*ben šaḥar*). The Venus star as the Morning and Evening Star is male in the morning and female in the evening.

10b. *the moon.* The term *lĕḇānāh,* "the white one," as a poetic designation of the moon is attested elsewhere in the Old Testament only in Isa 24:23 and 30:26, in each instance parallel with *ḥammāh,* "the hot one," as in the present instance. The gender of the moon and the sun fluctuate. In Mesopotamia both the lunar and solar deities, Sin and Shamash, were major gods. In Ugaritic myth the sun goddess Shapsh plays a very minor role while lunar deities are still more insignificant. We have from Ugarit a short hymn celebrating the marriage of the moon god, *yrḫ* (Yariḫ or Yarḫ) with a goddess *nkl* (Nikkal, from Sumerian NIN-GAL, "Great Lady") presumably also lunar in character.

10c. *Bright.* Cf. 9c where the identical form *bārāh* is rendered "favorite." LXX and Vulgate rendered the same in both places, "elect."

as the sun. The term *ḥammāh,* in addition to the passages mentioned above (10b), is used in Job 30:28 as a designation of the sun. The word is used as a common noun of the sun's heat in Ps 19:7[6E].

Stephan (19*f*) noted that in Arabic the sun is female and the moon male, but "like the moon," *zei el qamar,* is still a common attribute of a fair girl.

10d. Cf. 4a. Syriac here read *kirḇāḇôṯ,* "like myriads" and Quinta and Sexta or Origen's *Hexapla* reflect the reading *kimmĕguddālôṯ,* "like enlarged things."

Some critics (Siegfried, Haupt, Zapletal) supposed that this verse was displaced from an original position between the end of the present chapter and the beginning of the next as an introduction to the so-called "sword dance" of 7:1[6:13E]. Delitzsch, however, made this verse the beginning of the First Scene of the Fifth Act, 6:10–7:7[6E], which he entitled "Shulamith, The Attractively Fair But Humble Princess," in which he supposed that the humble beauty stepped out of the recesses of the royal gardens and the daughters of Jerusalem, overpowered by the beauty of her heavenly appearance, exclaim, "Who is this? etc." Harper, following Oettli, emphasized the past tenses, "saw," "blessed," "praised," and took this to refer to the reaction of the court ladies when they first saw the beauteous maid.

The riddle of this verse for exponents of the cultic interpretation is not difficult to guess. Wittekindt (9) cited the singularity of the beautiful and terrible Ishtar and her astral traits as the Venus star. Schmökel (49*ff*) imagined that the goddess, her cult image, or the priestess representing her, appears here on a podium in the temple in a cultic marriage and is greeted by the community with appropriate display of awe and reverence, and is praised in terms which a Palestinian peasant would scarcely apply to his bashful bride. The traits of beauty and terror which the Sumero-Akkadian cult songs regularly ascribe to the Goddess of Love and War are vividly depicted here, as recognized by F. X. Kugler (1927, 45*ff*).

10. The Targum ascribed these words to the nations who exclaimed:

> How brilliant are the deeds of his people in the dawn. Beautiful are her youths as the moon and her merits bright as the sun, and her dread was upon all the inhabitants of the land at the time that her four regiments went in the desert.

Midrash Rabbah, in a series of elusive exegetical twists and turns, applied every part of this verse to Israel, and related it to a number of other passages of Scripture.

Christian allegorists made a great deal of this verse. Honorius of Autun recognized here the Church in all phases of its existence: the dawn is the Patriarchal Dispensation, the moon the Mosaic Law drawing its light from the unseen sun and waxing gradually to fulness, and the sun is the full light of the Gospel revelation. Limited to the Christian Church, the words were applied in various ways by Christian expositors. The early Church in Judea was fair as the moon, but pale with the light of suffering, terror and martyrdom during the Ten Persecutions, till under Constantine it became like the sun, visible throughout the world in faith and glory, and terrible as an army when it became active against Heresy and Paganism which previously it had resisted only with passive endurance (Cornelius à Lapide). Some of the Fathers put these words in the mouth of the repentant Synagogue at the end of the world, others attributed them to the Angels who attend the Bridegroom. The Church looks forth as the dawn, passing from clouds of darkness to shine with the light of truth; she is fair as the moon in this life, waxing and waning in prosperity or adversity, but clear as the sun in the world to come. Applied to the Religious Life, there are degrees of brightness, beginners making their first steps like the morning light, progressing Christians setting a good example to sinners are like the moon shining in the night, while the Saints are the sun shining in the broad day. Or the dawn may represent humility, the moon chastity, and the sun charity. Littledale presents a variety of dilations on this verse, including, among the applications to the Virgin Mary, St. Ambrose's hymn *Veni Redemptor Gentium*:

> The Lord a Maiden's womb doth fill,
> But keeps her stainless Maiden still,
> The banners there of virtue shine,
> Where God is present in His shrine.

and George Herbert's quaint anagram on Mary=Army:

> How well her name an army doth present,
> In whom the Lord of Hosts did pitch His tent!

11a. *walnut*. The word '*ĕḡôz* occurs only here in the Bible, but in post-Biblical Hebrew it is a common generic term for "nut" and a specific term for the "walnut," *Juglans regia*, which flourishes widely in temperate areas of Europe and Asia. The region around the lake of Galilee, according to Josephus (*Wars* III x 8), was especially suited to the walnut, the temper of the air being so varied that it agreed with different sorts of trees including walnuts, which require the coldest air, and palms which grow best in warm air. Although the walnut thrives in Palestine-Syria, it was the expert opinion of I. Löw (*FJ*, II, 33) that it was not indigenous to the area. The allusion in Song of Songs 6:11 and Josephus' assertion that the walnut tree flourished in vast plenty in Galilee were the only references from pre-Talmudic times which Löw could cite. The fact that neither biblical nor Mishnaic-Talmudic times attest a place name indicating the presence of the walnut tree was, in Löw's view, no accident. In contrast with the numerous place names which refer to the pomegranate, the lack of place names containing the word for walnut might seem significant, but for the fact that there are numerous other trees and plants which do not figure in place-names. Löw regarded as naïve the effort of the *Onomasticon Sacra* to connect Gozan of Isa 37:12=II Kings 19:12 with *gôz*, "walnut."

Although the walnut grew in the Holy Land, those that came to market were apparently regarded as imported (cf. *FJ*, II, 31). The walnut apparently was not highly regarded among the Greeks before the introduction of a superior type from Persia, the royal nut *karuon basilikon*. The Romans regarded the walnut as of Persian origin and it has been generally assumed that the term '*ĕḡôz* came into Hebrew from Persian *kawz*. The form '*ĕḡôz*, however, would be difficult to explain as coming from Persian *kawz* since there is no initial consonantal cluster which would need to be broken up by a prosthetic *aleph*, '. Grimme (1914, 269) tried to explain the initial ' of '*ĕḡôz* as a means of indicating voiceless *g*, but other forms of the word show that this is not so. The word is represented in the Aramaic of the Babylonian Talmud as '*amgōzā*. In Armenian the word appears as *engoiz*, "walnut," and *en-*

guzi, "walnut tree." The form in Ossetian is *ängūz,* Georgian *nigozi,* Kurdish *egviz* (cf. H. Hübschmann, *Armenische Grammatik,* 393). It is apparent that the shorter forms, Persian *kawz,* neo-Persian *gōz,* Syriac *gauzā,* Arabic *jawz, jôz,* Turkish *koz,* are younger than the longer forms appearing in Hebrew, Aramaic, Armenian, Ossetian, Georgian and Kurdish. This is now confirmed by the appearance of the word in Ugaritic texts dating to the middle of the second millennium B.C. in the form *'rgz,* presumably *'erguz.* J. Aistleitner (*WUS,* 2095) conjecturally related Ugaritic *'rgz* to Hebrew *'ĕgôz* and M. Dahood (1963, 292) cited a Ugaritic phraseological parallel to the present passage of the Song of Songs, which will be considered below, after noting various indirect lines of evidence tending to confirm Aistleitner's conjecture that Ugaritic *'rgz* and Hebrew *'ĕgôz* represent the same word.

The Ugaritic *'rgz* with initial *'ayin* falls in with a group of such nouns sparsely attested in Hebrew as animal names, e.g. *'akbār,* "mouse," *'akkāḇîš,* "spider," *'aqrāḇ,* "scorpion," but common in Arabic, mostly as animal and plant names, e.g. *'uṣfūr,* "bird," *'uṣqūl,* "male locust," *'irmiḍ,* "seaweed," *'usbur,* "leopard," *'aslaq,* "male ostrich," *'ukbuz, glans penis, 'uljum,* "frog," "duck," "he-goat," "louse," *'umkuss,* "ass," *'anbar,* "amber," *'anwaz,* "marjoram," *'anqafīr,* "scorpion." On Arabic nouns of this type, cf. S. Fraenkel, 1878, and J. J. Hess, 1924. If Ugaritic *'rgz* means, "nut," "walnut," "walnut tree," or the like, as has already been surmised, it is clear that the forms attested in Hebrew (*'ĕgôz*), Aramaic (*'amgōzā*), Armenian (*engoiz*) are nearer to the original pattern of the word than the monosyllabic forms of Persian, Arabic, and Turkish. The loss of the initial ' in nouns of this pattern is illustrated by the Hebrew *ṣippôr,* "bird," which is cognate with Arabic *'uṣfūr,* Akkadian *iṣṣūru* and Ugaritic *'ṣr* (*'iṣṣūr*<*'iṣpūr*). The quality of the initial vowel in the Armenian, Ossetian, Kurdish, and Hebrew forms of the word may reflect the influence of the original initial laryngeal. The *r* of the Ugaritic form *'rgz* becomes *n* in the Armenian, Ossetian, and Georgian forms of the word, *m* in the Aramaic, and disappears in the Hebrew and Kurdish forms, while in Persian, Syriac, and Arabic the first two consonants disappear.

The evidence for the meaning of Ugaritic *'rgz* and connection with Hebrew *'ĕgôz* is admittedly indirect and circumstantial, but nevertheless impressive and nowhere contradictory. The word occurs several times in different contexts in Ugaritic. In a price list of various commodities including oil, wood, horses, chariot equipment, reeds, stones, and various vegetable products it is listed at "fifty *'rgz* for five," *ḫmšm.'rgz.b.ḫmšt* (1127.22). C. H. Gordon (*UT* 19.1916) noted that in this context (1127:20–22) it is associated with the juniper, *dprn.* In a hippiatric text (161[56].10) *'rgz* is one of the medicines prescribed for the sick horse. The same word is to be restored in another hippiatric prescription (160[55].4, 9). The medicine is poured in the horse's nose (presumably with a tube and with caution lest the horse snort and reverse the process) and thus would be an oil or other liquid. On the medicinal properties of nut oil, Löw (*FJ,* II, 48*f*) cites Galen, Bar Hebraeus,

Maimonides, and others. Nut oil was prescribed for various human ills, heart trouble, kidney stones, leprosy, sciatica, and hemorrhoids. Rubbing the teeth with a root of the nut tree was believed to clear the head and make the thoughts bright. The physician Tobiah Kohen (1652–1729), stimulated by Canticle's allusion to the fruits of the nut garden, investigated and discovered that nut juice as well as pulverized nut shells was a good emetic (*nux vomica*), that the hulls were good for the colic, and the juice of the hulls good for cleansing the mouth and throat (*FJ*, II, 49). It would thus appear that almost any juice or substance from the nut tree might be used as physic for horses, as for humans.

The word *'rgz* also occurs as a place name in two lists of towns of the kingdom of Ugarit (2041.16 and 2074.36). In 2041.16 *'rgz* follows after *ḫlb* and *šld*. This *ḫlb,* however, is not the great city Aleppo which lay well beyond the control of the kingdom of Ugarit, but a small town on the border with Mukiš. The town *šld* is the *Su-la-da* which the Hittite king Šuppiluliumaš ceded to Ugarit. I am indebted for this information to Professor Michael Astour who is preparing an index of Ugaritic geographical names. The town *'rgz* Professor Astour cannot yet pinpoint, but in a private communication he suggested a location to the south of Jebel Aqra' in the present-day Basīṭ district where most of the place names are now Turkish.

The Arab geographer Yāqūt mentioned a district of villages along the Euphrates between Aleppo and al-Birah which was called Nahr al-Jawz, "Walnut River." (Cf. Guy Le Strange, 1890, 463.) Professor Astour also called the writer's attention to the reference to the district of Nahr al-Jawz in Kamal ad-Dīn's *History of Aleppo,* translated by E. Blochet (1897, 51). For other place names containing the element *gôz* in Syria, cf. Löw, *FJ,* II, 34. The connection of Gozan of Isa 37:12 with *gôz,* "nut," suggested by the *Onomasticon*, was regarded by Löw (33) as naïve. It is of interest, however, that in II Kings 17:6 the Khabur river is called *nĕhar gôzān,* which is strikingly similar to the Arabic Nahr al-Jawz. There is no good reason to doubt that Gôzān (Guzanna of the cuneiform texts, modern Tell Halāf, excavated by Baron Max von Oppenheim) could be related to *gôz,* "walnut," with the afformative *-ān.* Walnut trees flourished remarkably in well-watered areas. W. Thomson reported seeing near the source of the Orontes in 1846 a magnificent tree said to have produced in the previous year a harvest of a hundred thousand walnuts (cf. *FJ,* II, 36).

The Ugaritic town *'rgz* apparently gave rise to the gentilic form *'rgzy* as a personal or family name (131[309].27). Löw noted (34) the Jewish family name Egozi attested in Constantinople in the sixteenth century. The Ugaritic *'rgzy* suggests that this name might be very old. The name Nussbaum, however, hardly preserves any unbroken connection with Egozi or Ugaritic *'rgzy.*

The common noun *'rgz* occurs twice in Ugaritic mythological texts. In one of the so-called Rephaim Texts which deal with the *rpum* (the biblical *rĕpā'îm,* denizens of the netherworld) there is mention of a sacrifice with eating and drinking and the remains of a phrase . . .]*il d'rgzm* (20[121].1.8) which would mean "god of the walnuts." Unfortunately, there is no parallel passage for the restoration of this provocative line. The other occurrence is of special interest for the present concern since it presents a striking verbal parallel to Song of Songs 6:11a. At the end of the Nikkal Hymn, which celebrates the marriage of two lunar deities, the West Semitic Yariḫ, "Moon," and the Mesopotamian Nikkal, the rhapsodist says (24[77].40–45):

ašr [i]lht [k]ṯrt	I sing the goddesses, Skilled Ones,
bnt hll snnt	Jubilantes, Swallows(?),
bnt hll b'l gml	Jubilantes of the Sickle-Lord
yrdt b'rgzm	Who go down to the walnut (grove),
bg bz tdm' llay	With violent voice weep for the Unfortunate
'm lẓpn il dpid	With Beneficent El Benign

The parallel between *yrdt b'rgzm* and Song of Songs 6:11a was seen by M. Dahood, 1963, 292. We will dispense here with philological arguments in support of the translation given above. Suffice it to note that readings and word division of the fifth colon are highly uncertain (cf. Herrmann, 1968, 20–23 for variant readings and interpretations of these lines and of the whole poem).

The problem of the sense of the manifestly related expressions of Song of Songs 6:11a, "To the walnut grove I went down" and the Nikkal Hymn's (24[77].42–43) "(who) go down to the walnuts," resides, in a nutshell as it were, in the mythological meaning of the nut in question. Wittekindt (178) alluded to the walnut grove which surrounds the shrine of Adonis at Afqa in the beautiful valley of the River of Adonis between Byblos and Baalbek in Lebanon; cf. J. G. Frazer, 1922, 28. Wittekindt further noted that the nut, like the apple, is a love-food and a symbol of the vulva, and he cited the association of the nut with Dionysus and Artemis. Artemis' cognomen *caryatis* was related to the nut-nymphs, the caryatids, who performed the voluptuous dances in the cult celebrations and lent their name to the female figures which served as supporting columns in architecture. For the cosmic symbolism of the nut in the Orphic mysteries and among Jewish mystics, Wittekindt referred to R. Eisler, 1910, 521*ff*.

Belief in the quasi-magical properties of the nut is ancient and persistent, as one may observe in the window displays and on the shelves of present-day "organic" food shops. Apart from their unquestionable nutritive value, nuts are probably subconsciously esteemed as a love-food by reason of their similarity to and symbolism of the gonads. Pliny (*Hist. nat.* xvii 136) explained the classical designation of the walnut *Juglans* as referring to Jove's glands. Walnuts were apparently a staple of the diet of the priests of Isis who were distinguished for their vigor and longevity. The remains of a sacred repast found in the Iseum at Pompeii included eggs, lentils, and walnuts, all suggestive of fertility; cf. Witt, 1971, 98, 298n69, and pl. 29.

The nut as a sexual symbol also represents the female genitalia. The learned Italian rabbi and physician Isaac Ben Samuel Lampronti (1679–1756) explained in his Talmudic encyclopedia *paḥad yiṣḥaq* (*Isaac's Fear* 2, 99a, cited after Löw, *FJ,* II, 56) that the nut represents Eve's *pudenda* (*'erwāṯāh šel ḥawwāh*). The nut tree, moreover, according to Lampronti, was the tree of knowledge in the Garden of Eden and before the sin, the nut had no shell, the rose had no thorn, and the serpent no poison. On the Gaonic traditions of the blessing of the virgin bride beginning with the formula "He who planted the nut/the bridal pair in the Garden of Eden," with fluctuation between "nut" (*'ĕgōz*) and the bridal pair (*zûḡ*), cf. Löw, 55*f,* and A. Marmorstein, 1948. Nuts were strewn about the bridal pair (TB Berakot 50b), and the custom mentioned by Löw in Hungary and South Russia of tossing nuts and sweetmeats at the bridegroom, when he is called up for the Torah reading on the Sabbath before or after his wedding, still persists in orthodox circles in the United States. Pregnant women were also fed preserved nuts, and nuts, honey, and sweetmeats were eaten at Purim, Sukkot, and at circumcisions (cf. Löw, 48).

The nut tree also had its sinister aspects. The ancient Romans thought that this tree poisoned the earth around it (Pliny *Hist. nat.* xvii 18) and a similar notion was affirmed by Isidor of Seville in the seventh century. The belief persisted among the Arabs that to tarry under the nut tree is dangerous. Judah the Pious in the *Book of Pious Ones* (*sēp̄er ḥăsîḏîm,* ed. R. Margalioth, Bologna, 1538, no. 1153, p. 572) explained that the demons are wont to gather in groups of nine on the leaves of the nut tree which have nine pinnae, hence the hazard of sleeping under this tree. (I am indebted to my colleague Sid Leiman for verification of this reference cited by Löw, II, 37.) Demons also gather on other kinds of trees (TB Pesaḥim 111a). The restriction on eating nuts on New Year's Day has been explained as motivated by concern for the clear audition of the tone of the ram's horn which would be impeded by the clearing of throats dessicated and irritated by nuts. The reinforcement of this restriction by the notation that the numerical value of the consonants in the word for "nut," is equivalent to the sum of the word for "sin" (as defectively spelled with the omission of the otiose final ') suggests that the real reason was something else (cf. Löw, 53).

The infernal associations of the nut have cosmic significance in Jewish mysticism. Eleazar of Worms observed that the numerical value of the letters of the phrase "to the nut garden," *'l gnt 'gwz* (501) comes close to the sum of "this is the depth of the chariot," *zh 'wmq hmrkbh* (500), so that the reference is to Ezekiel's vision. The three or four layers of the nut in Qabbalistic literature are variously interpreted. The inner cavity, according to the New Zohar (28b), represents the Deep (*tĕhôm*). The inmost part also is the garden of the Shekinah. One of the halls of Paradise is the "Nut Palace" (*hêḵal 'ĕgôz*) which is near the inmost shrine, "Bird Nest Palace" (*hêḵal qan ṣippôr*) where the Messiah waits. (A. Jellinek, III, xxvii and 136; J. D.

Eisenstein, 1928, 87b; cf. Löw, *FJ*, II, 43.) The nut symbolizes Paradise as embedded and enclosed in layers of shells, protected on all sides, unseen by prophet or angel eye. The kernel is the Shekinah, the heavenly bride, like an enclosed garden, to which the King descended (cf. Löw, 44*f* for these and other interpretations).

There is a great deal more lore on the cosmic symbolism of the nut cited by Löw which is of considerable intrinsic interest but too extensive and involved to be reviewed here. Perhaps enough has been adduced with respect to the cosmic symbolism of the descent into the Nut Grove to prepare the ground for the suggestion, to be further developed in subsequent comment on the present verse, that the Grove in question was located in the Qidron Valley, between the Temple Hill and the Mount of Olives, which in both Jewish and Muslim tradition is the entrance to the netherworld. This area is still called by the Jerusalem Arabs *Wādi al-Jôz*, "Nut Valley." How old this designation may be, the present writer has not been able to determine, but the cultic and mythological associations of this Valley and the garden there suggest that it may well be a survival from ancient days when the walnut flourished where now the gnarled old olive trees grow in Gethsemane.

grove. This form *ginnaṯ*, occurs elsewhere only in Esther 1:5, 7:7–8, with reference to the locale of the great banquet which Ahasuerus gave in the garden of the royal palace in Susa. The regular feminine form *gannāh*, construct *gannaṯ*, is used several times, e.g. Num 24:6; Isa 1:30, 61:11; Jer 29:5,28; Amos 4:9, 9:14; Job 8:16. The use of the term in Isa 1:29, 65:3, 66:17 is of particular interest because of the clear references to lascivious pagan worship. The Aramaic form *gannĕṯā*, "garden," corresponding to Greek *kēpos*, and the term *gnt' 'ylm*, "oak garden," the holy grove, *hieron alsos*, figured in the sacred rites at Palmyra (cf. J. T. Milik, 1972, 12). These two terms are juxtaposed in the condemnation of the fertility cult in Isa 1:29:

You shall be ashamed of the oaks on which you doted,
Abashed for the gardens which you chose.

11a. *I went down.* Any use of the verb *yrd*, "go down," suggests to exponents of the cultic interpretation descent to the netherworld, either of Tammuz's demise or Ishtar's descent to seek him. Whereas in 6:2a there is triple indication of this masculinity of the subject, there is here no way to tell the gender of the speaker.

11b. *To view.* The expression *rā'āh bĕ-* means to look at an object with any of a variety of different emotions, delight, grief, sympathy, remorse, suspicion, disdain; cf. Gen 34:1; I Sam 6:19; Eccles 2:1; Gen 21:16; Exod 2:11; Gen 29:32; Ezek 21:21. Cf. 1:6a. Graetz's emendation of *lir'ôṯ* to *lir'ôṯ*, "to pasture," was misguided.

valley. The term *naḥal*, Akkadian and Ugaritic *naḫlu*, designates a valley, ravine, or stream-bed which may be a torrent during the rainy season and bone-dry in the hot summer (cf. Job 6:15; Jer 15:18). The Arabic term is *wādi*. The valleys were naturally the first areas to respond to the rain and produce lush vegetation and thus were scenes of fervid fertility worship, as the prophets' tirades attest (Isa 57:3–10):

Come, you sons of a sorceress,
Spawn of whoring adulteress,
At whom you are gibing,
At whom are you gaping,
Poking out your tongue?
You rebel rabble,
Progeny of deceit,
Inflaming yourselves at the oaks,
Under every green tree;
Butchering babes in the valleys
(*bannĕḥālîm*)
Beneath the clefts of the cliffs.
On the valley (*naḥal*) banks is your part;
They, they are your lot.
To them you pour libations,
Offer up your grain gifts.
On a high and lofty hill you set your
couch,
And go up to sacrifice.
Behind the door you set the (phallic)
symbol,
Without me(?) you strip and mount.
You spread your bed,
And make alliance with them.
You love their couch,
On the "hand" you gaze.
You go to the "King" with oil,
Multiply your perfumes.
You send your emissaries afar,
You descend to the netherworld.
With your great strength, you are weary,
But never say, "Enough."
You find life in your "hand,"
And you do not weaken.

On "hand" as a euphemism for "phallus," cf. 5:4. In spite of the textual difficulties (perhaps deliberately corrupted to obscure obscenities) the import is clear. Here are the elements of fertility worship, human sacrifice, orgiastic sexual rites, perfume, libations, the quest reaching to the netherworld. The present interest, however, is centered on the term *naḥal*, twice used to designate the locale of these activities. This is the same term used in the Ugaritic myth in connection with the resurrection of Baal. The assurance that Baal is alive comes with the return of fertility in the valleys:

The heavens rain oil,
The valleys (*nḫlm*) run honey;
Thus I know that Mighty Baal lives,
That the Prince, Lord of Earth, exists.
(6[49].3.6–9)

The descent here to the valley to see whether the fruits, vines, and pomegranates have sprouted may now be understood in the light of the Ugaritic myth as quest for assurance that the dead Baal has revived.

Joüon supposed that the valley in question was the fertile part of the Jordan Valley, the Zor, or "The Jungle of the Jordan" (cf. Glueck, 1968, 77*f*). Robert, however, suggested that if the author thought of a specific valley, it must be the Qidron, and more exactly the "king's garden" (Neh 3:15) which was watered by the spring of Gihon. Nevertheless, it seemed to Robert more likely that the valley is here "un nom d'espèce" equivalent to a plural and refers to the valleys of Palestine in general, the garden of the groom being identified with the whole country. It appears that Robert's first guess was best.

As noted in connection with the walnut grove of the preceding line, the quest for the garden and valley has overlooked a striking bit of relevant evidence in the modern Arabic designation of the Qidron Valley as Wādi al-Jôz, "Walnut Valley." The garden there, between the Temple Hill and the Mount of Olives, is Gethsemane, "fertile garden," or *gē' šĕmānî(m)*, "fertile valley," as Jerome derived the name, as in Isa 28:1 where the reference is to the valley where the sots of Samaria celebrated. There was a garden (*kēpos*) there by reason of the winter-flow (*cheimarros*) (cf. John 18:1). In earlier time, before Hezekiah closed the upper outlet of Gihon and diverted the water to the west side of the city (II Chron 32:30), the fertility of this valley must have been prodigious. This valley, called Qidron (i.e. Dark, perhaps by reason of the turbid torrent, cf. Job 6:16), Hinnom (of uncertain meaning, explained homiletically by the rabbis with play on *ḥinnām*, "gratuitously," the valley which all enter for vanity and worldly lust), and Tophet (with the vowels of the word *bōšeṯ*, "shame," thus associating the term with the root *wpṯ*, "spit," in disgust at vile and heinous rites). On the etymology of *tōp̄eṯ*, cf. Albright, *YGC*, 237*ff*, and 275(ee). Albright's connection of the word with Hebrew *špt* and Ugaritic *ṯpd* is questionable. There is nothing to support the view that *mṯpd* means "fireplace" in the cliché *ṯn mṯpdm tḥt 'nt arṣ* which Albright rendered "the two fireplaces under the fountains of the earth," i.e. hot springs. The context suggests that *mṯpd* is a measure of distance. Arabic *ṯpd*, used of lining a garment or reinforcing a coat of mail with an inner lining, suggests the sense of layers or strata. The Hebrew and Aramaic *špd*, "bore, pierce," Arabic *sfd*, may be ruled out unless there is an abnormal permutation of the *ṯ*.

The Valley, Qidron, Hinnom, or Tophet, was notorious for the abominations carried on there by kings, priests, prophets, and gentry through the centuries, burning incense on the high places (tombs) and hills and under every green tree, burning children as offerings to Baal, and indulging in drunken orgies of venery (cf. II Kings 16:3, 21:6, 23:10; II Chron 28:3, 33:6; Jer 7:31*f*, 19:2,6, 32:35). No lye or soap could wash away the stain of guilt (Jer 2:20–24):

"Long ago you broke your yoke,
You burst your bonds.
You said, 'I will not serve.'
On every high hill,
Beneath every tree,
You sprawled as a whore.
I planted you a prize vine,
Wholly of purest seed.
But how you turned foul on me,
A strange vine!
Though you scrub with niter,
Lavish lye on yourself,
Your guilty stain I still see,"
Says the Lord God.
"How can you say, 'I am not defiled,
I have not gone after the Baals?'
See your traipsing to the Valley,
Look what you have done!
A swift camel criss-crossing her track;
A wild ass used to the desert,
In her heat sniffing the wind!
Her lust who could restrain?
None who seek her need be weary;
In her month they'll find her."

The infernal associations with this (Walnut) Valley are many. The entrance to the netherworld was here marked by two palm trees (TB Erubin

19a, Sukkot 32b). In Arab lore the area opposite the sealed Golden Gate of the Old City is Jahannum. Here in the Valley of Jehoshaphat will be the final Resurrection and Judgment (Joel 4[3E]:12):

Let the nations awake and come up
To the Valley of Jehoshaphat;
For there I will sit to judge
All the nations round about.

At the same time, the old pagan associations with Baal and his consort Ishtar, or Anat, Queen of Heaven, persist, transmuted and transferred to Christ and the Virgin Mary. In the twelfth century there was a church here dedicated to St. Mary of Josaphat. The spring Gihon is still called "Lady Mary's Spring," *'Ain Sittī Maryām,* and St. Stephen's Gate is "Lady Mary's Gate," *Bāb Sittī Maryām.* One tradition places the Garden of Gethsemane where the Tomb of the Virgin is now located and where the Franciscans maintain the Grotto of the Agony. The infernal aspects of this valley in no way diminish its sacred character. Here from ancient days were celebrated both the joys and agonies of life and death, the ancient tombs being the locales of fertility orgies, human sacrifice, and violent mourning. The sides of the valley are still covered with graves, but the primitive pagan rites have long since been transformed and transferred to the synagogue and the church, in the devout mourner's Qaddish and the chaste communal Qiddush, and in the Christian Eucharist sacrifice and memorial for one who went down to the Garden alone on behalf of all men. In the light of the preceding associations, the gold plated cross of nut wood in the treasury of the Greeks in the Church of the Holy Sepulchre (cf. Dalman, 1921, 325) assumes added significance.

verdure. The word *'ēḇ,* here in the construct plural *ibbê,* occurs elsewhere in the Hebrew Scriptures only in Job 8:12 where it refers to the lush growth of rushes in marshland. *NEB* accordingly rendered the present line "to look at the rushes by the stream," which misses the mark by a wide margin. The Akkadian cognate *inbu* has the meanings fruit tree, fruit, offspring, and (sexual) attractiveness and vigor, and is taken over into Aramaic in the sense of "fruit," as in Dan 4:9,11,18[12,14,21E]. Note in Dan 4:11[14E] the series "tree . . . branches . . . leaves . . . fruit." The modern Ethiopic (Amharic) cognate means "flower." In the present context it is clear that the reference is to new growth, the sprouting and blooming of the spring vegetation. *RSV* thus changed *KJ*'s "fruits" to "blossoms." Meek (*AT* and *IB*) preferred "verdure." *JB* rendered the line "to see what was sprouting in the valley." *JPSV* chose "to see the budding of the vale." *NAB* has "to look at the fresh growth of the valley." In view of the explicit reference to blossoming and flowering in the two succeeding lines, the rendering "fruits" is premature. Meek's choice of "verdure" seems preferable, for lack of a more exact and suitable poetic term.

The word *inbu* in Akkadian is fraught with association with fertility worship. The charm of the love goddess herself designated by the term: "She

(Ishtar) is wrapped in charm and loveliness, adorned with attractiveness (*in-bi*) and sex appeal and (decked out with) cosmetics." Fruits are the fitting offering to the fertility goddess: "I planted a sacred orchard in honor of Ishtar, I established regular offerings of fruit to be made in perpetuity for her." The term may also apply to male sexual power. Ishtar appealed to Gilgamesh (VI 8) "Come, Gilgamesh, be thou (my) lover! Do but grant me of thy fruit" (*in-bi-ka*). "Fruit" (*inbu*) is also an epithet of the moon god Sin, e.g. "The 'Fruit' was eclipsed"; "the 'Fruit' and the Sun will be angry" (cf. *CAD,* VII, s.v. *inbu,* 144–147). In Ugaritic the same term is one of the double names of the lunar goddess, *ib-nkl,* Ibbu-Nikkal, and *nkl-w-ib,* Nikkal-and/or (alias) Ibbu.

11. The Targum interpreted the verse thusly:

> Said the Lord of the World: "For the second Temple which was built by the hands of Cyrus, I caused my Presence to dwell in order to see the good works of my people and to see if perhaps the sages had increased and multiplied, those who are likened to the vine, and if their scions were full of good works like pomegranates."

Midrash Rabbah compared Israel to a nut-tree in several respects. As a nut-tree is pruned for its own benefit and renews its branches, as hair grows more quickly when cut and nails when pared, so whenever Israelites are shorn of their wealth it is for their own good and it is soon replaced and increased. As the shell of the nut protects its fruit, so the ignorant in Israel strengthen those who study Torah (Prov 3:18). If a nut falls in the dirt, one can pick it up and wipe or wash it so that it is fit to eat, so Israel, however much it may be defiled with iniquities all the rest of the year, makes atonement when the Day of Atonement comes (Lev 16:30). As a nut has two shells, Israel has two precepts (concerning the foreskin), circumcision and *pĕrîʿāh* ("uncovering," i.e. exposing the corona by splitting the membrane and pulling it down).

Because the nut tree has a smooth trunk, if one climbs to the top without proper caution he is likely to fall and break his neck, so one who rises to a position of power in Israel and is not careful how he exercises it, is also liable to fall and be punished. As nuts are a childrens' plaything and an amusement of kings, so is Israel in this world because of her sins (Lam 3:14), but in the time to come it will be different (Isa 49:23). As there are soft, medium, and hard nuts, so in Israel there are those who give alms unasked, or when asked, or refuse even when asked. As nuts cannot escape customs duty, but are betrayed by their rattling, so with Jews: wherever one goes he cannot deny that he is a Jew, because he is recognized (Isa 61:9). Into a sackful of nuts, one can still pack a lot of sesame grains and mustard seeds, so many proselytes have been added to Israel (Num 23:10). If one nut is taken from a pile, all the rest topple, so if one Jew is struck, all feel it (Num 16:22). As a nut has four quarters and a court in the center, so Israel camped in the wilderness with four standards in four camps and with the Tent of Meeting in the center (Num 2:17).

This verse was applied to scholars (TB Hagigah 15b) as likened to a nut which, though it be soiled with mud and filth, yet its contents are not contemned. So a scholar, although he may have sinned, yet is his Torah (learning) not contemned.

The nuts, fruits, vine and pomegranates provided Christian expositors a paradise of allegory. The Heavenly Bridegroom first went down to the Synagogue, according to the oath and promise to Abraham and David. The garden of nuts was taken to refer to the Jerusalem priesthood and the nut itself to the Mosaic Law, for the nut tree has bitter leaves and its fruit is covered with a bitter hull and a hard dry shell, but within is a pleasant kernel divided four ways by a wooden cartilage or membrane while it is green. So the Law was covered with a meaning hard to be understood, and mystical, like a harsh rind, yet within was hidden the sweetest and most wholesome fruit, Christ Jesus Himself who came down from heaven to be made known to the four quarters of the earth through the fourfold sense of the Gospel (Philo of Carpasia). The nut garden was related to the enclosed garden of 4:12 as the hallowed womb of the Virgin into which the Lord went down. Again, the nut garden represents the hearts of the Saints who retain divine wisdom in their bodies, like a kernel in the shell, for there are in the Church many constantly occupied with study of Holy Writ, tasting the sweetness of the Lord, and desiring to taste Him more, chewing the cud of sacred joy and growing ever stronger.

The vines flourish when children are brought up in the faith of the Church and the pomegranates bud when the perfect edify their neighbors by example, holy conversation, preaching, and exhibition of good works. Or again when local congregations are healthy and abounding in meditations and prayers and the contemplative, ruddy with charity and zeal, give forth beauty and fragrance to adorn the Church.

The nut, St. Augustine explained, unites three substances, the hull, the shell and the kernel. The hull denotes the flesh of the Savior which had in itself the harshness of his Passion. The kernel is the inner sweetness of his Godhead. The shell signifies the transverse wood of the Cross which by its interposition mediated earthly and heavenly things; cf. Col 1:20. Adam of St. Victor enshrined this interpretation of Augustine in the hymnal sequence *Splendor Patris et figura:*

Nux est Christus, cortex nucis
Circa carnem poena crucis,
Testa corpus osseum,
Carne tecta Deitas
Et Christi suavitas
Signatur per nucleum.

which Littledale put in poetic paraphrase,

Christ the nut, the hull His passion
Closing round His human fashion,
And His bones and frame the shell:
Hid in flesh, Divine completeness
And Christ Jesus' perfect sweetness,
In the kernel mark ye well.

11c,d. These lines are repeated, with slight variations, in 7:13c,d and an additional line "There will I give you my love." LXX supplies here, on the basis of 7:13e, "There I will give my breasts to you."

12. This verse is generally conceded to be the most difficult in the Canticle and it continues to vex translators and commentators. MT, woodenly rendered, seems to say: "I do/did not know my soul (it) set me chariots of my princely people." LXX and Vulgate finding the sense elusive, tampered with nearly every word of the verse and thus compounded the difficulty. LXX

took *nep̄eš* as the subject of the first verb and thus changed the first person to third, "my soul did not know." Who or what was intended as the subject of the verb "put" is not clear, but it is generally assumed that Solomon was meant. Vulgate paused after "I did not know" and then made *nep̄eš* the subject of the verb which was changed from the simple stem of *ś(w/y)m,* "put," to the causative stem of *šmm,* "be astounded," and then the *m*-preformative of *mrkb(w)t* was construed as the preposition *min,* and, like LXX, *'my ndyb* was taken as the proper name Aminadab, to produce *Nescivi; anima mea conturbavit me propter quadrigas Aminadab.*

A thorough history of the exegesis of this verse would be a major undertaking and a few samples of English renderings, including some recent efforts, will suffice to demonstrate the lack of consensus as to the meaning of the verse and will serve as a basis for brief consideration of the difficulties:

KJ Or ever I was aware, my soul made me *like* the chariots of Ammi-nadib.

AT Before I knew it, my fancy set me in a chariot beside my prince.

JB Before I knew . . . my desire hurled me on the chariots of my people, as their prince.

(A note explains, "This difficult verse seems to mean that by a spontaneous impulse Yahweh places himself at the head of his people.")

JPSV Before I knew it, My desire set me Mid the chariots of Ammi-nadib.

NEB I did not know myself; she made me feel more than a prince reigning over the myriads of his people.

NAB Before I knew it, my heart had made me the blessed one of my kinswomen.

Living Bible paraphrase Before I realized it I was stricken with a terrible homesickness and wanted to be back among my own people.

(A footnote suggests another possible reading: terrible desire to sit beside my beloved in his chariot.)

There is general agreement that *lô' yāḏa'tî,* "I did not know," here means "Before I knew (it)." It is not clear whether *nap̄šî,* "my soul," is subject of the verb "know" (as Luther, e.g., took it, "Meine Seele wusste es nicht") or the object, as *NEB* took it, "I did not know myself," or whether *nap̄šî* is the subject of the verb *śāmaṯnî,* "it put me." Whether the word *nep̄eš* here has the reflexive sense of "self," or designates desire or appetite (presumably sexual), is not crystal clear, to judge from the translations cited. *AT*'s choice of the rendering "my fancy" is an inspired piece of ambiguity since the term may denote hallucination, imagination, caprice, or love.

The syntactic relationship between the verb *śāmaṯnî,* "it put me," and the following *mrkb(w)t,* "chariot(s) (of)," is also problematic. LXX took the latter word as a second object of the verb, the accusative of the product, *etheto me armata.* Rashi also construed the syntax in this fashion, taking the verse to mean, "My soul made me to be chariots for the princes of the rest of the nations to ride upon me." Thus the words spoken by Israel apply to her ignominy in submission to foreign domination. Joüon and Buzy also construed the chariot as the second object of the verb, which Joüon explained as meaning that Yahweh, driven by his love, suddenly transformed himself into chariots to take Israel away from exile. Some manuscripts of the Hebrew supply the desiderated preposition *b-*, or the comparative particle *k-*, before *mrkb(w)t*, but this is not necessary in order to support the translations "in," "on," "among," or "like," since any of these meanings could be obtained from the adverbial accusative construction. Ibn Ezra saw the chariots as a figure for speed, "I did not know that I was hurrying on to thee with rapidity like the chariots of the great prince who is among my people."

A variety of emendations have been proposed to eliminate the troublesome chariots and otherwise alter the reading. The usual expedient has been to detach the last two letters of *mrkb(w)t* to supply the *baṯ*, "daughter of." As for the remaining consonants *mrk*, there are several ways they may be read. Graetz proposed *mēraḵ* (from *rkk*) in the sense of "tender," "soft," "weakly," and rendered du has mich weichlich(?) gemacht, "thou hast made me soft." Hirschberg (1961, 378) proposed a similar reading but with an entirely different meaning related to one of the uses of *rakka* in Arabic, the sense of talking confusedly (like a drunkard); this sense, according to Hirschberg, offering an excellent parallel to the first half of the verse. Gordis adopted the emendation proposed by N. H. Tur-Sinai (II, 358*f*) who read *šam tĕnî mōreḵ baṯ-ammî nāḏîb,* and accordingly Gordis rendered:

I am beside myself with joy,
For there thou wilt give me thy myrrh,
  O noble kinsman's daughter!

Some critics eliminate the vexatious verse in part or in its entirety by detecting and deleting glosses. Haupt took 12a to represent the sensible comment of a baffled reader who was a great deal more honest than many moderns in admitting "I don't understand it." Jastrow went all the way; after deleting the alleged confession of the confused reader, 12a, he eliminated the remainder of the verse as glosses further corrupted by the endeavor of some uncritical editor to combine them into a sentence which turned out so badly as to have provoked the comment of 12a, taken to mean "I don't understand it"; thus, as Gordis noted, there is nothing left not to understand. Ricciotti read *śāmaṯnî murhaḇ baṯ 'ammî,* "she put me in agitation, the daughter of my people," and Wittekindt read *šām nāṯĕnāh lî dôḏehā mĕḇōreḵeṯ baṯ 'āmmî,* "there she gave me her love, the blessed daughter of my people." M. Bogaert (1964, 244*f*) proposed minor changes in the vocalization of two words, reading *śamtanî* instead of *śāmaṯnî* and *'immî* instead of *'ammî.* Construing the suffix *-nî* as dative rather than accusative, Bogaert arrived at the following interpretation:

Je ne sais mon âme
Tu m'as fait l'honneur de (tes) palanquins.
A mon côté le prince.

Most of the "modern" renderings cited tamper with the text without explanation, so that only those familiar with the holy tongue can detect the emendation. *NEB*'s "myriads" is presumably arrived at by changing *markĕḇôṯ,* "chariot(s)," to *riḇĕḇôṯ* and *NAB*'s "blessed one" by switching the consonants *rkb* to *brk* and revocalizing. The Living Bible paraphrase is not hampered by the received text.

The expedient of taking unintelligible words as proper names has produced some bizarre results in the Bible and elsewhere. (Early efforts to interpret the Ugaritic texts were hampered by the "Negebite Hypothesis" which mistook a number of common words as proper names.) The erratic exegetical history of the present verse has been due in considerable measure to LXX and Vulgate rendering of *'my nd(y)b* as the proper name Amminadab. This mysterious figure with his chariot(s) has taken expositors on some highly fanciful excursions. The name Amminadab occurs several times in the Old Testament (Exod 6:23; Num 1:7, 2:3, 7:12,17, 10:14; Ruth 4:19,20; I Chron 2:10, 6:7[22E], 15:10,11), but is never borne by a personage of particular note or fame who might serve as the inspiration of any particular symbolism. The name has been taken to refer to different entities, the neighboring peoples of Israel, the mystical bridegroom, the groom in a peasant wedding. Buzy supposed it to be a corruption of Abinadab, the worthy who housed the ark at Gibeah before David transferred it to Jerusalem (II Sam 6:2–3) and that the groom is poetically compared to a chariot which transports the beloved bride.

Robert, in keeping with his general view, related the verse to the Exile and Return, or perhaps to the final judgment of the pagan world; in either case, God is seen as liberating his people from exile and leading the war chariots to the victory which will inaugurate the eschatological era. The explanation of Joüon, that Yahweh transformed himself into chariots to transport his people from exile, struck Robert as a strange image and the citations Isa 66:15; II Kings 2:11; and Song of Songs 8:5 in support of this hypothesis did not seem very appropriate. Robert suggested that Joüon might better have mentioned in this connection Isa 58:14 and especially Deut 32:11–13, although these analogies are still not very proximate to the bizarre image.

R. Tournay (1959a) treated this verse at considerable length. Tournay found it easy to account for the troublesome text by taking chariots of Amminadab as symbolic of Israel as the vehicle bearing the deity, reminiscent of the carrying of the ark of the covenant on a new cart by Abinadab and his sons (II Sam 6:3–4). Tournay considered that A. Taoussi was on the right track when he paraphrased the verse thus: "Le désir de mon âme me fait considerer comme étant le char royal lequel siège mon divin époux." The allegorizing interpretation, according to Tournay, is amply justified if one refers to the Chronicler who intends to describe the eschatological kingdom by recounting the idealized history of the Davidic kingdom. The splendor of the reign of David and Solomon prefigures the beauty of the bride of the Canticle. The perfect beauty of Miss Zion in the eschatological time is celebrated at the departure from exile (Lam 2:15; Ps 48:3[2E], 50:2; Isa 33:17,20,21). The allegorizing intention, in Tournay's view, is revealed in the light touch by which Abinadab becomes Amminadab, as with the change of *šûnammîṯ* to *šûlammîṯ*. In both cases a significant new name is produced, "the pacified" and "my people is noble/generous." Just two verses later the poet calls the bride "fille de noble" and this rapprochement was clearly intentional, according to Tournay. The allusion to the nuptial allegories of Ezekiel is allegedly limpid. The first interpreters of the Canticle were thus not mistaken and it was not without reason that the Alexandrine translation identified Amminadib and Abinadab.

One of the leitmotifs of the Canticle, according to Tournay, is the sleep which precedes the great eschatological awakening, the dawn of the messianic age (2:7, 3:2, 5:2, 7:10, 8:4). Thus when the bride says, "Je ne connaissais pas mon amour, mon désir," she means that she was not yet fully conscious of her inclination toward her beloved . . . nevertheless this love, though unconscious, made of Israel, by virtue of the covenant and the divine presence in Zion, the "god-carrying" people (le peuple "théophore"), a noble people, of royal origin, a kingdom of priests, a holy nation (Exod 19:6), called to an eternal alliance with God. The central purpose of the Canticle, in Tournay's view, is to prepare for the coming of the King-Messiah by shaking off torpor and indifference. In a succession of covenants (with Abraham, Moses, and David), Yahweh chose the Holy Land in which to dwell and thus Israel became the "théophore"; before the Exile the priests and Levites alone could carry the ark of the covenant (I Chron 15:2; cf. Num 1:49; Deut 10:8, 31:25; Joshua 3–4); now the whole people is as sacralized (Isa 61:6, 66:21). Israel is to respond to the divine love with total love and faith; that is the condition of her power, beauty, nobility, and happiness. A day will come when the promise will be accomplished with the coming of King-Messiah, Son of David, the new Solomon. Then will be consummated the complete union between God and His People. Far from being weakened, the realism of the Canticle is advanced by this entirely biblical interpretation, Tournay claimed. The extraordinary realism of the Incarnation, the union of the two natures, human and divine, in the person of the Christ-King surpasses anything the author of the Canticle could suggest. The "nation théophore," daughter Zion, virgin Israel, became in the person of the Virgin Mary, mother of the Messiah, the Virgin Christophore, the ark of the new covenant, the temple of the living God (p. 308).

Gerleman has taken this Amminadib and his chariots quite seriously and offered a tentative explanation. He translated 6:12 thus:

Ich weiss nicht, wie mir zumute wurde—
in solchen Zustand setzten mich die Wagen Amminadibs

I know not, how I came to feel—
in such a state Amminadib's chariots put me.

It is this same Amminadib, in Gerleman's view, who addresses the woman in 7:1[6:13E]. The brevity with which he is mentioned Gerleman interpreted as an indication that his appearance and role was well-known to the contemporary hearers of the poem, so that no further hints were needed. Gerleman suggested that Amminadib is the Israelite counterpart of Prince Mehy of Egyptian love lyrics, an obscure figure who travels in a chariot and is accompanied by an escort of youths (cf. Smither, 1948, 116). It is at least conceivable, according to Gerleman, that the exceptionally puzzling vs. 12 becomes more intelligible in the light of the notices about Mehy, and that Amminadib with his chariots played a role in the biblical wedding poem similar to that of the Egyptian Love Prince. Like Mehy, Amminadib appears to travel by chariot and to be attended by companions. Mehy is represented as a prince and the second element of Amminadib's name suggests a princely personage. The attempt to clarify this difficult verse can be made only with utmost reservation, Gerleman admitted, but he found it enticing to see in Amminadib a literary figure who plays in Israelite love poetry a role like Prince Mehy in the Egyptian Love Lyrics. He appears suddenly in his chariot accompanied by his attendants and the encounter with him leaves unrest and perplexity in his train.

Prince Mehy is certainly no *deus ex machina* to deliver us from the problems of this verse. The fact is that the very entity of our Amminadib as a personage is exceedingly dubious. It is possible, and indeed preferable, to take the two elements *'my* and *ndyb* as other than a proper name. The weight of Jewish tradition is against construing the elements *'my* and *ndyb* as a single word or as a proper name and it is, therefore, surprising that *JPSV* so rendered it; on the Masoretic reading as two words, cf. Delitzsch, 118.

Every effort should be made to get sense from the verse without emendation, if possible. Ginsburg in his notes on this verse came close to the solution, but missed. Ginsburg translated:

Unwittingly had my longing soul brought me
To the chariots of the companions of the prince.

The word *'ammî* Ginsburg rendered "the companions of" and explained that the word may here be used like *'îš,* "man," in the sense of companions, attendants, followers, the *-î* ending not being the possessive suffix, but *paragogic,* and a mark of the construct state. The remark about the ending of *'ammî* being *paragogic* provides a way out of the mess. The word *'my* is to be taken not as the noun *'am(m)*, "people," but as the preposition *'im(m)*, "with." Thus the sense of *'my ndyb* is "with (the) Prince." If a little bit of emendation is to be ventured, the final *-y* of *'my* may be changed to *h* and attached to the following word as the article, *hannāḏîḇ,* but this is not necessary. There is yet another way to achieve similar sense by reading instead *'ḥy,* "my brother," instead of *'my.* "My brother," "my princely brother," or "my brother the prince" would be a most appropriate title for the lover, particularly from the viewpoint of the cultic interpretation. The vehicle here termed *mrkb(w)t* is hardly a war chariot, but a cult apparatus of some sort, probably the same that is elsewhere called a "bed" (*miṭṭāh*) 3:7a, and a palanquin (*'appiryôn*) 3:9a, a part of the latter apparatus being termed *merkāḇ,* 3:10c. In one of the Sumerian sacred marriage songs treated by S. N. Kramer the male lover is addressed as "overseer of the chariot" (*SMR,* 96) which may offer a parallel to the present verse. (Cf. *SMR,* 152n25.)

12b. *chariot.* The chariot as a cult implement in processions and as an element in myth had a prominent place in the religions of the ancient Near East, from the Sumerians to the medieval Jewish mystics; cf. M. Civil, 1968, and G. Scholem, 1965a, especially ch. 4 on the Merkabah (Chariot) Hymns. In ancient Mesopotamia, according to Civil (3), "the bridge between the real chariot and the mythical one is the model chariot, which may be an humble clay object or a piece of jewelry, kept in a sacred place." In some of the passages in the text treated by Civil, it is difficult to decide whether the chariot in question is the actual vehicle or its model. Chariots are also frequently depicted in religious and mythological scenes in glyptic art, as well as in martial scenes. See Figure *11,* p. 552. The point of interest here is that in the text treated by Civil, after the description of the construction of the splendiferous chariot, commissioned by Išme-Dagan for Enlil, the god is represented as entering [the chariot] and embracing his consort, Mother Ninlil:

(Enlil) completed his great harnessing, he stepped in [. . .]
He emb[raced] Ninlil, the Mother, [his] wife.

Enlil later suggested a contest between the hoe and the plow, the implements of the working people, and his son Ninurta complied:

The King paid attention to Enlil's instructions,
Ninurta put the holy plow in good order, and plows the fertile field.
So that the silos and granaries of Enlil
May be piled high, he drops the fertile seed.
The youthful Hero proudly enters the resplendent Ekur.
The lord Ninurta offers a prayer to Enlil:
"Towards Išme-Dagan, the accomplished shepherd . . . , who has performed (this) service for you,
Towards the King who has built you the chariot, cast a pious glance!
Give to him, as spouse, Inanna your beloved eldest daughter,
Let them embrace forever!
Delight, sweetness, holy limbs,
May last a long time in his abundant life."

(Civil, 7)

It is manifest that the modal auxiliary "may," in the last line of Civil's translation was intended in the precative or optative rather than the contingent sense, and should have been placed at the beginning of the sentence. The making of the chariot for the god was obviously an important part of the ritual celebrated in the hymn cited above. The fertility motif is explicit in the agricultural activities, the ground breaking by the god Ninurta, and in the sacral sexual rites implied in the blessing of the marriage of King Išme-Dagan with the goddess Inanna, as reward for building the chariot. We are not told what role, if any, the chariot may have played in the earthly ritual, but the representations of chariots in archaic Mesopotamian glyptic scenes of non-martial festivities suggest that it may have served to transport the consorts at some stage of the exercises. The goddess Ishtar in her attempt to seduce the hero Gilgamesh (*ANET*, 83*f:* The Epic of Gilgamesh, *Tablet VI,* lines 7–12) offers him a splendiferous chariot:

Come, Gilgamesh, be thou (my) lover!
Do but grant me of thy fruit.
Thou shalt be my husband and I will be thy wife.
I will harness for thee a chariot of lapis and gold,
Whose wheels are gold and whose horns are brass.
Thou shalt have storm-demons to hitch on for mighty mules. . . .

12. The Targum said nothing of chariots or of Amminadib, but related this verse to the doctrine of the supererogatory merits of the saints and patriarchs; cf. AB 15, on Job 22:28–30:

> And when it was manifest before YHWH that they were righteous and occupied with the Torah, YHWH said by His WORD: "I will not again smite them, nor will I make an end with them, but will take counsel with Myself to do good to them to lift them on high in the company of kings, because of the merits of the saints of the generation, which resemble in their actions Abraham their father."

Midrash Rabbah likewise made no mention of Amminadib. R. Hiyya compared the nation to a princess who was gathering stray sheaves when the king recognized her and took her into his chariot, and then he applied this to Israel's situation in Egypt, one day working with bricks and mortar, contemptible in the eyes of the Egyptians, and the next day free and lording it over the whole world. Similarly the verse was applied to the change in fortunes of Joseph, of David, of Mordechai, and again of the Community of Israel. The story of Jusṭa the tailor of Sepphoris is recounted in further illustration of the surprising rags to riches. Jusṭa ingratiated himself with the king and was made governor of his home region. Of those who knew him before, some said, "This is the same man," while others said, "This is not the same man." Jusṭa passed the street and stopped to look at the stool on which he used to sit and stitch, and people knew that he was the same man. He said, "You are astonished at me, but I am still more astonished at myself"; and so they applied to him the present verse.

This difficult verse provoked a variety of interpretations by Christian expositors.

Some of the Fathers applied the verse to the Synagogue perplexed by the preaching of the Gospel. Amminadab, the great grandson of Judah, through whom Christ's genealogy is reckoned, interpreted as meaning "The willing one of my people," was taken to denote Christ who voluntarily became Man and a part of His people. The chariot was applied to the Gospel which suddenly sped throughout the world. The Vulgate rendering *quadrigas,* "four-horse cars" was referred to the fours Gospels and the four principal mysteries of the Gospel (Incarnation, Passion, Resurrection, Ascension). Nicholas of Lyra, a convert from Judaism, developed Rashi's interpretation with animus toward the Synagogue, Amminadab, "my ruling people," which because of the sin of idolatry was punished by the Captivity and made like a chariot for the conquerors to drive.

The chariot(s) provided considerable mileage in several directions. The devout soul was seen as the chariot drawn by the four Gospels as steeds moved by the Holy Spirit to bear the Bride to heaven itself. The Church itself was also made the chariots to convey faithful souls safely to the kingdom of heaven. Or, Christ, as the true Amminadab, drives the soul of the righteous like a chariot, guiding it with the reins of the Word lest it be hurried down the steep by the untamed steeds, anger, desire, pleasure, and fear.

Amminadab was also seen in a very different light as anti-Christ, the prince of this world oppressing and enslaving the Church and interfering with her freedom. Or, similarly, the individual soul may be the mere chariot of its unbridled will, hurried away at its pleasure, until God calls it to return. Few Christian expositors followed the line of the Targum which applied the verse to God's promise to change His dealings with His now repentant people. A strange twist was taken with Amminadab as representing the evil spirits, who are also in a sense God's people. These evil spirits are *free-willing* because they have refused God's service and have chosen to follow their own wicked devices; they sit like drivers on the necks of sinners and force them to crime. These same evil spirits made Pilate, Herod, Caiaphas, and their cohorts the chariots on which Christ was carried to His death. (Cf. Littledale.)

VII
(7:1–14)

1 a Leap, leap, O Shulamite!
b Leap, leap, and let us gaze on you.
c How will you gaze on Shulamite
d In the Dance of the two Camps?
2 a How beautiful your sandaled feet,
b O prince's daughter!
c Your curvy thighs like ornaments
d Crafted by artist hands.
3 a Your vulva a rounded crater;
b May it never lack punch!
c Your belly a mound of wheat
d Hedged with lotuses.
4 a Your breasts like two fawns,
b Twins of a gazelle.
5 a Your neck like an ivory tower,
b Your eyes the pools in Heshbon
c By the gate of Bat-Rabbim.
d Your nose like towering Lebanon
e Overlooking Damascus.
6 a Your head on you like Carmel,
b The locks of your head like purple,
c A king captive in the tresses.
7 a How fair, how pleasant you are!
b O Love, daughter of delights.
8 a Your stature resembles the palm,
b Your breasts the clusters.
9 a Methinks I'll climb the palm,
b I'll grasp its branches.
c Let your breasts be like grape clusters,
d The scent of your vulva like apples,
10 a Your palate like the best wine

b Flowing (for my love) smoothly,
c Stirring sleepers' lips.
11 a I belong to my beloved,
b And for me is his desire.
12 a Come, my love,
b Let us hie to the field,
c Let us lie in the cypress,
13 a Let us get to the vineyards.
b We will see if the vine sprouts,
c If the blossoms bud,
d If the pomegranate flowers.
e There will I give you my love.
14 a The mandrakes give scent,
b At our door is every delicacy;
c Things both new and old,
d My love, I have stored for you.

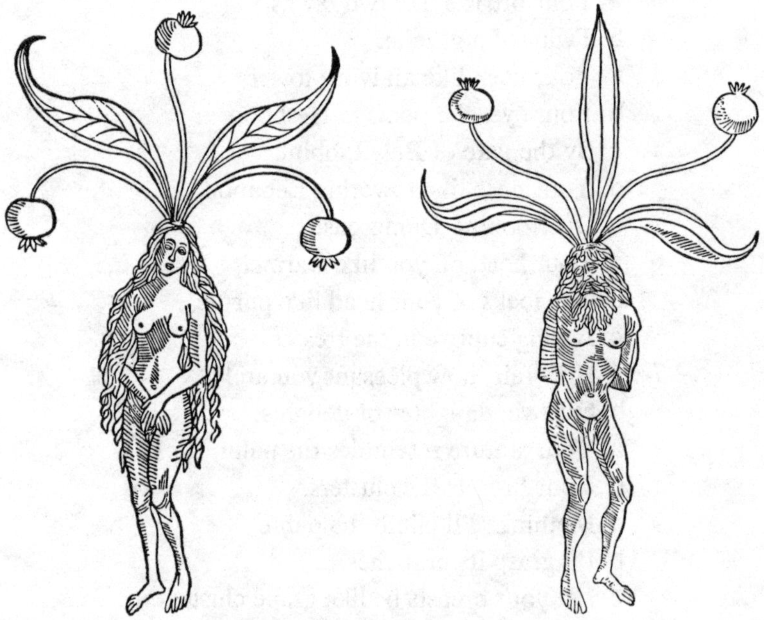

12. Mandrakes, male and female
7:14 The mandrakes give scent

NOTES

7:1a,b. *Leap, leap.* Reading *šĕḇî* or *šēḇî* for MT *šûḇî*. The double imperative is repeated for emphasis and rhythm, as in Judg 5:12 and in Ugaritic, *lk lk 'nn ilm,* "Go, go, ye divine servitors" (3['NT].4.76). The meanings ascribed to the word, or the emendations proposed, are inevitably dictated by theories of interpretation. The dramatic and melodramatic interpreters have no difficulty imagining situations calling for return, reentry, or encore. Delitzsch, for example, imagined that the daughters of Jerusalem, encouraged by Shulamite's unassuming answer in the preceding verse, here utter an entreaty which their astonishment at her beauty suggests. She is on her way from the garden to the palace and "the fourfold 'comeback' entreats her earnestly, yea, with tears, to return thither with them once more, and for this purpose, that they might find delight in looking at her." Ginsburg, in accordance with his melodramatic hypothesis, supposed that the Shulamite in her deeply rooted affections for her beloved shepherd is unmoved by all the persuasions, promises, and eulogies of Solomon and the courtiers, had just explained in the preceding verse how she came to be noticed and picked up by the king, and had started to leave. "But the king entreated her to return, that he might look at her once more. The Shulamite, pausing a little, turns round and modestly asks: 'What will you behold in the Shulamite?' That is, what can you see in a humble rustic girl?"

Budde, followed by many modern exegetes, in consideration of the subsequent allusion to dancing, assumed that the imperatives refer to twists, turns, maneuvers, or evolutions of the dance and proposed emendation of *šûḇî,* "return," to *sōbbî,* "revolve," i.e. "dance." The emendation is quite unnecessary, even in the interest of producing terpsichorean terminology, since it is possible to make a connection with some aspect of dancing whether the verb is connected with *š(w)b* (**ṯ(w)b*) "turn," "return," or with *yšb* (**wṯb*) which in Arabic has the meaning "leap." The meaning "return" is most congenial to those who interpret the entire Canticle as a series of allusions to the return of Israel from exile. Joüon saw in the imperative *šûḇî* an exhortation to Israel to leave the land of exile in order to return to Palestine, the appeal being addressed by the nations at the moment of Israel's triumphal return. Robert, RTF, agreed that it cannot be doubted that the return from exile is here envisaged, as he likewise imagined for 1:7–11, 2:7,13, 3:6, 4:8, 8:5. This expectation, according to Robert, haunts the mind of our author and in this he is in accord with the current literature for which Jeremiah and Hosea set the tone. The complete restoration cannot become operative unless their heart returns to God. The two ideas of restoration and conversion are closely connected, as shown by the wordplay in Jer 31:18 (cf. 15:19). According to Robert, in the quadruple repetition of *šûḇî* here, the nation is exhorted to shake off her bonds, and that depends only on her, since her liberation will be the result of her conversion (as Robert explained in his commentary on 2:7).

šûlammîṯ. The term occurs twice in this verse, first with the article, *haššûlammîṯ,* and then the preposition *b-,* vocalized as including the article with elision of the *h-, baššûlammîṯ*. The term is not found elsewhere in the Canticle nor in all of the Bible. It has been invoked heretofore in these NOTES (in the Anglicized form Shulamite) in citations of the views of commentators who take and use it as the regular designation of the otherwise anonymous Lady of the Canticle. LXX here rendered *hē Soulamitis* and *en tē Soulamitidi,* and Vulgate *Sulamitis* and *in Sulamite.*

There have been three basic interpretations of the form *šûlammîṯ,* with manifold variations. The first relates it to the name of Solomon and the meanings of the "root" *šlm*. The second equates it with *šûnammîṯ,* a female of the town of Shunem. The third interpretation regards the word as a name or epithet of the goddess Ishtar. These three views will be considered briefly.

In 1934 E. J. Goodspeed took up the suggestion of W. Erbt (1906) that the term *šûlammîṯ* is the feminine form of the name Solomon, just as Judith is the feminine of Judah. The simplicity and obviousness of this suggestion made Goodspeed wonder that it had not been dealt with before. Goodspeed further suggested that it may not be an accident that "the Shulamite" occurs in connection with the sword dance (accepting the Wetzstein-Budde theory in vogue at the time), and in the New Testament the lady who entranced Herod Antipas by her dancing was also named Salome, which is the feminine of Solomon. In response to Goodspeed's suggestion, H. H. Rowley (1939) noted that the interpretation of Shulamite as Solomoness was by no means new and, without seeking in any way to collect a complete list, cited thirty-one such suggestions, a few of which we may note here by way of illustration.

An anonymous Jewish commentator of the twelfth century put it thus: "The Shulammite was beloved of Solomon, for she was called after the name of her beloved. Alternatively, the meaning of *the* Shulammite is 'perfect, without spot.'" Similarly, the sixteenth-century commentator Joseph Ibn Yaḥya remarked: "And the calling of her 'Shulammite' was determined by reason of her devotion to the Holy One (Blessed be He) who is called Shelomoh." The Westminster Assembly annotators noted that "The word signifies peaceable or perfect, and is the Foeminine of Solomon, women being usually called after their husband's names"; cf. Isa 4:1. The learned Bishop Robert Lowth, in his *Lectures on the Sacred Poetry of the Hebrews,* opined that "The Subject of the Canticles appears to be the marriage feast of

Solomon; his bride is also called Solomitis, the same name with a feminine termination; though the latter Jews have strangely disguised and obscured it by a vicious pronunciation; for Solomon and Solomitis have evidently the same relation to each other as the Latin names Caius and Caia."

Rowley himself favored the derivation from Shelomoh but took exception to Goodspeed's assertion that this "confirms Budde's striking explanation of the Song in the most emphatic manner," noting that this interpretation does not confirm any of the several views but merely does not embarrass any of them. On any view of the significance of the Song, according to Rowley, it would be equally appropriate for the fair lady represented as the bride of Solomon to be called "Solomoness." The attachment of the article would be a real difficulty in Rowley's view, if the word were taken to be a true proper name, actually borne by, or given to, the lady of the Song, but would have no weight against the view that she was called "the Solomoness." As for the troublesome first vowel which many critics have regarded as secondary, assuming that the word was originally *šĕlōmîṯ,* or comparing the Greek form *Salōmē,* Rowley inclined to accept the long vowel supported by the Versions and MT (in spite of the nearly fifty manuscripts with defective spellings cited by Kennicott). Furthermore, Rowley was not convinced that it is relevant to adduce the various persons named *šĕlōmîṯ* in the Old Testament, since, even if that were the original form, it does not stand here in the Canticle as a proper name, but as a sort of title. Though tradition credited Solomon with a plethora of wives, the Old Testament does not record the name of his principal queen. Rehoboam's mother, Naamah the Ammonitess (I Kings 14:21), does not appear to qualify for that distinction. Rowley concluded from his study that "there would seem nothing incongruous in referring to Solomon's consort as 'the Solomoness,'" and that, indeed, "some such expression would seem necessary for the purpose."

Support for the view that *haš-šûlammîṯ* represents a feminine form of the name Solomon, "the Solomoness," may now be seen in the Ugaritic designation of Danel's wife as Lady Dantay (*mṯt dnty*).

The interpretation of *šûlammîṯ* as a variant form of *šûnammîṯ* relates the word to the town of Shunem through its supposed variant Shulem and thus, willy-nilly, to the fervid and beautiful Abishag who ministered to King David as a human heating pad in his chilly senility (I Kings 1:1–4,15) and later was the prize for which the hapless Adonijah forfeited his life (I Kings 2:17–25). (The other Shunamite mentioned in the Old Testament, an anonymous great lady with an aged husband and without a son, who provided a small room with bed, table, stool, and lamp for the prophet Elisha on his frequent visits to Shunem and who was rewarded for her kindness to the holy man with the birth of a son [II Kings 48:8–17], has not been considered a likely candidate for the feminine lead in the Canticle.) It is altogether possible that the forms Shunem and Shulem are equivalent variants, since interchanges of *l, n,* and *r* take place in various Semitic dialects, early and late, as in other languages. There is, however, no evidence that the change took place in the name of this particular town prior to the composition of the Canticle. The readings *Sounamitis* and *Sunamitis* of some manuscripts of the LXX and Vulgate, the evidence of Eusebius' *Onomasticon* that Shunem=Shulem, and the modern name of the town (Sûlam, near the plain of Jezreel; cf. Josh 19:18) are scant support for the equation of *šûlammîṯ* with *šûnammîṯ* in the Canticle.

"Were it not for the desire to connect the Song somehow with Abishag," Rowley opined, "no one would have dreamed of setting aside the MT on such trivial evidence. Yet there is nothing whatever in the Song to suggest Abishag, except this same slight evidence. It is true that Abishag was described as very beautiful, as is also the lady of the Song, but Abishag is not the only lady in the Old Testament to be described as beautiful, and it may be presumed that beauty was no rarer a phenomenon in Israel than among other peoples. Moreover, of any romance between Solomon and Abishag there is not the slightest evidence."

One could, of course, argue that Solomon's violent reaction to Adonijah's request suggests that Solomon had a special interest in Abishag. But if this were so, Adonijah was either unaware of it or else his own infatuation was so great that he cast reason and prudence to the wind. It seems more likely that Adonijah wanted Abishag as a sort of status symbol and consolation prize for his loss of the kingship and did not anticipate that Solomon would interpret the request as an indirect assertion of claim to the throne.

The mystery of the final fate of the beautiful Abishag is provocative of speculation and has stimulated some modern midrashic efforts to supply the missing sequel. It may well be imagined that a beautiful maiden worthy to warm the decrepit David and able to inspire a younger prince to risk his life for her, would not be left to languish for lack of love, especially in view of Solomon's notorious inclination to venery. It thus seems unrealistic to imagine that Abishag retained her virgin status to be reserved for a king of a higher order and to become the Type of the Bride of the Messiah (cf. G. Kuhn, 1926, 546*f*). A less implausible theory, but still wholly in the realm of fancy, is F. Dornseiff's suggestion that Solomon had Adonijah killed out of jealousy for Abishag and that the Canticle concerns this Court Lady (1936, 595).

Rowley concurred with Goodspeed, "that it is high time Abishag was banished from commentaries on the Song of Songs, into which she has been imported on such slender grounds." Against this view there is little that can be said.

The third type of explanation of the term *šûlammîṯ* takes it as the name or epithet of a goddess and thus espouses the cultic interpretation. Wilhelm Erbt (1906), under the influence of the Pan-Babylonian school of biblical research, appears to have been the first to offer this suggestion. Erbt regarded the Canticle as a collection of paschal songs of Canaanitish origin describing the love of the sun god Tammuz, called Dod or Shelem, and the moon goddess Ishtar under the feminine form of the name Shelem. O. Neuschotz de Jassy in 1914 identified Solomon with Osiris and his feminine counterpart, the Shulamite, with Isis, and Jerusalem, the City of Peace, with the abode of the dead. Following the publication by E. Ebeling of a series of Akkadian fragments belonging to a Tammuz liturgy, T. J. Meek identified the name Solomon with the divine name Shelem, equated with Tammuz (1924b, 53,57; 1922–23, 6*f*), and "the Shulammite" as a name of the goddess Shala, or Shulmanitu, allegedly a cognomen of Ishtar of Jerusalem. Similarly Wittekindt (6) connected the Shulamite with Šulmanitu as the name of Ishtar of Jerusalem. (Robert briefly mentioned Wittekindt's view and added "nous savons ce qu'il faut penser de ces fantasies.") Wittekindt further cited a report by I. Goldziher that in the vicinity of Nablus a stone was worshiped as marking the grave of the holy Sitt-al-Salamiye, which name he (Wittekindt) saw as a pagan survival related to the *šlmt* of the Canticle.

W. F. Albright (1931–32) placed by the side of the divine name *Šulmân* its feminine form *Šulmânîtu,* the name of an important goddess with a temple in the city of Assur. The name is written [d]*DI-tu* and [d]*DI nin-tu* which leave no doubt that the reading is *Šulmânîtu.* And if there were any doubt, it would be dispelled, according to Albright, by the fact that [d]*Šul* (*DUN*)*-ma-ni-tu* is said to be the goddess of the place *URU-DI-MA,* i.e. *URU-SILIM-MA* (*KAV,* nos. 73a, 7 and 145b, 6) which Böhl (1923, 76*ff*) supposed might refer to the city of Jerusalem, but was thought by Albright to be not a terrestrial town but a synonym for *URU-UL-LA,* i.e. "Hades." The form *Šulmânîtu,* according to Albright, can hardly be a gentilic from *URU-SILIM-MA,* the equivalence being quite obviously of learned origin (*SILIM=šulmu!*), but is an adjectival formation from *Šulmân,* meaning "the goddess (Ištar) belonging to Šulmân."

In 1950 and again in 1962, Albright asserted that the prototype of Shulamite "referred to the war goddess *Šulmânîtu,* female counterpart of the war-god *Šulmân;* the Hebrew form is presumably due to a conflation of *Šulmânît* with *Šunamîṯ,* the Shunamite woman, appellation of the last consort of King David" (1963, 5).

It is interesting that Schmökel, despite his drastic operations on the Canticle to conform it to his notions of the sacred marriage ritual, rejected the connection of the Shulamite with Shulmanitu. Unless we assume a deliberate corruption of the text by a redactor, we are here confronted with an insoluble mystery, Schmökel asserted. He found it tempting to rediscover in the last consonants of the name the Hebrew word *māweṯ,* "Death," and imagined an original reading like *bammāweṯ šĕ'ûlaṯ* which would mean "Thou by Death demanded" (Du vom Tod geforderte) as an allusion to Ishtar's descent to the netherworld, but he conceded that there is no possibility of demonstrating the correctness of this (1956,98n5).

Robert found it easy to explain the meaning of *haššûlammîṯ* on the basis of its morphology. The word, according to Robert, is an old form of the *qal* passive participle, like *yûlād* in Judg 13:8 with normal doubling of the *m* after the vowel *a* with the feminine adjectival afformative *ît*. The meaning thus is "the pacified one" (la pacifiée), the one who has rediscovered peace. Thus Aquila and Quinta interpreted it, *eirēneousa*. The peace in question was taken to be the eschatological peace, the benefit of which the second Solomon will procure for Israel in the new age.

It is manifest that the final word has not been written on the term *šûlammîṯ*. The present writer suspects that Robert's analysis (suggested already in 1909 by Joüon [274]: Le nom de Sulamite aurait donc un sens analogue à celui de Salomon [=*pacificus:* 8,11,12; Vulgate] et signifierait pacifique ou pacifiée, celle qui jouit de la paix) is not too far wrong, but for reasons which would be anathema to Joüon, Robert, Rowley, and others. The term "peace," and the epithets "pacific" and "pacified" may have a broad range of meanings. As applied to the volatile Virgin goddess of Love and War, it may suggest violent modes of pacification, either martial or venereal, or both. How the goddess might earn such an honorific title (perhaps a reverse euphemism, saying the opposite of what is intended) may be seen in an episode of Ugaritic mythology in which the Virgin Anat, after a great massacre of mankind in which her heart swells with laughter, joy, and victory, as she wades in blood and gore, is sent a beautiful message concerning "peace" by her brother and consort Baal. Baal tells his divine errand boys:

Like lads then [ent]er.
At Anat's feet bow and fall,
Do obeisance, honor her,
And say to Virgin Anat,
Repeat to the Progenitress of the Peoples,
"Message of Mighty Baal,
Word of the Mighty Hero:
Put war to the ground,
Set passion in the dust,
Pour peace amidst earth,
Bind love amidst the fields."
(3['NT].3.5–14)

The rest of Baal's message has to do with the great secret about his projected splendiferous house, but the allusion to war and peace presumably refers to the preceding violent episode by which she achieved victory, satisfaction, and pacification. Conceivably, some such episode may lie behind the title *šûlammîṯ*. As for the article before the word, it serves as the equivalent of the vocative particle (cf. Joüon, 137*f;* GKC 126e, note [e]). The distinction between proper name and epithet is not easy to maintain, since proper names often develop from epithets. The article may be applied to an epithet on the way to becoming a proper noun, or a proper noun with the article may be regarded as an epithet in cases like the Lebanon, the Nile, the Jordan, the Baal, the Christ, etc.

1b. *and let us gaze on you.* The introduction of the protasis with simple *wĕ-* before the verb amounts to a final or purpose clause, "in order that. . . ." The meaning of the expression "look at/on," *r'y b-* as in 6:11b, or *ḥzy b-*, as here, depends on the context; commonly the meaning is to look on with pleasure (cf. Job 36:25; Ps 27:4) or interest (cf. Isa 47:13, of stargazing). The words serve to call attention to the description which follows, their function being purely literary, as Robert remarked, with no basis for a historical connection such as envisaged by Joüon who imagined the nations watching Israel's departure from the land of exile.

1c. *How*. LXX, Vulgate, Luther, *KJ* took *māh* here as meaning "what?". *KJ*, "What will you see in the Shulammite?" Delitzsch similarly rendered, "What do you see in Shulamith?", ascribing the words to the modest maiden unconscious of her great beauty and unaware that anything particular is to be seen in her. Most modern English versions (e.g. *RSV, JB, JPSV, NAB*) render "Why?" Haupt compared the construction *māh teḥĕzû* with the late Arabic usage *mā tarā*, "just see," *mā taqūlu*, "say now," and rendered, "Look now at Shulamite." Similarly, *AT*, "Ah, gaze on the Shulammite." Le Hir took the *māh* here as negative, as in 8:4c, but made the whole clause interrogative, "Ne voyez-vous pas la Sulamite?", to which Robert objected that this sense cannot be joined with an interrogation (Joüon, 144h). It is possible, and indeed tempting, to construe *māh* here as negative or prohibitive, the construction being the same as in 8:4c *māh tā'îrû ūmāh tĕ'ôrĕrû*, "do not incite and do not excite." Thus the meaning would be "Gaze not on Shulamite." The rendering "How?" may have implications similar to the prohibition, suggesting that it is somehow improper, or dangerous to look on the Lady in certain situations; cf. 4:9, 6:5.

1d. *the Dance of the two Camps*. The unique expression, *k/bimḥōlaṯ hammaḥanayim*, "as/in the dance of the double camps" has been variously rendered in both ancient and modern versions. The forms *māḥôl* and *mĕḥôlāh*, apparently from the "hollow" root *ḥ(w)l*, "whirl," "dance," generally occur in association with terms for music, musical instruments, and singing on occasions of joy and in references to rejoicing in opposition to mourning; cf. (*māḥôl*) Jer 31:4,13; Pss 30:12[11E], 149:3, 150:4; Lam 5:15; and (*mĕḥôlāh*) Exod 15:20, 32:19; Judg 11:34, 21:21; I Sam 18:6, 21:12[11E], 29:5. Joüon supposed that the term *māḥôl* refers to singing in chorus and that *mĕḥôlāh* designates the collective dance, although susceptible to broader meaning approximating that of *māḥôl*. Moses heard the noise of the celebration from a distance (Exod 32:18), but it was only on approaching the camp that he saw the calf and the dancing. The LXX and Vulgate renderings as "chorus" suggest the instrumental and vocal accompaniment of the dance. The place Abel-meholah (Judg 7:22; I Kings 4:12, 19:16) presumably had some connection with funeral dancing.

Considerable light has been cast on the word in question by B. Landsberger's treatment of its Akkadian cognates (1960). Landsberger has convincingly argued that Hebrew *māḥōl, mĕḥōlāh* is to be derived from a geminated root **ḥll* rather than from a hollow root **ḥ(w/y)l* and is further to be connected with an Akkadian verb *elēlu* (B), to be distinguished from *elēlu* (A) which means "to become pure, to be free (of debts)." The form *elēlu* as a substantive is attested in texts of the first millennium B.C. in the sense of "jubilation" and *CAD* (IV, 80a,b) relates it to the *Šaf'el šūlulu,* "jubilate." There is also an Akkadian verb *mēlulu* and a noun *mēlultu* and Landsberger explained this form as a quadriliteral from **mhll,* corresponding to the *Pa'lel* pattern of Hebrew and related to the IXth stem of the Arabic verbal system, derived from the nominal form with *m-* preformative. The Sumerian equivalent of *mēlelu* E.NE.DI, literally "say this," Landsberger explained from the counting out which precedes a game (1960, 120). The noun *mēlultu* (Sumerian equivalent KI.E.NE.DI) is applied to a variety of games, cultic as well as non-cultic, such as skipping rope (*keppû*), gambling with knuckle bones (*kiṣallu*), and playing with dolls (*passu*) (121).

Akkadian *mēlultu* is frequently applied to the martial activities of the goddess Ishtar and to games and festivities in her honor. Lexical texts refer to the festival games of Inanna-Ishtar, *mēlultu ša Ištar* (cf. Landsberger, 1960, 123). The goddess' favorite sports are love and war; "battle is her game," *ša mēlultuša tuquntu,* and *ša melulša qablu* (p. 121).

J. M. Sasson has recently discussed the Akkadian term *mēlultu* and Hebrew *mĕḥōlāh* in connection with "The Worship of the Golden Calf" (1973b); bibliographical data on Akkadian *mēlelu* is given, p. 158n33.

Even a hurried look at the biblical passages which contain the word *māḥôl* or *mĕḥōlāh* suffice to suggest to Sasson that the usual translation "round dance" is, at best, imprecise. This alleged meaning is obviously based more on etymologizing from the supposed hollow root *ḥ(w)l,* which connotes "circling around," than on contextual exegesis. Judg 21:21 *laḥûl bimḥôlôṯ* lends support to such etymologizing (Sasson, 157n31). Perusal of the passages in which *māḥôl* and *mĕḥōlāh* occur indicate that instrumental music accompanied the celebration. On the basis of Ps 149:3; I Sam 21:12b[7bE], 29:5; Jer 31:3[4E], and the present passage of the Song of Songs, Sasson concluded that rather than a round dance the *māḥôl/mĕḥōlāh* consisted of antiphonal singing, a double group of performers including females, musical accompaniment, and ritual sporting. The term *maḥănayim,* "a double company," was one of the grounds for Sasson's understanding. The other evidence is the use of the verb *'ny,* "answer," "respond," in Exod 32:18; I Sam 21:12b[11bE], 29:5; Isa 27:2 and possibly in the superscription of Psalm 88. Sasson speculated that one should distinguish between the *Qal* and the *Pi'el* of *'ny* by translating, respectively, "responsive" and "antiphonal" singing.

Sasson ventured the cautious suggestion that *māḥôl/mĕḥōlāh* could be favorably compared with the Greek *hyporchēma,* a combination of instrumental music performed by men or women, boys or girls (p. 158), a connection proposed already by T. Reinack at the turn of the century; cf. Sasson, p. 159n38.

It is not unlikely that antiphonal singing was one of the features of *mĕḥōlāh,* along with instrumental music, dancing, and perhaps martial sports. The martial affinities of the Akkadian cognate *mēlultu* in connection with the war-goddess Ishtar are of particular interest in view of the application of *mĕḥōlāh* to the choral celebration of David's martial exploits, I Sam 21:12[11E], 29:5, and the construct relationship of *mĕḥōlāh* and *maḥănayim,* "two (army) camps," in the present passage. Although *mĕḥōlāh* is not actually used in the description of David's gymno-gyrations in the parade accompanying the transfer and installation of the Ark of Yahweh of Armies, II Sam 6:14,20, the term would have been quite appropriate to the celebration. Psalmody, dancing, dervish-style whirling, and martial games were features of the Hittite festival of the war god (cf. Goetze, *ANET,* 358–361; 1933, 163–166). Celebrations in honor of Hathor in Egypt included a ritual ball game in which the pharaoh sometimes participated. A celebration of Amenhotep III in worship of Hathor included acrobatics, music, and dancing (cf. C. E. de Vries, 1969, and White, 1969). Books twenty-three of the *Iliad* and eight of the *Odyssey* present evidence for martial sports in Mycenean Greece. Xenophon (*Anabasis* VI 1) mentions an armed dance performed after a sacrifice and feast. At Rome there was a sodality of minor priests dedicated to Mars who were called *salii,* "jumpers"; at the beginning and end of the season for military campaigns, in March and October, the *salii* paraded through the city, stopping at intervals to perform a war dance characterized by leaping, beating with daggers on shields, and shouting of ancient songs only partly intelligible (cf. Sasson, 156n24,26). The role of the Roman holy jumpers resembles that of the *kurgarru* performers in the Mesopotamian cultic games who played war games, sang and danced to battle songs, beating on clappers (*kiskilātu*), and shouting wild war cries. Cf. NOTE on 3:7–8.

The form *maḥănayim* is the dual of *maḥăneh,* "camp," used of various sorts of encampments, especially of military camps; cf. Gen 32:3,8,9,11 [2,7,8,10E], 33:8, 50:9; Exod 14:19–20, 29:14; Num 10:5–6; Deut 32:10, 15[9,14E]; Judg 7:10; II Kings 5:15; Ezek 4:2; Amos 4:10; Ps 27:3. Maḥanayim is also the name of a town of Gilead, near the river Jabbok, the modern Khirbet Maḥneh; cf. N. Glueck, 1939, 234*f.* Two etiologies of the name Maḥanayim are offered in Gen 32. Jacob on his return from the flight to escape Esau's wrath was met by divine messengers, or angels of God, and when he saw them exclaimed, "This is the camp of gods/God," so he called the place Maḥanayim, i.e. "two camps," Gen 32:3[2E]. Jacob's stratagem of dividing his entourage into two camps, so that if Esau attacked one, the other might escape, Gen 32:7–8, was apparently suggested by the place name, even though it is not mentioned in this connection. A number of modern translators and exegetes have assumed that the *maḥănayim* of the Canticle is none other than the place where the angels confronted Jacob. The presence of the article before the word, as with *šûlammîṯ,* is no serious impediment. Harper suggested that the article here defines the *dance,* not Maḥanayim.

Maḥanayim was manifestly a town of some significance, whether for political or religious reasons. Abner set up Saul's son as king there, II Sam 2:8, and David fled there from Absolom, II Sam 17:24,27. Maḥanayim was also a Levitical asylum for the manslayer, Josh 21:38. The association of a locale with dancing is seen in the name Abel-meholah. To connect the town Maḥanayim with dancing, however, requires a bit of fancy footwork on the part of the expositor. Delitzsch explained that Maḥanayim became in the post-biblical dialect a name for angels. "The dance of angels," he declared, "is only a step beyond the responsive song of the Seraphim, Isa 6," and he went on to invoke the association of the angelic choir and the heavenly host in old German poetry. Harper supposed "after Jacob's vision of the angelic host that Mahanaim became a holy place, if it was not one before, and that God was there praised in the dance (cf. Judg xxi 21), and that these dances had become famous either for their gracefulness or for their splendor." Renan averred that it is probable that the city of Maḥanayim had been the center of some non-Israelitish cult, and was still celebrated for its dancing girls.

Wetzstein described a dance (1868, 106; cf. Delitzsch, 171) in which the bride wielded a sword on the wedding day surrounded by a ring, one half of which is composed of men and the other of women; this has been taken to explain "the two companies." Budde took this "camp dance" to be the sword dance described by Wetzstein. The influence of Budde's sword-dance hypothesis continues and is even applied to passages outside the Canticle. Dahood invokes "the dance between the two camps" of the Canticle in connection with the "two-edged sword" of Ps 149:6, explaining that "while shouting the praises of God, the dancers brandished swords in a type of sword-dance known from Song of Solomon vii 1," and he further suggested that in Job 21:12 (reading *kĕṯōp̄* instead of *bĕṯōp̄*) the meaning is, "They take up the scimitar [cf. Ugaritic *ktp//ṣmd*] and lyre; they make joyful dance to the sound of the pipe" (cf. *PS III*, 358).

Wittekindt (p. 45) cited Gruppe to the effect that the sword dance belongs to the orgies of the Cybele festival. T. H. Gaster (1969, 813) suggested that the legend in which Maḥanayim appears as the place where Jacob saw "the camp of other worldly beings" (Gen 32:1–2) could be the starting point of an alternative interpretation which takes the dance as simply a Hebrew variant of the Wild Hunt, or the Furious Host, the latter in Greek and European folklore being associated with such goddesses as Artemis or Berchta and her troupe of ghostly dancers.

The versions, ancient and modern, reflect in various ways the shaky interpretations mentioned above. LXX rendered "the one coming like the chorus of the camps"; Vulgate *nisi choros castrorum;* Syriac "the one who descends like a chorus, and like a chorus of the camps"; Luther "The round dance at Mahanaim" (Den Reigen zu Mahanaim); *KJ* "As it were the company of two armies"; *RSV* "as upon a dance before two armies"; *AT* "in the Mahanaim dance"; *JB* "dancing as though between two rows of dancers"; *JPSV* "In the Mahanaim dance"; *NEB* "as she moves between the lines of dancers"; *NAB* "as at the dance of the two companies."

Some manuscripts read *b-* instead of *k-* before *mĕḥôlaṯ*, and this is adopted by many interpreters. The *k-* may also be taken as having temporal meaning, on the occasion of the dance, i.e. as she dances. Dussaud suggested an ellipsis, "like (in) the dance." Gordis took the *k-* as asseverative, attributing the words to the company in response to the maiden's question: "What will you see in the maid of Shulem?" The company responds: "Indeed, the counter-dance!"

Of emendations offered, none seems particularly arresting. Thilo proposed to read *kĕḥôlĕmôṯ hammaḥăzîm,* "like the dreamers of visions." H. H. Hirschberg (1961, 380) suggested that the meaning may be something quite different from a "sword dance" or "counter dance," and he related *mḥnym* to Arabic *maḥana,* "violate a girl," or, perhaps by error, to *mahana,* "cohabit with a woman," supposing that the dance is staged on the morning after the consummation of the marriage. The question asked by the coy bride in 7:1c,d thus becomes clear: "Just what do you see in the deflowered one, in her that is ravished by the coitus?", whereupon the guests begin a detailed description of her charms.

W. F. Albright (1963, 5*f*) has offered the following treatment of 7:1*f* in which "we have another transparent borrowing from a Northwest Semitic mythological theme." This passage was previously discussed by Albright in the G. L. Robinson Anniversary Volume (1935), but now nuanced slightly. Albright translated, with a modicum of emendation in the last stich:

> Come back, come back, O Shulammith,
> Come back, come back, let us watch thee!
> How do ye see Shulammith
> When <she dances> the dance of the two armies?

There can be no doubt, according to Albright, that the prototype referred to the war goddess Shulmanitu, female counterpart of the war god Shulman. Parallels in Mesopotamian literature are numerous and Albright limited his citation to a few striking examples. One of the epithets of Ishtar is "She Whose Dance Is Battle." Greenfield (1965, 257) objected that Albright's assumption that Akkadian *elēlu* can mean "to dance" is not supported by the lexica, to which Albright rejoined with citation of *CAD,* IV, 40 connecting *elēlu, šūlulu,* and *mēlultu* with dancing to music (from *ḥll-ḥwl*). In the thirteenth-century triumphal poem of Tukulti-Ninurta I, Ishtar appears as patroness of the warriors "who dance into the onslaught(?) of weapons." And in the Agushaya poem (iii 7–10) it is said of the goddess (Albright's translation, with citation of the Akkadian in transliteration and source reference):

> Her feast is the onslaught
> Of those who dance in battle,
> Ere the kindled fire flames up,
> They are reduced to ashes!

"We may safely suppose," Albright concluded, "that the Canaanite prototype of Shulmanitu-Shulammith is the goddess Anath, whose sanguinary play is so vividly portrayed in the Anath episode of the Baal Epic (VAB, B)."

Albright proposed in the article cited above (1963) to augment the last stich of 7:1 to read *k-tḥl mḥlt hmḥnym,* i.e. *kî tāḥōl mĕḥôlaṯ hammaḥănayim,* which emendation seems attractive but not compelling. More persuasive is his afterthought (*YGC,* 255n136) in which he takes his cue from the LXX reading *hē erchomenē,* "she who comes," which he would emend to *hē orchoumenē,* "she who dances." Thus the Hebrew should read *<mĕḥôleleṯ>bi-mḥôlaṯ maḥănayim,* "dancing in the dance of the two armies," with the corrected Greek text and variant Masoretic MSS. Attractive as this suggestion is, the restoration of the original reading, if we do not have it in the MT, may be more complicated. Conjectural textual restoration is always an uncertain venture.

If the word *maḥănayim* here refers to military camps or armies, as is widely assumed, then the dual form is an important feature which calls for an explanation. The solution to this long-standing puzzle may now be available to us in the exploit of the goddess Anat to which Albright alluded above with the suggestion that the Ugaritic goddess is the Canaanite prototype of Shulmânîtu-Shulamite. This episode supplies us with an explanation of the double armies and the dancing, and possibly of the peace and pacification motif in the title Shulamite as well.

In the second column of the so-called Anat Text, after obscure allusions to perfumes which need not detain us, it is related that:

She closed the housegates, did Anat,
Met the boys at the base of the mountain.
Then Anat fought in the plain,
Battled between the two towns,
Smote the people of the Sea-shore,
Attacked the men of the Sunrise.
Beneath her were heads like balls,
Above her like locusts were hands,
Like locust eggs heaps of warriors hands.
She attached heads to her back,
Girded hands to her waist;
Knee-deep she waded in soldiers' blood,
Hip-deep in warriors' gore;
With staff she drove the captives,
With the back of her bow the citizenry.
Then Anat went to her house,
The Goddess descended to her palace;
Not sated she fought in the plain,
Battled between the two towns,
She set chairs for the soldiery,
Arranged tables for the warriors,
Footstools for the heroes.
Much she fought and gloated,
Battled and gazed, did Anat.
Her liver swelled with laughter;
Her heart filled with joy,
Anat's liver with victory.
Knee-deep in warriors' gore,
Till sated she fought in the house,
Battled among the tables.
Soldiers' blood was wiped from the house;
Oil of peace was poured in a bowl.
She washed her hands, did Virgin Anat,
Her fingers, the Progenitress of Peoples;
Washed her hands of soldiers' blood,
Her fingers of warriors' gore.
Chairs to chairs, tables to tables,
Footstools she set to footstools,
She drew her water and bathed,
Dew of heaven, fat of earth,
Rain of the Cloud Rider—
Dew which the heavens pour,
Rain which the stars pour.

(3.[ʿNT].2.3–41)

Philological notes will be omitted here, but some commentary is necessary. The episode begins suddenly without explanation, unless something crucial is lost at the end of the preceding column and the beginning of the present one.

The "boys" who are encountered at the base of the mountain are presumably the personnel later termed soldiers, warriors, heroes, the victims of Anat's violence. The mountain base where the assault takes place is not identified. The renowned Mount Ṣapon, the abode of Anat's brother and consort, Baal, is the first possibility that comes to mind. Anat herself has the epithet Anat (of) Ṣapon, the other possibility is Anat's own abode termed *inbb* and *uġr* (3['NT].4.78). Whatever the identity of the mountain in the Ugaritic myth, it seems to be the counterpart of Mount Ebih in the Mesopotamian myth of Inanna and Mount Ebih, and in the Hymnal Prayer of Enheduanna in Adoration of Inanna of Ur, from which some parallels will be drawn anon.

The phrase translated "in the plain" (*b'mq*) might also mean "with power," as in Job 39:21a (cf. AB 15, NOTE ad loc.), but for reasons which will become apparent the sense "in the plain/valley" is preferred. The expression rendered "between the two towns" (*bn qrytm*) might also mean "the denizens of (literally "sons of") the two towns," and it would make no great difference. The important point to be noted here is that the dual form *qrytm* apparently designates two groups of military personnel whom the goddess assaults. The word **qiryāh* is usually taken to mean "town," but the more basic sense is "gathering," "meeting(-place)" (cf. Nöldeke, 1904, 61*f;* 1910, 131; Eitan, 1925, 421), so that the term here may be the equivalent of *maḥănayim,* "two (military) camps/companies." We have already alluded to the heads and hands which the goddess attached to her back and waist as trophies as a possible explanation of the expression *'ăyummāh k/bannidgālôt* in 6:4. There is no mention of dancing in this episode, but the references to the goddess' laughter and joy as she wades in blood and gore may be imagined to have choreographic aspects, amounting to a sort of victory dance. There are a number of enigmatic details which need not detain us or detract from the points which merit special emphasis for the present interests.

The writer has previously called attention to certain parallels between the episode cited above and the Egyptian myth about Sekhmet's slaughter of mankind and the exploits of the Indian goddess Kali (cf. 1956, 255 and *WbM,* s.v. "'Anat"). Some details may be repeated here, pending a detailed treatment of the motif of the violent virgin goddesses of love and war projected for the future.

In the Egyptian myth called "Deliverance of Mankind from Destruction" (*ANET,* 10*f*) we have a mythical episode with some striking parallels to the Ugaritic version of Anat's exploit. The sun god Re, suspecting that mankind is plotting against him, commissioned the goddess Hathor to destroy them. The goddess appeared in the form of Sekhmet, "She Who Prevails," and began to do such a thorough job of slaughtering mankind that Re became alarmed and wished the carnage to cease. But Sekhmet was enjoying her work and would not quit. The slaughter was finally halted by a ruse. The plain was flooded with beer dyed red and the goddess, thinking the ruddy liquor was blood, drank till she became too inebriated to fight, and thus mankind was saved from annihilation.

In the Indian myth, the goddess Kali, while destroying certain demons, waxed ecstatic with the joy of battle and slaughter and refused to desist so that the gods feared her continuing violence would destroy the world as she trampled on the slain and shook the earth in her victory dance. She was stopped only after her consort Shiva had thrown himself under her feet and she recognized with dismay that she was trampling the corpse of her consort. (There is also a sexual interpretation of this Shiva-Shava [corpse of Shiva] motif, Kali atop the lifeless body of her consort, but pursuit of this matter would divert from the present interest in the victory dance.) The representations of Kali in the popular religious art of India, especially in the garish prints sold around her chief temple in Calcutta, show her blue-black and beautiful, trampling on the pale corpse of Shiva, brandishing the sickle sword (which harks back to early dynastic times in Mesopotamia), and wielding a variety of other weapons with her multiple arms. She is decorated with gruesome trophies, a necklace of severed heads and a girdle of lopped hands, holds a freshly hacked gory head by the hair, and drinks blood from a skull, with corpses strewn in the background. (See Plate IX.) This is the horrendous aspect of the great Virgin Mother whose terror and beauty are hymned in the Tantras and thus apostrophized by her modern saint Vivekananda:

The flash of lurid light
Reveals on every side
A thousand, thousand shades
Of Death begrimed and black—
Scattering plagues and sorrows,
Dancing mad with joy,
Come, Mother, come!
For Terror is thy name,
Death is in Thy breath,
And every shaking step
Destroys a world forever.
Thou "Time," the All-Destroyer!
Come, O Mother, come!
Who dares misery love,
and hug the form of Death—
Dance in destruction's dance,
To him the Mother comes.
(Nivedita, 1950, 80)

The Thugs who were devotees of Kali and carried out mass murders to keep her supplied with blood (turning a neat profit on the side by robbing the victims before offering them to the goddess), were not allowed to look back on leaving the scene of a sacrifice. It was reported that once a Thug did hazard a look over his shoulder and saw the goddess playing ball with the corpses, tossing them up in the air and catching them as they fell (Hutton, 1857, 15). One may wonder whether a similar concern lies behind the question of 7:1c, "How can you look on Shulamite?", or perhaps the prohibition, "Gaze not, etc."

It is not feasible here to attempt any detailed treatment of the Mesopotamian parallels to Anat's assault on the citizens and soldiers at the base of the mountain, but a few observations may be made in passing. The myth of Inanna and Mount Ebih, presently in the process of recovery and editing, celebrates the goddess' conquest of the mountain and its rebellious people. It was apparently this great and bloody victory which gained for her the dominant position among the gods. The Hymnal Prayer of Enheduanna contains allusions to this exaltation which we now have in two English versions by leading specialists: S. N. Kramer, *ANET*^{3}, 579–582, and W. W. Hallo and J. J. A. Van Dijk, 1968, the latter a definitive edition of the text including variants, translation, study of its poetic structure and literary significance, notes and glossary. Some lines from the translation by Hallo and Van Dijk will serve to show the affinities with the myths of Anat, Sekhmet, and Kali sketched above.

9 Like a dragon you have deposited venom on the land
10 When you roar at the earth like Thunder, no vegetation can stand up to you.
11 A flood descending from its mountain, Oh foremost one, you are the Inanna of heaven and earth!

13 Raining the fanned fire ⌒ down upon the nation
17 Devastatrix of the lands, ⌒ you are lent wings by the storm,
21 When mankind ⌒ comes before you
22 In fear and trembling ⌒ at (your) tempestuous radiance,
23 They receive from you ⌒ their just deserts,
26 In the van of battle ⌒ everything is struck down by you.
27 Oh my lady (propelled on your wings) ⌒ you peck away (at the land).
34 Oh my lady, the Anunna, ⌒ the great gods,
35 Fluttering like bats ⌒ fly off before you to the clefts,
36 They who dare not walk(?) ⌒ in your terrible glance,
37 Who dare not proceed ⌒ before your terrible countenance.
38 Who can temper ⌒ your raging heart?
39 Your malevolent heart ⌒ is beyond tempering.
40 Lady (who) soothes the reins, ⌒ lady (who) gladdens the heart,
41 Whose rage is not tempered, ⌒ oh eldest daughter of Suen!
42 Lady supreme over the land, ⌒ who has (ever) denied (you) homage?

43 In the mountain where homage is withheld from you vegetation is accursed.
44 Its grand entrance you have reduced to ashes.
45 Blood rises in its rivers for you, its people have nought to drink.
46 It leads its army captive before you of its own accord.
47 It disbands its regiments before you of its own accord.
48 It makes its able-bodied young men parade before you of their own accord.
49 A tempest has filled the dancing of its city.
50 It drives its young adults before you as captives.

123 "That you are lofty as Heaven (An)—be it known!
124 That you are broad as the earth—be it known!
125 That you devastate the rebellious land—be it known!
125a That you roar at the land—be it known!
126 That you smite the heads—be it known!
127 That you devour cadavers like a dog—be it known!
128 That your glance is terrible—be it known!
129 That you lift your terrible glance—be it known!
130 That your glance is flashing—be it known!
131 That you are ill disposed toward the . . .—be it known!
132 That you attain victory—be it known!"

In their chapter on "Literary Structure and Parallels" Hallo and Van Dijk comment (p. 51) that the goddess "claims a special capacity which equips her to discipline mankind. She is, in fact, the 'Inanna of Battle,' a figure familiar not only from the *bab-bal-e* hymn sometimes so designated, but from numerous allusions to the particular delight she takes in the sights and sounds of conflict." (For the hymn "Inanna of Battle," *SRT* 9:1–21; cf. M. Lambert, 1961, 193, no. 55[!] and on Inanna's zest for violence, cf. B. Landsberger, 1960, 121*f* and 1961, 23.) "These descriptions," Hallo and Van Dijk observe, "recall the Sumerian goddess of love and fecundity much less than the Akkadian Ištar and her warlike West Semitic cognates, Aštarte and 'Anat." It is further remarked by Hallo and Van Dijk, apropos of lines 17 and 27, that we meet Inanna here "as the winged goddess, the flying Inanna who, in the guise of the storm(god), pounces on every unsuspecting culprit among the sinful nations." This metaphor, they note, is not unique to the poem of Enheduanna. In two unpublished duplicates of "The Curse of Agade" in the Yale Babylonian Collection the goddess is described as "flying out of her city to give battle" (p. 51n11) and "In a late bilingual text from Babylon, we read, in a description of her warlike pastime: 'in the battle I fly like a swallow, I heap up heads that are so many harvested rushes'" (p. 51n12). Hallo and Van Dijk go on to stress the motif of the winged goddess, but the present interest lies more in the motifs of the judgment of sinful people(s), the carnage, blood and gore, the piles of severed heads, i.e. in the parallels with the exploits of Anat, Sekhmet, and Kali.

A couple of biblical parallels may be noted in this connection. In Isaiah 34 the divine wrath and vengeance on the heathen nations, denoted collectively as Edom, is portrayed as a cosmic blood bath and holocaust. It is Yahweh's sword, rather than his person, that is soaked and smeared with blood and gore (vss. 2–10):

Yahweh is angry with all the nations,
Enraged at all their army,
He has devoted and given them to
slaughter.
Their slain will be piled up,
The stench of the corpses will rise;
The mountains will melt with their blood.
All the celestial army will rot,
The heavens be rolled like a scroll.
And all their army wither,
As wither leaves of the vine,
As the withering of the fig.
For my sword is soaked in heaven;
See now it descends on Edom,
On the people I devote to judgment.
Yahweh's sword is glutted with blood,
Gorged with gore,
With blood of lambs and he-goats,
Visceral gore of rams.
For Yahweh has a sacrifice in Bozrah,
A great slaughter in the land of Edom.
The wild bulls will go down together,
The bullocks with the bulls.
Their land will be soaked in blood,
Their dust smeared with gore.
For it is Yahweh's Vengeance Day,
Requital Year for Zion's Champion.
Her wadies will be turned to pitch,
Her dust to brimstone;
Her land will become burning pitch.
Night and day it will not be quenched;
Forever her smoke will rise.
Age on age it will lie waste;
Forever none shall traverse it.

In Isa 63:1–6, however, the famous "Grapes of Wrath" passage, it is Yahweh's clothing that is dyed red with the blood of Edom (playing on *'ādôm,* "red") which spurts up as the bodies are trampled like grapes in the wine press.

Who is this coming from Edom,
Crimson clad from Bozrah,
This one glorious in apparel,
Striding with mighty power?

"I who bespeak vindication,
Mighty to save."

Why is your clothing red,
Your garments like a vat treader?

"The trough I trod alone,
Of peoples, no one was with me.
I trod them in my anger,
Trampled them in my fury.
Their juice spurted on my garments,
All my clothing I stained.
For Vengeance Day was in my heart,
My Redemption Year had come.
I looked and there was no helper,
Appalled, but there was no support;
So my arm got me victory,
My fury supported me.
I trod the peoples in my anger,
Intoxicated with my fury,
I trampled their gore to the ground."

The emphasis here that Yahweh did all this alone, with no companions or helpers, may be motivated by concern to dissociate the episode from that attributed to the goddess Anat in pagan mythology. The Jews who fled to Egypt following the neo-Babylonian conquest were not so careful to dissociate Yahweh from Anat as evidenced by oaths made in the name of a deity *'nt yhw,* Anat-yahu.

A "Land of Maḫanaim" has been mistakenly discerned in a Ugaritic mythological fragment (1003.3–4) in the words . . . *tṣ]un barṣ mḫnm* which Virolleaud rendered "[Elle ('Anat, sans doute) so]rt(?) de la terre de Maḫanaim." This "Land of Maḫanaim" Virolleaud simply noted as "nouveau toponyme biblique," without further comment (*PRU,* II, 12), a view which has been tacitly accepted by eminent scholars. F. M. Cross (1973, 119) rendered:

In the Land of Mḫnm he (the dragon) swirled the sea.
His double tongue flicked the heavens;
His double tail swirled the sea.
She fixed the unmuzzled dragon;
She bound him to the heights of Leba[non].

It would indeed be significant for the present verse to relate the scene of Anat's victory over the Sea Dragon to a "Land of Maḫanaim." Unfortunately this alleged toponym must be discarded. As with many other mistakes in interpretation of Ugaritic poetry, this one also is the result of faulty stichometry. The parallelism suggests that the words *arṣ* and *mḫnm* are not in construct or bound relationship, but rather that *arṣ* ends one colon and *mḫnm* begins the other. The parallelism is thus between earth (netherworld), sea, and sky on the one hand and the three dual nouns *mḫnm, lšnm,* and *ḏnbtm* on the other. Arabic *maḫann-at,* "nose," offers a plausible cognate for *mḫnm* in the present passage. Thus we arrive at the following arrangement and translation of 1003.3–10:

. . . . .]un barṣ	. . . . . to/from earth.
mḫnm ṯrp ym	Snout swished the sea;
lšnm tlḥk šmm	Forked tongue licked sky;
tṯrp ym ḏnbtm	Swished sea twin tail.
tnn lšbm tšt	Dragon to gag she put;
trks lmrym lb[nn]	Bound (him) to Leb[anon's] heights.

Philological arguments will be sparing here. Suffice it to note simply that the verb *ṯrp* is to be connected with Syriac *trp,* "dip." Cross's analysis of *lšbm* as *lā šabūma,* "unmuzzled," though grammatically unexceptionable, seems unlikely in view of Anat's emphasis on the muzzling of the monster (3['NT].3.37),

lištbm tnn išbm[n]h,	Did I not muzzle the Dragon? I muzzled him.

Accordingly, we incline to the positive sense "Dragon to gag she put." The arguments by Barr (1973) against the connection of Ugaritic *šbm* with Arabic *šibām,* a device to prevent a kid from sucking, are unconvincing.

1. The Targum took the call to return as addressed to Israel to return to God, to Jerusalem, and to the Law:

> Return to Me, O Assembly of Israel, return to Jerusalem, return to the House of Teaching the Law, return to receive prophecy from the prophets who prophesy in the Name of the Word of YHWH. What good are you, false prophets, to mislead the people of Jerusalem with your prophecies (by) which you speak rebellion against the Word of YHWH and to defile the camp of Israel and Judah?

Midrash Rabbah explained the fourfold repetition of "return" as corresponding to the four powers that had subjugated Israel, and Israel both came under their sway unscathed and came away unscathed. The Shulamite was identified with the nation and related to peace in several ways. "That we may look at you" was taken as being addressed to Israel by the nations in taunt and flattery. The answer, "What will you see etc?" was Israel's reply, "Did you ever hear of Abraham, Isaac, and Jacob worshiping idols that their descendants after them should so worship?" The "dance of the two armies" was related to Jacob's encounter with the angels when he returned from the house of Laban, and there was discussion as to how many angels were involved in the dance, with the figure running as high as one hundred twenty myriads. The dance finally was referred to the dance of the righteous in the time to come, led by the Holy One.

This verse is cited in the Talmud (TB Baba Bartha 15b) in connection with R. Johanan's observation that the generation of Job was given up to lewdness. This information was deduced from Job 27:12, "Behold all of you have seen, and why have you become altogether vain?" These two verses have in common the verb *ḥzy,* "see." The suggestion that the reference in Job may be to prophecy, as in Isa 1:1, was scouted with the query, "If so, then why does it say 'Why have you become altogether vain?' " The object of gaze in the present verse is the dancing

Shulamite and this sort of girl-watching was apparently regarded as lewd. The verb *ḥzy* is used in Isa 57:8 with reference to fascination with phalloscopy.

Christian expositors found in this verse many items to allegorize. Nicholas of Lyra, taking his cue from the Targum, noted that Israel had returned from Captivity four different times: under Zerubbabel and Ezra in the time of Cyrus, a second return under Ezra in the seventh year of Artaxerxes, a third under Nehemiah, and the fourth when Judas Maccabeus cleansed and restored the desecrated sanctuary. Those who desired to look on the Shulamite were seen and heard as the Holy Trinity calling the errant Church, Jewish or Christian, or the individual soul, to return to God. Again, the four summonses to return were interpreted as the four Gospels calling to the Synagogue. "That we may look at you" was referred to the Synagogue after penitence, baptism, and confession of the Trinity. The calls to return meant to return from the four quarters of the world whither Israel had been scattered, a return to the true faith, to brotherly peace, acknowledgment of the Redeemer, and perfection in good works. This theme was developed with a vengeance against the Synagogue: "Return that we may look at you, standing to do penance for your sins, and acknowledging your crime in slaying and crucifying your King." The calls to return were also understood as addressed to individual souls of various sorts and conditions, from the erring to the perfect.

The choirs and camps too were put through rehearsals and maneuvers according to varying versions. Most edifying was the view of the two armies as not in rivalry, but met in perfect alliance within the Peaceful One, the Church Triumphant. There the two companies, Jew and Gentile in the Church Militant, and men and Angels in the heavenly Church Triumphant, move together till the great day of the final battle against the hosts of evil, when the two choirs will join in the mingled Song of Moses and the Lamb. Beyond that they move to the time when even the echoes of war are forgotten and only the new Song of eternal peace is heard from the lips of the Peaceful One as she sings the praises of the Prince of Peace, her Spouse. (Cf. Littledale for documentation.)

By way of modern historical allegory, Robert, after reviewing opinions of other commentators, concluded that the explication of the terms "dance" and "double choir" had to be sought elsewhere than in the context of the tableaux of pure imagination. The profound biblical character of the Canticle authorizes us to suppose, Robert asserted, that the author here makes subtle allusion to Jer 31:4,13 and Gen 32:2–22. Jeremiah 31 is a piece which approaches drama; it announces in magnificent terms the return from exile, the reunion of Israel and Judah in a single kingdom and the new covenant. In Jer 31:4 one sees the virgin Israel take up the timbrels long silent and go forth dancing joyously. Israel, regathered and satisfied with the good things of the land, utters cries of triumph on the heights of Zion: "Then shall the maidens rejoice in the dance, and the young men and the old together. I will turn their mourning into joy, etc." (Jer 31:13). The themes which this chapter develops are the same which the Canticle contrives to put in operation, according to Robert. It is thus normal to suppose that our author who has just now borrowed from Jer 31:16–21 the urgent exhortations to return, retains from this same chapter the figure of the dance, expressive of the joy of the repatriates. Then from the side of Gen 32:2–22, with reference to Jacob's return and the division of his entourage into two companies, Robert found it difficult to escape the conviction that the author of the Canticle saw an analogy between the two situations: Israel returning from the captivity of Babylon, and returning after seven years of servitude with Laban. The two companies of Gen 32 evoked for Robert thought of the post-exilic period. The reconstitution of the national unity was an essential element of the eschatological hope, to which Robert found reference also in 6:4. And now, again, he saw it expressed by allusion to the incident at Maḥanayim which seemed a prophecy in action of the complete restoration.

2a. *How beautiful*. Cf. 4:10, 7:7.

sandaled. Lit. "in sandals." The sandal left the top of the foot virtually bare and this was apparently regarded as especially captivating. Judith, when she went to seduce and slay Holofernes, anointed her face with oil, arranged her hair, put on a linen dress, and

> Her sandal ravished his eye,
> Her beauty captured his soul,
> And the sword severed his neck.
> (Judith 16:8–9)

Robert wondered whether the mention of sandals may conceal a hint. Isa 11:15 announces that on the day when Yahweh will assemble the dispersed of Israel, he will bring out those who are in Egypt by renewing for them the prodigies of the Exodus; he will divide the Nile into seven streams so that they will be able to cross over "in sandals." It is possible, Robert suggested, that our author wished to make allusion to this new exodus from Egypt, as in the preceding verse he allegedly referred to a new return from Mesopotamia. The text of Isaiah furnished the author with occasion to put the feet of the Shulamite in connection with the Nile; this detail has importance for Robert since in the succeeding verses the lady is described with reference to geography, going from the south to the north (from the ground up). The description of the groom in 5:10–16 runs in the opposite direction, from head to foot, and in 4:1–5 the praise of the bride's beauty starts with the eyes and goes to the hair, teeth, lips, cheeks, neck, and breasts, but lapses before reaching the midriff.

feet. LXX *diathemata sou* and Vulgate *gressus tui* thought of the movement of the dance. The noun *pa'am* is used as a synonym of *reḡel,* "foot," "step," and also in the sense of "stroke," "occurrence," "time" (in the sense of French "fois," German "mal"). In Isa 26:6 *pa'am* and *reḡel* stand in parallelism. In Ugaritic the cognate *p'n* is the regular term for "foot" and *rgl* is not used.

2b. *prince's daughter*. LXX and Old Latin read "daughter of Aminadab" and some interpreters seized on this to support the identification of the Shulamite as Israel, "daughter of my princely/noble people." The explanation of this term varies according to theories of interpretation. Delitzsch explained that *nāḏîḇ* means noble in disposition, and then noble by birth and rank. "Shulamith is here called a prince's daughter because she was raised to the rank of which Hannah, I Sam. ii. 8, cf. Ps. cxiii. 8, speaks, and to which she herself, vi. 12, points." Ginsburg opined that *baṯ nāḏîḇ* does not mean "a descendant of a titled family," but, according to common Hebrew idiom which applies "son" or "daughter" and other terms of human kindred to relations of every kind, expresses that she herself was of noble character. Harper thought it strange to call the peasant bride a nobleman's daughter and opined that on the dramatic view the term must mean "a born lady," i.e. one who would adorn any station. Siegfried thought that the term arose from a confusion with the Shunamite of II Kings 4:8 who is called "a great woman." Interpreters of the cultic persuasion cite the Gilgamesh Epic VI 6,88 where Ishtar is called "great (lady)," *rubūtu ᵈIštar.* Emendation of *nāḏîḇ* to *mĕḇōreḵeṯ,* "blessed," or *haššûlammît,* "the Shulamite," whether on metrical or other grounds, is wholly unwarranted.

2c. *Your curvy thighs.* Lit. "the curves of your thighs." The form *ḥammûqê* is hapax legomenon, but the verb *ḥāmaq* "turn (away)" occurs in 5:6 and elsewhere in the Old Testament only in Jer 31:22 (in the reflexive stem). In post-biblical Hebrew *ḥammûq* means "wheel" or "circle" and the Targum *kĕlîlā',* "crown," approximates this sense. LXX rendered *rythmoi,* but Symmachus *sundesmoi* and Vulgate *juncturae,* "joints," hence *KJ* "the joints of your thighs." The emendation by Graetz to *ḥassûqê,* "joints of" (Exod 27:10; I Kings 7:33), nevertheless appears unwarranted. Translators and commentators are generally agreed that the reference is to curvilinear symmetry. Luther apparently thought that the concern was for bilateral symmetry, "your loins match one another like two bracelets" (Deine Lenden stehen gleich an einander, wie zwei Spangen). Most modern versions agree that the term applies to the dancer rather than the dance and that the interest is in rotundity or curvature. *AT,* "the curves of your hips," *RSV, JPSV, NAB,* "your rounded thighs," *JB, NEB,* "the curve(s) of your thighs."

ornaments. The word *ḥălā'îm* is hapax legomenon, but similar forms occur in Prov 15:12 and Hosea 2:15, each time in juxtaposition with *nezem,* "ring." LXX rendered *hormiskos,* "collar," "necklace," and this sense has been adopted by a number of interpreters. Delitzsch rendered "The vibration of thy thighs like ornamental chains," and explained that "the manifold twistings and windings of the upper part of the body by means of the thigh-joint are meant." The *ḥammûqîm,* according to Delitzsch, "are not the beauty curves of the thighs at rest,—the connection here requires movement." Budde and Siegfried supposed that the evolutions of the dance sketched on the ground the curve of a collar. Robert objected that neither of these notions is satisfactory and suggested that it is a question of the hollow of the hip, its harmonious contour being compared to that of a necklace. Since in the subsequent context, according to Robert, every trait of the description is inspired by a geographical particularity of the Holy Land, one may ask if the author, in speaking of the hips of the bride, was not thinking of the outline of the Palestinian coast which resembles the soft curve of a necklace. One may, of course, ask, but it is doubtful that many will find a geographical allegory convincing here or conjure up a vision of the curves of the Palestinian coastline. Apart from the association of the word with *nezem,* "ring," there is nothing to suggest a connotation of curvature in the word *ḥălā'îm* itself. The curvation is expressed by the term *ḥammûq* and need not be intrinsic to the thing to which the curvy thighs are compared. In Arabic the root *ḥly* is used in the general sense of "adorn" and "adornment," without implication of curvature or rotundity. Thus it seems best to choose a general term like "jewels" or "ornaments."

2d. *Crafted by*. Lit. "work of."

artist. The form *'ommân* is hapax legomenon in the Old Testament, but the meaning is known from Akkadian *ummânu* and Aramaic *'ummân,* "artisan," "craftsman." A variant form *'āmôn* occurs in Prov 8:30 and Jer 52:15, rendered by *RSV* "master workman" and "artisans."

2. The Targum interpreted thus:

> Said Solomon in the spirit of prophecy before YHWH: How beautiful are the feet of Israel when they go up to appear before YHWH three times a year, in sandals of scarlet bringing their votive and free-will offerings, and their children that come from their loins are beautiful as the sparkling gems set in the Holy Crown which Bezalel, the craftsman (*'ummānā'*) of Aaron, fashioned.

Midrash Rabbah took its cue from *pa'am* in the sense of "festival season" and *nĕ'ālîm,* "barrings," "closings," rather than sandals, and this called forth several stories showing how persons who attended the festivals were protected from economic loss and depredations. The "closings" also were related to an agreement between two traders to take turns offering their wares in the same town to avoid depressing prices and to the Holy One's offer to Israel with respect to the two "closings" of Tabernacles and Passover. "You close before Me at Tabernacles and I close before you at Passover." That is, you close your work and I will open the heavens to bring rain and sun to make the crops grow. Then at Passover I will close (the heavens from raining) so that you can go out and reap, thresh, and winnow and do all that is required in the field and find it rich in blessing.

The reference to thighs suggested circumcision to which was attributed all the luxuries and delicacies which Israel enjoys in this world. The term *ḥălā'îm* suggested *ḥălāyîm,* "sicknesses," and evoked from Rabbi Nathan a story about a Cappadocian woman who had three sons die from circumcision, but the fourth was saved by delaying the operation.

This first part of the verse was applied to Israel's steps when going up to Jerusalem for festal celebration (TB Sukkah 49a,b). The prince was identified as father Abraham. The words of Torah were compared to thighs to teach us that as the thing is hidden, so should the words of Torah be hidden. The verse was regarded by Rabbi as unsuitable for public instruction or discussion (TB Mo'ed

Qatan 16a). From this verse it was also deduced that pits (for wine libations under the altar) existed from Creation (TB Sukkah 49a,b). The School of R. Ishmael taught that instead of *bĕrē'šîṯ,* "in the beginning," one should read *bārā' šîṯ,* "he created a pit (for libation!)."

This verse and its parts was treated in a variety of ways by Christian expositors. The steps or goings were applied to the Church's proclamation of the Gospel in distant lands, her feet shod with the readiness of the Good News of peace (Eph 6:15). The sandals served for some far-ranging exegetical excursions. One view was that they represent the departed saints typified by the skins of dead animals from which sandals are made, another that they refer to mortification of the flesh and voluntary promises of chastity, as one takes care not to step in the mire of sin. Again the Church, strengthened by the death of Christ, is shod against the evils that rise against her. The mystical sense of the sandals was related to the episcopal solid sole which guards the steps of the preacher from being defiled by earthly things. The Prince was seen as the Holy Ghost, or as Christ, the Prince of Peace who, in his mysterious relation to the Bride, was her Father (because she was born anew to Him in the water of Baptism) and also the Bridegroom. The LXX reading, "daughter of Nadab," was taken by Theodoret to refer to Nadab who died for offering strange fire (Lev 10:1) and explained as meaning that the Bride bore no legal fire into the sanctuary of God, but a new fire received from her Spouse (cf. Luke 12:49).

The thighs of the lady were allegorized as typifying the practical virtues which bear us along on our journey, temperance and holiness, or lowliness and purity, the twin supports of sanctification. The jewels or necklaces were seen as good works. The ornament was also applied to the motherhood of the Blessed Virgin and to Christ. The craftsman was the Almighty Himself. (Cf. Littledale.)

3a. *vulva.* The word (*šōr*<*šurr*) occurs elsewhere in Ezek 16:4 and Prov 3:8. In Ezek 16:4 it clearly refers to the umbilical cord which is cut. In Prov 3:8 it is probably an error for *šĕ'ēr,* "flesh," since a healthy navel seems a rather insignificant reward for piety. The form *šĕrîrê* in Job 40:16 is rendered "navel" by *KJ,* but is usually taken to mean "muscles"; cf. AB 15, ad loc. The Arabic cognate *surr* denotes properly the umbilical cord and then the scar or navel. The similar word *sirr,* however, in Arabic has the meanings "secret" and "pudenda," as well as "coition," "fornication," and the like, and a number of critics have taken the term here as a euphemism for vulva, related to Arabic *sirr.* Robert characterized this as pure fantasy, since *šēr* does not exist in Hebrew and the image which one tries to find does not accord with the context. Robert, however, had preconceived notions of the context which predisposed him to favor the navel over the vulva. To those who understood the "navel" as metonymy for "belly," Robert properly pointed out that belly is mentioned in the succeeding verse and that in this description the mention of each part of the body is accompanied by a single comparison. Since the movement of the description of the lady's charms is from the feet upward, the locus of the evermoist receptacle between the thighs and the belly would seem to favor the lower aperture. The liquid, too, would seem to make the navel unlikely since navels are not notable for their capacity to store or dispense moisture, despite the Arabian Nights' notion that an ideal female navel is like the bottom of a tiny coffee cup with a capacity of perhaps an ounce of oil; cf. p. 641.

crater. Both LXX and Vulgate render crater, "mixing bowl." The word *'aggān* in Exod 24:6 is applied to a basin for dashing blood on the altar. In Isa 22:24 it is put in the category of small vessels, "from bowls (*'aggānôṯ*) to crocks (*nĕḇālîm*)." In Akkadian *agannu* designates a bowl. The Egyptian term is *'ikn.* The word *aggos* applied to a vessel used for mixing wine (*Odyssey* xvi 13) is apparently the same word; cf. J. P. Brown, 1969, 158. The word may be represented in one of the several occurrences of *agn* in Ugaritic, but in 23[52].14–15, *agn* stands in parallelism with the Semitic word for fire *išt, 'l išt šb'd//w'l agn šb'dm,* "over the fire seven times," and thus represents the Indo-European loanword for "fire," Sanskrit *agni.* The expression *lriš agn* in 23[52].31,36 is ambiguous and has been taken to mean "from the top of the bowl" and "from the top of the fire"; cf., *EUT,* 80.

In any event, the nature of the vessel in question is now clear from archaeological and epigraphic data. It is a large, deep, two handled, ring-based bowl; cf. Honeyman, 1939, 79. The small sanctuaries from Palmyra have furnished a number of fragmentary examples. The single sanctuary of Ḫirbet Semrîn contained parts of at least nine stone craters, of which one intact example was found *in situ* in the banquet room of the sanctuary of Abgal; cf. Milik, 108. This intact specimen measures 49 cm. in height and 56 cm. inside diameter, with an internal depth of 42 cm, a sizable bowl. The inscribed rims of some of these bowls contain fragments of the formula: "This crater (*'gn' dnh*) so-and-so dedicated to such-and-such a deity." At Petra a bowl carved in the cliff is identified with the inscription: *[d]nh 'gn' qrb tymw br* [. .] *m br šmytt l'lh* [*'l*]*gy' 'lh' bšlm šlm,* "This is the *'aggān* which Taimu son of . . . dedicated to the god 'Ilâh-'al-Gai' in peace, peace"; cf. Milik, 109. On funerary reliefs the large bowl or jar from which the attendant dips with a pitcher to fill the drinking cup of the central figure is apparently to be identified as the *'aggān* or *kratēr,* the mixing bowl. See Figure 2, p. 212.

The effort by J. Reider (1925) to relate *'aggān* to Arabic *jaun,* supposed to mean, "disc" (of sun or moon) was shown by Kopf (1956, 293*f*), to rest on a misunderstanding of the Arabic dictionaries, *jaun* being a Persian loanword which relates to the reddish color and not the shape of the sun or moon.

rounded. The word *sahar,* here with the article, *hassahar,* is hapax. LXX rendered *torentos,* "turned," Vulgate *tornatilis,* used of artistically worked round objects. The Targum and Midrash Rabbah took the word to refer to the disc of the moon with reference to the seating arrangement of the Sanhedrin. Qimḥi accordingly understood the *'aggan hassahar* as a moon-shaped basin. If there is any connection with the moon, the question is what phase of the moon's circle and to which part or aspect of the vessel does it refer? Since we now know the shape of the *'aggān,* it is clear that the roundness implies more than the quarter circle of the crescent moon, at least a half or three-quarter moon, viewing the bowl from the side, and a full circle viewed from above. The emendation of *sahar* to *sōhar,* as applied to a prison in Gen 39:20, 40:5, on the assumption that the vessel was closed or covered, is unwarranted, as is also the change to *saḥar.* Since the stone exemplars of the *'aggān* found at Palmyra were obviously turned on some sort of lathe, it may be that the term *sahar* stands for the *nomen professionis sahhār,* "turner," as in the English name Turner for one who fashions objects on a lathe, and thus *'aggan hassah(h)ar* means "the turner's bowl," i.e. a well-turned bowl.

3b. *never.* The particle *'al* here may not have the usual prohibitive force, but serves, perhaps, as an emphatic negation, like Akkadian *ul,* similar to the use of *lô'* with the imperfect for emphatic, universal negation, as in the Ten Commandments, "you will not (ever) steal" (cf. Joüon, 114k). Most modern versions take it in this way. Luther, "dem nimmer Getränk mangelt"; *KJ* "*which* wanteth not liquor"; *AT,* "in which liquor is never lacking"; *RSV,* "that never lacks mixed wine"; *JB,* "with no lack of wine"; *NEB,* "that shall never want for spiced wine"; *NAB,* "that should never lack for mixed wine." A notable exception is *JPSV* with the rendering "Let mixed wine not be lacking." The interpretation of the particle *'al* as prohibitive turns the line into an apostrophe to our lady's navel or vulva, either as a receptacle or source for spiced wine.

Robert explained the navel and the crater as an allusion to a detail of the topography of Jerusalem and the notion that the city and the land is the navel of the earth; cf. Ezek 5:5, 38:12; Judg 9:37. Some of the famous temples of antiquity pretended to be the center of the earth and Jerusalem in apocryphal and rabbinic tradition was accorded that distinction (cf. Ethiopic Enoch 26:1–2; Jubilees 8:12–19; TB Yoma 54b, Sanhedrin 37a). Medieval maps represented Jerusalem as the center of the earth and in the midst of the Greek Choir of the Church of the Holy Sepulcher is a naïvely realistic reproduction of the navel of the world, concretizing the ancient opinion that salvation works in the middle of the earth in accordance with a servile application of Ps 74:12 and Ezek 38:12.

In the light of these explications, Robert believed that the expression *'aggan hassahar* becomes comprehensible. The Holy City is built on a spur which on the northeast is attached to Gareb, but to the east, south, and west is bordered by deep wadis (the Qidron, Hinnom, and ir-Rababy) which trace *grosso modo* an arc of a circle. This relief, Robert opined, suggested to the author of the Canticle at the same time the image of the navel and the comparison of a crescent sketching the form of a crater. Robert's rendering shows the influence of his theory, "Ton nombril est un cratère à demi formé."

punch. The term *mezeḡ* is hapax legomenon in the Old Testament, but occurs in Aramaic as *mězaḡ, mizḡā.* The variant form *meseḵ,* is found only in Ps 75:9[8E], but the verb *māsaḵ* is used in Isa 5:22, 19:14; Ps 102:10[9E];

Prov 9:2,5. The noun *mimsāḵ* is used in Isa 65:11 and Prov 23:30. In Ugaritic both the noun and the verb *msk* are employed. The Greek *misgō* or *mignumi,* and Latin *misceo* are manifestly related and already in 1815 Gesenius attributed the parallelism either to an original connection between Semitic and Indo-European or to chance (pp. 66*f*). For a treatment of this term along with other international terminology related to drinking, sacred and profane; cf. Brown, 1969, esp. 153–155 on *mezeḡ* and its congeners. Wine was mixed with water and with other wines and spices and the rabbis attempted to draw a distinction between the two terms *msk* and *mzg* (cf. TB Abodah Zarah 58b), *mzg* supposedly meaning to mix wine with water, but *msk* meaning to mix strong wine with weaker wine. Apropos of Isa 5:22 and Prov 23:30 Midrash Numbers Rabbah (10:8) comments "They used to mix (*msk*) strong wine with weak wine so as to get drunk with it." The terms *mezeḡ, meseḵ* and *mimsāḵ* are, for purposes of poetic parallelism, synonyms of *yayin* and *ḥemer,* as will be seen by comparison of Ps 75:9 and Prov 23:30. The rendering of *mezeḡ* as "punch" here is deliberate in view of the derivation of the term from the Sanskrit *pañchan,* Hindi *pānch,* "five," from the five ingredients which include spiced wine.

The notion that *mezeḡ* here is a metaphorical designation of semen or "seed (*zera'*)" (cf. Lev 15:18; Num 5:13), as supposed by Siegfried, Haupt and Haller, has no legitimation, as Robert noted. One must concur with Robert that the sense is metaphorical, but it does not follow that the wine figures the outpourings of spiritual love only. As Robert saw it, the sense is that Yahweh dwells in the Temple and the lovers seek mutually to captivate one another there (in the wine house 2:4), the figure giving to understand that Jerusalem is the place of perfect union and effusions of love.

If the vessel in question is the vulva, the spicy mixture probably does not refer to semen but to what the Indian erotologists call "love water" (*kamasulileh*) which in the ideal lotus woman is perfumed like the new-burst lily; cf. Edwardes, 1959, 59.

3a,b. The Targum found in the navel the illustrious Head of the Tribunal of the Sanhedrin:

> The Head of your College, by whose merit all the world is sustained—as a foetus is sustained by the navel in the inwards of its mother—sparkles with the Law, like the disc of the moon, when he goes forth to declare pure or impure, innocent or guilty; the words of the Law are never lacking in his mouth, as water never fails from the great River that issued from Eden.

Midrash Rabbah explained that the navel indicates the Sanhedrin and that Israel can never do without the Sanhedrin as an embryo cannot live without the navel. The *'aggan hassahar* was applied to the seating arrangement in a semicircle like the half moon. The mixed wine was taken to mean that the minimum membership of the local Sanhedrin is twenty-three, one third of the Jerusalem Sanhedrin, this deduced from the proportions of wine mixing, two parts water to one part wine.

Another explanation, playing on *mezeḡ*, "mixture," and *nizgāh* "need," invoked Ps 23:1.

Christian expositors, not unlike the Targumist who found allusion to the Head of the College, referred the navel to the order of holy preachers, fitly styled a goblet because when the people are taught from its mouth they are filled with spiritual wine. It is round because the preacher's tongue has to encompass all subjects with all classes of men. The goblet never lacks because it has to contain more than it gives. The Priesthood is compared to a goblet with mixed wine, because it is charged with the mystery of the Sacrament of the Body and Blood of Christ. The Priesthood also is the navel of the Church; it is a goblet that gives drink; and it is round because its sharp edges have been smoothed according to the divine will. The womb of Mary was also related to the round goblet in which was mingled the fullness of the Godhead. The navel and the goblet too typified the heart conscious of its weakness and holding the memory of its former sins. (Cf. Littledale.)

3c. *belly*. Some translators render *beṭen* here as "body," but that includes too much. The area in question is manifestly above the thighs and below the breasts. Robert asserted that this word can designate nothing but the mountain of Judah whose northern limit is marked by the fiftieth kilometer of the road from Jerusalem to Nazareth. Only the latter half of the assertion is unexceptionable.

mound. Again the symmetry is curvilinear. Winnowed grain is piled in heaps which naturally approximate hemispherical form. Whether the grain is sifted seems unimportant for the image. Delitzsch noted that in Arabic usage *'aramat*, the cognate of the present term *'ărēmāh*, applies to threshed and winnowed but yet unsifted grain, while *ṣubbah* is the term for the sifted heap. Apparently wishing only the finest for "Shulamith," Delitzsch assumed that the sifting was subsumed in the present sense of *'ărēmāh*.

wheat. Delitzsch, following Wetzstein, supposed that, in addition to the roundness of the grain heap, the comparison also refers to the color of wheat as describing the flesh color shining through the dress; "for fancy sees more than the eyes, and concludes regarding that which is veiled from that which is visible." In Delitzsch's imagination, the lady was presumably well veiled, although there is nothing, apart from the reference to the tunic in 5:3a, to indicate that she wears more than sandals, jewels, and perfume. The complexion of the first created man, according to Muslim tradition, was that of wheat and Delitzsch imagined that here wheat-yellow and subdued lily-white denotes at once health and purity. The blackness of 1:5 has presumably worn off and our lady's complexion is now a healthy cream color and a subdued lily-white. Robert, who imagined our danseuse's belly as an allusion to the mountain of Judah, noted apropos of coloration that except for a few weeks in the spring, when covered with ephemeral vegetation, the mountain has the tint of yellow gold which recalls that of ripe ears of grain. Further, agricultural prosperity is one of the characteristics of the eschatological era (Hosea 14:6–9[5–7E]) and Ps 72:16 even expresses the wish that at the messianic epoch the grain will shoot up on the mountain tops and wave in the breeze like the cedars of Lebanon.

3d. *Hedged.* This form *sûḡāh* is unique in the Old Testament, but the meaning is clear and well established in Aramaic and post-biblical Hebrew and Arabic. The root is sometimes listed by lexicographers as *s*(*w*)*g* II, but it is moot whether it should not be subsumed under the common biblical verb *s*(*w*)*g* I with an original meaning of "separate." The rabbinic use of *sĕyāḡ*, "fence," with reference to defending, fostering, and cultivating the Law is classic. Delitzsch observed that grain piles are frequently inserted with objects that move in the breeze to keep away birds and Buzy noted that wheat piles are often retained by a border of brambles held down by rocks. The hedge or fence encircling the belly somewhere between the waist and the broadest part of the hips was, presumably, purely decorative in view of its floral composition and not intended to bar or protect the primary erogenous zone. The elaborate girdles on Mesopotamian and Indian terracottas of the goddesses are generally worn below the navel and above the exposed and emphasized cuneate *mons Veneris;* cf. G. Dales, 1963.

lotuses. Cf. 2:1,16, 4:5, 6:2. The Targum took the *šôšannîm* here as "roses," *wārĕḏîn.* In the Indian *Hymns to the Goddess,* the "lotus-feet" of the goddess are frequently mentioned and her face is lotus-like, her three eyes as it were, full-blown lotuses, and in her hand she holds a knife, a skull, a lotus, and a sword (Avalon, 1952, 51). Her lotus-feet are worshiped by the universe, she is a lotus seated upon a lotus (p. 69); she dwells on the lotus (p. 113), but her waist is not lotus-girdled. She is slender of waist and beautifully girdled (p. 88); she glitters with a beautiful girdle round her hips (p. 143), a glittering gold waist-ornament on her large hips (p. 173).

3c,d. The Targum continued with the application of the belly or body to the Sanhedrin:

> . . . and seventy sages ranged around him (i.e. the Head of the Tribunal), like a round threshing floor, and their treasuries filled with the holy tithe, the votive and free-will offering which Ezra, the priest, Zerubbabel and Joshua, Nehemiah and Mordecai Bilshan (?) had set (*sayyĕḡû,* playing on the word *sûḡāh*) for them, the men of the Great Synagogue, who resembled roses, so as to enable them to be busy with the study of the Law day and night.

Midrash Rabbah found puzzlement in the choice of a heap of wheat for comparison of the lady's charms, since even a pile of cedar cones is prettier than a wheat pile. But an answer was found in consideration of the fact that the world can well do without cedar cones, but not without wheat. The cleft in the wheat (grain) evoked the cleft of the circumcision and further, as wheat (flour) absorbs water, so Israel sucks the wealth of the nations (Deut 7:16). This figure of Israel as the wheat, the Gentiles being chaff, was illustrated by a parable. The straw, chaff, and stubble argued among themselves each claiming that for its sake the ground had been sown. The wheat said to them, "Wait till the threshing time comes, and we will see for whose sake the field was sown." When the time came and they were all brought to the threshing floor, the farmer proceeded to winnow. The chaff was scattered to the winds; the straw he took and threw on the ground; the stubble he cast into the fire; the wheat he took and piled in a heap, and all who passed by when they saw it, kissed it, as it says (Ps 2:12), "Kiss the grain." The reference to the kissing of grain and the application of the famous crux of Ps 2:12, *naššĕqû-ḇar,* is of particular interest in the light of a puzzling Ugaritic ritual involving the hugging and kissing of grain.

After the murder of his son Aqhat by the Goddess Anat, the distraught father Danel uttered an imprecation reminiscent of David's reaction to the death of Saul and Jonathan, II Sam 1:21:

Seven years may Baal fail,
Eight the Cloud Rider,
No dew, no rain,
No upsurge of the Deeps,
No goodly voice of Baal.
(19[1 AQHT].1.42–46)

Danel then mounted his ass and went on an inspection tour of his grainfield(s).

The stalk he spied in the patch,
The stalk he spied in the foliage.
The stalk he hugged and kissed.
Ah me, that the stalk appear in the patch,
The stalk appear in the thicket,
That the hand of Hero Aqhat might gather thee,
Deposit thee in the granary.
. . . he approached the food-plot,
Saw the grain-ear in the food-plot,
The grain-ear appeared in the withered land.
The grain-ear he hugged and kissed.
Ah me, that the grain-ear appear [in the patch],
That the hand of Hero Aqhat might gather thee,
Deposit thee in the granary.
Hardly had the word left his mouth,
The utterance his lips,
When he/she lifted his/her eyes and she/they saw . . .
(19[1 AQHT].2.61–76)

Just what Danel and/or his daughter saw is unclear because the text becomes fragmentary and the stichometry and parallelism uncertain. Two "boys" approach and there is partial repetition of the account of the slaying of Aqhat (cf. H. L. Ginsberg's surmize, *ANET,* 153*f*). The hugging and kissing of the ears of grain are especially striking in the light of the reference to the kissing of grain in Midrash Rabbah. Danel's kissing the grain appears to be part of a divination ritual by which the mode of his son's death is revealed. It is interesting that the word *palt,* conjecturally rendered "patch," has a possible cognate in Arabic which relates to omens and portents. It is obvious that the grain-kissing episode in the Aqhat Epic requires further study, which cannot be undertaken here since it has no direct bearing on the Song of Songs.

For some of the Church Fathers the belly denoted the multitude of the faithful, since the womb signifies fecundity, and these were born not of blood, nor of the will of the flesh, nor of the will of man, but of God. The heap of wheat reminded of the grain of wheat of John 12:24. It is a heap, and not scattered grains, because the Church of all the faithful is formed by the union of many natures made one in the communion of one Baptism and the Sacrament of the Body and Blood of Christ. As a heap is broad at the base and grows progressively smaller toward the summit, so in the Church there are many self-indulgent at the bottom of the pile and very few who aim at the height of perfection. The heap is hedged with lilies because of the good works of the Saints. Some understood the heap of wholesome, nutritious wheat to represent the divines versed in Holy Scripture, who by their teaching win over many to purity and even vows of perpetual chastity. Again the lilies which fence the wheat were seen as the cloistered Orders of the Church. Or the heap of wheat to some symbolized the words of Holy Scripture and the lilies the pure and lovely thoughts which they supply for meditation. Applied to the Virgin Mary, the wheat reminds how she bore the One who was ground in the mill of Passion to become the Bread of Life, and how He was hedged around by her spotless virginity. (Cf. Littledale.)

4a,b. This verse repeats 4:5 but with omission of the attribute "Browsing on the lotus," probably because the lotuses are mentioned at the end of the preceding verse. Syriac, however, restored the supposedly missing line. Rothstein eliminated this verse as well as the first part of the next relating to the neck, since in the sword dance supposedly being executed by the bride, in the fashion of a Syrian peasant wedding, the breasts and neck were not especially featured. For Joüon the breasts symbolized the fecundity of Israel (cf. Gen 49:25 which mentions the blessings of breast and womb) and repeats the idea of 4:5 which allegedly announces the union of the two divisions of the tribes of Israel after the return from exile. For Robert the context was an invitation to rediscover beneath the image in question some physical characteristic of the Land of Palestine. Having just discovered Jerusalem as the navel and the mountain of Judah as the belly, and since the author moves from south to north, he was tempted to see the two breasts as Ebal and Gerizim which are veritable twin mountains.

4. For the Targum the two breasts were the two Messiahs:

> Thy two redeemers who are ready to redeem you, Messiah, son of David, and Messiah, son of Ephraim, are like Moses and Aaron, sons of Jochebed, who resemble two fawns, twins of a roe.

5a. *ivory tower*. The neck has already been compared to a tower, David's tower, in 4:4, and some critics think once is enough. Repetitions of this sort, however, are frequent and characteristic of the Canticle. In the description moving upward from foot to head, the neck is roughly in its proper place above the breasts and below the head. The material for the tower has seemed strange to some critics who would change the ivory to a proper name. H. Winckler proposed to read *śĕnîr* (cf. Deut 3:9) instead of *haššēn,* "the tooth" (1897, I, 294) and Horst added a letter to get *habbāšān,* "of Bashan." Bickell proposed to add *mĕṣuppeh hoḇnîm,* "covered with ebony," as an allusion to the black hair covering the neck. Others would add "set on a socket of porphyry," *mĕyussad 'al-'adnê-bahaṭ*. Several would transpose the first stich of vs. 6 "Your head on you like Carmel" with elimination of "on you," or alteration to "on it," but the transplant and surgery are ill-advised. As for the ivory tower, Cornelius à Lapide thought it a trifle fabricated, and Delitzsch supposed it to be a real tower covered externally with ivory slabs, a tower well known to all in Jerusalem and visible far and wide, especially when the sun shone on it; had it been otherwise, Delitzsch argued, the locality would have been more definitely mentioned. Ivory is not a very likely material for the construction or even the facing of a real tower: the "ivory palaces" of Ps 45:8 and the "ivory beds" of Amos 6:4, refer to ivory inlay of the furniture, as illustrated by archaeological finds of beautifully carved ivory inlay, e.g. on the bed of the King of Ugarit. Ginsburg remarked that the comparison between the beautiful symmetry, erect bearing, and ivory color of the neck, and between the elegant structure, lofty altitude, and white color of a tower, appears more striking and apposite in the light of the description of the towers of Jerusalem given by Josephus (*Wars* v, iv 4). The comparison of the neck with ivory was also drawn by Anacreon in his description of Bathyllus (*Ode* xxxix 28–29). The mention of ivory recalls the various precious materials of which the body of the male lover is composed in 5:10–16. From Ras Shamra we have an exquisite head done in ivory. See Plate VIII.

Robert, RTF, in accordance with his view that we have here geographical allegory, was of the opinion that it must refer to a place north of Samaria and, since Tabor could hardly be compared to an ivory tower, he speculated that it might be the mountain commonly called Little Hermon, *Nebi Daḥi.*

The current usage of *ivory tower* for the escapist, visionary, impractical, speculative, theoretical, abstract, esoteric attitudes and interests imputed to scholars, writers, poets, philosophers, artists, and aesthetes goes back to the French poet and critic C. A. Sainte-Beuve who referred to the turret room in which his fellow poet and novelist Alfred de Vigny wrote as his "tour d'ivoire." One may wonder how many of those who use the term are aware of its original biblical application to milady's neck.

5b. *pools.* LXX *limnai,* Vulgate *piscinae,* hence *KJ* "fishpools." The lady's eyes have already been termed "doves" in 4:1, while in 5:12 they are compared to doves by the brook(s). The expression of the comparative particle by LXX (*hōs*) and Vulgate (*sicut*) does not mean necessarily that it was written in the original; note the omission in 4:1a, 7:3a. (In 5:11,14,15, cited by Robert, it may not be a matter of simile, but of the materials of which the image or statuette was conceived as composed.) The equation or comparison of eyes with pools is natural enough as water acts as a mirror and the word itself in Semitic (*'ayn*) designates a water source and supply. Ovid used a similar comparison (*The Art of Love* ii 722):

Adspices oculos tremulo fulgare micantes Ut sol a liquida saepe refulget aqua.

Heshbon. The ancient city of Heshbon, an Amorite royal city (cf. Num 21:26–34) was located between Amman and Madaba, about seven miles north of Madaba, where the Nahr Ḥesbān flows into the Jordan not far above its entrance into the Dead Sea. It is well-supplied with water and the ruins of a huge reservoir of excellent masonry lie in the valley at the foot of the hill where the town stood. The comparison here implies two or more such pools or reservoirs. Excavations have recently begun at Heshbon by the Amman School of the American Schools of Oriental Research, under the supervision of Siegfried Horn. Aquila took *ḥešbôn* as the common noun which occurs in Eccles 7:25,27, 9:10, and in Sir 27:5, 42:3 and rendered *en epilogismō*. Winckler (1897, I, 294) proposed to read *ḥelbôn,* modern *Ḥalbūn* north of Damascus, mentioned in Ezek 27:18, as well as by Strabo, for its wine.

Robert here ignored the considerable detour eastward from the south–north geographical sweep which results in placing the eyes somewhat out of line with the neck and head. It would not help the theory to adopt Winckler's reading "Helbon," for that would put the eyes above the top of the head. With sufficient devotion, however, it would be possible to find an allegorical explanation, geographical or otherwise, for eccentric eyes.

5c. *Bat-Rabbim.* LXX read "in the gate of the daughter of many" and similarly Vulgate *quae in portae filiae multitudinis,* which, although it makes little sense, does confirm MT. The Targum, instead of *baṯ,* "daughter," read *bêṯ,* "house of," and some critics have done likewise. Blau's far-fetched conjecture *baṯ 'aqrabbîm* (cf. Num 34:4; Josh 15:3), as Delitzsch noted, is too far from Heshbon to serve as a parallel. Ginsburg rendered "By the populous gate," following Rashbam who explained that the gate is thus called "because through it a multitude of the inhabitants of the town go out and come in." If *ḥešbôn* of the preceding line is the place name, then *baṯ rabbîm,* whether corrupted or not, has to be taken as a cognomen or epithet of Heshbon. Pending further light on the term, it seems best to transliterate it as a proper name, without attempting to translate or interpret it.

5d. *nose.* The comparison of the lady's nose with the tower of Lebanon, or towering Lebanon, has bothered critics and some have attempted to avoid the difficulty by taking the word to mean "face" or "forehead" (thus Rashi). But the singular form here can only designate the nose and not the face. Critics are thus moved by this monumental nose to ponder notions of beauty and the limits of hyperbole. Dom Calmet found the comparison a bit strong, but noted that Orientals are not so delicate or moderate in expression. Guitton opined that Orientals lack proportion and moderation, citing the hyperbole of the speck and the log in the eye (Matt 7:4–5). Robert noted that hyperbole is frequent in biblical literature; sometimes, as in the Gospel parable, it is a pedagogical process intended to impress a teaching on the mind; sometimes, as in the Canticle, it translates an intense sentiment. This ardent and far-fetched (recherché) lyricism was further illustrated by Robert's interpretation of 5:10–16 as a description of the groom in terms of the architecture and furniture of the Temple. The whole question, Robert rightly observed, is to know what reality lies behind the figure of the tower. Critics generally have supposed that it was a real tower situated somewhere in the Lebanon or Anti-Lebanon mountains. David had garrisons in Syria (II Sam 8:6) and Solomon built military installations in the Lebanon (I Kings 9:19;

II Chron 8:6). Robert thought that the antecedent and subsequent context urge us to seek a geographical place and noted that several critics had already suggested Mount Hermon which towers over Damascus. The mountain, according to Robert, is here represented as an advance sentinel which, facing Damascus, dominates the routes of access to Palestine, and thus the Canticle is in defiance against a natural enemy which it naturally sees as coming from the northeast (cf. 4:8; Jer 4:6, 6:1,22). This enemy is not Damascus, which ceased to be a peril after the eighth century, nor even the Assyrian or Babylonian empire, which, in Robert's view, no longer existed at the time the Canticle was composed. Zech 9:1–7 witnesses that still in the Persian period the memory of the terrible invasions which had brought about the ruin of the nation had not been lost. And an analogous state of mind breaks through here, according to Robert; the powerful and haughty surveillance of Mount Hermon is a sort of defiance thrown out to those who are the successors of the traditional enemy and who continue to hold Palestine in servitude (cf. 4:8).

Apart from Robert's geopolitical hypothesis, it seems that he is right in taking the reference to be to the towering mountain rather than a man-made structure on the mountain, as Delitzsch understood it.

"The nose," Delitzsch noted, "gives to the face especially its physiognomical expression, and conditions the beauty. Its comparison to a tower or a lofty height is occasioned by the fact that Shulamith's nose, without being blunt or flat, formed a straight line from the brow downward, without bending to the right or left (Hitzig), a mark of symmetrical beauty combined with awe-inspiring dignity."

Whether a mountain tower or a towering mountain, if the writer regarded a prominent nose as a beautiful feature, he seems to have pressed his enthusiasm for salient features a bit far, with all due allowance for hyperbole. If our lady is superhuman in nature and size, then the dismay about her towering or mountainous nose disappears as the perspective and proportions fall into focus.

5. The Targum interpreted this verse thus:

> The Father of the Court (*'aḇ bêṯ dînā'*) who adjudicates your lawsuits is empowered over the people to compel them and to exact punishment of him who is found guilty by Court, as did Solomon, who made an ivory tower, and subdued the people of the House of Israel, and brought them back to the Lord of the World. Your Scribes are full of wisdom, like water channels, and they know how to compute the sums of the intercalary months and determine (leap) years and New Moons, and New Years, at the gate of the House of the Great Synagogue. And the Chief of the family of the House of Judah is like King David who built the fortress of Zion which was called "The Tower of Lebanon," so that all who stand on it may count all the towers which are in Damascus.

The neck reminded Midrash Rabbah of the episode in Gen 33:4 when Esau fell on Jacob's neck and kissed him. All the letters of *wayyiššāqēhû*, "and he kissed him," are dotted with the *puncta extraordinaria* and Rabbi Simeon ben Eleazar deduced the exegetical principle that when there are more dotted than undotted letters in a word one should concentrate on the undotted, and vice-versa. But since all the letters are dotted in the instance cited, the principle cannot be applied. The conclusion is somehow reached that Esau tried to bite Jacob rather than kiss him and that Jacob's neck turned to marble and Esau's teeth suffered. Thus "and they wept" refers to Jacob weeping for his neck and Esau for his teeth. From the reference to the ivory neck it is further deduced that when Pharaoh sought to slay Moses (Exod 2:15), the latter's neck became like ivory and the sword slipped off and beheaded the would-be executioner.

The eyes like the pools in Heshbon refer to the Sanhedrin. As the two hundred forty-eight members of the body all follow the eyes, so Israel can do nothing without the Sanhedrin. Heshbon, "reckoning," refers to decisions that depend on a (close) count, as when thirty-six vote innocent and thirty-five guilty. The gate of Bath Rabbim means the legal decision that originates in the gate (i.e. the Court) and spreads to the many. The word for "nose" was taken to refer to the forehead as the highest part of the head and thus to the Sanctuary. The Lebanon suggested plays on whiteness and Isa 1:18 was cited as proof that Israel's sins are forgiven.

Christian allegorical interpretations of this verse applied the neck to preachers and priests through whom the spiritual food passes to the laity, or the martyrs who put their necks under the yoke of Christ and never withdraw them; all these are ivory because of whiteness and purity. The tower reminds us that purity is allied with strength rather than weakness. Among other allegories, the ivory tower, as the spiritual neck of the Bride, was taken to refer to the knowledge of Scripture, and it is styled a tower because those who busy themselves with God's Word rise daily higher in spiritual progress. The soul also has its ivory neck, the pure observance of the precepts of God which is the bond and union between the faithful soul and Christ the Head. The neck too is the channel of speech through which the penitent confesses sins, and it is compared to a tower because it requires strength to acknowledge transgressions and not shrink back and cower in shame. The tower is ivory too because confession makes the soul white, firm, and clean.

The eyes like the fishpools of Heshbon were taken to refer to the Doctors of the Church who watch for the whole body and direct the way it should go; they are called fishpools because holy teachers wash the believers in the bath of life and refresh them with the drink from the fountain of salvation. The pools are beside the gate because none can enter the Church unless he is first washed in the water of Baptism and given to drink of the fount of saving doctrine. This was typified by the brazen sea which Solomon set at the Temple porch that the priests might wash themselves before entering the Temple to offer sacrifice, I Kings 7:23*f*. The gate was called "daughter of a multitude" because the Church gathers in the multitude of the Gentiles. Few of the Latin commentators developed the play on Hesbon as "thought" or "contemplation," but most rather related the word to *ḥēšeḇ*, "girdle," and interpreted it as "girdle of mourning" with reference to penitential sorrow as a special grace of the Bride.

The nose by which one distinguishes odors was referred to the holy teachers of the Church who know how to distinguish the sweet scent of the Catholic Faith from the deadly stench of heresy. The nose is like the tower of Lebanon because holy teachers occupy the highest place in the Church and also guard it from assaults of evil spirits. Damascus was the subject of wordplays on the first syllable as erroneously connected with the Hebrew word for "blood" and applied to the bloody powers of the world and the allurements of flesh and blood. The tower is against (*contra*) Damascus because those who are fortified by Christ always resist the devil. Lebanon in the sense of "frankincense" was applied to the Manhood of Christ. The nose as a lofty tower on the summit of Lebanon was also seen as a sentinel watching for the approach of any enemy of Israel (by Irimbert, abbot of Ambden, in the late twelfth century; this is also Robert's modern view). The tower looking toward bloody Damascus was also interpreted as referring to the Passion and shedding of Jesus' blood in Gethsemane and Calvary. Jerome applied the tower to Mary Magdalene and others to the Virgin Mary. The two orifices of the nose represent virginity and humility. Mary is the nose of the Church, like a tower lofty and sedate, and white in innocence. (Cf. Littledale.)

6a. *Your head on you.* This expression scarcely seems to require the attention that some commentators devote to it. LXX rendered literally and Vulgate omitted "on you." It is no great surprise to be informed that one says that the head is "on" a person (II Kings 6:31; Judith 14:18). Graetz, and others, supposed that "head" here refers to the hair of the head, because of the reference to tresses in the succeeding line.

like Carmel. Delitzsch commented that "After the praise of the nose it was natural to think of Carmel; Carmel is a promontory, and as such is called *anf el-jebel* ('nose of the mountain-range')." Mount Carmel is well wooded at the summit and it may be that the poet had in mind the lady's luxuriant tresses, cf. 4:1e,f. Graetz, following Ibn Janaḥ and Ibn Ezra, took *Karmel* to mean *karmîl* "crimson." Crimson hair seems no more strange than the purplish tresses of the following line. Delitzsch noted that if the hair of the head may be compared to the glistening of purple, then red and not black hair is meant.

6b. *locks.* The word *dallāh* is used elsewhere in the Old Testament only in Isa 38:12 where it is applied to the threads of a weaver's warp. The basic meaning of the root of the word, *dll,* is "hang down" or "dangle" which is appropriate to long hair and there is no reason to suppose that the word here designates ribbons rather than the hair itself.

purple. Cf. 3:10. The purple derived from the murex shellfish varied in shades and tones, from red to violet, to blue-black, as noted by Pliny *Hist. nat.* ix 135). The term "purple" is applied to hair in Lucian (*purphyreos plokamos*) and Anacreon (*porphyrai chaitai*). The use of henna for dyeing hair red is well-known. Although murex was used principally for dyeing textiles, it was also applied as a cosmetic to paint the face and dye the hair. J. C. de Moor has adduced evidence from the Ugaritic mythological texts for cosmetic use of murex for reddling the body, although nothing is said about the hair (cf. 1968, 214n2 for documentation of the Romans' cosmetic use of the murex). Schmökel (p. 99) in connection with this verse adduced the evidence of the statuette of Ishtar found by A. Parrot at Mari; the head of the statuette still showed reddish coloring.

The mention of purple following Carmel has perplexed critics. One would expect, as Joüon noted, something offering a similitude with the waving hair or having some connection with Carmel. Robert claimed that such a connection exists, but that it is of a geographical order. The allusion to Carmel is the last item in an enumeration going from south to north, and, once at Carmel, the author thinks of the Phoenician coast where abounds the murex from which the purple is extracted. But the characterization of the hair as like purple is not explained by this geographical hypothesis. The jump from Carmel to the shore from which comes the purple dye seems a rather forced leap without a compelling reason. Considerations of parallelism and "congruity of metaphor," to use a favorite term of Dahood's, suggests that, even if Carmel is not to be emended to *karmîl,* "crimson," the author intended a play on the name of the mountain and the color, a play which would be immediately appreciated only if the lady's hair was known to be crimson and/or purple. The red paint on the head of the statuette of Ishtar found at Mari suggests that the divine ideal of feminine beauty may have had dyed hair.

6c. *A king*. Syriac, Aquila, Symmachus, and Vulgate took the first word of this line, *melek,* "king," as the last word of the preceding line, as attributive to *'argāmān,* "purple," *purpura regis,* "royal purple." Several critics have adopted this division which makes the third line a trifle short, even though it is possible to make some sort of sense of the remaining two words, as applied to the tresses bound with ribbons rather than the king tangled in the tresses. Eliezer Ben Yehudah (1917) proposed to read *mallēḵ,* "your tresses," from the root *mll* which, as a verb implying motion, allegedly developed the sense "tresses." There is no ground for eliminating the word "king," in spite of the omission of the article. The male lover is elsewhere called "the king" in the Canticle, 1:4b,12a, 3:9b,11c.

tresses. The word *rĕhāṭîm* is used in Gen 30:38,41 and Exod 2:16 of gutters or troughs through or into which the water runs for watering flocks. The word is a derivative of the Aramaic verb *rĕhaṭ,* cognate with Hebrew *r*(*w*)*ṣ,* "run." LXX here rendered *en paradromais,* "in courses," and Vulgate *canalibus,* "in canals." The lady's hair is related to the action of moving water in 4:1*f,* with use of the verb *glš*. The emendations which have been proposed are unconvincing and scarcely worth reviewing.

Robert understood the king in question to be the king of Tyre. The allusion, in accordance with Robert's geographical hypothesis, comes naturally after the mention of the purple which designated the Phoenician coast. The king of Tyre is bound to the tresses of Israel; this expression recalls the alliance which existed between the two nations at the epoch of David and Solomon, and which manifested itself by the exchange of ambassadors and by the sending of materials and artisans for the construction of Ophel and the Temple, and by maritime expeditions made in common (cf. II Sam 5:11; I King 5:15[13E]*ff,* 9:10–14,26–28, 10:11,22).

6. The Targumist took a cue from the mention of Carmel to recall Elijah's contest with the prophets of Baal; *dallaṯ* was taken in the sense of the lowly poor (II Kings 24:14, 25:12; Jer 40:7) and the purple referred to their exaltation; the word *rĕhāṭîm* recalled Jacob's manipulation of genetics at the watering troughs (Gen 30:38,41):

> The king appointed over you as the head is righteous as Elijah the prophet who showed zeal for the Lord of Heaven and slew the false prophets on Mount Carmel, and restored the people of the House of Israel to the fear of YHWH God. And the lowly of the people who walk with bowed head because they are poor shall be clothed in purple, as Daniel was clothed in the city of Babylon and Mordecai in Shushan, on account of the merit of Abraham, who in former time ascribed Sovereignty to the Lord of the World, through the righteousness of Isaac whom his father bound in order to sacrifice him, and through the loyalty of Jacob who peeled the rods in the watering troughs.

Midrash Rabbah, like the Targum, referred Carmel to Elijah's victory, and the tresses to the poor. The captive king, however, was referred to the supreme King of kings who had bound Himself by oath to make His divine presence rest in the midst of Israel. Moses also was nominated as the captive king, the streams (*rĕhāṭîm*) being the waters of Meribah (Num 20:13) and Moses' regal status deduced from Deut 33:5 and Lev 24:2.

Christian expositors, following the Targum, interpreted the "head" as here meaning "king," i.e. Christ. Carmel was taken somehow to refer to "knowledge of circumcision" which the Head knew literally under the Law and spiritually under the Gospel (Littledale, 316 n1). The hair was interpreted as the innumerable company of Christian people which adorns the Church. The purple was seen as a prophecy of the death of the Bridegroom and of the faithful washed and dyed with His Blood. The LXX rendering of *dallaṯ* as *plokion*, "plait(s)," suggested to Theodoret the orderly sequence of Christian dogma as contrasted with the dishevelled opinions of Gentilism. The Vulgate rendering of 6c "as a king's purple bound in the canals" suggested dyed or washed hair and this served for a variety of allegories applied to Christ's Passion, His royalty, the prelates of the Church, the saints, the Church, and the Blessed Virgin. Littledale (pp. 319*f*) ends his summary of interpretations of this verse with the curious variant found in the Syriac and Arabic versions: "Thy hair is like a kingly purple awning spread above a racecourse (Syr.)/theatre (Arab.)." The obvious import of this seemed to Littledale "that the examples of the triumphant Saints, the witnesses of our struggle in the arena, serve to alleviate the burning heat of our trial, that we may endure to the end, and conquer."

7a. *How fair*. The exclamation *māh*, "how!" with the verbal form of *ypy* (**wpy*) "be beautiful," occurs also in 4:10 and 7:2 above. Adjectival forms of *ypy* are common throughout the Canticle, 1:8,15, 2:10,13, 4:1,7, 5:9, 6:1,4,10.

how pleasant. The term *n'm* is used in Ugaritic of both male and female beauty and charm. King Keret compared the beauty of his beloved to that of the goddesses Anat and Aštart when he asked her father to give her in marriage:

Give me lady Ḥurray,
Your beauteous firstborn progeny,
Whose charm is like that of Anat,
Like the beauty of Aštart her beauty.
(14[KRT].3.143–146; 6.288–293)

The term is applied to King Keret, *n'mn ġlm il,* "Handsome lad of El" (14[KRT].1.40–41; 2.61–62). The goddess Anat addressed the young hero Aqht derisively as *n'mn 'mq nšm,* "Handsome, strongest of men" (17[2 AQHT].6.45), when she threatened to trample him after she had failed in her efforts to seduce him in order to get his prized bow.

7b. *O Love.* LXX rendered *agapē,* "love," Vulgate *charissima,* "most dear one." Several modern versions follow this line of the Vulgate: *AT,* "beloved one"; *RSV,* "O loved one"; *JB, NAB,* "my love"; *NEB,* "my loved one"; but *KJ* and *JPSV* render "O love" and "O Love." The argument that the lover would not in the presence of his beloved burst forth with an apostrophe to love in the abstract (Joüon) is persuasive but not compelling. It seems most likely that *'ahăḇāh,* "love," is here to be taken as *abstractum pro concreto.* There is no need to emend to *'ăhûḇāh,* "loved one," in order to attain the sense "beloved," or "my love."

daughter of delights. It could scarcely be termed an emendation to follow Syriac and Aquila in dividing *batta'ănûgîm,* "with the delights," to *baṯ ta'ănûgîm,* "daughter of delight(s)." The error could have resulted from an auditory or scribal lapse or both. The root *'ng* is related to pleasures and delights of sundry sorts and it is silly to argue about the degree of sensuousness in the delights here intended. Harper's citation of Prov 19:10 and Micah 1:16, 2:9 to show that the term does not necessarily, or even generally, mean sensuous delights proves nothing. The term "daughter of delight" is strikingly similar to the French "fille de joie," but the connotation may not be the same.

7. The Targum explained,

> Said King Solomon: How beautiful you are, O Assembly of Israel, at the time when you bear upon you the yoke of My kingdom, at the time when I chasten you with afflictions for your guilt and you receive them with love and they seem in your sight as delights.

Midrash Rabbah referred the beauty and pleasantness to (Israel's) performance of religious precepts, positive and negative, and the exercise of charity, such as the distribution of tithes, leaving the corner of the field to be gleaned by the poor, avoiding mixtures (such as linsey-woolsey), avoiding uncircumcision, recitation of the *Shema',* use of the *mězûzāh* and *těfillîn, sukkāh,* palm branches, repentance and good deeds. Israel is fair in this world and pleasant in the world to come. The love and delights of the second half of the verse somehow evoked the love of Abraham to the king of Sodom (Gen 14:22) or of Daniel to Belshazzar (Dan 5:17).

Christian expositors applied this verse to the Church, fair in her faith and pleasant in her works, or to the Virgin Mother, fair in her maternity and pleasant in her virginity, and dearest in both to God who graced her with the delights of tending her Divine Son and meditating on her own marvelous destiny. (Cf. Littledale.)

8a. *Your stature*. Lit. "this thy stature." Latin and Vulgate omit the demonstrative and many commentators delete it on metrical grounds and translators generally ignore it. *RSV*, e.g. rendered "you are stately" and appended a note giving the Hebrew as "This your stature is." In Exod 32:1, however, *RSV* rendered "this Moses," while in Ps 104:25 "this the sea" was rendered "Yonder is the sea." The demonstrative is omitted in the present translation simply because "This, thy stature," "This figure of yours," or the like, makes poor poetry.

The term *qômāh* indicates the height of an object, such as a box or a table (Exod 25:10,23), or a man (I Sam 16:7), or of an anthropoid form compared to a tall vine or tree (Ezek 19:11, 31:3,5,10,14). In the *Shi'ur Qômāh*, "the most obnoxious document of Jewish mysticism" (cf. A. Altmann, 1967, 239), the term *qômāh* is used of the entire body of God, not just of his stature or height.

palm. The stately date palm, *tāmār* (*Phoenix dactylifera*) flourishes in warm moist areas and oases from Egypt to India. Iraq is presently, as in antiquity, the leading date-growing country of the world. Jericho was called "City of Palms" (Deut 34:3; Judg 1:16, 3:13; II Chron 28:15) and the oasis of En Gedi was also notable for its towering palms; cf. Sir 24:14, "I grew up like a palm tree in En Gedi." The comparison of a tall and slender lady to a tree, and especially a palm, is classic; cf. *Odyssey* VI 162*ff*. Stephan (76) cites examples of comparison to an unbending teak or tile tree and also to the palm:

O you, whose height is that of a palm tree in a serail.

For additional examples, cf. Ringgren, 1952, 92*f*.

Wittekindt (49*f*) stressed the connection of the palm with the fertility cult and as a standing attribute of Ishtar, recalling the palm ornamentation of the Temple in Jerusalem (Ezek 41:19; I Kings 6:29), the palm groves of Tyre dedicated to the love goddess (cf. Ohnefalsch-Richter, 1893, 149*f*), and the women of the Bible by the name of Tamar of whom erotic experiences are related (Gen 38:6; II Sam 13). Further, Wittekindt cited the pagan Arab worship of the date palm as a goddess, the Quran (Sura 19) which states that Mary was born under a palm, and even a report that whorehouses in Holland were painted with palm trees.

8b. *clusters*. The term *'eškôl,* plural *'eškôlôṯ,* usually designates a bunch or cluster of grapes and the Targum here added "of grapes," perhaps because of the "clusters of the vine" mentioned in the succeeding verse. The notion that the allusion is to a grape vine entwined around a palm tree (cf. Siegfried and Zapletal) seems rather far-fetched. The several references to the vine and the fig tree in poetic parallelism (I Kings 5:5[4:25E]; Jer 8:13; Micah 4:4; Hab 3:17; Ps 105:33) in no way suggest that the vine was entwined round the tree. The palm which reaches a height of eighty feet would in any event be unsuitable as a vine stake. It is manifest that the clusters here refer to the date clusters of the aforementioned date palm. That the term *'eškôl* can refer to clusters other than grapes is indicated by the specific reference to a cluster of henna in 1:14a. The comparison of the breasts to date clusters presumably intended a pair of clusters to match the dual form of the word for "breasts." A single large cluster of dates may carry over a thousand single fruits and weigh twenty pounds or more. It may be noted that the multiple breasts of the representations of Artemis of Ephesus look very much like a cluster of large dates, and it might be that the date clusters here were intended to suggest a similar condition of polymasty.

8. The Targum explained the verse thus:

> At the time when your priests spread their hands in prayer and bless their brothers of the house of Israel, the fingers of their outstretched hands resemble the branches of a palm tree, their stature like a date tree, and your congregation facing the priests, their faces bent to the ground like a cluster of grapes.

This verse provoked in Midrash Rabbah thoughts of idolatry and unchastity. Rabbi Ḥunia opined in the name of Rabbi Dosa ben Ṭebeth that God created two evil inclinations in His world, the inclination to idolatry and the inclination to unchastity. The inclination to idolatry has already been uprooted (in Israel). The inclination to unchastity, however, still exists. Says the Holy One, blessed be He: "If one can resist the inclination to unchastity, I reckon it to him as if he had withstood both." The discussion then moves to consideration of Mordechai and Esther and Hananiah, Mishael, and Azariah and their resistance to idolatry and unchastity.

Christian expositors related the palm to the Church, the soul, or the Cross of Christ. The Venerable Bede explained that the stature of the Church is the uprightness of her good works, because she, despising to be bent down towards the desires of earth, lifts her whole form upwards to attain heavenly things. The conqueror and victor, too, were decked or crowned with the palm, and thus the stature of the Bride is compared to a palm erect in love for heavenly things and pondering, while standing in the ranks of battle, that prize which is the victor's meed when the struggle is done. The palm is rough in its lower part, but displays its beauty and the sweetness of its fruit at the summit, and thus the Church or the faithful soul is fitly compared to it, as bearing harsh troubles on earth for the hope of a precious reward in heaven. The palm tree, according to Gregory the Great, is slender below and expands above, and similarly the holy soul begins in the depths with small things and grows slowly up to that which is greater, branching out at last to the full beauty of divine love. The palm is also elastic, springing up under any weight that may be laid on it; it also grows in dry and thirsty soil. The palm also suggested the Cross of Christ, for it grows to a great height and bears sweet fruit, and so the Cross of Christ prepared heavenly food for us.

The breasts were taken as the holy teachers of the Church who nourish with the milk of simple doctrine those who are reborn in Christ. These same breasts or teachers proclaim more perfect things to the perfect. The two breasts were also seen as the two Testaments, the two precepts of love, and the active and contemplative lives of Christianity.

The palm tree and the breasts were related to the Blessed Virgin in a variety of ways. Her outer bark was rough, in that she was weak in worldly honor, poor in temporal riches, yet possessed of great strength in the constancy of her soul. She was erect, shooting up to heaven in the resolution of her mind. At the summit she was firm by reason of her exalted virginity, lovely in flower, sweet in her fruitfulness, because she painlessly bore the Redeemer of the world. The breasts of Mary are her virginity and humility, in which Christ delights, and they are set before us as an emblem of victory, so that as she overcame the world, the flesh, and the devil, so too we may overcome according to her power. (Cf. Littledale.)

9a. *Methinks*. Lit. "I said." The verb *'mr,* "speak," is used also in the sense of "think," or "wish," cf. Gen 20:11, 44:28; Exod 2:14; Ruth 4:4; I Sam 20:4. There is in the expression itself nothing to suggest the intensity of passion which some commentators detect; this, however, may be legitimately deduced from the context. Delitzsch imagined that the remark was meant retrospectively, that, looking back, the lover can say that in view of the august attractive beauty the one thought filled him, to secure possession of her and of the enjoyment she promised. This could also apply to the present or the immediate future. The perfect here is used, as with verbs of cognition, with reference to the immediate past, or present.

I'll climb. The verb is cohortative or voluntative, indicating intensity of feeling. It would be quite legitimate to take this verb as subordinate to the preceding, as with Ginsburg, "I long to climb this palm tree."

Gerleman opined that the climbing of the palm has no erotic connotation, but is mentioned only because climbing the tree is the only way to harvest dates, and he cited Pliny's description of the climbing (*Hist. nat.* xiii 29). Ginsburg's reaction to the line indicates that he sensed a rather strong erotic suggestiveness:

> We earnestly request those who maintain the allegorical interpretation of the Song seriously to reflect whether this verse, and indeed the whole of this address, can be put into the mouth of Christ as speaking to the Church. Would not our minds recoil with horror were we to hear a Christian using it publicly, or even privately, to illustrate the love of Christ for his Church?

the palm. The definite article is not indicated in the vocalization of the Hebrew, but the sense requires it and the LXX supplied it. It would be a bit ludicrous in this instance to render, "I think I'll climb a palm."

9b. *grasp*. Or "lay hold on." The verb *'ḥz* with the preposition *b-* before the object implies, as Robert remarked, a certain vivacity or violence; cf. Exod 4:4; Judg 16:3; II Sam 4:10.

branches. The term *sansinnîm* occurs only here in the Old Testament, but a variant form *salsillôṯ* is found in Jer 6:9. The Akkadian cognate *sinsinnu* designates the topmost branches of the date palm. LXX *tōn hupseōn,* "the heights," may indicate a feeling for the proper sense and is not to be taken as reflecting a different reading *měrômāyw,* "its heights." Vulgate rendered *fructus ejus* and several commentators have adopted this sense. Robert explained that the term *sansinnîm* does not designate the fruit simply and directly, but the stalks with the fruit which they bear, and accordingly he rendered "les regimes." With Syriac, Symmachus, and Aquila, it seems best to render "branches." In Jer 6:9 the reference is to the branches or tendrils of the vine.

9c. *Let.* The precative particle *nā'* here comports with the cohortative or voluntative mood of the two preceding verbs and sustains the ardent, avid tone.

9d. *scent.* Odor, *rēaḥ,* is frequently mentioned in the Canticle as an erotic stimulant (1:3,13, 2:13, 4:10,11, 7:14). Several critics would read *rûaḥ,* "breath," but this does not alleviate the embarrassment.

vulva. Several MSS read the plural *'appayiḵ,* "thy face," instead of *'appēḵ,* "thy nose," and Gordis translated accordingly "the fragrance of thy face." Vulgate rendered *et odor oris tui,* "and the smell of your mouth." Some savants (e.g. Budde, Haupt, Staerk) supposed that the lover breathes through the nose because his mouth is smothered with kisses. Such would be natural enough, but even so the odor of one's breath, whether pleasant or offensive, comes more from the mouth than the nose. The emendation of *rēaḥ,* "scent," to *rûaḥ,* "breath," as noted above, does not relieve, but complicates, the problem, since the "breath of the nose" is used mainly of divine wind as a destructive force, as in Exod 15:8; II Sam 22:16=Ps 18:16[15E]. The mention of breasts in the preceding line suggests some more distinctively feminine zone than the nose or mouth. The word *ap* in Ugaritic is applied to the nostril(s) of a horse as the aperture through which medicine is administered, but it is also used of the nipple(s) of the breast(s) of the goddesses Asherah and Anat. In the poem called "The Birth of the Beautiful Gods" the newborn gods are dubbed "Suckers at the nipple(s) of the breast(s) of the Lady," *ynqm bap ḏd št* (23[52].61). The Akkadian cognate *appu* is used of the nose and also of the tip or crown of other parts of the body such as the nipple of the breast and the *glans penis.* Medicine was sometimes administered to an infant by putting it on the nipple of the mother (*ina appi tulī ummišu*). In 1:14 there is mention of a sachet of perfume between the breasts, but perfume on the nipples would be less effective than on the larger area.

It may be that the term *'ap(p)* here designates a spot more intimate even than the nipple of the breast. The word *ap* is applied in Ugaritic to the entrance of a city gate, as in the Aqht Epic where it is said:

Then Danel, Man of Rp',
The hero, Man of Hrnmy,
Went and sat in the entrance of the gate,
(*ytšu ytb bap tġr*)
Among the dignitaries in the forum.
He judged the case of the widow,
Adjudicated the cause of the orphan.
(17[2 AQHT].5.4–8)

It may be that Ugaritic *ap* in the sense of "opening," "entrance" is cognate with Akkadian *apu,* "hole," and *aptu,* "opening," "window," and has nothing to do with *appu,* "nose," "tip." In any case, the reference to the apple-like aroma of the lady's *'p* suggests an aperture or a tip other than nostril or nipple, perhaps the vulva or clitoris.

9. The Targum eschewed any suggestion of eroticism in the interpretation of this verse:

> Said YHWH, I will go and test Daniel and see whether he will be able to stand this trial, as Abraham stood like a palm branch in ten trials. And I will prove also Hananiah, Mishael, and Azariah, whether they are able to stand in their trials. I will redeem because of their merit the people of the House of Israel who are likened to a cluster of grapes. And the fame of Daniel, Hananiah, Mishael, and Azariah will be heard in all the earth and their fragrance be wafted like the fragrance of the apples of the Garden of Eden.

Midrash Rabbah took its cue from the Targum and elaborated on the examples of Daniel and his companions in their resistance to the idolatry which Nebuchadnezzar tried to impose.

This verse, Littledale noted, has originated, or at least encouraged, two opinions in the Church. One is that the Cross was made of four kinds of wood, cedar, cypress, olive, and palm, the last having formed the transverse beam:

Cedar the trunk, tall cypress holds His frame,
Palm clasps His hands, and olive boasts His name.

The other view based on this passage is that Christ literally went up to the Tree which was fixed erect in the ground before He was nailed to it. The more common view, nevertheless, is that He was laid on the Cross while it was still flat on the ground. The palm tree was taken also to represent the Church or the soul of the faithful. The Vulgate reading, "fruits" instead of "branches," suggested a variety of allegories. The fruits which the Lord gathered were salvation for mankind, glory for himself, resurrection, ascension, and authority as Judge. The palm as representing the Cross reminded of Christ's sorrows and Passion and, like Zaccheus, the Church ascends above the crowd to see her Lord who is hidden from such as reject the Cross. The palm was also seen as Christ the Tree of Life, the fruit being salvation. The use of palm branches in the rejoicing at the harvest festival (Lev 23:40; Neh 8:15) and in victory celebrations (cf. I Macc 13:51; II Macc 10:7) suggested Christ's triumphal entry into Jerusalem on Palm Sunday as typifying the celebration of the ingathering of the fruits of victory. Palm branches were also used in nuptial celebrations and this suggested the enthronement and marriage of the Lamb (Rev 7:9, 19:7).

The breasts as vine clusters, which when trodden yield their pleasant juice, suggested to Philo of Carpasia the holy men of God afflicted and tortured like grapes but producing the victory of salvation and gladness to God their Husbandman and to Christ and the Bride. The apple odor of the nose evoked for Philo the sweet savor of Christ both to the saved and the perishing (cf. II Cor 2:15). The nose also denoted the Orthodox Church which inhales the perfume of virtues with both nostrils, i.e. the two Testaments. Even though there is one nose, viz. one spirit, one faith, one baptism, one life eternal, and one God, yet there are two Churches, divided in name but not in faith or ultimate aim. The apples also were applied to the Church because they yield both food and drink, thus the sweet aroma of the Church in true faith and love possesses the mystic food and drink of the body and blood of Christ and dispenses it to others. Through the Cross, according to Gregory the Great, the Bride's breasts become grape clusters because the soul, nourished and inebriated by the two precepts of love, forgets what is past and reaches for what is ahead. The Vulgate reading, "mouth" rather than "nose," suggested to the Latin Fathers the preaching of the Word. Gregory took the apples to mean pomegranates, their ruddy hue typifying the example of the Martyrs as the Church's chief preachers. For Honorius the whole verse referred to the final glory of the redeemed; the Church Triumphant ascends the palm or reaches the Tree of Life because of the victory of the Cross (cf. Rev 2:7). (Cf. Littledale.)

10a. *palate.* LXX and Vulgate rendered "throat" (*laryx, guttur*) and similarly Luther, "Kehle"; *KJ* and *JPSV*[1] "the roof of thy mouth"; *AT* "palate"; Gordis, "thy kiss"; *RSV,* "thy kisses"; *JB,* "your speaking"; *NEB,* "your whisper"; *JPSV*[2] and *NAB,* "your mouth." According to the vocalization of the possessive suffix, the palate belongs to the female, but some commentators nevertheless ascribed the words to her rather than the male. Harper, e.g. asserted that the reference here as in 5:16 is to the sweet words of love which she whispers. Ginsburg objected strenuously to the attribution of these words to the maiden (by Rosenmüller, Döpke, De Wette, Noyes, Delitzsch, Hengstenberg, and others); it was incredible to Ginsburg that this modest woman would approve such expressions or continue with the words that follow. The palate is part of the speech mechanism and as such is used in poetic parallelism with mouth and lips (Prov 8:7; Job 33:2) but Ginsburg's assertion that it is used metonymically for speech is not supported by a single valid instance. In Job 6:30 the palate is mentioned not as an organ of speech, but of taste or discernment in testing the validity of speech. In Prov 5:3 the honey-dripping lips and smooth palate of the exotic wanton may refer both to her speech and her kisses. Gesenius (*HAHAT,* s.v. *ḥēk,* 312b) noted that in Canticles 7:11 "palate" seems put by way of delicacy for the moisture which accompanies a kiss, and he cited 5:16 and parallels from Arabic poetry. Delitzsch cited Lucretius' expression *jungere salivas oris* and Ovid's *oscula per longas jungere pressa moras,* but still understood the palate to refer to words of love which she whispers in his ear as he embraces her. *RSV*'s paraphrase "kisses" is the strongest evidence that the context suggests oral activity beyond mere verbal communication, since the revisers tended to resist erotic language and were not given to unwarranted suggestiveness in translation. The modern reader, however, scarcely needs to have the language of the Canticle clarified by paraphrase.

the best wine. The alteration of the expression *kĕyên haṭṭôḇ,* "like wine of the best," to *kayyayin haṭṭôḇ,* "like the good (i.e. best) wine," is entirely unwarranted, as is the emendation of *haṭṭôḇ* to *hāreqaḥ* on the basis of 8:2, "spiced wine." On this form of expression of the superlative, cf. GKC 126x,133h. The Canticle opens with allusion to kisses sweeter than wine.

10b. *Flowing.* LXX *poreuomenos* confirms the MT *hôlēḵ.* Vulgate *dignum* is puzzling and apparently influenced Symmachus' *harmozōn.* The verb *hlk,* "go," is used of the movement of liquids both in the Bible and in Ugaritic; cf. Eccles 1:7; Joel [3E] and especially Prov 23:31 where it is applied to smooth flowing wine, as here. The use of *hlk,* "go," rather than *yrd,* "go down," is appropriate to the drinking of wine in the recumbent position of the *mĕsibbāh* or symposium.

(*for my love*). The MT *lĕḏôḏî* is confirmed by the versions, but occasions considerable difficulty. The possessive suffix of *ḥikkēḵ,* "thy palate," indicates that the address is to the lady, thus *dôḏî,* "my love," seems inappropriate because it is used elsewhere in the Canticle only of the male lover. Budde emended *lĕḏôḏî* to *lĕḥikkî,* "for my palate." Many commentators assume an abrupt change in speakers, the Shulamite interjecting a single line which those who envisage a dramatic love triangle may interpret as an interruption addressed to the Shulamite's true love, the absent shepherd swain. Ewald proposed the reading *lĕḏôḏîm,* but Gordis suggested that *lĕḏôḏî* is an apocopated plural for *lĕḏôḏîm,* as in Isa 5:1 where *šîraṯ dôḏî* has the apparent meaning "love song." The meaning of *lĕḏôḏî,* according to Gordis, is "to lovers." The change to *dôḏay* suggested by a number of critics has nothing to commend it. *RSV* deleted the word, following the suggestion of Hitzig that it is due to vertical dittography from the following verse. Ewald's objection that the deletion leaves the line too short and incongruent with what follows seems at first blush compelling, but a syllable count shows that the line with omission of *lĕḏôḏî* still has the same number of syllables (six) as the preceding line and only a syllable less than the succeeding line. Thus it seems best to delete the word, with *RSV,* but with exception to *RSV*'s footnote to the effect that the Hebrew reads "down for my lover," since there is nothing in the MT corresponding to "down."

smoothly. LXX *eis eututēta.* Vulgate *ad potandum* may reflect a reading *lištôṯ,* "to drink," but more likely is an effort to make sense of the puzzling *lĕmêšārîm.* The term is similarly used in Prov 23:31 with reference to the flowing of wine, *yiṯhallēḵ bĕmêšārîm.* The suggestion that the line was added by a scribe reminiscent of the present passage seems rather unlikely in view of the variations in the two expressions, *hôlēḵ . . . lĕ mêšārîm,* and *yiṯhallēk bĕmêšārîm.* Possibly the meddling scribe had a poor memory, but it seems more likely that the variations are tokens of authenticity. Efforts to rectify matters by emendation have been absurdly inept. Graetz, e.g. supposed that the word should be divided *lmw-šrm,* but beyond that was at a loss: "Eine Heilung bin ich ausser Stande zu errathen." This is amply illustrated by his translation(?), "fliessend für meine Liebe ohne Falsch(?)."

Gordis rendered *mêšārîm* in 1:4 adverbially "as fine wine," but in his note suggested that the meaning may rather be "for thy manliness." In the present line, however, Gordis rendered *lĕmêšārîm* "that gives power," explaining in his note that this line and the following are descriptive of the power of wine to stimulate the strength of lovers' desire. According to Gordis, "The verse is to be rendered: Thy palate is like good wine, giving vigor to lovers, stirring the lips of the sleepers (with desire)." Another possibility Gordis suggested was that *lĕmêšārîm,* "for strength," may be a toast used in drinking wine, both here and in Prov 23:31, like the modern Hebrew *lĕḥayyîm,* "for life," Swedish "skoal," English "to your health," etc. Such a toast, Gordis noted, is to be found in the expression "may your hearts be alive," *yĕḥî lĕḇaḇḵem,* in Pss 22:27[26E] and 69:33[32E]. Our passage would then be rendered: "Thy palate is like good wine, going down for lovers with the toast 'for strength.' " But the first interpretation suggested is preferable in Gordis' view.

JPSV, here, as in 1:4, rendered *mêšārîm* as "new wine," relating it to *tîrôš,* and Aramaic *mēr*ā*ṯ,* following Ibn Ezra. On Dahood's proposal that *mêšārîm* here and Prov 23:31 means "throat," "gullet," cf. NOTE on 1:4e above.

In view of the well-attested senses of *mêšārîm,* there is no reason to dissent from the traditional rendering "smoothly" as appropriate to the flow or imbibition of fine wine or other highly rectified spirits.

10c. *Stirring.* The form *dôḇēḇ* is hapax legomenon. LXX rendered *hikanoumenos,* "sufficient," which may be an error for *hikanomenos,* from *hikanō,* "advance," as suggested by Robert who cited Arabic *dabba,* "move gently." Vulgate *ad ruminandum* seems to take its cue from the Aramaic sense of *dbb,* "murmur." Rashi, Ibn Ezra, Rashbam and many modern interpreters construed *dôḇēḇ* as factitive, "causing to speak," thus *KJ*'s "causing the lips of those that are asleep to speak." *AT* rendered "stirring my lips and teeth." Following Ewald, many interpreters have connected the form with the root **ḏ(w)b,* Hebrew *z(w)b,* Aramaic *d(w)b,* "flow," as reflected in *RSV, JPSV,* and *NEB* "gliding," and *NAB* "spreading." The choice between "speaking" or "flowing" is determined by the reading of the last word of the line, whether with MT "sleepers" or LXX and Vulgate "teeth."

sleepers' lips. LXX, Aquila, and Syriac read "my lips and teeth." Vulgate "his lips and teeth." MT "lips of sleepers," *śip̄ṯê yĕšēnîm,* is certainly the more difficult reading and one that taxes the ingenuity of exegetes. Wine is well known for loosening lips to eloquence, as Horace said: *Fecundi calices quem non fecere disertum?* "Whom have not potent cups made eloquent?" (*Epistle* I v 19). Inebriates also are given to muttering gibberish (cf. Prov 23:33b), awake or sleeping. Some have supposed that the reference here is to wine so fine that those who have indulged dream and mutter about it. The sweet-talk of lovers may at times be inane, but hardly to be related to the mutterings of a sot. Delitzsch remarked that "such a thing is known as sleeping through drink or speaking in sleep, but not of drinking in sleep." If "palate" here denotes not speech but kisses, deep and moist, smooth and sweet as the finest wine, then the reading "lips and teeth" makes better sense than "sleepers' lips." The sense "my lips and my teeth," or simply "lips and teeth," may be obtained by taking the final *-m* of the last word as the enclitic, emphatic particle. In Ugaritic the enclitic *-m* may be attached similarly to a noun following the possessive suffix, e.g. *aḫy-m,* "my brothers," as in 6[49].6.10–11:

aḫym ytn bʿl lpuy	My brothers Baal has made my smiters,
bnm umy klyy	My mother's sons my destroyers.

D. N. Freedman's suggestion here in favor of "lips and teeth" is simple and brilliant, eliminating both orthographic and grammatical impediments:

> in order to get the reading 'lips and teeth' which I think is right, you must also change the *yod* before *šnym* to a *waw,* which is not a serious matter. But then there is no need to worry about enclitic *mems,* since the reading "my lips and teeth" is good both in English and Hebrew (note the double-duty suffix on the first term: "my lips," which carries over to the "teeth" which is simply the dual form). Some revocalization is in order, but this is not serious either.

If, however, the "sleepers" are the dead whose lips move or ooze in the grave, as some Jewish sages supposed, one may think of the libations to one's ancestors in the funerary communion meals. Accordingly, we resort to the MT.

The passage above, 7:2–10, was central in the development of modern literary interest in the descriptive poem, or *wasf.* The following observations on feminine pulchritude supplement the discussion in the Introduction, pp. 54–84.

Stephan (20) offered the following summary of the treatment of the female form in The Thousand and One Nights:

> The description of the female body is comprehensively dealt with in the "Arabian Nights." The face shines like the full moon. Although the form is slim, yet the body is plump, likened to a silver bar or ivory, as soft as the tail of a sheep. The eyes fascinate and captivate like those of the gazelle, and are painted with stibium (*koḥl*). The lashes are long and so are the eyebrows. Like a bouquet of flowers are the cheeks—rosy apples, with a freckle, which enhances their beauty. The teeth gleam like pearls, the lips are as sweet as honey or sugar. The breasts are budding; they are well rounded, like pomegranates, seductive, and as white as ivory. The navel may hold an ounce of oil, and is like the bottom of a tiny coffee cup. The legs are round columns of choice marble, the thighs are cushions stuffed with feathers, and the nates are full and as heavy as a heap of sand.
>
> Although the comparison is not consistently carried out, one may grasp that the chief object of the narrator is to impress on his hearers that "she" is in every respect a very fine woman.

Further comparisons and descriptions Stephan (22) catalogued thus (we delete the Arabic script and transliteration):

> Her head is like a dove's head; she has gazelle-like eyes; the cheek is chubby; her ears are like the ears of noble horses; and her eyelashes fill her eye; her fingers are silver pencils; her back is straight like a lance; her breast is a marble flag, and the breasts are like well-rounded cups, or like honeyfilled pots; her belly is like bundles of silk; the navel is a tiny (coffee) cup and the abdomen is like a young dove filled (stuffed) and prepared; her stature is like a pot of oil, or like a sack of wheat. Both these metaphors are also applicable to the belly.

Among the parallels cited by Stephan the following gem is worthy of special note:

> Your breast is a marble flag,
> And your breasts (bosom) are (is) its watchman.
> And the belly is white and soft—
> I called it crystal.
> And the navel is of ivory;
> Happy he who turns on it.
> How great is the joy of the bachelor
> In the dark night . . .

10. The Targum continued the line of interpretation applied to the preceding verse:

> Said Daniel and his companions, "We will take upon ourselves the decree of the Word of YHWH, as Abraham our father took it upon himself, he who was like old wine. We will walk in paths established before him, as walked the prophets Elijah and Elisha on account of whose merits the dead rose like a man who slumbers; or like Ezekiel, son of Buzi, the priest, by the prophecy of whose mouth the sleeping dead were roused in the valley of Dura."

Midrash Rabbah, like the Targum, related this verse and the preceding one to Daniel and his companions. The "palate" suggested osculation rather than oration. The Holy One commanded his ministering angels: "Go down and kiss the lips of the ancestors of these men. For as they braved the fire for My sake; so have their sons braved the fire for My sake." The reference to the movement of sleepers' lips suggested that the lips of the dead quiver in the grave. Rabbi Samuel suggested that the lips are like a mass of heated grapes which ooze of themselves. The lips of a deceased scholar in whose name a traditional statement is reported in this world move slowly in the grave (TB Yebamot 96b–97a, Sanhedrin 90b). Others related the line to the lingering of the taste and scent of spiced or aged wine.

Christian expositors related this verse to the doctrine and preaching of the Church. The LXX reading, "Going straight for my Beloved, sufficient for my lips and teeth," suggested doctrine preferable to any perfumed wine or any pleasures of this life, given for the right guidance of believers and sufficient to be in part disclosed and proclaimed and in part guarded and hidden, the teeth being the barrier to withhold it (Theodoret). The Vulgate, "Worthy for my Beloved to drink, for His lips to ruminate," evoked the thought of the slow sipping of choice wine, allowing it to remain in the mouth to savor the flavor and bouquet, with reference to the sedulous meditation on the precepts of the Gospel in order to extract their full meaning and beauty. Albertus Magnus applied this text to meditation after Communion of the Eucharist.

The rendering of *KJ*, "Causing the lips of those that are asleep to speak," has been explained as the sweet wine of the Gospel which breathes new life into the dark sayings of the dead seers and prophets of the Old Testament, or dead through sin, roused from lethargy by the sweet voice of Christ. The more modern reading, "gliding over the lips of sleepers," has been applied to the tranquilizing influence of the Word and the pleasant after effects of meditating and ruminating on it. (Cf. Littledale.)

11. Cf. 2:16 and 6:3. Some critics would add *wĕḏôḏî lî*, "and my love is mine," after *'ănî lĕḏôḏî*, "I am my love's." But the reciprocal aspect of the "formula of mutual appurtenance," "my love is mine and I am his," is here amply supplied by the words "for me is his desire." LXX, Vulgate, and Syriac appear to have read *tĕšûḇāṯô*, "his return," for MT, *tĕšûqāṯô*, "his desire." The preposition here used with *ṯĕšûqāh*, "desire," is *'al-*, "upon," rather than *'el-*, "unto," which is used in Gen 3:16 and 4:7, and several critics would change *wĕ'ālay* to *wĕ'ēlay*. Robert remarked that the use of *'al-* here may be the result of graphic confusion under the influence of Aramaic which does not use the preposition *'el-*, but attributes its meaning to *'al-;* thus in a late composition, like the Canticle, Robert conceded the *'al-* might be the original reading.

Gordis commented on the radically different spirit in Gen 3:16 where Eve is punished by being made subservient to her husband and the present instance where virtually the same words are used to express the joyous desire of lovers for each other.

11. The Targum ascribed these words to the Holy City:

> Said Jerusalem, "All the time that I walk in the way of the Lord of the World, He makes His Presence dwell in my midst and His longing is for me. But at the time I rebel from His way He takes up His Presence from me and carries me away among the nations and these dominate me as a man dominates his wife."

Midrash Rabbah recalled the two other instances in which the world *tĕšûqāh* is used, in each case of a strong desire. The present instance relates to Israel's yearning for the heavenly Father. In Gen 3:16 it is the desire of a woman for her husband and in Gen 4:7 the penchant of Cain and his ilk for evil. Rabbi Joshua added the yearning of the rain for the earth, citing Ps 65:10 where the verb *wattĕšōqĕqehā*, "and thou waterest it," recalled the noun *tĕšûqāh*. A deservedly anonymous play was made on *tĕšûqāṯô* as a combination of *taš*, "weak," and *qawwēh*, "to hope," to deduce the good word that even though faint Israel hopes for salvation.

This third affirmation of the mutual appurtenance of the lovers (cf. 2:16 and 6:3) St. Ambrose took to mark the last stage of the Bride's progress in the love of God, the beginning, the advance, and now perfection. The LXX reading *hē epistropē autou* and Vulgate *conversio ejus* evoked a variety of homiletic turns. (Cf. Littledale for several samples too complex to be briefly summarized.)

12a. The two words of this line, *lĕḵāh ḏôḏî,* "come my love," were taken as the opening of the famous hymn of greeting to the Sabbath composed by Solomon Alqabeṣ. See above p. 175.

12b. *Let us hie to the field.* These words coincide with Cain's invitation to Abel, Gen 4:8, lost in the MT but preserved by the ancient versions. There is, however, no reason to imagine that we have here a reminiscence of Gen 4:8, since the purposes of the invitations are quite dissimilar. Joüon supposed that *śaḏeh,* "field," is here synonymous with *miḏbār,* "steppe," or "desert," mentioned in 3:16. This seems rather unlikely, as Robert noted, since the area in question produces grapes, pomegranates, and mandrakes, and the field is elsewhere called a garden (4:15–16, 5:1, 6:2,11). It should be noted, however, that in the present passage the "field" is the place to which the lovers go together and can scarcely be made a figure for our lady's charms. Nevertheless, in view of the uses of field, vineyard, garden, and the like, as figures for the female reproductive apparatus, it is understandable that the Palestinian Qabbalists related this passage to the ritualization of the Sabbath observance as a mystical sacred marriage. In emulation of the divine marriage, Torah scholars used to engage in marital intercourse on Friday night. The Shekinah-Sabbath-Bride in the mystical marriage ritual was the "field of holy apple trees," which as G. Scholem explains (1965b, 140), means the feminine principle of the Cosmos. On Sabbath Eve the King couples with the Shekinah-Sabbath-Bride, the holy field is fertilized, and from this sacred union the souls of the righteous are produced. Scholem remarks (p. 107) that the symbolism of the primordial mother is particularly charged with myth and exceedingly complex in structure and that he cannot here go into it more deeply.

A relevant item may be adduced from a Ugaritic ritual for a sacred marriage. In line 13 of the text called "The Birth of the Beautiful Gods" (23[52]) we have the pregnant words *wšd šd ilm šd aṯrt wrḥm,* which may be rendered either "The field is the field of the gods, the field is Asherah and Virgin," or "Harrow the divine field, the field Asherah and Virgin." There is scant basis for T. H. Gaster's rendering of the word *šd* as "breast" (*Thespis,* 242*f*), since we have in this text the spellings *zd* and *ḏd* instead of *ṯd* and there is no reason to add a fourth variant *šd.* Already in the initial publication of this text, Virolleaud made the suggestion that the first *šd* of the line may be related to *šdd,* "harrow" (1933, 139*f*), "Et laboure le champ des dieux, le champ d'Asherat et . . . Misericordieux (cf. *Raḥum*)." Reference to the field of the Mother Goddess Asherah and/or Anat (*rḥm* is here perhaps an epithet of Anat who is elsewhere called *rḥm 'nt* and *rḥmy* instead of the usual *btlt 'nt,* Virgin Anat) and possibly to the harrowing or cultivation of said "field" in a pre-Israelite ritual for a sacred marriage appears to confirm Scholem's observation that the Qabbalistic symbolism of the Shekinah-Sabbath-Bride as primordial mother and "holy field" is "charged" with myth.

Interpreters even moderately inclined to naturalism will inevitably think of the sexual connotations of the term "field" in ancient Near Eastern usage. "Let us go out to the field" could be as innocent or as suggestive as one may wish to make it. *JPSV* rendered openly, "Let us go into the open."

12c. *lie*. The verb *l(w/y)n* generally means to spend the night, with no implication in regard to presence or absence of sexual activity. Delitzsch set at ease those who might be concerned about this with the assurance that "they are married." It is difficult to find a suitable substitute for the unpoetic terms "lodge," or "spend the night." *AT* rendered "rest." *NEB*'s "lie" seems preferable in the present context.

cypress. Following Ewald, it seems preferable to take *kĕpārîm* not as "villages" but as the cypress or aromatic henna bushes from which the perfume *kōper* was made, cf. 1:4a. One does not go out to the field in order to lodge in a village, rather one comes from the field or open country to lodge in the village or leaves the village to go to the field. Taken as referring to villages, the plural form *kĕpārîm* also occasions some difficulty. Advocates of the shepherd hypothesis imagined that the Shulamite, spurning Solomon's suit, calls to her shadowy shepherd swain to come and return to their rural haunts. Delitzsch considered this comical since shepherds do not wander from village to village and Ewald's idea that the couple wished to bed in the henna bushes seemed to him too gipsy-like, even for a pair of shepherds; cf. Job 30:7 for aversion to alfresco amour. The plurality of the villages posed no problem for Delitzsch's understanding that the former vine dresser of the Galilean hills, now raised to the rank of queen, has an impulse for her earlier homely country life and invites Solomon on a tour of the village vineyards.

12. The Targum referred this field trip and rural retreat to the Exile and Diaspora:

> When the people of the House of Israel sinned, YHWH exiled them to the land of Seir, the field of Edom. Said the congregation of Israel, "I beseech Thee, Lord of all the world, receive my prayer which I pray before Thee in the cities of Exile and the districts of the nations."

Midrash Rabbah made a play on *kĕpārîm*, "villages," and *kôpĕrîm*, "infidels." "These are the cities of the heathen who deny the Holy One, blessed be He." In the Talmud (TB Erubin 21b) this verse is expounded in favor of rural life over urban. The Congregation of Israel spoke before the Lord of the universe, "Do not judge me as You judge those who reside in large towns, who indulge in robbery, adultery, in vain and false oaths." "Let us go out to the field" means "Come, and I will show you scholars who study Torah in poverty." The vineyards mean synagogues and schools, the budding vines and flowering pomegranates the students of Torah, Mishnah, and Gemara.

Christian expositors found in the field and villages considerable latitude for exegetical ingenuity. According to Ambrose, the Bride invites the Word of God to come to earth to take away the sins of the world. The field is the former desert bristling with the brambles and thorns of our sins and the village the place of exile of Adam and his heirs. The Church brings Christ to set Adam free and make the liberated exiles transform the barren land into the fertile and eternal plantation of the Vine. Cassiodorus explained that "Let us go out to the field" means "Let us preach to the world," and "Let us lodge in the villages" indicates that we should preach faith in God even to the Pagans, "for everyone knows that 'Pagan' derives from *pagus,* "village," and Pagans are fitly named because they are far from the city of God" (note the parallel with the rabbinic plays on *kĕp̄ārîm,* "villages," and *kôp̄ĕrîm,* "heathen," "infidels"). The figures of the "field" and the "villages" were also applied to the Church and its work, or to individual souls, in a variety of ways. Hugo of St. Victor, e.g. understood the villages to refer to villeins, or clowns, who are slow in understanding the rules of Christ's royal court. (Cf. Littledale.)

For modern interpreters who follow the tradition of the Targum and attempt to make the Canticle an historical allegory of Israel's Exile and Return, the field and villages present no problem. Joüon suggested that the field alludes to the vast regions which captive Israel had to traverse in order to re-enter the country of the vines, Palestine, and the villages mark the stages of their long journey. Robert wondered whether the enigmatic allusion to villages might not apply to the situation of the repatriates in the fifth century. According to Ezra 2:20–35 and Neh 7:25–38 the repatriates were settled mainly in localities near Jerusalem. If this hypothesis is correct, we have, according to Robert, a datum in this verse which could help fix the date of the Canticle!

13a. *get.* When the temporal phrase "in the morning" is absent, the verb *hškm* means "to get busy"; cf. AB 15 on Job 1:5. Although the phrase "in the morning" is absent here, there is implicit reference to night in the antecedent verb *l(w/y)n* which suggests that the subsequent action is to take place the following morning. The temporal setting of this action, however, is of secondary interest to the nature of the proposed activity. The allusions to field and flowers, pomegranates, mandrakes, and love give ample reason to suppose that the invitation intends something other than an early morning garden tour. Haupt commented, "This 'outing' must not be understood literally; it is a pleasure-trip in the garden of the bride," and "after the refreshing sleep they will be ready for new erotic achievements."

vineyard(s). On the sexual symbolism of vineyard, cf. 1:6d,e.

13b. *vine.* The symbolism of the vine is universal and well-known and too complex to attempt summation; cf. Goodenough, 1953–68, indexes. It is of interest to note that Baal's messenger(s)? in the Ugaritic fertility myths was dubbed "Vine and Field," *gpn-w-ugr.*

13c. *blossoms.* On *sĕmāḏār,* cf. 2:13,15.

13d. This line is repeated verbatim from 6:11d, q.v.

13e. *There.* The adverb *šām* usually has local reference, but may also relate to time, as regularly with its Arabic cognate *ṯumma.* For *šām* with temporal reference, cf. Eccles 3:17 and possibly Job 35:12. The ambivalence of the spatial and temporal relation lends itself to any of the various interpretations. Ginsburg supposed that the shepherd swain, gladdened that his beloved is restored to him, wishes to express his joy and affection, but she, anxious to get away from Solomon as quickly as possible, bids him wait till they are safely home amid the charms of nature. Similarly, Oettli commented, first freedom, then love, and Harper contrasted the "there" to the here and now. Robert, eschewing the naturalist school which finds erotic symbolism here, saw in the images of morning and vernal florescence the proximity of the eschatological future (as in 2:11–13 and 6:11) and the consummation of the new and definitive alliance between Yahweh and Israel. Accordingly, Robert rendered "Alors je te ferai le don de mes amours."

my love. LXX, Old Latin, Syriac, and Vulgate read here, as in 1:2,4, 4:10, *dadday,* "my breasts," instead of *dôḏay,* "my love." "There I will give you my breasts" is repeated in 6:11 of LXX.

13. The Targum interpreted this verse in an interesting way:

> The Israelites said one to the other, "Let us go early in the morning to the Synagogue and to the House of Study and research in the Book of the Law and let us see whether the time of salvation has come for the people of the House of Israel (who are likened to the vine) to be redeemed from their exile. Let us ask the Sages whether the merit of the Saints (who are filled with precepts like the pomegranate) is revealed before the Lord, whether the term has come to go up to Jerusalem to give there praise to the God of Heaven, and to bring burnt offerings and holy oblations."

Midrash Rabbah referred the vineyard to the House of Israel, citing Isa 5:7, the budding vine to the recitation of the *Shema'*, the vine blossoms to the synagogues and houses of study, and the pomegranates to busily learning Torah. "There I will give you my love" means that there (in the synagogues and houses of study) are produced the righteous, the prophets and prophetesses.

Christian expositors found a variety of applications for items of this verse. The early rising suggested Christ's resurrection, the vineyard visit and inspection, His defense and strict examination of the Church's progress. In the early morn of the new Gospel light, He marks the buds of faith and the development to young fruit which reaches maturity in the likeness of His Passion in the ruddy pomegranate, fit emblem of martyrs. The implicit allusions to night and morn suggested to Honorius the night of Antichrist's persecution of the Church and the early morn the beginning of the new age when the Synagogue will be converted and Christ and the Bride will visit the new Churches thus formed. The LXX and Vulgate reading "my breasts" suggested the nurture of sucklings to maturity and martyrdom. The vineyards were taken to denote the cloistered life, removed from urban strife, where the love of God could best be nourished in the soul, till the morn of the everlasting Day of Judgment. There the Church will give her breasts to Christ, presenting to Him in eternal glory the teachers of the Old and New Law. (Cf. Littledale for sources and more detail.)

14a. *The mandrakes.* This word, *dûḏā'îm,* occurs elsewhere in the Bible only in Gen 30:14–16. The versions identify it as the mandragora or mandrake. The word is usually related to the root *d(w)d,* "love," and the noun *dôḏ(îm)* which is frequently used in the Canticle. A possible cognate is attested in Ugaritic *ddym* which occurs six times in the Anat Text in an enigmatic message of Mighty Baal to his sister-consort, Virgin Anat, in which he bids her, among other things, to put *ddym* in the dust (*št b'prm ddym*). The message has been interpreted in diverse and diametrically opposite senses and need not detain us here. See above on 7:1. The association of mandrakes with fertility and with the love-goddess is of particular interest. Hesychius (*Lex* s.v. *Mandragoritis*) noted that *mandragoritis* was an epithet of Aphrodite. Rendel Harris suggested derivation of the name Aphrodite from a hypothetical *pĕrî dûdā'ē,* "fruit of Dôd" (p. 28; cf. Meek, 1922–23, 9n4 and Wittekindt, 53).

The mandrake plant, *Mandragora officinarum,* is native to the Mediterranean area. It belongs to the potato family and is related to the deadly nightshade *Atropa belladonna.* The fruit is a sort of berry about the size of a filbert nut which ripens in late spring. Reuben found *dûḏā'îm* in the time of the wheat harvest, Gen 30:14. The thick roots, two or three, forked or intertwined, were thought to resemble male and female genitalia. Digging for mandrake roots had its hazards and rituals, according to the ancient writers Theophrastus, Pliny, Dioscorides, and Aelianus. The plant was termed *cynopastus* (dog-dug) by Aelianus who related that it is not distinguished from other plants during the day, but at night it glows like a star (*De Natura Animalium* 14.27). A marker was fastened to the roots at night and the extraction was carried out at dawn. A dog which had been kept without food for some days was tied to the lower part of the plant and meat was tossed to it so that it lunged for the food and thus uprooted the plant. The hapless cur died in the process, and was buried on the spot with secret rites.

One of the causes for caution in the extraction of mandrake root is mentioned by Shakespeare in *Romeo and Juliet* (IV iii 47–48), "And shrieks like mandrakes' torn out of the earth, / that living mortals, hearing them, run mad." And again (*2 Henry VI* III ii 310) "Would curses kill, as doth the mandrake's groan." Mandrake diggers in medieval lore were cautioned to plug their ears with cotton and wax. Friday, Venus' Day, was the proper time for digging the roots. Their value as a love charm is clear from the story of Gen 30:14–16. Theophrastus noted that love charms were recited during the digging. Mandrake roots were used as talismans and fetishes to bring material prosperity, success in love, cure for sterility (as in the case of Rachel's infertility), and for sundry other purposes. Joan of Arc was accused at her trial of possessing mandragora. In Germany and other parts of Europe it was customary to place mandrakes under the nuptial bed (cf. *Handbuch des Deutschen Aberglaubens,* s.v. Mandragora). The aphrodisiac efficacy of the mandrake was allegedly appreciated by creatures other than man. The *Physiologus,* a bestiary of uncertain date, relates how the female elephant seeks out the mandragora plant, partakes of it, is inflamed, and going to the male, shares the plant with him so that he is immediately excited and copulates with her. This story is then given an allegorical application, to the Bible, the bull and cow elephants representing Adam and Eve and the mandrake the forbidden fruit. Shakespeare alludes to the supposed aphrodisiac powers of the plant in Falstaff's characterization of Shallow as "lecherous as a monkey, and the whores called him mandrake" (*2 Henry IV,* III ii 309–310).

As a drug, the mandrake is actually more of a soporific and narcotic than a stimulant. It was used in antiquity for anesthesia in surgery; a draft of mandragora wine reportedly produced deep sleep for three or four hours and complete insensitivity to knife or cautery. The active agents are the alkaloids atropine and scopolamine. In addition to its narcotic effect, it was also used as an emetic and purgative. W. M. Thomson (1865, 577) noted that the Arabs of Syria-Palestine believed the mandrake berries to be exhilarating and stimulating, even to insanity. They were said to produce dizziness, but Thomson claimed he had seen people eat them without experiencing any such effect. The Arabs call the mandrake berries "devil apples/eggs" (*tuffāḥ/ bayḍ el-jinn*), i.e. devil's testicles. St. Hildred of Bingen (twelfth century) observed that "In mandragora the influence of the devil is more present than in other herbs; consequently man is stimulated by it according to his desires, whether they be good or bad." (Extensive documentation is found in C. B. Randolph, 1905. Cf. also E. S. Gifford, 1962, 198–201, and T. H. Gaster, 1969, 200.) Shakespeare alluded to the narcotic effects of the mandrake:

Not poppy, nor mandragora,
Nor all the drowsy syrups of the world,
Shall ever medicine thee to that sweet
    sleep
Which thou owedst yesterday
    (*Othello,* III iii 330–33)

Give me to drink mandragora. . . .
That I may sleep out this great gap of
    time,
My Antony is away.
    (*Antony and Cleopatra,* I v 4–6)

John Donne's famous line "Get with child a mandrake root," despite the syntactic obscurity, takes note of its supposed efficacy in assuring conception. Stephan (24) cited the Gaza proverb *tuffâḥ il majal bijîb il-ḥabal,* "The mad apple brings pregnancy." Among the modern Palestinian names for the mandrake, Stephan cited *banj* which appears suspiciously similar to the Indian term *ḇhāṅg* which in northern Indian is applied by Hindu votaries of Tantrism to hemp, *Cannabis indica,* used as an aphrodisiac in the "left-handed" rites which are climaxed with the last of the five -M's, *maithuma,* sexual union. The hemp is prepared as a dessert in the shape of molasses, or as a beverage with sweet sherbet (cf. Bharati, 1965, 253,287,301). Stephan noted (24) that "Mandragora is thought to promote pregnancy. The leaves green cut and mixed with other vegetables, cooked in a pie, and given to a woman are said, however, to be a sure way to make her sterile. This is one of the secret recipes said to be used by women against each other."

give scent. The odor of mandrakes is reportedly pungent and distinctive and was presumably pleasant or exciting. While Occidental aesthetes may regard the scent as fetid rather than fragrant, it is well known that odors which may be offensive to some can be highly provocative to others. The belief that the plant has potency as an aphrodisiac could influence one's reaction to its odor. Just where the mandrakes were located with relation to the lovers, whether in the field, or at the door with other delectables, or by their couch, is not clear.

14b. *At our door*. The word for the opening is vocalized as plural which some critics would emend to a singular. The emendation is without justification, since such poetic plurals, or plurals of generalization are commonplace (cf. GKC 124c,e and Joüon 136j). Hitzig supposed that the locus above the doors referred to a floor above the family dwelling, or above the barn (a sort of loft), but Delitzsch, and similarly Harper, imagined a shelf or cupboard above the inner doors on which things were stored for some particular purpose. The preposition *'al-* was taken by a number of critics in the usual sense of "over," or "above," with reference to the common practice of putting good luck and fertility charms over doors. Wittekindt (54n3) cited the Talmudic reference to hanging fruits in the bridal tent (TB Abodah Zarah 12). The possible sexual symbolism of opening did not escape the naturalists. Wittekindt, e.g. noted that "door" is again a figure for *pudendum mulieris*. Joüon observed that *peṯaḥ* is often used of the door of a city or large building and thus becomes a synonym of *ša'ar*, "gate." To Robert it seemed that the author alluded to the "gate of hope" (*peṯaḥ tiqwāh*) of Hosea 2:17[15E]. The prophet supposes that Yahweh, after having brought back his unfaithful spouse to the desert, to betroth her to Him forever, reintroduces her to the country of vines, i.e. Palestine, whence he had expelled her because of her infidelities. The author of the Canticle, according to Robert, awaits the imminent realization of this prophecy; the nation purified by tribulation has returned to her husband, and the fruits which symbolize the refound love and restoration are there within reach.

delicacy. In 4:13,16 the expression is *pĕrî mĕḡāḏîm*, "fruit delectable," applied to our lady's groovy paradise, or "garden," with patent reference to her most intimate charms. Some critics would insert *pĕrî*, "fruit," after *kol-*, "all," and before *mĕḡāḏîm*. Outside the Canticle, this word occurs in the singular four times in the Song of Moses, Deut 33:13–16 with reference to the bounties of nature. In Syriac *maḡdā* means "fruit" while in Arabic *majd* means "glory," "honor," "nobility."

14c. *Things both new and old*. This expression recalls Lev 26:10 and Matt 13:52. Some translators and interpreters take the last clause as an asyndetic relative, e.g. *KJ*, "which I have laid up for thee." Graetz, Delitzsch, and Harper reasoned that the (supposed) relative clause refers only to the old fruits and does not include the new fruits that are only now ripening in the early summer between the barley and the wheat harvest. Harper observed, in support of his view that the abducted shepherdess' true love is the shadowy shepherd swain: "If Solomon were the bridegroom it is difficult to see how the shepherdess could have laid up fruits for him, as she had not been home since he carried her away." Meek, *IB,* V, suggested that the new as well as the old may refer to the Passover offering of the old harvest to ensure the productivity of the new. The sexual sense seems to have eluded many exegetes and was partly misapprehended even by Haupt who rendered:

The mandrakes are breathing their fragrance,
  at our door is most luscious fruitage,
Now ripe or ripened aforetime,
  which I, for thee, dearest, have treasured.

In his note Haupt explained that the "new as well as old" (fruitage) means this year's as well as that of former years, and means "the sweet remembrance of former kisses and caresses." Haupt missed the promissory note of novelty in the lady's treasure store; it is hardly a matter of remembrance of pleasures past, but the titillating prospect of erotic exploits new and old which she promises her lover.

Robert again sought to throw light on the present passage by searching the prophetic passages which connect the two extremes of Israel's religious psychology, to wit, the first period of fidelity in the wilderness and that of restored fidelity in a future more or less imminent. The prime text for Robert is Hosea 2:17–18[15–16E] which is echoed in Jer 2:2 and Isa 54:6–8, and indirectly the texts which speak of penitence of the unfaithful one without explicit allusion to the former state (Jer 3:21,22, 3:25 – 4:2; 31:21–22). The fruits old and new thus evoked for Robert the ideal past which the conversion of the bride will restore.

14d. *I have stored.* The verb *ṣpn* means to "hide," "treasure up." According to Robert, this is the response to the divine jealousy inscribed on the heart of Yahwism (Exod 20:5, 34:14; Deut 4:24, 6:15, 32:16,21; Josh 24:19; Ps 78:58); whether in the desert of yore or now, in the restored state of fidelity, the charms of the beloved have been and will be for her husband alone. The intermediate period, which covers almost the entire history of Israel, was one of aberrations, God does not wish to remember (Jer 31:34b).

14. The Targum ignored the mandrakes:

> And when it shall be the Lord's will to redeem His people from exile, it will be said to the King, the Messiah, "The term of the exile already has been completed, and the merit of the saints has become fragrant before Me like the aroma of balsam, and the Sages of the ages have been in attendance at the portals of Learning occupied with the words of the Scriptures and the words of the Law. Now rise and receive the Kingdom which I have reserved for you!"

Midrash Rabbah referred the mandrakes to the young men of Israel who do not know the taste of sin, and the delectable fruits to the daughters of Israel who stick to their husbands and know no other man. The mandrake episode of Gen 30:4*ff*, and the two baskets of figs in Jer 24:1*f* (the words for mandrakes and two baskets being very similar) were naturally recalled and given imaginative interpretations.

The last part of the verse referring to new and old things was attributed to God by Rabbi Abba ben Kahana, addressed to Israel. The Holy One, blessed be He, said: "You store up for Me by performance of precepts and good works while I store up for you treasures full of more good things than are in the world." God's store, however, was the greater, as Abba ben Kahana noted with citation of Ps 31:20[19E].

The aromatic, aphrodisiac and narcotic qualities of the mandrake gave Christian expositors multiple choice. The narcotic effect suggested to Theodoret deadness to the world, and sin, as well as tranquillity and freedom from disturbance and passion, attained by drinking the cup of holy doctrine. The medicinal use further suggested (to Gregory and Cassiodorus) the Saints, not only fruitful in good works, but able to heal others with the good odor of their example. The anesthetic use in surgical operations suggested the power of faith to bear the tortures of martyrdom. Philo Carpathius invoked the shape of the mandrake root to signify the buried saints of the Old Testament, hidden from the glory of God, but giving a sweet odor until the morn of Christ's resurrection when they received the gift of everlasting life as the reward of their fragrance. The Vulgate read "at our gates" as the end of the first stich rather than the beginning of the second. These gates were seen as the Apostles and their successors by whose teaching the regenerate gain entrance to the Church, the City of God. The mandrakes give forth their fragrance at the gates of the Church when the Apostles spread their sweet teaching. The gates provided many entrances and exits for expositors, whether applied to the Church or the individual soul—the gates of faith, hope, and charity, the gates of the Sacraments, the teachings of the Scriptures and the Saints, the strait and narrow gates, the gates of the five senses through which pass the thoughts from the body to the soul. The reference to things new and old evoked in most instances the example of the resourceful householder of Matt 13:52. (Cf. Littledale.)

VIII
(8:1–14)

1 a O that you were as my brother
b Who sucked the breasts of my mother!
c I would find you in the street and kiss you,
d And none would scorn me.
2 a I would lead you to my mother's house,
b Bring you to the chamber of her who bore me.
c I would make you drink spiced wine,
d The juice of my pomegranate
3 a His left hand under my head,
b His right hand embracing me.
4 a I adjure you,
b Jerusalem girls,
c That you neither incite nor excite
d Love until it is eager.
5 a Who is this ascending from the steppe,
b Leaning on her lover?
c Under the apple tree I aroused you;
d There your mother conceived you,
e There she who bore you conceived.
6 a Set me as a signet on your heart,
b As a signet on your arm.
c For love is strong as Death,
d Passion fierce as Hell.
e Its darts are darts of fire,
f Its flames . . .
7 a Mighty waters cannot quench Love,
b No torrents can sweep it away.
c [If a man gave all the wealth of
d his house for love, would he be despised?]
8 a Our sister is young
b And breasts she has none.

c What will we do for our sister
d On the day she is bespoken?
9 a If she be a wall,
b We will build on her a silver buttress.
c If she be a door,
d We will close her with a cedar board.
10 a I am a wall,
b And my breasts like towers.
c Thus have I become in his eyes
d As one producing peace.
11 a Solomon had vineyard
b In Baal Hamon.
c He gave the vineyard to keepers.
d A man would offer for its fruit
e A thousand silver pieces.
12 a My own vineyard is before me.
b The thousand is yours, O Solomon,
c And two hundred for those who guard its fruit.
13 a You who dwell in gardens,
b Companions are attentive.
c Make me hear your voice.
14 a Bolt, my love,
b Be like a buck,
c Or a young stag,
d On the spice mountains.

NOTES

8:1a. *O that.* The idiom *mî yittēn,* "who will give/place?", expresses a strong optative, as in Num 11:29; Deut 28:67; II Sam 19:1[18:33E]; Jer 9:1,2[8:22, 9:1E]; Ps 14:7; Job 6:8; cf. GKC, 151.

my brother. Lit. "like a brother to me." The particle *k-* some critics would delete as dittography of the object suffix of the preceding verb. The *k-* is not reflected in the LXX, Old Latin, or Vulgate. LXX mistakenly construed "my brother" as vocative, and similarly Luther, "O dass ich dich, mein Bruder der du meiner Mutter Brüste saugest." Gordis construed the *k-* as asseverative rather than comparative; cf. NOTE on 1:7d. As with many asseverative or emphatic expressions, the supposed emphasis is not crucial to the sense. Gordis rendered "Would thou wert indeed my brother," explaining that "like my brother" would not meet her problem, which is her desire to kiss her lover unashamedly in public.

The brother-sister relationship of the lovers has troubled commentators. Delitzsch opined that

> the close union which lies in the sisterly relationship thus appeared to her to be higher than the near connection established by the marriage relationship, and her childlike feeling deceived her not: the sisterly relationship is certainly purer, firmer, more enduring than that of marriage, so far as this does not deepen itself into an equality with the sisterly, and attain to friendship, yea, brotherhood (Prov. xvii.17), within. That Shulamith thus feels herself happy in the thought that Solomon was to her as a brother, shows, in a characteristic manner, that "the lust of the flesh, the lust of the eye, and the pride of life," were foreign to her.

This idealization of Platonic love has scant basis in the Canticle. Meek noted (*IB*) that brother is "suggestive of the fertility cult, with god and goddess sometimes thought of as brother and sister; on the other hand, the clause may express nothing more than the yearning of the girl for her beloved."

Robert, RTF, raised the question whether a girl could go further with a brother without being suspected of falling under the sanctions of Lev 18:9, 20:17. Various ways of attempting to resolve the difficulty, such as supposing the passage to be out of place (Budde) or that it happened in a dream (Kuhn), or that the relationship is purely Platonic (Delitzsch and Budde), or that modesty is in conflict with the violence of her desire (Dussaud), justly failed to satisfy Robert. Dussaud further supposed that we have here a vestige of primitive endogamy such as survived among some Arabs, as in the region of Mosul where marriage of a sister with her uterine brother is tolerated (cf. Jaussen, 1908, 45). These conjectures, Robert observed, are belied by what the Canticle says of the feelings of the girl toward her beloved (2:3–6, 3:1–4, 5:2–8) and by the pressing invitations which she addresses to him (4:16, 6:2–3, 7:10b–14). From all the evidence, she considers him as her spouse, without hesitation or any restriction. Accordingly, Robert decided that it was necessary to take leave of this indubitable datum and ask of allegorical exegesis an explication which the previous attempts have been unable to provide. Joüon felt that the emotion expressed here is too intense to have as its purpose simply the particular nuance of affection and that all the movement of the poem led to these two verses as a point of culmination. The bride wishes her divine husband to become like her, to have the same nature, to show himself to her as a veritable man, born like her of the same humanity. Thus there is a certain identity between Yahweh, the husband of Israel, and the Messiah. Robert regarded Joüon's hypothesis as most reasonable of all, if it is true that the Canticle has on the whole a strongly emphasized eschatology and that the purpose of 2:6–11 is to describe the accession of the Messiah.

The great question for Robert was to know what connection the author of the Canticle established between Yahweh and the Messiah. In spite of the fact that she seemed to identify the two, since she wished that her spouse (to wit Yahweh) were her brother, it was nevertheless clear to Robert that this could not be, since in his commentary on 3:7 he thought to have demonstrated that the appellation Solomon is addressed to the Messiah and not to God. Moreover, it is also quite impossible to identify the Messiah with the spouse, since one could not conceive how he shows himself in order to disappear immediately (3:1*ff*, 5:2*ff*) and is depicted by reference to the Temple (5:10–15). Thus the Messiah is distinct from the well-Beloved. Why then does the author use language that seems to confuse them? Astonishing as this may be, the attitude is simply classical, in Robert's view. Already in Isa 7:14, 8:8, the Messiah is called Immanuel, "God with us"; in Isa 9:56[6E] the Messiah receives among other transcendent names that of "Mighty God." Thus for the great prophet of the eighth century the Messiah will be the visible manifestation of the Majesty of the invisible God in the kingdom of the new age. A number of passages and a sizable literature are then cited on the personification of divine attributes, the arm, the Word, and especially divine Wisdom, and the Angel of Yahweh, to show that the biblical tradition, particularly the post-exilic tradition, conceived the Messiah, Wisdom, and the Angel of Yahweh as visible manifestations of the invisible God and tended more and more to make of it a hypostatic or quasi-hypostatic idea. Thus, for Robert, Canticles 8:1 fits easily into this cadre of thought. The spouse of the Shulamite, that is Yahweh, remains inaccessible. She wishes that he would assume the state of a brother so that she could see and hear him and enjoy his sensible presence and favors.

Despite the devout learning demonstrated in this construct, it collapses in the face of the widespread use of the brother-sister address common in love poetry, both human and divine, all over the ancient Near East, in Egypt (cf. Hermann, 1959, 75*ff*), in Mesopotamia (cf. Falkenstein, 1963, 16n27, and Held, 1961, 13), and in Ugaritic where Baal and Anat are commonly represented as brother and sister. The brother-sister terminology was also used by Anat when she attempted to seduce the hero Aqhat in order to obtain his marvelous bow. The goddess, having failed to gain her desire with an offer of immortality, tried sexual enticement:

Hear, O hero, Aqhat.
Thou art (my) brother and I [thy sis]ter
. . . . with satiety of thy flesh . . .
(18[3 AQHT].1.23–25)

Cf. AB 15 on Job 31:31b.

1b. Apropos of the expression "sucker of the breast of my mother" as parallel to "brother," it is of interest that Ugaritic uses "sons of my mother" as a parallel to "my brothers" (cf. 1:6c), and designates the family of the gods collectively as "breast suckers," *mrġtm ṯd.* (4[51].6.56). The beautiful gods sired by El are variously designated as "suckers of the nipple of the breast of Asherah/the Lady" (23[52].24,59,61), *ynqm bap zd/ḏd aṯrt/št.* Of Keret's son Yaṣṣib it is predicated (15[128].2.26–28):

He will suck the milk of A[she]rah,
Draw the breast of Virgin [Anat],
The wet nurses [of the gods].

See Plate XI.

The overriding question, according to Robert, is to know whether "my mother" here is to be taken literally or metaphorically. If one opts for the latter, then "brother" might simply mean compatriot, as in Exod 2:11, 4:18; Deut 15:12, etc. Wetzstein (1868, 93,108) pointed out that among the bedouin Arabs only the uterine brother and the father's brother's son have the right to kiss a maiden, and some commentators, accordingly, have taken "sucker of the breasts of my mother" to specify the uterine brother. Buzy explained that oriental custom did not permit a wife to exhibit public affection, but that of a sister and brother was more easily tolerated. Consequently the bride has just wished that her beloved were her brother so that she could love him more freely and give him, in whatever place she might meet him, the tokens reserved for love. On this Tournay observed (RTF, 283) that up to now the damsel has not given the impression that she cared much about public opinion (3:1–4, 5:6–8, 7:12–13).

1c. *find.* The verb *mṣ'*, "find," "meet," "encounter," recalls the quest and failure to find the absconded lover in 3:1–4, 5:6–8.

in the street. The term *ḥûṣ* designates the outside of a house, tent, camp, city, etc. In 3:1–4 the lady roams the streets and squares of the "city" in search of her lover. Commentators have been puzzled at the damsel's desire to encounter her brother out of doors. Robert explained that Israel awaits the Messiah outside the Temple to conduct him to the Temple for enthronement.

The cultic interpretation here finds support in the pattern of the Ugaritic myths of Baal and Anat. It is in the desert steppe land that Baal is mangled and killed by Mot (Death), and there Anat seeks and finds his body, buries him, and again seeks him on hearing the joyous news of his resurrection.

1. The Targum applied this verse to the advent of the Messiah:

> When King Messiah appears to the Congregation of Israel, they will say to Him: Come, be to us as a brother and let us go up to Jerusalem, and we will suck with you the judgments of the Law, as a suckling sucks at his mother's breast. All the time that I was taken away outside my land, as long as I was mindful of the Name of the Great God and gave up my life for His Divinity, the peoples of the earth did not scorn me.

Midrash Rabbah sought to clarify the brotherly relation with recollection of Cain and Abel, Ishmael and Isaac, Jacob and Esau, Joseph and his brothers. The one "who sucked the breasts of my mother" was applied to Joseph and Benjamin. Interestingly, *ḥûṣ* is explained as meaning the wilderness outside the inhabited land. The kissing recalled Aaron's kissing of Moses (Exod 4:27). Rabbi Phineas told a story of a sister who unashamedly embraced and kissed her brother after he escaped from a house fire.

Christian expositors found a variety of insights in this verse. The incongruity of the lady's wish with earthly love and marriage was taken by Cassiodorus as an incidental proof of the spiritual intent of the Canticle. The wish was seen by some as the Synagogue's prayer for the Incarnation of Christ. The mother of the Bride was identified as eternal Wisdom, the brother as Christ in human form. The breast sucking suggested the taste of heavenly things drawn from the two Testaments and the double precept of Love. The mother was also identified as the Synagogue, the substance of human nature, and as the Blessed Virgin through whose flesh came our Brother, Christ. Another view was that the mother is the Heavenly Jerusalem and that her breasts represent the new wine which Christ has promised to drink with us in His Kingdom, so that the wish is a prayer for the hastening of the Second Coming. "Outside" was understood as outside Jerusalem's gates where Christ suffered to sanctify the people with His own Blood, or as outside the bosom of the Father when He came to earth, or in the open, after the fulfillment of the hidden prophecies and types of the Old Testament, to mention only a few of the inside/outside oppositions. The kiss was understood in a variety of ways, as Christ's parting kiss of peace and love when he gave up the ghost on the Cross, or as the mystical kiss of eternal love in the heavenly Land. The scorn was applied to the lot of the Synagogue whose contumely will be changed to honor with conversion to the Gospel, or to the Church from the time of her suffering to the conversion of the Roman empire and great triumphs to come, or to the faithful soul no longer regarded with contempt after the condescension of so great a Deliverer. (Cf. Littledale.)

2a. Two virtually synonymous verbs are used here and are reflected in LXX and Vulgate. The two verbs by themselves, "I would lead you, I would bring you," do not seem quite sufficient as a poetic line and if joined with the following line make an overlong stich. One possibility would be to delete one of the verbs as a variant and combine the other with the succeeding phrase to produce a sensible and symmetrical line, "I would lead you to my mother's house." Comparison with 3:4d,e, 6:9b,c, and 8:5d,e, however, suggest that a parallel to 8:2a is missing. The corrupted remnant of the missing line is preserved in the last word of 8:2a, *tĕlammĕḏēnî,* which as it stands could mean either "she will teach me," or "thou (masc.) wilt teach me." *KJ* adopted the former expedient, "I would lead thee *and* bring thee into my mother's house, *who* would instruct me." *JPSV* followed a similar tack and made the verb a full line:

> I would lead you, I would bring you / To the house of my mother, / Of her who taught me———

but noted with reference to "taught" that emendation yields "bore" and referred to 6:9 and 8:5. Delitzsch construed the subject of the verb as second masculine, "thou wouldst instruct me," and explained it as the appeal of the wisdom-loving Shulamite to her spouse who was the personification of Wisdom. Similarly, Robert made the subject the Messiah, who as the hypostasis of Wisdom, when at last enthroned in the Temple, will teach his people the secrets of divine wisdom. Similarly *JB* rendered "and you would teach me," with the explanation that in the eschatological age, God himself will teach his people. *NEB* rendered "for you to embrace me," with an alternate choice: *or* "to teach me how to love you." *NAB* related the teaching to what follows:

> There you would teach me to give you spiced wine to drink, and pomegranate juice.

It appears that Kuhn was on the right track in omitting the *m* of *tlmdny* to obtain *tēlĕḏēnî,* "(who) bore me." We venture to go further and restore the missing line on the basis of 3:4d,e, 6:9b,c, and 8:5d,e.

2c. *spiced wine.* The partitive *min* is here used rather than the usual construction of the verb with two objects, the person and the material. The form *yayin* is here either an anomalous construct form, or the absolute form in the accusative case with *hāreqaḥ* in apposition. On spiced or perfumed wine, and other mixtures, cf. 4:10–14, 5:1, 7:3b and Brown, 1969. The term here used, *yayin hāreqaḥ,* corresponds to the *vinum conditura* of the Romans. Spices added both perfume and flavor to the mixture.

2d. *juice.* The term *'āsîs* designates what is pressed out, i.e. "juice," and is a poetic term for wine or other intoxicating juices; cf. Isa 49:26; Joel 1:5, 4[3E]:18; Amos 9:13.

my pomegranate. The ending of the form *rimmônî* appears to be the possessive suffix "my." The suffix in this construct could apply either to the juice or to the pomegranate, or to both. *KJ* rendered "of the juice of my pomegranate," *RSV* "of my pomegranates," *JPSV* "of my pomegranate juice." Several Hebrew MSS read *rimmônîm,* "pomegranates," and LXX B read "your pomegranates." Since the pomegranate was a symbol of fecundity, "my pomegranate" may be suggestive of eroticism; cf. 4:13a. Delitzsch explained that *rimmônî* applies to the pomegranate trees belonging to Shulamite and asserted that pomegranates are not to be thought of as an erotic symbol, but are named as something beautiful and precious. Rashi and Ibn Ezra thought that the pomegranate juice alluded to the Temple sacrifices and libations, and similarly Joüon. Kuhn supposed that the Shulamite was ready to give her blood for her spouse. Robert saw no reason to evade the symbolism already previously suggested by the author (cf. 4:13, 7:10), since the images in question signify the charms of the bride which subjugate her beloved and the enjoyment of which she surrenders to him alone.

2. The Targum applied this verse to the Messianic Banquet:

> I will lead you, O King Messiah, and bring you up to my Temple; and you will teach me to fear before YHWH and to walk in His ways. And there we shall partake of the feast of Leviathan and will drink old wine preserved in the grape since the day the world was created and from the pomegranates and fruits prepared for the righteous in the Garden of Eden.

Midrash Rabbah interpreted the verbs "I would lead you, I would bring you" to mean "I would lead You from the upper world to the lower" (apparently referring to the bringing of God to earth to give the Law). The mother's house was equated with Sinai, so called because there Israel became like a newborn child. "That you would instruct me" was applied to precepts and good deeds. The spiced wine referred to various collections of Mishnah, the pomegranate juice to tasty Talmudic narrative (*haggāḏôt*). The pomegranate also recalled the decoration of the high priest's garments (Exod 28:34).

Some Christian expositors interpreted this verse as relating to the Bride's anticipation of the joys of Heaven. Another view related the verse to the return of the Jews, led by the Church's preaching, to bring Christ back to the Synagogue, the mother of the Church, and there receive His teaching. The Bride will give Christ spiced wine by offering the Synagogue the strong wine of the Law blended and softened with the sweet tidings of the Gospel, and will give as the juice of her pomegranate the examples of the Martyrs glad to die for the Faith. Epiphanius and Philo of Carpasia saw in the mother of the Bride the earth as the parent dust from which human nature was formed, the mother's house being the grave where the Saints are stored till the Resurrection. The Bride is ready to go down with her Lord and did indeed go down with Him to conquer and spoil the realm of Death. Theodoret explained the mother's house as the Church, God's Temple, imitating the heavenly Jerusalem, and the wine as the church's wholesome doctrine, the pomegranate juice as the fruits of charity. The catena of the Three Fathers (Nilus, Maximus, and Gregory of Nyssa) applied the verse to the holy soul, the mother's house being the higher understanding wherein dwells the grace of the Holy Spirit of which she was born through Baptism. There she offers her Lord the knowledge she has of Him, as spiced wine mixed with various ingredients, contemplation of Him as revealed in His creatures and in Holy Scripture. The sweet yet tart juice of the pomegranate is the love which she offers her Lord, blended with reverence and longing for full possession. (Cf. Littledale.)

3. This verse reproduces verbatim 2:6, except for the omission of the preposition *lĕ-* between *taḥaṯ* and *rô'šî*. As with 2:6, the translation deliberately

avoids clear commitment as to the tense and mood of the action. Some critics have regarded this verse and the following as adventitious, since 2:6–7 appears to be in a contextual situation while 8:3–4 does not. The analogy of 2:5 and 8:2b,c supposedly explains the insertion at the latter point. Robert, however, argued that the apriori presumption of authenticity is more likely since repetitions of this sort are characteristic of the Canticle.

The Targum makes the Assembly of Israel here say:

> I am the chosen of all peoples. I bind *tefillin* on my left hand and on my head and fix the *mezuzah* to the right side of my door a third (of the way) from the lintel so that no demon can harm me.

4. The refrain here varies from 2:7 and 3:5, with replacement of the adjuration formula *'im . . . wĕ'im* by the negative *māh . . . ûmāh* (on the negative *māh,* cf. GKC 137b, n1) and omission of the allusion to the gazelles and hinds. The omission is appropriate to the change from adjuration to prohibition, since there is no place in the prohibition for reference to the objects by which an adjuration is made. Four MSS of the MT, most of the LXX MSS, and the Arabic, mistakenly supply the allusion to gazelles and hinds. Syriac and some LXX MSS conform to the parallel passages 2:7 and 3:5.

The Targum, having given slightly differing interpretations to 2:7 and 3:5, added further variety here:

> The King, the Messiah, shall say, I adjure you O (my) people, House of Israel, why are you warring against the peoples of the earth to escape the exile? Why are you rebelling against the forces of Gog and Magog? Wait a little longer till the peoples who come up to make war against Jerusalem are destroyed, and thereafter the Lord of the World will remember for you the love of the righteous, and let it be His will to redeem you.

The threefold repetition of this refrain suggested to Cardinal Hugo the alternations and successions of religious vocation and training, and three stages of nocturnal meditation. The omission of the reference to gazelles and hinds found in the two previous refrains was explained on the basis of the LXX interpretation as "powers" and "forces" as referring to the angelic host of Angels who are here addressed directly and so cannot be adjured by their own name; cf. Littledale. Delitzsch suggested that the omission may mean that here the natural side of love is broken and *erōs* rises to *agapē.*

5a. This line is identical with 3:6a. Comparison of 3:6a, 6:10a and the present line should make it clear that in each instance the question *mî zō't* "Who is this (female)?" refers to the Lady of the Canticle. Robert recognized this for the present line and for 6:10a, but took 3:6a to designate "une troupe indistincte."

from the steppe. Cf. 3:6a where LXX rendered MT, *apo tēs erēmon.* Here LXX has *leleukanthismenē,* "made white"; Old Latin *candida.* Rufinus rendered *dealbata.* Vulgate after *de deserto* adds *deliciis affluens.* Many critics have conjectured an original reading differing from MT. Delitzsch supposed that the Greek translator read *mitḥawweret̲* from the illegible consonants of his MS. Graetz conjectured an original *mĕnāheret̲*, Horst *mitbāreret̲*, and Rudolph *mabhîrāh*. It seems clear, however, that the deviations from MT were motivated by concern for blanching the black beauty of 1:5. Origen, who stressed the positive value of negritude in his commentary on 1:5, could not resist the opportunity provided by the Greek reading of 8:5a to whitewash the black beauty whom he had praised. Applying the paradoxical negritude and pulchritude to the individual soul that turns to repentance after many sins, Origen explained that she is black by reason of sins, but beautiful through her repentance. And finally, according to Origen, she who now says "I am black and beautiful" has not remained in her blackness to the end. The daughters of Jerusalem say later concerning her: "Who is this that comes up, having been made white?"

The imaginations of modern expositors were exercised to explain the desert or steppe land. Many thought of the wilderness of Judea which has to be traversed in approaching Jerusalem from the east. Renan imagined that the Shulamite, having resisted all of Solomon's temptations, supplicates her shepherd lover to take her home; she falls fainting into her true love's arms and he transports the sleeping maid back to Shulam and deposits her under the apple tree on the farm where she was born. Delitzsch supposed that the loving pair, Solomon and Shulamite, wander on foot through the Valley of Jezreel, a beautiful, well-watered, fruitful valley, which is here called *midbār*, "wilderness," as being uncultivated pasture land. Haupt translated "meadows" and explained in a note that the meaning is "pasture-land." The village of the bridegroom, according to Haupt, was probably situated on a hill so that the wedding procession came up from the meadows between the two villages. Ricciotti supposed that the reference is to the entry into Canaan at the time of the Exodus. Joüon thought that the allusion is to the return from exile and that the wilderness is simply the area around Jerusalem. Robert asserted that the desert here refers not only to the desert of Judea, but to the great Syrian desert which the Bride, Israel, must cross in returning from exile. As in 3:6, Robert related the scene to Hosea 2:16–25[14–23E] where the desert is the scene of Israel's conversion and return to her original love, and thence she departs, led by her husband, to retake possession of Palestine. On the mythological associations of the desert or steppe land, cf. 3:6.

5b. *Leaning*. The form *mitrappeqet̲* is hapax legomenon, but the root *rpq* is well known in post-biblical Hebrew, Aramaic, Arabic, and Ethiopic. The noun **marpiq* has the meaning "elbow" in neo-Hebrew, Jewish Aramaic, and Arabic. In Arabic the simple stem means "to be helpful, compliant," or "to bind a camel's leg to keep it from straying too far," and the eighth stem (Gt or, infixed -t) signifies "to support oneself with the elbow on a pillow," while the noun *rafīq* means "fellow traveler," and *rufqa*(*t*) "a company of fellow travelers," from the basic idea of mutual support. In Ethiopic the verb is used of reclining in order to eat, like Greek *anaklinestai* (cf. John 13:23). Because of the possible range of meanings of the word, it is impossible to tell whether the couple are walking arm in arm or reclining together on a litter. Commentators generally assume the former situation, but comparison with 3:6–10 suggests the latter circumstance.

5c. *Under the apple tree.* On the erotic and mythological associations of the apple (tree), cf. 2:3. Wittekindt (56*f*) observed that divine births often took place under trees sacred to the cult. Adonis was born from the Myrrh; Apollo, Artemis, and Mary under the palm. Romulus and Remus were found under the fig tree. Zeus married Europa under the plane tree at Gortyna and at Knossus he thus espoused Hera. Adonis as gardener was called Melus, Apple.

I aroused you. On the meanings and uses of this verb, cf. 2:7c. Connection of the verb with a similar root meaning "be naked" (Zapletal and Wittekindt), "under the apple tree I stripped you naked," is without justification. The suggestion of erotic excitation is generally avoided by relating the action to arousal from sleep or the awakening of a love other than physical or carnal. Virtually all interpretations go against the MT vocalization of the object suffixes of this verse which are all masculine. According to Delitzsch, we must change the punctuation of the text altogether, and throughout restore the feminine suffixes as those originally used, following the example of the Syriac Meek (*IB,* V) remarked "the MT is better." The MT vocalization of the suffixes as masculine must reflect an ancient tradition since it would have been simple and convenient to alter the vocalization to accord with the standard allegorical interpretation of the bride as Israel and the groom as Yahweh. The text as received would, in keeping with the allegory, represent Israel as arousing Yahweh under the apple tree where His mother conceived and bore Him! That this reading was preserved through centuries of allegorical interpretation suggests that it was so well established and known that it could not be changed but was left for moderns to correct.

5d,e. *There.* Delitzsch denied that the adverb implies that what follows took place under the apple tree. Shulamite, he objected, is not the child of bedouins, in which case she might have been born under the apple tree. The Bedouin often name a girl born at the watering place, or on a journey, or in the dew or snow, according to the circumstance. For Delitzsch, following Hitzig, the apple tree pointed the way to Shulamite's parental home, the birthplace of her love, not of her life. In spite of the offense or prejudice, the adverb can only refer to the apple tree as the setting of the arousal of the groom by the bride in the very spot where his mother had conceived him. The shade of the old apple tree continues a favored spot for alfresco amour, in popular song at least, preserving a tradition of great antiquity.

conceived. Vulgate *corrupta est violata est* accords with Aquila's, *diephtharē,* reading *ḥubbĕlāh* for MT *ḥibbĕlāh.* A number of misguided emendations have been proposed by modern critics, all involving change of the object suffixes from masculine to feminine. Zapletal proposed the reading *ḥubbalt kĕ'immēḵ*, "you were destroyed like your mother." Graetz rendered "dort, wo dich deine Mutter verwundet hat" (there, where your mother wounded you). The root *ḥbl* is commonly used of woman's travail and labor in child-birth (Isa 13:8, 26:17; Jer 13:21; Hosea 13:13), but it may also apply to the relatively painless and even pleasurable process of conception, as in Ps 7:15[14E], "Lo, he conceives (*yeḥabbēl*) evil, is pregnant (*hārāh*) with mischief, and gives birth (*yālaḏ*) to falsehood." In the present passage the repetition of the verb could refer to the same phase of the generative process, or to different phases, i.e. to conception in both instances, or travail in both, or to conception in the former instance and travail in the latter. Without knowledge of the affair in question, one can only speculate. Advocates of historical allegory, e.g. Ricciotti and Robert, appealed to Ezek 16:3,44–45 for the circumstances of the birth. The mother is the personification of the ancient populations of Canaan and the progeny is Israel, Yahweh's formerly unfaithful but finally repentant bride (the grammatical impediments being removed). Fidelity to the MT here would completely wreck all theories which make Israel the bride and Yahweh the groom. Whoever the mother may be, the offspring is plainly designated as male by the Hebrew text, a remarkable fact in view of traditional interpretations which militate against survival of such evidence.

Ginsburg's theory of interpretation permitted retention of the masculine suffixes of MT. The Shulamite addresses her shepherd swain:

> Under this apple tree I won thy heart,
> Here thy mother travailed,
> Here laboring she gave thee birth.

Ginsburg explained that "As they drew nearer home they beheld the endeared spot, the memorable shady tree under which the shepherd was born, and where their mutual love was first kindled." He goes on to imagine that "The solemn vow of love was then graven on the bark of the tree as a witness of their union," citing, among other parallels, Theocritus (*Idyl* xviii 47*f*):

> . . . and on the bark,
> In Doric shall be graven for all to mark,
> "To pay me honor—I am Helen's tree."

5. The reference to the desert suggested to the Targumist the netherworld and resurrection:

> Said Solomon the prophet, "When the dead shall come to life, the Mount of Olives will be cleft and all the dead of Israel come forth from beneath it; and even the righteous who died in exile will come by way of subterranean caverns and will come forth beneath the Mount of Olives. And the wicked who have died and been buried in the land of Israel will be cast up as a man throws up a stone with a stick. Then all the inhabitants of the earth will say,

'What was the merit of this people that have come up from the earth, myriads upon myriads, as (on) the day when they appeared beneath Mount Sinai to receive the Law?' At that hour Zion, mother of Israel, shall bear her children and Jerusalem shall receive her captive children."

Midrash Rabbah related the ascent from the wilderness both to the Exodus and to death, citing Num 14:35. The leaning on her beloved was interpreted by Rabbi Yohanan to mean that Israel leaves certain portions of the Torah for the future. The apple tree was related to Mount Sinai. The Torah was given in the month of Sivan at the time the apple tree produces its fruit. The mountain was uprooted and elevated and Israel stood beneath it (Deut 4:11). The mother in travail was related, among other things, to the sin with the golden calf (Exod 24:7, 32:4).

Christian allegorists found multiple meanings in all parts of this verse. The opening words were supposed to be spoken by the Synagogue in amazement at the rise of the Church from among the Gentiles. The ascent from the wilderness was applied also to the rise of the holy soul from the desert of earthly exile toward the heavenly joy of spiritual meditation in a three-stage pilgrim's progress from worldly vanity to humility to innocence. LXX's reading "made white" was welcomed as proof that the Black Beauty of 1:5 is at last made to match the whiteness of her mate (cf. 5:10). She is made white by the waters of Baptism and not by her own power or merit, or she is counted worthy to share the whiteness of her Bridegroom who is the Resurrection. The Vulgate's augmentation "abounding in delights," was taken by Cardinal Hugo as typifying Jesus' Ascension to the celestial throne, the preceding references to ascent, 3:6 and 6:10, being related to the Crucifixion and the early morning rise from the grave. It was also applied to the Assumption of the Blessed Virgin, as in the medieval hymn *Affluens deliciis,*

She, abounding in delights,
Child of David's kingly line,
Borne to the celestial heights
In the Bridegroom's arms divine,

Hastes to seek Him, as His love,
Thither, where He passed above,
Where the mystic lilies shine.

The arousal under the apple tree has been assumed to mean arousal from slumber. Littledale invoked the motif of the nursery tale of Sleeping Beauty awakened by the kiss of the Prince and cited several stanzas of Tennyson's "The Daydream."

And on her lover's arm she leant,
  And round her waist she felt it fold,
And far across the hills they went
  In that new world which is the old. . . .

"O eyes long laid in happy sleep!"
  "O happy sleep, that lightly fled!"
"O happy kiss, that woke thy sleep!"
  "O Love, Thy kiss would wake the dead!"

There is, however, nothing to suggest that anyone is asleep and the verb used may denote any kind of arousal, including sexual excitement. Theodoret recalled the reference to the apple tree in 2:3, but related the matter to regeneration through Holy Baptism. The apple tree was identified with the Cross of Christ and the Tree of Knowledge in the Garden of Eden through the legend that the Cross was made of a limb of that tree and was erected on the very spot where Adam was buried. John Donne referred to the legend in his "Divine Poems":

We think that Paradise and Calvary,
  Christ's Cross and Adam's tree, stood in one place.

The Vulgate rendering, "There thy mother was defiled, there she that bore thee was forced," was applied to the Synagogue which was deflowered and defiled under the Tree in crucifying her Lord and taking the curse of His blood on herself and her posterity. On the basis of the LXX the mother was seen as the Church, which brings forth the devout soul. (Cf. Littledale.)

6a,b. *signet.* The same word, *ḥôṯām,* is used in both lines. Budde's conjecture that the second line originally read *kaṣṣāmîd,* or some other word for arm band, finds no support in the Versions. LXX reads *hōs sphragida* in each instance and Vulgate *ut signaculum.* The word *ḥôṯām* is a loanword from Egyptian (*ḥtm*), as is also the word *ṭabbaʿaṯ* (*ḏbʿt*) of Gen 41:42 (cf. Schott, 1957, 181*f*). The signet or seal was made of metal or stone and worn on a cord around the neck (Gen 38:18) or as a ring on the (right) hand (Gen 41:42; Jer 22:24). With the beginning of writing in the fourth millennium B.C. seals were widely used, especially cylinder seals on clay tablets, but also stamp seals which were later used predominantly on clay or wax lumps attached to papyrus documents. The unbroken seal on letters, legal and official documents, or on a tomb, protected the contents. Storage jar handles were also stamped to indicate ownership. Thousands of seals and seal impressions have been recovered from the ancient Near East and the study of their decoration and inscriptions are fields of growing importance. Seals were made of precious and semiprecious metals and stones, elaborately and exquisitely engraved, and were thus among a person's most valuable possessions (cf. Sir 17:22) and at the same time one's legal signature and identification. Tamar's acquisition of her father-in-law's signet (Gen 38:18) kept her from being burned. The Pharaoh's signet ring made Joseph the royal deputy (Gen 41:42). The value set on one's signet is shown in the divine vow of Jer 22:24, "'As I live,' says Yahweh, 'though Coniah son of Jehoakim, King of Judah, were the signet on my right hand, I would rip you off.'" The promised election and exaltation of Zerubbabel, Hag 2:23, is expressed in the metaphor of Yahweh's signet, "'I will take you, O Zerubbabel, my servant, son of Shealtiel . . . and will put you on like a signet, for I have chosen you,' says Yahweh of Hosts."

heart . . . arm. Some critics have been bothered by the use of "arm," *zĕrôaʿ*, rather than "hand," *yāḏ*, and were moved to supply a more suitable ornament, a bracelet, or the like. Anatomical terms are somewhat loosely used in biblical poetry, and "arm" may be a poetic synonym for "hand." Ugaritic poetry offers an example which should teach us not to demand precision in such matters (14[KRT].2.63–64, 3.157–158):

He washed his hands to the elbow, His fingers up to the shoulder.

The wearing of amulets, charms, and other apotropaic devices on head, chest, arm or hand is an ancient and almost universal practice. E. A. Speiser (1965) has elucidated the Mesopotamian practice of wearing apotropaic objects bearing names referring to an associate or friend who thus accompanies and protects the wearer. The phylacteries (*tĕpillîn*) worn by orthodox Jews on the basis of Exod 13:9,16 and Deut 6:8, 11:18, are manifestly related to this notion and usage. P. D. Miller, Jr. (1970) has called attention to the striking apotropaic imagery in Prov 6:20–23:

Keep my son, your father's command,
Reject not your mother's teaching.
Bind them on your heart continually,
Tie them round your neck.

When you walk it will lead you;
When you lie down, it will watch over
 you;
When you wake it will talk with you.

In the present instance nothing is said of phylacteric function of the seal which represents love and symbolizes the lover's presence, but the following lines which emphasize Love's power over against that of Death suggest that there may be a blending of the functions of the signet with the memento and the phylactery.

As in the preceding verse, the second person object suffixes of MT are masculine. The bride thus addresses the groom as in vs. 5. It is noteworthy that here critics do not feel compelled to change the gender of the suffixes. It is permissible for the lady to ask to be worn like a seal or signet by her lover, but it did not seem proper for her to arouse him. The birth under the apple tree was the crucial reason for rejecting the masculine suffixes by critics who identify the male protagonist as Solomon or as God. Here, as throughout the Canticle, the female takes the lead in the courtship.

The wish to be as a jewel or ring worn by one's darling is commonplace in love songs, both exquisite and bawdy. In the Cairo Love Songs, the lover says:

I wish I were her Negro maid
who follows at her feet;
then the skin of all her limbs
would be [revealed] to me.

I wish I were her washerman,
If only for a single month,
then I would be [entranced],
washing out the Moringa oils
in her diaphanous garments . . .

I wish I were the seal ring,
the guardian of her [fingers],
then [. . .]

(Simpson, 1972, 311)

Stephan (8) cited in connection with 1:10 a line from a Palestinian love ditty, "O that I were a pearl necklace round her neck." In Tennyson's "Miller's Daughter" the lover says:

It is the miller's daughter,
And she is grown so dear,
That I would be the jewel,
That trembles in her ear.

Among the bawdy quatrains about a certain Lulu there is one that offers something of a parallel to the present verse:

I wish I was a diamond
Placed upon Lulu's hand . . .

6c. *love*. LXX *agapē,* Vulgate *dilectio*. Love is here personified in that the signet to be set on the heart and hand of the lady's lover represents her essence and power which is here revealed as Love.

strong as Death. It has been suggested that the word *môṯ*, "death," is here used simply to express the superlative, "Love is extremely strong"; cf. D. W. Thomas (1953, 221). It appears more likely that the allusion is to the god Mot, Death personified, king of the infernal realm, whose power mortals cannot deny or evade. The use of "death" as equivalent of the superlative may be attested in a Ugaritic letter (53[54].11–13) which reports "and the hand of the gods (presumably a plague or other calamity) is here, like Death, exceeding strong." The strength of Mot is once matched by Mighty Baal in a Ugaritic myth (6[49].6.16–22) in which the two fight to a draw and both are finally prostrate:

They push(?) like pachyderms(?)
Mot is strong, Baal strong;
They gore like buffalo,
Mot is strong, Baal strong;
They bite like serpents,
Mot is strong, Baal strong;
They kick like steeds,
Mot is down, Baal down.

On another occasion, after Baal had been mangled and devoured by Mot, the passion of Baal's Sister-Consort, Virgin Anat, made her more than a match for Mot's power (6[49].2.6–37):

As the heart of a cow for her calf,
As the heart of a ewe for her lamb,
So was Anat's heart toward Baal.
She seized Mot by the hem of his
garment,
Grabbed him by the end of his robe:
"Thou, Mot, give up my brother!"
Quoth divine Mot,
"What do you wish, Virgin Anat?"

I mangled Mighty Baal
Made him like a lamb in my mouth
Like a kid in my gullet . . .
As the heart of a cow for her calf,
As the heart of a ewe for her lamb,
So was Anat's heart toward Baal.
She seized divine Mot—
With sword she split him,
With sieve she scattered him,
With fire she burned him,
With millstones she ground him,
In the field she sowed him.
His flesh the birds did eat,
His parts the sparrows consumed;
Flesh to flesh did cry.

But even these drastic measures did not spell the end of Death who, in his turn, reappeared to challenge and devour Baal again, and this time Baal cravenly submitted without a fight.

The power of Death is not to be broken until the end.

Shall I rescue them from Sheol's grasp?
From Mot shall I redeem them?
Where are your plagues, O Mot?
Where your pestilence, O Sheol?
Compassion is hid from my eyes.
Hosea 13:14

But at the final feast,

Yahweh of Hosts will prepare
For all peoples on this mountain
A feast of dainties and wines,
Juicy dainties, mellowed wines;

And He will destroy on this mountain
The pall that shrouds all peoples,
The veil that covers all nations.
He will destroy Death forever,
Wipe the tears from all faces;
The reproach of His people he will
remove
From all the earth . . .
Isa 25:6–8

When man's perishable nature is clothed with immortality, then will come to pass the saying of Scripture,

Death is swallowed in victory.
Where, Death, is your victory?
Where, Death, your sting?
I Cor 15:54–55

When the old order passes, God will wipe the tears from every eye, and Death shall be no more, Rev 21:4. Meanwhile, the only force to pit against Death is Love.

6d. *Passion.* The term *qin'āh* is here rendered by LXX as *zēlos* and by Vulgate *aemulatio*. Luther rendered Eifer, "zeal." *RSV*'s retention of *KJ*'s "jealousy" was apparently influenced by consideration of the passages where the term *qin'āh* is applied to a man's suspicion that his wife may have been unfaithful (Num 5:14,29–30) and his venomous and vengeful rage toward her violator (Prov 6:34); cf. Ezek 16:38 where *qin'āh* is joined to blood and wrath as the reward of the adulteress. Yahweh is similarly provoked to jealousy and anger by Israel's idolatries (Deut 32:16,21; Ps 73:58), and is given the title *qannā' or qannô'*, using the nominal pattern applied to professions, as designating one especially zealous or jealous (Exod 20:5, 34:14; Deut 5:9). The term *qin'āh,* however, is used of emotions, other than jealousy, in a love triangle. In Eccles 4:4 it is used of envy and rivalry among neighbors. It is several times applied to the divine zeal and fury in battle on behalf of the elect, Isa 9:6[7E], 37:32, 42:13, 59:17, 63:15; Zech 1:14, 8:2. It is frequently used in parallelism or association with words for anger or similar passions; cf. Ps 119:139; Job 5:2; Isa 37:32; Prov 14:30; Ezek 5:13, 16:38,42, 23:25, 36:5, 38:19; Deut 29:19[20E]. It is clear that the word can designate a variety of strong emotions, anger, envy, jealousy, fury, and in the present context, the sexual instinct and ardor which is one of man's strongest propensities. *AT*'s choice of "passion" seems the most apt rendering in view of the parallelism with *'ahăḇāh,* "love."

fierce. LXX *sklēros,* Vulgate *dura.* The basic meaning of this root *qšy* is "hard," "tough," "severe," "obdurate," and the like, the opposite of *rkk,* "soft," "weak"; cf. II Sam 3:39. Love and passion are like Death and Hell, strong, fierce, and relentless.

Hell. LXX *Hadēs,* Vulgate *infernus.* The term *šě'ôl,* the usual Old Testament designation of the netherworld, is here rendered by the Germanic name in order to convey the superlative force of the comparison: strong, fierce, obdurate, relentless as the netherworld. The strength of "Hell" as a superlative and in oaths and curses has been vitiated by overwork, but may retain a modicum of its force in this instance.

6e. *darts.* The versions variously interpret the difficult word *rěšāpîm* here as wings, flames, fire, sparks. The word is cognate with the name of the god Rešep, an important chthonic deity related to the Mesopotamian Nergal and to Apollo of Greek and Roman mythology. The iconography of Rešep is best known from Egyptian sources where he appears commonly in martial attitude, brandishing a battle-ax and holding other weapons. Several times he appears with the nude fertility goddess who stands on her lion holding a lotus and a serpent and is flanked on her left by Rešep and on the right by ithyphallic Min. The ambivalent nature of the great goddess of love and war is thus graphically portrayed by this association with sexuality and fertility on the one side, and war, pestilence, and death on the other. For the connection of Rešep with pestilence, cf. Deut 32:24 and Hab 3:5, where the word *rešep* may be the name of the god rather than a common noun. Similarly in Job 5:7 (cf. AB 15, ad loc.) the sons of Rešep, usually taken to mean "sparks," may designate the plagues and pestilences that rise from Earth to afflict mankind; cf. Ps 78:48 where *rěšāpîm,* along with hail, frost and plague, are destroyers of crops and cattle. In a Cypriote inscription the god is called *ršp ḥṣ,* "Rešep of the arrow" (*CIS,* I, 10) and in a Ugaritic text (1001.1.3) he has the title "Lord of the arrow Rešep," *b'l ḥẓ ršp.* In Ps 76:4[3E] the term *rišpê qāšeṯ* is a poetic term for arrows, and probably flaming arrows (*AT* "fiery shafts of the bow") rather than merely "flashing arrows" (*RSV*). In the present passage the connection with fire is explicit. The fiery darts of Love are thus like the invincible arrows of Eros or Cupid. For a detailed study of Rešep and a bibliography, cf. W. J. Fulco, 1971, and D. Conrad, 1971.

6f. *Its flames . . .* LXX *p̄loges autēs* confirms MT *Kěṯîb,* but not the Qěrê. Vulgate *atque flammarum* passes over the possessive suffix which is permissible after its expression in the preceding *lampades ejus.* MT's vocalization, *šalhebeṯyāh* according to Ben Asher or, according to Ben Naphthali, *šalhebeṯ yāh,* indicates that final syllable *yāh* was construed as the short form of the ineffable name of Israel's God. In keeping with the established and recognized uses of divine names for the superlative sense (cf. J. M. P. Smith, 1927–28, 111*f;* 1928–29, 212*f,* and D. W. Thomas, 1953, 210*ff*), this "flame of the Lord" has been understood as "a most vehement flame" (*KJ, RSV*), "furious flames" (*AT*), "fiercer than any flame" (*NEB*). Ginsburg, however, insisted that the predicate does not state that the flames are vehement but rather "affirms that they emanate from the Eternal," citing I John 4:7, "love is from God." Thus *JB* rendered "a flame of Yahweh himself." The single word *šalhebeṯyāh,* with only four syllables, counting the anaptyctic penultimate syllable, is too short for a full line and various supplementations and emendations have been proposed, such as *šalhăḇôṯeyhā šalhăḇôṯ yāh* (Olshausen); or *lahăḇôṯeyhā šalhăbôṯ yāh* (Budde et al.), *šalhăḇôṯ yěqōd šalhăḇôṯeyhā* (Bickell), *lahăḇôṯeyhā lahăbôṯ ḥōm* (Wittekindt), or with a minor variation by Horst *lahăḇôṯ ḥammāh lahaḇôṯeyhā,* thus more than doubling the length of the line. It seems best to ignore the word as a gloss to *rĕšāp̄eyhā* of the preceding colon. To seize upon the final consonants *yh* as the sole reference to the God of Israel in the entire Canticle is to lean on very scanty and shaky support. Robert rendered "une flamme de Yahwé" but felt constrained to ask how a book which is wholly occupied with God and the love of God has been able to envelope its thesis in a continual mystery and only lift the veil in its conclusion.

6. The Targum ascribed this verse to Israel:

> The Israelites on that day shall say to their Lord, "We beseech Thee (lit. "with petition of Thee"), set us like a glyph (*gĕlūp̄*) of a signet ring on your heart, as the glyph of a signet ring on your arm, that we may never again be exiles. For strong as death is the love of Thy Divinity, and powerful as Gehinnom is the jealousy which the peoples harbor toward us. The enmity which they nurture toward us is like the coals of the fire of Gehinnom which YHWH created on the second day of the Creation of the World to burn therewith the devotees of foreign worship."

Midrash Rabbah offered a variety of interpretations of this verse. Rabbi Eliezer, for example, related the reference to the seal to Israel's acceptance of the Law at Mount Sinai, at which moment God called the Angel of Death and revoked his power over them. Others explained the freedom from the Angel of Death as referring to freedom from foreign domination or from tribulation. Rabbi Berekiah applied the seal on the heart to the recitation of the *Shema'* (Deut 6:6) and the seal on the arm to the application of the phylacteries. Rabbi Meir recalled the divine promise to Jehoiachin or Coniah (Jer 22:24). The love strong as death and jealousy cruel as Sheol were applied to the divine love of Israel (Mal 1:2) and resentment of her idolatry (Deut 32:16), to Isaac's love for Esau (Gen 25:28) and Esau's hatred of Jacob (Gen 27:41), or Jacob's love for Joseph (Gen 37:3) and the brothers' envy (Gen 37:11), or Jonathan's love for David (I Sam 18:1) and Saul's hatred (I Sam 18:9). The love and jealousy were, quite naturally, applied to the relation of man and wife (Eccles 9:9; Num 5:14). The love strong as death was finally related to the love which the generation of the destruction (the period of the Hadrianic Wars) exhibited in their martyrdom (Ps 44:23[22E]) and the jealousy to God's zeal for Zion (Zech 1:14).

In the Talmud (TB Ta'anit 4a) this verse is applied to improper or thoughtless requests. The Congregation of Israel made the thoughtless request of God, "Set me as a seal, etc." God replied, "My daughter, you ask me for something which at times can be seen and at other times cannot be seen. I, however, will make of you something which can be seen at all times, as it is said, 'Behold I have graven you on the palms of My hands' " (Isa 49:16).

Despite the masculine suffixes indicated in the vocalization of the Hebrew text, Christian interpreters generally ascribed these words to the Bridegroom rather than to the Bride. Philo of Carpasia explained the seal as the sign of the Cross which must be impressed on the heart and arm of the Bride so that the Church may learn to imitate its Head. The heart to Theodoret was the contemplative part of the soul, the arm the active portion and this was why the priests received the breast and shoulder of the sacrifices (Exod 29:27). Clement of Alexandria explained that as the seal is used to protect secrets from prying eyes, so the

Bridegroom, Christ, gives His Bride, the Church, a signet to seal the treasures and the mysteries of the Faith committed to her keeping. The Venerable Bede admonished the faithful to keep Christ as a seal on heart and arm by remembering all His words and actions in order to ponder and imitate them. Rupert, Abbot of Deutz, in keeping with the Hebrew text, took the words as spoken by the Bride and explained the heart and arm as the Scriptures written after Christ's own heart and as the record of His works which make known the might and greatness of His arm.

The love strong as death was taken either as God's love toward man, or of man's love toward God. Love is strong as death, Ambrose observed, because love slays guilt and sin and destroys the blows of death. God is love and when we love God's commandments we die to our vices and sins. Gregory the Great noted that as death affects the physical senses, destroying all the natural properties and desires of the external senses, so love forces men to despise all earthly inclinations. Philo of Carpasia was reminded of the joy with which the Martyrs faced torture and death.

The zeal or jealousy which is hard as Sheol, Hades, or Hell was variously explained as zeal for God and against sin, as referring to ecclesiastical censure and excommunication, or to Christ's descent into Hell to deliver the souls who had gone there before His Advent. Imitation of Christ moved the Saints to undergo suffering and death in emulation of Him. Christ's rivalry with Hell for the redemption of man was hellish hard, for as Hell will not relinquish those it has seized, Christ's love never lets go those it has embraced; cf. Rom 8:35. The jealousy was also applied to the hostility which the Synagogue exhibited toward the Lord and His disciples. The LXX reading *periptera,* "wingings around," was taken to mean that God's love serves as wings to lift the Bride from earth to heaven. The Vulgate reading *lampades,* "lamps," was seen as typifying the Saints who are aglow with the fire of the Holy Ghost. The vehement flame seen by modern interpreters in the word *šalheḇeṯyāh* is not in the LXX and Vulgate which take the word merely as amplification of the preceding phrase. The alleged occurrence of the Name of God was not exploited by early interpreters. The flame of the divine love was seen by Ainsworth as melting the hearts of men and purging the dross. Cocceius related it to the tongues of fire which descended on the Apostles at Pentecost. (Cf. Littledale.)

7a. *Mighty waters.* The expression *mayim rabbim,* traditionally rendered "many waters," occurs some twenty-eight times in the Old Testament and is echoed in the New in Rev 1:15, 17:1, 19:6. There are variants of the expression in Neh 9:11; Isa 43:16; Job 37:10, 38:34; Ps 69:2,14; Prov 18:4, using other attributes such as "strong," "broad," "deep," "flood of," instead of the adjective *rabbîm.* The phrase has been thoroughly treated by H. G. May (1955) who related many of the occurrences of the expression to the myth of the conquest of the insurgent waters borrowed from Canaanite and Babylonian sources. In the present passage May suggested that in the antithesis between "love" and "many waters" "the author may be saying something more penetrating than that love is a fire that cannot be put out by water. The many waters of the great deep and its rivers cannot extinguish or overcome it. Like the storm-God himself it remains unbowed in battle against its enemy." May further suggested that the preceding couplet (6e,f) is possibly to be translated:

Its thunderbolts are bolts of fire, furious flames.

May, however, admitted that this is not certain, "and perhaps too temptingly suggests the storm-God who was in conflict with the waters" (p. 18).

The crucial point here overlooked by May is the reference to Death. The waters in question are not those represented by Prince Sea or Chief River who was conquered by Mighty Baal in the West Semitic version of the myth preserved in the Ugaritic texts. The waters are rather those of Death and the Netherworld, as noted by N. J. Tromp, 1969, 64*f*. The watery character of the infernal abode of Death is well attested in the Bible, as in other ancient sources. A few biblical samples will suffice:

The breakers of Death engulfed me,
The torrents of Perdition assailed me,
The cords of Hell compassed me,
The snares of death confronted me.
II Sam 22:5–6=Ps 18:4–5

He reached from on high, he took me,
He drew me out of the Mighty Waters
II Sam 22:17=Ps 18:16

Jonah's prayer-hymn is graphic:

You cast me into the Deep,
Into the heart of the Sea.
The River compassed me,
Breakers and billows passed over me.
. . .
The waters engulfed me,

The Deep surrounded me,
Weeds wound round my head.
At the mountain bases I descended into
Earth,
And her bars closed on me forever.
But you brought up my life from the Pit,
O Yahweh, my God.
Jonah 2:3,5–6

(On the mountains which mark the entry and serve as lids to the netherworld, cf. M. Pope, 1964, 276n21, and Tromp, 144–148.) In Job 33:22 there is probably an allusion to the Waters of Death in the consonants *lmmtym:*

His soul draws near the Pit, His life to the waters of Death.
(Cf. AB 15 and Tromp, 65)

The meaning of the present couplet, 7a,b, is thus the same as 6c,d, that Love withstands even Death and the rigors of Hell. The assertion is thus stronger than translators and interpreters have realized and more is intended than is expressed by the paraphrase of the popular ditty:

Water can push and water can shove,
But water can't quench the fire of Love.

There's one thing I'm certain of:
Water can't quench the fire of Love.

As Paul expressed it in I Cor 13:8,13, "Love never fails . . . Thus Faith, Hope, and Love endure, these three; but of these Love is the greatest." In

Rom 8:38 Death is foremost among the forces which Paul declares powerless to separate us from the Love of God in Christ.

7b. *torrents*. The feminine plural form *nĕhārôṯ* Robert noted is several times used of the hostile powers Egypt and Babylon in announcements of the deliverance from captivity and of judgments of Yahweh in general (Jer 46:7–8; Ezek 32:2,14; Isa 42:15, 43:2, 44:27, 47:2; cf. Ps 74:15). This, however, has scant bearing on the present passage which asserts the power of Love to withstand even Death and the floods of the netherworld. The term *nāhār* is rarely used in connection with the waters of Death, but there is at least one other instance, Jonah 2:4[3E]; cf. Tromp 63.

The similarity of vocabulary between 8:6–7 of the Canticle and Isa 43:2 was regarded by Robert as astonishing. Both passages use the nouns *mayim, nĕhārôṯ, 'ēš* and *lehāḇāh,* "water," "rivers," "fire," "flame," and the verb *šṭp*. The prophet, announcing to Israel her imminent return to Palestine, gives this assurance in the name of God:

When you pass through the waters I will be with you,
And through the rivers, they will not overwhelm you.
When you walk through the fire you will not be burned,
The flame will not consume you.

The peace and security of the eschatological era is thus evoked for Robert in this verse which affirms that nothing can again disturb the tranquil and profound attachment of the Bride returned to her Beloved.

6a – 7b. O. Loretz (1971, 50) noted in this hymn to Love a certain parallel to Sophocles' hymn to Eros in a chorus of *The Antigone* (781–801):

Erôs, invincible in fight,
  Who ragest in the flocks, Erôs,
  Who hauntest, tender in repose,
A maiden's cheek at night;

Past the deep sea thy pinion flies,
Past where the hidden forest lies;
And none of gods immortal may
Escape thee; how shall humans, they
Whose breath endureth scarce a day?
  The Madman grasps his prize.

Though man be just, by thee his mood
Is warped to wrong and wrecked his life;
'Tis thou, even here, hast wakened strife
  'Tween kinsmen of one blood.

All-conquering is thy spell soft-eyed
That yearneth from the waiting bride;
Beside the eternal laws thy will
Is throned, where, irresistible
And deathless, Aphrodite still
  Mocketh her prisoners' pride.

(Sophocles, *The Antigone*. Translated by Gilbert Murray, London, 1941, 55*f*).

A more literal translation is offered by J. O'Brien, *A Guide to Sophocles' Antigone: A Student Edition*. Southern Illinois University Press, 1977:

Strophe (781–790)

O Eros unconquered in battle, Eros you who / destroy men's resources, Eros you who keep / night watch on the soft cheek of a maiden / you make your way over the deep sea and into wild / beasts' lairs. No immortal can escape you / nor can ephemeral man. And / whoever possesses you is mad.

Antistrophe (791–799)

You lure even the just to injustice— / to their own destruction. It is you too who have stirred up this strife among kinsmen. / The love-glare that shines from the eyes / of the fair bride is victorious. That love / is enthroned equally alongside / the great laws. For the unconquerable goddess / Aphrodite deceives her victims.

Loretz regarded it as striking that in spite of the thematic similarity, the Hebrew poet in his hymn (Loblied) to Love is silent about the Love-Goddess. This silence would not be so remarkable if it is the Goddess herself who thus speaks of her power.

7c,d. *all the wealth of his house.* LXX *ton panta bion autou,* "all his life," is most unlikely and unsupported by other versions. The phrase is found in vs. 31 in the following context, Prov 6:30–35:

Do they not despise a thief when he steals
  to satisfy his appetite when he is hungry?
If caught, he pays sevenfold, gives all the wealth of his house.
The adulterer lacks a mind; he who does it destroys himself.
Wounds and disgrace he gets and his dishonor will not be erased.
For jealousy poisons a man and he will not spare on the day of revenge.
No ransom will he accept, nor be appeased though you multiply bribes.

Wittekindt asserted that one can tell at first glance that the passage in Proverbs is later than that in Canticles from which it was borrowed and expanded in the manner of a midrash. Wittekindt eliminated the words "all" and "love" as additions to the text and "his house" as a gloss to "his wealth" (emending *hôn* to *hônô*) and related the resultant line, *Gäb* jemand sein Gut um sie, würde man ihn verspotten?, to the custom mentioned by Lucian in *De Dea Syra* that women prostituted themselves and donated the proceeds as offerings to the goddess. Budde surmised that the allusion may be to the custom of paying the purchase price for the bride. Harper regarded vss. 6–7 as the climax of the book and this declaration as the point toward which the author had been moving from the beginning of the book. This ethical conception of love, according to Harper, underlies all that goes before and thus the book should be thought of as a unity. The author had an ideal of love totally incompatible with the coarseness detected by those who regard the book as a collection of professional laudations of the sensuous side of marriage. This ideal, according to Harper, must have been an elevating influence of great importance for the moral life of a people for whom marriage was a mere matter of contract and the price given for the bride a subject of pride. Harper thus understood the preceding statement on the nature of love as leading immediately and inevitably to the condemnation of the common point of view (i.e. of marriage as purchase and contract) "in an arrow-like phrase, which having first transfixed the gorgeous and voluptuous Solomon, goes straight to the heart of the ordinary practice of the time." Thus Harper would make the Canticle a manifesto on marriage reform. Renan ascribed all of vs. 7 to "A Sage, who appears to draw a moral from the poem." "Great waters cannot quench love, rivers cannot extinguish it. If a man would seek to purchase love at the sacrifice of his whole substance, he would only reap confusion." Robert labeled only the last sentence as "Aphorisme d'un sage."

7d. It is not clear whether the antecedent of the masculine suffix was meant to be "a man" or "all the wealth of his house." *KJ, AT,* and *RSV* took the latter option and rendered "it," and so also *NEB:*

> if a man were to offer for love
> the whole wealth of his house,
> it would be utterly scorned.

JPSV and *NAB* took "a man" as the antecedent. Thus *NAB,*

> Were one to offer all he owns to purchase love, he would be roundly mocked.

Such a statement following the eloquent praise of the power of Love strikes one as an anticlimax. This, no doubt, was the consideration which led some translators to make the wealth rather than the man the object of scorn. Another expedient is to make the sentence interrogative. It is, of course, possible that the interrogative particle has been lost. A sentence can also be made interrogative by intonation, without an interrogative particle. P. Haupt rendered:

> Hang me close to thy heart like a signet,
> on thy hand, like a ring (do thou wear me!)
> For Love as Death is strong,
> and Passion as Sheol unyielding.
> Its flames are flames of fire,
> its flashes are flashes of lightning.
> Nothing is able to quench it,
> neither can any streams drown it.
> If one should resign for it all his possessions,
> could any man therefore contemn him?

No matter what one does with this last sentence, it is impossible to arrange it in any semblance of poetic symmetry, whether taken as a one, two, or three cola. O. Loretz (1971, 49) divided it into three unequal parts of eight, sixteen, and ten consonants. The syllable count would be more meaningful and it turns out to be exactly half the number of consonants for each line. The lack of symmetry or parallelism is patent:

> If one should give
> All the wealth of his house for love,
> One would only despise him.

The imbalance cannot be remedied, and the line must be pronounced prosaic and suspect.

7. The Targum interpreted the verse thus:

> Said the Lord of the World to His people, the House of Israel: "Though all the peoples, being likened to the waters of the Great Sea, were to gather themselves, they could not quench My love for you. And if all the kings of the earth were to join together, likened to the waters of a river flowing mightily, they could not sweep you from the world. And if a man gave all the wealth of his house to buy wisdom in the Exile, I would restore it to him double in the world to come. And all the spoil taken from the camp of Gog would be his."

Midrash Rabbah, like the Targum, equated the many waters with the nations of the world, citing Isa 17:12. The unquenchable love was similarly identified as God's love for Israel (Mal 1:2). The floods were seen as the other nations (Isa 7:20, 8:7). The treasure for which one might well give all his wealth was the Torah, and several illustrations of devotion to the Torah were given.

The usual patristic interpretation agreed with the Targum in identifying the many waters as those who persecuted the Saints and sought to separate them from the love of God. The Saints of the Old Covenant, the Patriarchs, Moses, Joshua, Samuel, David, Elijah, Daniel and his three companions were recalled. The miracle of the fire that did not burn (Dan 3:27) was seen as analogous to the waters that fail to quench; cf. Isa 43:2; Ps 69:1,2. The unquenchable fire reminded Cardinal Hugo of the "Greek Fire," a mixture of sulphur, naphtha, and quicklime which was ignited rather than quenched by water. The "Greek Fire" could be extinguished only by vinegar and from this Cardinal Hugo drew the lesson from Christ's refusal of the vinegar put to His lips (Matt 27:34), that temptation and suffering cannot hurt love, but the vinegar of hatred can quench it.

The last sentence of the verse was taken as self-explanatory by Cassiodorus, since there are no riches to be compared with love. Thus Paul gave up all worldly possessions, and counted them as refuse, in order to gain Christ; Phil 3:8. The LXX reading "they will contemn him with contempt" suggested to Theodoret the reward of those who are fools for Christ's sake; cf. I Cor 4:9–13. Philo of Carpasia pointed to Christ who gave up everything for love, was despised, mocked, spat on, scourged, and crucified. (Cf. Littledale.)

Herder (1778) opined, "I would almost close the book with the divine seal. It is even as good as closed, for what follows appears only as an appended echo." Delitzsch cited several "Fragmentists" of the nineteenth century who similarly cut off the remaining verses as not original, but he saw in vss. 8–14 "the continuation of the love story practically idealized and set forth in dramatic figures" which he made the second Scene of the fifth Act.

For after the poet has set before us the loving pair as they wander arm in arm through the green pasture-land between Jezreel and Sunem till they reach the environs of the parental home, which reminds them of the commencement of their love relations, he cannot represent them as there turning back, but must present to us still a glimpse of what transpired on the occasion of their visit there. After that first Act of the concluding scene, there is yet wanting a second to which the first points.

5b–7. Robert in his "critique littéraire" of this passage affirmed that it forms an ensemble which represents the conclusion of the book. He would begin the passage with 5b, "Sous le pommier je t'ai reveillée," connecting 5a with what precedes rather than what follows. The view that 5b is an isolated fragment (Bickell, Budde, Siegfried, Zapletal) Robert rejected, agreeing with Harper who saw in this passage a return to the thought of the antecedent context. Robert rejected the traditional vocalization of the MT which makes the Bride the speaker. It would be astonishing, Robert averred, that the conclusion of the book having such striking lyrical quality would not have been more lofty (n'eut pas plus d'envolée) and that the last word of the Shulamite would have been simply to solicit the fidelity and protection of her husband. On the contrary one understands the propriety and lofty import of this conclusion if it is the Husband who speaks, if he is identified with Yahweh and if the pressing exhortation which he formulates is a simple echo of the classical theme of prophetic preaching. A moment before, with allusion to Ezekiel 16, the incessant prevarications of the Bride were delicately recalled, according to Robert, and it is thus natural that in conformity with the views of that same chapter (vss. 60–63) our author envisages for the end of time the reestablishment of an intimacy which nothing can break, and that his prophecy takes the form of an exhortation addressed to the unfaithful one which pure divine pity has restored to her first state.

It is a test of the validity of Robert's preconceived hypothesis and his exegetical method that at the conclusion he is forced to go against the sense of the received text and alter it to suit his theory.

8a. *Our sister is young*. Or, "We have a little sister," with *KJ, RSV, JPSV, NEB*.

8b. If one renders 8a "We have a little sister," then it is better to make 8b a relative clause, "who has no breasts." *JPSV* rendered "Whose breasts are not yet formed." For a similar relative construction, cf. Job 19:12. The verecund may be assured by Delitzsch's Victorian affirmation that the description "she has no breasts" has neither in itself nor particularly for Oriental feeling anything indecent in it. The absence of breasts means, of course, that the damsel is allegedly not yet nubile. This allegation she pointedly contradicts in 10b.

8d. *bespoken*. The expression *lĕḏabbēr bĕ-* has different meanings according to context. It may denote disapproval and hostility, "to speak against," as in Num 12:1, 21:5,7; Ps 50:20. Tur-Sinai (II, 368) interpreted the clause *šeyyĕḏubbar-bāh* here as meaning "when incantations are pronounced upon her" (cf. Gordis, 32n120). The brothers would thus take measures to protect little sister. One may think also of malicious gossip and recall the "hillbilly" ditty in which the brothers' concern for sister's reputation dictates drastic action, "Smack her down agin, Pa . . . We don't want the neighbors talkin' 'bout our kin . . ." The expression is also used in the Bible for proposal of marriage (I Sam 25:39): "And David sent and spoke for (*wayḏabbēr bĕ-*) Abigail to take her to himself as wife." Brothers played a major role in the sister's courtship and marriage (Gen 24:29,50,55,60), and in the protection of her chastity (Gen 34:6–17; II Sam 13:20,32). Courtship and marriage was a family affair even among the gods, as seen in the Ugaritic hymn on the marriage of the two lunar deities (24[77].32–37):

Then Moon (*yrḫ*) betrothed Great Lady (*nkl*).
Her father set the scale standard,
Her mother the scale trays;
Her brothers arranged the balances,
Her sisters the scale weights.

8. The Targum made this verse a colloquy of the Angels:

> At that time, the Angels of Heaven shall say to each other, "We have one people on earth and her merits are manifest, but kings and potentates she has none to go forth and wage war against the camp of Gog. What shall we do for our sister in the day when the peoples speak of going up against her for war?"

Midrash Rabbah explained the little sister in two ways. Rabbi Azariah identified her with Israel. The princes (i.e. the guardian angels) of the nations will accuse Israel before the Holy One of idolatry, lewdness and bloodshed. And the Holy One will respond, "We have a little sister": as a child is not reproved because he is a child, so Israel may be defiled by iniquities throughout the year. But the Day of Atonement comes and atones for them (Lev 16:30).

Rabbi Berechiah applied the verse to Abraham, citing Ezek 33:24. A wordplay was made on the word *'āḥôt,* "sister," and the verb *'ḥy,* "unite, sew." It was Abraham who stitched together all mankind (cf. Midrash Genesis Rabbah 39:3). The reference to absence of breasts was applied to Abraham as a child who occupied himself with religious observances and good deeds even before he was obligated to do so. To Rabbi Johanan, however, the little sister suggested Sodom (Ezek 16:46). The little sister was also equated with the small number of exiles who returned from Babylon. The undeveloped breasts, the wall and the door, similarly evoked a variety of interpretations.

The Church Fathers were not in accord with regard to the identity of the speaker of this verse. The Greeks generally attributed it to the Bride and the Latins to the Bridegroom. Ambrose ascribed the words to the daughters of Jerusalem and Theodoret to the Saints of the Old Testament. The reference to breasts, or rather the lack of breasts, was applied to the immaturity and imperfection of the Church, or the individual soul, as yet incapable of producing progeny or supplying milk to babes. The undeveloped little sister was seen as a figure of the Gentile Church in its lowly beginnings, or as the Synagogue converted at last, but newborn through Baptism and thus the younger sister of the Church. Nevertheless, she is Christ's sister by descent from Abraham and will come eventually into her full glory. Again, the breastless little sister suggested the neophyte believer to be fed with the milk of faith, but as yet uninstructed in the two Testaments or the two great precepts of the Gospel.

The question of what could be done for the little sister was applied to the vexed relations of the Church and Synagogue. The ambiguity of the expression "the day she will be spoken to/for/against" allowed for considerable latitude of interpretation; it was applied to the interrogation of the Church by Nero and her persecutors and to God's addressing the Church or the faithful soul, whether through secret inspiration or open preaching. Gregory the Great applied the day of speaking to the Pentecost experience. On these and further elaborations. (Cf. Littledale.)

9a,c. *a wall . . . a door.* The question here is whether the parallelism is synonymous or antithetical. A wall protects, preserves, and repels. A girl like a wall is thus inaccessible and impregnable. A door (*deleṯ*) serves the dual function of opening a wall and closing the opening (*peṯaḥ*), for entering or barring entrance (cf. Gen 19:6; I Kings 6:31; II Kings 4:4, 6:32; Judg 3:23–25; II Sam 13:17–18; Prov 26:14). A girl like a door may be either closed or open, all the time or part of the time. Thus the exegesis of this verse is divided by the door, as open or closed. Tur-Sinai (1950, 351–388) argued that wall and door are here in synonymous parallelism and that no contrast is intended, and cited in support of this view an Akkadian incantation:

If he is a door, I will open thy mouth,
If he is a bar, I will open thy tongue.

Gordis (32*f*,97*f*) agreed with Tur-Sinai on the synonymous parallelism of wall and door and cited Ezek 38:11 where "wall" and "gate" are parallel with reference to defense, or the lack thereof. Robert likewise opposed the open door view as suggesting a person easy to seduce and took the door as a protective obstacle. The matter is moot. Whether the damsel as a door is open or closed, it is the relatives' concern to keep her closed until the proper time for opening. Protection of the virginity of a daughter or sister is a general familial concern. Parental worry on this score is no recent development, as witness Ben Sira's admonition (Sir 26:10,12):

Keep watch over a headstrong daughter,
For if allowed liberty, she will abuse it.
. . .
Like a thirsty wayfarer who opens his mouth
And drinks any water that is near,
She will squat before every tent peg,
And open her quiver to the arrow.

9b. *buttress.* LXX *epalxeis,* Vulgate *propugnacula,* Syriac *'elyān.* The term *ṭîrāh* apparently designated primitively a row of stones used to mark off a nomadic encampment; cf. Gen 25:16; Num 31:10; Ps 69:26[25E]; Ezek 25:4; cf. C. M. Doughty, I, 261. In Ezek 46:23 the terms *ṭûr* and *ṭîrāh* are applied to rows of masonry and in I Kings 6:36, 7:12 the term *ṭûr* is used of courses of stone and cedar beams in the Temple walls. The purpose of the building is to bolster the defenses of her chastity. The preposition *'al* thus has here its basic meaning "on, upon," and not the adversative sense, "against."

9b,d. *silver buttress . . . cedar board.* Some critics would delete *kesep̄,* "silver," on metrical grounds. The parallelism, however, favors its retention. Ginsburg suggested that the "silver turret" here mentioned refers to the prized silver horn worn in various ways by Levantine women; a married woman affixed it to the right side of her head, a widow to the left, and a virgin to the crown of her head. In a passage in which all the traits are symbolic, the silver certainly has its meaning, as noted by Robert who supposed that it signifies not simply solidity, but also richness, a construction requiring considerable expenditure. Gordis opined that the cedar board is not a punishment for unchastity, but like the *ṭîrāh* is a figure drawn from military operations connected with a siege. The use of "cedar" and "silver," he suggested, may hint at the gifts with which the suitors hope to overcome her resistance. It seems more likely that the silver buttress and cedar board refer to formidable and valuable devices, real or imaginary, for protection of cherished virginity, a kind of chastity belt.

9d. *close her*. The Versions apparently connected the MT form *nāṣûr* with the root *ṣ(w)r* III in the sense "fashion," "shape," "sketch," LXX *diagrapsōmen,* Vulgate *compingamus,* Targum *diktîḇā'*. More likely the proper relation is to *ṣ(w)r* I, "block," "enclose," "besiege," which is frequently used with the preposition *'al* of shutting up a city by siege. Gordis rendered "We will besiege her with boards of cedar." It seems better to translate *nāṣûr 'ālēyhā,* "we will close over her," in this instance as "we will close her (up)."

cedar. This wood was especially prized for strength and durability (cf. II Sam 7:2,7; I Kings 10:27; Isa 9:9[10E]; Jer 22:14–15). In the Ugaritic myth relating the building of Baal's splendiferous palace on Mount Ṣapān, the structure is termed "Cedar House," *bt arzm* (4[51].5.72), and the material is fetched from the Lebanon and Anti-Lebanon mountains. Lebanon and its trees, Siryon (and) its choicest cedars (4[51].6.18–21) are mentioned as well as silver, gold, and lapis lazuli (4[51].5.93–97), as the materials for the building.

board. The term *lûaḥ* is used of flat surfaces, tablets of stone (Exod 24:12), metal plates (I Kings 7:36), and planks of wood (Exod 27:8, 38:7; Ezek 27:5). Winckler (1906, III, 238–240) understood the term to refer here to a siege machine. Graetz rendered *mit einer Schranke,* "with a bar." The manifest meaning here is simply board(s) or planks, whether one reads the word as singular with MT, or as plural with some of the versions.

8–9. Critics are by no means unanimous as to the speaker(s) and the import of these lines. Delitzsch, after criticism of other views, asserted that it is Shulamite who here speaks. Thus the "sister" in question would have to be a younger member of her family. The common view has been that the speakers are the angry brothers of 1:6 who gave their sister the onerous assignment of vineyard keeping. The brothers speak or the Shulamite recalls their speech. This, according to Haupt, is what the brothers used to say when their sister was still an immature little girl. Joüon and Ricciotti identified the sister as Israel and the speakers as the other nations. Robert rejected this hypothesis as gratuitous and impossible to justify and proposed instead that the little sister is the Holy City, deemed little not because of her youth but because of the exiguity of her territory and resources; cf. Ezek 16:46,61, 23:4. The lack of breasts, accordingly, means that the city was without fortification.

Harper felt that 8–14 is one of the sections which weigh heavily in favor of the view that the Song is a series of dramatic lyrics rather than a connected drama in which it would be difficult to find a place for such a scene. Harper found, in Tennyson's "Maud," what he regarded as an almost exact analogy for the present passage, a group of separate but connected poems which the author himself termed a melodrama. In Part VII Maud's son, the hero of the poem, reports prenatal concern about his marital prospects in case he turned out to be a girl rather than a boy:

Men were drinking together,
Drinking and talking of me,
"Well, if it prove a girl, the boy
Will have plenty, so let it be."

Among the new fragments of "Divine Love Lyrics" reconsidered by W. G. Lambert (1975, 125), there is an exchange between the lovers which is similar to the present verse. The lady says:

As for me, my boy friend scares me,
As for me, my boy friend scares me:
(he says)
"I will lift you up like a wall, I will bring
you down like a ditch.
I will break you like a . . .
I will roll you over like a rotating harrow
from the shed . . [. .]
I will plaster you over like beauty . . .
[. ."]

The following lines convey the lady's retort addressed directly to her lover:

Come lord of beauty, I will . . [. . .]
Should you lift me up like a wall people
[will . . .] in my shade
Should you bring me down like [. . .]
Should you break me like . . [. . .]
Should you roll me over like . . [. . .]
Should you plaster me over like . . [. . .].

Unfortunately, the meaning of this badinage is unclear. The lady's statement that her lover scares her may be playful irony. At any rate, she is undaunted at the threats of rough treatment and appears to challenge him to do his worst, or best. In a Canaanite mythological fragment in Egyptian language recounting a sexual assault by Seth (i.e. Baal) on Anat, it is said that "Seth leapt her arse like the sacred ram of Amun" and that he copulated with her in fire and deflowered her with a chisel. This text has been called "The Rape of Anat by Seth" (cf. Albright, 1942, 197*f*), but there is no hint of resistance or displeasure on the part of the redoubtable Virgin and it is at least conceivable, in view of her violent nature, that she welcomed and reciprocated Seth's exceptional ardor.

9. The Targum applied this verse to Israel's devotion, to Israel's willingness to pay money to buy (the privilege of asserting) the unity of God's name:

> Then shall Michael, the chief of Israel, say: "If she is ready like a wall among the peoples and will give money to buy the Unity of the Name of the Lord of Worlds, then I and you will be with their Scribes surrounding them like scaffoldings of silver, and the nations will have no power to rule over her, as the serpent has no power to rule over silver. And even though she be poor in precepts, we will implore mercy on her behalf before YHWH and He will remember for her the merit of the Law which sucklings study, which is written upon the tablets of the heart and ready to oppose the nations like a cedar."

On the possible significance of this verse for the dating of the Targum, cf. Introduction, p. 94.

Midrash Rabbah treated this verse with the preceding, and at considerable length. Only a few samples may be noted here. The two verses were applied to Abraham and his pious deeds. Rabbi Yohanan referred the verses to Sodom and

Israel. Again the rabbis applied the verses to the exiles who returned from Babylon. The little sister refers to the returnees. The absence of breasts was related to five things lacking in the second Temple (fire from heaven, anointing oil, the ark, the holy spirit, and Urim-and-Thummim). "If she is a wall" was explained as meaning that if the Israelites had gone up from Babylon like a wall, the Temple would not have been destroyed a second time. "If she is a door, etc." was referred to the continuation of the three annual pilgrimages even after the Temple had been destroyed.

Early Christian commentators took the parallel clauses of this verse as synonymous rather than antithetical. The Bride of Christ, the Church or the individual soul, is both a wall and a door. The Church as a wall has twelve Apostolic gates affording the nations access to the City (Ambrose *Sermon 22* on Psalm 119). Christ is the door to salvation (John 10:9) and the Church also is a door. The cedar boards are to repel the heretic moths and worms. The door was also seen as representing the weaker converts who need fortification with the incorruptible timbers of the example of the Fathers, the broad boards of knowledge and love. Again as a door both opens and closes, members of the Church should know when to speak and when to shut the mouth. As the wall denotes firmness and durability, the door represents docility and obedience, admitting the Master of the house and His friends and excluding others.

Littledale observed that the notion that the two figures of wall and door are antithetical arose only in the seventeenth century and was adopted by most of the modern literalists; it is, however, according to Littledale, to be rejected on the very sufficient ground that the silver battlements and cedar panels answer to one another as costly decorations, and are not opposed in any way as rewards and punishments. Some interpreters saw in the preceding verse a discussion as to what should be done for the Blessed Virgin, in view of her vow of perpetual purity, when she shall be greeted by Gabriel. They saw here a pledge of those graces of shining and constant faith and incorruptible purity of body and soul of the one who was the temple through whose gate the King alone had passage.

10a. The little sister affirms her virginity with the symbolism of the impregnable wall.

10b. Far from being breastless, the maiden boasts towering *mammae*. The development of the breasts along with the appearance of the pubic hair are the signs of sexual maturity and readiness for marriage; cf. Ezek 16:7–8. In a short *balbale* song of Inanna, the companions of the goddess chant:

Lo, high[?] is our bosom,
Lo, hair has grown on our vulva,
At the lap of the bridegroom
let us rejoice . . .
(Kramer, *SMR*, 98)

10c. *Thus have I become*. The particle *'āz* usually has temporal reference, "then," but may also have logical sense, "thus," "therefore," or the like. The verb *hāyîṯî*, being in the perfect tense, has been taken to indicate past action, "then was I." The dramatic school of interpreters in particular stressed this view. Thus, according to Harper, the most obvious explanation is that the Shulammite explains her return to safety by saying:

"I have been, throughout, a wall and my breasts like towers, then was I in his (my oppressor's) eyes *as one finding peace"*: that is to say, he dealt with her as a king deals with a city he cannot capture, he made peace. This fits admirably with the view that the bride had been besieged by Solomon's attentions and that she had resisted them."

This type of interpretation Robert characterized as mistaken like its presuppositions and suggested a logical sense better suited to the context: if the city is provided with a wall and towers, it follows that she is secure. It is necessary then to give the verb present value, which is normal, the verb being stative here (Joüon 111:1). Robert is quite correct, apart from the concern about the city. As a stative *hāyîṯî* thus means "I have become and now am."

in his eyes. The suffix of *bĕ'ênāyw,* "in his eyes," has been troublesome since it has no antecedent anywhere in the vicinity. Some critics would emend to "your eyes," while others seize on the reading of LXX B, "their eyes," with reference to the brothers. For the dramatic and pastoral interpreters the suffix presents no problem, since it could be referred either to Solomon or to the shepherd lover. (Harper, after applying it to Solomon, offered the alternative: "If 'his' be taken to refer to the lover, then the meaning would be: 'When I had shewn my chastity and constancy, then I was in his eyes as one finding peace,' i.e. I was favoured in my lover's eyes.") Robert remarked that if it is proven (cf. *infra*) that vss. 8*ff* have no organic connection with the body of the book, then the suffix "his" can only point to Yahweh, which is the way Targum understood it, "in the eyes of her Lord."

10d. *As.* The particle *k,* according to Delitzsch, is here the *k veritatis,* i.e. the companion of the fact with its idea, or of the individual with the general and common. Robert rendered accordingly, "Aussi ai-je à Ses yeux vraiment trouvé la paix."

producing. The form *mwṣ't* may be construed either as the *Qal* participle of *mṣ'*, "find," or the *Hip̄'îl* (causative) of *yṣ'*, "go out," "one who brings forth, produces." Graetz rendered Friedensbotin, "messenger of peace," and in his note Friedensspenderin, "dispenser of peace." *RSV* rendered "one who brings peace," but with an alternative note: Or *finds*. Robert opted for *mṣ'*, "find," and commented that here, as often, the word has the nuance of happy accident (cf. 3:4, 5:8; Prov 1:28, 2:5, 3:13, 8:17,35).

peace. The pregnant term *šālôm* is here rendered in the usual way to emphasize the ambiguity. To catalogue variant interpretations of the expression *kĕmôṣē'ṯ šālôm* would be tedious and a few samples must suffice. Delitzsch regarded the expression "find peace in his eyes" as a variant of the common idiom "find favor (*ḥēn*) in his eyes," which is used especially of a woman gaining the affections of a man; cf. Deut 24:1; Jer 31:2*f;* Esther 2:17. (Delitzsch then proceeded to use this against those who regarded Solomon as the dirty old man attempting to seduce the chaste shepherdess, arguing that the expression must mean more than: "I brought it to this, that he left me further unmolested.") Joüon suspected here an allusion to the popular etymology of the name Jerusalem as City of Peace; cf. Ps 76:3[2E]. Gordis mentioned four possibilities, "as a fountain of well-being," "as one that has found peace," "as one to whom good fortune comes," and "as one finding grace or favor," and opted for the last. Among more recent renderings may be noted: "And under his eyes I have found true peace" (*JB*); "so in his eyes I am as one who brings contentment" (*NEB*); "So now in his eyes I have become one to be welcomed" (*NAB*). Winandy rendered "aussi suis-je à ses yeux comme ayant atteint l'âge adulte," in response to the attribution of immaturity in the preceding verses.

The nature of the peace produced or found by our lady has been variously interpreted. Delitzsch, in answer to the question why she should use here *šālôm,* instead of *ḥēn,* explained that it was in order to form a play on the name of Solomon, the man of rest and peace; cf. I Chron 22:9. That Shulamite had found *šālôm* with *Šĕlōmōh* (Solomon) Delitzsch insisted, cannot mean that uninjured she escaped from him, but rather that she had entered into a relationship with him which seemed to her a state of blessed peace. For Dussaud, her entry into the royal harem made her a source of happiness to her brothers. The "naturalist school" generally saw an opposition between the wall and the door of the preceding verse and carried this forward, so that the fortress which was for all others invincible now yields at the first assault of her true love: *šālôm* would thus be a synonym of surrender (as in Deut 20:11; Josh 11:19). Interpreters in the dramatic school made a great deal of this verse. Renan, for example, regarded it, along with 7:1, as the nub of the problem of the Canticle. According to Harper, as noted above, the peace here refers to Solomon's ceasing to besiege the city he could not capture. Joüon understood the lady as Jerusalem personified and the brothers as the benevolent Persians who wish her to rebuild so that she may have power and beauty in the day of her new alliance with her God. The spouse responds that her ramparts are already built and she has again become in the eyes of her beloved the city of peace. Ricciotti regarded vss. 8–10 and 11–12 as the logical sequence of vs. 7. The brothers were the idolatrous neighbors who showed hostility at the time of the rebuilding of the walls, but were overcome by Nehemiah. And now they offer again their help and suggest that it is not yet time for Israel to contract a spiritual marriage with God. But she replies that she is nubile and that Yahweh is the perfect spouse for her.

Robert, before trying to determine the meaning of vss. 8–10, averred that the first task is to ask whether they are authentic. He then offered four arguments for his negative conclusion that there is no intelligible connection with the antecedent context, that the personages introduced are not those of the Canticle, that the tone changes, and that the verses are either prose or defective in metre. Having admitted that the verses are a later addition composed in the genre of enigmas and not to be explained according to the themes of the Canticle, Robert attempted to find their historical background. After an extensive sketch of post-exilic Jewish history, Robert thought to have made vss. 8–10 and 11–13 intelligible. The brothers of Jerusalem are the Sadducees of the time of John Hyrcanus. The silver, Robert suggested, alludes to the three thousand talents which Hyrcanus robbed from the tomb of David. In vs. 10, Jerusalem personified protests that she has no need of human help for her security since she is under divine care. This appeal to blind confidence, in Robert's view, reflects the attitude of the Pharisees and their principal grievance against Hasmonean policy, in keeping with prophetic tradition (Isa 33:20–21, 37:35; Zech 2:9[5E], 9:8; cf. Psalms 20, 46, 48, 76:3–4[2–3E]).

The puzzling allusion to the production of peace by our lady recalls the episode in Ugaritic myth in which the Virgin Anat is requested to pour peace on earth. Cf. above, p. 600.

10. The Targum ascribed this verse to Israel:

> The Assembly of Israel answered and said: "I am mighty in the words of the Law like a wall and my children are strong as a tower. And in that time the Assembly of Israel will be finding favor in the eyes of her Lord and earth's inhabitants will be seeking her welfare."

R. Johanan (TB Pesahim 67a) explained the wall as meaning the Torah and the breasts as scholars. Raba, however, took the walls as the Community of Israel and the breasts as the synagogues and houses of study. Resh Laqish agreed with the exposition of Raba (TB Baba Bathra 7b–8a).

Christian interpreters took the little sister as the Gentile Church, or the Synagogue newly converted, or the elect soul, who says, *I am a wall* because I am founded on the sure Rock and cemented with the mortar of divine love, built up with living and select stones, the Saints of God. My breasts are like towers because I can nourish others with spiritual instruction and defend them. The wall of the Church was seen also as the Manhood of Christ and the towering breasts as the Apostles whose teachings are the weapons of Christian warfare. This verse has also been applied to various classes of Saints, and especially to Virgins whom Jerome advised when assailed by temptation to take these words upon their lips. Honorious saw here the Church Triumphant, built as the dwelling for God, chosen to repair the tower of Heavenly Jerusalem, built up by Christ. The breasts are the Church's Doctors who yield the milk of instruction. The Peace is Christ, the Prince of Peace. (Cf. Littledale.)

11a. The wording, except for the name, is the same as Isa 5:1, *kerem hāyāh lĕ . . .* , "A vineyard was to my beloved/to Solomon." The style is narrative, like the beginning of the Book of Job, "A man there was." Vulgate, instead of the name Solomon, gave the etymological interpretation *pacifico,* and similarly in the following verse.

11a,c. *vineyard.* Cf. 1:6 on *kerem,* "vineyard," and vineyard keeping. Haupt understood the vineyard to allude to a large harem, such as attributed to Solomon in I Kings 11:3.

11b. *Baal Hamon.* The name *ba'al hāmôn* means "Lord of a crowd" and Vulgate interpreted it thus, *quae habet populos,* rather than as a proper name. LXX offers variant spellings, *Beetlamōn, Beellamōn, Beelamōn.* Syriac ignored the problematic name and read *wĕ'inbēh saggī',* "and its fruit (was) plentiful," as in Dan 4:9[5:12E]. No place by this name is otherwise mentioned in the Hebrew Bible, but in Judith 8:3 it is noted that the heroine's husband succumbed to sunstroke in Bethulia and was buried "between Dothaim and Balamōn." There is a Tell Bel'ame about a mile south of Jenin (cf. F. M. Abel, *Géographie de la Palestine,* 1938, II, 357) which would fit the locale of the burial of Judith's husband, Manasseh, but whether this was also the site of Solomon's vineyard is uncertain.

Graetz proposed emendation of *hāmôn* to *ḥermôn,* Baal Hermon being mentioned in I Chron 5:23. Haupt suggested that we should perhaps read Baal-*ḥammôn,* designating an especially sunny and fruitfull hill (cf. Isa 5:1) which was sacred to the sun god Baal-ḥammôn; cf. *ḥammā,* "sun," 6:10; Isa 24:23, 30:26; Job 30:28. The deity Baal-ḥammon is mentioned in numerous Carthaginian votive inscriptions. There is evidence of a deity *ḫammān, ḫammôn* at Alalaḫ, Nuzi, and Ugarit; cf. C. H. Gordon, *UT* 19.971, *ḫmn.* A town *Ḥammôn* is listed in Josh 19:28 and another in I Chron 6:61(76E). According to Haller, Baal Hamon is simply an imaginative creation of the poet. Buzy similarly took it as a "nom de māchāl," in imitation of Baal Ḥaṣor. Gordis also suggested that it may be an imaginary locale, created to express the meaning "master of wealth" and cited Isa 60:5; Ps 37:16; Eccles 5:9[10E]; I Chron 29:16 for *hāmôn* in the sense of "wealth." Robert regarded it as more likely that the words *ba'al hāmôn* had meaning, as taken by Aquila, Symmachus, Jerome, and the Syro-hexaplar which render the phrase in the sense of "possessor of a crowd." According to Robert the country in question, dubbed "la populeuse" because of the great number of its inhabitants, is not Jerusalem, and above all not the Jerusalem of the future, as Joüon supposed (cf. Isa 19:20–21, 54:2), but the entire country of Palestine regarded as the vineyard of Yahweh (as in Ps 80:9–12[8–11E]); it is the Palestine of another time, however, since the verb *hāyāh* in effect sets us in the past. The historical situation supposed by Robert is again the conflict between the Sadducees and Pharisees in the time of John Hyrcanus, represented here under the name of Solomon.

The suggestion that the reading should be *ḥammôn* rather than *hāmôn* seems a likely solution although not for the reasons offered by Haupt. A place named *Ḥammôn* mentioned in Josh 19:28 is apparently the same locale mentioned in the Ma'ṣub inscription (*KAI* 19), lines 3 and 4, in the phrases *'l ḥmn* "god of Ḥammon," and *b'l ḥmn* which has been taken to mean "citizens of Ḥammon." These citizens of Ḥammon dedicated a portico (*'rpt*) "to Aštart in the shrine of the god of Ḥammon (*l'štrt b'šrt 'l ḥmn*). The sanctuary in question is apparently that located in the southwest part of the ruins of Umm el-'Awāmid in the Wādi Ḥamūl south of Tyre. The existence of a shrine of Aštart at Ḥammon and the association of Aštart with the motif of vineyard guarding in a Ugaritic text (2001.2.1) suggest that the vineyard guarding mentioned here and in 1:6 are allusions to an ancient myth or ritual related to the shrine of ʻAštart at Ḥammôn.

A recently published inscription from Palmyra (cf. M. Gawilkowski, 1971) mentions the god Bel-Ḥammôn and the goddess Manawat in connection with a (sacral) marriage. The text inscribed on a small limestone altar reads:

lbryk šmh lʻlmʼ	To the one whose name is blessed forever
ʻbd blḥmwn wmnwt	Bel-Ḥammôn and Manawat made
mn kys ʻtʻqb br	from the purse of ʻAteʻaqab son of
ḥyrn bgmws byrḥ	Ḥairan at the marriage in the month of
sywn šnt 4	Siwan, year 4
39	39 (June A.D. 128)

The term *gmws* here is the Greek *gamos* transliterated. Gawilkowski read *gmwt* and felt it necessary to assume omission of the possessive suffix: *bgmwt* (*hwn*), "lors de leur gamos" (p. 409). Harald Ingholt, however, pointed out to the writer that the troublesome letter is *s* rather than *t* and thus the supposed difficulty vanishes. The divine couple Belḥammôn and Manawat occurs in other inscriptions and each had a temple at Palmyra (cf. Gawilkowski, 409n3). This inscription calls attention to a troublesome formula in another inscription, *lbl blḥmwn wmnwt,* "to Bel Belḥammôn and Manawat," where Gawilkowski finds it difficult to understand the omission of a *w* before *blhmwn* if it is a matter of two distinct gods, Bel and Belḥammôn. This recalls the enigmatic *Bebellahamon* which occurs in a Latin inscription and which Starcky had translated as "Bel et Belḥammôn," but which du Mesnil du Buisson (1962, 199; cf. Gawilkowski, 412n1) took to be a corruption of Bel Belḥammôn. Gawilkowski assumed the identity of Bel and Belḥammôn. "Les adorateurs de Belḥammôn invitent donc au temple de celui-ci, à un banquet en l'honneur de Bel; l'identité des deux semble être la meillieure explication de cette démarche." There is yet another possibility which from the grammatical viewpoint seems simplest and most obvious, that Baal-Ḥammôn is a place name.

11–12. Commentators have devoted a great deal of attention to the agronomy and economy of this tenant farming and sharecropping arrangement. Delitzsch, for example, took pains to explain that the keepers have to pay a rent, not in fruits but in money, as the equivalent of a share in the produce. Isa 7:23 mentions a plot of a thousand vines valued at a thousand silver pieces, from which Delitzsch deduced that the vineyard here was also divided into portions with a definite number of vines in each plot. From the ratio of the numbers 1000 and 200 Delitzsch computed a 20 per cent average annual profit for the keepers. Gordis noted that in Talmudic times, a tenant farmer tilling a field received a half, a third, or a fourth of the crops as his share (TB Baba Bathra 110a; Gittin 74b), while here the keepers get only a fifth or a sixth (two hundred out of one thousand, or out of twelve hundred) for their labor. Conditions in pre-exilic Palestine, Gordis suggested, may have differed from those in Talmudic Babylonia, or, as seems more likely, farmers would receive a greater percentage because their work was harder than tending or guarding a vineyard.

Robert summarized several contradictory views and observed that the way out of the impasse is simply to recognize, once more, that the passage is allegorical: if the vine is Palestine, and if the "keepers" are the royal functionaries, it is not unlikely that each paid the royal treasury a thousand sheqels a year. Robert explained the vineyard as the land of Palestine, called Baal Hamon because of the plenitude of its population, with allusion to I Kings 4:20. The keepers are the Sadducean functionaries, evoking memory of the dozen officials mentioned in I Kings 4:7–19 and called in I Kings 10:15b "governors of the land." The "vineyard" Wittekindt understood as the hierodules, or sacred prostitutes, in the sanctuary of Baal Hamon (or *ḥermôn,* as related to *ḫarimtu,* "hierodule," or *ḫam(m)on* as the name of the fertility deity). The "keepers" were the eunuchs who supervised the hierodules. And the "silver" brought for the "fruit" was the payment for participation in the sacred rites, according to Wittekindt. The plain statement that a man would bring for the vineyard's "fruit" a thousand silver (pieces) is very suggestive in view of the recognized sense of vineyard as a metaphor for the female sexual partner. Solomon's financial skill may well have combined devotion to fertility worship and the need for revenue in a happy scheme of sacrificial support for church and state.

11. The Targum applied this verse and the following to Solomon's reign and the subsequent division of the kingdom:

> A people came up by lot of the Lord of the world with whom is peace. She is likened to a vineyard. He settled her in Jerusalem and delivered her to the rule of the kings of the House of David that they might guard her as a tenant guards his vineyard. And after the death of Solomon, King of Israel, she was left in the hand of Rehoboam, his son. Jeroboam son of Nebat came and divided the kingdom with him and led away from his hands ten tribes, according to the word of the mouth of Ahijah from Shiloh, who was a great man.

Midrash Rabbah identified the vineyard as Israel, on the basis of Isa 5:7. It was also applied to the Sanhedrin because that too was arranged in rows. Baal-Hamon was so named because the people thronged (*hāmû*) after Baal. The giving over of the vineyard to keepers was referred to the Captivity by Nebuchadnezzar. The mention of a thousand (pieces) of silver evoked the thousand craftsmen and smiths mentioned in II Kings 24:16. The remainder of the midrash on this verse loses sight of the starting point and goes off in a maze of discussions about armies, angels, embroidery (with stubby fingers), bloody flux, etc.

This verse afforded its share of edifying allegory to Christian expositors. The vineyard is the Church planted by the Peaceful King in Baal-hamon, the multitude of the nations. The keepers to whom the vineyard is given are the Apostles and Doctors who keep it with vigilance to prevent multiform sects from dividing and wasting it with diverse opinions. The thousand pieces of silver were understood as the saving fullness of God's law and commandments, or the payment given by the Lord as reward to the faithful laborers at the end of their toil, the perfect gift of wisdom and love. The man who spends his goods for the poor and leaves all that he has in order to obtain the fruit of the heavenly vineyard, brings a thousand pieces of silver for it; cf. Matt 13:44. The vineyard which has people (*quae habet populos*) is the whole Church which unites all nations, or, as some of the Fathers understood it on the basis of Isa 5:7, the Synagogue alone, "The vineyard of the Lord of Hosts is the House of Israel, and the men of Judah his pleasant plantation." If we neglect His vineyard, its stone wall will be broken down (Prov 24:31) and the plot that once had a thousand vines worth a thousand pieces of silver will be briars and thorns (Isa 7:23). Then we will be debtors, unable to pay the rent, and the Owner will be angry and will destroy the miscreants and turn the vineyard over to other keepers (Matt 21:33,41). (Cf. Littledale.)

12a. *My own vineyard.* The phrase *karmî šellî* is the same as in 1:6. In classical Hebrew a construction like this one would indicate emphasis on the preceding personal pronoun, but in neo-Hebrew the usage has lost all emphatic nuance. Joüon denied any emphasis or contrast here and was alleged to be in error by Robert who also declared equally mistaken those who saw a contrast between two vineyards, that of Solomon in vs. 11, and that of the person speaking in vs. 12. It could be, Robert suggested, that there are two persons in competition for the same vineyard.

before me. Commentators generally take *lĕp̄ānay* here as meaning "at my disposal"; cf. Gen 13:9, 20:15, 24:51, 34:10, 47:6; I Sam 16:16. Harper explained that the meaning here is "still in my possession, neither given away nor sold, and sufficiently guarded by me." Haupt translated and interpreted thus:

> In my sole charge is my vineyard, / nought else on earth do I care for.

The term "before me" he elucidated with reference to Prov 4:3 (*rak̲ wĕyāḥîd̲ lip̄nê 'immî,* "tender and unique to my mother"). The second hemistich Haupt restored conjecturally from Ps 73:25, on the assumption that some similar statement once stood in the text and was suppressed because "an orthodox Jew would have considered the application of this passage to a bride a blasphemy." *RSV* rendered, "My vineyard, my very own, is for myself"; *JB,* "But I look after my own vineyard myself"; *JPSV,* "I have my very own vineyard"; *NEB,* "But my vineyard is mine to give"; *NAB,* "My vineyard is at my own disposal." The vineyard in question can scarcely be any other than that of the Lady of the Canticle, the same mentioned as unguarded in 1:6. The crucial question here is whether the speaker is the bride or the groom. If the groom speaks, declaring dominion over his spouse's body, it is classic male chauvinism. If the female here asserts autonomy, this verse becomes the golden text for women's liberation.

12b. It is generally assumed that "the thousand," *hā'elep̄,* refers to the thousand silver (sheqels) just mentioned in the preceding verse. This is favored by the reference to "two hundred for the keepers of its fruit" in 12c, presumably in payment for their work. The mention of a thousand in connection with "vineyard," a metaphor for woman as a sex object to be cultivated, suggests that the number may also refer to members of Solomon's harem who were associated with him in the worship of Astarte, I Kings 11:3–10.

11–12. The meaning of these verses was taken in typically differing ways by commentators of the various schools. Graetz understood that Solomon wished to reserve the vineyard for himself and levied a heavy fine on poachers. But no matter how honest the guards, they could always be bought off if the price were high enough. This says openly; if only I have enough money, I can plunder your vineyard, Solomon, as often as I wish, in spite of your prepossession for it, and in spite of the guards you have set over it. Thus the Shulamite means to say, "Virtue must, and can, protect itself" (Die Tugend muss sich selbst beschützen—und vermag es auch). Delitzsch interpreted the vineyard as the totality of Shulamite's personal and mental endowments which she was free to dispose of, just as Solomon was free to dispose of his vineyard at Baal-Ḥammon; even so, she had freely and joyfully given herself to Solomon's possession. The keepers of the vineyard are Shulamite's brothers who, as protectors of her innocence, merit reward. Thus Shulamite makes the case of the vineyard in Baal Hamon a parable of her relation to Solomon on the one hand, and to her brothers on the other. From the figure two hundred, in relation to one thousand, Delitzsch deduced that the brothers were two in number, since each would get a tithe for the faithful rendering of the intact sum. For l'école naturaliste, as Robert termed it, the groom compares and contrasts his bride to Solomon's sizable harem. Wittekindt, representing the cultic school, took the name of Solomon to represent a fertility deity and the vineyard as the god's harem, the hierodules of the sanctuary. The keepers are the priests of the sanctuary who look after the fruit of the vineyard. The dramatic school saw in these verses the final triumph of the Shulamite who escaped from Solomon's clutches.

Among modern allegorists, Joüon found in these verses the principal idea of the poem. The vineyard represents the Kingdom of God on earth. The keepers are the Israelites who had previously not done their duty (cf. 1:6), but now propose to guard the vineyard zealously, so that Solomon (i.e. Yahweh) will have his due and the harvest will be abundant. Ricciotti regarded these verses as a parable on 8:7b. The historical Solomon, famed for his wealth, is mentioned to match the value of the love of Yahweh and also to warn against the perils of immorality and idolatry which were Solomon's downfall. Buzy anticipated Robert in judging these enigmatic verses as totally foreign to the general conception of the Canticle. Buzy saw here a little parable about a faithful attendant who assumed responsibility for a vineyard, conscientiously carried out his task, paid his annual dues to Solomon, and paid his workers a fair wage.

Robert regarded vss. 11–12, like 8–10, as an epigram appended to the Canticle by a Pharisee of the time of John Hyrcanus. The context is the same in both instances, but easier to identify in the latter. John Hyrcanus is compared to Solomon because of his policy of political aggrandizement, extravagance, and pretensions to royal dignity. The vineyard is the land of Palestine, called Baal Hamon by allusion to I Kings 4:20. The keepers are Sadducean bureaucrats, evoking reminiscence of the functionaries mentioned in I Kings 4:7–19 and in 10:15. Thus, in Robert's view, John Hyrcanus as pseudo-Solomon had pretensions to profit from this vast domain, but this in the eyes of faith was regarded as usurpation, since the owner is God. Robert saw God as speaking in vs. 12, asserting his inalienable rights and affirming that he does not need guards to protect his property. There is, in Robert's view, perfect unity of thought between the two epigrams. The second criticizes the bureaucracy (fonctionnarisme) as the first blames the excess of caution at the rebuilding of the walls. Both are human calculations which violate the principle of theocracy, injure God, and are perfectly useless, because the solicitude of the divine omnipotence suffices for the protection of the chosen people; cf. Ps 127:1.

12. The Targum referred this verse to the rupture of the kingdom after Solomon's death:

> When Solomon, King of Israel, heard the prophecy of Ahijah who was from Shiloh, he wished to kill him. But Ahijah fled from Solomon and went to Egypt. At that very moment it was told to Solomon through prophecy that he would rule over the ten tribes all his days, but after his death Jeroboam son of Nebat would rule over them, and two tribes, Judah and Benjamin, Rehoboam son of Solomon would rule.

Midrash Rabbah related a parable of Rabbi Hiyya applying this verse to the destruction of the Temple and the exile to Babylon as punishment for Israel's idolatry. The reference to the numbers one thousand and two hundred suggested connections with I Chron 12:33,38[32,34E] which mention two hundred chiefs of Issachar and a thousand commanders of Naphtali, with application to the rewards for learning Torah.

The vineyard, according to Theodoret, is the same which of old "I had not kept" (1:6), but has now been restored to me along with the thousand pieces of silver which I brought Him, because His only reason for requiring the fruit was His desire for my salvation. Cornelius à Lapide understood this vineyard to be distinct from that in Baal-Hamon which belonged to Solomon. The former vineyard typified the Synagogue, but this one is the Church. A new dispensation obtains now because the Church is permitted a share in the management of the vineyard not granted in the older dispensation which was bound by an immutable code received from the Lord of the vineyard. It is *mine,* according to Cocceius, not only because of its freedom from any owner but Christ, but also because the Communion of Saints is so perfect that each soul can claim all that the entire body possesses; every grace, blessing, promise, intercession, or thanksgiving ever made by one member of the Church belongs to all, and the aggregate which the whole Church enjoys is also the property of each single partner in that great firm, both in this world and the next.

The Latin Fathers generally assigned these words to the Bridegroom as response to a remark of the Bride that He had let out His vineyard to keepers; cf. Littledale for extensive samples. The Vulgate rendering *pacifici* for Solomon called forth a variety of interpretations. Vulgate *mille tui pacifici* is ambiguous, depending on whether *pacifici* is construed as genitive singular, "A thousand are of Thee, of the Peaceful One," or as nominative plural, "Thy peaceful ones are a thousand." The latter expedient was common among Western interpreters, with a variety of results: Thy peaceful Saints are a thousand; Thy peaceful ones shall have a thousand; They who are a thousand are Thine, O Peaceful One; A thousand fruits shall be Thine, O Peaceful One. (Cf. Littledale.)

13a. *You who dwell.* The versions are not in agreement as to the gender and number of the participle. MT *hayyôše̱be̱ṯ* is feminine singular with the article functioning as the vocative LXX *ho kaṯēmenos* offers the masculine singular, perhaps influenced by 5:1 and 6:2 which present the male protagonist as going to the garden. Syriac reads the masculine plural collective, *'aylēn děyāṯěḇīn,* "those who dwell"; Vulgate, *Quae habitas.*

in gardens. There is no need to emend the plural form *baggannîm,* "in the gardens," to singular, *baggan.* The plural may be regarded as the plural of extension of indetermination (Joüon, 136). Cf. 4:12, 5:1 where the bride is represented as a garden; 7:12–13 where she invites her lover to accompany her to the field and vineyard; and 6:2 where the lover goes down to his garden. In 2:14 the bride is pictured as a dove ensconced in a cliff cleft. If, for any compelling reason, the garden must be taken as a singular, specific garden, the *y* could be discounted as a *mater* introduced because of failure to recognize the final *-m* as the old enclitic, emphatic particle, or as the old case ending preserved before the enclitic *-m.*

13b. *Companions.* LXX A *heteroi* apparently read *'ăḥērîm* instead of MT *ḥăḇērîm.* Syriac omits the word, and so also Haller on metrical grounds. Wittekindt, only as a very daring hypothesis, proposed instead of "companions" to read "thy sorceries" (Deine Zaubersprüche), as in Isa 47:9,12 *ḥăḇārayiḵ,* with reference to Ishtar and the oracles in her shrines (Plessis, 258). Horst altered the noun *ḥăḇērîm* to the adjective *maḥămaddîm,* "desirable," to modify the gardens. Graetz read *ḥăḇēray,* "my companions," omitting the final *-m* as dittography from the first letter of the following word, and Harper opined that Graetz was probably right since the absence of an article with *ḥăḇērîm* is anomalous. Graetz's suggestion could be reinforced now that the enclitic *-m,* as used in Ugaritic, is recognized as occurring also in biblical poetry. The "companions" of the male protagonist are mentioned by the female in 1:7. Robert noted that the word *ḥāḇēr* is used in Ps 119:63 as a title for those who share the same zeal for the Law.

This was the post-biblical term for a member of a religious or charitable association, especially of those zealous for the observance of levitical laws. The term, however, could apply to any sort of association and the masculine form *ḥāḇēr ṭôḇ,* "a good friend," is even used as a euphemism for a woman of questionable virtue in TB Sabbath 63a. The term *ḥbr* is used in Phoenician, Punic, Palmyrene, and Nabatean inscriptions as a designation of members of cultic associations (cf. *DISO,* 82). A neo-Punic inscription (*KAI,* 159:5) juxtaposes the terms *ḥbr* and *mrzḥ* (on the latter term, cf. pp. (214–221), *wḥbrnm hmrzḥ,* "and their colleagues (belonging to) the Sodality." The term *ḥbr* is also used in Ugaritic in two very interesting texts dealing with ritual eating and drinking among the gods. In text 6.6[62.2]. 42–52, after a graphic description of Anat's mourning for her dead brother-consort, Mighty Baal, his burial with a series of sacrifices of seventy large animals, we have an apostrophe to an unidentified participant in the funeral feast:

ap ltlḥm [l]ḥm trmmt	You shall eat the [f]ood of oblation,
ltšt yn tġẓyt	You shall drink the wine of petition;
špš rpim tḥtk	Shapsh will rule(?) the Shades,
špš tḥtk ilnym	Shapsh will rule the Manes.
'dk ilm	Your colleagues (will be) the Gods,
hn mtm 'dk	Lo, the Dead (will be) your colleagues.
kṯrm ḥbrk	Koshar (will be) your companion,
wḫss d'tk	And Hasis your acquaintance.
bym arš wtnn	On the day of mourning and wailing
kṯr w ḫss yd	Koshar-and-Hasis will invite(?),
ytr kṯr wḫss	Koshar-and-Hasis will cheer(?).

Philological notes will be omitted as unnecessary for the Ugaritologist and Semitist and disconcerting to others. Suffice it to stress here the repeated references to sacrificial eating and drinking, the Shades (*Rephaim*) and Manes (*ilnym*), the Gods (*ilm*) and the (deified) Dead and especially the versatile Koshar, master of music and song, as well as of other arts and crafts, as associates, colleagues, and companions in the celebration.

The other passage (UG 5.2.1.1–9) which uses the term *ḥbr* with reference to participants in a divine banquet also mentions the artist and artisan-god Koshar in connection with music, song, and dance:

[. . .]*n yšt rpu mlk 'lm*	[Then] drank Rpu, King Eternal,
wyšt [ ] *gṯr wyqr*	Drank [ ], Strong and Noble,
il yṯb b 'ṯtrt	The god who dwells in Ashtarot.
il ṯpṭ bhdr'y	The god who rules in Edrei,
dyšr wyḏmr	He who sings and chants
bknr wṯlb	To the lyre and flute(?),
btp wmṣltm	To the tympanum and cymbals,
bmrqdm dšn	With castanets of ivory,
bḥbr kṯr ṭbm	With the goodly companions of Koshar.

The identity of Rpu King Eternal is disputed and need not be discussed here. Argument for connection with the cult of the dead will be offered elsewhere. The text ends with a benediction binding the future fortune of the city to the god, invoking his strength, power, might, paternal care, and glory in the midst of Ugarit for the days of the Sun and Moon and the pleasant years of El. The liturgical appendix to the Lord's prayer comes to mind at once.

are attentive. Some critics emend the participle *maqšîḇîm* to the imperative feminine singular with the first common singular object suffix, *haqšîḇînî,* to match the form *hašmî'înî,* "make me hear," of the following line. The masoretic punctuation connects *maqšîḇîm* with the following word *lĕqôlēḵ,* "are attentive to your voice," and so LXX took it, *hetairoi proseechontes tē phonē sou*. Vulgate however, separated the words, *amici auscultant: fac me audire vocem tuam*.

13c. *Make me hear*. Graetz and Budde read the suffix as *-nû,* "us," rather than *nî,* "me," to agree with the plural antecedent, *hăḇērîm,* "companions." It does not change the sense appreciably whether one reads "companions are listening for your voice; make me/us hear it," or "companions are listening, make me/us hear your voice." In any case, the speaker has to be included among the companions who are attentive for the voice of the lady who dwells in the garden.

The explications proposed for this verse are, as Robert remarked, scarcely more satisfying than the textual corrections. The same, unfortunately, applies to Robert's explication. A few samples will more than suffice to show the validity of Robert's appraisal. The address, "O thou at home in the gardens," denoted for Delitzsch that these gardens are Shulamite's home as a fundamental feature of her nature. The companions are not Solomon's, for she has come to the gardens with Solomon alone, leaning on his arm. The companions are the childhood playmates of the former shepherdess and vineyard keeper who listen for her dear voice which was wont to cheer their hearts and which they have not heard for a long time. The voice they wish to hear is her singing rather than merely her speaking, as deduced from 2:14. According to Harper, the bridegroom (the shepherd swain) here calls upon the Shulamite to let his companions, i.e. his friends who have come to congratulate him on his bride's safe return (from durance vile in Solomon's harem), hear her voice. Wittekindt saw here allusion to Ishtar and the solicitation of oracles from her. For Joüon the bride in the garden (in the Second Temple) invites the groom (the Messiah) to join her there. The companions are the angels, as in 1:7, who transmit to the Groom the desire of his beloved. Ricciotti related the voice of the bride here to the liturgical chants of the Temple. Gerleman opined that the companions here are probably the rivals for the favor of the maiden, who with her swain listen to her voice.

Robert admitted that it is incontestable that the present verse is inspired by images of the Canticle, even if it does not refer explicitly to 2:14. Nevertheless, Robert regarded this as no reason to attribute the verse to the author of the Canticle or to find here a prolongation of the situation described in the authentic poems. He saw it rather as a reflection or isolated prayer. If the LXX reading is correct, the prayer would be addressed to Yahweh who dwells in the gardens (4:16, 5:1), i.e. in Palestine. If the MT reading as a feminine participle is authentic, as Robert inclined to believe, then the reference is to Wisdom which the redactor identifies with the Bride on the basis of

Sira 24 (cf. Wis 8:2) which text shows divine Wisdom as dwelling in Israel and compares her to the most beautiful and useful Palestinian vegetation. Wisdom, thus, according to Robert, is besought to let her voice be heard by the companions, i.e. in accordance with Ps 119:63, the group of those fervent for the Law and for Wisdom (cf. Ps 119:12,26,33 and Robert, 1939, 14–18). According to Robert, the one who composed this prayer appears to have distinguished himself from the group and solicits light for himself as if he had to communicate it to others. This is the classical attitude of the Scribe or Sage (cf. Prov 18:4; Sir 39:5–6, 50:27; Isa 50:4–5). The redactor of this verse is thus, in Robert's view, a Scribe who identifies the bride of the Canticle with divine Wisdom and prays her to make him able to instruct others, asserting that they are avid to hear her teachings.

13. The Targum made this verse a prophetic prayer of Solomon on behalf of the Nation:

> Said Solomon at the end of his prophecy: "The Lord of the World is ready to say to the Assembly of Israel at the end of days: You, O Assembly of Israel, are likened to a little garden among the nations, sitting in the House of Study with the colleagues of the Sanhedrin and the rest of the people who listen to the voice of the Head of the Academy and learn from his mouth words of the Law. Make me hear the sound of Your words at the time when You sit to acquit or convict and I will be agreeable to all you do."

Midrash Rabbah on this verse related a parable comparing God to a king who grew angry with his servants and threw them into prison. He then took all his officers and servants and went to listen to the song of praise which they were chanting. He said to them: "My children, raise your voices, so that the companions who are by you may hear." So although Israel is occupied with work for six days of the week, on the Sabbath they rise early and go to the synagogue and recite the *Shema'* and pass in front of the ark and read the Torah and a passage from the Prophets, and the Holy One (blessed be He) says: "My children, raise your voices so that the companions standing by may hear [the companions denoting the ministering angels] and take heed not to hate one another, nor wrangle, or shame one another, in order that the ministering angels may not say before Me: 'Sovereign of the Universe, the Law which you gave Israel is not practised by them, and there is enmity, jealousy, hatred and wrangling among them,' but you in fact are fulfilling it in peace."

Theodoret, following LXX, made the Bride address the Groom: "O my Bridegroom, Thou who restest in Thy spiritual and Thy visible creation, planted like gardens, with them that do Thy will, there are others besides us, who gaze unceasingly on Thee, because not drawn aside by the fetters of the body, namely the ranks of the Angels, altogether immaterial. But I, who am bound by this chain, am in dread of change, and therefore, eagerly looking for Thy second Advent, I beseech Thee, make me to hear that desirable voice, 'Come, ye blessed of My Father, inherit the Kingdom prepared for you.'" Cassiodorus, following Vulgate, made the Groom address the Bride, the Church: "O Church, *that dwellest in the gardens,* which art busied in cultivating the plants of holiness, *Cause Me to hear thy voice,* that is, preach the Gospel to all thou canst, declare the precepts of My law, and also the promise of heavenly rewards. And *the companions hear thee,* for the angelic spirits delight to listen to thy voice, they whom I made thy companions by the shedding of My own Blood, whom I have appointed as thy helpers and guardians against evil spirits. And those others thy companions, the spirits of the just, whom I have taken out of thy congregation to Myself in heaven, they hear thy voice also, for they delight in thy preaching and in the salvation of their brethren."

Others saw the gardens as the Holy Scriptures, or the churches and shrines of the Martyrs, or the Convents of ascetic life. The Holy Scripture, according to Cardinal Hugo, is divided into four gardens: the herbs being the literal sense; the apples moral interpretation; the nuts denoting the difficult, yet sweet lessons of allegory; the spices are anagogical interpretation, the foretaste of heavenly things. The Religious Life likewise was divided into four gardens, herbs, apples, nuts, and spices. The kitchen-garden and pot-herbs denote the temporal administration, a garden to be kept small; the apples are ready and cheerful obedience; the nuts, hard outside but sweet within, are the austerities of the rule; the spices are the joys of devout contemplation. The truly cloistered soul dwells in all these gardens. (For these and further allegories, cf. Littledale.)

14. With minor changes, *bĕraḥ,* "be swift," for *sōḇ,* "turn"; the addition of the conjunction *wĕ-,* "and," before *dĕmēh,* "be like"; and the change of *beṯer,* "cleavage," to *bĕśāmîm,* "spices," this verse is a doublet of 2:17. LXX retained *koilōmatōn* here as in 2:17 for *beṯer*. The reading *beṯer* is also presupposed by the Ethiopic (*bēṯel*).

14a. *Bolt.* The imperative *bĕraḥ* is ambiguous as reflected by the versions, both ancient and modern. LXX *pheuge,* Vulgate *fuge,* "flee." Syriac *'thpk,* "turn," reflects *sōb,* as in 2:17. Modern versions generally take *brḥ* in the sense of "be swift," e.g. *KJ* and *RSV* "Make haste"; *AT* "Hasten"; *JB* "Haste away"; *JPSV* "Hurry"; *NAB* "Be swift." Contrariwise *NEB* "Come into the open." The direction of the movement of the verb *brḥ* may be specified by means of prepositions, "from," "to," or "with" (*'aḥărê* in I Sam 22:20). Without a preposition the meaning may also be "flee from," as in Judg 9:21, or "flee to," as in I Sam 27:4. Robert insisted that the derivatives of *brḥ* leave no doubt as to the authentic sense of the verb as "flee," and he cited *mibraḥ* "fugitive" (Ezek 17:21) and *bārîaḥ* as applied to "le serpent fuyard" (Isa 27:1; Job 26:13). According to Robert the uses of *brḥ* never lose sight of the place which one leaves and it is inexact to pretend that *brḥ* means only to hasten (*se hâter*) and can indifferently denote motion which approaches or goes away. This assertion could apply to Job 9:25 where *brḥ* is parallel to *qll* in the sense of "be swift" ("My days go swifter than a sprinter//They speed (away) and see no good"), but it is difficult to see how it could apply to the noun *bĕrîaḥ,* "bolt," and the graphic description of the action of a bolt in Exod 36:33, "He made the middle bolt to bolt through the boards from end to end." This bolt action was perhaps in the minds of the *KJ* translators in rendering *nāḥāš bārîaḥ* in Isa 27:1 as "the piercing serpent."

The possibilities for sexual entendre and phallic imagery in the verb *brḥ* with reference to the motion of a bolt appear to have been appreciated only by Haupt who rendered "Bolt, O my dearest, like a buck or gazelles or a pricket on the mountains of spices." In a note Haupt suggested that *bĕraḥ* has a double meaning, like *zĕk̲ōr* in Eccles 12:1. "It means not only to go off like a bolt, to spring away suddenly, but it has also an erotic meaning (cf. our term 'male screw,' etc.)." Haupt suggested that it may be taken as a denominative verb derived from *bĕrîaḥ,* "door-bolt, bar," or from Aramaic *barḥā,* "he-goat, buck."

14. The abrupt ending of the Canticle posed difficulties for modern exegetes. Hitzig explained that since the poet wished to close he had to clear the stage (die Bühne zu leeren). Delitzsch saw the verse "Flee my beloved," etc., as the opening of Shulamite's song, requested by Solomon. "Flee," of course, means "flee to me." The words of the song thus invite Solomon to disport himself, i.e. to give in to frolicsome and aimless mirth on these spicy mountains. The aim of the poet was to conclude the pleasant song of love that has reached perfection and refinement with an absolutely pleasant word. Solomon and Shulamite are now married and her summons is unlimited. It reconciles itself neither with the strength of her love nor with the tenderness of the relation, according to Delitzsch, that she should with so cheerful a spirit give occasion to her husband to leave her alone for an indefinite time. Thus we have to suppose that as she sings "Flee, my beloved" she goes forth leaning on Solomon's arm out into the country. With this song breaking forth in the joy of love and life, the poet represents the loving couple as disappearing over the flowery hills, and at the same time the sweet charm of the Song of Songs, leaping gazelle-like from one fragrant scene to another, vanishes away.

In the dramatic scheme of Renan 8:8–14 constitutes the Epilogue following the final act (6:4 – 8:7) and the last two verses by themselves alone form a short scene, in itself clear but occasioning surprise in the position in which it is found. At vs. 13 Renan envisaged a young man, accompanied by youths from the village, at the end of a pavilion at the bottom of the garden. He calls to his well-beloved and asks her to let him hear her voice. The well-beloved responds in the final verse and begs the young man to listen. The young man is the lover of the Shulamite and the young people are his paranymphs, or village companions. The lovers are now mutually pledged (8:6) and preparations are made for the wedding. The whole village becomes interested in the doings of the shepherd. There is here, Renan suggested, some allusion to those usages still to be found in countries where ancient manners have been preserved and which consist in imposing upon the fiancés a series of April-fool quests and attempts at deception. The response in which the Shulamite engages her lover to take flight, in Renan's view, can only be accepted as a mere pleasantry. This verse he viewed as superimposed in 2:17, and the whole of 8:8–14 he saw as an appendix of only secondary importance which will probably come to be regarded as hardly forming any part of the poem and that it will be omitted in the majority of representations. Thus Renan analyzed the Canticle as consisting of five complete acts, plus an epilogue which could be detached and discarded at will.

Harper cited Oettli's view that the bridegroom requested the bride to exhibit her lovely voice and that she desired him to demonstrate his elastic gait. The object of the verse, however, in Harper's opinion, was simply to end the poem with a repetition of the Song she had previously sung on request in 2:17. Notice has already been taken of Haupt's understanding of this verse in connection with the meaning of the verb *brḥ*. Wittekindt interpreted the verse, like its doublet in 2:17, as one of the torrid wooing songs of the Hierodule, replete with erotic double-entendre. The lover Tammuz is shepherd, gardener, and hunter who springs over the hills (2:8) and like Enkidu in the Gilgamesh Epic consorts with the gazelles. The god, like the goddess, lives in the Lebanon mountains and there hunts all kinds of animals. The Hierodule here orders the hunter to behave like his hunted animals. As they cavort in their love-making, so should he now pass the night with her until the morning wind blows. Gazelles, hinds, and bucks, as sacred to Ishtar, play a role in love-magic; cf. Ebeling, 41, line 18; 47, line 6*f*. To this may now be added the striking examples from R. Biggs, 1967, 13,21,22,23,24,26,33). The spice mountains (Balsamberge), according to Wittekindt, like the variant *beṯer* in 2:17, have no cosmic sense but refer rather to the maidens' spice-perfumed charms, the *mons Veneris*. Joüon in keeping with his allegorical exegesis saw the spice mountains as the hill of the Temple. The bride, representing the nation, makes a final appeal to the Messiah, "Haste" (accours). Thus for Joüon the Canticle ends with the same cry as the Apocalypse. The same, however, can be said of a Sumerian sacred marriage song which after the rubric designating it as a *balbale* of Inanna, repeats the refrain: "Let him come, let him come, . . . pray [?] let him come" (*SMR*, 98, 152n30).

The great error of all these interpretations, according to Robert, is to connect this verse not only with the expressions, but also with the thought and plan of the Canticle. In reality vs. 14 is an addition which is not even connected with vs. 13 and comes from a different author. Robert, in agreement with Ricciotti, explained that the scribe added this verse with the mistaken notion that in vs. 13 the bride was invited to let her voice be heard and not understanding that the appeal could remain without response, he repeated here 2:17, which seemed to him to be the response to a similar appeal formulated in 2:14. The fact that 8:13 is inspired by 2:14 gave to that interpretation a semblance of reason, but in transcribing 2:17 the maladroit reader who took *sōḇ* as an invitation to flight replaced it with the clearer term *běraḥ* and in place of the enigmatic *beṯer,* he wrote *běšāmîm* under the influence of 4:6,16, 6:12.

Robert, in support of his understanding of 8:8–14, presented a brief tableau of literary criticism. Authors have commonly and mistakenly thought that these verses represent the authentic conclusion of the Canticle and have judged it as written in verse like the rest of the book. The violence which one is obliged to apply to the text in order to produce acceptable meter, according to Robert, should make one suspect that it is not written in verse, but in prose. Moreover, Robert thought to have demonstrated in his exegesis of this finale of the Canticle, that the personages set on the scene are not the brothers of 1:6, but rather some Sadducees; not the groom, but, in vs. 11, the historical Solomon and, in vs. 12, John Hyrcanus who offers himself as a second Solomon; and finally not the Shulamite, but Palestine. Thus, in Robert's view, vss. 8–12 are best explained by events of the reign of John Hyrcanus. In vss. 8–10, 11–12 we have two distinct epigrams, but of the same context. They were composed by a Pharisee in a veiled and sarcastic fashion to criticize the laicization of the sovereign as contrary to the classical principles of theocracy. Verses 8–10 blame the luxury of the precautions deployed in the reconstruction of the walls of Jerusalem after the campaign of Antiochus Sidetes VII (134 B.C.); vss. 11–12 attack the monarchical pretensions of the regime. Verses 13–14, in Robert's view, were added separately at a later period. Verse 13 is the prayer of a pious sage (*ḥāḵām*) who identified divine Wisdom with the Shulamite. Taking up the expressions of the Canticle, he asks to be instructed by her in order to be able in his turn to instruct those who are in communion of faith with him. The expressions used, borrowed from 2:14, gave the idea to a still later scribe to add 8:14 which reproduces 2:17 with maladroit modifications.

Over against Robert's view we may consider that of his Protestant compatriot Lys who sees this last song as "un *flash back* sur la situation au point de depart et en mise au point actuelle." Whatever be the response one gives to the problem of the structure of the Canticle, one cannot ignore the fact that, even if it is only an anthology in the view of the final redactor (unless one takes him for an imbecile) the Canticle does not end: "l'amour authentique est toujours quête l'un de l'autre, il est tension constante ver l'unité de celui qui est chére par excellence et de la compagne qui est unique (p. 308).

14. The Targum applied this final verse of the Canticle to the ultimate redemption of Israel:

> In that hour shall the Elders of the Assembly of Israel say: "Flee, my Beloved, Lord of the Universe, from this polluted earth, and let your Presence dwell in the high heavens. But in time of trouble, when we pray to you, be like a gazelle which sleeps with one eye closed and one eye open, or like a young antelope which as it runs away looks behind. So look on us and regard our pains and afflictions from the high heavens, until the time when you will be pleased with us and redeem us and bring us up to the mountain of Jerusalem and there the priests will offer up before you incense of spices."

Midrash Rabbah made wordplays on *ṣĕbî*, "gazelle," and *ṣāḇā'*, "army," *bĕśāmîm*, "spices," and *baššāmayim*, "in the heavens," and *dmy*, "resemble" but also "pray." After several plays and parables too involved to summarize here, it ends with a striking parable which compares the greatness (better, redemption) of Israel to harvest, wine gathering, spices, and childbirth. In each case, premature completion of the action spoils the product and the results are good only when carried out in the fullness of time; cf. Micah 5:2[3E] and Isa 60:22. So, with respect to Israel's redemption, even undeserved it will come in due time, but if merited, God will hasten it. Like the Christian Apocalypse, the Midrash on the Song of Songs ends with the prayer: "So may it be God's will speedily in our days, Amen."

Why the Bride, who all along had sought union with her beloved, should now exhort Him to flee, was explained by Christian interpreters in sundry ways. Because of Christ's words, "If I do not go away, the Comforter will not come to you," and "It is expedient for you that I go away" (John 16:7), the Primitive Church desired her Beloved to *flee away* in His Manhood that she might more clearly comprehend Him according to His Godhead. Or it may be the voice of humanity saying with Peter, "Depart from me for I am a sinful man, O Lord" (Luke 5:8); or with the Centurion. "Lord, I am not worthy that Thou shouldst come under my roof" (Matt 8:8). *Flee* from hard and sinful hearts, from the unbelieving Synagogue to the faithful Church, from Thine earthly kingdom to the heights of heaven, and draw us with Thee from the perishing world. The roe (Greek *dorkas,* "clear-eyed") suggested that the Bride asks her Beloved to flee but not to lose sight of her during her toils, that she may always be comforted with the thought of His ever-watchful eyes. The "mountains of spices" were seen by Lyranus as the mountains on which stands the Heavenly Jerusalem and whence incense of perpetual adoration ascends before the throne of God. Littledale concluded his commentary with eloquent quotations from Augustine, Lyranus, and the Apocalypse: "O truly blessed kingdom, free from death, having no end, where no seasons follow one another for ever and ever, where the perpetual day without night knows not time, where the victorious warrior, united with the tuneful choirs of Angels, sings to God unceasingly the Song of Songs of Sion, while the crown evermore encircles his ennobled brow." *Make haste, then, my Beloved,* for "the Spirit and the Bride say, Come. And let him that heareth say Come." And Thou, O dear and worshiped Lord, art not deaf to the call, "He who testifieth these things saith, Surely I come quickly; Amen. Even so, come, Lord Jesus."

INDEX OF AUTHORS

Abel, F. M. 687
Abravanel, Don Isaac 90, 110
Adam of St. Victor 584
Adeney, W. E. 35, 252
Aelianus 648
Ainsworth, Henry 128, 246, 672
Aistleitner, J. 575
Alain de Lille 124, 242
Albertus Magnus 642
Albright, W. F. 27, 51, 252, 298, 300, 398, 470, 492, 530, 568, 581, 599, 605, 606, 682
Alcuin of York 239
Alfonso di Liguori 175, 285
Altmann, A. (1967) 252, 633
Ambrose of Milan 120, 121, 185, 237, 302, 328, 345, 370, 416, 418, 490, 514, 565, 574, 643, 645, 672, 679, 683
Amiet, P. xv, 252, 503, 552, 590
von Ammon, C. F. 136, 251
Anacreon 513, 522, 625
Andrae, Tor 252, 315
Angelome of Luxeuil 122, 239
Angenieux, J. 45, 46, 253
Aponius 122, 124, 128, 238*f*, 336, 344, 370, 374, 383, 402, 461, 463, 567
Apuleius 314
Aristanetus 522
Arnold, Edwin 85, 86, 87, 253
Astour, M. 220, 253, 340, 341, 576
Athanasius 117, 563
Athenaeus 444
Augustine 120, 185, 227, 228, 237, 383, 463, 584, 701
Avalon (pseudonym of Sir John Woodroffe) 253, 317, 333, 353, 482, 490, 563, 622
Avigad, N. 56, 253

Balkan, K. 253, 398
Barr, J. 253, 445, 612
Barre, H. 253
Barth, K. 208, 253
Barton, G. A. 146, 253, 483
Baruch, I. L. 174, 253
St. Basil 307
Baudissin, W. 476
Bauer, Hans 253, 505
Bauer, Theo 150
Baumgartner, W. 398
Bea, A. 200, 201, 253, 320
Bede, the Venerable 238, 358, 423, 554, 634, 672
Ben Dor, I. 410
Bennett, James 135, 136
Ben-Yehudah, E. xvii, 254, 376, 630
Benz, Ernst 254, 309, 310
Bernard of Clairvaux 123, 124, 125, 185, 240, 307, 329, 336, 342, 344, 349, 358, 360, 393, 399, 407, 409, 417, 420, 463
Bertholet, A. 68, 254, 475, 476
Bettan, I. 41, 198, 254, 387
Bewer, Julius A. 25, 254
Bezold, C. 376
Bharati, Agehananda 192, 254, 383, 649
Bickell, G. W. H. 448, 567, 624, 670, 677
Biggs, R. D. xvii, 381, 386, 479, 699
Bishop, E. F. F. 254, 320, 329, 396
Blackman, A. M. 254, 459
Blank, S. H. 198, 254
Blochet, E. 254, 576
Blommerde, A.-C. M. 254, 474
Boardman, J. 223, 226
Bogaert, M. 254, 586
Böhl, F. M. Th. 255, 599
Boling, R. G. 51
Bossuet, J. B. 40, 129, 130, 141, 248
Boyd, Bernard 255, 351
Breasted, J. H. 255, 338
Brekelmans, D. H. W. 255, 518
Brightman, T. 90, 128, 247
Brotz, Howard 255, 309
Brown, J. P. 255, 348, 349, 488, 489, 491, 492, 505, 618, 620, 659
Browning, Robert 36
Buber, S. 159, 255, 314

Buchanan, B. 27, 255
Budde, K. 255, 495, 504, 510, 518, 527, 534, 541, 567, 595, 596, 597, 604, 615, 636, 639, 655, 666, 670, 675, 677, 695
du Buisson, de Mesnil 256, 688
Burns, Robert 462
Burrowes, George 141, 256
Burrows, M. 22, 256
Buzy, T. R. D. 45, 190, 256, 323, 326, 518, 520, 543, 544, 568, 586, 622, 657, 687, 691

Cabaniss, A. 256, 416
Calkins, Raymond 196, 256
Dom Calmet, 372, 378, 388, 389, 404, 421, 427, 466, 542, 543, 626
Cannon, W. W. 40, 144, 256, 504
Caro, Joseph 177
Cassiodorus 121, 302, 319, 418, 524, 566, 646, 652, 658, 677, 696
Castelli, D. 36, 157
Castellio, Sebastian 126, 127, 192
Catullus 490
Celine, L.-F. 205
Celsus 113
Chariton 523
Charles, R. H. xvii, 315
Cherburg, Lord Herbert of 311
Cheyne, T. K. 21, 36, 257, 558
Chrysologus 185
Chrysostom 92, 465
Civil, M. 70, 71, 257, 488, 590
Clarke, Adam G. 85, 257
Clement of Alexandria 671
Clericus 184
Clermont-Ganneau, C. S. 220, 257
Cocceius, Johannes 128, 129, 248, 411, 524, 542, 566, 672, 692
Columella 458
Conrad, D. 257, 670
Cooper, J. S. 71, 72, 257, 431, 496, 497
Copley, Frank O. 257, 522, 523
Cornelius à Lapide 118, 128, 185, 302, 372, 416, 486, 520, 573, 624, 692
Cowley, A. E. 385, 389, 431, 600, 639, 650, 655, 661
Crawford, C. F. S. xv, 257, 481
Crawley, A. E. 257, 297
Cross, F. M. 258, 611
Cumont, F. 258, 611
St. Cyprian 116
Cyril of Alexandria 121, 170

Dahood, M. J. 258, 298, 303, 305, 321, 322, 345, 381, 435, 436, 445, 457, 518, 575, 577, 604, 630, 640
Dales, George F. 258, 468, 483, 527, 622
Dalman, G. H. 56, 57, 144, 258, 337, 367, 395, 435, 466, 469, 490, 518, 520, 546, 549, 567, 568, 582
Daly, Mary 206, 258
Dante 124, 374
Davidson, Samuel 136, 258
Dawson, W. R. 73, 258
von Deines, H. 258, 339
Delcor, M. 110, 258, 517
Delitzsch, F. 35, 40, 110, 142, 259, 303, 322, 331, 341, 345, 351, 354, 358, 367, 368, 374, 378, 387, 391, 393, 396, 401, 402, 404, 409, 410, 415, 427, 435, 441, 458, 459, 461, 463, 465, 466, 468, 472, 473, 475, 492, 498, 504, 508, 521, 527, 536, 539, 541, 543, 544, 545, 546, 557, 558, 560, 563, 567, 569, 570, 573, 589, 595, 604, 615, 621, 622, 624, 626, 627, 629, 635, 638, 641, 645, 650, 655, 659, 661, 662, 663, 677, 678, 681, 684, 685, 688, 691, 695, 698
Delrio, Martin 124, 127
Dempsey, R. B. 195, 196, 197, 259
Denis the Carthusian 185
Dhorme, É. 259, 406, 491, 519
Van Dijk, J. J. A. 259*f*, 335, 439, 609, 610
Di Lella, A. 110, 259
Dionysius the Carthusian 125, 244, 302
Donne, John 649, 655
Döpke, J. C. C. 132, 259, 638
Dornseiff, F. 259, 598
Dothan, M. 410
Doughty, C. M. 259, 680
Driver, G. R. 259, 323, 331, 435, 445, 532
Driver, S. R. 35, 36
Dubarle, A. M. 199, 259
Durand-Lefèbvre, Marie 260, 312, 313, 314, 321

Durham, J. 129, 249
Dussaud, R. 260, 318, 323, 357, 387, 391, 408, 445, 466, 468, 469, 484, 518, 543, 546, 558, 560, 568, 605, 655, 685
Dyer, Jacob A. 309

Ebeling, E. 146, 260, 547, 599, 699
Edmonds, J. M. 260, 311, 403
Ehrlich, A. B. 395, 448, 458
Eisenstein, J. D. 260, 578
Eisler, R. 260, 577
Eissfeldt, O. 42, 218, 219, 220, 260
Eitan, I. 260, 607
Eleazar of Worms 578
Emerson 480
Edwardes, A. 260, 383, 407, 410, 620
See Masters, R. E. L.
Empedocles 113
Emerton, J. A. 20, 234
St. Ephrem 185
Epiphanius 118, 185, 379, 393, 566, 569, 660
Erbt, W. 145, 150, 260, 323, 596, 598
Erman, Adolf 260, 459, 540
Euripides 506
Eusebius 367, 598
Ewald, H. G. A. 35, 37, 136, 198, 261, 520, 639, 640, 645
Exum, J. C. 46, 50, 261

Falkenstein, A. 70, 153, 261, 657
Farnell, L. R. 271, 379
Feuillet, Andre 180, 181, 182, 261, 320, 347, 369, 405, 406, 415, 416, 504, 512, 625, 655
Finkelstein, J. J. 225, 226, 261, 461
Fisher, L. R. 75, 77, 261, 459, 512, 536
Fitzgerald, Robert 400
Fletcher, John 328–29
Florus 472
Forbes, R. J. 261, 352
Fraenkel, S. 262, 575
Francis, Ann 131
Frankfort, H. 211, 261, 481
Franklin, Ben 82
Frazer, J. G. 262, 340, 577
Freedman, D. 262, 481
Freehof, Solomon B. 133, 262, 510, 511
Freud 133
Friedrich, F. 136
Fulco, W. J. 262, 670

Gadd, C. J. 27, 262
Galen 575
von Gall, A. F. 262, 331
Galico, Elisha 110, 245
Gaster, T. H. 262, 305, 320, 380, 436, 604, 644, 649
Gawilkowski, M. 262, 688
Gay, John 399
Gebhardt, Carl 26, 36, 144, 262
Gelb, I. J. 84, 262
Gerardo, P. 188, 244
Gerleman, G. 262, 323, 324, 339, 353, 356, 357, 376, 385, 389, 410, 428, 429, 442, 445, 463, 470, 472, 532, 540, 546, 561, 588, 589, 635, 695
Gerson, John 125, 185
Gesenius, W. 262, 380, 385, 389, 431, 466, 600, 620, 638–39, 650, 655, 661
Gifford, E. S., Jr. 262, 356, 400, 649
Gilbert of Hayland 124, 242, 532
Gillebert 447
Ginsberg, H. L. 199, 263, 339, 623
Ginsburg, C. D. xviii, 24, 35, 40, 104, 105, 108, 109, 110, 111, 112, 116, 118, 127, 128, 129, 130, 131, 132, 136, 137, 138, 139, 140, 198, 205, 298, 301, 302, 303, 329, 331, 334, 338, 340, 347, 356, 361, 374, 375, 389, 404, 415, 424, 445, 448, 464, 466, 470, 475, 479, 481, 482, 508, 513, 567, 589, 595, 615, 625, 626, 635, 638, 647, 664, 670, 680
Ginzberg, L. 56, 263, 314, 339
Gleave, H. C. 20, 235
Glueck, N. 263, 580, 603
von Goethe, J. W. 41, 263
Goetze, A. 263, 324, 603
Goitein, S. D. 263, 560, 561
Goldin, J. 160, 263, 323, 336, 339
Goldziher, I. 599
Good, E. M. 264, 488
Good, Mason 85, 132
Goodenough, E. R. 214, 264, 646
Goodspeed, E. J. 264, 596, 597
Goodyear, W. H. xv, 264, 455, 470
Gordis, R. 25, 26, 41, 85, 199, 264, 300, 301, 304, 305, 319, 330, 332,

376, 387, 409, 448, 458, 465, 469, 488, 511, 532, 547, 564, 568, 586, 605, 636, 638, 639, 640, 643, 655, 678, 680, 681, 685, 687, 688
Gordon, C. H. xxi, 300, 338, 343, 360, 575, 687
Goshen-Gottstein, M. H. 55, 56, 264
Gottwald, N. K. 25, 264
Graetz, H. 19, 25, 26, 104, 105, 264, 304, 332, 351, 375, 408, 414, 418, 419, 421, 445, 457, 458, 464, 466, 471, 474, 475, 490, 520, 541, 544, 560, 579, 586, 615, 629, 639, 650, 662, 664, 681, 684, 687, 691, 693, 695
Graham, W. C. 151, 193, 264
Granqvist, Hilma 144, 264
Grapow, Hermann 73, 265
Graves, Robert 265, 313, 403
Greenfield, J. C. 265, 294, 399, 435, 460, 568, 605
Greengus, S. 265, 481
Gregory of Elvira 238
Gregory of Narek 239
Gregory Nazianzen 117
Gregory of Nyssa 118, 122, 185, 237, 302, 374, 447, 462, 469, 471, 539, 565, 569, 660
Gregory the Great 118, 121, 122, 125, 238, 346, 358, 383, 393, 440, 563, 604, 632, 638, 647, 650, 675, 677, 681, 683, 684, 685, 690, 693, 695, 699

Harris, Rendel 266, 648
Hartmann, M. 266, 328
Philip of Harveng 122, 241
Haupt, P. 41, 54, 216, 356, 391, 406, 408, 410, 424, 427, 442, 445, 457, 466, 468, 484, 490, 518, 541, 545, 546, 567, 568, 573, 586, 601, 620, 636, 646, 651, 662, 676, 681, 686, 687, 690, 698
Haymo of Halberstadt 122, 239
Hazan, A. 35, 267
Heimpel, W. 72, 267
Held, M. 78, 79, 80, 83, 267, 480, 657
Hengstenberg, E. W. 126, 141, 267, 300, 306, 457, 558, 638
Heraclitus 113
Herbert, George 574
Lord Herbert of Cherbourg 311
von Herder, J. G. 40, 90, 131, 132, 136, 144, 251, 404, 677
Hermann, A. 72, 73, 74, 267, 324, 657
Herodotus 223, 339
Herrmann, W. 69, 74, 267, 535, 577
Herxheimer, S. 112
Hesiod 348, 400
Hess, J. J. 267, 575
Hesychius 648
St. Hildred of Bingen 649
Hill, W. D. P. 267, 311, 403
Hippolytus 114, 115, 185, 236
Hirschberg, H. H. 267, 297, 378, 379, 381, 433, 445, 491, 492, 586, 605
Hirzel, L. 136, 267
Hitzig, F. 136, 267, 403, 508, 639, 650, 663, 698
Hölscher, G. 39, 267
Homer 47, 113, 114, 348, 359, 400, 406, 444, 603, 618, 633
Honeymann, A. M. 267, 467, 618
Honorius 122, 241, 411, 573, 638, 647
Horace 336, 640
Horst, F. 66, 67, 68, 69, 268, 448, 466, 468, 469, 517, 518, 520, 535, 549, 567, 624, 662, 670, 693
von Hug, Johann Leonhard 132, 268
Hugo of St. Cher 124, 307, 563, 567, 661, 665, 677, 697
Hugo of St. Victor 646
Hutton, J. 268, 608
Huxley, F. 268, 398

Ibn Janaḥ 304, 629
Ibn Tibbon 105, 106, 243
Immanuel ben Solomon 105, 106, 107, 108, 136, 243
Ingalls, D. H. H. 268, 403
Ingholt, H. 218, 268, 688
Insler, Stanley 87–89
Irimbert 122, 629
Isaac of Antioch 315
Isidore of Seville 122, 238, 578
Isserlin, B. S. J. 268, 467

Jacob, G. 66, 268
Jacobi, J. F./T. C. 35, 112, 136

Jameson, A. (Mrs. Murphy) 268, 313
Jastrow, M., Jr. 41, 56, 268, 356, 381, 382, 433, 443, 469, 586
Jaussen, A. J. 268, 656
Jayadeva 85, 87, 253
Jellinek, A. 269, 316, 578
Jerome 20, 114, 118, 119, 120, 121, 237, 336, 346, 354, 367, 431, 441, 476, 484, 490, 528, 581, 629, 687
Jochims, U. 269, 558
John of the Cross 185, 186, 188, 244
Jones, Wm. 86, 464
Josephus 18, 35, 91, 139, 155, 574, 625
Joüon, P. xix, 90, 179, 189, 269, 318, 323, 329, 337, 350, 372, 381, 382, 384, 385, 388, 389, 393, 401, 404, 408, 415, 417, 421, 427, 433, 434, 437, 441, 447, 470, 477, 491, 511, 520, 538, 542, 543, 544, 547, 557, 564, 566, 569, 580, 586, 587, 595, 600, 601, 619, 630, 632, 644, 646, 650, 656, 660, 662, 681, 684, 685, 687, 690, 691, 693, 695, 699
Justus of Urgel 121, 238, 567

Kaiser, G. P. C. 134, 269
Kakati, Bani Kanta 269, 481
Kalidasa 87, 88, 89
Kautzsch, E. 385, 389, 431, 600, 639, 650, 655, 661
Kavanaugh, K. 188, 245
Keith, A. B. 86, 269
Kessler, R. 47, 48, 49, 50, 51, 269
Kimchi, David 109, 220, 294, 380, 395, 457, 458, 618
Kimchi, Joseph 220
King, C. W. 269, 312
Klasens, A. 73, 269
Kleuker, J. F. 132, 294
Knudtzon, J. A. 286, 324
See Weber, D.
Knutson, F. B. 75, 77, 261, 450, 512, 536
Koehler, L. xix, 398
Kohler, K. 37, 270
Koldewey, R. 270, 399
Kopf, L. 270, 618
Kramer, S. N. 69, 77, 78, 152, 153, 270, 304, 324, 325, 333, 334, 335, 359, 361, 362, 371, 372, 373, 377, 382, 384, 392, 414, 419, 422, 424, 425, 486, 491, 497, 499, 506, 507, 515, 516, 519, 555, 556, 562, 569, 590, 609, 683, 699
Krauss, S. 270, 435, 436
Krinetzki, L. 270, 300
Kronasser, H. 270, 317
Kugler, F. Z. 191, 271, 561, 573
Kuhn, Gottfried 90, 110, 271, 295, 406, 429, 432, 466, 470, 539, 544, 598, 655, 659, 660
Kurgal, A. 214, 271
Kurtz, D. C. 223, 226, 271
Kutscher, E. Y. 218, 271

deLagarde, P. A. 354
Lambert, M. 271, 610
Lambert, W. G. 80, 81, 82, 83, 84, 271, 482, 483, 496, 682
Lambrecht, P. 153, 271
Lampronti 578
Landsberger, B. 271, 437, 601, 602, 610
Landsberger, Franz 42, 150, 271
Langdon, S. 146, 271
Laroche, E. 271, 317
LaSor, W. S. 271, 301
Lassen, Christian 86
Laurin, R. B. 193, 194, 195, 272, 465
Lawson, R. P. 115, 117, 236, 297
Leemans, W. F. 28, 272
Lefèvre, A. 182, 272
Lehrmann, S. M. 197, 272
Leiman, S. Z. ix, 578
LeLasseur, D. xvi, 161, 272
Leo XIII 201
Leo Hebraeus 110, 244
Leslau, W. 173, 272
Le Strange, Guy 272, 576
Levi, Abraham 110, 243
Lewy, J. 272, 435
Lichtenstädter, Ilse 272, 536
Lieberman, Saul 99
Littledale, R. F. xix, 116, 118, 121, 122, 123, 124, 125, 126, 127, 128, 297, 302, 307, 319, 321, 328, 329, 330, 346, 350, 352, 355, 358, 360, 363, 370, 371, 374, 378, 383, 385, 388, 390, 393, 394, 397, 399, 402, 404, 407, 411, 417, 418, 420, 423, 431, 434, 441, 443, 447, 451, 461,

463, 465, 469, 471, 473, 474, 478, 479, 484, 485, 488, 490, 493, 495, 498, 499, 500, 510, 514, 517, 520, 524, 527, 528, 530, 531, 532, 534, 538, 539, 546, 548, 550, 554, 557, 558, 563, 565, 566, 567, 569, 571, 574, 584, 592, 613, 617, 621, 624, 629, 631, 633, 635, 637, 638, 643, 646, 652, 658, 660, 661, 665, 666, 672, 677, 679, 683, 686, 690, 693, 697, 701
Loewe, R. 93, 95, 96, 97, 98, 99, 100, 111, 116, 121, 272
Longus 505
Loretz, O. 37, 39, 53, 273, 490, 491, 674, 676
Loring, Richard Tuttle 182, 183, 273
Löw, I. 273, 367, 574, 575, 576, 578, 579
Löwisohn, S. 35, 111, 273
Lowth, Robert 130, 131, 596
Lucas, Abbot of Mount St. Cornelius 122
Lucian 476, 629, 675
Lucretius 522, 638
Luis de la Puente (=De Ponte) 128, 244
Luther, Martin 125, 126, 244
Lys, Daniel 201, 202, 203, 204, 205, 273, 295, 700

Maclean, A. J. 227
Madden, Sister Mary Daniel 227, 228
Maimonides 105, 139, 157, 576
Malamat, A. 273, 379
Marmorstein, A. 159, 273, 578
Masters, R. E. L. 260, 383, 407
See Edwardes, A.
Matthews, H. J. 104, 109, 274
Maximus of Tyre 113, 660
May, H. G. 151, 193, 274, 672–73
Mazar, B. 274, 354
Meek, T. J. 21, 34, 37–39, 146, 147, 148, 149, 150, 151, 152, 153, 274, 354, 359, 362, 372, 373, 386, 394, 395, 404, 432, 433, 445, 458, 488, 527, 539, 582, 599, 648, 651, 655, 663
van der Meer, F. 223, 227, 228, 274
Meier, E. 136
Mendelssohn, Moses 111
Milik, J. T. 191, 192, 214, 218, 274, 579, 618
Miller, A. 274, 320, 350, 415, 445, 469, 541
Miller. J. L. 21, 274
Miller, P. D., Jr. 274, 667
Millet, Kate 209
Milton 35, 94
Minucius Felix 213, 214, 220
Modi, J. J. 213, 274
de Moor, J. C. 275, 459, 532, 629
Morgenstern, Julian 157, 275, 498
Moses de Leon 162, 165, 167
Moses of Cordovero 110, 169
Moses of Narbonne 159
Moulton, R. G. 36, 274
Movers, T. C. 275, 333
Murphy, Roland E. 25, 37, 44, 188, 189, 190, 191, 200, 201, 275
Murray, Gilbert 674
Musajoff, Solomon 99, 275

Napier, B. Davie 197, 275
Neil, James 276, 297
Neuschotz de Jassy, O. 145, 276, 311, 555, 599
Neusner, J. 94
Nicolaus de Argentina 125, 360, 397
Nicolaus of Lyra 124, 125, 128, 411, 592, 613, 701
Nigidius 185
Nilus 238, 315, 660
Sister Nivedita (Margaret E. Noble) 276, 608
Nöldeke, Theodor 276, 459, 607
Nygren, A. 276, 384

Obadiah Sforno 109
O'Brien, J. 674
Oesterley, W. O. E. 152, 276
Oettli, S. 276, 566, 573, 647, 699
Ohnefalsch-Richter, M. 276, 633
Origen 34, 35, 89, 94, 95, 96, 97, 98, 112, 114, 115, 116, 117, 118, 119, 121, 185, 236, 297, 302, 309, 310, 337, 342, 344, 346, 358, 360, 369, 383, 569, 662
van den Oudenrijn, M. A. 199, 276
Ovid 22, 523, 524, 625, 638

Parchon 109

Parente, Paschal P. 183, 184, 185, 186, 188
Parez, Jacob 125, 244, 526
Parker, B. 277, 399
Parrot, A. 277, 379
Patai, Raphael xx, 153, 154, 155, 156, 157, 158, 159, 160, 161, 162, 163, 164, 165, 166, 167, 169, 170, 171, 172, 173, 174, 175, 176, 177, 178
Paton, L. B. 221, 223, 277
Pausanias 313, 340, 348
Payne, H. 214, 277
Peek, W. 223, 277
Pelikan, J. 244
Perella, N. J. 277, 297
Perles, F. 277, 435, 466, 490
Peter Damiani 178, 240, 371
Philo of Alexandria 154, 155, 157, 158, 161, 162, 171, 172
Philo of Byblos 362, 476
Philo of Carpasia 118, 122, 237, 302, 443, 517, 520, 534, 537, 539, 545, 567, 569, 584, 637, 652, 660, 671, 672, 677
Phipps, W. E. 115, 123, 124, 277
Picard, C. 277, 314
Plessis, J. 277, 693
Pliny 314, 319, 354, 362, 493–94, 505, 577, 578, 629, 635, 648
Plutarch 348, 441, 524
Polybius 441, 494
Polychronius of Apamea 119
Pope, M. 33, 75, 76, 77, 98, 171, 210, 211, 277, 278, 330, 348, 350, 368, 386, 448, 479, 481, 491, 492, 512, 517, 536, 591, 607, 617, 618, 646, 657, 670, 673
Porten, B. 218, 220, 278, 316
Porter, J. R. 278, 505
Psellus, Michael 122, 374, 441, 471
von Puffendorff, S. 313, 251
Pusin, Max N. 133, 134

Rabin, Chaim 27–33, 278
Rabinowitz, I. 110, 278
Radet, C. 278, 314
Ralbag (Rabbi Levi ben Gershon) 108
Ramsaran, John A. 86, 278
Randolph, C. B. 278, 649
Ranke, Hermann 73, 278
Rashbam (R. Samuel ben Meir) 103, 241, 361, 395, 458, 466, 508, 626, 640
Rashi (Rabbi Solomon ben Isaac) 89, 102, 103, 109, 240, 305, 308, 331, 380, 395, 457, 458, 462, 464, 466, 469, 508, 535, 586, 592, 626, 640, 660
Reider, J. 278, 618
Reisman, D. 278, 438, 439
Renan, Ernest 35, 141, 278, 332, 338, 350, 387, 401, 429, 445, 542, 543, 569, 604, 662, 675, 685, 698
Ricciotti, Giuseppe 179, 279, 320, 384, 404, 415, 432, 433, 437, 442, 445, 477, 511, 543, 586, 662, 664, 681, 685, 691, 695, 699
Richard of St. Victor 122, 441, 487
Riessler, Paul 144, 145
Ringgren, H. 158, 279, 488, 633
Rivera, P. Alfonso 188, 189, 279
Robert, A. 44, 45, 90, 179, 180, 181, 182, 183, 278, 318, 320, 323, 327, 329, 331, 332, 333, 337, 338, 347, 350, 351, 357, 361, 369, 372, 374, 375, 381, 382, 384, 385, 387, 388, 389, 390, 392, 393, 396, 401, 404, 405, 406, 408, 409, 410, 411, 415, 417, 418, 421, 424, 428, 432, 433, 437, 441, 442, 443, 448, 449, 450, 464, 468, 469, 470, 473, 476, 477, 483, 488, 490, 494, 498, 504, 512, 520, 526, 527, 528, 529, 538, 540, 541, 544, 545, 546, 547, 556, 557, 559, 564, 566, 568, 569, 571, 580, 587, 595, 596, 599, 600, 601, 613, 614, 615, 617, 619, 620, 621, 624, 625, 626, 627, 629, 630, 636, 643, 644, 646, 647, 650, 651, 655, 656, 657, 659, 660, 661, 662, 664, 674, 676, 677, 678, 680, 681, 684, 685, 686, 687, 689, 690, 691, 692, 693, 695, 696, 697, 699, 700
Rosenmüller, E. F. K. 110, 279, 541, 638
Rosenthal, Franz 50, 279
Roth, R. 280, 348
Rothstein, J. W. 280, 318, 490, 520
Rowe, A. 280, 400

Rowley, H. H. xx, 36, 110, 112, 127, 129, 144, 149, 151, 192, 193, 280, 596, 597, 598, 600
Rudolph, W. 280, 561, 662
Rundgren, F. 280, 441
Rush, A. C. 214, 280

Saadia 17, 89, 101, 102, 239, 466
Sabar, Yona 280, 339
Sainte-Beuve, C. A. 625
Salfeld, S. 109, 280
Salonen, A. 82, 280, 522
Sanders, J. A. 110, 111, 280
Sarna, N. M. 281, 518
Sasson, J. M. 84, 85, 281, 602, 603
Schechter, S. 92, 160, 281
Schmidt, N. 41, 149, 150, 151, 281
Schmökel, H. 24, 25, 42, 43, 44, 281, 320, 322, 323, 361, 409, 415, 417, 419, 429, 457, 476, 554, 555, 573, 599, 629
Schneemelcher, W. 115, 281
Schoff, W. H. 148, 149, 281
Scholem, Gershon 99, 101, 153, 158, 159, 167, 281, 590, 644
Schott, S. 73, 281, 324, 464, 472, 666
Seerveld, Calvin 37, 282
Segal, M. H. 21, 23, 24, 42, 282
Segert, Stanislav 39, 40, 282
Shakespeare 406, 480, 572, 648, 649
Shuraydi, H. A. 282, 537
Siegfried, C. 282, 318, 323, 415, 424, 434, 494, 498, 508, 518, 527, 541, 564, 567, 573, 615, 620, 634, 677
Simon, M. 282, 339
Simpson, W. K. 56, 74, 282, 667
Skaist, A. 282, 481
Skehan, P. W. 26, 110, 282
Smith, J. M. P. 283, 670
Smith, J. P. 135
Smither, P. 283, 589
Snaith, N. H. 151, 152, 283
von Soden, W. 70, 78, 85, 283
Sophocles 674
Speiser, E. A. 283, 306, 481, 548, 591, 666
Spenser, Edmund 127
Stade, B. 143, 283
Staerk, W. 283, 391, 415, 457, 484, 520, 541, 636
Starcky, J. 688
Steindorff, G. 283, 338
Stephan, S. H. 57, 58, 59–65, 284, 308, 311, 329, 381, 480, 486, 488, 508, 509, 512, 558, 566, 572, 633, 641, 642, 649, 667
Stephens, F. J. 70
Strabo 224, 494, 626

Taoussi, A. 284, 587
Tarn, W. W. 284, 315
See Griffith, G. T.
Tate, J. 112, 284
Tennyson 356, 665, 667, 681
Teitelmann, Francis 125, 244
St. Teresa of Avila 185, 186, 187, 188, 189, 244
Tertullian 211, 213, 214, 220, 461
Theocritus 26, 36, 311, 336, 403, 462, 476, 486, 664
Theodore of Mopsuestia 90, 119, 126, 184, 192, 237
Theodoret of Cyrrhus 97, 98, 99, 100, 116, 120, 121, 238, 336, 360, 423, 478, 545, 548, 565, 617, 642, 652, 660, 665, 671, 677, 679, 692, 696
Thilo, M. 284, 433, 605
Thomas, D. W. 284, 668, 670
Thomas Aquinas 124, 558
Thomas of St. Victor 124
Thomas of Villanova 125
Thomson, W. M. 284, 320, 400, 576, 649
Tigay, J. 75, 76, 77, 512, 536
Tishby, J. 165, 284
Tobiah ben Eliezer 239, 314
Tournay, R. 44, 180, 181, 182, 285, 320, 347, 369, 415, 504, 587, 588, 625, 655, 657
Toutain, J. F. 285, 314
Toynbee, J. M. C. 224, 285
Trever, John 368
Trible, Phyllis 205, 206, 207, 208, 209, 210, 285
Tristram, H. B. 285, 400, 475
Tromp, N. J. 285, 417, 673, 674
Trotti, J. B. 70, 73, 285, 355
Tur-Sinai, N. H. 285, 305, 332, 379, 380, 469, 586, 678, 680

Ulanov, Barry 176, 285
Umbreit, F. W. K. 136, 285

Urbach, E. E. 92, 116, 117, 285, 336

de Vaux, R. 17, 286, 558
Vaccari, A. 286
Virgil 329
Virolleaud, C. 286, 611, 644
Vogel, E. K. 286, 354
de Vries, C. E. 286, 603

Waldman, N. M. 479, 565
Wasson, R. G. 286, 403
Waterman, Leroy 24, 40, 151, 194, 286, 347, 350
Weber, D. 286, 324
See Knudtzon, J. A.
Wellhausen, J. 287, 315, 320
Wesley, John 130, 251
Wetzstein, J. G. 56, 90, 142, 144, 287, 362, 424, 429, 433, 435, 564, 596, 604, 621, 657
Whiston, Wm. 129, 130, 192, 249
White, E. F. 287, 603
Whitney, W. D. 280, 348
Widengren, G. 287, 441
Wilcocks, Thomas 127, 246
William of St. Thierray 121, 241
Wilson, C. T. 287, 329
Winandy, J. 287, 685
Winckler, Hugo 145, 287, 320, 441, 560, 624, 626, 681
Witt, R. E. 287, 314, 577
Wittekindt, W. 24, 42, 151, 152, 287, 312, 323, 328, 340, 341, 343, 368, 374, 404, 406, 415, 445, 457, 469, 474, 484, 549, 554, 555, 556, 560, 561, 573, 577, 586, 599, 604, 633, 648, 650, 663, 670, 675, 689, 691, 693, 695, 699
Woodroffe, Sir John 317
See Avalon, A.

Xenophon 603

Yadin, Y. 56, 287, 340, 376, 390, 469
Yamauchi, E. M. 153, 288
Yeats, W. B. 480
Yepheth ben ʻAli 109, 239, 319
Young, E. J. 198, 288

Zapletal, V. 145, 288, 320, 357, 394, 396, 457, 468, 469, 474, 518, 520, 534, 573, 634, 663, 664, 677
Zimmern, H. 288, 380
Zunz, Leopold 112, 288

INDEX OF TOPICS

Abdulhamid 61
Adad 483
Adonis 149, 152–53, 362, 368, 475, 491, 555, 577, 663
Afqā 491–92
allegory 112
All Souls 226
aloes 28
Amenhotep II 339
Amminadab 587–92
Ammiṣaduqa 225
Amun 428
Anahita 167
Anat 34, 75, 77, 150, 160, 163, 165, 167–68, 170, 195, 211, 219–20, 293, 299, 302, 325, 340, 353, 358, 382, 416, 419–20, 425, 477, 480, 525, 536, 553, 563, 582, 600, 605–11, 623, 632, 636, 644, 648, 657–58, 668, 682, 686, 694
Anatyahu 157
aphrodisiacs 378, 380–83, 403, 609, 648
Aphrodite 313, 333, 399, 475, 648
Apollo 663
appetite 381
apple 381
apple tree 663
Aqht 75, 293, 480, 623, 632, 657
Aqiba 19, 21, 26, 92, 100, 159, 221, 306
Artemis 398, 400, 577, 663
Asherah 51, 163, 165, 293, 325, 386, 459, 508, 636, 644, 657
Ashtart 75, 315, 325–26, 334, 340, 380, 426, 632, 687–88
asseverative *k* 559
Astarte 149, 151, 157, 178, 211, 315, 335, 362, 368, 386, 610, 691
Atargatis 170, 302, 399, 477
Athena 562
Attis 153
Azazel 315–16

Baal 51, 75–77, 149, 153, 160, 163, 165, 168, 195, 218, 220, 299, 325–26, 340, 358, 380, 382, 386, 391, 415–16, 420, 424–25, 436, 444, 459, 486, 506, 525, 535, 548, 553, 580, 582, 600, 607, 648, 657, 658, 668, 673, 681–82, 694
Baal-Hadad 293, 302
Baal-ḥammon 687–88
Baal Peor 217, 220
banquet house 19
Bāveru (Babylon) 28
Bāveru Jātaku 27
Bhāgavata Purana 86
black 307–18
black beauty 311, 662
black Demeter 313, 340
black goddess 191
black Jews 308
black madonna 312–13
blood drinking 220, 559
bowel movement 217, 519–20; Plate VI
Britannia 562

cake mold 379; Plate I
Dr. Tewfik Canaan 381
camphor 353
change of sex 437–39
chariot 82, 552, 585, 590
Chemosh 314
Cherubim 154–58
Chester Beatty Love Songs 74
Chief River 673
cross chest bands 210, 277
cuneiform tarts 222, 378
cunnilingus 407
"The Curse of Agade" 610
Cybele festival 604
cypress (perfume) 353

Dagan 340
dancing 602*f*
Danel 298, 623
date palm 633
death 18, 210, 668

"Deliverance of Mankind from Destruction" 607
Demeter 313, 398
depatriarchalizing 205–10
Devi 163
Diana 314
Dionysus 398, 506, 577
"Divine Love Lyrics" 80, 682
dog 81, 211–15, 648
Donatists 228
dove 399, 538
Dumuzi 77, 152–53, 325, 333–35, 361–62, 371, 392, 414, 419, 422, 424, 429, 497, 507, 516, 554, 556
Dura 192

El 52, 75, 163, 165, 211, 218–19, 221, 223, 303, 325–26, 340, 372, 380, 386, 396, 419–20, 425, 492, 507–8, 553, 657
Emesal dialect 69
enallage 297
En Gedi 354
enclitic *m* 446, 641
Enkidu 699
Enlil 483, 590
"Enmerkar of Erech" 361
Essenes 145
Eve 17, 394
exclusus amator 522
eye power 482

Falashas 173
fellatio 225
female symbol 222
fertility worship 145
field work 324*f*
fig 398
foot 110, 381
form criticism 66
Fri(g)day 175

garden 488
Gautama Buddha 398
gazelle 386, 406*f*, 696–98; Figure *8*
Geers Law 389, 512
Gematria 297, 308
Geshtinanna 334–35
Gilgamesh 340, 462, 547–48, 583, 591, 615, 699
Gita-Govinda 85–86, 538

gods, dying and rising 153
gopīs 86
Göttertypen 535
groove 490*f*
Gula 211

Hamantaschen 222
"hand" 110, 517; Plate V
harp, lyre 294
Harrapan civilization 27
Harun ar-Rashid 61
hashish 382
Hathor 73, 603, 607
Hatshepsut 73
Heliopolis 73
henna 353
Hera 359, 663
herm(phalloid) 226
Heshbon 625
hole 518
Holy Spirit 159
honey 487
Horus 73
"Hymnal Prayer of Enheduanna" 562, 609
"Hymn to Ishtar" 69
"Hymn to Ninurta" 70
hyporchēma 602

Ibbu-Nikkal 583
Inanna 69, 71, 77, 153, 167, 170, 324, 333–35, 361–62, 371, 381–82, 414, 419, 421–22, 425, 431, 437–40, 477, 496, 506–7, 516, 527, 554–55, 562–63, 569, 602, 608, 610, 683, 699
"Inanna of Battle" 610
"Inanna's Descent to the Nether World" 152
incest 211, 655–57
India 29, 32
Indus valley 27
irtu-song 146, 150
Ishḫara 210
Ishtar 43, 67, 69, 71, 81, 84, 145, 147, 149, 151, 153, 170, 191, 219, 222, 302, 312, 314, 316–17, 335, 341, 343, 353, 372, 374, 380, 399, 419, 421, 426, 429, 437, 439, 462, 476–77, 483, 496, 527, 554–55, 561–63, 569, 573, 579, 582–83,

591, 599, 602, 605, 610, 615, 633, 695, 699
"Ishtar's Descent to the Nether World" 419
Isis 311, 313–14, 398, 599
ivory tower 624

Jewish-Christian dialogue 93–101
John Hyrcanus 686, 692, 700
Judith and Holofernes 55, 614

k veritatis 684
Kali 90, 163, 191, 317, 353, 481, 562–63, 607–10
Kali-Durga 170
Kawṯar 491
Keret 75, 631–32
kispu 225–26
kissing 276, 297, 638, 657
Koshar 391, 444
Krishna 33, 86–87
Kumārsambhava 87

Lady Hell 561
Lady of the Steppe 477
lamed auctoris 295
lapis lazuli 544
letter to mother 27, 70–72, 489, 496, 530, 546
lice 259, 331
Lilith 169–71, 174–75
lion 34
lotus eating 406–7, 455
love sickness 382
Lu-dingir-ra 70–72, 489, 496, 530, 546

the five M's 383
Malcolm X 308
Manawat 688
mandrake 647–51
Manes 694
Manhannaim Dance 143
Marduk 81, 429, 483
mare ruse 336–40, Figure *5*
marriage canopy (*ḥuppāh*) 435–36, 441
Mary, the Virgin 89–90, 122, 125, 162, 168, 170, 172–73, 175, 178, 185, 188–91, 312, 314, 321, 349, 352, 358, 379, 394, 563, 574, 582, 629, 635
marzēaḥ 216–21, 348
Matronit 163, 165, 167–71, 174, 177
Mayumas festival 218
Mehy 589
Melqart 475
meter 37
"missionary position" 402
monkey business 27
Moses 160, 169, 172, 310, 332, 354
Moses' Cushite wife 308
Mot 150, 425, 506, 525, 658, 668
Munificentissimus Deus 190
murex 531
mushrooms 403
musk 353
Mut 428
Mut-Nefertari 73
myrrh 350
mystical marriage 183–84

Nabu 483
Nanna 422, 483
nard 348
navel/vulva 450*f*, 617, 636
necklace (layered) 465–69; Figure *7*, Plate III
Nergal 76–77, 483, 560
Nergol 214
Nikkal 293, 299, 448, 572, 577
Ningal 421–22, 483
Ninlil 483, 590
Ninurta 70, 76, 483, 590–91
Niqmepa 219
Nusku 483
nut nymphs 577
nuts 574–78

obscene gesture 398
odors 82, 84, 299*f*, 378, 381, 636
oil 300
Opet festival 428
Osiris 73, 145, 153, 224, 311, 599

Palmyra 218
Panammu II 33
Papyrus Harris 500 74
paraclausithyron 72, 552
Pārvatī 87–89, 163
peacocks 28
peeping Tom 392
polymasty 633; Plate X

pomegranate 491
potency (sexual, male) 479
Prince Sea 673
Ptah 73
pulchritude 54–84 *passim*
punch 620
Dr. Max N. Pusin 133–34

Qabbalah 161–62, 173, 175, 178
Qadesh 338
Qedar 319
Qidron valley 579
Queen of Heaven 379
Qumran 22, 26, 55
Quran 2:223 324
19 633
108 491

R. Abba ben Kahana 416, 462, 518, 652
R. Aqiba 19, 21, 26, 92, 100, 159, 221, 342, 511, 534
R. Johanan 296, 355, 362, 385, 407, 430, 434, 495, 497, 499, 516, 612, 679, 682, 686
R. Johanan ben Zakkai 336
R. Isaac Luria 176–77
R. Simeon ben Laqish 156, 537, 686
R. Simeon ben Yohai 162, 165, 173, 473
Rādhā 86–87
raisins 378–80
raw flesh feast 220, 559, 562
Re 607
repetitive parallelism 51–52
Rephaim 694
Rephaim Texts 219, 576
Reshep 670
resonant rib 402
"Ritual of Zarpanitum and Games of Marduk" 81
Romulus and Remus 663

Sabbath 171, 173, 175, 178
Sacred Apple Orchard 175
sacred marriage 42, 69, 81–82, 115, 178–79, 210, 212, 324, 359, 361–62, 373, 421, 491, 497, 506, 515, 519, 569
sacral meal 210
Samson's riddle 34
sandals 614
Sarah 55
Sarpanitum 483
Sekhmet 607, 609–10
Seth 682
Shakti 163, 165
Shalim 433
Shamash 572
Shapsh 416, 420, 553, 572
Shat-Ishtar 71, 495
sheila na gig 398
Shekinah 92, 96, 158–62, 171, 177, 644
Shekinah-Matronit 169
Shemesh 151
Shiva 163, 165, 608
Shulgi 371, 410, 506
signet 666
Sin 422, 572, 583
Solomon 23, 432
Solomon Alqabeṣ 175, 644
"Songs of the Orchard" 74
"The Songs of Extreme Happiness" 74
South Arabia 30, 32
Sumerian literature 69
Sumerian poetry 52
Susanna 55

Talpiyot 465–68
Tamil poetry 32
Tammuz 43, 67, 145, 147–49, 151–53, 199, 302, 322, 368, 372, 395, 415, 421, 429, 475–76, 491, 554, 579, 598–99, 699
Tantric worship 192
teeth 463
temple 96
Thesmophoria 379
"Thousand and One Nights" 66, 68
Thutmose III 338
Tirzah 558
Torah 96
Tree of the Knowledge of Good and Evil 17, 398
Turin Papyrus Love Songs 74
twinning (sheep) 461–62

Ur-Hoheslied 25
Al-'Uzza, "The Strong Female" 330, 458

Valley Festival 428
veil 330, 458
Venus' Day 175, 648
Victoria 170, 562
vineyard 324–26
"Vision of the Netherworld" 76, 535

walnut 574–79
waṣf 55–56, 67, 142, 144
windbreaking 82
wisdom 110, 154, 158, 163
women, equality and liberation 138–40, 205–9, 402

Yabneh 19
Yariḫ 293, 299, 340, 448, 572, 577
Yoga 167

Zeus 172, 359, 663
Zohar 162

INDEX OF WORDS

1. Akkadian
assinnu 437
ašīšu 380
dādu 299
dgl 376
dīdu 527
dudittu 527
ēkā 328
elēlu 601
ḫabaṣillatu 367
inbu 80, 582
kittu 306
kurgarrû 437
labābu 479
māru 80
mēlultu 602
mīšaru 306
nīš libbi 479
paṭarru 439
paṭru 439
sabarra 82
sāḫir dūri 419
ša 33
ša ana šinništimipparaqqadu 80
tappatu 82
zawarum 85

2. Arabic
ḫadara 303
ḏū 33
ḏurrat 33
rḍ' 527
rzḥ 221
surr 617
saqf 572
š(w)q 297
ṣḥḥ 531
'lm 301
marzaḥ 221
mirzaḥ 221
mirziḥ 220
mâšalla 61

3. Aramaic
'ar'ā' 93
bny mrzḥ' 218
dī 33
yĕsōd 176
ktš 176
nṭr 34
ṣĕmam 457
ṣamṣēm 457
qallûṯ 156
rb mrzḥ' 218
rummānā' 464

4. Greek
agapē 228
agallochon 28
aiōnion nymphōna 224
thiasos 216
kēpotafion 224
melitoutta 223
paradeisos 31
symposiarchēs 218
symposion 216
telopia 31
phoreion 31

5. Hebrew
'ēḇ 582
'ăḇāqāh 427
'ĕgôz 574–75
'aggān 618
'āḏām 207
'eḏen 546
'hbh 445
'ahaḇah 48
'ăhālôṯ 28
'āz 683
'ḥz b 635
'ăḥôṯî 48
'êḵāh 328
'êḵāḵāh 515
'āyōm 560
'al 619
'ommân 616
'mr 635
'ānāh 553
'appiryôn 31, 441, 443

'argāmān 444
'ry 34, 504
'ăšîšôṯ 378
'eškôl 633
'ăšer 295
b 298, 518
bāḇel 28
b(w)' 498
bāḥûr 547
bêṯ hayyayin 375
bêṯ marzēaḥ 216
bêṯ mišteh 216, 375
bêṯ mišteh hayyayin 375
běnôṯ ṣiyyôn 447
bqš 553
bar 570
bārô'eh 217
brḥ 697
bāṯ-nāḏîḇ 48
bāṯ ṣiyyôn 447
beṯer 409
gibbôr 433
gdl 540
gullāh 488
gll 542
glš 458–59, 565
gan(n) 488
gan/l nā'ûl 224
ginnaṯ 579
gešem 394
dbr 526
děḇāš 505
dāḡûl 532
dgl 561
deḡel 375
dôḇēḇ 640
dôḏ 80, 299
dûḏā'îm 647
dôḏî 47
dlg 389
dallāh 629
dll 629
dmy 341
dpq 512
hbl 664
hôrāh 421
hayyāp̄āh bannāšîm 47
hlk 639
hmy 519
hinnêh 358
haššûlāmmîṯ 48
hškm 646
w 448
zeh 389
zhr 304
zkr 226
zalzallîm 536
zāmîr 395
ḥăḇaṣṣeleṯ 367
ḥbq 384
ḥbr 694
ḥeḏer 303
ḥôaḥ 370
ḥûṣ 657
ḥôṯām 666
ḥēḵ 549
ḥălā'îm 615
ḥallôn 391
ḥly 381
ḥammāh 572
ḥmq 525
ḥāmaq 615
ḥnṭ 397
ḥpṣ 387
ḥere' 217
ḥrk 392
ḥărakkîm 392
ḥtm 489
ḥătunnāh 448
ṭnp 515
yônāṯî 48
yôšěḇôṯ 'al-millē'ṯ 538
ysd 546
yāp̄āh 355
yāp̄āṯî 47
w/yr' 319
yěrî'ôṯ 319
k 330
kî 68, 298
kallāh 48
kōp̄er 34, 493
kěp̄ārîm 645
karkôm 493
kōṯel 391
keṯem 534
l 518
lě 295, 299
libbaḇtînî 478
lěḇānāh 572
lěḏabbēr bě- 678
lûaḥ 681
l(w/y)n 645

lĕḥî 540
m 298
miḇhār 547
meḡeḏ 492
miḏbār 424
mûm 473
môṯ 668
mezeḡ 619, 620
māḥôl 601
maḥămaddîm 549
maḥănayim 603
miṭṭāh 431
mî 423
mî yittēn 655
mayim rabbîm 672
mêšārîm 305
min 426, 518
mēsēḇ 348
mēsiḇ 216
msk 620
mar'eh 401
marzēaḥ 218–20
marzēaḥ sĕrûḥîm 216
marzĕḥîm 217
merkāḇ 443
merqāḥîm 540
mšk 302
miškāḇ 431
maṯ'îmôṯ 461
miṯrappeqeṯ 662
niḏgālôṯ 560
nĕhārôṯ 674
naḥal 579
nṭr 34
n'l 488
nep̄eš 328, 525
nōp̄eṯ 486
niṣṣānîm 395
nṣr 34
nšq 297
sahar 618
sûḡāh 622
salsillôṯ 536
sela' 400
sĕmāḏār 398
sansinnîm 536, 636
sappîrîm 544
srḥ 216
sĕṯaw 394
sēṯer 401
'br 525
'ad 347
'adše 408
'(w/y)r 386, 498
'ôrēḇ 537
'ēymāh 560
'akkāḇîš 575
'akbār 575
'ly 424
'lm 301
'elem 301
'almāh 301
'lp 532
'im 505
'ēmeq 368
'ng 632
'āsîs 659
'ōp̄er 390
'aqrāḇ 575
ešeṯ 543
pag(g) 397
pāz 534
pḥd 437
pelaḥ 464
pĕlîliyyāh 217
pa'am 614
pardēs 31, 491
pĕrî 80
ṣo'āh 217
ṣĕ'eynāh 447
ṣe'ĕlîm 368
ṣĕḇî 390
ṣawwā'r 85
ṣwṣ 391
ṣawwārôn 482
ṣaḥ 531
ṣammāh 457
ṣippôr 575
ṣpn 651
qdr 319
qôl 512
qĕwuṣṣôṯ 512
qṭr 426
qînāh 37
qômāh 633
qin'āh 669
qānēh 493
qinnāmôn 494
qpṣ 389
qiryāh 607
qôrôt 360
qšy 669

rā'āh bĕ 579
r'y 447
rĕḏîḏ 527
rhb 564
rĕhāṭîm 630
rôḵēl 427
rzḥ 220
rēaḥ 636
rēa' 549
r'y 31, 405
rē'î 47
r'yh 106
ra'yāṯî 47
rpd 380
rpy 420
rĕp̄îḏāh 443
rpq 662
rāṣûp̄ 446
raqqāh 464
rqḥ 540
rĕšāp̄îm 670
śāp̄ām 541
še 31, 33, 295, 564
še 'ahăḇāh nap̄šî 47
šĕ'ôl 669
šb' 385
šgḥ 391
šûlammîṯ 596
šû'āl 403
šôšannāh 368
šāḥôr 307
šḥr 307
šaḥar 572
šaḥărûṯ 536
šṭy 479
šîr 293
šîr haššîrîm 294
šayyārāh 30
škr 507
šālôm 432
šlḥ 517
šelaḥ 490–91
šeleṭ 468–69
šlmh 320
šām 646
šēn 544
šqp 571
šōr 617
šārôn 367
šēš 546
tôḵ 444
tûraq 300
tîmĕrāh 426
tukkî 28
talpiyyôṯ 31, 465
taltallîm 536
tāmār 633
tammāṯî 48
tappûaḥ 371
tōp̄eṯ 581
trṣh 558
taršîš 543
tĕšûqāh 643

6. Latin
cepotafium 224
hortus 224

7. Persian
Farvardigan 221
haoma 191
pardēs 25

8. Sanskrit
aghal 28
soma 191

9. Sumerian
ell 439
gír ba-da-ra 439
ŠÀ.ZI.GA 17, 479

10. Tamil
akil 28
Bāveru 28
tōkai 28

11. Ugaritic
agn 618
an 553
ap 636
ary 34, 504
bqṯ 553
glṯ 459
gpn-w-ugr 646
d 33
dd 299
ddym 648
drt 33
d 33
hlk 639
w 448
ḥbr 694
ḥr' 217

ḫlb 576
ḫtn 448
k 330, 559
kpr 352
l 295
lan 553
-m 641
mḥmd 547, 549
mẓ' 418
msk 620
mrzḥ 81, 211, 214
mtq 549
nbt 486
n'm 631
nġr 34
sld 576
ś 33
'd 347
'(w/y)r 386
'lm 301
'm 345
'rgz 575–76
ġlp 531–32
p 445
palt 623
rimt 294
rbd 380
rḥm 325
rpum 576
šḥlmmt 425
šḥr 572
š(y)r 294
tply 536
trm 344
trq 300
ṯnt 217

INDEX OF SCRIPTURAL REFERENCES

Gen 1:2 460
2 203
2:16–17 207
18 199
20 138
21–23 207
24 199
2–3 205–6, 208–9
3:5 17
7 398
16 643
23–24 209
4:7 643
8 644
22 358
6:2 54
3 33
7:12 394
8:11 460
9:25 294
11:28 323
31 323
12:1 394
1–2 301
11 54
13 480
14 54, 356
14–15 56
13:9 690
14:18 433
22 632
15 410–11
6 478
7 323
12 560
13 395
13–14 397
16:2 498
11 309
18:2 161, 352
7 394
19:6 680
15 572
20:2 480
11 635
12 480
15 690
21:16 579

(*Gen*)
22:2 570
24 323
3 385
16 54, 301
28 301
29 678
30 542
37 385
43 301
50 678
51 690
55 678
60 678
65 527
67 421
25:13 309, 319
16 680
20 323, 370
23 519
28 388, 671
29–30 533
30 531
26:8 220
19 496
27:3 466
27 487
29 322
37 378
41 671
28:1 323
29:13 384
17 54, 356
27 442
32 579
30 566
:4 651
13 370, 571
14 648
14–16 647–48
32 345
38 361, 630–31
41 361, 630–31
31:12 345
20 323

(*Gen*)
24 323
27 293
42 437
46 556
47 460
53 437
32 603
1–2 604
2–22 613–14
3 603
8 603
9 603
11 603
25 572
27 572
33:4 627
8 603
13 512
34:1 579
6–17 678
10 690
35:18 525
37:3 671
11 671
13 406
16 328
38:6 633
14 331, 527, 532, 544
16 498
17 333
18 666
19 527
28 463
30 463
39:6 355
12–13 527
20 619
40:5 619
10 395–96
41:2 406
6 322
18 406
23 322
27 322
38 571
42 666
42:35 350

(*Gen*)
43:30 303
44:28 635
45:16 571
47:6 690
14 556
49:19 355
21 388
25 470, 624
26 421
50:2 397
9 603
26 397

Exod 1:4 395
16 225
2:3 403
11 579, 657
13 549
14 635
15 628
16 361, 630
3:8 486
17 486
4:4 636
18 657
22 407
27 658
28 471
6:23 587
26 471
27 471
9:9 427
23 342
10:22 399
11:4 397, 513
12:1 397
12 533
29 533
43 406
48 440
13:9 667
16 667
21 426–27
22 426
14:19 426–27, 462
19–20 603
24 426
27 533
15 94, 297, 464
1 296
1–2 397
2 514
6 51
8 636

(*Exod*)
16 560
20 601
16:4 556
16 556
21 556
26 556
17:1 380
8 380
19:2 380
6 588
11 393
20:1 393
2 407
5 651, 669
17 550
21:10 177
18 416
22:9 549
23:6 220
14–17 156
27 560
24:5 535
6 618
7 320, 373, 473, 565, 665
10 478, 545
12 681
25 149
2 309
3–7 492
7 539
8 159
10 633
23 633
26:1 444, 463
7 319
12 216
19 546
31 436
33 294
36 444, 463
27:8 681
10 615
11 546
16 444, 463
28:5 444, 463
6 444
8 444, 463
15 444
17 539
17–21 93
20 543
33 444, 463
34 660
29:14 603

(*Exod*)
27 671
30:5 485
18–21 540
23 350, 439, 493–94, 521
34 426
31:17 548
32:1 633
4 524, 665
6 156
14 524
18 601–2
19 601
33:27 420
34:13 176
14 651, 669
23–24 156
35:9 539
27 539
36:33 697
35 463
38:7 681
8 540
39:10–14 93
13 539, 543
40:32 540

Lev 2:1–2 426
15–16 426
10:1 617
11:15 536
13:31 307, 536
37 307, 536
48 332
14:5–6 496
50–52 496
15 537
9 443
13 496
18 620
16:8 316
30 583
18:6 406
6–18 322
9 655
19:10 556
18 204, 550
20:7 655
24 486
21:10 488
24:2 631
7 304
10 489
26:10 650

Num 1:7 587
18 568
44 434
49 588
52 376
2:3 587
2–3 376
10 376
17 583
17–18 376
25 376
34 376
3:32 294
36 546
4:8 463
20 155
5:2 473
12 139
13 620
14 669, 671
29–30 669
6:5 493, 540
24–26 434
7:3 563
12 587
17 587
59 157
9:15 320
10:5–6 603
14 587
18 376
22 376
25 376
11:5 489
8 556
29 655
12 309
1 308, 678
13:23 491
27 486
32 320
14:14 427
33 406
35 430, 665
15:24 357, 539
16:22 583
19:2 168, 531
17 496
20:5 492
13 631
21:5 678
7 678
17 296–97
20 572
26–34 625
29 314
23:10 583

(*Num*)
38 572
24:6 494, 579
25 327, 379
1 320, 566
1–2 217
1–9 156
3 327
4 566
6–8 217
9 220
31:10 680
32:12 320
33:14 380
41–50 401
34:4 626

Deut 1:33 427
3:9 475, 624
16 444
4:11 344, 665
24 651
48 475
5:9 669
6:3 486
5 204
6 671
8 667
9 385
15 651
7:3 301
5 176
13 334, 375
16 622
8:8 491, 556
10:8 588
17 294
11:14 375
18 667
22 385
12:15 390
17 375
22 390
13:7 322, 549
14:1 407, 550
5 390
14 536
15:7 389
12 657
22 390
16:16 156, 402
17:17 570
20:11 685
21:11 54
22:28 535
24:1 684
26:5 323

(*Deut*)
17–18 405
28:1 301
4 334
18 334
22 322
24 427
29 329
67 655
29:12 405
19 669
31:25 588
32 94, 296–97
4 157
5 473
10 603
11–13 587
15 297, 603
16 651, 669, 671
21 651, 669
24 670
25 560
34 489
48–52 477
33:2 537
5 631
13–16 492, 650
28 375
34:1–4 477
3 633

Josh 1:8 537
2:9 560
15 391
18 463, 465
21 463, 465
3–4 588
7:1 321
19 321
8:17 478
9:5 345
10:12 296
13 305
11:19 685
12:2 444
17 371
24 558
15:3 626
19 488
53 371
62 354
16:8 371
17:8 371
16 369

(*Josh*)
19:18 598
28 687
21:38 603
24:19 651

Judg 1:15 488
16 633
3:3 488
13 633
23–25 680
4:1 462
21 464
22 464
5 94, 297
1 296
4 514
7 31, 33, 51
12 293, 595
21 51
26 464
28 392, 572
30 325
6:1 462
17 33
25–30 176
38 513
7:10 603
12 33
22 601
8:26 33, 482
9:15 372
21 697
37 619
53 464
11:22 424
24 314
34 601
37 341
37–40 151
13:8 600
14:11 436
12 442
14 67, 505
18 67
15:2 54
4 403
16:3 636
9 303
12 303
19:22 512
20:40 426
21:19–21 151
19–23 437
21 601–2, 604

Ruth 2 556
3:3 300
9 62, 372
4:4 635
11 182
19 587
20 320, 587

I Sam 2:1 296
8 615
22 62
6:19 579
9:2 547
7 478
22 347
11:7 437
13:18 572
14:11 518
19 347
25–27 505
15:12 226
16:7 633
12 355
16 690
17:24 356
18:1 671
9 321, 671
16 601
19:15 431
20:4 635
17 385
38 556
21:12 601–3
22:17–18 408–9
20 697
25:20 401
25 300
39 678
26:19 304
27:4 697
28:14 330
29:5 601–3
30:12 464

II Sam 1:18 305
19 390
21 623
24 463
2:8 603
29 410
3:31 431
39 669
4:7 303
10 636
5:11 630
6:2–4 587

(*II Sam*)
13 426
14 603
16 572
19 378
20 378, 603
7:2 681
6 360
7 681
8:4 337
6 626
7 468
10:7 433
11:2 54
11 515
21 464
12:20 300
13 633
1 54, 356
10 303
17 488
17–18 680
20 678
32 678
14:25 356
27 54
16:22 62
17:24 603
27 603
18:14 469
18 226
30 408–9
19:1 655
22 94, 297
1 296
2 401
5–6 673
16 636
17 673
27 570
30 389
23:9 433
16 433
17 433
22 433

I Kings 1:1 488
1–4 597
3 54, 356
4 356
8 433
15 597
2:17–25 597
3:1 23
4:7–19 689, 692
12 601

(*I Kings*)
20 24, 360, 689, 692
5:1 24
3 390
4 24
5 24, 634
6 444
12 18, 22
13 22
15 630
6–7 538
6:2 442
3 545
7 545
9 547
10 547
15 360, 362
15–16 547
16 360
18 547
20 547
20–22 538
29 347–48, 541, 633
31 442, 526, 680
32 538
33 442
34 542–43
35 538
36 547, 680
7:6 442
7 441–42
12 547, 680
13 442
14 442
15–22 543
19 545
23 628
23–26 540
30 681
33 615
41 488
51 442
8:2 390
3 433
4 433
8 360
27 294
37 322
64 444
9:10–14 630
11 442
15 442
16 23
19 626

(*I Kings*)
26 442
26–28 630
28 23, 442
10:5 525
10 23
10–11 23
11 630
13 442
15 689, 692
16 442
16–17 23, 468
18 442, 446, 535
18–20 441–42
21 442
22 28, 630
23 442
23–24 91
27 23, 681
11:3 22, 567, 569, 686
3–10 691
7 315
14:3 345
17 22, 558
21 597
26 23
26–28 468
15:7 22
21 558
33 558
16:6 558
8 558
9 558
15 558
17 558
23 558
18:41 394
45 394
19:2 574
16 601
20:30 303
21:8 489
27 321
22:25 303

II Kings 1:2 392
2:11 587
3:22 531
4:4 680
8 615
8–17 597
39 464, 556
5:12 478

(*II Kings*)
15 603
21 474
6:11 33
17 337
31 629
32 680
8:9 478
29 381
9:2 303
22 347
30 356
11:10 468
12:10 518
14:7 400
9 370
15:25 399
16:3 581
17 446
17:6 576
18:27 217
20:2 393
13 300
21:6 581
23:5 347–48
10 581
11 327
13 315
24:14 631
16 689
25:12 631

I Chron 2:2 10, 587
11 320
5:23 475, 687
6:7 587
7:40 570
9:22 570
27 524
12:33 692
38 692
15:2 588
10 587
11 587
16 293
16:3 378
8 297
41 570
42 293
18:7 468
21:2 360
22:9 685
24 434
25 434
27 434
29 406
29:2 539, 546

(*I Chron*)
16 687

II Chron 1:15 346
3:1 181
7 360
14 444
4:2–5 540
6 540
6:28 322
7:3 446
8:6 627
9:17 535
21 28
12:9–11 468
23:9 468–69
28:3 581
15 633
32:30 581
33:6 581
35:13 417

Ezra 1:3 424
11 424
2:1 424
59 424
3:3 528
4:2 424
7 528
5 528
8 391
7:6 424
7 424
28 424
8:1 424

Neh 2:8 31, 491
3:15 490, 580
25 465
30 348
4:3 404
3–17 437
5:11 375
13 528
18 570
7:3 347
5 424
6 424
61 424
8:10 549
9:11 672
12 426–27
19 426–27
10:1 474
40 375
11:23 474
12:1 424

(*Neh*)
44 348
13:5 375
12 375

Esther 1:5 579
6 431, 446, 542, 546
11 54
2:3 300
7 54
8 407
9 300
12 300, 478
13 350
17 684
5 204
6 375
7:2 375
7 375
7–8 579
8 221, 375
8:6 515
9 568

Job 1:16 481
19 498
2:14 487
3:12 470
5:2 669
7 670
10 493
11 319
14 329
16 389
23 38
27 332
6:8 655
15 525, 579
16 319, 581
30 638
8:12 582
16 579
9:7 489
13 564
25 697
34 560
11:4 570
12 448, 479
15 473
17 329
13:21 560
14:12 386
17 350
15:33 395–96
16:12 513
17:13 380

(*Job*)
19:4 351
9 447
12 678
20:9 322
12 486
25 560
21:12 604
20 481
33 302
22:28–30 98
26:5 219
12 564
13 697
27:12 612
21 498
28:7 322
13–28 158
18 294
30:6 518
7 645
28 319, 572, 687
30 307
31:7 473
23 437
40 370
33:2 638
7 560
22 673
35:12 646
36:25 600
37:9 498
10 672
38:6 546
26 424
34 672
41 537
39:20 560
21 607
28 401
40:16 617
17 387
21 368
41:6 560
16 464
22 380
42:14 356
15 54, 356

Ps 2:12 623
3 295
7 533
4 295
8 375
7:15 664
9:9 305

(*Ps*)
10:5 408
7 486
14:2 572
7 655
17:8 372
18 94, 297
4–5 673
11 339, 342, 538
13 342
15 342
16 636, 673
27 570
30 389
19:6 436, 441
7 572
9 450
11 537, 549
20 686
4 304
6 560
22:6–9 432
10 470
15 519
27 640
23 297
1 621
2 328
27:3 603
4 600
29:5 443
5–6 477
11 432
30:12 601
31:20 652
33:14 391
34:8 374
9 298
15 539
35:14 319
36:8 372, 497
37:6 329
16 687
25 164
38:7 319
40:13 457
42:2 540
2–4 32
8 397
9 293
10 319
33 640
43:2 319
44 190
23 357, 534, 671

(*Ps*)
45:3 360
4 441
8 300, 625
9 28, 319, 350, 427, 487, 494
11 164
11–12 184
12 54
15 341
46 686
4 497
48 686
3 588
49:13 351
15 305
50:2 558, 588
20 322, 678
51:14 378
55:5 560
57:2 372
58:2 305–6
63:6 65
65:10 643
13 424
68:5 436
9 514
19 565
31 309
69:1 677
2 672, 677
5 457
14 672
26 680
31 293
71:6 519
72 432
4 404
7–8 432
12–14 404
16 621
73:20 386
25 690
26 513
58 669
74:12 619
15 674
19 400
75:3 305–6
9 619–20
76:3 433, 685
3–4 686
4 670
77:5 435
78:14 427
16 496

(*Ps*)
40 320
44 496
48 670
58 651
80 327, 559
2 181, 407
9 181
9–12 687
11 546
12 490
13 34, 504, 557
14 181
85:9–14 432
87:4 564–65
88 602
11 219
16 560
19 549
89:11 564
91:5 436
7 533
15 514
92 94, 296
9 51
95:7 405
96:10 305
98:9 305
99:4 305
100:3 405
102:10 619
104:18 401
25 633
28 556
105:8 469
33 634
106:19 320
28 217, 220
30 321
109:4 357
112:4 415
113–18 402
113:8 615
119:12 696
26 696
33 696
54 397
63 693, 696
103 549
139 669
120:5 319
121:4 407
5 372
6 360
122:7 469
8 550

(*Ps*)
125:5 432
127:1 418, 420, 692
128:6 432
131:8 190
132:9 488
133:2 300, 540
3 478
138:3 564
140:4 486
141:10 347
144:1 521
12 540
146:4 525
147:14 432
15 307
149:3 601–2
6 604
150:4 601

Prov 1–9 486
1:3 305
9 482
21 417
28 684
2:5 684
9 305
18 219
3:8 617
10 375
13 684
18 583
4:3 570, 690
5 201
3 486, 549, 638
15 489, 496
19 298
20 381, 384
6 201
3 564
19 408
20–23 667
25 356
30–35 675
34 669
7:6 392, 572
7 372
16 326, 380
17 28, 300, 319, 350, 427, 494
18 298, 508
20 350
8 158, 173
6 305

(*Prov*)
7 638
17 684
19 372
22 154, 537
26 347
30 616
35 684
9:1 447
2 620
5 510, 620
7 473
18 219
10:12 488
11:22 54
12:27 392
14:5 408
25 408
30 669
15:4 406
12 615
31 351
16:21 549
24 486
17:17 655
23 518
18:4 672, 696
19:2 381
5 408
9 408
10 632
20:2 560
30 300
21:14 518
16 219
22:2 159
23:30 620
31 305, 639–40
33 640
24:4 303
13 486
30 328
31 690
25:16 487
20 293
26:14 680
27:7 486
30:17 537
19 301
26 401
31:10 71, 139, 497
10–31 54, 176
15 537
29 370

Eccles 19, 80
1:2 294
7 639
16 521
2:1 521, 579
5 31, 491
8 440, 567
11 521
15 521
3:17 521
18 521, 570
4:4 669
5:9 687
7:2 375
25 626
27 626
28 139
9:9 671
10 626
11:10 536
12:1 698
6 489

Song of Songs 1:1 44, 53
2 49, 58, 95, 97, 104, 145, 147, 484, 508, 647
2–3 103
2–4 38–39, 44, 68, 180
2–11 46
2–17 95
2–2:6 46
2–2:7 107
2–2:17 106
2–3:5 102
2–3:6 95
3 53, 58, 62, 97, 131, 147, 534, 636
4 46, 53, 58, 62, 92, 98, 103, 108, 115, 147, 375, 417, 421, 508, 510, 630, 645, 647
5 23, 39, 57, 60, 63–64, 67, 96, 104, 167, 191, 195, 340, 458, 536,

(*Song of Songs*)
571, 621, 665
5–2:7 44
5–5:1 179
5–6 43–44
5–7 44
6 23, 34, 57, 150, 208, 404, 431, 536, 579, 646, 657, 681, 686, 688, 690–92, 700
7 38, 43–44, 47, 58, 65, 68, 93, 201, 693, 695
7–8 30, 85
7–11 595
8 23, 38, 43–44, 47, 58, 208, 355, 631
9 23, 37, 47, 58, 62, 164, 181
9–11 44, 66
9–14 44
9–5:2 42
10 23, 540
11 66
12 38, 53, 66, 216, 375, 431, 505, 630
12–2:5 44
12–2:6 46
12–14 23
13 47, 66, 470, 505, 636
14 24, 34, 47, 505, 512, 634, 636
15 24, 46–49, 51, 53, 58, 62, 66, 164, 195, 341, 457, 460, 512, 538, 662, 631
15–17 66

(*Song of Songs*)
16 47, 59, 66, 181, 355, 375, 441
16–17 44, 181, 402
17 23, 34, 82, 147, 369, 375, 417
1–2 128
1–4:6 128
1–5:1 141
2:1 58, 541, 556, 622
1–3 44, 66
1–3:6 95
1–6 46
2 164, 341, 571
3 47, 58, 60–61, 66, 80, 106, 148, 382, 571, 663, 665
3–6 656
4 46, 68, 85, 147, 221, 372, 387, 532, 620
4–5 44
5 49, 64–65, 222, 387, 529
5–6 195
6 44, 46, 147, 660
6–7 44, 661
6–11 656
7 44, 46, 48–49, 59, 181, 222, 318, 347, 401, 423, 512, 529, 571, 588, 595, 663
7–3:5 46
8 38, 47, 49, 64, 307, 512
8–3:3 44
8–9 44
8–16 44, 408
8–17 107

(*Song of Songs*)
9 23, 47, 53, 80, 181, 402, 470
10 47, 58, 147, 164, 341, 631
10–13 68
10–14 43
11–12 93
11–13 647
11–15 369
12 53, 147, 181, 402
13 47, 53, 61, 147, 164, 341, 378, 595, 631, 636
14 48, 57–58, 68, 147, 195, 546, 693, 695, 699
15 66, 123, 129, 181, 191, 378, 398
15–17 181
16 43, 46–47, 49, 60, 67, 92, 181, 534, 541, 557, 622, 643
17 30, 43, 47, 49, 53, 106, 147, 181, 347, 390, 415, 470, 697–99
17–3:3 44
3:1 47, 49, 53, 63, 65, 133, 148, 408, 511, 656
1–2 43
1–4 68, 393, 423, 465, 656–57
1–4:16 128
1–5 107, 195
1–5:1 106–7
2 47, 49, 53, 201, 588
2–3 23, 528

(*Song of Songs*)
2–4 409
3 43, 47, 62, 64, 107, 147
4 23, 43–44, 46–47, 85, 107, 133, 201, 322, 388, 417, 659, 684
5 44, 46, 49, 181, 222, 318, 385, 387, 389, 512, 529, 571, 661
6 23, 30, 49, 53, 65, 181, 190–91, 350, 435, 505, 571, 595, 644, 661–62, 665
6–4:7 102
6–5:1 45–46, 107
6–8 180, 450
6–10 28, 663
6–11 25–26, 43, 45, 67, 441
7 22, 48, 53, 104, 590, 656
7–4:1 95
7–5:1 95
7–8 30
7–9 432
9 22–23, 31, 53, 107, 297, 590, 630
9–11 429
10 318, 380, 387, 590, 629
11 22–23, 53, 147, 180, 297, 318, 630
4:1 24, 46–47, 49, 53, 58, 67, 164, 341, 355–56, 512, 527, 538, 558, 565, 625, 629, 631
1–2 49, 53, 64
1–5 43, 614
1–7 48, 67
1–8 45
2 356, 402, 566–67
2–5 95
3 49, 53, 58, 457, 527, 541, 566
4 23, 31, 194, 564, 624
5 49, 53, 114, 180–81, 351, 390, 406, 461, 541, 622, 624
6 49, 114, 181, 350, 408, 505, 699
6–7 95
6–8 30
7 43, 46–47, 58, 67, 164, 190–91, 195, 341, 355, 631
7–8:14 128
8 20, 24, 43, 52–53, 64, 68, 90, 147, 485, 595, 627
8–5:1 95, 102
9 48, 58, 66, 485, 565, 601
9–5:1 38
9–11 43, 66
9–15 45
10 39, 48–49, 57–58, 355, 480, 485, 508, 614, 631, 636, 647
10–5:1 46
10–14 505, 659
11 48, 58, 62, 147, 319, 463, 485, 541, 636
12 48, 53, 58, 61, 190–91, 224, 480, 485, 496, 554, 584, 693
12–14 31, 57
12–15 66
13 25, 31, 34, 61–62, 80, 650, 659–60
14 28, 439
15 58, 488, 491
15–16 644
16 41, 45, 47, 80, 85, 147, 488, 492, 508, 650, 656, 695, 699
5:1 34, 41, 45, 48, 58, 60, 107, 147, 222, 372, 480, 485, 488, 508, 554, 644, 659, 693, 695
1–5 522
1–6:8 129
2 42, 47–49, 60, 63–64, 72, 80, 132, 164–65, 195, 201, 341, 356, 399, 401, 536, 570, 588, 656
2–4 107
2–5 45, 524
2–6 43, 133
2–6:1 95
2–6:3 45–46, 102, 511
2–7 68, 95,

(*Song of Songs*)
510
2–8 37, 195, 656
2–8:5 108
2–8:14 106–7, 141, 179
2–9 179
3 23, 621
4 47, 58, 60, 225, 543, 580
5 23, 47, 350, 541
6 47, 49, 60, 65, 201, 615
6–7 85
6–8 45, 657
7 23, 29, 43, 145, 147, 419
8 43, 47, 49, 58, 64–65, 85, 128, 318, 381, 387–88, 510, 684
8–16 95
9 43, 47, 52, 58, 62, 65, 67, 70, 333, 355, 510, 534, 631
9–10 92, 128
9–16 45
10 24, 47, 58, 61, 67, 95, 100, 307, 375, 534, 665
10–15 656
10–16 43, 67, 70, 72, 75, 77, 99, 101, 294, 417, 510, 614, 625–26
11 53, 58, 307, 458, 512, 625
11–15 538
12 24, 60, 62, 65, 128, 457, 491, 625

(*Song of Songs*)
13 58, 128, 350, 368, 406, 463
14 58–59, 61, 93, 128, 483, 519, 625
14–15 23, 85
15 58, 372, 625
15–17 128
16 47, 58, 67, 318, 341, 373, 571, 638
6:1 43, 45, 47, 62, 92, 95, 333, 355, 508, 510, 534, 631
1–8:14 128
2 41, 43, 47, 66, 181, 488, 540–41, 622, 644
2–3 45, 656
2–7:11 95
2–12 95
3 43, 46–47, 49, 60, 66, 181, 405, 534, 643
4 22, 24–25, 43, 47, 53, 57, 66–67, 91, 164, 195, 341, 355, 375, 532, 607, 631
4–7 48
4–8:3 46
4–8:5 45
4–8:7 698
4–9 102
4–12 45
5 24, 43, 58, 64, 66, 195, 458–59, 479, 481, 601
5–7 49, 53, 67
5–9 43
6 53, 58, 461

(*Song of Songs*)
7 58, 457, 464, 567
8 22, 30, 68, 104, 429
8–9 53, 204
9 48, 52–53, 322, 399, 512, 659
9–7:10 129
9–10 64
10 43, 49, 53, 57, 62, 64, 66, 129, 355, 375, 424, 458, 532, 561, 631, 661, 665, 687
10–7:7
10–7:9 102
11 41, 49, 65, 68, 181, 424, 488, 600, 644, 646–47
11–12 43
12 53, 82, 181, 406, 615, 699
7:1 45, 48–49, 52, 57, 67, 129, 143, 145, 330, 432, 510, 589, 648, 685
1–6 44, 67
1–11 95
2 23, 49, 57, 65, 67, 91, 181, 355, 525, 631
2–6 45
2–7 48
2–10 641
3 93, 541, 625, 659
3–5 356
4 49, 53, 180, 194, 390, 461, 470
5 24, 93, 97, 129, 180, 194, 465, 467

(*Song of Songs*)
6 24, 58, 194
7 46, 57, 96, 358, 387, 614
7–10 43, 45, 66
7–8:3 46
8 53, 62, 65, 298, 352, 470
9 53, 58, 60, 63, 66, 85, 352, 371, 381–82, 536
10 47, 53, 65, 222, 305, 373, 588, 660
10–14 45, 656
11 43, 47, 49, 60, 405, 638
11–8:3 129
12 23, 34, 47, 147
12–8:4 102
12–13 175, 657, 693
12–14 41, 44, 369
13 49, 194, 378, 398, 508
14 47, 59, 95, 181, 222, 492, 636
8:1 29, 60, 62, 68, 147, 330
1–2 43
1–4 180
1–12 325
2 46, 48, 60, 65, 95, 322, 505, 639
2–6 538
3 45–46, 49, 384
3–4 44, 661
4 44–46, 49, 95, 181, 222, 318, 385–88, 409, 470, 512, 529,

(*Song of Songs*)
571, 588, 601
4–6 129
4–14 46
5 28, 43, 45, 47, 49, 52–53, 67, 96, 102, 134, 175–76, 310, 371–72, 424, 510, 571, 587, 595, 659, 662
5–7 43, 45
5–14 108
6 18, 59, 65, 68, 85, 96, 148, 180, 198, 208, 210, 226, 387, 490
6–7 45, 179, 182, 195
7 45, 62, 80, 134, 387
7–14 129
8 96, 125, 470
8–10 45, 67, 84, 94, 134, 179
8–12 45
8–14 45, 179, 698
9 96
10 53, 96, 470
11 22, 30, 34, 53, 68, 104, 147
11–12 45, 134, 179, 432
11–14 96
12 22–23, 30, 34, 53, 326, 431
13 43, 45, 68, 96, 488, 584
13–14 45, 179
14 30, 45, 47, 49, 53, 67, 96, 108,

(*Song of Songs*)
147, 195, 389–90, 409

Isa 1:1 612
18 458, 464, 532–33, 628
21 328, 539
29 297, 579
30 579
2:8 521
10 437
12–14 477
19 437
21 437
3:5 564
18–23 351
23 23, 527
4:1 596
4 318
5 427, 441
5:1 94, 147, 639, 686–87
1–7 326–27
5 488
7 407, 647, 689–90
11 375
12 375
17 406
22 375, 619
30 329, 415
6 604
7:14 301, 407, 436, 441, 656
20 677
23 690
8:7 677
8 656
22 415
23 542
9:1 415
5 656
5–6 432
6 669
9 681
10:33–34 477
11:4–5 404
10 534
10–16 559
15 614
13:8 664
14:9 219
12 572
13 499
16 391

(*Isa*)
16:7 379
8 490
11 519
12 379
17:5 556
8 176, 521
10 149, 476
12 677
18:4 531
4–6 396
5 395, 536
19:1 436
14 619
20–21 687
20:29 296
21:11 415, 418
16 319
22:24 618
23:15 293
24:9 293
16 369
18 437
23 572, 687
25:6–8 669
26:3 432
6 614
9 415, 512
12 432
14 219
17 664
19 219, 369
27:1 697
2 326, 602
4–11 326
9 176
28:1 581
1–3 375
7–8 375
7–9 217
9 470
25 33
29:4 301
5 525
30:7 564
26 572, 687
29 94, 293
32:4 531
9 370
16–19 477
17–18 432
19 477
33:15 305
17 588
18 560
20 588
20–21 686

(*Isa*)
21 588
34 610
13 370
35:1 367, 369
6 389
7 561
36:12 217
23 217
37:12 574, 576
24 546
32 669
35 686
38:12 629
40:2 473
3 389–90, 512
3–5 428
9–11 428
41:11 323
19 369
42:11 319
13 669
15 674
25 499
43:2 674, 677
5–6 428
6 498–99
14 478
16 672
23–24 493
24 439
44:3 496
20 406
27 674
45:19 305
24 323
46:3–4 428
8 380
47:2 402, 457, 674
9 693
12 693
13 600
48:18 432
49:1 519
2 372, 570
9 415
9–10 428
10 561
16 671
18 485
20–21 318
23 583
26 659
50:1 103–4
4–5 696

(*Isa*)
51:1 415
3 556
4 165, 407
9 564
16 372
17 388
22 318
52:1 389
7–9 428
8 528
9 415
11 570
12 428
15 389
17 432
53:2 360
10–12 428
54:2 319, 687
6–8 651
11 545
55:6 417
56:4–5 177
5 226
56–59 512
57:3–10 580
8 613
8–10 517
58 424
58:9 509
10 329
14 587
58–60 418
59 424
3 521
10 329
17 342, 669
60 424
1–2 415
3 301, 460
4 318
5 687
6 494
8 400, 423
13 362
16 298
17 432
19 385
22 701
61:6 588
9 583
10 449, 485
11 556, 579
62 418, 424
3–5 449
5 103, 485
6 418, 420,

(*Isa*)
528
8 375
63–66 512
63:1 423
1–6 533, 611
2 531–32
15 669
15–64:12 418, 424
16 407
65:1 415
1–7 224
3 225, 518
11 620
66:1 418, 424
3 304
12 432
15 587
17 82, 579
20 478
21 588

Jer 1:14 499
2:2 393, 424, 651
10 319
13 496–97
20–24 581
3 182
1 550
1–10 204
6 359
12–13 389
13 359
19 294
20 550
21 651
21–22 389
22 651
25–4:2 651
4:6 499, 627
11 531, 570
14 389
19 519
20 319
28 319
30 356, 463
5:6 476
28 543–44
6:1 572, 627
4 408
7 497
9 536, 636
17 420
20 439, 493–94

(*Jer*)
22 627
7:18 149, 175, 379, 556
23 405
31 581
34 485
8:7 396
13 634
21 319
9:1 655
2 655
10:9 444
20 319
11:4 405
12:7 404
10 327
13:21 664
24 498
14:2 319
15:9 525
18 579
19 596
16:5 214
6–9 216
8 375
17:2 176
8 490
13 496
19:2 581
6 581
21:14 477
22:14–15 681
18 149
24 297, 666, 671
23:1–8 334
24:1 651
7 405
25:32 498
29:5 579
13 415
28 579
31 613
1–6 559
2 684
3 302, 602
4 601
7–10 428
9 407
12 375
13 601
18 596
20 519
21 334
21–22 331, 651

(*Jer*)
22 182, 525, 615
27–28 559
31 559
33 405
33–34 389
34 651
32:35 581
37 428
33:6 432
12 331
34:5 149
35:2 375
2–5 347
5 375
6 375
14 375
38–39 309
38:12 542
40:7 631
43:12 331
44:17 149
17–19 175
19 379
46:7 423
7–8 674
8 423
22–23 477
48:17 328
28 400
49:7 216
19 476
28 319
29 319
50:38 560
44 476
51:11 468, 570
52:15 616

Lam 1:1 328
8 156
2:1 328
15 558, 588
19 537
3:14 583
4:1 328
2 328, 447
7 307, 531, 545
20 372
5:15 601

Ezek 1:7 395
16 543
3:13 297
26 549

(*Ezek*)
4:2 603
5:5 619
13 669
7:12 294
8:8 518
14 149, 302, 476
9:3 155
10:1–22 155
9 543
11:17–20 389
13:11 394
13 394
18 542
15:4 444
16 182, 678
2 104
3 323, 664
4 617
7 54, 103, 294, 470
7–8 683
8 62, 103, 372, 508
10–12 492
11–13 347
37–39 134
38 669
42 669
44–45 323, 664
46 679, 681
53–55 559
61 104, 681
17:6 216
7 540
10 540
21 697
23 372, 546
18:23–32 389
19:2 318
10 318
11 633
20:38 570
21:2 486
2–3 477
7 486
21 579
36 411
23 182, 204
2 318
3 351, 470
4 681
15 216
17 508
21 351, 470

(*Ezek*)
25 669
40 356
41 431
24:10 222
16 549
25:4 680
26:10 427
27:5 681
10 468
11 468
12–25 427
15 445
16 294
18 626
19 439, 493
21 319
22 493–94
28:13 543
31 477
3 633
5 633
6 372
10 633
12–17 372
14 633
32:2 674
14 674
33:11 389
24 571, 679
34 334
11–16 428
13 406
14–15 331
23–30 181
25 432
30–31 405
31 407
35:28 405
36:5 669
24 428
24–29 389
31–32 389
37:15–28 559
21 428
23 405
26 432
38:11 680
12 619
19 669
20 401
39:27–28 428
40:3 466
17 375, 446
48–49 545
41:19 633
42:3 446

(*Ezek*)
13 375
46:14 513
23 680
47:1–12 498
12 492

Dan 55
1:10 330
2:2 494
31 77
32 535, 543–44
34 473
34–36 497
35 473
37 294
3:3 494
7 494
10 494
27 677
4:9 582, 687
11 582
12 372
18 582
22 512
30 512
5:1–4 221
5 391
10 221, 375
17 632
21 512
7:9 77, 458, 537–38
10 532, 534
10:5 534, 536
6 543
11:35 570
37 302
45 441
12:10 570

Hosea 1–3 204
1:19–20 184
2 182, 327, 404
2:2 559
4 351, 470
4–7 318
5 424
7 419, 421
9 102
15 615
16–25 662
17 650
17–18 651
20 475

(*Hosea*)
24 405
3 550
3:1 222, 379
5 415, 559
4:10–14 375
5:6 415
15 415
7:4–5 375
11 401
14 375
16 375
9:1–2 375
2 375
4 375
6 370
10 375
14 528
11:4 302, 445
11 357
12:2 406
12 417
13:3 512
13 664
14 668
14:4 389
6 181, 371, 487
6–9 621
8 304, 372
9 362

Joel 1:5 659
10 375
12 491
20 540
2:2 415
10 319
16 441, 470
19 375
22 424
24 375
3:3 426
4:12 582
15 319
18 639, 659

Amos 3:5 446
4:9 322, 579
10 603
5:18 329
18–20 415
20 329
6:4 431, 625
4–6 359
4–7 214, 445
6:5 293

(*Amos*)
6 300
7 221
11 513
7:16 486
8:13 356, 544
9:7 320
13 659
14 579

Jonah 2:4 673–74
6 673
7 673
3:7 406
4:8 544

Micah 1:11 525
16 632
2:6 486
9 632
11 486
3:6 319
4:4 24, 634
5:2 701
3 406
4 432
6:2 390
7 533
7:5 549
19 297

Nahum 1:3 427
2:5 537
13 518

Hab 1:7 560
2:19 498
3:3 499
5 670
15 342
17 634

Zeph 1:9 389–90
15 415
3:10 309

Hag 1:6 507
2:17 322
23 666

Zech 1:8 531
14 669, 671
2:9 686
3:10 24
4:1 386
10 481, 483
6:2 307, 531

(*Zech*)
6 307
8:2 669
21–22 415
9:1–7 627
8 686
9 448
10 432
10–12 432
13 559
17 375
10:3 334
6–10 559
8 428
10 428
11:1–2 477
3 476
12:6 104
11 149
13:7 498
7–9 334
14:7 570
12 518

Mal 1:2 388, 671, 677
3:4 537
23 492
Matt 5:18 537
19 98
6:22 484
28 368
7:4–5 626
8:8 701
9:15 184
13:44 690
52 650, 652
19:21 542
21:2 448
7 448
33 690
41 690
22:30 165
37–40 204
25:1–13 184
27:34 677

Mark 9:3 532–33
13:28 398
14:5 349
51–52 527
15:23 505
16:1 222

Luke 1:35 312
48 407
5:8 701

(*Luke*)
7:37 349
10:30 557
12:27 368
49 617
13:26 418
14:26 542
15:6 510
7 473
22:38 441
23:11 532–33
43 557
24:1 222
13 416

John 2:10 507
3:28–29 184
29 436
4:14 497
34 500
6:44 303
7:34 417, 527
10:9 526, 683
12:3 493
6 349
24 623
32 303
13:23 663
35 204
15 397
15 510
16:7 701
18:1 581
19:30 509
34 533
39 350, 352, 495
39–40 222
41 509, 557
20:11–18 416
15 555
27 520
21:16 336

Acts 2:2 377
5:2 121
13:46 328

Rom 1:21 121
8:35 672
35–39 195
38 673
11:28 309
13:13 220

I Cor 3:9 557
4:9–13 677

(*I Cor*)
9:5 481
10:4 402
7 220
10–11 220
11:3 537
21 220
13:8 226, 673
13 673
15:54–55 669

II Cor 2:15 638
3:13 528
4:7 487
17 422
6:16 423
11:2 121, 302

Gal 4:26 423
6:14 530
17 346

Eph 2:20 548
5:23 199
23–25 184
25 203
27 474
6:15 617

Philip 2:6 473
3:8 677

Col 1:20 584
2:3 98
3:3 530
9 517

I Tim 2:9 457
2:11–15 205

Heb 1:1 390
3 533

I Peter 1:12 531
3:3 457
4:8 488

2:4–22 227
13 226

Jude 8–16 227
12 226

I John 4:7 670
19 204

Rev 1:13 532

(*Rev*)
13–16 77
14 458, 538
15 672
16 532–33
20 128
2:7 638
3:20 512
7:9 637
14 532
16:15 488
17:1 672
19:6 672
7 184, 637
8 487
9 184
13 532–33

II Esd 5:24 92
26 92
10:1 435

Tobit 3:7 435
4:7 228
5:20 481
7:16 481
11:19 442

Judith 5:6 323
18 323
8:3 687
10:19 55
14:18 629
16:8–9 614

Esther Additions 15:9 480

Wis 2:8 447
8:2 91, 696
3 158
9:14 121
15 526

Sir 9:5–9 55
14:22–24 145
16:18 54
17:22 666
23:19 539
24 696
14 354
19 176
30–31 498
25:17 307
20 55
21 55
26:2–3 54

(*Sir*)
9 356
10 680
12 680
14 55
14–15 54
18 546
27:5 626
30:18 227
36:10 559
39:5–6 696
40:29 391
42:3 626
11 216
43:20 498
47:6 533
14–17 91
15 18

(*Sir*)
50:5 391, 532
8 369
27 696
51:13–30 110

Baruch 6:72 444

Susanna 56 55

I Macc 2:29 145
4:57 468
9:37–42 437
39 427
13:29 468
51 637

II Macc 10:7 637

Jubilees 8:12–19 619
50:8 171
Enoch 8:1 315
46:1 458
106 77

Ethiopic
Enoch 26:1–2 619

III Macc 5:[2], 45 505

Acts of 8:8 467
Thomas 12–14 115

Apocalypse
of Peter 3:10 348

INDEX OF POST-BIBLICAL JEWISH REFERENCES

Dead Sea Scrolls
  Genesis Apocryphon 20.1–8 55
  Manual of Discipline (1QS 7:13) 517

Targum Onqelos
  Gen 15:19 320
  Num 24:21 320
  Judg 4:17 320

Mishnah
  Yoma vi 8 316
  Ketubot v 6 177
  Sotah ix 14 441
  Sanhedrin vii 6 217
  Abot vi 6 497
  Yadayim iii 5 19, 92

Tosefta
  Sandedrin xii 10 19

Babylonian Talmud
  Berakot 24a 402
    30a 466
    40a 398
    56b 497
  Shabbat 30b 542
    33b 336
    52b 484
    62b 348
    63a 348, 694
    88b 349, 373, 484, 526, 541
    119a 172
  Erubin 19a 581
    21–23 537
    21b 645
    54a 542
    81a 214
  Pesaḥim 67a 686
    111a 578
    117a 542
  Yoma 21a 397
    38a 362
    54a 155, 352
    54b 156, 619
    75a 489
  Sukkah 32b 582
    49a 616–17
    49b 616–17
    51b 156
    55b 357
  Rosh ha-Shanah 11b 390
  Ta'anit 4a 671
    25b 397
    26b 450
    29b 175
  Megillah 7b 217
  Moed Qatan 27b 156
    28b 214
    34? 616
  Hagigah 13a 487
    14a 537
    15b 306, 583
  Yebamot 96b–97a 642
    101b 473
    109x 440
  Ketubot 8b 216
    17a 55
    57a 478
    62b 171
    75a 402
    111a 388
  Nedarim 9a 512
  Nazir 3a 493
  Sotah 12a 403
    13 160
    14a 216
    49a 448
  Gittin 36b 349
    68b 440
  Qiddushin 76b 473
  Baba Qamma 88a 171
  Baba Bathra 160, 688
    7b–8a 686
    14 19
    14b 18
    15a 18
    15b 612
    68a 493

68b 493
99a 156
Sanhedrin 36b 473
37a 619
60b 217
64a 217
90b 642
100a 548
101a 19
Abodah Zarah 12 650
35a 299
44b 217
58b 620
Zebaḥim 116a 499
Niddah 19b 492
31b 402
47a 397

Palestinian Talmud
Ketubot ii 1 442
Horayot iii 4 512

Midrash
Eccles 5:10 214
Genesis Rabbah 3,4 99
11:8 173
15:7 398
20:8 218
28:11 513
39:3 679
93:7 469
Leviticus Rabbah 159
5:3 218
6:1 159
28:6 214
Mishle p. 93 159
Numbers Rabbah 10:3 218
10:8 62
15 376
Sifre
Numbers sec. 131 217
Deuteronomy sec. 355 160

Later Rabbinic Works
hêḵalôṯ rabbāṯî 99
hilḵôṯ ʿēḏûṯ 9.1 139
Pardes Rimonim, Gate 16, §6 169
Pirqe Rabbi Eliezer ch. 12 436
16 448
Shulhan ʿAruk 240 177
695.2 217
Tiqqune Hazohar 34, p. 77 165
Zohar i 12b 169
15a 442
21b–22a 169
27b 171
49b–50a 169
84b 169
156b 165
162a–6 164
ii 29a 170
50b 170
51a–b 170
89a 177
89a–b 169
iii 5a 165
7a 166
17a 165
17a–b 170
44b 166
59a 157
69a 165, 169
75a–b 170
88b 165
180b 168
186b 170
272 174
290b 164
296a 164, 169
Zohar Hadash Tiqqunim 28b 578
117a top 171

INDEX OF UGARITIC REFERENCES

2.4[68].9–10 51
2.4[68].20–21 521
3[ʻNT].1.3–25 293
3[ʻNT].1.18–20 294
3[ʻNT].2–3 353
3[ʻNT].2.3–41 606
3[ʻNT].2.33 521
3[ʻNT].3.1–2 294
3[ʻNT].3.1–5 299
3[ʻNT].3.5–14 600
3[ʻNT].4.76 595
3[ʻNT].4.78 607
3[ʻNT].5.19–20 303
3[ʻNT].5.34–35 303
4[51].1.24–38 444
4[51].1.44 533
4[51].2.14 559
4[51].4.27 559
4[51].4.35–39 223, 508
4[51].4.38–39 386
4[51].4.50–51 448
4[51].5.68–71 459
4[51].5.72 681
4[51].5.93–97 681
4[51].5.100–1 549
4[51].6.18–21 681
4[51].6.20–21 547
4[51].6.56 657
4[51].7.9–12 568
5[67].5.6–22 425
5[67].5.19–22 382
6[49].2.6–37 668
6[49].2.12–23 425
6[49].2.15–19 525
6[49].3.6–7 506
6[49].3.6–9 580
6[49].3.22–4.47 420
6[49].4.4–9 553
6[49].4.14–25 553
6[49].4.28–29 416
6[49].4.28–36 553
6[49].4.39–40 416, 553
6[49].4.44 416
6[49].4.44–47 553
6[49].6.10–11 322, 641
6[49].6.16–22 668
6[62].1.14 559
6.6[62.2].42–52 694
10[76].2.16 75
10[76].3.11 75
11[132].1.1–3 382
12[75].1.7 572
12[75].1.36–37 419
14[KRT].1.26 303
14[KRT].1.40–41 632
14[KRT].143–55 75
14[KRT].2.60*ff* 531
14[KRT].2.61–62 632
14[KRT].2.63–64 666
14[KRT].2.86 294
14[KRT].2.88–90 533
14[KRT].3.143–46 632
14[KRT].3.154*ff* 531
14[KRT].3.157–58 521, 542, 666
14[KRT].6.288–93 632
15[128].2.26–28 657
16[12G].3.12–16 506
17[2 AQHT].5.4–8 637
17[2 AQHT].5.15 559
17[2 AQHT].6.26–31 293
17[2 AQHT].6.45 75, 632
18[3 AQHT].1.23–25 657
18[3 AQHT].1.24 480
19[1 AQHT].1.42–46 623
19[1 AQHT].2.61–76 623
19[1 AQHT].2.63*ff* 298
19[1 AQHT].4.204*ff* 531
20–22[121–24] 219
20[121].1.8 577
22.2[124].4–5 517
23[52] 644
23[52].1 50
23[52].6 508
23[52].6–7 223
23[52].8–11 396
23[52].13 50, 325
23[52].14–15 618
23[52].15 191
23[52].23 50
23[52].24 50, 51

23[52].28 50, 325
23[52].31 618
23[52].32*ff* 52
23[52].36 618
23[52].37–39 82
23[52].39 559
23[52].41 61
23[52].44 61
23[52].46–47 517
23[52].47*f* 61
23[52].49–50 75, 549
23[52].49–51 297, 372
23[52].59 50, 51, 657
23[52].61 636, 657
23[52].61–63 325
23[52].64–71 426
23[52].68 325
23[52].69 325
23[52].73 325
23[52].76 303
24[77] 293
24[77].22–23 324
24[77].23 299
24[77].32–37 678
24[77].40–45 577
24[77].42–43 577
53[54].11–13 668
122:1 219
124:4–5 219
131[309].27 576
160[55].4 575
160[55].9 575
161[56].10 575
1001.1.3 670
1003.3–4 611
1003.3–10 612
1111.11 381
1121.1–5 343
1122.1–7 343
1123.7 343
1127.6–8 343
1127.20–22 575
1127.22 575
1129.8–9 435
2000.2.1 325
2001.1.5 459
2001.2.1 687
2001.2.13 380
2011.12 325
2032 219
2041.16 576
2050.9 381
2074.36 576
UG 5.1 211
UG 5.1.1.3–4 507
UG 5.2.1.1–9 694
UG 5.3 75
UG 5.3.1.1–5 536
UG 5.3.1.5 512
UG 5.3.1.7 459
UG 5.3.2.4–8 294
UG 5.7 340
RS 22.225.1–5 358
RS 24.245 294
RS 225.1–2 559